DATE DUE

			PRINTED IN U.S.A.

CLASSICAL AND MEDIEVAL LITERATURE CRITICISM

Guide to Gale Literary Criticism Series

For criticism on	Consult these Gale series
Authors now living or who died after December 31, 1959	*CONTEMPORARY LITERARY CRITICISM (CLC)*
Authors who died between 1900 and 1959	*TWENTIETH-CENTURY LITERARY CRITICISM (TCLC)*
Authors who died between 1800 and 1899	*NINETEENTH-CENTURY LITERATURE CRITICISM (NCLC)*
Authors who died between 1400 and 1799	*LITERATURE CRITICISM FROM 1400 TO 1800 (LC)* *SHAKESPEAREAN CRITICISM (SC)*
Authors who died before 1400	*CLASSICAL AND MEDIEVAL LITERATURE CRITICISM (CMLC)*
Black writers of the past two hundred years	*BLACK LITERATURE CRITICISM (BLC)*
Authors of books for children and young adults	*CHILDREN'S LITERATURE REVIEW (CLR)*
Dramatists	*DRAMA CRITICISM (DC)*
Hispanic writers of the late nineteenth and twentieth centuries	*HISPANIC LITERATURE CRITICISM (HLC)*
Native North American writers and orators of the eighteenth, nineteenth, and twentieth centuries	*NATIVE NORTH AMERICAN LITERATURE (NNAL)*
Poets	*POETRY CRITICISM (PC)*
Short story writers	*SHORT STORY CRITICISM (SSC)*
Major authors from the Renaissance to the present	*WORLD LITERATURE CRITICISM, 1500 TO THE PRESENT (WLC)*

ISSN 0896-0011

Volume 14

CLASSICAL AND MEDIEVAL LITERATURE CRITICISM

Excerpts from Criticism of the Works of World
Authors from Classical Antiquity through the
Fourteenth Century, from the First Appraisals
to Current Evaluations

Jelena O. Krstović
Editor

Dana Ramel Barnes
Jennifer Brostrom
James E. Person, Jr.
Associate Editors

 **Gale Research Inc.**

An International Thomson Publishing Company

NEW YORK • LONDON • BONN • BOSTON • DETROIT • MADRID
MELBOURNE • MEXICO CITY • PARIS • SINGAPORE • TOKYO
TORONTO • WASHINGTON • ALBANY NY • BELMONT CA • CINCINNATI OH

STAFF

Jelena Krstović, *Editor*

Dana Ramel Barnes, Jennifer Brostrom, James E. Person, Jr., *Associate Editors*

Marlene H. Lasky, *Permissions Manager*
Margaret A. Chamberlain, Linda M. Pugliese, *Permissions Specialists*
Susan Brohman, Diane Cooper, Maria Franklin, Pamela A. Hayes, Arlene Johnson, Josephine M. Keene,
Michele Lonoconus, Maureen Puhl, Shalice Shah, Kimberly F. Smilay, Barbara A. Wallace,
Permissions Associates
Edna Hedblad, Tyra Y. Phillips, *Permissions Assistants*

Victoria B. Cariappa, *Research Manager*
Frank Vincent Castronova, Eva M. Felts, Mary Beth McElmeel, Donna Melnychenko, Tamara C. Nott, Tracie A. Richardson,
Norma Sawaya, *Research Associates*
Alicia Noel Biggers, Melissa E. Brown, Maria E. Bryson, Julia C. Daniel, Michele McRobert, Michele P. Pica,
Amy Terese Steel, Amy Beth Wieczorek, *Research Assistants*

Mary Beth Trimper, *Production Director*
Mary Kelley, *Production Associate*

Cynthia Baldwin, *Product Design Manager*
Sherrell Hobbs, *Macintosh Artist*
Willie Mathis, *Camera Operator*

∞™ This book is printed on acid-free paper that meets the minimum requirements of American National Standard for Information Sciences—Permanence Paper for Printed Library Materials, ANSI Z39.48-1984.

Library of Congress Catalog Card Number 94-29718
ISBN 0-8103-4877-2
ISSN 0896-0011
Printed in the United States of America
Published simultaneously in the United Kingdom
by Gale Research International Limited
(An affiliated company of Gale Research Inc.)

I(T)P™   Gale Research Inc., an International Thomson Publishing Company.
ITP logo is a trademark under license.

10 9 8 7 6 5 4 3 2 1

Contents

Preface

Since its inception in 1988, *Classical and Medieval Literature Criticism* has been a valuable resource for students and librarians seeking critical commentary on the writers and works of these periods in world history. Major reviewing sources have assessed *CMLC* as "useful" and "extremely convenient," noting that it "adds to our understanding of the rich legacy left by the ancient period and the Middle Ages," and praising its "general excellence in the presentation of an inherently interesting subject." No other single reference source has surveyed the critical reaction to classical and medieval literature as thoroughly as *CMLC*.

Scope of the Series

CMLC is designed to serve as an introduction for students and advanced readers of the works and authors of antiquity through the fourteenth century. The great poets, prose writers, dramatists, and philosophers of this period form the basis of most humanities curricula, so that virtually every student will encounter many of these works during the course of a high school and college education. By organizing and reprinting an enormous amount of commentary written on classical and medieval authors and works, *CMLC* helps students develop valuable insight into literary history, promotes a better understanding of the texts, and sparks ideas for papers and assignments. Each entry in *CMLC* presents a comprehensive survey of an author's career, an individual work of literature, or a literary topic, and provides the user with a multiplicity of interpretations and assessments. Such variety allows students to pursue their own interests; furthermore, it fosters an awareness that literature is dynamic and responsive to many different opinions.

CMLC continues the survey of criticism of world literature begun by Gale's *Contemporary Literary Criticism (CLC)*, *Twentieth-Century Literary Criticism (TCLC)*, *Nineteenth-Century Literature Criticism (NCLC)*, *Literature Criticism from 1400 to 1800 (LC)*, and *Shakespearean Criticism (SC)*. For additional information about these and Gale's other criticism series, users should consult the Guide to Gale Literary Criticism Series preceding the title page in this volume.

Coverage

Each volume of *CMLC* is carefully compiled to present:

- criticism of authors and works which represent a variety of genres, time periods, and nationalities

- both major and lesser-known writers and works of the period (such as non-Western authors and literature, increasingly read by today's students)

- 4-6 authors or works per volume

- individual entries that survey the critical response to each author, work, or topic, including early criticism, later criticism (to represent any rise or decline in the author's reputation), and current retrospective analyses. The length of each author or work entry also indicates relative importance, reflecting the amount of critical attention the author, work, or topic has received from critics writing in English, and from foreign criticism in translation.

An author may appear more than once in the series if his or her writings have been the subject of a substantial amount of criticism; in these instances, specific works or groups of works by the author will be covered in separate entries. For example, Homer will be represented by three entries, one devoted to the *Iliad,* one to the *Odyssey,* and one to the Homeric Hymns.

Starting with Volume 10, *CMLC* will also occasionally include entries devoted to literary topics. For example, *CMLC*-10 focuses on Arthurian Legend and includes general criticism on that subject as well as individual entries on writers or works central to that topic—Chrétien de Troyes, Gottfried von Strassburg, Layamon, and the Alliterative *Morte Arthure.*

Organization of the Book

An author entry consists of the following elements: author heading, biographical and critical introduction, principal English translations or editions, excerpts of criticism (each preceded by a bibliographic citation and an annotation), and a bibliography of further reading.

- The **Author Heading** consists of the author's most commonly used name, followed by birth and death dates. If the entry is devoted to a work, the heading will consist of the most common form of the title in English translation (if applicable), and the original date of composition. Located at the beginning of the introduction are any name or title variations.

- A **Portrait** of the author is included when available. Many entries also feature illustrations of materials pertinent to the author or work, including manuscript pages, book illustrations, and representations of people, places, and events important to a study of the author or work.

- The **Biographical and Critical Introduction** contains background information that concisely introduces the reader to the author, work, or topic.

- The list of **Principal Works** and **English Translations** or **Editions** is chronological by date of first publication and is included as an aid to the student seeking translated versions or editions of these works for study. The list will focus primarily on twentieth-century translations, selecting those works most commonly considered the best by critics.

- **Criticism** is arranged chronologically in each entry to provide a useful perspective on changes in critical evaluation over the years. All titles by the author featured in the critical entry are printed in boldface type to enable the user to ascertain without difficulty the works being discussed. Also for purposes of easier identification, the critic's name and the publication date of the essay are given at the beginning of each piece of criticism. Anonymous criticism is preceded by the title of the journal in which it appeared. Publication information (such as publisher names and book prices) and parenthetical numerical references (such as footnotes or page and line references to specific editions of works) have been deleted at the editors' discretion to provide smoother reading of the text. Many critical entries in *CMLC* also contain translations to aid the users.

- A complete **Bibliographic Citation** designed to facilitate the location of the original essay or book precedes each piece of criticism.

- Critical excerpts are also prefaced by **Annotations** providing the reader with information about both the critic and the criticism, the scope of the excerpt, the growth of critical controversy, or changes in critical trends regarding an author or work. In some cases, these notes include cross-references to excerpts by critics who discuss each other's commentary. Dates in parentheses within the annotation refer to a book publication date when they follow a book title, and to an essay date when they follow a critic's name.

- An annotated bibliography of **Further Reading** appears at the end of each entry and lists additional secondary sources on the author or work. In some cases it includes essays for which the editors could not obtain reprint rights. When applicable, the Further Reading is followed by references to additional entries on the author in other literary reference series published by Gale.

Topic Entries are subdivided into several thematic rubrics in which criticism appears in order of descending scope.

Cumulative Indexes

Each volume of *CMLC* includes a cumulative **author index** listing all authors who have appeared in Gale's Literary Criticism Series, along with cross references to such biographical series as *Contemporary Authors* and *Dictionary of Literary Biography*. For readers' convenience, a complete list of Gale titles included appears on the page prior to the author index. Useful for locating an author within the various series, this index is particularly valuable for those authors who are identified with a certain period but who, because of their death date, are placed in another, or for those authors whose careers span two periods. For example, Geoffrey Chaucer, who is usually considered a medieval author, is found in *Literature Criticism from 1400 to 1800* because he died after 1399.

Beginning with the tenth volume, *CMLC* includes a cumulative index listing all topic entries that have appeared in the Gale Literary Criticism Series *Classical and Medieval Literature Criticism, Contemporary Literary Criticism, Literature Criticism from 1400 to 1800, Nineteenth-Century Literature Criticism,* and *Twentieth-Century Literary Criticism.*

Beginning with the second volume, *CMLC* also includes a cumulative nationality index. Authors and/or works are grouped by nationality, and the volume in which criticism on them may be found is indicated.

Title Index

Each volume of *CMLC* also includes an index listing the titles of all literary works discussed in the series. Foreign language titles that have been translated are followed by the titles of the translations—for example, *Slovo o polku Igorove (The Song of Igor's Campaign)*. Page numbers following these translated titles refer to all pages on which any form of the title, either foreign language or translated, appears. Titles of novels, dramas, nonfiction books, and poetry, short story, or essay collections are printed in italics, while those of all individual poems, short stories, and essays are printed in roman type within quotation marks. In cases where the same title is used by different authors, the author's name or surname is given in parentheses after the title, e.g. *Collected Poems* (Horace) and *Collected Poems* (Sappho).

Critic Index

An index to critics, which cumulates with the second volume, is another useful feature of *CMLC*. Under each critic's name are listed the authors and/or works on whom the critic has written and the volume and page number where criticism may be found.

A Note to the Reader

When writing papers, students who quote directly from any volume in the Literary Criticism Series may use the following general forms to footnote reprinted criticism. The first example pertains to material drawn from a periodical, the second to material reprinted from books.

Rollo May, "The Therapist and the Journey into Hell," *Michigan Quarterly Review,* XXV, No. 4 (Fall 1986), 629-41; excerpted and reprinted in *Classical and Medieval Literature Criticism,* Vol. 3, ed. Jelena O. Krstović (Detroit: Gale Research, 1989), pp. 154-58.

Dana Ferrin Sutton, *Self and Society in Aristophanes* (University of Press of America, 1980); excerpted and reprinted in *Classical and Medieval Literature Criticism,* Vol. 4, ed. Jelena O. Krstović (Detroit: Gale Research, 1990), pp. 162-69.

Suggestions Are Welcome

Readers who wish to make suggestions for future volumes, or who have other comments regarding the series, are cordially invited to write or call the editors.

Acknowledgments

The editors wish to thank the copyright holders of the excerpted criticism included in this volume and the permissions managers of many book and magazine publishing companies for assisting us in securing reprint rights. We are also grateful to the staffs of the Detroit Public Library, the Library of Congress, the University of Detroit Mercy Library, Wayne State University Purdy/Kresge Library Complex, and the University of Michigan Libraries for making their resources available to us. Following is a list of the copyright holders who have granted us permission to reprint material in this volume of *CMLC.* Every effort has been made to trace copyright, but if omissions have been made, please let us know.

COPYRIGHTED EXCERPTS IN *CMLC,* VOLUME 14, WERE REPRINTED FROM THE FOLLOWING PERIODICALS:

Commentary, v. VI, 1948 for "God, Job, and Evil"by Paul Weiss. Copyright 1948, renewed 1976 by the American Jewish Committee. All rights reserved. Reprinted by permission of the publisher and the author.—*Comparative Drama,* v. 16, Winter, 1982-83. © copyright 1982, by the Editors of *Comparative Drama.* Reprinted by permission of the publisher.—*English Studies,* Netherlands, v. 49, 1968. © 1968 by Swets & Zeitlinger B.V. Reprinted by permission of the publisher.—*Isis,* v. 78, December, 1987 for "Science as Handmaiden: Roger Bacon and the Patristic Tradition" by David C. Lindberg. Copyright © 1987 by the History of Science Society, Inc. Reprinted by permission of the publisher and the author.—*Modern Philology,* v. 66, May, 1969 for "The Crucifixion and the Second Coming in 'The Dream of the Rood'" by John Canuteson. © 1969 by The University of Chicago. Reprinted by permission of the University of Chicago Press and the author.—*Neuphilologische Mitteilungen: Bulletin de la Société Néophilologique,* v. LXX, 1969, v. LXXI, 1970, v. LXXXIX, 1988. All reprinted by permission of the publisher.—*Traditio,* v. XXII, 1966. Reprinted by permission of the publisher.—*Vivarium,* v. XII, May, 1974. Reprinted by permission of the publisher.

COPYRIGHTED EXCERPTS IN *CMLC,* VOLUME 14, WERE REPRINTED FROM THE FOLLOWING BOOKS:

Beare, W. From *The Roman Stage: A Short History of Latin Drama in the Time of the Republic.* Revised edition. Methuen & Co. Ltd., 1964. Reprinted by permission of the publisher.—Brothers, A. J. From an introduction to *Terence: The Self-Tormentor.* Edited and translated by A. J. Brothers. Aris & Phillips Ltd, 1988. © A. J. Brothers 1988. All rights reserved. Reprinted by permission of the publisher.—Copley, Frank O. From an introduction to *The Comedies of Terence.* Translated by Frank O. Copley. The Bobbs-Merrill Company, Inc., 1967. Copyright © 1967 Macmillan College Publishing Company, Inc. Reprinted with the permission of Simon & Schuster, Inc. from the Macmillan College text.—Croce, Benedetto. From *Philosophy, Poetry, History: An Anthology of Essays.* Translated by Cecil Sprigge. Oxford University Press, London. © Oxford University Press 1966. Reprinted by permission of the publisher.—Dawson, Christopher. From *Mediaeval Religion (The Forwood Lectures 1934) and Other Essays.* Sheed & Ward, 1934. Copyright, 1934, Sheed & Ward. Renewed 1962 by Christopher Dawson. Reprinted with permission from Sheed & Ward, 115 E. Armour Blvd, Kansas City, MO 64141.—Ducksworth, George E. From *The Nature of Roman Comedy: A Study in Popular Entertainment.* Princeton University Press, 1952. Copyright 1952 by Princeton University Press. Renewed 1980 by Dorothy A. Duckworth. Reprinted by permission of the publisher.—Forehand, Walter E. From *Terence.* Twayne Publishers, 1985. Copyright © 1985 by G. K. Hall & Company. All rights reserved. Reprinted with permission of Simon & Schuster Macmillan.—Frye, Northrop. From *The Great Code: The Bible and Literature.* Harcourt Brace Jovanovich, 1982. Copyright © 1982, 1981 by Northrop Frye. Reprinted by permission of Harcourt Brace & Company.—Gassner, John. From *Masters*

Roger Bacon

c. 1214/1220-1292

English philosopher.

INTRODUCTION

Considered one of the most profound of the Schoolmen (a group of writers and teachers from about the eleventh to the fifteenth century who were interested in logic, metaphysics, and thology), Bacon fused elements of classical humanistic philosophy with a Christian worldview as well as Judaic and Islamic scientific and mathematical knowledge to form a coherent philosophy which lasted into the Renaissance. Such was his knowledge that some scholars have considered "Doctor Mirabilis"—as Bacon was called—superior in philosophical significance to his distinguished descendent, Sir Francis Bacon.

Biographical Information

Information about the life of Bacon is slim and accounts conflict. His birthplace is believed to have been either Ilchester, Somersetshire or Bisley, Gloucestershire. He studied at Oxford during the tenure of the distinguished classicist and natural philosopher Robert Grosseteste, and by 1236 he had established himself at the University of Paris as one of the first professors of Aristotle's works. While in Paris, Bacon became interested in scientific experimentation, and in about 1247 he began pursuing optical, mathematical, and scientific studies in addition to the disciplines in which he had been trained, which included languages and philosophy. Four years later he returned to England, where he entered the Franciscan order. He returned to Paris, where his writings had come to the attention of John of Fidanza, known today as Bonaventure, head of the Franciscan order at that time. Biographers long held that Bonaventure, displeased with Bacon's writings, placed Bacon under confinement for about ten years, denying him books, paper, and writing instruments; but the story of this imprisonment today seems doubtful. Bacon's writings did come to the attention of Pope Clement IV, and, to Bacon's surprise, Clement wrote to request a fair copy of his doctrines. Now under the gaze of a protector of sorts, and hoping to be commended by the Pope, Bacon responded by writing his *Opus majus* (c. 1267-68). Then, thinking he might be misunderstood, he wrote a lengthy explanatory treatise, *Opus minus* (1267). Having composed these massive works in fifteen months, he dispatched them to Rome, along with a work on alchemy, *Tractatus de multiplicatione speciarum*, in about 1268. Clement died the same year, and it is unclear what he thought of Bacon's works–or, for that matter, if he read them; however, it is clear that his death and the accession of Gregory X to the papacy boded ill for Bacon, as Gregory was not sympathetic to works containing the unfamiliar

and the possibly heretical. Bacon left Paris for Oxford, where he completed his third major work, *Opus tertium* (1268), as well as Greek and Hebrew grammars, and began an ambitious, encyclopedic work, *Compendium philosophiae*. This uncompleted project contains a blistering attack on Bacon's rivals among the clergy, and upon his monastic superiors for their ignorance and pedantry. In 1278 the head of the Franciscan order, Jerome of Ascoli (later Pope Nicholas IV) held an assembly in Paris to investigate contemporary works of heresy in the Church. Bacon was present at this meeting, and his writings were judged to contain serious theological errors. Bacon was then confined for (it is presumed) about ten years. Upon his release, he wrote two further treatises, not considered highly noteworthy. He died in 1292 and, it is believed, is buried at Oxford.

Major Works

Grosseteste exercised the most decisive influence upon Bacon's philosophical and scientific views as expressed in his three major works. From Grosseteste Bacon also derived his strong belief in the importance of mathematics, as well as his interest in the study of Greek and oriental languages. Bacon's originality lies in two areas: first, he further developed some of the ideas in natural philosophy which he found in Grosseteste; secondly, he attempted to completely synthesize the natural science, philosophy, and religious teaching of his time. Embracing Aristotle's works on physics and metaphysics as harmonious with Christian teaching, Bacon believed in the ultimate unity of all knowledge, physical and metaphysical; he fulminated against his contemporaries who insisted upon a separation of the two, and against the bluff ignorance of his fellow scholars who belittled and disdained learning about the physical sciences. In this, he is important for transmitting Islamic science into the Latin West. At the same time, he did not seek to free science and reason from theology. As Christopher Dawson has written, "The unity of science in which he believes is a purely theological unity. To an even greater extent than the earlier Augustinians he is prepared to subordinate all human knowledge to the divine wisdom that is contained in the Scriptures. All knowledge springs ultimately from Revelation." In his Christian humanist worldview, Bacon, wrote Dawson, "admits the possibility of scientific progress, for there is no finality in this life, and knowledge must continue to increase with the rise and fall of the world religions. All signs, he believed, pointed to the approaching end of the age and to the coming of Anti-christ, and it was to arm Christendom for the struggle and to prepare the way for its renovation under the leadership of a great Pope and a great king that he propounded his schemes for the reform of studies and the utilization of the power of science."

Critical Reception

For centuries Bacon's works existed, for the most part, only in manuscript form in libraries in Oxford, London, Douai, Paris, and Italy. One scholar declared that "it is easier to collect the leaves of the Sybil than the titles of the works written by Roger Bacon." Several fragments, mostly related to alchemy, were published sporadically throughout the fifteenth through seventeenth centuries, and for all that period Bacon was commonly thought of as an alchemist. A better-informed scholarly interest in them began in 1733, when Samuel Jebb published an incomplete Latin edition of *Opus majus*. For over one hundred years, this was the only available edition of Bacon's major works–until J. S. Brewer published *Fr. Rogeri Bacon Opera Quædam hactenus inedita* (1859), containing *Opus tertium, Opus minus*, and the extant portion of *Compendium philosophiae*, in 1859. This was followed by a still-incomplete Latin edition in 1897, with the first principal English edition of Bacon's writings appearing in 1928. Perhaps the most intriguing of Bacon's works came to light around 1912, when Wilfrid M. Voynich, a specialist in rare books and manuscripts, purchased at auction an illustrated treatise on natural science which came to be called the Voynich Manuscript. This bizarre document, written entirely in cypher, presents an attempt by Bacon to explain and integrate aspects of natural science not otherwise understood by thirteenth-century scholars. Only a few studies of the Voynich Manuscript have been published in the twentieth century, but many books and articles on Bacon's overall accomplishment have appeared, with key explorations conducted by Dawson, Robert Steele, Lynn Thorndike, A. G. Little, and Etienne Gilson. Current Bacon scholarship, in regard to translations and critical studies, is dominated by Jeremiah Hackett, Thomas S. Maloney, and David C. Lindberg. Although the extent of Bacon's influence and his importance to the beginnings of science in the western world have still not been fully noted or understood, commentators agree that he played a major part in the intellectual arena of fourteenth- and fifteenth-century Europe.

PRINCIPAL WORKS

Quaestiones supra libros quatuor physicorum Aristotelis [*Questions on Aristotle's Physics*] (treatise) c. 1240-47

Quaestiones supra undecim prime philosophiae Aristotelis (treatise) c. 1240-47

Summa grammaticae (treatise) c. 1240-52

Communium naturalium (treatise) c. 1267-70

Opus majus (treatise) c. 1267-68

Tractatus de multiplicatione specierum [*Multiplication of Species*] (treatise) c. 1267-68

Communia mathematica (treatise) c. 1267

Epistola fratris Rogerii Baconis de secretis operibus naturae et de nullitate magiae [*Letter on the Secret Works of Art and the Nullity of Magic*] (treatise) c. 1267

Opus minus (treatise) 1267

Opus tertium (treatise) 1268

Compendium studii philosophiae [*Compendium of the Study of Philosophy*] (treatise) c. 1292

Compendium studii theologiae (treatise) 1292

Fr. Rogeri Bacon Opera Quædam hactenus inedita (treatises) 1859

Opera Hactenus Inedita Fratris Rogeri Baconis. 12 vols. (treatises) 1905-40

PRINCIPAL ENGLISH TRANSLATIONS

The Opus Maius of Roger Bacon (translated by Roger Belle Burke) 1928

Roger Bacon's Philosophy of Nature: A Critical Edition, with English Translation, Introduction, and Notes, of "De multiplicatione specierum" and "De speculis comburentibus" (translated by David C. Lindberg) 1983

Compendium of the Study of Theology (translated by Thomas S. Maloney) 1988

Three Treatments of Universals by Roger Bacon (translated by Thomas S. Maloney) 1989

CRITICISM

Anthony à Wood   (essay date 1674)

SOURCE: "Life of Roger Bacon (from Wood's *Antiquitates Univ. Oxon.*)," in *Fr. Rogeri Bacon Opera quædam hactenus inedita, Vol. I,* edited by J. S. Brewer, 1859. Reprint by Kraus Reprint Ltd, 1965, pp. lxxxv-c.

[*Wood was an historian whose works are primarily concerned with the City and University of Oxford. In the following excerpt from a chapter reprinted from his* Historia et Antiquitates Universitatis Oxoniensis *(1674), he provides a brief overview of Bacon's significance in advancing human knowledge.*]

Omitting a great number of disputes which occurred this year [A.D. 1292,] between the University and the town, I shall proceed to speak of a philosopher the most celebrated that England had hitherto produced; I refer to Roger Bacon, a Franciscan friar, of the University of Oxford. . . .

He composed a great many books on different subjects, on theology, medicine, perspective, geometry, [natural] philosophy, of which he divulged many secrets. He published a Latin, Greek, and Hebrew grammar; he treated of chemistry, cosmography, music, astronomy, astrology, metaphysics, logic, and moral philosophy. And besides these treatises, in which he disclosed the various methods of study pursued in his days, he made many discoveries which but for him might not even now have seen the light. In fact, all his works display so much solid erudition, so many physical *tentamina,* that when modern sciolists boast so much of their experiments we may match Bacon with Bacon; and with the father and founder of the Gresham school the son of our University, whose singular praise it is to have given birth to such a man, in an age so immature and unfavourable. Leland speaks highly in his praise, and prefers him to Cornelius Agrippa. Moreover, Bacon, as early as 1267, explained to Clement IV., in various works, a method for correcting the calendar, and sent him several writings at the same time, containing precious observations on mathematics and philosophy, which he believed would be useful to the catholic Church. If you consider his care and diligence in this respect, I mean in his attempt to reform the calendar, you will acknowledge that Bede, Roger Infans, Robert Grostete, and other Englishmen, and what is more, that Theophilus, Eusebius, Victorinus, Cyril, and others laboured to little purpose.

William Whewell   (essay date 1847)

SOURCE: "The Innovators of the Middle Ages," in *The Philosophy of the Inductive Sciences, Founded upon Their History, Vol. 2,* second edition, 1847. Reprint by Johnson Reprint Corporation, 1967, pp. 155-73.

[*Whewell was Master of Trinity College, Cambridge University, and the author of several distinguished works on the inductive sciences. In the following excerpt, he focuses upon* Opus Majus, *seeking "to point out . . . the way in which*

the various principles, which the reform of scientific method involved, are here brought into view."]

[Roger Bacon] was termed by his brother monks *Doctor Mirabilis.* We know from his own works, as well as from the traditions concerning him, that he possessed an intimate acquaintance with all the science of his time which could be acquired from books; and that he had made many remarkable advances by means of his own experimental labours. He was acquainted with Arabic, as well as with the other languages common in his time. In the title of his works, we find the whole range of science and philosophy, Mathematics and Mechanics, Optics, Astronomy, Geography, Chronology, Chemistry, Magic, Music, Medicine, Grammar, Logic, Metaphysics, Ethics, and Theology; and judging from those which are published, these works are full of sound and exact knowledge. He is, with good reason, supposed to have discovered, or to have had some knowledge of, several of the most remarkable inventions which were made generally known soon afterwards; as gunpowder, lenses, burning specula, telescopes, clocks, the correction of the calendar, and the explanation of the rainbow.

Thus possessing, in the acquirements and habits of his own mind, abundant examples of the nature of knowledge and of the process of invention, Roger Bacon felt also a deep interest in the growth and progress of science, a spirit of inquiry respecting the causes which produced or prevented its advance, and a fervent hope and trust in its future destinies; and these feelings impelled him to speculate worthily and wisely respecting a Reform of the Method of Philosophizing. . . .

The *Opus Majus* is a work equally wonderful with regard to its general scheme, and to the special treatises with which the outlines of the plan are filled up. The professed object of the work is to urge the necessity of a reform in the mode of philosophizing, to set forth the reasons why knowledge had not made a greater progress, to draw back attention to the sources of knowledge which had been unwisely neglected, to discover other sources which were yet almost untouched, and to animate men in the undertaking, by a prospect of the vast advantages which it offered. In the development of this plan, all the leading portions of science are expounded in the most complete shape which they had at that time assumed; and improvements of a very wide and striking kind are proposed in some of the principal of these departments. Even if the work had had no leading purpose, it would have been highly valuable as a treasure of the most solid knowledge and soundest speculations of the time; even if it had contained no such details, it would have been a work most remarkable for its general views and scope. It may be considered as, at the same time, the *Encyclopedia* and the *Novum Organon* of the thirteenth century. . . .

I must now endeavour to point out more especially the way in which the various principles, which the reform of scientific method involved, are here brought into view.

One of the first points to be noticed for this purpose, is the resistance to authority; and at the stage of philosophical history with which we here have to do, this means resistance to the authority of Aristotle, as adopted and interpreted by the Doctors of the Schools. Bacon's work is divided into Six Parts; and of these Parts, the First is, Of the four universal Causes of all Human Ignorance. The causes thus enumerated are: —the force of unworthy authority; —traditionary habit; —the imperfection of the undisciplined senses; —and the disposition to conceal our ignorance and to make an ostentatious show of our knowledge. These influences involve every man, occupy every condition. They prevent our obtaining the most useful and large and fair doctrines of wisdom, the secrets of all sciences and arts. He then proceeds to argue, from the testimony of philosophers themselves, that the authority of antiquity, and especially of Aristotle, is not infallible. "We find their books full of doubts, obscurities, and perplexities. They scarce agree with each other in one empty question or one worthless sophism, or one operation of science, as one man agrees with another in the practical operations of medicine, surgery, and the like arts of Secular men. Indeed," he adds, "not only the philosophers, but the saints have fallen into errours which they have afterwards retracted," and this he instances in Augustin, Jerome, and others. He gives an admirable sketch of the progress of philosophy from the Ionic School to Aristotle; of whom he speaks with great applause. "Yet," he adds, "those who came after him corrected him in some things, and added many things to his works, and shall go on adding to the end of the world." Aristotle, he adds, is now called peculiarly the Philosopher, "yet there was a time when his philosophy was silent and unregarded, either on account of the rarity of copies of his works, or their difficulty, or from envy; till after the time of Mahomet, when Avicenna and Averroes, and others, recalled this philosophy into the full light of exposition. And although the Logic, and some other works were translated by Boethius from the Greek, yet the philosophy of Aristotle first received a quick increase among the Latins at the time of Michael Scot; who, in the year of our Lord 1230, appeared, bringing with him portions of the books of Aristotle on Natural Philosophy and Mathematics. And yet a small part only of the works of this author is translated, and a still smaller part is in the hands of common students." He adds further (in the Third Part of the *Opus Majus,* which is a Dissertation on Language) that the translations which are current of these writings, are very bad and imperfect. With these views, he is moved to express himself somewhat impatiently respecting these works: "If I had," he says, "power over the works of Aristotle, I would have them all burnt; for it is only a loss of time to study in them, and a course of errour, and a multiplication of ignorance beyond expression." "The common herd of students," he says, "with their heads, have no principle by which they can be excited to any worthy employment; and hence they mope and and make asses of themselves over their bad translations, and lose their time, and trouble, and money."

The remedies which he recommends for these evils, are, in the first place, the study of that only perfect wisdom which is to be found in the sacred Scripture, in the next place, the study of mathematics and the use of experiment. By the aid of these methods, Bacon anticipates the most splendid progress for human knowledge. He takes up the strain of hope and confidence which we have noticed as

so peculiar in the Roman writers; and quotes some of the passages of Seneca which we adduced in illustration of this: —that the attempts in science were at first rude and imperfect, and were afterwards improved; —that the day will come, when what is still unknown shall be brought to light by the progress of time and the labours of a longer period; —that one age does not suffice for inquiries so wide and various; —that the people of future times shall know many things unknown to us; —and that the time shall arrive when posterity will wonder that we overlooked what was so obvious. Bacon himself adds anticipations more peculiarly in the spirit of his own time. "We have seen," he says, at the end of the work, "how Aristotle, by the ways which wisdom teaches, could give to Alexander the empire of the world. And this the Church ought to take into consideration against the infidels and rebels, that there may be a sparing of Christian blood, and especially on account of the troubles that shall come to pass in the days of Antichrist; which by the grace of God, it would be easy to obviate, if prelates and princes would encourage study, and join in searching out the secrets of nature and art."

It may not be improper to observe here that this belief in the appointed progress of knowledge, is not combined with any overweening belief in the unbounded and independent power of the human intellect. On the contrary, one of the lessons which Bacon draws from the state and prospects of knowledge, is the duty of faith and humility. "To him," he says, "who denies the truth of the faith because he is unable to understand it, I will propose in reply the course of nature, and as we have seen it in examples." And after giving some instances, he adds, "These, and the like, ought to move men and to excite them to the reception of divine truths. For if, in the vilest objects of creation, truths are found, before which the inward pride of man must bow, and believe though it cannot understand, how much more should man humble his mind before the glorious truths of God!" He had before said: "Man is incapable of perfect wisdom in this life; it is hard for him to ascend towards perfection, easy to glide downwards to falsehoods and vanities: let him then not boast of his wisdom, or extol his knowledge. What he knows is little and worthless, in respect of that which he believes without knowing; and still less, in respect of that which he is ignorant of. He is mad who thinks highly of his wisdom; he most mad, who exhibits it as something to be wondered at." He adds, as another reason for humility, that he has proved by trial, he could teach in one year, to a poor boy, the marrow of all that the most diligent person could acquire in forty years' laborious and expensive study.

To proceed somewhat more in detail with regard to Roger Bacon's views of a Reform in Scientific Inquiry, we may observe that by making Mathematics and Experiment the two great points of his recommendation, he directed his improvement to the two essential parts of all knowledge, Ideas and Facts, and thus took the course which the most enlightened philosophy would have suggested. He did not urge the prosecution of experiment, to the comparative neglect of the existing mathematical sciences and conceptions; a fault which there is some ground for ascribing to his great namesake and successor Francis Bacon: still less did he content himself with a mere protest against the authority of the schools, and a vague demand for change, which was almost all that was done by those who put themselves forward as reformers in the intermediate time. Roger Bacon holds his way steadily between the two poles of human knowledge; which, as we have seen, it is far from easy to do. "There are two modes of knowing," says he; "by argument, and by experiment. Argument concludes a question; but it does not make us feel certain, or acquiesce in the contemplation of truth, except the truth be also found to be so by experience." It is not easy to express more decidedly the clearly seen union of exact conceptions with certain facts, which, as we have explained, constitutes real knowledge.

One large division of the ***Opus Majus*** is ***On the Usefulness of Mathematics,*** which is shown by a copious enumeration of existing branches of knowledge, as Chronology, Geography, the Calendar, and (in a separate Part) Optics. There is a chapter, "in which it is proved by reason, that all science requires mathematics." And the arguments which are used to establish this doctrine, show a most just appreciation of the office of mathematics in science. They are such as follows: —That other sciences use examples taken from mathematics as the most evident: —That mathematical knowledge is, as it were, innate in us, on which point he refers to the well known dialogue of Plato, as quoted by Cicero: —That this science, being the easiest, offers the best introduction to the more difficult: —That in mathematics, things as known to us are identical with things as known to nature: —That we can here entirely avoid doubt and errour, and obtain certainty and truth: —That mathematics is prior to other sciences in nature, because it takes cognizance of quantity, which is apprehended by intuition, (*intuitu intellectus*). "Moreover," he adds, "there have been found famous men, as Robert, bishop of Lincoln, and Brother Adam Marshman, (de Marisco) and many others, who by the power of mathematics have been able to explain the causes of things; as may be seen in the writings of these men, for instance, concerning the Rainbow and Comets, and the generation of heat, and climates, and the celestial bodies."

But undoubtedly the most remarkable portion of the ***Opus Majus*** is the Sixth and last Part, which is entitled ***De Scientia experimentali.*** It is indeed an extraordinary circumstance to find a writer of the thirteenth century, not only recognizing experiment as one source of knowledge, but urging its claims as something far more important than men had yet been aware of, exemplifying its value by striking and just examples, and speaking of its authority with a dignity of diction which sounds like a foremurmur of the Baconian sentences uttered nearly four hundred years later. Yet this is the character of what we here find. "Experimental science, the sole mistress of speculative sciences, has three great Prerogatives among other parts of knowledge: First she tests by experiment the noblest conclusions of all other sciences: Next she discovers respecting the notions which other sciences deal with, magnificent truths to which these sciences of themselves can by no means attain: her Third dignity is, that she by her own power and without respect of other sciences, investigates the secrets of nature."

The examples which Bacon gives of these "Prerogatives" are very curious, exhibiting, among some errour and credulity, sound and clear views. His leading example of the First Prerogative, is the Rainbow, of which the cause, as given by Aristotle, is tested by reference to experiment with a skill which is, even to us now, truly admirable. The examples of the Second Prerogative are three: —*first,* the art of making an artificial sphere which shall move with the heavens by natural influences, which Bacon trusts may be done, though astronomy herself cannot do it—"et tunc," he says, "thesaurum unius regis valeret hoc instrumentum;" —*secondly,* the art of prolonging life, which experiment may teach, though medicine has no means of securing it except by regimen; —*thirdly,* the art of making gold finer than fine gold, which goes beyond the power of alchemy. The Third Prerogative of experimental science, arts independent of the received sciences, is exemplified in many curious examples, many of them whimsical traditions. Thus it is said that the character of a people may be altered by altering the air. Alexander, it seems, applied to Aristotle to know whether he should exterminate certain nations which he had discovered, as being irreclaimably barbarous; to which the philosopher replied, "If you can alter their air, permit them to live, if not, put them to death." In this part, we find the suggestion that the fireworks made by children, of saltpetre, might lead to the invention of a formidable military weapon.

It could not be expected that Roger Bacon, at a time when experimental science hardly existed, could give any *precepts* for the discovery of truth by experiment. But nothing can be a better *example* of the method of such investigation, than his inquiry concerning the cause of the Rainbow. Neither Aristotle, nor Avicenna, nor Seneca, he says, have given us any clear knowledge of this matter, but experimental science can do so. Let the experimenter (*experimentator*) consider the cases in which he finds the same colours, as the hexagonal crystals from Ireland and India; by looking into these he will see colours like these of the rainbow. Many think that this arises from some special virtue of these stones and their hexagonal figure; let therefore the experimenter go on, and he will find the same in other transparent stones, in dark ones as well as in light-coloured. He will find the same effect also in other forms than the hexagon, if they be furrowed in the surface, as the Irish crystals are. Let him consider too, that he sees the same colours in the drops which are dashed from oars in the sunshine; —and in the spray thrown by a mill wheel; —and in the dew drops which lie on the grass in a meadow on a summer morning; —and if a man takes water in his mouth and projects it on one side into a sunbeam; —and if in an oil lamp hanging in the air, the rays fall in certain positions upon the surface of the oil; —and in many other ways, are colours produced. We have here a collection of instances, which are almost all examples of the same kind as the phenomenon under consideration; and by the help of a principle collected by induction from these facts, the colours of the rainbow were afterwards really explained.

With regard to the form and other circumstances of the bow he is still more precise. He bids us measure the height of the bow and of the sun, to show that the center of the bow is exactly opposite to the sun. He explains the circular form of the bow, —its being independent of the form of the cloud, its moving when we move, its flying when we follow, —by its consisting of the reflections from a vast number of minute drops. He does not, indeed, trace the course of the rays through the drop, or account for the precise magnitude which the bow assumes; but he approaches to the verge of this part of the explanation; and must be considered as having given a most happy example of experimental inquiry into nature, at a time when such examples were exceedingly scanty. In this respect, he was more fortunate than Francis Bacon, as we shall hereafter see.

We know but little of the biography of Roger Bacon, but we have every reason to believe that his influence upon his age was not great. He was suspected of magic, and is said to have been put into close confinement in consequence of this charge. In his work he speaks of Astrology, as a science well worth cultivating. "But," says he, "Theologians and Decretists, not being learned in such matters, and seeing that evil as well as good may be done, neglect and abhor such things, and reckon them among Magic Arts." We have already seen, that at the very time when Bacon was thus raising his voice against the habit of blindly following authority, and seeking for all science in Aristotle, Thomas Aquinas was employed in fashioning Aristotle's tenets into that fixed form in which they became the great impediment to the progress of knowledge. It would seem, indeed, that something of a struggle between the progressive and stationary powers of the human mind was going on at this time. Bacon himself says, "Never was there so great an appearance of wisdom, nor so much exercise of study in so many Faculties, in so many regions, as for this last forty years. Doctors are dispersed everywhere, in every castle, in every burgh, and especially by the students of two Orders, (he means the Franciscans and Dominicans, who were almost the only religious orders that distinguished themselves by an application to study,) which has not happened except for about forty years. And yet there was never so much ignorance, so much errour." And in the part of his work which refers to Mathematics, he says of that study, that it is the door and the key of the sciences; and that the neglect of it for thirty or forty years has entirely ruined the studies of the Latins. According to these statements, some change, disastrous to the fortunes of science, must have taken place about 1230, soon after the foundation of the Dominican and Franciscan Orders. Nor can we doubt that the adoption of the Aristotelian philosophy by these two Orders, in the form in which the Angelical Doctor had systematized it, was one of the events which most tended to defer, for three centuries, the reform which Roger Bacon urged as a matter of crying necessity in his own time.

J. S. Brewer   (essay date 1859)

SOURCE: A preface to *Fr. Rogeri Bacon Opera quædam hactenus inedita, Vol. 1,* edited by J. S. Brewer, 1859. Reprint by Kraus Reprint, 1965, pp. ix-lxxxiv.

[*Brewer was Professor of English Literature at King's College, London, and Reader at the Rolls. By the authority of Queen Victoria's Treasury and under the direction of the Master of the Rolls, he edited a one-volume edition of Bacon's works which includes* Opus Minus, Opus Tertium, Compendium studii philosophiae, *and* Epistola fratris Rogeri Baconis de secretis operibus artis et naturae, et de nullitate magiae. *In the following excerpt, Brewer summarizes the significance of Bacon's contributions to science and philosophy.*]

Numerous proofs are at hand of his great regard for experimental philosophy. He considered it as the only security against vague theories, the chief remedy for the errors in speculation and practice prevalent in his age. If the world loves to contemplate the great lord chancellor of James I. retiring from the court or the parliament to his museum at Grays Inn or at Gorhambury, laying aside his chancellor's robe to watch the furnace or count the drops from the alembic, the example of the solitary friar, with more scanty means and fewer associates justifying the value of experiments, in a darker and less favourable age, is not less interesting. So far as the prize is to be given to mere invention, Roger Bacon has superior claims to Lord Bacon. But as the discoverer of a new method, which has changed the whole face of science, —(for he must he called a discoverer who vindicates a truth long forgotten, or presents it in such a light that all must see and acknowledge its importance), —in this respect Lord Bacon will always bear the palm alone. Roger Bacon did not live in an age when the value of Aristotle as the philosopher of nature could be appreciated at its true worth. He reprobated the mistranslations of Aristotle, but not Aristotle himself; he thought there were treasures still to be discovered in the books of his Physics and Natural History, and that better translations and more accurate texts would justify his admiration for the great Greek teacher. He still adopted the older distinctions of philosophy into pure and mechanical, and he ranked under the latter division many of those processes to which modern estimation has since given a higher name. Though in his practice a keen and sagacious experimentalist, in his exposition of science he adopted the deductive in opposition to the inductive method.

To say that his aspirations far outstripped all that he, or that science in its most perfect state, could be expected to realize, is to charge him with no greater error than what is common to all enthusiastic, all great discoverers in every age. In common also with minds of great and comprehensive grasp; his vivid perception of the intimate relationship of the different parts of philosophy, and his desire to raise himself from the dead level of any individual science, induced Bacon to grasp at and embrace the whole. The errors in all directions, of which he was fully cognizant, perhaps something of the encyclopædical tendency of the age in which he lived, still more his anxiety to make all learning directly subservient to theology, led him to undertake so gigantic a task, which hitherto has set at defiance the energy and ambition of the grandest and most daring intellects. The noblest minds in every age have felt the strong necessity of resisting the tendency to dissever the body of the sciences.

The Westminster and Foreign Quarterly Review
(essay date 1864)

SOURCE: "The Life and Writings of Roger Bacon," in
The Westminster and Foreign Quarterly Review, Vol.
LXXXI, No. CLIX, January, 1864, pp. 1-30.

[*In the following excerpt, an anonymous critic surveys
Bacon's career and outlines Bacon's character based on his
writings.*]

Roger Bacon is one of the few really great men who have
been equally neglected by their contemporaries and by
posterity. All who have looked into his writings, Leland
and Selden no less than Humboldt and Victor Cousin,
point to him as the most original thinker of the middle
ages. His anticipations of the course of scientific discovery,
yield only in importance to the justness of his conceptions
of the method and purposes of science itself. First among
the schoolmen, he pointed out the evils of that blind subservience to authority which is the cardinal defect of scholasticism. First in an age almost wholly devoted to metaphysical speculation and logical dispute, he realized the
value of the study of nature, and insisted on the importance of experiment as an aid to it. The language in which
this great reform is advocated, is in the highest degree
striking and original. There are passages which recall, if
they did not suggest, some of the most brilliant aphorisms
in the *Novum Organum* of his illustrious namesake. These
facts sufficiently mark the interval which separated Bacon
from the current thought of the thirteenth century; and
therefore we cannot be surprised that in his lifetime he
should have shared the ordinary fate of those who presume to differ from the world around them. What is remarkable is, that of all the mediæval doctors, the one who
approaches most nearly to the spirit of modern science
should have obtained the smallest share of postumous re-
nown. . . .

The *Opus Majus* is not only highly original in its general
conception and plan, it is an encyclopædia of mediæval
science, full of curious research and ingenious experiment.
Its style is more lively and sustained than that of any contemporary author. It is enriched with quotations from
Cicero, Pliny, Seneca, and the Latin poets—now and then
a phrase of Livy, or a line of Juvenal, is incorporated into
the text. In point of literary merit, we cannot pay it a
higher compliment than in saying that it invites criticism.
As for the *Compendia* and *Summulæ,* of the Dominican
doctors, one would as soon think of criticizing them as of
objecting to the style of *Euclid's Elements.*

This work is divided into seven parts. It opens with an introduction, which describes in detail the causes which
delay the progress of true knowledge. These are four in
number: —(1.) The influence of authority. (2.) The force
of custom. (3.) The ignorance of the vulgar. (4.) The pride
of false and seeming knowledge. The three first Bacon considers together, and in the first place; the fourth is important and deadly enough to require separate treatment.

The second part consists of an Essay, addressed to the
proof of the proposition, that all wisdom is implicitly contained in the Holy Scriptures, but that it can only be
evolved therefrom by the aid of the Canon Law and phi-

losophy. In the discussion of this subject Aristotle is made
to play a very important part. Indeed, Bacon does not hesitate to affirm that, in common with Pythagoras, Socrates,
and Plato, he was a specially inspired authority. The Dominican doctrine of the active intellect, the same, it will
be remembered, which Aquinas opposed to the theory of
Averroes, is vigorously criticized, and shown to be inconsistent with the idea of all human wisdom existing as a direct revelation from God. Having pointed out, in this
manner, the source of knowledge, and the instruments by
which alone it can be obtained, and so harmonized, after
a fashion, the rival claims of philosophy and faith, Bacon
next turns to grammar and language, studies necessary to
the understanding of the sacred and philosophical writings. His remarks on this subject are especially interesting.
He first observes that languages are connected with one
another, and that it is necessary to know several before we
can fully understand any. He justifies the study of philology by the joint authority of the Latin poets and the saints,
especially St. Jerome, whose enthusiasm was so great that
he filed his teeth, in order that he might give the proper
breathing to certain Oriental words.

Next follows a plea for a critical revision of the text of the
Bible. The Paris Vulgate is declared to be so hopelessly
corrupt, especially in its figures, that no educated man can
conscientiously read it or preach from it. But this is not
the worst. Bacon complains that the clergy, both regular
and secular, have taken upon themselves to make corrections at their pleasure. With so much effect have they exercised their powers of emendation, that they have succeeded in outdoing the blunders of the Paris copy itself.
"Clamo ad Deum et ad vos," he says, "de ista corruptione
litteræ." In the thirteenth century this appeal for a critical
revision is not a little noticeable, and it marks a turn of
mind quite peculiar to Bacon, and which was no doubt
owing to his habits of accurate scientific research.

A long treatise on grammar may seem somewhat out of
place in a strictly scientific treatise; but it should be remembered that it was not merely as models of literary
style that Bacon wished the ancient masters of philosophy
and eloquence to be studied. He considered that their writings contained many facts highly necessary for the observer and experimentalist. Notwithstanding his antipathy to
authority, he does not hesitate to accept facts on the authority of authors of established reputation. The effects of
this inconsistency will hereafter appear.

The fourth part of the *Opus Majus* is devoted to mathematics. Considerable acuteness is shown in describing the
relation of this study to the other natural sciences. Bacon
explicitly declares, not only that a familiarity with mathematics is necessary for the purposes of experiment, but
that it is necessary as a *preliminary* for such purposes—
that other branches of knowledge are grounded in numbers, and that an acquaintance with numbers must precede their rational study. These canons are applied at
great length to celestial and terrestrial physics, and also,
it must be confessed, to some physiological and metaphysical questions, with which mathematics have very little to
do.

Bacon tells us in the *Opus Minus,* that the fifth part of his greater work—the **"Treatise on Perspective"**—was, in his opinion, one of the most valuable portions of the whole. In this judgment we are not easily induced to agree. The **"De Perspectiva"** is very long, and somewhat encumbered with scholastic distinctions and divisions. It describes, in the first place, the instruments of sight, *i. e.,* those parts of the brain which are concerned in vision; the optic nerve and the anatomy of the eye; the nature of the medium through which light is transmitted, and some of the qualities of visible objects are next considered; then we have an analysis of what are called modes of vision—in fact, a description of the different lines which rays take in passing through media of varying density. The arrangement is not unscientific; several facts are recorded which prove accurate and original observation, but there is also a great deal of error which the slightest observation would have corrected. Bacon trusted rather too much to his "solid and true authorities."

In the sixth and last division of the **Opus Majus** Bacon enlarges on the dignity and importance of experimental science, "the mistress and ruler of all." He accurately distinguishes observation from experiment, and points out the greater certainty of the conclusions arrived at by that means than by a merely ratiocinative process. The latter, he pithily remarks, terminates the discussion, the former settles the fact. Instances are given of the errors which have arisen from the unfortunate habit of trusting to report rather than to experience: for example, there is the common belief that adamant can only be split by goat's blood, that hot water freezes sooner than cold, and many others. Nothing can be more admirable than the first twelve chapters of this Essay; but presently Bacon betakes himself to his "solid authorities," to Pliny, to Solinus, to Avicenna, to Basilius, Ambrosius, and the poets. Then we get the story of a man who lived several centuries by smearing himself with some ointment which he found in a jar, and who carried about with him a letter from the Pope to certify the truth of his statement; and the story of the kingfishers, who are able to quell the winter storms till such time as they have laid their eggs and their young are fledged. Bacon hopefully conjectures that these facts will be of great service in converting infidels who deny the truths of faith because they are not able to understand them.

It will be seen from this rapid sketch, that the **Opus Majus** is written on a plan conspicuously different from that of the commentaries and compendia most in vogue, and that it differs from them not more in the form in which it is cast than in the object kept in view. It must, nevertheless, be confessed that its value lies rather in the spirit in which it is written than in the facts it records, or in any merit which it may have as a scientific whole. The state of knowledge in Bacon's time was not such as to enable even the most far-seeing man to carry out the object proposed—that of methodizing and relating the various branches of human learning. So far as the **Opus Majus** aims at classifying the sciences, proceeding, as it did, on a misapprehension inevitable at the time, it produced and could produce no useful effect; but before any true philosophy could expand itself there was a false philosophy to be cleared away. "There are three very bad arguments which are perpetually in use: this has been shown to be so; this is customary; this is universal—therefore we must hold to it." This was the real incubus which weighed down the finest and most subtle intellects of the middle ages, and it is Bacon's especial merit to have laid his hand on the root of the evil, and to have been constant in his efforts to eradicate it. Though containing many striking passages and many remarkable anticipations, it is, we think, as a propaideutic work that the **Opus Majus** best justifies its name.

It is not known what Clement thought of the triple reply which his letter called forth. No allusion to the subject is to be found either in his own lengthy correspondence, or in Bacon's works. . . .

[In 1268] Clement died. The accession of Gregory X. after an interval of three years of intrigue and confusion, destroyed any chance of protection or countenance from the head of Christendom for the new philosophy. Nor was the state of things at home or abroad calculated to inspire hope of the co-operation of men in place and power, in a scheme of intellectual reform. The long contest between Henry III. and the popular party had lately turned in favour of the king by the death of de Montfort at Evesham three years before. But the dispossessed nobles were maintaining a guerilla warfare throughout the length of the country: at Chesterfield, at Kenilworth, in the Isle of Ely, at London, the king's troops were held in check. When at last, through the energy and good fortune of Prince Edward, the leaders of the insurrection had been finally driven from these strongholds, it was just a question whether the objects for which they had so long contended had not been surrendered also. In the midst of this confusion Prince Edward sets out on the Crusade, and while he is abroad, no one knowing whether he was alive or dead, the king dies.

It was at this critical time—in 1272—that Bacon wrote his fourth work—the **Compendium Studii Philosophiæ**. The confusion and misery around are accurately reflected from its pages. The treatise is designed to show the necessity of wisdom—the means by which it may be acquired, and the impediments to its acquisition. It is the last head, however, which chiefly occupies the author. The following passages seem to point directly to the state of England during the concluding years of Henry's reign: —

> The princes, barons, and soldiers mutually oppress and spoil one another, and ruin those who are below them by wars and exactions without end. . . . No one cares what is done or how, whether justly or unjustly, if only he can work his will; they are slaves withal to luxury and the pleasures of the palate, and to other deadly sins. The people thoroughly incensed by its rulers hates them, and therefore keeps no faith with them if it can be avoided. As to traders and artificers, there is no question of them, for in everything they say and do, boundless fraud, cheating, and lying prevails.

The same desponding tone is preserved throughout. The four great impediments on which he enlarges in the **Opus Majus**—authority, custom, popular opinion, and the pride of knowledge—are referred to, but the corruption of the times is made the first and principal count of the indictment. The picture he draws is sufficiently gloomy: —

> "Let us diligently consider," he says, "every state of society, and we shall find infinite corruption everywhere, which first of all shows in the head. The Court of Rome is torn in pieces by deceit and fraud; justice is no more; all peace is broken in upon; the scandals which arise are infinite. As a consequence, morals are perverted, and pride reigns supreme; avarice is rampant, envy eats into the heart of individual men, while all are ruled by the pleasures of the palate, and luxury depraves the whole of that Court. Nor is this enough. A Vicar of God is denied us through the negligence of his church, and the world is left without a ruler, as has lately been the case for several years, owing to the envy and desire of honour which rule the Court of Rome."

On the state of the clergy he is equally explicit—

> Let us consider the religious bodies; I exclude no order. Let us see how far each one has fallen from his proper state, and how the new orders have already lapsed terribly from their former dignity. The whole body of clergy gives itself up to pride, luxury, and avarice. Wherever the clerks are collected in any number, as at Paris and Oxford, they scandalize the whole lay body by their brawls and disturbances and other vices.

These extracts show the profound impression which the state of Europe and England produced upon Bacon's mind. They also indicate pretty clearly the deadening influence of cloister-life even upon a thinker as original as he. Nowhere does he betray the slightest thought or care for the great political revolution which was being enacted before his eyes. It is solely in its reference to the welfare of his philosophy that he deplores the anarchy which he describes. The wars of Henry and de Montfort are an "impediment to knowledge." The crusade in which Louis of France and Prince Edward were engaged, is an ineffectual means of advancing the works of wisdom. Bacon does not so severely confine himself to the subject in hand as to prevent his remarking on some of the other bearings of these events, if it had occurred to him to do so. It is evident that he had no thought for them. He considered reform in speculation to be the determinant of all practical improvements. "If men are corrupt in their studies, they will be corrupt in their lives." "Such as a man shows himself in the study of wisdom, so he must always be in life." Hence, his one, sole, all-including object was the proper direction of studies; speculative reform being the necessary preliminary of practical improvement.

The gloomy anticipations with which the *Compendium Studii* was written were shortly afterwards realized with respect to himself. In 1274, two years after the appearance of that work, Jerome of Ascoli succeeded to the generalship of the Franciscans, on the death of St. Bonaventura. The leaders of the Church party felt strongly that repressive measures should be taken to check the growing spirit of liberty. They could not see why men should want to know anything which Aquinas did not know, or why they should not accept, as their fathers had done, the *Book of Sentences* as a rule and code of faith. Accordingly, in 1277,

the Bishop of Paris, one Stephen Tempier, convened a synod, at which more than two hundred philosophical propositions were formally condemned. In the succeeding year, the Dominican Chapter held at Milan decreed severe punishments to those brothers who presumed to differ from the doctrine of St. Thomas. The Franciscan General was determined not to be outdone by his Dominican rivals in vigour of action. He assembled his own order at Paris in the same year as that in which the Synod of Milan was held; and brought Bacon before them, charged with entertaining new and dangerous views—"propter quasdam novitates suspectas." Neither his age, nor his learning, nor his undoubted fidelity to the Papal See, protected him—his doctrine was formally condemned, and he himself thrown into prison.

In prison he remained for fourteen years, to the great comfort of the religious world. At last, in 1292, he was released by the authority of a Chapter General of his order held at Paris, under the presidency of the humane Ganfredi. He was in his seventy-eight year. One would think he had had enough of writing. However, with an energy and determination which nothing could subdue, he immediately made use of his freedom to compose a fifth and last work—the ***Compendium Studii Theologiæ.*** This treatise adds little that is new either to Bacon's doctrine or his method: it is a commentary on the old text—a dying lament on the causes of human ignorance, the neglect of useful knowledge, and the unreasoning obedience to authority. . . .

It is unfortunate that Bacon's printed works afford such slender materials for a judgment on his personal character. A man so original in speculation must have had many curious points of contrast with ordinary Englishmen, in his habits and in his everyday mode of regarding various current events. But we are not able to fill-in those little touches which complete the character of the man. It is solely as a thinker that he exhibits himself to us. No writer with whom we are acquainted is so carefully reticent as regards his actions and feelings in all things which lie outside his philosophy. When he warms into gratitude, it is to Clement, for having deigned to notice his scientific labours; when he breaks out, as is too frequently the case, into a torrent of bitter invective, it is against ignorant grammarians, like Hugutio, Brito, and Papias, or against the leaders of the two new orders, or against the administrative abuses which rob the Church of its head and Science of its legitimate support. We have already remarked how curiously inobservant he seems to have been of political and social changes. To merely human interests—those which concern the sentient and suffering man—he was, to all appearance, more indifferent still; at least, we cannot recall a single passage which reveals a fellow feeling with the hopes and fears, the joys and griefs, which make up so large a part of actual existence. It is not because of their irrelevancy to the object of his writings that such subjects are avoided. The truth of the matter is this: Bacon cared very little about the human race as such, or about anything which did not directly bear upon his philosophical system. His whole nature was absorbed in speculation. He himself made considerable sacrifices to science, and he was prepared to sacrifice in its cause the interests of any other person or class whatever. The poor and ignorant—those for whom his vows as a Franciscan especially bound him to care—were precisely those with whom, as a thinker, he was least concerned. When it became a question between St. Francis on one side and Aristotle or Averroes on the other, Bacon had not much doubt which side to take.

A man of this temper may command our respect, but must fail to draw us to him by any closer feeling. To say the truth, the impression left by a persual of Bacon's writings is not favourable to him as a man. He is somewhat arrogant; he is intensely self-confident; he is apt to assume motives; he is frequently hasty in his judgments and unnecessarily severe in his criticisms. Above all, he is infected with a bitter class spirit. His contempt and aversion for those who are not members of his own intellectual aristocracy are boundless: in his eyes, the people which knoweth not the law is cursed indeed.

But whatever may be thought of Bacon in a moral point of view, there can be no doubt of his intellectual power. In what proportion truth and error are mingled in his doctrine is another matter. The consideration of this question demands a more detailed examination of his philosophical writings than our present limits allow.

E. H. Plumptre (essay date 1866)

SOURCE: "Roger Bacon," *The Contemporary Review,* Vol. II, May-August, 1866, pp. 364-92.

[*In the following excerpt, Plumptre offers a general estimate of Bacon's teaching on universals and of his views on ethical and political philosophy. The critic also discusses the relation in which Bacon stood to the religious life of Oxford and of England.*]

Few of the chance coincidences of history are more striking than the fact that the great philosophical reformers of the thirteenth and the seventeenth centuries, who fought the same battles against the same foes, who used almost the same weapons, should have also borne the same name. So strong is the resemblance of thought and feeling, that it would not be difficult to select passages from Roger, which, to nine readers out of ten, acquainted only with the latter, would seem to have been written by Francis, and it is quite conceivable that the students of a far off age may discuss the question whether there were two Bacons or one, as we discuss the question whether there were one or two Zoroasters. . . .

What gave to universals their universality, or determined the individuation of individual things? Was there one common material substance, differenced only into genera and species by the varying forms impressed upon it? What were these forms that constituted the essence of each single thing, making it what it was? Were they capable of being apprehended by themselves, apart from the individual objects in which they inhered? Was the "sensitive soul" of man essentially different from that of brutes, or was there present, with a soul like theirs, a divine light, a power supernatural? In such wandering mazes men might entangle themselves for ever, and the history of the Nominalist and Realist controversies shows how inexhaustible was the subtle tissue of speculations, how fierce and hot

the passions that gathered round it. All that we can note is that hero also Bacon's position was unique. His love of experimental science led him to feel that all true knowledge must begin from individual facts, and so he was guarded against living in a cloudland of universals, or thinking of the essential forms of species or genera, as themselves objects of contemplation, or fit to be the starting-point of *à priori* reasoning. So far he anticipates, often almost verbally, the Nominalism of Ockham. But, on the other hand, there was a mystical element in his character which brought him nearer to Augustine, and saved him from the scepticism into which Nominalism sometimes passed. He rejected the popular psychology of his time, and fell back on the higher teaching of William of Auvergne. "Man's mind by itself, the *intellectus passibilis,* has but a potential receptivity of true knowledge. It gets that from the *intellectus agens,* and this is none other than the 'light that lighteth every man,' no *part* of man's soul, but indwelling and abiding with it." He quotes, with obvious delight, the answer once given by his old master, Adam de Marisco, when pressed hard on this point by the Friars who disputed round him, that "the *intellectus agens* was none other than the raven of Elijah," sc., "*Deusvel angelus,*" a supernatural and divine visitant. Equally striking, as showing a capacity for profound thought in the mystical direction, is his acceptance of the doctrine that the distinction between Hell, Purgatory, and Heaven is not local, and that the change of the soul in passing from one to another is one of state rather than of place.

More striking and interesting for us are his views on ethical and political philosophy. Living when the three forces that governed all things were Despotism, Feudalism, and the Papacy, he, in his dreams of an ideal state, constructed an elective monarchy, with the right of deposition in the people. Acknowledging the whole sum of the Church's doctrine, he yet recognised that the ethical teaching of heathen thinkers had often presented a higher standard than that of Christian divines. While he lifts up his voice against contaminating the minds of youth by the base and prurient literature of ancient Rome, and protests against the blind reverence paid by the thinkers of his time to the very name of Aristotle, and to the bad translations by which alone they for the most part knew him, he yet has a far higher estimate than they of his worth, and that of others like him. It seems to him infinitely probable that he and Pythagoras, and Socrates and Plato, received special illuminations, by which they knew much concerning God and the salvation of the soul. "We Christians are beyond all comparison below them." "Read the Ethics of Aristotle, and we shall find that we are in an abyss of vices." "With the philosophers there is the noblest zeal for purity, and meekness, and patience, and fortitude, and all virtues." Nor is his admiration confined to the teachers of Greece and Rome. On the ground of ethics Moslems can meet as well as Greeks and Latins, and "their truths will be the strongest confirmation of ours." Averroes and Avicenna take their place side by side with Aristotle. The pure contemplation of the Ethics ($\theta\epsilon\omega\rho\grave{\i}\alpha$) connects itself apparently with the ecstasies of St. Francis, and he finds, in a *suspensio mentis,* the true and only method by which the soul can attach itself to its one Supreme Object.

In the space that yet remains I can only touch upon one other question, and note the relation in which Bacon stood to the religious life of Oxford and of England. May we think of him there also, as in physical or moral science, as in any measure a prophet of the future, the harbinger of a brighter day?

It would be idle to point to him as having done any work analogous to that of Wycliffe in the century that followed. There is no trace throughout his writings that he shrank from the Mariolatry which his Order, under Bonaventura, carried to its culminating point; no protest against papal authority, or the worship of images, or purgatory, nothing even (unless we except his sympathy with Bertholdt) to indicate opposition to the abuses of indulgences. He defendel the dogma of Transubstantiation on philosophical grounds (one of which, by the way, seems to limit the Sacred Presence to the elect), and sees in the Sacrament of the Altar the great stay and support of a devout life, by which men enjoy a foretaste of the beatific vision, and become partakers of the Divine nature. No Protestant can claim him as being in this sense a Reformer before the Reformation. And yet in no small measure there was in him, and must have been in those who at Oxford and Paris came under his influence, the germs of all true reform, of all true freedom in theology.

W. E. H. Lecky on Bacon's significance:

Roger Bacon, having been a monk, is frequently spoken of as a creature of Catholic teaching. But there never was a more striking instance of the force of a great genius in resisting the tendencies of his age. At a time when physical science was continually neglected, discouraged, or condemned, at a time when all the great prizes of the world were open to men who pursued a very different course, Bacon applied himself with transcendent genius to the study of nature. Fourteen years of his life were spent in prison, and when he died his name was blasted as a magician.

William Edward Hartpole Lecky in his History of European Morals from Augustus to Charlemagne, *Vol. ii, revised edition, 1879. Reprint by D. Appleton and Company, 1925.*

Foremost among the evils which he notes as requiring correction in the Church is the ignorance of the clergy of his time. They knew nothing of any text of Scripture but the Vulgate, and the copies of the Vulgate in use were shamefully corrupt and inaccurate. They were unable to correct the Vulgate by the Septuagint, still less to test the agreement of either with the Hebrew. Through this want of knowledge they fell into "infinite falsities and intolerable perplexities" as to the literal sense of Scripture, and these were only multiplied tenfold when they passed from the literal to the spiritual interpretation. They knew nothing of the natural history of the Bible, and so lost sight of many important truths. They were ignorant of Biblical archaeology, and so committed themselves to the most ridiculous interpretations. The one remedy for these evils was

to be found in a critical correction of the text, and a careful study of the original languages. The literal sense of Scripture might well furnish occupation for a man's lifetime. He himself had known one (it is possible that he adopts in this instance St. Paul's formula for speaking of himself) who had devoted forty years to it. With a wonderful insight into the effect of the teaching which was then looked upon almost as a new revelation, while Bonaventura was lecturing on the *Sententiae* of Peter Lombard, and Thomas Aquinas was enjoying the fame of his gigantic *Summa Theologiae,* Bacon had the courage to write that the way in which he had been trained under Grosseteste and Adam de Marisco was a far truer one; that the use of the *Sententiae* was one of the sins that filled theology with error; that all useful questions "in omnibus Summis et Sententiis" might be discussed with far greater profit from the text of Scripture. Characteristically enough, with this he mingles a personal complaint that the lecturers on the *Sentences* had the choice of hours, and a special chamber, while one who lectured on Scripture had to beg a vacant hour and lecture where he could. So, too, with a like protest against the substitution of authority for inquiry, while he maintains, on philosophical grounds, that the ideal of the Church required one perfect legislator, the *Vicarius Dei,* he yet refers to the fact that a Pope had once offered incense to idols, and protests against the blind prejudice that had led the University of Paris to condemn, forty years before, the very writings of Aristotle which afterwards became the text-book of all lecturers.

The structure of the books which he was writing—the haste, we may add, with which they were necessarily written—hindered him from giving any full exegesis of any part of Scripture, such as would have enabled us to judge how far he himself approached the standard of theological knowledge which he sets before others. But the incidental notices dropped here and there are sufficient to show that he knew enough to put to shame many thousands of the clergy, even of the nineteenth century, who talk complacently of the dark ages, and boast of their superior knowledge of the Scriptures. He had made himself acquainted with the whole history of the Septuagint translation, of Origen's *Hexapla,* of Jerome's great undertaking. He dwells on the fact that while Jerome's version was in general use, the Psalter, which the Western Church continued to use even in the thirteenth century, was not his, but the older Latin version made from the Septuagint. He knows the difference between the grammatical forms of Biblical Hebrew and Chaldee, rejects what he speaks of as the vulgar error of all theologians, that the Lamentations were written in the latter, and fixes on the one verse in Jeremiah (x. 11) which is so written. He explains that prophet's use of the mysterious Sheshak, in chap. xxv. 26, li. 41, as arising from his adoption of the cipher writing, which the later Jews knew as the Athbash,—sc., the use of an inverted alphabet,—and shows how in this manner, without incurring the wrath of the Chaldeans, he was able to prophesy the downfall of Babylon. He gives the derivations, and gives them rightly, of Arrhabon, Gehenna, Israel (in this case with a full discussion), Alleluia, Alma (with special reference to Isa. vii. 14), Jubilee, Mammon, Manna, Hosanna, Satan, and knows the name of Jehovah as the holy *tetragrammaton.* So in treating of the other sacred language, he gives a long list of all words of Greek origin in the Vulgate, with their derivations, discusses four or five interpretations of the mystical number of the beast, based upon the numerical value of the letters of the Greek alphabet, and rejects many false etymologies then current by applying the test of the quantity of Greek vowels. He had seen in the original text the fifty books of Aristotle's *Natural History.* He seems, however, to have formed a somewhat strange estimate of the labour required for mastering the two languages, and boasts that, with his method of teaching, any one, however ignorant of them before, might learn to read either in three days. Possibly the boy [Bacon's assistant] Joannes had learned the alphabet with a quickness which led his enthusiastic teacher to generalize hastily.

Yet more striking is his complaint of the preaching of his time, for, if the thirteenth century had any characteristic it could claim as its own, it was that it was a century of preachers. The two Mendicant Orders had devoted themselves to that as their special work. The Dominicans had used it as their designation, and were the *Fratres Praedicatores.* Their success as such had given them great influence all over Europe, and made practical ecclesiastics like Grosseteste eager to welcome them. And yet it is on their failure in this work that Bacon again and again dwells as utter and complete. The history of Wesleyanism in the eighteenth and nineteenth centuries did but reproduce that of the thirteenth. Young men without adequate training were admitted into the two Orders between the ages of fifteen and twenty. Unable to read their *Psaltery* or their *Donatus* when they came, they were at once set to the study of theology, as though that could be acquired by itself, when in truth it demanded, for its completeness, all human wisdom. The evil might be concealed by the personal excellence of individual preachers, or by the moral effects of their preaching. He is even obliged to admit that one simple friar who has never heard a hundred lectures in divinity may preach better than the most profound theologians. He feels that there is an earnestness and life in the Orders of which the secular, or parochial and cathedral, clergy of his time were for the most part destitute. Still less could he find what he yearned after in the bishops of his time, who were content to borrow the sermons of these very boy-friars, ignorant and ill-trained as they were, and so fell into a style of preaching in which there was neither loftiness of language nor depth of thought, but a folly infinitely puerile. Through this divorce of what God had joined together, the Church had suffered an immeasurable loss. In the preaching of a man like Bertholdt he saw an augury of better things; but he still yearned passionately, as many a noble and anxious heart has yearned since, for the reunion of the power to preach with the power to understand—of earnestness in maintaining truth with sympathy and insight—the union, in one word, of theology and life.

More interesting and suggestive even than his complaints as to the teaching of the Church is the utterance of his mind as to its worship. A keen susceptibility to the power of music, a strong sense of its value in the true education and *hygiène* of man's life, had been one of the points of sympathy between him and Grosseteste, and in his three great works he returns to the subject with all the ardour of a passionate affection. That which he recognised as the true music of the Church was such as stood aloof from all effeminate softness, from all barbarous wildness. What was required for the devotion of the faithful was not a soft and wanton warbling, nor the loud shouting of boors, but a sustained and grave melody, able at once to soothe the sense of hearing and gently raise the soul to the thoughts of a higher life. "Sounds have a wonderful power in their own nature to affect the mind; and therefore the Holy Spirit, who is the Master of the Church, inspiring all its members, has appointed the enharmonic form of music which has strength without harshness, and gives delight without voluptuousness." He complains bitterly that the taste of his time had given preference to a degenerate and effeminate *falsetto,* so that well-nigh all cathedrals and colleges had fallen into a corrupted use.

The thought of these corruptions did but carry his mind forward to the ideal perfection of the future. His imagination could conceive a time when, through a knowledge of its inner and secret laws, Church music should be able to stir all Christendom to devotion, and convert the heathen. His mind recalled many examples of its power. Elisha had bidden his servants bring a minstrel to him that he might prophesy. St. Francis had been helped, by the soft playing of the *cithara,* to pass into the ecstatic state in which he heard the harmonies of heaven. He waxes yet bolder in his praise. Music, if it be but of the right stamp, has power to reform the depraved—lead the drunkard to temperance— turn away the footsteps of the impure from the harlot's house—calm the passion of the wrathful. So Asclepiades had restored a madman to his reason; so David had freed Saul from his demoniacal possession. Of all dietetic exercises, singing, *teste Avicennâ,* was the most healthful for body and for spirit. Yes; its power extended over brute creatures. Stags were drawn on by soft music, and horses roused to battle by the sound of the trumpet. And all these things were to him but presages and foreshadowings of a more perfect excellence. If all this was done by common instruments and hackneyed tunes, what might not be, if, in accordance with the secret principles of the science, instruments should be made of consummate skill and perfection, and all the forms and elements of music combine to produce a true and unmarred delight? "Then, certainly, brute creatures would be drawn to submit themselves to our will, and be taken by our hands, astonished and led captive by that exceeding sweetness. And, in like manner, the minds of men would be raised to the highest pitch of devotion, to the fullest love of every virtue, and to all healthy and true activity." As if conscious that his enthusiasm carried him farther than most men could follow him, he is constrained to add that this power of music is not common; that the vulgar herd of philosophers do not aspire after it, neither meditating on the teaching of the ancients, nor applying themselves to the test of experiment; and therefore what he has written is not known to many. Not the less does he repeat his conviction that it is most true—worthy of all acceptance by every wise man. He submits it to the Pope that he, seeing this ineffable power of music, might apply it to the right government of the Church.

With this—the highest and noblest dream of the solitary thinker—I close the present sketch. Enough has been said, it is hoped, to give English readers, to whom his name was before associated only with a few scanty notices or grotesque legends, some notion of the life and character of one who may well claim a place among the highest group of English thinkers.

George S. Morris (essay date 1880)

SOURCE: "Mediaeval Anticipations of the Modern English Mind—John of Salisbury, Roger Bacon, Duns Scotus, William of Occam," in *British Thought and Thinkers: Introductory Studies, Critical, Biographical and Philosophical,* S. C. Griggs and Company, 1880, pp. 30-52.

[*Morris was Lecturer on Philosophy at Johns Hopkins University and an Associate of the Victoria Institute, London. In the following excerpt, he surveys Bacon's accomplishment as the work of a martyr to the cause of scientific and philosophical truth: a "wonder," whose profound works went unappreciated in the "darkness of the Middle Ages" and are superior to those of his descendent, Francis Bacon.*]

A more striking and personally interesting figure [than John of Salisbury] is that of Roger Bacon. Born in the year 1214, near Ilchester, in Somersetshire, his life extends through nearly the whole of the classic century of scholasticism. And yet, though a student and teacher in the schools, wearing the dress of a Franciscan monk, and acknowledging, with the rest of his contemporaries, the supremacy of the interests of faith (as including those of religion and morality, and hence of perfected and successful manhood itself), his image stands out in picturesque and impressive contrast with the intellectual life of his time. As a student at Oxford and Paris his commanding mental qualities obtained early recognition. He was the critic of his teachers, not a merely passive recipient of their knowledge. The genuine and the palpable could alone content him. First, what do the acknowledged authorities for our faith and knowledge, the Hebrew and Greek Scriptures, the works of Aristotle, the commentaries of the Arabians (then held in the highest esteem) really teach? That this could not be known through the Latin translations then current, Bacon was convinced. These translations were the imperfect work of ignorant bunglers. Instead, therefore, of wasting long, plodding years on the technicalities of grammar and logic—which, rightly considered, are, in Roger Bacon's view (with which John Locke agrees), but different names for an innate and unstudied art which every healthy mind naturally possesses—he would have scholars devote themselves first to a careful and thorough study of Hebrew, Greek and Arabic. They must be able to read these languages with ease and correctness for themselves. Only on this condition could they expect rightly to understand the Scriptures, or Aristotle or his Arabian commentators. Accordingly Bacon, while teaching at Oxford, devoted himself earnestly to the study of these languages, and spared no expense to procure for himself the best manuscripts. No wonder that, in the simple imagination of the people, or in the ignorant imagination of illiterate ecclesiastics, the story (repeated by Bayle) could find currency that he had discovered a receipt for

teaching any one "in a very few days Hebrew, Latin, Greek, and Arabic."

But all valuable and accessible knowledge is not, in Bacon's view, to be acquired through the interpretation of texts. There is another book, the book of nature, to be read, and by another method, made up of a combination of mathematics with experiment. In his appreciation of mathematics, as an instrument of scientific method, Bacon was far in advance of his age, and a herald of modern physical science, which, in the estimation of a living German historian of modern thought, first arrived at complete theoretical independence, and was ready to be separated from philosophy, when Newton formally stated, and successfully inaugurated the application of, its method, as consisting in the regulated "combination of induction with mathematical deduction" (Windelband, *Geschichte der neueren Philosophie,* I, 290). Roger Bacon, naturally, could not be expected to draw the line of distinction between philosophy and science, and their respective methods, for which the times were then not ripe. But in his *naïve* faith in the applicability of mathematics to all branches of knowledge he appears as the prototype of many English (and also Continental) enthusiasts of a later day, as Hobbes and Locke, Descartes and Spinoza, and in an important and essential sense even the author of the "Critique of Pure Reason" himself. Mathematics is for him, in his own language, the very "alphabet of philosophy." It is the "first among all sciences," not only in rank, but also as to the time of its "discovery." It is in some sense innate in man, and was known to the holy men at the beginning of the world. It is the "door and key" to all sciences, including that which we now exclude from the rank of a science, namely, magic. It alone furnishes absolutely valid demonstrations, and through its aid alone, therefore, can man arrive at the knowledge of truth without any admixture of error. We need it for the interpretation of Scripture even, and for the establishment of moral science. It is, in Bacon's words, an instrument in the hands of "the church of God for the common benefit of believers, the conversion of unbelievers, and the repression of those who cannot be converted." . . .

But the chief theoretical interest of Bacon lies in the knowledge of nature, in the discovery of her mechanical secrets, the consequent dispelling of the rude ignorance of which he complains as universal, and the improvement of man's present estate. Accordingly we read of his spending very large sums, perhaps the most of his large estate, in the purchase of instruments, and in making experiments. Of so great importance was this way and kind of knowledge to him, and so far did he carry his researches in this direction, that he was believed to possess magical secrets which nought but collusion with the devil could account for. Accordingly he was forbidden by his monastic superiors to "communicate to any one anything concerning his labors and the results of his investigations," and compelled to live an unwilling exile ten years in France. At last invited by a pope, who was favorable to him, to communicate to him what he knew, at the age of fifty-two he set about the composition of immense works, which he completed in a year and a half, and sent, along with certain mathematical instruments, by a trusty messenger, a pupil of his own, to Rome. "After the death of his papal patron" he became again the victim of "the envy and superstitious ignorance of his brother monks," at whose instigation he was accused of practicing the black art and teaching dangerous doctrines, and was compelled to pass ten years in a dungeon at Paris. A few years before his death the old man was at last released and permitted to return to his native England, where he died and where, at Oxford, he lies buried.

There is something deeply pathetic and even tragic in the fortunes of Roger Bacon. His fate was that which has so often, and from the very necessities of the case, befallen real greatness in the world. It stands alone, on heights unknown to its contemporaries, who look on it with ignorant contempt and reward it with sacrilegious buffetings. That is perhaps more true of him, which is alleged of Francis Bacon, that he "took a view of everything as from a high rock." His experience reminds one of Heine's saying: "Wherever a great mind utters its thoughts, there is Golgotha." Says Prof. Noack: "In view of his knowledge of languages and of the natural sciences Roger Bacon stood as a giant among his contemporaries." Many are the inventions and discoveries (as of gunpowder—though incorrectly) which have been ascribed to him, and still more startling are those which he predicted. It is reported that it was a passage stolen from Roger Bacon by some author known to Columbus that, arresting the attention of the latter, led him to the formation of his world-discovering plans. By his appreciation of mathematics, and the solidity of his own scientific work (*e. g.* in optics), Roger Bacon certainly is superior to his successor, Francis Bacon, Lord Verulam. On the other hand, the points of intellectual resemblance between the two Bacons are numerous and very striking. If Francis Bacon is by general admission an accurate representative of the English mind on one of its most striking sides, in Roger Bacon we must recognize a prophecy or evidence of the same English type shining out of the profounder darkness of the Middle Ages.

To his contemporaries Roger Bacon was a wonder. Hence the appellation which they gave him, *Doctor Mirabilis.*

Herbert Maxwell   (essay date 1894)

SOURCE: "Roger Bacon," in *Blackwood's Edinburgh Magazine,* Vol. CLVI, No. DCCCXLIX, November, 1894, pp. 610-23.

[*In the following excerpt, Maxwell summarizes Bacon's significance as an enlightener of the modern mind, emphasizing his role as a persecuted seeker of truth.*]

The coincidence that Roger Bacon bore, in a time before surnames had come into general use, the same surname that was to be carried to fame four centuries later by "the wisest, brightest, meanest of mankind," has cast into deeper eclipse the reputation of one of the most penetrating thinkers who have from time to time revolted against false teaching and unsound systems of science. Hardly for every hundred persons who have a general idea of the life and works of Francis Bacon of Verulam shall one, be found who could give an outline of those of Roger Bacon the Franciscan. Yet with the fruit of four additional centuries

of learning and civilisation at his command, the secret of the later Bacon's philosophy was none other than the earlier Bacon had imparted to ears that would not hear—that the road to knowledge lay, not through scholastic argument and self-confident routine, but by way of cautious induction and patient experiment.

There exists one other hindrance to popular familiarity with Roger Bacon's teaching, inasmuch as there hangs over his writings the veil of a dead language. A very small part of them have been translated out of the original Latin, nor is there, indeed, any pressing reason for undertaking this at the present day. It is pathetically interesting to follow the workings of a powerful mind tearing at the trammels woven by generations of mysticism and scholasticism, and sympathy is deeply starred for the dauntless spirit suffering persecution at the hands of prejudice and vanity; but the battle has since been fought and won, the truths contended for are now so unquestionable, the knowledge so painfully strained at has been brought within such easy reach of all who care to possess it, that, except as a study of faithful human endeavour, these writings are not now of great profit to the general reader. . . .

It has been commonly said of Roger Bacon that he lived three centuries before his time, but this is an observation founded on a misconception of human progress. None can say what he might have accomplished in direct invention and discovery had he not been hampered by ecclesiastical authority, and deprived, during the best years of his life, of the means of carrying out experiments. The part of his mission which he performed was to detect fallacies in accepted systems, and clear the way for workers in a happier age. Error had been accumulating in Europe through all the centuries following the fall of the Roman Empire. It lay deep as volcanic ash on buried Pompeii on every subject of human inquiry; and, if the truth were to be brought to light, some one must be found with hardihood to break the crust. Such pioneers are only too likely to meet a martyr's fate. Bacon's career, weighed as that of an individual, may be reckoned a failure, but only inasmuch as he failed to convince the world of the falsity of its system of learning. Regarded in its true light as an episode in the advance of knowledge, it must be deemed part of the mighty movement, destined in the lapse of years to overthrow the whole fabric of medieval scholasticism. The gospel he proclaimed fell as seed by the wayside; the clue which he uncovered seemed to slip unheeded from his dying hand: but still, the seed had been sown, the clue had been found, and it is to the despised Franciscan friar that the glory is due of having been the protomartyr of the new learning, at once the knell of dogma and the *réveille* of free inquiry. Roger Bacon was the first Englishman to claim freedom for human intellect and proclaim its scope.

John Henry Bridges   (essay date 1897)

SOURCE: An introduction to *The "Opus Majus" of Roger Bacon,* Vol. I, edited by John Henry Bridges, 1897. Reprint by Minerva G. m. b. H., 1964, pp. xxi-xcii.

[*A Fellow of the Royal College of Physicians and sometime Fellow of Oriel College, Oxford, Bridges was a scholar of*

Auguste Compte's work and himself a philosophical positivist. He edited a Latin edition of Opus Majus *which was first published in two volumes in 1897, but was withdrawn by the Clarendon Press after critics noted serious errors in the text due to Bridges's faulty reading of Bacon's manuscripts, his too-strict reliance upon Samuel Jebb's 1733 edition, and his omission of a key section of text located in the Vatican. (A corrected edition was published in 1900). In the following excerpt, Bridges, comments upon general characteristics of* Opus Majus *and compares Bacon's thought to that of Sir Francis Bacon and Auguste Compte.*]

The question presents itself, How far can the ***Opus Majus,*** with its two appendices, the ***Opus Minus*** and the ***Opus Tertium,*** be accepted as the final exposition of Bacon's philosophy and polity? It is spoken of by the author throughout as a *persuasio praeambula.* It is a hortatory discourse addressed to a busy statesman (for Clement IV, like most other popes of the thirteenth century, may be so called), urging him to initiate a reform of Christian education, with the direct object of establishing the ascendency of the Catholic Church over all nations and religions of the world.

A fundamental principle with Bacon was that truth of whatever kind was homogeneous. 'All the sciences,' he said, 'are connected; they lend each other material aid as parts of one great whole, each doing its own work, not for itself alone, but for the other parts: as the eye guides the whole body, and the foot sustains it and leads it from place to place. As with an eye torn out, or a foot cut off, so is it with the different departments of wisdom; none can attain its proper result separately, since all are parts of one and the same complete wisdom. Much light is thrown by passages like these, and there are many such, on the varied and at first sight heterogeneous character of the ***Opus Majus.*** A glance at the Index of this edition will give some notion of the multiplicity of the topics treated. History of philosophy, comparative philology, mathematics, astronomy, geography, optics, the physiology of sensation, all find a place; and all are subordinated to the service of the Catholic Church as the guardian of the highest interests of man. All these topics are handled so far and in such a way as to convince the Pope, or others in authority, of the width of the field to be cultivated, and of the importance of the object in view. Bacon's procedure is like that of a traveller in a new world, who brings back specimens of its produce, with the view of persuading the authorities of his country to undertake a more systematic exploration. To that further and more complete inquiry he proposed to devote the remainder of his life. He speaks of it in several passages of the present [edition of the ***Opus Majus***] under the title of ***Scriptum Principale.*** But, as we have reason to believe, of the twenty-five years of life that remained, more than half were sterilized by his imprisonment. When released, though he persevered, like Galileo, indomitably to the end, he was too old to think with his former vigour, and was capable only of such inferior work as the ***Compendium Theologiae,*** or the Commentary on the ***Secretum Secretorum.*** There remain the years between 1268 and 1278. They produced the ***Compendium Studii*** (published by Brewer), the ***Communia Naturalium,*** the ***Communia Mathematicae,*** and other fragments of the *Scriptum Prin-*

cipale. But, making large allowance for what may have been lost through neglect or through malignant hostility, or for what may yet remain to be discovered, the balance of probabilities indicates clearly enough that the ***Scriptum Principale*** was never brought to completion. The ***Opus Majus*** remains the one work in which the central thought of Bacon is dominant from first to last; the unity of science, and its subordination to the highest ethical purpose conceivable by man.

Another characteristic of Bacon's philosophy, to which it seems to me that sufficient attention has not yet been called, is the sense of historical continuity by which it is pervaded. Not indeed that Bacon stood alone in this respect. Comte, in a remarkable passage of his appreciation of the mediaeval Church, called attention, perhaps for the first time, to the awakening of the historic sense which the very constitution of that Church involved; rising as it did from the threefold root of Roman law, Greek thought, and Hebrew theocracy (*Philosophie Positive,* vol. v. p. 247, ed. Littré). As an example of this influence, he proceeds to quote the example of Bossuet, one of the first of European thinkers to form, in however imperfect a way, a broad and definite conception of the unity of history. But the example of Roger Bacon, writing four centuries earlier, is even stronger and more startling. Two centuries before the Renascence, he states explicitly what others may have implicitly thought, but would have shrunk from avowing even to themselves, that the whole course of intellectual development of mankind from the beginning of the world was not multiple but one, not discrete but continuous. He takes pains to synchronize the demi-gods, the heroes and the thinkers of Greece with the kings and prophets of Judaea. In his conception, philosophy, science, and religious truth had a common origin with the patriarchs: though separated in later centuries, they pursued a parallel course in Judaea and in Greece. The growth of science, no less than the growth of religion, was a process of continous evolution, taking place under divine guidance. It may be said that traces of such a doctrine as this may be found here and there in the early fathers, and especially in the writings of St. Augustine. But a comparison of the ninth and tenth books of *De Civitate Dei* with the second and seventh sections of the ***Opus Majus,*** will reveal a profound difference in the mode of treatment, even more than in the conclusions reached. What the earlier writer looks at as concessions wrung from an opponent, the later hails as the testimony of a friend. Augustine dwells on the points that separate the Christian from Porphyry and Seneca; Bacon on the points of union.

There are students of history even yet surviving to whom the centuries following the fall of the Western Empire seem a chasm hard to pass; so that they prefer, with Vico, to conceive of an ancient civilization which has run its course, and a new cycle as beginning. For Roger Bacon the apparent breach of continuity was in great part filled up by the long series of thinkers and students, who kept the torch of science alive in the Mahommedan schools of Mesopotamia and Spain. . . . Bacon made [much use] of such men as Thabit ben Corra, Alfarabius, Alfraganus, Alkindi, Alhazen, Albumazar, Avicenna, Hali, and Averroes. They are spoken of, and most truly, not merely as the principal channels through which Greek philosophy and science were introduced to the Western world, but as having increased the treasure entrusted to them; a treasure which the Westerns of the thirteenth century, 'unless they are dolts and asses,' will regard it as their duty to transmit with due interest to their posterity.

Hallam on Bacon's prescience as a scientist:

It seems hard to determine whether or not Roger Bacon be entitled to the honors of a discoverer in science. That he has not described any instrument analogous to the telescope, is now generally admitted; but he paid much attention to optics, and has some new and important notions on that subject. That he was acquainted with the explosive powers of gunpowder; it seems unreasonable to deny: the mere detonation of nitre in contact with an inflammable substance, which of course might be casually observed, is by no means adequate to his expressions in the well-known passage on that subject. But there is no ground for doubting that the Saracens were already conversant with gunpowder.

The mind of Roger Bacon was strangely compounded of almost prophetic gleams of the future course of science, and the best principles of the inductive philosophy, with a more than usual credulity in the supersitions of his own time. Some have deemed him over-rated by the nationality of the English; but, if we may have sometimes given him credit for discoveries to which he has only borne testimony, there can be no doubt of the originality of his genius.

Henry Hallam, in Introduction to the Literature of Europe in the Fifteenth, Sixteenth, and Seventeenth Centuries, *Vol. I, fourth edition, A. C. Armstrong and Son, 1886.*

At the close of these introductory remarks, some attempt may be made to assign Bacon's position in the history of human thought. It appears on the surface that he belongs to the order of thinkers, typified by Pythagoras rather than by Aristotle, who engage in speculation, not for its own sake alone, but for social or ethical results, that are to follow. His protests against the intellectual prejudices of his time, his forecasts of an age of industry and invention, the prominence given to experiment, alike as the test of received opinion and the guide to new fields of discovery, render comparison with his great namesake of the sixteenth century unavoidable. Yet the resemblance is perhaps less striking than the contrast. Between the fiery Franciscan, doubly pledged by science and by religion to a life of poverty, impatient of prejudice, intolerant of dullness, reckless of personal fame or advancement, and the wise man of the world richly endowed with every literary gift, hampered in his philosophical achievements by a throng of dubious ambitions, there is but little in common. In wealth of words, in brilliancy of imagination, Francis Bacon was immeasurably superior. But Roger Bacon had the sounder estimate and the firmer grasp of that combination of deductive with inductive method which marks the

scientific discoverer. Finally, Francis Bacon was of his time; with Roger Bacon it was far otherwise.

M. Hauréau, the historian of Scholastic philosophy, and also M. Renan, have suggested a parallel (or, it may be, have adopted it from Littré) between Roger Bacon and Auguste Comte. Some anticipation of the *Philosophie Positive* there assuredly is in Bacon's subordination of metaphysic to science, in his serial arrangement of the sciences, and in his avowal of a constructive purpose as the goal of speculative inquiry. But it is well not to push such comparisons too far. We shall best understand Bacon's life and work by regarding him as a progressive schoolman. Like the other great schoolmen of the thirteenth century, he set before himself the purpose of strengthening the Church in her work of moral regeneration, by surrounding her with every intellectual resource. But the forces that he brought to bear were not limited, like theirs, to the stationary dialectic of Aristotle; they were also, in great part, drawn from the progressive culture of natural and historical science. As compared with his successors of the Renascence, his purpose was loftier; for, in urging the continuous advancement of knowledge, he had higher things than knowledge in view. His aim, pursued in no spirit of utilitarian narrowness, yet steadily concentrated on the moral progress of mankind, was, *Induire pour aéduire afin de construire.*

Henry Osborn Taylor   (essay date 1911)

SOURCE: "Roger Bacon," in *The Mediaeval Mind: A History of the Development of Thought and Emotion in the Middle Ages,* Vol. II, Macmillan and Co., Limited, 1911, pp. 484-508.

[*In the following excerpt, Taylor offers a balanced examination of Bacon's attitude toward Scripture and the doctrines of the Church, his views of the state of knowledge in his time, and his interest in optics and experimental science.*]

Of all mediaeval men, Thomas Aquinas achieved the most organic and comprehensive union of the results of human reasoning and the data of Christian theology. He may be regarded as the final exponent of scholasticism, perfected in method, universal in scope, and still integral in purpose. The scholastic method was soon to be impugned and the scholastic universality broken. The premature attack upon the method came from Roger Bacon; the fatal breach in the scholastic wholeness resulted from the constructive, as well as critical, achievements of Duns Scotus and Occam.

Bacon is a perplexing personality. With other mediaeval thinkers one quickly feels the point of view from which to regard them. Not so with this most disparate genius of the Middle Ages. Reading his rugged statements, and trying to form a coherent thought of him, we are puzzled at the contradictions of his mind. One may not say that he was not of his time. Every man is of his time, and cannot raise himself very far out of the mass of knowledge and opinion furnished by it, any more than a swimmer can lift himself out of the water that sustains him. Yet personal temper and inclination may aline a man with less potent tendencies, which are obscured and hampered by the dominant intellectual interests of the period. Assuredly, through all the Middle Ages, there were men who noticed such physical phenomena as bore upon their lives, even men who cared for the dumb beginnings of what eventually might lead to natural science. But they were not representative of their epoch's master energies; and in the Middle Ages, as always, the man of evident and great achievement will be one who, like Aquinas, stands upon the whole attainment of his age. Roger Bacon, on the contrary, was as one about whose loins the currents of his time drag and pull; they did not aid him, and yet he could not extricate himself. It was his intellectual misfortune that he was held by his time so fatally, so fatally, at least, for the proper doing of the work which was to be his contribution to human enlightenment, a contribution well ignored while he lived, and for long afterward.

Bacon accepted the dominant mediaeval convictions: the entire truth of Scripture; the absolute validity of the revealed religion, with its dogmatic formulation; also (to his detriment) the universally prevailing view that the end of all the sciences is to serve their queen, theology. Yet he hated the ways of mediaeval natural selection and survival of the mediaeval fittest, and the methods by which Albert or Thomas or Vincent of Beauvais were at last presenting the sum of mediaeval knowledge and conviction. Well might he detest those ways and methods, seeing that he was Roger Bacon, one impelled by his genius to critical study, to observation and experiment. He was impassioned for linguistics, for mathematics, for astronomy, optics, chemistry, and for an experimental science which should confirm the contents of all these, and also enlarge the scope of human ingenuity. Yet he was held fast, and his thinking was confused, by what he took from his time. Especially he was obsessed by the idea that philosophy, including every branch of knowledge, must serve theology, and even in that service find its justification. But what has chemistry to do with theology? What has mathematics? And what has the physical experimental method? By maintaining the utility of these for theology, Bacon saved his mediaeval orthodoxy, and it may be, his skin from the fire. But it wrecked the working of his genius. His writings remain, such of them as are known, astounding in their originality and insight, and almost as remarkable for their inconsistencies; they are marked by a confusion of method and a distortion of purpose, which sprang from the contradictions between Bacon's genius and the current views which he adopted. . . .

There seems to have been nothing exceptional in Bacon's attitude toward Scripture and the doctrines of the Church. He deemed, with other mediaeval men, that Scripture held, at least implicitly, the sum of knowledge useful or indeed possible for men. True, neither the Old Testament nor the New treats of grammar, or physics, or of minerals, or plants, or animals. Nevertheless, the statements in these revealed writings are made with complete knowledge of every topic or thing considered or referred to—bird, beast, and plant, the courses of the stars, the earth and its waters, yea, the arts of song or agriculture, and the principles of every science. Conversely (and here Bacon even gave fresh emphasis and novel pointings to the current view) all knowledge whatsoever, every art and science, is needed for the full understanding of Scripture, *sacra doctrina,* in a word, theology. This opinion may hold large truth; but Bacon's advocacy of it sometimes affects us as a *reductio ad absurdum,* especially when he is proceeding on the assumption that the patriarchs and prophets had knowledge of all sciences, including astrology and the connection between the courses of the stars and the truth of Christianity.

There was likewise nothing startling in Bacon's view of the Fathers, and their knowledge and authoritativeness. Thomas did not regard them as inspired. Neither did Bacon; he respects them, yet discerns limitations to their knowledge; by reason of their circumstances they may have neglected certain of the sciences; but this is no reason why we should.

As for the ancient philosophers, Bacon holds to their partial inspiration. "God illuminated their minds to desire and perceive the truths of philosophy. He even disclosed the truth to them." They received their knowledge from God, indirectly as it were, through the prophets, to whom God revealed it directly. More than once and with every detail of baseless tradition, he sets forth the common view that the Greek philosophers studied the prophets, and drew their wisdom from that source. But their knowledge was not complete; and it behoves us to know much that is not in Aristotle.

> The study of wisdom may always increase in this life, because nothing is perfect in human discoveries. Therefore, we later men ought to supplement the defects of the ancients, since we have entered into their labours, through which, unless we are asses, we may be incited to improve upon them. It is most wretched always to be using what has been attained, and never reach further for one's self.

It may be that Bacon was suspected of raising the philosophers too near the Christian level; and perhaps his argument that their knowledge had come from the prophets may have seemed a vain excuse. Says he, for example:

> There was a great book of Aristotle upon civil science, well agreeing with the Christian law; for the law of Aristotle has precepts like the Christian law, although much is added in the latter excelling all human science. The Christian law takes whatever is worthy in the civil philosophical law. For God gave the philosophers all truth, as the saints, and especially Augustine, declare. . . . And what noble thoughts have they expressed upon God, the blessed Trinity, the Incarnation, Christ, the blessed Virgin, and the angels.

Possibly one is here reminded of Abaelard, and his thought of Christianity as *reformatio legis naturalis.* Yet Christ had said, He came not to destroy, but to fulfil; and the chief Christian theologians had followed Augustine in "despoiling the Egyptians" as he phrased it; the very process which in fact was making the authority of Aristotle supreme in Bacon's time. So there was little that was peculiar or suspicious in Bacon's admiration of the philosophers.

The trouble with Bacon becomes clearer as we turn to his

views upon the state of knowledge in his time, and the methods of contemporary doctors in rendering it worse, rather than better. These doctors were largely engaged upon *sacra doctrina;* they were primarily theologians and expounders of the truth of revelation. Bacon's criticism of their methods might disparage that to which those methods were applied. His caustic enumeration of the four everlasting causes of error, and the seven vices infecting the study of theology, will show reason enough why his error-stricken and infected contemporaries wished to close his mouth. The anxiousness of some might sour to enmity under the acerbity of his attack; nor would their hearts be softened by Bacon's boasting that these various doctors, of course including Albert, could not write in ten years what he is sending to the pope. Bacon declares that there is at Paris a great man (was it Albert? was it Thomas?), who is set up as an authority in the schools, like Aristotle or Averroes; and his works display merely "infinite puerile vanity," "ineffable falsity," superfluous verbiage, and the omission of the most needful parts of philosophy. Bacon is not content with abusing members of the rival Dominican Order; but includes in his contempt the venerable Alexander of Hales, the defunct light of the Franciscans. "*Nullum ordinem excludo,*" cries he, in his sweeping denunciation of his epoch's rampant sins. As for the seculars, why, they can only lecture by stealing the copy-books of the "boys" in the "aforesaid Orders." "Never," says Bacon in the *Compendium studii* from which the last phrases are taken, "has there been such a show of wisdom, nor such prosecution of study in so many faculties through so many regions as in the last forty years. Doctors are spread everywhere, especially in theology, in every city, castle, and burg, chiefly through the two student Orders. Yet there was never so great ignorance and so much error—as shall appear from this writing."

Bacon never loses a chance of stating the four causes of the error and ignorance about him. These causes preyed upon his mind—he would have said they preyed upon the age. They are elaborately expounded in pars i. of the **Opus majus:**

> There are four principal stumbling blocks (*offendicula*) to comprehending truth, which hinder well-nigh every one: the example of frail and unworthy authority, long-established custom, the sense of the ignorant crowd (*vulgi sensus imperiti*), and the hiding of one's own ignorance under the pretence of wisdom. In these, every man is involved and every state beset. For in every act of life, or business, or study, these three worst arguments are used for the same conclusion: this was the way of our ancestors, this is the custom, this is the common view: therefore should be held. But the opposite of this conclusion follows much better from the premises, as I will prove through authority, experience, and reason. If these three are sometimes refuted by the glorious power of reason, the fourth is always ready, as a gloss for foolishness; so that, though a man know nothing of any value, he will impudently magnify it, and thus, soothing his wretched folly, defeat truth. From these deadly pests come all the evils of the human race; for the noblest and most useful documents of wis-

dom are ignored, and the secrets of the arts and sciences. Worse than this, men blinded by the darkness of these four do not see their ignorance, but take every care to palliate that for which they do not find the remedy; and what is the worst, when they are in the densest shades of error, they deem themselves in the full light of truth.

Therefore they think the true the false, and spend their time and money vainly, says Bacon with many strainings of phrase.

"There is no remedy," continues Bacon, "against the first three causes of error save as with all our strength we set the sound authors above the weak ones, reason above custom, and the opinions of the wise above the humours of the crowd; and do not trust in the triple argument: this has precedent, this is customary, this is the common view." But the fourth cause of error is the worst of all. "For this is a lone and savage beast, which devours and destroys all reason, —this desire of seeming wise, with which every man is born." Bacon arraigns this cause of evil, through numerous witnesses, sacred and profane. It has two sides: display of pretended knowledge, and excusing of ignorance. Infinite are the verities of God and the creation: let no one boast of knowledge. It is not for man to glory in his wisdom; faith goes beyond man's knowledge; and still much is unrevealed. In forty years we learn no more than could be taught youth in one. I have profited more from simple men "than from all my famous doctors."

Bacon's four universal causes of ignorance indicate his general attitude. More specific criticisms upon the academic methods of his time are contained in his *septem peccata studii principalis quod est theologiae.* This is given in the **Opus minus.** Bacon, it will be remembered, says again and again that all sciences must serve theology, and find their value from that service: the science of theology includes every science, and should use each as a handmaid for its own ends. Accordingly, when Bacon speaks of the seven vices of the *studium principale quod est theologia,* we may expect him to point out vicious methods touching all branches of study, yet with an eye to their common service of their mistress.

> Seven are the vices of the chief study which is theology; the first is that philosophy in practice dominates theology. But it ought not to dominate in any province beyond itself, and surely not the science of God, which leads to eternal life. . . . The greater part of all the quaestiones in a *Summa theologiae* is pure philosophy, with arguments and solutions; and there are infinite quaestiones concerning the heavens, and concerning matter and being, and concerning species and the similtudes of things, and concerning cognition through such; also concerning eternity and time, and how the soul is in the body, and how angels move locally, and how they are in a place, and an infinitude of like matters which are determined in the books of the philosophers. To investigate these difficulties does not belong to theologians, according to the main intent and subject of their work. They ought briefly to recite these truths as they find them determined in philosophy. Moreover, the other matter of the

quaestiones which concerns what is proper to theology, as concerning the Blessed Trinity, the Incarnation, the Sacraments, is discussed principally through the authorities, arguments, and distinctions of philosophy.

Evidently, this first vice of theological study infected the method of Albert and Thomas, and of practically all other theologians! Its correction might call for a complete reversal of method. But the reversal desired by Bacon would scarcely have led back to Gospel simplicity, as may be seen from what follows.

> The second vice is that the best sciences, which are those most clearly pertinent to theology, are not used by theologians. I refer to the grammar of the foreign tongues from which all theology comes. Of even more value are mathematics, optics, moral science, experimental science, and alchemy. But the cheap sciences (*scientiae viles*) are used by theologians, like Latin grammar, logic, natural philosophy in its baser part, and a certain side of metaphysics. In these there is neither the good of the soul, nor the good of the body, nor the good things of fortune. But moral philosophy draws out the good of the soul, as far as philosophy may. Alchemy is experimental and, with mathematics and optics, promotes the good of the body and of fortune. . . . While the grammar of other tongues gives theology and moral philosophy to the Latins. . . . Oh! what madness is it to neglect sciences so useful for theology, and be sunk in those which are impertinent!

> The third vice is that the theologians are ignorant of those four sciences which they use; and therefore accept a mass of false and futile propositions, taking the doubtful for certain, the obscure for evident; they suffer alike from superfluity and the lack of what is necessary, and so stain theology with infinite vices which proceed from sheer ignorance. For they are ignorant of Greek and Hebrew and Arabic, and therefore ignorant of all the sciences contained in these tongues; and they have relied on Alexander of Hales and others as ignorant as themselves. The fourth vice is that they study and lecture on the *Sentences* of the Lombard, instead of the text of Scripture; and the lecturers on the *Sentences* are preferred in honour, while any one who would lecture on Scripture has to beg for a room and hour to be set him.

> The fifth fault is greater than all the preceding. The text of Scripture is horribly corrupt in the Vulgate copy at Paris.

Bacon goes at some length into the errors of the Vulgate, and gives a good account of the various Latin versions of the Bible. Next, the "*sextum peccatum* is far graver than all, and may be divided into two *peccata maxima:* one is that through these errors the literal sense of the Vulgate has infinite falsities and intolerable uncertainties, so that the truth cannot be known. From this follows the other *peccatum,* that the spiritual sense is infected with the same doubt and error." These errors, first in the literal meaning, and thence in the spiritual or allegorical significance, spring from ignorance of the original tongues, and from

ignorance of the birds and beasts and objects of all sorts spoken of in the Bible. "By far the greater cause of error, both in the literal and spiritual meaning, rises from ignorance of things in Scripture. For the literal sense is in the natures and properties of things, in order that the spiritual meaning may be elicited through convenient adaptations and congruent similitudes." Bacon cites Augustine to show that we cannot understand the precept, *Estote prudentes sicut serpentes,* unless we know that it is the serpent's habit to expose his body in defence of his head, as the Christian should expose all things for the sake of his head, which is Christ. Alack! is it for such ends as these that Bacon would have a closer scholarship fostered, and natural science prosecuted? The text of the **Opus minus** is broken at this point, and one cannot say whether Bacon had still a seventh *peccatum* to allege, or whether the series ended with the second of the vices into which he divided the sixth.

Bacon's strictures upon the errors of his time were connected with his labours to remedy them, and win a firmer knowledge than dialectic could supply. To this end he advocated the study of the ancient languages, which he held to be "the first door of wisdom, and especially for the Latins, who have not the text, either of theology or philosophy, except from foreign languages." His own knowledge of Greek was sufficient to enable him to read passages in that tongue, and to compose a Greek grammar. But he shows no interest in the classical Greek literature, nor is there evidence of his having studied any important Greek philosopher in the original. He was likewise zealous for the study of Hebrew, Chaldee, and Arabic, the other foreign tongues which held the learning so inadequately represented by Latin versions. He spoke with some exaggeration of the demerits of the existing translations; but he recognised the arduousness of the translator's task, from diversity of idiom and the difficulty of finding an equivalent in Latin for the statements, for example, in the Greek. The Latin vocabulary often proved inadequate; and words had to be taken bodily from the original tongue. Likewise he saw, and so had others, though none had declared it so clearly, that the translator should not only be master of the two languages, but have knowledge of the subject treated by the work to be translated.

After the languages, Bacon urged the pursuit of the sciences, which he conceived to be interdependent and corroborative; the conclusions of each of them susceptible of proof by the methods and data of the others.

> "Next to languages," says Bacon in chapter xxix. of the **Opus tertium,** "I hold mathematics necessary in the second place, to the end that we may know what may be known. It is not planted in us by nature, yet is closest to inborn knowledge, of all the sciences which we know through discovery and learning (*inventionem et doctrinam*). For its study is easier than all other sciences, and boys learn its branches readily. Besides, the laity can make diagrams, and calculate, and sing, and use musical instruments. All these are the *opera* of mathematics.

Thus, with antique and mediaeval looseness, Bacon conceived this science. He devotes to it the long *Pars quarta* of the **Opus majus:** saying at the beginning that of—

> the four great sciences the gate and key is mathematics, which the saints found out (*invenerunt*) from the beginning of the world, and used more than all the other sciences. Its neglect for the past thirty or forty years has ruined the studies (*studium*) of the Latins. For whoso is ignorant of it cannot know the other sciences, nor the things of this world. But knowledge of this science prepares the mind and lifts it to the tested cognition (*certificatam cognitionem*) of all things.

Bacon adduces authorities to prove the need of mathematics for the study of grammar and logic; he shows that its processes reach indubitable certitude of truth; and "if in other sciences we would reach certitude free from doubt, and truth without error, we must set the foundations of cognition in mathematics." He points out its obvious necessity in the study of the heavens, and in everything pertaining to speculative and practical *astrologia;* also for the study of physics and optics. Thus his interest lay chiefly in its application. As human science is nought unless it may be applied to things divine, mathematics must find its supreme usefulness in its application to the matters of theology. It should aid us in ascertaining the position of paradise and hell, and promote our knowledge of Scriptural geography, and more especially, sacred chronology. Next it affords us knowledge of the exact forms of things mentioned in Scripture, like the ark, the tabernacle, and the

temple, so that from an accurate ascertainment of the literal sense, the true spiritual meaning may be deduced. It should not be confused with its evil namesake magic, yet the true science is useful in determining the influence of the stars on the fortunes of states. Moreover, mathematics, through astrology, is of great importance in the certification of the faith, strengthening it against the sect of Antichrist; then in the correction of the Church's calendar; and finally, as all things and regions of the earth are affected by the heavens, astrology and mathematics are pertinent to a consideration of geography. And Bacon concludes *Pars quarta* with an elaborate description of the regions, countries, and cities of the known world.

Bacon likewise was profoundly interested in optics, the *scientia perspectiva,* which he sets forth elaborately in *Pars quinta* of the **Opus majus.** Much space would be needed to discuss his theories of light and vision, and the propagation of physical force, treated in the **De multiplicatione specierum.** He knew all that was to be learned from Greek and Arabic sources, and, unlike Albert, who compiled much of the same material, he used his knowledge to build with. Bacon had a genius for these sciences: his **Scientia perspectiva** is no mere compilation, and no work used by him presented either a theory of force or of vision, containing as many adumbrations of later theorizing. Yet he fails to cast off his obsession with the "spiritual meaning" and the utility of science for theology. He discussed the composition of Adam's body while in a state of innocence, a point that may seem no more tangible than Thomas's reasonings upon the movements of Angels, which Bacon ridicules. Again in his **Optics,** after an interesting discussion of refraction and reflection, he cannot forego a consideration of the spiritual significations of refracted rays. Even his discussion of experimental science has touches of mediaevalism, which are peculiarly dissonant in this most original and "advanced" product of Bacon's genius, which now must be considered more specifically.

The speculative intellect of the twelfth and thirteenth centuries was so widely absorbed with the matter and methods of the dominant scholasticism, that no one is likely to think of the eminent scholastics as isolated phenomena. Plainly they were but as the highest peaks which somewhat overtop the other mountains, through whose aggregation and support they were lifted to their supreme altitude. But with Bacon the danger is real lest he seem separate and unsupported; for the influences which helped to make him are not over-evident. Yet he did not make himself. The directing of his attention to linguistics is sufficiently accounted for by the influence of Grosseteste and others, who had inaugurated the study of Greek, and perhaps Hebrew at Oxford. As for physics or optics, others also were interested—or there would have been no translations of Greek and Arabic treatises for him to use; and in mathematics there was a certain older contemporary, Jordanus Nemorarius (not to mention Leonardo Fibonacci), who far overtopped him. It is safe to assume that in the thirteenth, as in the twelfth and previous centuries, there were men who studied the phenomena of nature. But they have left scant record. A period is remembered by those features of its main accomplishment which are not superseded or obliterated by the further advance of later times.

Weber on Bacon as a reformer of education:

As early as the thirteenth century, the Franciscan monk Roger Bacon, a professor at Oxford, recognized the serious imperfections in the system [of instruction offered in Christian schools], and conceived the plan of reforming it by the introduction of the sciences. His three works, **Opus majus, Opus minus,** and **Opus tertium,** the fruit of twenty years' investigation, to which he devoted his entire fortune, constitute the most remarkable scientific monument of the Middle Ages. Not only does he call attention to the barrenness of the scholastic *logomachies,* the necessity of observing nature and of studying the languages, but he recognizes, even more clearly than his namesake of the sixteenth century, the capital importance of mathematical deduction as an auxiliary to the experimental method. Nay, more than that; he enriches science, and especially optics, with new and fruitful theories. But his scientific reforms were premature in the year 1267, which marks the appearance of his **Opus majus.** His plan was submitted to the court of Rome, but owing to the intrigues of the obscurantist party, it fell flat, and procured for Roger twelve years of confinement. The seed sown by this most clear-sighted thinker of the Middle Ages upon the barren soil of Scholasticism did not spring up until three centuries later.

Alfred Weber, in History of Philosophy, *translated by Frank Thilly, 1896. Reprint by R. K. Publishers, 1987.*

Nothing has obliterated the work of the scholastics for those who may still care for such reasonings; and Aquinas to-day holds sway in the Roman Catholic Church. On the other hand, the sparse footprints of the mediaeval men who essayed the paths of natural science have long since been trodden out by myriad feet passing far beyond them, along those ways. Yet there were these wayfarers, who made little stir in their own time, and have long been well forgotten. Had it not been for the letter from Pope Clement, Bacon himself might be among them; and only his writings keep from utter oblivion the name of an individual who, according to Bacon, carried the practice of "experimental science" further than he could hope to do. It may be fruitful to approach Bacon's presentation of this science, or scientific method, through his references to this extraordinary Picard, named Peter of Maharncuria, or Maricourt.

In the **Opus tertium,** Bacon has been considering optics and mathematics, and has spoken of this Peter as proficient in them; and thus he opens chapter xiii., which is devoted to the *scientia experimentalis:*

> "But beyond these sciences is one more perfect than all, which all serve, and which in a wonderful way certifies them all: this is called the experimental science, which neglects arguments, since they do not make certain, however strong they may be, unless at the same time there is present the *experientia* of the conclusion. Experimental science teaches *experiri,* that is, to test, by observation or experiment, the lofty conclusions of all sciences." This science none but Master Peter knows.

By following the text further, we may be able to appreciate what Bacon will shortly say of him:

> Another dignity of this science is that it attests these noble truths in terms of the other sciences, which they cannot prove or investigate: like the prolongation of human life; for this truth is in terms of medicine, but the art of medicine never extends itself to this truth, nor is there anything about it in medical treatises. But the *fidelis experimentator* has considered that the eagle, and the stag, and the serpent, and the phoenix prolong life, and renew their youth, and knows that these things are given to brutes for the instruction of men. Wherefore he has thought out noble plans (*vias nobiles*) with this in view, and has commanded alchemy to prepare a body of like constitution (*aequalis complexionis*), that he may use it.

It may be pertinent to our estimate of Bacon's experimental science to query where the *experimentator* ever observed an eagle or a phoenix renewing its youth, outside of the *Physiologus?*

> The third dignity of this science is that it does not accept truths in terms of the other sciences, yet uses them as handmaids. . . . And this science attests all natural and artificial data specifically and in the proper province, *per experientiam perfectam;* not through arguments, like the purely speculative sciences, and not through weak and imperfect *experientias,* like the opera-

tive sciences (*scientiae operativae*). So this is the mistress of all, and the goal of all speculation. But it requires great expenditures for its prosecution; Aristotle, by Alexander's authority, besides those whom he used at home *in experientia,* sent many thousands of men through the world to examine (*ad experiendum*) the natures and properties of all things, as Pliny tells. And certainly to set on fire at any distance would cost more than a thousand marks, before adequate glasses could be prepared; but they would be worth an army against the Turks and Saracens. For the perfect experimenter could destroy any hostile force by this combustion through the sun's rays. This is a marvellous thing, yet there are many other things more wonderful in this science; but very few people are devoted to it, from lack of money. I know but one, who deserves praise for the prosecution of its works; he cares not for wordy controversies, but prosecutes the works of wisdom, and in them rests. So what others as purblind men try to see, like bats in the twilight, he views in the full brightness of day, because he is *dominus experimentorum.* He knows natural matters *per experientiam,* and those of medicine and alchemy, and all things celestial and below. He is ashamed if any layman, or old woman, or knight, or rustic, knows what he does not. He has studied everything in metal castings, and gold and silver work, and the use of other metals and minerals; he knows everything pertaining to war and arms and hunting; he has examined into agriculture and surveying; also into the experiments and fortune-tellings of old women, knows the spells of wizards; likewise the tricks and devices of jugglers. In fine, nothing escapes him that he ought to know, and he knows how to expose the frauds of magic.

It is impossible to complete philosophy, usefully and with certitude, without Peter; but he is not to be had for a price; he could have had every honour from princes; and if he wished to publish his works, the whole world of Paris would follow him. But he cares not a whit for honours or riches, though he could get them any time he chose through his wisdom. This man has worked at such a burning-glass for three years, and soon will perfect it by the grace of God.

There is a great deal of Roger Bacon in these curious passages; much of his inductive genius, much of his sanguine hopefulness, not to say inventive imagination; and enough of his credulity. No one ever knew or could perform all he ascribes to this astounding Peter, from whom, apparently, there is extant a certain intelligent treatise upon the magnet. And as for those burning-glasses, or possibly reflectors, by which distant fleets and armies should be set afire—did they ever exist? Did Archimedes ever burn with them the Roman ships at Syracuse? Were they ever more than a myth? It is, at all events, safe to say that no device from the hand and brain of Peter of Maharncuria ever threatened Turk or Saracen.

It is knowledge that gives insight. Modern critical methods amount chiefly to this, that we know more. Bacon did not have such knowledge of animal physiology as would assure him of the absurdity of the notion that an eagle or any animal could renew its youth. Nor did he know enough to realise the vast improbability of Greek philosophers drawing their knowledge from the books of Hebrew prophets. And one sees how loose must have been the practice, or the dreams, of his "experimental science." His fundamental conception seems to waver: *Scientia experimentalis,* is it a science, or is it a means and method universally applicable to all scientific investigation? The sciences serve it as handmaids, says Bacon; and he also says, that it alone can test and certify, make sure and certain, the conclusions of the other sciences. Perhaps he thought it the master-key fitting all the doors of knowledge; and held that all sciences, so far as possible, should proceed from experience, through further observation and experiment. But he has not said quite this.

He is little to be blamed for his vagueness, and greatly to be admired for having reached his possibly inconsistent conception. Observation and experiment were as old as human thought upon human experience. And Albert the Great says that the conclusions of all sciences should be tested by them. But he evinces no formal conception of either an experimental science or method; though he has much to say as to logic, and ponderously considers whether it is a science or the means or method of all sciences. Herein he is discussing consciously with respect to logic, the very point as to which Bacon, in respect to experimental science, rather unconsciously wavers: is it a science, and almost the queen? Or is it the true scientific method to be followed by all sciences when applicable? Bacon had no high regard for the study of logic, deeming that the thoughts of untaught men naturally followed its laws. This was doubtless true, and just as true, moreover, of experimental science as of logic. The one and the other were built up from the ways of the common man and universal processes of thought. Yet the logic of the trained mind is the surer; and so experimental science may reach out beyond the crude observations of unscientific men.

Manifestly with Roger Bacon the *scientia experimentalis* held the place which logic held with Albert, or queenly dialectic with Abaelard. He repeats himself continually in stating its properties and prerogatives, yet without advancing to greater clearness of conception. *Pars sexta* of the **Opus majus** is devoted to it: and we may take one last glance to see whether the statements there throw any further light upon the matter.

> The roots of the wisdom of the Latins having been placed and set in Languages, Mathematics, and Perspective, I now wish to re-examine these *radices* from the side of *scientia experimentalis;* because, without *experientia* nothing can be known adequately. There are two modes of arriving at knowledge (*cognoscendi*), to wit, argument and *experimentum.* Argument draws a conclusion and forces us to concede it, but does not make it certain or remove doubt, so that the mind may rest in the perception of truth, unless the mind find truth by the way of experience.

And Bacon says, as illustration, that you could never by mere argument convince a man that fire would burn; also that "in spite of the demonstration of the properties of an

equilateral triangle, the mind would not stick to the conclusion *sine experientia.*"

After referring to Aristotle, and adducing some examples of foolish things believed by learned and common men alike, because they had not applied the tests of observation, he concludes: "Oportet ergo omnia certificari per viam experientiae." He continues with something unexpected:

> *Sed duplex est experientia:* one is through the external senses, and thus those *experimenta* take place which are made through suitable instruments in astronomy, and by the tests of observation as to things below. And whatever like matters may not be observed by us, we know from other wise men who have observed them. This *experientia* is human and philosophical; but it is not sufficient for man, because it does not give plenary assurance as to things corporeal; and as to things spiritual it reaches nothing. The intellect of man needs other aid, and so the holy patriarchs and prophets, who first gave the sciences to the world, received inner illuminations and did not stand on sense alone. Likewise many believers after Christ. For the grace of faith illuminates much, and divine inspirations, not only in spiritual but corporeal things, and in the sciences of philosophy. As Ptolemy says, the way of coming to a knowledge of things is duplex, one through the *experientia* of philosophy, and the other through divine inspiration, which is much better.

Any doubt as to the religious and Christian meaning of the last passage is removed by Bacon's statement of the

> seven grades of this inner science: the first is through *illuminationes pure scientiales;* the next consists in virtues, for the bad man is ignorant; . . . the third is in the seven gifts of the Holy Spirit, which Isaiah enumerates; the fourth is in the beatitudes which the Lord defines in the Gospel; the fifth is in the *sensibus spiritualibus;* the sixth is in *fructibus,* from which is the peace of God which passes *omnem sensum;* the seventh consists in raptures (*in raptibus*) and their modes, as in various ways divers men have been enraptured, so that they saw many things which it is not lawful for man to tell. And who is diligently exercised in these experiences, or some of them, can certify both to himself and others not only as to spiritual things, but as to all human sciences.

These utterances are religious, and bring us back to the religious, or practical, motive of Bacon's entire endeavour after knowledge: knowledge should have its utility, its practical bearing; and the ultimate utility is that which promotes a sound and saving knowledge of God. The true method of research, says Bacon in the **Compendium studii,**

> . . . is to study first what properly comes first in any science, the easier before the more difficult, the general before the particular, the less before the greater. The student's business should lie in chosen and useful topics, because life is short; and these should be set forth with clearness and certitude, which is impossible without

experientia. Because, although we know through three means, authority, reason, and *experientia,* yet authority is not wise unless its reason be given (*auctoritas non sapit nisi detur ejus ratio*), nor does it give knowledge, but belief. We believe, but do not know, from authority. Nor can reason distinguish sophistry from demonstration, unless we know that the conclusion is attested by facts (*experiri per opera*). Yet the fruits of study are insignificant at the present time, and the secret and great matters of wisdom are unknown to the crowd of students.

It is as with an echo of this thought, that Bacon begins the second chapter of his exposition of experimental science in the sixth part of the **Opus majus,** from which we have but now withdrawn our attention. He anxiously reiterates what he has already said more than once, as to the properties and prerogatives of this *scientia experimentalis.* Then he gives his most interesting and elaborate example of its application in the investigation of the rainbow, an example too lengthy and too difficult to reproduce. In stating the three prerogatives, he makes but slight change of phrasing; yet his restatement of the last of them: —"The third *dignitas* of this science is that it investigates the secrets of nature by its own competency and out of its own qualities, irrespective of any connection with the other sciences," —signifies an autonomous science, rather than a method applicable to all investigation. The illustrations which Bacon now gives, range free indeed; yet in the main relate to "useful discoveries" as one might say: to ever-burning lamps, Greek fire, explosives, antidotes for poison, and matters useful to the Church and State. Along these lines of discovery through experiment, Bacon lets his imagination travel and lead him on to surmises of inventions that long after him were realised. "Machines for navigating are possible without rowers, like great ships suited to river or ocean, going with greater velocity than if they were full of rowers: likewise wagons may be moved *cum impetu inaestimabili,* as we deem the chariots of antiquity to have been. And there may be flying machines, so made that a man may sit in the middle of the machine and direct it by some devise: and again, machines for raising great weights." The modern reality has outdone this mediaeval dream.

S. A. Hirsch   (essay date 1914)

SOURCE: "Roger Bacon and Philology," in *Roger Bacon Essays Contributed by Various Writers on the Occasion of the Commemoration of the Seventh Centenary of His Birth,* edited by A. G. Little, Oxford at the Clarendon Press, 1914, pp. 101-51.

[*In the following excerpt, Hirsch offers a disinterested assessment of the philological theory and practice of Bacon, tracing possible sources and assessing his influence.*]

Roger Bacon held that the knowledge of languages was the first gate that led to the acquisition of wisdom. It was particularly indispensable to the 'Latins', whose entire acquaintance with theology and philosophy was derived from channels other than Latin. He did not recognize the study of languages to be important for its own sake; it was not a *scientia principalis*, like, for instance, mathematics.

It was, like logic, only accidental to philosophy. But he did not for that reason minimize its importance. Recognizing as he did that grammar, in the narrow sense of the word, as it was taught to boys, was to music what the work of the carpenter was to geometry, he yet demanded an independent and scientific research into the origins and the fundamental bases of languages.

It would be idle to say that Bacon has arrived at any striking results in the study of comparative philology, of the structure of the individual languages with which he was concerned, or of a comprehensive knowledge of their literary products. These subjects, and the topics connected with them, form nowadays separate disciplines, every one of which is treated on its own merits, and is calculated to engross the life-long attention of the student. It would be futile to expect Bacon to have reached anything approaching the standard of proficiency in these subjects which is demanded at the present day even of mediocrities. But it would be an error to imagine that many of the questions which have risen to such prominent importance in recent times did not agitate Bacon's mind to a large extent. They had certainly attracted his attention, and it cannot be denied that, given the status which such questions occupied at his time, the scanty apparatus at his disposal, and the meagre attainments of his contemporaries, he far surpassed the latter in his speculations upon the nature of language, in his insight into the structure of the several tongues that formed the subject of his researches, and his acquaintance with their literatures, in so far as they were accessible to him.

All such disciplines as are, in modern times, comprehended in the term 'philology' were termed by Bacon 'grammar'. Even such topics as the investigation of the origin of speech are declared by him to belong solely and exclusively to the science of grammar.

Bacon holds that a systematic investigation into the theory of 'signs' was indispensable to the knowledge of the composition of languages. He voices his usual complaint that this part of grammar had not been touched upon by the Latins, who did not even possess any translations of more ancient works on the subject. This was the more surprising, seeing that it was of the utmost utility in the study of all speculative truths of philosophy and theology.

In reference to the theory of 'signs', Bacon declares that his own investigations had led him to the same conclusions which his subsequent studies showed him to have been arrived at by Augustine. A sign may be either natural or imposed by the mind. Signs imposed by the mind either signify naturally, or are imposed at pleasure and voluntarily. The latter is the case in human language: words are imposed by the mind. Their signification is arbitrary, and a word signifies nothing before imposition. A word can be imposed upon itself, and thus become significant, e. g. 'white' may be used in the sense of the word 'white', or in the sense of a 'white' thing. When a word is applied to a thing outside the mind, it signifies the thing itself and nothing else (i. e. not the 'species' of the thing in the soul). A name imposed upon a thing outside the mind can at the same time signify other things outside the mind which can then be said to be 'co-intellected' or 'connoted'. The name

43

Fragment of Bacon's Opus Majus.

of an 'aggregate' or concrete thing signifies both the formal cause of the aggregation (i. e. the meaning of the concrete form) and the constituent elements of the aggregation. But a distinction must be made. The name signifies the aggregate primarily and principally, and the form and matter secondarily or mediately. It signifies the aggregate by imposition, and the matter and form naturally. A word cannot signify anything common to an 'ens' and a 'non-ens'. A word imposed upon a thing can lose its significance.

In coming to these conclusions on questions of the philosophy of languages Bacon has broken no new ground. He discusses the opinions of those who preceded' him, but in doing so he shows himself, as everywhere else, the keen critic of such speculations, through which he carefully steers his own course. He weighs, and partly controverts, the results arrived at by Aristotle, Boethius, Augustine, and Averroes. He chastises, in his usual manner, Richard of Cornwall, whom he calls *'famosissimus apud stultam multitudinem'*, as the worst and most stupid author of various erroneous notions.

The question of the origin of speech also agitated Bacon's mind. It is needless to say that he did not approach the question from the standpoint of anthropology and evolution in the way modern science has tried to obtain some understanding about it, and, thus far, with but scanty success. But within the compass and limitations into which his age and the state of knowledge accessible to him confined him, he meditated on the origin of languages, on the primitive language, on the language spoken by Adam, and the way the latter found names for the things. He ponders on what would happen if children were to grow up in a desert—whether they would have intercourse by speech, and how they would give expression to their mutual feelings when meeting under such circumstances. He was convinced that this part of 'grammar' was indispensable to theology, philosophy, and to all wisdom.

He was not himself aware, it seems, that his philological instincts would have led him to the consideration of such topics on their own merit. He measured all matters of research that offer by the uses to which they could be put in the service of philosophy and theology. Like so many other scholars of that age, and of subsequent ages, he acknowledged only utilitarian motives of that kind. They were certainly powerful incentives to direct him to the study of languages. Whether 'the first authors of languages had invented them', or whether the diversity of tongues was 'the work of God, at the division of languages at the erection of the tower of Babel after the Flood', or the result of 'diversity of locality', the variety existed, and his mind was exercised by the desire of inquiring into those languages in which were couched the documents from which theology and philosophy and all wisdom were derived.

Of these motives, the theological occupied to Bacon the first and foremost rank. At the conclusion of his speculations on signs and words in the ***Compendium Studii Theologiae*** he exhorts the reader not to lose sight of the manifold power of the word in figurative speech. The text of the Bible was full of it. The word, he says, had, besides its literal sense, three other meanings: the allegorical, the tropological, and the more hidden meaning (. . . *praeter sensum literalem potest vox significare tres alios sensus, scilicet allegoricum, tropologicum, et anagogicum*); and it was necessary to consider the way in which, in Holy Scripture, the literal sense concorded with the spiritual. Considerations of that kind were strengthened by Roger Bacon's propensity to mysticism.

Mysticism was, in Bacon's time, closely mixed up with religion, philosophy, magic, and physical science. He also believed in the mystical power of words; and, like so many others before and after him, he ascribed a spiritual meaning over and above the literal sense to every word of the Bible. Besides his philosophical elucidation of the meaning and application of words, and their grammatical formation, he seriously ponders on their occult influence.

> For the same knife cuts bread and wounds a man. In the same way, the wise man works wisely by means of words, and the magician magically. But their mode of action is different. The former makes use of a natural force; the work of the other was either nothing or else the work of the devil. . . . Since the creation of the world almost all miracles were performed by words. The word is the principal product of the rational soul, and its greatest delight. Words are possessed of great power when they are the result of profound thought, great longing, fixed intention, and strong confidence. By the co-operation of these four functions the rational soul is excited to give its impress and virtue to its own body, to things external, to its actions, and, above all, to the words which are produced from within, and receive therefore more of the virtue of the soul. Nature, says Avicenna, obeys the cogitations of the soul, as is shown by the hen on whose legs a spur grew by its feeling of triumph at the victory won by the cock. If thus nature obeys the cogitations of the sensitive soul, how much more will it obey those of the intellectual soul of those who are only one degree below the angels! Man's outward appearance and voice vary as the greater or lesser sanctity of the soul. A considerable increase in the power of either the good or the bad soul modifies the voice and the air affected by the latter. The air thus formulated by the voice, and having received a strong impetus from the rational soul, can be changed accordingly, and change, in its turn, the things it contains, be they agents or patients. It is the same with the body. Body and soul forming a unit, the body naturally obeys the cogitations of the soul; they modify its outer appearance. It again affects, and is affected by the air, which was itself affected by the voice. A further change is due to stellar influences. Whenever the voice is produced, the change wrought by it in the air is complicated by the effect of the constellations, and this again acts upon the things contained in the air. Everything depends, therefore, upon four influences: the voice formulating the air, the good or evil condition of the rational soul, the body, and the stars. When cogitating, intending, wishing, and strongly hoping for any change, a favourable condition of the heavenly bodies must be chosen in conjunction with the other in-

fluences; in the same way as a skilful physician selects suitable stellar conditions when desirous of working a cure. It was, as Avicenna says, in this way that the prophets and sages of old changed the matter of the world (*materiam mundi*), and produced rain, or drought, or other atmospheric changes by the power of words. In this consists the art of alluring or repelling men and beasts, snakes and dragons. This is the nature of every spell, and not the mere utterance of a word; the latter will have no effect unless the devil interferes. The other forces combined with the five conditions of the soul—strong thought, vehement wish, firm will, and either goodness or badness—are indispensable. The origin of songs, incantations, and various modes of writing must be traced to these influences.'

This combination of the power of words in general, and the spiritual sense underlying the words of the Bible in particular, made it imperative for Bacon to devote himself to the study of Hebrew and Greek, so as to be able to find hidden truths which would elude the eyes of those who knew these writings only from translations. It was only by a knowledge of Hebrew and Greek that it was possible to grasp the spiritual meaning of the 'text'. The 'text' was to Bacon what it was to his predecessors and contemporaries, and what it is to a great many people at the present day—the Latin translation. It would be possible, he holds, to study the literal meaning of the 'text', but this could be of very little avail for the knowledge of the spiritual sense.

> Suppose even the "text" to be correct to the letter, innumerable false and doubtful notions still remain on account of the ignorance of the languages from which the translations were made. But we theologians do not know even the alphabets. Consequently, we understand neither the text nor the expositions of the saints.

Bacon supported his standpoint with numerable examples. It was impossible for any one ignorant of the numerical value of the Greek and Hebrew letters to understand the interpretations given by the saints, as, for instance, Bede's gloss regarding the names of the Beast in the Apocalypse, the numerical value of the letters of each amounting to 666; or another passage of the Bible where the numerical value both of the Greek and the Hebrew letters coincided in revealing beautiful mysteries.

Another powerful motive to study languages was Bacon's disgust at the insufficiency of the existing translations. He sets forth that philosophy, religion, and science were laid down in documents which were written in languages that had fallen out of the ken of the majority of scholars of the day. Of the ancient languages, there was only one which had survived as the universal vehicle of thought and study in southern and western Europe. Latin could in Bacon's time still rightly be called a living language. But Bacon complained that the Latin world of priests and students, the 'Latinitas', had lost the knowledge of those very languages that formed the basis upon which everything that should interest them was reared. This would not have been so bad if the Latins were possessed of original and independent works on all branches of learning. But all wisdom had been revealed by God to nations other than Latin.

Philosophy was delivered on four distinct occasions. It was delivered for the first time in Hebrew, complete in all its details, by Adam and Noah; the second time, by Solomon; but Aristotle and Avicenna, who mark the other two epochs in the history of philosophy, were only able to deliver it incompletely, because they were heathens. Wisdom was delivered by these only and by none else; it certainly had not originated with the Latins.

> The Latins never originated a single text, either in theology or philosophy. All texts were composed in the first and second instance in Hebrew, in the third in Greek, and in the fourth in Arabic. . . . Waters drawn from the fountains were sweeter than those taken from turbid rivulets, and wine was purer and more wholesome when kept in the original cask than when poured from vessel to vessel. If, therefore, the Latins wished to drink the pure and wholesome liquor from the fount of wisdom, they must turn their attention to the Hebrew, Greek, and Arabic languages. It was impossible to recognize the proper form and beauty and wisdom in all their dignity except in the languages in which they were originally laid down. Oh, how delicious is the taste of wisdom to those who draw from the well of wisdom in its primary fullness and purity! All others are like those stricken with paralysis, who could not judge of the sweetness of food; like those born deaf, who are unable to enjoy the harmony of sound.

Translations cannot possibly replace the original documents.

> Jerome says that one language cannot possibly be represented by another. That which sounds well in one tongue becomes ridiculous when expressed in another. Homer became ridiculous when translated into Latin, and that most eloquent poet could hardly be said to speak at all.

The Latins derived their theology and philosophy merely from translations. But translations were unsatisfactory. Take, for instance, Logic. The logician will not find in his vernacular terms by which to express the sense of the original. He is therefore compelled to invent new terms. The result is that he will only be understood by himself. The same obtained in all other branches of knowledge. The translator must, consequently, borrow words from the language from which he translated. Such could neither be written, nor pronounced, nor understood, except by those who understood the language of the original.

In medicine the names of herbs, of spices, and other things were, for the most part, borrowed from the original languages. The same was the case with the holy text: all names of persons, localities, and numerous other things are either Greek or Arabic or Hebrew. Numbers of words were taken over from Lombardic, Spanish, and other languages that are akin to Latin. Bacon himself, when commenting in his lectures on a word which he took to be Arabic, was laughed at by his Spanish hearers, who told him that the word was not Arabic, but Spanish. Such ignorance brought the Latin teachers into contempt.

Translations were powerless to remedy the evil. The requirements necessary to procure a good translation—a thorough knowledge of the languages from which and into which the translation is made, and of the subject-matter—were possessed by very few indeed. All others were frauds. Robert Grosseteste belonged to the former class; but he only acquired the capacity of translating when he was an old man; and the Greeks whom he had gathered around him had translated very little. The translations furnished by Gerard of Cremona, Michael Scot, Alfred the Englishman, Hermann the German, and William the Fleming (William of Moerbecke) were sorry performances. The Bishop Hermann the German had told Bacon that he did not venture to translate books on logic from the Arabic, because he knew no logic. Not knowing logic, he could have no learning. But he did not even know much Arabic, and he was rather an assistant of translators than a translator himself. Michael Scot palmed off as his own, translations which were for the most part the work of a Jew, Andrew. Aristotle, whose works formed the foundation of all learning, had suffered most at the hands of these translators. Their versions of his logic, natural philosophy, and mathematics were such that no mortal could make head or tail of them. In consequence, the scholars squabble among themselves as to what Aristotle meant. It would have been much better if Aristotle had not been translated at all. Scholars laboured hard to understand him, and the more they laboured the less they knew. For this reason Grosseteste neglected the works of Aristotle, and dealt with several topics, guided only by his own experience and research, and certainly with greater success than if he had made use of those perverse translations. If, Bacon says, he could have his way, he would have all translations from Aristotle burned. It is sheer loss of time to study them, and it leads only to innumerable errors.

Ignorance of Greek and Hebrew, together with some other causes, were responsible for the corruption of the text of the Vulgate. The Paris text was the worst of all. Everybody, however illiterate some of them may be, and even 'married people', presumed to interfere with the text. They knew no grammar, they did not consult Priscian, and did not know that, on many points, Jerome was better informed even than he. Nevertheless, Jerome's translation did not always reproduce the true sense of the originals. People inveighed against him because he had dared to deviate from the Septuagint, and he was termed a falsifier and corrupter of the Scriptures. He therefore adapted himself to the previous versions, sometimes to that of Aquila, sometimes to that of Symmachus, but chiefly to the Septuagint, although he knew that these translations did not always agree with the originals. Jerome, moreover, admitted to have occasionally erred from undue haste.

All these reasons combined caused Roger Bacon to urge upon his contemporaries the study of the ancient languages. But he did not stop at exhortations. He threw himself into this pursuit with the same energy which characterized his efforts in the other fields of learning. It was especially the three languages—Arabic, Greek, and Hebrew, the mastery of which he considered to be a *conditio sine qua non* for all independent research in theology, philosophy, and science.

But Bacon was aware that no workman can effect anything without proper tools, which were in this case books and teachers. He says that it was necessary for the Latins to possess a short and useful treatise on the languages other than Latin, particularly on Greek, Hebrew, and Arabic; not only because all knowledge they possessed was borrowed from books written in these idioms, but because their own language (Latin) was based upon them.

A treatise of that kind should only contain the elements of grammar. It would be injurious to attempt too much at first. The student should not endeavour to master the learned languages completely, so as to know them in the same way as he knew and spoke his mother tongue; as he spoke English, French, and Latin. Nor was it necessary for the student to be able to translate scientific books. A third and lower standard was preferable, and this could easily be attained under a proper teacher, and with the help of good and concise manuals. But the student must be able to read Greek and Hebrew, and know the accidence according to Donatus. Once this was acquired, and a proper method followed, the construing and understanding of the words follow easily. The second degree, the capacity of translating, was much more difficult, although not so difficult as people imagined. But the first degree was very difficult indeed: it implied the capacity of speaking the language like the vernacular, and of using it for teaching and preaching and making speeches. The attempt to acquire all this would only frustrate its object; the student would soon despair, and not even reach the third degree.

> If a person were to apply himself from his youth for thirty years, he might attain all three degrees, or, at least, the two lower degrees. It is the first degree that offers all the difficulty, as we who have tried it know from experience.

The problem of finding competent teachers of the learned languages, although not a difficult one to Bacon in one sense, was far from easy in another. Bacon says that the best means was to learn Greek from the Greeks, and Hebrew from the Jews. Jews he declared to be everywhere, and their language was *in substance* the same as Arabic and Chaldaean. There were, besides, people in Paris, in France, and elsewhere who knew sufficient for the purpose. Greek accorded in most respects with Latin, and there were persons in England and France who knew enough. In many places in Italy the clergy and population were purely Greek, and it would be worth the trouble to go there for information.

And yet the matter was not so easy after all. Such of the inhabitants of southern Italy as were *veri Graeci* were not easily accessible. Some of these were still to be found in England, thanks to the efforts of Grosseteste; but the acquisition of the proper books and persons was a task that could only be undertaken by prelates and wealthy people.

But for educational purposes these Greeks and Hebrews were, for the most part, useless. They knew no grammar. As there were many laymen who spoke Latin very well and yet had no notion of the grammatical rules of that language, in the same way there were only very few Jews and Greeks who were able to teach the grammar of their languages in a methodical and rational manner. Among the

Latins there were many who could speak Greek, Arabic, and Hebrew, but how many of them knew, or could teach, the grammar of these languages? Not four.

Bacon must have early in life conceived the idea of supplying the deficiency, and providing his contemporaries and a future generation with, at least, elementary Grammars of the learned languages. He says that, although he had himself studied for forty years, from the time that he first learned the alphabet, he was yet convinced that within three months or half a year he could impart his own knowledge of the sciences and languages by oral teaching—provided he had first composed a text-book, and the student were earnest and willing. Under such conditions he would be able to teach in three days as much Hebrew as was wanted for reading and understanding all that was written by the saints and ancient sages in elucidation and correction of the sacred text. The student would, however, have to submit to the prescribed method. In three more days he would teach sufficient Greek for reading and understanding everything which pertains to theology, philosophy, and the Latin language. Whatever our opinion may be as to the sufficiency of three days for the attainment of even the most elementary degree, so much is certain that Bacon himself acted upon his suggestion that Grammars should be written.

There are no traces in Bacon's works to show that he was interested in the spread of a grammatical knowledge of modern languages. There can hardly be any doubt that he was an accomplished English and French scholar; and his remarks on the dialects of several European languages, and their grouping under distinct mother languages to which they are related, sufficiently prove that he had drawn them within the scope of his investigations. It is true he anim-adverts upon the commercial and international advantages which the commonwealth of the Latins might derive from the study of languages, but this fragmentary notice seems also to refer only to the general use which can be made of the ancient languages. In another passage he refers to the Russians as schismatic Christians, and says that, although they follow the rites of the Greek Church, their language is not Greek but Slavonic. He also makes some remarks regarding the mode of writing in use among the Tartars, and the writing in pictures in vogue with the Chinese. These observations, coupled with some illustrations in Norman French, and some allusions to modern Greek, about which more below, are all the references we find in his works to the languages spoken in his time.

Bacon considered Latin his mother tongue by the side of the language of the country in which he was born. The Latin he employs in all his writings is that of the thirteenth century, and is clear, grammatically correct, and belongs to the best specimens of mediaeval Latinity. He was thoroughly acquainted with a number of Roman authors, of whose works he makes ample use for the purpose of illustrating some rule of etymology or prosody. And although he complains that the advice given by Boethius and Bede to instruct youths in the writings of Seneca for the training of their morals was neglected, and that they were taught instead the fables and nonsense of Ovid, which are so full of irreligion and immorality; yet he himself did not hesitate to use Ovidian phrases and to cite his verses. Bacon's proficiency in Latin grammar will again be alluded to.

Bacon's intention was to compose grammatical manuals for the study of Arabic, Greek, Hebrew, and Chaldaean; for, after having indicated the necessity for the Latins to have a sufficient knowledge of the grammar of these languages, he prefaces his Greek Grammar and his grammatical treatises in the *Compendium Studii Philosophiae* with the remark that he dealt first with Greek grammar because it was the easiest, and more in agreement with Latin. This implies his intention of writing also an Arabic Grammar. There is no indication in any of Bacon's acknowledged works that he had accomplished his design. Nor can we at all be sure that his proficiency in Arabic was great enough. He says that he wrote Greek, Hebrew, and Latin, but not Arabic. But as he declares his intention of dealing with Arabic on the proper occasion (*locis suis*), we may rest assured that he had acquired some knowledge of that language also, albeit it amounted perhaps to no more than what he called the third degree.

With Greek it is altogether different. Here we have tangible proofs of Bacon's close application, and ample data by which to estimate the standard of his knowledge.

Let us consider the judgement passed by Bacon on his predecessors. Whenever he detects faults in their works, and attributes them to their insufficient knowledge of Greek, his remarks invariably proceed from his thorough mastery of the subject. On such occasions he does not assail the subject of his criticism with kid gloves; he shows him the mailed fist. He never derides, he scourges. Bacon enumerates the various directions in which the common crowd of Latin scholars wandered astray. In the first place, they took for Latin, or Greek, or Hebrew, or *vice versa,* words which were nothing of the kind. Secondly, they were at fault in their derivations, etymologies, and interpretations. Thirdly, their pronunciation and spelling were faulty. But it was only partly their fault. They were led into error by their foremost authors, Papias, Hugutio, and Brito. These were one and all liars. Hugutio was the worst; he was at pains to show that Latin texts were more reliable than Greek, and Greek more reliable than Hebrew, even though the Greek be a translation from the Hebrew, and the Latin translated from these languages. He wanted to saddle Jerome with the same absurdities of which he was guilty. He derived *dogma* from *doceo,* as if a word in an older language could have been derived from a younger; but, then, he thought *dogma* to be a Latin word. He derived the Hebrew word *Amen* from the Greek. Both Hugutio and Papias derived *parasceue* from the Latin *paro* and *coena = preparatio coenae.* Brito did not approve of this etymology, but he was no better; for he explained the word *Deus* as *dans aeternam vitam suis.* He said that $\theta\epsilon o$ meant fear. Hugutio and Papias said the same; and, Bacon regrets to say, Isidore likewise. These people were all Latins, and therefore ought either to have adduced their authorities or given the *rationale* of their derivations.

Bacon himself assented to other explanations of the word $\theta\epsilon o$. Either it was derived from $\theta\epsilon\omega$, 'to run' or 'to go round,' because God comprised and protected the universe; or from $\alpha\iota\theta\epsilon\iota\nu$, 'to burn,' because God was a fire, and consumed all wickedness (*aut dicitur ab 'ethin' quod est ardere; Deus enim est ignis consumens malitiam*); or from $\theta\epsilon\alpha\sigma\theta\alpha\iota$, 'to look,' because God considered and perfected all things before they were created. He says that these etymologies were correct and trustworthy, because they emanated from Johannes of Damascus, himself a Greek, and who was therefore able to interpret Greek words from the Greek.

Brito, *indignissimus auctoritate,* derived the Hebrew word *Gehenna* from *ge, terra,* and *ennos, quod est profundum,* an error shared by Hugutio. They both, with other *grammaticellae idiotae,* imagined the Hebrew word *arrabon* (Genesis xxxviii. 17) to be *arra bona* (*ut res quae datur pro coniugio, velre bona, non pro mala*). Other authors of Greek dictionaries also included this word, as if it were Greek. Hugutio and others showed what jackasses they were (*et in hoc ostendunt se esse asinos*) by averring that the purely Latin word *coelum* was *casa helios,* and Brito gave an alternative derivation of *tus, turis,* from $\theta\epsilon o$. Bacon relates that Johannes de Garlandia had told him that he had blamed our trio for spelling the word *orichalcum: auricalcum,* and deriving it fancifully from *aurum* and *calcum.* He further takes these authors to task for their blunders in spelling, scansion, and etymology, and adds to them a fourth culprit, Alexander Neckham, whom Brito quoted as an authority because he was his equal in making mistakes.

It cannot be denied that Bacon himself occasionally erred in the same way. Thus, in the **Opus Minus,** when describing Origenes' sixfold edition of the Bible, called *Hexapla,* he took this word to be a compound of *'hex' simul ordine conscripta, et 'aplum' idem quod simul.* Later, he must have become aware that *apla* does not mean *simul,* and we find in the Cambridge fragment of his Greek Grammar: *'hex' enim Graece idem est quod sex Latine, et 'aplum' idem quod simplex,* 'six translations in one', and not 'six versions simultaneously exhibited'. But he adheres to the erroneous derivation of the word. He gives the genitive of the word $\beta\omega\xi$ as $\beta\omega\acute{\epsilon}\kappa o$ after the analogy of $\nu\upsilon\xi$, $\nu\upsilon\kappa\tau o$, instead of $\beta\omega\kappa\acute{o}$. The false quantity in the word *mathesis* (*et ab hoc nomine mathesis media correpta*) he corrected himself. But such instances are extremely rare, and his corrections of the errors of his predecessors display his through acquaintance with Greek forms.

It is not only this intimate knowledge of the language, but also his keen critical powers that are proved by his inexorable condemnation of most of the existing translations. It would be superfluous to multiply examples; a few remarks will suffice. His horror of translations is particularly pronounced in reference to Aristotle, and he dwells upon one passage, which touches upon an important point of mediaeval controversy. He says that most of the commentators of Aristotle's *De Anima* (iii. 5) were under the impression that he meant to convey that the *intellectus agens* and the *intellectus possibilis* were both of them parts of the soul. This, he says, was an error; what Aristotle taught was that the *intellectus agens* came from without, and was not a part of the soul. The *intellectus agens* was, in the first place, God; and in the second place, the angels.

God's relation to the soul could be compared to that of the sun to the eye, and that of His angels to the stars. It was a mistake of *omnes moderni* to assume that the *intellectus agens* was a part of the soul; but those who were better informed did not share the error, such as the venerable Bishop of Paris, William of Auvergne, and Robert Grosseteste, and Adam Marsh; and when some presumptuous Franciscans asked the latter what the meaning was of *intellectus agens,* he answered that it was Elijah's raven. Bacon sets forth that the fault of these *moderni* lay in a misinterpretation of the translation of Aristotle's words. From the phrase *quoniam autem in omni natura est 'aliquid quod agat, et aliquid quod patiatur', ita erit in anima,* they concluded that the *agens* and the *patiens* were both in the soul, and that they formed parts of it. But if they had considered the whole of Aristotle's words in their context their tenor would have shown them the real meaning.

Having referred to a mistranslation in regard to the surfaces of plane and solid figures, he proceeds to point out a ridiculous mistake about the recurrence of a lunar rainbow. The words $\delta\iota\acute{o}\pi\epsilon\rho$ $\epsilon\upsilon$ $\epsilon\tau\epsilon\sigma\iota\nu$ $\upsilon\pi\epsilon\rho$ $\tau\alpha$ $\pi\epsilon\nu\tau\eta\kappa o\nu\tau\alpha$ $\delta\iota$ $\epsilon\nu\epsilon\tau o\chi o\mu\epsilon\nu$ $\mu\acute{o}\nu o\nu$ (*Meteor.* iii. 2) were translated so as to convey the meaning that a lunar rainbow could only occur twice in fifty years, whereas it is clear that Aristotle merely said that for upwards of fifty years the phenomenon had only been observed twice. It is unnecessary to give more examples of mistranslations from the Greek commented on by Bacon.

Of the Grammars of the four learned languages which it was Bacon's intention to write, we posses only a tolerably complete specimen of his Greek Grammar. This may be due to the circumstance that he wrote it first 'because it was easier, and more in accordance with Latin', and could not at a later time give full effect to his design. Or the reason may be that the fatality attaching to books played havoc with the others, and caused them to disappear. He desired his Greek Grammar to be useful to the Latins; a comparison of Greek and Latin grammar was therefore indispensable; and the grammar of all languages was the same *in substance,* the divergences being merely *accidental.* Besides, Latin grammar was modelled after that of Greek.

It is a characteristic peculiar to Bacon that he frequently repeats in one work, sometimes in an amplified, sometimes in an abbreviated form, and at other times even *verbatim,* that which he has dealt with elsewhere. This is particularly the case with Greek grammar. He deals with the subject in the **Opus Tertium;** a fuller treatment of the whole subject is preserved in part in the **Compendium Studii Philosophiae,** and a few brief remarks occur in the third part of the **Opus Majus.** The most elaborate treatise we posses is his Greek Grammar, a great portion of which is preserved in an Oxford manuscript, while a small fragment has been discovered in the University Library at Cambridge. Thus a chapter on certain long and short vowels, intended to correct some vulgar errors, is found in exactly the same form in the Greek Grammar and in the **Compendium Studii Philosophiae.** Another section in the Greek Grammar, dealing with the same matter, is nothing but an amplification of the sixty-third chapter of the **Opus Terti-**

um. Some points of orthography and scansion are dealt with in the *Compendium* and reproduced in the Greek Grammar, as is also another lengthy discussion on a similar topic. The lacuna in the Oxford manuscript at the end of Part II contained probably rules on punctuation, and may be filled in from the sixty-second chapter of the *Opus Tertium.* A further number of parallel passages will probably be found when the Toulouse manuscript, of which Samuel Berger has given some extracts, will have been published. For whether some parts of the contents of that work be ascribed to Roger Bacon, or to one of his followers, it is certain that the leading points originated with Bacon.

Such repetitions, such overlapping, are due to his own method of working, to a careless intercourse with friends, and to frauds of unscrupulous copyists. He says that many copyists were required, and many proofs had to be prepared, before the final copy could be completed in a finished form. He was very careful in the revision of the proofs, and it was often only the fourth or fifth that met with his final approval. But some of the copyists were not trustworthy, and occasionally kept the copies, or gave them away to strangers. Before delivering his works to the professional copyists, he was in the habit of composing several drafts of what he intended to publish; they were frequently disconnected jottings, written for the use of pupils, or at the request of friends. Not attaching much importance to them, he neglected them and did not retain them. But worst of all was the treachery of fraudulent copyists.

In the case of Bacon the further distinction must be made between cursory treatises on the subjects that came under his consideration and their exhaustive esoteric treatment that was to form his *Scriptum Principale.* His intention was to supply both classes of writings, and a repetition of the same matter must needs follow.

The Greek Grammar preserved in Corpus Christi College, Oxford, and published in 1902, is in the main a treatise on the comparative grammar of the Greek and Latin languages. Youths, when taught Latin, are first introduced to the elements of writing, reading, and construing easy sentences; the same method should be followed in Greek. Bacon therefore started with the Greek alphabet, classifying the letters, and giving their shapes, their names, and their numerical values. We must be rather doubtful as to the share the copyists bear in the shaping of the letters. They differ in form from those given in the manuscripts of the *Opus Majus* and in the Cambridge fragment. It is of interest to compare them with the characters exhibited in his specimen of Greek palaeography, at the end of the *Compendium Studii Philosophiae,* 'the earliest in all probability extant in Western Christendom,' and 'an instance of the minute accuracy with which he prosecuted these philological studies, and the care he had taken in examining manuscripts'.

The alphabet is followed by the accents and abbreviations in writing; the article, some directions regarding writing and reading, and, as reading lessons, the Greek text of '*Pater noster, Ave Maria, Credo, Magnificat, Nunc dimittis, et Benedictus, quae sunt fundamenta fidei*', with transliteration and translation. Then follow the letters of the alphabet and their numerical values. The names given to the numerals are, roughly, the same as in modern Greek: e. g. *ena, dio, tria, tessara,* &c.; *icossi, trianda, salanda, pindinda,* &c. Here Bacon takes the opportunity of complaining of the ignorance of bishops of even the letters of the Greek alphabet, which tends to interfere with a proper performance of an important rite of the Church. It is the duty of the bishop, when consecrating a church, to write with his pastoral staff the letters of the Greek alphabet in small heaps of sand or ashes. But, in their ignorance, they perverted the shape of the letters, with which, besides, they jumbled up the numerals.

Before proceeding with the rules of accidence, Bacon makes some remarks on idioms, on the necessity of comparing Greek and Latin grammar, on distinctions in reference to the 'voice', and on the difference between *elementum* and *litera.*

An idiom is the distinct way in which a race of men make use of a language, according to their customs (*Idioma est proprietas linguae determinata qua una gens utitur juxta suam consuetudinem*), another race using the same language in a different way. Each language has as many idioms as there are races that use it. All languages spoken between Apulia and Spain are *in substance* Latin, and diversified only as idioms. Chaldaean and Hebrew are idioms of the same language, in the same way as Picardian, Norman, Burgundian, Parisian, and French are idioms of the common language, French. It is the same with the Greeks; they had one language in substance, but various ways of using it. Of these, five idioms were especially famous: Attic, Aeolic, Doric, Ionic, and the idiom in use among the Boeotians. It was of the utmost importance to know this, because of its utility to the Latins. For, after all, Latin grammar was based upon that of Greek, and a comparison of Greek and Latin grammar is imperative for the understanding both of Greek and of Latin grammar; *and this consideration was the chief motive for writing the present treatise.*

In regard to the division of words, Bacon rejects some of Priscian's definitions and prefers those of Boethius, who was *majoris auctoritatis et in linguis et in scientiis.* A word (*vox*) is *articulate* when it can be written down in letters, whether it convey a meaning or not. It is then a λεξι. A letter, in writing and shape, is the smallest part of an articulate word; but its sound is an *element.* The sign α, when put down in ink, or by means of the style, is a *letter,* but the sound with which we express that letter by the voice is an *element.* Of course we must go back for such distinctions of Bacon's to the grammatical disquisitions of the Stoics. After this Bacon deals in detail with both Latin and Greek letters, with the classification of vowels and consonants, with spelling and similar matters.

The next chapter is devoted to a critical examination of a treatise on Greek grammar, which professes to be a translation of a work by Aristotle. Bacon proves that it could not have been written either by Aristotle or by any Greek; it was nothing but a compilation by some Latin author out of his own head. He investigates the order of sciences, in order to arrive at grammar. But grammar came first in the curriculum of instruction; it was therefore impossible for a pupil when learning grammar to understand the properties of other branches of learning which are taught at a later stage, and only a fool would begin his instruction in grammar with a division of other sciences. Everything set forth by that author, Bacon avers, was either false or futile or absurd; and this could be easily gathered from his (Bacon's) treatise on Metaphysics, and some other of his dissertations on the division of sciences. He would omit pointing out the errors the author committed in some of his high-sounding remarks on the effects of the celestial bodies on sound and voice. They had been refuted elsewhere, and, moreover, did not belong to grammar in the narrower sense of the word.

In a large section of his Grammar Bacon exposes numbers of errors in writing and speaking certain Greek words, particularly such as have a γ, although other words are also considered. The passage also deals with computation by means of Greek letters, and gives ample rules about the diphthongs. In his remarks about words with γ he follows an alphabetical order, but in regard to other words he states that he would not continue alphabetically, but put down the words as they occurred to him, as he intended to compose an alphabetical vocabulary of all Greek words that were in use with the Latin scholars.

We cannot say whether he completed it, but it is certain that he commenced it, for the grammatical treatise inserted in the **Compendium Studii Philosophiae** contains an alphabetical list of Greek words in common use with the Latins, another list of ecclesiastical terms, and a number of grammatical, logical, mathematical, and similar terms, without alphabetical order.

A lexicon in the possession of the College of Arms in London (Arundel, ix) was thought to be the vocabulary in question. But Dr. M. R. James, in a description and analysis of this manuscript, decides against the assumption. Dr. James is of opinion that there was no evidence to show that Roger Bacon was concerned with this lexicon; nor did the lexicon show any traces of borrowing from his works, and more especially his Greek Grammar. Dr. James supposes the author, or rather the compiler, to have been a member of Robert Grosseteste's circle; not Grosseteste himself, but a younger contemporary.

Another large portion of the Greek Grammar is taken up by Bacon's treatment of accentuation and prosody, and no wonder! The subject was of particular interest to him. Besides many other authorities he particularly refers to Augustine, who said that the rules concerning length and brevity of vowels belonged rather to the theory of music than to grammar. The musician provided the art, the grammarian was the mechanic. Not only song, but also metre, rhythm, and accentuation were properties of the human voice. Consequently length and brevity of the vowels, and everything appertaining to proper pronunciation, were parts of the science of music. But, Bacon complains, it would be much easier to impart to the people a sufficient knowledge of *Perspective*, although it be one of the important disciplines of which they knew nothing, than to teach them this particular branch of music, although everybody

learned the much slighted science of grammar from his youth.

Bacon follows up some definitions and rules with a list of errors commonly committed in metre in which Brito, Papias, and Hugutio come in for their customary share of vituperation. He corrects erroneous notions on the quantities of a number of words in use among the Latins, on quantities of vowels when followed by consonants, and on aspiration and accentuation.

Of the third part, which follows next, the first and second *distinctiones* and a portion of the third are missing in the manuscript. They must have contained the rules about the declension of nouns. What we possess of it is a continuation of the rules on the *genitive*. He mentions the system of declension, which is that of the κανόνε εισαγωγικοι of Theodosius, i. e. 35 masculine declensions, 12 feminine, and 9 neuter. He does not, however, quote Theodosius by name, but only says that the system is in use among the *Graeci moderni*. He himself prefers a simpler system of three declensions. An account of the *synaeresis* follows. Compound nouns, nine classes of derivative nouns, pronouns, and the verb are discussed at length.

In reference to the verb, Bacon assumes, after Priscian, thirteen conjugations, which he describes *seriatim,* and deals with the voices, moods, and tenses. He modifies his first intention of giving paradigms of all the classes of verbs. This, he says, was undesirable, first, on account of their number, and, secondly, because of the difficulty of understanding them; that this grammar was only elementary, and no beginner would be able to master them all. He refers students to his larger treatise, if they should want more information. The present one was written to serve the requirements of the Latins, so as to enable them to understand any Latin text, the expositions of the saints, the grammarians, the poets, and the other sages; and such students did not want to study all conjugations. He would therefore give only one conjugation in Greek letters, and another in Latin characters. He gives the forms of τυπτω, following one of those manuals in which the rules laid down by Dionysius Thrax and his immediate followers were rendered in the form of a catechism (ερωτηματα). He calls its author simply *Graccus*. No more has been preserved in the manuscript.

It is unnecessary to give a description of the Cambridge fragment of Bacon's Greek Grammar. It is evidently a draft of some passages occurring in the third part of the **Opus Majus,** or of his Greek Grammar. There is, however, one point of interest. In the interlineary reading lessons in the Oxford Grammar, the Greek text forms the lowest line, the transliteration in Latin characters the middle line, and the Latin translation the first line. Whenever the article occurs in the Greek text it is transliterated in the middle line, but in the first line it is only indicated by a blank space. But in the Cambridge fragment the Greek article is indicated by the syllable *ar = articulus,* e. g. *In nomine ar Patris, et ar Filii,* &c. It is noteworthy that the same method is followed in the Toulouse manuscript; and in the literal translation of the Hebrew Bible, a work of the second half of the thirteenth century, portions of which are extant in Oxford and Cambridge, this syllable is used not only to indicate the article but also the particle *eth;* for instance, *Creavit Deus* ar *celum et* ar ar *terram.*

It should also be observed that Bacon's pronunciation of Latin was that common on the Continent. Both his transliterations of Greek and of Hebrew show this. On rendering the Latin equivalents of the Hebrew vowels, he says that they have the sounds *quinque vocalium nostrarum* a, e, i, o, u, implying the sounds these letters have abroad.

This leads to the question of Bacon's pronunciation of Greek. It has already been observed that the names he gives of the numerals are, on the whole, those of the Greeks of his day. The same is the case with his pronunciation of Greek. Two centuries after Bacon, Johann Reuchlin, one of the representatives of the more successful renaissance of letters, introduced the style of pronouncing Greek which has since received the name of *Itacism,* and which was commonly called the Reuchlinian pronunciation, in distinction from the *Etacism,* introduced by Erasmus. Both modes of pronunciation were known to Bacon, and he gives the preference to the former, in spite of the tradition of the Latins.

Bacon's indebtedness to his Greek acquaintances should not be overrated. He owed them much, but he owed much more, in the first place, to the analytical powers of his vast intellect, and, in the second place, to his study of books on grammar.

The former enabled him to perceive the formation and construction of words and sentences when endeavouring by their means to arrive at the true meaning of the works he read. Hence his trenchant criticisms of such mistaken interpretations as might have been avoided if an adequate knowledge of the language had guided the reader or translator. His scrutiny of such Greek works as were accessible to him was carried on with conscientious care, both regarding the letter and the spirit. He was aware how limited a portion of Greek literature was at his disposal; and he never ceased to appeal for the search for and the acquisition of new books. He seems to have had no copy of Homer in the original; many other works he knew only from translations; but he had an intimate knowledge of the few Greek books that were within his reach, in particular some of the authentic and a few of the spurious works of Aristotle. His Latin reading had a much wider range. Hence it is that in his Grammar he demonstrates his observations on Greek orthography and prosody by quotations from Latin and not from Greek authors.

Bacon gives a list of the principal authorities on grammar consulted by him, and of the authors whose productions he refers to as standard works. He names Bede, Priscian, Donatus, Servius, Lucan, Juvenal, Statius, Horace, Persius, Juvencus, Arator, Prudentius, Paulinus, Prosper, Sedulius, Isidore, and Plinius. This list is not exhaustive, but he cites these 'as ancient and reliable authorities, who had a thorough knowledge of Greek grammar, and, consequently, of Latin grammar'. But he refuses to acknowledge Hugutio, Papias, and Brito as authorities. Priscian's name appears almost on every page of his Grammar, but he does not blindly follow him. He declares him to be more of a compiler than an author, saying that he reproduced the opinions of others, from which he selected what he deemed to be correct, but that he sometimes, though rarely, made mistakes, and should not be followed in every case. Servius, whom Priscian frequently cited, was a greater authority; so was Boethius; and whenever the latter differed from Priscian, his view should be adopted. But Bede's authority surpassed all of them. He was most learned in languages and grammar. Bacon thought him to have been older than Priscian. Neither among the 'Latin' poets nor among grammarians was there anybody greater than he; he was a much greater scholar than Priscian, both in theological and secular subjects.

Bacon also made use of other grammatical works, which he does not quote by the names of their authors, but simply alludes to as *Graeci auctores in grammatica eorum.* But whilst citing them, he deems it necessary, at the same time, to explain Priscian's rules, so as to save misunderstandings. Several of such manuals must have been included in those which Grosseteste had caused to be imported from Greece. The knowledge of some of these grammarians must have been rather feeble; for, misled by the similarity of the shape of some letters, they turned the *aorist* into *loriston,* and ο αυτό into ολιτο .

Some of the manuals that were used by Bacon undoubtedly followed the traditions of the Byzantine school. There are some points of likeness between his Grammar and those of Constantine Lascaris and Chrysoloras; but in other points they differ. Professor Heiberg urges that in the reading lessons the *Symbolum* particularly betrayed the Byzantine origin, because it tallies almost verbally with Lascaris, and Bacon reproduced even from his source the phrase εκ του πατρὸ εαπορευόμενον, without adding, as Lascaris did, the words και του υιου, according to the Latin dogma. But there are also important discrepancies; as stands to reason, considering Bacon's critical scrutiny of his predecessors; and, besides, he had probably access to some of the more ancient works upon which the later systems of grammar were based. We have already seen that Bacon rejected the κανόνε εισαγωγικοι of Theodosius (*c.* the end of the fourth century), Lascaris and Chrysoloras having other numbers. It is improbable that Bacon had any direct knowledge of Theodosius; if he had, he would have quoted him instead of the *moderni Graeci.* He seems, however, to have had some knowledge of Herodian (*c.* 160). He quotes him twice in his Grammar, and the latter passage displays a close acquaintance with at least a part of his works (. . . *sed necessaria est ratio scribendi quam hic volo inserere secundum quod in grammatica Graeca Herodiani diligenter interscripsi*).

The paradigms Bacon uses were, for the most part, the same which were in use from the earliest times. The verb τυπτω was used probably since the time of Dionysius Thrax (*c.* 100 B.C.); the paradigms for *verba contracta* and verbs in -μι, and at least some of the examples for the declensions, have remained the same ever since Theodosius, and the subjunctive is always given with εαν. The rare word βωξ was also a standard example; it was used by Herodian and Theodosius, and commented upon by Choeroboscus. The latter was also quoted in the aforementioned lexicon, whose author either had access to a copy of that author, or, as Dr. James presumes in reference to his citations from Pausanius the Atticist, derived his knowledge from some work in which Choeroboscus had been quoted. It has already been mentioned that Bacon had before him a grammatical catechism, similar to that of the Wolfenbüttel *Erotemata.* Dr. James informs us that a *liber de erotematibus* is also quoted in the Graeco-Latin Lexicon. It is therefore evident that such catechisms were known to the scholars that belonged to Grosseteste's circle.

From the introductory sentence in Bacon's Greek Grammar, it appears that he harboured the idea of including a Chaldaean Grammar in his *Opus Principale,* but there is no sign that it was written. He had a thorough knowledge of Biblical Aramaic, and knew the passages in the Bible written in that language. When reading the—for his age—modern expositions of more ancient commentators, he kept a critical eye on such passages as referred to Aramaic. In this way he was able to correct a gross misconception. These expositors had read in Jerome's prologue to the Book of Daniel that one 'pericope' of Jeremiah was written in Aramaic.

> All theologians understood that "pericope" to mean the Book of Lamentations; that word bearing the meaning of "small part", and the Book of Lamentations being the smaller of Jeremiah's books. These writers have themselves to thank for making such blunders; they will follow the vile and imaginary authority of Brito. Every Hebraist knew that the Book of Lamentations was written in Hebrew. Jerome's remark applied to one verse in the tenth chapter of Jeremiah (verse II).

Bacon reproduces the verse in the original Aramaic, with a Hebrew translation, and supplies both with an interlineary transliteration and a Latin translation. He observes that Chaldaean and Hebrew are merely different dialects of the same language; where the Hebrew says *Elohim* for *God, lo* for *no,* and *Samayim* for *heaven,* the Chaldaean says *Elaha* for *God, la* for *no,* and *Samaya* for *heaven.*

There are more data by which to gauge Bacon's attainments in Hebrew. We cannot tell whether he realized his wish of writing a Hebrew Grammar, but we know that he attempted it. The fragment discovered by the Reverend E. Nolan in the University Library at Cambridge is undoubtedly his work. The incentives to enter zealously upon the study of Hebrew were powerful for a man of Bacon's frame of mind. He was actuated at the same time by scientific, religious, and mystical motives. Science directed him to Greek and Arabic, religion led him, moreover, to Hebrew.

He was convinced that Hebrew was the language in which God had revealed to mankind His will and His wisdom.

> 'God has revealed philosophy to His saints, to whom He also gave the Law. He did so because philosophy was indispensable for the understanding, the promulgation, the adoption, and the defence of the Law, and in many other ways also. It was for this reason that it was delivered, complete in all its details, in the Hebrew language.' 'The whole wisdom of philosophy was given by God, who, after the creation of the world, delivered it to the patriarchs and the prophets. . . . They possessed wisdom in its entirety before the infidel sages obtained it, such as the famous poets, or the Sibyls, or the seven wise men, or the philosophers after them. . . . All their information about heavenly bodies, about the secrets of nature and the superior sciences, about sects, God, Christianity, the beauties of virtue, and the rectitude of the Laws, of eternal reward and punishment, resurrection of the dead, and all other questions, were derived from God's saints. The philosophers did not find them out; God had revealed them to His saints. . . . Adam, Solomon, and the others testified to the truth of the faith, not only in holy writ, but also in books of philosophy, long before there were any philosophers so-called.' 'Philosophy was developed by Noah and his sons, particularly by Shem; and all philosophers and great poets lived after them, and after Abraham. . . . Zoroaster invented the magic arts; he was the son of Ham, the son of Noah. Io, who was afterwards called Isis, the daughter of Inachus, the first king of the Argives, a contemporary of Jacob and Esau, taught the Egyptians to write. Minerva, the inventress of many things, lived about the same time. Under Phoroneus, Inachus's son, moral philosophy was first introduced among the heathens. Prometheus was the first teacher of philosophy, and his brother Atlas the first great astrologer. But he was preceded by the great astronomers, the sons of Noah, and by Abraham.

In this way, Bacon continues tracing the chain of transmission of philosophy, based upon the writings of his predecessors, mixing up biblical and mythological personages, and treating them after the method first introduced by Euhemerus of Crete.

All this wisdom, Bacon was fully persuaded, emanated primarily from the wisdom that was revealed by God in Hebrew. Besides, King Solomon, who was the second promulgator of philosophy, was possessed of great wealth, and was thus enabled to complete his philosophical work in Hebrew. No wonder, therefore, that Bacon was eager to gain a more intimate knowledge of the divine tongue.

There was another aspect of Bacon's religious convictions which turned his mind to Hebrew. It was his disgust at the corruptions that had crept into the text of the Bible, i. e. the Vulgate, which consists of the Latin translation of the Septuagint translation of the Psalms, and of Jerome's translation of all other books. The 'text' was overrun with errors, and worst of all in the Parisian copy. The eradication of errors from that translation was considered tantamount to the purging of 'the text of the Bible'. Even at the present day the term 'Biblical criticism', which denotes quite a different procedure, is sometimes applied to the correction of Jerome's translation. Before Bacon's time there had been no lack of *Correctoria* which attempted to restore the original form of the 'text'. It seems that in Bacon's time these attempts ran riot. He complains that everybody interfered with the text; whenever any one did not understand it, he altered it. Both the correction and the understanding of the text imperatively demanded the study of the original languages.

The mystical element in Bacon's nature also turned him to the study of Greek, and, much more so, to that of Hebrew. important mysteries were concealed in the numerical values of the letters; the spiritual meaning of the text was indissolubly bound up with the literal sense, and both suffered equally if the text was corrupt in most parts and dubious in many others.

As Bacon had turned to Greeks for instruction in Greek, so he consulted Jews for information on Hebrew. In both cases he points out the deficiency in grammatical knowledge on the part of most of that class of teachers. His estimate of the amount of knowledge attainable was the same for both languages; as is also his tripartition of the degrees of proficiency, his estimate of a sufficiency of three days of close application for the acquisition of the lowest degree, provided a manual had first been prepared, and the necessity of earnest study for thirty years, if a mastery of the highest degree were desired.

The extent of Bacon's knowledge of Hebrew may be gauged by those passages in his works in which he alludes to matters Hebrew, and by his fragmentary Hebrew Grammar. The evidence derived from the former source might induce us to form a low estimate of his Hebrew learning, but the question is whether we possess all the data from which to judge.

Two points offer themselves for consideration in this respect, both based on the fair assumption that Bacon was not behind his contemporaries in whatever knowledge of Hebrew they possessed. There was, in the first place, Bacon's elder contemporary, the *homo sapientissimus,* whom he described as a good Hebrew scholar, 'whose difficulties were very great on account of the want of Greek and Hebrew Bibles and dictionaries, which, it is true, existed in England and France, but were not accessible to him.' But if Denifle's assumption be correct, that this *homo sapientissimus* was the author of the *Correctorium Vaticanum*—whether his other assumption, that he ws identical with William de la Mare, be correct or not—he must have had such books at his disposal at a later date, for the *Correctorium* displays an intimate acquaintance with works of that kind. Its author had read the *Targum* (the old Aramaic translation); he quotes the *Peruš,* the 'Commentary', by which he either meant that of Rashi, or the commentary which existed before him, and was known under the name of *Peruš.* He knew the Mahberet, Menahem ben Saruk's Hebrew lexicon. He had consulted the Hebrew manuscripts of Spain, and distinguished between 'modern' Hebrew texts, 'old' Hebrew manuscripts of France, and 'old' Hebrew manuscripts of Spain.

It is unthinkable that Bacon, enjoying the personal acquaintance of a scholar of such eminence, and bent upon the same pursuits, should not have benefited by the opportunity, and made himself acquainted with some of the sources which the scholar he so much admired had made use of. It was only intercourse with Jews that could have brought such works to the notice of that author, and Bacon made ample use of that same medium of information.

This view is, in the second place, singularly supported by the latter portion of the afore-mentioned Toulouse manuscript. It contains a collection of letters, in which a questioner, or some questioners, ask for information on Hebrew subjects, and are answered by the other correspondent. The questioners did not know much Hebrew, some did not even know the Hebrew letters. It was quite different with the respondent. He not only knew Hebrew, but he also quotes the Rabbis, especially Rashi. Berger does not venture to say that this scholar who was consulted as an oracle was Roger Bacon, although there are many almost *verbatim* parallels in the latter's acknowledged writings. But if not Bacon, it was some one so closely connected with him that he might easily be taken for him. Both Denifle and Berger came to the conclusion that the respondent was the Franciscan friar, William de la Mare, whom they identified at the same time with Bacon's *homo sapientissimus,* and the author of the *Correctorium Vaticanum.* If William de la Mare was the respondent, it is clear that Bacon had been the master who was mainly responsible for the learning displayed in the letters. The concurrence of the responses with many passages in Bacon's works is too obvious to doubt it. And how can we be certain that the learned correspondent was not the master himself?

Roger Bacon deals, in his **Opus Majus,** elaborately with the subject of lunations, and explains that the Jews used the Metonic cycle of 19 years, or 235 lunations, and the mean lunation was therefore 29 days, 12 hours, and 793/1080 of an hour. He added a Hebrew table, which has not been preserved, and is full of praise for the Jewish way of fixing the calendar. In the Toulouse manuscript it is said that the calendar and the lunations had been more fully investigated by the Jews than by the Greeks or the Arabs. He, the respondent, had had some Hebrew books sent him from Germany by a learned Jew, who knew him only by reputation, and with whom he carried on a regular correspondence in Hebrew. If this was written by Bacon himself, it would corroborate his statement that he was able to write Hebrew. The respondent proceeds to say that these books were composed by Abraham, that they contained much information, and were provided with many tables. They were more useful on astronomical subjects than any which he had seen before. He had long desired to possess such Jewish books, and had written to a certain Jew in Toledo, in Spain, whom he knew, to procure them for him, but in that city no complete copy could be found. Berger conjectures that the book on the new moon was the *Kidduš Hàhodeš,* a treatise on the calendar, forming a portion of one of the larger works of Maimonides. The Abraham mentioned here must have been Abraham bar Hija, the author of *Sefer Ha-'ibbur.*

All this could very well have been written by Roger Bacon, and serve as evidence how hard he tried to obtain books, and how strong his desire was to obtain information from the Jews. It would show at the same time his acquaintance with such Hebrew works as are nowhere mentioned in his known writings. But suppose the correspondent to have been his pupil, the one passage on the calendar sufficiently indicates the source whence he had drawn his information. And it was only from Jewish students of Maimonides' works that this writer could have known of the division of the Pentateuchal injunctions into 'laws', 'testimonies', 'judgements', and 'precepts'. It is further noteworthy that these letters contain the Aramaic verse in Jeremiah, transliterated and translated into Hebrew and Latin in the same way as we find it in the *Opus Majus.* The description of the Hebrew final letters *(men aperia, men clausa,* &c.) is identical with that in the fragment of Bacon's Hebrew Grammar, as are also a few other grammatical points.

But apart from such indirect evidence, Bacon's acknowledged works amply show that he was competent to satisfy his own demands on a third-rank, and even a second-rank Hebrew scholar. Although he has added nothing to the stock of information, and not a single observation of his can perhaps be called original, he yet speaks with authority, and knowledge of the subject, when he explains derivations of words from the Hebrew, or exposes blunders made by some scholars. That he had a good notion of Hebrew grammar is sufficiently proved by his remarks in the third book of the *Opus Majus,* and by the fragment of a Hebrew Grammar discovered in Cambridge.

In the latter Bacon gives the names of the letters of the Hebrew alphabet and their sounds. He describes the ordinary and final letters in terms which answer to those used by the Jewish grammarians. True to his doctrine that there is only one grammar in *substance,* he tries perforce to find an analogy between Hebrew and Greek in his exposition of genders, cases, numbers, the article, diphthongs, and the preposition.

Accustomed as he was to classical and occidental languages, where each consonant is accompanied by a separate letter, which indicates the sound, he seems not to have had a clear understanding of the system in use in Hebrew. In that language only the consonants are written; the sound is only occasionally indicated by 'vowel letters', but usually by some strokes or points under or above the consonants, except in copies of the Bible designated for ritual use and books written for the learned, where such signs of vocalization are entirely absent. Such lack of understanding would be all the more strange if he really had been the Arabic expert he describes himself. He mentions the signs, and at the same time calls the letters *'aleph, ain, he, heth, iot, vaf,'* vowels, giving the word 'vowel' the same sense as in Latin and Greek: *a, e, i, o, u.* Thus, when the occasion arises, he inserts one of these letters where it is quite inadmissible, e.g. בנאך for בנך; אלאהים for אלהים, Bacon gives a fantastic explanation of the absence of vowel letters in the Bible. The Hebrews, he avers, omitted them because they did not want other nations to read their books, and when some 'wise philosophers who understood Hebrew' tried to translate the holy history, God punished them, as Josephus teaches us.

He ascribes to such secretiveness the circumstance that Babel is called Šešak, according to the explanation given by Jerome, who had himself followed the Rabbis. He fully understood the scheme of transposition of the letters of the Hebrew alphabet on which this interpretation rests.

As in Greek, so in his transliteration of Hebrew words Bacon gave the Latin vowels the sounds which they have on the Continent. The Hebrew vowels, he observes, have the sounds *quinque vocalium nostrarum, a, e, i, o, u,* implying the sounds these letters have abroad.

In Hebrew, there are two principal styles of pronunciation: the *Sephardic,* which was in vogue in Spain, Portugal, Italy, and the East, and the *Ashkenazi,* in use in central, north-east, and western Europe. Bacon follows, on the whole, the former mode of reading, which he must have derived partly from Jews, and partly from Jerome's commentaries. Might he not, perhaps, have seen a copy of the *Hexapla,* of which he gives so accurate a description, and been partly guided by the transliteration found there? He transliterates בַּ, בֶּ, בִּ, בֹּ, בֻּ, into *ba, be, bi, bo, bu;* once only ח and ט are rendered in the Cottonian manuscript *heis* and *teis;* in all other cases they are described as *cheth* and *teth,* and we always find *bet* and *tav.* Whatever pronunciation the Jews of England may have used before the Expulsion, it is evident that those consulted by Bacon had the *Sephardic* mode of reading.

It has already been noticed that Bacon considered it in the light of a religious duty to utilize Hebrew and Greek towards the establishment and understanding of an authentic text of the Vulgate translation. He sets forth that Jerome referred in his expositions to Hebrew and Greek at almost every word, and was always at pains to demonstrate his exegetical remarks by the languages. Bacon had adopted this principle, and adhered persistently to it. His intimate acquaintance with the text of the Hebrew Bible is especially conspicuous in a passage of the *Opus Majus,* in which he rectifies some of the innumerable errors of the Paris text, particularly in the matter of figures, e. g. that Arpahsad lived after the birth of Šelah 303 years, instead of 403 years; or that Re'u lived 35 years, instead of 32 years, &c. The whole passage is, as Mr. Bridges justly remarked, 'one of the many proofs of the care with which Bacon had collated the Septuagint and the Hebrew text.'

Much in advance of his age as Bacon was, he had yet as little idea of modern Bible criticism as he had of modern comparative philology. He urged the necessity of Hebrew for the correct understanding of the Bible, but he did not for a moment admit that it was allowable to alter a word of the Vulgate, even at the instance of a comparison with the original. He could not have approved of Stephen Harding's method of purifying the text. The latter knew no Hebrew, and therefore consulted the Rabbis; and he erased from the Latin text all such passages and verses as were not found in the original. The *Correctorium Parisiense* was the work of Hugo de Sto Caro, a man thoroughly familiar with the Hebrew language, who all along refers conscientiously to the Hebrew. The Dominicans continued his labours, in which they also displayed tolerable knowledge of Hebrew. But Bacon did not approve of such methods; to him it was not correcting the text, but corrupting it, and making it incurable; for it was not the question of applying Hebrew or Greek, but of the restoration of Jerome's text.

It was in this spirit that the author of the *Correctorium Vaticanum*—whether he was or was not the *homo sapientissimus* or William de la Mare—pronounced the warning that 'one must not be unfaithful to the Latin text on the testimony of the Hebrew or the Greek'. He opposed the correctors, especially Hugo de Sto Caro, who altered the Latin on the sole authority of the Hebrew, without the support of the manuscripts; and in the same sense he said, 'Beware of attaching yourselves too much to the Jews.'

This principle, not to be influenced by the Hebrew to such a length as to meddle with Jerome's text, closely linked Bacon to the author of that *Correctorium*. In adherence to this principle, Bacon praises and scolds at the same time a certain Andrew *(Andreas quidam),* whom he considers to have sinned in that way. I consider him to be identical with the Englishman Andrew, an Augustinian monk, who lived about 1150; he was a pupil of Hugo de Sto Victore, and is said to have written learned commentaries on the Bible and the Apocrypha. Bacon discusses the ambiguity of the Latin translation of Genesis ii. I, 2. The Latin words may be forced to mean: 'These are the generations of heaven and earth when they were created, on the day when God made heaven and earth. And all the vegetation of the field had not come forth yet,' &c. Or they may mean: 'These are the generations, &c., . . . on the day when God made heaven and earth and the vegetation of the field, before it had come forth on the earth, and all the herbs of the field before they were grown.' Bacon considers the latter meaning to be more in accordance with the Latin, but it would contradict the narrative of the first chapter of Genesis. He says that in the phrase *omne virgultum agri antequam oriretur in terra* the words *onme virgultum* were in the nominative, and in the sentence *omnemque herbam regionis priusquam germinaret* the word *terra* had to be supplied or understood as the subject to *germinaret.* Bacon adopts this interpretation, not only for the purpose of harmonizing the two chapters, but also in order to reconcile the Latin translation with the Hebrew text, and adds that the sense would be much clearer if we had the word *herba* in the nominative.

Bacon then mentions 'a certain Andrew' who had written the word *herba* in the nominative and inserted a negative particle to the verbs *oriretur* and *germinaret* 'quite in accordance with the Hebrew text'. How did Andrew, Bacon complains, dare to make his translation, which is not *nostra translatio,* appear as if it were ours, the authorized Latin text? His was neither a commentary nor a translation; it was nothing but a literal construing of the Hebrew. The worst of it was that many people attributed to Andrew an authority which he did not possess. Nobody since Bede had obtained the sanction of the Church to expound Scripture; and although Andrew was undoubtedly a well-read man, and probably knew Hebrew, yet for all that he enjoyed no authority; he could not be credited, but the Hebrew text must be consulted to see whether he was right or wrong. If he were right, credence was due to the Hebrew, but not to him; if wrong, he involved us in the danger of taking his text for ours. Neverthless, Bacon proceeds, Andrew had the great merit of inducing us to consult the Hebrew, whenever we meet with some difficulty in our translation. Thus, in our passage, and in many oth-

ers, but few people would have thought of the true meaning if it had not been for Andrew. We see how Bacon's love for the investigation of the Hebrew original neutralized his orthodoxy to a considerable extent.

In the same way as Bacon exposes misconceptions in reference to Greek, he also corrects false notions on Hebrew words. The seventh chapter of the **Compendium Studii Philosophiae** contains a list of words and names which were considered of Latin or Greek origin, but which were really derivations from the Hebrew. He sometimes exposes such absurdities in his usual robust style; for instance, as has already been remarked, when Hugutio and Brito and other idiotic grammarmongers explain *arrabon* and *Gehenna* as *arra bona* and *ge ennos.* All these instances exhibit Bacon as a thorough Hebrew scholar. The greater part of them refer to misunderstood passages in the writings of the exegetes, especially those of Jerome.

In one case, however, he discards his usual bitterness and contumely, and is even at pains to palliate the fault; and no wonder! It is this time an error committed by no less a person than Pope Gregory the Great. Bacon held Pope Gregory in great veneration, and fully believed that the latter's works, which were, after his death, in danger of being burned, were saved 'by a beautiful miracle of God'. Pope Gregory had quoted Job xlii. 4 thus: 'And he called the name of one *Dies,* and the second *Casia,* and the third *Cornustibii.'* These are meant to be the renderings of the Hebrew names, *Q'ssiah, Yemima,* and *Keren Happuk* (קציעה, ימימה, קרן הפוך). Gregory thought *Cornustibii = Cornus tibii,* a compound of two words denoting musical instruments (trumpet-fife), and observes that

> the translator rightly took care not to insert these names as they are found in the Arabic, but to show their meaning more plainly by translating them into Latin. For who does not know that *Dies* and *Casia* are Latin words! But as to *Cornustibii*—although it is not *cornus* but *cornu,* and the pipe of the singers is called *tibia* and not *tibium*—I suppose he preferred to state the thing as it was without keeping the gender of the word in the Latin, and to preserve the peculiarity of the language from which he translated. Or also, since he formed one compound word out of the two—*cornu* and *tibia*—he was at liberty to put both words, which are translated into Latin by one part of speech, in whatever gender he liked.

Bacon says that it was clear to any one able to compare the original Hebrew, that the text used by the Pope was corrupt; that the second part of the compound word was *stibii,* and not *tibii;* that the name was *Cornu stibii,* meaning a horn or receptacle for stibium. Bacon correctly traces the etymology of the name from the Hebrew, and adds that the term used here was the same as 2 Kings ix. 30, where we are told that Jezebel dyed her eyes with stibium. Bacon finds excuses for the Pope; the holy man's time was fully occupied, and he had not the leisure to collate many copies of the Bible to see what the Greek and Hebrew texts offered. Bacon reserves the indignation which he could not vent on the Pope for the 'crowd of modern theologians who disputed about things they did not understand, and persisted in defending Gregory's rendering'.

Bacon fell himself occasionally, though very rarely, into errors of the same description. Thus he warns his readers not to confound Horeb, the mountain of God, with the stone 'Oreb in R'phidim, from which Moses had drawn water; the former name being written with a *Heth,* but not the latter. As a matter of fact, the latter name is also written with a ח (Exod. xvii. 6), and Bacon evidently confused that rock with the rock of 'Oreb, צור עורב of Judges vii. 25.

Bacon nowhere mentions the Hebrew accents by name, the 'tonic accents' as they are called. As in Greek, he refers also to accentuation, aspiration, punctuation, and prosody in regard to Hebrew. He says that the Hebrew text contained many kinds of metre, and complains that the Latin translators lacked that sense for music which was possessed by the patriarchs and the prophets. 'The only way in which theologians could obtain a knowledge of Hebrew metres and rhythms was by recurring to the Hebrew original, and by studying that branch of music.'

But there is evidence to show that Bacon knew the accents. On mentioning Jerome's etymology of the name of Israel, as denoting 'Master with God', and not as others before Jerome had explained it as 'a man who saw God', Bacon enters into the reasons, which prove the latter derivation to be untenable. Since *Is* meant 'man', *Ra* 'seeing', *El* 'God', these commentators thought the patriarch's name to be a compound of these three words. Jerome, Bacon says, rightly objected to this derivation, because the name contained the five letters *Iod, Sin, Resh, Aleph, Lamet,* making up the name ישראל, 'Israel.' The other compound would have to consist of eight letters: *Aleph, Iod, Sin, Resh, Aleph, He, Aleph, Lamet,* forming the word אישראהאל. This would be 'Iserael', a word of four syllables, whereas the name had only three, because a dot under a letter denoted the vowel *i,* two (horizontal) dots *e,* and a stroke with a dot under it *a;* but the strongest argument was the sense of the word, which is explained in the verse itself. Bacon illustrates this further by reproducing the whole verse in Hebrew. The Cottonian manuscript not only gives the vowel points, but also most of the accents. Now it is well known that the copyists did not much relish copying Greek, much less copying Hebrew, and supplying of their own free will a Hebrew text with accents must have been the last thing any of them would have dreamed of doing. We may therefore safely assume that Bacon himself had added them. He dealt with this point in the ***Opus Majus;*** and in the ***Compendium Studii Philosophiae,*** where he repeats the discussion, he modestly declares that a fuller explanation of this difficulty would carry him too far, and he was, at present, neither obliged nor competent to enter into all the niceties of Hebrew grammar connected with the question.

Philology was only one of the many branches of learning that exercised Bacon's mind. Keeping this in view, and considering the scanty supply of books in their original languages which were at his disposal, and the conditions of linguistic proficiency of his time, his achievements must be looked upon as truly wonderful. He proved himself an independent thinker in his treatment of the philosophy of languages, but only within the groove in which the philosophers of his age moved: starting from *a priori* assumptions, and arriving at unverifiable conclusions. He showed himself a keen critic in passing in review the grammatical products which his contemporaries adopted as authorities, and on questions of etymology none of them was his equal.

His attainments, whether in classics or Semitics or comparative philology or the philosophy of languages, do not by a long distance approach the results of modern research and thought. It would be a sad testimonial to the progress of learning if they did; if six centuries and a half had failed to change the aspect of these disciplines beyond all recognition. It is so with all subjects of knowledge; given favourable circumstances, no one of them will remain the same, even after the lapse of a comparatively short period. This fact, instead of detracting from Bacon's greatness as a philologist, serves the more to throw his efforts into stronger relief Forty years ago Huxley said that 'our "Mathematick" was one which Newton would have to go to school to learn'. Then, at what shall Isaac Newton's 'mathematick' be rated, when those who come after us shall be celebrating the septingentenary anniversary of his birth!

William Romaine Newbold (essay date 1921)

SOURCE: "The Forerunner of Modern Science," in *The Cipher of Roger Bacon,* edited by Roland Grubb Kent, University of Pennsylvania Press, 1928, pp. 1-28.

[*Newbold was the Adam Seybert Professor of Intellectual and Moral Philosophy at the University of Pennsylvania until his death in 1926. He was a master at decoding ciphers, a lifelong passion, and he spent considerable time and industry deciphering the Voynich Manuscript—a discourse on natural science by Bacon, written in cipher, and purchased in or about 1912 by Wilfrid M. Voynich, a specialist in rare books and manuscripts. Newbold lectured on the Voynich Manuscript in 1921 before the College of Physicians of Philadelphia, and his remarks were published in the College's* Transactions *that same year. This same lecture was later published in his* Cipher of Roger Bacon *(1928). In the following chapter from that work, Newbold provides a detailed, enthusiastic overview of Bacon's accomplishment, hailing him as the forerunner of modern science.*]

Throughout the dark and turbulent stream of human history there runs a series, often obscured or interrupted but always recurring, of wholly beneficent discoveries, marking the successive steps in man's acquisition of control over the powers of nature. Some primitive creature first grasped a stone as a weapon, and thus made man a tool-using animal; another wielded a stick, discovering the principle of the lever; another chipped his stone, and introduced the cutting edge; another learned to smelt copper, and the age of metals dawned. Of these benefactors of the human race, few even of later times are known by name, and they receive but scanty honor. Not many statues are'erected to their memories, and seldom does anyone think of them with gratitude.

Still more seldom does anyone think of those men of genius, and there must have been many of them, who lived and labored for the advancement of knowledge, yet died in the bitter consciousness of failure. Some were intellectually unequal to the task they had set themselves; some saw their efforts frustrated by untoward circumstances; some succeeded in their efforts, but only to find themselves overwhelmed by incredulity, obloquy, even persecution. One such genius, whom his contemporaries could neither understand nor appreciate, is soon, I hope, to be accorded the honor which is his due.

Of all inventions, few if any have contributed more to the increase of knowledge than those of the microscope and the telescope. The telescope has extended the range of vision far out into the depths of space; the microscope has revealed the existence of the unimagined realm of the infinitely little, and often exposes to view the secret mechanism by which the processes of nature are accomplished. That both of these indispensable instruments were known to and probably discovered by Roger Bacon, and that by their means he made discoveries of the utmost importance, the Voynich Manuscript puts beyond the range of reasonable doubt.

Born near the beginning of the thirteenth century, Roger Bacon lived almost to its end He was a contemporary of that eccentric genius Emperor Frederick II; of Henry III, King of England, in whose unworthy cause Bacon's brothers fought and were impoverished; of his son, Edward III, "the English Justinian," who laid the foundations of the present system of English law and crystallized into being the English Parliament, ancestress of all the democratic governments of the present day. Bacon's life was passed at Oxford and Paris, the centers of the intellectual life of the age, and thus he became personally acquainted with its leaders—among them, to mention a few out of many, with Robert Grosseteste, scholar, statesman, Bishop of Lincoln; with Saint Bonaventura, the devout and mystical theologian, head of the Franciscan Order of which Bacon was a member; and in particular with Albertus Magnus, and probably with Thomas Aquinas. These two, the most renowned of the scholastic philosophers, were even then engaged in assembling the whole of knowledge, especially as recorded in the encyclopedic works of Aristotle, in order to show its harmony with the doctrines of the Catholic Church, and the system of philosophy which they built up is to this day, I believe, taught in every Catholic institution of learning.

In that age Bacon lived, but he was not of it. He belonged rather to our own time. The knowledge amassed with such toil by his contemporaries he contemptuously casts aside as little better than rubbish; it is founded, he holds, in the main upon reverence for authority, and reverence for authority but too often leads to little more than repetition of ancient errors. There is but one ultimate test of knowledge, experience, and but one way of organizing such knowledge into a science, namely, by showing its conformity to the laws of mathematics.

Thus Bacon lays down with an assurance which, in view of the embryonic condition of the physical sciences known to him, one can but compare to the intuition of a supreme genius, the fundamental principle of mathematical physics. Only less amazing are his bold applications of common-sense principles in the fields of textual criticism and of education, especially as regards the necessity of knowing the original languages of works usually read in translations, his appreciation of the need of endowing research work, his forecasts of the development of medicine in the direction of hygiene and preventive medicine, of the applications of chemistry to physiology, medicine, agriculture, and industry, and his visions of the contributions to human comfort which applied science ultimately was to make by producing a multitude of useful inventions.

Many of his theories, supposed facts, and forecasts were of course mistaken—how could they not be, in view of the poverty of the intellectual nourishment with which he had to feed his genius? The universities of Oxford and Paris were almost wholly given over to theology and the Aristotelian science and philosophy. Bacon mastered all that was then known of Aristotle, but Aristotle's method, for reasons which I shall presently explain, was of little assistance to him. At Oxford, Grosseteste, himself a scientific genius of no mean order, implanted in Bacon's mind many of the principles which were later regarded as original with his pupil, and also first introduced him to the languages and to the study of the non-Aristotelian science. Bacon learned Greek, and diligently sought out the existing remains of Greek and Roman science, and of the Arabic science which had been inspired by it and had recently been translated into Latin. Thus he learned the Greek arithmetic, the Hindu-Arabic system of notation and calculation, the Greek and Arabic optics, astronomy, astrology, alchemy, and medicine. He acquired considerable knowledge of Hebrew and Aramaic, and probably a little of Arabic. He even learned something of that strange Gnostic philosophy, the Kabbalah, which, after being handed down among the Jews by secret channels for a thousand years, was in Bacon's own lifetime being compiled into the *Zohar*.

In all these sources he found theories aplenty, but comparatively little of that empirical knowledge for which his soul hungered. So he sought it elsewhere. As Aristotle had done before him, he inquired among the artisans, farmers, old-wives, and other such simple folk. Each of them, however ignorant, knew something which the most learned scholars did not know. "From them," says Bacon, "I learned more and beyond all comparison more important things than from all my learned doctors."

Still unsatisfied, he ventured yet further from the beaten track, into fields in which no son of the Church could roam save at his peril. He studied the magic properties of herbs, the virtues of charms and incantations and the like, seeking out in all the forbidden books the secrets of Greek and Roman, Jewish and Arabic, magic and necromancy.

When writing to Pope Clement, in 1267, Bacon drew a sketch of the ideal scientist, ostensibly the portrait of an unnamed friend. The context indicates that Peter of Maharncuria was the friend in question; but one can scarcely doubt that, as he was drawing it for the Pope to contemplate and to admire, he must have hoped that the Holy Father would realize there was another man besides Peter who might have sat for that portrait. And as every line of the sketch can be shown to portray faithfully Bacon's own features, I need make no apology for quoting it in full. Bacon has been speaking of optics, and proceeds:

> I know of no man save one who deserves credit for his work in this science. In lectures and wordy battles he has no interest, but pursues his scientific work and in it finds contentment. So it is that all which other men are blindly trying to see, like bats in the twilight blinded by the setting sun, he contemplates in the full glare of day, because he is a master of experiment. Therefore by experiment he acquires knowledge of the products of Nature, of the things studied by medicine and alchemy, of all things indeed whether in heaven or on earth. He is in fact ashamed that any layman or old crone or soldier or rustic fresh from the country should know anything which he does not himself know. Hence he has peered into all the processes of smelters, of goldsmiths, of silversmiths, and of other workers in metals and minerals; he knows everything pertaining to war, weapons, and hunting; he has examined everything pertaining to agriculture, surveying, and other occupations of the countryman; he has even taken into consideration the experiments of witches and their fortune-telling and charms and those of magicians in general, likewise the tricks and illusions of legerdemain—so that nothing worth knowing might remain unknown to him and that he might know what to condemn as due to sorcery or magic. Hence without his aid philosophy cannot be perfected, nor can it be pursued with any good or trustworthy results. Moreover, as he is beyond price, so also does he put no price upon himself. If he wished to meet kings or princes on terms of equality he would easily find one to honor and enrich him; indeed, if he were willing to exhibit at the University of Paris what he has learned by his scientific work, the whole world would follow him. But because either of these courses would interfere with the splendid experiments which give him the highest pleasure, he disregards all honor and riches, the more willingly because he can acquire wealth by his science whensoever he will.

In the Gasquet *Fragment* Bacon gives a vivid picture of the difficulties with which a scientific investigator of the thirteenth century had to contend. After speaking of the dishonesty and untrustworthiness of most professional copyists, he proceeds:

> And inasmuch as besides copyists other persons are required who will keep watch on their dishonesty and negligence, who will not only correct the copies but are also expert in computations, calculations, and languages (for without these three nothing of moment can be accomplished, as will be made manifest from the books which I am sending your Glory), there is more labor in scientific work than any one unacquainted therewith could imagine. Furthermore, without astronomical, geometrical, and optical instruments, and those of many other sciences, nothing can be accomplished, for through these we acquire knowledge of many celestial objects and from them the causes of the things beneath them. But effects cannot be known without their causes, therefore without such instruments nothing of great moment can be known. One ought then to have them, and yet few of them have been manufactured among the Latin-using peoples. Also a plentiful supply of books is needed relating to all the sciences, historical records (*actorum*) as well as the works of learned men of old, and they are not to be found either in my possession or in that of any one else; one has to collect them from the libraries of scientific men in various countries. Furthermore, since authors contradict one another on many points and have made many assertions on merely hearsay evidence, it is necessary to ascertain the truth by experience of actual facts, as I prove in my treatise on the experimental sciences. For this reason I have very frequently sent beyond the sea and to various other countries and to the regular fairs that I might see the objects of Nature themselves with my eyes and test the reality of the created thing by sight, touch, smell, and sometimes by hearing, and by the certitude of experience, in cases in which the truth was not made self-evident to me by books, just as Aristotle sent many thousand men through various countries in order to learn the facts about things.

The general nature and range of Bacon's scientific work may be gathered from various passages in the books addressed to Pope Clement IV in 1267. He had been a hard student ever since he learned his letters, a period of about forty years, except that two of those years were devoted to the recovery of lost health. About twenty years were devoted especially to the study of science, and ten of the twenty to optics. During these twenty years he had spent on "secret" books, experiments, languages, instruments, astronomical tables, in forming friendships with scientists, in teaching his assistants the languages and the use of figures, tables, instruments, and the like, more than two thousand pounds, which, even if taken only as Parisian pounds, would be equivalent in purchasing power to about fifty thousand dollars of our money, an average of two thousand five hundred dollars a year.

The precise date of Bacon's entrance into the Franciscan Order is not known, but comparison of his various allusions to his past life indicates 1256 or 1257 as the most probable year. During the ten years preceding 1267 ill-health had made him an exile from the public lectures and debates of the University of Paris, in which he had formerly won no little reputation, and that same lack of health, combined with lack of money, isolation from his friends and collaborators, and the insistence of his superiors that he devote himself to other occupations, had compelled him not only to forego the composition of scientific works but also to leave incomplete and unused the "many useful and grand wonders of science" which he had brought together at great cost of time and money, partly from books and partly as the results of his own experimental work.

It is obvious that the greater part of the twenty years of work must have preceded, and the ten years of comparative idleness have followed, Bacon's entrance into the Order; the remaining ten years of the forty that have elapsed since his childhood were, presumably, those of his early education.

The motives which prompted Bacon, when forty years or more of age, to enter the Franciscan Order are entirely unknown, and I shall not venture to speculate upon their character. Whatever they were, the step must have proved highly detrimental to his scientific work. Undoubtedly his interest and belief in alchemy, astrology, and magic, must have brought him under grave suspicion of heresy, and his superiors could not have been disposed to encourage him in them. It is not probable that they absolutely forbade them but they refused him the authorization without which no Franciscan brother could write for publication, and they kept him, as above related, so busily occupied with uncongenial tasks, among which begging food for the support of the monastery at Paris was probably not the least uncongenial, that he had little time or energy for anything else. Bacon's frequent allusions make it abundantly evident how these restrictions galled his proud spirit, and one can imagine how eagerly he would have looked for some way of deliverance.

In the year 1265 a ray of hope dawned upon him. Guy de Foulques, or Guido Fulcodi, who had been Archbishop of Narbonne before his elevation to the Cardinalate, was in that year elected to the chair of St. Peter and assumed the name Clement IV. He was a man of superior ability, of pure life, high ideals, and determined will, had had a distinguished career as a soldier and statesman before his entrance into the Church, and had known of Bacon and displayed interest in his work before his election as Pope. Elated at the possibility of finding so powerful a protector, Bacon wrote him a letter, sent it by a friend, Sir William Bonecor, and authorized him to explain more at length to the Pope his purpose in writing it. That letter has been lost, but from the Pope's reply one may infer that in it Bacon spoke of his work and also offered the Pope certain remedies in connection with a crisis of some sort. The reply was written in June of 1266; the Pope asks Bacon to send the works which he understands Bacon had written and also to inform him as secretly as possible what the remedies in question were.

The despised and oppressed scholar was transported with joy. After only six months of preparation he wrote in one short year, notwithstanding the all-but-insuperable difficulties interposed by his poverty and by the opposition of his superiors, the three bulky works upon which his fame has hitherto mainly rested, the *Opus Majus,* the *Opus Minus,* and the *Opus Tertium.* With them he sent a fourth, which is supposed to be lost.

The purpose revealed in these works is one of sublime audacity. The obscure and oppressed friar, fully conscious, as he himself says, of his insignificance, of his manifold ignorance, of his tongueless mouth and scratchy pen, silenced, buried, erased in oblivion, endeavors in all earnestness to convert to his own point of view the Head of the Church, the Vicar of the Saviour, the Lord of the entire universe! To appreciate Bacon's daring, one needs a clear comprehension of the irreconcilable antagonism between the principles which he advocated and those that governed the age in which he lived.

I have said that the characteristics of Bacon's mind which made him alien to his own age and spiritually akin to ours are in particular his attitude towards authority and his appreciation of the importance of empirical evidence. Sweeping generalizations are often only partly true, but none the less they are indispensable if one is to express salient facts in brief, and I think that, if that qualification be borne in mind, the statement will not be found misleading.

In all ages the conduct of the mass of men is largely influenced by recognition of the authority of other men, but the extent to which authority is exercised, the individuals who are recognized as possessing it, and the reasons by which its recognition is justified, vary from age to age. In the thirteenth century European society was organized upon a feudal basis. Theoretically, supreme authority was conferred by God upon the King, by him upon the high nobility, and from them derived to the lower social orders. Every man was the "man" of some "lord"; his chief duty to society was that of obedience, within the prescribed limits, to his lord; the "lordless" man was an outlaw. The Church was organized upon similar principles, in a hierarchy comprising Pope, Cardinals, Bishops, Priests, Deacons, and "Religious." The habit of mind corresponding to this type of organization was reflected in the world of thought. The Church was accorded supreme authority in matters of belief. The truths it sanctioned were expressed not only in the Bible and in the decrees of Popes and of Councils, but also in the writings of the Fathers approved by the Church as "authorities," whose utterances might be quoted to prove or disprove any allegation of fact. In addition to the Fathers, certain secular and even non-Christian "authorities" were slowly winning recognition. Aristotle had but recently been accorded that rank, an influential group was striving for the recognition of Averroes and other Arabian philosophers, and Bacon complains that his own contemporaries, Alexander of Hales and Albertus Magnus, are already quoted as "authorities" in the University of Paris.

The only scientific method recognized by the Universities was essentially the method of Aristotle. Aristotle had taught that "science" in the proper sense is a body of necessary and eternal truths, consisting exclusively of certain self-evident principles together with the inferences which may be derived from them by syllogistic reasoning. Sense-experience is of importance as a means of access to the self-evident principles, but is of no independent authority whatsoever. Aristotle also recognizes the propriety of using in syllogistic reasoning, under certain circumstances and for certain defined ends, principles based upon authority, which he terms $\tau\alpha$ $\delta o\kappa o\upsilon\nu\tau\alpha$, and the method which employs them he terms "dialectic." But he expressly excludes from the scope of "science" both the principles and the conclusions deduced from them. The mediaeval Aristotelians, however, placed the authorities above mentioned on a level with intuitional truths as primary sources of knowledge, and sometimes sought to justify this modification in Aristotle's scheme upon Aristotelian or Platonic principles. But to sense-experience they conceded little more importance than Aristotle had done.

This overemphasis upon the deductive method is the fatal

defect in the Aristotelian theory of science. It is an excellent instrument for the classification of existing knowledge, but if not supplemented by experiment it will seldom lead to the acquisition of new knowledge. Wheresoever it has prevailed science has remained stationary, stagnant. And this is precisely the point in Aristotle's system against which Bacon directs his most telling blows. He by no means rejects the deductive method; he acknowledges its importance and employs it himself. But he does deny its adequacy, and he *places experience above it.* Experience is not merely a means of reaching intuitive principles; it is itself a source of certitude superior to that of intuition; it is indeed the *only* source of certitude; conclusions deduced from intuitional principles, even those of mathematics (!), must be verified by experience before they can be really believed. It is also the only instrument for the discovery of new truths, whether they do or do not ostensibly lie within the spheres of recognized sciences.

The principle of authority Bacon criticizes with equal severity. He accepts formally, and I think sincerely, the authority of the Church and the Bible, but rejects in principle that of the Fathers and the philosophers. He does not, of course, deny that in practice the individual scholar must rely to a large extent upon the opinions of his competent predecessors in forming his own. He had indeed, himself, no little respect for the Fathers and for Aristotle and is reluctant to differ from them, but he denies absolutely that their judgments are final. By numerous quotations he proves that even the greatest of the recognized authorities, such as Jerome and Augustine, repeatedly contradict both themselves and one another, and he does not shrink from the obvious conclusion that they are but fallible men. The principles laid down by such authorities must be tested by experience before they can be finally accepted.

The "experience" which Bacon thus recognizes as a third criterion of truth, in addition to the authority of the Church and the Bible, occurs in two forms, sensuous and spiritual. Sense-experience, which he often calls "experiment," includes both observation, and experiment in the narrower sense. That Bacon was aware of the importance of the experimental method is shown by his actual use of it, but it does not appear that he had ever attempted to define it and to distinguish it from mere observation.

By "spiritual experience," Bacon meant, in particular, that intuitional apprehension of spiritual truth which God accords by special revelation to certain individuals. His recognition of it is designed not merely to provide a place in his empirical scheme for his other two criteria, but also for the special revelations claimed by men of later ages. It is not unlikely that he had Abbot Joachim in mind, for whose claims, as it would seem, Bacon had no little sympathy. But he also included in "spiritual experience" that immediate intuition of generalizations which Aristotle had ascribed to the "poietic" or "operating" Reason, but which Bacon believed to be the immediate operation of the Divine Intellect in the depths of the purified human intelligence.

Bacon not only appeals to the Pope to accept his new principles as intrinsically sound, but also presses him to take at once certain steps to ensure their ultimate success. He

disclaims any desire to see them applied in any revolutionary way to existing institutions; he is quite willing that those who disagree with him should be free to act in accordance with their several convictions. But he implores the Pope to protect with his irresistible pontifical power Bacon himself and those who shared his views, that they may pursue their scientific work without fear of persecution, and also to provide them with the means essential to its prosecution—books, instruments, physical and chemical laboratories, and astronomical observatories. He sets before him all the inducements which he thought would influence him especially the great benefits which the Church would reap in finding the Faith buttressed by scientific knowledge and in arming herself with the weapons of war which science alone could provide wherewith to withstand the impending onslaughts of Antichrist.

While Bacon was well aware that his proposals were revolutionary and would be bitterly opposed by many, it may be doubted whether he realized the full sweep of the revolution to which their adoption might lead. He seems to have regarded his two ultimate criteria of truth, authority and experience, as coördinate principles, each independent of the other. His recognition of spiritual experience as an ultimate source of truth opens the way to private judgment in matters of faith; his assertion that it is a psychological impossibility to believe with full assurance anything not established by the evidence of the senses not only makes science independent of revelation, but implies the possibility of bringing revelation before the bar of science for judgment. It may be that Bacon, orthodox Churchman as he believed himself to be, never seriously contemplated the possibility of conflict between his ultimate sources of truth, but it is scarcely to be believed that in the animated debates of the University of Paris so vulnerable a point in his doctrines had been overlooked. Bacon must have known that this and many others of the beliefs to which he would convert the Pope, beliefs in astrology, for example, alchemy, and magic, in the influence of the stars upon the conception of Christ and the propriety of the Church's employing magic as a weapon against Antichrist, would be denounced by many and influential theologians as damnable heresies. He must have known that if the Pope listened to them rather than to him, his temerity in trying to convert the Vicar of Christ might well result in sending him to the stake.

The risk was great, but the issue was worthy of the risk. For the moment the mightiest power on earth—and no other power would suffice to inaugurate the reforms which Bacon had in view—was lodged in the hands of a man singularly enlightened, conscientious, strong of will. To win his approval might be difficult, but it was not beyond the range of possibility. Bacon saw the unique opportunity, and regardless of personal danger, seized it. If he had succeeded, he probably would have hastened by several centuries the dawn of modern science.

It is this that gives Roger Bacon his unique position in mediaeval thought. Of all the millions that lived between the downfall of the ancient culture and the dawn of modern science, he alone not only discerned clearly the intellectual evils of the age and pointed out the way of escape, but at the risk of his life strove to turn the tide of history into that new channel.

But Bacon failed. The *Opus Majus,* at least, reached the Vatican, for Monseigneur Pelzer recently discovered in the Vatican Library the actual copy despatched by Bacon to the Pope with his autograph notes upon the margin; but there is still nothing to show even that the Pope read the books, much less that he was favorably impressed by them. Only a few months thereafter, November 29, 1268, Pope Clement died, and with him died Bacon's hopes.

Of the next ten years of his life little is known. To these years are referred several of his works, notably (1272) the *Compendium of the Study of Philosophy,* in which the bitterness of a disappointed and despairing man finds vent in savage denunciation of clergy and laity, high and low alike, for their cupidity and viciousness. Nine years after Pope Clement's death the final blow descended. In 1277 the Bishop of Paris issued a sweeping condemnation of heresies alleged to be then prevalent at the University, especially astrology, magic, and Averroism. An anonymous reply, attributed with great probability by Father Mandonnet to Bacon, defends the study of science, including astrology and magic, and accuses the ecclesiastical authorities of ignorance and bigotry. Bacon had for years, by his repudiation of authority and pursuit of forbidden lore, been accumulating the materials for an explosion, and this audacious book was, in all probability, the spark that provoked it. In 1277 he was sentenced to prison by the Minister-General, Jerome of Ascoli, afterwards (1288-92) Pope Nicholas IV, and his doctrines were condemned as "dangerous." Only once thereafter, fifteen years after his sentence, his voice speaks again in *Compendium Studii Theologie,* recently published, dated 1292. Nothing is known as to the place or duration of his imprisonment, although it is quite generally assumed that he was released in 1290 or 1292, when, as is known, the newly elected Minister-General of the Order, Raymund Gaufredi, liberated other monks who had been sentenced at the same time and for similar offences. A confused and seemingly self-contradictory note in a manuscript of one of Bacon's alchemical works also attributes his release to Raymund. The best authority for the date of Bacon's death, John Rous, states that he was buried in the Grey Friars at Oxford, June 11, 1292.

The greater part of Bacon's scientific work probably was done, as I have shown, during the years 1237 to 1257. After he became a friar he must have been seriously hampered by lack of money and the opposition of his superiors even before his imprisonment; thereafter it is difficult to imagine how he could have carried on much important experimental work. As to the actual results attained by him during those years of labor, little evidence has hitherto been available. More than once he speaks of himself as being in possession of important secrets of science, which he feels obliged to conceal from the vulgar, and in many passages he specifies some of the marvellous achievements, possible or actual, of experimental science. Among them are explosives, incandescent lights, a small instrument for the multiplication of power, the use of mirrors and lenses to make small objects seem large and large small, distant objects to seem near and near distant, to make images appear in the air, and to set fire to distant objects by focussing the rays of the sun upon them. It is not impossible that these discoveries were known to him. But these statements are associated with others which cannot be so interpreted, as, for example, that a magnet attracts all metals as well as iron, that vinegar attracts a falling stone, that the severed parts of plants and animals exert reciprocal attraction one upon another. It is indeed quite evident that Bacon had been so deeply impressed by discoveries actually known to him that he had adopted an attitude of uncritical credulity as regards alleged achievements of science; he was, as he frankly admits, ready to believe anything of the kind if reported upon what he took to be good authority. He seems also to have been willing to accept as accomplished fact many achievements which were as yet merely inferred, from accepted principles, to be possible, and as the accepted principles were often quite wrong, some of Bacon's predictions and assertions seem, even in this age of invention, absurdly mistaken. One is not, therefore, justified in taking those of his statements which seem to imply knowledge of the microscope and telescope as affording trustworthy evidence that he had any empirical knowledge of those instruments.

There are, however, certain other considerations, hitherto generally ignored by writers on the subject, which make it probable that Bacon's statements suggesting empirical knowledge of the microscope and the telescope are something more than mere deductive forecasts. These considerations tend, indeed, to show that Bacon was the first man known to us, with the possible exception of his friend Peter of Maharncuria, who possessed the qualifications which the discoverer of those instruments should possess.

Bacon, of course, shared his contemporaries' knowledge of the magnifying properties of the simple lens and of concave, spherical, and parabolic mirrors. These had been known for centuries and are, for example, fully explained by geometrical principles in the chief authority used by Bacon, Alhazen. Some of these explanations had already been formulated in the terms still used, *e. g.,* that the apparent size of the object depends upon the size of the visual angle, and that the size of that angle is modified by convex and concave mirrors and by lenses.

But Alhazen treats these properties merely as capable of causing illusions of vision; neither he nor Vitellio betrays any consciousness of the possibility of applying them to the practical end of increasing the power of vision as regards very small or very distant objects. This idea was perfectly familiar to Bacon. He recurs to it in his works again and again. He believed that telescopes had been made in the past; that they had, for example, been used by Julius Caesar in order to spy upon his enemies in Britain from the coasts of France, and was eager to see them again constructed in order to aid the Church in her war against Antichrist.

The failure of Bacon's predecessors to refer to this important possible application of optical theory to practice is not to be explained by mere preoccupation with theory, for they devote considerable space to the no less practical application of theory to the construction of burning mirrors, but by the fact that the idea never had occurred to them. Yet the honor of first conceiving it does not belong to Bacon, but to his great teacher, Robert Grosseteste, who, in his treatise *On the Rainbow and the Mirror,* deduces this possibility from the laws of optics and states it in language that leaves nothing to be desired in clearness and breadth of generalization. In fact, the passage so often quoted to prove Bacon's knowledge of the microscope and telescope is nothing more than a condensed quotation from Grosseteste's work.

It would, then, appear that Bacon and his friend Peter had a definite conception of the end to be attained, an eager desire to attain it, and the greater part of the requisite theoretical knowledge. There remains one other essential condition, command of the practical mechanical skill without which such instruments could not be made. There can be no doubt that at that time such skill was rare in western Europe. Bacon himself says: "These instruments are not made among the Latin-using peoples and could not be made (*fierent*) for two hundred pounds; no, nor for three hundred." It was no doubt for this reason that Peter of Maharncuria made with his own hands the first concave parabolic mirror made in Europe and that Bacon himself was compelled to manufacture his own mirrors. It is likely that the spherical crystal lens which he sent the Pope as a gift, by John, was also his own handiwork. At all events one may infer that such a lens was a rarity which the Pope probably would not possess and could not easily procure, and also that Bacon either had or could procure others.

Since the first concave parabolic mirror was not made until 1268, it follows that Bacon could not have had a mirror of that type wherewith to experiment at an earlier date, but it by no means follows that he had no concave spherical mirror; on the contrary it is probable that the comparatively easy task of making the letter was successfully accomplished before the more difficult was undertaken. And if he possessed lenses and concave spherical mirrors, provided the latter were small portions of spheres of large radius, he had the materials, necessary to the discovery of the compound microscope, the refracting and the reflecting telescope. For, although a parabolic mirror makes a better reflector for a telescope than a spherical, one of the latter type may be so made as to give very satisfactory results. Sir Isaac Newton, indeed, who rediscovered the reflecting relescope, always used in his instruments a mirror of this kind.

If then Bacon had the fundamental theoretical principles, the requisite mechanical skill, a clear conception of the end to be attained, and a determination to succeed, it is not in the least improbable that he did succeed.

But the question is not one of mere probability. It has long been known that there exists direct, positive, and uncontradicted evidence to the fact that Bacon left in writing instructions for the making of a "perspective glass" or reflecting telescope, and that, in accordance with those instructions, Leonard Digges made such a telescope prior to 1571. Digges's telescope was constructed of mirrors set at due angles, one to the other, together with a lens "for the multiplications of beames," that is, for the magnification of the focal image produced by the concave mirror. It was

of sufficient power to bring out the details of objects not clearly distinguished by the naked eye at a distance of seven miles with a degree of distinctness which was satisfactory to its manufacturer and his friends.

Leonard and Thomas Digges belonged to a Kentish family of gentry which had played an honorable part in the history of England for more than two hundred years. They were themselves sound scholars, reputed the best mathematicians of their time in England and highly esteemed by such shrewd judges of character as Sir Nicholas Bacon and Sir Francis Walsingham. Their evidence, until discredited by more trustworthy evidence to the contrary, is entitled to full credence, and establishes the fact that Roger Bacon left intelligible instructions in writing for the construction of a reflecting telescope.

This conclusion is confirmed by the legend attached to Bacon's drawing of a spiral nebula in the Voynich manuscript, which, if it has been correctly deciphered, states that the object in question was seen "in a concave mirror," that is, a reflecting telescope. But this legend is so difficult to read that I would not adduce it as independent evidence of Bacon's possession of a telescope until the reading has been revised and verified.

That Bacon possessed a telescope I regard as an established fact, independently of the new evidence afforded by the Voynich manuscript. But for his possession of a compound microscope, or even of a simple microscope of sufficient power to enable him to make discoveries of real importance, there has been hitherto no evidence at all. At most one may say that, since he had lenses and was familiar with the idea of arranging them in such manner as to increase the size of the visual angle, there is no improbability in the hypothesis that he succeeded in so arranging them as to make the first compound microscope.

The doubt that has overhung the subject is now, in large part, dispelled by Mr. Voynich's discovery. That the author of the manuscript possessed both a telescope and a microscope, both of considerable power, is established by the drawings which it contains. That the author was Roger Bacon is established by the fact that the alphabets which I worked out from the Key on the last page of the manuscript, when applied to the cipher elements interpolated into the Key, spelled out the name *R Baconi*.

But whether the microscope with which he saw the spermatozoa and the cells which he has so clearly depicted in the drawings was of the simple or the compound type will remain an open question until the manuscript has been deciphered. Some students are of the opinion that a simple lens of high power would have sufficed; whether this is the case or not I must leave to the decision of those more competent to judge than I am.

It would appear, then, that it was only during the twenty years from 1237 to 1257 that Bacon enjoyed comparative freedom and possessed sufficient money for the prosecution of his scientific work. During those years he made what he regarded as scientific discoveries of the utmost importance, and it is extremely probable that the telescope and the microscope, in some form, were among them. There after, for thirty-five years or more, he worked, when permitted to work at all (for at least some of those years were passed in prison), under severe restrictions, closely watched by suspicious and hostile eyes. The majority of his contemporaries, and very many among those of position and power, would have seen in his achievements conclusive proof of commerce with the devil, and many, even of the more enlightened, would have found in his teachings equally good reasons for sending him to the stake. He must, therefore, as a mere ordinary precaution, have been compelled to keep these discoveries secret, either locked up in his own breast or at most communicated to a few trustworthy friends. What would have been his reaction against such circumstances as these? What course of action would they have driven him to adopt?

In the Voynich manuscript is found the answer to these questions, but any one familiar with Bacon's works could have predicted his course of action without this concrete evidence of what he actually did do.

Bacon's reticence about his discoveries, even before he entered the Franciscan Order, was not entirely, nor, I think, chiefly, due to fear of persecution; it was grounded in his most sacred convictions. He was profoundly religious; in everything he saw the hand of God. The mere fact that the secrets of Nature had then so long been hidden is to him conclusive proof that God wills it so to be. The solitary scholar who succeeds in lifting a corner of the veil has, he believed, been admitted by God to His confidence, and is thereby placed under the most solemn obligation conceivable to make no use of his knowledge which God would not approve. Especially must he be careful not to betray it to the vulgar. God has indeed Himself, with special regard for this contingency, directly inspired scientific men, when writing of their discoveries, to conceal them either in obscure language such as was used by philosophers, or in peculiar technical terms such as were used by alchemists, *or in cipher.*

That Bacon had devoted much study to the subject of ciphers is apparent from the eighth chapter of his **Letter on the Secret Works of Art and the Nullity of Magic,** in which he enumerates and describes no less than seven modes of concealing ideas. "The man is insane who writes a secret in any other way than one which will conceal it from the vulgar and make it intelligible only with difficulty even to scientific men and earnest students. On this point the entire body of scientific men have been agreed from the outset, and by many methods have concealed from the vulgar all secrets of science. For some have concealed many things by magic figures and spells, others by mysterious and symbolic words. For example, Aristotle in the *Book of Secrets* says to Alexander, 'O Alexander, I wish to show you the greatest secret of secrets; may the Divine Power help you to conceal the mystery and to accomplish your aim. Take therefore the stone which is not a stone and is in every human being and in every place and at every time, and it is called the Egg of the Philosophers, and Terminus of the Egg.' Innumerable examples of the kind are to be found in many books and divers sciences, veiled in such terminology that they cannot be understood at all without a teacher. The third method of concealment which they have employed is that of writing in different

ways, for example, by consonants alone, so that no one can read it unless he knows the words and their meanings. In this way the Hebrews and the Chaldaeans and Syrians and Arabs write their secrets. Indeed, as a general thing, they write almost everything in this way, and therefore among them, and especially among the Hebrews, important scientific knowledge lies hidden. For Aristotle in the book above mentioned says that God gave them all scientific knowledge before there were any philosophers, and that from the Hebrews all nations received the first elements of philosophy. . . . In the fourth place, concealment is effected by commingling letters of various kinds; it is in this way that Ethicus the astronomer concealed his scientific knowledge by writing it in Hebrew, Greek, and Latin letters in the same written line. In the fifth place, certain persons have achieved concealment by means of letters not then used by their own race or others but arbitrarily invented by themselves; this is the greatest obstacle of all, and Artephius has employed it in his book *On the Secrets of Nature.* In the sixth place, people invent not characters like letters, but geometrical figures which acquire the significance of letters by means of points and marks differently arranged; these likewise Artephius has used in his science. In the seventh place, the greatest device for concealment is that of shorthand, which is a method of noting and writing down as briefly as we please and as rapidly as we desire; by this method many secrets are written in the books of the Latin-using peoples. I have thought fit to touch upon these methods of concealment *because I may, perhaps, by reason of the importance of my secrets, employ some of these methods,* and it is my desire to aid in this way, at least *you,* to the extent of my ability."

It is quite characteristic of Bacon that this specious pretence of good-will really masks a deliberate intention to deceive, for the list contains not a hint which would aid any one in unravelling the system of ciphers which he himself uses; it is indeed drawn up expressly to mislead the would-be decipherer by directing his attention to forms of cipher which have no place in that system.

Finally, we know that Bacon was deeply concerned to hand down to future generations the results of his labors. The whole burden of the voluminous work addressed to Pope Clement in 1267 is for official recognition of that work, for complete reformation of the conditions under which it was prosecuted, for repression of ignorant opposition, for endowment of research. But long before his appeal to the Pope, Bacon had taken steps to ensure the perpetuation of his ideals. He had probably taken into his confidence a few friends of his own generation, but he had certainly looked beyond his generation. He mentions specifically two boys whom he had trained in his methods, and it is not unlikely that there were others. One of these two, John, Bacon says he found on the streets of Paris at the age of fifteen, penniless and starving. For six years he has provided him with food, clothing, and education, and now, at the age of twenty-one, he sends him to Rome to the Pope as his trusted representative and bearer of the most precious of his manuscripts, informing the Pope that John is more competent than any living scholar, however learned, to explain to him anything he may find difficult of comprehension. Bacon's object in training these boys, he himself explains, was that "they might be useful vessels in the Church of God in ordering aright, by the grace of God, the entire course of study of the Latin-using peoples." In other words, they were to be Bacon's torchbearers, handing on to the next generation the flame kindled and nurtured by him, the spirit of pure science as we understand it today.

It was then, in all probability, for John or for some other such trusted friend or friends that Bacon wrote this precious manuscript, which now, after more than six hundred years of concealment, has been rescued by the intuitive genius of Mr. Voynich from imminent peril of destruction, and has been brought to light for the instruction of our own generation. Twenty years of free and independent research, during which he had often experienced that rapture of discovery which he so feelingly describes, had been followed by long years of hampering restrictions, enforced silence, and daily intensified despair. He felt himself buried alive, and the fruits of his labors seemed destined to be finally buried with him in the Friary Church at Oxford. It was under these circumstances that he conceived the plan which was to thwart his opponents. He had long since devised and used a cipher of extraordinary ingenuity in which at once to record his discoveries and to conceal them from prying eyes. He resolved to embody in a single work, concealed in that cipher, his most important discoveries together with his own interpretation of their significance, to provide it with a key so constructed that it could be understood and used only with the aid of oral instruction, and to entrust the secret of its use to some faithful friend in the hope that in a more sympathetic age the fruits of his labors would come to light. That age was not to dawn as soon as he had hoped, and the secret probably died with the friend with whom he entrusted it. But at last, after the lapse of more than six hundred years, the dawn has come and the secret of the cipher has been unravelled. Difficulties, formidable difficulties, still bar the way to the reading of Bacon's manuscript, but they are less formidable than those which have been overcome. These also must be overcome before the full story can be told. But even with the text unread the drawings alone throw a flood of light upon the achievements of Roger Bacon. They confirm to the full the inference drawn by a few scholars from existing evidence, but denied by the majority, that he possessed and was probably the discoverer of the telescope and the microscope; they prove that he had seen anatomical and astronomical objects never seen by the human eye before, and not to be seen again for centuries, and show that he is here trying to weave them into and interpret them by a preconceived system of ideas drawn in the main from the Platonic tradition. Roger Bacon at last stands revealed as one of the greatest of the many men of genius born of the gifted English race: the true Forerunner of Modern Science.

Robert Steele   (essay date 1921)

SOURCE: "Roger Bacon and the State of Science in the Thirteenth Century," in *Studies in the History and Method of Science, Vol. II,* edited by Charles Singer, Oxford at the Clarendon Press, 1921, pp. 121-50.

[*Steele was one of the editors of the twelve-volume* Opera Hactenus Inedita Fratris Rogeri Baconis *(1905-40). In the following excerpt, he places Bacon within the context of his world and of his scholarly contemporaries, summarizing Bacon's contributions to knowledge in several fields of learning.*]

In estimating Bacon's position among the men of his own time it is important to remember, first of all, the complete originality of his scheme. His great work, unfinished though it most probably was, and almost beyond the powers of any one unaided scholar to complete, the ***Compendium Studii Philosophie*** or ***Theologie,*** as the case may be, was as distinct in kind as in form from the works of his great contemporaries. . . . [His] was an age of encyclopaedias, but none of them were independent in form. Albert's life-work consisted in a series of comments on the words of Aristotle, following the order of his text with occasional excursuses when the subject seemed to suggest them, but breaking no new ground, and making no rearrangement of his matter. The great work of St. Thomas is conditioned by the *Sentences,* following its order with more originality and power than Albert, but, after all, adopting another man's scheme. His physics are mere commentaries on the text of Aristotle. On the other hand, the encyclopaedia of Vincent of Beauvais owes nothing of its arrangement to Aristotle, and comparatively little to its early forerunners, and was, so far, original. But there its originality ceased: it was merely a collection of facts and dicta collected from approved authors by the industry of a small college of clerks, and arranged under convenient headings. It added nothing to human knowledge, no inspiration for the progress of thought.

Bacon's schematic arrangement was not only unparalleled among the writers of his time; it was absolutely new. Nothing like it had been devised since the time of Aristotle, and it had the advantage of not being obliged to combat a large number of exploded hypotheses. The whole system of human thought was re-cast, and the plan simplified to an extraordinary degree to meet the necessities of the age. It may be that the framework of his scheme owed something to Al Farabi's *de Scienciis,* or to Avicenna, but in its conception and execution its originality is manifest. His plan has already been described, its execution was to be marked by the most rigorous economy. Everything superfluous or unnecessary to the development of the argument was to be cut away; all the excrescences which dialectical skill had embroidered on the simplest notions were to be discarded. Bacon did not exclude the notion of special treatises ancillary to the main lines of his course, but he did not regard them as necessary to every pupil. He thought it more necessary, for example, that the results of geometry should be known as a whole, than that the pupil should be able to prove the fifth proposition and be ignorant of the sixth book of Euclid.

The foundation of his system was laid on an accurate study of language: 'Notitia linguarum est prima porta sapientie.' Latin, of course, was taken for granted like English or French (is it, by the way, noticed that English is spoken by a Norman family as early as 1270?). But Latin alone was no sufficient key to the treasury of knowledge:

its vocabulary was too limited, the masterpieces of the world's teaching were either not translated into it, or were so badly translated that they were wholly misleading to such teachers and taught as attempted to profit by them. We need not labour the point as Bacon had to do; the fact remains that no mediaeval translation of Aristotle or his commentaries is now consulted, except as a curiosity. Bacon's study of languages, *Grammatica,* included not only the modern Philology but also a strictly utilitarian Logic and Dialectic, sufficient for the study of mediaeval science which was to follow: 'Grammatica et logica priores sunt in ordine doctrine.' We have a great part of Bacon's teaching on the subject, scattered over many writings. His main work was destructive; the schools were lumbered with inefficient text-books and antiquated errors. After that came reconstruction, 'secundum linguas diversas prout valent immo eciam necessarie sunt studio Latinorum'; Greek, Hebrew, and Arabic. He recognized three stages in the knowledge of languages, looking at the question from the point of view of actual life, not of a teacher. The first was that of a man who recognizes that a word is Greek, Hebrew, &c., can read it and even pronounce it, knows approximately what grammatical forms it may take, and so on: something like a man who can read enough German to know the names of the streets and the directions on the tramcars, but cannot speak the language. This is the sort of knowledge of Hebrew or Greek which Bacon pledged himself to impart in three days, when writing in his *Opus Tertium* and elsewhere. The second stage of knowledge was the power to read and understand in an ordinary way. 'Certes,' he says, 'this is difficult, but not so difficult as men believe.' His third stage is only reached when the student can talk and write and preach in the foreign language as in his own. The only grammars actually preserved to our own day which have been identified are the Greek and a fragment of the Hebrew. It is doubtful whether he ever knew Arabic or composed a grammar of that language. He certainly knew Chaldaic enough to explain its relation to and difference from Hebrew. His Greek Grammar is a very remarkable one for the time, even if it be true that it is founded on a Byzantine original. As we have it, the work is not complete, and the study of Greek made no progress in this country for nearly two centuries and a half.

This, then, is his first distinction in the study of languages, that he laid down the principle that every language has an individuality of its own, and that the grammar appropriate for one of them, say Latin, would not lend itself to the study of another, such as Greek. It is a principle which was only recognized in practice towards the end of the nineteenth century, and is still disregarded by many writers. But he was also distinguished as a critic.

All human knowledge was, in his day, assumed to lead up to the study of theology—the queen of sciences. Whatever progress was made on the great lines of modern thought was made, not with that aim, but with the intention of facilitating the formation of right conclusions as to the relation between God and man. If we are to undervalue our predecessors on this account, we need not study the thought of the Middle Ages. Bacon's criticism of his contemporaries was actuated by the thought that they were

bad teachers because they were insufficiently taught, that they taught in error because they were unable to test the truth of the maxims they repeated. His zeal for truth, his application of the tests of truth, remain of value if his conception of the highest truths no longer satisfies us. His criticism was applied to the text of the Vulgate; the principles of textual criticism he laid down are of universal application.

A large part of Bacon's published work on the subject is taken up with the proofs of the corrupt state of the Vulgate text, made worse by the number of correctors, for the most part ignorant of both Greek and Hebrew. More than that, many of these corrections would not have been made if the correctors had even consulted a good Latin grammar. The scheme he proposes is an official attempt to restore the genuine text of the Vulgate as issued by St. Jerome from a comparison of the oldest manuscripts, which were to be collected, examined, and compared, while the readings were to be judged by the original Greek or Hebrew from which St. Jerome had made his translation. Here for the first time in the Middle Ages were the true principles of textual criticism laid down, principles valid for the work of every editor since his time.

After the science of language had been thoroughly mastered, so that the student was able to read the principal documents of scholarship in the original and follow their train of thought, Bacon next directed his attention to Mathematics. As we have already pointed out, this science was already reviving in western Europe. In Italy Leonardo Fibonacci had published his *Liber Abaci,* Campanus had re-edited Euclid and written on the sphere, de Lunis had begun the study which was to become algebra. In France Alexandre de Villedieu had written the *Carmen de Algorismo,* the popular treatise on Arithmetic; in Germany Jordanus Nemorarius on the theory of numbers, the geometry of the sphere and on triangles; while the English John of Halifax wrote *c.* 1232 the *De sphera mundi,* the most popular text-book on the subject of the Middle Ages, and his *Tractatus de arte Numerandi;* and Peckham's *Perspectiva communis* and Grosseteste's semi-mathematical tractates were also published.

Bacon's own reading, as evidenced by quotations in his *Communia Mathematica,* was considerable. Besides the general scholastic learning of his day he quotes from all the works of Euclid, the *Almagest* and *Aspects* of Ptolemy, Theodosius on the Sphere, Apollonius, Archimedes, Vitruvius, and Hipparchus. Boethius is his main stand-by. The Arabic writers were well known to him, and early mediaeval writers such as Adelard of Bath, Jordanus, Anaricius, Bernelinus, Geybert, and others are often quoted; indeed, we learn of a hitherto unknown work by Adelard from his writings. It would seem, however, that the general interest in mathematics of his time was strictly utilitarian. 'The philosophers of these days,' says he, 'when they are told that they ought to know perspective or geometry, or languages, and many other things, ask derisively, "What good are they?" asserting that they are useless. Nor will they listen to any account of their utility, and so they neglect and despise the sciences of which they are ignorant.'

His own view of the value of mathematics in education was a very high one. Like Plato, he saw in it the master key to all correct reasoning and all progress in knowledge. 'Mathematica est omnino necessaria et utilis aliis scientiis.' 'Impossibile est res huius mundi sciri, nisi sciatur mathematica.' 'Oportet ut fundamenta cognitionis in mathematica ponamus.' It was not so much mathematics for its own sake, as mathematics a handmaid to the natural sciences and theology. We have already referred to his classification of the subject as speculative and practical, following a study of the elements of the science. His remaining work is largely taken up by discussions of the meaning of continuity, infinity, dimensions, axioms, postulates, definitions, and the like, and he spends much time on the various ratios, arithmetical, geometrical, and harmonical. But in pure mathematics he was not an originator, he made no discoveries in geometry or the theory of numbers: his title to remembrance as a mathematician is his sympathy with it, his wide knowledge, and his insistence on its value as the foundation of a liberal education.

Bacon's work on optics was really a part of a larger scheme in his own mind—a study of the propagation of force at a distance. This he treated geometrically and used one variety of force as an example which was susceptible of measurement—light. Thus is explained the emphasis laid on the science of optics, or perspective, as he called it. His main treatises on it, the *Perspective* and the *Multiplication of Species,* were written before the *Opus Maius.* The scheme of the *Perspective* was not entirely new, of course; it had to include much that had been treated by his predecessor Alhazen, and, as a summary, to omit many of his detailed geometrical extensions of theorems. But on the other hand, it carried on the science a considerable way, as, for example, by proving that a concave spherical mirror would bring the reflected rays from different parts of its surface to a focus on different parts of its axis, and that to obtain a single focus the mirror must have a surface produced by the rotation of a parabola or hyperbola.

His study of the theory of optics went hand in hand with practical work; he caused to be constructed concave mirrors for use as burning-glasses, time after time, remarking on the diminishing cost as the craftsman grew more skilful; he was familiar with the use and properties of a convex lens both for magnification of objects, i. e. the simple microscope, and as a burning-glass; and there is every reason to suppose that he was acquainted with the combination of lenses which makes up the telescope, though he only used it for terrestrial objects and did not make it portable.

It is this combination which lies at the base of the legend of Bacon and Bungay's magic mirror which had grown up by 1385. 'Friar Roger Bacon took such delight in his experiments that instead of attending to his lectures and writings he made two mirrors in the University of Oxford: by one of them you could light a candle at any hour, day or night; in the other you could see what people were doing in the uttermost parts of the earth. The result was that the students either spent their time in lighting candles at the first mirror instead of studying books, or, on looking into the second and seeing their relations or friends dying

and lying ill, left Oxford to the ruination of the University—and so both mirrors were broken by the common counsel of the University.' This legend refers evidently to the burning-glass and telescope. The latter is shown to have existed by a statement printed in 1579 that Leonard Digges, then dead, 'was able by Perspective Glasses duely situate upon convenient Angles, in such sort to discover every particularities of the Countrie round about, wheresoever the Sunne beames might pearse . . . which partly grew by the aid he had by one old written book of the same Bakon's experiments, that . . . came to his hands'. This work of Bacon's is no longer known to exist.

We have already spoken of his devotion to Astronomy in the modern sense of the word. His account of the science in the *Opus Maius,* the *De Celestibus,* and the fragment of the *Opus Tertium* published by Duhem, not only shows that he was abreast of the best work of his time, but also forms the best epitome of the state of knowledge at the day. His continual labour in the construction of astronomical tables bore fruit in his attempt at the reformation of the calendar, of which we have given some account. His work on Chronology, sacred and secular, is closely connected with this subject.

Bacon also takes rank as one of the earliest mediaeval writers on Geography, and part of his treatise was reprinted for the first time by Purchas in 1625 from the *Opus Maius* manuscript. His study was founded in the first place on Ptolemy, checked by modern travel, and his first consideration is an approximate determination of the relative amounts of land and water on the globe. It was a passage of this part of his work which had a leading part in deciding Columbus to make an attempt to reach the Indies by the Atlantic route, as shown by his letter from Haiti to Ferdinand and Isabella. Bacon's description covers the known world with the exception of western Europe, and he insists on the habitability of the earth south of the equator, and on the extension of Africa to the south. We have only to compare this treatise with Albert's *De natura locorum* to understand the great advance Bacon has made.

His position in the history of Chemistry has yet to be fully investigated. The very large number of alchemical tracts which pass under his name show that his influence upon the students of the next century was very great. We are, naturally, at a loss to do more than form a reasonable conjecture as to the extent of his practical acquaintance with the operations of chemistry or alchemy, since his writings are devoted rather to theoretical than practical considerations. There was, of course, a large number of industries which depended on chemical reactions for their methods; brewing, dyeing, enamel-making, glass-making, metallurgy, lime-works, are but a few examples; but the eyes of inquirers were rarely turned towards these, and a superficial reason was given for the effects produced. What was really being sought by students was the general formula of the universe, adopting more modern terms, its integral equation, which, once found, would resolve any particular case by substituting suitable values for its constants. Whether he had made up his mind as to the existence of a universal primary matter in our modern sense, taking up the properties which made it a distinct material, is doubtful. The theories he held as to the action of the celestial bodies on this earth swayed him first one way, then another, while the dicta of Aristotle and Avicenna that no change can happen 'nisi fiat resolutio ad materiam primam', which he accepted without questioning, led him towards its acceptance. His doctrine of the multiplication of species was one of the most fruitful in his theory of alchemy. Just as celestial fire produced fire by means of a lens, so the celestial bodies might act on a suitable primary matter to produce their cognate metal, if their influence were as great. The science of weights was a branch of alchemy, because what distinguished the four elements in changeable matter from those in the super-celestial regions was their combination with the qualities of heaviness and lightness.

Alchemy, according to Bacon, was either speculative or practical. Speculative or theoretical alchemy treats of the generation of materials from their elements inanimate or animate. His list of inanimate things comprises metals, gems, stones, colours, salts, oils, bitumen, &c.; his animate things include vegetables, animals, and men. Alchemy was for him linked with Physics and Medicine in a chain of development. Among the treatises which give us the clearest views of his thought are the **Opus Minus** fragments and the **Opus Tertium:** by these the others are to be tried and accepted or rejected. A striking example of the effect of his teaching is to be found in the treatise *De lapide philosophici,* attributed to St. Thomas Aquinas but really written by Fr. Thomas, chaplain to Robert, son of Charles of Anjou, in 1296.

Nothing has yet been said of his relation to the peculiar science of his scholastic contemporaries—speculative philosophy. This was almost a creation of his own time, due to the fuller study of Aristotle now possible. The meaning of matter, form, and substance, the struggle between realist and nominalist, the question of species and individual, all involved questions of the highest religious importance, pantheism or theism. Here Bacon, leading the Oxford schoolmen of later years, rejects much of the controversy as useless. There is no answer to the question what causes individuality or what universality: God makes things as their nature requires. The second part of the **Communia Naturalium** alone is quite enough to place Bacon in a high place among mediaeval schoolmen: its clear treatment shows solid thinking as well as sound criticism.

Looking back on the whole activity of this remarkable scholar we may try to sum up the interest he has for the modern world. Perhaps to himself the question would have been otiose: he was, like many men of science to-day, prepared to accept results and methods without lingering over the history of how they came into being. But on the other hand, to the large and increasing number to whom the history of scientific thought and method is often almost as important as its results, Roger Bacon stands out prominently as the first English leader of scientific thought. More still, he has the special English quality of fighting a lone battle for his views, unsupported as he was by his own order, attacking its opponent's chiefs, and remaining unshaken to the end. His works, though not entirely neglected, have usually been treated as curiosities, while those of his two great contemporaries have been

held in reverence for centuries, and even to-day are receiving the full honours of scholarship in new editions from the manuscripts. The publication of his remains would be invaluable, if only as marking the development of a mediaeval thinker, ranging as they do over a period of forty years' activity from his early lectures at Paris. In them we can trace the process of emancipation from established ruts of thought and the entrance of new conceptions. We can follow his attempts to make a theory to explain the whole body of natural phenomena, the gradual elaboration of a mathematical theory of action at a distance, which, unfruitful at the moment, reappears in a fuller form in modern science. We see him as a pioneer of textual criticism, a critic of established authorities in whom the spirit of *Reynard the Fox* and the *Fablaux* is incarnated, a critic of received doctrines who applies to them in an ever-increasing degree the test of common sense and experiment. The work of such a one should be available to all the world of scholars: more than half of it in bulk is still locked up in single manuscripts difficultly legible and almost inaccessible.

Lynn Thorndike   (essay date 1923)

SOURCE: "Roger Bacon," in *A History of Magic and Experimental Science during the First Thirteen Centuries of Our Era,* The Macmillan Company, 1923, pp. 616-87.

Pope Clement IV, who requested of Bacon a written, fair copy of his philosophy and received Opus Majus *in return.*

[*In the following excerpt from a lengthy chapter in his important* History of Magic and Experimental Science, *Thorndike turns from a brief overview of Bacon's life to examine* Opus Maius, Opus Minus, *and* Opus Tertium, *Bacon's contributions in the development of modern experimental science, and his attitude toward magic and astrology. Throughout his essay, Thorndike scornfully emphasizes Bacon's gullibility and derivitiveness.*]

His Criticism of and Part in Medieval Learning

We turn from Bacon's life to his writings, and shall center our attention upon his three works to the pope. In them he had his greatest opportunity and did his best work both in style and substance. They embody most of his ideas and knowledge. Much, for example, of the celebrated "Epistle concerning the secret works of art and nature and the nullity of magic" sounds like a later compilation from these three works. Two of them are merely supplementary to the **Opus Maius** and are parallel to it in aims, plan, and contents. Its two chief aims were to demonstrate the practical utility of "philosophy," especially to the Church, and secondly, to reform the present state of learning according to Bacon's idea of the relative importance of the sciences. Having convinced himself that an exhaustive work on philosophy was not yet possible, Roger substituted this introductory treatise, outlining the paths along which future study and investigation should go. Of the thirty divisions of philosophy he considers only the five which he deems the most important and essential, namely, the languages, "mathematics," perspective or optic, "experimental science" (including alchemy), and moral philosophy, which last he regards as "the noblest" and "the mistress of them all." Treated in this order, these "sciences" form the themes of the last five of the seven sections of the **Opus Maius.** Inasmuch as Roger regarded himself as a reformer of the state of learning, he prefixed a first part on the causes of human error to justify his divergence from the views of the multitude. His second section develops his ideas as to the relations of "philosophy" and theology.

The mere plan of the **Opus Maius** thus indicates that it is not exclusively devoted to natural science. "Divine wisdom," or theology, is the end that all human thought should serve, and morality is the supreme science. Children should receive more education in the Bible and the fundamentals of Christianity, and spend less time upon "the fables and insanities" of Ovid and other poets who are full of errors in faith and morals. In discussing other sciences Bacon's eye is ever fixed upon their utility "to the Church of God, to the republic of the faithful, toward the conversion of infidels and the conquest of such as cannot be converted." This service is to be rendered not merely by practical inventions or calendar reform or revision of the Vulgate, but by aiding in most elaborate and far-fetched allegorical interpretation of the Bible. To give a very simple example of this, it is not enough for the interpreter of Scripture to know that the lion is the king of beasts; he must be so thoroughly acquainted with all the lion's natural properties that he can tell whether in any particular passage it is meant to typify Christ or the devil. Also the marvels of human science strengthen our faith in divine miracles. Bacon speaks of philosophy as the hand-maid of "sacred wisdom"; he asserts that all truth is contained in Scripture, though philosophy and canon law are required for its comprehension and exposition, and that anything alien therefrom is utterly erroneous. Nay more, the Bible is surer ground than philosophy even in the latter's own field of the natures and properties of things. Furthermore, "philosophy considered by itself is of no utility." Bacon believed not only that the active intellect (*intellectus agens*) by which our minds are illuminated was from God and not an integral part of the human mind, but that all philosophy had been revealed by God to the sainted partriarchs and again to Solomon, and that it was impossible for man by his own efforts to attain to "the great truths of the arts and sciences." Bacon alludes several times to sin as an obstacle to the acquisition of science; on the other hand, he observes that contemporary Christians are inferior morally to the pagan philosophers, from whose books they might well take a leaf. All this gives little evidence of an independent scientific spirit, or of appreciation of experimental method as the one sure foundation of scientific knowledge. We see how much of a medieval friar and theologian and how little of a modern scientist Roger could be. It must, of course, be remembered that he is trying to persuade the Church to support scientific research; still, there seems to be no sufficient reason for doubting his sincerity in the above statements, though we must discount here as elsewhere his tendency to make emphatic and sweeping assertions.

Writers as far back as Cousin and Charles have recognized that Bacon was interested in the scholasticism of his time as well as in natural science. His separate works on the Metaphysics and Physics of Aristotle are pretty much the usual sort of medieval commentary; the tiresome dialectic of the **Questions on Aristotle's Physics** is well brought out in Duhem's essay, "Roger Bacon et l'Horreur du Vide." Bacon's works dedicated to the pope, on the contrary, are written to a considerable extent in a clear, direct, outspoken style; and the subjects of linguistics, mathematics, and experimental science seem at first glance to offer little opportunity for metaphysical disquisitions or scholastic method. Yet, here too, much space is devoted to intellectual battledore and shuttlecock with such concepts as matter and form, moved and mover, agent and patient, element and compound. Such current problems as the unity of the intellect, the source of the *intellectus agens,* and the unity or infinity of matter are introduced for discussion, although the question of universals is briefly dismissed.

Two other characteristic traits of scholasticism are found in the **Opus Maius,** namely, continual use of authorities and the highest regard for Aristotle, *summus philosophorum,* as Bacon calls him. Because in one passage in his *Compendium Studii Philosophiae* Bacon says in his exaggerated way that he would burn all the Latin translations of Aristotle if he could, it has sometimes been assumed that he was opposed to the medieval study of Aristotle. Yet in the very next sentence he declares that "Aristotle's labors are the foundations of all wisdom." What he wanted was more, not less Aristotle. He believed that Aristotle had written a thousand works. He complains quite as much that certain works of Aristotle have not yet been translated into Latin as he does that others have been translated incorrectly. As a matter of fact, he himself seems to have made about as many mistakes in connection with the study of Aristotle as did anyone else. He thought many apocryphal writings genuine, such as the *Secret of Secrets.* an astrological treatise entitled *De Impressionibus Coelestibus,* and other writings concerning "the arcana of science" and "marvels of nature." He overestimated Aristotle and blamed the translators for obscurities and difficulties which abound in the Greek text itself. He declares that a few chapters of Aristotle's *Laws* are superior to the entire *corpus* of Roman law. His assertion that Robert Grosseteste paid no attention to translations of Aristotle is regarded as misleading by Baur. He nowhere gives credit to Albertus Magnus and Thomas Aquinas for their great commentaries on Aristotle which are superior to any that he wrote. He bases some of his own views upon mistranslations of Aristotle, substituting, for instance, "matter" for "substance"—a mistranslation avoided by Albert and Thomas.

Despite its theological and scholastic proclivities, Bacon's mind had a decidedly critical bent. He was, like Petrarch, profoundly pessimistic as to his own times. Church music, present-day sermons, the immorality of monks and theologians, the misconduct of students at Oxford and Paris, the wars and exactions of kings and feudal lords, the prevalence of Roman Law—these are some of the faults he has to find with his age. The **Opus Maius** is largely devoted, not to objective presentation of facts and discussion of theories, but to subjective criticism of the state of learning and even of individual contemporary scholars. This last is so unusual that Bacon excuses himself for it to the pope in both the supplementary treatises. Several other works of Bacon display the same critical tendency. The **Compendium Studii Philosophiae** enlarges upon the complaints and criticisms of the three works. In the **Tractatus de Erroribus Medicorum** he detected in contemporary medicine "thirty-six great and radical defects with infinite ramifications." But in medicine, too, his own contributions are of little account. In the **Compendium Studii Theologiae,** after contemptuous allusion to the huge *Summae* of the past fifty years, he opens with an examination of the problems of speculative philosophy which underlie the questions discussed by contemporary theologians. As far as we know that is as far as he got. And in the five neglected sciences to which his **Opus Maius** was a mere introduction he seems to have made little further progress than is there recorded; it has yet to be proved that he made any definite original contribution to any particular science.

After all, we must keep in mind the fact that in ancient and medieval times hostile criticism was more likely to hit the mark than were attempts at constructive thought and collection of scientific details. There were plenty of wrong ideas to knock down; it was not easy to find a rock foundation to build upon, or materials without some hidden flaw. The church fathers made many telling shots in their bombardment of pagan thought; their own interpretation of nature and life less commands our admiration. So Roger Bacon, by devoting much of his space to criticism of the mistakes of others and writing "preambles" to science and theology, avoided treacherous detail—a wise caution for his times. Thus he constructed a sort of intellectual portico more pretentious than he could have justified by his main building. To a superficial observer this portico may seem a fitting entrance to the temple of modern science, but a closer examination discovers that it is built of the same faulty materials as the neglected ruins of his contemporaries' science.

Merely to have assumed a critical point of view in the middle ages may seem a distinction; but Abelard, Adelard of Bath, William of Conches, and Daniel Morley were all critical, back in the twelfth century. Moreover, our estimate of any critic must take into account how valid, how accurate, how original and how consistent his criticisms were and from what motives they proceeded. Some of Bacon's complaints the reader of medieval literature has often listened to before. What student of philosophy in the twelfth and thirteenth centuries had not sighed at the invasion of the Roman law into school and church and state? What devotee of astronomy had failed to contrast its human interest and divine relationships with the dry drubbing of the jurists? What learned man had not expressed his preference for the wise and the experts (*sapientes*) over the vulgus or common herd? The great secrets of learning and the danger of casting pearls before swine were also quite familiar concepts. If Bacon goes a step farther and speaks of a *vulgus studentium* and even of a *vulgus medicorum,* he is only refining a medical commonplace or quoting Galen.

In Bacon's discussion of the four causes of human error his attack upon undue reliance on authority has often seemed to modern readers most unusual for his age. But all his arguments against authority are drawn from authorities; and while he seems to have got a whiff of the spirit of rationalism from such classical writers as Seneca and Cicero, he also quotes the *Natural Questions* of his fellow-countryman, Adelard of Bath, who in the early twelfth century had found the doctrine of the schools of Gaul as little to his liking as was that of Paris to Roger's taste, and whom we have heard reprove his nephew for blind trust in authorities. Bacon's fourth cause of human error, the concealment of ignorance by a false show of learning, might well have been suggested by Daniel Morley's satire on the *bestiales* who occupied chairs in the schools of Paris "with grave authority," and reverently marked their Ulpians with daggers and asterisks, and seemed wise as long as they concealed their ignorance by a statuesque silence, but whom he found "most childish" when they tried to say anything. Or by the same Daniel's warning not to spurn Arabic clarity for Latin obscurity; and his charge that it was owing to their ignorance and inability to attain definite conclusions that Latin philosophers of his day spun so many elaborate figments and hid "uncertain error under the shadow of ambiguity."

Bacon's criticisms have usually been taken to apply to medieval learning as a whole, but a closer examination shows their application to be much more limited. In the first place, he is thinking only of the past "forty years" in making his complaints; in the good old days of Grosseteste, Adam Marsh, William Wolf, and William of Shyrwood things were different, and scholarship flowed smoothly, if not copiously, in the channels marked out by the ancient sages; nor does Bacon deny that there was a renaissance of natural science and an independent scientific spirit still farther back in the twelfth century.

Secondly, except for his tirades against the Italians and their civil law, Bacon's criticisms apply to but two countries, France and England, and two universities, Oxford and Paris. Also those few contemporaries whom he praises are either his old Oxford friends or scattered individuals in France. Of the state of learning in Italy, Spain, and Germany he says little and apparently knew little. Amid his sighing for some prince or prelate to play the patron to science, he never mentions Alfonso X of Castile, who was so interested in the "mathematics" and occult science which were so dear to Bacon's heart; Roger even still employs the old Toletan astronomical tables of Arzachel instead of the Alfonsine tables issued in 1252, the first year of that monarch's reign. His lamentation over the sad neglect of astrology among the "Latins" is not borne out by our investigations of their interest in that subject, and indicates that he was ignorant of the work at the University of Bologna of the astrologer, Guido Bonatti, whose voluminous Latin treatise on that art based on wide reading in both classical and Arabian scholars did not indeed appear until after 1277, but must have already been in preparation when Bacon wrote, since Guido was born at some time before 1223. Bacon grieves at the neglect of the science of optic by his age, and says that it has not yet been lectured on at Paris nor elsewhere among the Latins except twice at Oxford; he does not mention the Pole, Witelo, who traveled in Italy and whose important treatise on the subject was produced at about this time.

While complaining of the ignorance of the natures and properties of animals, plants, and minerals which is shown by contemporary theologians in their explanation of Scriptural passages, Bacon not only slights the encyclopedias which several clergymen like Alexander Neckam, Bartholomew of England, Thomas of Cantimpré and Vincent of Beauvais had compiled; he also says nothing of the school at Cologne of Albertus Magnus, whose reputation was already established by the middle of the century, who personally investigated many animals, especially those of the north, and often rectified the erroneous assertions of classical zoologists, whom the historian of botany has lauded, whose students too were curious to know not only the theoretical botany that passed under the name of Aristotle, but also the particular characteristics of plants, and who in his five books on minerals discusses the alchemy and indulges in the same occult science and astrology which Bacon deemed so important. Yet Albert was a noted theologian and Biblical commentator as well as a student of nature.

In saying that Bacon does not mention Albert's work in natural science, I of course do not mean to imply that he never mentions Albert. He excuses his delay in answering the pope by declaring that the most noted Christian scholars, such as Brother Albert of the Order of Preachers, and Master William of Shyrwood, could not in ten years produce such a work as he transmits; and he incidentally observes that William is a far abler scholar than Albert. I am suspicious, however, of the integrity of the passage where

Bacon sneers at the theological teaching of "the boys of the two Orders, such as Albert and Thomas and the others who enter the Orders when twenty years or under." It seems incongruous for Bacon to speak of his probable senior, Albert, as a boy. Other passages in Bacon's works which have been taken to apply to Albert, though he is not expressly named, seem to me not to apply to him at all closely; and if meant for him, they show that Bacon was an incompetent and unfair critic. Not only was Albert only for a short time in Paris; he does not seem to have been in sympathy with the conditions there which Bacon attacks. Nor can I see that Bacon is meant in the passage at the close of Albert's *Politics,* where he declares that its doctrines, as in his books on physics, are not his own theories but a faithful reflection of peripatetic opinion; and that he makes this statement for the benefit of lazy persons who occupy their idle hours in searching writings for things to criticize; "Such men killed Socrates, drove Plato from Athens to the Academy, and, plotting even against Aristotle, forced him into exile." Such a passage seems a commonplace one. Both Adelard of Bath and William of Conches expressed the same fear of setting forth new ideas of their own, and medieval writers not infrequently in their prefaces apprehend with shrinking "the bite of envy" which both their Horace and personal experience had taught would follow fast on publication.

Thirdly, while Bacon occasionally makes bitter remarks about the present state of learning in general, it is the teaching of theology at Paris and by the friars that he has most in mind and that he especially desires to reform. Though himself a friar and master of theology, he had been trained and had then himself specialized in the three learned languages, Hebrew, Greek and Arabic, in optic and geometry, in astronomy and astrology, in alchemy and "experimental science," and in the writings of the classical moralists. Consequently he thought that no one could be a thorough theologian who did not go through the same course of training; nay, it was enough to ruin the reputation of any supposed scholar in Bacon's sight, if he were unacquainted with these indispensable subjects. Bacon held that it was not sufficient preparation for theology merely to study "the common sciences, such as Latin, grammar, logic, and a part of natural philosophy, and a little metaphysics." However, it was not that he objected to these studies in themselves, nor to the ordinary university instruction in the arts course; in fact, he complains that many young friars start in to study theology at once and "presume to investigate philosophy by themselves without a teacher." Bacon has a low opinion of the scholarship of Alexander of Hales, because his university education had been completed before the chief authorities and commentaries in natural philosophy and metaphysics had been translated. Against another friar generally regarded by the academic world as its greatest living authority Bacon brings the charge that "he never heard philosophy in the schools," and "was not instructed nor trained in listening, reading and disputing, so that he must be ignorant of the common sciences." Such passages show that to represent Bacon's writings as full of "sweeping attacks" upon "the metaphysical subtleties and verbal strifes" of his age is to exaggerate his position. There are not many direct attacks upon scholastic method in his works.

It is true that Bacon complains of the lack of good teachers in his day, saying in the ***Opus Minus*** that he could impart to an apt pupil in four years all the knowledge that it had taken himself forty years to acquire, and in the ***Opus Tertium*** that he could do it in a half or a quarter of a year, and that he could teach a good student all the Greek and Hebrew he need know in three days for each subject. But aside from the young friars who presume to teach theology, the teachers against whom he rails most are those in his favorite subject of "mathematics." Bacon could teach more useful geometry in a fortnight than they do in ten or twenty years—a hint that much time was given in those days to the study of mathematics. These boasts are not, however, as wild as they may at first seem; after all Roger did not know a vast amount of geometry and Greek and Hebrew, and he had no intention of teaching any more of mathematics and the languages than would be of service in his other sciences, in theology, and in practical life. He complained that "the ordinary mathematician does not consider that he knows anything unless he demonstrates it, and so he takes from thirty to forty years" to master the subject, and that "the text-books and the teachers of mathematics delight in multiplying conclusions to such an extent that one has to give years of unnecessary time to extracting the essentials," and "this is one reason why there are so few students of a science which is a prerequisite to all knowledge." Nor were such boasts unique in the age in which Bacon lived. Another professor and Franciscan friar, who wrote at least no later than the early fourteenth century, Bernard of Verdun, states that his little book on astronomy takes the place of "innumerable works and huge tomes," and makes it possible for anyone acquainted with geometry to learn in a short time not only the gist of books which two years of steady reading could scarce suffice to cover, but also many points which other books omit.

It is easy to discern the personal motives which actuated Bacon in his criticism. He was jealous of his more successful contemporaries and desperately anxious to secure the pope as his patron. If, as Macaulay said, Francis Bacon seeking the truth was a very different person from Francis Bacon seeking the seals, we must remember that Roger Bacon combined both attempts at once. He grieved to see the neglect by his fellow theologians of the subjects in which he was particularly interested, and to see himself second in reputation, influence and advancement to the "boy theologians." It angered him that these same narrowly educated and narrow-minded men should "always teach against these sciences in their lectures, sermons and conferences." And after all, as he tells the pope, he does not wish to revolutionize the curriculum nor overthrow the existing educational system, "but that from the table of the Lord, heaped with wisdom's spoils, I, poor fellow, may gather the falling crumbs I need."

Bacon's allusions to and dates for events in the history of medieval learning are sometimes hard to fit in with what we learn from other sources, and as we have seen he has been detected in misstatements of the doctrines of other scholars. His personal diatribes against the Latin translators of Greek and Arabian science seem overdrawn and unfair, especially when he condemns the first translators

for not knowing the sciences in question before they ventured to translate, whereas it is plain that the sciences could not be known to the Latin world until the translations had been made. Indeed, it may be doubted if Roger himself knew Arabic well enough to read scientific works therein without a translation or interpreter. Especially unjustifiable and ill advised seems his savage onslaught upon William of Moerbeke, whom we are told Aquinas induced to translate Aristotle from the Greek, who was like Bacon interested in occult science, and to whom Witelo dedicated his treatise on optics. As William held the confidential post of papal chaplain and penitentiary under Clement IV, and as he became archbishop of Corinth about the time that Roger was condemned to prison, there may have been some personal rivalry and bitterness between them.

It should be said to Bacon's credit that his own statements do not support the inference which others have drawn from them, that he was alone in the advocacy or pursuit of the studies dear to him. In the ***Opus Minus*** he says to the pope, with rather unusual modesty it must be admitted, "I confess that there are several men who can present to Your Wisdom in a better way than I can these very subjects of which I treat." And though the secrets of the arts and sciences are neglected by the crowd of students and their masters, "God always has reserved some sages who know all the necessary elements of wisdom. Not that anyone of them knows every detail, however, nor the majority of them; but one knows one subject, another another, so that the knowledge of such sages ought to be combined." Combine it Bacon does for the pope's perusal, and he is not ashamed to speak on its behalf, for though there are fewer Latins conversant with it than there should be, there are many who would gladly receive it, if they were taught. Thus he speaks not merely as an exponent of his own ideas, but as the representative of a movement with a considerable following at least outside of strictly theological circles.

Bacon has been given great credit for pointing out the need of calendar revision three centuries before the papacy achieved it; but he says himself that not only wise astronomers but even ordinary *computistae* were already aware of the crying need for reform, and his discussion of the calendar often coincides verbally with Grosseteste's *Computus*. When Cardinal Pierre d'Ailly over a century later again urged the need of reform upon Pope John XXIII he cited Grosseteste often, but Bacon seldom or never. The Parisian version of the Bible, against which Bacon inveighs as a corruption of the Vulgate, was in the first instance the work of a conscientious Hebrew scholar; and the numerous corrections and changes made in it since, though deplored by Bacon, show the prevalent interest in such matters. While Bacon holds that there are very few men who understand the theory of Greek, Hebrew and Arabic grammar, or the technique of the sciences which have to be studied from those languages, he admits that many men are found among the "Latins" who can speak those tongues and that there are even plenty of teachers of Greek and Hebrew at Paris and elsewhere in France and England. Thus Bacon was not so superior linguistically to his age as he has sometimes been depicted.

The treatment of geography in the **Opus Maius** is simply an intelligent compilation of well-known past writers, including the wretched work of Ethicus, supplemented from writings of the friars who had recently visited the Tartars. Roger Bacon's name has sometimes been connected with the discovery of America by Columbus on the ground that Columbus was greatly influenced by the *Imago mundi* of Pierre d'Ailly and that a chapter in that work on the extent of the habitable earth was copied in large measure without acknowledgment from Roger Bacon. Cardinal d'Ailly, however, can scarcely be censured for failing to mention Bacon in this context since he does cite him elsewhere and since in this passage all that he borrows from Roger are the statements of other writers whom Roger cites. That is, against Ptolemy's discouraging assertion that five-sixths of the earth's surface is covered with water he cites Aristotle, Seneca and Pliny to provie that the distance west from Spain to India is not great and the apocryphal book of Esdras to the effect that only one-seventh of the earth's surface is covered with water. But it is contended that the *Imago Mundi* was not published until 1487 and that Columbus did not read it until after his first voyage in 1492, which is to be regarded as a continuation of the search after new islands and lands in the western ocean already undertaken by various Portuguese sailors. It is interesting to note one argument for the propinquity of northwestern Africa to India employed by Bacon which d'Ailly, firm believer in astrology as he was, did not copy. Bacon argues that Aristotle and his commentator included northwestern Africa in "Spain," "since they say as proof of the narrowness of the sea between Spain and India that there are elephants only in those two places." And "Aristotle says that there cannot be elephants in those places unless they were of like complexion." —i. e., under the same constellations.

If in many respects Bacon's contribution to learning has been overestimated, there is one side of his thought which has seldom been emphasized but deserves some notice, namely, his historical attitude. In one sense history was a weak point with Bacon as with most of his contemporaries. He not only accepted the faulty accounts of the past current in his day, but was apt to pounce upon the most sensational and incredible details and use these to support his case. He had no notion of historical criticism. Unfortunately he thought that he knew a good deal about the history of philosophy, and his attitude to science is colored by his false ideas of the history of intellectual development. He of course knew nothing of evolution or of prehistoric man. For him intellectual history commenced with a complete divine revelation of philosophy to the patriarchs. Science then declined owing to the sinfulness of mankind, the invention of magic by Zoroaster, and further corruption of wisdom at the hands of Nimrod, Atlas, Prometheus, Hermes Trismegistus, Aesculapius, and Apollo. Complete knowledge and understanding were granted again by God to Solomon, after whom succeeded another period of sinful decline, until with Thales began the gradual upbuilding of Greek philosophy culminating in Aristotle. Then night set in again, until Avicenna revived philosophy among the Arabs. To him and Aristotle, however, as infidels, less complete knowledge was vouchsafed than to the representatives of God's chosen people. Of the compo-

sition and development of Roman law Bacon had so little notion that he thought it borrowed chiefly from Aristotle and Theophrastus, except that the Twelve Tables were derived from the laws of Solon. Though he saw the value of linguistics and textual criticism, and sought with true humanistic ardor for a lost work like the *Morals* of Seneca, he accepted as genuine works of antiquity spurious treatises like the *De Vetula* ascribed to Ovid. He believed that Paul had corresponded with Seneca and that Alexander's conquests were due to Aristotle's experimental science. We shall soon see how he used the astrological interpretation of history, which was the medieval counterpart of our geographical and economic interpretation. Yet Bacon deserves praise for so often opening his discussion of a problem by an inquiry into its historical background; he at least tried to adopt the historical point of view. And on the whole his historical method makes about as close an approach to modern research as do his mathematics and experimental science to their modern parallels.

Yet the introduction of mathematical method into natural science has often been attributed to Roger Bacon, in which respect he has been favorably contrasted with Francis Bacon. Therefore it will be well to note exactly what Roger says on this point and whether his observations were notably in advance of the thought of his times. It will be recalled that in his criticism of the teaching of mathematics Roger had shown little appreciation of the labors of those pure mathematicians who devoted a lifetime to painstaking demonstration and were satisfied with nothing short of it. The discussion in the **Opus Maius** opens with strong assertions of the necessity for a knowledge of mathematics in the study of natural science and of theology as well; and we are told that neglect of mathematics for the past thirty or forty years has been the ruin of Latin learning. This position is supported by citation of various authorities and by some vague general arguments in typical scholastic style. Grammar and logic must employ music, a branch of mathematics, in prosody and persuasive periods. The categories of time, place, and quantity require mathematical knowledge for their comprehension. Mathematics must underlie other subjects because it is by nature the most elementary and the easiest to learn and the first discovered. Moreover, all our sense knowledge is received in space, in time, and quantitatively. Also the certitude of mathematics makes it desirable that other studies avail themselves of its aid.

But now we come to the application of these glittering generalities and we see what Bacon's "mathematical method" really amounts to. Briefly, it consists in expounding his physical and astronomical theories by means of simple geometrical diagrams. The atomical doctrine of Democritus cannot be true, since it involves the error that the hypothenuse is of the same length as the side of a square. Geometry satisfies Roger that there can be but one universe; otherwise we should have a vacuum left. Plato's assertion that the heavens and four elements are made up each of one group of regular solids is also subjected to geometrical scrutiny. Mathematics is further of service in Biblical geography, in sacred chronology, and in allegorical interpretation of the dimensions of the ark, temple, and tabernacle, and of various numbers which occur in Scripture. But mathematics, according to Bacon, plays its greatest rôle in astronomy or astrology and in physics, and in his favorite theory of multiplication of species or virtues, or, as modern writers have flatteringly termed it, the propagation of force.

Astronomy and astrology had together long made up the world's supreme science; there was no originality in urging their importance, and unfortunately it was astrology rather than astronomy which seemed to Bacon by far the most important and practical part of mathematics. In physics he borrowed his discussion of weights and falling bodies from Jordanus, an earlier writer in the thirteenth century, and his optics from Alhazen and Grosseteste and from treatises which passed then under the names of Ptolemy and Euclid but were perhaps of more recent origin. Bacon's graphic expression of the multiplication of species by lines and figures we find earlier in Grosseteste's *De Lineis, Angulis, et Figuris*. It does not seem, therefore, that Bacon made any new suggestions of great importance concerning the application of mathematical method in the sciences, and historians of mathematics have recognized that "he contributed nothing to the pure science," of whose very meaning his notion was inadequate.

His Experimental Science

Let us next inquire what contributions, if any, Bacon made in the direction of modern experimental method. Jebb's edition of the *Opus Maius* in 1733 ended with the sixth part on "Experimental Science," which thus received undue prominence and seemed the climax of the work. Bridges' edition added the seventh part on "Moral Philosophy," "a science better than all the preceding," and the text as now extant, after listing various arguments for the superiority of Christianity to other religions, concludes abruptly with an eight-page devout justification and glorification of the mystery of the Eucharist.

Our preceding chapters have similarly rectified the place of Bacon's discussion of experimental science in the history of thought. We have already brought out the fact that he was not the first medieval man to advocate experimentation, but that writers before him contain "experiments," rely on experience rather than mere authority, and mention the existence of other "experimenters" and "experimental books." We have noted Petrus Hispanus' discussion of "the experimental method" (*via experimenti*), Albertus Magnus' experimental school for the study of nature, Robert Grosseteste's association of experimentation with physics, and William of Auvergne's association of experiment with natural magic. We have described experiments of Constantinus Africanus, Adelard of Bath, Pedro Alfonso, Bernard Silvester, and many others. We have yet to describe experimental books, many of which antedate Roger Bacon. His discussion will be found to do little more than duplicate and reinforce the picture of the medieval status of experimental method which we have already obtained from other and earlier sources. He is not a lone herald of the experimental method of modern science; he merely reveals and himself represents the merits and the defects of an important movement of his time.

Bacon's discussion of "experimental science" and of ex-

perimental method are not quite one and the same thing. He treats of "experimental science" in a separate section of the *Opus Maius,* and seems to regard it as something distinct from his other natural sciences, such as optics, alchemy, astronomy and astrology, rather than as an inductive method through regulated and purposive observation and experience to the discovery of truth, which should underlie and form an essential part of them all. Yet he also approaches the latter conception. But note that, while the sixth part on "Experimental Science" is not the last section of the *Opus Maius,* it is the last of the natural sciences to be discussed by him there rather than the first. It is not, like modern experimentation, the source but "the goal of all speculation." It is not so much an inductive method of discovering scientific truth, as it is applied science, the putting the results of the "speculative" natural sciences to the test of practical utility. "Other sciences know how to discover their first principles through experience, but reach their conclusions by arguments made from the principles so discovered. But if they require a specific and final test of their conclusions, then they ought to avail themselves of the aid of this noble science." "Natural philosophy narrates and argues but does not experiment. The student of perspective and the astronomer put many things to the test of experience, but not all nor sufficiently. Hence complete experience is reserved for this science." It uses the other sciences to achieve definite practical results; as a: navigator orders a carpenter to build him a ship or a knight tells a smith to make him a suit of armor, so the *experimentator* uses his knowledge of geometry to construct a burning-glass or outdoes alchemy at its own specialty of gold-making. In working out these practical inventions, however, the "experimenter" often happens on new facts and truths of which the speculative sciences have not dreamed, and in this way experimental science "by its own power investigates the secrets of nature." Thus Bacon begins to see the advisability of a close alliance between "experimental science" and natural science, but it is also clear that they are not yet identified. The artisans of the gilds and the alchemists—Bacon includes a discussion of alchemy in the same sixth section with his "experimental science," although in a way keeping the two distinct—seem to be engaging in this experimental science more than do the scholars of the books and schools. As William of Auvergne associated experimentation with magic rather than with science, so Bacon seems to regard natural science as largely speculative, and confirms the impression, which we have already derived from many other sources, that magicians were the first to "experiment," and that "science," originally speculative, has gradually taken over the experimental method from magic. This impression will be strengthened as we proceed to examine in more detail, first Bacon's "experimental science" and then what he has to say concerning magic. From now on, however, we shall credit Bacon with all the traces of experimental method that we can find anywhere in his writings, as well as in his separate section on "experimental science" in the *Opus Maius* and his further allusions to the same subject in the *Opus Minus* and *Opus Tertium.*

Bacon not merely emphasizes the importance of experience in arriving at the truth, but of all sciences regards his "experimental science" as the best criterion of truth. "All sciences except this either merely employ arguments to prove their conclusions, like the purely speculative sciences, or have universal and imperfect experiences"; while "It alone, in truth, has the means of finding out to perfection what can be done by nature, what by the industry of art, what by fraud"; for it alone can distinguish what is true from what is false in "incantations, conjurations, invocations, deprecations, and sacrifices."

But how is one to set about experimenting? On this point Bacon is disappointing. His explanation of the rainbow, which is his longest illustration of the value of experimental science, is based merely on ordinary intelligent observation and reasoning, although he adds at the close that tests with instruments are needed and that consequently he will not assert that he has reached the full truth of the matter. Elsewhere he speaks of astronomical experiments "by instruments made for this purpose," but seems to regard the unaided eyesight as sufficient for the investigation of terrestrial phenomena. Bacon has sent "over sea and to various other lands and to annual fairs, in order that I might see the things of nature with my own eyes." "And those things which are not present in our locality we may know through other sages who have experienced them, just as Aristotle by authority of Alexander sent two thousand men to different regions to experience all things on the face of the earth, as Pliny testifies in his Natural History." The one contemporary who most nearly fulfills Bacon's ideal of what an experimental scientist should be, does not spend his time merely in reading, attending lectures, and engaging in disputations, but "is ashamed to have some layman or old wife or knight or rustic know facts of which he is ignorant"; hence he goes out into the world and observes the doings of common workingmen and even takes hints from the operations of witches, enchanters and magicians. Bacon even accepts the notion which we have already often met in other writers, that valuable medicines can be discovered by observing what remedies various animals employ. It would seem that experimental method is in a low state of its development; if it takes lessons from common human experience and from the actions of brutes. Bacon sufficiently indicates, however, that it does not consist merely of observation and casual experience, but includes purposive experimentation, and he often speaks of "experimenters." Undoubtedly he himself experimented. But the fact remains that he gives no directions concerning either the proper environment for experimenting or the proper conduct of experiments. Of laboratory equipment, of scientific instruments, of exact measurements, he has no more notion apparently than his contemporaries.

It cannot be shown that Roger Bacon actually anticipated any of our modern inventions, nor that to him in particular were due any of the medieval inventions which revolutionized domestic life such as chimney flues and window panes, or navigation such as the rudder and mariner's compass, or public and ecclesiastical architecture such as the pointed vault and flying buttress and stained glass, or reckoning and writing such as the Hindu-Arabic numerals and paper, or reading and seeing such as lenses and eyeglasses, or warfare such as gunpowder. We probably are justified, however, in accepting such passages in his works as the following, not merely as dreams that have been brought true by modern mechanical inventions, but as further indications that an interest existed in mechanical devices, and that men were already beginning to struggle with the problems which have recently been solved.

> Machines for navigation can be made without rowers so that the largest ships on rivers or seas will be moved by a single man in charge with greater velocity than if they were full of men. Also cars can be made so that without animals they will move with unbelievable rapidity; such we opine were the scythe-bearing chariots with which the men of old fought. Also flying machines can be constructed so that a man sits in the midst of the machine revolving some engine by which artificial wings are made to beat the air like a flying bird. Also a machine small in size for raising or lowering enormous weights, than which nothing is more useful in emergencies. For by a machine three fingers high and wide and of less size a man could free himself and his friends from all danger of prison and rise and descend. Also a machine can easily be made by which one man can draw a thousand to himself by violence against their wills, and attract other things in like manner. Also machines can be made for walking in the sea and rivers, even to the bottom without danger. For Alexander the Great employed such, that he might see the secrets of the deep, as Ethicus the astronomer tells. These machines were made in antiquity and they have certainly been made in our times, except possibly a flying machine which I have not seen nor do I know any one who has, but I know an expert who has thought out the way to make one. And such things can be made almost without limit, for instance, bridges across rivers without piers or other supports, and mechanisms, and unheard of engines.

Since Bacon's authority concerning Alexander is unreliable and his conjectures concerning ancient scythe-bearing chariots unwarranted, we may also doubt if steamboats and automobiles had "certainly been made" in his day; but men may have been trying to accomplish such things.

Bacon says far more of the marvelous results which he expects experimental science to achieve than he does of the methods by which such results are to be attained. In the main marvelousness rather than practicability characterizes the aims which he proposes for *scientia experimentalis*. Indeed, of the three ways in which he represents it as superior to all other sciences, while one is that it employs sure proofs rather than mere arguments, two are that by it life may be greatly lengthened, and that from it a better knowledge of the future may be gained than even from astrology. Thus experimental method is especially connected with alchemy and astrology. Bacon declares that "it has been proved by certain experiments" that life can be greatly prolonged "by secret experiences," and he believes that Artephius was enabled by such methods to live for a thousand and twenty-five years. Or experimental science may predict the weather by observing the behavior of animals.

Some of Bacon's "experiments" are as fantastic as the aims are marvelous. "A good experimenter says in the book *De regimine senum*" that the following elixir will greatly prolong life: "that which is temperate in the fourth degree, and what swims in the sea, and what grows in the air, and what is cast up by the sea, and plant of India, and what is found in the entrails of an animal of long life, and those two serpents which are the food of the inhabitants of Tyre and Ethiopia." We also are told that "at Paris recently there was a sage who asked for snakes and was given one and cut it into small sections except that the skin of its belly on which it crawled remained intact; and that snake crawled as best it could to a certain herb by touching which it was instantly made whole. And the experimenter collected an herb of wonderful virtue."

Credulity, in contrast to the sceptical attitude of modern science is a characteristic of Bacon's experimental method. He declares, it is true, that experiment disproves many false notions such as that hot water freezes faster than cold, that adamant can be broken only with the blood of a goat, and that the beaver when hunted castrates itself to save its life; but we have already heard such beliefs questioned by Albertus Magnus and others. On the other hand, Bacon asserts that credulity is necessary to experimentation. "First one should be credulous until experience follows second and reason comes third. . . . At first one should believe those who have made experiments or who have faithful testimony from others who have done so, nor should one reject the truth because he is ignorant of it and because he has no argument for it." Taken as a plea for an open-minded attitude toward scientific investigation on the part of the ordinary man and of the ecclesiastical authorities, this utterance may be commended; but as a prescription for the scientific investigator it is dangerous. Many of Bacon's "experiments" are copied from books, and the reproach made against the Greek Empirics that they followed tradition, applies also to him. Describing a certain marvel of nature, he exclaims, "After I beheld this, there was nothing difficult for my mind to believe, provided it had a reliable author." In the midst of his discussion of experimental science we encounter the following instance of his gullibility:

> It is certain that Ethiopian sages have come into Italy, Spain, France, England, and those Christian lands where there are good flying dragons; and by an occult art that they possess, excite the dragons from their caves. And they have saddles and bridles ready, and they ride the dragons, and drive them at top speed through the air, in order to soften the rigidity and toughness of their flesh, just as boars, bears, and bulls are hunted with dogs and beaten with many blows before they are killed for eating. And when they have tamed the dragons in this way, they have an art of preparing their flesh . . . which they employ against the accidents of age and prolong life and inspire the intellect beyond all estimation. For no education which man can give will bestow such wisdom as does the eating of their flesh, as we have learned without deceit or doubt from men of proved trustworthiness.

Bacon's discussion of experimental science, therefore, on its positive side amounts to little more than a recognition of experience as a criterion of truth and a promulgation of the phrase "Experimental science" which, however, he himself ascribes to Ptolemy.

On the other hand, the credulity, the superstition, the element of marvelousness, which seem to vitiate the experimental tendencies of Bacon, are to be explained as the result of a real connection between experiment and magic. There is abundant evidence for this. Bacon, it is true, asserts that experimental science exposes and shuns all the follies of the magicians, but he admits that many persons confuse it with magic because of the marvels which it works, and he himself especially associates it with the occult sciences of alchemy and astrology. It makes gold such as neither the art of alchemy nor nature can produce; it can predict the future better than astrology. It teaches one to choose the proper constellations for his undertakings, and to use the right words at the proper times; it can construct "philosophical images and incantations and characters" which are vastly superior to those of magic; it can alter the world about us, and incline and excite the human will, though without coercion. Moreover, Bacon's ideal experimental scientist does not scorn to take hints from wizards, while Roger himself derives his hazel rod experiment from the magicians. The snake experiment of his sage at Paris sounds more like the trick of a Hindu conjurer than the procedure of a modern laboratory.

His Attitude Toward Magic and Astrology

Thus we are finally led to a consideration of the magic and astrology which were evidently so closely connected with Bacon's mathematics and experimental science. Roger admits a certain connection between magic and astrology, since he adopts Hugh of St. Victor's fivefold division of magic into *mantice, mathematica, sortilegium, praestigium* and *maleficium*. However, except for this superstitious *mathematica* he approves of astrology, whereas his attitude towards magic is uniformly one of condemnation and contempt. We shall therefore take up his treatments of the two subjects separately.

Bacon discusses or alludes to "magic" in a number of passages scattered through his works, and to it is more particularly devoted the "Letter on the secret works of art and nature and the nullity of magic," a treatise which faithfully reproduces his point of view whether actually penned by him as it stands or not. Bacon had evidently read a good deal about magic and gives a rather unusual account of its position in the Roman Empire and early Christian period, but one which is not so very far from the truth. His idea is that there were three great conflicting and contending forces in the early centuries of the Christian era, namely, Christianity, philosophy, and magic, and that each one of these was then in opposition to the other two, although there was no sufficient reason for the permanent hostility of Christianity and philosophy, which have since become allies. But at the time the result was that the philosophers often accused the Christians of practicing magic, and that the early Christians similarly confused philosophers with magicians, as indeed was often done by uneducated men of the time who were not Christians. Moreover, Bacon complains that this confusion still exists in his own time and that contemporary theologians, Gratian in his work on Canon law, and "many saints" have condemned many useful and splendid sciences along with magic.

Roger himself, however, not only regards magic as rife in antiquity, but as still prevalent in his own time. He often refers to contemporary magicians and witches, old-wives and wizards. He declares that every nation is full of their superstitions. He is another medieval witness to the currency of a considerable body of occult literature, of which he speaks especially in the second and third chapters of the *Epistola de secretis operibus,* and again in his commentary on *The Secret of Secrets.* "Books of the magicians" are in circulation which are falsely attributed to Solomon and the ancient philosophers and which "assume a grand-sounding style," but which "ought all to be prohibited by law, since they abound in so many lies that one cannot distinguish the true from the false." Such works as *De officiis spirituum, De morte animae,* and *De arte notoria* embody only "figments of the magicians." Yet these books of false *mathematici* and demons, ascribed to Adam, Moses, Solomon, Aristotle, and Hermes, have seduced not only youths but mature and famous men of Bacon's own time.

Bacon, indeed, despite the prevalence of magic both in antiquity and in his own time, regards it as essentially a delusion. It is "the nullity of magic" that he especially attempts to demonstrate both in the *Epistola de secretis operibus* and elsewhere in his works. He is medieval Christian enough, it is true, to grant that magic may perform marvels by the aid of demons. But he also accepts the orthodox belief that magicians cannot coerce the demons by their invocations, sacrifices, and employment of the properties of natural objects, and that the evil spirits in reality respond only with evil intent and as God permits. But his emphasis is not, like Augustine's upon the "host of wonders" which magicians work by demon aid. He seems to be sounding, not a religious retreat from magic, but a rational and scientific attack upon it. Nor does he dwell much on the criminal character of magic, although he calls the magicians *maledicti*—"of evil repute." What impresses him most about magic, and the charge which he most often brings against it, is its fraud and futility. Twice he speaks of things as "false and magical"; he mentions the "figments of the magicians"; and associates magic and necromancy, not like Albert with astronomy, but with deception. For him magicians are neither *magni* nor philosophers and astronomers; in half a dozen passages he classes them with old-wives and witches. He will not admit that they employ valid natural forces. He represents magic as using sleight-of-hand, ventriloquism, subtle mechanism, darkness and confederates to simulate results which it is unable to perform. He further represents the magicians as "stupidly trusting in characters and incantations," and affirms that "the human voice has not that power which magicians imagine it has." When words are employed in magic, "either the magician accomplishes nothing, or the devil is the author of the feat." Magical incantations and formulae are made haphazard and at anyone's pleasure; they therefore possess no natural transforming power, and if they seem to effect anything, this is really the work of demons. Similarly Bacon regards as worthless the assertion of the magicians and witches that sudden transforma-

tions may be produced by any man at any time of day. He dismisses "fascination by word alone uttered at haphazard" as "a stupid notion characteristic of magic and of old-wives and beneath the notice of philosophers." Here again nothing is accomplished, "unless the devil because of men's sins operates unbeknownst."

In certain passages, however, Bacon suggests that magic is not utterly worthless and that some truth may be derived from it. The experimental scientist whom he most admired "investigated even the *experiments* and lot-castings of old women"—note that they too were experimenters—"and their charms and those of all the magicians, and likewise the illusions and devices of all the conjurers"; and he did so not merely that he might be able to expose their deceptions, but also "so that nothing that ought to be known might escape him." And his experimental science not merely "considered all the follies of the magicians, not to confirm them but to shun them, just as logic deals with sophistry"; but also "so that all falsity may be removed and the truth of the art alone retained." Roger himself in the case of the split hazel rod discovered a natural phenomenon concealed by use of a magic incantation. Bacon also granted that the books of the magicians "may contain some truth." It also was apparently very difficult to distinguish them from other writings, since he states that many books are reputed magical which are nothing of the sort but contain sound learning; since he calls the magicians "corrupters of wisdom's records," and charges them not only with fraudulently ascribing various "enormities" to Solomon, but with misinterpreting and abusing "enigmatical writings" which he believes Solomon really wrote; and since he tells us that even true philosophers have sometimes made use of meaningless incantations and characters in order to conceal their meaning. He consequently concludes that experience will show which books are good and which are bad, and that "if anyone finds the work of nature and art in one of them, let him receive it; if not, abandon the book as open to suspicion."

Indeed, Bacon seems to think that magic has taken such a hold upon men that it can be uprooted only by scientific exposition of its tricks and by scientific achievement of even greater marvels than it professes to perform. Perhaps he realizes that religious censure or rationalistic argument is not enough to turn men from these alluring arts, but that science must show unto them yet a more excellent way, and afford scope for that laudable curiosity, that inventive and exploring instinct which magic pretends to gratify. He waxes enthusiastic over "the secret works of art and nature," and contends that the wonders of nature and the possibilities of applied science far outshine the feats of magicians. One reason why early Christian writers so often confounded philosophy and magic together was, in his opinion, that the philosophers by their marvelous exploitation of the forces of nature equalled both the illusions of magic and the miracles of the Christians. Science, in short, not merely attacks magic's front; it can turn its flank and cut it off from its base of supplies.

But Bacon's science is sometimes occult science. In the first place he shared the common belief of his time that "herbs and stones and metals and other things" possess "almost miraculous" powers. By thorough investigation of such occult virtues Artephius prolonged his existence to one thousand and twenty-five years. "Moreover, there are numerous things which kill every venomous animal by the slightest contact; and if a circle is drawn about such animals with objects of this sort, they cannot get out but die without having been touched. And if a man is stung by a venomous animal, he can be cured by a little powder scraped from such objects, as Bede writes in his *Ecclesiastical History* and as we know by experience. And so there are innumerable things which have extraneous virtues of this sort, of whose powers we are ignorant from mere neglect of experimentation." By calling such virtues "extraneous" Bacon seems to imply that they cannot be accounted for by the properties of the elements composing the objects, and perhaps further that they are of celestial origin. This points on to his belief in astrology.

But Bacon goes farther than that, for some of his "secret works of art and nature" we must regard as plain cases of magic procedure, and they would indeed be so classified by most of our authors. Bacon really goes about as far as Albertus Magnus in credulous acceptance of superstition, but will not admit, as Albert does, that such things are magic or very closely related to it. The incantations and characters, the fascination and marvelous transformations of magic Bacon condemns, but he does not condemn all incantations and characters, nor disbelieve in marvelous transformations and fascination. While he regards haphazard fascination as magic, he holds that just as certain bodily diseases are contagious, so if some malignant soul thinks hard of infecting another, and desires this ardently, and has full confidence in its own power to inflict such injury, "there is no doubt that nature will obey thought, as Avicenna"—who seems to have been the leading medieval authority on the subject of fascination—"shows in his eighth book on animals and in his fourth book on the soul: . . . and this much is not magic."

Bacon makes a close connection between fascination and the power of words and of the human voice, since in his opinion both are largely due to the rational soul. Words are the soul's most appropriate instrument and almost every miracle since the beginning of the world has been performed by using them. "For where the attention, desire and virtue of the rational soul, which is worthier than the stars, concur with the power of the sky, it is inevitable that either a word or some other instrument of marvelous power be produced which will alter the things of this world, so that not only natural objects but also souls will be inclined to those ends which the wise operator desires." Again in the **Opus Tertium** we are told that, while the magician accomplishes nothing by words, the wise man may for this reason. "When words are uttered with deep thought and great desire and good intention and firm confidence, they have great virtue. For when these four qualities these four qualities unite, the substance of the rational being is strongly excited to radiate its own species and virtues from itself into its own body and foreign matter." The rational soul influences the voice, which in turn affects the atmosphere and all objects contained therein. The physical constitution of the speaker also has some influence,

and finally the positions of the stars must by all means be taken into account. All this reasoning is equivalent to accepting the power of incantations, for as Bacon states, "They are words brought forth by the exertion of the rational soul, and receive the virtue of the sky as they are pronounced." Through their power bodies are healed, venomous animals put to flight, and other such effects produced. If incantations are made as described above, "then they are philosophical and the work of a sage wisely enchanting, as David the prophet says." Bacon, however, recognizes that he is dealing with a delicate matter in which it is hard to distinguish between philosophy and magic. Of his further discussion of characters and images, and effort to show that they need not be magical, we shall treat presently in connection with his astrology. In his introduction to *The Secret of Secrets* he holds that the prayers and sacrifices of Aristotle and other philosophers were licit and not idolatrous.

Thus Bacon fails in his attempt to draw the line between science and magic, and shows, as William of Auvergne, Albertus Magnus, and others have already shown, how inextricably the two subjects were intertwined in his time. His own science still clings to many occult and magical theories and practices, while he admits that the magicians often try or pretend to use scientific books and methods, and that it is no easy matter to tell which books and characters and images are which. The experimental scientist not only exposes the frauds of magic but discovers secrets of nature hidden beneath the husk of magical ceremony and pretense. Also some men employ the marvels of philosophy for wicked ends and so pervert it into a sort of magic. Finally in one passage he forgets himself and speaks of "those magnificent sciences" which properly employ "images, characters, charms, prayers, and deprecations" as "magical sciences."

Bacon's doctrine of the multiplication of species is a good illustration of the combination of magic and science which we encounter in his works. This theory has been praised by his admirers as the propagation of force subject to mathematical law; and he has been commended for describing the species which every agent causes in all directions not, like the idols of Lucretius, as material films which peel off from the agent and impress themselves on surrounding matter, but as successive effects produced in that matter. Bacon usually illustrates his theory by the radiation of light from the sun, and by a discussion of the geometrical laws of reflection and refraction; thus his theory seems at first sight a physical one. He believed, however, that the occult influences of the planets upon nature and man were exercised in the same way, and also such mysterious powers as those of the evil eye and of fascination. Indeed, he asserts that this multiplication of virtues is universal, and that spiritual beings as well as corporeal objects affect in this manner everything about them and may themselves be so affected by other objects and beings. Viewed from this angle, his theory seems a magical one of occult influence, though given a scientific guise by its assumption that such forces proceed along mathematical lines after the analogy of rays of light. This suggests that it is not fair merely to call Bacon's science superstitious; we must also note that he tries to make his magic scientific. But finally we must note that this doctrine was not original with Bacon; we have already met with it in Alkindi's work on stellar rays.

It is interesting to find Bacon's belief that the works of art and nature can exceed those of magic, and his charge that unscientific persons are confusing such works with magic, repeated by another writer. William of St. Cloud composed astronomical tables based upon his own observations during the period from about 1285 to 1321, in which he detected errors in the earlier tables of Thebit, Toulouse, and Toledo. This experimental astronomer, speaking of the powers of mirrors and lenses, such as those of Archimedes, those by which Caesar saw Britain from the shores of Gaul, and that by which Socrates discovered a dragon in the air, says: "These marvels and many others have been performed in ancient times, not by magic art, as some would have it, who are ignorant of the secrets of nature and of scientific industry, but solely by the force of nature and the aid of art."

We now turn to Bacon's attitude towards astrology, which we have already seen was an important factor in his "secret works of art and nature" as well as in his mathematics. He was aware that the *mathematici* or astrologers of the Roman Empire had been condemned by some of the church fathers, and were classed as practitioners of magic by more recent theologians and writers on Canon law. Like Isidore, Albertus Magnus, and other authors whom we have already discussed, Bacon gets around this by distinguishing two varieties of mathematics, one of which he says is magic, condemned by Cicero in his *De divinatione* and by other classical authorities as well as by the church fathers, the other a department of philosophy, a branch of which Augustine, Ambrose, Basil, Cassiodorus, and Gregory all approved. In the **Opus Maius** and **Opus Tertium** he states as usual that the "e" is long in the magical art of divination, while the vowel is short in the philosophical study; but in other writings he changed his mind and declared that "all the Latins" were wrong in this opinion and that the distinction was just the opposite. Bacon also cites Isidore's distinction between two kinds of "astronomy"; one natural science, the other superstitious. Roger himself sometimes uses the words "astrology" and "astronomy" indifferently; sometimes speaks of "astrology" as speculative and "astronomy" as practical; sometimes distinguishes between speculative and practical astrology, of which the last includes judicial astrology.

Four features, to Bacon's mind, distinguish the forbidden *mathematica* from legitimate judicial astrology. In the first place, it ascribes fatal necessity to the influence of the stars, whereas Bacon shows by an examination of the writings of Haly, Ptolemy, Avicenna, Messahala, and Isaac that learned and legitimate astrologers have never held any such tenet as fatal necessity, although common report may ignorantly ascribe such doctrine to them. In the second place, the practitioners of the magical variety of mathematics "invoke demons by conjurations and sacrifices to supplement the influence of the constellations, an execrable practice." Third, "they mar their astrological observations by the idlest sort of circles, figures, and characters, and by the stupidest incantations and unreasonable

prayers in which they put their trust." Finally they often resort to fraud, employing confederates, darkness, deceptive mechanisms, and sleight-of-hand. By such methods "in which they know there is illusion" and "in which there is no virtue of the sky operating," "they perform many feats which seem marvelous to the stupid."

While thus censuring the *mathematica* which is a subdivision of magic, Bacon declared that "it is manifest to everyone that the celestial bodies are the causes of generation and corruption in all inferior things." Had not Aristotle in his treatise on Generation and Corruption said that the four terrestrial elements are related to the heavens as tools to an artificer? Bacon regarded the stars as ungenerated, incorruptible, and voluntary in their movements, which were regulated by angelic intelligences. He also accepted the usual technique of the astrological art in explaining the operation of this celestial influence.

Bacon naturally subjected the human body to the constellations and was a firm believer in astrological medicine. If a doctor is ignorant of "astronomy," his medical treatment will be dependent upon "chance and fortune." Bacon holds not only that at conception and at birth one's fundamental "complexion," or physical constitution, is determined by the sky, but that with each changing hour our bodies are governed by a different planet whose characteristics the physician should know. Where Neckam had assigned six hours to the planet after which the day was named, that is, the first three and last three hours of the twenty-four, Bacon assigns it only four hours, namely, the first, eighth, fifteenth and twenty-second. Then, in order to bring the proper planet into control of the first hour of the succeeding day, he is obliged to have them follow each other in a different order in their rule of hours from that in which the days of the week are named. Bacon also distributes the parts of the body among the signs of the zodiac, and states that the physician must observe the moon carefully. He cites Hippocrates, Galen, the *Centiloguium* and Haly concerning the great influence of the stars both upon health and the administering of medicines. That the patriarchs of the Old Testament lived so much longer than men do to-day has been explained by many, Bacon says, as due to the stars. His explanation of the strange case of a woman of Norwich who ate nothing for twenty years and yet was during all that time in the best of health is that some constellation must have reduced the concourse of the four elements in her body to a self-sufficient harmony such as they seldom attain. Indeed, he goes so far as to hold that the resurrected body will have that harmony of the elements and so endure through eternity, no matter whether raised to the bliss of heaven or subjected to the consuming torments of hell.

Bacon even held that the stars by their influence upon the human body incline men to bad acts and evil arts or to good conduct and useful sciences. Such natural inclinations might, however, be resisted by effort of will, modified by divine grace, or strengthened by diabolic tempting. But while the individual by an effort of will may resist the force of the stars, in masses of men the power of the constellations usually prevails; and the differences in peoples inhabiting different parts of the earth are due to their being under different aspects of the sky. Recent bloody wars might have been avoided, had men harkened to warnings written in the sky. "Oh, how great profit to the church of God might have been procured, if the disposition of the sky for those times had been foreseen by the wise, and known to prelates and princes, and restricted by zeal for peace! Then there would not have been such slaughter of Christians nor so many souls sent below." The personality of the king, too, has such great influence upon his kingdom that it is worth while to examine his horoscope carefully.

Bacon was especially attracted by the doctrine of Albumasar concerning conjunctions of the planets, and derived comforting evidence of the superiority of the Christian faith to other religions from the astrological explanation of the origin of religious sects according to the successive conjunctions of the other planets with Jupiter. He was pleased by the association of Christianity with Mercury, which he calls the lord of wisdom and eloquence, of oracles and prophecies; it is dominant only in the sign Virgo, which at once suggests the Virgin Mary; and its orbit, difficult to trace because of epicycle and eccentric, typifies well the Christian creed with its mysteries that defy reason. Similarly the malign force of the moon, productive of necromancy and magic, fits Antichrist exactly; and Venus corresponds to the sensuality of Mohammedanism. Further astrological evidences of Christianity are the coincidence six years before the birth of Christ of an important conjunction of Saturn and Jupiter with a tenth revolution of Saturn, which last occurs only at intervals of 320 years, and always marks some great historical change like the advent of Alexander or Manes or Mohammed. Astrology further assures us that Islam can endure only 693 years, a prediction in close agreement with the number of the beast in the Apocalypse, 663 (sic); the small discrepancy of thirty years is readily accounted for by the dictum of the venerable Bede that "Scripture in many places subtracts something from the complete number, for that's the way with Scripture."

The astronomers, Bacon tells the pope, further assure us that even the Virgin Birth of Christ and His Nativity were in accordance with the constellations. They think that God willed so to order His works that certain future events which He foresaw or predestined should be revealed to the wise through the planets, in order that the human mind, recognizing God's marvelous works, might increase in love towards Him. They grant that it is impossible that the Creator be subject to a creature, or that the birth of Christ, in so far as it was supernatural, should be subject in any way to the influence of the stars, which in this respect could only be signs of the divine work. But in so far as the birth of Jesus was a natural event and His nature was human, they regard Him as under the influence of the constellations, like the rest of humanity. Their statements in such matters should, however, Bacon more cautiously adds, be brought into conformity with the doctrines of the Catholic faith.

Bacon believed that by means of astrology not only could the future be in large measure foretold, but also marvelous operations and great alterations could be effected through-out the whole world, especially by choosing favorable hours and by employing astronomical amulets and characters—in other words, by the arts of elections and of images. As the babe at birth receives from the stars that fundamental physical constitution which lasts it through life, so any new-made object is permanently affected by the disposition of the constellations at the moment of its making. Especially by images, "if they are engraved in accordance with the aspect of the sky in the elect times, can all injuries be repelled and useful undertakings promoted." Bacon not only cites as authorities concerning them Haly's commentary on the *Centiloquium* supposed to be by Ptolemy, Thabit ben Corra, and the spurious *Secret of Secrets* of Aristotle; but believes that Moses and Solomon both made use of them. The marvelous power of spoken words is also in part accounted for by Bacon by the celestial influence prevalent at the moment of utterance. "Although the efficacious employment of words is primarily the function of the rational soul," nevertheless "the astronomer can form words in elect times which will possess unspeakable power" of transforming natural objects and even inclining human minds to obey him. Thus Bacon's "astronomer" is really a magician and enchanter as well—one more of the many indications we have met that there is no dividing line between magic and astrology: divination is magic; astrology operates. Bacon was very desirous that the church should avail itself of the guidance and aid of astrology; and he feared the harm that Antichrist, whose advent Bacon with many others of his century seems to have believed was near at hand, or the Tartars with their astrologers, would be able to do Christendom, if the church neglected this art.

Having considered Bacon's position in regard to magic and astrology, we are now prepared to inquire what likelihood there is that his reported condemnation in 1278 for "some suspected novelties" was due to either. Briefly it may be answered to begin with that his views concerning these subjects were not novel; he shared them with Albert and other contemporaries, and there seems to be no good reason why they should have got him into trouble. His expressed attitude towards "magic" is so hostile that it seems unlikely that he would have been charged with it, when other clergymen like Albert and William of Auvergne spoke of it with less hostility and yet escaped unscathed. There is not a particle of evidence in his works that he even invoked spirits or attempted to do anyone an injury by occult methods, and this was the only kind of magic that was likely to be punished at that time. Towards astrology he was, it is true, more favorable than some of his contemporaries. With his views on astrological images and his attribution of religious sects to conjunctions of the planets theologians like Aquinas and William of Auvergne would refuse to agree, but Arabian astrology supported such doctrines, and the views of an approved Christian thinker like Albertus Magnus concerning astrology are almost identical with those of Bacon. We note elsewhere writings on such subjects as astrological medicine by Franciscans; and such a regulation as that of May 25, 1292, for Franciscans studying at Paris, that they should not spend the alms given them to buy books with for other purposes, nor cause curious books to be made, suggests that a number of them were prone to consult superstitious works as well as that the Order forbids this. And by "curi-ous books" are doubtless meant the sort that we have heard Bacon strongly censure.

Again therefore there is no reason why Bacon should have been singled out for condemnation. Such a notion has aris-en partly from misapprehension as to the views of Bacon's contemporaries and from misstatements such as the pas-sage in Charles' life of Bacon, where he declares that Car-dinal Pierre d'Ailly in his treatise on laws and sects con-demns the doctrine of an English doctor concerning reli-gions and the conjunctions of planets, and approves the contrary doctrine of William of Auvergne, but "does not dare" to name Bacon, to whom he alludes with the bated breath of terror and repugnance. All this, except the bare fact that d'Ailly criticizes this particular doctrine of Bacon, is sheer fancy on Charles' part. Had he consulted a complete fifteenth-century edition of d'Ailly's writings instead of merely such of his treatises as were included in an eighteenth-century edition of the works of Gerson, he would have known that elsewhere the cardinal cites Bacon on astrology by name with respect and admiration, and that the learned reformer even goes so far as to agree bold-ly and explicitly with Bacon's doctrine that Christ as a son of man was under the stars. That Bacon's astrology had not been condemned in 1278 is also indicated soon after his death by Pierre Dubois' approving mention of his dis-cussion of the utility of "mathematics."

It must be added, however, that there are passages in Bacon's own writings which are perhaps also partly re-sponsible for the growth of the idea that he was con-demned for magic or astrology. Briefly, these are the pas-sages where he himself says that there is danger of scien-tists being accused of magic. For instance, he tells us that "scarcely anyone has dared" to speak of astronomical im-ages in public, "For those who are acquainted with them are immediately called magicians, although really they are the wisest men." It also seems somewhat strange that Bacon should always be so condemnatory and contemptu-ous in his allusions to magic and magicians, when both William of Auvergne and Albertus Magnus allude to it as sometimes bordering upon science, in which case they do not regard it unfavorably. The suspicion occurs to one that Bacon perhaps protests a little too much, that he is con-demning magic from a fear that he may be accused of it. But are not his apprehensions exaggerated? Does he not overstate the hostility of canonists and theologians to his many splendid sciences, and their tendency to confuse them with magic? Thomas of Cantimpré in the *De natura rerum* and Albert in the treatise on minerals and in the *Speculum astronomiac* dared to discuss astronomical im-ages. And finally, whether there is any real ground for Bacon's apprehensions or not, if he is afraid of being ac-cused of magic, would not this very fear keep him from going too far and from thereby incurring condemnation in 1278 on this account?

Conclusion

Such were Roger Bacon's views bearing upon magic and experimental science and their relations to Christian thought, as set forth principally in his *Opus Maius* and the two other treatises to the pope which supplemented it.

Most medieval books impress one as literary mosaics where the method of arrangement may be new but most of the fragments are familiar. One soon recognizes, how-ever, that striking similarity in two passages is no sure sign that one is copied from the other. The authors may have used the same Arabic sources or simply be repeating some commonplace thought of the times. Men began with the same assumptions and general notions, read the same lim-ited library, reasoned by common methods, and naturally often reached the same conclusions, especially since the field of knowledge was not yet so extensive but that one man might try to cover it all, and since all used the same medium of thought, the Latin language. New discoveries were being made occasionally but slowly, perhaps also sporadically and empirically. A collection of industrial and chemical recipes in the thirteenth century may in the main be derived from a set of the seventh century or Helle-nistic age, but a few new ones have somehow got added to the list in the interim. Thomas of Cantimpré's encyclo-pedia professes to be no more than a compilation, but it seems to contain the first allusion we have to modern plumbing.

Bacon's chief book was a mosaic like the rest, but bears a strong impress of his personality. Sometimes there is too much personality, but if we allow for this, we find it a valu-able, though not a complete nor perfect, picture of medi-eval learning. Its ideas were not brand-new; it was not cen-turies in advance of its age; but while its contents may be found scattered in many other places, they will scarcely be found altogether anywhere else, for it combines the most diverse features. In the first place it is a "pious" pro-duction, if I may employ that adjective in a somewhat ob-jectionable colloquial sense to indicate roughly a combina-tion of religious, theological, and moral points of view. In other words, Bacon continues the Christian attitude of pa-tristic literature to a certain extent; and his book is written by a clergyman for clergymen, and in order to promote the welfare of the Church and Christianity. There is no deny-ing that, hail him as one may as a herald of modern sci-ence. Secondly, he is frequently scholastic and metaphysi-cal; yet thirdly, is critical in numerous respects; and fourthly, insists on practical utility as a standard by which science and philosophy must be judged. Finally, he is an exponent of the aims and methods of what we have called "the natural magic and experimental school," and as such he sometimes comes near to being scientific. So there is no other book quite like the *Opus Maius* in the Middle Ages, nor has there been one like it since; yet it is true to its age and is still readable to-day. It will therefore always remain one of the most remarkable books of the remarkable thir-teenth century.

George Sarton   (essay date 1927)

SOURCE: "Philosophic and Cultural Background: Roger Bacon," in *Introduction to the History of Science: From Rabbi Ben Ezra to Roger Bacon, Vol. II*, The Williams & Wilkins Company, 1931, pp. 952-67.

[In the following excerpt from a work originally published in 1927, Sarton surveys Bacon's achievement, arranged by

discipline, referring occasionally to his unfinished Compendium philosophiae.]

General appreciation—Bacon was essentially an encyclopaedist; that is, he was tormented with the idea of the unity of knowledge, and his life was a long effort better to grasp and to explain that unity. He denounced violently the evils of scholasticism, too violently in fact to obtain practical results. He realized the urgent need for philosophers and theologians to enlarge their basis of knowledge; they were not acquainted with the available scientific data and their mathematical and linguistic equipment was utterly insufficient. His greatest title to fame however, was his vindication of the experimental spirit. He was not himself an experimenter any more than he was a mathematician, but he clearly saw—better than anybody else in his time—that without experimentation and without mathematics, natural philosophy is very soon reduced to verbiage.

He also realized the utility of knowledge, and this was even more remarkable than to realize its unity, for the latter had been done instinctively by almost every philosopher. In the *Opus majus* and the *Opus tertium* he insists upon that utility repeatedly. This double point of view, unity (to be discovered experimentally and proved with the help of mathematics) and utility, led him to entirely new conceptions of knowledge, of learning, and of education.

Unfortunately he was of a quarrelsome disposition—a regular "kicker" or "mauvais coucheur"—and too temperamental to exert much influence upon his contemporaries; his immoderate criticism of the other leaders was bound to antagonize their followers instead of conciliating them. He detested Albert the Great and St. Thomas, not only because he was jealous of their tremendous success but also because he knew that their syntheses, though offered as complete and accepted as such, were incomplete in some essential respects. Moreover he was temperamentally opposed to them. Like the majority of his Franciscan brethren, he was an Augustinian (i. e., a Platonist), while they were Aristotelians. Bacon was a poorer philosopher perhaps than St. Thomas; that is, he was less able to construct a harmonious and authoritative synthesis; but he was a far better scientist; he was a poorer naturalist than Albert, but a better mathematician and physicist; he was a deeper encyclopaedist than both.

His accomplishments fell considerably short of his visions. Yet visions are very important, and we need seers as well as inventors. Bacon made few if any experiments, and no invention, not even gunpowder, can be definitely ascribed to him. He seems to have vaguely foreseen fundamental discoveries and inventions: the possibility of circumnavigating the world, of propelling boats by mechanical means, of flying, of taking advantage of the explosive property of powder, of improving sight by proper adjustments of lenses. One such anticipation would hardly deserve to be mentioned, but the combination of so many in a single head is very impressive.

As opposed to a dogmatic system like Thomism, Bacon's thoughts seem and are disconnected. His own philosophy was less a system than a method, a point of view. Hence its comparative failure was not surprising. St. Thomas founded a school, almost comparable in size and influence to the Academy and the Lyceum; Bacon founded none, but the majority of modern scientists feel more genuinely attracted to him than to any other mediaeval personality.

One should not confuse dogmatism with originality. Bacon's thought was less systematic, but on the whole more original than that of his great contemporaries. And the best proof of this is that he was a true harbinger of modern civilization, while St. Thomas (not to speak of the others) was destined to become the most perfect symbol of mediaevalism.

Of course, Bacon's originality—like any other—was limited. It consisted more in new arrangements and displacements of emphasis than in actual inventions. He borrowed materials from everywhere, and continued to a large extent the Oxford Franciscan tradition. He had no real followers and his fame increased but very slowly during the fourteenth and fifteenth centuries; much of it was a poor fame at that, a purely legendary one. . . .

The Opera of 1266-1267— . . . Bacon wrote a series of four works which were sent to Clement IV in 1268; the **Opus majus,** the **Opus minus,** the **Opus tertium,** and the **De multiplicatione specierum.**

The **Opus majus** was divided into seven parts: (1) Causes of error; (2) Philosophy vs. theology; (3) Study of languages; (4) Mathematics (including astronomy, music, geography, etc.); (5) Optics or perspective; (6) Experimental science; (7) Morals.

The **Tractatus de multiplicatione specierum** was probably written before 1266; it was possibly a part of the *Compendium philosophiae.* A copy of it was sent to the Pope together with the **Opus majus.** . . .

The **Opus minus** was both an introduction and a supplement to the Opus majus. We have only fragments of it. It contained additional notes on astrology (**De notitia caelestium**), on the main points of the **Opus majus,** on alchemy (**In enigmatibus; De rerum generatione ex elementis**), on medicine (**Remedia studii**).

The **Opus tertium** was a work of the same kind as the preceding, i. e., a sort of supplement to the **Opus majus.** It deals with the relations of the different sciences to one another, with physics (vacuum, motion, and space), mathematics, astronomy alchemy, etc.

Bacon's ideas on almost every subject may be found in the **Opus majus** and its supplements. In the following sections, reference to them as well as to the more special treatises mentioned, will always be implied.

Questions on the Aristotelian treatises—During his stay in Paris (c. 1236-1251), Bacon discussed the Physics of Aristotle (Bks. I to VI), the Metaphysics (Bk. I, XII, and possibly Bks. II and IV), the *De plantis* and the *De causis.* The result of that teaching was the publication, not of commentaries, but of "questions" relative to special topics. These questions are of the purely scholastic type.

Logic—Bacon was well acquainted with the Aristotelian

Organon and with the De sex principiis of Gilbert de la Porrée, but—and this is one of his originalities—he attached to logic only a subordinate importance. For him the main avenue to knowledge was not logic, but linguistic and mathematical ability. Logical ability he thought was almost instinctive, but languages and mathematics had to be learned. . . .

Mathematics—Bacon was not an original mathematician, and his knowledge of mathematics was very limited. But he was imbued with the Platonic idea of the transcendental, importance of mathematics and he helped the diffusion of that idea. He was equally convinced of the practical utility of mathematics in almost every study, and explained it at great length.

Though the best source of knowledge (outside of revelation) is experimentation, the latter must be completed by mathematical treatment to bear all its fruits. This was a sort of anticipative conception of mathematical physics; very vague indeed, yet very fine. . . .

Astronomy and astrology— . . . Bacon was well acquainted with Greek and Arabic astronomy and much interested in the subject, but like Grosseteste, he was never able to decide between Ptolemy and al-Bitrūjī; he found that Ptolemy's system gave a better account of the observed facts, but that al-Bitrūjī's was more consistent with the principles of natural philosophy. His influence can be traced in the work of the French Franciscan, Bernard of Verdun, and perhaps also in that of William of Saint Cloud. He had obtained some knowledge of the strange cosmological views (solid planetary spheres) of Ibn al-Haitham and of Muhammad ibn Ahmad al-Kharaqī.

He was deeply interested in astrology in which he believed implicitly. However he made a clear distinction between astrology and magic. Astrology itself he divided into two kinds; a legitimate kind, and a forbidden one, mere superstition. This was very sound, in spite of the fact that much if not all of Bacon's legitimate astrology was nothing but error and superstition from our point of view.

The theory of multiplication of species . . . had naturally an astrological aspect—for how were astrological influences transmitted through space? —which Bacon carefully amplified.

Calendar—Bacon continued Grosseteste's efforts to introduce a reform of the calendar which became more and more necessary as centuries went by. He devoted two special treatises to this question; the *Compotus naturalium,* written in 1263-1265, and the *De termino Paschali.* A *Kalendarium* ascribed to him was made by another Franciscan (?) at Toledo, 1292, or 1297. Bacon's *Compotus* is a complete and masterful treatise on the subject; it includes a full history of it wherein a large number of earlier authors—Greek, Arabic, Latin—are quoted and discussed, and an elaborate criticism of the ecclesiastical and lay calendars.

Mechanics—Bacon knew some of the mechanical writings of Jordanus Nemorarius (*De ponderibus; Elementa super demonstrationem ponderis?*) or of the latter's school, but in this field as in others he was chiefly influenced by Grosseteste. He investigated such subjects as force and its mathematical expression, and the impossibility of a vacuum. Following Adelard of Bath he explained the impossibility of vacuum by a theory of universal continuity. On the other hand he used it as an argument against the plurality of worlds.

He gave considerable thought also to the problems relative to what we would call action at a distance. How are mechanical forces, light, astrological influences, transmitted? He discussed these problems in the *Opus majus,* the *Opus tertium* and in a treatise ad hoc *De multiplicatione specierum,* which was sent by him to the Pope together with the *Opus majus.* Bacon called "species" what we would call "action" (I do not use a more definite term on purpose) and his *Multiplicatio specierum* was a study of the transmission of these actions, of the propagation of efficient causality.

Optics or "perspective"—Naturally that theory of multiplication of species was especially elaborated with a view to its optical applications. In this Bacon was walking in Grosseteste's footsteps; but he had a better knowledge of the Arabic writings, e. g., those of al-Kindī and of Ibn al-Haitham. In his turn he influenced John Peckham and William of Saint Cloud. His optics was essentially based upon that of the Ibn al-Haitham, with small additions and practical applications. He made experiments with mirrors and lenses, chiefly burning lenses, and foresaw vaguely both the compound microscope and the telescope. He influenced Leonard Digges, who died c. 1571. He had some understanding of spherical aberration and of its correction by the use of paraboloidal and hyperboloidal surfaces.

In opposition to Grosseteste he claimed that the passage of light through a medium cannot be instantaneous. Light is not an emanation of particles, but the transmission of a movement (*Opus majus*). However all this is too vaguely put to be considered an anticipation of the wave theory of light.

Bacon spent a consideration amount of money in these optical experiments. He sent a lens to the Pope to induce him to experiment himself (*Opus tertium*).

Alchemy—Gunpowder was discovered probably within Bacon's lifetime, but there is nothing to prove that he was the inventor. . . . He mentioned several times inflammable mixtures, such as were used for fireworks, and he described an explosive one which was probably gunpowder. He even suggested that its explosive power would be increased if the powder were enclosed in an instrument of solid material (*Opus tertium*).

His interest in alchemy is sufficiently proved by the fact that one of the four books of his *Compendium philosophiae* was to be entirely devoted to it, by the amount of space given to it in the *Opus minus* and the *Opus tertium,* and by the *Tractatus expositorius enigmatum alchemiae* which he communicated to Clement IV. He made a distinction between practical and speculative alchemy. He was opposed to the theory of the unity of matter (*Opus tertium*); his "primary matter" was not the primary constituent of all substances, but on the contrary a perfect and final blending of the elements. . . .

The most important of Bacon's chemical writings are the **Tractatus expositorius** and the **Epistola de secretis operibus naturae.** The ascription of the invention of gunpowder to him was based upon a cipher contained in this **Epistola.** However this cipher has no MS. authority whatever; it was probably nothing more than a copyist's blunder.

Geography—The geographical section of the **Opus majus** (in the mathematical part) contained information on the less known countries of the world, derived not only from ancient geographers and from Aethicus Ister but also from recent travelers, notably William of Rubruquis. Bacon insisted upon the habitability of the southern hemisphere. He explained to the Pope the importance of undertaking a complete and accurate survey of the world, and appended to his treatise a parchment mappemonde whereupon the coordinates of the principal places were fixed (this map is lost). He indicated the possibility of reaching the Indies by sailing westward from Spain, and assumed that these countries were considerably nearer than they are. This was known indirectly to Columbus (through Peter of Ailly's *Imago mundi*) and may have been one of his incentives.

Medicine—Bacon wrote a number of medical treatises which were derived essentially from the Arabic writings and proved little originality (except one of them). Believing as he did in astrology, he naturally insisted upon the astrological side of medicine.

The longest and best known of these writings, the **Liber de retardatione accidentium senectutis,** was also the poorest. It was written relatively early (it was probably his first publication) when his mind was still undeveloped. In spite of its mediocrity it was plagiarized c. 1309-1311 by Arnold of Villanova under the title *De conservanda juventute et retardanda senectute,* and Villanova's edition was translated into Italian and into English.

Experimental science—Bacon's greatness as an experimental philosopher has been very much exaggerated. He made few experiments himself and in a sense he never understood the experimental method as we now understand it. Much of the praise bestowed upon him is based upon his own irresponsible statements. Like his countryman, Francis Bacon, more than three centuries later, he gave many precepts which he never followed himself. But what of it? Was it not—in his time—an immense achievement to speak of the superior value, of the indispensableness, of experimentation as he did repeatedly?. ..

A whole part of the **Opus majus,** out of seven, was devoted to experimental science, and he came back to it in the two other Opera. He was careful to distinguish between external and internal experience (*scientia experimentalis, per sensus exteriores; scientia interior, intuitiva*), a distinction which was unfortunately lost by many of the later philosophers. Bacon was primarily interested in external or objective experience. To be sure some of the experiments proposed by him were fantastic, and in spite of his own efforts to separate experimentation from magic, he did not always succeed. However, the essential soundness of his experimental point of view is proved by his readiness to sacrifice theories to facts and to confess his own ignorance.

Philosophy—Bacon's philosophy is explained in his Aristotelian commentaries, in the Metaphysica de viciis contractis in studio theologiae (c. 1266)—we have only a fragment of it—in the **Opus majus,** and finally in his last work, the **Compendium studii theologiae** (1292). To appreciate it correctly, one must bear in mind that Bacon was not a philosopher stricto sensu; the apparent or real contradictions of his thought were due to the complexity of his nature, half seer, half scientist.

His main sources were Aristotle, St. Augustine, Ishāq al-Isrā'īlī, Ibn Gabirol, Ibn Sīnā, Ibn Rushd, Pedro Alfonso, Grosseteste, and other English Franciscans. He was an Augustinian (i. e., a Platonist), a bold realist and pluralist, antagonistic to Thomism. Yet he deeply admired Aristotle and claimed to have a purer knowledge of him than was available in the Latin translations used by his contemporaries; he probably referred to the knowledge he had obtained through Ibn Rushd, but his understanding of Aristotle was far from perfect; witness his own inveterate Platonism. For example, he took considerable pains to prove that Aristotle had not taught the theory of the eternity of the world (he had taught it of course).

He had a strong belief in the unity of knowledge, but that unity was accounted for by him as a subordination of all knowledge to theology. No knowledge would ever have been possible without divine revelation. It is interesting to compare these views with his experimental philosophy.

This mixture of mysticism and scientific positivism was Bacon's main characteristic; each ingredient would explain his growing impatience with metaphysical discussion; the combination of both was overpowering. Bacon was not a philosopher, but he was one of the greatest thinkers of all ages. . . .

Philology—Bacon, realizing the supreme importance of the texts written in Greek, Hebrew and Arabic, insisted upon the necessity of studying these languages. This was really the first door to knowledge; the only means of approaching the sources of ancient wisdom. The third part of the **Opus majus** was entirely devoted to explaining the utility of linguistic studies, **De utilitate grammaticae.** The first volume of the *Compendium philosophiae* was planned to deal with grammar and logic. We have two important extracts from it, a complete Greek grammar, and incomplete Hebrew one.

While the need of languages for theological, philosophic and scientific purposes was foremost in his mind, he pointed out also other uses, diplomatic, missionary, and commercial. In his arguments for the study of Hebrew he anticipated Reuchlin. He realized that the best means of studying it was with the help of a Jew. He had a genuine interest in comparative philology. He suggested that Arabic, Hebrew, and Chaldaean were dialects of the same language. However it is doubtful whether he had any but the most superficial knowledge of Arabic.

He denounced the imperfection of the Latin versions of Aristotle and of the Bible. He insisted upon the urgency of recovering St. Jerome's text, and explained how it could be done. He thus laid down some of the principles of textual criticism.

To return to his Greek grammar, his work had been prepared for by Grosseteste and John Basingstoke, yet he was the first scholar in western Christendom to complete such a grammar for Latin use. . . .

Biblical studies—It is very misleading to represent Bacon as a sort of anticlerical prophet. He spoke ill of many clerics, but was not by any means anticlerical; he was or tried to be very orthodox, and considered the study of the Bible as of fundamental importance. Indeed the moral necessity of knowing the Holy Scriptures as exactly as possible was his primary argument for the study of Hebrew and Greek. All knowledge is explicitly or implicitly set forth in the Bible, and no effort should be spared to make that knowledge as clear and available as possible. In short, Bacon was in many respects what we would call a "fundamentalist," preaching repeatedly a return to the Bible, away from modern works such as the Books of sentences of Peter the Lombard to which theologians were giving undue importance. Like the majority of his contemporaries, Bacon believed in the approaching epiphany of Antichrist, and he made a special study of that problem.

Attitude to Israel and to Islām—His Hebrew studies and his need of Jewish collaboration may have induced him to consider the Jews with more kindness than was usual. At any rate his toleration of them was very remarkable and may have helped to make him obnoxious to other people. He shared the belief of most Jews and of many of his own contemporaries that the Hebrew culture was the original one from which the Greek had been derived at a later time. (According to various Jewish traditions, Aristotle had obtained his knowledge from Jewish sources, or was himself of Jewish race, or had become a Jewish proselyte). In the **Opus tertium** he says a good word for the Jews who lived in Palestine at the time of the Crucifixon.

One of his arguments for the study of Hebrew and Arabic was the need of these languages to convert unbelievers to Christianity. He realized the utter futility of the Crusades with respect to their avowed purpose. Persuasion will succeed where violence must fail, but people cannot be persuaded unless they be evangelized in their own language (**Opus majus**). In this respect he makes one think of Ramon Lull; he was a very poor orientalist as compared with Ramon, but he was far more consistent in his distrust of material strength.

Baconian legends—The experiments made or suggested by Bacon, his visionary inventions, failed to be appreciated for a considerable time, or rather, what is worse, they were misunderstood, and there emerged gradually the legend of Friar Bacon, the wonderworker. All sorts of magical powers were ascribed to him. . . .

An entirely different legend dating from modern times represents him as a martyr of science and of the freedom of thought. This is doubly misleading, for Bacon was a scientist but not a free thinker, as this phrase is generally understood. He was a very original thinker, a forerunner of modern science; he was outspoken and uncautious, yet very orthodox, and in many ways, a fundamentalist. On the other hand, if he was imprisoned by order of his Franciscan superiors this was apparently a matter of internal

discipline. Granted that he suffered for the originality of his mind and the eccentricities of his character, his martyrdom is not established, and he was not in any sense a forerunner of the modern rationalists, nor even of the Reformers. For him, theology was still the crown of all knowledge, and the Bible its repository.

Christopher Dawson   (essay date 1934)

SOURCE: "Religion and Mediaeval Science," in *Mediaeval Religion (The Forwood Lectures 1934) and Other Essays,* Sheed & Ward Inc., 1934, pp. 57-94.

[*In the following excerpt, Dawson summarizes the significance of Bacon's thought and its originality, citing him as a key example of the pursuit of knowledge for its own sake.*]

[It] is difficult to overestimate the influence of Grosseteste's thought on the mind of one of the most remarkable figures of the thirteenth century, whose fame has indeed overshadowed that of his master—I mean Roger Bacon. It was from Grosseteste that Bacon derived not only his distinctive philosophical and scientific views, above all his conviction of the importance of mathematics, but also his interest in philology and in the study of Greek and the oriental languages, of which Grosseteste was one of the pioneers. But if Bacon owed far more to his predecessors than has usually been supposed, he was none the less a profoundly original mind. His originality is however to be found less in his scientific theories than in his personality, and in his general attitude to contemporary thought. To a far greater extent than Grosseteste he stands apart from the main current of scholastic philosophical study, he belongs rather to the tradition of the men of science who were responsible for the introduction of Arabic science into the West, such as Adelard of Bath, Gerard of Cremona and Plato of Tivoli. It is true that he speaks with contempt of the translators, but this is owing to a somewhat exaggerated sense of their linguistic incompetence and not from any doubt as to the value of Arabic science, which he regards as the main channel by which Christendom could recover the wisdom of the ancient world. He resembles Adelard above all in his critical attitude to Western scholasticism; indeed, he quotes the actual words of Adelard with regard to the danger of a blind reliance on authority. In Bacon's view, the four fundamental obstacles to the progress of philosophy are dependence on authority, the influence of custom, the ignorance of the populace and the false pretensions of those who esteem themselves to be learned. He cannot find words strong enough to express his contempt for "these new theologians" of the teaching orders who become masters in theology and philosophy before they have studied, and who console themselves for their ignorance by belittling the sciences and display their emptiness before the eyes of the ignorant multitude.

Yet although Bacon includes the great Dominicans, Albert and Thomas, in his wholesale condemnation, he is far far from hostile to the new learning. He dismisses Alexander of Hales, precisely because the latter had had no training in Aristotelian physics and metaphysics "which are the glory of our modern studies." The works of Aristotle are for him "the foundation of all wisdom," and he blames his contemporaries not for their cultivation of Aristotelian science, but for their misunderstanding and corruption of it.

Still less can we regard his attitude to scholasticism and authority as an attempt to free science and reason from their dependence on theology. In this respect he is distinctly reactionary in comparison with St Thomas. The unity of science in which he believes is a purely theological unity. To an even greater extent than the earlier Augustinians he is prepared to subordinate all human knowledge to the divine wisdom that is contained in the Scriptures. All knowledge springs ultimately from Revelation. The first and most perfect scientists were the patriarchs, and the philosophers of the Gentiles merely collected the crumbs that had fallen from the tables of Shem and Abraham and Solomon. He admits the possibility of scientific progress, for there is no finality in this life, and knowledge must continue to increase with the rise and fall of the world religions. All the signs, he believed, pointed to the approaching end of the age and to the coming of Antichrist, and it was to arm Christendom for the struggle and to prepare the way for its renovation under the leadership of a great Pope and a great king that he propounded his schemes for the reform of studies and the utilization of the power of science.

Thus Bacon was no devotee of knowledge for its own sake. His attitude is fundamentally far less rational and far less intellectualist than that of Aristotle or even that of St Thomas. But though this detracts from the philosophic value of his work, it does nothing to diminish his personal originality and his historical significance. For the greatness of Roger Bacon consists not in his scientific achievement, which was small, nor in his scientific method, which was inferior to that of his master, Peter of Maricourt, the obscure *Magister Experimentorum*. His greatness is to be found in the scientific vision and imagination which made him the discoverer of a new scientific ideal and the prophet of the new world of modern science.

F. Winthrop Woodruff   (essay date 1938)

SOURCE: "Roger Bacon as a Critic among the Schoolmen," in *Roger Bacon: A Biography*, James Clark & Co., Ltd, 1938, pp. 89-101.

[*In the following excerpt, Woodruff examines the role of Bacon as a critic of and among the Schoolmen, comparing his philosophical emphases with those of Thomas Aquinas, Alexander of Hales, and others.*]

Bacon was somewhat critical of the intellectual world around him, and it is important to consider his comments on some of the great individuals of his day. At first he seems to have studied with a docile spirit, and to have been appreciative of his teachers. Indeed to judge from his earlier writings there is little to distinguish him from the general tone of the time. For instance, in his treatise *Questions on Aristotle,* which belongs to his early Paris life, there is hardly a trace of that emphasis on the appeal to experience which is the great characteristic of his more famous works. As Professor Little, who has edited some of Bacon's less notable writings, puts it:

> They are not commentaries on the text, but discussions of questions arising from the text. They proceed in the scholastic manner with arguments pro and con and solution, and are almost entirely argumentative. Thus he begins his discussion "whether it is possible that living things can be generated by putrefaction" with "it seems that . . . not", followed by a series of abstract arguments. Then "on the other side it is the authority of the scientists". That single line is the nearest approach in the whole argument to an appeal to experience and it is an appeal to authority. (*Roger Bacon.* British Academy lecture.)

In the same essay, Professor Little calls attention to an important passage in *Opus Tertium* to show that Bacon himself divided his intellectual life into two parts. Bacon writes:

> During the last twenty years, in which I have laboured specially in the study of wisdom after leaving the beaten track (abandoning the ordinary methods), etc.

This was written in 1267, so we may consider that Bacon's method changed somewhere about 1247, in the latter part of his first sojourn in Paris. He then ceased to be a conventional scholastic with his emphasis on reasoning and appeals to authority, and began to stress the value of actual experiment. It was this attitude which caused him to get out of harmony with his age, and to become its foremost critic. But even in his early period his mind was not in tune with much that passed for intellectual eminence in the Schools.

We have mentioned that he formed an opinion of the celebrated Alexander of Hales, who was lecturing in Paris when Bacon first went there about 1240, and died in 1245. We will now see what he has to say on the subject of Alexander. In the *Opus Minus* he is listing the obstacles to the progress of study among the "Latins", that is, the Western part of Christendom. Obstacle three is that theologians are ignorant of the sciences they need to make use of. He mentions two "leading doctors" whom he blames for much of the trouble. One is already dead, the other living. The first is named and is Alexander of Hales, who entered the Order of Friars Minor in its early days. He says that from the very start the brethren and others exalted Alexander to the skies, they gave him authority over all their studies, and ascribed to him a great Summa or compendium of knowledge, which not he but others had compiled. Before he entered the Order and was gaining the reputation which led the Friars to think so highly of him, the principal books and translated commentaries necessary for a sound basis of study were not in use at the University, their use being in many cases forbidden. Hence Alexander could not but be deficient in natural Philosophy and Metaphysics, and quite unworthy of the trust that had been placed in him.

The other doctor, who is described as living, is not named. According to Brewer he is simply another Franciscan professor, but Professor Little and others have taken the view that no less a personage is referred to than the Angelic doctor Thomas Aquinas himself.

"Another who lives", writes Bacon, "became a Friar as a mere lad, he never read Philosophy, nor heard it in the school, neither did he study much before he became a Theologian, nor could he be taught in his own Order, because he himself is the first Master of Philosophy they have had. He taught others, hence what he knows himself is self-taught. And indeed I praise him more than all the crowd of students, because he is a very studious man, and he looks into the infinite, and has gone to expense, so that he is able to collect much that is useful from a sea of authors. But because he has not the foundation, since he was not instructed nor exercised in listening, reading, disputing, he is necessarily ignorant of the common sciences. Since he is no linguist, his learning cannot be of great value, for the reasons I have urged in treating the subject of languages. Again he knows nothing of perspective, and cannot know much about Philosophy. As for those matters which I have dealt with, experimental sciences, alchemy, and mathematics, he can have no reason to boast. For these are greater than the other sciences. And if he does not know the lesser, how can he know the greater? God is witness that I have only exposed the ignorance of these men for the sake of truth in study. . . . For the common people believe everything these have written, and adhere to them as though they were angels. They are referred to in disputations and lectures as 'authors'. And he that lives has the greatest name of any Doctor in Paris, and they take him as 'author' in the schools, which cannot be without confusion and the destruction of wisdom, because his writings are full of falsehoods and endless vanities. There was never such a scandal in this world. There are some useful things in his work, but not as people think. . . . These have neither heard nor read the common Sciences, especially natural Philosophy and Mathematics [an inclusive term as far as Bacon was concerned] . . . they know not the Sciences and Languages about which I write to Your Holiness, without which nothing can be known about Philosophy as the treatise shows."

To understand what Bacon meant by these severe strictures on those whose reputations were very much greater than his own, we must remember the bent of his mentality, and what a great trial it must have been to him to see the world about him satisfied with what for him was not enough. The work of men like Alexander of Hales seemed adequate to the age, because they expounded fully the religious truth that was necessary for man's salvation. There was no idea of divorcing knowledge from immediate spiritual profit, and the sources of profitable knowledge were thus identical with those of Divine Revelation. Bacon, as we have seen, shared this general view to some extent. Study was for spiritual profit, but God's revealed Word was not confined to the supernatural revelation for which one went to Scripture and Tradition. There was also a natural revelation of God in nature, so nature must also be

studied if the full message of God's truth was to be discovered and profited by. Moreover, he was shrewd enough to realise that Scripture and Tradition required a large amount of subsidiary natural knowledge for their adequate study. Reasoning based on a string of texts or extracts from the Fathers of the Church might well be misleading if not founded on a proper knowledge of the languages involved, and the conditions under which the writings were composed. Hence Bacon could not be satisfied with the imposing array of Scriptural and Patristic quotations with which the schoolmen about him were wont to "prove" their points. He sought, consciously, for something more basic, and seems to have had some vision of the great increase of knowledge that the use of his methods would bring. Hence the urgency of his appeals to the Pope for the reform of the Schools, hence the vehemence, one might say the impatience, of his language. Hence also his true greatness. But while we sympathise with him, we must not blind ourselves to the real virtues of those whom he criticised. They produced many a monumental work, they often displayed great industry and reasoning power, and explored every logical conclusion that could be drawn from the data of existing knowledge.

The foremost textbook of the Schools when Bacon came on the scene was the famous *Sentences* of Peter Lombard. This was later superseded by the *Summa* of Thomas Aquinas, but it enjoyed unrivalled sway for about a century. The *Sentences* consisted of propositions clearly set out with a large number of Scriptural and Patristic passages which had a bearing on the matter under discussion. In dealing with this most learned work, Bacon is most severe. His fourth obstacle to the progress of study among the Latins is indeed simply that there is an exaggerated respect paid to those who read the *Sentences*. The theologians, as he puts it, place the burden on this one horse; and, after reading this mere summary, set up as Masters of Theology; but not a thirtieth part of the sacred text of Scripture is to be found here expounded, so the student of the *Sentences* has only made a beginning in grasping the full treasure of the Bible, but, alas, simply being a reader of this book is enough to give a man a reputation for learning, and favoured treatment among religious people. The *Sentences* are preferred, he goes on, to the study of the Bible itself, and even the Holy Doctors are not referred to except as they are quoted in this all-pervading book. Thus the works of great moderns like Grosseteste and Adam Marsh are unfortunately neglected, to the great loss of true learning.

In the ***Opus Tertium,*** Bacon refers to the writings of a certain Professor of Paris as having four short-comings. First, childish vanity, then unutterable falsehood, thirdly, they are far too long, what he says could be said in a twentieth of the space, and lastly, the omission of all that is most useful and beautiful in Philosophy. The influence of this man he considers detrimental to both Philosophy and Theology. It seems that he is here referring to the same Professor that he was referring to in the passage previously quoted from ***Opus Minus.*** In both passages the Professor is linked with Alexander of Hales. Bacon's words in this connection are:

And he gave not only great detriment for the study of Philosophy, but of Theology, as I show in the *Opus Minus,* where I speak of the Seven Sins of the study of Theology, and the third Sin is mainly directed against him, in as far as there is more open discussion on his account, for there I note too, that he is the principal offender, though the other of a greater name is dead.

Now the dead man referred to is certainly Alexander of Hales, and the living must certainly be Aquinas if it is he that is meant in the other passage. It is difficult to believe that Bacon would have so failed to appreciate the great work of the Angelic Doctor, though if we consider the very different mentality of the two men and the fact that the age was only able to appreciate one of them, Bacon may have been tempted to be unduly critical of one whom he alone felt it his duty to criticise.

A comparison of the two men will not be out of place here; for if we understand the main differences between them we shall go far to understand the age in which they lived. Thomas Aquinas was considered the greatest intellect of his time, he studied the things that really mattered, and wrote in such a clear concise way that even the most difficult theological problems appear in his pages as clear as day. His reasoning is always lucid. He proves his contentions point by point in a series of short chapters, he announces first various difficulties against what he is going to say, then proclaims the truth and finally answers the difficulties one by one in the order in which he has given them. Such concise writing would have been impossible for Bacon, who always seems anxious to do his subject full justice by painting a long word picture. He cannot be concise. But it is not only in the manner of writing that these men differ, there is a great and noticeable difference in their subject-matter. Both share the same faith and believe in the vital place of Theology in human learning, but whereas for Bacon God's truth is to be found everywhere, Aquinas lays his emphasis on revealed truths. Bacon would never have thought of writing at length on such difficult theological topics as the knowledge of God, or the nature of the Angels. He was not concerned to make the mystery of the Blessed Trinity or that of the Incarnation of God in Man clearer by a long, reasoned exposition, whereas in the pages of Thomas Aquinas these matters hold the stage, and are indeed made to appear almost simple. Aquinas therefore was the greater man in that he spoke to his age a language that it was ready and able to listen to, he accomplished a great work in reconciling Aristotle's philosophy with the Christian Faith, and the truths proclaimed by the Church he made to appear perfectly sound and reasonable. Bacon, on the other hand, was a voice crying in the wilderness; compared with the great truths of the Faith, natural Science appeared a trivial affair unworthy of serious attention, but to Bacon the truths of Science were of the greatest importance to Theology, and he realized that the state of man in this world could not be satisfactory, even from a religious point of view, if any branch of truth were neglected.

Another great man of the age who entered into Bacon's life was Bonaventure, who was General of the Franciscans from 1257 until his death in 1274. It was shortly after Bon-

aventure's appointment as General that Bacon was recalled to Paris, and the difficulties that he found in pursuing his work were no doubt to some extent of Bonaventure's making. He is, however, not mentioned critically by Bacon, though we may deduce that Bacon had him in mind when he used the phrase "my Superiors"; the mentality of Bonaventure was in great contrast to that of Bacon, he also differed from Thomas Aquinas in not laying such great store on the works of Aristotle. . . .

In 1271 Bacon wrote his *Compendium of Philosophy,* which contained much severe criticism of the clergy and schoolmen of the time. It is thought that this may have been the cause, first of his unpopularity and then of his condemnation, but it seems more probable that a condemnation on account of novelties would have referred to his actual work rather than to his criticisms.

Bertrand Russell   (essay date 1945)

SOURCE: "Franciscan Schoolmen," in *A History of Western Philosophy, and Its Connection with Political and Social Circumstances from the Earliest Times to the Present Day,* Simon and Schuster, 1945, pp. 463-75.

[*A respected and prolific author, Russell was an English philosopher and mathematician known for his support of humanistic concerns. Two of his early works,* Principles of Mathematics *(1903) and* Principia Mathematica *(1910-13), written with Alfred North Whitehead, are considered classics of mathematical logic. His philosophical approach to all his endeavors discounts idealism or emotionalism and asserts a progressive application of his "logical atomism," a process whereby individual facts are logically analyzed. Regarding Russell, biographer Alan Wood states: "He started by asking questions about mathematics and religion and philosophy, and went on to question accepted ideas about war and politics and sex and education, setting the minds of men on the march, so that the world could never be quite the same as if he had not lived." In recognition of his contributions in a number of literary genres, Russell was awarded the Nobel Prize in literature in 1950. In the following excerpt, he provides a succinct overview of Bacon's life and significance as a philosopher.*]

Roger Bacon (*ca.* 1214-*ca.* 1294) was not greatly admired in his own day, but in modern times has been praised far beyond his deserts. He was not so much a philosopher, in the narrow sense, as a man of universal learning with a passion for mathematics and science. Science, in his day, was mixed up with alchemy, and thought to be mixed up with black magic; Bacon was constantly getting into trouble through being suspected of heresy and magic. In 1257, Saint Bonaventura, the General of the Franciscan order, placed him under surveillance in Paris, and forbade him to publish. Nevertheless, while this prohibition was still in force, the papal legate in England, Guy de Foulques, commanded him, contrary orders notwithstanding, to write out his philosophy for the benefit of the Pope. He therefore produced in a very short time three books, *Opus Majus, Opus Minus,* and *Opus Tertium.* These seem to have produced a good impression, and in 1268 he was allowed to return to Oxford, from which he had been removed to a sort of imprisonment in Paris. However, nothing could teach him caution. He made a practice of contemptuous criticism of all the most learned of his contemporaries; in particular, he maintained that the translators from Greek and Arabic were grossly incompetent. In 1271, he wrote a book called *Compendium Studii Philosophiae,* in which he attacked clerical ignorance. This did nothing to add to his popularity among his colleagues, and in 1278 his books were condemned by the General of the order, and he was put in prison for fourteen years. In 1292 he was liberated, but died not long afterwards.

He was encyclopædic in his learning, but not systematic. Unlike most philosophers of the time, he valued experiment highly, and illustrated its importance by the theory of the rainbow. He wrote well on geography; Columbus read this part of his work, and was influenced by it. He was a good mathematician; he quotes the sixth and ninth books of Euclid. He treated of perspective, following Arabic sources. Logic he thought a useless study; alchemy, on the other hand, he valued enough to write on it.

To give an idea of his scope and method, I will summarize some parts of the *Opus Majus.*

There are, he says, four causes of ignorance: First, the example of frail and unsuitable authority. (The work being written for the Pope, he is careful to say that this does not include the Church.) Second, the influence of custom. Third, the opinion of the unlearned crowd. (This, one gathers, includes all his contemporaries except himself.) Fourth, the concealment of one's ignorance in a display of apparent wisdom. From these four plagues, of which the fourth is the worst, spring all human evils.

In supporting an opinion, it is a mistake to argue from the wisdom of our ancestors, or from custom, or from common belief. In support of his view he quotes Seneca, Cicero, Avicenna, Averroes, Adelard of Bath, Saint Jerome, and Saint John Chrysostom. These authorities, he seems to think, suffice to prove that one should not respect authority.

His respect for Aristotle is great, but not unbounded. "Only Aristotle, together with his followers, has been called philosopher in the judgement of all wise men." Like almost all his contemporaries, he uses the designation "The Philosopher" when he speaks of Aristotle, but even the Stagyrite, we are told, did not come to the limit of human wisdom. After him, Avicenna was "the prince and leader of philosophy," though he did not fully understand the rainbow, because he did not recognize its final cause, which, according to Genesis, is the dissipation of aqueous vapour. (Nevertheless, when Bacon comes to threat of the rainbow, he quotes Avicenna with great admiration.) Every now and then he says something that has a flavour of orthodoxy, such as that the only perfect wisdom is in the Scriptures, as explained by canon law and philosophy. But he sounds more sincere when he says that there is no objection to getting knowledge from the heathen; in addition to Avicenna and Averroes, he quotes Alfarabi very often, and Albumazar and others from time to time. Albumazar is quoted to prove that mathematics was known before the Flood and by Noah and his sons; this, I suppose,

is a sample of what we may learn from infidels. Bacon praises mathematics as the sole (unrevealed) source of certitude, and as needed for astronomy and astrology.

Bacon follows Averroes in holding that the active intellect is a substance separated from the soul in essence. He quotes various eminent divines, among them Grosseteste, bishop of Lincoln, as also supporting this opinion, which is contrary to that of Saint Thomas. Apparently contrary passages in Aristotle, he says, are due to mistranslation. He does not quote Plato at first hand, but at second hand through Cicero, or at third hand through the Arabs on Porphyry. Not that he has much respect for Porphyry, whose doctrine on universals he calls "childish."

In modern times Bacon has been praised because he valued experiment, as a source of knowledge, more than argument. Certainly his interests and his way of dealing with subjects are very different from those of the typical scholastics. His encyclopædic tendencies are like those of the Arabic writers, who evidently influenced him more profoundly than they did most other Christian philosophers. They, like him, were interested in science, and believed in magic and astrology, whereas Christians thought magic wicked and astrology a delusion. He is astonishing because he differs so widely from other medieval Christian philosophers, but he had little influence in his own time, and was not, to my mind, so scientific as is sometimes thought. English writers used to say that he invented gunpowder, but this, of course, is untrue.

Frederick Mayer (essay date 1948)

SOURCE: "Religion and Science in Roger Bacon," in *The Personalist,* Vol XXIX, No. 3, Summer, 1948, pp. 261-71.

[*In the following essay, Mayer discourses upon Bacon's achievement, arguing that Bacon, far from being a dabbler in medieval magic, was a scholar who believed that the pursuit of scientific knowledge was complementary to Christian belief, not antithetical to it.*]

Until the sixteenth century only three of Bacon's minor works had been printed. The obscurity of his life and his labors in science, together with his aloofness from the affairs of his day, caused his name to be linked with magic. This impression of Bacon dominates Robert Greene's play: *Honourable History of Friar Bacon and Friar Bungay.* Greene had found a very popular theme that already had been worked out in the Middle Ages. Few of the great scholars like Gerbert of Aurillac, Albertus Magnus, and Roger Bacon escaped the suspicion of possessing magical powers.

Such a view can be understood by virtue of the superstitious bent of the Middle Ages. But the picture of Roger as a superman who never accepted the tendencies of the Middle Ages, as a modern in his ideals, is less excusable. We shall see that Roger Bacon experienced in many ways the limitations of his own age and that his ultimate aspirations aimed not at the overthrow of theology as "the queen of sciences" but at the establishment of a more solid and durable foundation for Christian theology.

Roger Bacon took part in the debates about the subjects

foremost in the minds of the scholastics. He too took a stand, for example, on the problem of universals. He combated the pantheistic tendencies of Averroism. Even his *Opus Majus* contained much metaphysical ballast. All this was not merely incidental to Roger Bacon's work in other fields; it formed an attempt to orient himself amidst divergent intellectual currents. A modern scientist, without being interested in the technical problem of philosophy, would adopt a certain kind of world view necessary for classifying and unifying his own discoveries and theories. Such was Bacon's position towards nominalism. "One individual," he maintained, "is of more account than all the universals in the world." Had not God created the world for the sake of individual persons rather than for universal man? Furthermore individuals could be observed; there was something substantial about them. Science only progressed in the direction of nominalism. When Roger Bacon discussed such a problem vital for his world view, one feels that he did not merely perform a good piece of verbal shadow boxing. On the other hand, he showed little patience with logical subtleties, with abstract concepts that could not be verified by observation and experiment. He told his students:

> Look at the things, try them, see how they act on you, how you act on them. As to the matter and form that may underlie them, leave that to God.

It seems to be a well-established fact that Roger Bacon accepted the official dogmas of the Church. He did not doubt the absolute authority of the Scripture, provided that a pure text could be found. Like Abélard he did not believe in the infallibility of the Church fathers. He knew that they were limited in their knowledge. However, this independent view was in complete accord with the opinions of the famous scholastic doctors. The *Sic et Non* of Abélard had caused a storm of indignation, but a century later such a writing would have produced no sentence of excommunication and would have caused no hardships for its author. Although Roger Bacon blamed the incorrect translations of Aristotle for much of the misunderstanding regarding his doctrines, he regarded Aristotle as the "great" philosopher and quoted frequently from his works. This did not prevent him from disagreeing when the occasion arose. His respect for the ancient philosophers was great. That they were not Christians made no difference to him. Thus he preferred Seneca's moral teachings to the doctrines of the Christian teachers and stressed the purity and integrity of the ancient philosophers. Even the Mohammedan thinkers got their share of praise for their excellence and accuracy in scientific observation.

For Bacon the summit of the scholastic mountain lay in theology. He advocated that children should obtain a thorough instruction in the Bible rather than in the current "fables of Ovid," because he thought the latter were harmful to the faith. Convinced of the practical value of the sciences, he wanted to apply them chiefly to pious instruction in order to raise the level of religious contemplation, and to destroy the faith of infidels. His view of the sciences as supporters and pillars of scriptural revelation would have strengthened the unity and solidarity of Christianity. Like other medieval scientists he emphasized that

sin constituted a formidable obstacle to the mastery of science.

Bacon mixed up history with fable and mythology without showing any sense of discrimination, asserting, for example, that Prometheus was the "first teacher of philosophy and his brother Atlas the first great astrologer." We cannot blame Roger Bacon for such inaccuracies in his historical knowledge, since history in the Middle Ages contained more fable than truth.

At the same time, Roger Bacon was limited in his researches by the prevalent methods and knowledge of his day. Science was based upon authority, revelation and, last but not least, upon superstition. With the discovery of Aristotle's physical treatises, the sciences that now have become autonomous were entirely derived from Aristotle's writings. It took centuries to get rid of some of Aristotle's ideas, such as the four elements that make up the universe and his denial of the sexuality of plants. In medicine the books of Galen were used, but the method of examination applied to the sick was unspeakably crude. The progress of the physical sciences came through the impetus of the Arabs given by their exact experiments. In mathematics alone they transmitted to Western Europe the fundamentals of trigonometry, the algebraic notation obtained from India, Mesopotamia and Egypt, the Greek contributions to plane and solid geometry, and the so-called Arabic numerals really derived from the Hindus, which, together with the invention of the zero by Arabic scholars, made possible a better system of arithmetical computation. Revelation especially played an important rôle in medieval geography. Since people did not travel extensively in the Middle Ages they assumed that the world was extremely small. The *Book of Genesis* served as an authoritative and infallible guide for the geological structure of the earth.

It can be readily seen that the spirit of medieval science was characterized by the willing acceptance of superstitions. The belief that the stars and other celestial bodies exerted an influence upon the destiny of human beings was accepted even in the most educated circles. It was thought that certain plants possessed occult powers, and that by the use of herbs and other objects found in nature one might be able to coerce the supernatural spirits. Above all, alchemy occupied the minds of the medieval scientists and they attempted to transmute the base metals into gold and to find the philosopher's stone which would act as a cure for all and reveal the secret of eternal youth. One might dismiss all this as base superstition, but we find that astrology and alchemy contributed to an expansion of scientific knowledge. That Roger Bacon was interested in alchemy and in astrology has been put to his disadvantage and to derogation from his genius. We have to realize that in the Middle Ages everything was linked with supernatural causes. Thus we find traces of astrology and alchemy in nearly every science of that time.

Roger Bacon was profoundly critical in regard to the knowledge of his contemporaries. In his *Opus Majus* he wrote about the four stumbling blocks to the comprehension of truth, consisting in frail and unworthy authority, long established customs, the influence of the ignorant crowd, and the hiding of one's ignorance behind the show of wisdom. These stumbling blocks bear a close resemblance to the four Idols of Francis Bacon. He became more specific when discussing the stumbling blocks of the theologians. To begin with, he asserted that in practice philosophy dominates theology. Theology should be less concerned with the things of nature, than with the mysteries of the faith, such as the Trinity. But Roger Bacon did not stop there. He reproved the theologians for their ignorance and neglect of the "exact" sciences such as optics, alchemy, mathematics and philology. Furthermore, Roger Bacon saw that the theologians were lecturing on the *summa* of Lombardus instead of going back to the original Scripture text. He believed that the Vulgate copy at Paris was extremely defective and that hence no one could get the literal meaning of the sacred text or its spiritual meaning.

At other times, Roger Bacon was fighting a private war with the translators, reproving them for ignorance of the meaning and contents of the books they translated and of the original language. Such is his criticism of Gerard of Cremona, who translated Euclid from the Arabic.

He lamented the state of education, with teachers turning their energies to speculation and to abstract theories instead of teaching practical sciences. When he remarked that he could teach a capable student in four years what he himself had learned in forty, he summarized the inefficiency of thirteenth century teaching methods. He deplored, moreover, the sad neglect of sciences like optics and physics.

Thus Roger Bacon experimented with burning glasses, gunpowder, the magnet, Greek fire, artificial gold, magic mirrors, and the philosopher's stone. Those subjects which are least important today as objects of scientific study, such as astrology and alchemy, Bacon thought were most valuable. He lashed his contemporaries for not studying enough astrology and for not heeding the influence of the stars upon the conduct of their lives. Even Thomas Aquinas did not deny that the celestial bodies exerted an indirect influence upon the lives of men without impairing freedom of the will. Roger Bacon stayed on the path of orthodoxy and left room for individual selection, but he was also convinced that astrology was an unexplored gold mine for the medieval scientist.

Reared in the educational system and dogmas of the Church, he looked to the heavens for the highest truths and there expected his scientific ideals to be realized. Of course, he was intensely interested in practical inventions, but they were less important for him than those that were marvelous and would confirm the expectations of his religious beliefs.

Yet Roger Bacon was not a supporter of sweeping generalizations. He knew that natural science was complex and could not be explained in terms of one hypothesis. Thus in alchemy he did not think of the elements as part of a universal primary matter, that it would be possible at all to reduce them to this indefinite principle which for other alchemists continued to be the only subsisting reality in a world of appearances. Primary matter constituted for them a magic formula which would solve all the ills of the world. Bacon thought, on the contrary, that the purity of matter could only be restored by the perfect, harmonious blending of the elements. Now this would have been a more complex process. In the same way he avoided a belief in the omnipotent sway of celestial bodies and left room for the action of free will in the individual.

Bacon's distrust of sweeping generalizations, his understanding of the complexity of the problems of natural science, was influenced by his acceptance of the Church dogmas, his connection with the scholastic theology and his conception of education. The theology and the Church teachings were highly complex in the thirteenth century. Many volumes were needed in order to clarify the facts of salvation. Catholic theology had become aware of an expansion of knowledge. It had assimilated, or attempted to assimilate, strange teachings propagated by infidels and unbelievers. It was a difficult task to harmonize advanced philosophy with the simple tenets of the faith. In order to accomplish this one had to know a great deal of philosophy.

Likewise the scientists of the Western World became aware of a body of knowledge accumulated by the Arabian scholars which opened up a multitude of new problems resulting in an extension of speculation and experimentation. The scientific researches of the Arabs likewise had to be harmonized with the articles of the Christian religion. Roger Bacon assumed that the truth of science could not disturb the calm equilibrium of his religious faith. His ideal was to use the weapon of the infidels, scientific study, for their own destruction. Ultimately he believed that Christianity should not conquer the world by force, but convert the infidels by the strength of their marvelous arguments based upon exact experimentation which would verify the miracles of Christian revelation.

It is clear that a knowledge of the external world could not be obtained in the thirteenth century by the use of mere allegory and number symbolism. There was sufficient interest in the study of nature independent of the articles of the faith. Although Roger Bacon made some exaggerated claims about his ability to impart knowledge to his students, about the ineptitude of contemporary teachers, this should not be taken to mean that in his opinion the road to knowledge was an easy one. On the contrary, he wanted a more intricate and analytical system of instruction to supplement the current knowledge of Latin, grammar, logic, and metaphysics, with a comprehensive study of the natural sciences. He attacked the friars who ventured to study theology without sufficient preparation. If anything, he envisaged an educational procedure more difficult, more complete and more factual than that of his own time.

In his systematic theories Bacon was well ahead of his contemporaries. For example, he formed the conjecture that the transit of light from the stars occupied time, though we cannot perceive it, and he supported the conception of the sphericity of the earth, a conception which indirectly influenced Columbus. However, Bacon was seldom original. He frequently acknowledged his debt to his predecessors, especially to Aristotle and to the Arabs. At times, he seemed to be borrowing from the extensive work of his teacher Grosseteste. But this does not mean that he could not apply the facts. His power in application, rearrangement and combination of previously established facts was unsurpassed in the Middle Ages. His imagination in regard to the possibilities of science rivaled that of Dante in the field of poetry. In this manner he overcame the limitations of his own day and of his own bitter fortunes. It is difficult to draw a line where Bacon's imagination stops and the mystic spirit starts. For he did not always remain on the solid ground of experience but aspired to find the higher realm of religious visions. He did not believe in religion in order to demonstrate his orthodoxy; a sincere belief in the doctrines of the faith was part of his nature and his Franciscan environment.

To counteract the monopolizing of education by dialectics and metaphysics, Roger Bacon urged the study of languages and mathematics. He was convinced of the utility of such a study for the secular rulers and for the Church; languages were indispensable for the student who wanted to read the original texts of theology and philosophy. Especially he commended the study of Hebrew, Greek, and Arabic and therefore composed a Greek and Hebrew grammar to facilitate the instruction of students. The highest stage of linguistic learning would be to speak a foreign language with the same facility as the mother tongue; a second degree of proficiency would be the ability to translate it, and a lower stage of linguistic knowledge would be mere capacity to read and understand the foreign language. For a student this would be sufficient, but it was Roger Bacon's ideal to master Greek, Hebrew, and Arabic like his mother tongue. There is no proof that he succeeded. It is doubtful whether he was so much better than the translators whose ignorance he decried, who were, however, in a better position to travel in foreign lands and learn the languages as they were actually spoken. Bacon's ideal was realized to some extent at the Council of Vienna in 1312. There the establishment of schools of oriental languages was ordered in the Universities of Paris, Oxford, Bologna, and Salamanca. Unfortunately, the decree of the Council proved to be unsuccessful. The students did not respond to the new courses, the teachers were underpaid and half-starving; thus there existed no strong stimulus for either teacher or student to devote himself to this field of research.

For Roger Bacon the study of philology possessed another attraction in the mystic power of words. he pondered about the "tyranny of words" from the standpoint of their magical value in coercing supernatural forces. His ideal was to get ultimately to the root of the spiritual meaning of the Bible. He envisaged a revision of the Bible, which had become corrupt through many changes and translations. This revision was to be carried out by a papal commission composed of outstanding scholars. Writing to Clement IV, he said: "I cry to you against this corruption of the Text, for you alone can remedy the evil."

Mathematics, Bacon prized even more than philology. He called it "the gate and key of the natural sciences, the alphabet of philosophy." In all sciences he found traces of mathematics and saw that the fundamental concepts in physical science, like matter and force, could be expressed by mathematical concepts. For him mathematics replaced logic as a fundamental discipline. The objection against logic was its abstraction and its faulty consideration of the real, because logic could not give us absolute certainty. Moreover, Bacon claimed that we do not need instruction in this field because we have a natural grasp of it and only have to learn its technical terms.

This represents Bacon's reaction against the excessive reliance upon argumentation. We can scarcely imagine to what extent logic dominated the instructional program of the universities. It was no accident that the masters of logic were the most arrogant, self-satisfied and dogmatic people of the age. They looked down upon experimentation and observation of natural phenomena.

Nevertheless Roger Bacon did not arrive at any striking results in his study of mathematics. What mattered was his appreciation and his understanding that mathematics formed the key for the physical sciences, and in this respect he resembles Descartes. But he also recognized that mathematics could not be the noblest natural science though it was fundamental. For him the queen of the natural sciences was the *scientia experimentalis,* experimental science. Established on the twin pillars of mathematics and experience, it has a very durable foundation.

Now experimental science has three prerogatives: (1) It confirms conclusions to which other scientific methods already point; (2) It reaches results which take their places in existing sciences, but which are entirely new; (3) It creates new departments of science.

It would be wrong to say, however, that Roger Bacon resembled the modern research scientist. In the first place he experimented with many subjects, such as alchemy, unrelated to exact measurement. He expected miraculous results from his experiments and he lacked the impartiality with which a modern scientist approaches his field of study. Finally, Bacon relied too much upon the validity of the sense organs and did not appreciate enough the need for exact measurements.

What was the function of the experimental method? How could it be applied? Here Bacon showed most clearly his connection with the prevalent ideals of the Middle Ages. By its application he expected to arrive at a more exact understanding of the spiritual meaning of the Bible, to convert infidels by proving the miracles of the Christian faith, to exterminate the errors of magic and to meet the challenge of the Antichrist who would descend upon earth fully equipped with the knowledge of experimental science and of mechanical inventions. If one understood the secrets of nature, it might be more possible to cope with the guile of Antichrist.

We have emphasized the fact that Roger Bacon remained within the limits of orthodoxy. At the same time he represented a change in ideals from the Patristic Age. The Church fathers had little patience with those who were bent upon experimenting and observing the working of nature, since this had little relation to the life beyond where man would live a different kind of existence. They saw in the beauty of nature the snares of the devil and in anything that appeared to be mysterious and inexplicable the work of demons or angels. On account of the authoritarian, otherworldly, attitude of the Church there could be little progress of the natural sciences in the Middle Ages. Progress of natural scientific study would only come from without by the recovery of antique writings. When these were introduced, together with the commentaries of the Arabian scholars, a new field of study was opened up. An orthodox scholar like Roger Bacon believed that everything was reasonable in the universe and reflected the rationality of the creator. For him science became a confirmation of the wisdom of God. Hence in the *Opus Majus,* after discussing the natural sciences, he turned in the concluding chapter to moral philosophy, "nobler than all the other branches of philosophy." Scientific study did not constitute an end in itself. It formed an avenue to salvation and was definitely subordinated to the knowledge of God.

Stewart C. Easton   (essay date 1952)

SOURCE: "The Universal Science of Roger Bacon," in *Roger Bacon and His Search for a Universal Science: A Reconsideration of the Life and Work of Roger Bacon in the Light of His Own Stated Purposes,* Columbia University Press, 1952, pp. 167-85.

[*In the following excerpt, Easton sketches the philosophy of science "which Bacon took for granted as his intellectual framework, but himself never stated in formal terms."*]

It has sometimes been supposed that the science of Roger Bacon is full of contradictions. He believed in revealed and experimental knowledge at the same time; he thought of theology as the queen of sciences and the crown of all knowledge. Even George Sarton, who has understood Bacon in many ways so well, seems to think that his 'fundamentalism' was somehow at variance with his scientific vision, a kind of atavism that he had not yet thrown off in spite of his 'modern' approach. . . .

I do not believe that it is necessary to make excuses for Bacon. His science, including his 'fundamentalism', seems to me remarkably consistent, and in accordance with the best knowledge of his time. He is not, however, a good apologist for himself because his gift for systematic analysis is greatly inferior to his imagination and vision. He does not clearly state his assumptions and postulates, which he largely took for granted, and are those of his time. He has not yet found it necessary to keep his religious beliefs and his natural knowledge in separate compartments; he is far, indeed, from the doctrine of the double truth, associated with the name of Averroes, that what is true in philosophy may contradict the revealed truths of religion and vice versa. Bacon's belief in revealed knowledge in no way vitiates his claim to be a scientific thinker. It may be alien to the modern viewpoint, but it is consistent with his own, and his theory of psychology supports it. The active intellect is God, or, in Adam Marsh's phrase, the 'raven of Elias', and the human soul is capable of receiving knowledge from this source through its own highest faculty, the *intellectus possiblis.*

In this chapter, therefore, rather than state the scheme adopted by Bacon in his work for the Pope—which has in any case been effectively done by Bridges in his introduction to his edition of the *Opus Majus*—we shall endeavour to sketch the philosophy of science which Bacon took for granted as his intellectual framework, but himself never stated in formal terms. Bacon was primarily a thinker (if not a systematic one) and his contribution to the details of scientific knowledge is meagre; it seems, therefore, fairer to make any judgment of his work dependent on our understanding of his achievements as a scientific thinker and philosopher. This intellectual scheme has been drawn entirely from Bacon's own statements, though in some details I have drawn out to their logical conclusions various remarks which are only suggestions. And I have used his illustrations, which are of so much interest to himself, as indications of the thought behind them, even when his thought is not explicitly stated. Since the whole of his work has been utilized for this purpose, specific notes and references will not usually be made unless there is some passage where Bacon himself states his theories in unequivocal terms, and consultation of this particular passage will be of value to the reader.

I. How can nature be known?

Before ever he starts to investigate, the scientist, faced with all the varied phenomena of nature, must, above everything else, have some form of belief. He must believe that knowledge of at least some part of nature is attainable; as a human being he will probably also have a belief in the potential usefulness of his endeavour. What he considers useful will likewise depend upon prior beliefs. If he thinks that the life of every man upon earth is of great value, then he may hope that his work will serve to prolong this life upon earth. If he believes that life should be pleasurable, then he will guide his research in such a way as to make the lives of his fellows more pleasurable. If, like Bacon, he accepts a goal of salvation in the next world through faith in a certain religion, he will order his scientific work in such a way that the number of believers, candidates for salvation, will be increased, that the understanding of existing believers will be deepened and their faith strengthened. No scientific worker can be without a belief, whether it is stated explicitly or taken for granted without question.

But he must also have a belief that there is a possibility of finding out the *truth* about a certain range of phenomena. Again, this need not be explicitly stated, even to one's self. We may reasonably deny the possibility of absolute truth, and say that truth is only what is perceived to work in practice. We may hold the theory that we can only perceive the appearances of things, but never the things-in-themselves. In this case we shall only investigate the appearances, and the relations between them. At least, then, the relationships are true, and the fact that the knowledge works is true.

Modern science in general has been based upon the realization that, in the natural world, we can never know either the 'what' or the 'why', but only the 'how'. By the examination of the successive stages of a process, and learning how to repeat them at will, we can in fact learn *how* the second stage follows the first. And we say glibly that the second is *caused* by it, though we have known ever since Hume that this is not really so. But we have ceased altogether to try to discover the other why, the 'for the sake of which', the final cause in Aristotle's metaphysical scheme. And though we have been able to disintegrate matter into electrical charges, we still hesitate to say that this is what matter is, because the principle of organization cannot be simply disregarded. Yet this limited knowledge of modern times is of immense practical value because we can repeat the 'cause' and 'effect' at will. And we can erect a theoretical science of causes and effects throughout the whole of nature. This is always subject to checking, and is entirely effective for practical purposes within the limited area to which it is applicable.

Now the medieval man had the use of a most remarkable aphorism, which does not seem to modern scientists to be true. But, even if true, it was not originally based on verifiable empirical facts; nor can it conceivably be proved. It is, in short, an entirely illegitimate and unscientific assumption. Yet this cardinal tenet of medieval science was regarded in the thirteenth century not as a pleasing moral aphorism, but as a scientific axiom, as true as any geometrical axiom from the system of Euclid, and as useful for deducing further data by the syllogistic method. 'Natura nihil facit *frustra*', said the medieval. Nature does nothing *in vain*.

If this beautiful and sublimely simple axiom can be accepted as true, at once the whole of natural knowledge becomes potentially available for man. It supplies the synthetic principle that can never be inferred empirically from the data. Nature, instead of being a collection of disordered and chaotic phenomena, only to be investigated in its separate parts, becomes an ordered whole, bound together by *purposes;* and these, being analogous to human purposes, are comprehensible to the human understanding. A parasite growing on a tree does not just happen to grow there because the seed took root in a favourable spot, which is all that can be verified by empirical methods. To a believer in purposes the parasite could be there because it did something for the tree, because it benefited the plants in the neighbourhood, because it fed the animals and birds that ate it, or conceivably for the purpose of decorating the baronial hall for Christmas festivities, or even to act as a symbol for man of mutual aid in the kingdoms of nature. It could, for the medieval, be any or all of these things. The doctrine allowed scope for the human imagination, and it really did explain natural phenomena in a way which was satisfying to human aspirations. To understand these phenomena it was only necessary to transfer our own knowledge of human purposes to the field of nature; if one went far enough and had enough knowledge, it was possible to know the whole of nature, even without personally examining every phenomenon. Universal science was not beyond the possibility of man. When Bacon was asked in the course of his Parisian lectures whether plants had a sense of touch, he could and did confidently reply in the negative. The sense of touch, he said, is useful for animals and human beings because they have the power of locomotion. What would be the use of a plant's ability to feel if it could not do anything about it, if it could not escape from its enemy? Nature would not give it this power *in vain*. Therefore the plant has no sense of touch.

Now to our science this question is insoluble. We cannot

identify ourselves with a plant, and therefore cannot know subjectively whether it feels. We know that it lacks a central nervous system, and therefore does not feel through the same mechanism as man or animal. On the other hand, we have observed plants that react in a specialized way to the near presence of certain animals. We call this an 'automatic reaction'; but this is only a verbal explanation, giving no positive information. We smile at the medievals for thinking that the question was even legitimate and could have an answer.

The modern ecologist, one of the few synthetic scientists of our day, has set himself the task of observing the behaviour of living creatures in relation to their environment. His fundamental hypothesis is that nature does preserve a balance amongst living creatures; from which it follows that much can be learned from this natural economy. He has discovered that if we change any important factor, there will be a chain reaction of events, any one of which may cause serious disturbance in fields far remote from the one in which the first change was made. Nature, as he puts it, seems to 'hang together'. He speaks of the various activities in nature as having a relation to others; his science is descriptive and normative, or practical. But it cannot really be speculative in the sense in which Baconian and medieval science was speculative, because there can be no verifiable laws in this modern science, no universals to which the ecologist can relate his particulars. If he speaks of the *function* of an animal or plant in nature, he is careful to explain that this implies no anthropomorphism; he is only stating what the plant or animal actually does in nature.

The medievals, in the absence of the tedious observation and inquiry that show how each part of nature is in fact dependent on another, contented themselves with simplifying science—and we may excuse them on the grounds of their ignorance. And if we ask them ironically how they are going to inform us of the purposes of natural phenomena which appear to have no connection whatsoever with man or with any living creature, they would reply that it is quite true that such purposes can never be determined by observation and inquiry. But this does not mean that they are unknowable, and that men may resign themselves to their ignorance. On the contrary, *this* information has been given by God in the form of revelation.

It should be understood that revelation was not to the medieval an alternative form of knowledge to empirically acquired data. It was an absolutely essential part of it if there were to be any final understanding of a phenomenon which included its purposes. It was one of the primary tasks of the scientific investigator to complete, and, as Bacon emphasized, to confirm, the knowledge given in summary or occult form in the Scriptures, and in the writings of the Saints and Fathers of the Church, and of anyone who had had direct access to the revealed knowledge.

The knowledge least accessible to man, the purpose of those heavenly bodies that seem at first sight to have nothing to do with man, was, according to Bacon, the first of all to be revealed, to the sons of Seth, the grandsons of Adam. The reason we cannot believe in astrology to-day is that we cannot conceive of any possible *mechanism* by which the stars, which our instruments may tell us are millions of light years away, could affect humble man. Billions of stars, galaxies, and nebulæ, which can only be seen at all by the aid of the most powerful telescope, according to our way of thinking can have no relation to man. In our search for efficient causes in the universe, cosmic rays have been discovered, and these make sense to us; and we proceed to investigate the means of their transmission. Our 'why' is answered by the statement that such or such a body gives off these rays by a recognizable process which we can even duplicate in the laboratory on a small scale. When the only stars that could be seen were those visible to the naked eye, it did not seem so impossible that there was a relationship between their movements and the vital processes of the human being, or even his path of life. Each planet, according to its position at a given moment in the sky, would have its effects on earth. For nature was one. Superiors ruled inferiors, and rays from the planets converged on the central earth.

This was the kind of knowledge that could only come originally from revelation. However far back into the past the observations went, they could not make astrology into an empirical science, whatever might be said of true astronomy. For the relations of the observed movements to man must necessarily be hidden. We see a star in the sky and observe its movements; but the correlation with man's activities or with parts of his body is a theoretical one and cannot be based solely on observation. But once the knowledge had been revealed, as long as it was not lost but preserved through the generations, it could be *checked* empirically. Bacon suggests that this should be done, and it is the heart of his *scientia experimentalis.* If the revealed knowledge (hypothesis) could be confirmed by observations in the world of sense, this would help to confirm faith in *all* revelation, including the truths of religion. It was not enough to accept the revelation on authority alone; since, as Bacon realized, we can never be really certain until a thing is demonstrated to be true by the evidence of our senses. But at the same time everything that had been revealed could not at once be demonstrated to be true by experience. It was necessary to accept certain kinds of statements on the basis of authority, on the presumption that they were true; this acceptance depended upon the nature of the authority. As we have seen, Bacon had no objections to prophesy if the source were satisfactory to him. He might have even accepted scientific revelations if they had come from Joachim or St. Francis, since they had lived the kind of lives which make revelation possible. It is not unlikely that Bacon himself hoped for a personal revelation. But in the absence of any sign that moderns were fit to receive them, it was safer to believe that all scientific knowledge had been revealed long ago, and there was no need to repeat the revelations. However, these original revelations had become distorted by translation from one language to another, and by being transmitted through unbelievers. The truly scientific method was surely to try to discover in all their pristine purity the revelations first given to the sons of Seth, to Solomon, to the Hebrew prophets, and so on down to Aristotle and Avicenna, each being a lesser authority than his predecessors.

Now in most scientific fields revelation of this kind was a necessity. The medieval man could only hope to learn a little from empirical inquiry in comparison with the enormous amount that he could never know; and heavenly purposes were completely hidden from him. If a man were suffering from a stomach ailment, the medieval scientist had not yet the technique to determine the interrelationships between the stomach and the rest of the body. Even to-day these relationships are very imperfectly understood. But a medieval would have thought it ridiculous to say that these relationships were confined to the body as we see it before us; for the body itself was composed of matter and form, of soul and body. And the soul-element could not be observed by means of the five senses. Though the soul separated from the body at death, it could not be seen escaping; it was a non-physical entity. Moreover, there were other non-physical entities existing in the world which could also be neither seen nor touched—angels and demons. And it was quite possible that these entities might have taken possession of the soul, being of similar substance. A demon could, like electricity, only be perceived in its outward manifestations, and, being evil in nature, it could cause all kinds of diseases if it were united with the soul. Furthermore, man himself was also part of the universe, a *minor mundus,* or lesser world, in himself. His temperament or *complexio* was ruled not only by the elements and humours within his bodily organism, but by his relationship with the heavenly bodies. Finally, these same heavenly bodies which ruled the temperament and the bodily organization of man were themselves intimately connected with the rest of the universe, and especially with the plants and minerals that might be used for his cure. A plant that was especially subject to the influence of the planet Venus might be the required remedy for a disease of the kidneys ruled likewise by Venus; or perhaps an extract of copper, the mineral under the influence of Venus, might be indicated. But again, this would depend upon the man's own make-up. If he were especially choleric, the remedy might be contra-indicated for him, while it might work for others. The time of the year the disease occurred, and the climate of the country, would also have their effects.

It can, therefore, be seen at once that medieval medicine would be far from simple, and an enormous amount of 'knowledge' would be needed, both for diagnosis and prescription. But it did not rest on nothing but ignorance. It was based upon the appreciation of the relation between man and the universe which had been revealed as a necessary supplement to our feeble empirical knowledge. A medieval man would have considered it wildly unscientific to treat man as an organism in isolation, analyse a few mechanisms, and call it knowledge or science. Where medieval medicine would no doubt break down would be in its real ability to predict, or effect apparent cures. And it is one of Bacon's more lasting titles to fame that he suggested empirical verification of the data of revelation. It was not due to any scepticism on his part of the fact of revelation. But he wanted to separate folk-lore and magic from the genuine data of revelation. The testing by experiment of the old wives' tale of the ability of goats' blood to crack diamonds is a case in point. Bacon's reverence for the text of Aristotle, and his irritation with the bad translations that were in circulation among the Latins, and his own consequent studies in philology, are a result of this belief. How could a corrupt text be used as deductive material for science, any more than an incorrect equation in mathematics? Ultimately the best experimental proof for the correctness of our mathematics is the verifiable fact that the George Washington Bridge has so far withstood the theoretically calculated strains put upon it in practice. The experiments in Bacon's time probably failed to confirm the deductions from the 'hypotheses' provided by revelation. But it was truly scientific of him to see the need for such experiments.

When Bacon stated that the first stage of knowledge was credulity, the second experience, and the third reason, he was not recommending credulity; he was merely stating the obvious fact in medieval, and, indeed, in all science. We must first believe those who claim to have made an experiment, or those who have received or heard of a revelation. This is not the belief of certitude, but the equivalent of what we should call a hypothesis, a provisional belief. As Bacon says, we only finally believe it after proving it by experience, and then the soul can rest in the light of truth. Bacon himself instanced the fact that a magnet attracts iron, an improbable fact, but nevertheless true. We first hear of it through an experimenter. When later he makes the famous statement that he will believe anything, however apparently incredible, as long as it comes from a good authority, this does not mean that he denies the necessity for proving it by experiment. But as an attitude towards the phenomena of the world, it is a more probable prelude to discovery than a severe scepticism which refuses to believe in anything until it has been proved. The importance of the method, of course, lies in the insistence of the scientist on the provisional nature of the belief. As we shall see later, Bacon does not deny the possibility of attaining provisional truth also through reasoning, the mathematical method; but again, even in this sphere, certitude only comes from experience. This means that experience is fundamental for both forms of knowledge:

Revelation and Belief.

Experience CERTITUDE

Natural philosophy

Mathematics.

Nature, as we have seen, can be known by revealed knowledge and certified by experience. Is this the only knowledge of nature? Can it be known, and is the knowledge trustworthy, by experience alone?

Bacon seems to take the knowledge obtained through the senses, as far as it goes, for granted. He is worried by no epistemological problem. It might, therefore, be considered surprising that he seems to have no conception at all of the so-called 'natural history method of inquiry', the inductive method favoured by his later namesake, the attempt to find 'laws' of nature from a series of planned experiments and observations.

The reason that I think Bacon would give to justify his omission would be that experimental knowledge by itself is worthless, but only gains philosophical validity from its position within a theoretical framework. This is the point

of view we should expect from a man who was primarily a thinker in search of universal knowledge. But even modern science would admit this. There is no limit whatever to the number of experiments one could make. But it is useless to make them unless there is some way of either interpreting them or using them. And this is precisely what Bacon suggests.

'The science of experience', he says, 'verifies all natural and artificial things . . . not by arguments as the purely speculative sciences do, nor by feeble and imperfect experiences as the operative sciences'. Then he goes on to describe the activities of Peter de Maricourt, and explains that Peter knows the natural sciences by experience—medicine, alchemy, astronomy, and astrology—and he makes inquiries even from old women, soldiers and farmers, and would be ashamed if he did not know as much as they. But lest all this should be construed as experiment for its own sake, Bacon adds that without this kind of work it would be impossible for *philosophy* to be completed.

It would, therefore, seem that the operative sciences by themselves have no great value for philosophy. But Bacon has great respect for those who make these experiments, since they will verify the speculative scheme. Moreover, they are of great practical use when controlled by a Christian ethical system.

2. The philosophy and ethics of the study of nature.

Bacon's conception of the origin of scientific knowledge might have led him to advocate only a return to the ancients to see what they had said, check it by experience, and call this a universal science. In the **Opus Majus,** indeed, he urges as strongly as he can the full study of the ancients and the more recent Arabs, and the establishment of a definitive Latin text of their works. But this is by no means the whole of his message. He might have been content if the science of the ancients had been complete, if the knowledge possessed by Solomon had been recovered in its entirety. Then all that was necessary would have been a checking with experience.

But Bacon's ambition was far greater than this. He wanted to create a theoretical framework which would take care of *all* branches of science, even those which had not been dealt with by the ancients in any of the books available to the Latins. And, above all, he wanted to make use of this knowledge. It has already been pointed out how Bacon viewed himself as another Aristotle, trying to do for his own time what Aristotle had done in his. Such a work was, in fact, necessary. Aristotle had done a gigantic work, nothing less than the founding of a systematic science out of a heterogeneous mass of philosophic speculations and a limited quantity of sense data, most of it observed personally by himself and his associates. Aristotle had had to formulate methods of describing and classifying these phenomena, he had even to show how to think about them— how, in short, to direct the human mind purposefully in its thinking so that concentration upon a limited set of data was possible. In this he had much help from his predecessors, especially from Plato, who had shown the possibilities of pure thought, untrammelled in the world of ideas, but without the limitations of form that are necessary to the practical scientist.

So Aristotle had to start from the very beginning and say: 'What do we mean when we say that a thing is?' —the categories of being—and take the principles of description he then formulates over into all the fields he can investigate. As a true Greek he searched for understanding and knowledge, and at his death he left a methodical body of knowledge, drawn up according to systematic and logical principles, capable of being understood by students in the ages that followed, once they had mastered the logic that informed it.

But in the fabric of this colossal theoretical work, surely unequalled in the history of mankind, two things were faulty—a metaphysics of being which does not account for man, and, as a consequence of this, a failure to unite the sciences of nature and the sciences of man. It is the sign of Bacon's genius that he saw both of these clearly and tried to remedy them.

The Christian Fathers had already seen that a metaphysics of being was insufficient to carry the scientific structure; it gave the principles that underlie all sciences, but it did not place man within the structure, and did not give him a purpose commensurate with all the works of the universe which he was capable of understanding. Since they believed that these very purposes had been revealed to them in their religion, they chose another metaphysics more in keeping with these high purposes. Then, since Neo-Platonism laid little stress on the sciences, and, indeed, to some degree emphasized the worthlessness of human knowledge, science was neglected as unimportant. It fell into the hands of practical men who used it, but were not capable of giving it its due place in a total view of the universe.

Bacon, as a Christian and a student of science, refused to accept this neglect of science by the Church as the proper policy for Christians. He explains at considerable length the reasons the Father neglected it, and tries to point out that this was due to the abuses of science or philosophy rather than to any inherent evil in it, or to their ignorance of it because translations were not available to them. But Bacon knows that the burden of proof is upon himself, and it is therefore essential that both the theoretical structure of his science and his precepts for its use be welded into a grand whole that is altogether Christian in its foundations.

It was necessary, then, that the two inadequacies of Aristotle should be repaired, and a different emphasis laid upon the whole. The underlying thought must no longer be: 'All men by nature desire to know', though Bacon had always admitted this desire. In his Parisian *Quaestiones* on the *Metaphysics* he had said that any orderly and discreet person would naturally desire to know, but not a disorderly and confused person. Moreover, the corporeal complexion of the person might prevent the natural appetite of the soul from expressing itself. Elsewhere he defends the natural desire against the argument that it is acquired for the sake of gain. It is interesting how little Bacon stresses the Greek ideal of knowledge for its own sake in his later

work. He had been entirely won over to the idea of the beauty and usefulness of knowledge. The beauty is seen by the student because even a little knowledge is part of the great whole, the wonderful works of God; the usefulness lies in its contribution to the last end of man. The Christian influence is unmistakable. Knowledge cannot be an end in itself, but must be a means to an end; intellect must ultimately be subordinated to the will. The acquisition of knowledge ceases to be a natural instinct, of no ethical value; or all knowledge would be given by nature, as Bacon had argued even when he was still only a philosopher. It becomes a moral virtue to seek for knowledge now that he has become a scientist. But now also the merit lies not in the mere search but in the application of the knowledge in accordance with ethical principles. Man must search for knowledge and apply it. Completed knowledge which is of surpassing beauty will incidentally benefit the soul; but its value is not exhausted thereby.

Now when Aristotle analyses the relationship between the sciences it is primarily a logical analysis. He sees the way in which each contributes to the other, and he recognizes that the relationship is one of subalternation. He even sees the hierarchy of higher and lower sciences. But the emphasis Bacon gives to this is subtly different. He knows the subalternational relationship, but he does not state it in logical terms. He emphasizes rather the manner in which each helps the other, providing its tools so that it may progress further. And the whole picture is changed by the insistence upon the supremacy of moral philosophy or ethics. The whole structure of universal science, beautiful as it is, might not be worth struggling for if it were not to be used.

Now this again is different in Aristotle. His *Ethics,* wonderful as it is, is not based on his knowledge of science, but upon his knowledge of the nature of man and his ordinary life as a citizen. Coming from a man who, as Mandonnet points out, must have studied in the Faculty of Arts, it is remarkable that Bacon could produce no better moral philosophy than he gives us in the last part of the *Opus Majus.* The reason for this is simple. Aristotle's *Ethics* cannot tell us what we are to *do* with our knowledge; it is in no sense the crown of his scientific achievements, but only another empirical inquiry, this time into the nature of man and his place in society. Like his work in biology and physics, it is primarily an inquiry into principles, derived mainly from experience by the inductive method. To tell us in detail on what principles science should be used would have required an entirely new system of ethics, and this, perhaps, never occurred to Aristotle; and Bacon had not the time, and probably had not the ability, to produce it. He knew that science must in some way be brought into relation with the Christian scheme of salvation. But as he had not done this thinking except in very general terms— it is, after all, possibly the most difficult question in modern ethics, and we have certainly not solved it to-day, though the need is far more urgent—all Bacon does in the *Opus Majus* is give us a few details on how science could benefit organized Christianity, and how it would help to a fuller understanding of the Scriptures. In doing this he neglects Aristotle, since Aristotle's ethics can only be properly understood within the framework of his philosophy and psychology. He prefers the moral platitudes of Seneca which are *ex parte* utterances derived from his own experience of life in the Roman Empire and the ethical philosophy of Stoicism. But it cannot be denied that Bacon saw the need for a system of ethics which was the culmination of his science, even if he did not produce it.

It is to be understood, therefore, that theoretical and practical knowledge, or what we should call pure and applied science, were no more separable for Bacon than they are for us. But he did not make the mistake of thinking that the practical application of pure science was an end in itself, nor did he assume without argument that its end was the greatest comfort and pleasure to be obtained by it for human beings. He gave thought to the problem of the ends of both forms of science. The pursuit of pure science resulted in, first, the perception of its beauty, and thus was good for the soul; but at the same time it resulted in practical inventions which would be good for the Church, and ultimately able to help in the conversion of more Christians, all able to share in the hope of salvation. The pursuit of practical science, as well as helping the Church, served again to confirm the faith by proving the truths of revelation, even such esoteric matters as the Holy Trinity, the Blessed Virgin, and the resurrection of the body—which truths could not be discovered by these means, but, having been revealed, could be confirmed.

Nevertheless, for purposes of analysis it may be well to distinguish between Bacon's ideas on the increasing of knowledge, or speculative science, and practical science, as he understood it. The key to his scientific system is, of course, to be found in his special science that he calls 'scientia experimentalis', which, as suggested in the introduction to this study, should probably be translated as the 'science of experience' rather than experimental science, which suggests some kind of experiments in our modern sense. In the Romance languages the derivatives of the Latin *experimentalis* retain this meaning to-day.

We have discussed already the mediating position experience holds between revealed and natural knowledge, as giving certitude to both. But this is only one of its functions. It must also add knowledge, and guide its application. Indeed, Bacon distinguishes clearly between the three 'dignities' or 'prerogatives' of this science. Only the first is concerned with what we should call to-day the 'experimental method', and is the function we have described already. When Bacon says that this science is the ruler of the separate sciences, and compares it with the navigator who gives orders to the carpenter, or the soldier who gives orders to the smith, he is describing the rôle of the third 'dignity', the principles which should guide the application and use of the special sciences.

The second dignity of the science of experience is concerned with the relating of the knowledge of one field of science with the others. It is one of the outstanding deficiencies of our modern scientific system that we lack precisely such a science as Bacon is here suggesting, though in the twentieth century steps have already been taken in the direction of providing one. In view of the enormous content of our special sciences to-day and the way in which each overlaps the other, we have a very great need

for it. But on the other hand this knowledge is now so specialized within each particular field that it may be for ever impossible to provide it. Already it was impossible in Bacon's day for one man to understand all fields, and Bacon himself ultimately saw this. When he appealed to the Pope to patronize a corps of scientists, each working in special fields but contributing his knowledge to the whole, he was suggesting the only possible measure that could be taken to provide the basis for this second dignity.

Since Bacon did not give it a name, but only called it the second dignity of the science of experience, let us call it simply 'synthetic science'. It could be a science within its own right, and perhaps some day it will be. Its function, according to Bacon, was to concern itself with those great truths which, though they belong to other sciences, lie outside the scope of their investigation. As an example of what he means he suggests that the behaviour of animals in the light of nature may have value in determining the medicines to be used by human beings who have forgotten these secrets of nature. If the animal eats a plant that will prolong his life, and the human being has forgotten the use of it, could he not be reminded of it, and profit from the example of the animals? Here we have a direct connection between the separate sciences of biology, medicine, and psychology which is very much used to-day, though in practice the specialist in one science will have to think out the application for himself, and may be in complete ignorance of the findings of his fellow specialist in his own different field of inquiry.

These particular sciences are recognized to-day as being closely connected, and even the specialist will be expected to know something of the work going on in at least these allied fields. Theoretical physics and agronomy are not so closely connected that they will be equally studied by the experts in the biological sciences. But it is at least possible that the remarkable visible effects in the soil of fantastically small quantities of such elements as boron, may be worth studying by physicians who may have insufficiently considered whether small doses may not have as important effects within the human body as large doses, even if they do not work in the same manner. And the fact that valuable minerals may be present in the soil in huge quantities but unavailable to the plant until certain agricultural practices have been carried out, might suggest certain useful experiments to dieticians and doctors on the conditions necessary for the proper intake of minerals and vitamins in the human body. It is even possible that the 'revealed' Christian Science of Mary Baker Eddy or ascetic practices recommended by the Hindu scriptures may have something to offer to the specialized studies of physiological and psychological therapy.

It was the ability of all the separate sciences (revealed, speculative, and practical) to contribute knowledge to the others that Bacon so continuously stressed. If he had foreseen our age of specialization he might have been even more emphatic. Was it so unscientific of him to suggest a special synthetic science, whose business it would be to examine the findings of the special sciences and co-ordinate them?

His plan for a compendium of scientific knowledge produced by co-operative effort under the patronage of prelates and princes, which would explain the state of each science in tabloid form for the benefit of non-specialists was a truly remarkable idea for his age, and is an excellent example of his practical thinking. He states concisely the seven conditions required for such a compendium as: (1) true, (2) well-chosen, (3) systematic, avoiding confusion, for instance, between natural things and metaphysics, (4) moderately short, (5) clear, though he admits the difficulty of combining clarity with brevity, (6) proved by trustworthy experience, (7) as perfect as possible.

It would be difficult indeed to produce such a work in our day without excessive oversimplification; but many undergraduate schools in the United States have adopted something not unlike it. And the whole effort of President Hutchins and his associates at the University of Chicago has been infused with ideas not far different from Bacon's, and with the same purpose in view.

The third 'dignity' of the science of experience is to Bacon the supreme one. We cannot call it by the name of any of our separate sciences, since one part of it concerns the uses to which the results of all the sciences are to be put. And this brings it at once within the sphere of the higher science of moral philosophy. But in so far as it belongs to what we call science, it is concerned with the practical application of all the other separate sciences. To-day this is the function of the engineer and technician in the widest sense of these terms. It is true that the engineer does command the services of all the pure scientists. The geometrician, to use Bacon's example, does not make a burning glass, though he studies the principles on which it must be built. The technician asks the geometrician only for the practical results of his findings, and then makes his mirror. Or the physician asks the astronomer for the results of his findings when he compounds a medicine.

But in Bacon's view the practical scientist or technician has yet a further task. This makes him, in Bacon's scheme, superior even to the mathematician, or to the synthesizer who takes the results of one science and applies them in another. The technician must see the *possibilities* in the work of each of these separate sciences. He must visualize from the work of the mathematicians the theoretical possibility of building a flying-machine; he must draw out to their conclusions their ideas which may have been applied only on a small scale. On seeing a burning glass he must realize that if one were built that were large enough, a mirror could be constructed on the same principles, which would burn up everything combustible at a great distance and annihilate armies. He must see that with a combination of mirrors it would be possible to see to the other side of the English Channel as Julius Caesar is said to have done. Since saltpetre in small quantities can make a shocking noise, it must be possible to use it in such a way that the noise would be greater than the human being could bear. The Palomar telescope and the blockbuster bomb would not be surprising to Bacon because they are only applications on a large scale of principles valid on a small. This ability of the engineer to see the possibilities both of existing discoveries and the theoretical principles on

which they are based is to Bacon the highest achievement of a scientist.

So the total of Bacon's science of experience is seen to make a great deal of sense if it is split up into its separate parts; and his theoretical scheme, with its hierarchy of sciences graded according to their contribution to practical life, seems valid within its own framework. Schematically it would appear as follows:

MORAL PHILOSOPHY

Third dignity—Use

Second dignity—Synthesis

First dignity—Verification

(Separate sciences)

Revealed science. Alchemy. Astronomy. Astrology. Agriculture, etc.

A modern pope might also agree that moral philosophy should be in the same position at the top to supply direction to the separate sciences. When Pius XII made a public statement regretting the necessity for the hydrogen bomb but supported research looking towards its production, Bacon would have approved his utterance. The engineers and technicians were lords in their own domain, but even they must bow to the superior wisdom of spiritual advisers who could state authoritatively whether their endeavours were directed to the ultimate good of mankind. Only those trained in moral philosophy could answer this question, not the scientists themselves.

A. C. Crombie   (essay date 1953)

SOURCE: "Grosseteste and the Oxford School," in *Robert Grosseteste and the Origins of Experimental Science, 1100-1700*, Oxford at the Clarendon Press, 1953, pp. 135-88.

[*In the following excerpt, Crombie demonstrates the influence of Robert Grosseteste's thought upon Bacon's scientific theories.*]

The writer who most thoroughly grasped, and who most elaborately developed Grosseteste's attitude to nature and theory of science was Roger Bacon (c. 1214-92) himself. Recent research has shown that in many of the aspects of his science in which he has been thought to have been most original, Bacon was simply taking over the Oxford and Grossetestian tradition, though he was able also to make use of new sources unknown to Grosseteste, as, for example, the *Optics* of Alhazen. Though it is improbable that Bacon heard Grosseteste's lectures at Oxford, he seems to have become a member of Grosseteste's 'circle' by 1249, and when he became a Franciscan friar he would, no doubt, have had access to his manuscripts. Baur has drawn attention to the many striking parallels between the science of Roger Bacon and that of Grosseteste. The chief point of resemblance to be noted is Bacon's 'grundsätzliche methodische Auffassung der Náturwissenschaft, und die Erklärung des Wirkens und Werdens in der Natur'. It has been suggested above that Grosseteste in his search for

Medieval tower on an Oxford bridge known traditionally as Bacon's Study.

experimental science, since without experience nothing can be sufficiently known. For there are two modes of acquiring knowledge, namely, by reasoning and by experience. Reasoning draws a conclusion and makes us grant the conclusion, but does not make the conclusion certain, nor does it remove doubt so that the mind may rest on the intuition of truth, unless the mind discovers it by the method of experience (*via experientiae*); for many have the arguments relating to what can be known, but because they lack experience they neglect the arguments, and neither avoid what is harmful, nor follow what is good. For if a man who has never seen a fire should prove by adequate reasoning that fire burns and injures things and destroys them, his mind would not be satisfied thereby, nor would he avoid fire, until he placed his hand or some combustible substance in the fire, so that he might prove by experience that which reasoning taught. But when he has actual experience of combustion his mind is made certain and rests in the full light of truth. Therefore, reasoning does not suffice, but experience does. . . . What Aristotle says therefore to the effect that the demonstration is a syllogism that makes us know, is to be understood if the experience of it accompanies the demonstration, and is not to be understood of the bare demonstration.

This experimental science [he went on] has three great prerogatives with respect to the other sciences. The first is that it investigates by experiment the noble conclusions of all the sciences. For the other sciences know how to discover their principles by experiments, but their conclusions are reached by arguments based on the discovered principles. But if they must have particular and complete experience of their conclusions, then it is necessary that they should have it by the aid of this noble science. It is true, indeed, that mathematics has universal experiences concerning its conclusions in figuring and numbering, which are applied likewise to all the sciences and to this experimental science, because no science can be known without mathematics. But if we turn our attention to the experiences that are particular and complete and certified wholly in their own discipline, it is necessary to go by way of the principles of this science which is called experimental.

The other prerogatives of experimental science, besides this first one of confirming the conclusions of deductive reasoning in existing sciences, as, for example, in optics, were, secondly, to add to existing sciences new knowledge at which they could not arrive by deduction, and thirdly, to create entirely new departments of science. By virtue of these two prerogatives the experimenter was able to make a purely empirical discovery of the nature of things. Of the second prerogative Bacon said:

This mistress of the speculative sciences alone is able to give us important truths within the confines of the other sciences, which those sciences can learn in no other way. Hence these truths are not connected with the discussion of principles but are wholly outside of these, although they are within the confines of these sciences, since

reality and truth began with the theory of science which he developed in his commentary on Aristotle's *Posterior Analytics,* and that he then made use of this theory in his detailed scientific studies. Roger Bacon in his major writings on natural science, as in the **Opus Maius, Opus Minus** and **Opus Tertium,** the **De Multiplicatione Specierum,** and the **Communia Mathematica** and **Communium Naturalium,** also first postulated a theory of science as a means of discovering reality and truth, and then used this methodological theory in detailed researches undertaken as an illustration of it as well as for their own sakes. In setting out this theory of science Roger Bacon, like Grosseteste, began with Aristotle's *Posterior Analytics* and he developed particularly those points to which Grosseteste had paid attention: the means of arriving at universals or causes by induction and experiment, and the use of mathematics as the most certain means of demonstrating the connexions between events.

Having laid down the fundamental principles of the wisdom of the Latins so far as they are found in language, mathematics and optics, [he said in Part VI of the **Opus Maius,** 'De Scientia Experimentali'] I now wish to unfold the principles of they are neither conclusions nor principles. . . . The man without experience must not seek a reason in order that he may first understand, for he will never have this reason except after experiment. . . . For if a man is without experience that a magnet attracts iron, and has not heard from others that it attracts, he will never discover this fact before an experiment. . . . Mathematical science can easily produce the spherical astrolabe, on which all astronomical phenomena necessary for man may be described, according to precise longitudes and latitudes [as in the device described by Ptolemy in the *Almagest,* viii]. But that this body, so made, should move naturally with the daily motion is not within the power of mathematical science. But the trained experimenter can consider the ways of this motion.

Other examples of the exercise of the second prerogative were seen in medicine and in alchemy. The third prerogative was exercised outside the bounds of existing sciences, as in the investigation of natural wonders and prognostications of the future.

The inductive process of the discovery, as well as the verification and falsification of principles or theories, Roger Bacon explained fully and clearly in the example he gave to illustrate the first prerogative, though he did not include discovery in the special meaning he gave to the phrase 'scientia experimentalis' in the passage concerning this prerogative quoted above. But, before discussing this 'example of the rainbow and of the phenomena connected with it', it would be well to turn briefly to his ideas about the use of mathematics and of optics.

Mathematics, Roger Bacon said, was the 'door and key' 'of the sciences and things of this world' and gave certain knowledge of them. In the first place 'all categories depend on a knowledge of quantity, concerning which mathematics treats, and therefore the whole excellence of logic depends on mathematics'. For 'the categories of *when* and *where* are related to quantity, for *when* pertains to time and *where* arises from place; the category of *condition* (*habitus*) cannot be known without the category of *where,* as Averroës teaches in the fifth book of the *Metaphysics;* the greater part, moreover, of the category of *quality* contains affections and properties of quantities, because all things that are in the fourth class of quality are called qualities in quantities . . . ; whatever, moreover, is worthy of consideration in the category of *relation* is the property of quantity, such as proportions and proportionalities, and geometrical, arithmetical, and musical means and the kinds of greater and lesser inequality.' This being the case it was plain that 'mathematics is prior to the other sciences', and since 'in mathematics only, as Averroës says in the first book of the *Physics* . . . , things known to us and in nature or absolutely are the same', the greatest certainty was possible in mathematics. 'In mathematics only are there the most convincing demonstrations through a necessary cause.' 'Wherefore it is evident that if, in the other sciences, we want to come to certitude without doubt and to truth without error, we must place the foundations of knowledge in mathematics.' 'Robert, Bishop of Lincoln and Brother Adam of Marsh' had followed this method and 'if anyone should descend to the particular by applying the power of mathematics to the separate sciences, he would see that nothing magnificent in them can be known without mathematics.'

As an example of the use of mathematics in making known 'the things of this world' Roger Bacon gave astronomy, which 'considers the quantities of all things that are included among the celestial and all things which are reduced to quantity'. He said that 'by instruments suitable to them and by tables and canons' the movements of the celestial bodies and other phenomena in the heavens and in the air might be measured and reduced to rules on which predictions might be based. In fact he carried on the work of Grosseteste towards the reform of the calendar, making use of Grosseteste's *Compotus* and also sharing his hesitation between the Aristotelian and Ptolemaic astronomical systems.

The special reason why Bacon held that 'in the things of this world, as regards their efficient and generating causes, nothing can be known without the power of geometry', and that 'it is necessary to verify the matter of the world by demonstrations set forth in geometrical lines', was that he accepted Grosseteste's theory of the 'multiplication of species' or power as the basis of all natural operations and the Neoplatonic theory of a 'common corporeity' as the first form giving dimensions to all material substances. Like Grosseteste, he held that the 'multiplication of species' was the efficient cause of every occurrence in the universe, whether in the celestial or terrestrial region, whether in matter or in sense, and whether originating from inanimate things or from the soul. And, he said, 'the force of the efficient cause and of the matter cannot be known without the great power of mathematics', for 'Every multiplication is either with respect to lines, or angles, or figures'.

In discussing the 'multiplication of species' Roger Bacon based conclusions on the same basic metaphysical principles that Grosseteste had used. The principle of the uniformity of nature he expressed as follows: 'the effects . . . will be similar to those in the past, since if we assume a cause the effect is taken for granted', and 'those which are of similar essence have similar operations'. The principle of economy he expressed in Grosseteste's own words: 'Aristotle says in the fifth book of the *Metaphysics* that nature works in the shortest way possible, and the straight line is the shortest way of all.' The type of such 'species' was visible light and therefore, like Grosseteste, he made a particular study of geometrical optics, through which he held that it was possible to obtain experimental knowledge of the laws of the operation of these species, which laws were the basis of all natural explanation.

Of the mode of propagation of 'species' Roger Bacon gave an account which resumed and extended some of the essential features of Grosseteste's 'wave' theory. He asserted first that for propagation between two points to occur at all the intervening medium must be a *plenum:* no propagation could pass through an absolute void.

> Democritus thought that an eye on the earth could see an ant in the heavens. . . . But we must here state that we should not see anything

if there were a vacuum. But this would not be due to some nature hindering species, and resisting it, but because of the lack of a nature suitable for the multiplication of species; for species is a natural thing, and therefore needs a natural medium; but in a vacuum nature does not exist. For vacuum rightly conceived of is merely a mathematical quantity extended in the three dimensions, existing *per se* without heat and cold, soft and hard, rare and dense, and without any natural quality, merely occupying space, as the philosophers maintained before Aristotle, not only within the heavens, but beyond.

He then went on to argue that the propagation was not instantaneous but took time. Alhazen had brought various arguments against Alkindi's attempt in *De Aspectibus* to prove that 'the ray passes through in a wholly indivisible instant'. After a long discussion based on such considerations as that 'a finite force cannot produce any result in an instant, wherefore it must require time', and that since 'the species of a corporeal thing has a really corporeal existence in a medium, and is a real corporeal thing, as was previously shown, it must of necessity be dimensional, and therefore fitted to the dimensions of the medium', Bacon concluded: 'It remains, then, that light is multiplied in time, and likewise all species of a visible thing and of vision. But nevertheless the multiplication does not occupy a sensible time and one perceptible by vision, but an imperceptible one, since anyone has experience that he himself does not perceive the time in which light travels from east to west.'

This multiplication of species through a medium, he continued, was not a flow of body like water but a kind of pulse propagated from part to part. In this, light was analogous to sound.

> For sound is produced because parts of the object struck go out of their natural position, where there follows a trembling of the parts in every direction along with some rarefaction, because the motion of rarefaction is from the centre to the circumference, and just as there is generated the first sound with the first tremor, so is there a second sound with the second tremor in a second portion of the air, and a third sound with the third tremor in a third portion of the air, and so on.

> [With light the species] forms a likeness to itself in the second position of the air, and so on. Therefore it is not a motion as regards place, but is a propagation multiplied through the different parts of the medium; nor is it a body which is there generated, but a corporeal form, without, however, dimensions *per se,* but it is produced subject to the dimensions of the air; and it is not produced by a flow from a luminous body, but by a renewing from the potency of the matter of the air. . . . As regards Aristotle's statement that there is a difference between the transmission of light and that of the other sensory impressions, . . . sound has the motion of the displacement of the parts of the body struck from its natural position, and the motion of the following tremor, and the motion of rarefaction in every direction, as was stated before, and as

is evident from the second book of *De Anima;* and . . . in the multiplication of sound a threefold temporal succession takes place, no one of which is present in the multiplication of light. . . . However, the multiplication of both as regards itself is successive and requires time. Likewise, in the case of odour the transmission is quite different from that of light, and yet the species of both will require time for transmission, for in odour there is a minute evaporation of vapour, which is, in fact, a body diffused in the air to the sense besides the species, which is similarly produced. . . . But in vision nothing is found except a succession of the multiplication. The fact that there is a difference in the transmission of light, sound, and odour can be set forth in another way, for light travels far more quickly in the air than the other two. We note in the case of one at a distance striking with a hammer or a staff that we see the stroke delivered before we hear the sound produced. For we perceive with our vision a second stroke, before the sound of the first stroke reaches the hearing. The same is true of a flash of lightning, which we see before we hear the sound of the thunder, although the sound is produced in the cloud before the flash, because the flash is produced in the cloud from the bursting of the cloud by the kindled vapour.

In the details of his researches into optics and cognate sciences Roger Bacon made use of a number of Grosseteste's ideas, though his work was more mature because of the new sources available to him and he usually added something original of his own. Besides Grosseteste, his chief sources in optics were Aristotle, Euclid, and pseudo-Euclid, Ptolemy, Diocles (Tideus), Alhazen, Alkindi, Avicenna, and Averroës. He took over and extended Grosseteste's explanation of the variation in the strength of rays according to direction, and according to the distance from the radiating source; examples, respectively, of the multiplication of species 'according to lines and angles' and 'according to figures'. The results he used in an interesting discussion of which the object was to

> verify the fact that on the surface of the lens of the eye, although it be small, the distinction of any visible object whatsoever can be made by means of the arrangement of the species coming from such objects, since the species of a thing, whatever be its size, can be arranged in order in a very small space, because there are as many parts in a very small body as there are in a very large one, since every body and every quantity is infinitely divisible, as all philosophy proclaims. Aristotle proves in the sixth book of the *Physics* that there is no division of a quantity into indivisibles, nor is a quantity composed of indivisibles, and therefore there are as many parts in a grain of millet as in the diameter of the world.

He showed then that it was possible to draw an infinite number of lines from the base of a triangle to the point at its apex.

Roger Bacon made use also of Grosseteste's explanation of the tides. He incorporated a section of *De Natura Locorum* in the section of the **Opus Maius** dealing with the effects of rays on climate, and he seems to be referring to

De Iride in the remark in the **Opus Tertium** that 'homines habentes oculos profundos longius vident'. He took over Grosseteste's theory of heat and expanded his remarks about the internal strain between the parts of a body, which produced an intrinsic resistance to movement in falling bodies because each part prevented those lateral to it from going straight to the centre of the earth. 'This conclusion, that a heavy body receives a strain in its own natural motion, is proved by cause and effect', he said, and motion under strain generated heat. He made use of Grosseteste's theory of double refraction to explain the operation of a spherical (and hemispherical) lens or burning-glass, adding: 'instruments can be made so that we may sensibly see propagations of this kind; but until we have instruments we can prove this by natural effect without contradiction. . . . Let us take a hemisphere of crystal or a glass vessel, the lower part of which is round and full of water.' This, he said, should be held in the rays of the sun, as Grosseteste described in *De Natura Locorum*. He took up also Grosseteste's suggestion as to the possibilities of using lenses for magnifying small objects, and he made experiments with plano-convex lenses while trying to use the laws of refraction to improve vision, a practical object such as he held to be the final justification of all theoretical science.

> If anyone examine letters or other small objects through the medium of a crystal or glass or some other transparent body placed above the letters, and if it be shaped like the lesser segment of a sphere with the convex side towards the eye, and the eye is in the air, he will see the letters much better and they will appear larger to him. For in accordance with the truth of the fifth rule regarding a spherical medium beneath which the object is placed, the centre being beyond the object and the convexity towards the eye, all conditions are favourable for magnification, for the angle in which it is seen is greater, the image is greater, and the position of the image is nearer, because the object is between the eye and the centre. For this reason this instrument is useful to old people and people with weak eyes, for they can see any letter however small if magnified enough.

To the eye and its functioning in vision Roger Bacon paid particular attention because, as he said, 'by means of it we search out certain experimental knowledge of all things that are in the heavens and in the earth'. His account of vision was one of the most important written during the Middle Ages and it became a point of departure for seventeenth-century work. Bacon's chief contribution was to try to explain the operation of the eye, of which his account was based largely on the writings of Alhazen and Avicenna, by means of the theory of 'multiplication of species'. Distinguishing like Grosseteste between the psychological act of vision which went forth from the eye, and the physical light which went from the visible object to the eye, he asserted that both the extramitted species of vision and the intramitted species of light from the visible object were necessary.

> The reason for this assertion is that everything in nature completes its action through its own

force and species alone . . . as, for example, fire by its own force dries and consumes and does many things. Therefore vision must perform the act of seeing by its own force. But the act of seeing is the perception of a visible object at a distance, and therefore vision perceives what is visible by its own force multiplied to the object. Moreover, the species of the things of the world are not fitted by nature to effect the complete act of vision at once, because of its nobleness. Hence these must be aided and excited by the species of the eye, which travels in the locality of the visual pyramid, and changes the medium and ennobles it, and renders it analogous to vision, and so prepares the passage of the species itself of the visible object. . . . Concerning the multiplication of this species, moreover, we are to understand that it lies in the same place as the species of the thing seen, between the sight and the thing seen, and takes place along the pyramid whose vertex is in the eye and base in the thing seen. And as the species of an object in the same medium travels in a straight path and is refracted in different ways when it meets a medium of another transparency, and is reflected when it meets the obstacle of a dense body; so is it also true of the species of vision that it travels altogether along the path of the species itself of the visible object.

To show how the eye focused the species of light entering it he described first the anatomical arrangement of its parts. Following Avicenna he said that the eye had three coats and three humours. The inner coat consisted of two parts, the *rete* or *retina,* an expansion of the nerve forming a concave net 'supplied with veins, arteries and slender nerves' and acting as a conveyor of nourishment; and outside this a second thicker part called the *uvea.* Outside the *uvea* were the *cornea,* which was transparent where it covered the opening of the pupil, and the *consolidativa* or *conjunctiva.* Inside the inner coat were the three humours, and so, for light entering the pupil: 'There will then be the *cornea,* the *humor albigineus,* the *humor glacialis* [lens], and the *humor vitreus,* and the extremity of the nerve, so that the species of things will pass through the medium of them all to the brain. . . . The crystalline humour [lens] is called the pupil, and in it is the visual power.

The theory of vision Bacon described was essentially that of Alhazen and in fact misunderstanding of the functions of the lens and retina remained the chief stumbling block to the formulation of an adequate theory of vision until the end of the sixteenth century. Of the theory that the lens was the only sensitive part of the eye Bacon wrote, using what became known as the method of agreement and difference, as Alhazen had done: 'For if it is injured, even though the other parts are whole, vision is destroyed, and if it is unharmed and injury happens to the others, provided they retain their transparent quality, vision is not destroyed.' But, in another passage inspired by one of Alhazen's chapters, he stressed the qualification.

> that vision is not completed in the eye, but in the nerve . . . for two different species come to the eyes and . . . in two eyes there are different judgements. . . . Therefore there must be something sentient besides the eyes, in which vision

is completed and of which the eyes are the instruments that give it the visible species. This is the common nerve in the surface of the brain, where the two nerves coming from the two parts of the anterior brain meet, and after meeting are divided and extend to the eyes. . . . But it is necessary that the two species coming from the eyes should meet at one place in the common nerve, and that one of these should be more intense and fuller than the other. For naturally the two forms of the same species mingle in the same matter and in the same place, and therefore are not distinguished, but become one form after they come to one place, and then, since the judging faculty is single and the species single, a single judgement is made regarding the object. A proof of this is the fact that when the species do not come from the two eyes to one place in the common nerve, one object is seen as two. This is evident when the natural position of the eyes is changed, as happens if the finger is placed below one of the eyes or if the eye is twisted somewhat from its place; both species do not then come to one place in the common nerve, and one object is seen as two.

In another passage Roger Bacon tried to show how the 'visible species' were focused on the end of the optic nerve without producing an inverted image. In common with all optical writers before Kepler he failed to understand that such an image was compatible with normal vision.

> If the rays of the visual pyramid meet at the centre of the *anterior glacialis* [lens], they must be mutually divided and what was right would become left and the reverse, and what was above would be below. . . . In order, therefore, that this error may be avoided and the species of the right part may pass on its own side, and the left to its side, and so too of other positions, there must be something else between the anterior of the *glacialis* and its centre to prevent a meeting of this kind. Therefore Nature has contrived to place the vitrous humour before the centre of the *glacialis,* which has a different transparency and a different centre, so that refraction takes place in it, in order that the rays of the pyramid may be diverted from meeting in the centre of the *anterior glacialis.* Since, therefore, all rays of the radiant pyramid except the axis . . . are falling at oblique angles on the vitreous humour . . . all those rays must be refracted on its surface. . . . Since, moreover, the vitreous humour is denser than the *anterior glacialis,* it follows, therefore, that refraction takes place between the straight path and the perpendicular drawn at the point of refraction, as has been shown in the multiplication of species. . . . Thus the right species will always go according to its own direction until it comes to a point of the common nerve . . . and will not go to the left. . . . The same is true of the species coming from all other parts.

Roger Bacon was mistaken in thinking that the vitreous humour had a higher refractive index than the lens, and in other respects his theory of vision was far from correct. Nevertheless, his attempt to solve the problem of how the image was formed behind the lens was a step in the right direction. He thought that the nerve was 'filled with a sim-ilar vitreous humour as far as the common nerve' so that the 'species' travelled along it without refraction, though caused by 'the power of the soul's force (*virtutis*) . . . to follow the tortuosity of the nerve, so that it flows along a tortuous line, not along a straight one, as it does in the inanimate bodies of the world'. In the common nerve the judgements of the 'visual faculty' (*virtus visiva*) were completed, so that it was the seat of 'ultimate perception' in vision. The other special senses were analogously accommodated. Where more than one special sense was involved the 'ultimate perception' occurred at a deeper level, in 'the common sense (*sensus communis*) in the anterior part of the brain'.

His knowledge of optics Roger Bacon used in the experimental-mathematical investigation of the cause of the rainbow which he gave in Part VI of the *Opus Maius* as an example of his method. His procedure, in fact, followed the essential principles of Grosseteste's methods of combined resolution and composition and of falsification, and it represents the first major advance made in the experimental method after Grosseteste. He began by collecting instances of phenomena similar to the rainbow, both as to the colours and the bow-like shape. He said:

> The experimenter, then, should first examine visible objects in order that he may find colours arranged as in the phenomenon mentioned above and also the same figure. For let him take hexagonal stones from Ireland and from India, which are called iris stones in Solinus on the *Wonders of the World,* and let him hold these in a solar ray falling through the window, so that he may find in the shadow near the ray all the colours of the rainbow, arranged as in it. And further let the same experimenter turn to a somewhat dark place and apply the stone to one of his eyes which is almost closed, and he will see the colours of the rainbow clearly arranged just as in the bow. And since many employing these stones think that the phenomenon is due to the special virtue of those stones and to their hexagonal shape, therefore let the experimenter proceed farther, and he will find this same peculiarity in crystalline stones correctly shaped, and in other transparent stones. Moreover, he will find this not only in white stones like the Irish crystals, but also in black ones, as is evident in the dark crystal and in all stones of similar transparency. He will find it besides in crystals of a shape differing from the hexagonal, provided they have a roughened surface, like the Irish crystals, neither altogether smooth, nor rougher than they are. Nature produces some that have surfaces like the Irish crystals. For a difference in the corrugations causes a difference in the colours. And further let him observe rowers, and in the drops falling from the raised oars he finds the same colours when the solar rays penetrate drops of this kind. The same phenomenon is seen in water falling from the wheels of a mill; and likewise when one sees on a summer's morning the drops of dew on the grass in a meadow or field, he will observe the colours. Likewise when it is raining, if he stands in a dark place, and the rays beyond it pass through the falling rain, the colours will appear in the shadow nearby; and frequently at

night colours appear round a candle. Moreover, if a man in summer, when he rises from sleep and has his eyes only partly open, suddenly looks at a hole through which a ray of the sun enters, he will see colours. Moreover, if seated out of the sun he holds his cap beyond his eyes, he will see colours; and similarly if he closes an eye the same thing happens in the shade of his eyebrows; and again the same phenomenon appears through a glass vessel filled with water and placed in the sun's rays. Or similarly if someone having water in his mouth sprinkles it vigorously into the rays and stands at the side of the rays. So, too, if rays in the required position pass through an oil lamp hanging in the air so that the light falls on the surface of the oil, colours will be produced. Thus in an infinite number of ways colours of this kind appear, which the diligent experimenter knows how to discover.

In a similar way also he will be able to test the shape in which the colours are disposed. For by means of the crystalline stone and substances of this kind he will find the shape straight. By means of the eyelids and eyebrows and by many other means, and also by means of holes in rags, he will discover whole circles coloured. Similarly, in a place where the dewfall is plentiful and sufficient to take the whole circle, and if the place where the circle of the rainbow should be is dark proportionately, because the bow does not appear in the light part, then the circle will be complete. Similarly, whole circles appear frequently around candles, as Aristotle states and we ourselves experience.

Since, moreover, we find colours and various figures similar to the phenomena in the air, namely, of the iris, halo, and mock-suns, we are encouraged and greatly stimulated to grasp the truth in those phenomena that occur in the heavens.

From an examination of these instances Bacon tried to reach a 'common nature' uniting the rainbow and similar phenomena, and in the course of his argument he considered several different theories and eliminated those contradicted by observation. To explain the variation in the altitude of rainbows he took over Aristotle's theory that the rainbow formed part of the circumference of the base of a cone of which the apex was at the sun and the axis passed through the observer's eye to the centre of the bow, and he confirmed this by showing by measurements with the astrolabe that the sun, the observer's eye, and the centre of the bow were always in a straight line. This explained why the altitude of the bow varied at different latitudes and different times of year, and why a complete circle could be seen only when the base of the cone was elevated above the surface of the earth, as with rainbows in sprays.

> The experimenter, therefore, taking the altitude of the sun and of the rainbow above the horizon will find that the final altitude at which the rainbow can appear above the horizon is 42 degrees, and this is the maximum elevation of the rainbow. . . . And the rainbow reaches this maximum elevation when the sun is on the horizon, namely, at sunrise and sunset.

In the latitude of Paris, he said, 'the altitude of the sun at noon of the equinox is 41 degrees and 12 minutes', and therefore in the summer, when the altitude of the sun is greater than 42 degrees, no rainbow can appear at noon. He discussed in some detail the times of year when rainbows could not appear in Scotland, Jerusalem, and other places.

Going on to discuss 'whether the bow is caused by incident rays or by reflection or by refraction, and whether it is an image of the sun . . . and whether there are real colours in the cloud itself', he said: 'to understand these matters we must employ definite experiments'. He pointed out that each observer saw a different bow which moved when he did in relation to trees and other fixed objects, whether he moved parallel to, towards, or away from the bow. There were, he said, as many bows as observers, for each observer saw his bow follow his own movement, his shadow bisecting its arc. Therefore the rainbow could not be seen by 'incident' (i. e. direct) rays, for if it were it would appear fixed in one place like the white and black patches on clouds.

> Similarly, when a colour is produced by incident rays through a crystalline stone, refraction takes place in it, but the same colour in the same position is seen by different observers. . . . Moreover, the image of an object seen by refraction does not follow the observer if he recedes, nor does it recede if he approaches, nor does it move in a direction parallel to him; which is evident when we look at a fish at rest in water, or a stick fixed in it, or the sun or moon through the medium of vapours, or letters through a crystal or glass.

Therefore, since there were only three kinds of 'principal rays' (direct, refracted and reflected), and since 'accidental rays . . . do not change their position unless caused by reflection', the rainbow must be seen by reflected rays. 'All the raindrops have the nature of a mirror', and things seen in a mirror moved when the observer moved, just as the rainbow did. 'There are, then, raindrops of small size in infinite number, and reflection takes place in every direction as from a spherical mirror.' Yet the rainbow could not be an image of the sun produced by such reflection, as Seneca had suggested, because spherical mirrors distorted the shape and changed the size and colour of objects seen in them.

Of the colours seen in the rainbow and in crystals, Roger Bacon said:

> If it be said that solar rays passing through a crystal produce real and fixed colours, which produce a species and have objective reality, we must reply that the phenomena are different. The observer alone produces the bow, nor is there anything present except reflection. In the case of the crystal, however, there is a natural cause, namely, the ray and the corrugated stone, which has great diversity of surface, so that according to the angle at which the light falls a diversity of colours result. And viewing them does [not] cause the colours to be present here, for there is colour before it is seen here, and it is seen by different people in the same place. But in the case of the bow the phenomenon is the result of

vision, and therefore can have no reality but merely appearance.

The theory that Albertus Magnus had advanced, that the colours of the rainbow were due to differences in density of cloud, Roger Bacon rejected on the grounds that there were no such differences in crystals, or in sprays or dew on the grass, where, nevertheless, similar colours were seen. Real colours such as those seen in hexagonal crystals he attributed to mixtures of white and black, as explained by Aristotle in *De Sensu et Sensibili.* Of the colours of the rainbow he said: 'We need give only the cause of the appearance.' 'It is thought by scientists that these colours are caused by the humours and colours of the eye, for these colours exist merely in appearance.'

Concerning the shape of the rainbow, Bacon considered and rejected two earlier theories. First, he said that it could not be produced by the raindrops themselves falling in a cone, for the circular shape appeared in irregular sprays. Secondly, he attacked Grosseteste's theory that the bow was produced by three separate refractions through successively denser layers of moist atmosphere. He said that only one refraction could take place in sprays, yet the same shape was formed as seen in the sky. Moreover, Grosseteste's statement that the refracted rays would spread out, 'not into a round pyramid [i. e. cone], but into a figure like the curved surface of a round pyramid', seemed to Bacon to contradict the law of refraction, according to which the rays would form a regular cone. Nor could the curvature be produced by the moisture, for according to Grosseteste this was not of such a form but was 'a rounded mass of conical form'.

'Another explanation must therefore be sought; and it can be stated that the bow must be in the form of a circular arc.' For the colours of the rainbow did not shift with varying incidence of light like those on the dove's neck, but 'the same colour in one circle of the bow appears from one end to the other, and therefore all parts must have the same position with respect to the solar ray and the eye'. This condition and the appearance of the rainbow would be satisfied if the rainbow were a circle with its centre on the line joining the sun and the eye. He concluded:

> everywhere [where there are raindrops] there are conditions suitable for the appearance of the bow, but as an actual fact the bow appears only in raindrops from which there is reflection to the eye; because there is merely the appearance of colours arising from the imagination and deception of the vision. . . . A reflection comes from every drop at the same time, while the eye is in one position, because of the equality of the angles of incidence and reflection.

Bacon's understanding of the part played by individual raindrops in the formation of the rainbow was a real advance, in spite of his rejection of refraction. He extended his knowledge of optics to try to explain halos, mock-suns, and other similar phenomena. His explanation of the halo is interesting because it was based on the explicit assumption that the sun's rays were parallel. He said in the *Opus Maius* that the halo was caused by rays going out from the sun 'like a cylinder in shape' and becoming refracted on

passing through a spherical mass of vapour in the atmosphere between the sun and the eye, so as to go to the eye in a cone. The reason for the shape of the halo was that 'All the rays falling on one circular path round that axis [joining the sun and the eye] are refracted at equal angles, because all the angles of incidence are equal'. But, he continued, 'just as many experiments are needed to determine the nature of the rainbow both in regard to its colour and its shape, so too are they required in this investigation'.

Taking up the same subject in the **Opus Tertium,** he said that each eye saw a different halo, which moved as it did. In this work he attributed the refraction of the sunlight to individual water-drops. He pointed out also that colours seen in a halo were in the reverse order to those seen in the primary rainbow, and that measurements with an astrolabe showed that the diameter of the halo subtended at the eye of the observer an angle of 42 degrees, the same angle as that subtended by the radius of the rainbow. The sentiments with which he concluded his account in the **Opus Maius** of the first prerogative of experimental science are a worthy expression of the ideals of the experimental method by one of its founders:

> Hence reasoning does not attest these matters, but experiments on a large scale made with instruments and by various necessary means are required. Therefore no discussion can give an adequate explanation in these matters, for the whole subject is dependent on experiment. For this reason I do not think that in this matter I have grasped the whole truth, because I have not yet made all the experiments that are necessary, and because in this work I am proceeding by the method of persuasion and of demonstration of what is required in the study of science, and not by the method of compiling what has been written on this subject. Therefore it does not devolve on me to give at this time an attestation impossible for me, but to treat the subject in the form of a plea for the study of science.

Etienne Gilson   (essay date 1955)

SOURCE: "Roger Bacon," in *History of Christian Philosophy in the Middle Ages,* Random House, 1955, pp. 294-312.

[*Gilson was a prominent and prolific Neo-Thomist philosopher. He was the founder and longtime director of the Institute of Mediaeval Studies in association with St. Michael's College, the University of Toronto. In the following excerpt, Gilson offers a detailed overview of Bacon's beliefs as a philosopher and as a reformer.*]

I. THE PHILOSOPHER

A mere glance at the philosophical works of Roger Bacon is enough to convince the reader that they were written under the predominant influence of Avicenna. The style is Avicennian; the titles are Avicennian (*Communia naturalium*); last, not the least, Bacon himself explicitly says that, to him, Avicenna was the leader and the prince of philosophy after Aristotle (*Avicenna dux et princeps philosophiae post eum, Opus majus*). Naturally, Bacon never doubted that, in following Avicenna, he was following Aristotle himself; he should remain to us a representative of those to whom, precisely, Avicenna was Aristotle, which, on some important points, Avicenna was not.

A. *Physics*

Like Albert the Great, Roger Bacon intended to compose an encyclopedia of all sciences, written in a free and direct way (*per modum expositionis*), without adhering to the text of Aristotle, nor even always to the order of his books. He wrote a grammar dealing with the various scientific languages necessary to the Latins; then he disposed of Logic; physics came next in order, to be followed by metaphysics and ethics, which is the end of learning because the cognition of truth is ordained to the doing of the good as to its ultimate end. Since the name "physics" means nothing else than "science of nature" (*physis*), it includes the science of the soul (*psychology*) together with that of other living beings. Bacon intends to deal with these sciences in a free way, without wasting his time on philosophical positions which, like those of Anaxagoras, Democritus, Empedocles, Melissus or Parmenides may have been interesting in their own times, but, today, sound perfectly sterile and ridiculous. Moreover, we should remember that more scientific knowledge could be contained in a single treatise the size of his *De coelo et mundo,* for instance, than there is in all the books of Aristotle. The moderns, who write on a single one of Aristotle's treatises commentaries longer than his complete works, are simply displaying their ignorance. They do not know what is necessary and what is not. The reason for this is simple: these men have never learned the sciences about which they write; they have never taught them in some famous school (*in studio solemni*); they have not even learned them under anybody, and thus, becoming masters without having been pupils, they spread their own errors among the rank and file of their students. Again, these men do not know mathematics, without which natural science cannot be acquired. In writing these things, Bacon had two men in mind, two masters famous in his own times (*duo moderni gloriosi*), the Franciscan Alexander of Hales and the Dominican Albert the Great. His remark, that Albert was presuming to teach natural science without having first learned it from any master in any university, may have been true, although we do not know what he had been taught at Padua. As will be seen, according to Bacon, man is essentially a "taught" animal. At any rate, the personal ambition of Bacon was only to retain the very substance of scientific knowledge, and, so to say, its "marrow" (*substantia medullaris*), beginning with the fundamental notions of matter and form, whose union makes up all substances.

Matter is an essence essentially different from all forms, either substantial or accidental. It is a common substance. This point is denied by those who imagine that, to conceive matter as a common substance is to conceive it as numerically the same in all composite beings, which is absurd. What is everywhere one and the same, and therefore numerically one, is the "essence" of matter, not its "being." In other words, matter has the same nature in all composite beings. To confuse this doctrine with that of David of Dinant, who taught that since matter is common

to all beings, it is infinite like God, and, therefore, is God, is precisely to confuse essence and being. Moreover, it is to forget that the passive receptivity of matter with respect to all forms may well be said to be infinite, but not at all in the same sense as the active potency of God is infinite; there is no resemblance whatever between the passive potency of matter and the active potency of God.

Bacon is clear on the point that, considered in its essence, matter is one. His conception of what the essence of matter actually is cannot be understood unless one remembers his significant attack against "all" his contemporaries, whom he accuses of positing matter as "numerically one in all things" (*Opus tertium,* Brewer ed.). This seems to imply that, in Bacon's own mind, matter was much more like the universal intelligible entity posited by Gabirol than the element of the physical composite posited by Aristotle. At any rate, the matter of which he speaks seems to be nothing else than the possibility (i. e., non-necessity) inherent in all beings that are not the necessary being, or God. Since this lack of necessity is common to all finite beings, they all are composed of matter and form. Since, on the other hand, each species of beings has its own specifically distinct sort of matter, the problem is to find out the cause for their distinction.

Considered in itself, the notion of universal potentiality is identical with the notion of the matter of any substance in general; it is the matter included in the most general of all genera (*genus generalissimum*); this universal genus, therefore, is that of substance in general. All that is a substance first has the matter of substance and the form of substance. In order to be made either a corporeal substance or an incorporeal substance, it must receive the form of either one of these two types of substances. The same remark applies to each one of the successive degrees of determination acquired by concrete beings. Every single being is made up of a hierarchy of matters determined by a corresponding hierarchy of forms. Moreover, every higher matter is as form to the lower ones, just as every lower form is as matter with respect to the higher ones. This twofold series of matters actuating, or perfecting, other matters, and of forms actuating other forms, plays an important part in the doctrine of Roger Bacon.

The three general species of matter are: spiritual matter (Intelligences and souls), the matter of celestial bodies, the matter of sublunary bodies. Spiritual matter is not subjected to quantity nor change; the matter of celestial bodies is subjected to motion; the matter of sublunary bodies is subjected to both motion and change. Consequently these constitute three specifically distinct types of matter. Incidentally, this confirms what has been said of matter and its divisions. Naturally, just as these matters are specifically distinct, their forms are specifically distinct. The division of beings by their forms is more manifest than their division by their matters, but the matter of a celestial body differs essentially from the matter of a stone by reason of its specific differences in the *genus* matter. This is an important point in physics because, if matter were everywhere one and the same in all physical bodies, as all modern philosophers assure us it is, there could be no distinct physical substances and, therefore, neither generations nor corruptions.

Natural beings are composed of form, matter and privation, which is, in matter itself, a craving, or blind desire, for the destruction of the old form and to the acquisition of a new one. Strictly speaking, privation is not a third principle; it is matter itself, in the restlessness born of its potentiality. As Alfarabi says, it is not of the essence of matter; rather, it is its accident.

A physical form acts upon matter by educing it from potency to act. The rank and file of theologians and philosophers make a big mistake in imagining, in matter, a kind of active potency which, under the stimulus of an external agent, actuates itself, and becomes form. The potentiality of matter truly is its craving for perfection which, as Aristotle says, it loves as the female loves the male and as the ugly loves the beautiful. This is the Baconian meaning of Augustine's doctrine of the "seminal reasons." A seminal reason, Bacon says, "is the very essence of matter which, being incomplete, can be brought to completion, as a seed can become a tree." In itself, it is a seed; inasmuch as it craves to be perfected and actuated, it is a "seminal reason." This aspiration inherent in matter is the seminal reason itself. In this sense, natural forms come to matter from both within and without. From within, because their coming fulfils the desire of an imperfect being; from without, because they are given to it by an external agent. Bacon is substituting the "mutability" attributed by Augustine to matter for the "seminal reasons." He is parting company with the Philosopher as well as with the Saint.

Since physical beings are made up of matters actuated by forms, Bacon can be counted among the supporters of the plurality of forms; but "form" has not the same meaning in his doctrine and in those of Aristotle, Averroes or Thomas Aquinas. Those who teach the oneness of substantial form imply that where there is a substantial form, there also is an actual being. Consequently, they refuse to posit a plurality of substantial forms in any being for the simple reason that, were it made up of several substantial forms, a being would be made up of several beings. Such is not the case with Roger Bacon. Following the tradition of Denis, he considers each substantial form as preserving within its own being all the inferior forms included in its own essence. When the advent of a higher form has been prepared by that of the lower ones, or when a higher form essentially includes lower ones, these lower forms remain present in the higher one, where they continue to exercise their operations. Yet when all is said and done, the unity of the composite being is safe, because the supreme form of the composite holds all the other ones within its own unity. The Scotist school will call these included forms "formalities."

Although its structure parallels a system of more or less general concepts, this universe is not made up of universals. Forms are more or less universal, but they themselves are not abstract universals. The proof of this is that their degrees of nobility do not follow their degrees of universality. Physical beings, which are the subject matter of natural science, are ruled by their natures. Now, as Avicenna says in his *Metaphysics,* nature is twofold in kind. There is universal nature, that is, the virtues and forces of the celestial bodies, which can be considered as one single nature because they cause all generations and corruptions in this sublunary world. And there is particular nature, which is the ruling virtue of each particular species as well as of each one of the individuals it contains. From the point of view of the operations of nature, the more universal goes first: nature proceeds from substance to body, then to animal. But from the point of view of nature's intention, the particular goes before the universal: nature does not stop at producing animal, it produces horse, or rather "horses," that is, not only a species, but completely determined individuals. What is true in philosophy is equally true in theology. Each individual is more noble than its own universal (*singulare est nobilius quam suum universale*). Now, Bacon says, since I deal with all matters in view of theology (*quia omnia quae tracto sunt propter theologiam*), let us observe that God has not made this world for man in general, but for individual persons; God has not created mankind; he has redeemed, not man in general, but singular persons; he has not prepared beatific vision for universal man, but for a certain number of personally chosen men. All this shows that "the singular is better than the universal." This is what Aristotle says in the First Book of his *Posterior Analytics:* Farewell, *genera* and *species!* How could they bring about anything? They are monsters.

This is a point which Bacon intends to enforce because he knows that the rank and file are against it. Ignorant persons, he says, love universals (*homines imperiti adorant universalia*). Hence their ceaseless questions about what turns species into individuals. This is the big and insoluble problem of the principle of individuation. In fact, it is a foolish question. Since the intention of nature is to produce individuals, nature itself, which makes individuals, is the cause of individuation. When such people ask us what can be the cause of individuation, since neither the species nor something added to the species can cause it, we should ask them in turn what is the cause of universality, since neither the individual nor something added to the individual can cause it! Theirs is a silly question, because it supposes that an individual can be caused by nothing else than a species, plus something. Singulars are made up of singular constituents just as universals are made up of universal constituents. God makes things as they should be: a man according to his nature and a donkey according to its own, a universal nature if many individuals are to agree in it and a singular nature if it is to be that of only one single individual. There is indeed a great deal of nonsense in this problem they raise about individuation.

This is a good example of how a doctrine can be at the origin of several other ones. The plurality of forms, as Bacon conceives it, anticipates the similar position of Duns Scotus. At the same time, his insistence on the singularity of all that is real will find an echo in many early fourteenth-century doctrines, most of them opposed to Scotism. The remark of Bacon, that what stands in need of an explanation is not singularity, but universality, will be taken up by the "Thomist" John of Naples as well as by the "nominalist" William of Ockham.

On nature, the four kinds of causes, chance and other classical problems, Bacon does not seem to have contributed much that was new. As has been said, his whole effort was to simplify problems, leaving out what was useless or had become obsolete in the philosophy of Aristotle. Seen from his own modern times, many things said by the Philosopher appeared to him superfluous. Moreover, the translations of his writings were often faulty. Even the masters who had publicly "read" his works in famous schools, when they went over their own notes, could not help wondering if natural philosophy could be learned from Aristotle, following his method and even with the help of his commentators. So, Bacon says, they turn to scientific studies and to mathematics, as well as to the writings of those who wrote on natural philosophy, such as Pliny, Seneca and many other ones; thus, indeed, they succeed in learning what they have failed to learn from Aristotle. Obviously, the main intention of Bacon went beyond that of Albert the Great, which had been to make Aristotle's doctrine intelligible to the Latins. One of the reasons for this was the difficulties he himself encountered in understanding it, as well as his partial dissatisfaction with Aristotle's neglect of mathematical method. He expressly states that the natural philosophy of Aristotle had begun to be taught about 1245, at the earliest, and this by few masters who had written nothing (*a paucis viris a quibus scripta non sunt facta*). He himself seems to be one of those men who, after learning and teaching Aristotle's natural philosophy, had turned their minds to the study of sciences and of other authors in the hope of finding there what they had failed to find in Aristotle. And this effort, too, has left its mark on the physics of Roger Bacon.

The more interesting part of his work is his theory of the multiplication, or propagation, of species. It is directly inspired of Robert Grosseteste and of the optics of the Arabs. The very notion of "species," in its meaning of physical or spiritual emanations flowing from beings and reaching other beings, is one of the most confused we find in mediaeval philosophy. Grosseteste and Bacon have attempted to give it a scientific meaning. Physics is about actions exerted by causes. As undergone, an action is called a passion. Now, let us call "species" the first effect produced by any efficient cause; that is, the medium through which it acts upon another being. A typical case of "species" is light, by which the sun illumines air and causes objects to become visible. Light is the "species" of the sun. It may be given other names: Virtue of the agent, Similitude, Image. Whatever the name, it is a "species," like heat, odors, tastes, etc. The notion of species, therefore, extends to all physical forces because it points out the medium of all natural actions. Optics revealed to Bacon, as to Grosseteste, the possibility of a universal science of the propagation of species and therefore the possibility of a geometrical explanation of all natural operations. By extending to the objects of the five senses what optics had established concerning the object of sight, they hoped to achieve a mathematical interpretation of all natural phenomena. The generalization of the notion of species was necessary to their purpose. This being done, the science of the propagation of species (*de multiplicatione specierum*) could be considered as applicable to all physical facts.

There was, however, a difficulty. It was not easy to fit this quantitative type of explanation in a qualitative physics of Aristotelian forms. But the world of Bacon was not quite the same as that of Aristotle. It was a universe full of efficient causes. To him, the efficient cause of the species is the form, and the purer the form, the more efficient it is. By a special disposition of universal nature, that is, ultimately, by the will of God who intends the welfare of the universe, the highest natures are held, in virtue of their very perfection, to multiply their own influence (*species*); in fact, they do practically nothing else. The absolutely highest of all beings, namely, God, produces no species; he creates *ex nihilo,* for his species, or Image, is a similitude naturally born of the Father: the Son of God, identical with him in substance. But all creatures, imitating their creator as best they can, communicate to others, not indeed their substance, but a being specifically similar in nature to their own. The species is the medium of this communication. It is not the active form itself: the species of fire is not fire, but it is its resemblance, that is, something like it: *propter quod non vocantur res, sed similitudines rerum.* This awkward notion, which Descartes will severely criticize as being neither clear nor distinct, permitted Roger Bacon to write the sketch of what we would today call a sort of general physics, that is, a mathematical exposition of the laws according to which all forces propagate themselves, first along straight lines; then following the laws of refraction; then again in a circular or pyramidal way, etc. This part of his physics, which Roger Bacon wrote several times under more or less different forms, was incorporated by him to his ***Opus majus,*** itself the sketch of his *Principal Work,* the great doctrinal synthesis of which he dreamed during his whole life, and never wrote.

B. *Man*

The problem of the human soul is studied by Bacon according to the same method and in the same spirit. His guide remains the same: Aristotle interpreted by Avicenna. He knows that the famous *De spiritu et anima* is not the work of Saint Augustine, but he still thinks that they who, "among other men have been and still are rather good scholars," always deserve to be consulted. In the doctrinal milieu where he lives, the traditional conception of the soul as a complete spiritual substance remains the natural one; the only question is for him, as it was for Albert, to maintain this substantial independence of the soul without destroying the substantial unity of man.

The intellective soul alone is immediately created by God; the vegetative and the sensitive souls are just like the other forms which efficient causes draw out of the potency of matter. That the intellective soul is created is a Christian truth, but it also is a philosophical one: *Tota philosophia clamat quod solus intellectus creatur.* The agreement between philosophy and theology is perfect on this point, since "all the theologians of England and all the philosophers teach it." The rank and file of the Parisian philosophers, whose errors on this point Bacon reports and refutes, are therefore sinning against both theology and philosophy.

An important consequence of this position is that, since it is created apart from the other powers animating the body, the intellectual soul is an individual substance composed of its own matter and of its own form; it is an individual in the full sense of the term: a *hoc aliquid.* This does not entail that the human soul is a separate Intelligence. Its *unibilitas,* i. e., its natural aptitude to be united with a body, renders it specifically different from pure Intelligences. Thus, of its own nature, it is both an individual substance and the immediate act, or perfection, of a physical body. The soul is not the separate mover of its body; it is its mover inasmuch as it is its act.

Since it is an individual substance, the intellectual soul is completely definable apart from its body; but since *unibilitas* is part of its specific definition, it is of the essence of the soul to be the act and perfection of its body. The difficulty is inherent in the problem itself. The soul of the Christian man must be both individually immortal, like a Platonic soul, and the form of its organic body, like an Aristotelian soul. We should not be surprised to find Bacon using both languages. Rather, we should note that the difficulty is less apparent in his doctrine than it was in that of Albert the Great. To him, this probably was one more of those cases when a higher substantial form gathers within its own perfection the lower forms together with their operations.

In accordance with this general position, Bacon holds that rational souls are composed of matter and form, like angels, for indeed the question is the same in both cases (*eadem enim est quaestio de angelis et de animalibus rationalibus*). The Aristotelian doctrine of the categories compels us to accept this conclusion, for indeed, all that is, is either substance or accident; if angels and souls were not substances, they would be accidents, which is absurd. Now all substances are made up of matter and form; consequently angels and souls are composed of these same principles of being. Here, like everywhere else, the subject of generation progressively achieves more and more perfect degrees of composition until it receives its highest degree from its highest form. Now, it is a Baconian principle that composite beings are made up of composite beings. The highest form of man must therefore be composite like the preceding ones. The only difference is that, in the case of the rational soul, instead of resulting from an operation of nature (generation), the highest form is directly created by God. This explains the relation of the soul to its body in the doctrine of Roger Bacon. "Since the rational soul is the ultimate perfection of the human embryo, which is composite, this soul must needs be composite, so that its form may perfect the form of the embryo, while its matter completes the matter of the embryo."

The powers of the soul are in it as parts are in a whole. Some say that they are accidents of the substance "soul"; others say that they are something intermediate between substance and accident; in fact, they are "virtual" or "potential" parts, as Boethius says. Such parts are not material fragments of a corporeal whole, but spiritual parts. Their distinction follows from that of their essences, which itself can be inferred from the diversity of their operations. "The soul is one substance composed of several parts, like the body. These parts are different in essence, like those of the body; nevertheless, the whole which re-

sults from these parts is one by essence, and it is truly one, because, just as, in the body, there results a form of the whole uniting all the parts in its essential unity, so also, in the soul, there results from many parts a substantial nature in which these parts have an essential unity."

All the problems related to free choice revolve around this question: are reason and will really distinct in the soul, or is their distinction a mere distinction of reason? Bacon holds that the soul is one single substance whose diverse operations are given various names, although, in reality, they cannot be isolated from each other. The same soul both knows and loves, because it knows in order to love, just as, in order to have something to love, it first needs to know. This is what theologians seem to forget in dealing with the notion of free choice. Augustine rightly says that it is a power of both reason and will (*facultas rationis et voluntatis*). Now, if we make reason and will to be two essentially distinct powers of the soul, free choice cannot be considered an essentially distinct power. Otherwise, its own essence would be made up of two other distinct essences, which is impossible. Consequently, free choice itself is a power of the soul whose operations are diverse but reciprocally ordered. This answer gives Bacon full satisfaction, including that of once more carping at theologians who, because they do not first ascertain the fundamental notions they use, multiply questions almost to infinity.

In a thus conceived human soul, the operations of the intellect cannot be considered apart from the dual aspect of the substance from which they flow. As has been said, the intellective soul is both a substance and a form. Considered as the form of its body, it performs its operations in conjunction with the body, negotiates with phantasms and, so to speak, uses them in order to know. As form, the intellective soul is the act of its body, inseparable from it and, consequently, mortal like it. On the contrary, considered as a substance, the soul is not passive, but active (*agens*); its intellectual operation does not belong to it *qua* form of a body, but as separated from it; it does not consist in negotiating with phantasms but, rather, in completely turning itself to its own essence, where it contemplates the intelligible models of things. As a spiritual substance, the soul is naturally immortal. Now, this is the part of the soul which is an active intellect (*intellectus agens*). Although created in conjunction with a body, which is a matter subjected to change and mutability, the intellective soul can contemplate exalted realities through innate models confusedly known. We call it agent intellect because it does not need sense knowledge. It remains in the soul after death. The possible intellect, however, that is, the inferior reason which negotiates with sensible things, and of which it is said that there is in it nothing that has not first been in the senses, does not seem to remain in the separated soul after death. The blending of the Augustinian distinction of *ratio inferior* and *ratio superior,* with the Aristotelian distinction of *intellectus possibilis* and *intellectus agens* is here apparent.

This, which Bacon has never recanted, does not contradict what he says elsewhere concerning an agent intellect separated from the soul. On the one hand, Bacon has always maintained that the duality of the soul (as absolute substance and as form) entailed the duality of its intellectual powers; on the other hand, like Albert the Great, Bacon never denied that, over and above the active intellect that is part of the soul, there was a universally acting intellect, wholly separated from the soul and from all that is, namely God. This is the separate agent intellect which Bacon has always maintained as the source and cause of all reality and intelligibility. The two positions were compatible in a doctrine where the agent intellect in man was just the aptitude of the soul, *qua* spiritual substance, to turn to pure intelligible realities.

Leaving aside the divine agent intellect, whose consideration belongs in metaphysics, let us return to Bacon's statement that our own intellect finds in itself an innate confused cognition of the intelligible models (*exemplaria*) which in God, are principles of both knowledge (Ideas) and operation (forms). Our own active intellect does not know these models in a distinct way, as separate Intelligences do, but in a confused way: "*exemplar. . . innatum et. . . confusum in intellectu animae scilicet agente.*" This is what enables our own agent intellect, whose intelligible models (*exemplaria*) are created, to illumine the phantasms and, after purifying them from material conditions, to impart them to the possible intellect. Hence, Roger Bacon had a notion of abstraction which practically identified it with an illumination of the phantasms by the light of the innate intelligible models created in the soul's agent intellect. That this agent intellect belongs to the soul *qua* substance is in perfect agreement with Bacon's psychology. The seat of these innate intelligibles must needs be separated by its very nature from corporeal matter. Although it speaks the language of Aristotle, this doctrine rests upon a notion of the soul derived from Plotinus through Augustine and Avicenna. Set forth by Gundissalinus, elaborated by William of Auvergne and considered by Bacon as common to practically all theologians, it runs throughout the whole thirteenth and fourteenth centuries. Despite the opposition of Saint Thomas Aquinas, it still will remain a fitting object of reflection, as late as the fifteenth century, for the Franciscan William of Vaurouillon.

C. *Being*

Metaphysics is the science of being, which is the first and the most universal of our notions. Being is neither equivocal nor univocal; it is analogical. This means that its notion is attributed to all that is, neither as signifying a mere community of name (*canis,* "dog," may mean either an animal or a constellation), nor as signifying a real community of being ("animal" is identical in all animals), but as a name which points out either the same thing or the same notion (according to cases) attributed according to an order of priority or of posteriority. In short, being is analogical because it belongs to all that is, not equally, but by priority or posteriority.

Being can be considered as a thing abstracted from other things; for instance, mathematicians abstract mathematical things from sensible things. Being can be considered as a notion abstracted from concrete reality; for instance, in physics, or natural science, "man" or "horse" are abstracted from the particular beings that bear these names. Being can be considered as a notion abstracted from other

notions, which is the case in logic, where second intentions are at stake: "species" is a second intention superadded to "man" or "horse." Being can be considered in its universality, that is, neither as restricted to singulars or to species, nor as abstracted from actual beings, and this is the kind of being studied by the metaphysician, whose proper function it is to determine the relations of priority and of posteriority of all things with respect to being. After studying these relations, the metaphysician is led to examine the notion of absolute Being, as neither abstracted nor restricted by any determination, but as separated from the rest by its own perfection, namely, God. Metaphysics then receives the name of theology.

Bacon refuses to introduce any real distinction between being and its properties. Being is substance, and thing, and one, precisely inasmuch as it is being. These notions point out various modalities in our own ways of conceiving being, but no distinct reality. For instance, to say that "being is one is to say that, inasmuch as it is, a being cannot be separated from itself." "Man," "a man," "this man," are so many expressions that signify the same metaphysical being *qua* being.

After considering the properties of being, metaphysics deals with its causes, not, however, without some qualification. All sciences deal with all the four causes, but each science is especially in charge of one of them, to which it relates the other three. Natural science principally deals with matter; mathematics with form; ethics with ends, and metaphysics with the efficient cause. Accordingly, the metaphysician demonstrates by the efficient cause, which is will. Naturally, this does not prevent him from resorting to forms and to ends in his demonstrations, for, indeed, the final cause is the noblest of all, and it is through its formal cause that the nature of a thing is best known. Yet, when all is said and done, all the demonstrations of the metaphysician ultimately lead him to the supreme efficient cause, which is God.

Being is either universal or singular. Universal beings are caused partly by creation, partly by nature. To create first means to produce something *ex nihilo,* and this is, for all things, the first way of coming into existence. In a second sense, to create means to distinguish and to order already existing singular things. Thirdly, the same term means to unite already distinguished and ordered beings, and this uniting is achieved in universals. The universal is "one in many"; it extends to many singulars. Let us observe, however, that only singulars are created in the proper sense of the term because they are the only completely determinated and subsisting beings. As to universals, they are created in, and together with, singulars; they are "concreated, not created". For the same reason, universals are not "natures" in the proper sense of the term; they are not tied up with any determinate individual; rather, they are everywhere in a state of indifference to individuals. In things, a universal is an essence that is one in many; in the soul, it is an "intention," or notion, that is found, not *in* singulars, but outside them. From the point of view of actual and natural existence, the true being of universals is in singulars; from the point of view of spiritual and cognitive existence, their true being is in the soul. As such, that is, in the soul, to be a universal and to be predicable are two different notions, but in reality they are one and the same thing. All the problems raised by Porphyry and by Boethius in their *Isagoge* are successively dealt with by Roger Bacon, in the same order, not even forgetting the problem added by Abélard: is it possible for universals to subsist after the destruction of all singulars? The object of metaphysical cognition, however, is not the universal as such, which, since universality is predicability, belongs to the order of logic; it is the being of essence considered in itself; for this is metaphysical being: namely, the essence, or quiddity, which is the complete reality of every being.

In investigating being and its causes, metaphysics has to posit a noncaused cause whose proper effect is esse, being. God is the first eternal efficient cause; acting by his will, he is the source whence all beings flow according to their natural order. He is one and eternal; great by his power, which is identical with the infinity of his essence; generous, as one who gives without needing to receive anything. Since he is perfect, God is endowed with knowledge: not, however, a knowledge derived from things, but one which is their cause. Although his knowledge is identical with his essence, God knows not only himself, but all beings, whose ideal forms are eternally contained in him. His cognition of other things is achieved through that of their formal principles, or exemplars, in which they are known more truly than in themselves. Possible beings are as well known to him as actual ones. Let us note that, since possibles are included in their eternal exemplars, they are not mere non-beings.

The word "exemplar" signifies a form present in the mind of an artisan. As a principle of cognition, it is called "Idea," or "species." As a principle of operation, it is called "form"; as a principle of both cognition and operation, it is called "exemplar." In God, there is only one exemplar, neither created nor made, in whose unity the multiplicity of all possible beings is contained.

God is immobile; he moves all things because he is their ultimate end. He can move them all because he knows them all through his own substance, which is the Idea of all that is. It is therefore an error to posit, under the sphere of the moon, a separate substance such as the "giver of forms" of Avicenna, at least if we understand it as a natural and necessary cause of all motions and cognitions in the sublunary world. Like Albert the Great, Roger Bacon maintains that God is the agent intellect of all that is, so much so that, in comparison with him, man is merely "possible." No doubt, angels have in themselves intelligible forms, but these are not the very forms which are to be found later on either in matter or in our intellects. All forms ultimately come from the divine Ideas, through the will and power of God. Angels can help us in knowing; they even are, with respect to our intellect, active separate substances, because our own intellect has not enough natural light; in this sense, it is fitting that angels should irradiate our intellect, according to their will, in order to help us in acquiring merits. Nevertheless, speaking in his own name as well as on behalf of the whole tradition, Bacon maintains that God is the prime and universal cause of all

created forms, such as these are found either in actual existence or in human cognitions.

2. THE REFORMER

Even while explaining Aristotle at the Faculty of Arts, Bacon had in view the great theological synthesis (*Opus principale*) which it was his intention to write. He knew that a considerable amount of research work was required for it; that the common effort of many theologians, besides himself, was necessary to bring it to completion, but Bacon was alone, and he never ceased to complain about what he considered a general decadence of philosophical and theological studies in his own times. His obstinate energy in denouncing the prejudices, the ignorance and the laziness of his contemporaries, as he himself saw them, must have contributed to bring upon him their enmity. His treatise **On the Vices Contracted in the Study of Theology** is a good specimen of what Bacon could write when in his controversial mood, but the **Longer Work** and the two shorter ones show that this was not with him a mood; rather, it was an obsession.

There is one single perfect wisdom, and one science which dominates all the others, that is, theology; but two other sciences are indispensable to unfold it: canon law and philosophy. In other words, the whole body of human knowledge is included in Holy Scripture, which is wisdom, and from whose roots the truth of all the other sciences has sprung. Thus, an interpretation of Scripture by canon law and philosophy would yield a perfect knowledge of divine truth. "All wisdom has been given by one God, to one world, for one purpose," namely man's salvation.

This unitarian conception of human learning, where philosophy, together with its many particular disciplines, is virtually included in revelation, gives its full meaning to the doctrine of God as agent intellect developed by Roger Bacon. First, there is no truth to be found outside of this divine wisdom; at least, whatever intimation of truth may be found elsewhere is sure to be found there in its state of perfection. Secondly, we know that even whatever truth the ancient philosophers have known has come to them from God, that is, from the divine light which illumined their minds.

Roger Bacon has two reasons to affirm this. Philosophers themselves agree that there is a possible intellect and an agent intellect. They also agree that the human "soul" (Bacon does not say "intellect") is "possible" because it is able to receive from on high an illuminating light. Moreover, Alfarabi and Avicenna agree that the active Intellect is no part of the soul; it is a separate substance essentially other than the possible intellect. Even Aristotle says, in his *De anima,* that the active Intellect is separated and unmixed. All those acquainted with philosophy also agree that such was the intention of Aristotle: "For when the University of Paris was convoked, I twice saw and heard its venerable president, Master William, bishop of Paris, of blessed memory, speaking in the presence of all, express the opinion that the active intellect cannot be a part of the soul; and Master Robert, bishop of Lincoln, and brother Adam of Marsh, and elders of this type supported the same view" (Burke's transl.). Last, not the least, does not

Augustine teach, in his *Soliloquies* and elsewhere, that the rational mind of man "is subject to God alone in its illuminations and in all principal influences," so much so that "we do not learn any truth except in the uncreated truth and in eternal laws." What all these famous theologians, and Bacon after them, were doing on this point, is clear: they were substituting the Christian Word of Saint John and Saint Augustine for the separate Intelligence of Avicenna.

If what Bacon says is true, he is equally well founded in maintaining that philosophy is, in our minds, an effect of the divine illumination. Philosophy was revealed to men in the beginning; the patriarchs and the prophets received it from God, and not only the law of God, but all the disciplines that make up philosophy (**Opus majus**). The pagan philosophers, who succeeded the prophets, inherited their wisdom, and Bacon tells at great length the fantastic tale of this transmission of divine learning from the Jewish prophets to the Greek philosophers. Its details are of no particular importance, but its conclusion is highly significant: "Therefore philosophy is merely the unfolding of the divine wisdom by learning and art. Hence there is one perfect wisdom which is contained in the Scriptures, and was given to the Saints by God; to be unfolded, however, by philosophy as well as by canon law" (**Opus majus**).

Bacon did not think he was the first one to know the rules of sound theological and scientific methods. The two predecessors he liked to mention were Robert Grosseteste and Peter of Maricourt. He liked Robert Grosseteste first because, without being in the least ignorant of Aristotle's books, the bishop of Lincoln had desired to learn from other authors and from his own experience; then because, with Adam of Marsh and others, he had learned to explain mathematically the causes of all phenomena, and shown that mathematics is necessary, not only to all natural sciences, but to theology itself: *per potestatem mathematicae sciverunt causas omnium exponere.* But if he received from his English masters the taste and respect for mathematics, it was to a Frenchman that he owed the feeling, so vivid in him, of the necessity for experiments. His real master on this point, and the one he was forever praising, was Peter of Maricourt, the author of a treatise on the magnet which W. Gilbert quoted even in the early seventeenth century and which at that time was still the best work on magnetism. Peter proclaimed, in his *Letter on the Magnet* the necessity of completing the mathematical method by the experimental method. It was not enough to know how to calculate and reason, one should also be clever with one's hands. With manual skill (*manuum industria*) one can easily correct an error that he would not discover after an eternity of trying by the sole resources of physics and mathematics. Roger Bacon seems to have been deeply impressed by that new method and by the learning Peter of Maricourt owed to it. He calls him the master of experiments: *dominus experimentorum,* and draws us a really striking portrait of this solitary scholar, of whom we know so little. Those, with a few other still more obscure names of isolated seekers, were the masters whose methods he claimed to take up again and whose effort he wanted to promote.

It is, therefore, important to stress first the role mathematics were to play in the constitution of science. One can learn nothing of the things of this world, either celestial or terrestrial, unless he knows mathematics (*impossibile est res hujus mundi sciri, nisi sciatur mathematica*). That is evidently true of astronomical phenomena, but since terrestrial phenomena depend directly on the stars, no man can understand what happens on earth if he is ignorant of what is happening in the heavens. Moreover, it is certain, and Robert Grosseteste had perfectly proved it, that all natural actions are propagated and performed in conformity with the mathematical properties of lines and angles. There is, therefore, no need to press this point.

As to experiment, it is much more necessary, for the superiority of the evidence it brings with it is such that even mathematical evidence can sometimes be upheld by it. "There are, in fact, two ways of knowing: reasoning and experiment. Theory concludes, and makes us admit the conclusion, but it does not give that assurance free from all doubt in which the mind rests in the intuition of truth, so long as the conclusion was not arrived at by way of experiment. Many people have theories on certain subjects, but as they have not had experience of them, these theories remain unutilized by them and incite them neither to seek a certain good, nor to avoid a certain evil. If a man who has never seen fire were to prove by conclusive arguments that fire burns, that it spoils and destroys things, his listener's mind would remain unconvinced, and he would not keep away from fire until he had put his hand or some combustible object in it, to prove by experience what theory had taught him. But once having made the experiment of combustion, the mind is convinced and rests on the evidence of truth; reasoning, therefore, is not enough, but experiment does suffice. That is clearly evident even in mathematics, whose demonstrations are the surest of all." If someone possesses a conclusive demonstration in these matters, but without having verified it by experience, his mind does not follow it, is not interested in it, and he disregards the conclusion until an experimental proof makes him see the truth. Then only will he accept that conclusion with perfect tranquillity.

Experiment as Roger Bacon conceives it is twofold. The one is internal and spiritual, whose highest degrees lead us to the summits of the inner life and of mysticism; the other is external and we acquire it by means of the senses. It is the latter which is the source of all our veritably certain scientific knowledge and, in particular, of the most perfect of all sciences, experimental science.

Experimental science (*scientia experimentalis*), whose name seems to appear for the first time in the history of human thought under the pen of Roger Bacon, prevails over all the other kinds of knowledge by a triple prerogative. The first is that, as we have said, it engenders a complete certitude. The other sciences start from experiences considered as principles and deduce their conclusions from them by way of reasoning; but if they wish to have in addition the complete and particular demonstration of their own conclusions, they are forced to seek it from experimental science. This is what Roger Bacon proves at great length in a series of chapters devoted to the theory of the rainbow. The second prerogative of that science is that it can take up at the point where each of the other sciences ends and demonstrate conclusions that they could not attain by their own means. An example of discoveries that are found at the limit of the sciences without being either their conclusions or their principles is the increased length of human life, which will crown medicine, but which speculative medicine alone could not achieve. The third prerogative of experimental science is not relative to the other sciences, but consists in the proper power which enables it to peer into the secrets of nature, to discover the past, the future and to produce so many marvelous effects that it will secure power to those who possess it. This is what the Church should take into consideration, in order to be sparing of Christian blood in its struggle against the unbelievers. This science would enable us to foresee the perils that will attend the coming of Anti-Christ, perils which it would be easy for the Church to prevent, with the grace of God, if the princes of the world and the popes would favor the study of experimental science and carry on the search for the secrets of nature and of art.

Roger Bacon's *Opus majus* does not present itself as an exposition of Christian wisdom, for the learning necessary to it still remains to be acquired. Bacon only intends to urge the pursuit of research, and especially the practice of experiment. This is the theme he goes over tirelessly: here reasoning does not prove anything, everything depends on experience (*Nullus sermo in his potest certificare, totum enim dependet ab experientia*). Beyond describing this method, of which he is sure, Bacon can give us only samples of its fecundity. This accounts for the encyclopedic character of his main work, in which we come across successively: the analysis of the conditions required for a serious study of scientific languages, an exposition of the mathematical method with examples of its application to sacred and profane sciences, a treatise on geography, a treatise on astrology and its uses, one on vision, a description of the experimental method and an ethical doctrine borrowed from Seneca and other ancient moralists. All these speculations attest a very extensive erudition, a lively taste for concrete facts and a sound appreciation of the conditions necessary to promote scientific progress. His errors themselves often betray a mind ahead of his time. For instance, his vivid interest in alchemy and in astrology, which he shared with many of his contemporaries, should not be considered as the mark of an abnormally adventurous spirit; Bacon simply knew more about these things than most of the theologians of his times, with the possible exception of Albert the Great. Had he been able to write it up, the theology he had in mind, although unusual in its form and in its method, would have been rather traditional in its content. More than the doctrine itself, the spirit that animated it gives it interest and assures it a lasting place in the history of ideas. Remembering the miserable conditions in which he lived, his poor health, the difficulties which hindered him not only from making experiments, but even from writing, one feels astonished at this unhappy genius who, alone in the thirteenth century, dreamed of a universal Republic of Christians, united under the authority of the popes, and directed, guided, saved by the truth of an all-comprehensive Christian Wisdom.

Julius R. Weinberg   (essay date 1964)

SOURCE: "Philosophy in Thirteenth Century Christendom," in *A Short History of Medieval Philosophy,* Princeton University Press, 1964, pp. 157-81.

[*In the following excerpt, Weinberg succinctly summarizes Bacon's philosophy and its significance.*]

In his *Opus Majus,* a lengthy exposition of the need to improve philosophical study, Roger Bacon (born about 1214 or a little later; died after 1292) expresses points of view which link him to Avicenna and the older Augustinian doctrines and at the same time reveal his intense interest in the development of mathematics and experimental science.

The eternal light of Wisdom, he tells us, directs the Church, regulates the Commonwealth of the Faithful, brings about the conversion of infidels, and curbs evil men. But many things prevent men from receiving the benefits of divine Wisdom. There are four such hindrances to understanding: following unsuited authority, the bad effects of custom, the acceptance of the opinions of the uninformed masses, and the concealment of ignorance in the display of apparent wisdom. Bacon does not refrain from including some of the best intellects of his time within the scope of his scorn.

Theology is the one supreme science and it must be explained by philosophy and Canon law. The reasons for this preeminence of theology are as follows: All truth comes from Christ, and so all the truths which philosophers have discovered come from the divine Light. The doctrines of Al-Farabi and Avicenna and of Aristotle concerning the active Intellect must be interpreted in this way. Augustine supports this doctrine. And Bacon tells us that William of Auvergne as well as Robert of Lincoln were of the same opinion. This active Intellect from which all illumination comes is God.

Scripture attests to the same view: all philosophy is reducible to divine Wisdom. And it was necessary that the fundamental truths which philosophers discovered be revealed to man from the beginning.

The whole aim of philosophy amounts to this, that through a knowledge of creatures, men be led to a knowledge of the Creator. In the *Opus Majus* there is an argument to establish the existence of God. It is a postulate for every reasonable person that there can be no infinite regression of causes, for an actual infinity is inconceivable and, indeed, impossible; hence, we must stop at some cause to which no other cause is antecedent. This ultimate cause cannot be its own cause since nothing can bring itself into existence; hence, the first cause had no cause and therefore always existed and will always exist. Such a thing will not be capable of nonexistence.

But though this argument be cogent, the full understanding of all that is involved requires a knowledge of mathematics and physical science, for a knowledge of the physical world requires a study of the category of quantity which is involved in all kinds of change. Mathematics, moreover, should be studied before other sciences because it is the easiest, it is more knowable both for the human mind and in itself. It is the most certain of the sciences, for while the other sciences—metaphysics, physics, and moral science—use the demonstration which proceeds from the fact that something is the case (*demonstratio quia*), mathematics uses demonstrations which proceed from the definitions of essences (*demonstratio propter quid*).

In his discussion of experimental science, Bacon argues that of the two ways of knowing, by argumentation and by experience, experience is more fundamental. And he goes so far as to suggest that, even in mathematical demonstrations, the experience of the conclusion is more certain than the mere demonstration without experience. Experience, however, is of two kinds: one derived by way of external senses, the other through interior illumination. The former, although indispensable to acquiring knowledge, human and philosophical, is not sufficient even for gaining full certainty regarding corporeal things; hence, even in natural philosophy, interior illumination is necessary. Interior illumination has seven degrees: the barely scientific, the illumination which instills the virtues, the Gifts of the Holy Ghost "which Isaiah enumerates," the beatitudes, the spiritual senses, the peace of God, and, finally, raptures. Bacon concentrates much of his attention on the experimental sciences which are acquired by external experience and the first degree of interior illumination.

The last part of the *Opus Majus* is devoted to moral philosophy. In this part, Bacon discusses the existence and attributes of God, God's creative and providential function, the celestial Intelligences and angels, the immortality of the human soul, and the beatitude of man. This beatitude is the highest good of which man is capable, and morality and revelation are indispensable to its acquisition.

As the continuator of his teacher Robert Grosseteste, Bacon exhibits the characteristic tendencies and interests of a point of view which combines elements of Augustinian illumination with an interest in physical and especially optical studies. This combination of ideas is to be explained, in the most general terms, by the parallel which Grosseteste found between God as the Light which illumines men's minds and physical light which is the physical counterpart of the divine Light and the first material creation of God.

Joseph Kupfer   (essay date 1974)

SOURCE: "The Father of Empiricism: Roger Not Francis," in *Vivarium*, Vol XII, No. 1, May, 1974, pp. 52-62.

[*In the following essay, Kupfer examines Bacon's credentials as the true father of empiricism for awarding "utility, observation, and 'experience' the central place in his philosophy of science and knowledge."*]

Although Roger Bacon's life spanned most of the Thirteenth century, his philosophy of science carried his thought into what has been loosely dubbed the "Modern period". And although often credited with heralding this Modern period of philosophy Francis Bacon's emphasis on experiment is itself anticipated by his cousin's empiricism. Living three centuries earlier than his more celebrated scion, Roger Bacon's view of the scientific method is more fittingly regarded as the harbinger of the empirical tradition. Anticipating the Renaissance and Enlightenment interest in the melioration of the human condition Bacon awards utility, observation, and "experience" the central place in his philosophy of science and knowledge. Reacting against much of the scholastic emphasis on the deductive method, he abandons the quest for deductive certainty in science. In so doing he avoids the Cartesian dilemma: certitude about relations of ideas, as in mathematics, but skepticism in knowledge of the empirical. Roger Bacon's partial but illuminating analysis of scientific procedure and theory ushers in the so-called Modern period of philosophic and scientific speculation. It is from him and not Francis that the Twentieth century derives the "scientific critical attitude."

I. Idolatry

Early in the *Opus Majus* Bacon enumerates four "obstacles" to the acquisition of truth: the submission to unwarranted authority; the influence of custom and the popular; and conceit or desire for esteem. While respecting the authority of the church fathers and Aristotle, Bacon rejects their judgments as conclusive. "The principles laid down by such authorities [explains William Newbold in *The Cipher of Roger Bacon,* 1928] must be tested by experience before they can be finally accepted." Thus does Roger anticipate Francis Bacon's warning about the Idols of the Theatre. As astute a scholar as Lewis White Beck stresses [in *Philosophic Inquiry,* 1952] *Francis'* articulation of this danger and neglects Roger's:

> In the first half of the seventeenth century, scholasticism, the philosophy of the Church, was challenged from two sides. [Francis] Bacon . . . objected to its Idols of the Theatre, to what he regarded as its slavish acceptance of ideas based on authority, and against it he insisted upon the importance of new observations of nature and man. In this respect, [Francis] Bacon was an empiricist, objecting to the authoritarianism and the empty logic by which many of his opponents believed they could demonstrate scientific and philosophical truths, *a priori*.

What most who place Francis Bacon as the forerunner of the empiricist tradition fail to realize is that he is still actually fighting in the Seventeenth century the battle begun by Roger in the Thirteenth century.

The rejection of authority opens the door to reliance upon evidence and observation. New evidence can discredit old hypotheses. The theories of the authorities are subject to the test of experience. [Emile Charles has written] " . . . elle [authority] ne fait rien comprendre, elle fait seulement croire, . . ." Authority can only provide belief in an idea, suggest an hypothesis, but can not give the verification which experience confers. This emphasis upon experience, in fact, yields a new notion of authority and credibility. Because of our confidence in the scientific inquiry of others, their reports, and the continued openness of hypotheses to further testing, we can rely more upon the findings and claims of other inquirers: "Things that do not belong in our part of the world we know through other *scientists* who have had experience of them" (my italics).

While habitual ways of thinking are more powerful than authority in subverting the quest for knowledge, popular prejudice and custom are the strongest of the three main forces. "For authority merely entices, habit binds, popular opinion makes men obstinate and confirms them in their obstinacy." Like Francis' Idols of the Cave, customary beliefs serve Roger as a *foil* for the truth. Compare the cousins on this head:

> Therefore let not your Wisdom [Pope Clement IV] be surprised, nor your Authority consider it improper if I labor against popular custom and common precedents. For this is the only way of arriving at a consideration of truth and perfection.

Francis counsels us to do the same with our most cherished beliefs:

> Let every student of nature take this as a rule, —that whatever his mind seizes and dwells upon with peculiar satisfaction is to be held in suspicion, and that so much the more care is to be taken in dealing with such questions to keep the understanding even and clear.

The consistency of popular or desirable belief in leading us astray, then, serves as an optimum point of departure for both Bacons.

The fourth cause of error, that of concealing from ourselves our own ignorance and error because of pride, must be corrected by the scientific method because it

> . . . is the beginning and the source of the other causes of error already mentioned. For owing to excessive zeal in regard to our own feeling and the excusing of our ignorance there arises at once the presumption of weak authority, relying on which we extol what is ours and censure what is another's. Then since every man loves his own labors, we willingly form ours into habit.

Bacon's professional suspicion of man's psychological tendencies, again fore-shadowing Francis' warnings about Idolatry, are the reverberations of his scientifically critical attitude.

Roger pre-empts Francis Bacon's rejection of the deductive method and the authority which advocated it as the means of discovering scientific and philosophic truths. Roger stresses the importance of studying language and mathematics, but opposes the scholastic tradition from which he is emerging by holding that experience is the only means of verifying thought. [As A. G. Little has written, in *Roger Bacon,* 1929] "This was opposed to the general trend of thought in his day, which would that logic as the principal door to knowledge." [And Charles has stated] "La méthode scolastique est mauvaise; il en faudrait une autre; c'est la préoccupation constante de Bacon. . . ." Bacon believed logic to be given man by nature, the only part of which that required learning was its terms. Thus, it is a natural tool or instrument of thought, but not the means to gaining knowledge of the empirical world.

For Newbold the Thirteenth century over-emphasized the deductive method—a defect in the Aristotelian theory of science. Newbold sees logic as the means of classifying existing knowledge, but not sufficient for the acquisition of new knowledge. "And this is precisely the point in Aristotle's system against which [Roger] Bacon directs his most telling blows. He by no means rejects the deductive method; he acknowledges its importance and employs it himself. But he does deny its adequacy, and he places experience above it." [In the essay "Roger Bacon," published in A. G. Little's *Roger Bacon Essays,* 1914, M. Muir has written] "He said that scholastic science was too greatly concerned with intellectual definitions . . . and neglected the accurate observation of these events." The conclusions deduced from our axiomatic principles must be warranted by experience before they can be accepted. Bacon rebels against the scholastic dual reliance on the deductive method and authority, advocating in their stead attention to sense experience: "Ainsi, à ces deux instruments de la science scolastique [reason and authority], Bacon oppose l'expérience, et il est, je crois, le premier qui ait caractérisé par leur methode les sciences de la nature, en les appelant les sciences expérimentales."

II. Two Experiences

Bacon distinguishes between two sorts of "experience": inner illumination and sensed impressions. Both are necessary to scientific inquiry and the former temporally precedes the latter. The spiritual experience is a necessary condition for the organization of the "ordinary" sense experience. [As Charles wrote in 1861:]

> Il faut donc le secours d'une autre faculté, l'illumination intérieure, sorte d'inspiration divine, par laquelle l'auteur veut désigner la connaissance directe de certains principes que les sens ne peuvent nous révéler.

Thus do we come to grasp the first principles which Aristotle maintains must be prehended in immediate intuition by "operating" reason. Bacon posits the *Intellectus Agens* (God or Angels) which illuminates the human intellect. [According to Little:]

> The human intellect is not merely passive, but it is incapable of arriving at real knowledge until its responsive powers are called into action by some stimulus from above. . . . The response of the human intellect to the illumination or inspiration of the divine *Intellectus agens* results in 'experience'.

Without this inspiration, the senses cannot yield us knowledge of the "monde matériel."

An extensive criticism of Bacon's notion of illumination and how it relates to his philosophy of the experimental science is offered by Carton. What exactly is the relation of this interior experience to the external sense experiences? Are the senses merely validating eternal truths actually given by means of inspiration, fleshing out a Divine relation, or does the revelatory experience itself pertain directly to the senses? Carton argues for the view that Bacon is in reality a mystical thinker, his "inner experience" being "hermétique"—the senses barely of secondary significance. Bacon's "two experiences", however, reflect his Augustinian frame of reference. The soul or mind of man is unable to discover truths without the aid of a participating God. Moreover, the external sensible world is not discrete or cut-off from that of the spiritual. The two form a continuity of experience: the "revealed" and the sensible are aspects of the one God-created reality. We deduce theorems from our first immediately intuited principles. Once such theorems have been confirmed by sense experience, the revelation or illumination need not come again to every scientist. This hardly seems in conflict with the way science does indeed work. Once a law or theory has been offered its inspirational genesis is not a prerequisite for other scientists.

The sense experience itself is the stuff of which Bacon's philosophy of science is made. "That Bacon was aware of the importance of the experimental method is shown by his actual use of it [writes Newbold] but it does not appear that he had ever attempted to define it and distinguish it from mere observations." By this "second sort" of experience, then, Bacon is referring to that which occurs during observation or experiment. A. G. Little sums up Bacon's view of the two types of experience and their relation to Bacon's revolt against the *a priori* method: "These two kinds of experience are alike in this, that they proceed by immediate contact with reality, not by reasoning."

III. The Experimental Science

" . . . without experience nothing can be sufficiently known."

Bacon distinguishes reasoning from experience as a means of acquiring knowledge, but sees their mutual dependence.

> For there are two modes of acquiring knowledge, namely by reasoning and experience. Reasoning draws a conclusion and makes us grant the conclusion, but does not make the conclusion certain nor does it remove doubt so that the mind may rest on the intuition of truth, unless the mind discovers it by the path of experience. . . . "

Experience must provide the test of our deduced theorems, thereby validating our immediate intuitions. Without observation via the senses, the mind has no warranted beliefs about the external world: " . . . Roger Bacon [writes Muir] insists on the need of observation and experiment for attaining to real knowledge of natural events." Argument, reasoning alone, is insufficient to yield us knowledge.

While Bacon often speaks of the experimental science as a discipline, as a science separate and distinct from other sciences, he is manifestly aware of its relation to these other sciences as a *procedure* without which they cannot function. The experimental science has three "dignities" or "prerogatives"; it "certifies" all other sciences by observation; it supplements other sciences [according to Little] by "taking account of facts which lie within their sphere but outside their actual cognizance;" and thirdly, experimental science itself investigates the secrets of nature. Bacon seems to indicate that experimental science has a

field or realm of inquiry uniquely its own, but does not make this clear.

Bacon maintains that the scientific attitude is one of openness to new hypothesis. The inner illumination remarked above may indeed be the preparation for such openness. We cannot experiment without hypothesis and once we experiment, reasoning about the date is essential:

> Hence in the *first* place there should be a *readiness to believe,* until in the second place experiment follows, so that in the third reasoning may function (my italics).

Following the testing of this hypothesis, (which may be one's own or that of another scientist) the causes at work are to be analyzed. We are to use our observations, moreover, as the basis of these causal explanations: "Bacon [writes Muir] at least tried to look first at external realities, and to base his intellectual explanation of material change on observed facts."

Bacon sees the work of scientists as constituting the work of a *professional community.* One scientist adds to the warrant or verification of a hypothesis or theory posited by another: "Therefore in the beginning he must believe those who have made the experiment, or who have reliable information from experimenters, to which one adds the finding of his own experiments." If we reject an authority it is not on the basis of our own preconceived theory or mode of reasoning, but on the grounds that his claims do not bear up under experimental investigation. It is within this community of scientists that hypotheses are more or less accredited, *more* or *less* disproved.

Bacon approaches an articulation of the contemporary concept of degrees of verification when he says that ". . . . truths and virtues are infinite, and there are innumerable gradations in each truth and virtue; . . . additions can fitly be made to the statements of real authorities, and correctly applied in many cases." These additions are to be made on the basis of experiment. The Enlightenment and Renaissance view of progress and revision is again hinted at when Bacon remarks that the "younger, that is those of a later age, in the progress of time possess the labors of their predecessors."

Because experience, observation, is the final court for any theory, Bacon's philosophy of science provides for a corpus of theory which is self-correcting and ever openended. [According to Little] " . . . he saw clearly that when theories are inconsistent with known facts, the theories must be sacrificed and the facts saved."

While Bacon's "method" was not a very carefully worked out one, "L'observation n'est pas pour lui un accident, un hasard: c'est un système nouveau. . . ." On this point [Raoul] Carton agrees: "Très précisément, notre étude a pour objet de dégager les caractères et de fixer l'allure de l'expérience des sens comme méthode. . . ." The method consists in studying the following in their respective order: the simpler things before the more complex; the general before the particular; and the easier before the more difficult. Believing inanimate objects less complicated than animate ones, Bacon insists on their examination first. "The compounding of substances [writes Muir], which are generated from their elements, therefore, should precede the investigation of the generation of animate things."

These experiments will not only reveal the wonders of nature but will help shatter the Idols of the Cave and Theatre. The efforts of the experimental science can loosen the hold of authority and customarily held belief. That Bacon was, himself, caught up in the drama of science can be seen from the following: "For after I saw this [experiment with the magnet], there has been nothing difficult for my intellect to believe, provided it had a trustworthy authority." But Bacon has a criterion for the "trustworthiness" of authority—reliance upon the scientific method—with which he begins the destruction of faith in "bad" authority. Is this not precisely what we today base the overwhelming majority of our beliefs upon—"trustworthy authority" of one sort or another—the basis of which lies in the strength of the method of verification and our confidence in that method.

Bacon's empiricism has teleological elements: understanding an object's purpose is crucial in grasping its causal relations. "The utility of everything must be considered [writes Muir]; for this utility is the end for which the thing exists." Thus, ascertaining a thing's "purpose" is part of the scientific procedure.

This scientific procedure, beginning with the inner light (illumination or inspiration) culminates in the success of prediction. The objects under investigation are ultimately rendered *useful* through their inclusion in the hypothesis and its verification. A warranted hypothesis is significant not in itself, but because it is useful. It enables us to relate objects of our experience in fruitful ways. [In 1924 Carton wrote] "C'est dire que la méthode de certification comprend deux moments extrêmes, un dernier où nous rapportons les choses à nos fins pour les utiliser dans des œuvres plus particulièrement opératives ou de puissance. . . ."

Bacon prefigures the Renaissance concern for mankind's progress and the American pragmatists such as Dewey and Lewis. Scientific reasoning is ultimately concerned with leading from one sensuous experience, through observation and experiment, hypothesis and verification, to other experiences. He may have been the first to flirt with a pragmatic notion of truth—as Carton puts the matter: "Dès lors en effet que la vérité est essentiellement dispensatrice d'intérèt, elle est d'autant plus noble at possède d'autant plus de prix qu'elle est plus utile. . . ." More salient than this, however, is Bacon's pervasive belief that science will increase man's physical and spiritual powers, leading to his increased happiness.

IV. Mathematics

Bacon offers several reasons for the claim that all sciences require the use of mathematics. He argues that, firstly, all the other sciences use mathematical examples, and since examples clarify the subject matter of the particular science, ignorance of the examples implies lack of full comprehension of the subject. To this reason, Bacon adds, "Secondly, because comprehension of mathematical truths is innate, as it were, in us," but then seems to back off just a bit:

> Wherefore since this [mathematical] knowledge is *almost* innate, and as it were precedes discovery and learning, or at least less in need of them than other sciences, it will be first among sciences and will precede others disposing us towards them; since what is innate or almost so disposes toward what is acquired (my italics).

This presupposes that mathematical truths apply to the external sensible world, and that what is innate and that which is acquired refer to the same universe. Perhaps his awareness of this presupposition is what prompted Bacon to consider mathematical truths verifiable by experience and quasi-innate.

An understanding of mathematics is essential to the other sciences because of its primacy among the sciences (in the order of acquisition) and because it is the easiest to acquire. It is not beyond anyone's grasp, maintains Bacon, and the "natural road" for inquiry is from the simplest to the more difficult.

Our capacity for an "intimate" and more thorough knowledge of mathematics than the other sciences again marks it as a starting point of inquiry. These other sciences, moreover, *require* the use of mathematics for their verification.

> This amounts to showing that other sciences are not to be known by means of dialectical and sophistical argument as commonly introduced, but by means of mathematical demonstration entering into the truths and activities of other sciences and regulating them . . . this simply amounts to establishing definite methods of dealing with all sciences, and by means of mathematics verifying all things necessary to the other sciences.

Although Bacon argues that mathematics is the foundation and first effort of the mind, he nevertheless applies the experiential criterion to it, also. It might seem a bit inconsistent—to subject near-innate knowledge to experiential verification—but for Bacon the innate and the externally received experience are part of an organic whole and are mutually dependent. As with the two sorts of experience, illumination and sense-experience, so with the almost innate mathematical knowledge and acquired knowledge of the external world. Experience remains crucial to knowledge. "This is also evident in mathematics, where proof is most convincing. But the mind of one who has the most convincing proof in regard to the equilateral triangle will never cleave to the conclusion without experience. . . ." He goes on to cite Aristotle's claim that mathematical proof be accompanied by "its appropriate experience."

Bacon's apparent inconsistency of claiming of the one hand that mathematical truths are demonstrable with certainty by necessary and proper causes, and urging on the other that even mathematical truths require experiential verification is further dispelled by viewing mathematics as the framework and method according to which our empirical investigations are ordered. Experimental science must proceed on the basis of mathematical notation, which by itself is insufficient to yield truths about reality.

Like the "experimental method" proper, mathematics functions as a dimension of the investigation required by the various particular sciences. Although Bacon himself speaks of both experimental science and mathematics as *sui generis* sciences his characterization of them belies his labelling. The former represents the sensible-observable component of the method of scientific inquiry, and the latter the logico-exemplary feature of science. Note the significance of "completing" in the following statement by Étienne Gilson: ". . . it was to a Frenchman that he [Roger Bacon] owed the feeling, so vivid in him, of the necessity for experiments. His real master on this point . . . was Peter of Maricourt . . . Peter proclaimed, in his *Letter on the Magnet* the necessity of completing the mathematical method by the scientific method."

Mathematics, then, is a tool of the experimental scientist, who always has his mathematical structure in mind: "Bacon often insists on the need of mathematics in the investigation of physical occurrences [writes Muir]. He tried to form a general science which should bring the actions of bodies, and of natural agents, under the principles of mathematics." We do not verify the conclusions of mathematics directly so much as we verify the predictions reached through the application of those conclusions. Newbold nicely state Bacon's conception of the relation between mathematics and experiment: ". . . there is but one ultimate test of knowledge, experience, and but one way of *organizing* such knowledge into a science, namely, by showing its conformity to the laws of mathematics" (my italics). This suggests that Bacon was recommending the hypothetico-deductive model of Plato: in doing analysis we work from experiment towards our first principles; then, in synthesizing, or organizing, we demonstrate our experimental findings as following from our first principles.

Mathematics and deductive theorizing are necessary to organize and complete the finding of our empirical observations. Bacon's insight lies not only in his rejection of the exclusive reliance upon the deductive method of the schools, but in his acceptance of that method as a *facet* of the scientific procedure. The Medieval and Modern periods are thus bridged in Bacon's philosophy of science, and

Bacon, as depicted in a fifteenth-century manuscript.

it is therefore from Roger Bacon that the Modern period gets its impetus.

Jeremiah M. G. Hackett   (essay date 1980)

SOURCE: "The Attitude of Roger Bacon to the *Scientia* of Albertus Magnus," in *Albertus Magnus and the Sciences, Commemorative Essays 1980,* edited by James A. Weisheipl, Pontifical Institute of Mediaeval Studies, 1980, pp. 53-72.

[*Hackett has written extensively on Bacon's works. In the following excerpt, he examines four of Bacon's works to discern the identity of the "unnamed master" derided by Bacon in his writings and to determine the reason for Bacon's objections to the science of this mysterious authority.*]

Since the rediscovery of the works of Roger Bacon in the nineteenth century, it has been customary to see the *Doctor mirabilis* as a controversialist, early scientist, philosopher, and theologian. Many scholarly judgments have been passed on the merits of his work. Some would see him as a schoolman who never quite reached the stature of an Aquinas or a Bonaventure. Others would see him as a very significant representative of an important stage in the history of science and philosophy. The life and work of Roger Bacon span the whole educational background of the thirteenth century. Like his contemporary Albertus Magnus, whom he may have known at Paris during the years 1245-1248, he was a *savant* with an enormous encyclopaedic mind. The breadth and depth of their understanding of the whole tradition of learning in their time was very great. To take one example, the reception of the new translations of Aristotle in the university milieu of the first half of the thirteenth century found two diverse interpreters in Roger Bacon and Albertus Magnus. It is well known that Albertus Magnus was renowned as a commentator on Aristotle; it is not so well known, even though the point has been made forcefully in some modern Bacon scholarship, that Roger Bacon stands out as a great example of one who had mastered the new translations of Aristotle in the early years of the thirteenth century. Furthermore, Roger Bacon had completed his *Questiones* on Aristotle's books well before Albertus Magnus came to Paris to take his doctorate in theology.

Perhaps the popular image of Bacon today and the view of his work as mere magic or mere alchemy has been due in no small way to attitudes towards Bacon during the Renaissance. However, the "scientific" work of Bacon was not without its defenders during that period; the *apologia* of John Dee is a case in point. An examination of all of Bacon's writings shows that his works on magic and alchemy form a small though significant part of his work. His criticism of magic stands out as a clear-headed attempt to distinguish magical practice from the art and science of nature. The greater part of Bacon's philosophical work is concerned with the interpretation of Aristotle. There is scarcely a page in his scientific work which does not owe something to the logic, ethics, metaphysics, and natural philosophy of Aristotle. In speaking about the philosophy of Roger Bacon, it is best to avoid traditional labels and to seek out just what he said. . . .

Bacon wrote with great haste and against serious impediments, and within a year and a half, produced the works for the Pope which are nowadays known as the **Opus maius** (1266-1267), **Opus minus** (1266-1267), and **Opus tertium** (1266-1267). These writings contain Bacon's plans for the reform of education and society. They include an uneven mixture of philosophical comment, polemic, and some scientific work. These works have been seen as the inept ravings of a tired old man. Rather, however, they seem more like a conscious effort to study the state of learning in the universities of the mid-thirteenth century, and to suggest positive means for reform in education.

Bacon believed that two men were responsible for the failures in the educational system of his time. He names one of them in regard to the teaching of theology as Alexander of Hales. The second master, who bears the brunt of the most sarcastic remarks to come from Bacon, is not personally named; he has come to be known in modern scholarship as "the unnamed master." According to Bacon, he is the one who made himself an authority and a writer of many books on the topic of natural philosophy (*ille, qui fecit se auctorem*, and *ille qui composuit tot et tam magna volumina de naturalibus* etc.). Although the "unnamed master" is often thought to be Albertus Magnus, at least in some contexts, there is no universal agreement about the identity of the person intended by Bacon, and almost no appreciation of the reason for Bacon's ire. . . .

The purpose of this paper is twofold: to determine as unmistakably as possible the "unnamed master" who has perverted the whole of philosophy in "the past forty some years," and to spell out the precise reasons for the "innumerable errors" that have resulted from the "authority" of this one man, as Bacon evaluated the situation. The procedure will be to examine the works of Bacon, beginning (in reverse order of composition) with the works wherein Albert is mentioned by name to the earlier works in which "that man who has made himself an authority" is, in fact, unnamed. Thus the order of works to be considered are the **Compendium studii philosophiae** (ca. 1271-1272), the **Opus tertium** (1266-1267) to Pope Clement IV, the **Opus minus** (ca. 1266-1267) to the same pope, and finally the first part of **Communia naturalium,** a work begun early in the 1260s and completed at a later date. From this examination not only should the identity of the "unnamed master" be clear, but also the reason for Roger Bacon's objections against the "science."

Compendium studii philosophiae (CA. 1271-1272)

We may begin with those passages which explicitly name Albert and Thomas together. These are found in a late work entitled **Compendium studii philosophiae.** We know from internal evidence that this was written circa 1271-1272. In this work Bacon mentions that he had sent a tract on these matters to "the predecessor of the present pope"; thus he wrote it in the region of Pope Gregory X (1271-1276). The **Compendium** shows a remarkable development in tone from that of the three works which he wrote specifically for Pope Clement IV. The topic remains the

same, viz. the new "boy theologians" who read the *Sentences* have ruined the traditions of study, which were characteristic of the faculty of arts, and of great prelates such as Robert of Lincoln (Grosseteste). The emphasis has become explicit in identifying the crux in the decline of studies. In the **Opus maius, Opus minus,** and **Opus tertium,** Bacon had not placed the decline in study in the actual context of the conflict between the regular and secular clergy. Bacon shows in the **Compendium studii philosophiae** that he is writing his new ideas as a propagandist who reflects on the current state of university affairs. Here, he makes an effort to situate the problem of studies in historical pattern. Thorndike has rightly drawn attention to the historical awareness of Bacon, who is somewhat unique in discussing the question of the reception of Aristotle in the west in the thirteenth century.

From the opening pages of the **Compendium studii philosophiae** on, Bacon sets out this problem in detail. The work is concerned with the ways and means of achieving speculative and practical wisdom. The schools are the ideal place for this endeavour. Again, Bacon is presenting the utility of the sciences for theology. Thus, his overall purpose in this work is unmistakably practical. One of the goals of science for Bacon is the proper direction and reform of society. Very systematic about learning, he thinks that studies should be based on a definite method and not on arbitrary decision. In the opening part of the **Compendium,** he states that method has to do with the study of things through the discovery of rational causes. It is a search which is based on authority, reason, and experience. Bacon once again mentions the normal impediments to learning. The worst impediment, the fourth fault which he gives in the first part of the **Opus maius,** is the false appearance of knowledge. According to Bacon, the schools at that time (ca. 1271-1272) are rife with this error. He names those responsible for this condition—the young students of the two orders. This deficient state of studies is reflected in the corruption of society as a whole: the papacy has been vacant for a number of years; religious have lapsed into a decadent state. The Italian civil lawyers are responsible for drawing students from the schools, and for being mechanical in their approach to the study of philosophy. On the whole, he reserves his wrath for the "boy theologians" of the two orders; in chapter v he begins a long tirade against them. It is here that the explicit reference to Albert and Thomas occurs.

He speaks of the "boys" as the embodiment of all the error in studies. These young men have arisen in the *studia* and have made themselves into masters and doctors of theology and philosophy. However, they have learned nothing of value on account of their state of life. They neglect the arts; they do not know all the parts of science and philosophy; they presume to know theology even though they lack the human knowledge which is needed for that task.

> These are the boys among the students of the two orders like Albert and Thomas, and others, who enter the orders when for the most part they are twenty years of age and less.

He adds that these boys were put to read theology after their profession even though they did not have any formal training in reading the Psalter or in reading Priscian. And this has been the case since the establishment of the many *studia*.

Is this reference to Albert and Thomas as boys quite as self-contradictory as Thorndike would have us think? Is it not clear from the context that the author merely takes them as examples of the many boys who did enter the orders at an early age? In his comments on the "boy" theologians, Bacon is, at least, consistent. He returns to the same criticism in his anonymous texts against the "unnamed master." According to Bacon the latter did not teach (*legit*) in *artes* before becoming a theologian. Therefore, even though he was self-taught, he must necessarily be ignorant of the sciences. Bacon continues in the ***Compendium:***

> And so it was proper that they should not profit in any way, especially since they did not seek to have themselves instructed by others in philosophy after they had entered [the orders], and especially since they presumed to investigate philosophy by themselves without a teacher. Thus, they became masters in theology and philosophy before they were students (*discipuli*). Therefore, infinite error regins among them. . . .

This accusation could be levelled against Albert, and indeed against many of the friars who went out to preach.

Bacon further places blame for the mere "appearance of wisdom" on the apparent sanctity of the two orders. However, the real reason for the lack of wisdom in the centres of Christian culture was the manifest neglect of studies by the secular masters. According to Bacon, contemporary secular masters had betrayed the great tradition of study associated with Robert Grosseteste, Adam Marsh, and William of Shyreswood. The new secular masters do not teach the *Sentences,* or incept in theology, or lecture, preach, or dispute except by means of the *quaternos puerorum in dictis ordinibus,* as is evident at Paris and elsewhere. Bacon consciously discusses the important conflict between the seculars and the mendicant orders, and sees therein the reason for the decline in study.

> Therefore, truly it has already been brought to the notice of the public at Paris for the past twenty years that an unspeakable conflict has arisen among the religious because the seculars revolted against the regulars and the religious revolted against the seculars. And they called each other heretics and disciples of antichrist. . . . And they have not ceased up to this time.

Bacon is not altogether detached in regard to this conflict. It can be seen from Bacon's own words that he was engaged in discussion with the "boy" theologians. He allows that though they are not immune from the corruption of the study of wisdom, they are guarded from the accusation of heresy and the name of the antichrist in that they are members of a holy order.

At this point in the ***Compendium,*** Bacon reveals a personal conviction which may well shed some light on his motive for joining the Franciscan Order. He says that God has punished the secular masters who blasphemed against the grace of God which is now given to the religious, in-cluding his own Franciscan Order. He holds strongly to the view that the whole Church regards the religious state in life as higher than the secular, although he readily admits that the Parisian masters disagree with him:

> But the masters at Paris teach what is plainly contrary and they confirm it with many sophisms.

Bacon is irritated that the seculars solicit the power, support, and authority of pope and prelates to defend themselves. He answers that there are two kinds of authority; the authority of office and the authority of spiritual perfection. For Bacon, the latter is the more perfect kind. Bacon, thus, manifests a tension in his own teaching concern. On the one hand, he has great respect for the tradition of the earlier secular masters. On the other hand, he now despises the position which the new secular masters have taken in the university. Thus, one can say that Bacon's becoming a Franciscan was a much more intense experience than it is generally held to be.

Opus tertium (1266-1267)

Bacon is writing in the context of the anti-mendicant controversy. Thus, there is an evident absence of names from all three works which were written for Clement IV. Yet it is certain that anyone acquainted with the problems which Bacon criticises would know immediately the names which Bacon held responsible for the decline in study. In this respect, it is to be expected that Bacon would refrain from an explicit mention of Albert in the three works for the pope. He does make an explicit reference to Albert in the ***Opus tertium.*** Apart from the above-mentioned reference from ***Compendium studii philosophiae,*** this is the only explicit reference to Albert in Bacon's later works. Bacon does praise Albert in the ***Opus tertium,*** but such praise is merely a stage in an argument intended to show that the science of Albert does not measure up to Bacon's strict standards. At first it would seem that Bacon is showing respect for a great mind. As the argument develops, however, it is evident that Bacon is drawing a contrast between the wisdom of this man and the system of knowledge based on his own theory of perspective. Wishing to explain his delay in writing to the pope, Bacon says that the works which His Holiness requested had not yet been written as the clerk of the pope had believed. Bacon blames his failure in writing on the difficult nature of the subject matter:

> . . . which you can certify through the better known *sapientes* among the Christians, one of whom is brother Albert of the Order of Preachers, while the other is Master William of Shyreswood, the treasurer of the church of Lincoln in England, a far wiser man than Albert. For no one is greater than he in *philosophia communi.*

> If Your Wisdom were to write to them concerning the matter of the works which I sent to you, and concerning which I will touch on in this third writing, you will see that ten years will pass before they will send to you those very things I have already written. You will certainly find a hundred places [among my writings] to which they would never attain through those things

which they know now, even up to the end of their life. For I know their science well (*Cognosco enim eorum scientiam optime*). And I know at least that neither of the aforementioned, neither the first nor the last, would be able to send to you the works which I have written within the amount of time that has elapsed since your mandate. One should not wonder therefore at my delay in this area of philosophy. For the wisdom of perspective alone, which I will write, could not be written by anyone within a year. But why do I hide truth in this matter? I assert, therefore, that you will find no one among the Latins who would render this area of wisdom within one year or indeed in ten years.

This text poses a problem. Bacon usually contrasts the terms *sapientes* and *vulgus*. Here he calls Albert one of the *sapientes,* yet in another text Bacon refers to the "unnamed master" as the best teacher among the *vulgus.* And he adds that he was the most studious among them. He uses the term *sapientes* again in the **Opus tertium** in those texts which treat of the "unnamed master." A reading of these texts will show that Bacon's words of praise for Albert are severely qualified. In a reference which is placed soon after the above passage from the **Opus tertium,** Bacon takes up the topic of the completion of philosophy in the Latin language.

> The fifth objection is the strongest and the gravest for me; but it is solved through the fourth. It states that it is already thought by the *vulgus studentium,* and by many who are sincere scholars, although they are deceived, that philosophy was given to the Latins, and was completed and composed in the Latin language. And they hold that it was accomplished in my time and spread about at Paris, and the composer of it was held to be an authority (*in tempore meo et vulgata Parisius et pro auctore allegatur compositor eius*). For just as Aristotle, Avicenna, and Averroës are held [as authorities] in the schools, so too is he. And he still lives and has great authority in his lifetime, such as no man ever had in teaching.

Various allegations which Bacon brings against this man will be noted later. The key issue for Bacon is that he (the unnamed master), or rather his followers at Paris, claim that he has rewritten the whole of philosophy in Latin, and that it is now final and complete. Bacon's fourth objection, alluded to in the above quotation, deserves consideration:

> . . . the fourth [objection] is that the author of these works omitted those parts of philosophy of great utility and immense beauty and without which it is not possible to know those things which are commonly taught, concerning which I will write to Your Glory.

> And so there is nothing of use in his writings. But there is much in them which is of the greatest detriment to learning. One should not be surprised that his writings have been justly neglected since he heard no part of philosophy and was not taught by anyone. And he was not educated in the *studium* in Paris, nor in any place where a *studium* of philosophy flourished. He did not

teach nor dispute nor exercise himself in conferring and disputing with others. Nor did he have a revelation, since living otherwise, he did not prepare himself for this. And gathering false, vain, and superfluous things, he put aside the practical but necessary things, which things do not indicate a revelation. But through himself he presumed to treat of those things he did not know.

> I have not said these things about this aforementioned author without cause, since not only is it of service to my proposal, but it is to be mourned that the study of philosophy has been corrupted through him more than through all who ever existed among the Latins. For while others failed, they did not presume authority. But this one wrote his books *per modum authenticum.* And so the whole mob at Paris refers to him as to Aristotle, or Avicenna, or Averroës, and other *auctores.* And this man gave great injury not only to the study of philosophy but to theology, as I show in the **Opus minus,** where I speak of the seven sins in the study of theology. And the third sin is especially against him, as I discuss it openly because of him. For I remark on two people there, but he is the principal one in this matter. The other one, who however has died, has a greater reputation. And these things follow clearly from the **Opus majus** and the **Opus minus,** since in respect to matters both human and divine, concerning which he is accustomed to adjudicate, I show that all vain, false, and superfluous things are multiplied, while singularly renowned, great, and useful things are left aside. And these things will be apparent with sufficient clarity from this third writing.

Bacon is most explicit here. No one has ever composed philosophy in Latin. It was originally given to the Hebrews and renewed through the Greeks, especially through Aristotle, and was renewed in the Arabic language through Avicenna:

> It [philosophy] was never composed in Latin, but was only translated from foreign languages, and the better parts were not translated. And nothing is perfect of those sciences which have been translated. The translations are perverse and are not understandable in many sciences, especially in the books of Aristotle.

At this point, Bacon moves to a favourite theme: "only one [of the Latins] knew sciences, that is the bishop of Lincoln [Grosseteste]; only Boethius knew all languages. . . ." He says that there are not even four Latins who know Hebrew, Greek, and Arabic grammar. He does not deny that many translators were at work on the Arabic and Greek texts. Later, in the **Opus tertium,** he refers to them by name, and he claims friendship with some of them. But he criticises them for not knowing the grammar of these languages in the manner in which they know their Priscian in Latin.

Bacon then proceeds to talk about the importance of mathematics and Perspective (*Perspectiva*). He is particularly emphatic on the central importance of Perspective. All things are known through mathematics; and the laws of the multiplication of species are known through Perspective. Perspective, then, provides the key to a universal science. It, and not a purely philosophical treatment of physics, is the way to a knowledge of generated things. In Bacon's precise language, Perspective is not just the means of knowing those things which are common elements in a theory of vision, but it is also the key to all sensible things and to "the whole machine of the world, both in the heavens and in inferior things" (*totam mundi machinam, et in coelestibus et in inferioribus*).

Bacon continues the argument:

> However, this science is not yet taught at Paris, nor among the Latins, except twice at Oxford in England, and there are not three people who know the power of this science. Whence that one, who made himself an authority, concerning whom I have spoken above, knew nothing of the power of this science, as appears in his books, because he did not write a book about this science, and he would have done it if he had known it. Nor did he say anything about this science in the other books. However, it ought to be the case that the exercise of this science would be fulfilled in all the others, since all things are known through its power. And so he was not able to know anything about the wisdom of philosophy. But those who know these things are few, just like those who know mathematics, and they cannot be had without great expense. Similarly the instruments of this science, which are very inaccessible and of greater expense than the instruments of mathematics, cannot be had without great expense.

The remarks about money make some sense as Bacon argues strongly in his later works that scientific endeavour is impossible unless some great power such as a king or the pope will support it. And to a great extent, the polemic of the works to the pope is a persuasive attempt to get the pope to finance and set up an organised study in the natural sciences. Bacon evidently knew the public prestige of this competitor, the "unnamed master." Hence, he needed to argue that his own science was much better for the good of society and the Church. The centrepiece of any such study of the natural sciences would concern itself with Perspective and the multiplication of species, which for Bacon is the *summa et principalis radix sapientiae*.

> But he who multiplied volumes ignores these roots. For he touches on no aspect of them. And so it is evident that he ignores the natural things, and all things which are concerned with philosophy. And he not only himself is ignorant [of these things] but the whole *vulgus philosophantium,* which errs through him, is ignorant of these matters. For if you will write to him about what he would write concerning these roots, you will find him unqualified in these matters.

Thus, no authority, ancient or modern, wrote about these things; but he, Bacon, worked for ten years before he was able to speak to some people about them. And he notes here that he is putting the fruits of his labours into writing on the occasion of the pope's mandate. Bacon's main concern with the multiplication of species and with Perspec-

tive meant a widening of the treatment of *Perspectiva* from that of the normal school text of the time. One can recognise this great difference by comparing the brief account of *Perspectiva* in the *De ortu scientiarum* of Robert Kilwardby with the extended mathematical and physical explanation by Roger Bacon. It is obvious from the later scientific tracts of Bacon that his ten-year search for new forms of knowledge outside of the common study of the faculty of arts concerned itself with the study of mathematics, perspective, and *scientia experimentalis.* Bacon, then, claims to have found a new foundation for the sciences. This claim is, perhaps, best stated by Bacon in his *Communia naturalium.*

Bacon repeats the same claim in the **Opus tertium** about *scientia experimentalis* and about alchemy. All of this is significant in that it points to the question of astronomy as the real issue which brought about Bacon's conflict with his order. This aspect has been briefly presented by Theodore Crowley in his study of the problem of the soul in Bacon's philosophical commentaries. In general, Bacon accuses the "unnamed master" of ignoring the basis of all of these sciences:

> But he indeed who composed so many great volumes about the natural things, concerning whom I have spoken above, ignores these basic matters (*fundamenta*), and so his building is not able to stand.

Only one further reference to this "unnamed master" need be mentioned from the **Opus tertium.** It has not, to my knowledge, been used before in regard to the identification of the "unnamed master," but it is important in that it comments on the notion of method. Speaking about his pupil John, whom he is sending to the pope with his works, Bacon claims that John alone of all the Latins knows this *Perspectiva* and mathematics of which he speaks. The others do not know it because they do not know Bacon's method:

> . . . nor that one great master (*magister magnus*), nor any of those whom I have mentioned above, because they do not know my method.

His criticism of the great master is due to the fact that both masters use a different philosophical method.

Opus minus (1266-1267)

Since Bacon refers to the **Opus minus** in regard to the "unnamed master" in the **Opus tertium,** it is important to examine the context of his argument in the former work. The first sin against theology which displeases Bacon has to do with the place of philosophy in the study of theology. He claims that philosophy has taken on a dominant role in theology. The latter science should be a *scientia dei.* But in the books on the *Sentences* theologians do not generally consider theology and prophecy since most of the questions in the *Sentences* have to do with purely philosophical matters. The theologians thereby are led to neglect the text of scripture.

The second sin is that theology omits the greater sciences and is quite content with the vulgar sciences. The latter included the grammar of the Latins, logic, natural philosophy according to its worst part, and a certain part of metaphysics. Bacon's point is that these sciences have no practical application. They treat of pure knowledge, and they are without any practical purpose. The greater sciences, which Bacon proposes here and which include mathematics, perspective, moral science, and experimental science, have to do with the practical good of the body, and the soul, and fortune. For that reason, they are more actual and effective.

The third sin, which Bacon relates to the fault of the "unnamed master," is concerned with the same questions as the second. He says that the theologians even neglect the four common sciences which were in general use in the schools at the time he wrote the three works for the pope. According to Bacon, those who wrote *summae* in theology did not know either the natural philosophy or metaphysics in which they now glory. This remark is significant and the reference is unmistakable. He says that all the error of study arose because of these two men, Alexander of Hales and the "unnamed master." Bacon states that he saw these two men who made *summae* with his own eyes, and thus he knew that they never saw or heard the sciences in which they now glory. He argues that they never had a chance to hear or teach the natural sciences. One of them is now dead, the other is still alive. The one who is dead was a good man, a great archdeacon, and a master of theology in his time, and because of this, he was made a great friar when he entered the Order of Friars Minor. This order was new in the world and it had neglected studies, but it still gave to this man authority over all its study. They also ascribed to him a great *summa* which is more than the weight of one horse. Bacon's argument against this man, which is also a point he holds against the second master, is that he had not lectured on metaphysics or on natural philosophy. The books on these subjects, according to Bacon, had been excluded from the arts faculty when Alexander was a student. And soon after that, these books were condemned and forbidden at Paris. Then, when the university, which had been dispersed in 1229, had reassembled in 1231, Alexander had become an old man:

> Whence, as I will say briefly, he ignored these sciences which are now in common use, that is, natural philosophy and metaphysics, in which is found all the glory of the study of the moderns.

Bacon does link Alexander with the "unnamed master." Both are responsible for the decline in study. Alexander is responsible for the fall in the study of theology; the "unnamed master" is the one responsible for the decline in the study of philosophy. In the end, Bacon says that the *studium* at Paris lacked these sciences. He then introduces his remarks on the "unnamed master":

> The other one who lives (*Aliter qui vivit*) entered an Order of Friars as a boy. He never taught (*legit*) philosophy anywhere, nor did he hear it in the schools, nor was he in a *studium solemne* before he was a theologian, nor was he capable of being taught in his own order, as he was the first master of philosophy among them. And he taught others; whence from his own study he had what he knows. And truly I praise him more

than all of the common students, because he is a most studious man, and he saw many things, and had money (*habuit expensum*). And so he was able to collect many useful things in the infinite sea of authors (*auctorum*). But since he did not have a foundation (*fundamentum*), for he was not instructed or exercised in hearing, reading, or disputing, it was inevitable, therefore, that he did not know the common sciences (*scientias vulgatas*). And again, since he did not know the languages, it is not possible that he would know anything great, on account of the reasons which I write concerning the knowledge of languages. And again, since he ignores perspective, just as others of the common students do not know it, it is impossible that he should know anything of worth about philosophy. And he is not able to glory in the tract which I have composed concerning *scientia experimentalis,* alchemy, and mathematics, since these [sciences] are greater than the others. And if he does not know the lesser he cannot know the greater. God, however, knows that I have only exposed the ignorance of these men on account of the truth of study. For the *vulgus* believes that they [Alexander of Hales and the "unnamed master"] know everything and it adheres to them like angels. For these ones are quoted (referred to) in disputations and lectures as *auctores.* And especially that one who lives; he has the name of *doctor Parisius,* and he is referred to in the *studium* as *auctor;* which cannot be done without the confusion and destruction of wisdom, since his writings are filled with falsehoods and infinite vanities. Never before did such abuse appear in this world.

Bacon then lists some of the other faults which he later discusses in the *Opus tertium,* and which we have already examined. One should note that Bacon himself intended the cross-reference in these works.

Communia naturalium

That Bacon develops his natural philosophy in contradistinction to the thought of the "unnamed master" is clearly seen from a very important introduction to the *Communia naturalium.* This is a purely theoretical work which Bacon probably began in the early 1260s and which he probably completed towards the end of the decade. Like many of Bacon's writings, the text received many revisions. This work lacks the polemic and persuasive character of much of the work which Bacon wrote for Pope Clement IV. He intended the work as a tight *compendium* of the common features of the different areas of natural philosophy. He explicitly leaves it to later times and to others to develop work in the individual special sciences. He leaves us in no doubt that perspective is first among the special sciences. He argues that concision and precision are more important in natural philosophy than are all the volumes of Aristotle and much of the research of the thirteenth century. Thus, he says that there is more value in one book of Aristotle, namely the *De celo et mundo,* than there is in all the other volumes of the *naturalia.* In this respect, he adds:

> And so some moderns are in error beyond measure who exceed the quantity of the volumes of Aristotle and give a greater quantity to one of

their own books than Aristotle deigned to present in all [his] books. Truly, therefore, they are convicted of great ignorance on account of which they do not know how to stand in regard to necessary things, although they not only gather most vain things but multiply infinite errors. The root cause of this is that they have not examined the sciences on which they write nor did they teach them in a *studio solemni,* nor did they even hear them. Whence they were made masters before they were disciples, so that they err in all things on account of themselves and they multiply the errors among the *vulgus.*

Again, they are not able to know the *libri naturales* and the common books without knowledge of the seven other special sciences, or even without mathematics. But two glorious moderns (*Sed duo moderni gloriosi*) [have tried to do so], just as they have not heard the sciences about which they speak, nor have they read them or are they exercised in the other ones, as appears from their writings, therefore, it is evident that they are confounded everywhere by errors and vanities. Indeed, their error is multiplied in the natural sciences and in the other common sciences since the translations which they use are perverse and nothing of value can be said from them.

Some lines after this, Bacon makes the following remark which shows that he was consciously defending a particular school of thought, namely that one which is associated with Robert Grosseteste. He argues that these latter sought the sources of natural science in places other than the works of Aristotle and in the practice of mathematics:

But the other men mentioned, namely, those who heard these sciences, and read and examined them, seeing that through the text of Aristotle and his commentators they were not able to know natural philosophy, turned themselves to the seven other natural sciences, and to mathematics, and to other authors of natural philosophy as to the books of Pliny and Seneca and of many others. And so they came to the knowledge of natural things, concerning which Aristotle in his common books and his expositor were not able to satisfy by [their] study of the natural things.

Whom does Bacon include among the "other men"? He includes Grosseteste, Adam Marsh, Peter of Maricourt, John of London. He also includes Campanus de Novara and Master Nicholas, the teacher of Lord Aumury de Montfort. These names are not given in the **Communia naturalium,** but they are the ones he praises in the **Opus tertium** for their knowledge of mathematics and science. One should also include William of Shyreswood in this group, for he is mentioned together with Grosseteste and Adam Marsh throughout these later works of Bacon.

Conclusion

It will be evident from the present review of the texts in Bacon which refer to Albertus Magnus and to a certain "unnamed master" that there is an unmistakable coincidence in these texts. Of the two explicit references to Albert, one is openly critical; the other is a statement of

praise which soon changes into critical contrast of Albert's method with that of Bacon. The implicit texts, directed against the "unnamed master," continue the very same argument. The "unnamed master" does not know perspective, and therefore his science is without a foundation. And that charge, according to Bacon, applies to every aspect of his *scientia.* His science lacks a foundation for *scientia experimentalis,* and alchemy. Thus, Bacon, in accordance with his method of experience (*scientia experimentalis*) and by reason of his mathematicization of reality, makes a fundamental methodic objection to the science of Albert. The crux of the question is whether or not mathematics is universal and all encompassing. Does it give the principles of explanation to each area of investigation or are the different areas of knowledge specific in that each of them has its own principles of explanation? Albert's own concern for and criticism of the thirteenth-century *amici platonis* in many places in his works shows that he was involved in controversy with contemporaries who favoured mathematics as the key to a proper understanding of natural science. Bacon's criticism of Albertus Magnus, which is a central part of his *persuasiones* to the pope, should not be dismissed lightly as the pedantry of an old crank, but should be seen for what it is. It is the polemic and persuasive side of a very important debate on the principles of philosophic and scientific method in the schools of thirteenth-century Europe.

One question remains unanswered. Did Bacon include other well-known scholars in his criticism? Who, for example, is the second of the "two glorious moderns" (*duo moderni gloriosi*) mentioned in the **Communia naturalium?** This would not seem to be a reference to Alexander of Hales. It would appear to be a reference to a master who has commented on the works of Aristotle, and especially on his metaphysics and natural philosophy. Since his name is linked in the text to that of the "unnamed master," it could well be a reference to Thomas Aquinas. He, indeed, was the head of the *vulgus studentium* at Paris, who spread (*vulgata*) the newly published works of Albert during this time. His fame as a representative of the standpoint of Albert was well established by the time Bacon had written the **Communia naturalium.** One has to grant that there are problems in regard to scribal changes of personal names in the works of Bacon. Still, one ought not to dismiss the linking of the names of Albert and Thomas, as given in the **Compendium studi philosophiae,** as merely the result of scribal error. For Bacon, they both represented a method of philosophizing which differed from his own.

Finally, it must be said that Bacon quite consciously avoided direct condemnation of Albert by name in his later work, especially in his work to Pope Clement IV. The presence of internal reference in the **Opera** to Pope Clement IV is Bacon's way of criticising the *scientia* of Albertus Magnus without engaging in direct personal name-calling. By means of a system of cross-references Bacon builds up a portrait which would be recognizable to any thirteenth-century reader acquainted with school debates.

David C. Lindberg   (essay date 1987)

SOURCE: "Science as Handmaiden: Roger Bacon and the Patristic Tradition," in *Isis,* Vol. 78, No. 294, December, 1987, pp. 518-36.

[*Lindberg has written extensively on Bacon's accomplishment and is the editor of* Roger Bacon's Philosophy of Nature: A Critical Edition with English Translation, Introduction, and Notes of "De multiplicatione specierum" *and* "De speculis comburentibus" *(1983). In the following excerpt, he seeks to demonstrate that "Bacon was not a modern, out of step with his age, or a harbinger of things to come, but a brilliant, combative, and somewhat eccentric schoolman of the thirteenth century, endeavoring to take advantage of the new learning just then becoming available while remaining true to traditional notions, patristic in origin, of the importance to be attached to philosophical knowledge."*]

In the middle of the thirteenth century Roger Bacon found himself in a situation roughly analogous to that of Hugh of St. Victor in the first half of the twelfth, but considerably graver. Each perceived the threat of scholarship divorced from biblical studies and theology. But if, early in the twelfth century, the handmaiden named "philosophy" appeared ready to dally with the pleasures of insubordination, by the middle of the thirteenth a full-scale rebellion did not seem out of the question. The translations of the twelfth and early thirteenth centuries had brought to Christendom an enormous body of Greek and Islamic learning, impressive in scope and depth, but much of it claiming no religious function or allegiance. A first reading of the Aristotelian corpus, for example, was not religiously reassuring: the eternity of the world was proclaimed; divine providence and personal immortality were denied; and authority in matters of belief was claimed for reason rather than revelation. And if the danger of an autonomous, secularized philosophy was not enough to worry about, there was the equally appalling opposite risk—namely, that the new learning would be judged impious and condemned without an adequate hearing, its potential benefits thus forever lost. That the latter was a genuine risk had become apparent with the banning of Aristotelian natural philosophy at Paris early in the century. This, then, is the dilemma that dominated the intellectual life of the thirteenth century and determined the shape of Bacon's career.

Bacon had no intention of giving up the new knowledge. As a master of arts, knowledge was his business, and surely his natural impulse was to enlarge, rather than to diminish, the body of teachable arts and sciences. Besides, to Bacon the utility of the new sciences of mathematics, astronomy, optics, and medicine was too obvious to permit even the thought of giving them up. Bacon's goal, then, had to be to reclaim secular learning for the faith—to demonstrate that, purged of a few errors, it was benign and useful. This was not an altogether novel goal, of course; it was a vigorous restatement, or perhaps recasting, of the traditional (Augustinian) ideal of knowledge in the service of religion, at a point in history when there was a great deal more purported knowledge, some of it quite unruly, to be pressed into servitude.

The chronology of Bacon's career is still open to dispute. It seems that he lectured in the faculty of arts at Paris during the 1240s, producing a series of Aristotelian commentaries. Late in that decade or early in the next he returned to Oxford, began the investigations of mathematical and experimental science that would ultimately distinguish him from the great mass of arts masters, and eventually joined the Franciscan Order. We do not know when or how his plan for a reform of learning originated, but during the 1250s he seems to have been at work on pieces that would be fitted together in the 1260s to form the great *opera* for Pope Clement IV. It will be enlightening to examine the program of scholarship set forth in these works.

Bacon opens the ***Opus maius,*** the largest and most systematic of the works for the pope, with a discussion of four obstacles to the apprehension of truth—sources of error that have suppressed knowledge of the utmost beauty and value. "Out of these deadly pestilences arise all of the afflictions of the human race; for [on account of them] the greatest, most useful, and most beautiful teachings of wisdom, as well as the secrets of all arts and sciences, remain unknown. Worse yet, men blinded by the darkness of these four [errors] do not perceive their own blindness." The first cause of error is "adherence to flawed and unworthy authority," by which the ignorant are doomed. The second is the persistence of custom, which consistently favors the false over the true. The third is popular prejudice, which produces obstinacy and confirms men in their error. Bacon hastens to add that he has no objection to the "solid and true" authority of the church, the saints, and other experts in the pursuit of wisdom—a claim that he proceeds to demonstrate by appealing to such (no doubt) "solid and true" authorities as Seneca, Aristotle, Cicero, and Jerome, all of whom scorn reliance on custom and vulgar opinion.

The fourth, and most serious, cause of error is the tendency to cloak ignorance in a show of wisdom; this fault, universal in mankind, is a "wild beast, which devours and destroys all reason." This source of error is not only dangerous in itself, but also contributes to the other three, for it leads us to rely on weak authority, to convert our own achievements into custom (if we can), and to disseminate our madness as popular prejudice. It is owing to such unfortunate tendencies that Aristotle is rejected on many points in favor of Plato, despite Aristotle's manifest superiority as a philosopher; and that the philosophical works of Avicenna and Averroes have been banned at the University of Paris. Recognizing this fourth cause of error, we should not allow the ignorant to suppress books; rather we must liberally permit works to be read, trusting that ultimately, with divine help, truth will prevail.

To buttress his case, Bacon sets forth a series of historical examples of opposition to the truth. The law was given to Moses, but was scarcely received with enthusiasm by the pharaoh and the Egyptians, or even by the children of Israel. Christ and the apostles met opposition because of the novelty of their message and the ignorance of their audience. Again, many of those now acknowledged to be doctors of the church, such as Jerome, were first considered heretics: "Similarly, resistance to the truth has confronted all the doctors of sacred Scripture; for in their restoration of learning, they always encountered contradiction and hindrances. Nonetheless, truth grows and will continue to grow until the Antichrist comes."

Bacon's campaign in defense of the new learning unfolds in Part 2 of the *Opus maius,* where he assembles arguments to demonstrate the legitimacy and value of philosophy. Bacon was not a particularly systematic thinker, and the arguments tumble helter-skelter from his pen. Looming over them, however, is the Augustinian conception of one perfect wisdom, contained (in kernel, at least) in Scripture and expounded by philosophy (or, as Bacon puts it, by canon law and philosophy). Just as writers on canon law are contributing to the development of the leaves, flowers, and fruit of a truth "whose roots and trunk are to be found in sacred Scripture," Bacon argues, so "philosophy is nothing except the unfolding of divine wisdom by teaching and writing."

Philosophy and biblical exegesis enjoy an intimate and complex linkage. On the one hand, exegesis of the literal sense requires a knowledge of the nature of things, acquired from philosophy. On the other (and this is where Bacon places the emphasis), the true natures of creatures are revealed in Scripture, and there the philosopher must look for them if he is to succeed at the business of philosophy. Bacon uses the rainbow as an example:

> Scripture apprehends [the natures of] creatures far more certainly and more truly and better than philosophical labor could search them out. Instead of an infinity of examples, let the rainbow serve for the moment. The philosopher Aristotle confuses us with his obscurities, nor do we obtain any useful knowledge [of the rainbow] from him. And this should not surprise us, since his principal imitator, Avicenna, . . . acknowledges that he himself does not clearly understand the nature of the rainbow. And the reason for this is that [these] philosophers were ignorant of the final cause of the rainbow and, being ignorant of the purpose of the rainbow, they were ignorant of the things that serve this purpose. . . . But the final cause of the rainbow is the dissipation of the aqueous vapor, as is shown in the book of Genesis.

Nor is the ability of Scripture to supply vital philosophical perspective or information an isolated phenomenon. Bacon argues that every creature, "in itself or in its similitude, as a universal or an individual, from the highest of the heavens to their furthest limits, appears in Scripture," placed there to assist our understanding; philosophy, which has no purpose other than to unfold the natures and properties of created things, is thus founded at every point on biblical exegesis.

To support these contentions Bacon appeals to the authority of the church fathers: Augustine, Jerome, Cassiodorus, and others. Augustine's *De doctrina Christiana* is several times quoted or paraphrased: "whereever the Christian finds truth, it is his Lord's"; truth is to be reclaimed from the philosophers, "as from unjust possessors." Bacon quotes Cassiondorus in defense of the quandrivium, and Jerome in defense of eloquence. And he introduces Bede's

admonition to Christians that they seize all that is useful in the liberal arts and apply it to sacred purposes.

Philosophy is also justified by its pedigree. Bacon argues that it was revealed in its fullness to the patriarchs and prophets, "the only true philosophers, who knew all things." God also gave them increased longevity to provide time for the completion of that which had been revealed to them. This knowledge was passed down through various ancient sages to Plato and Aristotle, the latter "aspiring to that perfection of philosophy possessed by the ancient patriarchs." Bacon acknowledges that philosophy, as it has come down to his own age, is incomplete; but far from justifying its rejection, this merely obligates us to "supply what the ancients lacked."

The divine origin of philosophy is proved by the presence of the principal articles of the faith in the writings of pagan philosophers—doctrines such as the existence of God, the resurrection of the dead, and the immortality of the soul. Moreover, virtue is taught by pagan authors, whose teachings can be "reduced to contempt for riches in place of covetousness, disregard for honors in place of pride, scorn for pleasures in place of lust and gluttony, and activity and receptivity of the soul in place of anger, envy, and sloth." Philosophy is justified, finally, by its utility in proving the faith and persuading the unbeliever.

Philosophy, then, is a divine gift, an instrument of biblical exegesis and theology, and a weapon against the infidel; it is integral to the pursuit of wisdom, and its cultivation is obligatory. But Bacon cannot simply argue that all knowledge, in principle, serves the faith and leave it there; he must also demonstrate that, in fact, the new learning will submit to faith's command. To this task he devotes the remainder of the *Opus maius.*

Part 3 of the *Opus maius* is an appeal for the study of grammar and foreign languages. The need is obvious, because the original languages of the Bible were Hebrew and Greek, and philosophy has been acquired from Hebrew, Greek, and Arabic sources. Since "it is impossible for the peculiarities of one language to be preserved in another," our understanding will necessarily remain incomplete until we have mastered the original languages. Bacon launches into a discussion of faulty translations and the errors that have arisen through linguistic ignorance; he complains about the Paris edition of the Bible and takes his readers on a brief excursion through the Hebrew and Greek alphabets.

Bacon concludes this part with a systematic presentation of reasons for the study of languages. They are required, first, for the government of the church: so that foreign words employed in the divine office and the administration of the sacraments will be properly pronounced and comprehended; so that the church will be able to rule successfully over foreign peoples; and so that numero-alphabetical studies of the Hebrew, Greek, and Latin Scriptures, which can predict the events of the end of the age, will be encouraged. Linguistic studies are also required for the government of the Christian commonwealth, in its commercial and diplomatic dealings with various nations. Finally, languages are necessary for missionary activity and for the repression of those who refuse conversion.

If Bacon had no difficulty defending grammatical and linguistic studies, mathematics would seem to present a somewhat stiffer challenge. Bacon believes that mathematics is one of four sciences so basic as to constitute the foundation for all others. (The remaining three are language, perspective, and experimental science.) However,

> the gate and key of these [four] sciences is mathematics, which holy men discovered at the beginning of the world . . . and which has always been used by holy and wise men more than any other science. Its neglect for the past thirty or forty years has ruined the whole educational system of the Latins, since he who is ignorant of it cannot know the other sciences or the things of this world. . . . And what is worse, men ignorant of it do not perceive their own ignorance, and therefore they do not seek a remedy. And, on the contrary, knowledge of this science prepares the mind and elevates it to sure knowledge of all things, so that if one grasps the basics of wisdom concerning this science and applies them correctly to knowledge of other sciences and things, one will be able to know all things that follow, without error or doubt, easily and powerfully.

Bacon devotes hundreds of pages to the elaboration of this claim, and we will not attempt to follow the argument in detail. One of his most serious points is that causal demonstration, the most powerful form of demonstration in the realm of natural things, requires a mathematical cause; therefore, the mathematician has significant advantages over the physicist or natural philosopher, who knows only the physical effects.

Many other points follow. Bacon resorts again to authority (citing Boethius, Ptolemy, and Aristotle) to show the ubiquity of mathematics in all branches of philosophy. All sciences, he argues, employ mathematical examples. Mathematics is the most innate of all the sciences, and the most easily learned. Mathematics was the first of the sciences to be discovered. Mathematics alone yields certainty, and only as other sciences make use of it can they find secure foundations: "A series that is full of doubts and sprinkled with opinions and obscurities cannot be certified or made manifest or verified except through another science, known, verified, clear, and certain to us, as in a conclusion reached through premises. But only mathematics . . . remains certain and verified to the limits of certitude and verification. Therefore, all other sciences must be known and certified through mathematics."

Bacon proceeds to examples that demonstrate the necessity of mathematics for astronomy, astrology, meteorology, and optics, and the utility of these sciences for the church. Astronomy teaches us how to correct the calendar. Optics furnishes mirrors and other optical devices, through which we can inspire terror in unbelievers and defend Christendom against invasion. Astrology enables us to predict the future, as well as understand the complexion of the human body and the course of disease. And all of these disciplines assist in biblical exegesis:

> We see that the literal sense rests on an understanding of the natures and properties of creatures, so that through suitable adaptations and similitudes the spiritual senses might be elicited. For thus it is explained by the saints and all of the ancient sages. . . . Wherefore, the theologian requires an excellent knowledge of creatures. But it has been shown that without mathematics nothing can be known; therefore, mathematics is altogether necessary for sacred knowledge.

The third special science to be treated is *perspectiva,* or the science of vision. *Perspectiva,* Bacon points out, is the most beautiful of the sciences because vision is the noblest of the senses, best revealing the differences of things and offering "sure experiences of all that is in the heavens and on earth." He maintains at one point that *perspectiva* is especially useful for the pursuit of wisdom and that without it nothing can be accomplished in the other sciences. He admits at another that although other sciences may have greater utility, none has greater charm and beauty. In either case it is an admirable science, neglected by the Latins, and therefore deserving of special attention. We might add that it was also the science Bacon knew best, and he could not pass up the opportunity to display his knowledge.

As Bacon develops the science of *perspectiva* in Part 5 of the ***Opus maius,*** he mainly sticks to technical detail with little attention to practical application. However, vision leads inevitably to an analysis of sense perception, with its psychological and epistemological implications. Vision also leads to the laws of radiation, including the radiation of force, thus presenting us with principles of causation (including astrological causation). Further practical applications are noted in the ***Opus tertium,*** where Bacon argues that nothing is more frequent in Scripture than references to light, color, vision, and mirrors; the biblical exegete therefore requires *perspectiva.* For example, the apostle Paul's remark about "now" seeing "through a glass darkly, but then face to face" (I Cor. 13:12), reveals the apostle's own ignorance of the principles of reflection. Moreover, optical instruments can reveal things distant and hidden; small things can be made to appear large, and large things small; and a man, through multiple reflections, can be made to appear as a multitude. Such wonders as these are useful in converting the infidel, who is more apt to be persuaded by visible demonstrations than by preaching; and the same wonders can be employed to terrorize those who refuse conversion.

Bacon turns finally to what he calls "experimental science," an ill-defined category that embraces both a methodology applicable to all sciences and a body (or several bodies) of practical knowledge and lore, presumably gained by experimental or experiential means. As a methodology it certifies the conclusions of rational argument, providing the assurance that can only come from a direct confrontation with reality. For example, no rational argument can ever certify the injurious nature of fire as putting your hand in a fire can. Experimental methodology also dispels myth and refutes faulty authority: "Although argument does not suffice for the certification of truth, authority suffices far less. . . . Therefore, this science [experimental science] wishes to teach that nothing is to be examined by argument or by authority unless there is some [confirming] experience."

In order to guard against misunderstanding, I must note that "experimental science," as a methodology, denotes an extremely broad range of activities. Although it certainly includes the use of instruments to poke nature and probe her secrets, its more general sense is simply that of "experience." And even experience is defined in the broadest possible way, to include reports of other people's experiences and the internal experience of divine illumination.

Experimental science also discovers truths within the boundaries of other sciences not attainable by those sciences alone—that is, truths that cannot be reached demonstratively, by deduction from the first principles of the discipline. For example, although the principles of the spherical astrolabe are supplied by the mathematician, the actual production of one requires the special skills of the experimental scientist. Again, there are secrets for the prolongation of life, unknown to the art of medicine, which experimenters have discovered; they "have lain in wait for beasts, in order to discover the powers of herbs, stones, metals, and other things by which they restored their bodies in many, shall we say, miraculous ways."

Finally, experimental science discovers natural powers wholly outside the other sciences. Bacon has in mind the marvelous powers of plants and stones, the wonders of fireworks, the phenomena of magnets, and other mysterious virtues. Experimental science also offers astrological predictions without astronomical intricacies; it produces useful inventions, which will save the church from the infidel and the Antichrist; it investigates magical practices and distinguishes philosophical truth from superstitious belief; and, like every other science Bacon has examined, it contributes to biblical exegesis and conversion of the unbeliever.

Conclusions

Viewed from the perspective of traditional Christian discussions of the uses of secular learning, going back to Augustine and before, Bacon's much-trumpeted modernity disappears without a trace. He was not the champion of autonomous, secularized natural science against a repressive church. Quite the contrary: the growing autonomy and secularization of science were among the things he feared. But he also feared suppression of the new learning. He was endeavoring, therefore, to steer a middle course between two equally dangerous extremes. In this he reflects, in microcosm, the dilemma of the thirteenth century.

Against those who feared the new learning and would condemn it if they could, Bacon presents traditional arguments about the usefulness of the arts and sciences for determining the literal sense of Scripture. He argues that philosophy in its fullness was given to the patriarchs and prophets and that we must aspire to recover their perfect wisdom. He notes the presence of certain articles of the faith in pagan writings. He quotes Augustine and Jerome and Cassiodorus, who called upon Christians to reclaim

philosophy from its pagan possessors and put it to its proper use. Bacon proceeds to identify sources of error that help to explain the disrepute in which the new learning is held by the ignorant; unworthy authority, custom, popular prejudice, and pretended wisdom, not to speak of bad translations, have led to attacks on Aristotle and his commentators by those who do not understand what they are attacking. And finally, Bacon displays considerable originality in the discovery of new uses, beyond biblical exegesis, to which the church can put the new learning. Calendar reform, astrological predictions, the prolongation of human life, the discovery of nature's secret powers, and the invention of optical devices—all are of vital importance for the government of Christendom, conversion of the infidel, and defeat of the Antichrist. Nobody saw the religious possibilities of the new learning more vividly (which is not to say more accurately) than did Bacon.

But the possibilities that he saw *were* religious ones. Bacon may have endeavored to enlarge the range of useful studies beyond that contemplated by Hugh of St. Victor, and certainly beyond anything Augustine would have condoned; but he shared their determination to define utility in religious terms. In none of his writings is there so much as the hint of a preference for an autonomous philosophical enterprise. There is "one perfect wisdom," he argued in the **Opus maius,**

> and this is contained in sacred writ, in which all truth is rooted. I say, therefore, that one science is mistress of the others—namely, theology, for which the others are integral necessities and which cannot achieve its ends without them. And it lays claim to their virtues and subordinates them to its nod and command. Or better, there is only one perfect wisdom, which is totally contained in sacred Scripture and expounded by canon law and philosophy.

Wisdom (the "way of salvation") is vitally in need of philosophy and the sciences, both for its achievement and for its exposition. Bacon emphatically rejects the opinion that knowledge is valuable for its own sake: "For every investigation of man that is not directed toward salvation is totally blind and leads finally to the darkness of hell."

But how would one reply to the proposal that Bacon's claims about the religious utility of philosophy were rhetoric or subterfuge, offered only to placate the authorities and purchase enough freedom for the philosophical enterprise to proceed without interference? I would counter by suggesting that such a proposal could spring only from an iron determination to view Bacon as a modern, since it is not supported by a shred of evidence. Besides, there are persuasive arguments to the contrary. In the first place, Bacon was not known for tact or political acumen; he was capable of referring to one of the leading theologians of his own order as "the worst and most stupid author of those errors, . . . the most infamous among the stupid multitude." He was also prepared to violate the rules of his Order when he found it in his interest to do so; and he had the courage (or foolhardiness) to align himself with the radical "spiritual" wing of the Franciscan Order despite the significant dangers of such a stance. Furthermore, if Bacon's purpose were simply to create breathing room for philosophy, he need only have argued that philosophy serves the faith. But he claimed much more: he developed the Augustinian notion that no rational activity can hope to succeed unless founded on Christian faith and set to work on the data of revelation; the pathway even to nature's secrets, he insisted, leads through biblical studies.

The refusal to take Roger Bacon at face value is part and parcel of the refusal to accept the Middle Ages on its own terms; the opinion that forces heroism and martyrdom onto Bacon is the same opinion that demands incompatibility, if not confrontation, between medieval religion and medieval natural philosophy. Bacon's entire career was motivated by quite a different view of the matter. Bacon was certainly an early and enthusiastic defender of the new learning, but not as a body of knowledge distinct from, or antagonistic to, the faith. His defense, though ingenious in its details and impressive in its fervor, was the obvious one: the new learning could, despite various perils, be made to serve the faith and submit to its command. This was the Augustinian formula stretched to fit the burgeoning intellectual life of the thirteenth century.

To put it somewhat crudely, then, Bacon's campaign did not look forward to modern science, but backward to the patristic tradition. It does not follow, however, that Bacon was a reactionary. Although traditional in his conviction that knowledge is to be pursued only insofar as it serves religious functions, Bacon evinces an unusual command of the sciences and an unprecedented determination to bring them into the religious fold. Whereas Augustine had been fundamentally pessimistic about the utility of secular disciplines, Bacon was inclined to suppose that everything could be of religious use. If Augustine was prepared to accept a little secular learning, Bacon wanted it all. Bacon therefore stretched the Augustinian formula to cover a vast array of sciences having, on the surface, no obvious theological or religious utility—an array that would certainly have dismayed Augustine. And it was Bacon's success in thus wielding the Augustinian formula that helped to overcome resistance to the new learning, to establish it in the universities and the religious orders of the thirteenth century, and ultimately to introduce it into the intellectual life of Europe. Bacon's traditionalist strategy thus proved a vehicle for fundamental change.

Nonetheless, we must be careful not to exaggerate Bacon's importance. The campaign that we have been examining was certainly not his alone; the integration of newly acquired Greek and Arabic learning into Christian thought was the central intellectual problem of the century, and it attracted Europe's finest minds. Moreover, new strategies soon appeared alongside Bacon's. The purpose of this paper, in any case, has not been to identify heroes and recount heroic deeds, but to take a man who has become the symbol of a medieval attitude that never existed and to see him for what he was. In the process, we stand to deepen our understanding of his age.

Jeremiah Hackett   (essay date 1988)

SOURCE: "Averroes and Roger Bacon on the Harmony of Religion and Philosophy," in *A Straight Path: Studies*

in *Medieval Philosophy and Culture—Essays in Honor of Arthur Hyman,* edited by Ruth Link-Salinger and others, The Catholic University of America Press, 1988, pp. 98-112.

[*In the essay below, Hackett seeks to demonstrate that Bacon managed to reproduce the essential teaching of Averroes's treatise* Kitab fasl al-maqal (The Decisive Treatise Determining the Nature of the Connection between Religion and Philosophy); *he posits that the two men shared essentially the same belief regarding the harmony of religion and philosophy.*]

The relationship between religion and philosophy has had a long and controversial history. One of the landmarks on that journey is Averroes's *Kitab fasl al-maqal (The Decisive Treatise Determining the Nature of the Connection between Religion and Philosophy).* The aim of this paper is to propose and argue the thesis that Roger Bacon in the thirteenth century, in his *Opus maius,* managed to reproduce the essential teaching of Averroes's treatise. There is no explicit reference in Bacon to *The Decisive Treatise.* Yet, it can be shown that Bacon presents an interpretation of "the harmony of religion and philosophy" similar to that of Averroes. Further, it is clear that Bacon did use other works of Averroes to formulate this position, especially Averroes's *Exposition on the Poetics* of Aristotle.

The Bacon had held views associated with Averroes did not escape the notice of the learned Renaissance philosopher Agostino Nifo. Nifo understood Bacon's intention in the *Opus maius* quite well. He saw him as a critical defender of the natural philosophy and metaphysics of Aristotle as interpreted by Avicenna and Averroes. Yet, in modern times Roul Carton, among others, does not correlate significant references to Averroes on Bacon's part. This has led, I believe, to seeing Bacon as one of the representatives of "L'Augustinisme Avicennisant" with emphasis on "Avicennisant." We should take Bacon on his own terms and in the light of his own stated intentions. It will be evident to the reader that the *Opus maius* is the classic text for a major polemic in the Latin West in the mid-thirteenth century on the "harmony of religion and philosophy." Indeed, this issue pervades all seven parts of the *Opus maius.* One can say that Bacon in this work confronts a polemical situation in the Christian West analogous to that faced by Averroes in the Islamic West.

Averroes on the Harmony of Religion and Philosophy

It may be useful to give a brief review of the main tenets of Averroes's position in *The Decisive Treatise.* George Hourani remarks that "in the *Fasl al-maqal,* Ibn Rushd was primarily giving a legal retort to a condemnation of philosophy which had been spelled out by Ghazali and was now being pressed in the West by the Ash'arite schoolmen." This work was thus primarily a persuasive response to a situation in Islam concerning the relationship of philosophy to the *sharīcah*—the law. This can be seen clearly from the introduction to the treatise: "The purpose of this treatise is to examine, from the standpoint of the Law, whether the study of philosophy and logic is allowed by the Law, or prohibited, or commanded—either by way of recommendation or as an obligation." In Hourani's words, "The final juridical arbitrer is said to be the *Shar.*" This term is translated by Hourani to mean scripture when it refers to a text, and law when it refers to a course of commands and prohibitions. "*Shar* is lawgiving Scripture or Scriptural Law. The Scripture referred to is primarily the Qur'ān and secondarily the traditions; the ultimate lawgiver is God, through the mouth and deeds of his prophet, Muhammed (who is referred to as "the law-giver," the *Ash-hari*)." Doctrinal problems are solved by Islamic consensus, the doctrine of *ijmac*.

Difficulties arose, however, concerning *ijmac. In practice, it meant the consensus of the learned (the 'ulama).* On matters of conduct, the teacher (the *imām*) set the standard. Under the Ash'arites, however, an attempt was made to enforce a strict standard of doctrine. It would seem that Averroes was fighting against the imposition of such a conformity in doctrine. He set out to defend the rights of a small minority of philosophers. The crucial issue concerned the right of qualified philosophers to interpret scripture according to their particular methods. The philosophers were mainly accused of explaining away the literal sense of scripture by means of a false use of allegorical interpretation. Averroes objected and claimed that in matters of doctrine there is no fixed set standard: it is impossible to know the views of all Islamic scholars. There is room, therefore, for some uncertainty.

The main contention of Averroes in *The Decisive Treatise* is that if teleological study of the world is philosophy, and if the law commands such a study, then it commands philosophy. It is Hourani's view that Averroes does not try to prove the permissibility of all philosophy. He seeks only to prove that the Qur'ān encourages a scientific, teleological study of the world, which is part of philosophy. This is, of course, an important claim: it is a claim for scientific knowledge or demonstration as set out by Aristotle. I would argue, however, that Averroes's goal includes this but is more comprehensive. *The Decisive Treatise* deals mainly with the different levels of assent or what one may call the degrees of knowledge. Throughout the treatise, Averroes is attempting to show the relationships among demonstration, dialectical reasoning, and rhetorical reasoning in reference to the assent to religion.

I cannot give a detailed account of *The Decisive Treatise* here. I can merely summarize the main theses.

1. According to Averroes, the law commands the use of demonstrative argument for that class of the learned who have the capacity for it. It is not more heretical than legal reasoning. And because it did not originate in Islam, Muslim scholars must learn it from others. By means of demonstrative argument, one can attain a "natural knowledge" of the author of nature.

2. The art of the demonstrative syllogism and the truth of scripture do not ultimately conflict. If there is an apparent conflict, the allegorical meaning of scripture must be interpreted by means of demonstration. Further, the man of science, just like the ordinary person, must accept the literal meaning of scripture when that meaning is obvious. The meaning of allegorical interpretation is the extension of the significance of an expression from real to metaphori-

cal significance, keeping to the rules of the Arabic language. Moreover, unanimity in doctrinal matters is not attainable. Experts can be excused in making an error; the nonexpert cannot.

3. The philosophical interpretation of scripture should not be taught to the masses. The main aim of scripture is to instruct the masses; the best means toward that end is the rhetorical argument. There are, therefore, three means for teaching true science and right practice leading to happiness in the future life. And there are three classes of persons corresponding to these three ways: (a) philosophers, the practitioners of demonstration; (b) dialecticians, either lawyers or theologians; and (c) the masses, including those who are educated. The correct means of instruction for the masses is given in the Qu'rān.

Bacon's Opus maius

According to Lynn Thorndike, the distinguished historian of experimental science in the Middle Ages, "The mere plan of the *Opus maius* . . . indicates that it is not exclusively devoted to natural science. 'Divine wisdom,' or theology, is the end that all human thought should serve, and morality [i. e., moral philosophy] is the supreme science."

This remark mirrors a very accurate judgment of the scope of the *Opus maius*. It is primarily concerned with the place of learning—science and philosophy—in the study of theology and in the Christian life. One might say that it is a very detailed analysis of the harmony of religion and philosophy. One might also add a necessary qualification. The word "philosophy" for Bacon includes not only metaphysics, logic, and ethics, but also the liberal arts.

What is the nature, method, and procedure of the *Opus maius?* Is it a work of strict systematic theology, a *Summa theologiae* after the manner of an Aquinas? No. Bacon himself tells us plainly that it is an *opus preambulatum,* an introductory work. Given, therefore, that it is not a strictly systematic work in either philosophy or theology, what kind of work is it?

The *Opus maius* of Roger Bacon is essentially a legal-persuasive defense of a position. It is a *persuasio,* a work of moral philosophical persuasion in content and form. And it was intended as such by Bacon on the basis of what he understood to be a theory of persuasion that he had learned from Averroes, especially, among other Islamic writers. The importance of secretive writing on Bacon's part cannot be overlooked. He makes it abundantly clear to the reader in many of his later works that he is cloaking his references and meaning from the masses (the *vulgus*).

The first part of the *Opus maius* is a sustained polemic against "the sophistical authorities of the irrational multitude, men who are authorities in an equivocal sense." This means the common run of students and teachers at Paris. They are set in opposition to the Wise (*Sapientes*), including older scholars such as Robert Grosseteste and others associated with Lincoln and Oxford. Yet, despite his sometimes disparaging remarks about Albertus Magnus, Bacon does include him among the *Sapientes*. In my view, there is much evidence to show that the *vulgus philosophantium et theologorum* attacked by Bacon included the new school of Latin Aristotelianism that arose in Paris around 1260, and developed under the leadership of Boethius of Dacia and Siger of Brabant. It also included the younger generation of theologians such as Aquinas, Bonaventure, and Richard of Cornwall.

These are "the false authorities," "the modern teachers of the people":

> Although many important portions of philosophy have been translated, [they] make no use of them, and delight in small and trivial works while neglecting the two better works on Logic, one of which has been translated with a commentary of Al-Farabi [i. e., the *Rhetoric* of Aristotle and the *Didascalia* of Al-Farabi], and an exposition of the second made by Averroes has been translated without the text of Aristotle [i. e., Averroes's exposition of the Poetics]. Far more do they neglect all the rest possessing still greater value such as the nine sciences of mathematics, and the six great natural sciences, comprehending in them many others, and the four very excellent divisions of moral philosophy. And they seek wretched solace for their ignorance in Gratian and the other recognised masters who had no knowledge of the parts of philosophy, even as these men have not. They take refuge also in the bald statements of certain sacred writers since they do not understand the reasons stated above. For the sacred writers after Christ did not take advantage of the great value of philosophy . . . [and] the host of modern students neglect important sciences, although they were introduced after the time of Gratian.

In Bacon's view, in explicit dependence on Averroes, the masses will always follow principles contrary to philosophy. And this includes the common teachers and students of philosophy, law, and theology. He puts the matter as follows: "For the wise have always been divided from the multitude, and they have veiled the secrets of wisdom not only from the world at large but also from the rank and file of those devoting themselves to philosophy." Bacon's polemic consists of an attempt to replace "the sophistical authorities" with real authorities—namely, "the commands and precepts of God, and his Scriptures, of Canon Law, the Saints, the Philosophers and the Ancient Sages."

At this point, Bacon introduces a historical note. He points out that the human mind is not self-sufficient and that philosophy builds on the correction of one's predecessors:

> And Avicenna, the leader and prince in philosophy after him, as the Commentator [Averroes] calls him in the chapter on the rainbow in his commentary on the *Metheora* of Aristotle, and as the works arranged by him [the Commentator] from Aristotle into a complete system of philosophy make clear, declared that he was ignorant of the nature of the rainbow, even as the aforementioned Commentator confesses. . . . Just as Averroes, the greatest after these, refuted Avicenna in many particulars, so too our men of science correct him in more instances and rightly so, since without doubt he erred in many places, although he spoke well in others. . . .

But not only the philosophers, but even the sacred writers have been subject to human infirmity in this respect. For they retracted many of their own statements.

I labor this point in order to stress the fact that for Bacon it is Averroes, not Avicenna, who is really the new *dux philosophorum*. Yet, in Bacon's view, the torch of philosophy has now passed to the "Christian philosophers" of his own day. Moreover, Bacon himself is very explicit about his views on the general Christian reaction to both Avicenna and Averroes:

> For Averroes, a still greater man after these [i. e., Aristotle and Avicenna], as well as others condemned Avicenna beyond measure. But in these times whatever Averroes has said has received the approval of the wise. Yet, he too for a long time was neglected and rejected, and called in question by philosophers famous in their work until gradually his wisdom became clear and generally approved, although on some matters he spoke less convincingly. For we know that *in our own times* [i. e., 1237-67] objection has long been raised in Paris to the Natural Philosophy and Metaphysics of Aristotle as interpreted by Avicenna and Averroes, and on account of dense ignorance their books and those using them were excommunicated for quite long periods. Since the facts are as stated, and we moderns know that every addition and increase in wisdom they have made is worthy of all favor, though in some matters they are superfluous, and in certain others need correction, and in some explanation. It is clear to us that those who during their individual lives have hindered the evidence of truth and usefulness offered to them by the men mentioned above have erred too far, and have been very harmful in this respect. But they have done this to extoll their own wisdom and to palliate their own ignorance.

It will be evident from this initial polemic that "the cause of Averroes" is very close to Bacon's concern in his **Opus maius** and indeed throughout his later works.

The second part of the **Opus maius** presents Bacon's views on the relationship of philosophy to theology and is deserving of a study in itself. Bacon begins by stating:

> Therefore, having reviewed the four causes of all human error in general outline and having completely set aside this persuasion, I wish in this second distinction to point out that there is *one perfect Wisdom,* and that this is contained in the Sacred Scriptures, from whose roots all truth comes forth. I say, therefore, that one science is the mistress of the others, namely, theology, to which the remaining sciences are completely *necessary* and without which it is not capable of reaching its fulfillment. Theology claims the strength of these sciences for her own law, to whose nod and rule the other sciences subordinate themselves. Or better, there is one perfect wisdom, which is totally contained in the Scriptures, and which ought to be unfolded through Canon Law and philosophy.

In this manner, Bacon places philosophy alongside canon

law as the means by which the truth of scripture is to be interpreted. Wisdom is presented as a way to salvation, and philosophy as a doctrine of wisdom is subordinated to the wisdom of sacred scripture, and by implication to theology. Moreover, all law, including the natural law, canon law, and the common law is said to derive from the law of sacred scripture.

It would appear, then, that Bacon has completely abolished philosophy as an independent discipline by taking it up into theology so completely. This, however, as we shall see, would be an extreme interpretation. It does not take into account the positive things that Bacon says about the role of philosophy in the interpretation of scripture. Indeed, he makes scientific, demonstrative philosophy as indispensable a tool for the interpretation of scripture as does Averroes.

Bacon begins his correlation of philosophy and theology by using the position of St. Augustine in the *De doctrina Christiana.* Much of what he says is based on the church fathers and on scholars of the early Middle Ages. The position is that Christians have a duty to take over pagan wisdom and use it for knowledge of God:

> We must show, moreover, both in general and in particular that the power of philosophy is not foreign to the wisdom of God, but is included in it. After this has been made clear by authorities, examples, and arguments of a general nature, a fuller exposition will then be made covering the four or five divisions of philosophy in regard to the power of the separate sciences and arts.

This is precisely what Bacon achieves in the *Opus maius.* Having argued with St. Augustine that the liberal arts are an essential introduction to the study of theology, Bacon adds:

> And if this is the case with these [the liberal arts], much more so are metaphysical subjects in agreement with divine speech. For metaphysics has the place of one part of theology among the philosophers, which with moral philosophy and the theology of physics is called the divine science by them as is apparent from the first book of Aristotle's *Metaphysics* and the ninth, tenth, and eleventh book of Avicenna's *Metaphysics.*

In this manner, all philosophy but especially metaphysics, ethics, and physics are in agreement with theology. For Bacon, furthermore, all truth belongs to Christ, and although the philosophers may be said to possess truth, yet, in fact, they possess it on account of a divine illumination. Bacon's identification of the agent intellect with God explicitly refers to Al-Farabi as a source. Yet Bacon seems to be emphasizing the notion of the agent intellect as a separate substance, a doctrine prominent in Avicenna and Averroes.

Above all, Bacon thinks that the whole aim of philosophy is that "the Creator may be known through the knowledge of the creature." Again, he thinks that "the end of speculative philosophy is the knowledge of the creator through creatures, and moral philosophy establishes the dignity of morals, just laws, and persuades us of our future happiness in a profitable and glorious manner as far as lies in the power of moral philosophy."

Bacon in chapter 8 takes up the problem of scriptural interpretation once again:

> Moreover, all sacred writers and wise men of old in their expositions take a literal sense from the natures of things and from their properties in order that they may bring out spiritual meanings through convenient adaptations and similitudes. This Augustine declares in the second book of *De doctrina Christiana.*

Bacon proceeds to argue that the whole purpose of philosophy is "to evolve the natures and properties of things." Moreover, philosophy in and of itself is no match for the wisdom of scripture. The example that Bacon gives is that of the rainbow, a topic central to his notion of a *scientia experimentalis* in part six of *Opus maius.* According to Bacon, scripture alone tells us about the final cause of the rainbow; the philosophers for their part fail in this. But to understand the nature of the production of the rainbow, one has need of philosophical and scientific method. And a person will not be able to understand the allegorical meaning of the rainbow until the scientific method of the philosopher provides a coherent understanding of the literal meaning of a phenomenon such as a rainbow.

Bacon presses on with his subordination of philosophy to theology by showing that God revealed philosophy to the ancient patriarchs and prophets at the beginning of time. Thus, philosophy was revealed to these holy men *ab origine.* Bacon continues with a long account of the history of wisdom and salvation.

In all of this Bacon seeks to guard the essential unity of wisdom:

> Hence, it follows of necessity that we Christians ought to employ philosophy in divine things, and in matters pertaining to philosophy to assume many things belonging to theology, so that it is apparent that there is one wisdom shining in both.

Bacon argues that Christians *de necessitate* must use philosophy for the interpretation of scripture. Philosophy, therefore, provides the Christian with the methods of proof in religion. And in recognizing its own inadequacy, it allows itself to be sublated into theology. One should note, however, that for Bacon, the Christian philosopher as such is not a theologian. Rather, the Christian philosopher is a competent scholar who draws from the well of all past philosophers:

> The sacred writers not only speak as theologians, but as philosophers, and frequently introduce philosophical subjects. Therefore, Christians desiring to complete philosophy ought in their works not only to collect the statements of the philosophers in regard to divine truths, but should advance far beyond to a point where the power of philosophy as a whole may be complete. And for this reason, he who completes philosophy by the truths of this kind must not on this account be called a theologian, nor must he transcend the bounds of philosophy. For he

can handle freely what is common to philosophy and theology and what must be accepted in common by believers and unbelievers. There are many such matters besides the statements of the unbelieving philosophers, which belong as it were within the limits of philosophy.

Toward the end of the second part of his *Opus maius,* Bacon points to philosophy as the indispensable means of dialogue between persons of different belief-systems. Then, following Avicenna, he argues that the speculative philosopher seeks out moral philosophy as its goal or end. The term "moral philosophy" must be taken here in a very broad sense: it includes philosophy of religion, law, and what today is called ethical theory. In this sense, both *The Decisive Treatise of Averroes* and Bacon's *Opus maius* are works in moral philosophy.

In part 3 of the *Opus maius,* Bacon discusses the role of language in the study of theology. First, language is important because the Latins have received their wisdom from other languages, especially from Hebrew, Greek, and Arabic. Secondly, theology has need for the theory of meaning and for a theory of signification. This is especially the case in language that refers to God. By its very nature it will require analogical predication.

In the fourth, fifth, and sixth parts of the *Opus maius,* Bacon discusses the uses of mathematics in physics and theology. In the introduction to the fourth part, Bacon gives a *reductio* of logic to mathematics. In mathematics, alone, according to Bacon, is found the way to the fullness of truth without error. This is because "in it it is possible to have demonstration through a proper and necessary cause. And demonstration makes the truth to be known. As Averroes points out, that which is true in itself or *simpliciter* and that which is true for us are the same." Mathematical knowledge by means of a demonstrative argument is the sine qua non for a discussion of physics. Indeed, a variety of physical phenomena mentioned in scripture, such as the rainbow, cannot be understood without demonstrative argumentation. It is very clear in part 4, especially in regard to astronomy, that Bacon is directing a polemic against some theologians and lawyers. In part 5 Bacon makes a study of perspective and light. And in part 6, among other matters, he gives the causal study of the rainbow as an example of the first prerogative of *scientia experimentalis.* The whole point is to show that a mathematico-causal analysis of physical phenomena is required before the literal sense of some texts of scripture can be understood. It is on the basis of such understanding that a true allegorical reading can be understood.

Averroes: A Source for the Moralis philosophia of Bacon

Modern scholars of Bacon's *Moralis philosophia* have not done justice to Bacon's dependence on Averroes. It is clear that Bacon made wide use of Averroes in this field. For both authors, the perfection of the active mind in virtue and the happiness of the other life constituted full perfection. It has not been sufficiently emphasized by scholars that Averroes is cited by Bacon as a major source for moral philosophy in the wide sense which that term has for him. He certainly means more than ethics. In fact, the kernel of moral philosophy, apart from the teaching on

happiness, the state, and virtue, is the teaching on the kinds of assent needed for religion:

> And so if I will cite authorities from places other than those which are contained in books of morals, it ought to be considered that these ought to be placed appropriately in this science. Nor can we deny that those things are written in the books of this science, since in Latin we only have the philosophy of Aristotle, Avicenna, and Averroes in parts, and they are the principal authorities in matters of this kind.

The most important material from Averroes that Bacon cites is the exposition on the *Poetics* of Aristotle. Yet this should not blind us to the fact that Bacon reproduces an interpretation of happiness that in many respects resembles that of Averroes. Further, it is evident that he is engaged in a polemic that places him in direct opposition to some representatives of radical Aristotelianism in regard to this question. In brief, Bacon again subordinates the achievement of virtue in this life, in so far as that is possible for philosophy, to the goal of happiness in the next life. Moral philosophy as such is transcended and taken up into moral theology. Again, the moral philosopher presupposes the teaching of the metaphysician, especially concerning those truths about God and creatures that can be known by philosophy on its own.

In all of this, it is a clearly stated assumption on Bacon's part that the *Sapientes* have access to a wisdom hidden from the masses (the *vulgus*). As philosophers who can use demonstrative argumentation, and as those who are illumined by the active intellect or God, they have access to a superior wisdom. It is their function, therefore, to convey the truth to the masses in a covert manner:

> For other sciences descend to other questions in matters such as what is the nature of each thing, and of what kind, and how much, and such matters according to the ten predicaments. For the moral philosopher ought not to explain all the secrets of God, angels, and other beings, but only those which are necessary for the multitude of people in those things where all have to agree lest they fall into questions and heresies, as Avicenna teaches in the *Roots of Moral Philosophy.*

When Bacon comes to persuasion about true religion and morality, he argues forcefully that the demonstrative syllogism, although of value for the philosopher in the search for truth, is useless for the task of persuading the masses. The role of the moral philosopher is not just a matter of style; it is a matter of truth. According to Bacon, the theory of rhetoric belongs to logic; its practice belongs to moral philosophy. Because of this, there is only one method open for the persuasion of the masses, that of the rhetorical argumentation. The rhetorical argument is the best means available to lead ordinary persons to a knowledge of "happiness in this life and the next."

In Bacon's view, there are three kinds of rhetorical argument. The first kind has to do with persuasion about religion. This kind has to do with what is provable and with levels of assent to religious truth. The second kind has to do with forensic oratory, and is found in Cicero. The third kind is concerned with things that sway persons toward what Bacon calls the *operabilia*. He maintains that these actions, so closely tied to human moral action as such, are "more difficult to know than are the objects of speculative knowledge." He defines them: "these are the highest truths concerning God and divine worship, eternal life, the laws of justice, the glory of peace, and the sublimity of virtue." In brief, they are the things that go to make up the subject matter of *Moralis philosophia*.

Bacon calls the first two kinds of rhetoric "rhetoric absolutely speaking." The third kind, he says, "is properly called poetic argument by Aristotle and other philosophers, since true poets use it to sway men to the honesty of virtue." According to Bacon, the *vulgus philosophantium* at Paris in the mid-1260's did not know how to compose this kind of argument. He says that diligent scholars, however, who know the recent translations of the *Rhetoric* and Averroes's exposition on the *Poetics* by Hermannus Alemannus, and the works of Horace, Avicenna, and Al-Ghazali, can produce this kind of argument. These works, which are listed by Bacon many times, as if for the maximum emphasis, show the explicit sources used by Bacon. Yet, in the end, for an understanding of the limits of interpretation in regard to scripture, especially in terms of the fourfold sense of scripture, including the allegorical, Bacon returns to the foundation of Christian practice—that is, the *De doctrina Christiana* of St. Augustine. He says that "the whole of book two is concerned with the present subject matter and almost everything I have said here is found in that book in a philosophical mode."

He ends part 5 of the *Opus maius* by arguing that the scriptures have a great variety of meanings, and have need of being interpreted by rhetorical and poetical modes. This does not destroy the literal sense; rather, it takes it up and perfects it. Even granted the inner illumination of the mind, there is still need for philosophy and science to disclose the hidden meaning of scripture. Without the aid of language, science, and philosophy, the literal meaning will never be understood and the allegorical meaning will not be correctly interpreted. Thus, literalism would reign.

Above all, Bacon manages to skewer the dialecticians, whether they be philosophers, lawyers or theologians. He announces in part 6 of the *Opus maius* that the *ars prima et originalis* of persuasion is not fully known to the Latins. Moreover, the art of persuasion is not just a matter of style; it is also a matter of truth. And the *ars fontalis* of this moral persuasion is given in logic. In this way, Bacon in a very profound manner, realized that the *Poetics* and *Rhetoric* of Aristotle were not mere appendage, but rather, an essential part of logic.

In working out his synthesis of religion and philosophy, it is clear that Roger Bacon made a creative use of Greek, Islamic, and Latin sources. It is also clear that the *Opus maius* sets out to defend the philosophy of Aristotle as interpreted by Avicenna and Averroes. Above all, Bacon comes to the defense of Averroes, even though he has reservations about some teachings.

Throughout the *Opus maius,* Bacon succeeds in reproducing what is essentially Averroes's position on "the harmony of religion and philosophy" as found in *The Decisive Treatise* and other works. Thus, the *Opus maius* reproduces Averroes's position in content and form. That is, Bacon's major work, like *The Decisive Treatise* is a *persuasio,* a work in legal-moral persuasion. And in this respect, it is unique in the philosophical literature of the Latin West in the thirteenth century. The content of the *Opus maius* closely resembles that of *The Decisive Treatise*. The essential themes of the latter are reproduced, from the role of philosophy in theology to demonstrative argument, and the role of rhetoric in moral persuasion. Can one say, then, that the *Kitab fasl al-maqal* is the unnamed book that inspired the form and content of the *Opus maius?* In answer, I suggest that the evidence points in that direction, even if evidence of textual borrowing or explicit citation is not available.

FURTHER READING

Coulton, G. G. "The Universities." In his *Studies in Medieval Thought,* pp. 130-50. New York: Russell & Russell, 1965.
> Surveys the lives and accomplishments of several figures prominent in the *Universitates* of the Middle Ages, including Alexander of Hales, Thomas Aquinas, Boneventura, and Bacon. Coulton emphasizes Bacon's stature as a founder of empirical rationalism. This work was originally published in 1940.

Crowley, Theodore. *Roger Bacon: The Problem of the Soul in his Philosophical Commentaries.* Dublin: James Duffy & Co., 1950, 223 p.
> In-depth study of Bacon's philosophy of the soul, revealing Bacon as a thinker deeply attached to Aristotelian thought mixed with neo-Platonism through various channels, but free of Augustinian influences.

Hackett, Jeremiah M. G. "Moral Philosophy and Rhetoric in Roger Bacon." *Philosophy and Rhetoric* 20, No. 1 (1987): 18-40.
> Introductory examination of the relationship between moral philosophy and rhetoric in Bacon's work.

Hirsch, S. A. "Early English Hebraists: Roger Bacon and His Predecessors." *The Jewish Quarterly Review* XII (October 1899): 34-88.
> Recounts Bacon's efforts to promote the study of the Hebrew language as an important vehicle for learning.

Lindberg, David C. "Lines of Influence in Thirteenth-Century Optics: Bacon, Witelo, and Pecham." *Speculum* XLVI, No. 1 (January 1971): 66-83.
> Examines the question of Bacon's tangled influence upon Witelo and John Pecham as a theorist of optics.

———. Introduction to *Roger Bacon's Philosophy of Nature: A Critical Edition, with English Translation, Introduction, and Notes, of "De multiplicatione specierum" and "De speculis comburentibus,"* pp. xv-lxxxi. Oxford: Clarendon Press, 1983.
> Thorough scholarly introduction to Bacon's two treatises on the multiplication and action of light and the generation of species out of the potentiality of matter.

———. "Roger Bacon and the Origins of *Perspectiva* in the West." In *Mathematics and Its Applications to Science and*

Natural Philosophy in the Middle Ages: Essays in Honor of Marshall Clagett, edited by Edward Grant and John E. Murdoch, pp. 249-68. Cambridge: Cambridge University Press, 1987.

Examines Bacon's role in "the process of assimilation, and its accompanying struggles, in the formation of the discipline of optics or *perspectiva*."

Lutz, Edward. "Roger Bacon's Contribution to Knowledge." *Franciscan Studies*, No. 17 (June 1936): 1-82.

Sympathetic overview of Bacon's life and work, focusing upon Bacon's writings on the sacred sciences, philosophy, languages, mathematics, natural sciences, as well as his influence.

Maloney, Thomas S. "Roger Bacon on the *Significatum* of Words." In *Archéologie du signe*, edited by Lucie Brind'Amour and Eugene Vance, pp. 187-211. Papers in Mediaeval Studies, Vol. 3. Toronto: Pontifical Institute of Mediaeval Studies, 1982.

Considers the notions of signification, supposition, appellation, and copulation in Bacon's logical treatises and their significance in the development of medieval semantics.

————. "The Extreme Realism of Roger Bacon." *The Review of Metaphysics* XXXVIII, No. 4 (June 1985): 807-37.

Examines *Questiones supra libros prime philosophie Aristotelis, Questiones alatere supra libros prime philosophie Aristotelis* and *Liber primus communium naturalium Fratris Rogeri* to determine whether Bacon was a nominalist, a moderate realist, or an extreme realist ("or indeed whether he developed a position uniquely his own") on the problem of universals.

————. Introduction to *Three Treatments of Universals*, by Roger Bacon, translated by Thomas S. Maloney, pp. 1-30. Binghamton, N.Y.: Medieval & Renaissance Texts & Studies, 1989.

Expands upon the arguments Maloney presented in the *Review of Metaphysics* in 1985 (see above) in regard to Bacon's views on universals.

Parkhurst, Charles. "Roger Bacon on Color: Sources, Theories, and Influence." In *The Verbal and the Visual: Essays in Honor of William Sebastian Heckscher*, edited by Karl-Ludwig Selig and Elizabeth Sears, pp. 151-201. New York: Italica Press, 1990.

Discourses upon Bacon's theory of optics, specifically concerning his contributions to color theory. Beginning with a little-known text on the senses, *De sensu et sensato*, Parkhurst argues that Bacon made contributions to late medieval color doctrines which were to "open new ways of organizing colors for useful ends, and which had an immediate impact upon the art of painting that is still reverberating."

Petry, Ray C. "The Reforming Critiques of Robert Grosseteste, Roger Bacon, and Ramon Lull and their Related Impact upon Medieval Society: Historical Studies in the Critical Temper and the Practice of Tradition." In his *The Impact of the Church upon Its Culture: Reappraisals of the History of Christianity*, 95-120. Chicago: University of Chicago Press, 1968.

Views Grosseteste, Bacon, and Lull as innovators who sought to effect reformation within the Church of their era. Petry examines various elements of their theology to substantiate his thesis.

Sharp, D. E. "Roger Bacon." In her *Franciscan Philosophy at Oxford in the Thirteenth Century*, pp. 115-71. New York: Russell & Russell, 1964.

Intensive discourse upon the central concerns of Bacon's writings. Sharp discourses upon Bacon's theory of becoming, types of becoming, matter in its static aspect, form in its static aspect, and such concerns as natural theology and angelology, among others.

Thorndike, Lynn. "Roger Bacon and Experimental Method in the Middle Ages." *The Philosophical Review* XXIII, No. 3 (May 1914): 271-98.

Scornful reassessment of Bacon's originality and significance on the seventh centenary of the scholar's birth.

Additional coverage of Bacon's life and career is contained in the following source published by Gale Research: *Dictionary of Literary Biography*, Vol. 115.

The Book of Job

c. Fifth Century B.C.?

(Also rendered as *Iyyov* and *iyyôbh.*) Hebrew poetry and prose.

INTRODUCTION

The Book of Job is best known as one of the Poetic Books of the *Old Testament* of the *Bible*. While the work has been the subject of theological discussion and teaching since ancient times, it has also inspired extensive exegetical and philosophical commentary by modern secular critics. The story's depiction of the undeserved hardship experienced by a virtuous and pious man has served both as a means of advocating traditional morals and as a springboard for complex philosophical exchanges regarding the problem of human suffering. Combining elements of folklore, wisdom literature, prophetic literature, poetic drama, tragedy, lament, hymn, diatribe, proverb, and judiciary procedure, *The Book of Job* defies strict literary classification. Paul Weiss has commented: "*The Book of Job* is surely one of the very great works of literature of the world. It touches the core of existence; it probes to the root of the problems of good and evil, the destiny of man, the meaning of friendship, the wisdom and goodness of God, and the justification of suffering."

Plot and Major Characters

Critics divide *The Book of Job* into three sections: a prose prologue (1:1-2:13), a poetic dialogue (3:1-42:6), and a prose epilogue (42:7-17). The prologue provides an idyllic picture of a semi-nomadic sheik named Job who is virtuous, prosperous, and immensely happy. Soon thereafter, however, a meeting of the celestial court takes place in which God (Yahweh) praises Job. This incites a challenge from the satan (the Hebrew term for the adversary, an antecedent of Satan), who suggests that Job's piety is simply a product of his good fortune. The satan instigates a wager with Yahweh that Job will curse God if he is made to suffer. A chain of calamities befalls Job, and every component of his wealth and security is destroyed, culminating in the death of his children. After Job successfully eschews blasphemous speech and behavior, another test is proposed by the satan, and Job is inflicted with a loathsome skin disease. At the prologue's conclusion, the three friends Eliphaz, Bildad, and Zophar arrive to comfort Job, sitting with him in silence for seven days. Following the prologue is a diverse poetic section incorporating elements of lament, debate, soliloquy, and hymn. Job lashes out against the injustice of his suffering and is answered by each of the three friends, who castigate him for challenging God and suggest that his misfortune must be a punishment for some hidden sin. Job steadfastly rejects their arguments, insisting that he is innocent and pleading for a fair hearing from God. The dialogues are followed by a poem on wisdom and the speeches of Elihu, a younger friend who also intervenes in defense of God. In the final poetic section, called the theophany, God answers Job with a series of questions and declarations of omnipotence spoken from a whirlwind, after which Job repents. In the epilogue, Yahweh rebukes Job's friends and restores Job's property and wealth.

Textual History

Considerable discussion and debate surrounds the origin of *The Book of Job* and the means through which it achieved its final form. Although the *Talmud* names the prophet Moses as the author of *The Book of Job,* most scholars consider it to be an anonymous work. *The Book of Job* is classified as a work of Hebrew literature, but some scholars have pointed to evidence of Arabic influences within the Hebrew text. Archaeological discoveries made during the twentieth century have also led researchers to speculate that the story of Job may have evolved from other cultural traditions, including the wisdom literature of the Edomites, Egyptian Pessimism, and Babylonian Skepticism. According to modern scholars, the chief exegetical question surrounding *The Book of Job* concerns its literary integrity. Commentators maintain that the prose prologue and epilogue contrast significantly with the poetic dialogue at the book's center, suggesting that the book was written by more than one author. One widely espoused, although inconclusive, theory suggests that the book's prologue and epilogue evolved from an ancient oral folktale, perhaps dating back to the semi-nomads of the second millennium B.C. A later poet or scribe who, some critics believe, lived during the postexilic period of the fifth century B.C. may have been the first to write the Hebrew text in its complete form, adding the poetic dialogue in the center of the traditional story as a means of addressing the problem of evil more closely. Although numerous English translations of *The Book of Job* have been produced, virtually all are ultimately derived from one of three sources: the Greek Septuagint text, which is a translation of the Hebrew *Bible* made in the second or third century B.C. for the benefit of Greek-speaking Jews in Egypt; the Hebrew Masoretic text, which was compiled by rabbis in or around the second century B.C. from manuscripts surviving the fall of Jerusalem; and the Latin Vulgate *Old Testament*, St. Jerome's fourth-century Latin translation of the Hebrew text.

Major Themes

The Book of Job has incited diverse interpretations ranging from explorations of its basic morality to extensive philosophical discussions concerning human suffering and divine justice. Traditional religious teaching has emphasized the patience of Job in the face of suffering, reaffirming the conventional concept that, through divine justice, faith will ultimately be rewarded. The view of suffering as a potentially purifying, and even desirable, experience has also been a subject of discussion surrounding the work, particularly in the writing of such medieval theologians as Pope Gregory I and Thomas Aquinas. Critics approaching the work from a secular perspective, however, have commented that the popular image of Job as an example of faith and patience actually ignores the fact that he is depicted as a rebellious and even blasphemous figure in the central poetic section of work. In modern times particularly, scholars have suggested that the apparent injustice and randomness of God's treatment of Job raise the possibility that Job is in fact faithful without a good reason to be so. Much debate also surrounds the enigmatic relationship between God and Job. When God finally speaks to Job from the whirlwind, he gives no explanation for Job's affliction, but instead offers a poetic description of his own omnipotence, describing the natural wonders of the creation and questioning Job's right to challenge him. Some critics have asserted that God's response fails to address the serious questions raised by Job concerning justice, leaving the reader with an amoral conception of the universe. Others have interpreted God's evasion of Job's questions as a denouncement of an anthropocentric view of the world, asserting that the essential theme of *The Book of Job* is the human inability to comprehend a deity who functions outside the realm of worldly justice.

Critical Reception

While *The Book of Job* has been continuously reinterpreted over the centuries, it has traditionally been presented in religious teachings as a morality tale in which Job is upheld as a model of patience, endurance, and humility. During the sixth century, for example, Pope Gregory I emphasized Job's piety in his *Moralia in Iob* (*Morals on the Book of Job*), considered an important early example of ecclesiastical writing on the subject of Job. Moses Maimonides, one of the foremost intellectual figures of medieval Judaism, included a section on *The Book of Job* in his twelfth-century work *Dalālat al-hā'rīn* (*Guide of the Perplexed*), portraying Job as an upright and pious man who was flawed by a lack of wisdom, which impeded his capacity to accept the actions of God. Throughout the Middle Ages, the Biblical story of Job was superseded in popularity by a more familiar pseudepigraphal book entitled *Testament of Job*, considered by such critics as Lawrence Besserman to be the principal example of the "apocryphal tradition" of writings about Job. In the *Testament of Job*, Job is presented as both a saint and a heroic king of Egypt. During the Reformation, John Calvin presented a series of 159 sermons on *The Book of Job* in which he emphasized Job's integrity and resistance to the temptation to reject God. Job's exemplary response to misfortune was also praised during the nineteenth century by the theologian and philosopher Søren Kierkegaard. While theologians have traditionally interpreted *The Book of Job* as a vindication of conventional morality concerning divine justice, secular scholars of the twentieth century have given greater attention to Job's defiance in the middle section of the

book, occasionally arguing that the work in fact denounces the notion that human suffering is justifiable. Writers outside the realm of theology, for example Carl Jung, have invoked the book as a forum for examining broad philosophical and psychological questions concerning suffering, evil, and faith outside the context of any specific religion. Widely considered one of the most celebrated books of the *Bible*, *The Book of Job* has also been an inspiration for such diverse works of art and literature as Johann Wolfgang von Goethe's *Faust*, William Blake's *Inventions to the Book of Job*, Fyodor Dostoyevsky's *The Brothers Karamazov*, and Archibald MacLeish's *J.B.*

PRINCIPAL ENGLISH TRANSLATIONS

The Book of Job, in the *Wycliffe Bible* (translator unknown) c. 1390

The Book of Job, in the *Great Bible* of 1539 (translated by Miles Coverdale) 1539

The Book of Job, in the "Authorized," or "King James" *Bible* (translated by a committee under the auspices of King James I) 1611

A Critical and Exegetical Commentary on The Book of Job: Together with a New Translation (translated by Samuel Rolles Driver and George Buchanan Gray) 1921

The Book of Job, in the Revised Standard Version of the *Holy Bible* (translated by the International Council of Religious Education) 1952

The Anchor Bible: Job (translation by Marvin H. Pope) 1965

The Book of Job, in *The New English Bible: The Old Testament* (translated under the supervision of the Joint Committee on the New Translation of the *Bible*) 1970

The Book of Job: Commentary, New Translation, and Special Studies (translated by Robert Gordis) 1978

The Book of Job (translated by Stephen Mitchell) 1987

CRITICISM

John Calvin   (sermon date 1554-55?)

SOURCE: "Sermon 1: The Character of Job," in *Sermons from Job*, translated by Leroy Nixon, 1952. Reprint by W. B. Eerdmans Publishing Company, 1979, pp. 3-17.

[*Calvin was an influential French theologian and Protestant reformer. Among his most famous writings is the* Christianae Religionis Institutio, *(1536;* Institutes of the Christian Religion). *Although primarily known as a theologian, Calvin was also a devoted preacher whose sermons were most often delivered extemporaneously, a fact which has prevented the preservation of his early sermons. In 1549, however, a group of his devotees hired Denis Reguenier as a secretary to record his addresses. Calvin's usual method of preaching was to speak on entire books of the*

Bible *consecutively. The 159 sermons on* The Book of Job, *for example, were delivered between 1554 and 1555. In the following sermon, he considers the nature of Job's "integrity" and examines the book's theme of "spiritual temptation" to reject God during a time of suffering.*]

There was in the region of Uz a man by the name of Job, perfect and upright, who feared God, and kept himself from evil.—*Job* 1:1

To really profit by the contents of this book, we must first know the scope of it. The story which is here written shows us how we are in the hand of God, and that it belongs to Him to order our lives and to dispose of them according to His good pleasure, and that our duty is to submit ourselves to Him in all humility and obedience, that it is quite reasonable that we be altogether His both to live and to die; and even if it shall please Him to raise His hand against us, though we may not perceive for what cause He does it, nevertheless we should glorify Him always, confessing that He is just and equitable, that we should not murmur against Him, that we should not enter into dispute, knowing that if we struggle against Him we shall be conquered. This, then, in brief, is what we have to remember from the story, that is, that God has such dominion over His creatures that He can dispose of them at His pleasure, and when He shows a strictness that we at first find strange, yet that we should keep our mouths closed in order not to murmur; but rather, that we should confess that He is just, expecting that He may declare to us why He chastises us. Meanwhile we have to contemplate the patience of the man who is here set before our eyes, according as Saint James (5:11) exhorts us. For when God shows us that we have to suffer all the miseries that He will send us, we surely confess that it is our duty; however, we allege our frailty and it seems to us that this ought to serve us as an excuse. For this cause it is good that we have examples who show us that there are men frail like us, who nevertheless have resisted temptations, and have persevered constantly in obeying God, although He afflicted them to the limit. Now we have here an excellent example of it.

Besides, it is not all that we should consider the patience of Job, but we have to look at the result, as Saint James also mentions; for if Job had remained confounded, although there was a virtue more than angelic in him, it would not have been a happy ending. But when we see that he was not disappointed in his hope, and inasmuch as he was humbled before God he found grace, seeing such an ending, we have to conclude that there is nothing better than to subject ourselves to God, and to suffer peaceably all that He sends us until by His pure goodness He delivers us. However, beyond the story we have to regard the doctrine which is comprehended in this book: namely, from those who come under the pretense of comforting Job, and who torment him much more than did his own illness, and from the answers he gives to repulse their calumnies, by which it seems they wish to crush him. First, we have to note with respect to our afflictions, although God sends them and they proceed from Him, yet the devil brings them on us, as also Saint Paul warns us that we have to fight against spiritual powers. (*Ephesians* 6:12). For when

the devil thus lights the fire he also pumps the bellows, that is to say, he finds men who are his own to continually prick us and to lengthen and augment the illness. So then, we see how Job, beyond the illness which he endured, was tormented, even by his friends, and by his wife, and above all by those who came to tempt him spiritually. Now I call it spiritual temptation when we are not only beaten and afflicted in our bodies; but when the devil so works in our imaginations that God is a deadly enemy to us, and we can no longer have recourse to Him, and we know that He never has to be merciful toward us. All the propositions put forward by the friends of Job tended to persuade him that he was a man reproved by God and that he was certainly mistaken in trusting that God should be propitious toward him. Now these spiritual struggles are much more difficult to bear than all the evils and all the adversities that we can suffer when we are persecuted. All the same God releases the bridle to Satan that he may draw with him his servants, who make such assaults upon us as we shall see that Job endured.

So much for one item. However, we have also to note that in the whole dispute Job maintains a good case, and his adversary maintains a poor one. Now there is more, that Job maintaining a good case pleads it poorly, and the others bringing a poor case plead it well. When we shall have understood this, it will be to us as it were a key to open to us the whole book. How is it that Job maintains a case which is good? It is that he knows that God does not always afflict men according to the measure of their sins; but that He has His secret judgments, of which He does not give us an account, and yet we must wait until He may reveal to us why He does this or that. He was, then, entirely persuaded that God does not always afflict men according to the measure of their sins, and by that he has testimony in himself that he was not a man rejected by God, as they wished to make him believe. This is a case which is good and true, though it is poorly pleaded; for Job here now throws himself off balance and uses excessive and exaggerated propositions, so that he shows that he is desperate in many respects. And he is even so heated that it seems that he wishes to resist God. So here is a good case that is pleaded badly. Now on the contrary those who sustain the poor case, that God always punishes men according to the measure of their sin, speak beautiful and holy sentences; there is nothing in their propositions that we ought not to receive as if the Holy Spirit had pronounced it; for it is pure truth, these are the foundations of religion, they discuss the providence of God, they discuss His justice, they discuss the sins of men. Here, then, is a doctrine which we have to receive without contradiction, and yet the result that these people try to put Job into despair and to destroy him completely is bad. Now by this we see when we have a good foundation that we must consider how to build thereon, in such a way that all may harmonize, as Saint Paul says (I *Corinthians* 3:10), that he built, since he founded the Church upon the pure doctrine of Jesus Christ; and yet that there is such a conformity that those who will come after him will use as foundation neither straw nor thatch, nor worthless material; but that there be a good foundation, firm and solid. So, in all our life we have to consider that if we are founded in good and just reason, each one must be on his guard not to bend or turn this way or that way; for there is nothing easier than to pervert a good and just case, according as our nature is vicious and we experience every bit of it. God will have exercised the grace toward us that our case will be good, and yet we shall be pricked by our enemies so that we cannot keep ourselves in bounds and we cannot simply follow what God orders for us without adding to it in any fashion whatever. Seeing, then, that we are so easily carried away, all the more ought we to pray to God that when He shall have given us a good case, He may lead us by His Holy Spirit in all simplicity, that we may not pass beyond the limits that He has established for us by His Word. However, also we are admonished not to apply the truth of God to bad use; for we profane it by this means; like these people, though they speak holy words (as we have already declared, and as we shall see more fully) yet however they are sacrilegious; for they corrupt the truth of God, and they abuse it falsely; they apply to a bad end that which is good and just in itself. So then, when God has given us knowledge of His Word, let us learn to receive it in such fear that it may not be to darken the good nor to make the bad attractive; as often those who are the most keen, and the most wise will let themselves go and will abuse the knowledge which God has given to them, in fraud, in malice, and they will upset everything, so that they only tangle themselves up in knots. Seeing that the world is addicted to such vice, all the more have we to pray to God that He may give us the grace to apply His Word to such use as He intends; namely, a pure and simple use. This is what we have to observe in summary.

Now since we understand what the book deals with we have to pursue things more at length, so that what we have mentioned briefly we may deduce according to the procedure of the narrative. It is said: *"There was a man in the land of Uz, named Job, a man perfect, and upright; and fearing God, and withdrawing himself from evil."* We cannot and we do not know how to divine at what time Job lived, except that it can be perceived that it was very ancient; some Jews have even estimated that Moses was author of the book, and that he had given this example to the people in order that the children of Abraham who were descended from his race might know that God had shown grace to others who were not of this line, and that they might be ashamed if they did not walk purely in fear of God; seeing that this man, who had not had the mark of the covenant, who had not been circumcised but was Pagan, conducted himself so well. Now because this is not at all certain, we must leave it in suspense. But let us take what is without any doubt, namely, that the Holy Spirit has dictated this book to this use, namely, that the Jews might know that God has had people who have served Him, although they were not separated from the rest of the world, and although they had not the sign of the circumcision, who nevertheless have walked in all purity of life. The Jews, knowing this, have had occasion to be all the more careful to observe the Law of God, and, since He had exercised the grace and given them the privilege of gathering them from among all the foreign nations, that they had to dedicate themselves entirely to Him. And also it is perceived through the book of *Ezekiel* (14:14) that the name of Job was renowned among the people of Israel; for we have seen that in the 14th chapter that it was said,

"Though Noah, Job and Daniel were found among the people who were to perish, they would save only their own souls, and the rest of the people would be destroyed." Here the Prophet speaks of three men, indeed, as of those who were known and renowned among the Jews, as we have already mentioned. So we see the intention of the Holy Spirit: namely, that the Jews might have a mirror and a pattern to recognize how they had to observe the doctrine of salvation which was given them, since this man who was of a foreign nation had so preserved himself in such purity. And it is the principal thing that we have to retain from the name which is here mentioned, when it is said that he was of the land of Uz. It is true that this land is located by some rather in the East; but there is in the Lamentations of *Jeremiah* (4:21) the same word, used to indicate a part of Edom. We know that the Edomites were descended from Esau. It is true that they still had the circumcision, but inasmuch as they had wandered from the Church of God, there was no longer any sign of the covenant. If we take it, then, that Job was of Uz, he was an Edomite, that is to say, of the lineage of Esau. Now we know what is said by the Prophet (*Malachi* 1:2), that although Esau and Jacob were twin brothers, indeed from one womb, God had chosen Jacob by His pure goodness and had rejected Esau, and had cursed him with all his lineage. That is how the Prophet speaks of it in order to magnify the mercy of God toward the Jews, showing them that He had elected them not on account of any dignity that was in their persons, seeing that He has rejected the elder brother of Jacob, to whom belonged the birthright, and that He had chosen him who was the lesser, and the inferior. So then, although this man was descended from the lineage of Esau, yet we see in what integrity he lived, and how he served God, not only with respect to conversing with men in uprightness and equity; but by having a pure religion which was not polluted with the idolatries and superstitions of unbelievers. As for the name "Job," it is true that some translate it as "weeping" or "crying;" but others take it as "a man of enmity," not that he hated, but that he was as it were a target, at which one could shoot. Yet we ought not to doubt that this man, whose country is here noted, whose name is expressed, really was, that he lived, and that the things which are here written have happened to him; in order that we may not think that this is an argument contrived by a man, as if under a pen-name there was here proposed to us that which never happened. For we have already alleged the testimony of Ezekiel, and that of Saint James, who well show that Job truly was, and also when history declares it, we cannot erase what the Holy Spirit so notably wished to say.

Besides we have to note pertaining to that time that, although the world was alienated from the true service of God, and from the pure religion, nevertheless there was much more integrity than there is today, even in the Papacy. In fact, we see how from the time of Abraham, Melchizedek had the Church of God, and sacrifices which were without any pollution. And so, although the greater part of the world was wrapped in many errors, and false and wicked fantasies, yet God had reserved some little seed to himself, and there were always some who were retained under the pure truth, indeed, waiting for God to establish His Church; and that He should choose a people, namely, the successors of Abraham, in order that they might know that they were separated from all the rest of the world. Now it is very true that Job lived during that time, but the Church of God was not yet as trained up as it has been since; for we know that while the children of Israel lived in Egypt it seemed that everyone was to be annihilated. And we even see to what extremity they came in the end, when Pharaoh commands that the males should be killed; and in the desert it still seems that God had rejected them; when they have come into the country of Canaan, they have great battles against their enemies, and even the service of God is not yet established there, nor the tabernacle, as would be required. God then, not yet having set up a form of the Church which could be seen, wished that there might always remain some little seed among the Pagans, in order that He might be adored, and that it might also be to convict those who had turned away from the right road, as the Pagans; for He needed only Job to be judge of an entire country. Noah has also condemned the world, as Scripture speaks of it, since he always kept himself pure and walked as before God, although everyone had forgotten Him, and all had gone astray in their superstitions. So then, Noah is judge of all the world to condemn unbelievers and rebels. So it was with Job, who condemned all those of that region, because he served God purely, and others were full of idolatries, of infamies, of many errors; and this came to pass because they would not condescend to recognize Who was the true and living God, and how, and in what manner He wished to be honored; yet God has always had this consideration (as I have said) that the wicked and unbelievers should be rendered inexcusable. And for this He willed that there might always be some people who would follow what He had declared to the ancient Fathers. Such was Job, as the Scripture speaks to us of him, and the present narrative shows well how he purely served God and that he conversed among men in all uprightness. It is said, *"He was a perfect man."* Now this word in Scripture is taken as a general term when there is neither falsehood nor hypocrisy in a man, but what is inside is shown outside, and that he does not keep a shop in the rear to turn himself away from God, but he displays his heart, and all his thoughts and affections, he asks only to consecrate himself to God and to dedicate himself entirely to Him. This word has been rendered "perfect" by both the Greeks and the Latins; but because the word "perfection" was later improperly expounded, it is much to be preferred that we should have the word "integrity." For many ignorant people, who do not know how this perfection is taken, have thought, "There is a man who is called perfect, it follows then that we can have perfection in ourselves, while we walk in this present life." They have obscured the grace of God, of which we always have need; for those who will have walked the most uprightly still must have their refuge in the mercy of God; and if their sins are not pardoned them, and God does not support them, behold, they all perish. So then, although those who have used the word "perfection" have well understood it, yet since there have been those who have turned it to a contrary sense (as I have said) let us retain the word "integrity." Here then is Job who is called "entire." How? It is because there was no hypocrisy or falsehood in him, for he did not have a double heart; for the Scripture, when it wishes to state the vice opposite to this virtue of integrity, says, "heart and heart," that is to say, "double heart." Let us note, then, that in the first place this title is attributed to Job to show that he had a pure and simple affection, that he did not have one eye on one side and the other on the other, that he did not serve God only half, but he tried to give himself entirely to Him. It is true that we shall never have such integrity that we would reach this goal, as would be to be desired; for those who follow the right road, still go hobbling along, they are always weak, they drag their legs and droop their wings. So, then, is it with us, as long as we shall be surrounded by this mortal body; until God may have delivered us from all these miseries, to which we are subject, there will never be in us an integrity which is perfect, as we have said. Nevertheless, we must come to this openness, and we must renounce all pretense and falsehood. Besides, let us note that true holiness begins within; even if we should have the finest appearance in the world before men, even if our life were so well ruled that everyone should applaud us, if we have not this openness and integrity before God, it will be nothing. For the fountain must be pure, and then the streams trickle down from it pure; otherwise the water could well be clear, and yet it will not cease to be bitter or to have some other evil corruption in it. We must, then, always begin by what is said, namely, "God wishes to be served in spirit and in sincerity of heart," as he says in Jeremiah (5:3). [In an endnote the editor notes: "I think Calvin means *Jeremiah* 3:10 and *John* 4:24."] We must, then, learn in the first place to conform our hearts to the obedience of God.

Now after Job has been called "entire," it is said, "He was upright"; this uprightness is referred to the life which he has led, which is as it were the fruits of this root, that the Holy Spirit had put first. Did Job, then, have his heart upright and whole? His life was simple, that is to say, he walked, and lived with his neighbors without harming anyone, without injuring or molesting anyone, without applying his study to fraud or to malice, without seeking his profit at the expense of another. This, then, is the meaning of the "uprightness," which is here added. Now by this we are admonished to have a conformity between the heart and the outward senses. It is true (as I have said) that we can well abstain from doing evil, we can well have fine appearance before men, but it will be nothing, if before God there is hidden hypocrisy and fiction, when we examine this root, which is within the heart. What is necessary, then? that we should begin at this end, as I have said; yet to have good integrity, the eyes, and the hands, and the feet, and the arms, and the legs must respond, that in all our life we may declare that we wish to serve God, and that it is not in vain that we protest that we wish to keep the integrity within. And that is also why St. Paul exhorts the *Galatians* (5:25) to walk according to the spirit if they live according to the spirit as if he said, "It is true that it is necessary that the Spirit of God should dwell in us, and that He should govern us; for it would be nothing to have a beautiful life, which pleased men, and which was in great esteem, unless we were renewed by the grace of God. But what then? We must walk, that is to say, we must show in fact, and by our works how the Spirit of God reigns in our souls, for if our hands are polluted either by larcenies, or by cruelty, or other injuries, if the eyes are infected by evil and immodest glances, by coveting the goods of another, or by pride, and by vanity the feet run to evil (as the Scripture speaks of it) [in *Proverbs:* 1:16], by this we shall show well that the heart is full of malice and of corruption; for there are neither feet, nor hands, nor eyes which are led by themselves; the leading comes from the Spirit and from the heart." So then, let us learn to have the conformity that Scripture shows us in this passage, when it is said, "Job, having this integrity and openness, also lived uprightly," that is to say, he conversed with his neighbors without any injury, without seeking his particular profit, but he kept equity with all the world. And this is also wherein God wishes to prove whether or not we serve Him faithfully; not that He has need of our service, or of all that we can do for Him; but when we do good to our neighbors, and we keep loyalty to each one, as even nature teaches us, by this we render testimony that we fear God. We shall see many, whom we make great zealots, if it is only a matter of disputing and holding many conversations, to say that they study to serve God and to honor Him; but as soon as they have to do with their neighbors, it is known what is in their heart; for they seek their own advantage, and they have no conscience against drawing to themselves and cheating when they will have the power to do so by any means whatever. Those, then, who seek their advantage and profit—there is no doubt that they are hypocrites, and that their heart is corrupted; however beautiful zealots they may be, God declares that there is only filth and poison in their heart. And why? If there is openness, it is necessary that there should be uprightness, that is to say, if the affection is pure within, when we converse with men, we shall procure the good of each one, so that we shall not be addicted to ourselves, and to our particular interest, but we shall have the equity which Jesus Christ said is the rule of life, and the whole sum of the Law and the Prophets—that we should not do to anyone except what we would wish done to us. So then, let us note that in this praise of Job there are many people who are condemned when the Holy Spirit declares that this man had not only an integrity before God, but also uprightness and openness among men. This openness that He pronounces will serve sentence and condemnation against all those who will be full of malice, against all those who ask only to ravish and to entrap the goods of another, who ask only to pillage the substance of others. These are condemned by this word.

Now it follows, *"He feared God, he was a God-fearing man, and he withdrew from evil."* Also when Job had the praise of having kept uprightness and equity among men, it was very necessary that he walked before God; for without this the rest would be considered nothing. It is true that we cannot live with our neighbors (as I have already said) without doing evil to anyone, procuring the good of each one, except we regard God; for those who follow their nature, though they may have beautiful virtues (it will seem), yet are preoccupied with love of themselves, and compelled only by ambition, or some other consideration, so that all appearance of virtue which is in them, is corrupted by this; but although we may not be able to have this uprightness without fearing God, yet these are two distinct things: (1) serving God, and (2) honoring our

neighbors, as also God has distinguished them in His Law, when He willed that it should be described in two tables. Let us note, then, that as by putting before us the word "uprightness" the Holy Spirit wished to declare how Job conversed among men, also when He says, "He had fear of God," He wishes to bring out the religion which was in him. Now by this we are admonished that to rule our life well we must regard God and then our neighbors; let us regard God, I say, in order to give ourselves to Him, in order to render Him the homage which is due Him; let us regard our neighbors in order to acquit ourselves of our duty toward them according as we are admonished to help them, to live in equity, and uprightness; and since God has joined us to one another, let each one be advised to employ all his faculties to the common good of all. That is how we have to regard both God and men to rule our life well, for he who regards himself—it is certain that there is only vanity in him; for if a man wishes to order his life so that it seems to men that there is nothing to find fault with in him and meanwhile God disavows him, what will he gain when he will have taken much trouble to walk in such a way that everyone magnifies him? There is only pollution before God, and the sentence written by Saint Luke (16:15) must be fulfilled: "He who is high and excellent before men is only abomination before God." Let us note, then, that we never shall be able to order our life properly, if we have not our eyes fixed on God, and toward our neighbors. On God, any why? In order that we may know that we are created to His glory, to serve and adore Him; for although He may not have to do with us as our neighbors will have to and though this may bring Him neither hot nor cold, yet He wished to have reasonable creatures, who would recognize Him, and, having recognized Him, would render to Him what belongs to Him. Besides, when it is spoken of the fear of God, let us note that it is not a servile fear (as it is called) but it is for the honor that we owe Him, as He is our Father and our Master. Would we fear God? It is certain that we should ask only to honor Him, and to be entirely His own. Would we recognize Him? We must do it according to such attributes as He declares of Himself: namely, our Creator, and He Who sustains us, and Who shows such a fatherly goodness that we surely must be His children if we do not wish to be too ungrateful to Him. Also we must recognize the mastery and superiority which He has over us, in order that, rendering to Him the honor which is due Him, each one of us may learn to please Him in everything and by everything. That is how under the word "fear of God" all religion is comprehended, namely, all the service, and the homage that creatures owe to their God. Now it was a very excellent virtue in Job to fear God thus, seeing that all the world had turned away from the right road. When we hear this, let us learn that we shall have no excuse, though we may converse among the worst outcasts in the world, if we are not given to the service of God; as we ought to be. Now it is well to note this, because it seems to many people, when they are among thorns, that they are thereby acquitted and fully excused; and if afterwards they are corrupted, if they are hurled among wolves (as they say), that it is all right, and that God will pardon them. On the contrary, here is Job who is called a God-fearing man. In what country? It is not in Judea, it is not in the city of Jerusalem, it is not in the Temple; but it is in a polluted place, in the midst of those who were entirely perverted. Being then, among such people, yet he was preserved, and he lived in such wise that he walked purely with his neighbors, although all were then full of cruelty, outrages, pillaging, and like things. Let us note that this will return to us with all the greater shame, if on our part we do not, consider how to reserve ourselves purely for the service of God, and for our neighbors, when he gives us such occasion for it as we have, namely, that daily the Word of God is preached to us, that we are exhorted, that it sets us right when we have failed. We surely must, then, be attentive to what is here shown us.

Now in conclusion let us note well what is here added to the text, *"He kept himself from evil."* For this is how Job surmounted all difficulties and battles which might have hindered him from serving God and from living uprightly with men: it is because he recalled to himself that he well knew that, if he had given himself license to do like others, he would have been a man completely addicted to vice, he would have been an enemy of God. Job, then, did not thus walk in the fear of God, in such openness and integrity without many battles, without the devil's having schemed to pervert him and to lead him to all the corruptions of the world; but he withdrew from evil, that is to say, he held himself back. What, then, must we do? Though we are in the Church of God, yet we shall see many evils; and (though it should be) there will never be such openness or purity, that we would not be mixed among many despisers, debauchees, who will be firebrands from hell, deadly pests to infect everything. We must, then, be on our guard, seeing that there are great scandals and all manner of lewdness, by which we would be immediately debauched. What must we do then? We must withdraw from evil; that is to say, we must fight against such assaults after the example of Job; and when we shall see many vices and corruptions ruling in the world, though it may be necessary for us to be mixed among them, nevertheless we must not be polluted by them and we must not say, as is customary, that we must howl among the wolves; but rather we must be advised after the example of Job to withdraw ourselves from evil, and to withdraw from it in such a way that Satan may not be able to make us give ourselves to him by means of all the temptations which he will put before us; but we must allow that God should purge us of all our filth and infections, as He has promised us in the Name of our Lord Jesus Christ, until He may have withdrawn us from the stains and pollutions of this world, to join us with His Angels, and to make us partakers of the eternal felicity to which we ought now to aspire.

Now we shall present ourselves before the face of our God.

Voltaire   (essay date 1764)

SOURCE: "Job," in *Voltaire's Philosophical Dictionary, Volume III,* translated by William F. Fleming, 1903. Reprint by The Lamb Publishing Company, 1910, pp. 314-19.

[A principal figure of the French Enlightenment, Voltaire promoted the highest ideals of the Age of Reason, particu-

Bible, twelfth century. Job's seven sons and three daughters are behind Job, who kneels. Below: Job seated on a dungheap, with his wife standing opposite.

larly the ideal of faith in man's ability to perfect himself. He was also a formidable satirist who was both feared and denigrated by the victims of his biting wit. Voltaire's works encompass diverse genres including drama, poetry, history, essays, literary criticism, political and social treatises, autobiography, and contes—short adventure tales. Also among his esteemed works are philosophical works including Letters philosophiques *(1734;* Letters Concerning the English Nation) *and* Dictionaire philosophique *(1764;* Philosophical Dictionary). *The following is an excerpt from the* Philosophical Dictionary, *in which Voltaire presents a humorous overview of* The Book of Job, *commenting on the moral failure of Job's friends and arguing that the work is Arabic in origin.]*

Good day, friend Job! thou art one of the most ancient originals of which books make mention; thou wast not a Jew; we know that the book which bears thy name is more ancient than the Pentateuch. If the Hebrews, who translated it from the Arabic, made use of the word "Jehovah" to signify God, they borrowed it from the Phoenicians and Egyptians, of which men of learning are assured. The word "Satan" was not Hebrew; it was Chaldæan, as is well known.

Thou dwelledst on the confines of Chalda. Commentators, worthy of their profession, pretend that thou didst believe in the resurrection, because, being prostrate on thy dunghill, thou hast said, in thy nineteenth chapter, that thou wouldst one day rise up from it. A patient who wishes his cure is not anxious for resurrection in lieu of it; but I would speak to thee of other things.

Confess that thou wast a great babbler; but thy friends were much greater. It is said that thou possessedst seven thousand sheep, three thousand camels, one thousand cows, and five hundred she-asses. I will reckon up their value:

LIVRES.

Seven thousand sheep, at three livres ten
   sous apiece 22,500

Three thousand camels at fifty crowns apiece . 450,000

A thousand cows, one with the other, cannot
   be valued at less than 80,000

And five hundred she-asses, at twenty francs
   an ass 10,000

The whole amounts to 562,500
   without reckoning thy furniture, rings and jewels.

I have been much richer than thou; and though I have lost a great part of my property and am ill, like thyself I have not murmured against God, as thy friends seem to reproach thee with sometimes doing.

I am not at all pleased with Satan, who, to induce thee to sin, and to make thee forget God, demanded permission to take away all thy property, and to give thee the itch. It is in this state that men always have recourse to divinity. They are prosperous people who forgot God. Satan knew not enough of the world at that time; he has improved himself since; and when he would be sure of any one, he makes him a farmer-general, or something better if possible, as our friend Pope has clearly shown in his history of the knight Sir Balaam.

Thy wife was an impertinent, but thy pretended friends Eliphaz the Temanite, Bildad the Shuite, and Zophar, the Naamathite, were much more insupportable. They exhorted thee to patience in a manner that would have roused the mildest of men; they made thee long sermons more tiresome than those preached by the knave V—e at Amsterdam, and by so many other people.

It is true that thou didst not know what thou saidst, when exclaiming—"My God, am I a sea or a whale, to be shut up by Thee as in a prison?" But thy friends knew no more when they answered thee, "that the morn cannot become fresh without dew, and that the grass of the field cannot grow without water." Nothing is less consolatory than this axiom.

Zophar of Naamath reproached thee with being a prater; but none of these good friends lent thee a crown. I would not have treated thee thus. Nothing is more common than people who advise; nothing more rare than those who assist. Friends are not worth much, from whom we cannot procure a drop of broth if we are in misery. I imagine that when God restored thy riches and health, these eloquent personages dared not present themselves before thee, hence the comforters of Job have become a proverb.

God was displeased with them, and told them sharply, in chap. xlii., that they were tiresome and imprudent, and he condemned them to a fine of seven bullocks and seven rams, for having talked nonsense. I would have condemned them for not having assisted their friend.

I pray thee, tell me if it is true, that thou livedst a hundred and forty years after this adventure. I like to learn that honest people live long; but men of the present day must be great rogues, since their lives are comparatively so short.

As to the rest, the book of *Job* is one of the most precious of antiquity. It is evident that this book is the work of an Arab who lived before the time in which we place Moses. It is said that Eliphaz, one of the interlocutors, is of Teman, which was an ancient city of Arabia. Bildad was of Shua, another town of Arabia. Zophar was of Naamath, a still more eastern country of Arabia.

But what is more remarkable, and which shows that this fable cannot be that of a Jew, is, that three constellations are spoken of, which we now call Arcturus, Orion, and the Pleiades. The Hebrews never had the least knowledge of astronomy; they had not even a word to express this science; all that regards the mental science was unknown to them, inclusive even of the term geometry.

The Arabs, on the contrary, living in tents, and being continually led to observe the stars, were perhaps the first who regulated their years by the inspection of the heavens.

The more important observation is, that one God alone is spoken of in this book. It is an absurd error to imagine that the Jews were the only people who recognized a sole God; it was the doctrine of almost all the East, and the Jews were only plagiarists in that as in everything else.

In chapter xxxviii. God Himself speaks to Job from the midst of a whirlwind, which has been since imitated in Genesis. We cannot too often repeat, that the Jewish books are very modern. Ignorance and fanaticism exclaim, that the Pentateuch is the most ancient book in the world. It is evident, that those of Sanchoniathon, and those of Thaut, eight hundred years anterior to those of Sanchoniathon; those of the first Zerdusht, the "Shasta," the "Vedas" of the Indians, which we still possess; the "Five Kings of China"; and finally the *Book of Job,* are of a much remoter antiquity than any Jewish book. It is demonstrated that this little people could only have annals while they had a stable government; that they only had this government under their kings; that its jargon was only formed, in the course of time, of a mixture of Phoenician and Arabic. These are incontestable proofs that the Phoenicians cultivated letters a long time before them. Their profession was pillage and brokerage; they were writers only by chance. We have lost the books of the Egyptians and Phoenicians, the Chinese, Brahmins, and Guebers; the Jews have preserved theirs. All these monuments are curious, but they are monuments of human imagination alone, in which not a single truth, either physical or historical, is to be learned. There is not at present any little physical treatise that would not be more useful than all the books of antiquity.

Søren Kierkegaard   (essay date 1843)

SOURCE: "The Lord Gave, and the Lord Hath Taken Away, Blessed Be the Name of the Lord," in *Edifying Discourses, Volume II* translated by David F. Swenson and Lillian Marvin Swenson, Augsburg Publishing House, 1944, pp. 7-26.

[*Kierkegaard was a Danish philosopher and theologian who is widely regarded as the founder of Existentialist philosophy. He was primarily concerned with ethical questions as they were experienced by individuals, and he observed three possible approaches to life: the aesthetic, the ethical, and the religious. According to his thought, the religious path would allow the greatest freedom for the self but would necessarily involve suffering. The human response to misfortune is the subject of the following essay, originally published in his* Opbyggelige Taler *(1843;* Edifying Discourses), *in which he upholds the figure of Job as "a teacher of mankind," focusing on the significance of the passage* Job 1:20-21.]

> Then Job arose, and rent his mantle, and shaved his head, and fell upon the ground and worshipped, and said: Naked came I out of my mother's womb, and naked shall I return thither: the Lord gave, and the Lord hath taken away; blessed be the name of the Lord. [*Job 1:20-21*]

Not only do we call that man a teacher of men who through some particularly happy talent discovered, or by unremitting toil and continued perseverance brought to light one or another truth; left what he had acquired as a principle of knowledge, which the following generations strove to understand, and through this understanding to appropriate to themselves. Perhaps, in an even stricter sense, we also call that one a teacher of men who had no doctrine to pass on to others, but who merely left himself as a pattern to succeeding generations, his life as a principle of guidance to every man, his name as an assurance to the many, his own deeds as an encouragement to the striving. Such a teacher and guide of men was Job, whose significance is by no means due to what he said but to what he did. He has indeed left a saying which because of its brevity and its beauty has become a proverb, preserved from generation to generation, and no one has been presumptuous enough to add anything to it or to take anything away from it. But the expression itself is not the guidance, and Job's significance does not lie in the fact that he said it, but in the fact that he acted in accordance with it. The expression itself is truly beautiful and worthy of consideration, but if another had used it, or if Job had been different, or if he had uttered it under different circumstances, then the word itself would have become something different—significant, if, as uttered, it would otherwise have been so, but not significant from the fact that he acted in asserting it, so that the expression itself was the action. If Job had devoted his whole life to emphasizing this word, if he had regarded it as the sum and fulfillment of what a man ought to let life teach him, if he had constantly only *taught* it, but had never himself practiced it, had never himself acted in accordance with what he taught, then Job would have been a different kind of man, his significance different. Then would Job's name have been forgotten, or it would have been unimportant wheth-

er anyone remembered it or not, the principal thing being the content of the word, the richness of the thought it embodied.

If the race had accepted the saying, then it would have been this which one generation transmitted to the next; while now, on the contrary, it is Job himself who guides the generations. When one generation has served its time, fulfilled its duty, fought its battle, then Job has guided it; when the new generation, with its innumerable ranks and every individual among them in his place, stands ready to begin the journey, then Job is again present, takes his place, which is the outpost of humanity. If the generation sees only happy days and prosperous times, then Job faithfully goes with them, and if, nevertheless, an individual in his thought experiences the terrible, is apprehensive because of his conception of what life may conceal of horror and distress, of the fact that no one knows when the hour of despair may strike for him, then his troubled thought resorts to Job, dwells upon him, is reassured by him. For Job keeps faithfully by his side and comforts him, not as if he had thus suffered once for all what he would never again have to endure, but he comforts him as one who witnesses that the terror is endured, the horror experienced, the battle of despair waged, to the honor of God, to his own salvation, to the profit and happiness of others. In joyful days, in fortunate times, Job walks by the side of the race and guarantees it its happiness, combats the apprehensive dream that some horror may suddenly befall a man and have power to destroy his soul as its certain prey.

Only the thoughtless man could wish that Job should not accompany him, that his venerable name should not remind him of what he seeks to forget, that terror and anxiety exist in life. Only the selfish man could wish that Job had not existed, so that the idea of his suffering might not disturb with its austere earnestness his own unsubstantial joy, and frighten him out of his intoxicated security in obduracy and perdition. In stormy times, when the foundation of existence is shaken, when the moment trembles in fearful expectation of what may happen, when every explanation is silent at the sight of the wild uproar, when a man's heart groans in despair, and "in bitterness of soul" he cries to heaven, then Job still walks at the side of the race and guarantees that there is a victory, guarantees that even if the individual loses in the strife, there is still a God, who, as with every human temptation, even if a man fails to endure it, will still make its outcome such that we may be able to bear it; yea, more glorious than any human expectation. Only the defiant could wish that Job had not existed, so that he might absolutely free his soul from the last vestiges of love which still remained in the plaintive shriek of despair; so that he might complain, aye, even curse life; so that there might be no consonance of faith and confidence and humility in his speech; so that in his defiance he might stifle the shriek so that it might not even seem as if there were anyone whom it defied. Only the effeminate could wish that Job had not existed, so that he might relinquish every thought, the sooner the better; might renounce every emotion in the most abhorrent impotence and completely efface himself in the most wretched and miserable oblivion.

The expression which, when it is mentioned, at once reminds us of Job, immediately becomes vividly present in everyone's thought, is a plain and simple one; it conceals no secret wisdom that must be unearthed from the depths. If a child learns this word, if it is entrusted to him as an endowment, he does not understand for what purpose he will use it; when he understands the word, he understands essentially the same thing by it as does the wisest. Still, the child does not understand it, or rather he does not understand Job; for what he does not comprehend is all the distress and wretchedness with which Job was tested. About that the child can have only a dark premonition; and yet, happy the child who understood the word and got an impression of what he did not comprehend, that it was the most terrible thing imaginable; who possessed, before sorrow and adversity made its thought cunning, the convincing and childishly vivid conviction that it was in truth the most terrible. When the youth turns his attention to this word, then he understands it, and understands it essentially the same as do the child and the wisest. Still he perhaps does not understand it, or rather, he does not understand Job, does not understand why all the distress and wretchedness should come in which Job was tried; and yet, happy the youth who understood the word and humbly bowed before what he did not understand, before his own distress made his thought wayward, as if he had discovered what no one had known before. When the adult reflects on this word, then he understands essentially the same by it as did the child and the wisest. He understands, too, the wretchedness and distress in which Job was tried; and yet perhaps he does not understand Job, for he cannot understand how Job was able to say it; and yet, happy the man who understood the word, and steadfastly admired what he did not understand, before his own distress and wretchedness made him also distrustful of Job. When the man who has been tried, who fought the good fight through remembering this saying, mentions it, then he understands it, and understands it essentially the same as the child and as the wisest understood it; he understands Job's misery, he understands how Job could say it. He understands the word, he interprets it, even though he never speaks about it, more gloriously than the one who spent a whole lifetime in explaining this one word.

Only the one who has been tried, who tested the word through himself being tested, only he interprets the word correctly, and only such a disciple, only such an interpreter, does Job desire. Only such a one learns from Job what there is to learn, the most beautiful and blessed truth, compared with which all other art and all other wisdom is very unessential. Therefore we rightly call Job a teacher of mankind, not of certain individual men, for he offers himself to every man as his pattern, beckons to everyone by his glorious example, summons everyone in his beautiful words. While the more simple-minded man, the one less gifted, or the one less favored by time and circumstances, if not enviously yet in troubled despondency, may sometimes have wished for the talent and the opportunity to be able to understand and absorb himself in those things which scholars from time to time have discovered, may also have felt a desire in his soul to be able to teach others, and not always be the one to receive instruction, Job does not tempt him in this way. How, too, could human wis-

dom help here? Would it perhaps seek to make that more intelligible which the simplest and the child easily understood, and understood as well as the wisest! How would the art of eloquence and fluency help here? Would it be able to produce in the speaker or in some other man what the simplest is able to do as well as the wisest—action! Would not human wisdom rather tend to make everything more difficult? Would not eloquence, which, despite its pretentiousness, is nevertheless unable to express the differences which always dwell in the heart of man, rather benumb the power of action, and allow it to slumber in extensive reflection! But even if this is true, and even if, as a result of this, the speaker endeavors to avoid intruding disturbingly between the striving individual and the beautiful pattern which is equally near to every man, so that he may not increase sorrow by increasing wisdom; even if he takes care not to ensnare himself in the splendid words of human persuasiveness, which are very unfruitful, still it by no means follows that the reflection and the development might not have their own significance. If the one reflecting had not hitherto known this word, then it would always be an advantage to him that he had learned to know it; if he had known it, but had had no occasion to test it, then it would always be an advantage to him, that he had learned to understand what he perhaps might some time have to use. If he had tested it, but it had deceived him, if he even believed that it was the word which had deceived him, then it would be advantageous to him that he had previously reflected upon it, before he fled from it in the unrest of the strife and the haste of battle! Perhaps the reflection would sometime become significant to him; it might perhaps happen that the reflection would become vividly present in his soul just when he needed it in order to penetrate the confused thoughts of his restless heart; it might perhaps happen that what the reflection had understood only in part, would sometime gather itself regenerated in the moment of decision; that what reflection had sowed in corruption would spring up in the day of need in the incorruptible life of action.

So let us endeavor to understand Job better in his beautiful words: *The Lord gave, the Lord hath taken away; blessed be the name of the Lord!*

In the land toward the east there lived a man whose name was Job. He was blessed with lands, innumerable herds, and rich pastures; "his words had lifted up the fallen, and had strengthened the feeble knees"; his tent was blessed as if it rested in the lap of heaven, and in this tent he lived with his seven sons and three daughters; and "the secret of the Lord" abode there with him. And Job was an old man; his joy in life was his pleasure in his children, over whom he watched that no evil might come upon them. There he sat one day alone by his fireside, while his children were gathered at a festival at the oldest brother's house. There he offered burnt offerings for each one individually, there he also disposed his heart to joy in the thought of his children. As he sat there in the quiet confidence of happiness, there came a messenger, and before he could speak there came another, and while this one was still speaking, there came a third, but the fourth messenger brought news concerning his sons and daughters, that the house had been overthrown and had buried them all.

"Then Job stood up and rent his mantle and shaved his head, and fell down upon the ground and worshipped." His sorrow did not express itself in many words, or rather he did not utter a single one; only his appearance bore witness that his heart was broken. Could you wish it otherwise! Is not that one who prides himself on not being able to sorrow in the day of sorrow put to shame by not being able to rejoice in the day of gladness? Is not the sight of such imperturbability unpleasant and distressing, almost revolting, while it is affecting to see an honorable old man, who but now sat in the gladness of the Lord, sitting with his fatherly countenance downcast, his mantle rent and his head shaven! Since he had thus surrendered himself to sorrow, not in despair but stirred by human emotion, he was swift to judge between God and himself, and the words of his judgment are these: "Naked I came forth from my mother's womb, and naked shall I return thither." With these words the struggle was decided, and every claim which would demand something from the Lord, which He did not wish to give, or would desire to retain something, as if it had not been a gift, was brought to silence in his soul. Then follows the confession from the man whom not sorrow alone but worship as well had prostrated on the ground: "The Lord gave, and the Lord hath taken away. Blessed be the name of the Lord!"

The Lord gave, the Lord took. What first arrests the attention is that Job said, "The Lord gave." Is not this word irrelevant to the occasion; does it not contain something different from what lay in the event itself? If a man in a single moment is deprived of everything dear to him, and deprived of the most precious of all, the loss will perhaps at first so overwhelm him that he will not even trust himself to express it, even if in his heart he is conscious before God that he has lost everything. Or he will not permit the loss to rest with its crushing weight upon his soul, but he will put it away from him, and in his heart's agitation he will say, "The Lord took." And thus to humble one's self before the Lord in silence and humility is indeed worthy of praise and emulation, and in the struggle such a man saves his soul though he loses all his gladness. But Job! At the moment when the Lord took everything, he did not say first, "The Lord took," but he said first, "The Lord gave." The word is short, but in its brevity it perfectly expresses what it wishes to indicate, that Job's soul is not crushed down in silent submission to sorrow, but that his heart first expanded in gratitude; that the loss of everything first made him thankful to the Lord that He had given him all the blessings that He now took from him. It did not happen with him, as Joseph predicted, that the abundance of the seven fruitful years would be entirely forgotten in the seven lean years. The nature of his gratitude was not the same as in that long vanished time when he accepted every good and perfect gift from the hand of God with thanksgiving; but still his gratitude was sincere, as was his conception about the goodness of God which now became living in his soul. Now he is reminded of everything which the Lord had given, some individual thing perhaps with even greater thankfulness than when he had received it. It was not become less beautiful to him because it was taken away, nor more beautiful, but still beautiful as before, beautiful because the Lord gave it, and what now might seem more beautiful to him, was not the gift

but the goodness of God. He is reminded again of his abundant prosperity, his eyes rest once more upon the rich pastures, and follow the numerous herds; he remembers what joy there was in having seven sons and three daughters, who now needed no offering except that of thankfulness for having had them. He is reminded of those who perhaps still remembered him with gratitude, the many he had instructed, "whose weak hands he had strengthened, whose feeble knees he had upheld." He is reminded of the glorious days when he was powerful and esteemed by the people, "when the young men hid themselves out of reverence for him, and the old men arose and remained standing." He remembers with thankfulness that his step had not turned away from the way of righteousness, that he had rescued the poor who complained, and the fatherless who had no helper; and therefore, even in this moment, the "blessing of the forsaken" was upon him as before.

The Lord gave. It is a short word, but to Job it signified so very much; for Job's memory was not so short, nor was his thankfulness so forgetful. While thankfulness rested in his soul with its quiet sadness, he bade a gentle and friendly farewell to everything at once, and in this farewell everything disappeared like a beautiful memory; moreover, it seemed as if it were not the Lord who took it, but Job who gave it back to Him. When therefore Job had said, "The Lord gave," then was his mind well prepared to please God also with the next word, "The Lord took."

Perhaps there might be someone who on the day of sorrow was also reminded that he had seen happy days, and his soul would become even more impatient. "Had he never known happiness, then the pain would not have overcome him, for what is pain, after all, other than an idea which he does not have who knows nothing else, but now happiness had so educated and developed him as to make him conscious of the pain." Thus his happiness became pernicious to him; it was never lost but only lacking, and it tempted him more in the lack than ever before. What had been the delight of his eyes, he desired to see again, and his ingratitude punished him by conjuring it up as more beautiful than it had formerly been. What his soul had rejoiced in, it now thirsted for again, and his ingratitude punished him by painting it as more desirable than it had previously been. What he had once been capable of doing, that he now wished to be able to do again, and his ingratitude punished him with visions that had never had reality. Thus he condemned his soul to living famished in the never satisfied craving of want.

Or there awakened a consuming passion in his soul, because he had not even enjoyed the happy days in the right way, had not imbibed all the sweetness from their voluptuous abundance. If there might only be vouchsafed to him one little hour, if he might only regain the glory for a short time so that he might satiate himself with happiness, and thereby learn to disregard the pain! Then he abandoned his soul to a burning unrest; he would not acknowledge to himself whether the enjoyment he desired was worthy of a man; whether he ought not rather to thank God that his soul had not been so extravagant in the time of joy as it had now become in his unhappiness; he was not appalled by the thought that his desires were the cause of his perdition; he refused to be concerned by the fact that more wretched than all his wretchedness was the worm of desire in his soul, which would not die.

Perhaps there might be another man who at the moment of loss also remembered what he had possessed, but who had the audacity to try to prevent the loss from becoming intelligible to him. Even if it were lost, his defiant will would still be able to retain it as if it were not lost. He would not endeavor to bear the loss, but he chose to waste his strength in an impotent defiance, to lose himself in an insane preoccupation with the loss. Or in cowardice he immediately avoided humbly attempting to understand it. Then oblivion opened its abyss, not so much to the loss as to him, and he did not so much escape the loss in forgetfulness as he threw himself away. Or he lyingly sought to belittle the good which he had once enjoyed, as if it never had been beautiful, had never gladdened his heart; he thought to strengthen his soul by a wretched self-deception, as if strength lay in falsehood. Or he irrationally assured himself that life was not so hard as one imagined, that its terror was not as described, was not so hard to bear, if one, as you will remember that he did, began by not finding it terrifying to become such a person.

In fact, who would ever finish, if he wished to speak about what so frequently has happened, and will so frequently be repeated in the world? Would he not tire far sooner than would passion of that ever new ingenuity for transforming the explained and the understood into a new disappointment, wherein it deceives itself!

Let us rather, therefore, turn back to Job. On the day of sorrow when everything was lost, then he first thanked God who gave it, defrauded neither God nor himself, and while everything was being shaken and overthrown, he still remained what he had been from the beginning—"honest and upright before God." He confessed that the blessing of the Lord had been merciful to him, he returned thanks for it; therefore it did not remain in his mind as a torturing memory. He confessed that the Lord had blessed richly and beyond all measure his undertakings; he had been thankful for this, and therefore the memory did not become to him a consuming unrest. He did not conceal from himself that everything had been taken from him; therefore the Lord, who took it, remained in his upright soul. He did not avoid the thought that it was lost; therefore his soul rested quietly until the explanation of the Lord again came to him, and found his heart like the good earth well cultivated in patience.

The Lord took. Did Job say anything except the truth, did he use an indirect expression to indicate what was direct? The word is short, and it signifies the loss of everything; it naturally occurs to us to repeat it after him, since the expression itself has become a sacred proverb; but do we just as naturally link it to Job's thought? For was it not the Sabeans who fell upon his peaceful herds and killed his servants? Did the messenger who brought the news say anything else? Was it not the lightning which destroyed the sheep and their shepherds? Did the messenger who brought the news mean something else, even though he called the lightning the fire from heaven? Was it not a wind-storm from out of the desert which overturned the house and buried his children in the ruins? Did the messenger mention some other perpetrator, or did he name someone who sent the wind? Yet Job said, "The Lord took"; in the very moment of receiving the message, he realized that it was the Lord who had taken everything. Who told Job this? Or was it not a sign of his fear of God that he thus shifted everything over to the Lord, and justified Him in doing it; and are we more devout, we who sometimes hesitate a long time to speak thus?

Perhaps there was a man who had lost everything in the world. Then he set out to consider how it had happened. But everything was inexplicable and obscure to him. His happiness had vanished like a dream, and its memory haunted him like a nightmare, but how he had been cast off from the glory of the one into the wretchedness of the other, he was unable to understand. It was not the Lord who had taken it—it was an accident. Or he assured himself that it was the deceit and cunning of men, or their manifest violence, which had wrested it from him, as the Sabeans had destroyed Job's herds and their keepers. Then his soul became rebellious against men; he believed he did God justice by not reproaching Him. He fully understood how it had happened, and the more immediate explanation was that those men had done it, and furthermore it was because the men were evil and their hearts perverted. He understood that men are his neighbors to his injury; would he perhaps have understood it in the same way if they had benefited him? But that the Lord who dwells far away in heaven might be nearer to him than the man who lived next to him, whether that man did him good or evil, such an idea was remote from his thought. Or he fully understood how it had happened, and knew how to describe it with all the eloquence of horror. For why should he not understand that when the sea rages in its fury, when it flings itself against the heavens, then men and their frail accomplishments are tossed about as in a game; that when the storm rushes forth in its violence, human enterprises are mere child's play; that when the earth trembles in terror of the elements and the mountains groan, then men and their glorious achievements sink as nothing into the abyss. And this explanation was adequate for him, and, above all, sufficient to make his soul indifferent to everything. For it is true that what is built on sand does not even need a storm to overthrow it; but would it not also be true that a man cannot build and dwell elsewhere and be sure his soul is safe! Or he understood that he himself had merited what had befallen him, that he had not been prudent. For had he rightly calculated in time, it would not have happened. And this explanation explained everything by first explaining that he had corrupted himself and made it impossible for him to learn anything from life, and especially impossible for him to learn anything from God.

Still who would ever finish if he tried to explain what has happened and what will frequently be repeated in life? Would he not become tired of talking, before the sensual man would weary of deluding himself with plausible and disappointing and deceptive explanations? Let us therefore turn away from that which has nothing to teach us, except in so far as we knew it before, so that we may shun worldly wisdom and turn our attention to him from whom there is a truth to be learned—to Job and to his devout words, "The Lord took." Job referred everything to the Lord; he did not retard his soul and extinguish his spirit in reflections or explanations which only engender and nourish doubt, even if the one who dwells on them does not realize it. In the same instant that everything was taken from him he knew that it was the Lord who had taken it, and therefore in his loss he remained in understanding with the Lord; in his loss, he preserved his confidence in the Lord; he looked upon the Lord and therefore he did not see despair. Or does only that man see God's hand who sees that He gives; does not that one also see God who sees that He takes? Does only that one see God who sees His countenance turned toward him? Does not that one also see God who sees Him turn His back upon him, as Moses always saw only the Lord's back? But he who sees God has overcome the world, and therefore Job in his devout word had overcome the world; was through his devout word greater and stronger and more powerful than the whole world, which here would not so much carry him into temptation but would overcome him with its power, cause him to sink down before its boundless might. And yet how weak, indeed almost childishly so, is not the wild fury of the storm, when it thinks to cause a man to tremble for himself by wresting everything away from him, and he answers, "It is not you who do this, it is the Lord who takes!" How impotent is the arm of every man of violence, how wretched his shrewd cleverness, how all human power becomes almost an object of compassion, when it wishes to plunge the weak into the destruction of despair by wresting everything from him, and he then confidently says, "It is not you, you can do nothing—it is the Lord who takes."

Blessed be the name of the Lord! Hence Job not only overcame the world, but he did what Paul had desired his striving congregation to do: after having overcome everything, he stood. Alas, perhaps there has been someone in the world who overcame everything, but who failed in the moment of victory. The Lord's name be praised! Hence the Lord remained the same, and ought He not to be praised as always? Or had the Lord really changed? Or did not the Lord in truth remain the same, as did Job? The Lord's name be praised! Hence the Lord did not take everything, for He did not take away Job's praise, and his peace of heart, and the sincerity of faith from which it issued; but his confidence in the Lord remained with him as before, perhaps more fervently than before; for now there was nothing at all which could in any way divert his thought from Him. The Lord took it all. Then Job gathered together all his sorrows and "cast them upon the Lord," and then He also took those from him, and only praise remained in the incorruptible joy of his heart. For Job's house was a house of sorrow, if ever a house was such, but where this word is spoken, "Blessed be the name of the Lord," there gladness also has its home. And Job indeed stands before us, the image of sorrow, expressed in his countenance and in his form; but he who utters this word as Job did still bears witness to the joy, even if his testimony does not direct itself to the joyous but to the concerned, and yet speaks intelligibly to the many who have ears to hear. For the ear of the concerned is fashioned in a special manner, and as the ear of the lover indeed hears many voices but really only one—the voice of the beloved, so the

ear of the concerned also hears many voices, but they pass by and do not enter his heart. As faith and hope without love are only sounding brass and tinkling cymbals, so all the gladness in the world in which no sorrow is mingled is only sounding brass and tinkling cymbals, which flatter the ear but are abhorrent to the soul. But this voice of consolation, this voice which trembles in pain and yet proclaims the gladness, this the ear of the concerned hears, his heart treasures it, it strengthens and guides him even to finding joy in the depths of sorrow.

My hearer, is it not true? You have understood Job's eulogy; it has at least seemed beautiful to you in the quiet moment of reflection, so that in thinking of it you had forgotten what you did not wish to be reminded of, that which indeed is sometimes heard in the world in the day of need, instead of praise and blessing. So let it then be forgotten, you will deserve, as little as I, that the memory of it should again be revived.

We have spoken about Job, and have sought to understand him in his devout expression, without the speech wishing to force itself upon anyone. But should it therefore be entirely without significance or application, and concern no one? If you yourself, my hearer, have been tried as Job was, and have stood the testing as he did, then it truly applies to you, if we have spoken rightly about Job. If hitherto you have not been tested in life, then it indeed applies to you. Do you think perhaps that these words apply only under such extraordinary circumstances as those in which Job was placed? Is it perhaps your belief that if such a thing struck you, then the terror itself would gave you strength, develop within you that humble courage? Did not Job have a wife, what do we read about her? Perhaps you think that terror cannot get as much power over a man as can the daily thralldom in much smaller adversities. Then look you to it that you, as little as any man, do not become enslaved by some tribulation, and above all learn from Job to be sincere with yourself, so that you may not delude yourself by an imagined strength, through which you experience imaginary victories in an imaginary conflict.

Perhaps you say, if the Lord had taken it from me, but nothing was given to me; perhaps you believe that this is by no means as terrible as was Job's suffering, but that it is far more wearing, and consequently a more difficult struggle. We shall not quarrel with you. For even if this were true, the quarrel would still be unprofitable, and increase the difficulty. But in one thing we are in agreement, that you can learn from Job, and, if you are honest with yourself and love humanity, then you cannot wish to evade Job, in order to venture out into a hitherto unknown difficulty, and keep the rest of us in suspense, until we learn from your testimony that a victory is also possible in this difficulty. So if you then learn from Job to say, "Blessed be the name of the Lord," this applies to you, even if the preceding is less applicable.

Or perhaps you believe that such a thing cannot happen to you? Who taught you this wisdom, or on what do you base your assurance? Are you wise and understanding, and is this your confidence? Job was the teacher of many. Are you young, and your youth your assurance? Job had also been young. Are you old, on the verge of the grave? Job was an old man when sorrow overtook him. Are you powerful, is this your assurance of immunity? Job was reverenced by the people. Are riches your security? Job possessed the blessing of lands. Are your friends your guarantors? Job was loved by everyone. Do you put your confidence in God? Job was the Lord's confidant. Have you reflected on these thoughts, or have you not rather avoided them, so that they might not extort from you a confession, which you now perhaps call a melancholy mood? And yet there is no hiding place in the wide world where troubles may not find you, and there has never lived a man who was able to say more than you can say, that you do not know when sorrow will visit your house. So be sincere with yourself, fix your eyes upon Job; even though he terrifies you, it is not this he wishes, if you yourself do not wish it. You still could not wish, when you survey your life and think of its end, that you should have to confess, "I was fortunate, not like other men; I have never suffered anything in the world, and I have let each day have its own sorrows, or rather bring me new joys." Such a confession, even if it were true, you could still never wish to make, aye, it would involve your own humiliation; for if you had been preserved from sorrow, as no other had, you would still say, "I have indeed not been tested in it, but still my mind has frequently occupied itself seriously with the thought of Job, and with the idea that no man knows the time and the hour when the messengers will come to him, each one more terrifying than the last."

Josiah Royce   (essay date 1898)

SOURCE: "The Problem of Job" in *Studies of Good and Evil: A Series of Essays upon Problems of Philosophy and of Life,* D. Appleton and Company, 1898, pp. 1-28.

[*Royce was an American philosopher whose writings encompass the fields of mathematical logic, psychology, metaphysics, religion, and social ethics. He is noted for developing an idealist philosophy emphasizing individuality and the human will rather than intellect. In the following excerpt from his essay "The Problem of Job" in* Studies of Good and Evil *(1898), he examines the problem of suffering as depicted in* The Book of Job, *employing the tenets of philosophical idealism, by which God may be viewed as an entity that is interconnected with humans rather than as a separate being.*]

In speaking of the problem of Job, the present writer comes to the subject as a layman in theology, and as one ignorant of Hebrew scholarship. In referring to the original core of the Book of Job he follows, in a general way, the advice of Professor C. H. Toy; and concerning the text of the poem he is guided by the translation of Dr. Gilbert. What this paper has to attempt is neither criticism of the book, nor philological exposition of its obscurities, but a brief study of the central problem of the poem from the point of view of a student of philosophy.

The problem of our book is the personal problem of its hero, Job himself. Discarding, for the first, as of possibly separate authorship, the Prologue, the Epilogue and the addresses of Elihu and of the Lord, one may as well come at once to the point of view of Job, as expressed in his speeches to his friends. Here is stated the problem of which none of the later additions in our poem offer any intelligible author develops all his poetical skill, and records thoughts that can never grow old. This is the portion of our book which is most frequently quoted and which best expresses the genuine experience of suffering humanity. Here, then, the philosophical as well as the human interest of our poem centres.

Job's world, as he sees it, is organized in a fashion extremely familiar to us all. The main ideas of this cosmology are easy to be reviewed. The very simplicity of the scheme of the universe here involved serves to bring into clearer view the mystery and horror of the problem that besets Job himself. The world, for Job, is the work of a being who, in the very nature of the case, ought to be intelligible (since he is wise), and friendly to the righteous, since, according to tradition, and by virtue of his divine wisdom itself, this God must know the value of a righteous man. But—here is the mystery—this God, as his works get known through our human experiences of evil, appears to us not friendly, but hopelessly foreign and hostile in his plans and his doings. The more, too, we study his ways with man, the less intelligible seems his nature. Tradition has dwelt upon his righteousness, has called him merciful, has magnified his love towards his servants, has described his justice in bringing to naught the wicked. One has learned to trust all these things, to conceive God in these terms, and to expect all this righteous government from him. Moreover, tradition joins with the pious observation of nature in assuring us of the omnipotence of God. Job himself pathetically insists that he never doubts, for an instant, God's power to do whatever in heaven or earth he may please to do. Nothing hinders God. No blind faith thwarts him. Sheol is naked before him. The abyss has no covering. The earth hangs over chaos because he orders it to do so. His power shatters the monsters and pierces the dragons. He can, then, do with evil precisely what he does with Rahab or with the shades, with the clouds or with the light or with the sea, namely, exactly what he chooses. Moreover, since he knows everything, and since the actual value of a righteous man is, for Job, an unquestionable and objective fact, God cannot fail to know this real worth of righteousness in his servants, as well as the real hatefulness and mischief of the wicked. God knows worth, and cannot be blind to it, since it is as real a fact as heaven and earth themselves.

Yet despite all these unquestioned facts, this God, who can do just what he chooses, "deprives of right" the righteous man, in Job's own case, and "vexes his soul," becomes towards him as a "tyrant," "persecutes" him "with strong hand," "dissolves" him "into storm," makes him a "byword" for outcasts, "casts" him "into the mire," renders him "a brother to jackals," deprives him of the poor joy of his "one day as a hireling," of the little delight that might come to him as a man before he descends hopelessly to the dark world of the shades, "watches over" him by day to oppress, by night to "terrify" him "with dreams and with visions"—in brief, acts as his enemy, "tears" him "in anger," "gnashes upon" him "with his teeth." All these are the expressions of Job himself. On the other hand, as, with equal wonder and horror the righteous Job reports, God on occasion does just the reverse of all this to the notoriously and deliberately wicked, who "grow old," "wax mighty in power," "see their offspring established," and their homes "secure from fear." If one turns from this view of God's especially unjust dealings with righteous and with wicked individuals to a general survey of his providential government of the world, one sees vast processes going on, as ingenious as they are merciless, as full of hints of a majestic wisdom as they are of indifference to every individual right.

> A mountain that falleth is shattered,
> And a rock is removed from its place;
> The waters do wear away stones,
> Its floods sweep the earth's dust away;
> And the hope of frail man thou destroyest.
> Thou subdu'st him for aye, and he goes;
> Marring his face thou rejectest him.

Here is a mere outline of the divine government as Job sees it. To express himself thus is for Job no momentary outburst of passion. Long days and nights he has brooded over these bitter facts of experience, before he has spoken at all. Unweariedly, in presence of his friends' objections, he reiterates his charges. He has the right of the sufferer to speak, and he uses it. He reports the facts that he sees. Of the paradox involved in all this he can make nothing. What is clear to him, however, is that this paradox is a matter for reasoning, not for blind authority. God ought to meet him face to face, and have the matter out in plain words. Job fears not to face his judge, or to demand his answer from God. God knows that Job has done nothing to deserve this fury. The question at issue between maker and creature is therefore one that demands a direct statement and a clear decision. "Why, since you can do precisely as you choose, and since you know, as all-knower, the value of a righteous servant, do you choose, as enemy, to persecute the righteous with this fury and persistence of hate?" Here is the problem.

The human interest of the issue thus so clearly stated by Job lies, of course, in the universality of just such experiences of undeserved ill here upon earth. What Job saw of evil we can see ourselves to-day whenever we choose. Witness Armenia. Witness the tornadoes and the earthquakes. Less interesting to us is the thesis mentioned by Job's friends, in the antiquated form in which they state it, although to be sure, a similar thesis, in altered forms, is prevalent among us still. And of dramatic significance only is the earnestness with which Job defends his own personal righteousness. So naïve a self-assurance as is his is not in accordance with our modern conscience, and it is seldom indeed that our day would see any man sincerely using this phraseology of Job regarding his own consciousness of rectitude. But what is today as fresh and real to us as it was to our poet is the fact that all about us, say every child born with an unearned heredity of misery, or in every pang of the oppressed, or in every arbitrary coming of ill fortune, some form of innocence is beset with an evil that the sufferer has not deserved. Job wins dramatic sympathy as an extreme, but for the purpose all the more typical, case of this universal experience of unearned ill fortune. In every such case we therefore still have the interest

that Job had in demanding the solution of this central problem of evil. Herein, I need not say, lies the permanent significance of the problem of Job—a problem that wholly outlasts any ancient Jewish controversy as to the question whether the divine justice always does or does not act as Job's friends, in their devotion to tradition, declare that it acts. Here, then, is the point where our poem touches a question, not merely of an older religion, but of philosophy, and of all time.

The general problem of evil has received, as is well known, a great deal of attention from the philosophers. Few of them, at least in European thought, have been as fearless in stating the issue as was the original author of Job. The solutions offered have, however, been very numerous. For our purposes they may be reduced to a few.

First, then, one may escape Job's paradox by declining altogether to view the world in teleological terms. Evils, such as death, disease, tempests, enemies, fires, are not, so one may declare, the works of God or of Satan, but are natural phenomena. Natural, too, are the phenomena of our desires, of our pains, sorrows and failures. No divine purpose rules or overrules any of these things. That happens to us, at any time, which must happen, in view of our natural limitations and of our ignorance. The way to better things is to understand nature better than we now do. For this view—a view often maintained in our day—there is no problem of evil, in Job's sense, at all. Evil there indeed is, but the only rational problems are those of natural laws. I need not here further consider this method, not of solving but of abolishing the problem before us, since my intent is, in this paper, to suggest the possibility of some genuinely teleological answer to Job's question. I mention this first view only to recognize, historically, its existence.

In the second place, one may deal with our problem by attempting any one, or a number, of those familiar and popular compromises between the belief in a world of natural law and the belief in a teleological order, which are all, as compromises, reducible to the assertion that the presence of evil in the creation is a relatively insignificant, and an inevitable, incident of a plan that produces sentient creatures subject to law. Writers who expound such compromises have to point out that, since a burnt child dreads the fire, pain is, on the whole, useful as a warning. Evil is a transient discipline, whereby finite creatures learn their place in the system of things. Again, a sentient world cannot get on without some experience of suffering, since sentience means tenderness. Take away pain (so one still again often insists), take away pain, and we should not learn our share of natural truth. Pain is the pedagogue to teach us natural science. The contagious diseases, for instance, are useful in so far as they lead us in the end to study Bacteriology, and thus to get an insight into the life of certain beautiful creatures of God whose presence in the world we should otherwise blindly overlook! Moreover (to pass to still another variation of this sort of explanation), created beings obviously grow from less to more. First the lower, then the higher. Otherwise there could be no Evolution. And were there no evolution, how much of edifying natural science we should miss! But if one is evolved, if one grows from less to more, there must be something to mark the stages of growth. Now evil is useful to mark the lower stages of evolution. If you are to be, first an infant, then a man, or first a savage, then a civilized being, there must be evils attendant upon the earlier stages of your life— evils that make growth welcome and conscious. Thus, were there no colic and croup, were there no tumbles and crying-spells in infancy, there would be no sufficient incentives to loving parents to hasten the growing robustness of their children, and no motives to impel the children to long to grow big! Just so, cannibalism is valuable as a mark of a lower grade of evolution. Had there been no cannibalism we should realize less joyously than we do what a respectable thing it is to have become civilized! In brief, evil is, as it were, the dirt of the natural order, whose value is that, when you wash it off, you thereby learn the charm of the bath of evolution.

The foregoing are mere hints of familiar methods of playing about the edges of our problem, as children play barefoot in the shallowest reaches of the foam of the sea. In our poem, as Professor Toy expounds it, the speeches ascribed to Elihu contain the most hints of some such way of defining evil, as a merely transient incident of the discipline of the individual. With many writers explanations of this sort fill much space. They are even not without their proper place in popular discussion. But they have no interest for whoever has once come into the presence of Job's problem as it is in itself. A moment's thought reminds us of their superficiality. Pain is useful as a warning of danger. If we did not suffer, we should burn our hands off. Yes, but this explanation of one evil presupposes another, and a still unexplained and greater evil, namely, the existence of the danger of which we need to be thus warned. No doubt it is well that the past sufferings of the Armenians should teach the survivors, say the defenseless women and children, to have a wholesome fear in future of Turks. Does that explain, however, the need for the existence, or for the murderous doings of the Turks? If I can only reach a given goal by passing over a given road, say of evolution, it may be well for me to consent to the toilsome journey. Does that explain why I was created so far from my goal? Discipline, toil, penalty, surgery, are all explicable as means to ends, if only it be presupposed that there exists, and that there is quite otherwise explicable, the necessity for the situations which involve such fearful expenses. One justifies the surgery, but not the disease; the toil, but not the existence of the need for the toil; the penalty, but not the situation which has made the penalty necessary, when one points out that evil is in so many cases medicinal or disciplinary or prophylactic—an incident of imperfect stages of evolution, or the price of a distant good attained through misery. All such explanations, I insist, trade upon borrowed capital. But God, by hypothesis, is no borrower. He produces his own capital of ends and means. Every evil is explained on the foregoing plan only by presupposing at least an equal, and often a greater and a preëxistent evil, namely, the very state of things which renders the first evil the only physically possible way of reaching a given goal. But what Job wants his judge to explain is not that evil A is a physical means of warding off some other greater evil B, in this cruel world where the waters wear away even the stones, and where hopes of man are so much frailer than the stones; but why a God

who can do whatever he wishes chooses situations where such a heaped-up mass of evil means become what we should call physical necessities to the ends now physically possible.

No real explanation of the presence of evil can succeed which declares evil to be a merely physical necessity for one who desires, in this present world, to reach a given goal. Job's business is not with physical accidents, but with the God who chose to make this present nature; and an answer to Job must show that evil is not a physical but a logical necessity—something whose nor-existence would simply contradict the very essence, the very perfection of God's own nature and power. This talk of medicinal and disciplinary evil, perfectly fair when applied to our poor fate-bound human surgeons, judges, jailors, or teachers, becomes cruelly, even cynically trivial when applied to explain the ways of a God who is to choose, not only the physical means to an end, but the very *Physis* itself in which path and goal are to exist together. I confess, as a layman, that whenever, at a funeral, in the company of mourners who are immediately facing Job's own personal problem, and who are sometimes, to say the least, wide enough awake to desire not to be stayed with relative comforts, but to ask that terrible and uttermost question of God himself, and to require the direct answer—that whenever, I say, in such company I have to listen to these half-way answers, to these superficial plashes in the wavelets at the water's edge of sorrow, while the black, unfathomed ocean of finite evil spreads out before our wide-opened eyes—well, at such times this trivial speech about useful burns and salutary medicines makes me, and I fancy others, simply and wearily heartsick. Some words are due to children at school, to peevish patients in the sickroom who need a little temporary quieting. But quite other speech is due to men and women when they are wakened to the higher reason of Job by the fierce anguish of our mortal life's ultimate facts. They deserve either our simple silence, or, if we are ready to speak, the speech of people who our selves inquire as Job inquired.

A third method of dealing with our problem is in essence identical with the course which, in a very antiquated form, the friends of Job adopt. This method takes its best known expression in the doctrine that the presence of evil in the world is explained by the fact that the value of free will in moral agents logically involves, and so explains and justifies, the divine permission of the evil deeds of those finite beings who freely choose to sin, as well as the inevitable fruits of the sins. God creates agents with free will. He does so because the existence of such agents has of itself an infinite worth. Were there no free agents, the highest good could not be. But such agents, because they are free, can offend. The divine justice of necessity pursues such offenses with attendant evils. These evils, the result of sin, must, logically speaking, be permitted to exist, if God once creates the agents who have free will, and himself remains, as he must logically do, a just God. How much ill thus results depends upon the choice of the free agents, not upon God, who wills to have only good chosen, but of necessity must leave his free creatures to their own devices, so far as concerns their power to sin.

This view has the advantage of undertaking to regard evil as a logically necessary part of a perfect moral order, and not as a mere incident of an imperfectly adjusted physical mechanism. So dignified a doctrine, by virtue of its long history and its high theological reputation, needs here no extended exposition. I assume it as familiar, and pass at once to its difficulties. It has its share of truth. There is, I doubt not, moral free will in the universe. But the presence of evil in the world simply cannot be explained by free will alone. This is easy to show. One who maintains this view asserts, in substance, "All real evils are the results of the acts of free and finite moral agents." These agents may be angels or men. If there is evil in the city, the Lord has *not* done it, except in so far as his justice has acted in readjusting wrongs already done. Such ill is due to the deeds of his creatures. But hereupon one asks at once, in presence of any ill, "Who did this?" Job's friends answer: "The sufferer himself; his deed wrought his own undoing. God punishes only the sinner. Every one suffers for his own wrongdoing. Your ill is the result of your crime."

But Job, and all his defenders of innocence, must at once reply: "Empirically speaking, this is obviously, in our visible world, simply not true. The sufferer may suffer innocently. The ill is often undeserved. The fathers sin; the child, diseased from birth, degraded, or a born wretch, may pay the penalty. The Turk or the active rebel sins. Armenia's helpless women and babes cry in vain unto God for help."

Hereupon the reply comes, although not indeed from Job's friends: "Alas! it is so. Sin means suffering; but the innocent may suffer *for* the guilty. This, to be sure, is God's way. One cannot help it. It is so." But therewith the whole effort to explain evil as a logically necessary result of free will and of divine justice alone is simply abandoned. The unearned ills are not justly due to the free will that indeed partly caused them, but to God who declines to protect the innocent. God owes the Turk and the rebel their due. He also owes to his innocent creatures, the babes and the women, his shelter. He owes to the sinning father his penalty, but to the son, born in our visible world a lost soul from the womb, God owes the shelter of his almighty wing, and no penalty. Thus Job's cry is once more in place. The ways of God are not thus justified.

But the partisan of free will as the true explanation of ill may reiterate his view in a new form. He may insist that we see but a fragment. Perhaps the soul born here as if lost, or the wretch doomed to pangs now unearned, sinned of old, in some previous state of existence. Perhaps Karma is to blame. You expiate to-day the sins of your own former existences. Thus the Hindoos varied the theme of our familiar doctrine. This is what Hindoo friends might have said to Job. Well, admit even that, if you like; and what then follows? Admit that here or in former ages the free deed of every present sufferer earned as its penalty every ill, physical or moral, that appears as besetting just this sufferer to-day. Admit that, and what logically follows? It follows, so I must insist, that the moral world itself, which this free-will theory of the source of evil, thus abstractly

stated, was to save, is destroyed in its very heart and centre.

For consider. A suffers ill. B sees A suffering. Can B, the onlooker, help his suffering neighbor, A? Can he comfort him in any true way? No, a miserable comforter must B prove, like Job's friends, so long as B, believing in our present hypothesis, clings strictly to the logic of this abstract free-will explanation of the origin of evil. To A he says: "Well, you suffer for your own ill-doing. I therefore simply cannot relieve you. This is God's world of justice. If I tried to hinder God's justice from working in your case, I should at best only postpone your evil day. It would come, for God is just. You are hungry, thirsty, naked, sick, in prison. What can I do about it? All this is your own deed come back to you. God himself, although justly punishing, is not the author of this evil. You are the sole originator of the ill." "Ah!" so A may cry out, "but can you not give me light, insight, instruction, sympathy? Can you not at least teach me to become good?" "No," B must reply, if he is a logical believer in the sole efficacy of the private free will of each finite agent as the one source, under the divine justice, of that agent's ill: "No, if you deserved light or any other comfort, God, being just, would enlighten you himself, even if I absolutely refused. But if you do not deserve light, I should preach to you in vain, for God's justice would harden your heart against any such good fortune as I could offer you from without, even if I spoke with the tongues of men and of angels. Your free will is yours. No deed of mine could give you a good free will, for what I gave you from without would not be *your* free will at all. Nor can any one but you cause your free will to be this or that. A great gulf is fixed between us. You and I, as sovereign free agents, live in God's holy world in sin-tight compartments and in evil-tight compartments too. I cannot hurt you, nor you me. You are damned for your own sins, while all that I can do is to look out for my own salvation." This, I say, is the logically inevitable result of asserting that every ill, physical or moral, that can happen to any agent, is solely the result of that agent's own free will acting under the government of the divine justice. The only possible consequence would indeed be that we live, every soul of us, in separate, as it were absolutely fire-proof, free-will compartments, so that real coöperation as to good and ill is excluded. What more cynical denial of the reality of any sort of moral world could be imagined than is involved in this horrible thesis, which no sane partisan of the abstract and traditional free-will explanation of the source of evil will to-day maintain, precisely because no such partisan really knows or can know what his doctrine logically means, while still continuing to maintain it. Yet whenever one asserts with pious obscurity, that "No harm can come to the righteous," one in fact implies, with logical necessity, just this cynical consequence.

There remains a fourth doctrine as to our problem. This doctrine is in essence the thesis of philosophical idealism, a thesis which I myself feel bound to maintain, and, so far as space here permits, to explain. The theoretical basis of this view, the philosophical reasons for the notion of the divine nature which it implies, I cannot here explain. That is another argument. But I desire to indicate how the view in question deals with Job's problem.

This view first frankly admits that Job's problem is, upon Job's presuppositions, simply and absolutely insoluble. Grant Job's own presupposition that God is a being other than this world, that he is its external creator and ruler, and then all solutions fail. God is then either cruel or helpless, as regards all real finite ill of the sort that Job endures. Job, moreover, is right in demanding a reasonable answer to his question. The only possible answer is, however, one that undertakes to develop what I hold to be the immortal soul of the doctrine of the divine atonement. The answer to Job is: God is not in ultimate essence another being than yourself. He is the Absolute Being. You truly are one with God, part of his life. He is the very soul of your soul. And so, here is the first truth: When you suffer, *your sufferings are God's sufferings,* not his external work, not his external penalty, not the fruit of his neglect, but identically his own personal woe. In you God himself suffers, precisely as you do, and has all your concern in overcoming this grief.

The true question then is: Why does God thus suffer? The sole possible, necessary, and sufficient answer is, Because without suffering, without ill, without woe, evil, tragedy, God's life could not be perfected. This grief is not a physical means to an external end. It is a logically necessary and eternal constituent of the divine life. It is logically necessary that the Captain of your salvation should be perfect through suffering. No outer nature compels him. He chooses this because he chooses his own perfect selfhood. He is perfect. His world is the best possible world. Yet all its finite regions know not only of joy but of defeat and sorrow, for thus alone, in the completeness of his eternity, can God in his wholeness be triumphantly perfect.

This, I say, is my thesis. In the absolute oneness of God with the sufferer, in the concept of the suffering and therefore triumphant God, lies the logical solution of the problem of evil. The doctrine of philosophical idealism is, as regards its purely theoretical aspects, a fairly familiar metaphysical theory at the present time. One may, then, presuppose here as known the fact that, for reasons which I have not now to expound, the idealist maintains that there is in the universe but one perfectly real being, namely, the Absolute, that the Absolute is self-conscious, and that his world is essentially in its wholeness the fulfillment *in actu* of an all-perfect ideal. We ourselves exist as fragments of the absolute life, or better, as partial functions in the unity of the absolute and conscious process of the world. On the other hand, our existence and our individuality are not illusory, but are what they are in an organic unity with the whole life of the Absolute Being. This doctrine once presupposed, our present task is to inquire what case idealism can make for the thesis just indicated as its answer to Job's problem.

In endeavoring to grapple with the theoretical problem of the place of evil in a world that, on the whole, is to be conceived, not only as good, but as perfect, there is happily one essentially decisive consideration concerning good and evil which falls directly within the scope of our own human experience, and which concerns matters at once familiar and momentous as well as too much neglected in philosophy. When we use such words as good, evil, perfect, we easily deceive ourselves by the merely abstract

meanings which we associate with each of the terms taken apart from the other. We forget the experiences from which the words have been abstracted. To these experiences we must return whenever we want really to comprehend the words. If we take the mere words, in their abstraction, it is easy to say, for instance, that if life has any evil in it at all, it must needs not be so perfect as life would be were there no evil in it whatever. Just so, speaking abstractly, it is easy to say that, in estimating life, one has to set the good over against the evil, and to compare their respective sums. It is easy to declare that, since we hate evil, wherever and just so far as we recognize it, our sole human interest in the world must be furthered by the removal of evil from the world. And thus viewing the case, one readily comes to say that if God views as not only good but perfect a world in which we find so much evil, the divine point of view must be very foreign to ours, so that Job's rebellious pessimism seems well in order, and Prometheus appears to defy the world-ruler in a genuinely humane spirit. Shocked, however, by the apparent impiety of this result, some teachers, considering divine matters, still misled by the same one-sided use of words, have opposed one falsely abstract view by another, and have strangely asserted that the solution must be in proclaiming that since God's world, the real world, in order to be perfect, must be without evil, what we men call evil must be a mere illusion—a mirage of the human point of view—a dark vision which God, who sees all truth, sees not at all. To God, so this view asserts, the eternal world in its wholeness is not only perfect, but has merely the perfection of an utterly transparent crystal, unstained by any color of ill. Only mortal error imagines that there is any evil. There is no evil but only good in the real world, and that is why God finds the world perfect, whatever mortals dream.

Now neither of these abstract views is my view. I consider them both the result of a thoughtless trust in abstract words. I regard evil as a distinctly real fact, a fact just as real as the most helpless and hopeless sufferer finds it to be when he is in pain. Furthermore, I hold that God's point of view is not foreign to ours. I hold that God willingly, freely, and consciously suffers in us when we suffer, and that our grief is his. And despite all this I maintain that the world from God's point of view fulfills the divine ideal and is perfect. And I hold that when we abandon the one-sided abstract ideas which the words good, evil, and perfect suggest, and when we go back to the concrete experiences upon which these very words are founded, we can see, even within the limits of our own experience, facts which make these very paradoxes perfectly intelligible, and even commonplace.

As for that essentially pernicious view, nowadays somewhat current amongst a certain class of gentle but inconsequent people—the view that all evil is *merely* an illusion and that there is no such thing in God's world—I can say of it only in passing that it is often advanced as an idealistic view, but that, in my opinion, it is false idealism. Good idealism it is to regard all finite experience as an appearance, a hint, often a very poor hint, of deeper truth. Good idealism it is to admit that man can err about truth that lies beyond his finite range of experience. And very good idealism it is to assert that all truth, and so all finite experience, exists in and for the mind of God, and nowhere outside of or apart from God. But it is not good idealism to assert that any facts which fall within the range of finite experience are, even while they are experienced, mere illusions. God's truth is inclusive, not exclusive. What you experience God experiences. The difference lies only in this, that God sees in unity what you see in fragments. For the rest, if one said, "The source and seat of evil is only the error of mortal mind," one would but have changed the name of one's problem. If the evil were but the error, the error would still be the evil, and altering the name would not have diminished the horror of the evil of this finite world.

But I hasten from the false idealism to the true; from the abstractions to the enlightening insights of our life. As a fact, idealism does not say: The finite world is, as such, a mere illusion. A sound idealism says, whatever we experience is a fragment, and, as far as it goes, a genuine fragment of the truth of the divine mind. With this principle before us, let us consider directly our own experiences of good and of evil, to see whether they are as abstractly opposed to each other as the mere words often suggest. We must begin with the elementary and even trivial facts. We shall soon come to something deeper.

By good, as we mortals experience it, we mean something that, when it comes or is expected, we actively welcome, try to attain or keep, and regard with content. By evil in general, as it is in our experience, we mean whatever we find in any sense repugnant and intolerable. I use the words repugnant and intolerable because I wish to indicate that words for evil frequently, like the words for good, directly refer to our actions as such. Commonly and rightly, when we speak of evil, we make reference to acts of resistance, of struggle, of shrinking, of flight, of removal of ourselves from a source of mischief—acts which not only follow upon the experience of evil, but which serve to define in a useful fashion what we mean by evil. The opposing acts of pursuit and of welcome define what we mean by good. By the evil which we experience we mean precisely whatever we regard as something to be gotten rid of, shrunken from, put out of sight, of hearing, or of memory, eschewed, expelled, assailed, or otherwise directly or indirectly resisted. By good we mean whatever we regard as something to be welcomed, pursued, won, grasped, held, persisted in, preserved. And we show all this in our acts in presence of any grade of good or evil, sensuous, aesthetic, ideal, moral. To shun, to flee, to resist, to destroy, these are our primary attitudes towards ill; the opposing acts are our primary attitudes towards the good; and whether you regard us as animals or as moralists, whether it is a sweet taste, a poem, a virtue, or God that we look to as good, and whether it is a burn or a temptation, an outward physical foe, or a stealthy, inward, ideal enemy, that we regard as evil. In all our organs of voluntary movement, in all our deeds, in a turn of the eye, in a sigh, a groan, in a hostile gesture, in an act of silent contempt, we can show in endlessly varied ways the same general attitude of repugnance.

But man is a very complex creature. He has many organs.

He performs many acts at once, and he experiences his performance of these acts in one highly complex life of consciousness. As the next feature of his life we all observe that he can at the same time shun one object and grasp at another. In this way he can have at once present to him a consciousness of good and a consciousness of ill. But so far in our account these sorts of experience appear merely as facts side by side. Man loves, and he *also* hates, loves this, and hates that, assumes an attitude of repugnance towards one object, while he welcomes another. So far the usual theory follows man's life, and calls it an experience of good and ill as mingled but exclusively and abstractly opposed facts. For such a view the final question as to the worth of a man's life is merely the question whether there are more intense acts of satisfaction and of welcome than of repugnance and disdain in his conscious life.

But this is by no means an adequate notion of the complexity of man's life, even as an animal. If every conscious act of hindrance, of thwarting, of repugnance, means just in so far an awareness of some evil, it is noteworthy that men can have and can show just such tendencies, not only towards external experiences, but towards their own acts. That is, men can be seen trying to thwart and to hinder even their own acts themselves, at the very moment when they note the occurrence of these acts. One can consciously have an impulse to do something, and at that very moment a conscious disposition to hinder or to thwart as an evil that very impulse. If, on the other hand, every conscious act of attainment, of pursuit, of reinforcement, involves the awareness of some good, it is equally obvious that one can show by one's acts a disposition to reinforce or to emphasize or to increase, not only the externally present gifts of fortune, but also one's own deeds, in so far as one observes them. And in our complex lives it is common enough to find ourselves actually trying to reinforce and to insist upon a situation which involves for us, even at the moment of its occurrence, a great deal of repugnance. In such cases we often act as if we felt the very thwarting of our own primary impulses to be so much of a conscious good that we persist in pursuing and reinforcing the very situation in which this thwarting and hindering of our own impulses is sure to arise.

In brief, as phenomena of this kind show, man is a being who can to a very great extent find a sort of secondary satisfaction in the very act of thwarting his own desires, and thus of assuring for the time his own dissatisfactions. On the other hand, man can to an indefinite degree find himself dissatisfied with his satisfactions and disposed to thwart, not merely his external enemies, but his own inmost impulses themselves. But I now affirm that in all such cases you cannot simply say that man is preferring the less of two evils, or the greater of two goods, as if the good and the evil stood merely side by side in his experience. On the contrary, in such cases, man is not merely setting his acts or his estimates of good and evil side by side and taking the sum of each; but he is making his own relatively primary acts, impulses, desires, the objects of all sorts of secondary impulses, desires, and reflective observations. His whole inner state is one of tension: and he is either making a secondary experience of evil out of his estimate of a primary experience of good, as is the case when he at once finds himself disposed to pursue a given good and to thwart this pursuit as being an evil pursuit; or else he is making a secondary experience of good out of his primary experience of evil, as when he is primarily dissatisfied with his situation, but yet secondarily regards this very dissatisfaction as itself a desirable state. In this way man comes not only to love some things and also to hate other things, he comes to love his own hates and to hate his own loves in an endlessly complex hierarchy of superposed interests in his own interests.

Now it is easy to say that such states of inner tension, where our conscious lives are full of a warfare of the self with itself, are contradictory or absurd states. But it is easy to say this only when you dwell on the words and fail to observe the facts of experience. As a fact, not only our lowest but our highest states of activity are the ones which are fullest of this crossing, conflict, and complex interrelation of loves and hates, of attractions and repugnances. As a merely physiological fact, we begin no muscular act without at the same time initiating acts which involve the innervation of opposing sets of muscles, and these opposing sets of muscles hinder each other's freedom. Every sort of control of movement means the conflicting play of opposed muscular impulses. We do nothing simple, and we will no complex act without willing what involves a certain measure of opposition between the impulses or partial acts which go to make up the whole act. If one passes from single acts to long series of acts, one finds only the more obviously this interweaving of repugnance and of acceptance, of pursuit and of flight, upon which every complex type of conduct depends.

One could easily at this point spend time by dwelling upon numerous and relatively trivial instances of this interweaving of conflicting motives as it appears in all our life. I prefer to pass such instances over with a mere mention. There is, for instance, the whole marvelous consciousness of play, in its benign and in its evil forms. In any game that fascinates, one loves victory and shuns defeat, and yet as a loyal supporter of the game scorns anything that makes victory certain in advance; thus as a lover of fair play preferring to risk the defeat that he all the while shuns, and partly thwarting the very love of victory that from moment to moment fires his hopes. There are, again, the numerous cases in which we prefer to go to places where we are sure to be in a considerable measure dissatisfied; to engage, for instance, in social functions that absorbingly fascinate us despite or even in view of the very fact that, as long as they continue, they keep us in a state of tension which makes us, amongst other things, long to have the whole occasion over. Taking a wider view, one may observe that the greater part of the freest products of the activity of civilization, in ceremonies, in formalities, in the long social drama of flight, of pursuit, of repartee, of contest and of courtesy, involve an elaborate and systematic delaying and hindering of elemental human desires, which we continually outwit, postpone and thwart, even while we nourish them. When students of human nature assert that hunger and love rule the social world, they recognize that the elemental in human nature is trained by civilization into the service of the highest demands of the Spirit. But such students have to recognize that the elemental

rules the higher world only in so far as the elemental is not only cultivated, but endlessly thwarted, delayed, outwitted, like a constitutional monarch, who is said to be a sovereign, but who, while he rules, must not govern.

But I pass from such instances, which in all their universality are still, I admit, philosophically speaking, trivial, because they depend upon the accidents of human nature. I pass from these instances to point out what must be the law, not only of human nature, but of every broader form of life as well. I maintain that this organization of life by virtue of the tension of manifold impulses and interests is not a mere accident of our imperfect human nature, but must be a type of the organization of every rational life. There are good and bad states of tension, there are conflicts that can only be justified when resolved into some higher form of harmony. But I insist that, in general, the only harmony that can exist in the realm of the spirit is the harmony that we possess when we thwart the present but more elemental impulse for the sake of the higher unity of experience; as when we rejoice in the endurance of the tragedies of life, because they show us the depth of life, or when we know that it is better to have loved and lost than never to have loved at all, or when we possess a virtue in the moment of victory over the tempter. And the reason why this is true lies in the fact that the more one's experience fulfills ideals, the more that experience presents to one, not of ignorance, but of triumphantly wealthy acquaintance with the facts of manifold, varied and tragic life, full of tension and thereby of unity. Now this is an universal and not merely human law. It is not those innocent of evil who are fullest of the life of God, but those who in their own case have experienced the triumph over evil. It is not those naturally ignorant of fear, or those who, like Siegfried, have never shivered, who possess the genuine experience of courage; but the brave are those who have fears, but control their fears. Such know the genuine virtues of the hero. Were it otherwise, only the stupid could be perfect heroes.

To be sure it is quite false to say, as the foolish do, that the object of life is merely that we may "know life" as an irrational chaos of experiences of good and of evil. But knowing the good in life is a matter which concerns the form, rather than the mere content of life. One who knows life wisely knows indeed much of the content of life; but he knows the good of life in so far as, in the unity of his experience, he finds the evil of his experience not abolished, but subordinated, and in so far relatively thwarted by a control which annuls its triumph even while experiencing its existence.

Generalizing the lesson of experience we may then say: It is logically impossible that a complete knower of truth should fail to know, to experience, to have present to his insight, the fact of actually existing evil. On the other hand, it is equally impossible for one to know a higher good than comes from the subordination of evil to good in a total experience. When one first loving, in an elemental way, whatever you please, himself hinders, delays, thwarts his elemental interest in the interest of some larger whole of experience, he not only knows more fact, but he possesses a higher good than would or could be present to one who was aware neither of the elemental impulse, nor of the thwarting of it in the tension of a richer life. The knowing of the good, in the higher sense, depends upon contemplating the overcoming and subordination of a less significant impulse, which survives even in order that it should be subordinated. Now this law, this form of the knowledge of the good, applies as well to the existence of moral as to that of sensuous ill. If moral evil were simply destroyed and wiped away from the external world, the knowledge of moral goodness would also be destroyed. For the love of moral good is the thwarting of lower loves for the sake of the higher organization. What is needed, then, for the definition of the divine knowledge of a world that in its wholeness is perfect, is not a divine knowledge that shall ignore, wipe out and utterly make naught the existence of any ill, whether physical or moral, but a divine knowledge to which shall be present that love of the world as a whole which is fulfilled in the endurance of physical ill, in the subordination of moral ill, in the thwarting of impulses which survive even when subordinated, in the acceptance of repugnances which are still eternal, in the triumph over an enemy that endures even through its eternal defeat, and in the discovery that the endless tension of the finite world is included in the contemplative consciousness of the repose and harmony of eternity. To view God's nature thus is to view his nature as the whole idealistic theory views him, not as the Infinite One beyond the finite imperfections, but as the being whose unity determines the very constitution, the lack, the tension, and relative disharmony of the finite world.

The existence of evil, then, is not only consistent with the perfection of the universe, but is necessary for the very existence of that perfection. This is what we see when we no longer permit ourselves to be deceived by the abstract meanings of the words good and evil into thinking that these two opponents exist merely as mutually exclusive facts side by side in experience, but when we go back to the facts of life and perceive that all relatively higher good, in the trivial as in the more truly spiritual realm, is known only in so far as, from some higher reflective point of view, we accept as good the thwarting of an existent interest that is even thereby declared to be a relative ill, and love a tension of various impulses which even thereby involves, as the object of our love, the existence of what gives us aversion or grief. Now if the love of God is more inclusive than the love of man, even as the divine world of experience is richer than the human world, we can simply set no human limit to the intensity of conflict, to the tragedies of existence, to the pangs of finitude, to the degree of moral ill, which in the end is included in the life that God not only loves, but finds the fulfillment of the perfect ideal. If peace means satisfaction, acceptance of the whole of an experience as good, and if even we, in our weakness, can frequently find rest in the very presence of conflict and of tension, in the very endurance of ill in a good cause, in the hero's triumph over temptation, or in the mourner's tearless refusal to accept the lower comforts of forgetfulness, or to wish that the lost one's preciousness had been less painfully revealed by death—well, if even we know our little share of this harmony in the midst of the wrecks and disorders of life, what limit shall we set to the divine power

to face this world of his own sorrows, and to find peace in the victory over all its ills.

But in this last expression I have pronounced the word that serves to link this theory as to the place of evil in a good world with the practical problem of every sufferer. Job's rebellion came from the thought that God, as a sovereign, is far off, and that, for his pleasure, his creature suffers. Our own theory comes to the mourner with the assurance: "Your suffering, just as it is in you, is God's suffering. No chasm divides you from God. He is not remote from you even in his eternity. He is here. His eternity means merely the completeness of his experience. But that completeness is inclusive. Your sorrow is one of the included facts." I do not say: "God sympathizes with you from without, would spare you if he could, pities you with helpless external pity merely as a father pities his children." I say: "God here sorrows, not with but in your sorrow. Your grief is identically his grief, and what you know as your loss, God knows as his loss, just in and through the very moment when you grieve."

But hereupon the sufferer perchance responds: "If this is God's loss, could he not have prevented it? To him are present in unity all the worlds; and yet he must lack just this for which I grieve." I respond: "He suffers here that he may triumph. For the triumph of the wise is no easy thing. Their lives are not light, but sorrowful. Yet they rejoice in their sorrow, not, to be sure, because it is mere experience, but because, for them, it becomes part of a strenuous whole of life. They wander and find their home even in wandering. They long, and attain through their very love of longing. Peace they find in triumphant warfare. Contentment they have most of all in endurance. Sovereignty they win in endless service. The eternal world contains Gethsemane."

Yet the mourner may still insist: "If my sorrow is God's, his triumph is not mine. Mine is the woe. His is the peace." But my theory is a philosophy. It proposes to be coherent. I must persist: "It is your fault that you are thus sundered from God's triumph. His experience in its wholeness cannot now be yours, for you just as you—this individual—are now but a fragment, and see his truth as through a glass darkly. But if you see his truth at all, through even the dimmest light of a glimmering reason, remember, that truth is in fact your own truth, your own fulfillment, the whole from which your life cannot be divorced, the reality that you mean even when you most doubt, the desire of your heart even when you are most blind, the perfection that you unconsciously strove for even when you were an infant, the complete Self apart from whom you mean nothing, the very life that gives your life the only value which it can have. In thought, if not in the fulfillment of thought, in aim if not in attainment of aim, in aspiration if not in the presence of the revealed fact, you can view God's triumph and peace as your triumph and peace. Your defeat will be no less real than it is, nor will you falsely call your evil a mere illusion. But you will see not only the grief but the truth, your truth, your rescue, your triumph."

Well, to what ill-fortune does not just such reasoning apply? I insist: our conclusion is essentially universal. It discounts any evil that experience may contain. All the horrors of the natural order, all the concealments of the divine plan by our natural ignorance, find their general relation to the unity of the divine experience indicated in advance by this account of the problem of evil.

"Yes," one may continue, "ill-fortune you have discovered, but how about moral evil? What if the sinner now triumphantly retorts: 'Aha! So my will is God's will. All then is well with me.' " I reply: What I have said disposes of moral ill precisely as definitely as of physical ill. What the evil will is to the good man, whose goodness depends upon its existence, but also upon the thwarting and the condemnation of its aim, just such is the sinner's will to the divine plan. God's will, we say to the sinner is your will. Yes, but it is your will thwarted, scorned, overcome, defeated. In the eternal world you are seen, possessed, present, but your damnation is also seen including and thwarting you. Your apparent victory in this world stands simply for the vigor of your impulses. God wills you not to triumph. And that is the use of you in the world—the use of evil generally—to be hated but endured, to be triumphed over through the very fact of your presence, to be willed down even in the very life of which you are a part.

Eleonore Stump on the perspective of St. Thomas Aquinas (1225-1274) on *The Book of Job*:

[We] take the attitude we do toward *Job* because of the values and worldview we bring to the book. Because *we* assume, unreflectively, that temporal well-being is a necessary constituent of happiness (or even the whole of it), we also suppose that Job's losses undermine or destroy his happiness. Consequently, we wonder how God could count as good if he allowed these things to happen to a good person such as Job, or we take stories of undeserved suffering to constitute evidence for thinking there is no God. Aquinas, on the other hand [in his *Expositio super Job*], begins with the conviction that neither God's goodness nor his existence are in doubt, either for the characters in the story of *Job* or for the readers of that story. Therefore, on his view, those who go astray in considering sufferings such as Job's do so because, like Job's comforters, they mistakenly suppose that happiness and unhappiness are functions just of things in this life. And so Aquinas takes the book of *Job* to be trying to instill in us the conviction that there is another life after this one, that our happiness lies there rather than here, and that we attain to that happiness only through suffering. On Aquinas's view, Job has more suffering than ordinary people not because he is morally worse than ordinary, as the comforters assume, but just because he is better. Because he is a better soldier in the war against his own evil and a better servant of God's, God can give him more to bear here; and when this period of earthly life is over, his glory will also be surpassing.

Eleonore Stump in Reasoned Faith: Essays in Philosophical Theology in honor of Norman Kretzmann, *Cornell University Press, 1993.*

But to the serious moral agent we say: What you mean when you say that evil in this temporal world ought not to exist, and ought to be suppressed, is simply what God means by seeing that evil ought to be and is endlessly thwarted, endured, but subordinated. In the natural world you are the minister of God's triumph. Your deed is his. You can never clean the world of evil; but you can subordinate evil. The justification of the presence in the world of the morally evil becomes apparent to us mortals only in so far as this evil is overcome and condemned. It exists only that it may be cast down. Courage, then, for God works in you. In the order of time you embody in outer acts what is for him the truth of his eternity.

A. B. Davidson and C. H. Toy　(essay date 1911)

SOURCE: "Job," in *The Voice out of the Whirlwind: The Book of Job,* edited by Ralph E. Hone, Chandler Publishing Company, Inc., 1960, pp. 87-103.

[*Davidson was editor of* The Book of Job *for the Cambridge Bible for Schools and Colleges, and Toy was a distinguished American scholar of Hebrew. In the following essay, originally published as "Job" in the* Encyclopaedia Britannica, *Eleventh Edition (1911), the authors outline the progression of events in* The Book of Job, *commenting: "Two threads . . . run through the book—one the discussion of the problem of evil between Job and his friends, and the other the varying attitude of Job's mind towards God. . . ." The authors also consider various theories concerning the book's origin.*]

[*The Book of Job*], in the Bible, the most splendid creation of Hebrew poetry, is so called from the name of the man whose history and afflictions and sayings form the theme of it.

As it now lies before us it consists of five parts. 1. The prologue, in prose, ch. i.—ii., describes in rapid and dramatic steps the history of this man, his prosperity and greatness corresponding to his godliness; then how his life is drawn in under the operation of the sifting providence of God, through the suspicion suggested by the Satan, the minister of this aspect of God's providence, that his godliness is selfish and only the natural return for unexampled prosperity, and the insinuation that if stripped of his prosperity he will curse God to His face. These suspicions bring down two severe calamities on Job, one depriving him of children and possessions alike, and the other throwing the man himself under a painful malady. In spite of these afflictions Job retains his integrity and ascribes no wrong to God. Then is described the advent of Job's three friends— Eliphaz the Temanite, Bildad the Shuhite, and Zophar the Naamathite who, having heard of Job's calamities, come to condole with him. 2. The body of the book, in poetry, ch. iii.-xxxi., contains a series of speeches in which the problem of Job's afflictions and the relation of external evil to the righteousness of God and the conduct of men are brilliantly discussed. This part, after Job's passionate outburst in ch. iii., is divided into three cycles, each containing six speeches, one by each of the friends, and three by Job, one in reply to each of theirs (ch. iv.-xiv.; xv.-xxi.;

xxii.-xxxi.), although in the last cycle the third speaker Zophar fails to answer (unless his answer is to be found in ch. xxvii.). Job, having driven his opponents from the field, carries his reply through a series of discourses in which he dwells in pathetic words upon his early prosperity, contrasting with it his present humiliation, and ends with a solemn repudiation of all the offences that might be suggested against him, and a challenge to God to appear and put His hand to the charge which He had against him and for which He afflicted him. 3. Elihu, the representative of a younger generation, who has been a silent observer of the debate, intervenes to express his dissatisfaction with the manner in which both Job and his friends conducted the cause, and offers what is in some respects a new solution of the question (xxxii.-xxxvii.) 4. In answer to Job's repeated demands that God would appear and solve the riddle of his life, the Lord answers Job out of the whirlwind. The divine speaker does not condescend to refer to Job's individual problem, but in a series of ironical interrogations asks him, as he thinks himself capable of fathoming all things, to expound the mysteries of the origin and subsistence of the world, the phenomena of the atmosphere, the instincts of the creatures that inhabit the desert, and, as he judges God's conduct of the world amiss, invites him to seize the reins, gird himself with the thunder and quell the rebellious forces of evil in the universe (xxxviii.-xlii.6). Job is humbled and abashed, lays his hand upon his mouth, and repents his hasty words in dust and ashes. No solution of his problem is vouchsafed; but God Himself effects that which neither the man's own thoughts of God nor the representations of the friends could accomplish: he had heard of him with the hearing of the ear without effect; but now his eye sees Him. This is the profoundest religious deep in the book. 5. The epilogue, in prose, xlii. 7-17, describes Job's restoration to a prosperity double that of his former estate, his family felicity and long life.

With the exception of the episode of Elihu, the connexion of which with the original form of the poem may be doubtful, all five parts of the book are essential elements of the work as it came from the hand of the first author, although some parts of the second and fourth divisions may have been expanded by later writers. The idea of the composition is to be derived not from any single element of the book, but from the teaching and movement of the whole piece. Job is unquestionably the hero of the work, and in his ideas and his history combined we may assume that we find the author himself speaking and teaching. The discussion between Job and his friends of the problem of suffering occupies two-thirds of the book, or, if the space occupied by Elihu be not considered, nearly three-fourths, and in the direction which the author causes this discussion to take we may see revealed the main didactic purpose of the book. When the three friends, the representatives of former theories of providence, are reduced to silence, we may be certain that it was the author's purpose to discredit the ideas which they represent. Job himself offers no positive contribution to the doctrine of evil; his position is negative, merely antagonistic to that of the friends. But this negative position victoriously maintained by him has the effect of clearing the ground, and the author himself supplies in the prologue the positive truth, when he communi-

cates the real explanation of his hero's calamities, and teaches that they were a trial of his righteousness. It was therefore the author's main purpose in his work to widen men's views of the providence of God and set before them a new view of suffering. This purpose, however, was in all probability subordinate to some wider practical design. No Hebrew writer is merely a poet or a thinker. He is always a teacher. He has men before him in their relations to God, and usually not men in their individual relations, but members of the family of Israel, the people of God. [In a footnote, the critic adds: "Exceptions must be made in the cases of Esther and the Song of Songs, which do not mention God, and the original writer in Ecclesiastes who is a philosopher."] It is consequently scarcely to be doubted that the book has a national scope. The author considered his new truth regarding the meaning of affliction as of national interest, and as the truth then needful for the heart of his people. But the teaching of the book is only half its contents. It contains also a history—deep and inexplicable affliction, a great moral struggle, and a victory. The author meant his new truth to inspire new conduct, new faith, and new hopes. In Job's sufferings, undeserved and inexplicable to him, yet capable of an explanation most consistent with the goodness and faithfulness of God, and casting honour upon his faithful servants; in his despair bordering on unbelief, at last overcome; and in the happy issue of his afflictions—in all this Israel may see itself, and from the sight take courage, and forecast its own history. Job, however, is not to be considered Israel, the righteous servant of the Lord, under a feigned name; he is no mere parable (though such a view is found as early as the Talmud); he and his history have both elements of reality in them. It is these elements of reality common to him with Israel in affliction, common even to him with humanity as a whole, confined within the straitened limits set by its own ignorance, wounded to death by the mysterious sorrows of life, tortured by the uncertainty whether its cry finds an entrance into God's ear, alarmed and paralysed by the irreconcilable discrepancies which it seems to discover between its necessary thoughts of Him and its experience of Him in His providence, and faint with longing that it might come into His place, and behold him, not girt with His majesty, but in human form, as one looketh upon his fellow—it is these elements of truth that make the history of Job instructive to Israel in the times of affliction when it was set before them, and to men of all races in all ages. It would probably be a mistake, however, to imagine that the author consciously stepped outside the limits of his nation and assumed a human position antagonistic to it. The chords he touches vibrate through all humanity—but this is because Israel is the religious kernel of humanity, and because from Israel's heart the deepest religious music of mankind is heard, whether of pathos or of joy.

Two threads requiring to be followed, therefore, run through the book—one the discussion of the problem of evil between Job and his friends, and the other the varying attitude of Job's mind towards God, the first being subordinate to the second. Both Job and his friends advance to the discussion of his sufferings and of the problem of evil, ignorant of the true cause of his calamities—Job strong in his sense of innocence, and the friends armed with their theory of the righteousness of God, who giveth to every man according to his works. With fine psychological instinct the poet lets Job altogether lose his self-control first when his three friends came to visit him. His bereavements and his malady he bore with a steady courage, and his wife's direct instigations to godlessness he repelled with severity and resignation. But when his equals and the old associates of his happiness came to see him, and when he read in their looks and in their seven days' silence the depth of his own misery, his self-command deserted him, and he broke out into a cry of despair, cursing his day and crying for death (iii). Job had somewhat misinterpreted the demeanour of his friends. It was not all pity that it expressed. Along with their pity they had also brought their theology, and they trusted to heal Job's malady with this. Till a few days before, Job would have agreed with them on the sovereign virtues of this remedy. But he had learned through a higher teaching, the events of God's providence, that it was no longer a specific in his case. His violent impatience, however, under his afflictions and his covert attacks upon the divine rectitude only served to confirm the view of his sufferings which their theory of evil had already suggested to his friends. And thus commences the high debate which continues through twenty-nine chapters.

The three friends of Job came to the consideration of his history with the principle that calamity is the result of evil-doing, as prosperity is the reward of righteousness. Suffer-ing is not an accident or a spontaneous growth of the soil; man is born unto trouble as the sparks fly upwards; there is in human life a tendency to do evil which draws down upon men the chastisement of God (v. 6). The principle is thus enunciated by Eliphaz, from whom the other speakers take their cue: where there is suffering there has been sin in the sufferer. Not suffering in itself, but the effect of it on the sufferer is what gives insight into his true character. Suffering is not always punitive; it is sometimes disciplinary, designed to wean the good man from his sin. If he sees in his suffering the monition of God and turns from his evil, his future shall be rich in peace and happiness, and his latter estate more prosperous than his first. If he murmurs or resists, he can only perish under the multiplying chastisements which his impenitence will provoke. Now this principle is far from being a peculiar crotchet of the friends; its truth is undeniable, though they erred in supposing that it would cover the wide providence of God. The principle is the fundamental idea of moral government, the expression of the natural conscience, a principle common more or less to all peoples, though perhaps more prominent in the Semitic mind, because all religious ideas are more prominent and simple there—not suggested to Israel first by the law, but found and adopted by the law, though it may be sharpened by it. It is the fundamental principle of prophecy no less than of the law, and, if possible, of the wisdom of philosophy of the Hebrews more than of either. Speculation among the Hebrews had a simpler task before it than it had in the West or in the farther East. The Greek philosopher began his operations upon the sum of things; he threw the universe into his crucible at once. His object was to effect some analysis of it, so that he could call one element cause and another effect. Or, to vary the figure, his endeavour was to pursue the streams of tendency which he could observe

till he reached at last the central spring which sent them all forth. God, a single cause and explanation, was the object of his search. But to the Hebrew of the later time this was already found. The analysis resulting in the distinction of God and the world had been effected for him so long ago that the history and circumstances of the process had been forgotten, and only the unchallengeable result remained. His philosophy was not a quest of God whom he did not know, but a recognition on all hands of God whom he knew. The great primary idea to his mind was that of God, a Being wholly just, doing all. And the world was little more than the phenomena that revealed the mind and the presence and the operations of God. Consequently the nature of God as known to him and the course of events formed a perfect equation. The idea of what God was in Himself was in complete harmony with His manifestation of Himself in providence, in the events of individual human lives, and in the history of nations. The philosophy of the wise did not go behind the origin of sin, or referred it to the freedom of man; but, sin existing, and God being in immediate personal contact with the world, every event was a direct expression of His moral will and energy; calamity fell on wickedness, and success attended right-doing. This view of the moral harmony between the nature of God and the events of providence in the fortunes of men and nations is the view of the Hebrew wisdom in its oldest form, during what might be called the period of principles, to which belong Prov. x. seq.; and this is the position maintained by Job's three friends. And the significance of the book of Job in the history of Hebrew thought arises in that it marks the point when such a view was definitely overcome, closing the long period when this principle was merely subjected to questionings, and makes a new positive addition to the doctrine of evil.

Job agreed that afflictions came directly from the hand of God, and also that God afflicted those whom He held guilty of sins. But his conscience denied the imputation of guilt, whether insinuated by his friends or implied in God's chastisement of him. Hence he was driven to conclude that God was unjust. The position of Job appeared to his friends nothing else but impiety; while theirs was to him mere falsehood and the special pleading of sycophants on behalf of God because He was the stronger. Within these iron walls the debate moves, making little progress, but with much brilliancy, if not of argument, of illustration. A certain advance indeed is perceptible. In the first series of speeches (iv.-xiv.), the key-note of which is struck by Eliphaz, the oldest and most considerate of the three, the position is that affliction is caused by sin, and is chastisement designed for the sinner's good; and the moral is that Job should recognize it and use it for the purpose for which it was sent. In the second (xv.-xxi.) the terrible fate of the sinner is emphasized, and those brilliant pictures of a restored future, thrown in by all the speakers in the first series, are absent. Job's demeanour under the consolations offered him afforded little hope of his repentance. In the third series (xxii. seq.) the friends cast off all disguise, and openly charge Job with a course of evil life. That their armoury was now exhausted is shown by the brevity of the second speaker, and the failure of the third (at least in the present text) to answer in any form. In reply Job disdains for a time to touch what he well knew lay under all their exhortations; he laments with touching pathos the defection of his friends, who were like the winter torrents looked for in vain by the perishing caravan in the summer heat; he meets with bitter scorn their constant cry that God will not cast off the righteous man, by asking: How can one be righteous with God? what can human weakness, however innocent, do against infinite might and subtlety? they are righteous whom an omnipotent and perverse will thinks fit to consider so; he falls into a hopeless wail over the universal misery of man, who has a weary campaign of life appointed him; then, rising up in the strength of his conscience, he upbraids the Almighty with His misuse of His power and His indiscriminate tyranny—righteous and innocent He destroys alike—and challenges Him to lay aside His majesty and meet His creature as a man, and then he would not fear Him. Even in the second series Job can hardly bring himself to face the personal issue raised by the friends. His relations to God absorb him almost wholly—his pitiable isolation, the indignities showered on his once honoured head, the loathsome spectacle of his body; abandoned by all, he turns for pity from God to men and from men to God. Only in the third series of debates does he put out his hand and grasp firmly the theory of his friends, and their "defences of mud" fall to dust in his hands. Instead of that roseate moral order on which they are never weary of insisting, he finds only disorder and moral confusion. When he thinks of it, trembling takes hold of him. It is not the righteous but the wicked that live, grow old, yea, wax mighty in strength, that send forth their children like a flock and establish them in their sight. Before the logic of facts the theory of the friends goes down; and with this negative result, which the author skilfully reaches through the debate, has to be combined his own positive doctrine of the uses of adversity advanced in the prologue.

To a modern reader it appears strange that both parties were so entangled in the meshes of their preconceptions regarding God as to be unable to break through the broader views. The friends, while maintaining that injustice on the part of God is inconceivable, might have given due weight to the persistent testimony of Job's conscience as that behind which it is impossible to go, and found refuge in the reflection that there might be something inexplicable in the ways of God, and that affliction might have some other meaning than to punish the sinner or even to wean him from his sin. And Job, while maintaining his innocence from overt sins, might have confessed that there was such sinfulness in every human life as was sufficient to account for the severest chastisement from heaven, or at least he might have stopped short of charging God foolishly. Such a position would certainly be taken up by an afflicted saint now, and such an explanation of his sufferings would suggest itself to the sufferer, even though it might be in truth a false explanation. Perhaps here, where an artistic fault might seem to be committed, the art of the writer, or his truth to nature, and the extraordinary freedom with which he moves among his materials, as well as the power and individuality of his dramatic creations, are most remarkable. The rôle which the author reserved for himself was to teach the truth on the question in dispute, and he accomplishes this by allowing his performers to push their false principles to their proper extreme. There

is nothing about which men are usually so sure as the character of God. They are ever ready to take Him in their own hand, to interpret His providence in their own sense, to say what things are consistent or now with His character and word, and beat down the opposing consciences of other men by His so-called authority, which is nothing but their own. The friends of Job were religious Orientals, men to whom God was a being in immediate contact with the world and life, to whom the idea of second causes was unknown, on whom science had not yet begun to dawn, nor the conception of a divine scheme pursuing a distant end by complicated means, in which the individual's interest may suffer for the larger good. The broad sympathies of the author and his sense of the truth lying in the theory of the friends are seen in the scope which he allows them, in the richness of the thought and the splendid luxuriance of the imagery—drawn from the immemorial moral consent of mankind, the testimony of the living conscience, and the observation of life—with which he makes them clothe their views. He remembered the elements of truth in the theory from which he was departing, that it was a national heritage, which he himself perhaps had been constrained not without a struggle to abandon; and, while showing its insufficiency, he sets it forth in its most brilliant form.

The extravagance of Job's assertions was occasioned greatly by the extreme position of his friends, which left no room for his conscious innocence along with the rectitude of God. Again, the poet's purpose, as the prologue shows, was to teach that afflictions may fall on a man out of all connexion with any offence of his own, and merely as the trial of his righteousness; and hence he allows Job, as by a true instinct of the nature of his sufferings, to repudiate all connexion between them and sin in himself. And further, the terrible conflict into which the suspicions of the Satan brought Job could not be exhibited without pushing him to the verge of ungodliness. These are all elements of the poet's art; but art and nature are one. In ancient Hebrew life the sense of sin was less deep than it is now. In the desert, too, men speak boldly of God. Nothing is more false than to judge the poet's creation from our later point of view, and construct a theory of the book according to a more developed sense of sin and a deeper reverence for God than belonged to antiquity. In complete contradiction to the testimony of the book itself, some critics, as Hengstenberg and Budde, have assumed that Job's spiritual pride was the cause of his afflictions, that this was the root of bitterness in him which must be killed down ere he could become a true saint. The fundamental position of the book is that Job was already a true saint; this is testified by God Himself, is the radical idea of the author in the prologue, and the very hypothesis of the drama. We might be ready to think that Job's afflictions did not befall him out of all connexion with his own condition of mind, and we might be disposed to find a vindication of God's ways in this. There is no evidence that such an idea was shared by the author of the book. It is remarkable that the attitude which we imagine it would have been so easy for Job to assume, namely, while holding fast his integrity, to fall back upon the inexplicableness of providence, of which there are such imposing descriptions in his speeches, is just the attitude which is taken up in ch. xxviii.

It is far from certain, however, that this chapter is an integral part of the original book.

The other line running through the book, the varying attitude of Job's mind towards God, exhibits dramatic action and tragic interest of the highest kind, though the movement is internal. That the exhibition of this struggle in Job's mind was a main point in the author's purpose is seen from the fact that at the end of each of his great trials he notes that Job sinned not, nor ascribed wrong to God (i. 22; ii. 10), and from the effect which the divine voice from the whirlwind is made to produce upon him (xl. 3). In the first cycle of debate (ix.-xiv.) Job's mind reaches the deepest limit of estrangement. There he not merely charges God with injustice, but, unable to reconcile His former goodness with His present enmity, he regards the latter as the true expression of God's attitude towards His creatures, and the former, comprising all his infinite creative skill in weaving the delicate organism of human nature and the rich endowments of His providence, only as the means of exercising His mad and immoral cruelty in the time to come. When the Semitic skin of Job is scratched, we find a modern pessimist beneath. Others in later days have brought the keen sensibility of the human frame and the torture which it endures together, and asked with Job to whom at last all this has to be referred. Towards the end of the cycle a star of heavenly light seems to rise on the horizon; the thought seizes the sufferer's mind that man might have another life, that God's anger pursuing him to the grave might be sated, and that He might call him out of it to Himself again (xiv. 13). This idea of a resurrection, unfamiliar to Job at first, is one which he is allowed to reach out of the necessities of the moral complications around him, but from the author's manner of using the idea we may judge that it was familiar to himself. In the second cycle the thought of a future reconciliation with God is more firmly grasped. That satisfaction or at least composure which, when we observe calamities that we cannot morally account for, we reach by considering that providence is a great scheme moving according to general laws, and that it does not always truly reflect the relation of God to the individual, Job reached in the only way possible to a Semitic mind. He drew a distinction between an outer God whom events obey, pursuing him in His anger, and an inner God whose heart was with him, who was aware of his innocence; and he appeals from God to God, and beseeches God to pledge Himself that he shall receive justice from God (xvi. 19; xvii. 3). And so high at last does this consciousness that God is at one with him rise that he avows his assurance that He will yet appear to do him justice before men, and that he shall see Him with his own eyes, no more estranged but on his side, and for this moment he faints with longing (xix. 25 seq.).

After this expression of faith Job's mind remains calm, though he ends by firmly charging God with perverting his right, and demanding to know the cause of his afflictions (xxvii. 2 seq.; xxxi. 35, where render: "Oh, that I had the indictment which mine adversary has written!"). In answer to this demand the Divine voice answers Job out of the tempest: "Who is this that darkeneth counsel by words without knowledge?" The word "counsel" inti-

mates to Job that God does not act without a design, large and beyond the comprehension of man; and to impress this is the purpose of the Divine speeches. The speaker does not enter into Job's particular cause; there is not a word tending to unravel his riddle; his mind is drawn away to the wisdom and majesty of God Himself. His own words and those of his friends are but re-echoed, but it is God Himself who now utters them. Job is in immediate nearness to the majesty of heaven, wise, unfathomable, ironical over the littleness of man, and he is abased; God Himself effects what neither the man's own thoughts of God nor the representations of his friends could accomplish, though by the same means. The religious insight of the writer sounds here the profoundest deeps of truth.

Doubts whether particular portions of the present book belonged to the original form of it have been raised by many. M. L. De Wette expressed himself as follows: "It appears to us that the present book of *Job* has not all flowed from one pen. As many books of the Old Testament have been several times written over, so has this also" (Ersch and Gruber, *Ency.*, sect. ii. vol. viii.). The judgment formed by De Wette has been adhered to more or less by most of those who have studied the book. Questions regarding the unity of such books as this are difficult to settle; there is not unanimity among scholars regarding the idea of the book, and consequently they differ as to what parts are in harmony or conflict with unity; and it is dangerous to apply modern ideas of literary composition and artistic unity to the works of antiquity and of the East. The problem raised in the book of Job has certainly received frequent treatment in the Old Testament; and there is no likelihood that all efforts in this direction have been preserved to us. It is probable that the book of Job was but a great effort amidst or after many smaller. It is scarcely to be supposed that one with such poetic and literary power as the author of chap. iii.-xxxi., xxxviii.-xli. would embody the work of any other writer in his own. If there be elements in the book which must be pronounced foreign, they have been inserted in the work of the author by a later hand. It is not unlikely that our present book may, in addition to the great work of the original author, contain some fragments of the thoughts of other religious minds upon the same question, and that these, instead of being loosely appended, have been fitted into the mechanism of the first work. Some of these fragments may have originated at first quite independently of our book, while others may be expansions and insertions that never existed separately. At the same time it is scarcely safe to throw out any portion of the book merely because it seems to us out of harmony with the unity of the main part of the poem, or unless several distinct lines of consideration conspire to point it out as an extraneous element.

The arguments against the originality of the prologue—as, that it is written in prose, that the name Yahweh appears in it, that sacrifice is referred to, and that there are inconsistencies between it and the body of the book—are of little weight. There must have been some introduction to the poem explaining the circumstances of Job, otherwise the poetical dispute would have been unintelligible, for it is improbable that the story of Job was so familiar that a poem in which he and his friends figured as they do here would have been understood. And there is no trace of any other prologue or introduction having ever existed. The prologue, too, is an essential element of the work, containing the author's positive contribution to the doctrine of suffering, for which the discussion in the poem prepares the way. The intermixture of prose and poetry is common in Oriental works containing similar discussions; the reference to sacrifice is to primitive not to Mosaic sacrifice; and the author, while using the name Yahweh freely himself, puts the patriarchal Divine names into the mouth of Job and his friends because he regards them as belonging to the patriarchal age and to a country outside of Israel. That the observance of this rule had a certain awkwardness for the writer appears perhaps from his allowing the name Yahweh to slip in once or twice (xii. 9, cf. xxviii. 28) in familiar phrases in the body of the poem. The discrepancies, such as Job's references to his children as still alive (xix. 17, the interpretation is doubtful), and to his servants, are trivial, and even if real imply nothing in a book admittedly poetical and not historical. The objections to the epilogue are equally unimportant—as that the Satan is not mentioned in it, and that Job's restoration is in conflict with the main idea of the poem—that earthly felicity does not follow righteousness. The epilogue confirms the teaching of the poem when it gives the divine sanction to Job's doctrine regarding God in opposition to that of the friends (xlii. 7). And it is certainly not the intention of the poem to teach that earthly felicity does not follow righteousness; its purpose is to correct the exclusiveness with which the friends of Job maintained that principle. The Satan is introduced in the prologue, exercising his function as minister of God in heaven; but it is to misinterpret wholly the doctrine of evil in the Old Testament to assign to the Satan any such personal importance or independence of power as that he should be called before the curtain to receive the hisses that accompany his own discomfiture. The Satan, though he here appears with the beginnings of a malevolent will of his own, is but the instrument of the sifting providence of God. His work was to try; that done he disappears, his personality being too slight to have any place in the result.

Much graver are the suspicions that attach to the speeches of Elihu. Most of those who have studied the book carefully hold that this part does not belong to the original cast, but has been introduced at a considerably later time. The piece is one of the most interesting parts of the book; both the person and the thoughts of Elihu are marked by a strong individuality. This individuality has indeed been very diversely estimated. The ancients for the most part passed a very severe judgment on Elihu: he is a buffoon, a boastful youth whose shallow intermeddling is only to be explained by the fewness of his years, the incarnation of folly, or even the Satan himself gone a-mumming. Some moderns on the other hand have regarded him as the incarnation of the voice of God or even of God himself. The main objections to the connexion of the episode of Elihu with the original book are: that the prologue and epilogue know nothing of him; that on the cause of Job's afflictions he occupies virtually the same position as the friends; that his speeches destroy the dramatic effect of the divine manifestation by introducing a lengthened break between Job's challenge and the answer of God; that the language and

style of the piece are marked by an excessive mannerism, too great to have been created by the author of the rest of the poem; that the allusions to the rest of the book are so minute as to betray a reader rather than a hearer; and that the views regarding sin, and especially the scandal given to the author by the irreverence of Job, indicate a religious advance which marks a later age. The position taken by Elihu is almost that of a critic of the book. Regarding the origin of afflictions he is at one with the friends, although he dwells more on the general sinfulness of man than on actual sins, and his reprobation of Job's position is even greater than theirs. His anger was kindled against Job because he made himself righteous before God, and against his friends because they found no answer to Job. His whole object is to refute Job's charge of injustice against God. What is novel in Elihu, therefore, is not his position but his arguments. These do not lack cogency, but betray a kind of thought different from that of the friends. Injustice in God, he argues, can only arise from selfishness in Him; but the very existence of creation implies unselfish love on God's part, for if He thought only of Himself, He would cease actively to uphold creation, and it would fall into death. Again, without justice mere earthly rule is impossible; how then is injustice conceivable in Him who rules over all? It is probable that the original author found his three interlocutors a sufficient medium for expression, and that this new speaker is the creation of another. To a devout and thoughtful reader of the original book, belonging perhaps to a more reverential age, it appeared that the language and bearing of Job had scarcely been sufficiently reprobated by the original speakers, and that the religious reason, apart from any theophany, could suggest arguments sufficient to condemn such demeanour on the part of any man. (For an able though hardly convincing argument for the originality of the discourses of Elihu see Budde's *Commentary*.)

It is more difficult to come to a decision in regard to some other portions of the book, particularly ch. xxvii. 7-xxviii. In the latter part of ch. xxvii. Job seems to go over to the camp of his opponents, and expresses sentiments in complete contradiction to his former views. Hence some have thought the passage to be the missing speech of Zophar. Others, as Hitzig, believe that Job is parodying the ideas of the friends; while others, like Ewald, consider that he is recanting his former excesses, and making such a modification as to express correctly his views on evil. None of these opinions is quite satisfactory, though the last probably expresses the view with which the passage was introduced, whether it be original or not. The meaning of ch. xxviii. can only be that "Wisdom," that is, a theoretical comprehension of providence, is unattainable by man, whose only wisdom is the fear of the Lord or practical piety. But to bring Job to the feeling of this truth was just the purpose of the theophany and the divine speeches; and, if Job had reached it already through his own reflection, the theophany becomes an irrelevancy. It is difficult, therefore, to find a place for these two chapters in the original work. The hymn on Wisdom is a most exquisite poem, which probably originated separately, and was brought into our book with a purpose similar to that which suggested the speeches of Elihu. Objections have also been raised to the descriptions of leviathan and behemoth (ch.

xl. 15-xli.). Regarding these it may be enough to say that in meaning these passages are in perfect harmony with other parts of the Divine words, although there is a breadth and detail in the style unlike the sharp, short, ironical touches otherwise characteristic of this part of the poem. (Other longer passages, the originality of which has been called into question, are: xvii. 8 seq.; xxi. 16-18; xxii. 17 seq.; xxiii. 8 seq.; xxiv. 9, 18-24; xxvi. 5-14. On these see the commentaries.)

The age of such a book as *Job*, dealing only with principles and having no direct references to historical events can be fixed only approximately. Any conclusion can be reached only by an induction founded on matters which do not afford perfect certainty, such as the comparative development of certain moral ideas in different ages, the pressing claims of certain problems for solution at particular epochs of the history of Israel, and points of contact with other writings of which the age may with some certainty be determined. The Jewish tradition that the book is Mosaic, and the idea that it is a production of the desert, written in another tongue and translated into Hebrew, want even a shadow of probability. The book is a genuine outcome of the religious life and thought of Israel, the product of a religious knowledge and experience that were possible among no other people. That the author lays the scene of the poem outside his own nation and in the patriarchal age is a proceeding common to him with other dramatic writers, who find freer play for their principles in a region removed from the present, where they are not hampered by the obtrusive forms of actual life, but are free to mould occurrences into the moral form that their ideas require.

It is the opinion of some scholars, *e.g.* Delitzsch, that the book belongs to the age of Solomon. It cannot be earlier than this age, for Job (vii. 17) travesties the ideas of Ps. viii. in a manner which shows that this hymn was well known. To infer the date from a comparison of literary coincidences and allusions is however a very delicate operation. For, first, owing to the unity of thought and language which pervades the Old Testament, in which, regarded merely as a national literature, it differs from all other national literatures, we are apt to be deceived, and to take mere similarities for literary allusions and quotations; and, secondly, even when we are sure that there is dependence, it is often uncommonly difficult to decide which is the original source. The reference to Job in Ezek. xiv. 14 is not to our book, but to the man (a legendary figure) who was afterwards made the hero of it. The affinities on the other hand between Job and Isa. xl.—lv. are very close. The date, however, of this part of Isaiah is uncertain, though it cannot have received its final form, if it be composite, long before the return. Between *Job* iii. and Jer. xx. 14 seq. there is, again, certainly literary connexion. But the judgment of different minds differs on the question which passage is dependent on the other. The language of Jeremiah, however, has a natural pathos and genuineness of feeling in it, somewhat in contrast with the elaborate poetical finish of Job's words, which might suggest the originality of the former.

The tendency among recent scholars is to put the book of

Job not earlier than the 5th century B.C. There are good reasons for putting it in the 4th century. It stands at the beginning of the era of Jewish philosophical inquiry—its affinities are with Proverbs, Ecclesiasticus, Ecclesiastes, and the Wisdom of Solomon, a body of writings that belongs to the latest period of pre-Christian Jewish literary development. . . . Its points of connexion with Isa. xl.-lv. relate only to the problem of the suffering of the righteous, and that it is later than the Isaiah passage appears from the fact that this latter is national and ritual in scope, while Job is universal and ethical.

The book of *Job* is not literal history, though it reposes on historical tradition. To this tradition belong probably the name of Job and his country, and the names of his three friends, and perhaps also many other details impossible to specify particularly. The view that the book is entirely a literary creation with no basis in historical tradition is as old as the Talmud (*Baba Bathra,* xv. 1), in which a rabbi is cited who says: Job was not, and was not created, but is an allegory. This view is supported by Hengstenberg and others. But pure poetical creations on so extensive a scale are not probable in the East and at so early an age.

The author of the book is wholly unknown. The religious life of Israel was at certain periods very intense, and at those times the spiritual energy of the nation expressed itself almost impersonally, through men who forgot themselves and were speedily forgotten in name by others. Hitzig conjectures that the author was a native of the north on account of the free criticism of providence which he allows himself. Others, on account of some affinities with the prophet Amos, infer that he belonged to the south of Judah, and this is supposed to account for his intimate acquaintance with the desert. Ewald considers that he belonged to the exile in Egypt, on account of his minute acquaintance with that country. But all these conjectures localize an author whose knowledge was not confined to any locality, who was a true child of the East and familiar with life and nature in every country there, who was at the same time a true Israelite and felt that the earth was the Lord's and the fullness thereof, and whose sympathies and thought took in all God's works.

James Strahan   (essay date 1913)

SOURCE: An introduction to *The Book of Job,* T. & T. Clark, 1913, pp. 1-30.

[*In the following excerpt from the introduction to his critical study* The Book of Job Interpreted, *Strahan interprets* The Book of Job *as a visionary author's response to an era of change in Israel which called for clarification and strengthening of the nation's theology, theodicy, and morality, particularly in regard to the problem of human suffering.*]

Pervaded by the thought and feeling of a period in some ways singularly resembling our own, the ***Book of Job*** is the most modern of all Hebrew writings, though some readers may naturally find themselves more at home in Ecclesiastes. The post-exilic age which produced the great drama of spiritual doubt transcended by faith was, on the one hand, heavily oppressed by that increase of knowledge

Pictorial exegesis of The Book of Job *from the* Floreffe Bible, *c. 1155.*

which brings increase of sorrow; and it is doubtless true that, [as stated by A. B. Davidson], 'when the Semitic skin of Job is scratched, we find a modern pessimist beneath.' But the age felt, on the other hand, that its richer culture and its wider outlook only constituted a fresh call to realise the union of the spiritual and eternal with its manifestation in time. The greatest thinkers of the period sought to conquer its pessimism with a higher, nobler, purer faith. Perceiving that the God of history was breaking with the past only to fulfil Himself in new and more wondrous ways, they endeavoured to enlighten the bewildered mind and establish the wavering faith of their nation by guiding it into a deeper knowledge of His will and a closer fellowship with Himself. Spiritual revolutions, however, are never effected without pain. 'Periods of religious transition, when the advance has been a real one, always have been violent, and probably will always continue to be so. They to whom the precious gift of fresh light is given are called upon to exhibit their credentials as teachers in suffering for it. They, and those who oppose them, have alike a sacred cause; and the fearful spectacle arises of earnest vehement men contending against each other as for their own souls, in fiery struggle; . . . and, at last, the old faith, like the phoenix, expires upon the altar, and the new rises out of the ashes', [according to James Anthony Froude].

In the *Book of Job* nothing less than a campaign of centuries is dramatically compressed into a single decisive battle. The Israelites of the pre-exilic time, mastered by a mighty monotheism that had not yet reached the stage of enlightenment at which the origin and existence of evil become an urgent speculative problem, have a facile explanation of all sufferings. To them, as their scriptures mirror their minds to us, there is no mystery of pain. God being all in all, and every event, morally or materially hurtful as well as beneficial, being traced to His immediate action, He rules the affairs of men with a justice so rigid and exact that it is always well with the righteous and ill with the wicked. The divine government accomplishes that which the best human government can only attempt—it rewards the deserving and punishes the guilty. The causal nexus between goodness and prosperity, sin and suffering, is never broken. Health, wealth, peace, comfort, long life are the lot of the true servants of God; sickness, poverty, trouble, disaster, early death the portion of the wicked. One's outward condition is always tell-tale, success being the indication of God's favour, failure of His anger. Accident and partiality are alike unknown. Famine, earthquake, pestilence, defeat in war are the punishment of sin; abundance of corn, wine, and oil, a peaceful home, and a numerous progeny, the reward of righteousness. In the field of destiny, which is this earth, men reap what they have sown. No light of immortality has yet been shed upon human lives; there is no judgment in Sheol, where all things are alike to all. The present life, rounded and complete in itself, alone counts for anything, and between the cradle and the grave men receive what they merit. A man's life and his lot in life *must* correspond, otherwise God would be unjust.

There can be no doubt that the doctrine of retributive justice is clearly and emphatically taught by all the early prophets, whose religious subject, however, is not the individual Israelite, but the nation Israel. According to them, every event is a revelation of God's righteousness. The physical has no meaning in itself; it is nothing but a medium for the display of the moral. God deals with His people by an unchanging, calculable law, and His external treatment of them manifests His real attitude towards them. The righteous nation is always exalted, the wicked always cast down. The equation between conduct and lot is perfect, the balance of justice so true that it needs no redress in an after-life. The course of events is God's adequate self-expression, His providence made visible. The early prophetic faith might be expressed in Schiller's words, *Die Weltgeschichte ist das Weltgericht,* 'The history of the world is the judgment of the world.'

From the time of Josiah the doctrine of retributive righteousness was embodied for Israel in the Book of Deuteronomy, which was the practical outcome of a strenuous endeavour to apply prophetic ideas to life. 'Do well and fare well' is the burden of all the exhortations of the ideal legislator who speaks in the divine name. 'Behold, I set before you this day a blessing and a curse; the blessing if ye shall hearken unto the commandments of Jahweh your God, which I command you this day: and the curse if ye shall not hearken unto the commandments of Jahweh your God.' [*Deuteronomy* 11:26-28].

The sunny creed which connected unbroken earthly happiness with religious fidelity was a relic of Israel's golden age. It was the faith of a strong, hardy, youthful race, which had, by the blessing of its God, triumphed in the struggle for life. But it was evidently exposed to some grave objections. First, so long as good conduct was the surest passport to divine favour and worldly success, the natural accompaniment of religion was a frankly utilitarian morality. If the basis of God's relations with His people was a covenant, in which He promised that upright living would be recompensed by temporal prosperity, virtue was practised for the sake of the results, and men felt that they had the right to remonstrate if ever the reward of their good deeds was withheld. A second objection is still more serious. If prosperity was regarded as the evidence of God's favour, it is apparent that religion was still the possession of the rich, the free, the healthy, the happy, while it had no message for the poor, the broken, the defeated, the wretched. 'So long as the community flourished, the fact that an individual was miserable reflected no discredit on divine providence, but was rather taken to prove that the sufferer was an evil-doer. . . . Such a man was out of place among the happy and prosperous crowd that assembled on feast days before the altar; . . . the unhappy leper, in his lifelong affliction, was shut out from the exercises of religion as well as from the privileges of social life. So the mourner, too, was unclean, and his food was unclean, as his food was not brought into the house of God; the very occasions of life in which spiritual things are nearest to the Christian, and the comfort of religion is most fervently sought, were in the ancient world the times when a man was forbidden to approach the seat of God's presence. To us, whose habit it is to look at religion in its influence on the life and habits of individuals, it seems a cruel law; nay, our sense of justice is offended by a system in which misfortunes set up a barrier between a man and his

God. But whether in civil or in profane matters, the habit of the old world was to think much of the community and little of the individual life; and no one felt this to be unjust even though it bore hardly on himself.'

It is certain that the Prophetic and Deuteronomic faith in the success of righteousness, containing as it did a large element of truth, took a firm hold of the national consciousness, as is proved by the fact that it became the burden of many of the Psalms and of the whole Book of Proverbs, as well as the perpetually recurrent moral of all the Hebrew histories. Orthodoxy teaches that the man whose delight is in the law of the Lord 'shall be like a tree planted by the rivers of water . . . and whatsoever he doeth shall prosper' [*Psalms* 1:3]. 'I have been young, and now am old; yet have I not seen the righteous forsaken, nor his seed begging bread' [*Psalms* 37:25]. 'Behold, the righteous shall be recompensed in the earth: how much more the wicked and the sinner!' [*Proverbs* 11:31].

Yet long before these confident words of poets and sages were written, the decline and fall of the State of Judah began to evoke the first murmurs of dissent from the traditional creed. The times were out of joint, and the victories of the heathen sorely tried the faith of the people of God. Brave, loyal, heroic men suffered manifoldly and tragically. The accepted theology appeared to be in violent conflict with facts; God's doings could not be harmonised with His attributes; He seemed to have broken His covenant, to be unfaithful to His promises, untrue to Himself. Men brooded on these mysteries till their faith shook and their reason almost reeled.

The Hebrew prophets themselves—God's confidants, sensitive to every whisper of His spirit, every leading of His providence—were the first Hebrew sceptics. Their doubt was faith perplexed, faith tried, faith bewildered, faith tortured. The strength and purity of their progressive ethical monotheism constrained them to ask questions, to expostulate with God, to complain in the anguish of their hearts. Their very faith became a cruel problem, a wellnigh intolerable burden. They could not shut their eyes to the moral confusion of the world, and the mysterious silence, the apparent indifference, of God appalled them. 'Righteous art Thou, O Jahweh,' says one of them, 'when I plead with Thee: yet would I reason the cause with Thee: wherefore doth the way of the wicked prosper? wherefore are all they at ease that deal very treacherously?' [*Jeremiah* 12:1]. 'Wherefore,' cries another, 'lookest Thou upon them that deal treacherously, and hidest Thy face when the wicked swalloweth up the man that is more righteous than he?' [*Habakkuk* 1:13]. And in the long centuries of misrule that follow the destruction of the Jewish State, plaintive voices become more and more common: 'Thou hast cast off and rejected, Thou hast been wroth with Thine anointed. . . . O Jahweh, where are Thy former mercies, which Thou swarest unto David in Thy faithfulness?' [*Psalms* 89:39, 49].

An old and consecrated dogma never lacks defenders, and many attempts were still made to buttress the traditional belief which connected all suffering with sin. If it could not be denied that ideal justice, which theoretically rewarded the righteous and punished the wicked, was in practice often painfully impartial, it was maintained that in the end the balance was always adjusted. In *Psalms* 37, 49, and 73, where the difficulty is felt, relief is sought in the idea that occasional aberrations from the ordinary course of providence are not permanent; that before the close of life, well-doers and evil-doers alike receive their due reward, while the righteous see it and are glad, their faith being thereby re-established. Yet such a theodicy was felt by many to be unsatisfying, for the simple reason that it was not true. And thus the intellect of the nation, enlarged and enlightened by observation and experience, came into sharp conflict with the devotional spirit of religious acquiescence. There was no possibility of theological progress on the old lines, for it had become abundantly evident that God *does* require the innocent to suffer with the guilty. At such a crisis there was no possibility of standing still; not to go forward was to go backward. If faith was afraid to face the facts of life, faith must perish.

But in the days of storm and stress a new era begins. One seer after another arose in Israel, not to defend the ancient tradition, but to offer a new solution of the mystery of suffering. The greatest of these was the unknown prophet of the Exile, and after him came the author of the ***Book of Job.*** Absolutely convinced that the simple creed of the nation's childhood was inadequate for its manhood, they felt themselves constrained to render to their people that greatest of all services—the purifying and ennobling of its spiritual faith.

The writer of the ***Book of Job*** is a born dramatist. It is of the essence of his active mind to recognise and state all the arguments which make for and against the conclusion which he himself has reached; and he finds a rudimentary form of dramatic art the fittest medium for a full and adequate discussion of the burning question of his age. Out of the rich store of the nation's legends he chooses the case of a blameless, upright, God-fearing sheikh, the greatest of the sons of the East, who was suddenly cast from the height of prosperity to the lowest depth of misery. Stripped of his wealth, bereft of his family, struck down with a loathsome disease, doomed to an early and painful death, regarded as a common criminal by those near and dear to him, this man presents an absolute contradiction to the ideal union of moral rectitude and worldly happiness. By means of a daring prologue in Heaven, the poet claims the divine sanction for his own view that the suffering of the righteous man is not the punishment of sin but the trial of faith. Job himself, though ignorant of this aspect of the case, at first bears his unparalleled misfortunes with exemplary patience; but, having been educated in the old faith, and necessarily regarding the calamities which have overtaken him as signs of God's anger, he is gradually forced to the agonising conclusion that God is unjust.

Job's three friends represent religious society and its verdicts. So long as they dare to trust their instincts, they are kind and gentle, but their sympathy is soon chilled by their creed. Holding the old dogma of retribution, not, like the early prophets, in its national aspect, but, like Ezekiel (ch. 18), in its individual bearing, they apply their grim tenet to their friend with an ever-increasing rigour and vigour. The poet gives them full scope, and uses all the resources of his genius in stating the old doctrine which he wishes to discredit. He does not forget that he belongs to a nation which has cherished that theory for centuries as an orthodox belief. Eliphaz the seer, Bildad the traditionalist, Zophar the ordinary zealot, have all of them great thoughts of the absolute power, the perfect wisdom, the ideal justice of God. They contend that they are striving to keep the nation's sacred heritage pure and intact. What they do not see is that the new conditions in which they live imperatively demand a modification of the nation's faith. Their fundamental error is that they refuse to admit patent facts, and it is the fruitful cause of others. Constituting themselves special pleaders on behalf of God, they become so enmeshed in scholastic jargon that they cease to be conscious of the poignant realities with which they trifle. They sacrifice their friend to their creed. *Tantum religio potuit suaderc malorum.* 'Of all the cruelty inflicted in the name of orthodoxy there is little that can surpass the refined torture due to this Jewish apologetic. Its cynical teaching met the sufferer in the anguish of bereavement, in the pain and depression of disease, when he was crushed by sudden and ruinous losses. . . . Instead of receiving sympathy and help, he found himself looked upon as a moral outcast and pariah on account of his misfortunes; when he most needed divine grace, he was bidden to regard himself as a special object of the wrath of Jehovah. If his orthodoxy survived his calamities, he would review his past life with morbid retrospection, and persuade himself that he had indeed been guilty above all other sinners' [W. H. Bennett in *The Book of Chronicles*].

Job is thus placed in an extraordinary dilemma. If the old doctrine of retribution is true—and he cannot yet doubt that it is—his good conscience is incompatible with the goodness of God, and he must sacrifice the one or the other. If, on the one hand, he trusts his moral sense, he is driven to distrust God; and if, on the other, he trusts God and his creed, he is compelled to deny his own integrity. In the awful conflict which becomes inevitable, will his creed or his conscience win the day?

Job is true to himself. His consciousness of his own innocence is clearer to him than the justice of God. He opposes his moral sense to the verdict of his friends, the judgment of society, the traditions of his race. He is not, like Athanasius, alone with God against the world; he is in the more tragic position of being alone against God and the world.

It is evidently one of the main purposes of the poet to assert the moral rights of personality. He realises two things with equal sureness—the meanness and the dignity of man. Job knows that he is but a driven leaf, a thing of nought, petty, ephemeral, infinitely to be pitied. But he knows also that he is a moral being; and, as he cannot deny his primal certainties, he vindicates his rights against wanton infringements not only at the hands of man, but also at the hands of a despotic God. He does not for a moment assert that he is sinless, but he knows that he has committed none of the crimes of which he is suspected, and no argument can induce him to declare himself guilty against his better knowledge. Omnipotence may crush him in an instant, but cannot compel him to violate his conscience. In reading the ***Book of Job*** one is constantly reminded of

Pascal's words [in *Pensées*]: 'L'homme n'est qu'un roseau, le plus faible de la nature, mais c'est un roseau pensant. Il ne faut que l'Univers entier s'arme pour l'écraser. Une vapeur, une goute d'eau, suffit pour le tuer. Mais quand l'Univers l'écraserait, l'homme serait encore plus noble que ce qui le tue, parce qu'il sait qu'il meurt, et l'avantage que l'Univers a sur lui. L'Univers n'en sait rien.' Job's friends have a kind of fanatical belief in the greatness of God and the worthlessness of man. The former doctrine Job accepts, but his words are an eternal protest against the latter. The spirit of man asserts the absolute character of its highest convictions against any array of external reasons. 'It was a momentous step when the soul in its relations to God ventured to take its stand upon itself, to trust itself ' [according to Wellhausen in *History of Israel*]. 'The doctrine of man's dignity receives in the person of Job its noblest exposition in all ancient literature' [according to R. H. Charles in his *Critical History of the Doctrine of a Future Life*].

It is Job's loyalty to his moral nature that leads him to a higher faith—to the belief in a God who owns the moral claims of the creature upon the Creator. So long as he doubts whether God is infinitely good as well as great, he is in spiritual darkness. If God is to be judged by the outward phenomena which seem to be the expression of His mind, His rule must be accounted the régime of an omnipotent despot whose arbitrary will is the sole moral law. But against such a conception Job's whole being triumphantly asserts itself. The God for whom his heart yearns, the God of righteousness and love, must be the true God. He *knows* that above all the dark things of earth such a God lives, that He is the Witness of his innocence, and that He will one day be his Vindicator. Though indisputable facts point to an awful God who has become his Enemy, his heart assures him of a gracious God who is his Friend and has never ceased to love him. And the strangest thing in the drama is his appeal to the God of Heaven against the God of earth. The antinomy indicates that he is groping after a higher conception of God. All his wild words, in some of which he comes perilously near to anathematising God, are directed against a pitiless and undiscriminating Force. And his new faith, which is not fabricated in the schools of logic, but forged in the furnace of affliction, is faith in a God who loves and can be loved.

In nothing is the ***Book of Job*** more modern than in its impressive protest against absolutism in theology, its plea for a reasonable service based upon the moral affinity and the mutual understanding of God and man. Is humanity to worship an Almighty Being, though His justice may not be as human justice, nor His mercy as the mercy of man, who may, in fact, for aught we know, be a despotic and revengeful Tyrant? Job's friends said 'Yes,' and therefore he regarded them as sycophants, trembling worshippers of might instead of right, cowards cringing before the unknown Cause of all things, good and bad alike, in nature and in providence. Before such a Deity of absolute power, who did not realise his moral ideal, Job steadily refused to bow. When Hamilton and Mansel unwittingly revived in Britain the doctrine of Job's friends, it was Stuart Mill who repeated, in different language, Job's fiery protest: 'I will call no being good who is not what I mean when I apply that epithet to my fellow-creatures; and if such a being can sentence me to hell for not so calling him, to hell I will go.' But if the theological difficulties of the ancient East and the modern West are essentially the same, the heart's intuitions are also everywhere alike, and 'in the person of Job the poet struggles towards the only conception of God which has hope for the universe' [according to A. M. Fairbairn in *The City of God*]. At the altar of that God the East and the West will meet.

There is yet another possible solution of the enigma of suffering innocence; and when Job is at the height of his great argument, he catches a glimpse of it. His theology is charged with white-hot emotion, and emits lightning flashes of prophecy. As if it were not enough to dispute with men, he dares to face that 'strange hero—Οανατοσ.' It is one of the presuppositions of the drama that this world is the only field in which divine justice is exercised, and there is at first no suggestion that the wrongs of the present may be righted in an after-life. But when it becomes apparent to Job that he can never get justice in this world, his mind leaps instinctively to the thought of a posthumous vindication. From the depth of despair he suddenly rises to grapple with the last enemy, to put his foot on the neck of Death. For at least one supreme moment he stands convinced that as a disembodied spirit he will be recalled from Sheol to hear himself justified and to see his Vindicator. It is true that what he expects is not immortality, but simply a favourable verdict which he will be summoned to receive after death. Seed-thoughts, however, grow, and one man's germinal faith—'apart from my flesh shall I see God'—may ultimately become all mankind's invincible hope of eternal life in the presence of God.

In his perplexity Job again and again expresses the passionate desire to come before God, to plead his cause, and to hear the explanation of his sufferings. He is confident that if God will speak, it will not be to condemn but to justify him. At length he is in a measure gratified. The divine speech . . . from the whirlwind is at once the crowning audacity and the literary glory of the poem. 'It transcends all other descriptions of the wonders of creation or the greatness of the Creator which are to be found either in the Bible or elsewhere' [according to Samuel Driver]. One may admit that in a sense it is disappointing. It does not account for Job's afflictions, and it throws little fresh light upon the moral anomalies of the divine government of the world; it leaves the universe still (in Carlyle's ironical phrase) 'a little abstruse.' But it admirably serves the poet's purpose of bringing his hero back to a sane and true conception of the character of God. If it does not answer the questions raised by the inquisitive intellect, it satisfies the hungering heart. It turns Job's brooding mind from the problem of evil to the problem of good. It plies him with humbling interrogations as to his knowledge of the infinite resources of the Divine Mind. It suggests to him that He who lavishes so much thoughtfulness and kindness upon inanimate and animate nature, cares still more for man. It uses the argument of Isaiah, 'Lift up your eyes on high, and see: who hath created these? . . . He giveth power to the faint' [*Isaiah* 40:26, 29], and of the Sermon on the Mount, 'Be-hold the birds of the heaven. . . . Consider the lilies, . . . shall he not much more clothe you, O ye of little faith?' [*Matthew* 6:26, 28, 30].

The searching but none the less tender irony of the speech has often been strangely misunderstood. Renan, [in his *History of the People of Israel*], thinks that it simply 'crushes the pride of the man who pretends to understand anything of the works of God.' Professor Cornill, who holds that the true solution of the problem of the poem is found in the speeches of Elihu, says that in the divine speeches not the slightest attempt is made to refute or persuade Job, 'but with an unparalleled brutality, which is usually palliated and styled divine irony, but which, under such circumstances and conditions, should much rather be termed devilish scorn (*teuflischer Hohn*), his mouth is simply stopped.' In that case the poet, as Duhm observes [in *The New World*], proves himself to be an entirely incapable thinker. The genius of Ewald [in *The Book of Job*] long ago divined the real meaning of the great utterance. 'The most suitable manner for these divine speeches is that of irony, which combines with concealed severity and calm superiority the effective and benevolent incisiveness of a higher insight that is used in bright sportiveness, a manner of speech which shows, without wounding or crushing, clearly and tellingly the disproportion of the human in its one-sidedness to the truly divine, of the clouded human understanding to the clear, complete wisdom, of powerless human defiance to true power. If the perfectly divine reveals itself in opposition to the limited and human, it is always like an involuntary irony in relation to the latter, even when it punishes and destroys: but in this case there is also a condescension which is really in its inmost nature of the most gracious character.' The hero is not in the end overwhelmed by the poet with diabolical scorn; like Gerontius, he is 'consumed, yet quickened, by the glance of God.' 'He humbles himself in the very dust; not, however, with painful resignation, but in the elevating assurance that God has acknowledged him, and that he must regard all the elements of his lot as evidence of an all-wise and loving will, [Kautsch].

The Book of Job was a great teacher's appeal to the heart of the Hebrew-speaking race in an age of transition, and in the measure in which its teachings were received it clarified the nation's theology, theodicy, and morality. (i.) In a period of intellectual unrest the faith of many Jews apparently reduced itself to a belief in a vague inscrutable Power, sublime, inaccessible, unfeeling, not to say blundering, on which they hesitated to bestow the ancient name of Israel's God. If the poet himself was for a time bound and cramped by such a conception, his spirit was ultimately liberated, and his message to his nation is, that by fidelity to its moral ideals it will recover the vision of a living personal God, the Witness and Vindicator of righteousness, the Light of those who seek Him, the Strength of those who find Him. Given such a conception of God, it matters little by what name He is called. The modern mind is tempted to depersonalise God, preferring 'the Divine' . . . , 'the something not ourselves that makes for righteousness,' to the eternally righteous Ego, who, having given us minds to know Him and hearts to love Him, reveals Himself that He may satisfy the instincts He has created. Renan thinks that what the writer of Job, who 'displayed great freedom of thought,' still needed to learn was, that 'no special will governs the world, and that what happens is the result of a blind effort tending upon the whole toward good.' It is a pity that the supreme Hebrew master of irony could not have replied to the patronising savant. He would probably have numbered him among Job's 'tormenting comforters.' At any rate, he would not have worshipped a Blind Effort. 'Dark as the problem of evil is, it would be immeasurably darker if we were compelled to believe that there is no infinite Righteousness and Love behind, from which a solution of the problem may ultimately be hoped for, [according to J. Orr in *The Christian View of God and the World*].

(ii.) The writer sought to purify Israel's theodicy. If he could deliver the national conscience from its age-long obsession by the belief that all pains are penalties, all afflictions evidences of the wrath of Heaven,—if he could prevent the massing of sin and suffering together as one complex blot upon human life, and so prepare for a higher conception of the meaning of sorrow,—he felt that he would not have lived in vain. If he could portray a Servant of God, perfect, upright, eschewing evil, and yet enduring unparalleled sufferings, what might not the next development in the nation's religion be? Of that the writer could probably have no presentiment, and doubtless he thought it enough if he lived his own life and did his own work well. But he builded better than he knew. Job's (and Israel's) forlorn doubt—the maze, the struggle, the labour, the anguish of it all—formed a true *praeparatio evangelica*. 'If the Jew was to accept a Messiah who was to lead a life of sorrow and abasement, and to be crucified between thieves, it was necessary that it should be somewhere or other distinctly taught that virtue was not always rewarded here, and that therefore no argument could be drawn from affliction and ignominy against the person who suffered it.' [J. B. Mozley, *Essays*].

(iii.) The poet endeavoured to refine his nation's ethics. In days of oppression and dishonour there were doubtless many Jews who impatiently asked, 'Must we serve God for nought?' And if not a few of them proved unfaithful, the cynical world thought it only natural. But the writer of Job dramatically rallies his people to a purer faith and a nobler morality. He commends that service of God which is not synonymous with prudence, expedience, utility, enlightened self-interest; which is rendered not merely in cheerful and happy times, but in the darkest and dreariest hours. He has discovered that man's love of God is of the higher, diviner order, not when life is smooth and prosperous, but when it is full of sorrow and strife. 'Doth Job serve God for nought?' asks the cynic; 'touch his bone and his flesh, and he will renounce Thee to Thy face.' But it is the cynic who is disillusioned. And the poet's appeal to his people is, Let your faith rise in eternal refutation of the cynicism which would kill the soul of a nation. Nowhere is the poem more modern than here. Paley defined virtue as 'the doing good to mankind, in obedience to the will of God, and for the sake of everlasting happiness.' Substitute 'lifelong' for 'everlasting,' and this is the Satan's definition. No greater service can be rendered to a nation than the displacement of utilitarian by ideal ethics.

'Schemes of conduct grounded on calculations of self-interest . . . do not belong to Moral Science, to which, both in kind and purpose, they are in all cases *foreign* and, when substituted for it, *hostile.*' [Coleridge, in Seth's *English Philosophers*.] To love and serve God for His own sake, as man's moral and spiritual Ideal, and thereby to quench the accusing spirit of sceptical cynicism, are the principles of action which are inculcated in the ***Book of Job***, and there are none higher. They are the principles which made the Hebrews, with all their faults, the foremost nation in history, and they are the principles which make nations great to-day. 'A people cannot be regenerated by teaching them the worship of enjoyment; they cannot be taught a spirit of sacrifice by speaking to them of material rewards. It is the soul which creates to itself a body; the idea which makes for itself a habitation. . . . Say to men, *Come, suffer; you will hunger and thirst; you will, perhaps, be deceived, be betrayed, cursed; but you have a great duty to accomplish:* they will be deaf, perhaps, for a long time, to the severe voice of virtue; but on the day that they do come to you, they will come as heroes, and be invincible' [Mazzini, *Essays*].

Morris Jastrow, Jr.   (essay date 1920)

SOURCE: "The Folktale of Job and The Book of Job," in *The Book of Job: Its Origin, Growth and Interpretation,* J. B. Lippincott Company, 1920, pp. 25-63.

Altarpiece, c. 1480-83. Cycle of scenes from the nonbiblical life of Job, including the visit of an angel (upper left) and Job and the minstrels (lower right).

[*In the following essay from his critical study and translation* The Book of Job: Its Origin, Growth and Interpretation, *Jastrow views the poetry section of* The Book of Job *as a philosophical discussion in which the traditional explanation for human suffering presented in the older folktale of* Job *is questioned.*]

The ambition of the student of Biblical Literature to try his hand at an interpretation of the *Book of Job* appears to be as irresistible as the longing of every actor—even though he begins his career with low comedy—to end as Hamlet. [In a footnote, the critic adds: "The list of interpretors of Job extends from Theodore of Mopsuestia who in the fifth century of our era endeavored to show that Job is a tragedy after the pattern of the Greek drama, to the year 1918 in which Dr. H. M. Kallen made the same futile attempt. The interpreters include the greater lights and smaller satellites among Biblical scholars from the Jewish commentators of the Middle Ages: Ibn Ezra, Kimchi and Rashi, to Ewald, Renan, Dillman, Duhm, Budde, Graetz, Cheyne, Szold, Genung, Delitzsch, Siegfried, Peake, Cox, Barton, Strahan, Blake, Ehrlich, Driver, Gray and Buttenwieser in the nineteenth and twentieth centuries."] The difficulties with which the book bristles from its challenge, as the intensely human problem with which it deals explains the fascination which it has ever exercised on every one who can sympathize—and who can not?—with the pathetic effort of the human soul to pierce the encompassing darkness and mystery of human life. Carlyle calls it "A noble book; all men's book" [in *Heroes and Hero Worshippers*, II]. It makes, in truth, a universal appeal, and this is the more remarkable because there is no other book in the Biblical collection which is so puzzling the moment one endeavors to penetrate beneath the surface, as there is none in regard to which so many misunderstandings are still current. It may be said without exaggeration that every thing about the book is puzzling. The language is difficult and in many cases almost hopelessly obscure, the text has come down to us in a very corrupt form, in part due to the obscurity of the language, the arrangement is most complicated, the setting is as strange as it is non-Jewish, and what adds to these difficulties, the entire book has been manipulated in the interest of conventional orthodoxy, so that its original import can only be discovered by a most exacting study.

We must at the outset recognize that the *Book of Job* in its original form was a skeptical composition—skeptical in the sense of putting a question mark after the fundamental axiom in the teachings of the Hebrew prophets of the ninth and succeeding centuries, that the government of the universe rests on justice. We will see that there is no single author in the modern sense to any part of the book. The group that produced the original book, while not denying the existence of a watchful Creator, is not satisfied with the mere repetition of a pious phrase,

"God's in His heaven,
All's right with the world!'"

They wish to test the phrase. Anatole France tells us in that charming narrative of his childhood—Le Petit Pierre—in which one suspects that he has used the Goethean device of combining "Wahrheit und Dichtung"—

that he declined to follow his mother's suggestion to put an interrogation mark after the title of his earliest composition "What is God," because, as he insisted, he purposed to answer the question. Since then, he tells us, he has changed his mind and is inclined to put a question mark after everything that he writes, thinks or does. The unknown thinker to whom we owe the first draft of the *Book of Job* is one of the great questioners of antiquity, and those who followed in his wake in enlarging the book often add two interrogation marks to statements that were accepted as a matter of course by the age in which they lived.

The personage of Job is merely an illustration of a man who endured in patience. The folktale is a peg on which to hang the discussion of the problem involved in Job's sufferings. This problem is resolved into the question— Why should the just man suffer? Job is "Everyman," and what happened to him represents merely on a large scale what on a smaller one may be taken as typical of the common human experience. For who has not at some time in his life suffered innocently and felt convinced of his martyrdom? Even the most fortunate experience disappointments which seem to involve injustice towards them. We are all at some time buffeted by the waves of fortune, and when we look about us we behold on all sides the sea strewn with the wrecks of human careers, as a result of the merciless fury of the elements aroused to anger through no cause that can be reconciled with the conception of a moral and just Neptune. In the larger field of human history—the fate of nations and countries—cunning, deceit, brute power, oppression of the masses seem to be the forces in control.

"Right forever on the scaffold,
Wrong forever on the throne."

A "gentle cynic" like Koheleth can deal lightly with a topsy-turvy world in which he sees "a righteous man who perishes by his righteousness, and there a wicked man rounding out his life in his wickedness." [*Ecclesiastes,* 7:15] The one who is willing to take things as they come can reach the conclusion that there is "nothing better for a man than to be happy and enjoy himself in his life" [*Ecclesiastes,* 3:12]. Not so the writers in the original *Book of Job,* who are neither gentle nor cynical. For them the fact that wickedness usurps the place of justice, and "where the righteous should have been, the wicked was" [*Ecclesiastes,* 3:16] constitutes the most serious problem of life, since it involves the possibility that at the head of the universe stands a blind and cruel fate in place of a loving Father of mankind. The questioner scans the heavens and finds the supposed throne of mercy without an occupant; and the discovery bears heavily on his disturbed soul.

This, then, must constitute our point of departure in any endeavor to penetrate into the meaning of the philosophic poem in its earliest form, that its spirit is skeptical. *The Book of Job* arose out of a circle which was not content with the conventional answer to the question why the innocent suffer in this strange world. Hence the manifest sympathy of the writers to whom we owe the Symposium (chapters 3-27) with Job. The three "friends" introduced as participants in the discourse are merely foils to press home the arguments of Job against the assumptions of the prevailing orthodoxy. Job is the Alpha and Omega in the situation, the climax and the anti-climax.

But the objection may be interposed, why designate *Job* as a book that questions the current view that suffering is for a good cause, when we have the speeches of the three companions who in answer to Job's complaints uphold the orthodox point of view? Besides there are the discourses of Elihu (chapters 32-37) in defence of orthodoxy, and the magnificent series of poems (chapters 38-41), put into the mouth of God Himself. Is not the orthodox point of view triumphant? Does not Job repent and only after his repentance is rewarded for his sufferings by having health, wealth and happiness restored to him? Why not judge the book from this angle? Such indeed was the prevailing view taken of *Job* till the advent of modern Biblical criticism, and even among the critical students there are at present some—and in the former generation there were more—who look upon the *Book of Job* as written for the purpose of vindicating the story of Job, instead of questioning the basis on which that story rests.

If we take the book as it stands in our ordinary Bible translations, there is no escape from the conclusion that *Job* is a powerful argument for the maintenance of Jewish orthodoxy of post-exilic days, but the fatal objection to the conclusion is that we *cannot* take the book as it stands. As we have it, the production is far removed from its original draft. It is not a unit composition, as little as is the Book of Koheleth. It is composite not to the same degree as the Pentateuch is a gradual growth, but of the same order. It consists of a trunk on which branches have been grafted. In the course of its growth from the first draft to its final form it covers a considerable period, just as the compilation of the five books into which the Psalms are divided stretches over several centuries. It received in the course of its growth large additions the purpose of which was to *counteract* the tendency of the original draft, precisely as was the purpose of the additions to Koheleth.

Now in order to establish this, let us try to make clear to ourselves how a Symposium such as we have in *Job* based on the story of *Job* may have arisen. We must take as our starting-point not an individual author—for there were no authors in any real sense of the word among the Hebrews till some time after the contact with Greek culture—but rather a circle in which the problem suggested by the folktale would form the subject of discussion. Some thinker in such a circle, gifted with insight into human nature and an observer of what was happening in the world around him, raised the question whether such a story as that of Job was a true one, that is, in the sense of representing what would really happen if misfortune should overtake a thoroughly good and virtuous and God-fearing man. Would such a man act in the manner indicated in the folktale, like Job accept the evil in the same spirit as the good and bow his head in silent resignation? The third chapter in which Job begins by cursing the day on which he was born, and ends by complaining that God will not grant release to those who long for death more than for hidden treasures,

"Who rejoice at the thought of the mound,"

furnishes the answer. "There you have the real Job," exclaims the thinker. That is the way in which a man who feels keenly the injustice of being made a butt of misfortune would feel. To be deprived of family possessions and station and finally to be tortured with loathsome disease would change the pious and God-fearing man into a violent accuser of the Deity. Throughout the Symposium, Job is represented as protesting against his cruel and unjustifiable treatment. He wrings our soul with pity by his bitter outcries. Those who write the speeches which they put into his mouth visualize for us the sufferings of Job beyond human endurance. Ever and again he breaks out in his anguish and indulges in indictments against Divine injustice that know no bounds.

A second question put by our thinker, who analyzes the story that was repeated from generation to generation, was even more pertinent. What about God? What an awful Deity to permit a man "perfect and removed from evil" (1, 2) to be thus wracked on the wheel! The introduction of the scene between Yahweh and Satan only enhances the callousness of the former in heaping misfortunes on an innocent head, just for the satisfaction of winning a wager. What a shocking and immoral story, we can fancy the thinker saying, to tell children and to impress upon their elders. Even if Job had acted as he is represented in the folktale, what is there to be said in justification of God? The good "Sunday School" story is thus transformed under the searching test of those who approach it from a more critical angle, into a most objectionable tale. Its supposed lesson to suffer without murmuring is punctured by the two questions thus raised in regard to it, the one of a psychological nature, the other of a theological order. How can one reconcile the conduct of Yahweh in the story with the conception of God taught by the Hebrew prophets of the century and a half preceding the downfall of Jerusalem (586 B.C.), as a Being ruling the world and the destinies of mankind by laws of justice, tinctured with mercy? That is the problem as it appeared to the circle within which at some time a thinker arose, who put his two questions and who stimulated his fellow thinkers to discuss the theme involved in what on the surface appeared to be an altogether proper and impressive folktale.

The Symposium in which arguments and counter arguments are exchanged by Job and his friends is the outcome of these discussions. The purpose of the Symposium is not to elaborate the story, but to illuminate the religious problem which may, in other words, be briefly defined as the search for the reason of suffering and evil in a world created by a supposedly merciful, just and loving Creator. One must enlarge the problem to one of suffering *and* evil, for the one implies the other. The counterpart to Job, the innocent sufferer, is the wicked man who escapes punishment. Our thinker is unsparing in his search, for no less typical than Job's case of what is happening daily is the con-current instance of the wrongdoer who eludes the fate that is his due. The one who heaps up ill-gotten gain enjoys his wealth without even a twinge of conscience at forcing others to tread the mill, so that he may acquire substance. The tyrant on the throne, the thief who robs his fellow, the murderer who mounts over the prostrate body of his victim, the dishonest dealer who defrauds his customers by false scales, the brutal employer who grinds the faces of the poor—are they not all around us, happy and prosperous while the weak and defenseless perish? Such is the terrible indictment that we encounter in the utterances put into the mouth of Job. Here is a problem indeed, well worthy of discussion. Where is God while innocent suffering and terrible injustice is going on in His world? Is a solution possible?

The circle in which the problem thus extended into a general discussion of the reason for suffering and evil in the world was tossed to and fro must have consisted of bold thinkers who had freed themselves from the shackles of traditional views to plunge fearlessly into the maelstrom of doubt and rationalism. They knew of the counter arguments that would be brought forward in orthodox circles against the position taken by Job. In order to illuminate the problem from all sides, the three friends of the folktale are introduced as the representatives of the prevailing orthodoxy, but it is evident throughout the Symposium that although the speeches put into the mouth of Eliphaz, Bildad and Zophar are from the literary point of view fully as impressive as those of Job, the sympathy of the writers is on the side of Job. It is only when we come to the four speeches of a fifth personage—Elihu—that we obtain compositions in which the attempt is made to divert our sympathy, but Elihu takes no part in the Symposium proper.

We are led to a post-exilic date for the existence of such a circle of free thinkers, sufficiently bold and advanced to tackle the most perplexing problem that arises when religion passes from the earlier stages in which the chief attribute of the gods is strength, arbitrarily exercised, to the highest level in which ethical motives enter into the conception of the Divine government of the universe. With the appearance of the great series of prophets, about the middle of the ninth century, B.C. the Hebrews definitely advance to this level, for the burden of the teachings of Amos, Hosea, Micah and Isaiah is that Yahweh, the national deity of the Hebrews, is a Power "making for righteousness." He does not act arbitrarily, but rewards or punishes according to the good or bad deeds of his people. The obedience that He exacts is to dictates of justice. He knows no favorites and cannot be bribed by sacrifices or homage to divert just punishment from wrongdoers. The pre-exilic prophets do not stress the universal sway of Yahweh. For them Yahweh is still, or at least primarily, the God of the Hebrews. In this sense the Hebrews are His chosen people, but the corollary that a God of justice and righteousness must be a unifying force, in control of the universe and exercising His sway over all nature and all mankind, was in due time drawn, though it is not until the exilic period that a genuine ethical monotheism was preached by the successors of the earlier prophets, by Ezekiel, by the anonymous prophets whose utterances are embodied in the second part of Isaiah [Chapters 40-66, with some scattered utterances also in the first 35 chapters], by Zephaniah and Zechariah.

We must descend well into the fifth century before Judaism, as we know it, became part and parcel of the life of the people. In the Symposium God is viewed as a power of universal scope. There is no longer any trace of the former nationalistic limitations; and it is just because the doctrine of the prophets involved the rule by this universal Power of the destinies of mankind by self-imposed laws of righteousness and justice, that the problem as to the cause of innocent suffering and unchecked evil in the world becomes real and intense. For religions of the older type, the difficulty did not exist. The gods were arbitrary. They could not be held to account. It was man's sole endeavor to keep them in good humor and favorably disposed by doing what would please them. If despite gifts and homage, the gods were disposed to manifest their anger by sending disease, by catastrophes and miseries of all kinds, there was nothing to be done but to wait until their displeasure had passed away. The circle from which the ***Book of Job*** emanated could therefore not have arisen in Palestine, where the book originated, before the fifth century, B. C. and scholars are generally agreed to proceed far into this century for the first draft of our book. The discussions on the vital problem may have gone on orally for some time before the thought rose of giving a written form to them, and we are probably safe in fixing upon 400 B. C. as the approximate date for the Symposium.

The problem of the ***Book of Job*** is thus one which directly arises out of the basic doctrine of post-exilic Judaism; and it was inevitable that the question would some time be raised, whether what the prophets taught of the nature of God which the people accepted as guidance in their lives was compatible with the facts of experience. Is there a just and loving Providence at the helm of the universe? If so, why does man live in a vale of sorrow? As the Psalmist asks:

> "Why standest Thou afar off, O Yahweh,
> Why hidest Thou Thyself in times of trouble?"
> [*Psalm* 10: 1]

The questioning spirit arises in the circles of the orthodox and pious quite as much as among those who boldly challenge conventional views, but the significance of the Symposium consists in the thorough manner in which for the first time the problem is discussed in the light of a particularly significant example of a contrast between what *ought* to be in a world that is supposed to be ruled by justice, and what *is*. Occasionally in other literatures of the ancient East, the problem is touched upon. So, for example, in a remarkable Babylonian poem of a king of Nippur, who despite his piety is smitten with disease. Tabiutul-Enlil, as the king is called, is represented as indulging in reflections on the prevalence of suffering in the world.

> "I had reached and passed the allotted time of
>   life.
> Whithersoever I turned—evil upon evil;
> Misery had increased, justice had disappeared."

But under the limitation of the Babylonian conception of the gods, who although not insensible to justice, yet exercise their power according to their pleasure and in arbitrary fashion, the poem goes no farther than to suggest that the ways of the gods are unfathomable, and that without apparent cause man's fate is subject to constant change.

"What, however, seems good to oneself, to a god
   is displeasing,
What is spurned by oneself finds favor with a
   god;
Who is there that can grasp the will of the gods
   in heaven?
The plan of a god full of power (?)—who can un-
   derstand it?
How can mortals learn the way of a god?
He who was alive yesterday is dead to-day.
In an instant he is cast into grief,
Of a sudden he is crushed.
For a moment he sings in joy;
In a twinkling he wails like a mourner.
Like opening and closing, their (*i.e.* mankind's)
   spirit changes;
If they are hungry, they are like corpses;
Have they had enough, they consider themselves
   equal to their god.
If things go well, they prate of mounting to heav-
   en;
If they are in distress, they speak of descending
   into Irkalla."

In the Upanishads of ancient India, from about the seventh and following centuries, the tragedy of life is the
constant theme, and the spirit in which life is viewed is
preëminently philosophical, but we have sporadic reflections rather than a genuine attempt to get at the core of
the problem. In this respect the Symposium of *Job* is
unique. Its philosophy is not academic but intensely
human. It brings the problem home to us in a way that betrays its origin in a circle which responded sympathetically to the hard experiences of life from which few escape,
a circle that was alive to the consciousness of frequent failure, despite all endeavors to follow the dictates of an ethical code of life and that grasped the bitterness of seeing
wrong triumphant while virtue is trampled under foot.
The Symposium is all the more remarkable because despite its rebellious tone, its boldness is kept within the limits of an honest search for truth, undertaken in a profoundly serious frame of mind. Its pessimism is free from
any tinge of cynicism or frivolity; its skepticism is never
offensive, because it keeps close to intense sympathy for
suffering mankind as typified by Job. The Symposium,
quite apart from its literary qualities, stands out for these
reasons in the world's literature as one of the boldest attempts to attack a problem which to-day, after two thousand years and more, still baffles religious minds.

A further condition for a proper understanding of the
book that follows from what has just been set forth, is the
separation of the story of Job from the philosophical discussion occasioned by the story; and here we touch upon
the most significant of misunderstandings in regard to our
book which is still widely prevalent. To the average person
who has been accustomed to think of the ***Book of Job*** as
a unit composition, written by one person as a book generally is in our days, there is only *one* Job. In reality there
are two, the Job of the story and the Job in the discussions
with his three companions. The only connection between
the two Jobs is the similarity in the name.

An uncritical tradition is responsible for the confusion, for
the compilers of the book in its original form did all that
lay in their power to distinguish between the two. Even ex-

ternally the Job of the story is separated from the Job in
the discussions. The story of the pious, patient, taciturn
Job is told in prose [Chapters I and 2 and the conclusion
of the story (though modified from its original form) chapter 42, 7-17. The distinction is made evident in the Revised
Version, as in other modern translations.], whereas the
other Job who is impatient, and rebellious, voluble in the
denunciation of the cruel fate meted out to him, and blasphemous in his charges of injustice against the Creator of
the universe in control of the destinies of mankind is made
to speak in poetry, as are his friends. Apart from this, the
Job who when misfortunes follow upon disasters in close
succession exclaims—

"Yahweh has given, and Yahweh has taken,
Blessed be the name of Yahweh."
[*Job* 2:21]

cannot possibly be the same as the one who at the outset
of the Symposium between him and his companions gives
vent to his embittered soul in the most vehement terms:

"Perish the day on which I was born,
And the night when a male was conceived."
[*Job* 3:3]

Can there be a more striking contrast than between the
Job in the story who, when called upon by his unsympathetic wife to do away with himself and thus put an end
to his sufferings, asks:

"Should we indeed receive the good from God,
   but the evil we should not receive"?
[*Job* 2:10]

and the Job in the discussion, whose piercing cry of despair resounds through the ages:

"Why did I not die at the womb,
Come forth from the lap and perish?
Why did knees receive me?
And why were there breasts to give me suck?"
[*Job* 3:11-12]

One must admire the persistency of the uncritical tradition which thus succeeded in confusing the two Jobs, in
the face of the contradiction between the one as not "sinning with his lips," (2, 10) despite all that he had to endure, and the unbridled blasphemy of the other Job who
exclaims to God,

"I will not restrain my mouth;
I will give voice to my despair.
I prefer strangling of my soul,
Death rather than my pains.
I refuse to live any longer;
Cease, for my days are vanity."
[*Job* 7:11 and 15-16]

Nor does the Job of the discussion stop short of accusing
God of deliberate injustice. He goes so far as to suggest
that it is God's nature to be cruel, to take pleasure in seeing the innocent suffer:

"If I were in the right, my mouth [*i.e.,* my complaints against fate] would condemn me;
If I were entirely right, He would twist the verdict.

. . . . .

The guiltless and the wicked He destroys.
If a scourge should suddenly strike one dead,
He would laugh at the death of the innocent."
                                        [*Job* 9:20-23]

Can a denial of a *merciful* Providence go further? The Job of the story has sublime faith in God's justice, despite all appearances to the contrary. The Job of the discussions conceives of God as strong and powerful, but as arbitrary and without a sense of justice. Such are the two Jobs, the one as far removed from the other as heaven is from earth—

"Look here, upon this picture, and on this."

The contrast between the story and the setting in the discussion extends to the portrayal of the three friends and to the conception of God. In the story, as told in the opening two chapters, the friends are intensely sympathetic. They are shocked at the appearance of Job; they are so deeply moved by the misfortunes that have overwhelmed him and by the sufferings that he endures as to be incapable of speech. Their sympathy is expressed by their silence. But note the contrast when we come to the Symposium. Their sympathy changes to harshness in a steadily ascending scale, Eliphaz, the first to speak, begins, to be sure, in an apologetic strain, excusing himself as it were for venturing to offer a suggestion to Job as to the cause of his suffering, but only to advance to a rebuke that is none the less stinging for being put in the form of a question:

"Can man be more righteous than God?
Can a man be purer than his Maker?"
                                        [*Job* 4:17]

The implication is clear, and with subtle skill Eliphaz advances to a more direct charge that Job must have committed some great wrong which brought on his hard fate.

"I have seen the foolish take root;
But his habitation of a sudden is swept away.
His sons far from salvation,
And crushed, with none to save [them]."
                                        [*Job* 5:3-4]

Eliphaz uses the milder term "foolish," but he means "wicked;" and he wishes to leave no doubt in Job's mind that his only hope is to confess his guilt and to throw himself on the mercy of God.

If Eliphaz in his first speech is somewhat restrained, not so Bildad and Zophar, who introduce their arguments with sharp invectives, and whose example is followed by Eliphaz in his subsequent speeches. There is no trace of friendly sympathy in Bildad's greeting:

"How long wilt thou babble thus?
Thy words are a mighty wind."
                                        [*Job* 8:1]

and there is downright hostility in Zophar's opening taunt:

"Should one full of words remain unanswered?
Should a babbler be acquitted?"
                                        [*Job* 11:1]

The friends in the story of Job become the accusers in the discussion. One after the other declares that Job—in fla-grant contradiction to the assumption throughout the story—is a wicked sinner whose punishment is merited because of his unrepentant nature, which manifests itself in the charges of injustice that he hurls against the Almighty as the cause of his ills and woes. We almost lose sight of the main discussion in the great variety of the taunts, rebukes and charges brought by the three companions against Job.

There are also two conceptions of God. The Yahweh of the story is a different being from the Elohim in the discussions. [In a footnote the critic adds: "Elohim, varying with El, is a generic designation like our 'God' or 'Deity,' in contrast to Yahweh, the name of the old national deity of the Hebrews. So personal was the name Yahweh that it became customary to avoid the pronunciation and to substitute for it 'Adonai' meaning 'Master,' 'Lord.' The substitute was not due to the holiness of the name Yahweh, as the later tradition assumed, but on the contrary to its distasteful association with a deity limited in scope to one people and restricted in jurisdiction to the territory controlled by that people. The later documents in the Pentateuchal compilation use 'Elohim,' *i.e.,* Deity, which is impersonal, just as we might to-day prefer 'Almighty' to the term 'God,' because of the strong implication of personality in the current use of God."] Yahweh is proud of Job's piety and has supreme confidence that His "servant Job" will endure the test to which he is put at the instigation of Satan. Yahweh boasts of Job as one might take pride in a fine achievement.

"Hast thou observed my servant Job? There is
none like him in the earth—pious and upright."

"There's a fine fellow," Yahweh says to Satan. See what a splendid creature I have made of him! One is tempted to say that the dialogue between Yahweh and Satan has a touch of bonhomie in it that is in refreshing contrast to the severe and forbidding picture we receive of the Deity in the philosophical poem. Goethe in the prologue to Faust, based on the two introductory chapters of *Job,* has caught this spirit in the scene between the Almighty and Mephistopheles, though he has also intensified it by a thorough modernization of the scene itself.

The use of a generic designation of the Deity like Elohim to avoid the personal quality involved in the more specific name Yahweh—is intentional; and similarly, El, Eloah and Shaddai are employed as synonyms of Elohim, because they conjure up the picture of a Being of universal scope and power whom one approaches in awe, and whose decision once made is unchangeable. The God portrayed by the friends is stern and unbending, while for Job He becomes a cold tyrant, indifferent to appeals for mercy even when they come from those whose lips are clean and whose hearts are pure.

How, then, are we to account for the two Jobs, the two varying portrayals of the three companions and the two conceptions of God? It is only necessary to put the question in order to show the obviousness of the answer that the story of Job is *independent* of the philosophical poem; and if independent also older. Three passages in Ezekiel come to our aid in establishing the existence in early days of a current tradition about a man of great piety whose name was Job [*Ezekiel* 14, 14; 16, 18 and 20]. The prophet, in order to drive home his doctrine that, on the one hand, God does not punish His people without cause, and that, on the other, punishment for wrongs and crimes cannot be averted by the existence of some righteous members of the community—as in the case of Abraham's plea to save Sodom and Gomorrah for the sake of the few righteous in the multitude of sinners,—declares that even if such men as Noah, Daniel and Job were living in the midst of the sinful nation, their virtues would only secure their own deliverance from the four scourges—the sword, famine, evil beasts and pestilence—decreed for Jerusalem. The juxtaposition with Noah and Daniel shows that Job, like these two men, had come to be regarded as a model and *type* of piety and human excellence. Ezekiel, is anterior to the *Book of Job,* as he is by four centuries earlier than the Book of Daniel, in which the traditional Daniel is utilized as a medium for encouraging pious Jews, suffering under the tyranny of Antiochus Epiphanes (175-164 B.C.), to remain steadfast in their faith. The tradition about Job survives, however, the composition of the book which is called by his name, for in the Epistle of James (5, 11), Job is incidentally referred to as an example of piety and patience. As late as the days of Theodore of Mopsuestia, (died c. 428 A. D.) . . . the story of the patient Job who becomes in the popular conception a holy prophet was still current in a form which suggests to Theodore that the author of the *Book of Job* had taken some undue liberties with the original tale. The Arabs have preserved traditions about Job, which point to the growth of the popular tale even after it had been given a literary form among the Hebrews.

We are, therefore, justified in concluding that from an early age, Job had become a popular figure among the Hebrews. In accordance with the tendency of folktales the story received additions from time to time, and it also shared the fate of popular tales in being carried from one people to another.

It does not follow that the tale of the pious man who became the prototype for the virtuous man not to be moved from his position by any misfortunes that might sweep over him originated among the Hebrews. Indeed, the name Job—for which there is no satisfactory Hebrew etymology and which we do not encounter elsewhere in the Old Testament—points to a foreign origin; and if, as we may properly assume, the statement in the prologue to the *Book of Job* that he lived in the land of Uz, which lies to the east of Palestine, was part of the popular tale as it circulated among the Hebrews, it becomes even more definite that Job was not a Hebrew, as little as the three companions were Hebrews. [Shown by the names and by the statement of their homes in parts of Arabia.] The entire setting of the story is in fact non-Hebraic. Job is described as "greater than any of the sons of the East," (1, 3) in a manner to suggest that he belongs to that vague region known as "East," but without any suggestion of a connection with the "sons of Israel"; and it is rather surprising that in the adaptation of the tale to the purposes of the discussion, which we must perforce assume, a more Hebraic atmosphere should not have been given to it. In the dialogue between God and Satan, the specific Hebraic name Yah-

weh is introduced, but Job himself is represented as using the general name Elohim, (1, 5 and 2, 10) as is also his wife (2, 9.) It is only in his pious submission to the Divine will, that the name Yahweh is introduced in what is probably a quotation from a "Yahweh" prayer. That such a touch as Job himself bringing sacrifices without the mediation of a priest, as demanded by the Pentateuchal codes, should have been retained in the adaptation may be taken as a further proof of the unconscious influence exerted by the non-Hebraic origin of the tale—an influence strong enough to have kept out of it any reference to specific Hebraic rites or customs. [In a foot note the critic adds: "The term used for sacrifices is the most general that could have been selected. The annual festival that brings Job's family together (1, 4-5) is similarly of a most general character—without any warrant in any of the Pentateuchal codes."]

We are thus led to the conclusion that the story of *Job* was a tale that became current in ancient Palestine and wandered, as tales do from place to place, subject to modification as it passed down the ages, altered to some extent in its adaptation to different localities, but retaining enough traces of its origin to preserve its distinctive character as a general illustration of the spirit in which misfortunes and sufferings should be received and endured. The story of a pious man who maintains his firm faith and his simple piety under most distressing circumstances, who bore all trials in patience was what we would nowadays call a good "Sunday School" tale—one that might be told with profit to encourage the young and to edify their elders. Tales of this character are common enough in antiquity. The "good man" is a type in folktales as common as is his counterpart—the "bad man." It is not surprising, therefore, to encounter "Jobs" elsewhere, as, for example, in India where [in *Indian Fairy Tales,* 1879] we have the tale of an "upright king" who loses his possessions and sells his boy, his wife and finally himself in order to carry on his works of charity, and to whom all is restored in the end because he had endured the burdens of misfortunes in patience and without complaint.

Similarly, in the story of the pious king of Nippur, . . . who, like Job, is smitten with sore disease and is finally restored to health through the intervention of the gods, there are analogies with the philosophical discussions in *Job* that are most suggestive, but even such literary analogies furnish no warrant for assuming a direct influence from the outside on our Biblical book. The problem suggested by the sufferings of Job is a perfectly natural one, so that if we find it discussed elsewhere it would merely point to a stage of intellectual development in which people—or at least the choice spirits—were no longer entirely satisfied with the conventional view that sufferings are due to sin.

It is not necessary to assume that a definite literary form was given to the tale among the Hebrews before it was incorporated into the *Book of Job,* though, on the other hand, one cannot dogmatically assert that this could not have been the case. Stories in the ancient East, as to a large extent still in the East of today, are recited, not read. Our specifically Western attitude towards mental productivity can hardly conceive of literature except as embodied in a definite written form, whereas until the East came under the influence of the West through contact with Greek civilization in the second half of the fourth century B. C., the oral transmission without a definite literary form was the regular mould of literature to which the written form, if it existed at all, was entirely secondary and incidental—memoranda to serve as a prop in the further oral transmission. Under such conditions a story or even a book might have existed for ages before it received what we would call a book form. One of the chief reasons why the modern critical study of the Bible aroused such hostility when its results began to be disseminated among the lay public and why it is still eyed with suspicion in many circles, is because we thoughtlessly—almost unconsciously—apply our modern and Western conceptions of literary composition to an age to which they do not apply. As I have pointed out elsewhere, we can hardly conceive of a book without a title and an author, whereas these two features are precisely the ones which are lacking in ancient compositions until we reach the age of Greek literature, which may be said to have invented the author.

The written form, when it arose in the ancient Orient, was not due to the promptings of the literary instinct, or to an ambition on the part of certain individuals to be known as authors, but purely as a preservative method to prevent tales and traditions that no longer enjoyed a full spontaneous existence among the people from perishing or from being distorted. Writing begins when genuine production comes to an end. As long as a tale retained its full popularity, as long as a tradition formed, as it were, part and parcel of the life of the people there was no urgent necessity to give the tale or tradition a written form. It lived in the minds and the hearts of the people. And so with the exhortations of a prophet, with the decisions of a lawgiver, or even with the prayers of a Psalmist, giving expression to emotions shared by the entire group. There was no occasion for the definite written form until with the advent of a new age with new interests and new problems, the tale no longer made its appeal, the tradition was no longer living, the exhortation was in danger of becoming a memory, the law needed reinforcement, and the prayer through the development of the cult was embodied into a fixed ritual.

It is also immaterial whether such a man as Job ever existed, just as it is of no consequence whether there was such a man as Noah or Daniel. A rabbi of the Talmudic age [Talmud Babli, Baba Bathra], betraying a critical spirit which is quite exceptional, declares in one place that Job is a product of popular fancy; and it is at all events clear that he as well as Noah and Daniel, as likewise Abraham, became a mere *type* of steadfast piety, just as to a later age David and Solomon, despite the historical character of much—though far from everything—that is told of them become types, David of the pious king to whom an unhistorical tradition subsequently ascribed the Psalms, and Solomon of the wise king to whom Biblical productions embodying the wisdom of the age were assigned. This tendency to transform traditional or historical personages into types is a by-product of the spirit peculiar to the ancient East, which only gradually reaches the point where the individual stands out in sharp outline from his surroundings.

G. W. F. Hegel on the idea of confidence in *Job* (1832):

[Faith and confidence are] the line of thought that is represented in the book of *Job,* the only book whose connection with the standpoint of the Jewish people is not sufficiently recognized. Job extols his innocence, finds his destiny unjust; he is discontented, i.e., there is in him a contradiction-the consciousness of the righteousness which is absolute, and the want of correspondence between his condition and this righteousness. It is recognized as being an end of God's that He makes things go well with the good man.

What the argument points to is that this discontent, this despondency, ought to be brought under the control of pure and absolute confidence. Job asks, "What doth God give me as a reward from on high? Should it not be the unrighteous man who is rejected thus?" His friends answer in the same sense, only they put it in the reverse way, "Because thou art unhappy, therefore we conclude that thou art not righteous." God does this in order that He may protect man from the sin of pride.

God Himself at last speaks: "Who is this that talks thus without understanding? Where wast thou when I laid the foundations of the earth?" (38:2, 4). Then comes a very beautiful and magnificent description of God's power, and Job says, "I know it; he is a man without knowledge who thinks he may hide his counsel" (42:2 f.). This subjection is what is finally reached; on the one hand, there is the demand that it should go well with the righteous, and, on the other, even the feeling of discontent when this is not the case has to be given up. It is this resignation, this acknowledgment of God's power, that restores to Job his property and the happiness he had before. It is on this acknowledgement of God's power that there follows the re-establishment of his happiness. Still, at the same time, this good fortune is not regarded as something that can be demanded by finite man as a right, independent of the power of God.

This confidence in God, this unity, and the consciousness of this harmony of the power, and at the same time of the wisdom and righteousness of God, are based on the thought that God is determined within Himself as end, and has an end.

G.W.F. Hegel in The Dimensions of Job, *edited by Nahum N. Glatzer, Schocken Books, 1969.*

Paul Weiss   (essay date 1948)

SOURCE: "God, Job, and Evil," in *The Dimensions of Job: A Study and Selected Readings,* edited by Nahum N. Glatzer, Schocken Books Inc., 1969, pp. 181-93.

[*Weiss was a leading American philosopher whose works include* Nature and Man *(1947),* Man's Freedom *(1950),* Modes of Being *(1958),* The World of Art *(1961),* Art and Religion *(1963),* The Making of Men *(1967), and* Right and Wrong: A Philosophical Dialogue between Father and Son *(1967). In the following essay, originally published in* Commentary *in 1948, he considers* The Book of Job *"one of the great works of literature," emphasizing its treatment of broad, universal problems that are not confined to any specific religion.*]

Great literature is a universe framed in words. Offering a scheme of things more dramatic, more intelligible, more beautiful, more self-revealing than the universe in which we live, it at once inspires, restrains, and enriches the wise man, providing him with an endless source and a satisfying measure of spiritual growth.

The Book of Job is surely one of the very great works of literature of the world. It touches the core of existence; it probes to the root of the problems of good and evil, the destiny of man, the meaning of friendship, the wisdom and goodness of God, and the justification of suffering.

We may call ourselves atheists. We may swear by the latest anthropological pronouncements that all values are relative except those that make anthropologists respectable. We may claim to have no use for anything other than the discoveries or rules of economics, history, politics, music, or physics. This will in no way prevent us from being radically informed and perhaps transformed by the book of Job. That book depends for its power on no prior commitment to any particular religion-or to religion at all.

The problem it deals with is unconfinable within any limited doctrine, philosophy, or creed. We must try to read it with the kind of sympathetic objectivity and resolute courage we normally reserve for our favorite modern writers-a Dostoevsky or a Freud, a Blake or a Kierkegaard—but then I think we will find in it much to despise as well as much to admire.

Though written in a magnificent style and sustaining brilliant insights, the book of Job is not a pleasant tale. It is not reasonable, and it violates our sense of what is right and wrong. Its value lies primarily in that it forces to the fore the mystery of human existence, where the righteous sometimes suffer and the evil apparently prosper mightily.

To get the most out of the book of Job, it is desirable, I think, to state the story in such a way as to stress traditionally neglected features. One will then be able to look in a fresh way at the perennial problem of evil, and perhaps even to make a little progress in grasping what existence means to man.

In outline the story is rather simple. A childishly conceived God, a childlike God in fact, boasts about Job to His angel Satan as a child might about a dog. Satan shrewdly observes that men well cushioned against the world of tragedy and disease, poverty and contempt, have no great temptation to abuse the source of their goods. God is provoked by this sensible remark. He sets Himself to prove that Job will stand firm though he lose all that is precious. God does not want to show that Job will stand firm in goodness, virtue, or decency. All that He wants to show is that if Job is cut off from the fat of existence he will not blaspheme in the face of God.

God, from a strictly legalistic point of view, is shown in the end to be right and Satan to be wrong. Job does not

blaspheme in God's face. But of course no one could possibly do this, for that would be at one and the same time to see God and not to see Him, to know Him and not to know Him, to face Him and to turn away. But if it is simple blasphemy that is in point, there is no doubt but that God lost and Satan won, for Job blasphemed again and again, sincerely, roundly, and wholeheartedly.

What shocks us and should shock us is not Job's blasphemies, but God's. With a callousness, with a brutality, with a violence hard to equal in any literature, secular or divine, God, just to make a petulant point, proceeds to do almost everything the most villainous of beings could want. Not only does He kill, in one fell swoop, without excuse, explanation, or warrant, all of Job's cattle, but He follows this up by killing all Job's servants and then all his sons and daughters.

The inhumanity of the author (or of his God, if one prefers) has been almost matched by the insensitivity of those commentators who accept the prologue to the book of Job and do not feel a need to underscore an abhorrence of God's project and performance. Putting aside the question of whether Job's health and happiness are justifiably jeopardized because Satan is unconvinced by God's boasts, and ignoring the rights of cattle to love, there is the fact that the servants, if not the sons and daughters of Job, are human beings as vital, as precious, as worthy of life, dignity, and a defense against Satan as Job himself.

The author of the book of Job thought of Job as a pawn between God and Satan. But less than Job, infinitely less, was the value he set on Job's servants and children. He thought of them as rightfully used and even abused just to make Job uncomfortable, to try his faith, to confound Satan.

It is really amazing that Job should find, not the death of his servants or of his children, but that of his body cells, the most trying of experiences. Our modern torturers know better. They know that the core of a decent man can be more readily and vitally touched by killing his dependents than by making him sick or wracking him with pain.

Three friends come to comfort Job. He entertains them with a long lament and a set of curses calculated to make the heart curl. To this they reply with little human sympathy. They are friends of an eternal law, not of a suffering spirit. Still, it is with considerable justice and good solid traditional wisdom that they observe that Job is not as pure as he thinks he is. His sufferings, they insist, are undoubtedly deserved.

In the epilogue, God reproves the three friends, apparently for believing that human suffering comes from God and that it is bestowed on those who do wrong. If the reproof is just, we should tremble for the souls of those who assure us that God is on the side of what we have learned is the right. The refusal to affirm that good men are the nurslings of God, to be fittingly rewarded before their days are done, is today often called a lack of faith in religion. Actually, it is one of the characteristics of God as He appears in the book of Job.

Job is not a pleasant person, rich or poor, in health or in

sickness, with children or without. His answer to his friends was that he was at least as good as any—which he undoubtedly was, except for saying so. He insists, a little too violently, that there is no wickedness in his heart and that his conduct is above reproach. He suffers damnably because of the searing pain to which he is subjected. But he suffers also at least as much because he is overwhelmed with shame. He is in anguish because he is looked on with contempt by the children of those he despised. And even more than cure and peace, he wants to argue with God and make God show due cause. But whatever his faults, his sufferings were real. And his question, whether taken to refer to him alone, to someone else, or to an indefinite number of men, demands an answer: Why should a good man suffer?

After an interlude in which Elihu, a brash youngster, repeats in principle what his elders said, God comes out of a whirlwind and confronts them all. He answers that He is omnipotent and therefore evidently possessed of a wisdom no man can rightly measure or rightly judge, a proposition that will not withstand logical scrutiny, and, so far as it does, cannot please those who think of God as having the same ideas of goodness and justice as man. The story ends with God reproving the friends (without making clear the exact nature of their fault), and with an inadequate attempt by God to make amends to Job by making him wealthy and respected once again, and by endowing him with a new set of children.

The *Book of Job* does not explicitly answer the question it so unmistakably asks. Instead, it forces one to try to answer the question oneself and therefore to re-examine what one had previously believed about God and man, and the nature of good and evil.

There are at least ten different kinds of evil, though philosophers have been inclined to mention only three. Since there are no well-turned designations and definitions for most of them, we must make up a set as we go along. With some warrant in tradition, we can perhaps designate the different kinds of evil as *sin, bad intention, wickedness, guilt, vice, physical suffering, psychological suffering, social suffering, natural evil, and metaphysical evil.*

The most characteristically human evils are the first two, for they are privately inflicted. Of these, the more radical is the religious, what we normally speak of as *sin.* It can be defined in such a way as to be applicable both to those who, like the followers of Confucius and Marx, are without a God, and to those who, like Job, firmly believe in one. He sins who is disloyal to a primary value accepted on faith. Blasphemy is one form of sin and treason another; treason being in fact but practical blasphemy in the realm of the state. These and other forms of sin but begin a process of alienation from the land of consistent living and almost always end in a deserved spiritual and sometimes physical death.

All men take some supreme value to serve as the pivot and justification of the things they think and do. It is one which they have not rationally justified and can perhaps not rationally defend. On the contrary, it is usually what is needed in order to justify their use of reason and their

activities. When they go counter to it, they go counter to themselves. He sins who denies his people, just as surely as does he who violates the fiats of his God.

The book of Job affirms—I think correctly—that it is not necessary for a man to sin (see 23:12; 13:15). Job was a righteous man, a man who lived up to the demands of his God, who feared God and shunned evil, who was *tam,* perfect, without blemish. This God affirms as well as Job. It never is denied.

Over against the theologians' belief that no mortal since the days of Adam can be without sin, is the testimony of the book of Job. It is not necessary that a man sin. But though we do not have to sin, all of us do. We are faithless again and again to the things we most cherish and which give our lives meaning and unity. The only thing "original" or unavoidable about sin is that each man sins in his own way.

Job is not a sinner. Since he suffers, suffering and the multiple evils of the world ought not to be attributed to man's failure to avoid sin. It is foolish to hope that a perfect world could be achieved if only men were true to God, the state, or science. He who claims that the solution of the problems left behind by the atomic bomb depends on man's willingness to subscribe to a single or triune God, to democracy or federalism, to physics or pragmatism, goes counter to the insights of the *Book of Job.*

An apparent hair's breadth from sin and yet a world away is *bad intent,* ethical evil, the setting oneself to break an ethical command. Like sin, this is privately achieved. It is a matter of the inward parts. Unlike sin, it has a this-worldly reference always, and is concerned with the good as open to reason. The man of bad intent fails internally to live up to what reason commends.

He who wants to cheat the orphan and the widow, who steals, lies, kills, is one who violates what reason endorses as right. He who is not religious does not necessarily find these prospects more delightful than does he who is. A religious man may in fact at times be more unethical than an irreligious one, for a religion may demand of its adherents that, on behalf of it, they defy their reason and destroy the lives, property, and prospects of others.

The history of religion is in good part a story of the improvement of the morals of the gods. Throughout the ages we have edited supposed divine words to make them conform to what we know to be ethically correct. He who would avoid all ethical evil must not cling too close to the practices and faith of his fathers.

It is conceivable that a man might be without evil intent, though it is hard to believe that there ever was a man so insensitive that he never was tempted by the smell of novelty, a challenge to his daring, or the promptings of his conceit and flesh to think pleasantly of what his reason tells him is wrong.

Evil intent and suffering do not necessarily go together. There are those who intend to do good to others and those who intend to be good to themselves. Often it is the former who get the grit while the latter enjoy the grain. And *Job* affirms that there is no afterlife in which the balance will be righted (see 7:9).

The brutal fact of the matter is that God's good is not identical with what we take to be ethically good. This is evident occasionally to Job:

> Though I be righteous, mine own mouth shall
>   condemn me;
> Though I be innocent, He shall prove me per-
>   verse.
>
> (9:20)

But it is also affirmed by God. Despite Elihu's claim that

> The Almighty, whom we cannot find out, is ex-
>   cellent in power,
> Yet to judgment and plenteous justice He doeth
>   no violence.
>
> (37:23)

God cries to Job out of the whirlwind:

> Wilt thou even make void my judgment?
> Wilt thou condemn Me, that thou mayest be jus-
>   tified?
>
> (40:8)

If the *Book of Job* be any guide, we must oppose those contemporary prophets who affirm that God's wisdom is ours, and that what we take to be good, God will eventually endorse.

Every man has evil intentions, if only for passing moments. Fortunately for our society and civilization, most of us do not allow such intentions to pass the threshold of the mind and be expressed in practice. Privately and occasionally unethical in intent, we publicly and regularly do much that is good. Though we may not escape the first and second forms of evil, most of us avoid the third, *wickedness,* the evil of carrying out evil intentions.

Job, who was a little too sure that he was righteous and well intentioned, was quite right in insisting that he was not wicked (see 29:14). Those who are wicked are the enemies of mankind. Yet they seem to prosper (21:7-13). Why should this be so?

Philosophers such as Maimonides (twelfth century) and Gersonides (thirteenth-fourteenth centuries) thought the answer was to be found in the theory that God's providential care did not extent to individuals. They held that men prospered or suffered as the outcome of natural laws, and regardless of whether or not they conformed to a religious or ethical demand. But their theory does not cover the issue. Putting aside the fact that the story of Job had God and Satan actually interfering with the lives and fortunes of individual men, there is the fact that the participants have no doubt but that God could apportion health, wealth, children, and reputation in any way He wished. To the question, why is it that God did not reward the good and punish the bad, the answer given in the book of Job is that God has His own business, that he does not use our standards, that He has His own reasons, that His idea of the good is beyond the reach of man's knowledge.

The philosophers and the Bible are not, however, altogether opposed. It is possible to hold that God does not inter-

fere with the detailed workings of the world and that He has His own standards of what ought to be and what ought to be done. The philosophers, I think, are right in affirming that God does not—in fact, cannot—interfere with the ways of the world. But the author of the *Book of Job* is right in thinking that God does not allow man's standard of true virtue, right action, and real justice to dictate to Him what He is to do. With scathing scorn God asks Job:

> Knowest thou the ordinances of the heavens?
> Canst thou establish the dominion thereof in the
>   earth?
>
> (38:33)
>
> Doth the hawk soar by thy wisdom?
>
> (39:26)

He who is wicked does not necessarily incur the wrath of God. Nor does he necessarily suffer. If a man ought to avoid wickedness, the reason cannot be that he would thereby escape either the anger of God or natural ills. We do not know what God will be angry about and whether, if He were, He could or would do anything to those who aroused Him.

A man ought to avoid wickedness because otherwise he stands in his own light. It is of his nature to need his fellows and to be obligated to preserve and enhance the good that is theirs. He who is wicked opposes himself, since he does what the very completeness of his nature requires that he should not do. He may gain the whole world, but since he thereby loses himself, it cannot be himself whom he profits.

It is not true that the wicked prosper. They may be at their ease, they may have pleasure, property, admiration, honor, security. They may be unconscious of any wrong. Everyone may account them happy. Yet it would be wrong to say that they really prosper, since they defeat themselves, forcing themselves as they do further and further away from the status of a complete man.

The wicked never really prosper. But do not the good suffer? And if they do, can the suffering be justified?

The answer to this question requires, I think, some grasp of the fourth form of evil, guilt.

A man ought to intend to do the good and ought to avoid injuring others. But he ought also not neglect the plight of any. Every single being deserves to be helped, cherished, loved. Yet he who concentrates on one here must slight others there. Each has only finite energy, finite funds, finite interest; none can be everywhere. Each thus fails to fulfill an obligation to realize the good completely. Not necessarily wicked, each is necessarily guilty, humanly evil—one who fails to do all that ought to be done.

Eliphaz correctly charges Job with a neglect of hosts of needy (22:7). He spoils the charge by supposing that Job deliberately neglected the needy. To be sure, so long as he had a shekel and another did not, Job was chargeable as selfish, as having a narrow vision, as being unwilling to extend himself. But since his actions were not rooted in a deliberate malicious intent, he could not be rightly said to be wicked. He was, however, guilty.

Even if Job gave up all that he owned, he would still be

guilty. He would be guilty of failing to fulfill an infinite obligation to do good to every being everywhere. Just as no man can claim that his poverty frees him from a duty to repay a loan, so no one can claim to be without guilt because unable to fulfill this infinite obligation. Job, even if he had given up all his possessions, which he was far from doing, would still have been infinitely guilty of neglecting the needs of most of mankind.

A guilty man deserves to be punished. Were there a God and were He just, did He measure punishment according to human standards of right and wrong, everyone would be subject to infinite punishment. Anything less than this would be an undeserved bounty, warranting paeans of thanks to any God that there might be. It is some such view as this, I think, that is characteristic of much of Jewish thought. Job, in his belief that he deserved to prosper, goes counter to the dark, somber, and reasonable temper of most Jews to the effect that men deserve nought but punishment. Every reward for the Jew is an unwarranted blessing, a sign of the infinite mercy of a just God.

Job deserved punishment. He was in fact a guilty man who was made to suffer less than he ought. Zophar rightly says to him:

> Know therefore that God exacteth of thee less
>   than thine
> iniquity deserveth.
>
>   (11:6)

But what Zophar did not say or see is that Job is no more guilty than anyone else, that his suffering was no evidence of his being more wicked, of his having unethical thoughts, or of his being irreligious. And what none of them sees or says is that the point could be made without referring to God at all. Despite our guilt, we have the good fortune to live in a universe where only some of us suffer and then only part of the time.

A fifth form of evil is *vice,* the habit of doing what injures others. This, though it looms large in the writings of ethicists and is of great interest to educators and lawmakers, is not dealt with in the book of Job. We must therefore regretfully pass it by, but not before we remark that it is produced by men and not by God, that it is independent of intent, and that it need not entail suffering.

The sixth, seventh, and eighth forms of evil can be dealt with together as different modes of suffering. Men suffer in their bodies, *physically;* in their minds, *psychologically;* and as both together, *socially.* Job suffered in all three ways (7:5; 30:17; 7:13 ff.; 19:9, 13, 17 f.).

Torn in his body, by his mind, and from his fellow man, Job has no place to rest. In him evil has found a lodging; there it festers and grows. His sufferings are real, painfully real, or everything we could possibly know is nought but an allusion.

Those philosophers who assure us that such sufferings are like ugly spots in paintings, which disappear when seen as part of the beautiful whole they make possible, overlook a slight point: it is a living man who suffers.

The suffering may seem like nothing from the perspective of the world. But it is all the world to him who suffers. It is real, it is vital, it is ultimate; it must be reckoned with. As the story of Job makes abundantly clear, it has nothing necessarily to do with other forms of evil. It is to be conquered, not by improving our morals, but by improving our bodies, our minds, and our societies.

Good men will undoubtedly help us advance in medicine, psychology, and politics more than those who are bad. But it will not be because they are religiously or ethically good that they will make progress in these fields, but because they are good as doctors, psychologists, and sociologists.

It is not necessary that men should suffer. Some remain healthy throughout their days, others are perpetually at peace with themselves, and still others are perfectly at home with their fellows. It is hard to see why any one man might not enjoy all three types of good. In any case, it is one of the tasks of all to make this true of each.

Beyond these evils, usually neglected in this anthropocentric age, is a ninth, a *natural* evil, an evil embodied in the wild, destructive forces of nature. Cataclysms of all kinds, earthquakes, tidal waves, and hurricanes, "the *leviathan* and the *behemoth*," are forces of destruction which

> esteemeth iron as straw
> and brass as rotten wood.
>
>   (41:19)

They ought not to be. They do not arise, however, because there is something bad in man. The wind does not blow violently, the earth does not rock, because men sin or kill. To suppose that nature is geared to the goodness and badness of men is to suppose either a mysterious harmony between ethics and physics, or that spirits can really move mountains.

It is God, according to the **book of Job,** who is responsible for the forces of nature.

> Out of whose womb came the ice?
> And the hoar-frost of heaven, who hath gendered it?
>
>   (38:29)

It is God

> Who hath cleft a channel for the waterflood
> Or a way for the lightning of the thunder,
> To cause it to rain on a land where no man is.
>   (38:25 f.)

But then, either God is responsible for natural evils, or He has His own mysterious reasons for allowing what He does, or the universe and its evils are independent of Him. The first of these alternatives is untenable. If God is responsible for the occurrence of evils, it must be because He is not good and therefore not God. We must take one or both of the remaining alternatives, unpalatable though they are to the traditionally minded. The former says that God is not necessarily on the side of what men term the right, while the latter says that God does not interfere with the workings of the universe. As we saw earlier in discussing wickedness, these two are compatible: men and God may not only have different standards of goodness but may be quite independent in nature.

God has His own standards of goodness and does not disturb the natural order of things. If "providence" be understood to refer to an irresistible divine force supporting what men take to be good, there is then no providence. But God could offer material which the universe might utilize in its own way, and God could preserve whatever goods the universe throws up on the shores of time. If He did, He would exhibit a providential concern for the universe and its inhabitants, but one that does not conflict with the brutal fact that there are both human and natural evils.

No one of the foregoing nine forms of evil is necessary. It is conceivable that none of them might be. To be sure, wherever there are men, there is the evil of guilt; but men need not exist. To be sure, if we have a universe of interplaying things, there will be destructive natural forces, but the universe might conceivably reach a stage of equilibrium. Each atom might vibrate in place and interfere with nothing beyond. What could not be avoided by the things in any universe whatsoever is the tenth kind of evil, *metaphysical* evil, the evil of being one among many, of possessing only a fragment of reality, of lacking the reality and thus the power and good possessed by all the others.

Any universe whatsoever, created or uncreated, is one in which each part is less than perfect precisely because it is other than the rest, and is deprived therefore of the reality the rest contain. God might have made, could He make anything at all, a better universe than this, for He could have eliminated or muted some of the forms of evil that now prevail. But He could not have made this universe in detail or as a whole completely free of all defect. No matter how good and concerned God might be, and no matter how few of the other nine types of evil happen to exist, there is always metaphysical evil to mark the fact that the universe is not God and God not the universe.

Much of the foregoing can be summarized in four questions and answers:

Why do bad men prosper? They do not.

Why does God not make bad men suffer more than they do? He does not interfere with the workings of the universe on the whole or in detail.

Why do good men suffer? Suffering and goodness have quite dissimilar causes.

Is God on the side of the right? God has His own standards. But to be religious is to have a faith that His standards will eventually be ours.

Samuel Terrien   (essay date 1957)

SOURCE: "The Fear and Fascination of Death," in *Job: Poet of Existence,* The Bobbs-Merrill Company, Inc. 1957, pp. 40-65.

[*Terrien is a French-born American theologian, educator, and pastor whose writings include* The Psalms and Their Meaning for Today *(1952),* Le Livre de Job: Commentaire *(1963;* The Book of Job: A Commentary*), and* The Elusive Presence: Prolegomenon to an Ecumenical Theory of the Bible *(1978). In the following excerpt from his* Job: Poet of Existence, *he discusses Job's experience of despair and*

isolation in relation to the concept of death in The Book of Job.]

How does man answer the riddle of self and existence? Not in being a marvel of obedience and submission, as Job was in the prose tale when he said, "What? shall we receive good at the hand of God, and shall we not receive evil?" (2:10), but on the contrary in refusing to bless the name of the Deity, in revolting against the faith of his childhood and of his community, in separating himself even from his dearest and most intimate friends, in losing willfully even more than he had lost unwillingly, in repudiating his reputation of honor among his fellow men.

If in the poem Job had spoken glowingly of accepting the will of God, he would have received approval from his community. Indeed, this is exactly the line of conduct which his three friends recommend that he should take. In the prologue, Job had lost his posterity—that is to say, his only hope in immortality—his wealth and his health, but not his reputation as an extraordinary man, a man of faith. He could have safeguarded this reputation. He could have enhanced it. He could have made it even more legendary than it was. But no. Job fell into despair.

This is the supreme irony of the human situation. Faith that does not know despair prevents man from ever forcing the riddle of self and existence; but despair kills faith and, when carried to the extreme, may bring about self-annihilation. Job falls into despair as soon as he rejects simple trust in a loving God. The faith he has expressed in the prologue becomes in the dialogue an unfaith. It becomes an unfaith because Job, in the dialogue, insists not on the love of God but on his own rights and achievements. Without knowing it, he answers in the negative the satan's question of the prologue, "Doth Job fear God for nought?" Throughout the poetic discussion, he repeats again and again, "My right is still with me. I am perfect but God declares me crooked. I am clean and even if my clothes were white as snow, God would throw me down in a ditch and splash them with mud. I shall never abandon the certitude of my integrity. He may kill me but I shall wait for him. I shall maintain my right before him until the end."

Death is therefore the ultimate risk one takes in order to prove one's worth; and Job is tossed about, throughout the dialogue, between the fear of death and its fascination. Before he reaches this dilemma, however, he begins elementally with the fear of life and the attraction of nothingness.

Job's religion has failed, but not altogether. In the prologue his wife, moved by compassion more than contempt, taunted him, saying, "Curse God and die!" She was proposing in effect a theological method of euthanasia. In the poem, however, if Job no longer blesses God, he does not curse him either. He merely asks to be put out of his misery, yet he never takes any practical measure toward suicide. He calls for death and even "non-being" but he does not curse God. He only curses life, envies the dead and makes his first philosophical quest.

i

Let the day perish wherein I was born,

and the night in which it was said, There is a
   man child conceived.
Let that day be darkness;
   let not God regard it from above,
   neither let the light shine upon it.
Let them claim it for their own, darkness and
   shadowy gloom;
   let a cloud settle upon it;
   let an eclipse grasp it as a prey.
That night—let obscurity possess it;
   let it not be joined unto the days of the year;
   let it not come into the number of the months.
That night—let it be barren from loneliness,
   let no shriek of delight be heard therein.

Let them curse it that curse the day,
   who are ready to raise up Leviathan.
Let them fade, the stars of the twilight thereof;
   let it wait for light but have none,
   neither let it see the eyelids of dawn open.
For it shut not up the doors of my mother's
   womb,
   nor hid sorrow from mine eyes.

ii

Why died I not in my mother's womb?
   why did I not expire as soon as I was born?
Why hath there been two knees to receive me,
   and two breasts to suckle me?
For now should I lie down in stillness,
   I should be asleep and at rest.
With kings and counsellors of the earth
   who built desolate places for themselves;
Or with princes that had gold
   and silver heaped in their tombs;
Or as a hidden untimely birth I had not been;
   as infants which never saw the light.

There the wicked cease from troubling;
   and the weary be at rest.
There the prisoners are left at ease;
   they hear not the voice of the jailer.
The small and great are there alike;
   and the slave is free from his master.

iii

Wherefore is light given to him that is in misery,
   and life unto the bitter in soul;
Which long for death but it cometh not;
   and dig for it more than for hid treasures;
Which rejoice exceedingly,
   and are glad, when they can find the grave?
Why is light given to a man whose way is hid,
   whom God hath hedged in as a beast?

For my sighing cometh before my bread,
   and my roarings are poured out like waters.
For the thing which I greatly feared is come
   upon me,
   and that which I was afraid of hath befallen
   me.
I have neither peace nor tranquillity;
   instead of rest cometh my torment.

This poem should be viewed in its present context: it is
more than a cry from the depths; it is a disruption of seven
days and seven nights of silence (2:13). The three friends
have come from afar to comfort the sufferer, and their silence should not be interpreted as a mark of hostility or

even condemnation. The poet quite clearly endorses the
validity of the note in the prose tale, "And none spake a
word unto him: for they saw that his grief was very great"
(2:13).

In the opening lament, moreover, Job does not address his
friends at all, nor even by the slightest implication does he
acknowledge their presence. Indeed, the initial poem deserves to be called a soliloquy, for its very mood bespeaks
the hero's most grievous suffering: his solitude.

The theme of man's isolation in the universe appears many
times in the poem: it is already subjacent to the opening
chords. For the first result of true pain, whether it be physical or mental, moral and spiritual, is the breakdown of
communication with other men, even with intimates. The
oriental bonds of community have already been symbolically and therefore actually broken in the note of the tale:
"And he sat down among the ashes" (2:8), just outside the
village or the encampment. The silent proximity of friends
did not succeed in renewing the ancient ties. "They recognized him not" (2:12). Suffering and disease had wrought
their changes. Thus the poem opens with the curse of life.

In the first strophe (3:3-10), Job wishes that he had never
been born. Nights and days are mythopoetically endowed
with personal existence (as in Ps. 19:3). If only the day of
Job's birth—nay, the night of his conception—had never
come to pass, if it had not been called into being by those
heavenly creatures which are, according to ancient mythology, the masters of the calendar, if Leviathan had been
stirred up (vs. 8), then chaos would have overcome the
created order and Job would not have received life. The
pain he now endures would never have excruciated him.

Here the poet hints at the spiritual disintegration which
is beginning to pervert Job's personality. Under the impact
of suffering, the hero begins to lose a sense of perspective
on life. He almost suggests that the world, as far as he is
concerned, might just as well have been nonexistent since
it produced only sorrow for him—a thought that has been
echoed often in other literatures, as for instance by Shakespeare in *King John:*

    A wicked day and not a holy day!
    What hath this day deserv'd? what hath it done,
    That it in golden letters should be set
    Among the high tides in the calendar?
    Nay, rather turn this day out of the week,
    This day of shame, oppression, perjury:
    Or, if it must stand still, let wives with child
    Pray that their burdens may not fall this day,
    Lest that their hopes prodigiously be cross'd.

It would be too easy to condemn Job's lack of concern for
the fate of others, and to regret that pain, leading to isolation, in turn may induce irresponsibility. The poet was
aware of the dangers of egocentricity, which is the natural
fruit of grief, for he has taken up the theme again in the
course of the work.

Some might find it tempting, at least among non-Latin
Westerners, to censure Job's outburst as a display of Mediterranean self-pity. Modern psychology, however, has
called attention to the therapeutic significance of literary
expostulation. There is a seed of healing in the articulate

exteriorization of grief. Alone "the damned don't cry," said Eugene O'Neill in *Mourning Becomes Electra*.

The second strophe (3:11-19) introduces a new motif as it passes from the hatred of life to the love of death. The ancient Hebrews did not believe in natural immortality. Perhaps in revulsion against the Egyptian funerary rituals which were destined to insure an after-death resurrection and which consumed, ironically enough, most of the energies of the living, Israel accepted for more than a thousand years the early Semitic idea of near annihilation. Life after the grave was not believed to be life, indeed, but a gray sort of partial survival, without joy and without peace. Thus, the Old Testament generally calls for a long life upon this earth and the Psalmists in particular pray with passion that death be postponed, since "the dead cannot praise the Lord." Only with the latest books of the Hebrew Bible did the idea of a full existence with God after death gain access to the religious mind of Judaism (Isa. 25-26; Dan. 12). Conceived through the symbol of the resurrection of the flesh—as the seat of personal identity, emotion, thought and power—this idea of immortality was radically different from either the early Semitic belief in partial survival in the grave or the Hellenic concept of a natural permanence of the human soul. It represented a rebirth through an act of divine re-creation. This late Old Testament motif found its way into the faith of the early Christian Church.

At the outset of the second strophe, Job reveals a view of the afterlife which stands in sharp contrast with that of the Old Testament in general and is equally distant from the later Judeo-Christian faith in resurrection. The sequence of thought is similar to that of Sophocles, who could say a century later in *Oedipus at Colonus,*

> Not to be born is the most
> To be desired; but having seen the light,
> The next best is to go whence one came
> As soon as may be.

For Job at the threshold of the argument, to die is to find an exit from present hell. More, for a prisoner or a slave, it is to receive freedom and even to enjoy the company of the great men of the past. Death is the only genetrix of man's hollow desires for liberty, fraternity, equality. Emily Dickinson, who said,

> Unto the dead
> There is no geography,

might have added, "but a knowledge of history," sublimated in cold promiscuity with the kings and counselors of the earth.

Here is a view of attractive death which is not unlike that of some Egyptian wisemen. The author of the "Dialogue Between the Man Weary of Life and His Soul," for example, was almost tireless in describing the attractiveness of the afterlife:

> Death is in my sight today
>   (Like) the recovery of a sick man,
>   Like going out into the open after a
>   *confinement.*
> Death is in my sight today
>   Like the odor of myrrh,
>   Like sitting under an awning on a

breezy day.

> Death is in my sight today
>   Like the odor of lotus blossoms,
>   Like sitting on the bank of drunkenness.
> Death is in my sight today
>   Like the *passing away* of rain,
>   Like the return of men to their houses
>   from an expedition.
> Death is in my sight today
>   Like the clearing of the sky,
>   Like a man *fowling thereby* for what he
>   knew not.
> Death is in my sight today
>   Like the longing of a man to see his
>   house (again),
>   After he has spent many years held
>   in captivity.

> Why surely, he who is yonder
> Will be a living god. . . .

Let it be made clear that Job did not accept the Egyptian idea of a resurrection. He toyed with such a hope several times in the course of the poem, but he rejected it even in the famous passage on the living Redeemer (19:25-26). Nevertheless, the second strophe reveals the vigor of his nonconformism. Such a romantic interpretation of death represents man's need for an ultimate security. After Job, many were those who cried,

> Would that the womb could have been the tomb
> of me.

At the moment of extremity in the struggle, here and now, the romantic hero can always command, as did Cleopatra,

> Give me my robe; put on my crown; I have
> Immortal longings in me. . . .

But this represents final self-deceit. In *Job*, the will "to end it all" does not spring from the attraction of nothingness. "Death is not the opening of a gate," wrote Geoffrey Moore on Swift, "but the closing of a wound." And thus, although Job would not say, with a modern poet like Donald Hall,

> Life is hell, but death is worse,

he is only "half in love with easeful death." He is fascinated, yes, but not enough to follow the advice of his distraught spouse in the prologue. The Joban hero, even in the poem, maintains the will to live. And he can do so because he still stands in a personal rapport with a personal Deity. To be sure, this God is at best a *deus absconditus,* a hidden God, and at worst a hostile God. But Job never brings himself to dismiss the reality of a living God from his world. He feels desperately his isolation precisely because he can ignore neither man nor God.

In the third strophe, therefore, God at last is named (3:20-26). The question "why?" is more theological than philosophical. It is not spoken by a man out of mere intellectual curiosity. It is thrown at the void that surrounds him by a man who has known intimate communion with a God he loved and who now discerns in the character of that same God a dimension of hate. Indeed, it is not the philosophical problem of evil which moves the poet. It is rather the deeply religious anxiety that rises from a doubt over

God's intentions for man. At the same time, Job's return to the awareness of God is simultaneous with his fascination for death, but little by little the awareness of God, even of a hostile God, chases away the thought of extinction. But the attraction for nothingness is not a superfluous element in the pilgrimage of suffering. Indeed, this fascination itself may well have lost its power through its very exercise. "Only those who have grasped their non-being," says Julius Caesar in Thornton Wilder's *Ides of March,* "are capable of praising the sunlight."

Furthermore, Job's quest appears at a moment when the egocentricity he expressed in the first strophe is no longer running the risk of deteriorating into social irresponsibility. Just as he becomes again aware of God, so also he rediscovers, however indistinctly, his solidarity with the mass of sufferers; and it is in their name that he speaks as a champion for their cause. His self-centeredness finds a channel into a concern for the lot of aching humanity.

Richard B. Sewall   (essay date 1959)

SOURCE: "The Book of Job," in *The Vision of Tragedy,* revised edition, Yale University Press, 1980, pp. 9-24.

[*Sewall is an American critic and educator whose critical study* The Vision of Tragedy, *originally published in 1959, was lauded by critics and declared an "academic bestseller." In the following essay from that work, Sewall discusses the concept of tragedy in* The Book of Job *in relation to several works of fiction, concluding that* Job *may be considered a somewhat "dangerous" or rebellious work in the context of traditional Hebrew literature.*]

We look at a work of literature and call it "optimistic" or "pessimistic" or "epic" or "tragic." The book is there before us, and we find the term to describe it. But the work comes first. It is not right to say that without the vision of life embodied in the Old Testament, and notably in *The Book of Job,* the term "tragedy" would have no substance, for the Greeks invented the term and gave it a great deal of substance. But knowing what we do now about the full depth and reach of tragedy, we can see with striking clarity in the writings of the ancient Hebrews the vision which we now call tragic and in *The Book of Job* the basic elements of the tragic form. The cultural situation, the matrix out of which *Job* came, is the very definition of "the tragic moment" in history, a period when traditional values begin to lose their power to comfort and sustain, and man finds himself once more groping in the dark. The unknown Poet's "action," his redoing of the orthodox and optimistic folktale of the pious and rewarded Job, is (as we can say now) a classic example of the dynamics of tragedy, of vision creating form. And the great figure of his creation, the suffering, questioning, and unanswered Job, is the towering tragic figure of antiquity. More than Prometheus or Oedipus, Job is the universal symbol for the western imagination of the mystery of undeserved suffering.

Of all ancient peoples, the Hebrews were most surely possessed of the tragic sense of life. It pervades their ancient writings to an extent not true of the Greeks. "Judaism," writes Paul Weiss [in "The True, the Good, and the Jew," *Commentary,* October, 1946], "is Moses in the wilderness straining to reach a land he knows he never can. For the Christian this truth is but the necessary first act of a Divine Comedy. The history of the universe for the Christian is in principle already told. For the Jew history is in the making. It has peaks and valleys, goods and bads, inseparably together and forever." The Hebraic answer to the question of existence was never unambiguous or utopian; the double vision of tragedy—the snake in the garden, the paradox of man born in the image of God and yet recalcitrant, tending to go wrong—permeates the Scriptures. No case is ever clear-cut, no hero or prophet entirely faultless. The Hebrews were the least sentimental and romantic of peoples. The Old Testament stories are heavy with irony, often of the most sardonic kind. And yet their hard, acrid realism appears against a background of belief that is the substance of the most exalted and affirmative religion, compared to which the religions of their sister civilizations, Egyptian, Babylonian, and even Greek, presented a conception of the universe and man both terrible and mean. The Hebraic view of God, man, and nature, wrought through the centuries out of hard experience and exalted vision, presented to the Poet of Job a rich and full-nerved tradition, containing all the alternatives, for evil as well as good, but founded on the belief in a just and benevolent Creator, in man as made in His image, and in an ordered universe.

Throughout their history as it is unfolded in the Old Testament, the Hebrews showed a strong critical sense, a ten-

William Blake's illustration to The Book of Job.

dency to test all their beliefs, even Jehovah Himself, against their individual experience and sense of values. This skepticism is at the root of much of their irony, and it implies, of course, a very high estimate of individual man. They had a sufficient confidence in their own native and immediate insights to set themselves, if need be, against their God. This was an affirmation about man, the Deity, and the relationship between the two, which the Babylonians and Egyptians surely never achieved, nor, as a people, did the Greeks. The Hebrews saw man not only as free and rational but free, rational, and righteous even before God. The eating of the apple was in a sense an act of the free critical intelligence. Why should there have been even one prohibition, arbitrary and unexplained?

The failure in actual experience of the orthodox teaching that God would reward the righteous and punish the wicked gave rise in later times to a whole literature of dissent, ranging from the disturbed and melancholy psalms, the ambiguous attitude toward the Deity in stories like Jonah, to the complaints of Ecclesiastes and the full-scale protests of Job. It is hard to see why Simone Weil said of the Hebrews [in "The Iliad, or, The Poem of Force," in *Politics,* November, 1945] that they "believed themselves exempt from the misery that is the common human lot" and that only in parts of *Job* is "misfortune fairly portrayed." Their belief in Jehovah and their hope for a Messiah served rather to intensify their sense of present inequity and to increase the anxiety which permeates this protest-literature.

But another aspect of the Hebraic tragic vision gives it its peculiar depth and poignancy, and it is the very clue to *Job.* It comes from the conception of Jehovah as a person, to be communed with, worshiped, feared, but above all to be loved. In the transactions of the Greeks with their gods, no great amount of love was lost. There was no doctrine of Creation, nor a Creator to be praised (as in psalm after psalm) for his loving-kindness and tender mercies. The Greek gods were fallible, imperfect, finite, and, above all, laws unto themselves; to rebel against them might be disastrous but it involved no inevitable spiritual dilemma or clash of loyalties. But Jehovah, in the eyes of the orthodox Hebrew, was righteous, just, and loving—and a being to whom one could appeal in the name of all these virtues. The protest embodied in *The Book of Job* came not from fear or hate but from love. Job's disillusionment was deeply personal, as from a cosmic breach of faith. However critical of the Deity, Job spoke not in arrogance and revolt but in love, and in this at least he was the true representative of an ancient piety.

The unknown Poet of *Job,* however, saw the old story of Job not as illustrating the ancient piety—that is, a good man blessing the Lord even in his afflictions and being rewarded for his constancy—but as throwing it into grievous question. All the latent doubts and questionings of his race came to a head. Job had trusted in The Covenant and followed The Code; God had watched over him; God's lamp had lighted his way through the darkness, His friendship had been upon his tent. Job was the beloved patriarch of a large family and a man of consequence in the community. And then, suddenly and unaccountably, the face of the universe changed. It was not only that he suffered misfortunes, lost his property, family, position, and health. Mortal man must face losses; the proverbial wisdom of the Hebrews had taught for generations that man was born for trouble, as the sparks fly upward. The shock of the story for the Poet did not lie there, if we may judge by how he retold it. The succession of catastrophes that befell Job, as the folk story recounts them, was systematic, the result of a wager between God and Satan to test Job. Job, who could know nothing of the wager, suffered at the hands of a God whom to worship and to love had been his daily blessing and who had turned suddenly hateful and malign. There was no mortal cause for his sufferings, nothing in his past to account for these repeated, calculated blows. If he had sinned, he had not sinned that much.

From the depth of an ancient skepticism and a sense of justice which dared to hold Deity itself to account, the Poet saw the story, as we would say, in the light of the tragic vision. The primitive terror loomed close. The resolution of the folk story, by which Job for his piety and suffering was rewarded by twice his former possessions and a new family, was unacceptable. The Poet saw Job's suffering as a thrust of destiny that raised the deepest issues, not to be accounted for by a heavenly wager and bought off by a handsome recompense. The suffering had been real; it could not be taken back; and it had not been deserved.

What to do about it? One can imagine in earlier times the primitive response of propitiation or lament, the wailing at the wall, the sharing of communal grief over inexplicable suffering. In later times, psalmists caught the mood in the most beautiful of melancholy and anguished lyrics; rabbis taught men to regard such suffering as punishment for secret sin or as God's way of testing man's loyalty. So Eliphaz (5:17) interpreted Job's suffering [in *The Authorized Vision*]: "Behold, happy is the man whom God correcteth: therefore despise not thou the chastening of the Almighty." Again, none of the ancient Hebrew writers responded to the fact of undeserved suffering more sensitively than Ecclesiastes or was truer to the realities of human misery: "The truest of all men was the Man of Sorrows," wrote Melville [in *Moby-Dick*], "and the truest of all books is Solomon's, and Ecclesiastes is the fine hammered steel of woe." But it was not for Ecclesiastes to discover the full possibilities of the "boundary-situation," to hammer from the hard steel of woe the full dimensions of the tragic form. He observed, and contemplated, and recorded movingly what he saw. But he stopped, halfway, with pathos—the single-voiced lament, the lyric expression of a reserved and passive acceptance.

The Poet of *Job* chose still another way, and with him tragic vision is fulfilled in tragic form. His response was dynamic and positive. He saw in Job's story the possibilities of a significant action, not only the lamentable blows that fell upon Job but the counterthrust that makes drama. He imagined Job as striking back in the only possible way when the adversary is Destiny—that is, with words. The Poet did not deal in plotted physical action, as in a Greek play; rather, he conceived of ideas, or inner realities, functioning like actions and as fully freighted with consequences. Although Job and his Counselors do not budge from the ash- heap (which 2:8 suggests as the setting of the drama) and do not exchange blows or even threats of blows, they are actually at death-grips. Each side sees survival at stake. The parts of the drama—character, incident, minor actions—are not clearly articulated as in plays to be performed, but the vital tension and forward movement of formal drama are clear. This method of the Poet's—sustained tension throughout the thrust-and-parry of ideas, the balancing of points of view in the challenge-and-response of argument—is the inner logic, or dialectic, of the tragic form as it appears in fully developed drama.

It is a way, of course, of making an important—and "tragic"—statement about the nature of truth. In tragedy, truth is not revealed as one harmonious whole; it is many-faceted, ambiguous, a sum of irreconcilables—and that is one source of its terror. As the Poet contemplated Job's case, he saw that the single-voiced response—the lament or the diatribe—was inadequate. The case was not clear; at its center was a bitter dilemma, every aspect of which, in the full and fair portrayal of human suffering like Job's, must be given a voice. The Counselors were partly right, and Job was partly wrong. Job was at once justified in complaining against his God, and deeply guilty. There was no discharge in that war. The dramatic form above all others conveys this sense of the jarring conflict of ideas-in-action, gives each its due, and shows how each qualifies and interacts on every other. It conveys directly what Jung called "the terrible ambiguity of an immediate experience" [in *Psychology and Religion*]. Comedy presents ambiguities but removes their terror; in tragedy the terror remains.

This method, like the tragic vision which was a part of the Poet's racial inheritance, was not new in the literature of the Hebrews. *Job* is merely the fullest development of a racial way of expression observable in the earliest writings. For example, after the single-voiced and full-throated praise of the Creator and the Creation in the first chapter of Genesis, the story of Adam and Eve and the Fall moves into a different mode. Many voices are heard, including the Serpent's. This is one way of saying that even this case was not entirely clear. Kierkegaard, who had a lively sense of the tragic aspect of the Old Testament, shows how Adam and Eve, though guilty, were in part justified. The Almighty had "goaded" them. The story of Abraham and Isaac, which moves forward in a kind of tragic dialectic, has frightening undertones, as Kierkegaard's famous discussion in *Fear and Trembling* shows. Moses, Jonah, and many of the Old Testament heroes and prophets argued with Jehovah, questioned his judgment, criticized his harshness or (as with Jonah) his leniency, in actual dialogue. In such ways the Hebrews surrounded even their most sacred religious figures and truths with an aura of ambiguity and qualification. Ideas, or truth, were not regarded apart, as abstractions or final causes. They were ideas-in-action, lived out and tested by men of flesh and blood. Thus like men they were in a constant process of becoming. Even Jehovah, as we see him in the Old Testament, evolved.

So the Poet of *Job*, true to his tradition, set his protago-nist—Job, or the "Job-idea"—free to run the dialectical gamut, to test it not only against Jehovah but against all the standard human formulations that had traditionally resolved such situations. He gave Job human adversaries as well as divine, to try him at every point. Thus the movement of statement-and-reply between Job and the Counselors, now swift, now slow, gives the sense not of the static opposition of ideas in a debate but of men in action, temperamental and passionate. Job is in turn bitter and despairing, angry and defiant, pensive and exalted. The Counselors, in their turn, console, plead, argue, scold, and threaten. Nothing is left untouched in the furious spirals of the debate. The method allows for the fullest "existential" exploration of the concerns—the nature of man and the universe—without which, after the achievement of *Job* and the Greeks, tragedy is purely nominal. Again, what tragedy seems to be saying—what *Job* and the Greeks made it say—is that we come closest to the nature of man and universe in the test-situation, where the strength or weakness of the individual, to endure or let go, is laid bare. Only then does the final "yea" or "nay" have meaning. When Job in his extremity puts ironically the question of the pious psalmist, "What is man, that thou are mindful of him?" the Poet gives no pat answer. The answer is the total *Book of Job,* all that Job says and becomes, all that the Counselors say and do not become, all that the Voice from the Whirlwind says about man and his place in the universe. The answer is the full drama, not in any one of its parts—least of all in the pious and comforting resolution of the folk story in the last chapter.

No analysis can convey more than the bare structure of the Poet's meaning. But the heart of his meaning, and surely the chief source of the tragic meaning for subsequent artists, is contained in the so-called Poem of Job, all that occurs between Job's opening curse (ch. 3) and 42:6, the last verse before the folk-story conclusion. This is the agon, the passion-scene, where the discoveries are made of most relevance to average, suffering, questioning humanity.

Job in the opening curse is in the torment of despair. The shock of his calamities has more than unbalanced him; it has prostrated him. For "seven days and seven nights" he has sat among the ashes, for "his grief was very great." His world has collapsed, his inherited values have been discredited. He faces at least four possible choices. He may follow the advice of his wife to "Curse God, and die." He may come to terms with his fate and accept it as deserved—the advice which his Counselors later give him. He may accept his fate, whether deserved or not, and contemplate it, like Ecclesiastes, with melancholy equanimity. Or he may strike back in some way, give vent to his feelings and carry his case wherever it may lead. The Poet does not present Job in his tragic moment as weighing these alternatives openly, although in "seven days and seven nights" he has had time to consider them all. But we get no sense of a closely reasoned choice. All we know is that he did not commit suicide (although the thought of it recurs to him later), that he "opened his mouth" and talked, and that he took this action through some mysterious dynamic within himself. There was no goddess whispering encouragement at his shoulder or divine vision leading him on. He was "unaccommodated man," moved in his first moment of bitterness to give up the struggle, but for some reason making a "gesture" first. It is this action, and the action which follows from it, which establishes Job as hero. It had what Aristotle called "magnitude": it involved Job totally, and he was a man of high estate on whom many people depended; it involved Job's world totally, since it questioned the basis of its belief and modes of life; it transcended Job's world, horizontally as well as vertically, as the perennial relevance of Job's problem, from his time to ours, shows. And it involved Job in total risk: "Behold he will slay me; I have no hope."

Although there is little in literature as black as the opening verses of Job's curse, in the speech as a whole there is a saving ambiguity which predicts the main movement of the Poem. This movement, in brief, is from the obsessive egotism (like Lear's or Ahab's) that sees particular misfortune as a sign of universal ruin (and even wills it, for revenge or escape or oblivion) toward a mood more rational, outgoing, and compassionate. Job's first words are of furious, not passive, despair. He has been wounded in his pride, humiliated as well as stricken. He curses life and the parents who gave him life. He would have his birthday blotted from the calendar; he would have all men go into mourning on that day and the light of heaven be darkened. He rages in the worst kind of arrogant, romantic rebellion. Yet gradually there is a change, however slight. The furious commands of the opening verses change to questions: "Why died I not from the womb? why did I not give up the ghost when I came out of the belly?" The plaintive tone leads to one more contemplative, as he thinks not of universal darkness but of rest with all those who have gone before, "the kings and the counsellors of the earth . . . princes that had gold, who filled their houses with silver." He has a word for the weary and oppressed, the small as well as the great. The first-person pronoun changes to the third: "Wherefore is light given to him that is in misery, and life unto the bitter in soul . . . ? Why is light given to a man whose way is hid, and whom God hath hedged in?" Although he returns in the last three verses to a mood of anguish and dread, it is more like the response to a spasm of pain—"For the thing which I greatly feared is come upon me, and that which I was afraid of is come unto me"—than the nihilism of the opening verses.

Thus Job does not abandon life, and as he rallies and reorganizes he opens up new and redeeming reaches of life. In the reverse of the way they expect, the Counselors assist in the process. Their arguments sting and thrust, kindle new energies in him, and compel him to ever greater expressive efforts. The dialectic works beneficently with Job. Eliphaz's first speech (ch. 4) is a curious combination of scolding ("Behold, thou hast instructed many . . . But now it is come upon thee, and thou faintest"), of mystical witness ("Now a thing was secretly brought to

me . . . in thoughts from the visions of the night"), and of the proverbial comforts about suffering as the common lot and as a corrective discipline. At the end of the speech Job is thoroughly aroused. He will not abide such half-faced fellowship. He will not be accused of impatience by men who have never had their own patience put to the test. He asks of them neither material aid nor deliverence "from the enemy's hand." What he wants is instruction. "Teach me, and I will hold my tongue: and cause me to understand wherein I have erred." This is a great gain over the nihilism of the Curse. To be sure, as often happens in the long sequences to come, Job relapses in the second half of his answer to Eliphaz (ch. 7) into self-pity and lamentation: "My days are swifter than a weaver's shuttle, and are spent without hope." But the speech ends in a surge of vigor, in defiance not so much of the Counselors as of Jehovah himself.

It is in this passage (7:11-21) that he commits himself to the ultimate risk: "Therefore I will not refrain my mouth; I will speak in the anguish of my spirit; I will complain in the bitterness of my soul." Later, in his first reply to Zophar (ch. 13), it is clear that he understands the full terms of the risk: "Though he slay me, yet will I trust in him: but I will maintain mine own ways before him." But by now Job has come to see his own ways and his own complaints in a different light. He sees his misfortunes not as unique but as typical of man's lot. In one phase of his being, at least, he is becoming a partisan of the human race. "What is man, that thou shouldst magnify him"— only to torment him? He never forgets his own personal grievances, but his thoughts turn ever more outward; he does not, [in the words of T. S. Eliot] "rest in his own suffering." He discourses upon God's capricious ways with all mankind: "He increaseth the nations, and destroyeth them" (12:23); upon the flourishing of the wicked and the oppression of the poor (chs. 21, 24); upon the element of chance in all life (ch. 21). For all his frequent lapses into despair, as sudden pain strikes him or as his thoughts turn back to happier times or forward to an uncertain future, he speaks as one having shouldered the burden of humanity.

But this growing sense of partisanship—like Ahab's [in *Moby-Dick*], "for all that has maddened and tormented the whole race from Adam down"—is only one phase of Job's experience, the structure of which, as the Poet presents it, represents an ordering of experience which many subsequent tragedies have imitated and all of them shared in part, some emphasizing one aspect, some another. It was not until Job gained some mastery over his despair, chose his course, and began his defense, that the full meaning of his position grew upon him. This realization was to be the source of his greatest suffering, beside which his physical afflictions were easy to bear. In justice he could decry the miseries of the human lot and the baffling ways of the Almighty, but he could not forget that it was Jehovah's hands that had (as he says) "made me and fashioned me together round about . . . [and] granted me life and favour, and thy visitation hath preserved my spirit." He was on the horns of a terrible dilemma—the clue to the nature of his suffering. He saw that what he had done, though justified, was wrong. He had been justified in asserting his innocence and in speaking out for all men who had been afflicted as he had. But it was wrong, as the Counselors repeatedly and rightly dinned into his ears, to defy the God whom he loved. If he could have regarded the idea of Justice abstractly, his suffering would not have involved this peculiar anguish. It was the Person in the impersonal that Job loved and could not repudiate—and which monomaniac Ahab hated and spat upon. It is this agony of dilemma, of the knowledge of the ambiguity of every choice, that, since *Job* and the Greeks, has defined tragic suffering. The capacity for such suffering (and even Ahab "has his humanities") has ever since been the mark of the tragic figure—he who is caught between the necessity to act and the knowledge of inevitable guilt. Job felt duty-bound to challenge God, Orestes to kill his mother, Hamlet to kill his uncle; and all of them knew guilt. Job had progressed from the experience of mere pain and distress to the experience of suffering.

In the course of the long ordeal, the Poet reveals many personal qualities in Job that have since been appropriated into the tradition of formal tragedy. "The ponderous heart," the "globular brain," the "nervous lofty language" which Melville saw as the qualities of the tragic hero are all in Job. After *Job* and the Greeks, it became part of the function of tragedy to represent, and make probable, figures of such stature. What would break lesser folk—the Counselors, or the members of the chorus—releases new powers in Job. His compulsion toward self-justification sends him far and wide over all the affairs of men, and deep within himself; and the agony of his guilt propels him ever nearer his God. He sets himself in solid debate against the Counselors: "I have understanding as well as you: I am not inferior to you." He answers their arguments in the full sweep of a massive mind, rich in learning and in the closest observation of human life. He resists every temptation to compromise or turn back, like Ahab denying Starbuck, or Hamlet thrusting aside his friends. As he gains in spiritual poise (though his course is very uneven), his mental processes become more orderly. He talks increasingly in legal terms. The universe becomes, as it were, a local court of justice where his "cause" can be "tried." "Behold now, I have ordered my cause; I know that I shall be justified." In one mood he complains that there is no "daysman," or umpire, to judge his case; in another he calls upon God to act as judge against Himself. He speaks of his "witness" and his "record" and longs to have his case recorded in a book—like Othello or Hamlet, wanting his full story told.

Nothing is more revealing of Job's (and the tragic hero's) stature than the contrast which the Poet develops between Job and the Counselors. Job outstrips them in every way. By chapter 28 Job has achieved an ironic reversal of roles: the Counselors who came to teach him are now being taught by him—and on the subject of Wisdom. He fails to convince them of the injustice of his suffering or even of the possibility of a flaw in their pat theology. But in failing to change their minds he demonstrates the littleness of minds that cannot be changed. He grows in stature as they shrink. He knows that he has achieved a vision, through suffering, beyond anything they can know. He has mystical insights, as when he sees into the time, perhaps long after his death, when his Vindicator "will stand up upon the earth," and when "without my flesh I shall see God." On his miserable ash-heap (and this is what the Counselors never see) Job rises to heights he never reached in the days of his worldly prosperity, when in his presence "the aged arose and stood up, the princes refrained talk-

ing." His summing up, the Oath of Clearance (chs. 30-31), is orderly and composed. He is the master of his spirit. When the Voice from the Whirlwind begins its mighty oration, the Counselors seem not part of the picture at all. They return in the folkstory conclusion (41:7) only to be rebuked: "the Lord said to Eliphaz the Temanite, My wrath is kindled against thee, and against thy two friends: for ye have not spoken of me the thing that is right, as my servant Job hath."

So far, the meaning of *Job* for the tragic tradition is this: A new dimension of human experience, a new possibility, has been explored and rendered probable. Vision, working on the raw materials of experience, has hammered out a form. New value has been found where it was least expected—in the clearest possible case of unjustified suffering. Suffering itself, as the Poet of Job defines it, has been made to yield knowledge, and the way has been plotted out. After this achievement by the Poet of *Job* and after the similar achievement by Aeschylus in what may have been the same ear of antiquity (the fifth century), the "tragic form" was permanently available. No subsequent artist whose imagination was attracted to this mode of writing could ignore it.

It has seemed to many that in the final stages of *Job*—the speech of Elihu, the Voice from the Whirlwind, Job's repentance, and the folk-story ending—tragic meaning, as the Poet has so far defined it, is swallowed up in mystical revelation or orthodox piety. In one sense it is true that the final phase of Job's experience carries him beyond the tragic domain, and the book as a whole is a religious book and not a formal tragedy. The revelation granted Job, and his repentance, would seem to deny the essence of his previous situation—the agony of dilemma, of the opposing compulsions of necessity and guilt. Certainly no such unequivocal Voice speaks to Antigone or Hamlet or Hester Prynne, who conclude the dark voyage in the light of their own unaided convictions, and live out their dilemmas to the end. But in these final scenes the tragic vision of the Poet is still active. Ambiguities remain, and the central question of the book is unanswered. Also, in the treatment of Job's pride, in the final revelation of how Job learned humility, in the irony with which the "happy ending" of the folk story is left to make its own statement, the Poet includes much that is relevant, as we can now see, to the tragic tradition.

At the end of his Oath of Clearance, Job had achieved a state of what Aristotle called catharsis. He had challenged the Almighty, made his case, and purged his spirit. He was in a Hamlet-like state of readiness. In taking him beyond catharsis into abject repentance and self-abhorrence, the Poet makes of him a religious rather than a tragic figure; but the Poem as a whole makes an important statement about pride, which the Greeks were to make repeatedly, though from a different perspective. According to the Poet, and to the Greek tragedians, pride like Job's is justified. It has its ugly and dark side, but it was through pride that Job made his spiritual gains and got a hearing from Jehovah himself. The Lord favored Job's pride and rebuked the safe orthodoxy of the Counselors. The pride that moved Job is the dynamic of a whole line of tragic heroes, from Oedipus to Ahab. It is always ambiguous and often destructive, but it is the very hallmark of the type.

Although the speech of Elihu (chs. 32-37) is generally regarded as not the work of the original Poet of *Job*, and although it repeats tiresomely much of what the other Counselors had said, it has the distinction of dealing not so much with Job's past sinfulness as with his present pride. Elihu, young, fiery, and a little pompous, is shocked that the Counselors have allowed Job in his pride to have the last word, and he sets out to humble him. Job's eyes have been blinded by pride, and his ears deafened: "For God speaketh once, yea twice, yet man perceiveth it not . . . he openeth the ears of men, and sealeth their instruction, that he may withdraw man from his purpose, and hide pride from man." "Why dost thou strive against him?" Elihu suggests a way of learning humility that is a curious blend of religious insight and the wisdom of tragedy. Job must see in God's chastisement not only discipline and a just judgment, but he must see that in his affliction there is "delivery"—through suffering he may learn: "He delivereth the afflicted by their affliction, and openeth their ear in oppression." But not only this: Job must see with his own eyes. More than the other Counselors, Elihu turns Job's eyes outward. As if to prepare Job for the revelations of the Voice from the Whirlwind (in this respect Elihu's speech is a firm dramatic bridge between Job's "Oath of Clearance" and the climactic chapters of the book), Elihu asks him to contemplate the magnificence of the external universe. "Stand still," he says, "and consider the wondrous works of God." He rhapsodizes on the lightning, the thunder, and the wind; and he sees God's concern for men even in the snow, ice, cold, and rain,

> Whether it be for correction, or for his land,
> Or for lovingkindness . . .
>
> [Translation from the American Standard
> Version]

The main movement of Job's experience, from the morbid concern for his own suffering toward membership and partisanship in the human family, is extending even farther outward. He must now experience the Infinite or the Absolute. Even though in formal tragedy there is no such apocalypse as Job presently experiences, the direction is the same. Through suffering, as Aeschylus wrote, men learn—not only their littleness and sinfulness but the positive and creative possibilities of themselves and the world they live in. They learn them, in *Job* as in later tragedy, not from Counselors or friends, but directly, on their pulses. As in the long debate with the Counselors Job made many discoveries about himself and the human realm, so now the Voice from the Whirlwind opens up for him the vast economy of the universe. In this new perspective, the question "Why did I suffer?" loses its urgency.

The question loses its urgency—Job never asks it again—but it is never answered. To the Poet, in contrast to the teaching of the Counselors or *The Book of Proverbs* or the first Psalm, the universe was not reasonable and not always just. He did not see it as a sunny and secure place for human beings, where to prosper one only has to be good. Even after the Voice ceased, Job was no nearer an understanding of what justice is than when he began his

complaints. Unjustified suffering must be accepted as part of a mystery; it is not for man to reason why. The universe is a realm of infinite complexity and power, in which catastrophe may fall at any time on the just as well as the unjust. There may be enough moral cause-and-effect to satisfy the members of the chorus or the Counselors. But all the hero can do, if he is visited as Job was, is to persevere in the pride of his conviction, to appeal to God against God, and if he is as fortunate as Job, hear his questionings echo into nothingness in the infinite mystery and the glory.

Even the folk-story ending contains a tantalizing ambiguity. Few people go away happy at the end of *Job,* or if they do they miss the point. Of course, the sense of frustration is largely eliminated by Job's rewards. God is good; justice of a sort has been rendered; the universe seems secure. We are inclined to smile at how neatly it works out—the mathematical precision of the twofold restoration of Job's possessions and his perfectly balanced family, seven sons and three daughters—a sign perhaps that we are in the domain of something less elevated than Divine Comedy. But

---

Ernest Renan on *Job* as a "cry of the soul" (1859):

In order to comprehend the poem of *Job,* it is not sufficient to fix its date; it must be restored by means of the sentiment of the race that created it, and of which it is the most perfect expression. Nowhere do the aridity, the austerity, and the grandeur that characterized the original works of the Semitic race show themselves more nakedly. . . . In it entire sides of the human soul are in default; a kind of grandiose stiffness gives to the poem a hard aspect, which resembles a tone of brass. But never has the position, so eminently poetical, of man in this world, his mysterious struggle against an inimical power which he sees not, his alternatives justified equally by submission and revolt, inspired so eloquent a plaint. The grandeur of human nature consists in a contradiction which has struck all sages and has been the fruitful mother of all elevated thought and of all noble philosophy: on the one hand, conscience declaring right and duty to be supreme realities; on the other, the experiences of every day inflicting upon these profound aspirations inexplicable contradictions. Hence that sublime lamentation which has endured since the beginning of the world, and which to the end of time shall bear toward heaven the protestations of the moral man.

The poem of *Job* is the most sublime expression of that cry of the soul. In it blasphemy approximates the hymn, or rather is itself a hymn, since it is only an appeal to God against the lacunae conscience finds in the work of God. The pride of the nomad, his religion-at once cold, severe, and far removed from all devotion-his haughty personality, can alone explain that singular mixture of exalted faith and of audacious obstinacy.

Ernest Renan in The Dimensions of Job, *edited by
Nahum N. Glatzer, Shocken Books, 1969.*

the universe seems secure only to those who do not question too far. Can a new family make up for the one Job lost? What about the faithful servants who fell to the Sabeans and Chaldeans? These questions the folk story ignores, and its reassuring final picture also makes it easy to forget Job's suffering and his unanswered question. Although the irony of the folk conclusion seems unmistakable, it was no doubt this easy piety, like the pious emendations to the bitterness of Ecclesiastes, that made *The Book of Job* acceptable to the orthodox for centuries. Actually, it is a "dangerous" book. Although the Hebrews had their recalcitrant figures, capable, like the Poet of Job, of deep penetration into the realm of tragedy, they are rightly regarded as the people of a Covenant, a Code, and a Book. This is one reason, perhaps, why they never developed a tragic theater, where their beliefs and modes of living would be under constant scrutiny. Their public communication was through synagogue and pulpit; their prophets and preachers proclaimed the doctrine of obedience to divine law, and the rabbis endlessly proliferated the rules for daily life. The rebellious Job was not typical. For the most part, their heroes were lonely, God-summoned men whose language was that of witness to the one true light.

Eugene Goodheart   (essay date 1961)

SOURCE: "Job and the Modern World," in *Judaism*, Vol. 10, No. 1, Winter, 1961, pp. 21-28.

[*Goodheart is an American critic and educator. In the following essay he contrasts modern interpretations of Job's suffering in several fictional works with the original intent of* The Book of Job.]

Behind much of the modern literature of suffering is the greatest single work of the Bible, *The Book of Job.* We hear echoes of *Job* in books as different from one another as *The Brothers Karamazov, Jude the Obscure* and *The Castle.* If, however, we return to *Job* from a reading of these works, we have the strange experience that the view of life that it presents is almost as alien to the modern sensibility as the story of the sacrifice of Isaac or the gospels of Christ. The Jobean element on *The Brothers Karamazov* or *Jude the Obscure,* for instance, represents the exploitation of what is most accessible in *Job* to the modern sensibility: the sense of gratuitous suffering, the impassioned indignation, but in the rhythm of *Job* the suffering and the indignation have significance that radically distinguishes *Job* from the modern works I have just mentioned. (The only modern writer who has affinities with *Job* is Shakespeare and particularly the Shakespeare of *King Lear.* It is significant that the multiple author of *Job* is frequently characterized by critics and scholars anachronistically as the Shakespeare of the Bible.)

I am going to try to recapture the essential intention of *Job* and distinguish the ethos of its sensibility from the ethos of the modern sensibility. But first I want to rehearse the main action of the book.

Job is the perfect and upright man whom God, on a dare from Satan, victimizes in the most outrageous fashion in order to test his faith. Job first loses his material prosperity, then his family and finally experiences the most acute physical suffering. He endures—up to a point; his patience is proverbial. Finally however, there is a great outburst of indignation. In an anguish of flesh and spirit, he challenges divine justice. Now that the torrent has been loosed, nothing can stop it. Friends of his come to console him, and each one presumes to discover a purpose in Job's afflictions. Perhaps he is suffering for the sins of his fathers or those of his children. Each consolation has the undeniable stamp of sophistry (for what do his friends know of God's purposes?), and Job's refusal to be consoled is simply another vindication of his integrity, his integrity even in defiance of his fate. We are never left with the slightest doubt of Job's character. He remains throughout perfect and upright.

Such has been the force of Job's indignation that God, turning aside the false pieties of the comforters, feels called upon to declare himself. And yet the Voice Out of the Whirlwind, despite the undeniable magnificence of its utterance, neither explains nor justifies God's treatment of Job. Job's indignant questions go unanswered. Indeed, the immediate impression is that questions are treated as impertinences, almost beneath the notice of the divinity which the magnificent poetry of the Voice is celebrating. And yet just as mysteriously as the Voice has spoken, Job with the perfect economy of movement that characterizes not only *Job,* but the whole of the Bible, abhors himself and repents in dust and ashes.

In light of the multiple authorship of *Job* can we talk about it as a unified work? There is obviously a conflict of intentions. The prose passages that concern God and Satan have the effect of rationalizing Job's afflictions: the prologue makes them into a test of Job's faith, and the epilogue subverts the scepticism of the poetry by seeing to it that justice is done. Job's anguished claim that the virtuous are unrewarded and the vicious unpunished is, as it were, denied by the epilogue. The fact of multiple authorship, however, does little damage to the coherence of the book; its inconsistencies are like the inconsistencies of a Gothic cathedral, many hands conspiring in their individuality to create a unified impression. Moreover, the conflict of intention is superficial. One might say that the poetic passages represent a deepening, rather than a contradiction of the original conception of the Job story. If the greatness of Job lies chiefly in the poetic passages, that greatness is not to be understood as belonging solely to its scepticism: that is, to its sense of the gratuitous cruelty of the universe. The greatness of *Job* lies as well in its triumphant religious clarity, and here the intentions of the narrative and the poetry virtually coincide. The greatness of *Job* is in the way in which it answers a question which every age must ask and which was asked in the nineteenth century by Dostoievsky in *The Brothers Karamazov.*

Towards the end of *The Brothers,* Dmitri dreams that he is riding in his carriage on the steppes and that he suddenly comes upon a woman and her child. They have been victims of fire and they are wandering away from their village, homeless. Dmitri asks the coachman why the child is crying, and the coachman, good empirical-rationalist that he is, answers that their house has burned down. But

Dmitri is asking another kind of question. Not what has happened, but why it has happened. Why was the world made in such a way that houses must burn down and the innocent must suffer. Dmitri's question is the question that Job asks himself, a question that must be asked again and again in every age. Indeed, the test of the integrity of an age is its capacity to ask the question and to seek the answer.

What kind of answer does *Job* give to the question? The answer certainly is not to be found in any explicit statement in the book. The book is not a philosophical treatise, it is a dramatic poem and its significances lie in character and situation, in the relationships between characters, in the relationship between character and situation. And yet having said this, the problem of interpretation is as formidable as ever. For so much of the meaning of *Job* seems to be—at least for the modern reader—in what is left out. For instance, we want to know what went on in Job's mind during the time that the Voice speaks out of the whirlwind. What is the human and psychological burden of the simple phrase: "then Job abhorred himself and repented in dust and ashes."

Has Job reluctantly surrendered to his ineluctable fate? Is his refusal to persist in his indignation the result of a sudden perception that his faith is being tested, that his utterance during his period of patience ("though he slay me, yet will I trust in him") is in danger of being betrayed by his indignation and that he must inhibit the indignation if he is to remain a moral man? Or is his surrender simply an act of cowardice, an unwillingness to assume the role of the romantic hero? In his submission, from another point of view, the only moral alternative, the others being suicide or dissipation or a romantic refusal to accept his fate?

It is possible to make out a case for the heroism of Job's final action. One might say that Job is accepting, not God's cruelty, but the limits that God has set upon Job's capacity to understand its meaning. God's imposition is so final that further evidence would be even morally superfluous. For what could Job hope to gain from continued indignation? Job is not confronted by Adam's choice of knowledge and suffering vs. ignorance and happiness. When Adam eats of the tree of knowledge, he is not defying his destiny, he is creating it. And one could interpret Adam's action as an heroic one. But in *Job* no price is put on the kind of knowledge that Job desires. It cannot be won even by suffering, for that kind of knowledge is fate, fate which has already been created and for which mystery is its necessary condition. Thus, the only honorable course for Job-in this interpretation-is to make his peace with God. The alternatives, suicide and dissipation, share a common characteristic: both involve a surrender of one's integrity, an unmaking of self. But Job in his act of submission remains true to himself. He responds to God's cruelty by his stern refusal to disintegrate. He is uncompromised at the end, free of the mealy-mouthed pieties of his comforters. One might say that the book demonstrates the superiority of Job's morality to the cruelty of divine justice.

The biblical narrative-I have in mind particularly *The Pentateuch*—in its spare and elliptical character invites the kind of interpretation I have just made. The modern reader feels a demand to supply the psychological and moral detail of actions that are so sparingly rendered. In Kierkegaard's *Fear and Trembling* and Mann's *Joseph and His Brothers* we are given glimpses of the characters of Abraham, Isaac and Joseph, glimpses that we never get in the Bible. What is the value of such glimpses? In what sense do they constitute interpretations of the Bible? They illustrate, it seems to me, a power which all great works have and which the Bible has supremely, the power to change its life in every age and thus to remain alive. Each interpretation invests the work with new life. This, of course, cannot be accomplished by the interpretation itself. There must be something in the work which elicits the life-giving interpretation. The work must present the kind of experience—we call it universal experience—of which each age has its own conception or version. So that the interpretation may not only have the value of adding life or significance to the work, it may also be a way that the imagination of the age reveals itself, a way in which it clarifies its own conception. Thus Kierkegaard's interpretation of the Abraham story becomes an opportunity for Kierkegaard to express the dilemmas of religious belief in the modern world—and the leap of faith that is necessary to transcend those dilemmas.

When a work is used in this fashion, it is in danger of having its spirit violated. Sometimes the experience that the work embodies is no longer accessible to the interpreter, and he fastens on to an aspect of the work that is accessible in order to make something entirely new. Here is an instance of the way in which Kierkegaard interiorizes the story of the sacrifice of Isaac, changing it from a drama of deed to a drama of motive:

> . . . Then Abraham lifted up the boy, he walked with him by his side, and his talk was full of comfort and exhortation. But Isaac could not understand him. He climbed Mount Moriah, but Isaac understood him not. Then for an instant he turned away from him, and when Isaac again saw Abraham's face it was changed, his glance was wild, his form was horror. He seized Isaac by the throat, threw him to the ground, and said, "Stupid boy, dost thou then suppose that I am thy father, I am an idolater. Dost thou suppose that this is God's bidding? No, it is my desire." Then Isaac trembled and cried out in his terror, "O God in heaven, have compassion upon me. If I have no father upon earth, be Thou my father!" But Abraham in a low voice said to himself, "O Lord in heaven, I thank Thee. After all it is better for him to believe that I am a monster, rather than that he should lose faith in Thee."

How the Biblical narrative has been altered by the act of conceiving the inner lives of Abraham and Isaac! Brilliant as Kierkegaard's reading is, it is a typical instance of the modern refusal to accept the mystery of the story, it is an instance of the modern need to rationalize it by fleshing it out with the psychological and moral detail of our own experience. As in the story of the sacrifice, the truth of *Job* lies not in what is absent or hidden; it lies chiefly in what the work reveals.

Let me return for a moment to the last sentence of my

summary of the action of *Job*. "And just as mysteriously as the Voice has spoken, Job with the perfect economy of movement that characterizes not the book, but the whole of the Bible, abhors and repents in dust and ashes." This certainly does not seem like an explanation of Job's action, but it is to my mind better than an explanation. Properly understood, it represents the manner by which we are to intuit the meaning of Job's submission to God.

What fails to satisfy us about the submission is the mystery of it. We either disbelieve it or mistrust it and our first impulse is to make it visible. We must solve the mystery—for the idea of the mysterious gives us a sense of the unresolved. But if we read *Job* with the kind of suspension of disbelief that Coleridge advocated as the necessary condition of an imaginatively critical reading, we may have a perception of the utter rightness of the book, the rightness of the impression that it makes upon us despite our moral and intellectual resistance to it. The rhythm of the work, its discords, the resolution of the discords and the final harmony to which the Book conspires and which it reaches depend completely on the mysterious—that is, on nothing that we can explain by modern rationalism or psychology. If we try to get behind the action to psychology, the interpretation, however internally coherent it might be, is bound to fail to correspond with our sense of the book's rhythm, where it seems to me the intrinsic meaning lies. Our experience of the rhythm of the book certainly does not justify the interpretation that Job, by submitting, is slyly affirming himself in his moral integrity against God's gratuitous cruelty.

Let me state the issue somewhat differently. Aristotle distinguishes among four kinds of causes, among which are the efficient cause and the final cause. Normally speaking, the efficient cause-that which makes something move—is motive, psychological motive, the final cause is the purpose of the action. In Aristotelian terms the movement in *Job* is created not by an efficient cause but by the final cause. The action of Job abhorring himself and repenting is significant not for any motives in Job, but for its movement towards *Someone* beyond Job. The mere presence of God is sufficient to command or explain Job's action. It is for this reason that the lack of psychological or moral detail is not a function of the primitivism of the writer, but rather a function of the book's meaning—a way the book has of indicating that its meaning is not in Job's psychology, but in Job's relationship to God.

While a psychological attention to *Job* might produce interesting interpretations, it would do violence to the integrity of the work. Nothing must subvert out sense of the authenticity of Job's final gesture. To understand it as cowardice or a sly assertion of superiority over God is to mistake the rhythm of the work. Job "abhors himself and repents in dust and ashes." The phrase is burdened by no hidden motives; it bears the pressure only of the Voice of God, of Job's hearing it and of his consequent seeing of it with his mind's eye. And here it seems to me we have the essential difference between the sensibilities of the biblical and the modern worlds.

The modern protest occurs in a world in which the voice of God is not heard. All that is heard is the echo of protest.

The result is that the protest is magnified and amplified. Since there is no answering voice the protest is limited only by the limits of the energy of the protest. When we contemplate the great outcries of romantic heroes in nineteenth-century literature—of the Byronic hero, of the Dostoievskian hero, of the Hardyian hero—we are contemplating Job's indignation raised to the hundredth power. If we have come to the modern romantics from Job we may even be struck by a sense of the absurd and the grotesque, of the extravagant posturing of the Jobean characters in modern literature: a sense which may even defeat our ability to sympathize with their suffering.

Notes from the Underground is a graphic instance of what has happened to the Jobean protest in the modern world. Early in the novel there is a contemptuous attack on the tragic view (which is the view of *Job*) from the romantic standpoint.

> With people who know how to avenge themselves and to stand up for themselves in general, how is it done? Why, when they are possessed, let us suppose, by the feeling of revenge, then for the time being there is nothing else but that feeling left in their whole being. Such a gentleman simply dashes straight for his object like an infuriated bull with its horns down, and nothing but a wall will stop him. (By the way: facing the wall, such gentlemen—that is, the *straightforward* persons and men of action—are genuinely nonplused. For them a wall is not an evasion, as for us who think and consequently do nothing; it is not an excuse for turning aside, an excuse which we always are very glad of, though we scarcely believe in it ourselves, as a rule. No they are nonplused in all sincerity. The wall has for them something tranquilizing, morally soothing, final—perhaps even something mysterious—but of this wall more later.)

We turn a page and find this about the wall.

> As though such a stone wall really were a consolation and really did contain some word of conciliation, simply because it is true as that two times two makes four. Oh absurdity of absurdities! How much better it is to understand all, to recognize all—all the impossibilities and the stone wall; not to be reconciled to one of those impossibilities and stone walls if it disgusts you to be reconciled to it; by the way of the most inevitable, logical combinations to reach the most revolting conclusions on the everlasting theme: that you yourself are somehow to blame even for the stone wall, though again it is as clear as day you are not to blame in the least, and therefore grinding your teeth in silent importance to sink into luxurious inertia, brooding on the fact that there's no one for you even to feel vindictive against, that you have not and perhaps never will have, an object for your spite, that it is a sleight of hand, a bit of jugglery, a cardsharper's trick, that it is simply a mess, no knowing what and no knowing who. But in spite of all these uncertainties and juggleries, there is still an ache in you, and the more you do not know, the worse the ache.

The stone wall represents the laws of nature. In the novel,

science indifferently performs the role of God, defining, as it were, the human condition. But what a difference between the arithmetic of the stone wall and the creative power of a living God. Naturally, the underground man refuses to be reconciled to the stone wall, though he lacks the courage to run his head against it. In his imagination where all his courage resides, he can conceive grandiose defiant gestures and refuse to submit to the inevitable. And this is what the romantic protest amounts to: a refusal to submit to the inevitable, a curiously mixed hatred of and disbelief in the inevitable. The objective world dissolves into the psychological confusions of the underground man. The stone wall is at once reality and illusion: inimical to and identical with the underground man, impossible to transcend and yet impossible to accept, the torment with which he is undeservedly afflicted and yet which he himself has created. The novel is obsessed by paradox and dilemma, a testimony to what happens to man when he can no longer experience life beyond the self—when the private self is hypostatized as the real world.

The psychological orientation of so much of modern literature, indeed of modern culture, reflects the inevitable egotism of a Godless universe. It is inconceivable that Job could have persisted in his indignation after he had heard the Voice of God, not because the Voice had intimidated him, but because it has defined the limits of his protest, and by extension of his egotism. Job learns that his suffering is not the world—that there is a great world, an infinitely greater world, beyond his suffering. If the writer of *Job* had given us a glimpse of Job's thoughts and feelings at the end, he would have destroyed the superb balance that is created between God's self-assertion and Job's submission. The values of *Job* are perfectly distributed by the economy of its imaginative attention.

The submission of Job is an act of freedom and paradoxically an act which is made possible by the divine power that limits him. The only modern work I know that has a similar perception of the meaning of freedom—in the interaction of self and otherness—is *King Lear*. The transformation that takes place in Lear from monumental vanity to the most compassionate concern for the welfare of others has something of the rhythm of Job's self-exaltation in his suffering and his final acquiescence in the inevitable. The transformation is incredibly painful—there is even more pain in *Lear* than in *Job*—but it is also magnificent, full of that grace that redeems and purifies. If we remember the religious connotation of the word grace, then we will have the right sense of the hero's will—of Job's and Lear's will—a supple strength, unlike the fixed, disembodied and abstract strength of the romantic hero's will. The power to endure catastrophe gracefully is an heroic power and a power that the modern spirit has yielded to self-exaltation through suffering.

What a presumption of Archibald MacLeish [in his drama *J. B.*] to have magnified the suffering of Job and minimized the counter-balancing presence of God. If MacLeish had intended satire, he might have revealed not only the suffering of the modern person, but the poverty of his suffering in his impulse towards self-magnification. But MacLeish takes his version of *Job* seriously-indeed, with a desperate seriousness. God and Satan are reduced to circus performers and the smug J. B., an unwitting Babbitt, vice-president of Organization Incorporated, becomes the center of significance. And the most flagrant demonstration of MacLeish's failure to be inspired by the original text is in the way in which he resolves the misfortunes of his organization man. All pretense at a concern with the man-God relation disappears. J. B. and his wife come together again after a short estrangement, and we are supposed to respond to the triumph of life in the new "inter-personal" relations that J. B. establishes with his wife. Love conquers all-this time with the hygienic sanction of revisionist Freudian psychology. MacLeish is simply incapable of imagining life beyond the squalid domesticities of middle class existence.

One cannot reproach MacLeish for what is a cultural failure. We cannot demand that a man envisage God in an epoch in which, as Nietzsche has remarked, God is dead. But we can demand of those gifted with the intelligence and the imagination to conceive works of art that they learn contempt for such an epoch, that they learn to regard the petty egotisms of men as less than world-shaking. There is at least one great writer of our century who had a vision of the other world which recalls the vision that we find in the Bible, D. H. Lawrence. Lawrence understood *Job* better than any modern I know. In a letter to a young novelist he writes as follows:

> I think the greatest book I know on the subject of egotism is the *Book of Job*. Job was a great splendid egotist. But whereas Hardy and the moderns end with "Let the day perish—" or more beautifully—"the waters wear the stones; thou washest away the things which grow out of the dust of the earth; thou destroyest the hope of man:
>
> Thou prevailest for ever against him, and he passeth: thou changest his countenance and sendest him away."—the real book of Job ends—"Then Job answered the Lord and said:
>
> I know that thou canst do everything, and that no thought can be withholden thee.
>
> Who is he that hideth counsel without knowledge? Therefore have I uttered that I understood not: things too wonderful for me, which I know not.
>
> Hear, I beseech thee, and I will speak: I will demand of thee, and declare thou unto me.
> I have heard of thee by hearing of the ear; but now mine eye seeth thee.
>
> Wherefore I abhor myself, and repent in dust and ashes." If you want a story of your own soul, it is perfectly done in the *Book of Job*—much better than in *Notes from the Underground*.
>
> But the moderns today prefer to end insisting on the sad plight which was really Prometheus Unbound, only the Prometheus Bound and terribly suffering on the rock of his own egotism.

It has been said of Kafka, whose profound despair puts him at the opposite pole of a writer like Lawrence, that his perception of the relations between man and God in *The Trial* and *The Castle* has affinities with the perception of *Job:* the human and divine spheres are incommensurable and it is the moral tragedy of man that the ultimate significance of his life is forever unavailable to him, in a word, he is doomed to experience life as meaningless.

Nothing could be further from the vision of *Job* than Kafka's despair. Though the human and divine spheres are indeed incommensurable in both Kafka and *Job,* the biblical work, indeed the whole of the Bible, conceives the two spheres as interpenetrable.

> Hear, I beseech thee, and I will speak:
> I will demand of thee, and declare
> thou unto me.
> I have heard of thee by the hearing
> of the ear; but now mine eye seeth thee.

What a world of difference between Job and Kafka's heroes, who hear only the silence of despair and see only the abyss of suffering and vacuity.

If Job has learned from hearing things that were too wonderful for him we must at least learn that we have failed to hear them. Then perhaps the experience of *Job* will become available to us.

Robert Gordis   (essay date 1965)

SOURCE: "The Lord out of the Whirlwind," in *The Book of God and Man: A Study of Job,* The University of Chicago Press, 1965, pp. 117-34.

[*Gordis is an American rabbi, theologian, and editor who has written broadly on Jewish culture and theology. In the following essay he focuses on God's speeches in* The Book of Job, *examining various critical perspectives concerning their authenticity and form and emphasizing the importance of allusion in Hebrew literature.*]

As Elihu's words end, a storm is seen rising in the east. The Lord himself appears in the whirlwind and addresses Job in two speeches, after each of which Job offers a brief reply [*Job*, 38: 1-40:2, 40:3-6, 40:6- 41:26]. These chapters are among the greatest nature poetry in world literature. Their purpose, however, is not the glorification of nature, but the vindication of nature's God.

The contention of the Friends that Job must be a sinner because he is a sufferer is treated with the silence it deserves. Nowhere does God refer to the misdeeds of which he had been accused by the Lord's "defenders." This silence is richly significant on several counts. It speaks eloquently of God's rejection of the conventional theology expounded by the Friends, which begins in untruth and ends in cruelty. (Eliphaz, who begins the dialogue with courtliness and consideration [chaps. 4, 5], ends by wildly accusing Job of every conceivable crime [chap. 22].) Later, when God and Job are reconciled, the Lord passes severe judgment upon the Friends: "The Lord said to Eliphaz the Temanite, 'My anger is kindled against you and against your two friends, for you have not spoken the truth about Me as has My servant Job' " (42:7); but at the present

juncture, silence is the most effective refutation of their position.

The Lord consciously refrains from referring to Job's suffering, not from callous indifference but, on the contrary, from exquisite tact and sensibility. Job's agony cannot be justified by the platitudes of conventional religion, nor can it be explained away as imaginary. If man is to bear his suffering at all, the entire problem must be raised to another dimension. This is the burden of the words of the Lord spoken out of the whirlwind.

Can Job comprehend, let alone govern, the universe that he weighs and now finds wanting? Earth and sea, cloud and darkness and dawn, sleet and hail, rain and thunder, snow and ice, and the stars above—all these wonders are beyond Job. Nor do they exhaust God's power. With a vividness born of deep love and careful observation, the poet pictures the beasts, remote from man, yet precious to their Maker. The lion and the mountain goat, the wild ass and the buffalo, the ostrich, the wild horse, and the hawk, all testify to the glory of God (chaps. 38, 39).

The creatures glorified by the poet are not chosen at random. For all their variety they have one element in common—they are not under the sway of man, nor are they intended for his use. The implication is clear—the universe and its Creator cannot be judged solely from the vantage point of man, and surely not from the limited perspective of one human being. This call to rise above the anthropocentric view will be emphasized even more strikingly in the Lord's second speech. Job is overwhelmed and confesses his weakness:

> Job answered the Lord, saying,
> Behold, I am of small account; how can I answer
>   You?
> I lay my hand to my mouth.
> I have spoken once, and I will not reply again;
> Twice, but I will proceed no further.
>   [*Job* 40:3-5]

God, however, ignores Job's surrender and with torrential force launches into His second speech. He begins by asking whether Job is ready to subvert the entire order of the universe so that he may be vindicated:

> Will you deny My justice,
> Put Me in the wrong, so that you may be in the
>   right?
>   [40:8]

The climax of this divine irony, infinitely keen yet infinitely kind, is now reached: God invites Job to assume His throne and take the reins of majesty and power into his own hands. If he is able to humble the arrogant and crush the evildoers, God himself is prepared to do obeisance to him!

> Have you an arm like God;
> Can you thunder with a voice like His?
> Deck yourself in majesty and dignity,
> Clothe yourself with glory and splendor.
> Scatter abroad your mighty wrath,
> And as you see each proud sinner—abase him!
> As you look on each arrogant one—bring him
>   low,

And tread down the wicked in their place.
Bury them all in the dust,
Press their faces into the grave—
Then I, too, will render thee homage,
When your right hand will have brought you
    victory.

[40:9-14]

Here on the one hand is God's moving acknowledgment that the world order is not perfect, and on the other, an affirmation of the complexity of the universe and of the conflicting interests which divine concern must encompass and reconcile. All these elements man must reckon with before he presumes to pass judgment on the universe and its Governor.

Thus God has conceded that there are flaws in His creation, and evils which He has not conquered. Yet the world is not evil merely because there is evil in it. Evil is not dismissed as illusory or unimportant, but neither is it permitted to usurp a position of dominance in the universe.

Then follow exultant descriptions of two massive beasts—*Behemot,* the hippopotamus (40:15-24), and *Leviathan,* the crocodile (40:25-41:26). These are not literal, exact delineations, but poetic pictures rich in hyperbole. It is possible that, carried along by his enthusiasm and exultation, the poet borrowed images from ancient oriental myths which tell of the creative god who fights and conquers primordial beasts of terrifying dimensions. But he is not interested in imaginary creatures from the dim mythological past—he is concerned with the actual present, with the vast universe as it is governed by its Maker. The hippopotamus and the crocodile are real beasts and their choice for inclusion in these paeans of praise is by no means accidental.

The first speech of the Lord has glorified creatures like the mountain goat, the ostrich, the horse, and the hawk. To be sure, they were not created for man's use, yet they do possess a beauty and grace that man can appreciate. The poet now goes a step further. The hippopotamus and the crocodile can lay no claim to beauty, but on the contrary, are physically repulsive. When the poet glorifies these beasts he is calling upon us to rise completely above the anthropocentric point of view which, however natural for man, distorts his comprehension of the world. Precisely because they are unbeautiful by human standards, these monstrosities, fashioned by God's hand, are a revelation of the limitless range of God's creative thought. Since His ways are not man's ways, how can man's thoughts grasp God's thoughts—and what is more, pass judgment upon Him?

Job replies briefly and for the last time (42:1-6). It is noteworthy that exactly as in his closing responses in the first and second cycles of the dialogue, he employs the device of quoting his opponent's words, using them as a basis for his own reply:

Then Job answered the Lord,
I know that You can do all things
And that no purpose of Yours can be thwarted.
You have said,

"Who is this that hides My plan without knowledge?"
Indeed, I have spoken without understanding,
Of things too wonderful for me which I did not
    grasp.
You have said,
"Hear, and I will speak;
I will ask you, and do you inform Me."
I have heard of You by hearsay,
But now my own eyes have seen You.
Therefore I abase myself
And repent in dust and ashes.

[42:1-6]

With these words of submission, the dialogue ends.

No reader can fail to be stirred by the power and beauty of these magnificent poems in praise of the wonders of nature and of nature's God. Herder undoubtedly had these chapters in mind, along with other biblical passages, when he wrote in his famous *Vom Geist der Ebräischen Poesie:*

> I have been particularly struck by its (the Jewish people's) perfect sympathy with brutes and the whole animate creation and was delighted even in childhood to find that it treated the brute animals (so called because they are dumb) as the brothers of man who want nothing but the power of speech. The wild beasts that the Hebrew language calls 'living creatures' *are* the living, because domestic animals are in comparison, as it were, still and dead. I was delighted when I found the voice and language of brutes so forcefully expressed in the language; when the prophet coos with the crane and the turtle dove, and mourns with the ostrich in the wilderness. I rejoiced at finding the form of the stag, the lion and the ox, sometimes their strength, stateliness, and velocity, at others, the acuteness of their senses, their habits of life and their character described and painted in appropriate terms. I wished that in place of some of the sacred songs we had more of its fables, parables and riddles respecting the brute creation, in short, more of the poetry of nature; for this seems to me to be among this people the most happy and the most perfect simplicity.

Granted the magnificence of the God speeches, several important questions arise. Most readers have been struck by the fact that these chapters make no reference whatsoever to the theme of man's suffering, with which the rest of Job is concerned. This has led some critics to assume that the work was left unfinished and that another poet added these chapters which, however beautiful in themselves, are irrelevant. Some of these scholars assume that the book originally was confined to a discussion of Job's misfortunes and that it grew to its present size via successive editions.

This view, rightly stigmatized by [R.H. Pfeiffer in *Le Problème du Livre de Job*] as "gratuitous," is generally rejected on several grounds. One argument is based on the literary greatness of these chapters. [S. R. Driver, in *Introduction to the Literature of the Old Testament*], after paying high tribute to the literary quality of the God speeches, makes the wise comment, "It is difficult to believe that there could be found a second poet of equal scope (as the author of the Dialogue) to retouch the work of the first." Another argument is based on the fact that throughout the dialogue Job has demanded that God answer him; the book would be highly unsatisfactory without some reply from the Lord. Most scholars, therefore, accept the view that the God speeches are authentic, although many critics have deleted one or more sections: the passage on the ostrich (39:13-18) in the first speech of the Lord, or the descriptions of the hippopotamus and the crocodile which constitute the bulk of God's second speech.

The section on the ostrich has been rejected principally because it does not appear in the Septuagint. The fact is, however, that the Greek translation of Job represents a very drastic abridgment of the text, being fully one-sixth shorter. This is undoubtedly due to the manifold difficulties of the Hebrew text, which frequently proved too great for the Greek translator, and for that matter, for all interpreters to the present day. Moreover, the long poetic passages which employ the Semitic device of parallelism would seem repetitious and hence uncongenial to a Greek reader. Since the description of the ostrich is particularly difficult, there would be every inducement for the translator to eliminate it from his version even if it existed in the original. Moreover, it should be noted that the ostrich passage leads directly into the description of the horse (39:19 ff.), the authenticity of which is not doubted.

Many critics have sought to delete the sections on *Behemot* and *Leviathan*. Several arguments concerning style have been adduced in this connection, some readers maintaining that the second speech is inferior to the first as literature. This is a highly subjective point of view which I do not share. Only a great poet could paint the vivid picture of the hippopotamus, lying at his ease in the Nile among the lotus leaves, swallowing an entire river in one mouthful (40:24)! There is undeniable power, too, in the portrait of the mighty crocodile, encased in his coat of mail and impervious to the harpoon as he swims through the waters, stirring them up and leaving behind him a trail of white foam like an old man's beard (41:22).

Some critics have pointed out that the passages on the hippopotamus and the crocodile are not couched in the question form which is characteristic of the descriptions in the first speech. There is, however, no reason for assuming that the poet would monotonously employ a single rhetorical form throughout four long chapters (chaps. 38-41). On the contrary, as a gifted poet he would be far more likely to vary his style. Moreover, an analysis of the text discloses a regular pattern—each God speech consists of sections alternating between the question form and the direct statement, thus retaining both the force of repetition and the interest of variety.

Considerations of content have probably been most influential in leading critics to delete these sections. It has been argued that God's second speech adds nothing to the discussion and that Job's second recantation is also an unnecessary duplication. If these paragraphs are deleted (and the remaining material transposed) we are left with only one speech for God, and Job's two responses can be combined into one.

If we penetrate to the full meaning of the poet it becomes clear, I believe, that the proposed solutions are unnecessary and have served only to create new problems. As has already been indicated, the second speech is far from being a repetition of the first: it represents a higher level in the argument, an ascent from God's creative power as manifested in creatures that are independent of man, to God's creative joy in creatures that are positively dangerous and repugnant to man.

Job's responses are not redundant either, nor can they easily be combined. The final verse in Job's first reply ends with the words, "I will proceed no further" (literally, "I shall not continue to speak"). This is entirely appropriate if Job now subsides into silence, but not if we append another passage, as some critics would have us do. Moreover, each of the two responses is informed by a different spirit, with a crescendo of emotion in each corresponding to the progression of thought in the two God speeches. Job's first answer strikes the note of submission and silence; it is only in the second that he attains a measure of repentance and acceptance. Job is convinced by God's words, but not easily: two stages are required for the argument.

It is, of course, impossible to "prove" that none of the passages in these chapters was interpolated by a later hand and that the sections are all in their proper sequence. What is clear is that if we fully understand the meaning of the received text and take into account the architecture of the book as a whole, we find the entire section highly relevant in content and thoroughly appropriate in form.

The question of the authenticity of the various passages in these chapters, though interesting, is far less important than another basic issue: What are the meaning and relevance of the God speeches? Unless we solve this problem, *Job* has eluded us. In all the magnificent nature description of the God speeches there is no concern with the problem of suffering and sin. Are we then to assume that the author of *Job,* after giving ample testimony of his intellectual powers, threw up his hands and permitted his masterpiece to end in a total collapse of thought? Obviously we should not "impose the strait-jacket of Aristotelian logic and consistency on an Oriental poet of great imagination and insight" [as stated by Pfeiffer], for the Hebrew genius had its own canons of thought and concept of beauty; but we have a right to expect that the tragic theme of the book not be totally abandoned.

A modern philosophical writer raises the issue clearly when he asks, "What did God reveal to him that suddenly rent asunder the cover of darkness over Job's soul and made divine truth shine forth before him in all its splendor?" He then answers, "The poor logic and weakness of God's arguments and speeches against Job are truly astonishing. Actually, He does not reply at all. He explains nothing. He only makes sport of the little worm Job; He only unfolds before him gigantic images of creation as seen in nature and taunts him: Canst thou do this? Dost thou at least understand how this is done?" [Chaim Zhitlowsky in *Job and Faust*].

That an author of transcendent genius should be guilty of

a total abdication of logic and reason, particularly when dealing with the theme of his lifework, is not merely astonishing—it is unbelievable. To adopt such a view of the poet is a confession of failure.

This effort to impugn the author's intellectual powers is at times associated with an attack on his moral character. Thus a twentieth-century biblical scholar [Pfeiffer] comes to the conclusion that "the author's wonder before the magnificence of nature, which conveys but a faint idea of the power and wisdom of the Creator, contrasts with *his contempt for miserable human beings, in whom God is no more interested than in wild animals*" (my italics).

Now the **Book of Job** is incontrovertible proof that the tragic fate of one human being preoccupied the poet for years. Is this compatible with the notion that he, or his God, would exhibit nothing but "contempt for miserable human beings"? There is not the slightest warrant in the text for attributing to God such an attitude, either toward man or toward the other animals. The entire section expresses God's deep joy in the wild creatures of the field, crag, and desert, and His care for them and their young. Even if God's concern for man were no greater than for the wild animals, that would be interest indeed!

A subtler but even more far-reaching attack on the integrity of the poet is inherent in another approach to the God speeches, [for example, that of K. Fullerton in "The Original Conclusion of Job"]. According to this view, the heart of the book is to be sought in Job's passionate protest against God's cruelty and injustice, which is the burden of the first two cycles of the dialogue (chaps. 3-19). As for the remainder of the book, nearly all of it is unauthentic: the third cycle is not only disorganized, but critically suspect of having been tampered with by orthodox apologists; the Elihu chapters are obviously interpolated; chapters 38-41, the second God speech and Job's second reply, are also to be deleted. In this view, only the first God speech (38:1-40:2) and the first confession of Job (40:3-5) are genuine. Coming immediately after chapters 3-19 they form the original conclusion of the book.

What is significant, according to this theory, is that these authentic sections in the God speeches were deliberately written by the poet ambiguously, with tongue in cheek. They were intended by the author for two totally different classes of readers, the traditionalists and the skeptics. The pious believer would find a conventional religious answer in God's reaffirmation of His power and in Job's submission, while the critical thinker would derive from the same lines the heterodox conclusion that the world as a whole and man's suffering in it constitute a riddle to which there is no solution. The motive for adding these God speeches with their *double entendre* was to get a hearing for the dialogue in circles that it would not otherwise have reached.

This ingenious theory rests upon no objective evidence in the text, either for the extensive interpolations or for the conscious deception. It should be noted, too, that by this theory the **Book of Job** would not be a case in which an author is misunderstood by his readers, but one in which he consciously seeks to mislead them. Moreover, several basic questions remain unanswered: What could the au-

thor of **Job** hope to accomplish if he disguised his true meaning so effectively that conventional readers would find only conventional answers? How does this kind of deception comport with the poet's preoccupation with Job's integrity and love of truth throughout the book? What need is there for the long and passionate dialogue by Job and his friends if no reference is made to the theme of their discussion thereafter and no solution to the problem is offered except the cold and impersonal conclusion that life is a meaningless riddle?

Another striking interpretation of the intent of the God speeches, and by that token of the book as a whole, has recently been advanced by E. M. Good who, [in *Irony in the Old Testament*], interprets the book as exhibiting "the irony of reconciliation." Good finds that after the God speeches Job "repents for a sin he now knows perfectly well and it has nothing to do with external suffering." His sin has consisted of "his being satisfied to know all about God at second hand and for elevating himself to Deity's rank." In conclusion, "God finds man guilty and acquits him. That is the fundamental irony of the **Book of Job** and of biblical faith." Unfortunately, this interpretation, acute as it is, does not carry conviction. Neither element of the irony that Good finds in the God speeches appears in the text either explicitly or by implication. Nowhere does God declare Job to be guilty and nowhere does He acquit him of his "guilt." Not only is no sin imputed by God to Job but, on the contrary, he is explicitly vindicated in the jointure following the poetic dialogue when the Lord informs the Friends, "You have not spoken the truth about Me as has My servant Job" (42:7, 8).

Whatever may have been the case with the Greeks, it was no act of *hybris,* of insolence or arrogance, for a Hebrew to demand justice of his God: the patriarch Abraham, whose faith was exemplary, voiced the challenge, "Shall not the Judge of all the earth do right?" (*Genesis* 18:25.)

Differing in spirit but not in substance is the view of the God speeches that seems to be presented by the American poet, Robert Frost. When a modern writer uses a biblical or classical theme we cannot be certain whether he is setting forth his understanding of the original source or is simply utilizing the familiar material as a framework for his own independent vision. A case in point is afforded by Frost's "A Masque of Reason." In an ironic passage God thanks Job for "liberating" Him from ethical enslavement to the human race by denying His righteousness. Job has thus freed his Maker from the obligation of observing the moral law that men have imposed upon Him when they demand that the good must prosper and the wicked suffer. In governing the world, God is now free to disregard the moral imperative.

Frost seems here to go beyond the contention that man's reason cannot demonstrate a universal and inevitable correspondence between his actions and his destiny. It is not merely that the moral standards of God are beyond man's comprehension but that morality is man's own invention, one he has sought to foist upon God. Actually, God is "beyond good and evil," free to rule His world untrammeled by the necessity of seeing justice done.

Intriguing as this view may be to some modern minds, it does not represent the thought of the ancient Hebrew poet, whose God could not so easily abrogate the law of justice in the world. Throughout the dialogue, as we have seen, Job has steadfastly insisted upon an arbiter, a witness to speak for him (9:33; 16:19). He has expressed his passionate conviction that a Redeemer exists who will vindicate him. He has demanded that his cause be engraved on a monument to last into the future. In spite of all provocations and temptations, Job has held fast to two convictions—that his agony is unjustified and that there must be justice in the world.

In the brief passage (42:7-10) by which the poet links his dialogue to the traditional epilogue, the Lord twice declares to the Friends, "You have not spoken the truth about Me as has My servant Job" (42:7, 8). Far from denying Job's insistence that justice must somehow inhere in the universe, the Lord vigorously confirms it. Job has spoken the truth not only about his unmerited suffering but "about Me," the nature of God. Thus the ***Book of Job*** demonstrates what could have been inferred a priori—a God without justice is no God to an ancient Hebrew.

To be sure, reconciling Job's two basic convictions is a difficult task. Therein lies the major problem in understanding the book as a whole and the God speeches in particular. But it does not help matters to attribute to the author of ***Job*** an incapacity for rational thought, a devious mentality, or a callous indifference to human suffering. A convincing explanation of the meaning of the God speeches must disclose their relevance to the themes of human suffering and God's justice, and, by that token, to the other sections of the book. Most students of ***Job*** have therefore attempted, in a variety of ways, to relate the God speeches to the earlier dialogue.

One widespread view maintains that God wins Job over by picturing His limitless might as seen in Creation. But this answer does not hold water. Job has frequently conceded God's might himself during the earlier debate with the Friends. If this be the point of the God speeches they are entirely unnecessary; Job himself has given more than one description of God's power as reflected in the world of nature. It is not God's might but His righteousness that Job calls into question:

> However wise and stouthearted a man might be,
> Has he ever argued with God and emerged un-
>   scathed?
> If it be a matter of power, here He is!
> But if of justice, who will arraign Him?
> Who would remove God's rod from me,
> So that my dread of Him would not terrify me.
> Then I would speak, and not fear Him,
> For He is far from just to me!
>   [***Job*** 9:4, 19, 34, 35]

> Who does not know in all this,
> That the hand of the Lord has made it?
> With God are wisdom and strength,
> His are counsel and understanding.
>   [12:9, 13]

> Remove Your hand from me,
> And let not the dread of You terrify me;

> Then You may call and I shall respond,
> Or I shall speak, and You answer me.
>   [13:21-22]

> Oh that I knew where to find Him,
> That I could come to His dwelling!
> I would lay my case before Him,
> And my mouth would not lack for arguments.
> Would He contend with me merely through His
>   great power?
> No, He would surely pay heed to me.
>   [23:3, 4, 6]

If Job suddenly surrendered before the spectacle of power which he had so passionately challenged in his cry for justice, it would be a stultifying conclusion to a brilliant debate. Were this the intent of the God speeches one would be driven to Cornill's view [in *Introduction to the Canonical Books of the Old Testament*] that they are of "unparalleled brutality, which is usually palliated and styled divine irony, but which, under such circumstances and conditions, should much rather be termed devilish scorn."

This conclusion is so thoroughly contradictory to the theme of the book and the entire tenor of biblical thought that scholars have been driven to the opposite extreme: it has been suggested that the message of the God speeches is that God remains near to man in his suffering. Throughout the dialogue, Job has contended that his Maker oppresses him while remaining indifferent to his misfortune. This unconcern is disproved by the mere fact that God appears to Job in the whirlwind and speaks to him. Job has won because he has succeeded in compelling God to answer him, and his vindication is marked by his experiencing the nearness of God. Thus one writer [Zhitlowsky] movingly declares, "It is as though a child who, lost and alone at night in a dense forest, scratched by thorns, terrified by the ghosts he sees in every tree, in every bush, were suddenly to hear the steps and the voice of his father, were to feel himself lifted up in the paternal arms and carried home. Who listens then to the scolding words of the father, and what difference does it make what happened! He is safe, close in the paternal embrace. . . . This was certainly also the psychology of Job, 'Formerly I merely heard about Thee, now mine eye beholds Thee!'—and an end to all questions." Another, more theologically oriented scholar finds in the God speeches the voice of a suffering God and sees in the ***Book of Job*** a foreshadowing of the need for a Christ.

To be sure, the idea that God shares in the suffering of His creatures does find expression in biblical thought. It is an extension of the doctrine of the covenant between God and man which unites their destiny in an indissoluble bond: "I shall be your God, and you shall be My people" (Leviticus 26:12, and often). On the one hand, this common link between God and Israel becomes the basis for the prophets' castigation of the wayward people who violated the covenant at Sinai. On the other hand, the notion of the bond is used by the prophets in their intercessions on behalf of sinful Israel, since the destruction of the nation would represent a profanation of the divine name.

From the concept that God and man are linked together by mutual responsibilities under the covenant, religious faith makes the bold leap to the conviction that God Himself suffers when man is in agony.

This theme is articulated in both the *Prophets* and the *Psalms:*

> In all their affliction He was afflicted,
> And the angel of His presence saved them;
> In His love and in His pity He redeemed them;
> And He bore them, and carried them all the days
>   of old.
>
> [*Isaiah* 63:9]

> He shall call upon Me, and I will answer him;
> I will be with him in trouble;
> I will rescue him, and bring him to honor.
>
> [*Psalms* 91:15]

> The Lord is nigh unto all them that call upon
>   Him,
> To all that call upon Him in truth.
>
> [*Psalms* 145:18]

In post-biblical thought this theme was further broadened to include the conviction that God shares in the exile and suffering of Israel, as well as in its redemption. To cite one rabbinic utterance, "When Israel went into exile, the Divine Presence went with them." In Christianity, the doctrine of the suffering God assumed a central role which needs no elaboration here.

The biblical doctrine of God is, however, characterized by polarity. Side by side with this emphasis on the nearness of God is the frequent stress on the vast gulf between God and man in creative power, in wisdom, and in moral quality. It is God's perfection and man's imperfection that lie at the root of the differences in their natures: man is changeable and perverse, but God is trustworthy and constant in His purpose; man is capable of falsehood and cruelty, while God is merciful and just. The divine transcendence and the consequent mystery of God's being are expressed in Moses' encounter with the Unseen God and his fruitless request to "see His face" (*Exodus* 33:12-23). They underlie the prohibition in the Decalogue against making an image of the Deity (*Exodus* 20:3; *Deuteronomy* 5:8). They are basic to the vision of Isaiah, whose God cannot be seen by human eyes because of man's sinfulness (6:5), though He is exalted through man's righteousness:

> Man is bowed down,
> Man is brought low,
> And the eyes of the lofty are humbled;
> But the Lord of Hosts is exalted through justice,
> And God the Holy One is sanctified through
>   righteousness.
>
> [*Isaiah* 5:15, 16]

Biblical religion is the result of the creative tension between God's covenant and His transcendence, the sense of man's intimacy with God and the recognition of the vast difference between them. Both elements of this polarity find matchless expression in the Eighth Psalm. Here the pettiness and the grandeur of man are both related to the greatness of God; it is not God descending to man, but man ascending to God!

> When I behold Your heavens, the work of Your
>   fingers,

> The moon and the stars that You have made,
> What is man that You are mindful of him,
> And the son of man, that You have regard for
>   him?
> Yet You have made him little lower than divine
> And crowned him with glory and honor.
>
> [*Psalms* 8:4-6]

The tension between these two themes was expressed by the Hasidic teacher Rabbi Bunam: "A man should carry two stones in his pocket. On one should be inscribed, 'I am but dust and ashes.' On the other, 'For my sake was the world created.' And he should use each stone as he needs it."

This sage counsel to draw upon each element of the polarity of God and man as needed was anticipated and followed by the author of *Job.* The conviction that God is near was deeply imbedded in Job's spirit during his days of well-being. In his final pathetic soliloquy he recalls with longing his previous intense intimacy with God:

> Oh, that I were as in the months of old,
> As in the days when God watched over me,
> When His lamp shone upon my head
> And by His light I walked through darkness;
> As I was in my days of vigor
> When God was an intimate in my tent,
> When the Almighty was still with me,
> And my children were all about me.
>
> [*Job* 29:2-5]

In an earlier plea as well, he recalled this loving fellowship:

> Your hands fashioned and made me
> Altogether—yet now You destroy me!
> Remember that You made me of clay
> And will return me to the dust.
> In Your love You granted me life;
> Your command kept me alive.
>
> [10:8, 9, 12]

More than once he passionately pleads for a restoration of this relationship, which had expressed God's erstwhile love, now unaccountably turned to cruelty:

> If a man die, can he live again?
> All the days of my service I would wait,
> Till my hour of release should come.
> You would call and I would answer You;
> You would be longing for the work of Your
>   hands.
>
> [14:14, 15]

We may gain an insight into man's yearning for fellowship with God in a significant observation by Gershom Scholem. In his classic work on Jewish mysticism [*Major Trends in Jewish Mysticism*], he points out that there are three main stages in monotheistic religion: (1) the *primitive,* when the communion between God and the worshiper is immediate and no abyss exists between them; (2) the *creative,* when consciousness of the transcendence of God develops, so that the distance between God and man is acutely felt as absolute; and (3) the *mystical,* which Scholem calls the "romantic" period, when the attempt is made to bridge the abyss by evolving new means of communion and by re-establishing unity between man and his

Maker. The observation may be made that the third stage thus reverts to the first or mythical level, but with significant differences. At all events, the first and third periods are mutually illuminating.

Whether or not this suggestive thesis is accepted, it is clear that nowhere in the God speeches in *Job* is it indicated, even by implication, that God is near to man and his suffering. On the contrary, it is the transcendental aspect of the Deity which finds expression here. With all the power at his command the poet underscores the tremendous chasm between Job and his Maker.

To be sure, Job is comforted by God's speaking to him, by the knowledge that he is not ignored. That sin separates man from God is clear from the very beginning of the Bible, when Adam, after his sin, is thrust out of the Garden of Eden. Hence, if suffering is the result of sin, at least part of the penalty lies in the sense of alienation from God. It is this estrangement from God which Job feels so keenly, and it is in the re-establishment of their relationship that he finds evidence of his vindication.

But if it were merely a matter of God's manifesting His fellowship with Job, His appearance itself, perhaps augmented by a few words of sympathy, would have sufficed. Actually, the God speeches express no sympathy for Job's suffering, which, as we have previously indicated, is nowhere referred to. Nor is the length of God's rejoinder to be ignored: not merely that God speaks, but what He says, is crucial. The content of God's words must therefore have a bearing upon the basic issue of evil in a world created by a good God.

The beauty of these chapters is not their sole excuse for being: they are distinctly germane to the issue at hand. What is needed is a recognition of the extensive role which allusiveness (the use of indirection and implication rather than categorical assertion) plays in the Hebrew literature of all periods. The ancient reader could be counted upon to understand a hint and, what is more, to revel in the intellectual pleasure of gathering the meaning from an indirect presentation of the theme under discussion. This rhetorical usage by the poet is particularly effective here, where he is concerned with issues that transcend the mundane and the experiential, so that a hint is far more eloquent than an outright statement. Not denotation, but connotation, is the heart of poetry in general, and of the God speeches in particular.

All of man's explanations of human suffering, varied and imperfect, have been set forth by the Friends and Elihu and have been countered by Job. The human protagonists are now silent. Any deeper word must be spoken by God, who makes His point by implication, but nonetheless effectively on that account. The vivid and joyous description of nature is not an end in itself: it underscores the insight that nature is not merely a mystery, but is also a miracle, a cosmos, a thing of beauty. From this flows the basic conclusion at which the poet has arrived: *just as there is order and harmony in the natural world, though imperfectly grasped by man, so there is order and meaning in the moral sphere, though often incomprehensible to man.*

The analogy is compelling, not only on the logical and psychological level, but aesthetically. For the poet, the harmony of the universe is important as an idea and as an experience. When man steeps himself in the beauty of the world his troubles grow petty, not because they are unreal, but because they dissolve within the larger plan, like the tiny dabs and scales of oil in a painting. The beauty of the world becomes an anodyne to man's suffering—and the key to truth. In Robert Louis Stevenson's words [in his essay "The Lantern Bearers" in *The Travels and Essays of Robert Louis Stevenson*], "The true realism, always and everywhere, is that of the poets: to find out where joy resides, and give it a voice far beyond singing. For to miss the joy is to miss all. In the joy of the actors lies the sense of any action. That is the explanation, that the excuse."

The force of the analogy and its implications are not lost upon Job, and it is before this truth that he yields. He repents his attack upon God, in which he failed to reckon with the limitations in his own understanding. Thus he is able to submit to God's will in a spirit of genuine acceptance.

In the author of *Job* we have a superb example of the creative artist at work, as Havelock Ellis describes him:

> Instead of imitating these philosophers who with analysis and syntheses worry over the goal of life and the justification of the world, and the meaning of the strange and painful phenomenon called Existence, the artist takes up some fragment of that existence, transfigures it, shows it: There! And therewith the spectator is filled with enthusiastic joy, and the transcendent Adventure of Existence is justified. All the pain and the madness, even the ugliness and commonplace of the world, he converts into shining jewels. By revealing the spectacular character of reality he restores the serenity of his innocence. We see the face of the world as of a lovely woman smiling through her tears.

The poet's ultimate message is clear: Not only *Ignoramus,* "we do not know," but *Ignorabimus,* "we may never know." But the poet goes further. He calls upon us *Gaudeamus,* "let us rejoice," in the beauty of the world, though its pattern is only partially revealed to us. It is enough to know that the dark mystery encloses and in part discloses a bright and shining miracle.

Marvin H. Pope   (essay date 1965)

SOURCE: An introduction to *Job,* translated by Marvin H. Pope, Doubleday & Company, 1965, pp. XV-LXXXIV.

[*In the following excerpt from his introduction to* The Anchor Bible: Job, *Pope examines several points of critical debate surrounding The Book of Job: the question of textual integrity, the form and origin of the book, the place of the work in the literary canon, and the philosophical and educational intentions of the book's author(s).*]

To summarize the contents of the *Book of Job* raises the question of its literary unity and integrity. The same issue is raised by the problem of classifying the work in its liter-

William Blake's illustration to The Book of Job.

ary form because the whole suggests a sort of piecemeal composition.

The problem of literary integrity is most immediately evident in the incongruities and inconsistencies between the Prologue-Epilogue and the Dialogue. The Prologue presents to us the traditional pious and patient saint who retained his composure and maintained his integrity through all the woes inflicted on him and refused to make any accusation of injustice against Yahweh, but rather continued to bless the god who had afflicted him. In the Dialogue we meet quite a different Job whose bitter complaints and charges of injustice against God shock his pious friends who doggedly defend divine justice and persistently reaffirm the doctrine of exact individual retribution. In view of these attitudes, the Epilogue, in which the friends, not Job, are rebuked for not having spoken the truth about Yahweh comes as something of a shock. In the Dialogue Job effectively demolishes the friends' doctrine that wickedness is always punished and virtue always rewarded. But in the final settlement in the Epilogue this dogma is sustained by the highly artificial manner in which Job is both compensated for his pains and restored to health and prosperity. There are other minor incongruities, for example, in the Prologue-Epilogue Job is scrupulous in his observance of the sacrificial cultus, but the Dialogue betrays not the slightest interest in this particular concern and in his final apology for his life Job makes no claim on this account. The names used for God are different in the Prologue-Epilogue and the Dialogue; the former uses Yahweh and Elohim while the latter employs variously the terms El, Eloah, Elohim, and Shaddai. The temper and mood of the Prologue-Epilogue and of the Dialogue are quite distinct: the Prologue reflects a rather detached and impersonal attitude toward the cruel experiment to test the basis of Job's piety; by contrast the Dialogue is highly charged with emotion and the anguish of a tortured soul. The literary forms are also different: The Prologue-Epilogue is in prose, though in its epic style a number of lines have such poetic quality that we have ventured to arrange portions of the Prologue as poetry; the Dialogue is in poetry throughout. In view of these incongruities, critics have generally regarded the Prologue-Epilogue and the Dialogue as having diverse authorship and origin, although some have thought the author of the Dialogue composed the Prologue-Epilogue as the setting for his work. Most critics, however, regard the Prologue-Epilogue as part of an ancient folk tale which the author of the Dialogue used as the framework and point of departure for his poetic treatment of the problem of suffering. Whether this ancient folk tale was in written form or transmitted orally, it had probably attained a relatively fixed form and content which the author of the Dialogue could not modify in any radical fashion. It has epic style and the charm and flavor of an oft told tale. *Ezekiel* xiv 14, 20 indicates that there was a legendary figure named Job, of great antiquity—like Noah and Danel (the ancient prototype of the biblical Daniel now known to us from the Ugaritic epic). The great antiquity of the literary motif of the righteous suferer has been established by S. N. Kramer's recovery of a Sumerian poetic essay dating from ca. 2000 B.C. dealing with the same problem as the ***Book of Job*** and giving an answer very much like that offered in the Epilogue [S. N. Kramer, "Man and his God: A Sumerian Variation on the 'Job' Motif," in *Wisdom in Israel and in the Ancient Near East*]. How much of the ancient folk tale is preserved by the Prologue-Epilogue and what modifications the author of the poetic Dialogue had to make in the old story is impossible, at this time, to determine. Probably very little of the old tale has been lost because the Prologue and Epilogue together present a fairly complete story. It may be that the older prose tale included an episode in which the friends counseled Job (as his wife had done) to curse God and die. This would explain God's censure of the friends and praise of Job in the Epilogue. It is not likely that the rebuke to the friends was added to reconcile the Prologue-Epilogue with the Dialogue, for, although it is clear that Job had the better of the argument, the Epilogue betrays no awareness that the doctrine of retribution had been refuted or even questioned.

The essential unity of the Dialogue (iii-xxxi) has not been seriously questioned. Though textual and exegetical difficulties abound in this section, a marked unity in style and consistency in the opposing viewpoints suggest a single author. It is clear that the author's sympathy is with Job, but he attempts to be fair to the friends' viewpoint, sparing no effort to present their arguments fully. Some of the difficulties in the Dialogue, particularly in Job's speeches, appear to have been produced by pious tampering with the text by well-meaning meddlers who felt compelled to mitigate Job's shocking charges against God. Considerable effort and ingenuity appears to have been expended in this effort and sometimes a very clever twist is given to the sense, but generally the attempt is unsuccessful and betrayed by the context. In some cases it would appear that failing to alter the sense, effort has been made to obscure it. The Masoretes on occasion indulge in this activity by imposing a tendentious vocalization on the consonantal text. The most extensive meddling with the text has occurred in chapters xxiv-xxvii where Bildad's third speech is vestigial and Zophar's is missing altogether. Here, Job suddenly expounds the friends' viewpoint which he had all along denied. Some critics have considered this dislocation accidental, but it was more likely a deliberate attempt to refute Job's argument by confusing the issue. The commentaries suggest various rearrangements of chapters xxiv-xxvii, but the order we have adopted appears the simplest and most satisfactory.

The poem on Wisdom (xxviii) is almost universally recognized as extraneous. Its style and language, however, show similarities to those of the rest of the Dialogue and some scholars have regarded it as an independent composition by the same author, though not an integral part of the *Book of Job.* It is hardly appropriate in Job's mouth since the burden of its message—that wisdom, the secrets of the universe and of divine providence are inaccessible to man—does not comport with Job's desire to bring God into court, as it were, and question him. The poem has some affinities with the Theophany and might have been better interpolated there. Despite its extraneous character, we may be grateful that the poem has been preserved, for it is one of the finest in the Old Testament.

The Elihu speeches (xxxii-xxxvii) are rejected as interpolations by many critics who regard them as having scant value either as literature or as a solution to the problem of evil. Their style is diffuse and pretentious, a large part of the content of the four discourses being devoted to prolix and pompous prolegomena. For the most part Elihu's arguments merely echo what the friends have already said repeatedly, yet he has the effrontery to offer them as if they were novel and decisive. If Elihu has anything distinctive to contribute, it is the elaboration of the idea that suffering may be disciplinary (xxxiii 14-33), already suggested by Eliphaz in his first speech (v 17). In spite of these considerations, a few critics regard Elihu's diatribes as the climax of the work and the author's best word on the problem of evil. There are, of course, many phraseological parallels between the Dialogue and the Elihu speeches, but these are easily explicable as imitation by the author of the Elihu speeches. It is difficult to believe that the author of the Dialogue would repeat the argument of the friends through the mouth of Elihu and represent it as something new. It seems more likely that the author of the Elihu speeches, shocked at Job's blasphemous accusations against God, and disappointed at the failure of the friends to silence him, and perhaps equally dissatisfied with the content of the divine speeches, felt impelled to attempt some vindication of divine justice. The author could not, of course, make the attempt after Yahweh had spoken and had humbled Job, but he had to get into the argument before the Theophany. His lavish apologies for presuming to speak at all, and his reassurances to Job that he is after all only

a man and not God, may reflect more his own misgivings about intervening ahead of the deity than concern for deference to his elders. Elihu sets the stage for the divine discourses by anticipating and bolstering the weak points in their argument. This could be regarded as the foresight of a single author or the hindsight of an interpolator. The strongest evidence that the Elihu speeches are interpolated is the fact that Elihu is completely ignored in the Epilogue. It is true that the Satan is also passed over in the Epilogue, but he had already completed his role in the Prologue and had no part in the Dialogue. If the Elihu speeches were an integral part of the Dialogue, and if a single author valued them as highly as Elihu did, one would expect some recognition of this in the attribution of praise and blame in the Epilogue.

Yahweh's speeches from the storm have been regarded as secondary by some critics who reason that the author of the Elihu speeches could not have known them, else he would not have dared intrude. We have already noted, however, that Elihu could scarcely be permitted to speak after the divine discourses. Moreover, Job's challenge, "Here is my signature, / Let Shaddai answer me," demands a divine response and not repetition of a discredited dogma by a young upstart. Yahweh's first speech has been praised as a work of genius unequaled in world literature, surpassing all other attempts to describe the greatness of God and the marvels of his creation. Critics who do not regard it as an original part of the work give a much less enthusiastic appraisal of the poem's literary and theological value. Some see in it only brutal irony and utter lack of concern for man's predicament.

The authenticity of Yahweh's second speech is less widely accepted than that of the first. The poems on the mythological monsters Behemoth and Leviathan (generally misunderstood as the hippopotamus and the crocodile) which make up almost the entire second speech are commonly considered spurious and inferior. Nevertheless, the second speech also has its champions, and some critics regard it as the climax of the book and a more original form of the divine reply than the first speech. A second speech by Yahweh after Job had been humbled and silenced seems like nagging, but it could be regarded as driving the lesson home. Job is only silenced at the end of the first speech (xl 3-5); after the second speech he is not only subdued but repentant (xlii 6).

The discrepancies between the Epilogue and other parts of the book have already been noted. Most striking is the fact that in the Epilogue the friends are rebuked, not Job, as is the case in the divine speeches. Kaufmann explains [in *The Religion of Israel,* 1960] the inconsistency by suggesting that the friends were reprimanded because they had taken the easy way of contending with conventional clichés and empty phrases, while Job had challenged God out of a moral duty to speak the truth before him. Job had indeed already charged the friends with asserting a lie in order to curry favor with God, and had warned them that God would rebuke such hypocritical sycophancy. Job's rehabilitation, in which he receives a bonus for his pains, appears to confirm the very doctrine of retribution which Job had so effectively refuted in the Dialogue. This incongruity, however, was unavoidable. In the old folk tale on which the *Book of Job* was based, as in its Mesopotamian prototypes, the hero must certainly have been restored and rewarded in the end. The author was naturally limited by the prefabricated materials with which he had to work and could not have taken a great deal of liberty with a familiar story. How else could the book have brought to a conclusion? It would certainly not do to leave Job in his misery after God had vindicated him, although the doubling of his material possessions is a highly artificial device and incompatible with Job's realistic observations in the Dialogue.

The Book of Job in its present form can hardly be regarded as a consistent and unified composition by a single author. Nevertheless, there is a considerable degree of organic unity despite the incongruities. Even the Elihu speeches, though probably interpolated, are blended into the whole with such skill that some scholars have seen Elihu as a reflex of the author of the Dialogue.

A good deal of the considerable discussion of the literary form of the *Book of Job* has been unprofitable. The naïve view that it represents sober history need not be taken seriously, but it may very well be that there was a historical personage behind the story. Rabbi Simeon-ben-Laqish opined that Job never existed and that the story is simply a poetic comparison or parable (*māšāl*) (cf. Midrash Rabba Gen lxvii; Talmud Babli, Baba Bathra 15a). The term is very fitting since Job is in a sense the type of any and every man who experiences the mystery of seemingly senseless and undeserved suffering. The notion that Job, like the Suffering Servant of Yahweh in Isaiah lii 13-liii 12, represents the nation Israel in a sort of historical allegory is intriguing. Certainly, if the work was composed in the exilic or early post-exilic period, as many critics believe, it would be difficult if not impossible for the author to ignore the parallel between the sufferings of the individual and the nation. There is, however, not the slightest suggestion of interest in the fate of the nation Israel betrayed anywhere in the book. The choice of a descendant of Esau as the representative righteous sufferer would rule out any likelihood that the narrator had in mind the nation Israel or Judah.

Theodore of Mopsuestia in the fourth century regarded the *Book of Job* as being modeled on the Greek dramas. Theodore Beza [in *Job Expounded*] considered the book as a tragedy and Milton regarded it as an epic. The Homeric epics have been compared, but actually have little in common, with *Job.* More appropriate is the comparison with the tragic dramas of Aeschylus, Sophocles, and Euripides, but even here the similarity is less in form than in an occasional ideological parallel. H. M. Kallen has argued [in *The Book of Job as a Greek Tragedy Restored,* 1918] that the *Book of Job* actually has the form of a Greek tragedy, including the chorus and the denouement by means of the *deus ex machina* (Yahweh from the storm). The dialogues of Plato have been mentioned for comparison, but there is scant similarity between the long poetic monologues of the so-called Dialogue of the *Book of Job* and the brief, precise, and analytical conversations of Plato's Dialogues.

In point of fact, there is no single classification appropriate to the literary form of the *Book of Job.* It shares something of the characteristics of all the literary forms that have been ascribed to it, but it is impossible to classify it exclusively as didactic, dramatic, epic, or anything else. The book viewed as a unit is *sui generis* and no single term or combination of terms is adequate to describe it. Definition of literary form generally presumes literary unity and this point is still disputed with regard to the *Book of Job.*

It is scarcely possible to speak of the author of any biblical book in the modern sense of the word, for virtually all biblical books are composite in some degree, as were most literary productions in the ancient Near East. Many different hands and minds must have contributed to the formation of the Gilgamesh Epic, before it reached its more or less standard or canonical form. *The Book of Job,* in the opinion of most biblical scholars, bears evidences of such compositeness. Yet, in the heart of the book, in the Dialogue (chs. iii-xxxi), there is a characteristic literary excellence which suggests the influence of a single personality. This person we can know only through his work, and it is altogether likely that he will remain forever anonymous, like the author of the great poems of the latter half of the Book of Isaiah. There can be no question that we are confronted with a poet of genius, for his work has been acclaimed as one of the great masterpieces of world literature. He must have been a profoundly religious person, sensitive to the tragic predicament of humanity, especially to individual suffering. The poet had himself probably experienced physical and mental agony, since it is hard to understand how one could have written thus without personal knowledge of suffering. The sincerity and depth of the poet's thought and feeling, his keen insight into human nature, the vivid beauty and the raw realism of his metaphors and similes give his work the power to move men's minds and hearts in every time and place.

There is no certainty that the author was an Israelite. Some parts of the book may suggest familiarity with the prophetic, and didactic writings of the Old Testament, but there is nothing very specific or definite. Job's bitter outcry recalls some of the biblical psalms of lamentation (Psalms xxxviii, lxxxviii, cii). Lamentation, however, was a common literary genre in the ancient Near East. There are figures of speech in the *Book of Job* that comport with a Palestinian background, but again there is nothing that could not be taken as reflecting some other part of the ancient Semitic world as well. The author appears to be acquainted with Egypt and perhaps had traveled widely. In any event, his familiarity with world literature is evidenced by numerous allusions to mythological motifs now known from ancient literature of Mesopotamia and Syria. We may be sure that the author belonged to the intellectual elite of his day. Recent studies of ancient Near Eastern Wisdom Literature indicate that "wisdom" had a strongly international and cosmopolitan flavor. The seeker of wisdom in the ancient world, even as today, tended to ignore geographical boundaries and political barriers. The author of the *Book of Job* cannot be precisely placed temporally or geographically, but this is of no great consequence for he speaks to and for all humanity about a problem that has perplexed thinking and feeling men in all times and places.

Ginsberg [in *Conservative Judaism,* Vol. 21, No. 3, 1967] has affirmed "that the author was a Jew, 100 per cent." (It is not clear whether the percentage applies to Ginsberg's certainty or to the author's Jewishness, or to both.) One good reason why the author can be only a Jew, according to Ginsberg, is his horror at the injustice in the world, as expressed, for example, in xxi 6. "Now this reaction is possible only in Israel," Ginsberg asserts. Without wishing to detract from ancient Israel's merited praise for concern about social justice and sensitivity to injustice, at least on the part of some gifted spokesmen, it does not seem reasonable to deny the possibility of this basically human reaction to non-Israelites. The section on Parallel Literature below, condensed as it is, may serve to mitigate the assurance of Ginsberg's assertion. Ginsberg, of course, is thoroughly familiar with the Parallel Literature and mentions it in connection with the assertion cited, but finds the horrified reaction to injustice exclusively Israelite.

The Book of Job finds its place in the last of the three divisions of the Hebrew scriptures, the Sacred Writings, or Hagiographa. Despite the unsettling character of the book, its right to be included in the Canon was never challenged, except by Theodore of Mopsuestia. Among the Writings its position has varied somewhat. The Talmud gives the order of the Writings as *Ruth, Psalms, **Job,** Proverbs, Ecclesiastes, Song of Songs, Lamentations, Daniel, Esther, Ezra, Chronicles.* In Codex Alexandrinus the order is *Psalms, **Job,** Proverbs,* but Cyril of Jerusalem, Epiphanius, Jerome, Rufinus, and the Apostolic Canons attest to the order ***Job,** Psalms, Proverbs.* In Jewish usage the poetic trilogy is designated by two sets of initials corresponding to the two orders, ***Job,** Proverbs, Psalms ('mt),* and *Psalms, **Job,** Proverbs (t'm).* The Latin Church Fathers mention other orders, but the order favored by St. Jerome, with ***Job*** in the initial position, was fixed by the Council of Trent and this official order of the Vulgate has been generally followed in modern western versions of the Scriptures.

. . . . .

It has been generally assumed that the purpose of [**The Book of Job**] is to give an answer to the issue with which it deals, the problem of divine justice or theodicy. This question is raised inevitably by any and every instance of seemingly unmerited or purposeless suffering, and especially the suffering of a righteous man. Job's case, whether real or imaginary, poses the problem in the most striking possible way. A man of exemplary rectitude and piety is suddenly overwhelmed with disasters and loathsome disease. How can such a situation be reconciled with divine justice and benevolent providence? It must be admitted first and last that the **Book of Job** fails to give a clear and definitive answer to this question. This, however, does not mean that the book is to be discounted as a magnificent misadventure or a conspicuous failure. The problem of theodicy continues to thwart all attempts at rational solution. Virtually every basic argument that has been adduced in connection with the problem is touched on in the **Book of Job.** Of the various attitudes suggested in the different parts of the book, it is difficult to say which, if any, was intended as decisive.

The Prologue presents Job's woes as imposed by the Satan with the permission and approval of Yahweh in order to determine whether Job's piety was completely unselfish. Some interpreters find the question of theodicy resolved here in advance. The reader is given a glimpse behind the scenes and made privy to the plot within the celestial council. The action is prompted by Yahweh himself when he calls the Satan's attention to Job as a paragon of virtue and provokes him into questioning the basis and the genuineness of Job's piety. Yahweh himself sets the limits of the testing and Job endures all with magnificent calm and without protest or complaint. Thus is proved to gods and men that disinterested virtue and piety are possible. The victory is seen in Job's confession of unshakable trust:

> Yahweh gave, Yahweh took away.
> Blessed be Yahweh's name.

and

> Shall we accept good from God,
> And not accept evil?

Some interpreters have regarded this as approaching the profoundest insight of both the Old Testament and the New, the doctrine of vicarious atonement by an innocent victim, as the Suffering Servant of the Lord (Isaiah lii 13-liii 12), or the Cross of Christian faith. Helpful as this insight may be, it derives from the hindsight of Christian faith and experience rather than from any hint in the biblical story. It is one thing for a rational person to choose to suffer or risk suffering for a cause, but it is quite another to become the victim of suffering which appears to have no meaning. We are informed in the Prologue that Job was innocent. The question naturally rises, why the devilish sadistic experiment to see if he had a breaking point? (This is reminiscent of a pessimistic Mesopotamian myth which represents the production of human deformities as a drunken diversion of the gods at the end of a spree celebrating the creation of mankind as slaves for the gods.) H. H. Rowley [in *Bulletin of John Rylands Library* 41 (1958)] has given an interesting and useful answer to this difficulty. In assuring us that Job's sufferings were innocent, the author makes an important contribution to the problem. Job, of course, was not aware that God reckoned him as righteous. If he had known he was merely being tried, it would have been no real test and there could be no meaning in this for the man who has to suffer without knowing why. The issue at stake in the testing of Job was not simply the winning of a wager, idle or diabolical, but the vindication of mutual faith of God in man and man in God. The Job of the Prologue thus agrees with the distorted sense of xiii 15,

> Though he slay me, yet will I trust in him.

He would have been willing to be damned for the glory of God. One may admire such faith without raising the question how this sort of damnation may reflect on the character of God or redound to his glory.

In the Dialogue the question is treated in a radically different fashion. The friends argue that Job must have sinned and earned his woes because God is just and rewards and punishes. Any apparent exception to this rule is unreal, or only temporary. But Job vehemently denies that he has sinned, at least not seriously enough to merit such misery as has been inflicted on him. Justice, he argues, often appears abortive in the world and for this God must be held responsible. Hence Job infers that God has no concern for justice or for human feelings. The Dialogue thus makes little contribution to the solution of the problem. Actually it is scarcely appropriate to call this section of the book a dialogue. There is not here the give-and-take of philosophical disputation aimed at the advancement of understanding and truth. Rather each side has a partisan point of view which is reiterated *ad nauseam* in long speeches. There is no real movement in the argument. Attempts to find progression in the debate and subtle differences in the character and personality of the three friends are labored and unconvincing. It is true that the friends grow progressively vehement in their indictment of Job. Their exasperation appears to mount round by round as Job steadfastly refuses to accept their argument—that God is always just and therefore he must be guilty—or their advice—that he admit his guilt and plead for mercy. As the exchange continues, Job grows more serene in his despair, as he gropes and grasps for an answer. He wishes to argue his case with God, but he cannot find God nor force him to grant a fair hearing. Job asks for an umpire to ensure fair treatment. It has been suggested that in Job's appeal to a mediator, an umpire or witness, we have a sort of prophetic testimony to the necessity for a Christ, a being both human and divine who could effect a reconciliation between God and Job. This theory appears to have some merit and validity, but it is doubtful whether this person should be described as messianic. It appears likely that behind Job's appeal to a mediator, an umpire or witness (ix 33) lies the ancient Mesopotamian idea of a personal god whose function and duty it was to look after his client's interest and plead his cause before the great gods in the divine assembly. This conception appears to be related more closely to the belief in guardian angels than to messianism, although the figure of the Messiah as Paraclete seems to derive from this sphere of ideas rather than from royal ideology. Job reverts to his appeal to an umpire or friendly witness in xvi 19, 21 (the verb in the latter passage being cognate with the term rendered "umpire" in ix 33). Job uses what seems to be legal jargon, and his tribulations take on the aspect of a legal process. All that he demands is a fair trial, the right of friendly witness, and of defense counsel.

Beginning with a plea to be allowed to escape his misery through death, Job in chapter xiv considers the possibility of an afterlife. This thought is entertained only momentarily, however, as he dismisses it and resigns himself to the inevitability and finality of death. It is often assumed that a hope of recompense in a future life would have sustained Job and solved his problem. Certainly it would have mitigated the difficulty considerably. But whether the prospect of future bliss gives one the strength and consolation to bear present pain, a pain that is meaningless and unjustified, is questionable.

The famous passage, xix 25-27, has been commonly regarded as the climax of Job's quest. Unhappily, these lines are extremely difficult, the text having suffered irreparable damage. It is clear that Job expects to be vindicated, but it is not certain whether he expects his vindication to come in the flesh or after his body has disintegrated. The traditional Christian understanding of the passage is based more on the interpretation of the Vulgate than on the Hebrew. Jerome thought that Job here prophesied the resurrection of the body but this is contradicted by xiv 12 and by several other passages (iii 11-22, vii 9-10, x 18-22, xvi 22, xvii 1, 13-16, xxi 23-26). Many critics, ancient and modern, have recognized that Job refers to his hope for vindication in the flesh (as expressed in xiii 15-16, xxiii 7, 10) and to his hope for restoration (as in ch. xxix). This passage has to be interpreted in the light of Job's other utterances, as well as of the immediate context. In spite of textual difficulties, it should be apparent that the vindicator on whom Job pins his hopes is not God, but the person elsewhere called an umpire (ix 33) and a witness (xvi 19, 21). This vindicator or redeemer, like the umpire or witness, would defend his case, acquit him of guilt, and restore him to favor with God. Job does not, as has been alleged, surrender all claim on God and put his trust in a sort of heavenly high priest. Rather he continues to press his demand for vindication which must come sooner or later. In spite of all his protests and railings against God, Job never completely gives up his conviction that justice must somehow triumph. Even if his flesh rots away and his body turns to dust, in his mind's eye he sees his ultimate vindication and expects to be conscious of it when it comes, though it be beyond this life in the dust of the netherworld.

As a last resort, Job appeals to the ancient test of the oath. The taking of an oath was the last word in assertion of innocence, tantamount to acquittal, since it was assumed that the terror of the sanctions of the self-imprecations would deter anyone from swearing falsely. After the oaths there is no more the friends can say. It is now up to God to strike down the blasphemer or acquit him.

Some scholars have assumed that the intent of the Dialogue is to refute once and for all the doctrine of exact individual retribution, or terrestrial eschatology, as it has been called, the doctrine that righteousness always brings prosperity and wickedness misfortune, in this life. The corollary of this doctrine is, of course, that prosperity is proof of divine favor and misfortune of sin. This dogma is doubtless a great comfort to the healthy and the prosperous, but a cruel taunt to the sick and the poor. This corollary doctrine is often expounded in the Old Testament, especially as applied to Israel and the nations (cf. *Exodus* xxiii 20 ff.; *Leviticus* xxvi; *Deuteronomy* xxviii; *Jeremiah* vii 5-7, xii 14- 17), but also to the individual (cf. *Psalms* i, xxxvii, xlix, lxxiii; *Isaiah* lviii 6-14; *Jeremiah* xvii 5-8; *Ezekiel* xviii). This view has been called "orthodox," with the implication that it is normative for the Old Testament. Now it must be admitted that there is considerable justification for the use of the term "orthodox" as applied to such statements as the famous utterance of *Psalm* xxxvii 25,

> I was once young, and now have grown old;
> And I never saw a righteous man forsaken
> Or his offspring begging bread.

Righteousness certainly ought to be rewarded and wickedness punished and it sometimes happens thus. All too often, however, the very opposite seems to be the case, as

Qoheleth observed (*Ecclesiastes* iii 16, viii 14). There ought to be no exceptions, and Job's comforters argue that there are in fact none. But Job refutes their doctrine thoroughly, not only with reference to his own case but to the world at large. The friends would have been well advised to maintain their discreet silence as they had in the Prologue, since the premise of their argument had already been nullified by the certification from the highest authority that Job was blameless. The author of the Dialogue could not allow either the victim or his miserable comforters to share this knowledge, else there would have been no basis for the disputation. The poet appears to give equally of his great talent to the rhetoric of both sides of the argument, but there can be no mistaking the fact that his sympathies are with Job and that the speeches of the friends are skillfully presented to show how wrong-headed traditional piety can be. The view of the friends was indeed venerable orthodoxy. The recovery of Mesopotamian Wisdom Literature now makes it clear that the position of the friends is essentially what was normative in Mesopotamian thought for centuries before Israel emerged in history. This doctrine is certainly asserted many times in the Old Testament, but to take it alone as normative is to overlook a great deal that contradicts it. The fates of Abel, Uriah, and Naboth, for example, were not recounted to suggest that they got merely what they deserved. Jeremiah, who is credited, along with Ezekiel, with refining the doctrine of individual retribution (*Jeremiah* xxxi 30) complains of its lack of application to himself. The thorough refutation of the doctrine in ***Job*** and *Ecclesiastes* did not eradicate the fallacious dogma. It persisted and was confuted again by Jesus of Nazareth (cf. Luke xiii 1-5; John ix 2) who urged men to love their enemies and pray for those who persecute them in order that they may be sons of the heavenly Father who makes his sun rise on the evil and the good, and sends rain on the just and the unjust (*Matthew* v 43 ff.).

The contributions of the Elihu speeches, such as they are, have already been noted. It is hard to see how some critics can regard them so highly. Kaufmann suggested [in *The Religion of Israel*] that Elihu is a reflex of the poet himself, while Gordis goes further [in *The Book of God and Man*] and regards the Elihu speeches not only as an integral part of the book but as the last and best word of the poet who in his later years put his more mature insights into the Elihu speeches and inserted them before the great climax of the divine speeches. (Gordis sees in the name Elihu a play on Eliyahu [Elijah] and an evocation of the theme of forerunner of the Lord, as in *Malachi* iv 5-6. The appearance of Elihu just before the theophany in the whirlwind evokes for Gordis the theme of Elijah's assumption and its attendant messianic ideology.) As for Elihu's verbosity, Gordis notes that the history of literature offers many instances in which a writer's style grows more complex and difficult with advancing years, and he cites as examples Shakespeare's *Tempest,* Yeats's later poems, Joyce's *Finnegan's Wake,* and especially Goethe's *Faust,* which gestated over a period of some sixty years and was written over a period of thirty years. As for the substance of Elihu's argument, Gordis notes that Elihu denies the conclusions both of Job and the friends and declares that even though suffering may not be a penalty for sin, yet God's

justice remains unassailable. A "virtually new" idea which Gordis finds in the Elihu speeches is one that had been advanced in another form by Deutero-Isaiah who maintained that national suffering was not the consequence of national sin, but, on the contrary, an integral element in the moral education of the human race. Elihu, however, goes substantially further, according to Gordis, and sees suffering as discipline and warning to the righteous, not only against sins actual and patent, but also against sins both potential and latent (xxxiii 16-30, xxxvi 9-12). This view of suffering as discipline, however, is not novel, and it had already been introduced by Eliphaz in his first speech, v 17 ff. It is hard to find anything new in Elihu's bombast. Whether composed by the author of the Dialogue, or by someone else, the Elihu speeches seem to represent one more futile attempt to support the same discredited traditional view which the friends had asserted.

Either the book ends in magnificent anticlimax, or we must see the highlight in the divine speeches. Job has silenced the friends with a series of terrible oaths affirming his innocence and has challenged God to answer. The content of the divine answer from the storm is something of a surprise and, on the face of it, a disappointment. The issue, as Job had posed it, is completely ignored. No explanation or excuse is offered for Job's suffering. As Job had expected, God refuses to submit to questioning. But, contrary to expectation, God does not crush him, or brush him away, or multiply his wounds. Rather he subjects Job to questioning. God's queries are ironical in the extreme, almost to the point of absurdity. Job had already expressed his awe and wonder at God's power in hymns among the most beautiful in the Old Testament. Man's finitude and helplessness Job had fully acknowledged. He had questioned not divine omnipotence but justice and mercy. The complete evasion of the issue as Job had posed it must be the poet's oblique way of admitting that there is no satisfactory answer available to man, apart from faith. God does not need the help or advice of impotent and ignorant men to control the world, any more than he needed such to create it. God cannot be summoned like a defendant and forced to bear witness against himself. No extreme of suffering gives mere man license to question God's wisdom or justice as Job had done. It is apparently on this very point that Job repents and recants (xlii 3b, c). Note that Job does not mention the question of his innocence and integrity which we may assume he would still maintain. It is noteworthy, too, that Yahweh makes no charge against Job except that he had spoken out of ignorance. Nothing is said that would imply that Job deserved his misery. The absence of any charge of guilt must be considered tantamount to vindication. This is at least part of what Job had sought to silence the friends who had argued that he must be guilty and would be proved so if God were to speak. The Prologue already informed us that Job was blameless. Here we have the complete refutation of the argument of the friends that suffering is itself proof of sin. This is perhaps the basis for the reprimand of the friends in the Epilogue, that they asserted a lie in the foolish belief that they had to defend God. (The only other way to understand their rebuke is to assume that in the old folk tale the friends had taken quite a different attitude and, like Job's wife, had urged him to curse God and die.) The fundamental question, If not for sin, why then?, is completely ignored. The reason for this is not too difficult to understand, in view of the fact that virtually all the arguments the human mind can muster had already been thrashed out in the Dialogue. The problem still baffles the philosopher and theologian, and we are thrown back on faith. It is quite understandable that readers, critical or otherwise, are left with a feeling of chagrin at the seemingly magnificent irrelevance of much of the content of the divine speeches. Some critics resort to surgery in the attempt to improve the divine reply, but this leads to more and more drastic cutting till scarcely a torso is left. The zoological as well as the meteorological marvels show the divine power and providence. Even the apparent stupidity of the ostrich testifies to the divine wisdom and providential care. The monsters Behemoth and Leviathan, dread powers of evil from ancient pagan Semitic myths, subdued or slain in primeval conflicts before creation of the world, are the final proof of the divine power and providence. Given but a glimpse or a whisper of God's power and glory and loving care for his creation, Job realizes that he had spoken from ignorance and rashly. His resentment and rebellious attitude disappear.

The fact that the Epilogue upholds the discredited doctrine of exact retribution has already been noted. This was doubtless a feature of the ancient folk tale that could not be altered. It is hard to imagine how else the story could end. It would scarcely do to leave Job in his misery after he had been vindicated. Perhaps the most significant line in the Epilogue is xlii 10 which seems to put Job's restoration in a temporal and perhaps causal nexus with his intercessory prayer for his friends. After all the hard things they had said to him—for his own good, as they doubtless felt—it would not have been easy to forgive them and pray for them. The possible implication of this line may be related to the idea elaborated at the end of the famous eulogy of the Suffering Servant, *Isaiah* liii 10-12:

> Yahweh willed to crush and afflict him;
> If his life were offered in expiation,
> He will see progeny and prolong his life,
> Yahweh's pleasure will prosper through him.
> After travail of soul he will be satisfied
> With the knowledge that he was righteous,
> Though he bore the sins of many.
> So will I allot him a share with the great,
> With the mighty he will share the spoil;
> Since he emptied himself to the death,
> And was reckoned among the transgressors;
> Yet he bore the sins of many
> And for transgressors made intercession.

While the Job of the Dialogue apparently has no thought of suffering vicariously for the friends, or for anyone else, the Job of the Epilogue is placed in the line of development of the Christian doctrine of the Cross, though still a long way from it (cf. xxii 27-30).

A modern man reflecting on the ***Book of Job*** from the vantage point of two millennia of human experience must marvel at the religious insights to be found therein.

Viewed as a whole, the book presents profundities surpassing those that may be found in any of its parts. The issues raised are crucial for all men and the answers attempted

are as good as have ever been offered. The hard facts of life cannot be ignored or denied. All worldly hopes vanish in time. The values men cherish, the little gods they worship—family, home, nation, race, sex, wealth, fame—all fade away. The one final reality appears to be the process by which things come into being, exist, and pass away. This ultimate Force, the Source and End of all things, is inexorable. Against it there is no defense. Any hope a man may put in anything other than this First and Last One is vain. There is nothing else that abides. This is God. He gives and takes away. From Him we come and to Him we return. Confidence in this One is the only value not subject to time.

But how can a man put his faith in such an One who is the Slayer of all? Faith in Him is not achieved without moral struggle and spiritual agony. The foundation of such a faith has to be laid in utter despair of reliance on any or all lesser causes and in resignation which has faced and accepted the worst and the best life can offer. Before

---

G. K. Chesterton on Job as a precursor of Christ (1916):

I do not know, and I doubt whether even scholars know, if the book of ***Job*** had a great effect or had any effect upon the after development of Jewish thought. But if it did have any effect it may have saved them from an enormous collapse and decay. Here in this book the question is really asked whether God invariably punishes vice with terrestrial punishment and rewards virtue with terrestrial prosperity. If the Jews had answered that question wrongly they might have lost all their after influence in human history. They might have sunk even down to the level of modern well-educated society. For when once people have begun to believe that prosperity is the reward of virtue, their next calamity is obvious. If prosperity is regarded as the reward of virtue it will be regarded as the symptom of virtue. Men will leave off the heavy task of making good men successful. They will adopt the easier task of making out successful men good. . . .

The book of ***Job*** is chiefly remarkable . . . for the fact that it does not end in a way that is conventionally satisfactory. Job is not told that his misfortunes were due to his sins or a part of any plan for his improvement. But in the prologue we see Job tormented not because he was the worst of men, but because he was the best. It is the lesson of the whole work that man is most comforted by paradoxes. Here is the very darkest and strangest of the paradoxes; and it is by all human testimony the most reassuring. I need not suggest what a high and strange history awaited this paradox of the best man in the worst fortune. I need not say that in the freest and most philosophical sense there is one Old Testament figure who is truly a type; or say what is prefigured in the wounds of Job.

G. K. Chesterton in The Dimensions of Job, *edited by Nahum N. Glatzer, Schocken Books, 1969.*

this One no man is clean. To Him all human righteousness is as filthy rags. The transition from fear and hatred to trust and even love of this One—from God the Enemy to God the Friend and Companion—is the pilgrimage of every man of faith. Job's journey from despair to faith is the way each mortal must go. Almost invariably there must be initial shock and disappointment to bring a man to the realization of his predicament. Time and again it has happened, to individuals and to groups. A people that regarded itself as chosen by God and especially favored has suffered cruelly. The Son of Man who was obedient to death was put to the ultimate test. Here, as with Job, we are confronted in the most striking way with the apparently ruthless Slayer who brings to nought the life of even the most devoted servant. Only by faith can such seeming defeat be turned to victory and the anguished cry, "My God, why have you forsaken me?" give way to resignation and trust, "Father into your hands I commend my spirit." The scribal sage who altered Job's defiant protest "He may slay me, I'll not quaver" to read "Though he slay me, yet will I trust in him" did so advisedly in the knowledge that this was the attitude to which Job must be driven at last since there is no escape and no other refuge. The Psalmist (lxxiii 25-26) put it thus:

> Whom (else) have I in heaven?
> (When) with you, I care not for earth.
> (Though) my flesh and mind waste away,
> My mind's rock and my portion is God forever.

Northrop Frye   (essay date 1981)

SOURCE: "Myth Two," in *The Great Code: The Bible and Literature,* Harcourt Brace Jovanovich, 1982, pp. 169-98.

[*A Canadian critic and editor, Frye is the author of the highly influential and controversial* Anatomy of Criticism *(1957), in which he argued that literary criticism can be scientific in its method and results, and that judgments are not inherent in the critical process. Believing that literature is wholly structured by myth and symbol, Frye views the critic's task as the explication of a work's archetypal characteristics. In the following essay from his critical study* The Great Code: The Bible and Literature *(1981), he views* The Book of Job *as a "U-shaped narrative which incorporates elements of prophetic literature."*]

We may take the ***Book of Job,*** perhaps, as the epitome of the narrative of the Bible, as the Book of Revelation is the epitome of its imagery. The order of Old Testament books in most copies of the AV [Authorized Version], following the Septuagint but keeping the Apocrypha separate, seems very arbitrary at first, but it makes its own kind of sense. The books from Genesis to Esther are concerned with history, law, and ritual; those from ***Job*** to *Malachi* with poetry, prophecy, and wisdom. In this sequence Job occupies the place of a poetic and prophetic Genesis. It is again a U-shaped story: Job, like Adam, falls into a world of suffering and exile, "repents" (i.e., goes through a *metanoia* or metamorphosis of consciousness), and is restored to his original state, with interest. In contrast to Genesis, there is no breach of contract to attract theological lawyers, and Job's ordeal is not a punishment but a testing.

His friends come to see him in his misery: they may be "miserable comforters" (16:2), but they are neither foolish nor malignant. They have nothing to gain from coming to see him, and their motivation seems decent enough (see 2:13). The discussion naturally focuses on a question of causality: What has brought about Job's disasters? The friends struggle hard to contain the issue within the rather simpleminded Deuteronomic framework of law and wisdom that they understand, or feel that they understand. Job must somehow have disturbed the balance of divine justice, and the balance must right itself. If that is not the answer, there is no human answer, and we must resign ourselves to the mystery of God's ways, with the hope that they make better sense than they appear to do. At first glance Job's final acquiescence (42:3) seems to be agreeing with this, which implies that the friends have been right all along, even though they are expressly said not to be (42:7).

Job is "righteous in his own eyes" (32:1) only from the point of view of his friends: he is not protesting innocence but saying that there is a vast disproportion between what has happened to him and anything he could conceivably have done. In other words, the situation cannot be contained within the framework of law and wisdom, and no causal explanation is good enough. All four speakers, or five counting Elihu (who is thought to be a later addition), are deeply pious men, and the one type of explanation that cannot occur to them is the one that has already been given to the reader: that God had made a kind of wager with Satan on Job's fidelity. Such a notion would have seemed to them not only frivolous but blasphemous, suggesting as it does that God has a stake and a concern of his own in the matter.

The fact that God's speech at the end of ***Job*** makes no reference to the pact with Satan, and that Satan disappears totally from the action after the second chapter, is not a real difficulty, as we see if we look at our table of demonic images. Behemoth and Leviathan are metaphorically identical with Satan; what is different is Job's perspective. We noted that the Biblical account of creation is ambiguous in the sense that darkness and chaos are at first outside the created order and are then dialectically incorporated into it, with the separation of land from sea and the division of light from darkness. Hence Leviathan and Satan may be thought of either as enemies of God outside his creation, or as creatures of God within it. In the ***Book of Job,*** and consistently only there, the latter perspective is adopted: Satan the adversary is a tolerated visitor in God's court, and Leviathan is a creature of whom God seems to be rather proud.

At the beginning, however, the role of Satan is the traditional one of cynical accuser, and his appearance in the poem sets up the whole legal framework of prosecution, defense, trial, and judgment which is the "fallen" or Satan-initiated vision of the human situation. Job is confident that he has a defender on his side (19:25; the AV's "redeemer" is perhaps over-Christianized, but the general sense of Job's word *go'el* is not too different from this), but he also wishes, like the hero of Kafka's *Trial,* which reads like a kind of "midrash" on the ***Book of Job,*** that his accuser would identify himself, so that Job would at least know the case against him. He wishes for his accuser to write a book (31:35) and we have suggested that Byron may have been right in calling history "the devil's scripture." The case against Job is simply that he lives in a world in which a good deal of power is held by Satan. Job, like the good Samaritan in Jesus' parable, comes from the country of an *Erbfeind* of Israel (assuming that Uz is in Edom), and, however genuine his piety, he is, like Israel in Egypt, in a world exposed to an arbitrary process of nature and fortune. If a soldier is asked why he kills people who have done him no harm, or a terrorist why he kills innocent people with his bombs, they can always reply that war has been declared, and there are no innocent people in an enemy country during a war. The answer is psychotic, but it is the answer that humanity has given to every act of aggression in history. And Job lives in enemy territory, in the embrace of heathen and Satanic power which is symbolically the belly of the leviathan, the endless extent of time and space.

The magnificent conclusion of Job's summarizing speech (29-31) is the climax of the poem, and nowhere in literature is there a more powerful statement of the essence of human dignity in an alien world than we get from this miserable creature scraping his boils with a potsherd. One issue in the great test is that of identity or property: how much can a man lose of what he has before the loss begins to affect what he is? God had previously drawn a rough line between Job's possessions and his "life" (2:6), but here we begin to see what "life" means for humanity: a consciousness that is neither proud nor abased, but simply responsible, and accepts what responsibility is there. God has clearly won his wager. The imagery suggests a man in the prime of his life: Job is no aged and impotent king whose daughters can be appropriately swallowed by a monster. The friends, who are old, have spoken; Elihu, who is young, has yet to speak: they are the continuing cycle of the voice of law and wisdom. Job lets Elihu's speech go by without comment on either its cocksureness or its genuine if not altogether original eloquence. He has heard it all before: it is all true, and all nonsense. He is waiting for a different kind of voice altogether. And suddenly, out of the whirlwind, it comes.

At first we are very disappointed. God seems to be only echoing Elihu, saying that he made the world and that Job did not, and that consequently Job has no right to be questioning his ways. We begin to wonder if some quaking later editor has decided to botch the whole enterprise, in order to justify the ways of man's superstition and slave morality to God. But even if such an editor exists, he has left too much of the original poem for us to come to terms with him: he is, in short, too facile a hypothesis. The fact that God's speech is thrown into a series of rhetorical questions to which "no" is the only answer seems to give it a bullying and hectoring quality, and certainly there is no "answer" to Job's "problem." But did we ever seriously think that so great a poem would turn out to be a problem with an answer? To answer a question, we suggested at the beginning, is to accept the assumptions in it, and thereby to neutralize the question by consolidating the mental level on which the question was asked. Real questions are

stages in formulating better questions; answers cheat us out of the right to do this. So even if we remain dissatisfied with God's performance, a God who was glibly ready to explain it all would be more contemptible than the most reactionary of divine bullies.

We remember that Job himself was groping toward a realization that no causal explanation of his alienated plight was possible. In a sense God is speaking out of Job's own consciousness here: any causal explanation takes us back to a First Cause, that is, the creation. The rhetorical questions really mean, then, in this context: don't look along the line of causes to the creation: there is no answer there, and no help there. How Job got into his position is less important than how he is to get out of it; and it is only because he was not a participant in creation that he can be delivered from the chaos and darkness within it. God's speech, if we are right about its general meaning, makes no sense without the vision of Behemoth and Leviathan at the end, which is the key to it. The fact that God can point out these monsters to Job means that Job is outside them, and no longer under their power.

The Book of Job is usually classified among the tragedies, but it is technically a comedy by virtue of its "happy ending," with Job restored to prosperity. In its conventional comic form of renewal, this kind of conclusion is seldom very convincing: people who lose their daughters are not really consoled with new daughters; conditions that cause suffering can be changed, but the scars of the suffering remain. Once again, a renewal or future restoration is most intelligible as a type of present transcendence. But the transcendence can hardly be to a different state of being altogether, as in waking from a dream: if the restored world were discontinuous with the world of the boils and uncomprehending friends, there would be no point in the poem.

The sequence of resolutions at the end follows the usual Biblical pattern. First is the restoration of the human community: we are told that God turned the captivity of Job when he prayed for his friends (42:10), even though what the friends have said "in God's behalf," to use Elihu's phrase, is not acceptable. The reintegration of the human community is followed by the transfiguration of nature, in its humanized pastoral form. One of Job's beautiful new daughters has a name meaning a box of eye shadow. Perhaps if we were to see Job in his restored state we should see, not beautiful daughters or sixteen thousand sheep, but only a man who has seen something that we have not seen, and knows something that we do not know.

For all the conventional Oriental formulas of self-abasement, some kind of confidential message seems to pass between God and Job, of which we overhear only such fragments as "I abhor myself" and "I have heard of thee by the hearing of the ear; but now mine eye seeth thee" (42:5-6). The first statement seems to mean primarily that what we should call Job's egocentric perception has disappeared along with its objective counterpart, the leviathan. The second one, even though it continues to use the first personal pronoun, makes the shattering claim to a direct vision of God that the Bible, even in the New Testament, is usually very cautious about expressing. A previous statement to the same effect (19:26-27) seems to have been retouched by an editor. The one reference to Job in the New Testament: "Ye have heard of the patience of Job, and have seen the end of the Lord" (James 5:11) carries on the same figure of a leap from hearing to seeing, but puts it in a Christian setting: what the readers of James have "seen" is the coming of Christ. But Job seems to have gone the entire circuit of the Bible's narrative, from creation and fall through the plagues of Egypt, the sayings of the fathers transmitting law and wisdom, the flash of prophetic insight that breaks the chain of wisdom, and on to the final vision of presence and the knowledge that in the midst of death we are in life.

We have somewhat expanded our earlier remark that the **Book of Job,** though classified as wisdom literature, needs the prophetic perspective to understand it. Job follows, not the horizontal line of precedent and prudence, but the U-shaped progression of original prosperity, descent to humiliation, and return. The prophetic element in the book is thus connected with its narrative shape. This in turn reminds us of the Bible's concern for narrative or *mythos* generally, which may be fictional, as here or in the parables of Jesus, or closer to the historical categories vaguely called "non-fiction." The emphasis on narrative, and the fact that the entire Bible is enclosed in a narrative framework, distinguishes the Bible from a good many other sacred books. The Buddhist sutras employ relatively little narrative, and the Koran consists of revelations gathered up after Mohammed's death and arranged in order of length, with no discernible narrative principle in their sequence. The narrative framework of the Bible is a part of its emphasis on the shape of history and the specific collision with temporal movement that its revelation is assumed to make. In a sense, therefore, the deliverance of Job is a deliverance from his own story, the movement in time that is transcended when we have no further need of time. Much the same thing would be true of the relation of Jesus to the Passion narrative, which is the kernel of the Gospels. The inference for the reader seems to be that the angel of time that man clings to until daybreak (*Genesis* 32:36) is both an enemy and an ally, a power that both enlightens and cripples, and disappears only when all that can be experienced has been experienced.

René Girard   (essay date 1985)

SOURCE: "The Case of Job," in *Job: The Victim of His People,* translated by Yvonne Freccero, The Athlone Press, 1987, pp. 3-18.

[*Girard is a French scholar whose critical studies include* Mensonge romantique et vérité romanesque *(1961;* Deceit, Desire and the Novel), *and* La Violence et le sacré *(1972;* Violence and the Sacred). *In the following excerpt from his critical study* Job: The Victim of His People, *originally published in 1985 as* La route antique des hommes pervers, *he examines the role of the community in Job's suffering.*]

What do we know about the **Book of Job?** Not very much. The hero complains endlessly. He has just lost his children and all his livestock. He scratches his ulcers. The misfor-

William Blake's illustration to The Book of Job.

tunes of which he complains are all duly enumerated in the prologue. They are misfortunes brought on him by Satan with God's permission.

We think we know, but are we sure? Not once in the Dialogues does Job mention either Satan or anything about his misdeeds. Could it be that they are too much on his mind for him to mention them?

Possibly, yet Job mentions everything else, and does much more than mention. He dwells heavily on the cause of his misfortune, which is none of those mentioned in the prologue. The cause is not divine, satanic nor physical, but merely human.

Strangely enough, over the centuries commentators have not paid the slightest attention to that cause. I am not familiar with all the commentaries, naturally, but those I do know systematically ignore it. They seem not to notice it. Ancients and moderns alike, atheists, Protestants, Catholics or Jews—none of them questions the object of Job's complaints. The matter seems to have been settled for them in the prologue. Everyone clings religiously to the ulcers, the lost cattle, etc.

And yet exegetes have been warning their readers for some time about this prologue. This short narrative is not on the same level as the Dialogues and should not be taken seriously. Unfortunately they do not follow their own advice. They pay no attention to the parts of the Dialogues that clearly contradict the prologue.

The new element I am suggesting is not buried in an obscure corner of the *Book of Job*. It is very explicit and is apparent in numerous and copious passages that are not in the least equivocal.

Job clearly articulates the cause of his suffering—the fact that he is ostracized and persecuted by the people around him. He has done no harm, yet everyone turns away from him and is dead set against him. He is the scapegoat of his community:

> My brothers stand aloof from me,
>   and my relations take care to avoid me.
> My kindred and my friends have all gone away,
>   and the guests in my house have forgotten me.
> The serving maids look on me as a foreigner,
>   a stranger, never seen before.
> My servant does not answer when I call him,
>   I am reduced to entreating him.
> To my wife my breath is unbearable,
>   for my own brothers I am a thing corrupt.
> Even the children look down on me,
>   ever ready with a gibe when I appear.
> All my dearest friends recoil from me in horror:
>   those I loved best have turned against me.
> *The Jerusalem Bible* 19: 13-19,

Even the fact that Job's wife complains of his foul breath reminds us of the tragic goat, a significant detail found in many primitive myths.

This allusion to a real goat should not be misunderstood. When I speak of a scapegoat I am not referring to the sacrificial animal in the famous rites of Leviticus. I am using the expression in the sense in which we all use it, casually, in reference to political, professional or family matters. This is a modern usage not found, of course, in the *Book of Job*. But the phenomenon is present in a more primitive form. The scapegoat is the innocent party who polarizes a universal hatred, which is precisely the complaint of Job:

> And now ill will drives me to distraction,
>   and a whole host molests me,
> rising, like some witness for the prosecution,
>   to utter slander to my very face.
> In tearing fury it pursues me,
>   with gnashing teeth.
> My enemies whet their eyes on me,
>   and open gaping jaws.
> Their insults strike like slaps in the face,
>   and all set on me together.
> (16: 7-10)

The text teems with such revealing passages. Since I cannot quote them all, I will choose those that are most striking in relation to my topic. One such passage introduces a subgroup that plays the role of permanent scapegoat in Job's society:

> And now I am the laughing stock
>   of my juniors, the young people,
> whose fathers I did not consider fit
>   to put with the dogs that looked after my flock.
> The strength of their hands would have been useless to me,
>   enfeebled as they were,
>   worn out by want and hunger.
> They used to gnaw the roots of desert plants,

> and brambles from abandoned ruins;
> and plucked mallow, and brushwood leaves,
>   making their meals off roots of broom.
> Outlawed from the society of men,
>   who, as against thieves, raised hue and cry against them,
> they made their dwellings on ravines' steep sides,
>   in caves or clefts in the rock.
> You could hear them wailing from the bushes,
>   as they huddled together in the thistles.
> Their children are as worthless a brood as they were,
>   nameless people, outcasts of society.
> And these are the ones that now sing ballads about me,
>   and make me the talk of the town!
> To them I am loathsome, they stand aloof from me,
>   do not scruple to spit in my face.
> Because he has unbent my bow and chastened me
>   they cast the bridle from their mouth.
> That brood of theirs rises to right of me,
>   stones are their weapons . . .
> (30: 1-12)

Historians do not know whether this group of scapegoats is a racial or religious minority, or some kind of subproletariat subjected to the same sort of regime as the lowest castes in India. It is not important. These people are not interesting in themselves; they are there only for Job to compare himself with them and define himself as the scapegoat of these scapegoats, persecuted by those who could least indulge in persecution, the victim of absolutely everyone, the scapegoat of scapegoats, the victim of victims.

The more obstinately Job remains silent on the subject of his lost cattle and his other good reasons for complaint, the more he insists on portraying himself as the innocent victim of those around him.

It is true that Job complains of physical ills, but this particular complaint is easily linked to the basic cause of his lament. He is the victim of countless brutalities; the psychological pressure on him is unbearable.

Some would say that Job's life is not really threatened, and that there is no question of killing him. He is protected by his friends. This is absolutely false. Job thinks they are after his life, and he may think that it is particularly his life they are after. He expects to die soon, and not from the illness that his doctors are struggling to diagnose. He thinks he is going to die a violent death: he imagines the shedding of his own blood:

> Cover not my blood, O earth,
>   afford my cry no place to rest.
> (16: 18)

I am content with the interpretation of these two lines given in *The Jerusalem Bible* footnotes: 'Blood, if not covered with earth, cries to heaven for vengeance [. . .] Job, mortally wounded, wishes to leave behind a lasting appeal for vindication: on earth, his blood; with God, the sound of his prayer . . . '

The translation of the two lines and the footnote conform exactly to what is found in the other great translations. The language of the footnote, granted, is somewhat ambiguous. By whom is Job wounded to death? It could just be by God rather than by men, but it certainly is not against God that the blood of the victim cries for vengeance; he is crying to God for vengeance, like the blood of Abel, that first great victim exhumed by the Bible. Yahweh says to Cain: 'Listen to the sound of your brother's blood, crying out to me from the ground' (*Genesis* 4: 10).

But against whom is the blood that is shed crying for vengeance? Who would seek to stifle the cries of Job, erase his words to prevent them from reaching God? Strangely enough, these elementary questions have never been asked.

Job constantly reverts to the community's role in what has happened to him, but - and this is what is mysterious - he does not succeed in making his commentators, outside the text, understand him any better than those who question him within the text . . . No one takes any notice of what he says.

The revelation of the scapegoat is as nonexistent for posterity as it is for his friends. Yet we are really trying to be attentive to what Job is saying; we pity him for not being understood. But we are so afraid of holding God accountable for all man's misfortunes, especially if we do not believe in him, that ultimately the result is the same. We are just a little more hypocritical than Job's friends. For all those who have always appeared to listen to Job but have not understood him, his words are so much air. The only difference is that we dare not express our indifference, as his friends did:

> Is there no end to these words of yours,
> to your long-winded blustering?
>
> (8: 2)

The victim's role that Job claims is bound to be significant within a collection of texts like the Bible where victims, always and everywhere, are prominent. On further reflection, it becomes apparent that the reason for the astonishing similarity between Job's discourse and what we call the penitential *Psalms* can be found in the perspective common to victims surrounded by numerous enemies.

Raymund Schwager's book [*Brauchen wir einen Südenbock*] provides an excellent reference on the topic of the tragic Psalms. These texts describe, in an extremely condensed form, the situation found in Job's complaints: an innocent victim, usually of a lynching, is speaking. Raymund Schwager is not mistaken: a scapegoat in the modern sense is describing the cruelties he is made to endure. There is one enormous difference. In the *Psalms,* only the victim speaks; in the Dialogues of *Job*, other voices make themselves heard.

Because the texts I have just mentioned best describe Job as scapegoat, they are also those which most resemble the Psalms. In fact they are so similar that they are interchangeable. Each focuses on the surrogate victim, that powerful element shared in common by so many biblical texts yet mysteriously ignored by everyone. There is no doubt that the intellectual expulsion of this scapegoat vic-

tim is the continuation of the physical violence of antiquity.

An excellent way to dispel the erroneous influence of the prologue, and come to terms with what *Job* is really about, is to reread the *Psalms:*

> To every one of my oppressors
>   I am contemptible,
> loathsome to my neighbours,
>   to my friends a thing of fear.
>
> Those who see me in the street
>   hurry past me;
> I am forgotten, as good as dead in their hearts,
>   something discarded.
>
> I hear their endless slanders,
>   threats from every quarter,
> as they combine against me,
>   plotting to take my life.
>
> (*Psalms* 31: 11-13)

. . . . .

Why has Job become the object of hatred for his community? No direct answer is given. Perhaps it is better this way. If the author were to identify a precise element or mention a certain incident as the possible origin, no matter what, we would immediately think we knew the answer and stop questioning. In reality we would know less than ever.

But we must not assume that the Dialogues are completely silent. They are full of indications, if we know where to look for them. In our search for an explanation of the choice of Job as a scapegoat, we should not ask just anyone. His 'friends', for example, have nothing interesting to say on the subject. They want to make Job responsible for the cruelties he is made to endure. They suggest that his avarice was his undoing; perhaps he was harsh to his people and used his position to exploit the poor and the weak.

Job appears to be virtuous but maybe, like Oedipus, he has committed a hidden crime. Or perhaps his son or some other member of his family has done so. A man condemned by the voice of the people could hardly be innocent. But Job defends himself so vigorously that no accusation holds. The indictments gradually fade away.

Some commentators reproach Job for his vigorous self-defence. He lacks humility and his friends are right to be scandalized. Such a reproach completely misunderstands the nature of the debate. Job's indignation must be put in its proper context, as he himself defines it, to be understood.

He does not say that he has never sinned, he says he has done nothing that deserves his extreme disgrace; just yesterday he could do no wrong and was treated like a saint, now everyone is against him. It is not he who has changed but the people around him. The Job that everyone detests cannot be much different from the man everyone revered.

The Job of the Dialogues is not just somebody who made a lot of money and then lost it all. He is not just a person who goes from splendour to misery and decides to talk over with his friends the attributes of God and the metaphysics of evil. The Job of the Dialogues is not the Job of the prologue. He is a great leader who at first commands the respect of the people and is then abruptly scorned by them:

> Who will bring back to me the months that have
> gone,
>   [. . .]
> when my feet were plunged in cream,
>   and streams of oil poured from the rocks?
> When I went out to the gate of the city,
>   when I took my seat in the square,
> as soon as I appeared, the young men stepped
>   aside,
>   while the older men rose to their feet.
> Men of note interrupted their speeches,
>   and put their fingers on their lips;
> the voices of rulers were silenced,
>   and their tongues stayed still in their mouths.
> They waited anxiously to hear me,
>   and listened in silence to what I had to say.
> When I paused, there was no rejoinder,
>   and my words dropped on them, one by one.
> They waited for me, as men wait for rain,
>   open-mouthed, as if to catch the year's last
>   showers.
> If I smiled at them, it was too good to be true,
>   they watched my face for the least sign of
>   favour.
> In a lordly style, I told them which course to
>   take,
>   and like a king amid his armies,
> I led them where I chose.
>
> (29: 2-25)

Before he became a scapegoat Job lived through a period of extraordinary popularity bordering on idolatry. We see clearly from this passage that the prologue has no relevance at all. If Job had really lost his cattle and his children, his reminiscence about the past would have provided the opportunity to mention that loss. But there is no reference to it . . .

The contrast between past and present is not from riches to poverty, or from health to sickness, but from favour to disfavour with the very same people. The Dialogues are not dealing with a purely personal drama or a simple change of circumstance, but with the behaviour of all the people towards a statesman whose career has been destroyed.

The accusations against Job, no matter how questionable, are very revealing. Primarily, the fallen potentate is reproached for abusing his power: an accusation that could not be made against any ordinary landowner, however rich. Job reminds us of the *tyrant* of the Greek cities. Eliphaz asks him: Why has Shaddai turned against you?

> Would he punish you for your piety,
>   and hale you off to judgement?
> No, rather for your manifold wickednesses,
>   for your unending iniquities!
> You have exacted needless pledges from your
>   brothers,
>   and men go naked now through your despoil-
>   ing;
> you have grudged water to the thirsty man,

> and refused bread to the hungry;
> you have narrowed the lands of the poor man
>   down to
>   nothing
>   to set your crony in his place,
> sent widows away empty-handed
>   and crushed the arms of orphans.
>
> (22: 4-9)

We modern readers eagerly accept the vision of the prologue because it fits our own world, or at least our idea of it. Happiness consists of having as many possessions as possible without ever becoming ill, of enjoying an eternal frenzy of consumer pleasure. In the Dialogues, on the other hand, the only thing that counts is Job's relationship with the community.

Job portrays his triumphal period as the autumn of his life—in other words, the season that immediately precedes the icy winter of persecution. The disgrace was probably recent and very sudden. The extreme infatuation with Job suddenly turned into extreme disgust. Job seems to have had no warning of the sudden change that was about to take place:

> My praises echoed in every ear,
>   and never an eye but smiled on me;
> because I freed the poor man when he called,
>   and the orphan who had no one to help
>   him . . .
>
> So I thought to myself, 'I shall die in honour,
>   my days like a palm tree's for number.
> My roots thrust out to the water,
>   my leaves freshened by the falling dew at
>   night.
> My reputation will never fade,
>   and the bow in my hands will gain new
>   strength.'
>
> (29)

The mystery of *Job* is presented in a context that does not explain it but at least allows us to situate it. The scapegoat is a shattered idol. The rise and fall of Job are bound up in one another. The two extremes seem to be connected. They cannot be understood separately, and yet one is not the cause of the other. We sense an ill-defined but very real social phenomenon in the probable unfolding of events.

The one thing in common between the two periods is the community's unanimity: first in worship, then later in loathing. Job is the victim of a huge and sudden reversal of public opinion that is obviously unstable, capricious and void of all moderation. He seems hardly more responsible for the change in this crowd than Jesus is for a similar change between Palm Sunday and Good Friday.

For this dual unanimity to exist, the mimetic contagion of the crowd must be at work. Members of the community influence each other reciprocally; they imitate each other in fanatical worship and then in even more fanatical hostility.

. . . . .

In the last of the three Dialogues Eliphaz of Teman, one of the three friends, clearly alludes to the existence of predecessors of Job who were both powerful upstarts and scapegoats:

> And will you still follow the ancient trail
>   trodden by the wicked?
> Those men who were borne off before their time,
>   with rivers swamping their foundations,
> because they said to God, 'Go away!
>   What can Shaddai do to us?'
> Yet he himself had filled their houses with good
>   things
>   while these wicked men shut him out of their
>   counsels.
> At the sight of their ruin, good men rejoice,
>   and the innocent deride them:
> 'See how their greatness is brought to nothing!
>   See how their wealth has perished in the
>   flames!'

(22: 15-20)

The 'ancient trail trodden by the wicked' begins with grandeur, riches and power but ends in overwhelming disaster. We have just observed these same two phases, the identical scenario, in the experience of Job.

Some day soon Job may well figure on the list of these anonymous men, who are hinted at only because their name has been 'erased'. He is one of those whose career is likely to end badly because it began too well.

Just as I have done, Eliphaz contrasts and, inevitably, compares the two phases. He recognizes that they form a whole and cannot be interpreted separately. Something in the rise of these men contributes to their fall. Our every intuition is voiced in the words of Eliphaz. Job has already travelled quite a distance along the 'ancient trail [of] the wicked'. He has reached the beginning of the final stage.

The events recalled by Eliphaz seem distant and therefore unusual, but not so unusual as to prevent the observer from recognizing in them a recurring phenomenon. The path has already been traced: many men have already taken it and now it is Job's turn. All these tragic destinies share the characteristic profile of the shattered idol. Their destiny, like Job's, is inevitably determined by the transformation of a crowd of worshippers into a crowd of persecutors.

Eliphaz could not allude to events in the *past,* if the disasters of wicked men were imaginary. He must be evoking an experience that everyone knows because it belongs to the entire community. The violent downfall of the wicked is alive in everyone's memory. These reversals leave too deep an impression to be forgotten, and their stereotypical character makes them easy to remember.

In the eyes of Eliphaz and of the community, the 'wickedness' of these victims is clearly demonstrated, just like Job's guilt. Once they have been denied by the crowd, former idols can never justify themselves; the poor unfortunates are condemned once and for all. The unanimity that is now formed against Job must have also been formed against them in earlier times.

The same process is beginning again and Eliphaz's warning is justified. Job would do well to pay attention to the words of this wise man. But how can he do so without adjuring himself and admitting his guilt?

Perhaps Eliphaz reproaches himself for having been too friendly with the criminal he considers Job to be. He speaks quite openly of the trial of popular 'justice' which, far from being a reprehensible act of disorder, seems legitimate to him, infallible and, quite literally, divine. His conscience is clear and he finds everything to be in order. The order is perfect, and the three 'friends' are happy that it has been forcefully reaffirmed.

Are 'wicked' men always the victims of crowd violence? Could it be a question of anything else? Reread the last four lines of the quotation. They allude to a violent form of social expulsion:

> At the sight of their ruin, good men rejoice,
>   and the innocent deride them:
> 'See how their greatness is brought to nothing!
>   See how their wealth has perished in the
>   flames!'

In the context of a rural society, the 'rejoicing of good men' and the 'derision of the innocent' are not without consequence. We must consider the formidable effect of unanimous condemnation in such an environment. To bring about the disasters ascribed to him, a god need only leave it to these good men, who are always ready to act in the name of his vengeance.

In the middle of the crowd we find the victim and all his possessions. The mob has already divided up what can be shared; perhaps they drew lots to avoid fights. What cannot be shared—which includes their former owner—will be consumed in great fires of joy.

The disaster that awaits 'the wicked' at the final stage, at the end of the 'ancient trail', must resemble those primitive feasts which, in spite of their moderated and ritualistic nature, remind us of a crowd phenomenon. Such social dramas always end with the simulated drowning or immolation of a scapegoat. Former ethnologists sensed the existence of a more extreme violence behind the ritual forms they observed. Many contemporary scholars regard them as victims of their own romantic and colonialist imagination. Yet I think that the earlier ethnologists were right. No doubt they had their prejudices, but we also have ours; the fervent Rousseauian dogma of today ignores the massive evidence that contradicts it, and thus hardly inspires confidence.

There are many other passages to suggest that the central event of the text, the terrible experience that is just beginning for the hero, is a recurring phenomenon of collective violence that is particularly, but not exclusively, directed against the 'mighty' and the 'tyrants'. This violence is always interpreted as an act of divine vengeance, as a god's punitive intervention.

I will cite only one example. It is found in the speech of Elihu, the fourth speaker in *Job*. This character is not generally thought to belong to the original Dialogues. His speech is probably the work of a reader who was scandalized by the impotence of the first three guardians of public order. Elihu despises the fact that the other three are rooted in tradition and strives to succeed where they have failed.

He thinks he is more able simply because he is younger and because he despises the past. He too tries to reduce Job to silence but succeeds only in restating, in a less attractive style, what the other three have already said. He belongs to a stage in which the archaic tradition is more feeble. Nevertheless, some of what he says makes the hidden topic of the Dialogues clearer than ever.

The theme of Job 'the oppressor of his people' has already been mentioned by the three friends; Elihu sets even greater store by it. The people's violence shines through his political and religious statements.

We are told that God, in an instant:

> smashes great men's power without inquiry
>   and sets up others in their places.
> He knows well enough what they are about,
>   and one fine night he throws them down for
> men to
>   trample on.
> He strikes them down for their wickedness,
>   and makes them prisoners for all to see.
>
>   (34: 24-6)

I am quoting from *The Jerusalem Bible:* the identity of God and the crowd are clearly suggested in the translation. God overthrows the great, but the crowd *tramples* on them. God makes prisoners of the victims, but his intervention is *for all to see.* It takes place in the presence of that same crowd, which perhaps does not remain completely passive before such an interesting spectacle. It is hardly surprising that the power of the great is smashed 'without inquiry'. The crowd is always ready to lend God a hand when he decides to take action against the wicked. Other great men are immediately found to replace those who have fallen. God himself sets them up in their places, but it is the crowd that worships them - only to discover later, of course, that they were again wrongly chosen and were no better than their predecessors.

Vox populi, vox dei. As in Greek tragedy, the rise and fall of great men constitutes a truly sacred *mystery* and its conclusion is the part most appreciated. Although it never changes, it is always anticipated with great impatience.

Moshe Greenberg   (essay date 1987)

SOURCE: "Job," in *The Literary Guide to the Bible,* edited by Robert Alter and Frank Kermode, Cambridge, Mass.: The Belknap Press of Harvard University Press, 1987, pp. 283-303.

[*An American professor of the* Bible *and of Hebrew and Semitic Languages and Literatures, Greenberg has published works that include* The Religion of Israel *(1963) and* Introduction to Hebrew *(1964). In the following essay he offers an analysis of* The Book of Job, *examining problems of inconsistency within the text and considering several possible interpretations of the work's meaning.*]

The prophet Ezekiel mentions Job alongside Noah and Daniel as a paragon of righteousness (*Ezekiel* 14:12-20);

William Blake's illustration to Job, *38, 7: "When the morning stars sang together, and all the sons of God shouted for joy."*

from this we know that Job was a byword among the sixth-century B.C.E. Judahite exiles whom the prophet addressed. But from Ezekiel and from the late passing reference to Job's patience (or perseverance) in *James* 5:10-11 one would never guess the complexity of the character set forth in the book that bears his name. Indeed the book's representation of Job seems to some modern scholars so disharmonious as to warrant the hypothesis that two characters have been fused in it: "Job the patient," the hero of the prose frame of the book; and "Job the impatient," the central figure of the poetic dialogue. In the prose story, Job the patient withstands all the calamities inflicted on him to test the sincerity of his piety and is finally rewarded by redoubled prosperity. The moral is: piety for its own sake is true virtue and in the end is requited. It is this old story—often called a folktale—that is supposed to have been known to Ezekiel's audience. Later, the hypothesis continues, a far more profound thinker (perhaps a survivor of the Babylonian Exile and its crisis of faith) used the temporary misfortune of the hero as the setting for his poem, in which the conventional wisdom of the tale is radically challenged.

This theory is based on expectations of simplicity, consistency, and linearity that are confuted by the whole tenor of the book. Reversal and subversion prevail throughout—in sudden shifts of mood and role and in a rhetoric of sarcasm and irony. The dialogue contains much response and reaction but no predictable or consistent course of argument. When to these disconcerting features are added the exotic language (loaded with Aramaisms and Arabisms) and the uncertain state of the text in many places—from apparent corruption of words to unintelligible sequences of verses—the confidence of some critics in their ability to reconstitute the original text by rewriting and rearrangement seems exaggerated. This essay discusses the book as we have it.

The chief literary (as distinct from theological or literary-historical) problem of *Job* is its coherence: do the prose and the poetry or the speeches of Job and his Friends hang together? How are they related? We must gain an awareness of the complexities of interplay among the elements of the book. The truncation of the third round of speeches and the integrality to the book of Elihu's speeches have been treated by most critics as problems to be solved by a theory of textual dislocation or adulteration. I shall try to describe how these elements in their present shape work upon the reader. This is not to assert the infallibility of the text in hand, but rather to confess our inability to justify on grounds other than individual predilection the alternatives proposed to it. It also reflects a conviction that the literary complexity of the book is consistent with and appropriate to the nature of the issues with which it deals.

The background of the dialogue is established in chapters 1 and 2 in five movements. The first movement introduces the magnate Job, one of the "dwellers in the east" (1:3)—that is, east of the Land of Israel—in the uncertainly located country of Uz (connected with Aram to the north in *Genesis* 10:23, but with Edom to the south in *Lamentations* 4:21). He is a "blameless and upright man, one who fears God and shuns evil" (1:1). His wealth and family are described in numbers typifying abundance—seven sons and three daughters, seven thousand small cattle and three thousand camels, and so forth. The happiness of the family is epitomized in the constant round of banquets held by the children; Job's scrupulousness is shown by his sacrifices on their behalf, lest in a careless moment they "bless" (euphemism for "blaspheme") God in their hearts (1:5).

In the second movement, the action that shatters this idyll starts. "One day," at a periodic assembly of the divine court (1:6), God singles out Job for praise to the Adversary (the antecedent of the later Satan and anachronistically so called in the King James Version; in Hebrew Scriptures an angel whose task is to roam the earth and expose human wrongdoing). This commendation virtually invites the Adversary to suggest that since God has built a protective hedge around Job, his piety may not be disinterested ("for nothing," 1:9): only deprive him of his possessions and see whether he won't "bless" God to his face! God accepts the challenge and empowers the Adversary to carry out the test.

The third movement takes place "one day" as a round of the children's banquets begins and they are gathered in the house of the eldest son (1:13). A terrible chain of calami-

ties befalls Job: one messenger after another arrives to report the destruction of every component of Job's fortune, culminating in the death of his children. Job goes into mourning, but with a blessing of God on his lips (the Adversary is thwarted, but his expectation is literally realized!). The movement concludes, "In all this Job did not sin or impute anything unsavory to God" (1:22).

The scene of the fourth movement is heaven again. "One day," at the periodic assembly of the divine court (2:1), God repeats his praise of Job to the Adversary, adding, "and he still holds on to his integrity, so you incited me to destroy him for nothing" (2:3). The Adversary proposes the ultimate test: afflict Job's own body and see whether he won't "bless" God. God agrees, with the proviso that Job's life be preserved, and the Adversary hurries off to inflict a loathsome skin disease on Job, driving him to constant scratching with a sherd as he sits in the dust (the Greek translation reads, "on the dungheap far from the city"). His wife protests: "Do you still hold on to your integrity? 'Bless' God, and die" (2:9). Job remonstrates with her: "Should we then accept the good from God and not accept the bad?" (2:10). The question is rhetorical, but in every rhetorical question lurks the possible affirmation of what is ostensibly denied. Moreover, by bluntly calling what he has received from God "bad," Job has moved from his nonjudgmental blessing of God after the first stage of his ruin. The movement concludes with a variant of the preceding conclusion: "In all this Job did not sin with his lips." Is "with his lips" a mere equivalent of "did not impute anything unsavory to God," or did the talmudic sage correctly perceive in it a reservation: with his lips he sinned not, but in his heart he did. Is the impatient Job of the poem already foreshadowed in the closing stage of the narrative?

The last movement brings the three Friends of Job (also of Abrahamitic, extra-Israelite stock) into the picture. Coming from afar to comfort Job, they assume his condition—they sit on the ground with him, having torn their clothes and thrown dust on their heads. They keep him company in silence for seven days until he starts to speak.

The contrast between the simple folktale and the artful poem must not be overdrawn. In fact the artistry in the narrative is considerable. The representation of time in the first to the fourth movements progresses from duration to instant. In movement one, the regularity of happy, uneventful lives is expressed by verbs in the durational mode: "would go and would make a banquet," "would send word," "always used to do." The decision in heaven to test Job and its earthly realization in calamities (the second and third movements) occur each on separate days. Moreover, temporal disjunction is accompanied by disjunction of agent: although the Adversary is empowered to ruin Job, he is not mentioned in the subsequent story of disasters. But in the climactic fourth movement, the pace is stepped up and the events are concentrated. Events in heaven and their effect on earth occur on one and the same day; God licenses the Adversary to afflict Job's body, and the Adversary sets to work immediately and in person, as though eager to win his wager. The parallelism of the second stage of Job's trial to the first is expressed with the intensification and focusing that are characteristic of the second verset of poetic parallelism.

Dialogue and elements of poetic diction permeate the prose tale, further diminishing the contrast between the frame and the poem. Only the last movement of the story is speechless—owing to the courteous silence of the Friends. The first movement ends with Job's internal dialogue of concern lest his children blaspheme in secret. The second movement and the corresponding first half of the fourth movement consist almost entirely of dialogue between God and the Adversary, with the latter employing markedly elevated speech: parallelism ("roaming the land and walking about in it," 1:7; "the work of his hands you blessed, and his cattle abound in the land," 1:10); proverbs ("Skin for skin; all a man has he will give for his life," 2:4), emphatic repetition ("a hedge about him and about his household and about all he has," 1:10). The chain of calamities in the third movement is conveyed entirely through reports of messengers all of which exhibit the same pattern. The details of the accounts of disaster are artfully disposed: human and natural destroyers alternate, and the loss of Job's children is delayed to the end. Job's acquiescence in God's decree, with its parallelism, its compression, and its balanced lines, is poetry proper:

> Naked came I forth from the belly of my mother
>   and naked shall I return thither:
> The Lord gave, and the Lord took away;
>   blessed be the name of the Lord.
>
> (1:21)

The terrestrial scene of the fourth movement is dominated by the sharp exchange between Job and his wife in which an ironic touch is visible. Job's wife unwittingly advocates the Adversary's cause to Job (" 'Bless' God, and die") while expressing her exasperation with her husband in the very terms used by God to praise him ("still hold on to your integrity"). Such reuse by one character of the language of another is a constant feature of the poem; its occurrence here in the narrative is another bond between the two parts of the book.

The preliminary narrative establishes Job's virtuous character and so provides us with inside information known to heaven and Job alone. Our judgment on what Job and his Friends will say about his character must be determined by this information. We also know—what neither Job nor his Friends do—that Job's sufferings are designed to test him. These circumstances are fertile ground for irony; their impact on our reception of the arguments put forward in the poetic dialogue is an open and intriguing issue. If we now follow the debate step by step, we will get a clearer sense of the artful interplay between statements and positions, of the elements of progression in the arguments, and of the overarching ironies of the book as a whole.

After brooding over his fate for seven days, Job breaks his silence with a bitter diatribe against his life and its symbol, light (chap. 3). He wishes that the day of his birth would be reclaimed by primeval darkness and imagines the peace he would have enjoyed in Sheol had he been stillborn. Why does God give life to the wretched, whom he has "hedged about" (that is, obstructed—a reversal of the meaning of the very phrase used by the Adversary to describe Job's security)? He recollects his lifelong fear of calamity (one thinks of his anxious sacrificing on behalf of his children) which did not avail to prevent it.

This outburst takes the Friends by surprise. They had come to commiserate and encourage, not to participate in a rebellion against God's judgment. Their first spokesman, Eliphaz, opens softly (chaps. 4-5), reminding Job of his custom of cheering victims of misfortune, and gently chiding him for breaking down under his own calamities. He preaches the doctrine of distributive justice: no innocent man was ever wiped out, while the wicked reap their deserts. He reports a revelation made to him "in thought-filled visions of the night" (4:13); man is by nature too base to be innocent before God—even the angels are not trusted by him! Short-lived as he is ("cut down from morning to evening," 4:20), man cannot acquire the wisdom to comprehend his fate. Will Job seek vindication from some (other) divine being? Only fools let vexation kill them; "taking root" for a moment, they suddenly lose everything they own through their blindness to the truth that "man is to misery born as the sparks fly upward" (5:7). In Job's place, Eliphaz would turn to God, who works wonders and benefactions and who constantly reverses the fortunes of men. It is a lucky man whom God disciplines, for if the man—here Job—accepts it and repents, he has good hope of being healed and of living prosperous and happy to a ripe old age. All this has been proved by experience.

In this first exchange, each party starts from advanced positions. Job vents his death wish with untempered passion, becoming the spokesman of all the wretched of the earth. Eliphaz's carefully modulated reply sets the pattern for all subsequent speeches of the Friends: a prologue, demurring to Job, followed by a multithematic advocacy of the conventional view of God's distributive justice. Most of the themes of the Friends' argument are included in Eliphaz's speech: man's worthlessness before God; man's ephemerality and (consequent) ignorance; a call to turn to God in penitence; praise of God; the disciplinary purpose of misfortune; the happiness of the penitent; the claim to possess wisdom greater than Job's.

The rhetoric of debate pervades the speech of Eliphaz and all that follow. Themes are introduced by expressions of interrogation ("Is/Does not . . . "), demonstration ("look, behold"), exhortation ("Remember! Consider! Know!"), and exception ("but, however"). Among the rhetorical questions peppering Eliphaz's speech, on exhibits the unconscious irony typical of many in the Friends' speeches: "Call now, will anyone answer you;/to which of the divine beings will you turn?" (5:1). Eliphaz is scoffing, but in the event Job will not only call upon a heavenly witness, arbitrator and vindicator; he will ultimately be answered by the greatest and holiest of them all.

A constant difference between the general and particular observations of Job and the Friends is already evident in this first exchange. Both parties pass back and forth from the particular case of Job to the general condition of mankind. But in Job's speeches his particular misfortune governs his vision of the general; his unmerited suffering opens his eyes to the injustice rampant in society at large.

In the Friends' speeches, on the other hand, the general doctrine of distributive justice governs their judgment of Job's case: he must be wicked in order to fit into their scheme of things. Job's empirically based generalities reflect reality; the Friends' perception of the particular is as fictive as the general doctrine from which it springs.

Echoes of Job's speech may be heard in that of Eliphaz. Job's "roarings" (3:24) reflect his anguish; Eliphaz speaks of the "lion's roar" (4:10). Birth and misery figure prominently in Job's speech; Eliphaz combines them in his epigrammatic "man is born to misery." Countering Job's wish for a direct passage from birth to grave, Eliphaz holds out hope of a penitent Job reaching the grave happy and in ripe old age. Such echoes and allusions pervade the dialogue, arguing against a commonly held opinion that the poem of *Job* consists of a series of disconnected monologues.

Job begins his reply to Eliphaz (chaps. 6-7) with a reference to *ka'as,* "vexation" (which Eliphaz warned kills fools, 5:2); overwhelming vexation has caused Job to speak so intemperately (6:2-3). He is the victim of God's terrors; to hold out hope to him is mockery, for his only wish is to be speedily dispatched ("crushed" he says in 6:9, using Eliphaz's language in 5:4). He is not made of stone so as to be able to tolerate his suffering any longer (6:12; in 5:17-18 Eliphaz called it God's benign discipline). He is disappointed that his Friends have deserted him. As when thirsty travelers seek out a wadi and find it has run dry in summer heat, so now when Job looks to his Friends for support they fail him. All he asks of them is to pay attention to his case, show him his fault, and stop producing vapid arguments. Job turns Eliphaz's theme of man's ephemerality to his own use: man's life is like a hireling's term of service; his only relief is night and wages. But Job's life is a hopeless agony; night brings him only the terrors of his dreams and night visions (a bitter echo of Eliphaz). Since human life is so brief, it is a wonder that God fills it with such suffering. Job parodies a verse in Psalms: "What is man, that you are mindful of him: / mortal man, that you take note of him?" (8:4; cf. 144:3: "Lord, what is man, that you should care about him, / mortal man, that you should think of him?"). This is skewed sardonically into:

> What is man, that you make much of him,
>   that you fix your attention upon him—
> inspect him every morning,
>   examine him every minute?
>
> (7:17-18)

If only the "watcher of men" would look away for a while and let Job live out his few remaining days in peace!

Establishing here the pattern for the following dialogues, Job's answer is longer than his predecessor's. He has been goaded by Eliphaz's pious generalities and oblique rebuke into itemizing his experience of God's enmity and its universal implications. In this way all the replies of the Friends arouse Job to ever-new perceptions of his condition and of the divine governance of the world.

Job's complaint scandalizes Bildad, the next interlocutor (chap. 8). "Will the Almighty pervert justice?" he asks rhetorically (v. 3), and proceeds to ascribe the death of Job's children to their sins. Thus Bildad lays bare the implications of the speeches of both his predecessors. Job ought to supplicate God contritely rather than assert a claim against him. Since we are so short-lived, it behooves us to consult the ancient sages; they teach that as it is nature's law that plants wither without water, so the course of the godless leads to perdition (the moral law). God will not repudiate the blameless or support the wicked; hence if Job repents, a joyous future, better than his past, is in store for him.

In his reply (chaps. 9-10), Job exploits the forensic metaphor in the rhetorical questions of Eliphaz and Bildad ("Can mortals be acquitted by God?" 4:17; "Will the Almighty pervert justice?" 8:3). It expresses the covenantal-legal postulate of ancient piety with its doctrine of distributive justice, shared by all the characters in the dialogue. God refuses to follow the rules, Job asserts: "Man cannot win a suit against God!" (9:2). God indeed works wonders (echoing Eliphaz)—mainly in displays of his destructive power in nature (a parody of Eliphaz's doxology). Such aggression he directs against any who seek redress from him for calamity inflicted on them undeservedly. In language suffused with legal terms, Job denounces God's disregard of his right: he terrorizes Job into confusion; even if Job could plead, his own words would be twisted against him. Contrary to Bildad's assertion, God indiscriminately destroys the innocent and the guilty, for "he wounds me much for nothing" (9:17; ironically, Job has unwittingly stumbled on the true reason for his suffering). If God would allow him, Job would demand of him a bill of indictment. He would charge him with unworthy conduct: he spurns his creature while smiling on the wicked; he searches for Job's sin, though he knows Job is not guilty. He carefully fashioned Job and sustained him through the years—only to hunt him down with a wondrous display of power (themes of Psalm 139 are sarcastically reused here).

It is now Zophar's turn (chap. 11). After denouncing Job's mockery and self-righteousness, he speaks as one privy to God's counsels: if God would answer Job, he'd show him his ignorance; the fact is that God has treated Job better than he deserves. God's purpose is unfathomable:

> higher than heaven,
>   deeper than Sheol,
> longer than the earth,
>   broader than the sea.
>
> (vv. 8-9)

Job should pray to God and remove his iniquity; then he will enjoy the hope, the light, the peace and the sound sleep of the righteous.

Each of the three Friends having had his say, Job now delivers his longest answer yet (chaps. 12-14). Goaded by Bildad, he mockingly acknowledges their monopoly of wisdom, but claims he is no less wise. A shower of irony and sarcasm follows. Borrowing terms from Bildad's invocation of the ancient sages and Zophar's celebration of God's boundless wisdom, Job grotesquely invokes the dumb creatures of sky, sea, and earth to teach the commonplace, "With him [God] are wisdom and power; his are counsel and insight" (12:13), followed by another parodic doxology depicting divine power exercised with sheerly destructive results in the social realm. In this context the stock praise of God that he "uncovers deep things out of darkness, brings deep gloom to light" (12:22; cf. *Daniel* 2:22) suggests that he tears the lid off submerged forces of death and chaos, allowing them to surface and overcome order. As for the Friends, they are quacksalvers, liars, obsequiously partial to God; they ascribe false principles to him and ought to be in dread of his ever subjecting them to scrutiny. Job, despite his ruined state, will stand up to God, convinced God must recognize integrity.

> Let him slay me; I have no [*or* in him I will]
>   hope;
>   yet I will argue my cause before him.
> Through this I will gain victory:
>   that no godless man can come into his pres-
>   ence.
>
>   (13:15-16)

This burst of confidence collapses into the mournful realization of his vulnerability to God's terrors. Again he asks to be allowed to converse with God, to be informed of his sin (13:20-23; cf. 6:24, 10:2). Again he complains of God's enmity, wonders at his petty keeping of accounts and his persecution of "a driven leaf" (13:25). Again he implores God to let him live out his term of service in peace, for, unlike a tree, which after being felled can still renew itself from its roots, man once cut down sleeps eternally in Sheol.

But must containment in Sheol be final? Might it not be a temporary shelter from God's wrath? "If a man dies, can he revive?" (14:14)—hope wells up in the question, and the fantasy of reversal continues: When wrath subsides, God would call and Job would answer, God would long for his creature. But this anticipation of a doctrine whose time was not yet ripe, this flight of a mind liberated by the collapse of its concept of order, is a momentary flash. Job falls back into despondency.

When the first round of dialogue began, Job rejected life; by its conclusion, he is clinging to it and longing for renewed intimacy with God. Lamentation, anger, despair, and hope succeed each other in waves, but a clear gathering of energy is visible in his speeches. The Friends, hurt by Job's challenge to their concept of the moral order, have turned from comforters to scolds, each harsher than his predecessor. Eliphaz only implies that Job is a sinner; Bildad openly proposes that his children have died for their sins; Zophar assures Job that his suffering is less than he deserves. Yet each ends with a promise of a bright future if Job will only acknowledge his guilt and implore God's forgiveness. Though they provide no direct comfort to Job, by blackening his character they rouse him out of the torpor of despair and kindle in him the desire to assert himself.

Eliphaz opens the second round (chaps. 15-21), deploring Job's mockery of his Friends' counsel. His pernicious arguments undermine piety. Is Job Wisdom personified ("Were you born before the mountains?" at 15:7 evokes *Proverbs* 8:25 in reference to Dame Wisdom); dose *he* have a monopoly of it (cf. 12:2-3)? Job's ridicule of sapiential

tradition rankles with Bildad and Zophar as well ("Why are we thought of as brutes?" 18:3; "reproof that insults me," 20:3). One would think Job had listened in on God's council when in fact it was to Eliphaz that insight into man's true condition was vouchsafed in a night vision (15:14-16 repeats with slight variation the oracle on man's baseness in Eliphaz's first speech, 4:17-21). Eliphaz proceeds to depict the life and exemplary fate of the wicked as taught by the sages. This theme, briefly touched upon previously, is elaborated at length throughout the second round of the Friends' speeches. Since they cannot persuade Job to withdraw his arraignment of God, his very perseverance in his claims appears to them to convict him of sin. Hence they endeavor, in this round, to frighten him into recanting by describing in detail the punishment of the wicked. That these descriptions, ostensibly generic, contain items identical with Job's misfortunes, is of course not accidental. The poet exhibits virtuosity in playing variations on this single theme. He has Eliphaz focus on the tormented person of the wicked man (chap. 15); here the most blatant allusions to Job's condition occur. Bildad concentrates on the destruction of his "tent" and progeny:

> Light has darkened in his tent;
>   his lamp fails him . . .
> Generations to come will be appalled at his fate
>   [and say],
>   "These were the dwellings of the wicked;
>   here was the place of him who knew not
>   God."
>
>   (18:21)

Zophar (chap. 20) develops an alimentary figure: the ill-got gain of the wicked are sweets he tries to swallow but must vomit, or they will turn to poison in him and kill him.

Job answers the monitory descriptions of the fate of the wicked with pathetic descriptions of his misery (chap. 16). In response to Eliphaz he figures God as an enemy rushing at him like a hero, setting him up as his target—inverting Eliphaz's picture of the wicked playing the hero and running defiantly at God (15:25-26). He has been afflicted despite his innocence, and this very thought moves him to plead that the wrong done to him not be forgotten ("Earth, do not cover my blood," 16:18). In a transport of faith he avers he has a witness in heaven who will arbitrate between him and God, then descends again into despair.

Responding to Bildad's depiction of the wicked man's loss of home and kin, Job relates (chap. 19) how God has stripped him of honor; how friends, wife, and servants have abandoned him till only his flesh and bones remain attached to him. He implores the compassion of his Friends, wishes for a permanent record of his arguments, and consoles himself with the assurance that although he is forsaken in the present, his redeemer-kinsman (*go'el*) lives and will in the end appear to vindicate him.

In his reply to Zophar (chap. 21), concluding the second round of dialogue, Job bids his Friends be silent and listen to something truly appalling (Job spurns as specious the horror over the pretended destruction of the wicked described by Bildad, 18:20), namely the real situation of the wicked. Contrary to the Friends' doctrine, the wicked live long and prosper, surrounded by frolicking children; they die without pangs. They flaunt their indifference toward God with impunity. How often is their light extinguished (contrary to Bildad's claim)? Their children will pay for their sins?—why doesn't God pay *them* back! The Friends have reproached Job with insolence toward God: "Can God be instructed in knowledge— / he who judges from the heights?" (21:22; the verse seems to cite the Friends, but it is a pseudo-citation since in fact they never said this; in the heat of debate Job ascribes to the Friends what can at most have been implied in their speeches). Job answers: What sort of judge distributes well-being and misfortune according to no standard? The Friends have admonished: "Where is the tent in which the wicked dwelled?" (see the end of Bildad's speech, 18:21); Job retorts: every traveler (that is, worldly-wise person, not necessarily old) knows that even in death the wicked are honored.

In the second round the Friends dwelt one-sidedly on the punishment of the wicked, intending Job to see in the wicked a mirror of himself. What they succeed in doing is to move him to particularize his own suffering and—equally one-sidedly—the success of the wicked, thus at once proving he is not one of them and confirming again God's perversity. In this round, too, Job experiences sporadic moments of hopefulness and intimations of vindication. Significant of things to come in round three is the frequency (especially in Job's last speech) with which Job cites the Friends or anticipates their responses to him. In the first speech of this round he says that were he in their place he would mouth the same sort of platitudes (16:4); in his last speech he begins to show he can do it.

Eliphaz returns to the arena yet a third time (chap. 22). Is your righteousness of any interest to God? he asks Job (v. 3); the implication seems to be that Job's clamor for a hearing is arrant presumption (Eliphaz cannot know that God indeed has a stake in Job's righteousness). In fact, he continues, you are very wicked—behaving in a cruel and callous manner toward the weak and defenseless. Eliphaz has been driven to this extreme by his tenacious adherence to the doctrine of distributive justice, the threat to which may be gauged by his incredible accusation. In the sequel, Eliphaz misconstrues Job's pseudo-citation (21:22) to mean that God cannot see through the cloud-cover to judge mankind; but, he affirms, the wicked are punished. Job must return to God, give up his trust in gold (another fabricated charge), and pray to God; reformed, he will be God's favorite, capable of interceding with him on behalf of the guilty. Once again Eliphaz suggests he knows God's counsels; he cannot know that in the end his prediction will come true when Job prays to avert God's wrath from Eliphaz and his companions!

Job replies in a soliloquy (chaps. 23-24) indirectly relating to Eliphaz. He would like to find God, not in order to repent, but to argue his case before him, for he is sure he would be cleared; but he finds him nowhere. He would emerge as pure gold from a test, and God knows it, yet the deity capriciously harasses him. A list of crimes committed by the wicked now appears, intertwined with a description of the downtrodden, and ending with the cutting

reproach "Yet God does not regard it unseemly!" (24:12). After describing a trio of "rebels against the light"—murderer, thief, and adulterer, who shun the light of day—the speech becomes unintelligible till its last defiant line: "Surely no one can give me the lie / or set my words at naught" (24:25).

Bildad's third speech (chap. 25) is a mere six verses, a doxology consisting chiefly of a repetition (for the second time; see 15:14-16) of Eliphaz's threadbare oracle (cf. 4:17-21). The following speech of Job contains a doxology that might well continue this one (26:5-14); indeed many critics have taken it for the misplaced end of Bildad's speech. But an alternative interpretation is commendable for its piquancy: "Bildad's speech is short and sounds like what Job says in reply precisely because Job cuts him off and finishes the speech for him." Such mimicry accords with the tenor of the beginning of Job's speech, in which he derides Bildad's rhetorical impotence and suggests that even his banalities are not his own ("Whose breath issued from you?" 26:4). Job demonstrates with great flourish that he can better anything Bildad does. When the Friends are reduced to repeating one another and Job can say their pieces for them, we know that the dialogue has ended.

And indeed Zophar has nothing to say in this third round. To be sure, critics have identified his "lost speech" in the next speech of Job: 27:13 is a variant of the conclusion of Zophar's last speech (20:29)—picking up as it were where he ended—and the subsequent description of the doom of the wicked continues Zophar's specific theme of dispossession. That these two passages are connected can hardly be in doubt, but is the latter an alien intrusion into Job's speech? Its context permits another explanation.

After waiting in vain for Zophar to speak, Job (chap. 27) resumes his address (aptly not called a reply) with an oath invoking (paradoxically) "God who has deprived me of justice" (v. 2). He affirms his blamelessness against his Friends' vilification. He will hold on to this integrity (an echo of 2:3, 9) as long as he lives, for God destroys the impious who contend with him. He offers to teach his Friends "what is with God" (27:11)—perhaps a reference to wisdom (cf. "It is not with me," 28:14, and "[What do] you understand that is not with us?" 15:9), in respect of which the Friends held themselves superior to Job (15:9-10). For now, they must stop talking the nonsense that their own experience contradicts (27:12). As an example of such nonsense Job then offers what Zophar might have said had he spoken, in a second display of expert mimicry.

Still formally part of Job's speech is the sublime poem on wisdom that follows (chap. 28)—the wisdom by which the world is governed, by which the meaning of events is unlocked. Man knows how to ferret precious ores out of the earth; he conquers the most daunting natural obstacles in order to obtain treasure. But he does not have a map to the sources of wisdom. The primeval waters, Tehom and the sea, do not contain it; farsighted birds of the sky do not know its place; Death (the realm next to divinity) has heard only a rumour of it. God alone, whose control of the elements of weather exemplifies his wide-ranging power, comprehends it. For man he has appointed, as its functional equivalent, the obligation to fear God and shun evil—wherewith he adjusts himself to the divine order.

The topic of this poem and its serene resignation seem out of place at this juncture. Critics generally excise the poem from its context, though some ascribe it nonetheless to the author of the dialogue. It is a self-contained piece having only tangential connections with its environment; but these may account for its location. The mention of silver in the first line links the poem to the preceding description of the wicked man's loss of his silver (27:16-17). More substantial is the possible connection with Job's undertaking to teach his Friends "what is with the Almighty" (27:11), preparatory to which they should stop talking nonsense. If, as was suggested above, this is a reference to wisdom, which is with God alone, then the Friend's parade of assurance that they know the reason for Job's suffering is sheer presumption. As the medieval exegete Nahmanides put it, "He instructed them to say, 'I don't know.'" A closer paraphrase might be: abandon your futile doctrine; it is a reproach to you and will not gain you God's favor. This is Job's last word to his Friends.

Job's speech in chapters 27 and 28 is framed by phrases that echo his initial characterization in the prose tale. At the beginning, the expressions "I will maintain my integrity / I will hold on to my righteousness" (27:5-6) recall God's praise: "he still holds on to his integrity" (2:3). At the end, the human equivalent of wisdom is "to fear the Lord and shun evil" (28:28), the very traits of which, according to the story, Job was a paragon. Between these appears Job's arraignment of God and his friends, and the denial that wisdom is accessible to man. Taken together, these evidence the sheer heroism of a naked man, forsaken by his God and his friends and bereft of a clue to understand his suffering, still maintaining faith in the value of his virtue and in the absolute duty of man to be virtuous. The universe has turned its back on him, yet Job persists in the affirmation of his own worth and the transcendent worth of unrewarded good. Perhaps this is the sense of the difficult passage in 17:8-9:

> The upright are appalled at this [Job's fate];
>   The innocent man is aroused against the impious [Job's Friends];
> The righteous man holds to his way [despite it all];
>   He whose hands are pure grows stronger.

If such is the gist of this complex speech, it marks a stage in Job's reconciliation with God, undercutting the climax in chapter 42. But did the ancient poet share our predilection for the single climax? He has depicted Job attaining to peaks of confidence several times, only to relapse into despondency. The same may hold true for Job's making his peace with his fate and with God.

Job's final speech, a long soliloquy (chaps. 29-31), reverts even more explicitly to his former state as "the greatest of all the dwellers in the east." He recollects pathetically his past glory, the awe in which he was held, his regal patronage of the needy and helpless (a pointed refutation of Eliphaz's gratuitous accusations); how he looked forward to living out his days in happiness, surrounded by his family and honored by society "like a king among his troop,

as one who comforts mourners" (29:25). Instead he now drinks bitter drafts of insult from a rabble "whose fathers I would have disdained to put among my sheepdogs" (30:1). Once again he describes his suffering—God's cruel enmity toward him—ending his lament with a line contrasting with the conclusion of the previous picture: "My lyre is given to mourning, / my pipe to accompany weepers" (30:31).

In the last section of the soliloquy (chap. 31), Job forcefully affirms his blamelessness in a form derived from the terminal curse-sanctions of covenants. The biblical models are *Leviticus* 26 and *Deuteronomy* 28: if Israel obeys the stipulations of the Covenant, it will prosper; if not, it will suffer disaster upon disaster. Attention is directed to this traditional pattern by allusion to a "covenant" Job made with his eyes not to gaze on a maiden (31:1). In the immediate sequel he spells out the classic covenantal doctrine by which he has guided his steps: "Surely disaster is appointed for the iniquitous: / trouble for the wrongdoer" (31:3). (In the retrospective light of this conception, all of Job's speeches assume the character of a "covenant lawsuit" in reverse: man accusing God, instead of God accusing man [Israel] as in the books of the Prophets). In the thin guise of self-curses Job recites a catalogue of his virtues—the code of a nobleman who does not allow his status to weaken his solidarity with the unfortunate. The virtues come in bundles and are interrupted by an only occasional self-curse ("If I did not practice such and such a virtue, may this or that calamity overtake me"), indicating that the pattern (in which normally the curses are prominent) is more form than substance—a vehicle serving the double purpose of marking a conclusion (the function of covenant curses) and of manifesting the unbroken spirit of Job. The latter is underlined by Job's wish that his Litigant produce a bill of indictment: he would display it as an ornament, so sure is, he that it would prove him righteous!

Having played out their parts, the Friends fell silent; now Job falls silent, and the scene assumes the form it had before the dialogue began. But there is a tension in the air: will the Litigant respond?

Resolution of the tension is delayed by the sudden appearance of a new character: angry at the Friends for their inability to answer Job otherwise than by declaring him a sinner, and at Job for justifying himself against God, brash young Elihu the Buzite takes possession of the stage (chaps. 32-37). He excuses his intervention by citing the impotence of his elders and delivers himself of three highly wrought speeches, full of obscure language and not always to the point. Though insisting he will not repeat what has been said (32:14), he does go over familiar ground; new are the grandiloquence and the occasional argument in favor of positions already taken. Thus to Job's charge that God does not answer, Elihu replies (off the point) that God speaks to man through dreams and illness designed to humble man's pride and turn him from his bad course (Eliphaz said as much in 5:17-18, but without elaborating the suffering and later confession and thanksgiving of the penitent). He counters Job's complaint of God's injustice by affirming, tautologically, that the sole ruler of the earth cannot do wrong, since it is of the essence of rulership to be just. From the transcendence of God Eliphaz had argued that man's works cannot interest him (22:2-3); Job had reasoned from the same fact of transcendence that even if he sinned, it could scarcely matter to God (7:20); Elihu advances the thought that the good and evil that men do cannot affect God, but only other men. Hence—if we understand 35:9 rightly—human misery has its cause in human evil; yet God is not indifferent, and in the end he punishes the guilty. Elihu's last speech opens with an interpretation of the suffering of the virtuous as disciplinary, and concludes with a rhapsodic paean to God's greatness as evidenced in the phenomena of rain, thunder, and lightning.

Elihu has indeed championed God's cause without condemning Job (except in 34:8 Job makes common cause with the wicked); his ornate eloquence has contributed color but little substance to the debate. Critics consider his speeches redundant and hence from another hand or at least outside the original plan of the book. But if repetition is an indication of unoriginality, considerable tracts of the dialogue of Job and his Friends would have to be declared secondary. The pattern of alternating dialogue is absent in Elihu's section, but it has already lapsed in the last spell of Job's oratory. Elihu's style is different from that of his predecessors, but might not that difference be intentional, to distinguish impetuous youthfulness from more deliberative age? Our author may simply have sought another character through which to display rhetorical invention. Indeed, can a better reason be given for the extension of the dialogue for three rounds than the delight of the poet in the exercise of his gift? This very motive animates the ancient Egyptian composition called "The Eloquent Peasant," whose thematic similarity to Job has been observed: a peasant who has been robbed pleads his cause before the governor; the king, who is told of the peasant's eloquence, deliberately delays judgment of the case so as to enjoy more and more of it. By this device the author gains scope for exercising his skill in playing variations on a few themes. (A modern editor's evaluation of the piece recalls evaluations of Elihu's speeches: "The peasant's speeches are, to modern taste, unduly repetitive, with high-flown language and constant harping on a few metaphors.") Be that as it may, the unconventional representation of youth outdoing age bespeaks the author of the rest of the poem, whose hallmark is subversion of tradition. Elihu has marginally surpassed the Friends in affirming that God does speak to man, that not all suffering is punitive, and that contemplation of nature's elements opens the mind to God's greatness—a line of apology for God that does not entail blackening Job's character. We are on the way to God's answer from the storm.

The chief problem raised by God's answer to Job (chap. 38-41) is to relate the panorama it paints of God's amazing creativity to the issues the interlocutors have been wrestling with.

In opening his speech (chaps. 38-39), God exchanges roles with Job: till now, Job has demanded answers from God; now God sets unanswerable questions to Job about the foundations of the universe. Does Job know anything about the fashioning and operation of the cosmic elements—earth, sea, the underworld, and darkness? Has he knowledge of, can he control, the celestial phenomena of snow, hail, thunder, and lightning, or the constellations? From these spectacles of nature God turns to wilderness animals and their provisioning: the lions, who lie in ambush for their prey; the raven, whose young cry to God for food; the mountain goats, whose birth only God attends; the wild ass, who roams far from civilization; the wild ox, who mocks man's attempt to subjugate him; the silly ostrich; the war horse, with his uncanny lust for battle; the soaring falcon and eagle, who sight their prey from afar. None owe man anything; the ways of none are comprehended by him.

How different this survey of creation is from that of Genesis I or the hymn to nature of Psalm 104. Here man is incidental—mainly an impotent foil to God. In *Genesis* I (and its echo, *Psalms* 8) teleology pervades a process of creation whose goal and crown is man. All is directed to his benefit; the earth and its creatures are his to rule. In *Psalm* 104 nature exhibits a providential harmony of which man is an integral part. But the God of Job celebrates each act and product of his creation for itself, an independent value attesting his power and grace. Job, representing mankind, stands outside the picture, displaced from its center to a remote periphery. He who would form a proper judgment of God cannot confine himself to his relations with man, who is, after all, only one of an astonishing panoply of creatures created and sustained in ways unfathomable to the human mind.

Instead of confessing his ignorance and, by implication, his presumptuousness, in judging God, Job replies (40:3-5) that he is too insignificant to reply; that he can say no more. This response, as Saadya Gaon observed in the tenth century [in *Iyyov 'im Targum u-Ferush Ha-gaon Rabbenu Saadya*], is ambiguous: "When one interlocutor says to his partner, 'I can't answer you, 'it may mean that he acquiesces in the other's position, equivalent to 'I can't gainsay the truth'; or it may mean he feels overborne by his partner, equivalent to 'How can I answer you when you have the upper hand?' " In order to elicit an unequivocal response, God speaks again.

In language identical with that of the first speech, God declares he will put questions to Job: "Would you impugn my justice, / condemn me, that you may be right?" (40:8). Job has dwelt on the prosperity of the wicked, attributing it to divine indifference or cruelty. God invites Job to try his hand at righting wrongs, if he has the hand to do it: "Have you an arm like God's? / Can you thunder with a voice like him?" (40:9). If he can do better, God will sing his praises. Once again, Job's ignorance and impotence are invoked to disqualify him from arraigning God; only one who comprehends the vastness and complexity of God's work can pass judgment on his performance. To drive home Job's powerlessness, two monstrous animals are described that mock the Genesis notion of man's rule of terrestrial and sea creatures. Behemoth, a land animal, is briefly described: his muscles are powerful, his bones like metal bars. Leviathan, a denizen of the waters, is a living fortress, whose parts evoke shields and military formations; flames and smoke issue from him; no weapon avails against him; his tracks are supernally luminous; he lords it over the arrogant.

The effect of this parade of wonders is to excite amazement at the grandeur and exotic character of divine creativity. By disregarding man, the author rejects the anthropocentrism of all the rest of Scripture. God's governance cannot be judged by its manifestations in human society alone. Had the moral disarray evident in society been tolerated by a mere human ruler, other humans of like nature and motives would have been entitled to judge him as vicious. But no man can comprehend God, whose works defy teleological and rational categories; hence to condemn his supervision of human events because it does not conform to human conceptions of reason and justice is improper.

Man's capacity to respond with amazement to God's mysterious creativity, and to admire even those manifestations of it that are of no use or benefit to him, enables him to affirm God's work despite its deficiencies in the moral realm. Such deficiencies, like so much else in the amazing cosmos, stand outside human judgment. Chapter 28 has already anticipated the conclusion at which Job must arrive in the face of God's wonders: for mankind wisdom consists of fearing God and shunning evil; more than that he cannot know.

Job now submits unequivocally (42:2-6). He confesses his ignorance and his presumptuousness in speaking of matters beyond his knowledge. Now that he has not merely "heard of " God—that is, known of him by tradition—but also "seen" him—that is, gained direct cognition of his nature—he rejects what he formerly maintained and "is consoled for [being mere] dust and ashes" (v. 6). Lowly creature that he is, he has yet been granted understanding of the inscrutability of God; this has liberated him from the false expectations raised by the old covenant concept, so misleading to him and his interlocutors.

The Adversary has lost his wager. Throughout his trial Job has neither rejected God (he has clung to him even in despair) nor ever expressed regret for having lived righteously (cf. *Psalms* 73:13-14). He thus gave the lie to the Adversary's insinuation that his uprightness was contingent on reward. Yet this last word of the poet does not pull all things together. God's answer does not relate to the issues raised in the dialogue; it seeks rather to submerge them under higher considerations. Although the poet rejects the covenant relation between God and man with its sanctions of distributive justice, he offers no alternative. In effect, he puts the relation entirely on a footing of faith—in the language of the Adversary, "fearing God for nothing" (1:9).

The narrative epilogue (42:7-17) relates Job's rehabilitation. God reproaches Eliphaz, the chief and representative of the Friends, for not having spoken rightly about him as Job did. God thus seconds Job's protest in 13:7-10:

> Will you speak unjustly on God's behalf?
>   Will you speak deceitfully for him? . . .
> He will surely reprove you
>   if in your heart you are partial toward him.

God forbids a conception of himself as a moral accountant, according to which the Friends interpreted Job's suffering as punishment and Job ascribed injustice to God. Since the prayer of the injured on behalf of those who injured him is the most effective intercession (cf. Abraham's intercession for Abimelech, *Genesis* 20:7, 17), God orders the Friends to seek Job's intervention with him on their behalf (ironically, Eliphaz promised Job this power, 22:30). With this act of mutual reconciliation, Job is restored to his material and social position: his possessions are doubled (cf. Bildad's promise, 8:7), and he has children equal to the number of those reported dead by the messenger. Unlike 1:2, 42:13 does not state that the children "were born to him"; Nahmanides infers from this difference that the original children were restored, having been only spirited away by the Adversary—a laudably humane, if unpersuasive, piece of exegesis. The story pays unusual regard to Job's daughters, noting their incomparable beauty, their exotic names—which may be rendered "Day-bright" (so ancient tradition understood *Yemima*), "Cassia" (a perfume-herb), and "Horn of Eye-Cosmetic"—and their equalization with their brothers as heirs, an egalitarian touch worthy of our unconventional author. Job dies at a ripe old age surrounded by four generations of his family (cf. 5:26, 29:18).

Critics have deemed this conclusion, yielding as it does to the instinct of natural justice, anticlimactic and a vulgar capitulation to convention; the common reader, on the other hand, has found this righting of a terribly disturbed balance wholly appropriate. In its reversal, the conclusion is of a piece with the rest of the book, so consistently subverting expectations and traditional values. Thus the story is set in motion by the Adversary's undermining the value of covenant-keeping piety, casting doubt on its disinterestedness. This instigates the immoral exercise of dealing the deserts of the wicked to pious Job in order to try his mettle—a perverse measure that cannot be avoided if doubts about his motives are to be allayed. Job, true to his character, blesses God even in adversity; however, soon thereafter he awakens to the moral disarray in the world and comes near blasphemy by accusing God of indiscriminate cruelty. Job despairs, yet continues to look to God for vindication. The Friends came to console, but exhaust themselves in vexatious arguments with Job; seeking his repentance, they incite him to ever bolder protest. They propose to teach him traditional wisdom; he ends by teaching them the inaccessibility of true wisdom. Job calls on God to present his bill of indictment, believing and not believing he will respond, and eager to present his defense. God does actually respond, but not to Job's questions; and Job has no answer at all. God rebukes Job for presumptuousness, but he also rebukes the Friends for misrepresenting him. Finally, when Job has resigned himself to being dust and ashes in the face of the cosmic grandeur revealed to him, God reverses his misfortune and smiles on him to the end of his life.

The piquancy of these incessant turns of plot, mood, and character is heightened by the overarching ironies resulting from the union of the frame story and the dialogue. We see a handful of men striving vainly to penetrate the secret of God's providence, guessing futilely at the meaning of what they see, while we know that behind this specific case of suffering is a celestial wager. The effect of keeping the background setting and the foreground dialogue simultaneously in mind is almost vertiginous. For example, the Friends appears so far right in insisting, and Job so far wrong in denying, that God discriminates in his visitations—for a reason none can know. All are wrong in asserting that whether Job (man) sins or not is of no account to God. Job's sardonic charge that he is persecuted just because he is righteous is truer than any of the human characters can know. At the same time, the surface meaning of the dialogue is not invalidated: appearances do support Job's contention that God is indifferent to those who cling to him and smiles on the wicked; the Friends' depiction of society as a perfectly realized moral order is really nonsense. The beacon of the righteous is not hope of reward but the conviction that, for man, cosmic wisdom is summed up in the duty to fear God and shun evil, whether or not these virtues bear fruit. The misfortunes of the righteous ought not to imply a condemnation of God, in view of the grandeur and mystery of God's creative work at large.

Vacillating between the "truth" of the story and the arguments of the dialogue, the reader may be inclined to harmonize the two: the suffering of the righteous is, or may be, a test of the disinterestedness of their virtue. This of course can never be known to the sufferers or their neighbors; the case of Job is a stern warning never to infer sin from suffering (the error of the Friends), or the enmity of God toward the sufferer (the error of Job). Although such a harmonization may offer some consolation to Job-like suffering, it is not spelled out in the book. With its ironies and surprises, its claims and arguments in unresolved tension, the **Book of Job** remains the classic expression in world literature of the irrepressible yearning for divine order, baffled but never stifled by the disarray of reality.

The poetry of **Job** is a sustained manifestation of the sublime, in the classical sense of "exhibit[ing] great objects with a magnificent display of imagery and diction" and having "that force of composition . . . which strikes and overpowers the mind, which excites the passions, and which expresses ideas at once with perspicuity and elevation" [according to Robert Lowth in *Lectures on the Sacred Poetry of the Hebrews*]. It embraces an extraordinary range of objects of universal interest: emotions of serenity and terror, hope and despair; the contrasting characters of men; doubts about and affirmations of cosmic justice; the splendors and wonders of animate and inanimate nature. To be sure, these appear elsewhere in biblical literature, but only in the **Book of Job** are these expressed with such concentration, such invention and vivid imagery.

The poet makes use of the various genres of biblical lyric and sapiential poetry: the personal complaint of Psalms in Job's self-descriptions; the moral character portraits of Proverbs (the lazybones, the drunkard) in the depictions of the righteous and the wicked; the psalmic hymns in the doxologies, which in **Job** are sometimes straightforward and sometimes parodic. However, Job's brilliant descriptions of weather and animal phenomena and the evocation of man's exploration and exploitation of earth's resources

have only rudimentary antecedents in earlier biblical poetry.

Innovative imagery pervades the book: the tree cut down that renews itself from its roots (14:7-9) as a metaphoric foil for man's irrevocable death; humanity's kinship with maggots (17:14) and jackals (30:29) as an image of alienation and isolation; the congealing of milk (10:10) as a figure for the formation of the embryo; the movement of a weaver's shuttle (7:6), of a runner in flight, or of the swooping eagle (9:25-26) as similes for the speedy passage of a lifetime; God's hostility figured as an attacking army (19:12); God's absence represented in the image of a traveler's unfound goal in every direction (23:8; a striking reversal of the expression of God's ubiquity in Ps. 139:7-10).

The diction of the poems is distinguished by lexical richness, with many unique, unusual, and "foreign" expressions, lending color to the non-Israelite setting and characters. For example, *'or*, besides its normal Hebrew sense of "light," seems to bear dialectical Aramaic senses of "evening" (24:14) and "west wind" (38:24); and there are many other terms that occur only in this book. There is much expressive repetition of sound (alliteration, assonance); the explosive *p* sound, for instance, dominates 16:9-14, a passage in which Job pictures himself as a battered and shattered object of God's pitiless assaults. Verbal ambiguity is abundantly exploited: *be'efes tiqwah* in the weaving image of 7:6 can mean "without hope" or "till the thread runs out"; in 9:30-31, the opposites *bor*, "soap," and *shahat*, "muck," are homonyms of two synonyms meaning "pit," thus conveying the suggestion "out of one pit into another." Contrariwise, the same expression recurs in different contexts, effecting cohesion while at the same time producing variety: the pair "vision / dream" serves as the vehicle of oracular experience (33:15), nightmares (7:14), or a figure of ephemerality (20:8); the pair "dust (dirt) / clay" expresses the qualities of insubstantiality (4:19), lifeless malleability (10:9), worthlessness (13:12), and multitude (27:16).

What quality in poetry makes it the preferred vehicle for this author's vision? Poetry was the form taken by sapiential observation and speculation throughout the ancient Near East. With its engagement of the emotions and the imagination, it was the usual mode of persuasive discourse. Through its compression, poetry allows stark, untempered expression that, while powerful in impact, awakens the kind of careful reflection that leads to the fuller apprehension of a subject. Moreover, the density of poetic language, compelling the reader to complement, to fill in gaps, fits it peculiarly for representing impassioned discourse, which by nature proceeds in associative leaps rather than by logical development. Spontaneous debate, too, is characterized by zigzag, repetitive, and spiral movement in which sequence is determined more by word and thought association than by linearity. Someone listening in to debate must supply the connections in a manner not very different from the complementing required for the comprehension of poetry. Such passionate argument is precisely reflected in the poetry of **Job**, as each interlocutor links theme to theme without troubling to arrange them according to logical sequentiality, and by that very liberty enriching the connotations and multiplying the facets of the argument.

The poetry of *Job* is continually astonishing in its power and inventiveness. Its compression allows multiple possibilities of interpretation, corresponding to the open, unresolved tensions in the author's vision of reality. It is a beautifully appropriate vehicle for a writer bent on compelling us to see things in new ways.

Martin Buber on Job as representative of Israel (1942):

I cannot ascribe [*Job*] which clearly has only slowly grown to its present form—in its basic kernel to a time later (or earlier) than the beginning of the [Jewish] Exile. Its formulations of the question bear the stamp of an intractable directness—the stamp of a first expression. The world in which they were spoken had certainly not yet heard the answers of *Psalm* 73 or Deutero-Isaiah. The author finds before him dogmas in process of formation, he clothes them in grand language, and sets over against them the force of the new question, the question brought into being out of *experience:* in his time these growing dogmas had not yet found their decisive opponents. The book, in spite of its thorough rhetoric—the product of a long-drawn-out literary process—is one of the special events in world literature, in which we witness the first clothing of a human quest in form of speech.

It has rightly been said that behind the treatment of Job's fate in this discussion lie "very bitter experiences of a supraindividual kind." When the sufferer complains, "He hath broken me down on every side, and I am gone" (*Job* 19:10), this seems no longer the complaint of a single person. When he cries, "God delivereth me to the ungodly, and casteth me into the hands of the wicked" (16:11), we think less of the sufferings of an individual than of the exile of a people. It is true it is a personal fate that is presented here, but the stimulus to speaking out, the incentive to complaint and accusation, bursting the bands of the presentation, are the fruit of suprapersonal sufferings. Job's question comes into being as the question of a whole generation about the sense of its historic fate. Behind this "I," made so personal here, there still stands the "I" of Israel.

Martin Buber in The Dimensions of Job, *edited by Nahum N. Glatzer, Schocken Books, 1969.*

Edwin M. Good   **(essay date 1990)**

SOURCE: "Is Job Religious for Nothing?" in *In Turns of Tempest: A Reading of Job,* Stanford University Press, 1990, pp. 189-203.

[*Good is a Cameroonian-born theologian whose writings include* Irony in the Old Testament *(1965) and* Job and the Literary Task: A Response *(1973). In the following essay he offers an analysis of the first section of* The Book of Job.]

Perhaps *Job* 1-2 is a folktale. In some respects it reads like one: the "once upon a time" beginning, with its quick, deft encapsulation of the hero's circumstances and character, the formulaic structural points ("It was the day when," 1.6, 13; 2.1), the refrains of the messengers' speeches ("And I escaped all alone to tell you," 1.15, 16, 17, 19), the formal greetings between Yahweh and the Prosecutor (1.7; 2.2), the repeated formula defining Job, given by the narration and twice by Yahweh ("scrupulously moral, religious, one who avoids evil," 1.1, 8; 2.3).

The only reference to Job outside the *Book of Job* might suggest that he was the subject of a folktale. The prophet Ezekiel refers to him twice as one of the three most righteous ancient worthies: "Even if these three men—Noah, Daniel, and Job—should be in [Jerusalem], they would by their righteousness save only themselves" (*Ezekiel* 14.14; JPS). Yahweh goes further in 14.20, saying that Noah, Daniel, and Job "would save neither son nor daughter." Noah saved his sons from the Flood (*Genesis* 6-9), and if daughters-in-law counted in those days as daughters, he saved daughters too. Daniel we know not from the *Book of Daniel* in the Hebrew Bible but from Canaanite epic texts recovered since the 1920's from the ancient city of Ugarit (modern Ras Shamra) in Syria containing a tale about a king named Dan'el who has, but does not save, a son. [In an endnote, the critic adds: "For Ezekiel, spells the name in that way, *dan'ēl*, rather than *danīyyē'l* as in Daniel. Scholars agree that Ezekiel's Dan'el has nothing to do with the *Book of Daniel*, whose hero is contemporary with Ezekiel and hardly comparable to Noah and Job. The Canaanite Dan'el story (the title is usually given as *Aqhat*, the name of Dan'el's son) is translated in Coogan, *Stories from Ancient Canaan,* and in *Ancient Near Eastern Texts Relating to the Old Testament,* ed. by James B. Pritchard."] For Ezekiel, Job is the epitome of "righteousness" in the culture's lore. In our story, however, Job does not "save" either son or daughter but loses them all. There is some incongruity between Ezekiel's perception of Job and what happens in the book.

Perhaps, because we are dealing with a folk hero, we are engaged not with a folktale but with an epic. Nahum Sarna has argued [in "Epic Substratum"] that the original tale was written in poetry, a characteristic of ancient epics. Job's high social stature and gravity of circumstance, moreover, are comparable to those of an epic hero. The presence of prose, together with the brevity of these opening chapters, is the major difference between the Hebrew story and the Canaanite epic tales from which Sarna derives his analogy, and both characteristics may make us think of folk story rather than epic. The style of Job's story is pure in its simplicity, and I remain unpersuaded that it was ever poetry. [In an endnote, The critic adds: "I do not believe that the speeches in chaps. 1-2 are in poetry, disagreeing with Pope (*Job*, pp. lv-lvi), who notes, though he does not expand the point, that he has set the speeches as poetry."] As we will see later in this chapter, we are not dealing with naive, unsophisticated storytelling. If calling the story a folktale makes readers expect naiveté (and some scholars who have called it a folktale have thought it naive), it is best to call it something else. But I do not feel required to designate the genre more closely than to call it a story or narration.

The story has six episodes, the first of which is general and introductory.

1. Job's character and circumstances (1.1-5)
2. First scene in Yahweh's court (1.6-12)
3. Job's first calamity (1.13-22)
4. Second scene in Yahweh's court (2.1-7a)
5. Job's second calamity (2.7b-10)
6. The coming of the friends (2.11-13)

Episodes 1 and 6, told as omniscient narration, present a certain symmetry. The first portrays Job's character and habitual activity, including a ritual of sacrifice, and the last shows a stereotypical, ritual action of the friends.

The middle four episodes alternate between Yahweh's court and Job's troubles in the land of Uz. All four are carried by dialogue: the two scenes in Yahweh's court consist of two sets of questions and answers between Yahweh and the Prosecutor followed by an imperative spoken by Yahweh. [In an endnote, the critic adds: "See Alter, *Narrative,* chap. 4, on the ways in which narration in the Hebrew Bible frequently rides upon dialogue."] They are framed by date- and scene-setting sentences at the beginning (1.6; 2.1) and exit sentences at the end (1.12b; 2.7a). The two scenes of calamity are presented in a simpler frame: in 1.14-19, the messengers' reports form one cumulative speech, to which Job responds hymnically (v. 21); in 2.9-10, Job and his wife have one speech each. Yet these two episodes are also asymmetrical. The first calamity is told from the point of view of Job's own position, sitting at home learning the story from successive messengers. By contrast, the second calamity proceeds by objective narration combined with dialogic comment.

The balance of these middle episodes is disrupted in the move from episode 4 to episode 5. Episodes 2-4 begin with the same formula, which suggests a customary occurrence: "It was the day when." . . . They also end with similar conventional formality. The Prosecutor makes his exit from Yahweh's presence in 1.12b and 2.7a, and Job engages in conventional mourning behavior in 1.20-22. But episode 5 plunges abruptly into action with no structural prelude, dropping the regularity maintained through episodes 2-4. The new narrative technique signals that Job's second calamity presents a new set of circumstances.

Within its apparent symmetry, then, the tale drives from one situation to a wholly different one, from a beginning in what seems stability to an end in change and uncertainty. At the beginning and in both scenes in Yahweh's court, Job is described as "one who avoids evil" (*ra',* 1.1, 8; 2.3). At the end, the friends come because of "all the evil [*ra'ah*] that had come upon him" (2.11). The recurring "days" also point to changed circumstances. The "feast days" in episodes 1 and 3 (1.4, 5, 13) and the customary meeting "days" of Elohim's sons in episodes 2 and 4 (1.6; 2.1) give way at the end of episode 6 to seven days of silence (2.13), a number that echoes the annual feasts of the seven sons (1.4). The feast days have turned into death—deeply ironic if those parties of Job's children were birthday dinners—the meeting days have produced Job's suffering, and now the days pass in silence. We find not a resolution of the problem but its intensification. Evil formerly avoided is now present; days have reversed their character.

On the other hand, we might seem to see a resolution. A recurring motif in the tale is blessing (see the annotation to 1.5). Job's religiousness, a question on which much turns, consists partly in his scrupulous sacrificing on the chance that his children have sinned in blessing the deity (1.5) and partly in a conventional piety that blesses Yahweh's name and avoids sin thereby (vv. 21-22). The first scene between Yahweh and the Prosecutor turns on two allegations of the Prosecutor: that Job is religious because Yahweh has blessed him with prosperity (1.10), and that if Job should come to think that Yahweh has stopped blessing him, he will bless Yahweh in another sense (v. 11). In fact, with the calamity, Job does "bless" Yahweh (v. 21), and he avoids sin by doing so (v. 22). The second scene in Yahweh's court, like the first, centers on the Prosecutor's expectation that Job will bless Yahweh (2.5), and with Job's second calamity in episode 5, his wife urges him to "bless Elohim and die" (2.9). Job does not bless anyone and again avoids sin (2.10). [In an endnote, the critic adds: "The qualification 'did not sin *with his lips*' in 2.10 may be important. It could imply that he did sin otherwise, but nothing in the text suggests it. Yahweh himself says twice that 'there's certainly no one like him on the earth' (1.8; 2.3). At the same time, 2.10 follows 2.3, and perhaps something has happened in the interim."]

From that point of view, it seems that Job has decisively avoided whatever problem has been posed. Yet the means by which he does so is strangely reversed. Twice the Prosecutor has put Job in a situation where he is sure he will bless Yahweh; once Job has avoided difficulty by blessing, and once, it seems, he has avoided difficulty by not blessing. It is not yet clear what the problem of the story is. If it is that of an evil that a good man wishes to avoid and does not, the story deepens the problem and does not resolve it. If it is the problem of a good man who is given a religious test, the problem is resolved, or seems to be resolved. We need to circle back over the story for a closer look.

The first paragraph underscores Job's extraordinary qualities. He is fecund and rich, which in his culture signified excellence. Many children—ten are many and in a decimal system are symbolically "perfect"—promise prosperity in old age. Children assured retirement security in those days, unless one had much wealth of one's own. Job has it, expressed again in stylized perfect numbers: thousands of sheep and camels that add up to ten thousand, hundreds of oxen and asses that add up to ten hundred, and—a nice breaking of the numerical symmetry—"a great many slaves."

There is more than external wealth and prosperity. We know that Job is "scrupulously moral, religious, one who avoids evil" (1.1), and in the second paragraph we see something of what that means. His family is unusual. That seven brothers would enjoy one another's company enough to have regular parties together might not seem surprising, though the fact, stated baldly, proposes a familial harmony that cannot be unremarkable. Quite exceptionally, the parties include the sisters. In those days one did not, it seems, deal socially with women, even one's sisters, as equals. The siblings' harmony appears nearly revolutionary.

Yet the oddly negative factor turns up. Job is so scrupulous that he wishes to forestall any religious fault that his children might incur in their feasts. "Perhaps my children have blessed Elohim sinfully in their hearts" (1.5). For the ancient Hebrews as for the Greeks, the heart was the seat not of emotion but of thought, decision, and intention. [In an endnote, the critic adds: "Pedersen (*Israel,*) refers to the heart as the operative soul, the person in action, and he believes that thinking and deciding too narrowly describe the heart's functions. But 'thought' seems most accurate if we do not confine it to its narrowest logical sense."] It had what we think of as the brain's function (the emotion we feel in the heart, they located in the bowels). They did not, moreover, distinguish an inner, genuine self (the heart) from an outer, ostensible self (the body, perhaps). Job worries, then, not about internal sin as opposed to external but about intended sin as opposed to inadvertent sin. The children may be purified of such thoughts by the religious intervention of the proper sacrifice.

What does that mean? Evidently Job is, in our day's jargon, a caring father. Equally evidently, he is entirely confident only of his own piety, not of his children's. If inadvertent sin concerns him, he need only remind his children to make the proper sacrifices. But he does it for them, apparently not trusting them to think of such precautions or to safeguard their intentions. His only thought about their intention is that they might "have blessed sinfully." An ambiguity is present. "Bless," as I said in the annotation, is only one possible meaning of the word (*brk*). Another is "curse," which, combined with "sin" (*ht'*), seems on the surface the better meaning. We are faced here, and in several places in this part of the story, by a crucial word with diametrically opposed, simultaneous meanings.

Job further assumes that his sacrifices, the expiations of a scrupulously moral and religious father, will ward off the punishments for intentional sin from his children. The father's religious deed produces the religious effect on the children, without their needing to do anything of their own. That means, I think, that Job's religion is a magical one. I do not criticize that but only label it. [See Good's chapter on Job in *Irony* for further discussion]. Every religion I know anything about is magical, assuming that certain religious actions, whether external or internal, physical or spiritual, if done properly, produce certain religious effects.

The first episode, then, exhibits a hero remarkable spiritually and materially, and religiously conventional, however profoundly if not excessively scrupulous. The religiosity that Job employs in 1.5 sets up the situation that arises in the next episode.

The scene changes to the divine court on assembly day. Just as Job's sons are in close contact with their father, so are the "sons of Elohim," [In an endnote the critic comments: "The implicit polytheism may trouble some readers. I cannot in all conscience claim that the **Book of Job** is monotheistic."] especially the one with the Hebrew title

haśśatan, "the Satan," which I have translated "the Prosecutor". He is not the Devil, not a principle of evil, but a member of the divine court whose apparent duty is to bring malefactors to the bar of divine justice. He is, then, no interloper in the assemblage of Elohim's sons but someone with every right to be there.

Yahweh evidently thinks so. He asks pleasantly after the Prosecutor's career, and the latter gives a curiously evasive answer. Can he conceal anything from Yahweh? Well, yes. Not only does this story imply polythesim, it also assumes no divine omniscience. Yahweh is interested less in the details of the Prosecutor's comings and goings than in one fact: there is a person with whom the Prosecutor will never have professional dealings. Yahweh incautiously boasts: "Have you given thought to ['set your heart on'] my servant Job? There's certainly no one like him on the earth, a scrupulously moral man, religious, one who avoids evil" (1.8). The description advances beyond what we have seen before. In 1.3 Job was "one of the greatest people of the East"; here there is "no one like him on the earth."

Both Yahweh and Job deal with hearts. Job made sacrifices on the possibility that something untoward had happened in his children's hearts, but he did not ask them about their hearts. Yahweh asks the Prosecutor about his heart: "Have you set your heart on my servant Job?" The Prosecutor's function is to think about people, to decide whether their faults, including those most concealed, deserve punishment. Yahweh wonders whether he has done his job and suggests that someone is proof against his investigations.

The Prosecutor responds with some heat. "Is Job religious for nothing?" (1.9) The rhetorical question implies a negative answer: "Of course not; he is religious for some reason." Yahweh has made sure that he would be religious by "hedging around him" with protection, by "blessing" him (*brk*—that word again), so that "his possessions burst out over the earth" (v. 10). The Prosecutor exaggerates Job's situation with the contradictory images of a protective hedge and of possessions bursting out. It is unfair of Yahweh to ensure by his own efforts so responsive a piety and then to boast about Job as if the man were responsible for it. The whole basis of the divine government of the world is challenged. If Yahweh is really in charge—and the crucial verb "bless" underscores that he is—then human beings have no possibility of responsibility. If they can be responsible, Yahweh is not in charge.

The Prosecutor has a still more powerful way of challenging the divine claims. He proposes that the deity "touch all [Job] has" (v. 11) and goes on: "If he doesn't curse you (*brk*) to your face—." Rhetorically, that clause is a curse upon the speaker, with the result clause omitted. Yahweh's hand is drastically forced. Faced with a curse (If A does not happen, may a horrible B happen to me), Yahweh has no choice. In that world, a spoken curse was an objective event, which ineluctably and with no moral entailments set in train a succession of events that had to work itself out to its end. By the risky expedient of putting himself under a curse, the Prosecutor has tied Yahweh in a knot from which only Job can extricate him. It is a crucial addition to the chain of curses and blessings I noted above.

This reading overturns the long interpretive tradition around this transaction between Yahweh and the Prosecutor, which has seen the transaction either as a test that Yahweh is persuaded to permit or as a wager between him and the Prosecutor. The tradition has been bedeviled, moreover, by reading the Prosecutor's remark in terms not of its own rhetorical form but of its paraphrase into an "equivalent." "If Job does not curse you to your face" equals "Job certainly will curse you to your face." For reasons that escape me, most interpreters have missed the additional meaning present in the sentence: "or else I will be cursed." If inflicting suffering upon Job is a test, it is meaningless, because Yahweh was seduced by the Prosecutor into permitting it (which lends a certain plausibility to identifying him as the Devil). If Job suffers because of a mere wager, the suffering is even more meaningless. Betting plays too close to the edges of blind chance, and our culture distrusts that. Suffering resulting from an illegitimate test or from a wager is by definition unjust. Nothing with the deity's fingerprints on it is supposed to be unjust.

When the sufferings result from the Prosecutor's curse *upon himself,* the situation is changed. The curse does not bind Yahweh in moral problems at all; Yahweh is helpless to stop the working of the curse, though he can, it seems, put limits on the worker ("but on him don't put your hand," 1.12). And the Prosecutor puts himself at hazard with his curse. We are not dealing with an underhanded trick of a Devil or with an unobservant deity who allows his most faithful servant to be the object of an experiment. We are dealing with a frontal challenge to magical religion, a religion that allows Yahweh's favorite to be religious for his own ends, not for Yahweh's. In one sense, the Prosecutor is angry not at the righteous Job but at Yahweh's system of order.

I cannot overemphasize the point that the transaction between Yahweh and the Prosecutor is not "I bet he'll do it" or "Let's see if he flunks." The Prosecutor could take no more serious step than the curse, and he himself stands to lose the most. He leaves unspoken the specific result that he calls down on himself, as is usual in such self-curses, but it cannot be trivial, and the lack of a stated result may be more powerful than its presence. The next loser is likely to be Yahweh, if Job hurls a curse in Yahweh's face. We do not yet know what Job stands to lose.

We must pause here over two things. I have spoken as if the Prosecutor expects from Job a *curse* similar to his own. We are faced again with that ubiquitous word *brk,* which inconveniently refuses to bear but one meaning. The Prosecutor says, "If he does not *brk* you to your face—." Everyone thinks that *brk* here is a euphemism for "curse," just as everyone thinks the word had to mean that back in verse 5. But no one blinks at interpreting the same verb as "bless" in the preceding sentence. We must relax our certainty that we know what this word means.

The other point is that the ambiguous, indeterminate *brk* appears in a sentence that is formed as a curse. Of that there is no question. We may not with the same confidence be able to assert the English equivalents of all of the words. "If he does not *brk* you to your face—."

Observe the next exchange. "Put out your hand and touch all he has," says the Prosecutor (v. 11). "All that he has is in your hand," replies Yahweh (v. 12). The Prosecutor wants Yahweh's hand to do the deed, but Yahweh shifts it to the Prosecutor's hand and imposes a limitation: "On him don't put your hand" (v. 12). The limitation is formal, indeed redundant; the Prosecutor has already specified what is to be touched: "all he has" (v. 11). Perhaps Yahweh states the limitation to remind the Prosecutor who gives the orders in this universe. The command might seem a bit hollow, given that Yahweh and his power are under constraint of a curse. Still, the formality of rank is observed, and the universe is not yet absurd.

Are we sufficiently on our guard to realize how ominous the opening of episode 3 is? "It was the day" (v. 13)—the formula that began episode 2. It is the prime heir's feast day. We can easily let the fact pass as mere fact, the formulaic beginning lulling us into inattention and its significance not sinking in until the terrible message of verse 19. Yet the narrative technique continues to mask the fact. We, the readers, hear the series of messages from Job's point of view, know only what Job knows. We are drawn inside the story and into its ignorances.

The series of messages, bursting over Job like those fireworks where one shower of stars explodes into another and that into a third, is notable both for its patterned formality and for its completeness. In the first and third messages, the agents of destruction are marauding neighbor peoples; in the second and fourth, they are natural phenomena thought of in that world as being under the deity's control. The messenger calls the lightning that burned up the sheep and the servants "Elohim's fire" (v. 16); the messenger cannot know that it is from the Prosecutor, and I suspect that we, being immersed in the story, forget it. The first and fourth messages have identical structures: (1) description of the situation; (2) narration of the catastrophe; (3) death of the *ne'arīm;* (4) escape. The second and third messages omit the description and begin immediately with the catastrophe. Such crossing and interlocking repetitions are the force of this formulaic style. The repetitious patterning makes the statements so terrible.

The catastrophes are total. In the first three, Job's wealth is taken, category by category (the elimination of his slaves is spread over all the events), in the fourth, his posterity is wiped out. Only in the fourth is the messenger allowed the exclamation of emotion: *hinnēh,* "Ah!" (v. 19). The very formula leaves us with a momentary ambiguity: "It [the house] fell on the *ne'arīm,* and they're dead." Each successive messenger has used *ne'arīm* to mean Job's slaves who were killed (vv. 15, 16, 17). The fourth messenger has stated the circumstance, that Job's sons and daughters were having their feast, and when he says that the house fell on the *ne'arīm,* perhaps we are at first relieved: "Oh, only the slaves." The relief is momentary, for we quickly realize that *ne'arīm* can include the sons, and we must then assume that here, unusually, it also includes the daughters. On further reflection, we may be ashamed that we have underplayed the humanity of slaves. Perhaps the messenger is being kind to Job, muting the impact of the bald statement by his formulaic repetition.

Are we prepared for Job's response? It is so utterly conventional, and the little hymn he sings (v. 21) is so banally repetitive. Verbal repetition ("Naked . . . and naked") and the repetitive word order (adjective-verb-adverbial expression) call attention to the opposed verbs ("came out . . . return") in the first two lines. The antonymous verbs in the third line ("gave . . . took") emphasize the repeated divine name. The final blessing formula, at last, puts the lie to the Prosecutor's curse in the same terms. "If he does not *brk* you—" said the Prosecutor. Job says, "May Yahweh's name be *mebōrak.*" There is that verb again, and perhaps we are too sure that it means "blessed" here.

Job's actions and words are completely appropriate. He fulfills all of the acts expected of a mourner, tearing his robe, shaving his head, falling prostrate on the ground, singing a hymn. It is exactly what he ought to do. Conventionalities are the most important religious acts, because they channel responses to unusual events and prevent them from overwhelming people. That is what religion is for. Job's mourning behavior, however formalized and conventional, has stood him in the best possible stead. He has avoided "sin" (v. 22), and Yahweh's boast has been vindicated. Now perhaps we will find out the unspoken result clause of the Prosecutor's curse.

Instead, we find the Prosecutor among Elohim's sons on the next assembly day (2.1). The god still has his sons, though Job has lost his. What happened to the curse? Was its unspoken result so mild as to leave its object undamaged? Or did the catastrophe drop between the two senses of *brk?* "If he does not *brk* you to your face—" said the Prosecutor. When Job said, "May Yahweh's name be *mebōrak,*" he did *brk* Yahweh, whatever the Prosecutor might have meant. Magic is magic, the right word was said, and no catastrophe need befall the Prosecutor.

The preliminaries identical to those in 1.6-8 passed, Yahweh adds to his previous description of Job the triumphant statement of his success: "He is still holding to his integrity, even though you urged me against him to swallow him up for nothing" (2.3). Three points of this speech need attention. Job's "integrity" (*tummah*) is etymologically related to his scrupulosity. . . . Job's basic character has not changed, and Yahweh still boasts about him. Second, Yahweh talks as if *he* had done the deed against Job at the Prosecutor's instigation, doing so with a nice pun on *haśśatan* in "you urged me" . . . . Third, it was "for nothing" (*hinnam*), a word the Prosecutor used in 1.9: "Is Job religious *hinnam,* for nothing?" Repeating the word, Yahweh turns it back on the Prosecutor: Job did not do his religion "for nothing," but you did something against him "for nothing."

The Prosecutor's response, like his earlier one, is heated. "Skin up to skin!" There seems to be scorn in that strange, probably proverbial statement, and beyond that it is difficult to determine what is in it. Most scholars propose variants on the notion of equal exchange. The preposition (*be'ad,* "up to") refers to boundaries, signifying a different idea of exchange. The Prosecutor uses it in his next sentence: "Everything the man has he will give over, right up to [*be'ad*] his life." It is not merely equal exchange. Job cannot give anything equivalent to his skin, for there is nothing equivalent to it. The limit on what Job can give in exchange for his life is his life. "Skip up to skin," then, means that the point at which you stop paying for skin is the point at which the price demanded is skin. Job will give anything short of life to remain alive—to give up life to stay alive is self-evidently absurd.

Now the Prosecutor's proposal is more drastic: "Touch his bone and his flesh"—his very person, his boundary of possible exchange, his life. And again the same self-curse: "If he doesn't *brk* you to your face—."

For the second time, the Prosecutor lays himself on the line, and again the operative word is that ambiguous *brk.* Again the situation is not tainted with morality or its absence; a curse on oneself is too serious for that. Does Job's earlier survival with his piety intact make us expect that it will triumph a second time, or do we expect him to fail? Either is possible.

As before, Yahweh shifts the deed to the Prosecutor's hands and emphasizes his own proviso, implied in "right up to his life." "Protect his life" is more than the rather inactive "spare his life" in most translations. The verb *šmr* has to do with guarding, and the Prosecutor is being told not merely to avoid killing Job but positively to guard him, indeed, to watch over him. That may be a kindly proviso. At the least Job is to remain alive. Yet we will see later that Job thinks the god watches him more closely than he likes, and he objects to the scrutiny. The lurking feeling remains that, though Yahweh cannot refuse the curse, his limitation on the Prosecutor's execution of it can be interpreted ironically as an effort to maintain the show of his own scrupulosity. He does not refuse to allow Job's suffering, and he surely does not expect the Prosecutor to slide away from the issue. Given the miscarriage of the Prosecutor's prior curse, a second following on it is nearly predictable. At least, if Yahweh cannot predict it, we must dismiss any notion of divine omniscience from the story. In any case, he does not object to the Prosecutor's touching Job's "bone and his flesh."

The catastrophe occurs, and Job is smitten with personal suffering. We might think the order of events curious, tending as we do to think of physical suffering as having less magnitude than mental or psychic suffering. Yet the story clearly proposes a crescendo of difficulty, and Job's suffering in his own person implies a greater pain than the psychic suffering he has endured at the deaths of his children.

Mental suffering is also involved, however. Job's scraping himself with a broken sherd of pottery to alleviate his pain (v. 8) is one sign. There is very little dignity in scraping one's horrid sores with a dirty potsherd. Moreover, he sits not in the midst of loving family and attentive friends, but as an outcast from social contact, in the ash heap, the garbage dump (he will lament that with vivid images in chap. 30). There are no hymns in Job's mouth this time.

Now we hear, for the only time, a character whose implied

presence is very strong, both in this part of the story and at its end: Job's wife (2.9). Her explicit presence is rather meager. Job will refer to her in 19.17 as disliking his breath, and she is a strange part of one of his self-curses in 31.10. Otherwise, she is the mother finally of twenty children. Her one line of dialogue has not made her a favorite with readers of the book: "You're still holding to your integrity? Curse [*brk*] Elohim and die?" The question repeats word for word what Yahweh had said about Job to the Prosecutor (2.3), and the imperative urges Job to do both what the Prosecutor has cursed himself about and what Job worried in 1.5 that his children might have done, to "*brk* Elohim."

The first sentence, which most interpreters translate as a question, contains no interrogative mark and could as well be the statement "You're still holding to your integrity." If the sentence is understood positively, as it is when Yahweh says it, the imperative *barēk* might very well mean something positive. If the first sentence expresses sarcasm, *bark* is negative. That ambiguous verb allows several alternative readings of the second sentence: farewell: Say goodbye to Elohim and die; rebellion: Throw the whole thing in Elohim's face and take the consequence of death; encouragement: Go on holding to your integrity, stand fast in your piety even to death; pity: Curse Elohim and be released from your suffering.

Job's response makes clear that he hears a negative meaning: "You're talking like a fool" (v. 10). He would not say that if he thought his wife were being supportive—unless his own mind has changed drastically since he said, "May Yahweh's name be blest" (1.21). Given the pain that has intervened since that hymn, it is quite possible that he has changed. We must investigate the next sentence: "We receive good from Elohim and do not receive evil."

As far as I know, I alone have translated this sentence as an indicative. Everyone else makes it an interrogative: "Should we accept only good from God and not accept evil?" [*Tanakh: A New Translation of the Holy Scriptures According to the Traditional Hebrew Text*]. That is an interpretive decision, not a translational one. The Hebrew sentence has no interrogative marker, but one may legitimately translate it interrogatively if one thinks that the question gives the most sensible meaning.

The sentence allows at least three understandings. As a rhetorical question it has one meaning, and as a statement it acquires two more. The question proposes that it is irrational to accept what is pleasant from the deity and to refuse what is unpleasant. Both "good" and "evil" are to be expected and accepted, and one does not "curse Elohim" but "blesses" him for either, as Job did in 1.21. Self-evidently, the deity is the author of both good and evil, and one ought not be surprised to receive either at his hands. According to the interrogative interpretation, the world and the god's actions have no clear moral structure, but the god is in charge of all that happens in the world.

If the sentence is a statement, it may have two other meanings. Statement 1 is that, because humans receive only good from the deity and not evil, such evil as there is must come not from the deity but from some other source.

There is no single origin of all events, and the god is not in command. Statement 2 is that, because everything humans receive from the deity is good, not evil, any unpleasantness, being from Elohim, is good, however contrary to appearances. In either case, there is no reason to "curse Elohim" for it. Under Statement 1 Elohim is not responsible for the evil; under Statement 2 the apparent evil is not to be understood as evil. The two statements hold as self-evident that the deity has nothing to do with evil. Statement 1 maintains the god's moral purity but denies him total control of the world. Statement 2 maintains that, despite evidence to the contrary, the god controls the world, and the world is nothing but good.

That everything that happens comes from the deity was a common assumption in the book's world. If Job intends the question or the second statement, he shares that assumption. Yet the story lays a question against it, by showing us what Job does not know, that this evil has come not from Yahweh but from the Prosecutor. What has happened as a result of the Prosecutor's self-curse is not necessarily attributable to Yahweh, even if Yahweh accepts the blame, as he does implicitly in 2.3.

Whatever may be the import of Job's statements, the narration shows that he avoids sin again—with his lips. I have already referred to the question whether that specification glances sidelong at the integrity of his inward disposition. "Job did not sin with his lips" may suggest that he sinned with something else. On the other hand, the only thing Job is portrayed as doing besides talk is scraping himself with a potsherd. Surely he could not sin doing that. Thus "Job did not sin with his lips" refers to the only significant thing he has done, and it could mean that he did not sin at all. To be sure, Job, might have had a sinful thought that did not pass his lips as words. Yet the story's only apparent reference to Job's inner thoughts, in 1.5, does not specify that Job "said" those words within himself. It seems that the story is not concerned with the hero's inward, unexpressed thoughts. But suddenly that casual, passing phrase "with his lips" has become centrally important, and ambiguous in terms of the Prosecutor's curse, which galvanized all of this action.

At least Job has not cursed Yahweh to his face, though his wife has urged him to do so, and the provocation has been great. More than that: in this episode he has not used the crucial verb *brk* at all, in any of its senses. The Prosecutor, it appears, has failed, and because we see and hear no more of him, we may suppose that whatever catastrophe he called down on himself in his curse came about. His disappearance has greatly troubled some interpreters. But if we take his self-curse seriously, as I believe we must, his absence is not strange. The curse eventuated, by implication, in his banishment or destruction.

It is necessary to look back at the problem of blessing and curse, especially but not solely as it is embodied in that ambivalent Hebrew word *brk*. The fact that at every occurrence the verb may mean "bless" or "curse" or both at the same time strains every unambiguous interpretation of the story. The blessing/cursing is central to it, carries the episodes from one place to another, motivates nearly everything that is done, both as to the words that appear in the text and as to the verbal actions the characters take. For example, the conjunction of *brk* with *ht'* in 1.5 might require that *brk* mean "curse," yet I think it plausible to join *ht'* and *brk* in a hendiadys meaning something like "sinful blessing," intending the wrong deed despite using the right words, or using the wrong words while intending the right deed. If *ht'* means "to miss," as it sometimes does (*Proverbs* 8.36; *Job* 5.24), the sentence might be translated, "Perhaps my children have missed blessing [failed to bless] Elohim in their hearts." It seems possible to consider all three ideas simultaneously.

It is easy to take as self-evident that *mebōrak* in the hymnic context of 1.21 must mean "bless." Indeed, that is the sense that the line takes best. Still, the hymn emphasizes the duality of the divine activity, "giving and taking," and the duality of *brk* mirrors on the human level the deity's duality. I twist about through this difficulty not to propose that the meaning of *brk* evaporates into nothing, but rather to help readers liberate their imaginations, wherever the word appears, to focus on its depth, not its shallowness, on its multiplicity, not its illusory simplicity. The very centrality of *brk* prevents smug certainty that we know the meaning of this story. It means in addition to our knowing, and perhaps in spite of and in opposition to it.

Some interpreters believe that Eliphaz, Bildad, and Zophar were introduced into the story when the poetic dialogue was composed, in order to provide a transition to the dialogue. They must somehow be gotten on stage. To say that the friends appear in the story only to be in the dialogue, however, is to attribute more than we can be sure of to the intention of an author whom we cannot consult. I do not know whether Eliphaz, Bildad, and Zophar were in the original story or not, having no access to that "original." The story we read now introduces them by the device of their hearing about evil (*ra'ah*) and, being friends (*rē'īm*), deciding to come. The pun is justification enough, and we need no permissions from an author's supposed intention.

What kind of gesture do they make toward a man otherwise isolated from human contact, who sits on his ash heap with only a seemingly unsupportive wife for company? Surely their coming to "console and comfort him" is friendly. On the other hand, their gestures in verse 12, weeping, tearing their robes (compare 1.20), and sprinkling dust on top of their heads, are those of mourning the dead, which would hardly encourage a man in pain. If Moses Buttenwieser is right that these gestures ward off from the friends the curse they perceive has fallen on Job, the ritual puts distance between the friends and Job. And though they are at least present for those seven days and nights of silence, the silence itself may signify another funeral rite.

Still, they have come because of evil (2.11), and evil was what Job so assiduously avoided. Now he has it, and the formalities of mourning underscore the fact. They have "raised their eyes" to see, and seeing have not recognized, so they have "raised their voices, weeping." Job is, it seems, as good as dead, even though he has not cursed Elohim.

The story, then, both resolves and does not resolve the issue it raises. The danger that Job might curse Yahweh is past. The Prosecutor has been defeated, and his forthright challenge, "Is Job religious for nothing?" (1.9) has been met. Job, it seems, *is* religious for nothing, holds to his integrity and to his piety even when the magic goes out of his life. He apparently requires neither special hedges as protection nor evidences of wealth and prosperity to persuade him to do religiously what he is supposed to do. With the Prosecutor's disappearance, the debate in Yahweh's court about Job's piety appears to be settled.

Yet not every loose thread is tied. Evil, formerly absent from Job's life, is now present. The friends have yet to begin their consoling and comforting, and there is the rising tension of those seven days and nights of silence. The debate in the land of Uz about the divine control of the world has barely begun.

FURTHER READING

Besserman, Lawrence L. *The Legend of Job in the Middle Ages.* Cambridge: Harvard University Press, 1979, 177 p.
    Traces the development of the legend of Job during the Middle Ages.

Bloom, Harold, ed. *The Book of Job.* New York: Chelsea House Publishers, 1988, 152 p.
    Collection of critical essays on *The Book of Job* with an introduction by Bloom.

Borges, Jorge Luis. "The Book of Job." In *Borges and His Successors: The Borgesian Impact on Literature and the Arts,* edited by Edna Aizenberg, pp. 263-75. Columbia: University of Missouri Press, 1990.
    Considers three significant interpretations of *The Book of Job*: as a "fable of stoicism," an examination of the origin of evil, and an illustration of "the inscrutability of God and the universe."

Brandon, S. G. F. "The Book of Job: Its Significance for the History of Religions." *History Today* XI, No. 8 (August 1961): 547-54.
    Offers a historical discussion of *The Book of Job,* asserting that the work "illustrates mankind's earliest attempt to discuss the problem of innocent suffering in relation to the idea of a just and omnipotent deity."

Cook, Albert. "Job: The Root of the Thing Is Found in Me." In his *The Root of the Thing: A Study of Job and The Song of Songs,* pp. 11-99. Bloomington: Indiana University Press, 1968.
    Includes discussion of the concepts of integrity, emotion, parallelism, language, and imagery in *The Book of Job.*

Daiches, David. "The Book of Job: God under Attack." In his *God and the Poets: The Gifford Lectures, 1983,* pp. 1-25.
    Discusses the themes of divine justice and the problem of evil in *The Book of Job.*

Dillon, E. J. "The Poem of Job." In his *The Sceptics of the Old Testament: Job, Koheleth, Agur,* pp. 1-84. London: Isbister and Company, 1895.

Offers an analysis of *The Book of Job,* including discussion of the date of the work, the structure of the text, theological and philosophical implications of the work, and Hebrew philosophy.

Driver, Samuel Rolles, and Gray, George Buchanan. *A Critical and Exegetical Commentary on The Book of Job: Together with a New Translation.* New York: Charles Scribner's Sons, 1921, 360 p.

Offers detailed information concerning the origin and history of *The Book of Job.*

Feuer, Lewis S. "The Book of Job: The Wisdom of Hebraic Stoicism." In *Biblical v. Secular Ethics: The Conflict,* pp. 79-97, edited by R. Joseph Hoffmann and Gerald A. Larue. Buffalo, N.Y.: Prometheus Books, 1988.

Argues that "[the] great contribution of the Book of Job to wisdom is that it refuted utterly the theology of guilt that the prophets advocated."

Fisch, Harold. "Job: Tragedy Is Not Enough." In his *Poetry with a Purpose: Biblical Poetics and Interpretation,* pp. 26-42. Bloomington: Indiana University Press, 1988.

Considers the question of whether *The Book of Job* should be considered a tragedy.

Froude, James Anthony. "The Book of Job." In his *Short Studies on Great Subjects,* Vol. I, pp. 281-338. London: Longmans, Green, and Co., 1892.

Discusses the origin and major themes of *The Book of Job.*

Glatzer, Nahum N. *The Dimensions of Job: A Study and Selected Readings.* New York: Shocken Books, 1969, 310 p.

Presents critical essays on *The Book of Job* from the perspectives of Judaic, Christian, and Humanist traditions. Nahum includes discussions of the issue of theodicy, the ways of God, and lessons concerning faith in *The Book of Job,* by such critics as Martin Buber, Ernest Renan, J. G. Herder, G. K. Chesterton, and G. W. F. Hegel.

Good, Edwin M. "Job: The Irony of Reconciliation." In his *Irony in the Old Testament,* pp. 196-240. Philadelphia: The Westminster Press, n.d.

Considers ironic aspects of *The Book of Job*'s depiction of suffering, the friends of Job, and God.

Henry, H. T. "Mediæval Comment on Job IV:12." *American Catholic Quarterly Review* 42 (1 July 1971): 371-96.

Presents an overview of significant medieval commentary on *The Book of Job,* focusing on translations and interpretations of *Job* IV:12.

Janzen, J. Gerald. In his *Interpretation: A Bible Commentary for Teaching and Preaching: Job.* Atlanta: John Knox Press, 1985, 269 p.

Offers detailed chronological commentary on the text of *The Book of Job.*

Jung, C. G. *Answer to Job.* The Collected Works of C. G. Jung, Vol. 11, Bollingen Series XX. Princeton: Princeton University Press, 1973, 121 p.

Addresses the problems of evil and man's ambiguous image of an omnipotent God.

Kallen, Horace M. *The Book of Job as a Greek Tragedy.* 1918. Reprint. New York: Hill and Wang, 1959, 163 p.

Attempts to demonstrate that *The Book of Job* is drama in the tradition of Greek tragedy.

Kraeling, Emil G. *The Book of the Ways of God.* New York: Charles Scribner's Sons, 1938, 270 p.

Provides an interpretive and exegetical overview of *The Book of Job.*

Lowth, Robert. "Lecture XXXIII, 'The Poem of Job Not a Perfect Drama'." In *Eighteenth-Century Critical Essays,* Vol. II, edited by Scott Elledge, pp. 695-703. Ithaca, N.Y.: Cornell University Press, 1961.

Examines the form and design of *The Book of Job* and argues that the work should not be interpreted as a tragic drama.

Pack, Robert. "Betrayal and Nothingness." In his *The Long View: Essays on the Discipline of Hope and Poetic Craft,* pp. 251-76. Amherst: The University of Massachusetts Press, 1991.

Presents a comparative examination of the motif of nothingness in *The Book of Job* and *King Lear.*

Penchansky, David. *The Betrayal of God: Ideological Conflict in Job.* Louisville, Ky.: Westminster/John Knox Press, 1990, 124 p.

Examines compositional aspects of *Job* and explores the idea that "*Job* embodies a powerful example of the disparate text, an act of literature that is characteristically unstable, a place of conflict."

Rowley, H. H. "The Book of Job and Its Meaning." In his *From Moses to Qumran: Studies in the Old Testament,* pp. 141-83. New York: Association Press, 1963.

Examines major themes within *The Book of Job,* and concludes that the author's intent was to depict suffering as a path to "enrichment of the fellowship of God."

Safire, William. *The First Dissident: The Book of Job in Today's Politics.* New York: Random House, 1992, 305 p.

Considers Job as a prototype of the political dissident, exploring parallels between the work and modern political situations.

Scherer, Paul, and Terrien, Samuel, eds. "The Book of Job." In *The Interpreter's Bible,* Vol. III, edited by George Arthur Buttrick and Nolan B. Harmon, pp. 877-905. Nashville: Abingdon Press, 1954.

Presents a critical overview of *The Book of Job,* discussing the book's literary form, exegetical background, date, language, poetic structure, and theological significance. Includes a bibliography.

Snaith, Norman H. *Studies in Biblical Theology: The Book of Job: Its Origin and Purpose,* second series. Naperville, Ill.: Alec R. Allenson, n.d., 116 p.

Presents a critical analysis of *The Book of Job* and argues that the book is the work of a single author.

Sparks, George Downing. "The Hebrew Prometheus; or, The Book of Job." *The Sewanee Review* XI, No. 1 (January 1903): 49-63.

Interprets *The Book of Job* as a poem "charged with the spirit of revolt."

Stevenson, William Barron. *The Poem of Job: A Literary Study with a New Translation.* Rev. ed. London: Oxford University Press, 1947, 123 p.

Focuses on the poetic section of *The Book of Job,* discussing the thematic development of the poem and considering its literary merit.

Tsevat, Matitiahu. "The Meaning of the Book of Job." In *Hebrew Union College Annual,* edited by Elias L. Epstein, pp. 73-106. Cincinnati: Hebrew Union College–Jewish Institute of Religion, 1966.

> Examines structure and themes within *The Book of Job.*

"The Book of Job." In *Westminster Review* IV (July & October, 1853): 417-50.

> Evaluates German contributions to criticism of *The Book of Job.*

Wiesel, Elie. "Job: Our Contemporary." In his *Messengers of God: Biblical Portraits and Legends,* pp. 211-35. New York: Summit Books, 1976.

> Interprets the figure of Job as a personification of "man's eternal quest for justice and truth."

Wilcox, John T. *The Bitterness of Job: A Philosophical Reading.* Ann Arbor: The University of Michigan Press, 1989, 243 p.

> Discusses origins and structure, the speeches of God, and meaning in *The Book of Job.*

The Dream of the Rood

c. Eighth Century

Old English poem.

INTRODUCTION

The Dream of the Rood has been heralded by scholars as the finest expression of the Crucifixion theme in Old English poetry. Though it focuses on a motif common in Old English poetry, *The Dream of the Rood* is unique in describing it from the viewpoint of the Cross and within the context of a dream vision. The poem thus becomes a philosophical one, and, as John V. Fleming has asserted, "the vehicle of an ascetical-theological doctrine which sketches in a brilliantly imaginative way the aspirations of the monastic cadre of Anglo-Saxon society." Although it is only 156 lines long, its depth and complexity have made *The Dream of the Rood* a popular topic of critical study in the twentieth century.

Plot and Major Characters

Characteristic of Old English poetry, *The Dream of the Rood* is divided into three parts: the Dreamer's initial reaction to his vision of the Cross, the monologue of the Rood describing the Crucifixion, and the Dreamer's conversion and resolution to seek the salvation of the Cross. The poem opens with the vision of the Dreamer, which establishes the framework for the rest of the poem. He sees the Cross being raised up, covered in gold and jewels, yet he notices a stain of blood on its side. The Rood begins to speak and recounts its experience as an instrument in the Crucifixion of Christ. The Cross recalls how it was cut down in the forest and taken by its enemies to support criminals, then details its emotions as it realizes it is to be the tree on which Christ will be crucified. The Rood and Christ become one in the portrayal of the Passion—they are both pierced with nails, mocked and tortured, and finally killed and buried; soon after, like Christ, the Cross is resurrected, then adorned with gold and silver. The Cross announces that because of its suffering and obedi-

ence, it will be honored above all other trees; it then commands the Dreamer to tell others what he has seen and heard. In the end, the Dreamer's hope of a heavenly home is renewed and he vows to seek again the glorious Rood.

Major Themes

Many critics have noted the poet's use of heroic diction and imagery in *The Dream of the Rood* and the representation of the Crucifixion as a battle. The poet develops the theme of triumph achieved through suffering as both the Cross and Christ undergo a transformation from defeat to victory. Bernard F. Huppé has summarized this view, remarking that "the Crucifixion is pictured as a battle and both Christ and the Cross as warriors, whose deaths are victories, and whose burials are preludes to the triumph of their Resurrections." Scholars assert, however, that this heroic treatment of the theme of the Crucifixion was unique for Christian poetry. While it has been generally assumed that, in using such language, the poet was trying to appeal to an audience acclimated to heroic verse, some critics have contended that he had inherent knowledge of the imagery of warfare and naturally used it in his poetry. Another key approach to the poem has been through liturgical influence; although it is uncertain how well-acquainted the poet was with religious and ecclesiastical services, some commentators have pointed out that *The Dream of the Rood* draws on the language of Christianity. Howard R. Patch has maintained that, in composing the poem, its author "could hardly rid his mind of all the echoes of the hymns and responsive utterances and the liturgical offices which he was accustomed to hear at various times during the church year."

Textual History

The source as well as the authorship of *The Dream of the Rood* remain unknown. Authorship of the poem has been credited by many critics to Cynewulf (c. 770-840), author of the epic poem *Elene*, and by others to Caedmon (fl. 658-680). The earliest evidence of the text of *The Dream of the Rood* is found on the Ruthwell Cross, a large freestanding stone cross, which is inscribed with passages from *The Dream of the Rood* rendered in the Northumbrian dialect. Scholars have been unable to concur upon a date for the cross, proposing any time from the fifth to the twelfth century, although many have agreed that the eighth century— the Golden Age of Northumbria— is the most probable date. The most complete text of *The Dream of the Rood* is found in the Vercelli Book, a manuscript of Old English prose and poetry unanimously assigned to the second half of the tenth century. Some commentators believe that *The Dream of the Rood* is possibly a later version of a lost poem by Caedmon; this theory is supported by one scholar's speculation that the Ruthwell Cross was inscribed on the upper panel with the phrase "Caedmon made me." However, this assertion has been called into question by others who have been unable to find any convincing traces of Caedmon's name on the cross.

Critical Reception

Positive criticism of *The Dream of the Rood* has been abundant. Charles W. Kennedy has called it "one of the most beautiful of Old English poems," and J. A. Burrow has praised it as "one of the first and one of the most successful treatments in English of the theme of the Crucifixion." Although most critics agree on the merit of *The Dream of the Rood*, certain aspects, such as the origin of the final lines of the poem, have prompted significant debate. Most scholars support the conclusion, drawn by A.S. Cook, that the last few lines were added by someone other than the original author when the poem was transcribed for the Vercelli Book; Bruce Dickins and Alan S. C. Ross have contended that "the latter half [of the poem] does not afford any metrical or linguistic evidence which necessitates the assumption of an early date, and in quality it seems to us definitely inferior." However, other critics, including Burrow, have maintained that the lines are indeed a part of the original poem despite their mediocrity, arguing that "it is not difficult to see that the themes of the earlier part are developed consistently and meaningfully." Despite the many uncertainties remaining about the poem, scholars agree that *The Dream of the Rood* is clearly one of the best poems of the Passion ever composed, for, as M. Bentinck Smith has written, it "above all others, betrays the spirit of tender yet passionate veneration, of awe and adoration for 'the wondrous cross on which the Prince of glory died'."

PRINCIPAL ENGLISH EDITIONS

The Dream of the Rood: An Old English Poem Attributed to Cynewulf   (edited by Albert S. Cook)   1905
The Dream of the Rood   (edited by Bruce Dickins and Alan S. C. Ross)   1934
The Dream of the Rood   (edited by Michael Swanton)   1970

CRITICISM

Stopford A. Brooke   (essay date 1898)

SOURCE: "Poems Attributed to Cynewulf or His School," in *English Literature: From the Beginning to the Norman Conquest*, 1898. Reprint by Macmillan and Co., Limited, 1921, pp. 180-202.

[*Brooke was an Anglo-Irish clergyman, poet, critic, and educator whose* Primer of English Literature *(1876) was popular with generations of students. In the excerpt below, he contends that Cynewulf, who is often credited as the author of* The Dream of the Rood, *wrote the epic poem as "his farewell to earth."*]

The **Dream of the Rood** is in the *Vercelli Book*. There is great discussion concerning its authorship. A large number of critics allot it to Cynewulf, but they lessen the weight of their opinion by giving other poems to Cynewulf which have nothing in them of the artist. Ten Brink and Zupitza both maintained against Wülker the authorship of Cynewulf. No assertion can be made at present on the subject. It is a matter of probabilities.

I not only think it probable that Cynewulf wrote it, but I believe it to be his last poem, his farewell to earth. It seems indeed to be the dirge, as it were, of all Northumbrian poetry. But I do not believe that the whole of the poem was original, but worked up by Cynewulf from that early lay of the Rood, a portion of which we find in the runic verses on the Ruthwell Cross. That poem was written in the "long epic line" used by the Cædmonian school, and I think that when in our **Dream of the Rood** this long line occurs, it belongs to or is altered from the original lay. The portions by Cynewulf are written in the short epic line, his use of which is almost invariable in the *Elene*.

What he did, then, was probably this. Having had a dream of the Cross in his early life which converted him and to which he refers in the *Elene*, he wished to record it fully before he died. But he found a poem already existing, and well known, which in his time was attributed by some to Cædmon, and which described the ascent of Christ upon the Cross, His death and burial. He took this poem and worked it up into a description of the vision in which the Cross appeared to him. Then he wrote to this a beginning and an end of his own, and in the short metre he now used.

This theory, whatever its worth may be, accounts for the double metre of the poem, does away with the strongest argument—that derived from metre—against Cynewulf's authorship, explains the difficulty of the want of unity of feeling which exists between the dream-part and the conclusion, and leaves to Cynewulf a number of passages which are steeped in his peculiar personality, which it would be hazardous to allot to any one but himself.

The introduction is quite in his manner, with the exception of two long lines. The personal cry—"I, stained with sins, wounded with my guilt," is almost a quotation from his phrases in the *Juliana* and *Elene*. The impersonation of the tree, the account of its life in the wood, is like the beginning and the manner of some of the *Riddles.* The subjective, personal element, so strong in his signed poems, is stronger in his parts of this poem. It would naturally be so if the poem were written, when he was very near to death, as his retrospect and his farewell. It is equally natural, if this view of the date of the poem be true, that he would enshrine at the last, by means of his art, the story of the most important hour of his life, and leave it as a legacy to the friends of whom he speaks so tenderly. "Lo," it begins—

> Listen, of all dreams, I'll the dearest tell,
> That at mid of night, met me (while I slept),
> When word-speaking wights, resting, wonned in sleep.
> To the sky up-soaring, then I saw, methought,
> All enwreathed with light, wonderful, a Tree;
> Brightest it of beams! All that beacon was
> Over-gushed with gold; jewels were in it,
> At its foot were fair; five were also there
> High upon the shoulder-span, and beheld it there, all the angels of the Lord
> Winsome for the world to come! Surely that was not, of a wicked man the gallows.

These two last lines may belong to the original poem, which Cynewulf was working on. Now he goes on himself: —

> But the spirits of the saints saw it (shining) there,
> And the men who walk the mould, and this mighty universe!
> Strange that stem of Victory! Then I, spotted o'er with sins,
> Wounded with my woeful guilt, saw the Wood of glory,
> All with joys a-shining, all adorned with weeds,
> Gyred with gold around! And the gems had gloriously
> Wandered in a wreath round this woodland tree.
>
> Nathless could I, through the gold, come to understand
> How these sufferers strove of old—when it first began
> Blood to sweat on its right side. I was all with sorrows vexed,
> Fearful, 'fore that vision fair, for I saw that fleet fire-beacon
> Change in clothing and in colour! Now beclouded 'twas with wet,
>
> Now with running blood 'twas moist, then again enriched with gems,
> Long the time I lay, lying where I was,
> Looking, heavy hearted, on the Healer's Tree—
> Till at last I heard how it loudly cried!
> These the words the best of woods now began to speak—
> "Long ago it was, yet I ever think of it,
> How that I was hewèd down where the holt had end!
> From my stock I was dissevered; strong the foes that seized me there;
> Made of me a mocking-stage, bade me lift their men outlawed,
> So the men on shoulders moved me, till upon a mount they set me."

These lines seem to me partly Cynewulf's and partly of the old poem. He has introduced personal modifications to fit them into his dream. Now, he scarcely touches the old work: and the lines run on to a length which contrasts strangely with those of the conclusion to the dream itself: —

> "Many were the foemen who did fix me there!
> Then I saw the Lord, Lord of folk-kin he,
> Hastening, march with mickle power, since he would up-mount on me."

"But I—I dared not, against my Lord's word, bow myself or burst asunder, though I saw all regions of earth trembling; I might have felled His foes, but I stood fast: —

> Then the Hero young, armed himself for war,— and Almighty God he was;
> Strong and staid of mood stepped he on the gallows high,
> Brave of soul in sight of many, for he would set free mankind.
> Then I shivered there—when the Champion clipped me round;
> But I dared not, then, cringe me to the earth.

A Rood was I upreared, rich was the King I lifted up; Lord of all the heavens was he, therefore I dared not fall. With dark nails they pierced me through and through; on me the dagger-strokes are seen; wounds are they of wickedness. Yet I dared not do them scathe; they reviled us both together. Drenched with blood was I, drenched from head to foot—blood poured from the Hero's side when he had given up the ghost. A host of wrathful weirds I bore upon that mount. I saw the Lord of peoples serve a cruel service; thick darkness had enwrapt in clouds the corse of the King. Shadow, wan under the welkin, pressed down the clear shining of the sun. All creation wept, mourned the fall of the King: Christ was on the Rood. I beheld it all, I, crushed with sorrow. . . . Then they took Almighty God: from that sore pain they lifted him; but the warriors left me there streaming with blood; all wounded with shafts was I: —

> So they laid him down, limb-wearied; stood beside the head of his lifeless corse.
> Then they looked upon him, him the Lord of Heaven, and he rested there for a little time.
> Sorely weary he, when the mickle strife was done! Then before his Banes, in the sight of them,
> Did the men begin, here to make a grave for him.
> And they carved it there of a glittering stone,
> Laid him low therein, him the Lord of victory.
> Over him the poor folk sang a lay of sorrow
> On that eventide!

And there he rested with a little company." Here the old work ends, and Cynewulf, touching in what he had learnt from the Legend of Helena and the Cross, is told by the Rood to tell his dream to men, to warn them of judgment to come, and to bear, if they would be safe, the Cross in their hearts.

Now the Rood ceases to speak, and Cynewulf's personal conclusion follows. Its first lines are retrospective. They tell how he felt in early manhood, immediately after the dream which was the cause of his conversion. He felt "blithe of mood," because he was forgiven, "passionate in prayer, eager for death"—a common mixture of feelings in the hearts of men in the first hours of their new life with God. "Then, pleased in my heart, I prayed to the Tree with great eagerness, there, where I was, with a small company, and my spirit was passionate for departure." But he did not die, forced to out-live many sorrows—"Far too much I endured in long and weary days." Then he turns from the past to the present—"Now I have hope of life to come, since I have a will towards the Tree of Victory. There is my refuge." Then he remembers all the friends who have gone before him, and sings his death-song, waiting in joy and hope to meet those he loved at the evening meal in Heaven. "Few are left me now," he says, "of the men in power I knew": —

> Few of friends on earth; they have fared from
> hence,
> Far away from worldly joys, wended to the Lord
> of Glory!
> Now in Heaven they live, near to their High Fa-
> ther,
> In their brightness now abiding! But I bide me
> here,
> Living on from day to day, till my Lord His
> Rood,
> Which I erst had looked upon, long ago on
> earth,
> From this fleeting life of ours fetch my soul
> away—
> And shall bring me there, where the bliss is
> mickle,
> Happiness in Heaven! There the High God's folk
> At the evening meal are set; there is everlasting
> joy!

At last, with a happy reversion to that earlier theme he loved—the deliverance of the Old Testament saints from Hades—he turns from himself, now going home, to the triumphant homecoming of Jesus; soaring, as his custom was, into exultant verse:

> Hope was then renewed,
> With fresh blossoming and bliss, in the souls
> who'd borne the fire!
> Strong the Son with conquest was, on that (soar-
> ing) path,
> Mighty and majestical, when with multitudes he
> came,
> With the host of holy spirits, to the Home of
> God—
> And to all the Holy Ones, who in Heaven long
> before
> Glory had inhabited—So the Omnipotent came
> home,
> Where his lawful heirship lay, God, the Lord of
> all.

This is the close of the **Dream of the Rood** and the closing song of the life and work of Cynewulf. We see him pass away, after all storms and sorrows, into peace.

The most vigorous part of the poem is the old work, but its reworking by Cynewulf has broken it up so much that its simplicity is hurt. The image of the towering Tree, now blazing like a Rood at Hexham or Ripon with jewels, now veiled in a crimson mist and streaming with blood, is conceived with power; but, as imaginative work, it is not to be compared with the image of the mighty Rood in the *Crist* which, soaring from Zion to the skies, illuminates with its crimson glow heaven and earth, the angels and the host of mankind summoned to judgment. The invention of the Tree bringing its soul from the far-off wood, alive and suffering with every pang of the great Sufferer, shivering when Christ, the young Hero, clasped it round, longing to crush His foes, weeping when He is taken from it, joining in the wail of burial, conscious that on it, as on a field of battle, death and hell were conquered, is full of that heroic strain with which Cynewulf sympathised, and the subject was his own. It was he, more than any other English poet, who conceived and celebrated Christ as the Saviour of men, as the Hero of the New Testament.

Howard R. Patch   (essay date 1919)

SOURCE: "Liturgical Influence in *The Dream of the Rood,*" in *PMLA,* Vol. XXXIV, No. 2, 1919, pp. 233-57.

[*In the following essay, Patch explores parallels between* The Dream of the Rood *and church liturgical texts "in order to gain a further knowledge of the poet's working method and to assist in reproducing a sense of the connotativeness of the poem."*]

Scholars have long made an earnest search for analogues to **The Dream of the Rood,** but the very remoteness of the parallels thus afforded so far is a unique testimony to the high degree of originality in the poem. Closer in some ways than any of them, in that it gives us a dialogue with the cross, the "Disputation between Mary and the Cross" might have been cited; but here again comparison shows that the **Dream** is a poem standing apart in the unusually fine quality of its inspiration and in its genuine feeling. The poet seems to have had little to work on for a basis, either as a source or as a guide. Yet we know that he was deeply religious and we can be sure that he must have been thoroughly acquainted with those parts of the ecclesiastical service which were devoted to the celebration of the cross. In writing such a poem he could hardly rid his mind of all the echoes of the hymns and responsive utterances and the liturgical offices which he was accustomed to hear at various times during the church year.

No hymn or piece of liturgy seems to have furnished him a model, and nothing could be more different in spirit and manner than his work and the type of hymn probably accessible to him. The poet writes primarily as a narrator; subjective expression in the form of complaint or panegyric comes in only incidentally, although perhaps all the more spontaneously. But he naturally would express himself in the idiom of the church. And it is the purpose of this study to trace such resemblances as may be found and to detect allusions which seem to have been deliberate, in order to gain a further knowledge of the poet's working method and to assist in reproducing a sense of the connotativeness of the poem. Its meaning for contemporary readers or hearers will thus be shown deepened; we may arrive at some conclusions regarding its relation to certain other Anglo-Saxon treatments of parts of the theme; and our conclusions may have some bearing on the general problem of the attribution of the poem.

What were the liturgical forms familiar to the poet? We may safely conjecture the general outlines from those of a somewhat later period. In regard to the hymns the difficulty is greater because presumably the hymns follow no traditional scheme. Yet even here, beautiful as the hymns are, the phrases in speech and figure are often stereotyped formulae which were freely passed around; and by reviewing the common stock of a later time we can assume with fair safety that the figures were known in some earlier form. Wholesale borrowing from an early favorite is one of the most striking features in the growth of hymnology. And if the **Dream of the Rood** shows a use of the phrase or formula turning up generally elsewhere, it seems extremely likely that the Anglo-Saxon poet was the debtor. I shall attempt to point out all such borrowings, and in doing so I shall include many slighter reminiscences or casual parallels which I should not mention in a strict category. Since the chief point consists in the number of the parallels, so far as the hymns are concerned, I shall put them in the body of the discussion rather than in the footnotes.

> Þuhte me þæt ic gesawe syllicre treow
> on lyft lædan leohte bewunden,
> beama beorhtost. Eall þæt beacen wæs
> begoten mid golde; gimmas stodon.
>
> *DR,* ll. 4-6.

As scholars have noted before, these lines afford a tantalizing parallel to some similar lines in the *Elene,* which I shall quote, together with the Latin of the *Acta Sanct.,* to see whether any conclusions may be reached in regard to the resemblance.

> Geseah he frætwum beorht
> wlitig wuldres treo ofer wolcna hrof
> golde geglenged: gimmas lixtan.
> wæs se blaca beam bocstafum awriten
> beorhte and leohte.
>
> *Elene,* ll. 88-92.

> Intendens in caelum vidit signum crucis Christi
> ex lumine claro constitutum, et desuper litteris
> aureis scriptum titulum.
>
> Holth., *Elene,* p. 4, l. 85.

The parallel to the *Elene* at first seems remarkable and among the points of similarity may be noted the following: "ic gesawe" (geseah he); "syllicre treow" (wuldres treo); "beama beorhtost" (se blaca beam); "begoten mid golde" (golde geglenged); "gimmas" (gimmas). Yet there are certain points in which the **Dream** is closer to the Latin: "on lyft" (in caelum); "leohte bewunden" (ex lumine claro constitutum); the use of "beacen" in this connection (signum). And some of the ways in which it resembles the *Elene* fade in importance when more carefully examined. "Ic gesawe" is necessary in the **Dream** as part of the obvious schematism (see also ll. 21, 33, 51, pointed out by [Albert S.] Cook in his edition, p. 17, n. 14.) The use of "treow" is natural in either case as an epithet for the cross, since it is the usual gloss for *lignum* and *arbor* of the hymns.

The use of "beama" here may have more significance. But

we may note that it is also to be found in a similar passage in the *Riddles:*

> Ic seah on bearwe beam hlifian
> tanum torhtne.
>
> *Rid.,* 54, ll. 1. ff.

One may add *Rid.,* 56, l. 7; and *Crist* (Part III), l. 1089.

It may be objected that "beacen" of the **Dream** cited as a parallel to *signum* in the Latin is also found in the *Elene,* l. 100: "Swa he þæt beacen geseah." But there it is the equivalent of some form of "viso autem signo" and has nothing to do with the lines I have quoted. It is necessary to add that "beacen" is not much evidence either way, since as "signum" it is common enough in the hymns: Mone, I, p. 174, l. 7 (Crux insignis palmæ signum); Daniel, IV, p. 276, l. 9 (Crux est signum, quod est dignum); IV, p. 185 and Mone, I, p. 145 (signum salutis); Daniel v, p. 183 (triumphale signum); Dreves, IX, p. 26, No. 25, 1a (signum Christi triumphale); XXXIX, p. 21, No. 9, 4a (signum triumphale); XLVIII, p. 57, No. 58 (venerabile signum). Most striking of all is the appearance in the liturgical phrase: "Hoc signum crucis erit in caelo." This phrase is an almost sufficient explanation for the entire passage in the **Dream** and with this in mind there is hardly any need to call on Constantine's vision. The way it could be expanded may be suggested by the use of the same idea in the Irish *Altus Prosator:* "Xristo de celis domino descendente celissimo profulgebit clarissimum signum crucis et vexillum."

My conclusions regarding the similarity to the *Elene,* then, are these: the episode in the **Dream** may possibly be based on one having nothing to do with the story of the *Inventio;* the verbal parallels may be due to the general similarity in situation (we have already seen the parallels in the *Riddles* and I shall refer to *Daniel,* ll. 496 ff. later); in at least two expressions the **Dream** is closer to the Latin. The detail of gold and gems in both the **Dream** and the *Elene* is certainly of the highest importance, but I shall reserve that for special study. If anything can be deduced at present it is that if the **Dream** alludes to the episode in the *Inventio,* it went straight to some source approximating the Latin, while the *Elene* utilized both the **Dream** and the *Inventio* story. What version of the *Inventio* may have been known to the poet of the **Dream** it is, of course, impossible to say; but he may have found his source in some form used in the *lectio* for the feast of the *Inventio.* For instance, in the York Breviary (Surtees Soc., II, col. 272, lectio ij) we have: "Et intuens in celum: vidit signum crucis Christi." In a different version the shining of the cross may have been added, which is a regular detail in Constantine's vision.

> Begoten mid golde; gimmas stodon
> fægere æt foldan sceatum, swylce þær fife wæron
> uppe on þam eaxlgespanne.
>
> *DR,* ll. 7-9.

On this passage Serrazin bases his argument for the intimate connection with the *Elene:* "Dass aber Constantinus, nach K's Darstellung das Kreuz schon in der kostbaren Verzierung gesehen haben soll, welche ihm erst nach der

Auffindung zuteil wurde, ist ein offenbarer Anachronismus, der sich nur dadurch erklärt, dass dem Dichter das visionäre Kreuz Constantins so vor dem geistigen Auge schwebte, wie es dem Traumseher erschienen war." Ebert's comment in another connection but on the same general idea is applicable here—that such a conclusion assumes that the poet of the ***Dream*** or of the *Elene* could see no other passage on the subject and no example of such a cross other than the one first described.

The chief problem is whether there were such crosses in England at the time in question. Ebert cites two allusions, both of which are however somewhat inferential: the *Ded. S. Crucis* of the *Pontificale* of the Archbishop of York— here "in splendore cristalli" may well refer to the "crux de christallo," carried in the English Church in Eastertide until Ascension Day, which after all may not have been a jewelled cross; in Tatwine's *Riddle* the word "nitescere" may describe the shining beryl or merely the light of a gold cross. Supporting evidence is derived from Ebert's examples of gemmed crosses of the time, but it must be said that the force of the total argument is slight compared with what we should have. If we are to believe that the poet actually saw such a cross, would he not have been so much impressed by such a rarity as to have devoted much more of his description, indeed the whole poem, to its details? Would not a *crux gemmata* have seemed a rarity in England in the eighth or ninth centuries, as we might infer from the material so far adduced?

It seems well worth while to collect the evidence to show that there were many such crosses in the British Isles and that the poet did not need to depend on a vision for the details. Precious stones, possibly jewels, were used in ornamenting the early churches; most interestingly for us in the Priory at Hexham:

> Porro beatae memoriae, adhuc vivens gratia Dei,
> Acca episcopus, qui magnalia ornamenta hujus
> multiplicis domus de auro et argento, lapidi-
> busque pretiosis et quomodo altaria purpura et
> serico induta decoravit, quis ad explanandum
> sufficere potest.

Pope Gregory sent the famous cross of Columcille to Iona as early as 590. We may note that the jewelled cross was common in Europe in the early period: still extant are those in the mosaics in Italy, dating from the fourth to the eighth century. They are plain Roman or slightly pattée, and both the crossbeam and the upright are jewelled. Some of them have specifically five jewels on the crossbeam: that in S. Apollinare in Classe in Ravenna; that in the catacomb of Pontianus; and that in S. Giov. Laterano in Rome. The number varies, however, in other crosses of this type: for example, that in the apse of S. Pudenziana; that in S. Paolo fuori le mura; and that in the apse of S. Teodoro. The evidence shows that this cross was widely popular. It came from a Byzantine source, apparently, and spread over Europe, not merely in the form of mosaics but in other decorative forms. And with the Oriental influence so powerful in Celtic and early English Christianity, it seems more than likely that it penetrated to the British Isles. The form appears in the plain English altar cross,

and the jewelled type is reproduced in the well-known Cross of Cong.

But what evidence we have indicates that this particular form arrived later than the period with which we are concerned. And even if it were known earlier, one might well question why, if this was the cross the poet had in mind, he laid so much emphasis on the five jewels of the crossbeam and neglected the greater number on the upright. Furthermore, there is no reason for supposing that the number on the crossbeam was likely to have been just five.

But another type of cross was familiar in England at the very time when the poem was probably composed, and it affords a more satisfactory explanation of the passage. I refer to the Celtic cross, which may be most readily recalled in the forms in stone: the arms of equal length and pattée, usually placed in a circle. Sometimes in each angle is a dot or small cross, making—with the circle or boss at the center—five units of ornamentation. This last characteristic is extremely common in the Celtic cross of English and Scottish territory. In the stone representations it will be found that whatever the variation in the arrangement of the dots, crosses, or bosses, importance seems to be attached to the number five.

The significance of these crosses for us may now be clear, and their importance will be greater if we can find any replicas of the type using precious stones. Fortunately there is good evidence that the same type was used in the jewelled cross; and this too maintains the quincunx, sometimes with the jewels in place of the dots or crosses and sometimes with a gem at the end of each beam. The form appears in the ornamentation of the box of St. Molaise; and in the pectoral cross formerly considered the property of St. Cuthbert. Here it is comprehensible what the poet means by the five jewels on the "eaxlgespan," since they would form the chief points of color and decoration. And here we have another link between a "Cynewulfian" poem and Celtic Christianity.

The general explanation of the use of the number five in the bosses has been the symbolism of the five wounds. Thus [W. O.] Stevens and J. R. Allen have held this view. Bayley, engaged in propounding another thesis however, glances at it with hostility: "The five knobs or bosses erroneously supposed to represent the 'five wounds of Christ,' are of frequent occurrence." For the jewels on the cross, Cook quotes another interpretation from the *Legenda Aurea*: "And in sign of these four virtues the four corners of the cross be adorned with precious gems and stones. And in the most apparent place is charity, and on the right side is obedience, and on the left side is patience, and beneath is humility, the root of all the virtues." This suggestion is supported by the use of the same virtues in the ladder figure of the cross in Alanus de Insulis. An Anglo-Saxon reading of the significance of such elements, although it does not touch on the number, gives a similar idea:

> Þurh þæt gold we understandað geleafan and
> god in gehygd; þurh þæt seolfor riht lice spræce
> and getingnysse on Godes lare; ðurh þa
> deorwurðan gymstanes halige mihte.

The jewels, then, may have symbolized certain virtues.

On the other hand, Durandus tells us in the *Rationale:* "Crux in medio altar significat passiones quam Christus in medio tre subsit." We should expect the wounds to receive special attention since they are given so much emphasis in the hymns and the liturgy. The five crosses cut in the altar stones and the five signs of the cross are taken as similarly symbolical. With these may be associated the five grains of incense in the liturgy, and the five stones in David's bag. And if the symbolism was not a matter of some special study and opinion, but the laity in general was expected to know it and derive benefit from it, the evidence for a symbolism other than that of the five wounds would have to be pretty general. Five is not a steady number for the virtues, which are usually classified as four or seven. It seems fairly safe, therefore, to believe that in the **Dream** the poet mentions the five jewels not only because they were prominent in the actual cross that he knew, but because they represented the sacred wounds, an interpretation of some power.

At this point we may note that the *Elene,* though it mentions jewels, gives no specific number. Here again, then, if there is any relation between the two poems, the **Dream** is probably the earlier, or at least it is not indebted to the *Elene.* Some difficulties remain in the lines of the **Dream:** the meaning of "fægere æt foldan sceatum" is not quite clear. Perhaps a hint may be found in the passage of the *Daniel* (ll. 500-501):

Ac he hlifode to heofontunglum,
swilce he oferfæðmde foldan sceatas.

The "foldan sceatas" are the corners of the earth, to which the cross reaches as it spreads over the sky. "Stodon" in the **Dream,** describing the position of the jewels, is fairly strong, possibly meaning something like "stood out." The whole passage I should then read as follows: "Gems stood out (on the cross) shining fair to the corners of the earth; five of these there were, above, on the shoulder-span." The five, as we have seen, were very likely those of the Celtic cross, grouped in a quincunx at the junction of the beams.

Fracoðes gealga.

DR, l. 10.

Cook notes this expression as "a comparatively infrequent designation of the cross." But see *Crist and Satan,* ll. 511, 550; *Menologium,* l. 86; A. S. Hymns (Surtees Soc.), p. 78 (Vexilla regis), l. 4, "patibulo" glossed "gealgan"; F. E. Warren, *The Leofric Missal,* Oxford 1883, p. 141 (crucis patibulum); Dreves, IX, p. 27, 5b (In ligno transverso sacri patibuli); Chevalier, *Poésie Lit. du Moy. Age,* p. 176, LVI (152); Prudentius, p. 248, l. 641; *Benedictionale S. Æthelwold* (X cent., MS., *Archaeologia* XXIV, p. 108, "per beatae crucis patibulum.")

"Ne wæs þæt . . . fracoðes gealga" might be a reference to the cross of one of the thieves, which would naturally be in the mind of anyone in connection with the *Inventio Crucis.* But "fracoð" is not paralleled in the *Elene;* the two sinners are called "scaðena" in the A. S. prose (*EETS,* XLVI, p. 13), one of them "sceaþæ" in twelfth century prose (*EETS,* CIII, p. 32, l. 25); the gloss of *latro* in Wuelcker's *Vocabularies* is usually *sceaþa,* sometimes *þefe;* and

the whole sentence may be simply a case of Anglo-Saxon understatement.

Syllic wæs se sigebeam.

DR, l. 13.

"Sigebeam" occurs several times in the *Elene,* as Cook has noted, but the kenning is familiar in the hymns and the liturgy. "Beam" is usually the gloss of *trabes;* but the reference to the cross in this compound is so direct that we can hardly be arbitrary in considering it the equivalent of *lignum.* For the hymns we may note the following uses: Mone, I, p. 137 (Salve lignum triumphale); Daniel, V, 183, st. 3; Mone, I, p. 159, ll. 13 (triumphale lignum); Morel, *Lat. Hymnen,* p. 27, l. 85; Dreves, XXXI, p. 94, No. 74, st. 7 (O crux, lignum triumphale). For the kindred expression, sigebeacen, sigorbeacen, or sigores tacen, found only in the *Elene,* note the following: Daniel, V, p. 183 (Ave, triumphale signum); Dreves, IX, p. 26, No. 25, 1a (Signum Christi triumphale); XXXIX, p. 21, No. 9, 4a (signum triumphale). Compare Prudentius, p. 38, l. 83 (Dic tropeum passionis, dic triumphalem crucem); Mone, I, p. 142, ll. 35 (signum victoriæ); *York Missal,* Surtees Soc., II, p. 103 (signum triumphale). Cook, *DR,* p. 16 (also *Crist,* notes) takes the Anglo-Saxon expressions as referring to "the victorious sign seen by Constantine," but the use in the hymns shows that unnecessary.

Geseah ic wuldres treow
wælum geweorðod   wynnum scinan.
DR, ll. 14-15.

Cook (p. 17) compares the *Elene* ll. 88-90, which I have already quoted. Here we may note especially the phrase "wlitig wuldres treo" ("geseach ic" in *DR* I have dealt with in the other connection). Both passages, however, may profitably be compared with one in the *Vexilla regis* with its Anglo-Saxon translation:

Arbor decora et fulgida
Ornata regis purpura.

treow wlitig *ond* scinende
gefrætewod cynges mid godewebbe.

Purpura is regularly glossed "godewebb" (see Napier, *O. E. Glosses*) which means a purple cloth or any rich material. "Wædum" may hold some reminiscence of this expression. Certainly it has nothing to do with the *vexillum,* which is glossed "guþfana," and which, it is interesting to note, did not appear in the Sarum and York use. The suggestion offered by Stevens that "wædum" "may be a recollection of the veiling of the rood on Good Friday," although it receives some support from line 22, is rendered doubtful by the context here, which has entirely to do with "wynnum," "golde," and "gimmas." On the other hand, line 22 may be read with the meaning "purpura" for "wædum" and it does not lose in clearness or significance thereby.

Geseah ic þæt fuse beacen
wendan wædum and bleom: hwilum hit wæs
     mid wætan bestemed,
besyled mid swates gange,   hwilum mid since
     gegyrwed.

DR, ll. 21-23.

We have here what seems one of the clearest allusions to the liturgy, to the method of changing the style of the cross between Lent and Easter. Ebert has noted certain foreign cases of using the blood-red cross and asserts without evidence that the custom held among the Anglo-Saxons of the eighth century. He gives this point in another connection and does not deal with "wendan wædum and bleom." Rock, however, has shown the use of the red cross during Lent in England; in the north the use was apparently general, and this may be reflected in the Anglo-Saxon "mid wætan bestemed" and part of the reference in "bleom."

This should be supplemented further by the possibility that there is some borrowing from the hymns in the very vividness of the detail in the **Dream:** Mone, I, p. 143, No. 109 (O crux, arbor inclita, Cristi membris praedita et sacrata sanguine); Chevalier, *Poésie Lit.*, p. 181, LXV, 174 (Beata crux cum gloria, Celso sacrata sanguine); Mone, I, p. 142, 43 (crux cruore consecrata); Dreves, XIV, p. 82, No. 72; XXXIX, No. 9, p. 21 (crucem tuo sanguine consecratam colimus); LI, p. 86, No. 81, st. 4; Daniel V, p. 184, st. 3; Merrill, *Lat. Hymns*, p. 67; Daniel, II, p. 101, No. 62; Merrill, p. 19, Pange lingua (Quem sacer cruor perunxit, fusas agni corpore); cf. Anselm, *Pat. Lat.* CLVIII, col. 937, Orat. XLII (Ave crux . . . ejus pretiosissimo sanguine cruentata); Mone, I, p. 140, l. 3 (fulgens Christi sanguine); I, p. 125, No. 99, ll. 25-26 (Per sanguinem sacerrimum, rigasti crucis postem); I, p. 186, ll. 30 (Vidit in ara sacram crucis ostiam, Sanguinis undam, laticem de latere, Sancto fluente); Daniel IV, p. 322 (Crux alma . . . torrente Christi sanguinis ebria); Mone I, p. 159, No. 122, ll. 31; Morel, *Lat. Hymn.*, p. 28, No. 45, l. 8; Dreves, IV, No. 46, p. 34; IX, p. 27, 3a (O altitudo atque profundum crucis purpuratae in Christi sanguine); IX, p. 28, No. 29, 1a (Rubens agni sanguine); XV, p. 46, No. 24 (Agni rubens sanguine); cf. *York Missal,* Surtees Soc., II, p. 102 (Fuit haec salutis ara Rubens Agni sanguine); Dreves, XLIII, p. 23, No. 32, st. 2 (Tu decora sic consiste, Lota sacro sanguine); Prudentius, p. 86 (Hinc cruoris fluxit unda, lymfa parte ex altera: Lymfa nempe dat lavacru*m*, tu*m* corona ex sanguine est).

While such expressions as the above account for "mid wætan bestemed," the change implied in the "hwilum . . . hwilum" clauses needs further explanation. As I have said, the plain red cross was carried during Lent, but on Palm Sunday a more ornamental cross appeared, as the Tracts of Maydeston tell us:

> Post distributionem palmarum exeat processio cum cruce lignea. . . . Deinde lectio euangelio feretum cum reliquijs preparatum. in quo corpus Christi in pixide dependat obuiam venientem cum cruce argentea. . . . Statim vero visa cruce argentea recedat crux lignea.

And on Easter day . . . , the "crux de christallo" was used, which was borne until Ascension-tide. With this progressive change in mind, we may better understand what the poet means when he says that he saw the cross change in garb and color, sometimes it was stained with the flowing of blood and sometimes adorned with treasure.

> Geseah ic þa Frean mancynnes
> efstan elne mycle þæt he me wolde on gestigan.

þær ic þa ne dorste ofer Dryhtnes word
bugan oððe berstan, þa ic bifian geseah
eorðan sceatas.

              (DR, ll. 33-37)
    gestah he on gealgan heanne.
              (l. 40)
Bifode ic þa me se Beorn ymbclypte; ne dorste
  ic hwæðre bugan to eorðan,
feallan to foldan sceatum, ac ic sceolde fæste
  standan.

              (ll. 42-43)

It is hard to believe that these passages have not something to do with the striking lines in the *Pange lingua* of Fortunatus:

> Flecte ramos, arbor alta, tensa laxa viscera
> Et rigor lentescat ille, quem dedit nativitas,
> Ut superni membra regis miti tendas stipite,
>
>   (ll. 24 ff.)

The cross explains why it was unable to bend. And the last line of the Latin seems to be echoed in the **Dream** by "Geseah ic weruda God þearle þenian" (ll. 51-52). Another line from Fortunatus, "Sola digna tu fuisti ferre pretium saeculi," although it was a generally popular sentiment, seems to appear in the following:

> Me þa geweorðode wuldres Ealdor
> ofer holtwudu, heofonrices Weard,
> swylce he his modor eac Marian sylfe
> ælmihtig God for ealle men
> geweorðode ofer eall wifa cynn,
>
>   **(DR,** ll. 90-94)

The figure in ll. 34 and 40 is paralleled in *Crist and Satan* (ll. 549 ff.) and in the hymns: Chevalier, *Poés. Lit.*, p. 176, LVI, 152 (Cum ascendisset Dominus Super crucis patibulum); Prudentius, p. 248, ll. 641 (Crux illa nostra est, nos patibulum ascendimus); *Liber Hymnorum,* I, p. 85, l. 22. The figure of l. 42 is paralleled: Mone, I, p. 181, st. 7 (O virtus crucis mundus attrahis amplexando tuis hinc inde brachiis); Dreves, IX, p. 27, 5b:

> transverso sacri patibuli
>   docemur
>   expansis manibus
>   crucifixi
>   dextros et sinistros
>   amplecti.

The most interesting parallel of all, however, is found in the third reading for the feast of St. Andrew in the York Breviary (Surtees Soc., vol. II, col. 88, lectio iij):

> Cum pervenisset beatus andreas ad locum ubi crux parata erat: videns eam a longe exclamabat voce magna dicens: salve crux: que in corpore Christi dedicata es: *et ex membris ejus tanquam margaritis ornata,* ps̄. Omnes gentes, an̄. *Antequam te ascenderet dominus noster o beata crux: timorem terrenum habuisti:* modo vero amorem celestem obtinens pro voto susciperis. ps̄. Exaudi deus deprecationem. an̄. Amator tuus semper fui: *et desideravi te amplecti.* o bona crux. ps̄. Exaudi deus orationem.

The Italics are mine. The passage affords us another connection with the northern liturgy and also one with the story of St. Andrew.

Gyredon me golde and seolfre.

DR, l. 77

This line has been taken as a reference to the story of the *Inventio.* We may note, however, that "golde and seolfre" is not paralleled in the *Elene* (ll. 1023 ff.), where we have "golde and gimcynnum." In the Latin (*Acta Sanct.,* Holth., *Elene*) we have gold and jewels with a silver box, and also in Eusebius. But the Anglo-Saxon Prose, which may indicate the Irish original, tells us: "bewyrcan het mid golde . . . mid seolfre . . . mid deorwurþum gimmum." At this point, then, the **Dream** is again closer to a possible common original than to the *Elene.*

Is me nu lifes hyht
þæt ic þone sigebeam secan mote.

DR, ll. 126-7

The Christian "hope" is common in hymns of the cross, although not exactly in these terms: Daniel, IV, p. 185 (Crux sancta . . . vera spes nostra), Mone, I, p. 145, *A. S. Hymns,* Surtees Soc., p. 156; Daniel I, p. 225, No. CXCVII, 2 (Spes et certa redemptio): Chevalier, *Repert. Hymnolog.,* IV, p. 88, No. 36454 (Crux, ave, spes unica inventionis); No. 36462 (Crux sancta . . . spes nostra); Dreves, IX, p. 26, No. 25, 1a (spes et nostra gloria); No. 26, 2a (sanctae crucis, spes nostra); XV, p. 46, No. 24 (spes praeclara); XV, p. 47, No. 25 (spes mihi viventi); XXI, p. 22, No. 15 (spes unica); XLVIII, p. 57, No. 58 (unica spes hominum). See also the liturgy: *York Brev.,* col. 552 (crux, ave, spes unica), also col. 270; *Hereford Brev.,* HBS, XL, II, p. 159. See a late hymn, Wackernagel, *Das deutsche Kirchenlied,* Leipzig, 1864, I, p. 252, No. 428 (magna spes credentium). See Anselm, Migne, *Pat. Lat.,* CLVIII, col. 939 (Tu es enim spes mea).

Incidentally it may be worth noting in relation to these lines and to l. 138 that the *lignum vitae* figure is extremely common: Mone, I, p. 181, st. 6 (Crux vitae lignum, Vitam mundi portans); I, 174, l. 8; Dreves, IX, p. 26, No. 25, 1b (lignum vitae); XV, p. 46, No. 24 (arbor vitae); XXI, p. 22, No. 15 (arbor vitae); XXXI, p. 94, No. 74, st. 6 (lignum vitae); XXXIV, p. 28, No. 24 (arbor ave vitae); XXXIX, No. 9, p. 21, 3b (vitale lignum); XL, p. 33, No. 14 (lignum vitae).

And ic wene me
daga gehwylce hwænne me Dryhtnes rod,
þe ic her on eorðan ær sceawode,
of þysson lænan life gefetige,
and me þonne gebringe þær is blis micel.

DR, ll. 135 ff.

Stevens cites these lines as indicating that the poet deifies the cross: "In endowing the cross with personality, the poet of the **Dream of the Rood** outstrips any other writer." While we may agree with this comment in part (although we have noted how the poet borrows details and utilizes allusions), the opinion should be modified by observing the frequency of the figure in the hymns: compare Mone, I, p. 181, st. 7:

O excelsa crux,
ima perforans,
vinctos, quos absolvis,
ad summa erigis.

Also: Mone, I, p. 140, ll. 53; I, p. 142, ll. 43 (Per te nobis . . . sempiterna gaudia det superna gratia); Daniel, V, p. 183, st. 3 (Tu nos hinc per modum scalae Ducas ad coelestia); V, p. 304, No. 608, ll. 3 (Qui fidelis introducis Ad coelestem Patriam), l. 8 (Nos transfer ad gloriam); Dreves, XV, p. 47, No. 25 (In te confisum me ducas ad paradisum—addressed to Christ). See Anselm, *Pat. Lat.,* CLVIII, col. 942 (et vitam aeternam nobis attulisti); *Greg. Sac., HBS,* p. 275 (per crucis lignum ad paradisum gaudia redeamus). See also the "lignum vitae" figure discussed above, especially Mone, I, p. 145, also in *A. S. Hymns,* Surtees Soc., p. 156; and cf. **DR,** l. 148 with *A. S. Hymns,* p. 83 (Redempta plebs captivata Reddita vitæ praemio).

Most of the conclusions given in the foregoing discussion need not be repeated. Many of them are extremely tentative, hardly more than shadowing as they do possible influence, and not attempting to arrive at the actual source. But to draw the matter together we may note the following points which seem to have received general support in the investigation: in the **Dream of the Rood** there are several clear allusions to the liturgy; even the phrases at times seem to be borrowed, especially from the hymn *Pange lingua;* we have observed several parallels in the **Dream** to Part Three of the *Christ;* if there is any connection between the **Dream** and the *Inventio,* it exists between the former and some document approximating the source of the *Elene* rather than the *Elene* itself. If the results of our search for liturgical influence are surprisingly small, the study has served to show all the more how little the poet of the **Dream** has relied on the conventional material accessible to him and yet with what effectiveness he has brought in reflections of the ecclesiastical services which he knew.

Margaret Schlauch   (essay date 1940)

SOURCE: "*The Dream of the Rood* as Prosopopoeia," in *Essays and Studies in Honor of Carleton Brown,* edited by Percy W. Long, New York University Press, 1940, pp. 23-34.

[*Here, Schlauch praises the poet's unique use of prosopopoeia (discourse by inanimate objects), stating that he "was not following a literary tradition concerning the Rood; he was making an innovation with the originality of genius."*]

As succeeding generations of scholars have studied the body of Old English lyric poetry and given tribute to its enduring literary qualities, an almost incredulous amazement has been expressed repeatedly concerning the originality of form and the extraordinary emotional intensity manifested in it. These qualities are particularly striking in the anonymous verse monologues which make up a considerable part of the whole lyrical offering. It is generally admitted that these poems show exceptional skill and mastery of technique; they are not the fumbling efforts of untaught beginners. For poems such as *Wanderer, Seafarer,* and *Banished Wife's Lament,* classical models have been suggested more than once. These lyrics represent persons as speakers. As partial explanation of their genesis, it has been pointed out [by Rudolf Imelmann, *Forschungen zur altenglischen Elegie,* 1920] that any cultivated Englishman of the time would have known and admired such declamatory passages as the speech of Æneas (most famous of exiles) to Dido and Dido's own lament at the involuntary perfidy of her guest in Vergil, and the more lachrymose epistolary monologues in Ovid's *Heroides.* Hilda Reuschel [in *Beiträge zur Geschichte der deutschen Sprache und Literatur* LXII (1938)] has recently suggested that Ovid's personal expressions of an exile's woe in the *Tristia* and *Epistolae ex Ponto* may have contributed to the very wording of Old English lyrics. The originality of treatment by Anglo-Saxon writers is generally conceded, but it is undisputed that Latin models were near at hand and well loved.

As a literary type, **The Dream of the Rood** stands somewhat apart from the other elegiac monologues in Old English. Here for the major part of the poem the speaker is an inanimate object, not a person. The discourse of the Rood is enclosed in another one, that of the dreamer who heard it speak; but the inner monologue is the essence of the poem. To endow the Cross with power of locution was to use a device of unexampled effectiveness in making vivid an event about which, for all devout Christians, the entire history of the world revolved. The object most intimately associated with that breath-taking moment when 'the veil of the temple was rent in twain from the top to the bottom; and the earth did quake, and the rocks were rent' might well be given speech with profound literary effectiveness. Yet this was not commonly done at the time. The Old English poet was not following a literary tradition concerning the Rood; he was making an innovation with the originality of genius.

Concerning the independence of models manifested by this author, A. S. Cook remarks in his introduction to the poem:

> The second part, the address of the cross, is unique in its composition. The notion of representing an inanimate object as speaking to him who stands in its presence, and communicating information or counsel, is as old as the Greek epigram. This was originally an inscription on a monument, a statue, or a votive offering preserved in a temple, and not seldom represented the work of art, or the dead who reposed beneath the monument, as addressing the passer-by.

As literary analogues Professor Cook cites some of the Greek epigrams from the *Anthology* and several in Latin in which a dead person, or the statue of a dead person, speaks briefly from the tomb. He also refers to an epigram which Ovid puts into the mouth of a parrot (*Amores,* II, 6) and another, perhaps spurious, at the beginning of *Heroides,* IX. Such simple statements in the first person singular were inscribed on bells, swords, and house fronts. Beyond these, however, he offers no literary parallels before the Old English period. If this were all, the originality shown by the author of the **Dream of the Rood** would indeed be all but unbelievable.

Now I have no desire to diminish the glory of the Old English poet, whose literary gifts remain beyond dispute no matter how many models he may have had. But I do wish to point out that Professor Cook has neglected to consider

a number of poems in Latin which bridge the period from the Greek *Anthology* to eighth-century England and perceptibly diminish the appropriateness of the term 'unique' as applied to the speech of an inanimate object—even if it is to be the Rood—in the literature still extant in the eighth century. Moreover, I should like to point out that even without any models in Latin, a gifted writer might have found the suggestion for such a poem as the **Dream of the Rood** in Latin rhetorical texts of the time which discussed prosopopoeia, or discourse by inanimate objects. The poems suggested so far as direct sources or models for the **Dream** differ from it most conspicuously in being third person narratives instead of monologues. Thus [Adolf] Ebert proposed a fourth-century poem *De Cruce* by Cyprian, also called *De Pascha,* as a direct inspiration for the Old English poem; but this is allegorical exposition with but a slight modicum of narrative *in the third person.* Such texts are pertinent in a general way, since they exemplify interest in the Cross as a theme, but they leave out of account the interesting aesthetic problem of the innovation in Rood literature: the use of elegiac monologue.

In the golden age of Latin literature there was already a marked development of imaginary discourses by inanimate objects. This was a device particularly favored by the elegiac poets. Among the better known examples of this and later ages are: the discourse of the Tress of Berenice by Catullus; the apologia or *exculpatio* of a courtesan's doorpost in a dialogue also written by Catullus; a similar theme, *Verba Januae conquerentis* by Propertius; the discourse attributed to his book of *Tristia* by Ovid; a panegyric on the emperor composed by Ausonius and put into the mouth of the Danube River; a discourse delivered by a statue of Dido and another by the petrified Niobe, also by Ausonius. An anonymous writer of the days of decline and fall represents the City of Rome itself speaking in its desolation:

> Vix scio quae fueram, vix Romae Roma recordor,
> > Quae populo, regnis, moenibus alta fui.
> Cesserunt arces, cecidere palatia Divum,
> > Jam servit populus, degeneravit eques.
> Quae fueram totum quondam celebrata per orbem,
> > Vix sinor occasus vel miminisse mei.

Elizabeth Hazelton Haight [in her *Romance in the Latin Elegiac Poets,* 1932] has pointed out the popularity of this literary device among the Roman elegiac poets. Speaking of *The Lock of Berenice* by Catullus, she says:

> The fact that the speaker in this elegy is a Talking Tress associates it with all those poems in which inanimate objects (tombstones, statues, doors) are given voice. The common device of the Speaking Door Catullus uses in another poem, which is not a monologue, but a dialogue, between House Door and Poet Catullus. . . . The House Door poem [of Propertius, she continues later] (I, 16) may have been suggested by Catullus LXVII. It is not specifically stated to be the door of Cynthia's house, but may be the door of any courtesan. . . . House Door speaks a monologue about its disgrace in having sunk from the portal of a consul whither triumphal

cars drove, to the barred door of a Light o' Love where all night excluded lovers chant their lamentation.

Of such themes the speaking tree, or the wooden statue which recalls that it was once a tree, presents the closest classical parallel to the monologue passage in the *Dream of the Rood.* A poem long attributed to Ovid, *De Nuce,* represents a nut tree as complaining about the hurts and indignities to which it is exposed because passers-by shake it and throw stones at it in order to obtain the ripened nuts. The tree protests its innocence, and laments the failure of the gods to act as husbandmen and protect the trees which were formerly in their charge.

> 1 Nux ego iuncta viae, cum sim sine
>   crimine vitae,
>   a populo saxis praetereunte petor.
>   obruere ista solet manifesta poena nocentes,
>   publica cum lentam non capit ira moram.
>   nil ego peccavi: nisi si peccare vocetur
>   annua cultori poma referre suo.

Fertility is a curse, not a blessing; if it were sterile it would be unmolested: 'Certe ego, si numquam peperissem tutior essem.' It has suffered mutilation not because of hatred but because of desire for the booty:

> 37 at mihi saeva nocent mutilatis
>   vulnera ramis,
>   nudaque deiecto cortice ligna patent.
>   non odium facit hoc, sed spes inducta
>   rapinae.
>   sustineant aliae poma: querentur idem.

The tree also laments because it is suffering from thirst, because it is not permitted to bring its fruit to maturity, because winter, hated by most creatures, is necessarily welcome to it on account of the peace it brings, and because it cannot escape from threatened wounds ('nec vitare licet mihi moto vulnera trunco'). These manifold ills cause it to desire death:

> 159 o! ego, cum longae venerunt taedia vitae,
>   optavi quotiens arida facta mori!
>   optavi quotiens aut caeco turbine verti
>   aut valido missi fulminis igni peti!
>   atque utinam subitae raperent mea poma
>   procellae,
>   vel possem fructus excutere ipsa meos!

The poem ends with a direct exhortation to the traveler by the wayside: if I have deserved this punishment or been harmful in any way, burn me or cut me down at once; if not, leave me in peace and pass on!

The resemblances of this poem to the *Dream of the Rood* are largely generic, because both are laments and both are spoken by trees. The chief difference lies in the important circumstance that Nux complains of its own misfortunes, whereas the Rood solicits pity for the crucified Christ whom it bore. Certain verbal parallelisms result from the similarity of theme: 'ac ic sceolde fæste standan' and 'hyldan me ne dorste' (ll. 43b and 45b) recall 'nec vitare licet mihi moto vulnera trunco, / quem sub humo radix vinclaque firma tenent?' (ll. 169 f.). The general statements 'Feala ic on þam beorye yebiden hæbbe / wraða wyrda' (ll. 50 f.) and 'Sare ic wæs mid soryum yedrefed' (l. 59a)

seem to echo the equally general sentiments of Nux such as 'sic ego sola petor, soli quia causa petendi est: / frondibus intactis cetera turba viret' (ll. 45 f.). There are specific references in both poems to the wounds suffered by the tree. Rood says: 'eall ic wæs mid strælum forwundod' (l. 62b), and Nux refers to its 'mutilatis vulnera ramis' (l. 37). Nux protests its innocence: 'nil ego peccavi: nisi si peccare vocetur / annua cultori poma referre suo' (ll. 5 f.). There is at least an implied protestation of innocence in the Rood's repeated emphasis on its inability to do otherwise than carry out the Lord's will (ll. 35 and 42) even though its part in the crucifixion made it seem for a time most loathsome to men ('leodum laðost,' l. 88a).

In the *Dream of the Rood* a few lines are devoted to a description of the tree's life in the forest, and an account of the day when men came and bore it away on their shoulders (ll. 28-33). In Latin literature too the wooden statue of a god sometimes refers to the time when it was transformed from a block of wood into an image. The most conspicuous examples are to be found in the group of poems giving speech to the god Priapus, of which Horace's satire (I, 8) *Canidia* is probably most famous:

> 1   Olim truncus eram ficulnus, inutile
>   lignum;
>   Cum faber, incertus scamnum faceretne
>   Priapum,
>   Maluit esse deum. Deus inde ego, furum
>   aviumque
>   Maxima formido. . . .

Not all of the Latin *Priapea* are composed in the first person, but many which are contain a few lines on the transformation from tree to image, and many stress its tutelary function.

Familiarity with the Ovidian *De Nuce* on the part of the author of the *Dream of the Rood* is by no means improbable. The poem was commonly included among the authentic works of Ovid. The earliest English manuscripts known to contain it postdate the Norman Conquest, but this does not preclude knowledge of it in England at an earlier date, since collections of the Ovidian poems are extant in continental manuscripts from the eleventh and twelfth centuries. The collection of *Priapea* was not lost in the Middle Ages; it was preserved partly, no doubt, because the poems were attributed to Vergil. A ninth-century manuscript of Murbach, Germany, contains these poems together with other short ones traditionally ascribed to Vergil. The text of Horace's *Canidia* was also known in Europe before the time of the Conquest, though there is no record of an 'Oratius totus' in England before 1170.

Besides these Latin discourses by trees or wooden images, there are, as Professor Cook has pointed out, a few riddles which bear a remote resemblance to the *Dream of the Rood.* Number 17 by Eusebius (eighth century) represents the Cross as speaking briefly in the first person, but the discourse is a form of enigmatic definition, entirely lacking in the narrative element so conspicuous in the *Dream:*

> Per me mors adquiritur, et bona vita tenetur;
> Me multi fugiunt, multique frequenter adorant;

Sumque timenda malis, non sum tamen horrida
  justis;
Damnavique virum, sic multos carcere solvi.

It is because of their continuity with this distinctly classical tradition that some of the Old English riddles composed in the first person singular show similarity of phraseology with the **Dream of the Rood;** for instance, number 72, which concerns a spear, begins 'I grew in the mead, and dwelt where earth and sky fed me, until those who were fierce against me overthrew me when advanced in years.' (Compare this with 'me vilem et e rude fuste / Manus sine arte rusticae dolaverunt' in number 63 of the *Priapea.*) The riddles are not, however, the sole or nearest source of inspiration available. Discourse by an inanimate object, making use of narrative, was a form known and practised according to the precepts of mediaeval rhetoric.

That form was known as prosopopoeia, and was usually discussed in conjunction with ethopoeia, or imaginary monologue attributed to a human but fictitious character. The two cannot be very well separated, since prosopopoeia assumes that an object feels and speaks like a person.

Priscian, following his source Hermogenes, gives the following brief description of the two germane forms under the heading of *adlocutio,* which is the ninth of his topics:

> Adlocutio est imitatio sermonis ad mores et suppositas personas accommodata, ut quibus verbis uti potuisset Andromache Hectore mortuo: conformatio vero, quam Graeci προσωποποιίαν nominant, est, quando rei alicui contra naturam datur persona loquendi, ut Cicero patriae reique publicae in invectivis dat verba.

The example from Homer—the discourse of Andromache—had been used by Hermogenes; the Ciceronian instance of prosopopoeia—the discourse by the City of Rome to Cicero—was Priscian's substitute for a similar but less familiar instance from Greek oratory in which the sea is made to speak. After a brief definition of *simulacri factio . . . ,* or the attribution of speech to the dead, Priscian makes some general remarks on the appropriateness of certain types of speeches to certain circumstances and individuals. He classifies all monologues into three groups according to their style or emotional tone: *orationes morales, passionales,* and *mixtae.*

> Passionales sunt, in quibus passio, id est commiseratio perpetua inducitur, ut quibus verbis uti potuisset Andromache mortuo Hectore; morales vero, in quibus obtinent mores, ut quibus verbis uti potuisset rusticus, cum primum aspexerit navem; mixtae, quae utrumque habent, ut quibus verbis uti potuisset Achilles interfecto Patroclo; habet enim et passionem funeris amici et morem de bello cogitantis. Sed operatio procedit per tria tempora, et incipit a praesentibus, recurrit ad praeterita et transit ad futura: habeat autem stilum suppositis aptum personis.

As prosopopoeia the **Dream of the Rood** appears to be an *oratio passionalis* (a specific Cross speaks, not one of a class; moreover, the aim is certainly to evoke 'commiseratio perpetua'). Emporius used the term pathopoeia for such impassioned fictitious orations. The **Dream** observes

the suggested time sequence of present-past-future by means of the introduction in which a dreamer recounts his vision of the Cross as an event in the present time, by the Rood's narrative account of the Crucifixion in the past, and by the closing references to a future life. The Rood says:

> 119 Ac ðurh ða rode sceal   rice yesecan
>   of eorðweye   æyhwylc sawl,
>   seo þe mid Wealdende   wunian þenceð.

The dreamer adds:

> 135   7 ic wene me
>   daya yehwylce   hwænne me Dryhtnes
>   ród,
>   þe ic her on eorðan   ær sceawode,
>   on þyssum lænan   life yefetiye,
>   7 me þonne yebrinye   þær is blis mycel.
>   dream on heofonum. . . .

In discussing imaginary monologues, some writers like Emporius limited themselves to ethopoeia, stressing the general advice that discourse must be made to harmonize with the characteristics . . . of the type of person being presented. Isidore of Seville echoes Priscian in his definition of prosopopoeia; he quotes the same example from Cicero's speeches: 'Etenim si mecum patria mea . . . loqueretur. . . .'

Another type of Latin discourse may be found represented in the **Dream of the Rood,** subordinate to the narrative embodied in prosopopoeia. Although not intended as an exculpation or speech of defense from an implied charge, the Rood's narrative contains certain phrases suggesting a desire to dissociate itself from the cruel tragedy to which it served as instrument. For a time it suffered reproach for this:

> 87 Iu ic wæs yeworden   wita heardost,
>   leodum laðost,   ærþan ic him lifes wey
>   rihtne yerymde,   reord berendum.

But throughout the narrative the Rood's helplessness has been emphasized. Just as the voluntary character of Christ's sacrifice is underscored in certain locutions, so the involuntary function of the Cross appears in such phrases as: 'þær ic þa ne dorste ofer Dryhtnes word / buyan oððe berstan' (ll. 35 f.); 'Bifode ic þa me se Beorn ymbclypte; ne dorste ic hwæðre buyan to eorðan' (l. 42); 'Ac ic sceolde fæste standan' (l. 43b); '. . . hyldan me ne dorste' (l. 45) and 'Ic þæt eall beheold. / Sare ic wæs mid soryum bedrefed' (ll. 58 f.).

Literary defense from a charge, whether overt or implied, was known as *purgatio.* All of the longer mediaeval rhetorics discussed it. Cassiodorus, for instance, shows it graphically charted as a subdivision of a technique of defense known as *concessio* ('I admit that I did this, but . . .'), which in its turn is a subdivision of *qualitas assumptiva* in the class known as *iuridicalis.* His definition is:

> Purgatio est, cum factum quidem conceditur, sed culpa removetur. Haec partes habet tres: inprudentiam, casum, necessitatem.

This definition of *purgatio* is to be found with but slight verbal changes in Martianus Capella and Isidore of Seville. Alcuin elaborates it by presenting hypothetical cases:

> Purgatio est, per quam eius qui accusatur non factum ipsum, sed voluntas defenditur: ea habet partes tres, inprudentiam, casum, necessitudinem. Inprudentia est, cum scisse aliquid is, qui arguitur, negatur, ut . . . [an example follows taken from a typical *controversia*]. Casus autem infertur in concessionem, cum demonstratur aliqua fortunae vis voluntati obstitisse, ut . . . [example follows]. Necessitudo autem infertur, cum vi quadam reus id quod fecerit fecisse defenditur, hoc modo . . . [an example of shipwrecked persons who involuntarily violated the law of Rhodes about its harbor: 'vi et necessitate sumus in portum coacti'].

The Cross indicates repeatedly that it performed its dolorous function 'vi et necessitate'; it is for this reason that parts of its speech sound like a *purgatio* using the technical plea of *necessitudo*. The approximation to this particular form of *concessio* or defensive pleading also explains the resemblance to Middle English and other poems in which the Cross tells of its unwanted function as part of its defense in a disputation with Mary. Professor H. R. Patch has already called attention [in his "Liturgical Influence in *The Dream of the Rood*," *PMLA*, XXIV (1919)] to the slightly argumentative tone which anticipates the disputes between Mary and the Cross. Mary is mentioned in the Old English poem, but the defense, if such it may be called, is directed not to her but to the dreamer. The epithet *reus* is probably more appropriately applied to the Cross in the later disputation than in the *Dream of the Rood,* but a knowledge of rhetoric may have caused the author to bring out the element of *concessio* in its speech.

The Latin poems and rhetorical theory here presented are intended to illuminate the literary genesis of the *Dream of the Rood* rather than to supply specific sources for lines and phrases. Its relationship to the general body of literature of devotion to the Cross, as demonstrated by Ebert, Stevens, Patch, and Williams, is not to be doubted. But if Cyprian's allegorical exposition *De Cruce*, the hymns of Fortunatus and acrostic poems glorifying the Cross give important evidence for the prevalent appeal of the theme, its poignant effectiveness of form can be better accounted for by pagan theory and practice of prosopopoeia. The Ovidian *De Nuce* is not in any sense a source for the *Dream of the Rood,* but its existence helps us to understand the element of tradition which shapes the work of even a great innovator like the Old English author. After all, his greatest innovation was in the style and intensity which made of his poem an *oratio passionalis* (pathopoeia) in every sense of the word. Emporius had said that there were three levels of discourse possible in the composing of this (as any other) type of speech; 'vasta, humilis, temperata.' These three, as he was well aware, were but three variant terms for the ancient Greek schools of oratory: Asiatic, Attic, and Rhodian. The English poet chose and successfully handled an *oratio vasta*, the only appropriate one for a monologue by the Rood. That he did this is truly his chief literary glory. No amount of defining of rhetorical tradition, and no number of literary analogues on any level, can lessen that great distinction.

Charles W. Kennedy   (essay date 1943)

SOURCE: "Poetry in the Cynewulfian Manner," in *The Earliest English Poetry: A Critical Survey,* Oxford University Press, Inc., 1943, pp. 235-66.

[*In the following excerpt, Kennedy discusses glorification of the Cross in* The Dream of the Rood, *attributing to the poem "pre-eminent distinction as a superb lyric presentation of a religious adoration which finds its symbol in the Cross."*]

In three Old English poems veneration of the Cross receives stressed and memorable expression: the *Elene, Christ III,* and *Dream of the Rood.* Of these, *Christ III* and the *Dream* have most in common both in spirit and detail. Cynewulf's *Elene . . .* is a narrative of the Invention of the Cross, which attains its greatest poetic distinction in two incidental passages, the descriptions of Constantine's battle against the Huns, and Elene's seajourney. In the lines which deal with the Cross itself, the *Elene* makes little display of that lyric emotion which is so continuously characteristic of the *Dream of the Rood,* and which colors at least two passages in *Christ III.* Of the three poems, it is the *Dream of the Rood* which, among all Old English religious poems, has pre-eminent distinction as a superb lyric presentation of a religious adoration which finds its symbol in the Cross.

The veneration with which Old English poets glorify the Cross as the greatest of all symbols cannot be considered in itself a derivative, solely or even chiefly, of the poetic imagination. Whether or not they were professional churchmen, the religious poets were obviously well versed in doctrine and patristic learning, and reflected in their poems much that was conventional in professional exegesis, and in mystical interpretation of ecclesiastical detail. Cynewulf, in the epilogue to *Elene,* refers to the care with which he had gathered, weighed, and sifted details of the Cross legend, until greater knowledge had brought him deeper understanding. It seems unlikely that this statement refers merely to the Crucifixion, or to the Invention of the Cross. His phrasing is suggestive, rather, of a pious concern with the corpus of mystical interpretations by which the medieval mind extended the symbolic significance of the Cross, linking its wood to the tree of life, and its shape to the shining sign of the Son of Man, which at the Judgment shall illumine and transcend the universe.

This adoration of the Cross is revealed both in patristic commentary, and in the hymnology of the medieval Church. It was illustrated in Alcuin's imitation of Fortunatus in the composition of cruciform acrostics and hymns to the Holy Cross. Even beyond the walls of the Church the cross became a frequently recurring symbol, and stone crosses, often skillfully adorned with carving and inscription, served not merely as mortuary monuments but as boundary marks, oratories, and places of public worship.

It is on one such cross, the Ruthwell Cross near Dumfries on the Scottish border, that we find inscribed, as a part of the decoration, brief passages from the *Dream of the Rood.* Through this inscription the *Dream of the Rood,* with little warrant, was for a time associated with the name of Caedmon.

The theory that Caedmon was author of the fragments of the **Dream** inscribed on the Ruthwell Cross rested on two postulates. Daniel Haigh in 1856 dated the Cross as of the seventh century, and suggested that the runic lines on the Cross are fragments of a lost poem of Caedmon of which the **Dream of the Rood** is a later version. Ten years later Stephens supported this theory of Caedmonian authorship by his assertion that an almost obliterated inscription on the upper runic panel included the words, 'Caedmon made me.' But repeated and careful examinations of the Cross have rendered these theories untenable. Critical studies of the beasts, flowers, and foliage in the ornamentation suggest a date definitely later than the seventh century, possibly as late as the year 1000. The language of the inscription is regarded by [Albert S.] Cook as of equally late date. Vietor, after thorough examination of the Cross, was unable in 1895 to find any convincing traces of the name of Caedmon.

It was Dietrich who first called attention to a number of reasons for attributing the poem to Cynewulf. He attempted to connect the **Dream of the Rood** with the *Elene,* since the theme of each was the Cross, and conjectured that the poet was inspired to write of the Invention of the Cross by the influence of the vision which he narrates in the **Dream.** He called attention to a similarity in tone between the personal passages of Cynewulf's signed poems and certain lines of a personal nature which end the **Dream of the Rood,** and found additional support for his theory in correspondence of diction between the **Dream** and the authentic Cynewulfian poems. He concluded that the **Dream** was written by Cynewulf toward the end of his life.

The question of the authorship of the **Dream of the Rood** must be determined in the light of the following facts: that the diction of the **Dream** is, on the whole, Cynewulfian; that Cynewulf had written and signed another poem on the Cross in which he handled the vision of Constantine with evident appreciation of its beauty; and that a somewhat extended passage at the end of the **Dream** is remarkably similar in substance and tone to the personal passages which conclude the *Christ* and *Elene.* These facts, taken in conjunction, tend to make probable the theory that Cynewulf wrote this lovely lyric of the Cross.

In its blending of lyric grace and religious adoration, the **Dream of the Rood** is one of the most beautiful of Old English poems. The poet employs the frame of the medieval dream-vision within which to set the glorious image which appeared to him in the midnight when mortal men lay wrapped in slumber. It seemed to him that he beheld the Cross upraised on high, enwreathed with light and adorned with gold and gems. Throughout Creation the angels of God beheld it; holy spirits gazed upon it, and men on earth. Stained as he was by sin, it was granted him to see the Tree shining in radiant splendor. In his dream the Cross flamed with changing color, now decked with gold and precious jewels, now wet with blood:

> Lo! I will tell the dearest of dreams
> That I dreamed in the midnight when mortal
> men

Were sunk in slumber. Meseemed that I saw
A wondrous Tree towering in air,
Most shining of crosses encompassed with light.
Brightly that beacon was gilded with gold;
Jewels adorned it, fair at the foot,
Five on the shoulder-beam, blazing in splendor.
Through all creation the angels of God
Beheld it shining—no cross of shame!—
But holy spirits gazed on its gleaming,
Men upon earth, and all this great creation.
Wondrous the Tree, that token of triumph,
And I a transgressor, stained with my sins!
I gazed on the Rood arrayed in glory,
Fairly shining and graced with gold,
The Cross of the Savior beset with gems;
But through the gold-work outgleamed a token
Of the ancient evil of wretched souls,
Where the Cross on its right side once sweat
   blood.
Saddened and rueful and smitten with terror
At the wondrous Vision, I saw the Rood
Swift to vary in vesture and hue,
Now wet and stained with the Blood outwelling,
Now fairly gilded and graced with gold.

The convention of the dream-vision provides the poet with a device whereby he is able to shape his material to superb advantage. It is characteristic of the convention that his vision should come vividly to life with endowment of human thought and feeling, and human speech. The Cross becomes the narrator of the Crucifixion and Passion of Christ, and the tragic description by this device takes on elements of dramatic emotion which could come in no other way. As the poet in dream gazes with rueful heart upon the Rood, it begins to speak, recalling its tragic history. Once, long years before, it grew as a forest tree on the edge of a wood. But impious hands hewed it from its stock and shaped it into an instrument for the punishment of malefactors. As it stood on a hilltop outlined against the sky, it became a spectacular symbol of the world's evil. Then fear and horror fell upon it. For it beheld the Lord of all the world hasting in heroic mood to ascend upon it for the redemption of Man. The terror of the Cross, as it foresaw its destiny to serve as the instrument of the Passion of Christ, is a superbly imaginative touch rendered in the simplest terms. Though struck with horror it could not in disobedience reject the fate appointed. When Almighty God clasped it with willing arms it trembled with terror, yet dared not bend or break. It must needs stand fast holding the Lord of all creation, and wet with His blood. A stark vigor of imagination fuses with lyric emotion to make the description notable:

> Natheless, as I lay there long time I gazed
> In rue and sadness on my Savior's Tree,
> Till I heard in dream how the Cross addressed
>   me,
> Of all woods the worthiest, speaking these
>   words:
> 'Long years ago—well yet I remember—
> They hewed me down on the edge of the holt,
> Severed my trunk; strong foemen took me,
> To a spectacle shaped me—a felon's cross!
> High on their shoulders they bore me to hilltop,
> Fastened me firmly, foes enough, forsooth.
> Then I saw the Ruler of all mankind

In brave mood hasting to mount upon me.
Refuse I dared not, nor bow nor break,
Though I saw earth's confines shudder in fear;
All foes I might fell, yet still I stood fast.
Then the Hero young—it was God Almighty—
Put off His raiment, steadfast and strong;
With lordly mood in the sight of many
He mounted the Cross to redeem mankind.
When the Hero clasped me I trembled in terror,
But I dared not bow me nor bend to earth;
I must needs stand fast. Upraised as the Rood
I held the High King, the Lord of heaven.
I dared not bow! With black nails driven
Those sinners pierced me; the prints are clear,
The open wounds. I dared injure none.
They mocked us both. I was wet with blood
From the Hero's side when He sent forth His
　　spirit.
Many a bale I bore on that hill-side,
Seeing the Lord in agony outstretched.
Black darkness covered with clouds God's body,
That radiant splendor; shadow went forth
Wan under heaven; then wept all creation,
Bewailing the King's death; Christ was on the
　　Cross.'

The last few lines of this passage furnish superb illustration of the imaginative realism which underlies the simplicity of the poet's phrasing. The darkness which falls upon the earth at the consummation of the Passion he inherits from Biblical source. But he puts it to striking and reverent use in a contrast between the darkness of obscuring cloud and the radiant splendor of the body of Christ hanging on the Cross. The weeping of all Creation at the Savior's death may well have come into the poet's mind from Gregorian homily, or from memories of the Balder legend and its reference to the mourning of all nature at Balder's death. But the stroke which completes the passage is his own, a brief half-line of pregnant compression in which all the drama and density of mankind are gathered up in the symbol of eternal love transcendent over evil: 'Christ was on the Cross.'

There follows, in the speech of the Rood, a description of the Deposition and Burial. The Cross stained with Christ's blood, and wounded with the arrows of the war-wolves who had slain Him, was hewed down and covered over in a deep trench—'a fearful fate.' But later friends and thanes of God recovered it and decked it with silver and gold. The Rood which was once the bitterest of tortures was honored by the Prince of glory above all forest trees, even as He had honored His mother, Mary, over all the race of women. The dreamer is then commanded to reveal his vision to men. The speech of the Cross ends with rehearsal of the Ascension, and prophecy of the Day of Judgment to come.

This vision of the Cross and its narrative of the Crucifixion find closest parallel in mood and detail in *Christ III,* where the more extended description of the Crucifixion and the shining image of the Cross transcendent in the Day of Judgment produce a unique fusion of realism and symbolism. Wherein, then, lies the unique emotional appeal of the *Dream of the Rood?* It springs, in considerable degree, from the inherent value of the poetic device which the poet has adopted, the dream-vision, within the conventions of

which the Crucifixion, as told by the Cross, receives uniquely personalized rehearsal. The resultant note of emotional fervor, in which the triumphant and the tragic are so closely blended, is a superlative derivative of the spirit of religious devotion effectively supplemented by elements of literary form.

The lines which follow, and which conclude the poem, unite highly personal reflection with a prophetic delineation of the joys of the blessed in the life to come. In mood and diction these lines are so suggestive of the personal passages of Cynewulf's signed poems that, even though the runes are lacking, we are tempted to regard the poem as his. If the *Dream of the Rood* is not Cynewulf's, it is the work of a poet who has imitated with singular faithfulness all the characteristics of the personal mood invariably associated with the Cynewulfian signature. Even in *Elene* and *Christ II* there is no more exquisitely sensitive and personalized revelation of religious faith and hope than that which graces the ending of the *Dream:*

> Then in solitude I prayed to the Rood fervently and with joyful heart. My soul was eager to be gone; I had lived through many an hour of longing. Now have I hope of life, that I may turn to the triumphant Cross, I above all men, and revere it well. Thereto I have great desire, and my hope of succor is set upon the Cross. I have not now in this world many powerful friends. They have departed hence out of the pleasures of this earthly life, and sought the King of glory; they dwell now with the High Father in heaven, and abide in glory. And every day I look forward to the hour when the Cross of my Lord, of which I had vision here on earth, may fetch me out of this fleeting life and bring me where is great joy and rapture in heaven, where God's people are established forever in eternal bliss; and set me where I may hereafter dwell in glory, and with the Saints have joy of joys. May the Lord befriend me, He who on earth once suffered on the Cross for the sins of men.

Ker on the mystery of *The Dream of the Rood* (1904):

The religious poetry of Northumberland is not to be dismissed as mere paraphrase of mediaeval commonplaces. *The Dream of the Rood* is a poem on a common theme—the cross regarded as a tree, the noblest of the forest—

Crux fidelis inter omnes arbor una nobilis.

But the rendering in the English poem is not commonplace. It is hard to describe it justly, but there is one simple beauty in it which makes a vast imaginative difference; it takes the story as if it were something new, and thinks of it as a mystery acted in some visionary place, not on any historical scene. It is not the solemnity of Passion Week in the ritual of the Church, but a sorrow unheard of before, scarcely understood.

W. P. Ker, in his The Dark Ages, *Thomas Nelson and Sons Ltd., 1955.*

Whether written by Cynewulf himself, or by some singularly faithful imitator, the intimate biographic appeal of such a passage brings conviction to ear and mind that here is an authentic and extended parallel to the signed revelations of the Cynewulfian poems.

Rosemary Woolf   (essay date 1958)

SOURCE: "Doctrinal Influences on *The Dream of the Rood*," in *Medium Aevum,* Vol. XXVII, No. 3, 1958, pp. 137-53.

[*In the following essay, Woolf assesses* The Dream of the Rood*'s emphasis on Christ's supremacy and suffering, stating that the poet "reflected exactly the doctrinal pattern of thought of his time."*]

The unique quality of the treatment of the Crucifixion in the **Dream of the Rood** has been long admired, and memorably commented upon. It is unique, not only in Old English poetry—that would not be remarkable since so little survives—but in the whole range of English, and perhaps even western, literature. It is almost certain that this uniqueness of conception is the Anglo-Saxon poet's own, and that he did not have before him a source which he followed closely. There is a compactness and intensity in the poem that would be startling in an Anglo-Saxon translation or paraphrase; nor is its individuality more easily accounted for by the hypothesis that it was originally the work of a Roman rather than of an Anglo-Saxon Christian. Nevertheless all literary and historical probability is against the supposition that nothing but the poet's personal inspiration lies between the gospel narrative and the **Dream of the Rood.** But, whilst the poem is obviously not a Biblical paraphrase in conventional style, yet it is influenced hardly at all by Latin hymns, nor by certain antiphons of the liturgy, such as lie behind the treatment of the Crucifixion in the *Crist.* The influences to be considered are in fact not of the kind that can be isolated in any specific text, but rather those of the religious thought of the poet's period, in particular its philosophic view of the person and nature of Christ and definition of the Redemption. The most remarkable achievement of the poem is its balance between the effects of triumph and suffering, and their paradoxical fusion in the Crucifixion is suggested first by the alternation between the jewelled radiant cross and the plain and blood-covered cross in the prelude, and secondly and much more subtly and powerfully by the two figures of the heroic victorious warrior and the passive enduring cross. At the time when the poet wrote, the Church insisted on the co-existence of these two elements in Christ, divine supremacy and human suffering, with a vehemence and rigidity deriving from more than two centuries of heretical Christological dispute, and which abated only when the orthodox view was no longer questioned. In the soteriological doctrine of the time there also co-existed the two ideas of a divine victory and a sacrificial offering, though here not as the result of a carefully formulated orthodox dogma, but simply because as yet the nature of the Redemption had not become a central subject of theological speculation, and contradictory views were

therefore stated not only by different writers but also often in different works of the same writer. The author of the **Dream of the Rood,** then, in emphasizing at once both triumph and suffering in a way that would have been inconceivable in the Middle Ages, reflected exactly the doctrinal pattern of thought of his time, though this fact, of course, by no means detracts from the brilliance with which this thought, so difficult of imaginative comprehension, is transmuted into a poetic form which brings home its meaning to the understanding in a way that is beyond the dry precision of philosophical language.

The stress that will be laid on the Crucifixion as a scene of triumph or a scene of suffering depends upon the stress that is laid on Christ as God or Christ as man. These two possible emphases developed in the late fourth century in the theological schools of Alexandria and Antioch, and both led to Christological heresy. The Monophysites, whose philosophic definition of Christ sprang from the speculative mode of thought of Alexandria, correctly insisted on the unity of Christ's person, but at the cost of a tendency to confuse His two natures: the result was that they overstressed His divinity, for in this confusion His humanity, unsafeguarded by an essential distinctiveness, might seem to be absorbed as a drop of water by the ocean. The undesirable but logically inevitable conclusion of such a philosophic view was either that the Godhead must be thought of as passible—as the Eutychians of the fifth century were accused of maintaining—or Christ must be said to have been immune from the ordinary human experience of suffering, and in the sixth century some of the more extreme Monophysites scarcely avoided this Docetic belief. The heresy of the school of Antioch takes its name from Nestorius, although modern scholarship has shown him to have been at least partly maligned. The Nestorians had the moral and literal way of thought which characterized all Antiochene studies. They, unlike the Monophysites, correctly distinguished between the two natures of Christ, but at the cost of almost denying the unity of His person, and hence of overstressing Christ's humanity. The Nestorians were notorious for their rejection of the term *Theotokos* (God-bearer) as a descriptive title of the Virgin, and in their most obviously extreme statements held that the indwelling of God in Christ was not different in kind, although of course in degree, from His indwelling in the prophets. To stress that Christ was subject to all the natural pains of human nature was therefore particularly characteristic of the Nestorians. This summary has stressed what is extreme and exaggerated in the Christology of the two heretical schools, for it was this that was remembered and feared by the orthodox. The difference between the moderate and unfanatical thinkers of both sides was more a matter of emphasis than of deep dogmatic division, and each side when speaking cautiously and charitably could reach agreement with the other, as they did at the time of Cyril's Formulary of Reunion (433), but the effect in the heat of hostile argument or in private eccentric speculation was that the Monophysites seemed to deny that Christ was fully man, and the Nestorians to deny that Christ was fully God.

The Church in Rome insisted on a middle way between these two extremes, and the dispute was first settled to the philosophic satisfaction of the west at the Council of Chalcedon (449). There the Council accepted a number of documents as orthodox, besides composing its own *Definitio Fidei.* Of these documents the one of most lasting importance was the *Tome* of Leo I. In this the Pope established a razor-edge position between Alexandria and Antioch, maintaining the true western tradition that there was in Christ one person and two natures, the person undivided and the natures unconfused. He also defined the correct manner of speaking of Christ's life on earth, so that this bare definition might be expressed in terms of narrative or exegesis. From Antioch he borrowed the principal of 'recognizing the difference', that is of dividing, as the Nestorians had commonly done in their scriptural commentaries, all the acts of Christ's life into those which appertained to His humanity and those which appertained to His divinity. In His humanity, for instance, He hungered, thirsted, felt fatigue, and suffered: in His divinity He healed, forgave, and accomplished all His miracles—or, to quote a popular and pointed example, in His humanity Christ wept for the death of Lazarus, but in His divinity He raised him. This method preserved admirably the doctrine of the two natures without confusion, but for full orthodoxy it required the corrective and corollary of the principle of *communicatio idiomatum,* which Leo adopted from Alexandria. The philosophic basis of this principle was that, since Christ's person was a unity, the properties of both natures could be ascribed to it, provided, of course, that the word used for Christ's person was a concrete not an abstract noun (e. g. God, not Godhead). The method was therefore to attribute to Christ under a divine title one of the limitations of humanity: authority for this could be found in the works of St. Paul himself, who had written in a much quoted text, 'If they had known it they would not have crucified the Lord of Glory' (1 Cor. ii. 8). The unity of Christ's person was thus emphasized in a manner which from a literary point of view produced a startlingly paradoxical effect.

Although Leo's *Tome* established for centuries the orthodox way of describing Christ's life, it did not at the time put an end to Christological dispute, but rather stimulated further dissension. With the doctrinal issue aggravated by motives of imperial policy, Rome and Byzantium remained opposed until the Oecumenical Council of 682, when the Monophysite and Nestorian controversy was finally determined, though only at the cost of the schism of the churches of Egypt and Asia Minor. Even in the west Christological orthodoxy did not then remain undisturbed, for in the eighth century the Adoptionist heresy (the view that Christ was Son of God by adoption only) became strong in Spain and France, and Alcuin was one of those who defended western orthodoxy against it.

Theological disputation may at first sight seem remote from Anglo-Saxon England of the late seventh century. But whilst the fact that the Anglo-Saxon ecclesiastics of this period came of a people only comparatively recently converted, and without any tradition of philosophical thinking, no doubt led to their accepting western orthodoxy unquestioningly, it did not necessarily mean that they accepted it ignorantly. It was not the policy of the Pope to keep them innocently unaware of heretical dangers, but rather to instruct the Anglo-Saxon church against them; nor could they have read the works of any of the great Fathers and remained ignorant of the eastern heresies. The Anglo-Saxons were in fact in an ideal position for upholding the western tradition. On the one hand it is clear that they had sufficient grasp of theological teaching to understand the issues involved, but on the other hand they had neither the fanaticism of spirit nor the confidence of a long tradition of independent scholarship, which might lead them into disagreement with Rome.

In the year 679 the Christological heresies were particularly brought to the attention of the Anglo-Saxon Church. The Pope, in preparation for the Oecumenical Council, wished to assure himself of the invariable orthodoxy of all the countries in the west. In accordance with this wish, Theodore of Tarsus, Archbishop of Canterbury, in 679 summoned the Synod of Hatfield, and in the presence of the papal legate inquired diligently of the bishops and doctors there assembled what doctrine they held, and found that they were all of the Catholic faith. This Council condemned the great heretics, including Nestorius and Eutyches, and read and accepted the documents of the Lateran Council of 649, which, of course, included Leo's *Tome.* Theodore also set down the declaration of faith of the Council in a Synodical letter 'for the instruction and faith of aftercomers', and a copy of this was given to the legate to take back to Rome. At the Oecumenical Council itself the faith of the Anglo-Saxon Church was attested by Wilfrid, on the first occasion when the Anglo-Saxons were represented at such a Council. The papal legate at Hatfield had been John, the arch-chanter or precentor of St. Peter's, who had spent the previous year under the guidance of Benedict Biscop in the monastery at Wearmouth, instructing the monks in the Roman manner of singing the monastic office, and during that time a copy of the documents of the Lateran Council, which he had brought with him, was made at Wearmouth. It is inconceivable that during this time he left unheeded the other half of his commission from the Pope, and failed to discuss and instruct in western Christology. Similar guidance and instruction must have been given by Theodore and his colleague Hadrian of Naples, both of whom are known to have made extensive journeys through England. Theodore himself had been brought up in the geographical centre of the dispute, and was so learned and skilled in the Monophysite controversy that the previous Pope had wished him to lead the Roman legation to Constantinople.

It was not, however, solely from the teaching of such men as Theodore and Hadrian, or from the assembly at Hatfield, or from the documents of the Councils deposited in England, that knowledge of the heretical doctrines of the person and nature of Christ would reach the Anglo-Saxon Church, but also from the works of the great Fathers, Ambrose, Jerome, Augustine and Gregory the Great. In separate tracts and in their exegesis of the New Testament the later Fathers constantly refuted the Nestorian and Monophysite heresies, and various key texts in the gospels became conventional starting points for an attack on the wicked Nestorius or the madness of Eutyches. These anti-heretical arguments based on scriptural texts are repeated by Bede, whose own commentaries on the four gospels were written in the first quarter of the eighth century. There is little in Bede's commentaries that is original, but neither are they simply translations, and Bede must be supposed to have selected from the works of his authoritative predecessors those arguments and explanations which he thought most relevant and important, and all his four commentaries are extraordinarily full of refutations of the earlier heretics. From the combined evidence of the historical information and of Bede's commentaries it is clear that the heresies of Nestorius and Eutyches were a living issue in England for at least the fifty years from about 675-725. Since the identity of the author of the ***Dream of the Rood*** is not known, it cannot be conclusively proved from evidence outside the poem that he knew of the Christological controversy. But the burden of proof is undoubtedly on anyone who would maintain that an educated man of this period could remain unaware at the very least that the greatest theological care and precision was required in any statements about Christ's life, and in particular about His Crucifixion, and that an equal stress must be laid on Christ's divinity (against Nestorius) and Christ's humanity (against Eutyches).

The tension between divinity and triumph on the one hand and humanity and suffering on the other might also arise from the doctrine of the Redemption as it was taught at this period. No comprehensive and consistent soteriological theory was evolved until that of Anselm in the eleventh century, and this point—no doubt because it had not been associated with heresy—was not treated with the same philosophic depth and perception with which the Fathers had analysed the person of Christ, and on it they were often ambiguous and self-contradictory. Apart from the typically eastern idea of humanity being cleansed and immortalized through its assumption by the divinity, which though important is not relevant here, two other main ideas can be clearly distinguished. The earlier is that which was commonly held by the eastern church, and it was dualistic, though of course not Manichaean. According to it, the nature of the Redemption was that God, by His Incarnation and Passion, released or redeemed mankind from the devil, who, by the Fall had acquired a just claim to man. Christ's death was seen either as a bait or an offering, and through his acceptance of it the devil was outwitted and overcome. The issue was therefore between God and the devil, and the result was God's defeat of the devil. Although this idea was of eastern origin, it was repeated by the great western Fathers, Leo, Augustine and Gregory 1. They, however, following the New Testament, and in particular the Epistle to the Hebrews, also stressed the Crucifixion as an offering or sacrifice made on behalf of man by Christ as man, the spotless for the guilty. The emphasis in the New Testament on man being redeemed by the blood of Christ could scarcely be ignored, and a recognition of this was aided by the growing devotion to the Eucharist. Gregory I contributed much to the Catholic doctrine of the mass, and in self-contradiction stated both theories of the Redemption, developing a theory of Christ's suffering and death as a sacrificial offering which is Anselm's view in rudimentary form; though elsewhere he also speaks of the Crucifixion in terms of conflict and triumph, repeating Gregory of Nyssa's grotesque image of Christ's humanity being a bait swallowed by Leviathan.

These two theories were not normally combined, but if they were associated in thought a tension and paradox would be inevitable. In one view the stress is on Christ's divinity: God enters the world to free man from the devil, and the moment of His triumph is the Crucifixion; in the other view the stress is on Christ's humanity: God becomes man that as man He may offer to God the due sacrifice which man is unable to offer for himself, and the Crucifixion is the supreme moment of pain and abasement. It must, however, be added that these two views were not entirely mutually exclusive, but rather what was central in one became secondary in the other. Thus in the theory of the 'devil's rights' it was not forgotten that the result of the defeat of the devil was the restoration of the former relationship between God and man, and in the 'satisfaction' theory it was remembered that the further result of God being reconciled to man was that the devil lost his former possession of the whole human race. For this reason it was not ridiculous that both ideas should be implied or stated within one passage or poem.

The ***Dream of the Rood*** then was written at a time when both Christology and soteriology laid this double stress on the Crucifixion as a scene of both triumph and suffering, and the author has succeeded in fulfilling what might seem to be an artistically impossible demand. Without such a brilliant conception as that of the poet's, the two aspects would inevitably have become separated, as they were usually in the Middle Ages. The Crucifixion in both mediæval art and mediæval literature is usually a scene of utmost agony: in accordance with the doctrine of 'satisfaction', Christ as man offers His suffering to its farthest limit, until the body hangs painfully from the Cross without blood or life. The note of triumph is necessarily reserved until the Harrowing of Hell, when Christ, approaching as the King of Glory, conquers the devil, often using His Resurrection cross as a weapon of war and plunging it into the mouth of the defeated Leviathan. The timing of this, of course, exactly expresses the pattern of the mediæval doctrine of the Redemption, the sacrifice being primary, the defeat of the devil secondary.

The image of the Crucifixion as a conflict and Christ as a warrior is very appropriate to the dualistic theory of the Redemption, for the essence of this image is that there should be an opponent to be overcome, and that the hero should be triumphant; as a symbol of the 'satisfaction' theory it would lose its force and appear crude and irrelevant. In the Middle Ages, therefore, the image of Christ as a feudal knight is rarely used, and, when it is, is normally accompanied by a statement of the theory of the 'devil's rights'. A clear example of this may be seen in *Piers Plowman* (*Passus* xviii, B Text), where Christ is represented as contestor and victor in a tournament, and releases man justly from the devil's power since 'gyle is bigyled' (l. 358) and Christ's soul given in reason (ll. 325, 337-42), the ideas of the bait and the offering being here combined. We might conjecture that the image of the Crucifixion as a battle would otherwise have almost died out, had it not been given a new force by the association of courtly love with chivalry, so that Christ becomes the lover-knight, loving his lady (mankind) to the point of death, and deserving thereby to win her love in return. The *examplum* of the lover-knight, of which the most moving form is in the section on love in the *Ancren Riwle* and Henryson's *Bloody Serk,* makes this much-stressed point of Christ's love for man with beauty and clarity.

The presentation of Christ in the **Dream of the Rood** as a young warrior advancing to battle has been much commented upon as an example of the common Anglo-Saxon convention of treating Christian subject matter in heroic terms. The conception of Christ as a warrior is, however, not peculiar to the Anglo-Saxon imagination. In visual art, for instance, it was a common Mediterranean theme, of which one of the most striking extant examples is a mosaic in the Chapel of the Palace of the Archbishop at Ravenna. There Christ, dressed in Roman military style, stands strongly, the symbolical animals subdued beneath His feet, and a cross of the Resurrection style swung over His shoulder as though it were a weapon. The effect is of a triumphant hero. The armour of Christ probably derives from the description of the divine warrior-redeemer in Isaiah lix. 17, whilst the animals beneath His feet are an illustration of Psalm xci. 13. Whilst it is not improbable that the Anglo-Saxons knew the *Christus Miles* theme, it cannot be proved that they did, for, although there is a Christ standing over the animals on both the Ruthwell and Bewcastle Crosses, the original was probably in the hieratic style, in which Christ, dressed in a long mantle, seems to stand as a ruler with serenity and power over the prostrate animals. The concept of the Crucifixion as a battle, however, was not restricted to the visual arts. The idea of a military conflict had been common in the patristic statements of the theory of the 'devil's rights', and became, no doubt therefrom, a commonplace of early Latin Christian poets and hymn-writers, and with it was associated the idea of kingly victory. This derived supposedly from Psalm xcvi. 10, which in the *Psalterium Romanum* read: 'Dicite in gentibus quia dominus regnavit a ligno'. Versions in which *a ligno* did not appear were dismissed by the early church as malicious alterations of the Jews, so admirably did this reading express their doctrine of the Crucifixion. The idea that Christ reigned from the tree was given popularity by the famous hymn of Venantius Fortunatus, *Vexilla Regis Prodeunt,* a hymn undoubtedly used by the Anglo-Saxon Church, and was given iconographical expression in the earliest crucifixes and representations of the Crucifixion. In these Christ, a young man of noble appearance, stands firmly on the Cross, His feet supported by a *suppedaneum,* and on His upright head a halo or royal crown. All these are but illustrations of a common imaginative theme of the early church, which must have been known to the Anglo-Saxons, and which presents such striking affinities to both conception and tone of the *geong hæleð* in the **Dream of the Rood,** that it would be perverse to prefer the theory of coincidence to that of influence.

In the **Dream of the Rood** the heroic quality of Christ is suggested by the three actions ascribed to Him: He advances to the Cross with bold speed, strips Himself, and ascends it. All these emphasize the confidence of divine victory and the voluntariness of Christ's undertaking the Crucifixion. They are therefore absolutely consonant with the teaching of the early church, and in intense contrast to the mediæval treatment of the Crucifixion. The

mediæval picture of Christ exhausted and stooping beneath the weight of the Cross is so well-known and so moving that it is easy to forget nowadays that this is not a literal illustration of the gospel narrative, but a mediæval interpretation which, though the Christian may well believe it to be true, is at most faintly implicit in the gospels themselves. There is a discrepancy in the gospel accounts of the carrying of the Cross. In the first three gospels the Cross is said to have been borne by Simon of Cyrene, whilst in St. John Christ carries it Himself. According to the orthodox exegesis, which Bede follows, the discordant statements are reconciled by the view that the Cross was first carried by Christ and later by Simon. But it is interesting to notice that Bede, again following an authoritative tradition, makes only an abstract and moral deduction from this: Simon is allegorically a Christian obeying Christ's command to take up his cross and follow Him, and literally a gentile in order to signify the gathering in of the whole world into Christ's Church. The naturalistic deduction that Christ was too exhausted to carry it farther Himself, which accorded so well with the mediæval doctrine of the Crucifixion, was not made until later. It was therefore not a wilful divergence from the gospel narrative to represent Christ advancing without the Cross (although that the Cross is already in position and watches Christ advancing to it seems to be the poet's own variation). In the mosaics of San Apollinare Nuovo at Ravenna, for instance, Christ Himself advances with His hands outstretched in a gesture of sacrificial self-offering. The poet has taken advantage of this tradition to heighten the heroic and voluntary nature of the Crucifixion.

The stripping of Christ is not described in any of the gospels. The soldiers divide His garments amongst themselves, but their actual removal is not given as an essential detail of the narrative. The Middle Ages, of course, imagined that Christ's robes were torn from Him by the soldiers, as a further stage in their grotesque brutality, and the manner in which this caused the wounds of His flagellation to reopen was often gruesomely described. Since Matthew and Mark a few verses before the description of the Crucifixion tell of the previous stripping of Christ, when the purple robe was placed upon Him, it is plausible to imagine the scene preparatory to the Crucifixion analogously. But the author of the **Dream of the Rood** was following a patristic tradition, to be found, for instance, in Ambrose's commentary on Luke, of Christ as kingly victor removing His clothes: 'Pulchre ascensurus crucem regalia vestimenta deposuit'. Though to this is added an Old Testament parallel, that as Adam defeated sought clothing, so Christ conquering laid down His clothing. In the **Dream of the Rood** Christ is very clearly a hero stripping Himself for battle in a description which has been compared with an analogous scene in the *Aeneid* (v. 241 ff.), where Entellus strips himself, and stands imposing of appearance, ready for his encounter with Dares: a resemblance, of course, of heroic description to heroic description, not of derivative to source. Christ's stripping of Himself, then, is voluntary and heroic, and so also therefore is His nudity. In the Syrian tradition of Christian art, in which nakedness was considered shameful, Christ on the Cross for the sake of reverence and decorum was dressed, with hieratic effect, in the long *collobium.* But Hellenic

Christian art retained the idea of the nudity of the hero, and therefore represented Christ as naked, or almost naked, upon the Cross, without this in any way conflicting with the idea of the Crucifixion as a royal and heroic triumph; and it is this conception which also lies behind the phrase *ongyrede hine* in the **Dream of the Rood.** It is interesting to notice that in the Middle Ages writers and artists adhered in this point to the gospel account and to the outward form of Hellenic art, but saw the enforced nakedness of Christ as a humiliation added to torment, and it was sometimes imagined that the Virgin intervened to save her Son from such shame by covering Him with her veil.

Christ's mounting the Cross is the climax and end of the description of the Crucifixion in heroic terms. Again in the gospels the method of attaching Christ to the Cross is not described, and exegesis, as in Bede, normally only expounds the allegorical significance of the Crucifixion, and is not primarily concerned with turning the gospel story into a continuous naturalistic narrative. Of the great Fathers, only Ambrose in the passage referred to above describes Christ ascending the Cross as victor. In Latin hymnody there were two conventional expressions, *crucem ascendere* and in *crucis stipite levatur.* The poet, perhaps following Ambrose, and certainly with the same intention in mind, makes use of the Old English equivalent of *crucem ascendere: gealgan gestigan.* This is the consummation of his theme, and Christ ascends the Cross of His own will, in contrast to the later mediæval representations in art and mystery plays, where the body of Christ is nailed to the Cross as it lies on the ground, and the thrusting of its base into the socket is an additional agony for Christ. The young hero's advance, and ascent of the Cross, is thus at once painless and heroic, and is therefore a most admirable symbol of the divine nature of Christ and the earlier definition of the Redemption.

In any narrative stressing the divinity of Christ, the greatest difficulty lies in the description of Christ's death, a difficulty which is not only literary but theological. To this the poet's image of Christ resting and asleep after His great struggle is a most brilliant poetic solution: 'Aledon hie ðær limwerigne . . . ond he hine ðær hwile reste, meðe æfter ðam miclan gewinne' (ll. 63-5). It had been a fairly common view that at the moment of Christ's death, the Godhead forsook the body, and that the obviously anguished cry of *Eli, Eli, lamma sabacthani,* was the lament of the human body as it felt the divinity depart. Such a conclusion was dangerously near to the Apollinarian heresy (that in Christ the place of the rational soul was taken by the Divinity), but the alternative, which seemed to involve the theologically impossible statement that God could die, and that it was the dead body of God which was removed from the Cross, was not immediately acceptable, and it is little wonder that Christian writers faltered before a so apparently incomprehensible paradox. At the same time there was an insistence on the voluntary nature of Christ's death—that, unlike the thieves and all other human beings, He had died at the exact moment that He chose. That Christ inclined His head before death, not after, was thought to demonstrate this, as also the comparatively short duration of His agony. The text of John x. 18 was orthodoxly associated with this, as can be seen

from Bede's commentaries on Mark and John. This theological uneasiness over the death of Christ is negatively reflected in early representations of the Crucifixion, in all of which Christ is shown alive; in the west it is not until the Middle Ages that Christ is shown hanging dead upon the Cross. The author of the **Dream of the Rood** similarly does not speak of Christ's death: the climax of the poem is simply, *Crist wæs on rode,* and His death is thereafter described as a sleep, in terms which with cathartic effect suggest exhaustion, release and temporary rest. In describing Christ's death as a sleep the poet was probably not original. The image had already been used of Christ; for instance, by Augustine in his commentary on St. John, and by Bede in imitation. Both intend by it to emphasize the voluntary nature of Christ's death: just as He slept when He wished, so He died when He wished, though Augustine also draws a further allegorical point, that just as Eve was born from the side of Adam as he slept, so the Church was born from the side of Christ in His flowing sacramental blood as He slept in death on the Cross. But, though the poet may have borrowed the image, the use he makes of it in suggesting a body still potentially instinct with life in his own. Modern usage may have reduced the image of death as a sleep to a sentimental euphemism—a danger perhaps inherent in the Homeric and late classical usage—but in its earliest Christian form, in Christ's words to Jairus, its point is not to evade the terror and finality of the word death, but to assert the power of God to bring the dead to life, and therefore its use in the **Dream of the Rood** is sublimely appropriate.

Whilst the effect of the poet's treatment of Christ the warrior is indeed fine, it is not here that his brilliance of invention lies, but rather in his emphasis on Christ's human nature, which is found in his treatment of the Cross. Wonder at the mere device of making the Cross speak has perhaps been exaggerated, for, as scholars have sufficiently shown, there are adequate parallels in the Anglo-Saxon Riddles and in Latin literature to the convention of ascribing speech to an inanimate object, and to this can be added the point that in at least one dramatic passage in the Fathers in a Pseudo-Augustinian sermon, the Cross itself is actually imagined as speaking. It is the use made by the poet of this device that rather deserves admiring praise: his identification, in part, of the Cross with Christ.

In reaction from the forms of Monophysitism, which so stressed the divinity of Christ that He was thought to be naturally free in both body and consciousness of all human experience of discomfort and pain, orthodox commentators stressed that like other men He hungered and thirsted. He must therefore also have felt the pain of the Crucifixion, though of course in His humanity, not in His impassible Godhead. The sufferings of Christ in His human nature the poet suggests most movingly by the sufferings of the Cross. The Cross shares in all the sufferings of Christ, so that it seems to endure a compassion, in the sense in which that word was used in the Middle Ages to describe the Virgin's identification of her feelings with those of her Son in His Passion. The real emotional intensity of Christ's agony is thus communicated without the reasonable and insoluble bewilderment arising of how impassibility and passibility could co-exist in one consciousness.

The Cross not only experiences the extremities of pain but, having within itself the power to escape them, endures with a reluctance heroically subdued. This reluctance must primarily be referred to the other aspect of the Cross, that of the loyal retainer, and its steadfastness then gains an impressive force, since by a tremendous and ironic reversal of the values of the heroic code, it has to acquiesce in and even assist in the death of its lord, forbidden either to protect Him or avenge Him. To see the Cross's reiterated statements of obedience solely as another reflection of Christ's human nature would undoubtedly be to narrow and misinterpret the range of emotion expressed, much of which consists of the anguish of being the cause of death to another, particularly since the other is by implication its lord, to whom it feels that mixture of love and loyal duty, which was the proper feeling of a retainer. It is, moreover, theologically undesirable to over-emphasize the reluctance of the Cross as being also a feeling of Christ. The Church, in opposition to Monothelitism, had defined the coexistence of two wills in Christ, but had added that there was no conflict between them, since the human will conformed itself voluntarily to the divine. There was also a view, which sprang from a sense of decorum rather than from philosophic reasoning, that even if moderate fear were not in itself evil, it would nevertheless be unfitting that Christ should in any way experience it and recoil from the Crucifixion, thus detracting from the voluntariness of the act. Nevertheless there was one notable passage in the gospels, the account of the Agony in the Garden, which in its literal sense precisely ascribed to Christ that revulsion from pain and death which is an inherent element in human nature. There is a sense of strain in Bede's commentaries on this scene in all three gospels. On the one hand, following Ambrose and Jerome, he does not interpret the cup, as it was commonly interpreted in the Middle Ages, as the cup of Christ's sufferings, but refers it to the Jews, who having the law and the prophets can have no excuse for crucifying one whom they should have recognized. On the other hand the passage interpreted literally provided the strongest evidence against the Gnostics and Phantasiasts who had denied the reality of Christ's human body—a point which Bede makes in exclamatory style—whilst the actual texts, 'The spirit is willing but the flesh is weak' and 'Not my will but thine be done' had similarly become *loci classici* for the refutation of the Monothelites; and in his commentary on the first of these in Matthew and Mark, Bede, following a common tradition, allows that Christ in His human nature shrank back from death:

> Facit hic locus et adversus Eutychianos, qui dicunt unum in mediatore Dei et hominum Domino ac Salvatore nostro operationem, unam fuisse voluntatem. Cum enim dicit *Spiritus quidem promptus est, caro autem infirma,* duas voluntates ostendit: humanam, videlicet, quae est carnis, et divinam, quae est deitatis. Ubi humana quidem propter infirmitatem carnis recusat passionem, Divina autem ejus est promptissima. (*P.L.* xcii, 277.)

Whilst, therefore, the parallel must not be pressed too far,

nor in any way exclusively, it is difficult not to see a correspondence between the antithesis of the divine and human wills in this passage from Bede and the contrast in the poem between the hero who hastens to his death and the Cross enduring only with reluctance.

It might at this point be urged that the reflection in the **Dream of the Rood** of the divine and the human in the young hero and the Cross has been overstated, and that the figure of the warrior might symbolize no more than Christ's glorious humanity. But it was precisely this element in Christ which had been ignored in Leo's *Tome* and by subsequent commentators. All actions had been assigned to the two categories of divine and human, and the possibility of a third category—actions possible to a sinless humanity—had not been mentioned. It is therefore certain that anybody who understood the Christological doctrine at all would think in terms of this rigid distinction, which may appear unfamiliar and exaggerated to the modern reader.

The treatment of the young hero and the Cross has so far been seen to fulfil the principle of 'recognizing the difference', but the distinction between divinity and humanity, triumph and suffering, is reunited by the stylistic form of the *communicatio idiomatum.* It is interesting to compare the style of the **Dream of the Rood** with that of the description of the Crucifixion in the *Crist.* Since the latter is a complaint, the main point is the contrast between man's sin and Christ's goodness, man's ingratitude and Christ's love. The characteristic of the style is therefore a series of antitheses, which are stylistically pointed by the alliteration:

> Ic wæs on worulde wædla,   þæt þu wurde
>   welig on heofonum,
> earm wæs ic on eðle þinum,   þæt þu wurde
>   eadig on minum.
>
>   (1495-6)

This, of course, is not native to Anglo-Saxon style, but derives from the Easter liturgy, particularly the *Improperia* of Good Friday, conceivably with the stimulus of a sermon intermediary. The effect of the *communicatio idiomatum* is likewise not native to Anglo-Saxon style, for it provides the shock and astonishment of violent paradox. The strangeness of both these styles to Anglo-Saxon literature is immediately evident if we think of them as characteristics of metaphysical poetry: the antitheses being found in their most polished and pointed form in Herbert's 'The Sacrifice', and the potentialities of the *communicatio idiomatum* most fully exploited in such an objectively meditative sequence as Donne's *La Corona.* But although the Anglo-Saxons lack the stylistic poise of the Metaphysicals, it might well be maintained that they managed these stylistic forms with greater assurance than did the writers of the mediæval lyric.

In the thirty lines of dramatic description of the Crucifixion in the **Dream of the Rood** there are ten examples of the *communicatio idiomatum,* and each one stimulates a shock at the paradox, a shock which grows in intensity as the poem progresses. Those towards the end are particularly striking: 'Genamon hie þær ælmihtigne god' (60), 'Aledon hie limwerigne . . . beheoldon hie ðær heofones dryhten' (63-64), 'gesetton hie ðæron sigora Wealdend' (67). The habit of variation in Anglo-Saxon poetic style and the richness of synonym in Anglo-Saxon poetic diction, assist the poet in each instance to use a fresh word or phrase to emphasize some attribute of God, His rule, majesty, omnipotence; and at the early date of the *Dream of the Rood* there can be no question of such periphrases having become so conventional as to be weakened in meaning. The theological point that the Christ who endured the Crucifixion is fully God and fully man is thus perfectly made, and with it the imaginative effect which is the natural result of the *communicatio idiomatum* is attained, the astonishment at the great paradox of Christianity that God should endure such things.

There is a further and related point of contrast to be made between the description of the Crucifixion in the *Crist* and in the *Dream of the Rood*. Since the first takes its form from the antiphons of the liturgy, it anticipates the mediæval lyrics and mystery plays, in which the audience or readers are made to feel participants in the action, by Christ's direct address to them, and the making of their actions and feelings one half of the stylized antitheses. The didactic and devotional intention of this is plain, but it also serves another useful literary purpose, though probably unintentionally: it removes the difficulty of the customary instinctive reaction of the audience—which is, to identify themselves with the character in the play or poem with whom they sympathize. There can be no danger of them unconsciously identifying themselves with Christ in His torment because they feel themselves present in their own person. Their own feelings and situation are dramatically relevant to what is being said or done in the literary work. Now this is not so in the *Dream of the Rood*, where the dreamer, with his consciousness of the tragic and terrifying contrast between his own sinfulness and the glory of the Cross, is forgotten once the Cross begins to speak. However, particularly in the Anglo-Saxon period, a treatment of the Crucifixion in which the hearer was led by his intense sympathy for Christ's pain to identify himself with Christ in the poem, would obviously be unfortunate, since it would carry with it the implication that Christ's consciousness was solely human and therefore comprehensible to fellow human beings. But to imagine Christ's consciousness at the Crucifixion in terms of human experience would be to revert, though no doubt unsuspectingly, to the Gnostic heresy which was even more obviously un-Christian than the extremes of Nestorianism and Monophysitism, that before the Passion began Christ's divinity left Him. By the semi-identification of the Cross with Christ, the poet enables his hearers to share in an imaginative recreation of Christ's sufferings, whilst the problem which bewilders the mind—the nature of Christ's consciousness—is evaded.

The general feeling and vocabulary of the *Dream of the Rood* suggest affinities with the school of Cynewulf rather than of Cædmon. But it is evident from the early date of the Ruthwell Cross, on which modern archæologists and art historians are agreed, that the *Dream of the Rood* must have been an offshoot of the school of Biblical poetry begun by Cædmon. Yet, when Bede speaks of Christ's Passion as one of Cædmon's subjects, one inevitably thinks of the style of the section of the *Heliand* which describes the Crucifixion (5534-715), rather than of the *Dream of the Rood*. But the poem must have been written round about the year 700, and that the poet did not simply write a Biblical paraphrase in native style must surely be accounted for by the fact that he was steeped in the doctrine of the Church, and thus gave to his treatment of the Crucifixion the full richness and subtlety of its theological significance. The exigencies of a complex and rigid doctrine, far from hampering the poetic magination, have here provoked a magnificent response: a profound and dramatic meditation that could never have been inspired by unchartered freedom. It is, in fact, this poetic transformation of the philosophic and theological views of the Crucifixion that gives to the poem its unique quality, and adds depths below depths of meaning under the apparently lucid surface.

Robert E. Diamond (essay date 1958)

SOURCE: "Heroic Diction in *The Dream of the Rood*," in *Studies in Honor of John Wilcox*, edited by A. Dayle Wallace and Woodburn O. Ross, 1958. Reprint by Books for Libraries Press, 1972, pp. 3-7.

[*In the essay below, Diamond analyzes the use of heroic language in* The Dream of the Rood.]

Many people who have read *The Dream of the Rood* have been struck by the poet's use of certain heroic phrases in describing the crucifixion. The tree from which the cross was made is said to have been cut down by bold enemies (*strange féondas*, 30b). The Lord is referred to as a young hero (*geong hæleþ*, 39a). He is said to be bold and brave (*strang and stíþmód*, 40a). The cross is said to be wounded with arrows (*stræÌum forwundod*, 62b). The Lord is said to rest for a while after the mighty conflict (*æfter þám micelan gewinne*, 65a). When the poet says that the Lord hastens with great courage (*efstan elne micele*, 34a), he uses a phrase strongly reminiscent of the one used to state that Beowulf hastened to do battle with Grendel's mother (*efste mid elne*, 1493). The executioners of the Lord are twice called warriors (*hilderincas*, 61, 72), the very compound used in *Beowulf* to refer to Beowulf twice (1495, 1576) and to Grendel once (986). The Lord is referred to as a famous ruler (*mæran þéodne*, 69a). This same phrase is used six times in *Beowulf* to refer to Hrothgar, four times to Beowulf, and once each to Heremod and Onela. The Lord is referred to as a prince (*æðelinge*, 58a). In *Beowulf*, this word is used three times to refer to Beowulf (1596, 2374, 2424), once to Scyld (33), once to Wæls (888), and once to one of the warriors at Heorot (1244). After the descent from the cross, the followers of the Lord sing a dirge for Him (*sorhléoð galan*, 67b). This is the same phrase that appears in *Beowulf* where Hrethel sings a dirge (*sorhléoð gæleþ*, 2460) for his son Herebeald.

It must be apparent at the outset that this heroic language is strangely out of place in a poem about the crucifixion of the Lord. When the poet describes Christ as a bold hero hastening courageously to the mighty struggle, he directly contradicts the story of the crucifixion as related in the gospels; but, more important, he does a kind of violence to the spirit and doctrines of Christianity. The central paradox of Christianity is the everlasting victory through the apparent momentary worldly defeat and humiliation. Our poet seems to have reversed the softening tendency which so often creeps into heroic poetry: for example, in the Serbian heroic song of the Battle of Kossovo, the hero rejects an earthly kingdom in favor of the heavenly kingdom; and one of the heroic figures of the *Mahabarata*—Arjuna—appears in the heroic narrative frame of the didactic poem, the *Bhagavad Gita,* bewailing the senseless slaughter of the approaching battle. There seems to be a point in the heroic poetry of many peoples where the softening tendencies of a more ethical society begin to supersede the old heroic standards of vengeance and glory in battle. In *The Dream of the Rood,* however, the situation is just the reverse: supposedly a Christian poem, presumably informed by the spirit and doctrines of Christianity, it displays in some passages a seemingly atavistic reversion to the heroic spirit.

How can we account for this apparent inconsistency of tone in *The Dream of the Rood?* Scholars and critics have generally assumed that the poet was trying to make his Christian subject matter attractive to an audience that was accustomed to hear heroic poetry. But England had been solidly Christian probably for quite a long time when the poem was composed. It seems likely that the poet lapsed into heroic language not so much in order to please his audience as because he was accustomed to compose in such language. This brings us, of course, to the subject of traditional diction in Old English poetry. Whether or not *The Dream of the Rood* and other such poems were composed orally or with pen in hand can probably never be settled to anyone's satisfaction, but they reflect a kind of oral-formulaic diction, handed down from generation to generation, added to a little here and a little there, comprising a common stock of formulaic phrases which enabled the poets to express almost any idea in correct verses, without casting about for a felicitous turn of expression. A poet who was accustomed to compose songs on heroic subjects would quite naturally apply all the old heroic epithets and formulas to his matter. If he set himself to compose a song on a Christian subject, it was natural that diction reflecting an earlier society should creep in. And, as time went by, a stock of Christian formulas was developed. Many were, of course, formed on older models, using, for example, epithets for kings to refer to the first two persons of the Trinity.

Such a poet, then, is in some sense a captive of his traditional diction. There are not an infinite number of ways to express an idea in correct verses; there are only the traditional ways. While the poet can rely on the traditional diction to help him out of tight places in composing, he is also caught in the net of tradition, so to speak—he cannot compose in any other way. This applies not only to his actual choice of words, but to the themes and narrative technique of his work. The tradition in which the poet was composing was a narrative tradition. Dogmatic or introspective subject matter would most likely be passed over in favor of something that gave the poet a story to tell. To call the thing by its right name: the poets tended to choose subjects from Christian story that were rather sensational.

A good example is the Cynewulf poem on the acts of Saint Juliana, which relates a succession of lurid events. Whereas hagiography does not lend itself particularly well to the kind of narrative treatment the Anglo-Saxon poets customarily gave their work, the Apocryphal book of Judith is admirably suited to this kind of narrative treatment and makes an excellent heroic poem. The setting and the proper names are all that distinguishes Judith of Bethulia from a Germanic heroic figure. In *The Dream of the Rood,* the central section of the poem, describing the actual crucifixion, the section where most of the heroic diction occurs, is handled in this narrative manner. The story of the events of the crucifixion is told in a series of swift-moving actions, with little delay.

A strong indication that the poem was composed in the traditional oral-formulaic style is the number of repeated verses. Checking every verse against the entire corpus of Old English poetry reveals that 67 of the 311 verses are repeated elsewhere at least once. This is 21.5 percent, more than one in five. Of course, this poem has a great number of hypermetric verses, 64 to be exact. As one can rarely find a hypermetric verse repeated in its entirety, it is interesting to examine the figures for the normal verses only: 27 percent of the normal verses are repeated elsewhere. This is more than one in four. Such a high percentage of repeated verses would be unthinkable in a poem composed in the modern way. This is not to deny originality to the poet of *The Dream of the Rood:* the dazzling conceit of the cross which tells its own story is not dimmed by the fact that the poet used traditional diction. Within the framework of the tradition in which he was composing, he displayed great inventiveness.

What kind of society can give rise to poems which represent such a strange blend of heroic and Christian elements? It would be no more accurate to say that *Beowulf* is a heathen poem with Christian coloring than that *The Dream of the Rood* is a Christian poem with heathen coloring. Both poems are clearly the work of believing Christians, composed in the traditional style for Christian audiences who were accustomed to certain standards and conventions of composition. They both represent a blend of traditional and Christian elements.

Perhaps we can account for the persistence of the traditional style of poetic composition by assuming that Anglo-Saxon England, while firmly Christian, still preserved many of the conditions of the heroic age. That epoch, from which the traditional style of composing and many of the themes of the poetry can be traced, is usually assumed to be over by the time most of the extant Anglo-Saxon poetry was composed. It is interesting to note, however, that the Cynewulf-Cyneheard episode, related in the Chronicle as having taken place in the year 786, occurred fifty years *after* the death of Bede. Here we have a typically heroic situation, with the loyalty to the comitatus taking precedence over kinship loyalty—half a century *after* the death of the man whose career surely represents the pinnacle of Christian civilization in Anglo-Saxon England. If the comitatus and the meadhall were still functioning so vitally, we can assume that there were two kinds of societies simultaneously in pre-Conquest England: one centering around the great monasteries; and the other a military society depending on the comitatus relationship. We know that oral composition was practiced in the monastic society—from Bede's account of Cædmon and his vision; and we know that heroic themes were sometimes of interest to the poets of this society—from Alcuin's letter mentioning Ingeld. As clerical communities constantly recruit members from lay society, young men who were in contact with the military society and its style and taste in poetry must have been drawn into the monastic centers—and they must have brought the traditional style of poetry with them. If they had not done so, none of the poems would have been preserved, for meadhall composing was for entertainment and not to be written down. It is natural that when the traditional style came to the monastic centers, it should be used for the most part to compose poems on Christian subjects.

It seems likely, then, that the contact between these two societies, the military and the religious, or, if you prefer, these two important and dominant segments of Anglo-Saxon society, gave rise to poetry which preserves the old clichés and formulas of heroic poetry but applies them to Christian subjects.

J. A. Burrow   (essay date 1959)

SOURCE: "An Approach to *The Dream of the Rood*," in *Old English Literature: Twenty-two Analytical Essays,* edited by Martin Stevens and Jerome Mandel, University of Nebraska Press, 1968, pp. 253-67.

[*In the following essay, first published in 1959 in* Neophilologus, *Burrow contrasts the emphasis and detail in* The Dream of the Rood *with that in several Middle English Crucifixion lyrics.*]

The Dream of the Rood is one of the first and one of the most successful treatments in English of the theme of the Crucifixion. It is successful because it is more than just a biblical paraphrase in the Caedmonian tradition. For one thing, the biblical narrative is treated with a greater freedom of emphasis and selection; for another, it is integrated into a new, non-biblical form, involving dreamer, vision, and speaking Cross. The present essay attempts to analyze and illustrate these two aspects of the poem, and to suggest how its characteristic pattern of emphasis, its "point of view," emerges in both. For the poem seems to me remarkable among Old English poems in the closeness of its organization. The organizing principle is, partly, the point of view or religious sensibility characteristic of the early Middle Ages as against the late. I think, therefore, that comparison with some later medieval English poems of the Crucifixion throws light, by contrast, on the Old English poem. It will illustrate how strikingly treatments of the same traditional theme can reflect varieties of sensibility in author and audience in the distribution of emphasis and selection of detail, and how different narrative forms serve these varying emphases—as, for example, the "goût de la pathétique" (taste of the pathetic), which [E.] Mâle finds characteristic of fourteenth and fifteenth century treatments of the Crucifixion [in his *L'art réligieux de la fin du Moyen Age en France,* 1925], has its most represen-

tative literary expression at that period in the monologue of the "mater dolorosa" (sorrowful mother) by the Cross. I will quote one or two such Middle English examples in order to suggest what is significantly absent in the Old English poem, and to throw into relief its own peculiar unity of form and emphasis.

The form of the poem offers a suitable point of departure, in the striking use of the figure "prosopopoeia." Miss [Margaret] Schlauch has already pointed this out [in her "*The Dream of the Rood* as Prosopopoeia"] as a formal innovation in the tradition of Crucifixion literature, tracing its background in the poetic practice and rhetorical theory of classical and post-classical Latin writing. I would like, here, to consider it from another point of view, as a controlling factor in the total meaning of the poem; for it seems to me that the identity and situation of the narrator, the "consciousness" through which the events of the Crucifixion are observed, is as significant here as—to draw a long comparison—in Henry James' *What Maisie Knew,* where Maisie's mind is made "the very field of the picture." It controls both what we see and how we see it, just as it does in the later Crucifixion lyric, where the same kind of device is frequently used, to different effect.

The use of prosopopoeia in descriptions of the Crucifixion is still to be found in the later Middle Ages (Miss Schlauch points out that Geoffrey of Vinsauf's most extensive illustration of the figure in his *Poetria Nova* consists of a speech by the Cross); but the dramatic forms which are most frequent and characteristic in the Middle English Crucifixion lyric would, in rhetorical terms, be called "ethopoeia"—fictional dramatic speech not of an inanimate object but of a human being. This ethopoeia takes three main forms—monologue of the "mater dolorosa," dialogue between Mary and Christ on the Cross, and monologue by the crucified Christ. I will give a short passage to illustrate each, taken from Carleton Brown's collections. Dialogue between Mary and Christ:

> Ihesus: Maiden and moder, cum and se,
> Þi child is nailed to a tre;
> Hand and fot he may nouth go,
> His bodi is wonden al in wo. . . .
>
> Maria: Mi suete sone þat art me dere,
> Wat hast þu don, qui art þu here?
> Þi suete bodi þat in me rest,
> Þat loueli mouth þat i haue kist—
> Nou is on rode mad þi nest.

This passage illustrates how fully this form of ethopoeia lends itself to the humanizing pathos which is characteristic of late medieval religious feeling. The tone is set by the repetition of *child* and *sone,* by the nest image of the last line, and by the use of the characteristic epithet *suete,* which could even, at this period, be applied to the Cross itself:

> Swete be þe nalys,
> And swete be þe tre,
> And sweter be þe birdyn þat hangis upon the.

The same note is struck in the monologue form, the "lamentacio dolorosa" (sorrowful lamentation) of Mary, which is often only formally distinguishable from the true dialogue:

> Suete sone, þi faire face droppeþ al on blode,
> And þi bodi dounward is bounden to þe rode;
> Hou may þi modris herte þolen so suete a fode
> Þat blissed was of alle born and best of alle gode.

In the monologue of Christ, by contrast, there is often a greater austerity of effect, as in this beautifully complete short lyric from the fifteenth century:

> I have laborede sore and suffered deyth
> And now I rest and draw my breyth;
> But I schall come and call ryght sone
> Hevene and erght and hell to dome;
> And thane schall know both devyll and mane
> What I was and what I ame.

But this is strictly a post-Crucifixion lyric, spoken from the tomb. In the many monologues from the Cross, as in Herbert's *Sacrifice,* which follows this traditional medieval form, we find again the "goût de la pathétique," without, however, the peculiar resonance which comes from stressing the family relationship between Christ and Mary:

> Þi garland is of grene
> Of floures many one;
> Myn of sharpe þornes
> Myn hewe it makeþ won.
>
> Þyn hondes streite gloved
> White and clene kept;
> Myne wiþ nailes þorled
> On rode and eke my feet.

In this, as in the other examples, the dramatic form serves directly to intensify the human immediacy of the Crucifixion scene, to excite "dolour" and "drede." In such poems, as Mâle puts it, speaking of the iconography of the Passion in the fourteenth and fifteenth centuries, "la sensibilité, jusque-là contenue, s'y exalte" (the sensibility, up to that point contained, becomes exalted). I would like now to turn back to **The Dream of the Rood** with the previous quotations in mind, and consider how, there, the prosopopoeia serves, unlike the ethopoeia of the Middle English lyrics, to "contain" the human pathos and immediacy of the scene.

The vision opens, after a short introductory passage, with twenty lines introducing the Cross. Nothing in Middle English quite matches this passage. The Cross here is neither the *swete tre* of which the fourteenth-century poet speaks, nor the physical instrument of the Miracle plays, but a cosmic hieratic image of both. The *swete tre* becomes the *syllic treow,* raised to the sky, bathed in light, adorned with gold and jewels, worshipped by *eall þeos mære gesceaft;* the instrument of torture, alternating with it, soaked in blood—*mid wætan bestemed*—is correspondingly represented in non-naturalistic terms. Both forms of the *fuse beacen* recall liturgical practice, as [H. R.] Patch has shown [in his "Liturgical Influence in the *Dream of the Rood,*" *PMLA* XXXIV (1919)]; neither makes any direct appeal to the human or the natural. The gap between the dreamer and the Cross, at this point in the poem, is absolute:

> Syllic wæs se sigebeam and ic synnum fah
>
> (13)
>
> Forht ic wæs for þære fægran gesyhþe
>
> (21)

With the opening of the speech of the Cross, however, there is a sudden shift in the tone and scale of the poem. The cosmic vision is left behind, and the Cross speaks as a natural tree:

> þæt wæs geara iu—ic þæt gyta geman—
> þæt ic wæs aheawen holtes on ende,
> astyred of stefne minum.
>
> (28-30)

The colloquial informality of this opening—without apostrophe or introduction—is in striking contrast to the impersonal liturgical grandeur of what has gone before. The congregation of worshippers, *halige gastas, menn ofer moldan, and eall þeos mære gesceaft,* is for the time being lost from sight, and there is nothing surprising when the Cross addresses the dreamer as if they were alone and on equal terms—*hæleþ min se leofa.* This sudden and unexplained transition from the public-hieratic to the private-colloquial would be possible only within the conventions of the vision form—it anticipates effects in *Piers Plowman.* It makes the mediating consciousness through which the action of the crucifixion is to be described a more complex thing than anything in the Middle English lyric. It is not a simple dramatic figure, but a double persona, strongly differentiated, belonging in its two forms to the two widely separate worlds (as they are presented at this point) of nature and the supernatural. The result in the narrative which follows is a kind of double focus, which I wish to consider next.

In the opening lines of its speech, already quoted, the Cross introduces itself in its natural environment, a wood, from which it is cut down to be used in executions for no other reason than that it stood *holtes on ende.* The tree is an ordinary one suddenly drawn into a world of violence. The suddenness and the violence, together with the passivity of the Cross itself, are conveyed in the compressed paratactic syntax, the lengthened line, and the rapid sequence of verbs of action in the passage immediately following:

> Genaman me þær strange feondas,
> geworhton him þær to wæfersyne, heton me
>   heora wergas hebban.
> Baeron me þær beornas on eaxlum, oþþæt hie
>   me on beorg asetton,
> gefaestnodon me þær feondas genoge.
>
> (30-33)

(The repetition of þær, to which [B.] Dickins and [A.S.C.] Ross tentatively assign the meaning "then," seems rather intended to suggest the confused telescoping of events at this point.) These lines dramatically establish the second, natural, persona of the Cross, and as such it functions throughout its account of the crucifixion as a representative of common humanity and consequently of the dreamer himself. Like the dreamer in face of his vision, the Cross is afraid:

> Bifode ic þa me se beorn ymbclypte; ne dorste
>   ic hwæþre bugan to eorþan.
>
> (42)

and, again like the dreamer, with a verbal reminiscence of line 20, it is "troubled with sorrows"—*sare ic wæs mid sorgum gedrefed* (line 59)—just as, with the other crosses, it later stands weeping (70). In this form, in fact, the Cross represents the common "crystyn creature" of the Middle English *Meditations on the Supper of our Lord:*

> Now, crystyn creature, take goode hede,
> And do þyn herte for pyte to blede;
> Loþe þou nat hys sorowes to se
> Þe whych hym loþed nat to suffre for þe.

But the Cross here does not only see with the dreamer—in its second, non-natural persona it suffers with Christ:

> þurhdrifan hi me mid deorcan næglum; on me
>   syndon þa dolg gesiene,
> opene inwidhlemmas. Ne dorste ic hira ænigum
>   sceþþan.
> Bysmeredon hie unc butu ætgædere.
>
> (46-48)

Here the wounds of the Cross are carried over by transfer from Christ with whom it suffers (*unc butu ætgædere*). So, in 47b, there is an obscurer transfer which suggests a kind of "dream condensation" between Christ and the Cross. The motif which it states—that the Cross could strike down the crucifiers but dare not since Christ does not wish it—recurs elsewhere in the poem (36-37: *Ealle ic mihte feondas gefyllan, hwæþre ic fæste stod*); and it is linked with the idea, repeated three times, that the Cross could have refused to bear Christ by bending or breaking (35-36, 42-43, 45). These themes seem to me more than simply a natural extension of the animism implicit in prosopopoeia. They refer properly to Christ. It was Christ who could have struck down his enemies, and Christ who could have refused the ordeal, if he had not willed it otherwise (a theme to which we will return later).

Thus the Cross, in its own narrative, functions doubly as a surrogate both for the dreamer and for Christ; and these two functions correspond to the double transcendental-natural image of the Cross established at the beginning of the poem. The consequences of this in the poem are curious. It might be expected that the Cross would, as it were, bridge the gap between the natural and supernatural worlds by virtue of belonging to and speaking for both. One might look, that is, for the kind of naturalism which I have illustrated from the Middle English religious lyric, or even for the direct pathetic realism of the Miracle play. There is indeed a trace of such an effect—in the way the Germanic idea of comitatus loyalty is implied in the scene of the Deposition, where the *beornas* bury their *æþeling* and sing him a *sorhleoþ*—but the general impression is quite different. The gap between the natural and the supernatural is felt as absolute. There is here a striking difference of effect between the prosopopoeia of the Old English poem and the various ethopoeic forms of the Middle English lyrics. In the later poems the central scene is humanized through the speeches of Christ and Mary—the emphases fall on the physical suffering of Christ, his *won hewe,* his body *dounward bounden to þe rode,* and on his natural relation as the *suete sone* of Mary. In *The Dream of the Rood,* by contrast, the reader and the dreamer expe-

rience the human suffering and passive naturalness of Christ only in so far as these are transferred to the Cross itself, *blode bestemed,* and shared by it. For the Cross in its main role, as representative of the "crystyn creature," Christ remains completely opaque:

> Geseah ic þa frean mancynnes
> efstan elne mycle þæt he me wolde on gestigan.
>
> (33-34)

These lines, in which Christ is for the first time introduced, follow immediately after the passage quoted above in which the *strange feondas* set up the tree as a cross. The passivity of the Cross in those lines throws into sharp relief the sudden dynamic appearance and mysteriously voluntary actions of Christ—he hastens *elne mycle, wishing* to ascend the Cross.

There is no concession here to circumstantial realism, no attempt to render the scene naturalistically in the late medieval way. The figure of Christ acts in absolute independence of its environment. The presence of the *feondas* is hardly felt at all from this point onwards in the poem—the moment of crucifixion itself is described in a series of non-realistic verbs which, as Patch has shown, recall the Latin hymns: *he me wolde on gestigan, gestah he on gealgan heanne* (*ascendere* (to climb)), *me se beorn ymbclypte* (*amplexere* (to embrace)). There is no sense of the weight of the body dragging *dounward* such as we find in later plastic and literary works; Christ is presented ceremonially in positive deliberate action, just as a little later:

> he hine þær hwile reste,
> meþe æfter þam miclan gewinne.
>
> (64-65)

The trope—death as sleep—was probably traditional in Old English verse (it is used of the dead Grendel, *guþwerig Grendel,* in *Beowulf* 1586); but it is characteristic of *The Dream of the Rood* that its use here should be fully meaningful, suggesting the willedness, and also the impermanence, of Christ's death. This emphasis harmonizes with the manner in which the crucifixion itself is described, and with those passages, already mentioned, in which it is Christ's will, *Dryhtnes word,* which controls the Cross itself.

The death-as-sleep trope is also used in the Middle English *Christ Triumphant,* quoted above; but, on the whole, the non-naturalistic mode which we have been illustrating in *The Dream of the Rood* is as alien to the Middle English lyric as it is to the Miracle plays. The nearest thing to *The Dream of the Rood* in Middle English literature is to be found in Passus XVIII (in the B text, from which I will quote) of *Piers Plowman.* The differences both in form and approach are clear enough—there is nothing in the Old English poem which anticipates Langland's fluid allegorical method (except, possibly, in 52-54, where, if one follows Dickins and Ross in taking *scirne sciman* as parallel with *wealdendes hræw,* there is a suggestion of Langland's allegory of light and darkness—but the phrase may belong to the following clause). Nevertheless, there is a striking similarity of emphasis between the two poets, for in some ways Langland stands outside the main Middle English tradition. There is little of pathos or passivity in his account of the crucifixion. Christ is a knight jousting with the powers of evil, who rides "pricking" to Jerusalem; or he is light conquering the darkness of hell. His death is described in words which recall the sleep metaphor, *the lorde of lyf and of lighte tho leyed his eyen togideres.* Correspondingly, there is little direct concession to the "goût de la pathétique"—the trial, the buffetings and the nailing to the Cross are treated sparely in less than twenty lines. We may recall the words of Repentance in his prayer to God earlier in the poem:

> And sith with þi self sone in owre sute deydest
> On godefryday for mannes sake at ful tyme of þe daye,
> Pere þiself ne þi sone no sorwe in deth feledest;
> But in owre secte was þe sorwe, and þi sone it ladde,
> *Captiuam duxit captiuitatem* (he led captivity captive).
>
> (V, 495-498)

These lines seem to me as relevant to **The Dream of the Rood** as they are irrelevant to the greater part of the lyric poetry and drama which was being written in Langland's own day. The Old English Christ feels no sorrow in death; there too the sorrow is *in owre secte,* in the dreamer and in the Cross as his representative. For Langland, Christ at the Passion jousts in *Piers armes* (glossed as *humana natura* (human nature)) *for no dynte shal hym dere as in deitate patris* (in the divinity of (his) father). This allegorical image stresses sharply, as Langland stresses throughout, the distinction between the natural and the supernatural Christ; in his poem the inviolable *deitas patris* (the divinity of the father) is never for a moment lost sight of, just as in **The Dream of the Rood** it is continually recalled:

> Ongyrede hine þa geong hæleþ, þæt wæs God ælmihtig.
>
> (39)

Dickins and Ross are surely wrong in suggesting . . . that the second half of this line is an "addition" or an "expansion." The whole line, as it stands, stresses the dichotomy which, we have already seen, is stressed throughout the poem. It is perhaps significant, in this connection, that Christ is referred to as such only once in the account of the crucifixion—otherwise he is either on the one hand *geong hæleþ, beorn, guma, æþeling,* or on the other *Frea mancynnes, Dryhten, heofona Hlaford, Wealdend, rice Cyning, God ælmihtig.* The two sets of terms express the contrast between *humana natura* and *deitas patris,* the contrast which is summed up in line 39.

So far in this essay I have attempted, by considering the account of the crucifixion in the first part of **The Dream of the Rood** and comparing it with later treatments of the same subject, to define the point of view characteristic of the Old English poem, and to suggest how this point of view emerges both in the prosopopoeic form and in details of language and style. It is this overall unity of form and meaning which seems to me remarkable in the poem—not the point of view itself, which, abstractly stated, was by no means unusual at that period. In fact the contrast I have drawn with the Middle English lyric corresponds very closely to the well-established general lines of con-

trast between the religious art of the early and late Middle Ages. Visual representations of the crucifixion in the earlier period lay the emphases very much where **The Dream of the Rood** lays them, on the *deitas patris* of Christ on the Cross, and, again like the Old English poem, make little of the natural pathos. Similarly, the characteristics of the Middle English religious lyric extend to the visual art of the period. In the late Middle Ages, as Mâle has shown, painting, sculpture, lyric and drama "ont évidemment leur origine dans le même sentiment . . . la sensibilité, jusque-là contenue, s'y exalte" (evidently have their origin in the same sentiment . . . the sensibility, up to that point contained, becomes exalted). They share the same naturalism, the same stress on the sufferings of Christ, the same "goût de la pathétique." Again, the contrasts with which I have been concerned have their parallels (perhaps even, to a certain extent, their explanations) outside the arts altogether, in the history of the philosophy and theology of the period. The pervasive Platonism in the religious thought of the early Middle Ages matches the supernaturalism implicit in **The Dream of the Rood;** and it is perhaps significant that traces of ultimately Aristotelian ideas are to be found in the most naturalistic of the Miracle cycles. Perhaps, too, the strength of the Franciscan, anti-Aristotelian tradition in Langland's thought has something to do with the peculiarities of his passus on the crucifixion. But these are matters where "the bottom is a long way down," and it is enough here to point out that the attitudes and emphases which I have been discussing are not peculiar to **The Dream of the Rood.** For the purposes of the present essay there remains one further topic of more immediate relevance.

The account of the crucifixion in **The Dream of the Rood** ends with the burying of the crosses (line 75)—not quite half way through the poem as it stands in the Vercelli Book. The rest of the poem consists of a homiletic speech by the Cross to the dreamer (78-121), with which the vision ends, and a coda in which the dreamer describes his unhappy life on earth and his hope of a *heofonlic ham* (122-156). Dickins and Ross, who regard the Vercelli text as an expanded and composite version of an earlier work, are suspicious of this part of the poem. They argue that it "does not afford any metrical or linguistic evidence which necessitates the assumption of an early date," that "in quality it seems to us definitely inferior," and that "it is perhaps significant that the passages found on the Ruthwell Cross all correspond to passages in the first half of the Vercelli text." The first of these arguments makes no claim to be conclusive, and the last is very weak—would it not, after all, be natural to choose passages from the speech of the Cross for inscription on a cross, rather than passages of a generally didactic or personally reminiscent kind? The case seems, therefore, to rest on the argument from inferiority, and this too is open to strong objection. The inferiority, to modern taste, of the latter part of the poem is hard to dispute; but the argument from this fact to an assumed composite origin, although quite a common procedure in the criticism of Old English verse, begs so many questions that I feel justified in considering briefly the latter part of **The Dream of the Rood** as a legitimate component in the whole poem.

It is, as I have admitted, inferior; but, despite some laxness of rhythm and diffuseness of expression, it is not difficult to see that the themes of the earlier part are developed consistently and meaningfully. With the conclusion of the account of the crucifixion (75), the tone of the speech of the Cross begins to change. It no longer speaks as a representative of common humanity to which the supernatural world is opaque (part, as we have seen, of the effect of the earlier passages), becoming again unambiguously an initiated member of that world, as it was in the opening vision, honored above natural trees as Mary is honored above women (90-94). The Cross reassumes its original persona, and, as it does so, the themes and images of the opening lines return—first in a brief reference to the Invention:

> Hwæþre me þær Dryhtnes þegnas
> freondas gefrunon,
> gyredon me golde and seolfre.
>
> (75-77)

and then, almost immediately, in full restatement:

> Is nu sæl cumen
> þæt me weorþiaþ wide and side
> menn ofer moldan and eall þeos mære gesceaft,
> gebiddaþ him to þyssum beacne
>
> (80-83)

where the verbal reminiscences seem deliberately to stress the recapitulation (line 82 is identical with line 12, for example). The Cross, thus reestablished in its original transcendent form, ends its speech appropriately enough by explaining to the dreamer the mysteries of salvation.

The poem, however, does not end here; there is a further thematic development, which appears in the closing soliloquy of the dreamer. In order to appreciate this, the reader must recall the opening section of the poem, as the poet himself recalls it in lines 75-83. That section, as we have seen, turned on the sharply marked contrast between the natural and the supernatural:

> Syllic wæs se sigebeam and ic synnum fah

and it is only in terms of this contrast that the dreamer's identity is defined at this point. He appears as a generalized, passive figure, prostrate in face of his vision, which in its turn is static, though brilliantly decorative, like a tableau:

> Hine þær beheoldon halige gastas,
> menn ofer moldan and eall þeos mære gesceaft.
>
> (11-12)

The last part of the poem offers a deliberate contrast to these effects. The dreamer takes on an independent personal identity, with a past in which he has suffered *feala ealra langunghwila* and the death of powerful friends; and it is these snatches of elegiac autobiography which provide the personal background for a new dynamic religious feeling:

> ic wene me
> daga gehwylce hwænne me Dryhtnes rod
> þe ic her on eorþan ær sceawode
> on þysson lænan life gefetige
> and me þonne gebringe þær is blis mycel.
>
> (135-139)

Instead of gazing at the Cross, he prays to it:

> Gebæd ic me þa to þan beame bliþe mode
> elne mycle.
>
> (122-123)

It is in keeping with this development in the dreamer's attitude that the last lines of the poem should be crowded with verbs expressing *movement* (the only movements in the opening vision are the symbolic transformations of the Cross):

> . . . ic þone sigebeam *secan* mote
>
> (127)
>
> . . . hie forþ heonon
> *gewiton* of worulde dreamum, *sohton* him wuldres Cyning
>
> (132-133)
>
> . . . ic wene me
> daga gehwylce hwænne me Dryhtnes rod
> þe ic her on eorþan ær sceawode
> on þysson lænan life *gefetige*
> and me þonne *gebringe* þær is blis mycel
>
> (135-139)
>
> . . . þa he mid manigeo *com*
> gasta weorode on Godes rice
>
> (151-152)

These passages contrast sharply with the static, hieratic imagery of the opening vision, for they represent the third and last stage in the development of the poem, where the opening tableau takes on life and motion after the central scene of the Crucifixion. The theme is the activity of Grace, released through the death of Christ; the language is the abstract language of motion—seeking, travelling, fetching, coming, bringing—abstract, that is, in the sense that it has little to offer in the way of visual "imagery." Perhaps it is for this reason that the last part of the poem is the least memorable, at any rate for most modern readers. It has to compete on unequal terms with the visual and dramatic concreteness of the visions of the Cross and of the Crucifixion.

The poet himself may have felt this, for at the very end of the poem (148-156) he attempts, as it were, to dramatize the personal religious themes of the last part in an account of Christ's Harrowing of Hell. There seems no reason to accept Cook's contention that this is an addition. The transition from the personal present to the historic past is skillfully managed, and it is hard to see where the supposed addition might begin:

> Si me Dryhten freond,
> se þe her on eorþan ær þrowode
> on þam gealgtreowe for guman synnum
>
> (144-146)

The relative clause effects the shift in tense and person, from the present to the past and from the dreamer to mankind (*guman*) which is confirmed in the following lines:

> He us onlysde and us lif forgeaf,
> heofonlicne ham

The further transition to the Harrowing of Hell (*Hiht wæs geniwad* . . .) is natural at this point as an amplification of Christ's "releasing" power. It is also convincing in the general economy of the poem. The last lines are not vivid, as is the treatment of the same theme by Langland (who draws on the Miracle play tradition)—though there is a compensating syntactic effect in the sequence of parallel clauses leading up to *þær his eþel wæs*—but they do have a specific relevance. This lies not so much in the traditional doctrinal association between the Harrowing and the Crucifixion, as in the story's tropological significance at this point in the poem, its relevance to the dreamer's "moral state"—his personal *hiht* (see line 126) which is the distinguishing theme of the closing soliloquy.

This personal theme is implicit in *The Dream of the Rood* from the first. The essential principle of development lies here, in the dreamer himself, just as it does in *Piers Plowman.* At the beginning of Langland's Eighteenth Passus, before the vision of the Crucifixion, the dreamer is *wolleward and wete-shoed* and *wery of the worlde;* when it is over he wakes joyfully calling to his wife and daughter to pray to the Cross:

> Crepeth to the crosse on knees & kisseth it for
> a iuwel,
> For goddes blissed body it bar for owre bote.

So the dreamer in the Old English poem moves from fear and sorrow to hope, and it is this simple emotional sequence which links the closing soliloquy with the opening vision and sets the tone of the central Crucifixion scene.

Highet analyzes the originality of *The Dream of the Rood*:

The Dream of the Rood is a poem describing a vision of the Cross and of the Crucifixion. It is more individual than any other work of its time: although it is as intense as the fighting heroic poems, its intensity is that of a stranger, more difficult spiritual world. . . . But the poem contains some elements which are unlike anything in earlier English literature, and which are harbingers of the Middle Ages: the sensuous beauty of the descriptions—the rood drips with blood and glows with jewels, as though in the rose-window of a Gothic cathedral; the setting of the whole as a dream—that characteristic mark of medieval otherworldliness; the cult of the Cross—which was established in the eighth century, and was a novelty for the western church; and the adoration of Christ, neither as a powerful king nor as a moral teacher, but as a supreme and beloved person. As far as can be traced, the poem is neither a translation nor an adaptation, but an entirely original utterance, the mystical cry of one enraptured soul.

Gilbert Highet, in his The Classical Tradition: Greek and Roman Influences on Western Literature, *Oxford University Press, 1949.*

Stanley B. Greenfield   (essay date 1965)

SOURCE: "Christ as Poetic Hero," in *A Critical History of Old English Literature,* New York University Press, 1965, pp. 124-45.

[In the following excerpt, Greenfield centers on the prominent role of Christ in The Dream of the Rood, *emphasizing "the poem's double stress on the triumphant and suffering Christ."]*

[Christ] is, by the nature of His Passion, eminently central to the ***Dream of the Rood,*** the finest expression of the Passion in Old English poetry. This 156-line narrative-lyrical adoration of the Cross survives in the Vercelli Book, and part of it appears in Northumbrian runic inscription in the margins of the east and west faces of the eighth-century Ruthwell [rivl] Cross in Dumfriesshire, Scotland. Two lines reminiscent of the poem also appear on the late tenth-century Brussels Cross. The relation between the Ruthwell inscription and the Vercelli text is not clear: is the former a condensation of an original Anglian poem of about A.D. 700, preserved in its West Saxon tenth-century form in the Vercelli MS, or is the manuscript poem, even in its earliest shape, an expansion of the Cross inscription? There is also a problem with the longer poem itself: lines 79 and following seem to be in a different style from the Crucifixion segment that precedes, and are possibly an addition by a later redactor. Even so, the ***Dream of the Rood*** is a coherent and unified poem as it stands, compact and intense in its emotional effect.

> Listen! I'll tell the sweetest dream,
> That dropped to me from midnight, in the quiet
> Time of silence and restful sleep.
>   I seemed to see a tree of miracles
> Rising in the sky, a shining cross
> Wrapped in light. . . .
>   It was a tree of victory and splendor, and
>   I tainted,
> Ulcered with sin. And yet I saw it—
> Shining with joy, clothed, adorned,
> Covered with gold, the tree of the Lord
> Gloriously wrapped in gleaming stones.
> And through the gold I saw the stains
> Of its ancient agony when blood spilled out
> On its right-hand side. I was troubled and afraid
> Of the shining sight. Then its garments changed,
> And its color; for a moment it was moist with
>   blood,
> Dripping and stained; then it shone like silver.
>   [ll. 1-23]

This beginning not only sets the mood and tone of wonder and sinful remorse but its image of the double-visaged cross, gemmed on the one hand and stained with blood on the other, functions as a symbolic prelude to the triumph and suffering that are doctrinally and poetically at the poem's core. In the body of the poem, the Cross itself is made to speak and to describe from its particular point of view the Crucifixion, a rhetorical device known as *prosopopoeia.* The Cross's speech begins in riddle fashion describing quickly and succinctly its origins as a tree, its felling and shaping into a rood, and its "planting" in the hillside. Then:

>   I saw the Lord of the world
> Boldly rushing to climb me
> And I could neither bend, nor break
> The word of God. I saw the ground
> Trembling. I could have crushed them all,
> And yet I kept myself erect.
>   [ll. 33b-38]

This advance of Christ upon the Cross is not, of course, the usual picture of Christ carrying the Cross to Calvary, but it has traditional sanction. More important, it shows Christ the hero freely willing His own Crucifixion, heightening this "leap's" heroic and voluntary nature. Stripping Himself for battle—again an action within Patristic tradition, and again emphasizing Christ's heroism and voluntarism—Christ climactically mounts the Cross, an admirable symbol of the Divinity of Christ and of the earlier Middle Ages' conception of the Redemption:

> I trembled as His arms went round me. And still
>   I could not bend,
> Crash to the earth, but had to bear the body of
>   God.
> I was reared as a cross. I raised the mighty
> King of Heaven and could not bend.
> They pierced me with vicious nails. I bear the
>   scars
> Of malicious gashes. But I dared not injure any
>   of them.
> We were both reviled, we two together. I was
>   drenched with the blood that gushed
> From that hero's side as His holy spirit swept to
>   Heaven.
>   Cruel things came to me there
> On that hill. I saw the God of Hosts
> Stretched on the rack. Clouds rolled
> From the darkness to cover the corpse,
> The shining splendor; a livid shadow
> Dropped from Heaven. The creation wept,
> Bewailed His death. Christ was on the cross.
>   [ll. 42-56]

Crist wæs on rode: the breathtaking account of the Crucifixion ends on this simplistic yet highly emotional note. But we may observe in this passage two things at least. First, the Cross's presentation of itself as a loyal retainer in the epic mode, with the ironic reversal that it must acquiesce and even assist in the death of its Lord, and cannot aid or avenge Him. Second, the Cross's trembling and suffering, taking upon itself the Passion of Christ. By its passive endurance it becomes a surrogate for Christ, representing that other aspect of the Crucifixion which was to predominate in the later Middle Ages, the humanity of Christ. Its suffering as a "thane" also foreshadows the Dreamer's own reflections toward the end of the poem where, after the vision has ended, he describes himself as an exile in this world, deprived of friends, longing for a new "patron" (God, of course) in a manner similar to the speaker's of *The Wanderer.*

The Cross of the poem continues its speech describing the Deposition and Burial:

> They carried away almighty God,
> Raised Him out of His torment. I was aban-
>   doned of men,
> Standing bespattered with blood, driven through
>   with spikes.
> They laid down the weary-limbed God, stood
>   and watched at His head,
> Beholding Heaven's King as He lay in quiet
>   sleep,

> Exhausted with hardship and pain. And they
>   started to carve a sepulchre,
> With His slayer watching. They chiselled the
>   tomb of the brightest stone
> And laid the Lord of victories there.
>   [ll. 60b-67a]

Christ's death is pictured here as a sleep, a catharsis of exhaustion, release, and temporary rest—a depiction probably not original with the poet, yet exquisitely handled by him. (The concept of death as a sleep has become a commonplace in speech and literature, but its use in the *Dream of the Rood* is as effective as is Donne's later handling of it in his sonnet "Death be not proud.") This passage stylistically fuses the human and divine doctrinal aspects of the Crucifixion by its use of the paradoxical *communicatio idiomatum: "They carried* away *almighty God," "They laid* down the *weary-limbed God . . . beholding Heaven's King," "And laid* the *Lord of victories* there." Miss [Rosemary] Woolf's comment [in her "Doctrinal Influences on *The Dream of the Rood,*" *Medium Aevum* XXVII (1958)] on this device and its doctrinal-esthetic result is worth quoting:

> In the thirty lines of dramatic description of the Crucifixion . . . there are ten examples of the *communicatio idiomatum,* and each one stimulates a shock at the paradox, a shock which grows in intensity as the poem progresses. . . . The habit of variation in Anglo-Saxon poetic style and the richness of synonym in Anglo-Saxon poetic diction, assist the poet in each instance to use a fresh word or phrase to emphasize some attribute of God, His Rule, majesty, omnipotence. . . . The theological point that the Christ who endured the Crucifixion is fully God and fully man is thus perfectly made, and with it the imaginative effect which is the natural result of the *communicatio idiomatum* is attained, the astonishment at the great paradox of Christianity that God should endure such things.

No known source has been found for the *Dream of the Rood.* Some liturgical influence there may have been, but the fine tensions of the poem between the Divinity and triumph of Christ on the Cross on the one hand and His humanity and suffering on the other, probably owe their inspiration to the poet's awareness of the Christological disputes of the seventh-eighth centuries about the human-divine nature of the Savior, and from the doctrine of the Redemption as taught at this time. The poem's double stress on the triumphant and suffering Christ argues that the poet knew well the difficult theological line he was treading and, *mirabile dictu,* succeeded in keeping his balance in the brilliant fusion he effected in his use of the Cross as narrator within the dream vision. As an emotional sequence of words and ideas, the *Dream of the Rood* also moves brilliantly from the fear and sorrow of the Dreamer at the beginning to the hope he visualizes at the end:

> He broke our bonds and gave us life
> And a home in Heaven. And hope was renewed
> In bliss for those who'd burned in Hell.
> The Son triumphed on that journey to darkness,

Smashing Hell's doors. Many men's souls
Rose with Him then, the Ruler of all,
Rising to Heaven and the angels' bliss
And the joy of the saints already enthroned
And dwelling in glory, welcoming almighty
God returning to His shining home.

Anderson discusses the appeal of *The Dream of the Rood:*

[Nowhere] else in Old English literature, except in Bede's *Ecclesiastical History,* do we find the same combination of lyrical freshness, tenderness, and simple religious feeling. The poem has its charm for the layman as well as for the confirmed medievalist. Such is hardly the case with many even greater poems produced under the immediate inspiration of the medieval Church. The intimate subjective quality of *The Dream of the Rood,* however, a quality which is so prominent and withal so unusual for the age, has much to do with the excellence of the work. The poem unfolds itself in the form of a vision—the most remarkable example in Old English literature of a type that was to become famous in Middle English literature.

George K. Anderson, in his The Literature of the Anglo-Saxons, *Princeton University Press, 1949.*

John V. Fleming (essay date 1966)

SOURCE: "*The Dream of the Rood* and Anglo-Saxon Monasticism," in *Traditio,* Vol. XXII, 1966, pp. 43-72.

[*Below, Fleming examines the characters, language, and themes of* The Dream of the Rood, *calling the poem "a carved celebration of the monastic ideals" of English Benedictinism.*]

The earliest text of *The Dream of the Rood* consists of a few lines of runic inscriptions carved around the edges of a North English high cross now at Ruthwell in Dumfriesshire. It represents no more than a fragment of the text as we find it in the Vercelli MS, a short passage describing the Crucifixion and the ordeal of the Cross. The precise relationship between the Ruthwell runes and the Vercelli poem is a matter of conjecture and dispute. To some critics the Ruthwell inscriptions represent an 'earlier poem,' of which the Vercelli text is an expansion or a later revision or both. It is a question to which I shall wish to devote some attention in due course. For the present, I would suggest that the runic inscriptions provide a valuable clue to the interpretation of the Vercelli poem along lines so far left unexplored; for the runes form a part of a rich iconographic program, developing a unified meaning closely connected with the figurative meaning of *The Dream of the Rood.*

This 'unified meaning' of the iconographic scheme of the Ruthwell Cross has also been much discussed. Baldwin Brown thought that the Ruthwell carvings celebrated the Triumph of the Cross. A more recent student [P.G. Medd]

concludes that 'the theme which emerges is that of *conversion.*' In light of the brilliant article on the Ruthwell Cross ["The Religious Meaning of the Ruthwell Cross," *Art Bulletin* 26 (1944)] by Meyer Schapiro, however, it seems clear beyond question that the 'unified meaning' of the Ruthwell carvings is eremitic. The figures of John the Baptist, the desert saints, Paul and Antony, the central Christ *in deserto,* together with less obvious icons of the ascetic life, form a carved celebration of the monastic ideals which were at the heart of both the Celtic and the early English (Roman) churches. I shall argue in this article that *The Dream of the Rood* is also such a celebration, a product of the English Benedictinism which was the chief cultural institution of the Age of Bede, presenting a figurative statement of the main principles of early Benedictine asceticism and a typically monastic view of salvation.

The religious meaning of *The Dream of the Rood* lies only thinly veiled beneath the surface of the Old English poetic diction which its author was obliged to use. It is a diction to some extent archeological and 'Germanic,' the language of the high style of Old English Christian poetry, which gives it its peculiar and often misleading heroic and Teutonic ring. This language has been thought to reflect the values of that kind of Germanic warrior society which Tacitus called the *comitatus,* still alive in the Anglo-Saxon poetic consciousness generations, indeed centuries after the Christianization of England. Typically, *comitatus* values of loyalty and community have been thought to animate such tragic and dramatic high points in Old English literature as the Finnsburh lay in *Beowulf* and the Cynewulf and Cyneheard episode in the *Chronicle,* and to provide the philosophic background for the plight of the 'exile' or 'lordless man' in *The Wanderer, The Seafarer,* and elsewhere. Indeed, one might argue that *The Dream of the Rood* is a kind of Christian 'answer' to the problems posed by the stringencies of a *comitatus* society.

The language of the *comitatus* applies to all the characters in the poem: the Cross, Christ, the Dreamer himself. Most obviously the episode of the Crucifixion is a heroic drama in which Christ seems to be associated with the Germanic warrior:

> Geseah ic þa frean mancynnes
> efstan elne mycle þæt he me wolde on gestigan.
> (33-34)
>
> . . . . .
> Ongyrede hine þa geong hæleð, (þæt wæs god
> ælmihtig),
> strang ond stiðmod. Gestah he on gealgan
> heanne,
> modig on manigra gesyhðe, þa he wolde mancyn
> lysan.
> (39-41)

But the Cross, too, has a dramatic role in terms of the *comitatus* in its prosopopoeic voice, for it has suffered just those two calamities that provide the main tensions of 'Germanic' tragedy: disruption from the *comitatus,* and disloyalty, at least apparent, to its lord. For the forest tree, part of the *comitatus* of the Lord of all created things, is cut down by *strange feondas,* removed from its place in the created order, degraded, humiliated. It is in its role as Christ's retainer that the Cross's frustration at being forbidden to strike back at its lord's enemies becomes most poignant. Charlemagne in pious legend is supposed to have cried out, upon hearing the tale of the Crucifixion retold, 'If I had only been there with my Franks!' The Cross says:

> þær ic þa ne dorste ofer dryhtnes word
> bugan oððe berstan, þa ic bifian geseah
> eorðan sceatas. Ealle ic mihte
> feondas gefyllan, hwæðre ic fæste stod.
>
> (35-38)

What was foolishness to the Greeks was treason to the *Germanen.* The Cross, in the poetic role of a warrior in Christ's band, must become the *bana,* or technical slayer, of its own lord. For this paradoxical disloyalty, the Cross receives the traditional reward of the faithful retainer ('gyredon me golde ond seolfre.' [77]) And the final inversion of the values of the *comitatus* comes in the homily of the Cross to the Dreamer, in which it makes the point that the path to salvation for all men lies in following the *bana* of their Lord. Cynewulf's men in the *Chronicle* episode are prepared to fight to the death even against their own kinsmen rather than follow the slayer of their lord: *hio næfre his banan folgian noldon.* Yet such is the blasphemy of Christians.

If the Cross and Christ are actors in a heroic drama, the Dreamer likewise participates in the apparent Germanic design of the poem. Though the point is not greatly elaborated, it is clear that he is a lordless man, a traditional elegiac exile.

> Nah ic ricra feala
> freonda on foldan, ac hie forð heonon
> gewiton of worulde dreamum . . .
>
> (131-133)

Elsewhere the Dreamer is *ana* and *mæte werede* (123-124). The resolution of his lordlessness is his transference of hope for protection from 'freonda on foldan' to a 'Friend' in heaven: 'Si me dryhten freond' (144). Such a compressed sketch hardly does justice to the considerable poetic gifts displayed in the development of the themes of community and exile in the poem, but I hope it will serve to draw attention to the ideographic framework around which an Anglo-Saxon poet chose to structure a particular kind of Christian poem.

It would be a mistake, however, to consider these carefully developed themes as some kind of archeological remains, pagan echoes in a Christian poem; for it is by no means only in the Teutonic poetry of the Anglo-Saxon period that the ideas of exile and community are to be found. They are two of the preeminent concerns of the principal ecclesiastical and cultural institution of Anglo-Saxon England: Benedictine monachism. In a brilliant essay ["Le Monachisme du haut moyen âge (VIIIe-Xe siècles)," in *Théologie de la vie monastique,* 1961] which modestly but authoritatively provides the guideposts for the study of Western monachism in the period from the eighth to the tenth centuries, Jean Leclercq has written thus:

> Il semble que l'on puisse grouper les principales idées théologiques illustrées par les Vies des saints moines des époques dites mérovingienne et carolingienne autour de deux thèmes majeurs, ceux de l'exil et du paradis, correspondant aux deux domaines de l'activité monastique: l'ascèse et de la mystique, la pratique des vertus et l'union de l'esprit à Dieu.

The twin concerns of early Benedictine thought here abstracted by Leclercq are the concerns as well of the poet of *The Dream of the Rood:* the 'lordless man' and the *comitatus,* the exile and the society for which he yearns.

One of the most felicitous of the notable poetic gifts demonstrated by the author of *The Dream of the Rood* is his ability to present us with a kind of double focus in which to view the ambiguities of the Crucifixion, the role of the Cross, and the response of the Dreamer. If we may imagine the Cross rising, as it does between the old Law and the New, between the themes of exile and *comitatus,* themselves the two sides of one coin, we shall discern that the Dreamer combines two roles: he is both the first person voice of an Old English poem, clothed in the elegiac and heroic language of traditional English poetry, and he is the Benedictine voice of a poem on the monastic life. For as the lordless man moves from exile into his true *comitatus* through the Cross, the monk moves through a spiritual exile to a mystical union with Heaven. The movement of the poem, we should note, is not so much *around* the Cross as *through* it, just as the Dreamer sees *þurh þæt gold* to a deeper meaning of the Crucifixion and that it is *ðurh ða rode* that he will be saved. In this respect *The Dream of the Rood* is an amplification of the little Latin motto which epitomizes the aspirations of the monastic life: *Per crucem ad lucem.*

We have already seen that the Dreamer is in some respects a typical 'lordless man.' He is alone; he lacks powerful friends; he moves toward a 'stoic' understanding. Unlike the Wanderer or the Seafarer, the Dreamer does not seem to be engaged in any kind of travel of a literal kind, though his state of exile might conceivably imply some kind of journey. Now Dorothy Whitelock suggested some fifteen years ago [in "The Interpretation of the *Seafarer,*" in *The Early Cultures of Northwest Europe,* 1950] that *The Seafarer* is not an exercise in Germanic seamanship with a stiff upper lip but an entirely Christian poem about actual *peregrinatio,* and G. V. Smithers, in a similar vein, has more recently produced impressive arguments [in his "The Meaning of *The Seafarer* and *The Wanderer,*" *Medium Aevum* 26 (1957)] to show that the language of both *The Seafarer* and *The Wanderer* in their imagery of exile and peregrination, is allegorical, spiritual. It would be fruitful to include in a study of *The Dream of the Rood* those two brilliant elegies which have so much in common with it, and to pursue the lines suggested by Whitelock and Smithers guided by recent work in monastic history and in the allegorical vocabulary of early monastics. Yet it would not be directly to my point, for despite the important characteristics which they share, *The Dream of the Rood* is different from the elegies in at least two important respects. It is in the first place overtly and obviously Christian, full of a wide range of specifically Christian allusions. It is also clearly allegorical, set in the allegorical framework *par excellence* of the dream vision. Secondly, it differs from the elegies in the nature of its philosophical resolution, for it provides an explicit answer for the 'lordless man' which goes beyond Boethian fortitude.

There is vigorous movement in the poem, movement from exile to community. The Dreamer begins alone and in the dark midnight (to midre nihte,/syðþan reordberend reste wunedon); the end of the poem leaves him in joy and hope, anticipating a life of radiant glory *on wuldre.* On the one side of the Cross the Dreamer is alone, *ana;* on the other he is inspired to eschatological anticipations of life in the eternal community of the saints (mid þam halgum). The whole force of the poem is directed toward the concept which finds expression in its final half-line: *þær his eðel wæs.* Christ's *eðel* is, of course, Heaven. It is the same homeland to which all who 'would be perfect' must hurry. Professor Smithers has drawn attention to a striking citation from Ælfric in the tenth century expressing the concept of our alienation from our true homeland (urum eðele) and finds a convincing 'single source' for it in the Fourth Dialogue of St. Gregory. But what these two great Benedictines, the one borrowing the words of the other, give voice to is a concept of Christian 'pilgrimage' as old as St. Paul, which finds expression as well in the *Regula Benedicti.* The monk is temporarily alienated from what Benedict calls the *patria,* and his Rule is addressed to those *ad patriam caelestem festinans.* Paul the Deacon, whose commentary on the Rule is one of the most valuable guides to Benedictine thought and practice in the Age of Bede, writes thus:

> Et debet [monachus] etiam expectare tempus; in quo exeat anima de corpore suo; exeat ad loca sua et proprietatem suam. hoc est in paradisum; quod est locus noster. et ad cives et parentes suos; hoc est angelos.

This *locus noster* is the *eðel* of *The Dream of the Rood,* the homeland to which the Cross is the key, and exile the path. In the telling phrase of a Benedictine commentator of the high Middle Ages, the monk moves 'per exterioris exilii finem . . . ad interne patrie claritatem.' *Per crucem ad lucem.* The monk should daily, *cotidie,* meditate expectantly on his last day, the end of his exile, just as the Dreamer awaits the eschatological Cross *daga gehwylce.*

The language used by the poet to describe the heavenly homecoming which is the end of exile might seem at first far removed from treatises on ascetic theology, and critics have found in the description an echo of the Germanic feast-hall as it appears elsewhere in Old English poetry.

> þær is blis mycel,
> dream on heofonum, þær is dryhtnes folc
> geseted to symle, þær is singal blis.
>
> (139-141)

The heavenly feast does indeed neatly complete the *comitatus* theme in the poem, but there is no need to turn to pagan Germania for an explanation. The imagery is just as strikingly reminiscent of the forceful, masculine vision of Heaven in a little dialogue on the monastic life attributed to Alcuin, 'ubi spiritualiter quiescens, bibes et epules perpetualiter in regno Christi et Dei'. The same point can be made of other 'Germanic' elements in the poem.

The historical episode of what might be called the Wagne-

rian school of Anglo-Saxon studies is happily over, but its monuments remain. We would be the poorer without them, for among those keen Germanicists who set out to explore our earliest literature in 'the search for Anglo-Saxon paganism' were some of the philological giants upon whose backs all dwarf-like literary critics must stand. Occasionally their zeal for Germania did positive violence to the text of *The Dream of the Rood*—as with the critic who translated 'ongyrede hine geong hæleþ' as 'the young hero put on his armor,' presumably because that is what a Germanic warrior was likely to do faced with a battle—but they have quite properly drawn attention to the interesting possibilities of approaching the poem through the *comitatus* theme. On the whole, however, the search for Germanic echoes in the poem has produced only untenable 'finds.' In a standard history of Old English literature [E.E. Wardale, *Chapters on Old English Literature,* 1935], recently republished, we are told that ' "All creation wept, lamented the fall of the King," is an echo of the description of the death of Baldor, the sun god, for whose untimely end all nature lamented . . .' [Bruce] Dickins and [Alan S.C.] Ross [*The Dream of the Rood,* 1954] repeat this farfetched suggestion, even though in later editions they add a citation to Curtius which completely undermines the identification of this 'source' by demonstrating the pervasiveness of the weeping-Nature trope. The author of *The Dream of the Rood* is being no more pagan than John Donne.

Of all the 'Germanic' elements in the poem, none has been more often commented upon than Christ's description as a *geong hæleþ* and the heroic treatment of the Crucifixion generally. In fact, the regal and heroic attitude of Christ is perhaps the least convincing of the proposed Teutonic elements in the poem. As Rosemary Woolf says [in her "Doctrinal Influences on *The Dream of the Rood,*" *Medium Aevum* 27 (1958)] the conception of a warrior Christ is 'not peculiar to the Anglo-Saxon imagination.' If we must speculate, it is not unlikely that the Anglo-Saxons picked up the idea, insofar as it is an idea and not the implication of Old English poetic diction, from the same source they picked up their other ideas about Christianity: the Benedictines who came to them as missionaries. Alcuin of York, who does not seem otherwise to be tainted by the religion of Woden, speaks of the Crucifixion, repeatedly and at length, in very much the style of *The Dream of the Rood,* stressing the power and vigor of Christ on the Cross. Of attempts to read a 'Germanic' meaning into such a view [Hans Bernhard] Meyer says rather pointedly [in his "Crux, Decus es Mundi: Alkuins Kreuz und Osterfrömmigkeit," in *Paschalis Sollemnia,* 1959],

> man braucht für die Idee des freiwillig leidenden und siegenden Königs nicht die germanische Volksseele zu bemühen. Es genügt, die exegetischen und homiletischen Werke der Kirchenväter zu lesen.

The *geong hæleþ* is no more 'Germanic' for the poet of *The Dream of the Rood* than he is for St. Ambrose. If it is dangerous to search for a 'Christ figure' in the hero of *Beowulf,* it is no less so to seek a 'Beowulf figure' in the Christ of *The Dream of the Rood.*

To what extent there was any real 'Germanisierung des Christentums' the scope posited by Dibelius and other keen Germanicists will probably remain a matter of some dispute, but it seems clear from the careful work of Michael Seidlmayer [*Weltbild und Kultur Deutschlands im Mittelalter,* 1953] that the most 'significant' examples of the Germanization of the Church can be limited to three: (1) the maintenance of class distinction within the cloister; (2) the acceptance, within severe limitations of the Germanic prerogatives of revenge; and (3) the institution of the secular Emperor, by quasi-sacramental anointings, as protector of the Church. The second of these concerns *The Dream of the Rood* tangentially, for it seems clear that its author is keenly aware of the brittle demands of Germanic revenge. His interest in them is ancillary to his principal matter, however, and the course he follows is not to Germanicize the Christian, but to Christianize the Germanic.

An attempt to get away from a Germanicizing reading of the poem has recently been made by Rosemary Woolf in her article, cited above, on the poet's Christology. She argues that the core poem (roughly the Crucifixion episode, stripped of its later accretions) is a carefully orthodox formulation of Christ's dual nature and the contrasting aspects of the Crucifixion—'divinity and triumph on the one hand and humanity and suffering on the other'—and that it was written in full knowledge of and to some extent in answer to heretical opinions which had partially characterized the Monophysite position at the Council of Chalcedon and which, as she shows, were of concern to English theologians in the late seventh and early eighth centuries. The poet's remarkable achievement is the fusion of a 'double stress on the Crucifixion as a scene of both triumph and suffering.' She goes on:

> Without such a brilliant conception as that of the poet's, the two aspects would have become separated, as they were usually in the Middle Ages. The Crucifixion in both mediaeval art and mediaeval literature is usually a scene of utmost agony: in accordance with the doctrine of 'satisfaction,' Christ as man offers His suffering to its farthest limit, until the body hangs painfully from the Cross without blood or life.

She later says that

> particularly in the Anglo-Saxon period, a treatment of the Crucifixion in which the hearer was led by his intense sympathy for Christ's pain to identify himself with Christ in the poem, would obviously be unfortunate since it would carry with it the implication that Christ's consciousness was solely human and therefore comprehensible to fellow human beings . . . would be to revert, though no doubt unsuspectingly, to the Gnostic heresy.

My basic sympathy with Miss Woolf's approach should be obvious; yet in rejecting her central conclusions I must debate her on at least two points. In the first place there seems implicit in her argument the curious notion that the statement of orthodoxy is invariably a rebuttal to heresy, in this case that 'Chalcedonian' Christology predicates an urgent concern with Monophysitism. I fully agree that much of the poet's remarkable achievement is the fusion

of a 'double stress on the Crucifixion as a scene of both triumph and suffering,' but it is the manner of this fusion rather than the fact of it which is remarkable. Generally speaking, orthodoxy is, after all, the rule, not the exception.

The other point concerns stylistic history. Miss Woolf seems to me narrow and misleading in her characterization of the Crucifixion of 'mediaeval art and mediaeval literature' as 'usually a scene of utmost agony.' Since she uses the terms 'mediaeval' and 'Middle Ages' to refer to an unspecified epoch which excludes 'the Anglo-Saxon period,' she is presumably referring to certain emotional tendencies in *late* Romanesque or *late* Gothic painting, to a stylistic convention which becomes dominant only many centuries after *The Dream of the Rood* could have been composed. Much of her own evidence supports the fact that neither in plastic nor pictorial art of the period during which the poem could conceivably have been written (and certainly not from the late-seventh century, when she would date it) is it possible to produce significant examples of the Crucifixion which are expressive at all, let alone expressive of 'utmost agony.'

As for the 'Gnostic' treatment of a pathetic Christ, it must be pointed out that it is precisely in England and precisely during 'the Ango-Saxon period' that such tendencies do appear. According to Thoby, the swaying corpse of the dead Christ begins to appear in English miniatures of the eleventh century. To the eleventh century as well belongs the incipient 'Gnostic' cult of the *adoratio crucis,* the sacred wounds, the nails which pierced Christ's flesh, and (in rudimentary form) the Sacred Heart. One of the lovely little painted books of the Old English period—B. M. MS Cotton Titus D 27—combines a sequence of these emotional devotions with a pictorial treatment of the Crucifixion which is entirely 'Chalcedonian,' heroic, with Christ open-eyed, triumphant, regnant.

The sole surviving English rood fragment *in situ* over a pre-Conquest chancel arch, at Bitton in Somerset, shows a typically heroic Christ with feet 'side by side on the cross, above a serpent or some such creature, and the Bitton Rood is typical of the treatments of the Crucifixion in the visual arts not only in England but in all of Western Christendom until well after the Conquest, the so-called 'Benedictine' type. The question of the development of the late Gothic or 'pathetic' crucifix is complex and as yet unresolved, though various theological influences have been suggested which may in part account for it—the preaching techniques of the friars, the development of the doctrine of 'Satisfaction' mentioned by Miss Woolf, etc. It is a question that hardly concerns *The Dream of the Rood,* however, except to reinforce the fact that the poet is clearly working within the stylistic mainstream of his own age.

Such discussion, which might seem more properly to appertain to the disciplines of theology and art history than literary criticism, seems to me necessary because of the fact that Woolf's doctrinal approach to the poem leads her to a position sometimes at odds with the text. For example, regarding the 'Gnostic' identification which an audience might make with the tortured human nature of Christ, she maintains that the author of *The Dream of the*

Rood 'does not speak of Christ's death: the climax of the poem is simply, *Crist wæs on rode,* and His death is thereafter described as a sleep.' In point of fact, of course, the first half-line of the 'climax' (56a) is *cwiðdon cyninges fyll,* where *fyll* means 'death,' or something stronger, like 'slaughter.' Line 49b (. . . *he hæfde his gast onsended*) is hardly less direct about speaking of His death. The overt statement 'Deað he þær byrigde' (101a), in the part of the poem which Woolf does not consider *echt,* merely recapitulates what has already been said. This is not to deny that the poet uses the death-as-sleep figure, but it has a poetic rationale of its own which has nothing to do with the poet's putative 'theological uneasiness' in speaking of the death of Christ, which as we have just seen he does on multiple occasions in the clearest of terms. Following St. Ambrose on Luke, the poet has described the Crucifixion in the mood of an athletic contest, violent and incidentally exhausting.

It remains possible, of course, to see in **The Dream of the Rood** a response to the Christological debates of the fifth century, but by the same token it would be possible to argue that virtually every treatment of the Crucifixion for half a thousand years is such a response. For my part, I find it difficult to believe that **The Dream of the Rood** is a polemical or controversial document of any kind. The poet's chief concern is not to handle a tricky bit of Christology without lapsing into Monophysitism, Nestorianism, or Gnosticism, and those critics who are unwilling to dismiss more than half the Vercelli text as 'surely a later addition by a writer of the school of Cynewulf ' may wish to seek an artistic purpose which has little to do with academic heresies, perhaps indeed little to do immediately with Christ or the Cross, in that part of the poem that deals with the Dreamer, the *ic* of the very first line, the speaker with whom the poem begins and ends.

I wish to suggest that the thematic intimacy between Christ and His Cross in **The Dream of the Rood** is not the poet's means of narrowing the theological focus of the Crucifixion episode to preclude Christological difficulties, but rather his method of widening that scope to bridge the gap between Christ and the Dreamer. The Cross becomes a kind of mediator, in the first instance, between the Dreamer and his Lord. A number of critics have sought a relationship between the Old English poem and the great liturgical hymn *Crux fidelis:* they both present images of 'faithful' crosses. There is no doubt that the Cross is faithful to Christ, but that is only half the story; and Dionysius the Carthusian, writing at the end of the Middle Ages but with the same ascetic point of view which I find everywhere revealed in **The Dream of the Rood,** says that the Cross is *fidelis* to mankind, for whom it is the key to Heaven. In **The Dream of the Rood** the Cross becomes the common denominator between Christ and the Dreamer, the essential experience which they share, and it is in terms of the exposition of the relationships between Christ, the Cross, and the Dreamer that the structure of the poem is to be explained.

Although no very careful study has been made of the compositional unity of the Vercelli text, it is commonly assumed to be a composite work, dividing at line 78. War-

dale speaks of it as a reworking of an 'original poem,' and Dickins and Ross say that 'the Vercelli text is probably composite.' [Albert S.] Cook [*The Dream of the Rood,* 1905] found the concluding lines of the poem an 'inartistic addition,' and as we have just seen Rosemary Woolf considers half the text a 'later addition.' Now it is not my purpose to produce a detailed defense of the unity of the Vercelli text, which remains problematical, but I should like to make the point that no arguments of any substance have in fact been advanced against it. Dickins and Ross find it 'perhaps significant' that the runic text on the Ruthwell Cross, undoubtedly linguistically more ancient than the Vercelli text, corresponds to a passage in the early part of the poem. The second part of the poem (i. e., after line 78) seems to them 'in quality . . . definitely inferior' But the Ruthwell runes are, after all, a *part* of a scheme of lapidary decoration. The inscription begins with the Crucifixion episode, omitting 38 lines of the Vercelli text, providing a poetic statement which is appropriate (a) to a tall cross, the sculptured decoration of which includes (b) a Crucifixion, and the central panel of which is (c) a victorious Christ *in deserto.* Even what is on the Ruthwell Cross represents considerably less half the number of lines of corresponding text in the Vercelli poem. This does not necessarily mean, however, that the Vercelli text is an expansion of the runic text, for the runic text may well be a series of lines taken from a larger work for epigraphic purposes. The Ruthwell runes in any case cover the entire workable space on the Cross shaft, so that there would not have been room for further 'quotations' from the second half of the poem even had they been relevant. The runes are actually rather cramped into the available space, unlike the uncrowded Latin inscriptions which accompany the carvings. The most recent study of the cross [Frank Willett, "The Ruthwell and Bewcastle Crosses—A Review," *Memoirs and Proceedings of the Manchester Literary & Philosophical Society,* 98 (1956-57)], partly on this account, goes so far as to suggest that 'the Ruthwell Cross inspired the poem inscribed upon it' and that 'the poem is inserted upon the cross in such a way as to suggest that it was not part of the original design, but was added later.' Epigraphy is not an art form generally characterized by brilliant original poetry, and I find Willett's suggestion improbable; but it does underscore a major weakness in the assumption that the Ruthwell text is necessarily the distant ancestor of the Vercelli poem.

Whether or not that part of the poem after line 78 is 'definitely inferior' to what has preceded it remains a matter for private critical appraisal. There is undeniably a marked difference of tone in the two 'halves.' Having finished the episode of the Crucifixion, the Cross goes on to a frank homily explaining the implications of spiritual crucifixion to a Dreamer who, as J. A. Burrow has nicely pointed out [in his "An Approach to *The Dream of the Rood,*" *Neophilologus* 43 (1959)], is 'the principle of development in the poem.' Without the Dreamer the poem would be more truly 'Caedmonian,' that is, it would be an inspired biblical redaction. With him it becomes a poem of philosophical pretensions, the vehicle of an ascetical-theological doctrine which sketches in a brilliantly imaginative way the aspirations of the monastic cadre of Anglo-

Saxon society, a society no longer one composed primarily of warriors.

A stylistic argument against the unity of authorship could conceivably be based on metrical grounds. The earlier part of the poem is characterized by lavish use of hypermetric lines, giving it an almost stanzaic effect, and these virtually disappear in the second part. On the other hand it would seem that these differences, essentially rhetorical, mirror the tonal differences between the *narratio* of the Crucifixion episode and the homiletic *explanatio* which follows it.

It should be apparent that arguments so far advanced against the compositional unity of the Vercelli text (when, indeed, any have been advanced) are rather assumptions based on subjective reactions to the 'quality' or appropriateness of the poetry in different parts of the poem. My own argument does not depend in the final analysis upon the compositional integrity of the Vercelli text. It is possible that a 'Vercelli poet' has reworked an 'earlier poem' about the Crucifixion, in which case he has produced a larger poem of extraordinary thematic unity in which the earlier Crucifixion episode fits like Cinderella's foot. The Crucifixion episode in *The Dream of the Rood* serves precisely the same function within the Vercelli text that it does within the iconographic schedule of the Ruthwell Cross: as part of an exposition of the eremitic life. That the only two texts of the Crucifixion episode—the Brussels inscription is more an misremembered quotation than a separate 'text'—should be used for the same artistic purposes by the Ruthwell masons and the author of the Vercelli poem strongly suggests, to my mind, that that was the purpose for which it was written.

The second 'half' of the Vercelli text is as important as the first; it is the spiritual history of the Dreamer who provides the 'essential principle of development' in the poem even as does the Dreamer in *Piers Plowman*. One could add other parallels: Boethius in the *Consolatio*, the Dreamers of *Pearl, The Book of the Duchess*, and many more. The Dreamer of the Old English poem belongs to that numerous tribe of *personae* of medieval vision poems who experience an education, moving with greater or lesser speed from incomprehension to understanding. In *The Dream of the Rood* the Cross is in the center of the poem, as it is at the center of the Christian religion; but it is neither the whole poem nor the whole religion.

The dramatic movement of this poem, as opposed to the dramatic *episode* of the Crucifixion, concerns the Dreamer's response to his vision. As Burrow puts it, the Dreamer

> moves from fear and sorrow to hope, and it is this simple emotional sequence which links the closing soliloquy with the opening vision and sets the tone of the central Crucifixion scene.

With one point only in Burrow's fine statement would I quarrel: the sequence is neither simple nor essentially emotional. It is, however, the undoubted movement of the poem—*per crucem ad lucem*—informing it with a thematic unity which argues persuasively against those unquestioning in their belief that the concluding section of the poem is a 'later addition.'

The poem in its entirely develops an ambiguity of the mo-

nastic vocation which is the ambiguity of the Crucifixion episode, for the 'cross' of monastic theology in the early Benedictine centuries, like the Cross of *The Dream of the Rood,* presents a double focus, suggesting both the spiritual crucifixion and daily martyrdom of asceticism and the martial and triumphant glory of the successful *militia*. In the visions of the cross which are a fairly common motif in early monastic hagiography, the spiritual and indeed specifically monastic implications of the 'cross' sometimes find explicit statement. A case in point comes from the life of a great French abbot of the early eighth century. St. Leutfrid, founder of the monastery which came to be known as La-Croix-St.-Lefroy. Engaged in a journey one day, Leutfrid came to a crossroads where, to his puzzlement, his horse stopped, refusing to go on further. After a few moments he became aware of a glorious vision of the Cross in the sky, a portent which he understood as a command to found a monastery on that spot: 'quod locus ille futuris temporibus crucifixi domini Iesu Christi veros cultores habiturus esset, qui crucis mortificationem et in corde et in corpore suo evidenter gestaturi essent.' For Leutfrid the corporeal vision of the Cross was a spiritual injunction to the *mortificatio crucis* of the cloister, the spiritual crucifixion. But the cross was also the battle standard of that glorious and heroic warfare of which St. Benedict speaks in the Prologue of the *Regula,* the other side, so to speak, of the monastic life. When a precisely similar revelation of the Cross appears in another saint's Life of the period, it is the aspect of the *militia Dei* which is stressed: 'Intellexit protinus quod locum sibi Dominus delegisset, in quo multos sub Christi vexillo militantes divina dignatio congregaret.'

An understanding of the ascetic implications of the cross will perhaps be helpful in analyzing the lines in which the Cross gives its final charge to the Dreamer to be constantly aware of that last terrible moment when Christ Himself will come to take a reckoning of his deportment in this life.

> Ne mæg þær ænig unforht wesan
> for þam worde þe se wealdend cwyð.
> Frineð he for þære mænige hwær se man sie,
> se ðe for dryhtnes naman deaðes wolde
> biteres onbyrigan, swa he ær on ðam beame
> dyde.
>
> (110-114)

Such an invitation to martyrdom may seem a jarring note in a poem which I maintain is about the monastic life—in spite of its thematic similarity to episodes in Anglo-Saxon hagiography. (We may cite the example of St. Boniface who, according to Leclercq, united the major monastic aspirations of exile, preaching, and martyrdom, impelled in part by nocturnal 'visions.') Yet the passage becomes less startling when examined from the point of view of the metaphoric vocabulary of the early monastic writers, both Celtic and Benedictine. The spiritual concept of the bloodless or ascetic martyrdom which finds its commonplace statement in Isidore's *Origenes* (7.11.4) has been carefully traced by the monastic scholar Louis Gougaud. The idea that martyrdom is a state of spiritual readiness to die for the faith, that is, to make a final act of self-denial, whether or not it actually culminates in physical death, is implicit in pre-Benedictine monachism, finds its first explicit statement in a famous letter of Sulpicius Severus about St. Martin, and is quickly taken up by the first major Benedictine commentator, Gregory the Great. The influence of the idea is apparent in the martyrologies of the early Benedictine centuries, where the distinction between 'martyrs' and 'quasimartyrs' is not conspicuous. Notable Anglo-Saxon martyrs include, for instance, SS. Guthlac and Etheldreda, both of whom died in bed so far as we know.

So-called 'bloodless martyrdom' or 'daily crucifixion' is a metaphor for the monastic life, and in early monastic vocabulary 'the acceptance of the cross is meant to signify the renunciation of all property, and a complete separation from one's kindred.' Such a state of separation characterizes the traditional 'lordless man' of Old English poetry (*anhaga, wineleas,* etc.), as it does the Dreamer in ***The Dream of the Rood*** ('Nah ic ricra feala/freonda on foldan'). In Old English, indeed, the very word *martirdom* means, in addition to its common modern meaning, the state of exile, of being 'lordless.' The *onhaga* of the Boethian poem 'Resignation' describes his state as a *martirdom.* That the monastic life is a martyrdom, a spiritual image of Christ's crucifixion, that the monk is one 'se ðe for dryhtnes naman deaðes wolde/biteres onbyrigan' is a point frequently emphasized by the great Benedictine reformers of the high Middle Ages who, in seeking to revitalize the Black Monks with the ascetical zeal of their glorious heritage, produced the first comprehensive treatises on the monastic life which went beyond glosses to the Benedictine Rule. For example, Peter of Celle argues in his *De disciplina claustrali* 'Quod claustrum sit vicarium Crucis,' building an intriguing allegory to show, among other things, that just as Christ, impaled on the Cross, had control of one member of his body only—His tongue, which he used to pray—so ought the monk to hobble all bodily activity save the praise of God with his mouth. And Ailred of Rievaulx, the great Cistercian saint whose works typify the spirituality of the second golden age of English Benedictinism, could tell his monks in chapter that their order was the very Cross of Christ:

> Jam ipsa crux Christi sit quasi speculum Christiani. In ipsa cruce Christi conveniant, et inquantum participat cruci Christi, intantum sibi praesumat gloriam Christi . . . Ordo noster crux Christi est.

Just as early monasticism was a daily crucifixion it was also an apostleship, and there is nothing that militates against a 'Benedictine' reading of ***The Dream of the Rood*** in the evangelical commission which the Cross gives the Dreamer: 'Nu ic þe hate . . . þæt ðu þas gesyhðe secge mannum.' (95-96) The expanse of the cloister was very wide in the Age of Bede. The Anglo-Saxons had received the Faith from Benedictine missionaries; and they were likewise monks—'foris apostoli, intus monachi'—who set out from England to conquer the old racial homelands. The chief pastoral functions in the Celtic Church, preaching and administering the sacraments, had been executed by monks, and in the Northumbrian (Roman) churches even such 'pure' Benedictine establishments as Wearmouth and Jarrow had considerable pastoral duties.

With this ideographic background in mind, we must look again at the intricate relationships by which the poet links Christ, the Cross, and the Dreamer, a series of poetic associations which I have argued are not his means of narrowing the poem's theological implications but rather his way of broadening them. There is no doubt, as many critics have noted, that there is an extraordinary identification of Christ and His Cross in the poem. Their intimate identification stems not from a fortuitous 'meeting' at the Crucifixion, but from a long, perhaps even labored, series of parallels. Both share a significant act of volition. That of the Cross is explicit, that of Christ implicit. Both are 'heroic.' They suffer the same ordeal, and the Cross appropriates the *stigmata* of Christ as its own wounds: 'Þurhdrifan hi *me* mid deorcan næglum. On *me* syndon þa dolg gesiene.' (46) The Cross says: 'Bysmeredon hie unc butu ætgædere,' (48) and the dual *unc* grammatically underscores the relationship between them in the Crucifixion episode. They are seen in intimate and isolated association, a heroic and redemptive stasis. Alone they suffer for the sins of men ('for mancynnes manegum synnum/ond Adomes ealdgewyrhtum' [99-100]) suspended, as in the common pictorial representation of a later period, between Heaven and earth. The Cross shares Christ's defeat, but it is soon to share His glory too, and their careers continue as in parallel columns. Christ is buried, and the Cross is dumped into a wretched hole with the gibbets of the thieves. Christ's resurrection was the visible sign of his victory over death, a victory which the Cross now fully shares. In one of the very few explicit echoes of the Invention legend, the Cross is exhumed from its pit. In this thematic identity of Christ and the Cross we may perhaps see the mental habit which lies behind the quasi-dramatic Good Friday 'deposition' as it appears for the first time in England in the *Regularis Concordia* at the end of the tenth century, in which a cross, crucifix, or eucharistic host becomes a surrogate for the corpse of Christ. But this remarkable identification is only half the poet's achievement, for he is just as concerned to establish a relationship, which is at first not identity but contrast, between the Cross and the Dreamer.

The splendor of the radiant *objet d'art* which is the Dreamer's first apprehension in his palimpsest view of the Cross creates an immediate 'tension' in the poem. 'Syllic wæs se sigebeam, ond ic synnum fah,' (13) says the Dreamer. The Cross is 'on lyft lædan, leohte bewunden' (5), and 'begoten mid golde' (7). The Dreamer is said to be *licgende.* But when the Dreamer sees through the gold of the Cross to the gory gibbet of Calvary, it is to the apprehension not of contrast but of identity. The Dreamer says, 'Eall ic wæs mid sorgum gedrefed' (20), and the Cross, 'Sare ic wæs mid sorgum gedrefed' (59). The Dreamer is 'forwunded mid wommum' (14); the Cross 'mid strælum forwundod' (62). Now these resemblances are no mere verbal parallels; they are true identities, understood spiritually. For the wounds and sorrows which the Cross shares with Christ are the wounds and sorrows, paraphrasing the text, of the stains of sin which characterize the Dreamer. It is this implicit realization by the Dreamer in line 21 which accounts for his fear, a fear which paradoxically grows from an understanding that there is no great gulf between him and the Cross, as his first glittering view of it seemed to suggest, but just the opposite. Even as Christ and the Cross bear together the *stigmata,* so in another sense do the Dreamer and the Cross, for the wounds of Christ are the *earmra ærgewin,* and *mancynnes manegum synnum ond Adomes ealdgewyrhtum,* the 'wounds' of the Dreamer.

The meaning of the poem must lie in the penitential submission by which, just as Christ has taken up the sins of men, men must take up the Cross of Christ. It is in this submission that the most satisfying explanation of the reference to the Annunciation in the poem is to be explained:

> Hwæt [says the Cross], me þa geweorðode wuldres ealdor
> ofer holmwudu, heofonrices weard!
> Swycle swa he his modor eac, Marian sylfe,
> ælmihtig god for ealle menn
> geweorðode ofer eall wifa cynn.
>
> (90-94)

We may wish to recall that the Annunciation appears in the iconographic scheme of the Ruthwell Cross immediately above the Crucifixion on the righthand panel, where it underscores the theme of humility or submission. 'Be it unto me according to Thy will,' was Mary's choice, and this is also the choice of Christ and the Cross. In the penitential economy of *The Dream of the Rood,* such submission becomes the sole *hyht* of the Dreamer.

We cannot, of course, claim that this perception is uniquely 'monastic.' The monastic vocation is, after all, merely the Christian vocation *par excellence.* Yet it seems to me that we may conclude that the theology of salvation in *The Dream of the Rood* is not commonplace in its expression; for though the redemptive work of Christ is explicitly spelled out ('He us onlysde ond us lif forgeaf,/heofonlicne ham' [147-148]), it is the Cross which actively urges itself as the agent of man's salvation ('*ic hælan mæg/æghwylcne anra, þara þe him bið egesa to me*' [85-86]). It is likewise the Cross, not Christ alone, which will come to fetch the Dreamer from this world. The ascetic theorem of this cross-centered poem is that 'ðurh ða rode sceal rice gesecan/of eorðwege æghwylc sawl,/seo þe mid wealdende wunian penceð' (119-121). For though it is undoubtedly the Dreamer who is the 'principle of development' in the poem, it is the Cross that is the vehicle of the development, spanning the gulf between exile and Heaven, between the 'lordless man' and his *comitatus,* between the Dreamer and his Lord. The function of the rood in this poem is succinctly stated by Gretser in his discussion of the 'spiritual' meaning of the Cross, a meaning with which St. Ailred would have been in full agreement. 'Eximius [he says] inter cæteros crucis fructus est & iste, quod crux Christo nos conformat & similes efficit.' The exiled forest tree, *déraciné* 'holtes on ende,' finds its fulfillment only in the paradoxical submission to becoming the *bana* of its own Lord. The Cross's experience is an educational one; it moves from uncomprehending obedience in distasteful duty to glorification with the risen Christ and the authoritative knowledge which characterizes its homily to the Dreamer. As Christ is the Cross's 'teacher,' making an instrument of healing of a machine for executing criminals, so the Cross is the 'teacher' of the Dreamer, leading him from fear to hope to the eschatological contemplation of eternal joy. The Cross's first view of the Crucifixion, of its

'loyalty' as it were, was a limited one, and so is the Dreamer's first view of the Cross as a radiant ecclesiological *objet.* He must see þurh þæt gold to the ascetic implications which lie behind the repeated adversative sense of *hwæðre* with its contrasts of 'degradation and glory, or earthly impulse and spiritual duty.'

We must now examine the Dreamer's response to the 'message' of the Cross, the importance of which I have repeatedly stressed. That response is immediate and dramatic.

> Gebæd ic me þa to þan beame bliðe mode,
> elne mycle, þær ic ana wæs
> mæte werede. Wæs modsefa
> afysed on forðwege, feala ealra gebad
> langunghwila. Is me nu lifes hyht
> þæt ic þone sigebeam secan mote
> ana oftor þonne ealle men,
> well weorþian.
>
> (122-129a)

The true meaning of these lines, however, has apparently been lost in the difficulties of translation which they present. According to Dickins and Ross *hyht* and *secan* do not here have their usual meanings of 'hope' and 'go to,' but by taking '*hyht* as 'joy' and *secan* as 'resort to' the sense is better: 'resorting to the Cross is the joy of my life, now that I alone (by reason of my vision) am in a more favorable position for adoring it than other men.' This paraphrase (it can hardly be called a translation) is remote from the text, making difficulty where none exists (the meaning of *hyht* and *secan*) but avoiding difficulty where it does exist (the meaning of *ana*). According to Hans Bütow, *ana* refers to the Cross, and the passage is to be translated: 'Nun ist mir des Lebens Hoffnung,/Dass ich das Siegeskreuz suchen mag,/ Es allein, öfter als alle Menschen,/Wohl su verehren . . .' This also seems to be the opinion of Sister Anna Mercedes Courtney, the most recent editor of the poem, who translates the passage: 'It is now my life's hope that I may/Search out that victory tree,/May honor it well, alone, more often than all men.' Such translations are grammatically impossible, and in my opinion we are on much surer ground to take *ana* on its face value, with A. S. Cook in his fine edition as 'alone, *nsm. wk,*' in both lines 123 and 128. The Dreamer says: 'It is now the hope of my life that I, alone more often than other men, may go to the cross, worship it fittingly.' The Dreamer is a monastic, a spiritual exile and a solitary. He is one of the Anglo-Saxon monks who rejoiced in the name of *crucicolae,* 'worshippers of the Cross.' The hope of his life is 'to go to the Cross,' to practice the asceticism which is the path to his celestial homeland, *per crucem ad lucem.* In line 128 *ana* means just what it means in line 123, 'alone,' not 'only.' The state of the Dreamer is that of the Cross hewn down from its forest, that of the icons of Christ, John Baptist, SS. Paul and Antony on the Ruthwell Cross: the Dreamer is *in deserto.* It was W. P. Ker, one of the first and best of the poem's critics who argued [in his *The Dark Ages,* 1904] that the vision is treated 'as a mystery acted in some visionary place, not on any historical scene.' The terminology which the poet uses to 'place' the Dreamer is likewise not geographical; it is spiritual. That the Dreamer should claim a unique channel of grace for himself alone in the Cross, by reason of his vision or anything else, would be dangerously advanced spiritual pride. That he should argue the aspirations of his monastic profession is entirely logical.

The implication that the Cross is the recourse of one who is 'ana oftor þonne ealle menn' is a recapitulation of the major theme of the poem. The Dreamer, pressing the inversion of the *comitatus* metaphor, now finds his 'mundbyrd' in his Lord's *bana* and no longer dreads his lack of powerful earthly friends. Such a statement, in addition to being thematically relevant, grows naturally out of what precedes it. The Dreamer describes a movement from *langunghwila* to *hyht,* two poles spanned by the Cross. He had suffered *langunghwila,* but the vision has restored an urgent spiritual energy. His *hyht* lies in going to the Cross, that is, in monastic asceticism. In the terms defined by Leclercq the voice of this poem moves from *askesis* to mysticism, from the penitential recourse to the Cross as a remedy for *langunghwila* to the 'soul's union with God'—*waes [min] modsefa afysed on forðwege.*

But what is the meaning of *langunghwila?* I have criticized Dickins and Ross, perhaps too severely, for their handling of lines 126b-129a; yet it is they alone who have given a satisfactory explanation of the hapax legomenon *langunghwila* in the immediately preceding half-line. They suggest that 'the precise sense of *lanyuny-* in this passage is *accidia.*' *Accidia* represents an opposing influence to the mystical energy of 124b-125a and is antithetical to *hyht* in 126b. The Krapp-Dobbie punctuation is misleading, for the verb *gebad* should be read as a perfect form: 'I had endured many of all spells of *accidia.* [But] now . . .' The construction 'feala ealra . . . langunghwila' is cumbersome, but its sense is clear.

Accidia takes on, in the later Middle Ages, the generalized meaning of 'sloth,' and it is probably most familiar in the listing of the seven capital vices. There is no doubt, however, as the citations in Du Cange attest, of its specifically monastic provenance. Dickins and Ross quote the definition in Cassian's *Institutes* ('anxietas sive taedium cordis'); and a recent study of the monastic vocabulary of the Latin translations of the *Vita Antonii,* probably the second most influental monastic document, after the *Regula* itself, of the entire Middle Ages, puts this definition in focus. A principal meaning of *accidia* in the monastic milieu which produced the Ruthwell Cross is the anxiety of a monk as to whether the sacrifices he has made—the abnegation of self in abandoning property, friends, and relations—is really worth it. It is a sapping of spiritual energy which comes from anxiety about the *vita peregrini,* the life of exile, spiritually *in deserto.* The Cross has revealed in its narrative that it, too, experienced incomprehension about its role; in this it is paralleled by the Dreamer who has suffered *langunghwila.*

It is this passing glimpse of the Dreamer's former *langunghwila* that more than anything else in the poem 'personalizes' him, or at least provides him with the condition which adds a dramatic emphasis to the revelation of the Cross. For once he hears the Cross's homily, his 'personality' undergoes a radical change. He regards the rood no longer 'sorgum gedrefed' but 'bliðe mode;' and he spe-

cifically refers to his 'lordless' state (131b f.) very much in the manner of the 'secular' Old English elegy, only to say that it no longer matters. In an ascetic (or Boethian) sense, he has changed his loyalty from one *comitatus* to another, from *visibilia* to *invisibilia.* As with the Cross, so it is with the Dreamer, a period of doubt and torture gives way to one of comprehension, of joy, even of glory—already achieved by the Cross and the Dreamer's former earthly friends, and by the Dreamer whose aspiration is *wunian on wuldre* (135, 143) eagerly awaited. Yet I cannot find that this transformation is essentially an 'emotional' one. The emotional language which the cloistered voice of the poem adopts, like the sensuous imagery describing the aspects of the Cross, is meant to move the reader from visceral engagement to the contemplation of insubstantial mysteries. He is talking about 'conversion,' in its principal medieval sense of ascetic profession, the putting off of the visible things of the world for the invisible things of God.

The Dreamer is speaking in no vague or woolly sense when he says 'Is me nu lifes hyht/þaet ic þone sigebeam secan mote.' His response to the vision of the Cross is at first penitential, dwelling in a series of adversative phrases on the spiritual distance between him and the saving *sigebeam;* then, after the Cross's homily, joyful, indeed mystical. For it is penitential 'going to the Cross' that is the cure for *accidia.* Surprisingly, we know little about the actual penitential practices in the cloisters of the earlier Middle Ages in spite of the large number of surviving penitential texts. Leclercq has observed that the sources for practically all monastic studies of the period must be hagiographic, enshrined in the monumental *Acta Sanctorum O.S.B.* of Mabillon; and these *Lives* do contain at least one episode which is revealing for the study of **The Dream of the Rood.** It concerns the life of the gentle St. Lambert († *ca.* 700).

Lambert, Bishop of Maastricht, was deprived of his see through the political tyranny which eventually led to his martyrdom. In great humility of spirit, he retired to the (Benedictine) monastery at Stavelot where he practised notable acts of mortification. His biographer related that one night when all the other monks were asleep St. Lambert, as was his wont, arose to pray, creeping through the dormitory, sandals in hand lest he disturb any of the sleeping brethren. Stumbling in the dark, he dropped one of the sandals with a clatter which awoke the convent. This, of course, was a quite serious offence, as it violated the major silence of the *Regula.* The abbot, having no idea that the culprit was the distinguished refugee Lambert, and ignorant of the circumstances of the infraction, called out in the dark that the guilty one, whoever he was, should 'go to the Cross' as penance. This the saintly Lambert did with the humility and deference to the abbot's authority which accounts for his biographer's inclusion of the story.

Lambert's biographer, the monk Sigeburt, had an interest in archeology and monastic practice, and it is he who best explains this reference to 'going to the Cross,' in the *Vita* edited by the Bollandists.

> Haec crux lapidea [he says] inter oratorium et dormitorium erat statuta. Filii Israel in deserto ob taedium longi itineris ac laboris murmurantes et pro hac noxa percussione ignitorum serpenti-

um pereuntes, sanabantur ab aspectu aenei serpentis, in figura crucifigendi Filii hominis, a Moyse pro signo exaltati. Ad hunc modum credibile est, hanc quoque crucem pro signo positam fuisee, ut ad aspectum illius hi, qui erant Christi, carnem suam crucifigerent cum vitiis et concupiscentiis, et si qui pertaesi longi laboris in via Dei lassescerent, ad aspectum crucis ex morte Christi longanimitatem spei resumerent, et sic ignita antiqui serpentis venena effugerent. [Et infra rursum ait:] Ad quam addicti regulariter poenitebant, si qui graviusculis culpis delinquebant.

There is much that is familiar in this passage. We have already seen a similar echo of the Pauline doctrine of spiritual crucifixion in the anecdote from the life of St. Leutfrid. As for St. John's typological interpretation, it is a favorite text of monastic authors of the Middle Ages, who were able to make a ready identification between the children of Israel *in deserto* and their own spiritual state. According to Bede (*Hist. Abb.* 9), pictures of the brazen serpent and the Crucifixion were among the paintings with which Benedict Biscop adorned the monastery at Wearmouth in a scheme intended to show the perfect fulfillment of the Old Law in the New. For the monk, the tropological significance of the text and its cognate in John 12.32 is that it is by humiliating himself before the exalted, crucified Christ that he comes to share Christ's glory, the *exaltatio caelestis*. This is, figuratively, the course followed by the Cross itself in *The Dream of the Rood;* so also the Dreamer, like St. Lambert, faces the penitential meaning of the Cross 'to midre nihte/ syþþan reordberend reste wunedon' (2-3), and moves from fear, guilt, *langunghwila*, the *tenebrae*, to the joy and implied brightness of the *patria caelestis*. To 'go to the Cross' was a common penitential practice in early monasteries. It reflects the same mental habit linking penance with the 'cross' which partially explains the widespread custom, even among the laity, of praying, standing or prostrate, with the arms outstretched in the form of a cross.

If I am correct in my argument that the 'cross' of the poem is essentially figurative, an emblem of diverse suggestion which generates the ascetical and penitential energy of the poem, we should not be surprised that [H.R.] Patch's early attempt [in his "Liturgical Influence in *The Dream of the Rood,*" *PMLA* 24 (1919)] to approach the text by way of actual ceremonies involving the cross in the Anglo-Saxon liturgy met with such limited success, or that the legend of the Invention and other aspects of the abundant medieval Cross-lore have little to offer toward the poem's explication. Attempts to find the poem's 'sources' in cross legends have been unsuccessful for the most part because the poet is interested in the cross as redemption, not as relic. There remain, nevertheless, some unexplored clues in the text, which are perhaps explicable by means of the 'monastic' liturgy. For example, there is a promising liturgical echo in the lines in which the Dreamer seeks the protection of the Cross: 'and min mundbyrd is/geriht to þaere rode' (130-131). Dickins and Ross translate *mundbyrd* as 'hope of protection,' but that is not necessary if we take *geriht* as an adjective: 'My protection is firm in the Cross.' This would seem to be an echo of the collect, dubiously

ascribed to Alcuin, in the *Missa de Sancta Cruce,* which became the standard Friday votive mass in the ninth century: 'Deus . . . concede, quaesumus, eos qui ejusdem sanctae crucis gaudent honore, tua quoque ubique protectione gaudere.' *The Dream of the Rood* (126b-131a) presents the same pattern of a desire to honor the Cross followed by the hope of enjoying its protection. Incidentally the lines spell out what Rosemary Woolf has nicely called 'a tremendous and ironic reversal of the values of the heroic code,' for it is Christ's *bana* as we have seen who now becomes the Dreamer's *mundbyrd*. As with so much in the latter portion of the poem, the lines are a kind of expanded poetic recapitulation of themes introduced in the Crucifixion episode. Such passages may indeed seem 'definitely inferior' according to critical canons which prize poetry only for its concision, paradox, and indirect suggestion, but they are characteristic of practically all surviving Old English poetry, including, of course, large chunks of *Beowulf.* In *The Dream of the Rood* they form a part of the structure of a poem with numerous medieval analogues, in which an at first uncomprehending visionary is brought to eventual knowledge as the poem moves from metaphoric to explicit statement.

There may be a liturgical explanation as well for another passage in the poem which has puzzled the poem's editors. The poet says (118) that no man 'þe him aer in breostum bereð beacna selest' need fear the Doom. Dickins and Ross say, 'This might mean "on his breast" and refer to an actual cross, or "in his breast" and be metaphorical. The latter seems the more probable.' In fact the cross is at once 'actual' and 'metaphorical,' for it is the cross signed by the minister at baptism. We have clear testimony from Alcuin concerning the pectoral unction which was part of the baptismal rite practiced by the English monk-missionaries on the Continent.

> Pectus quoque codem perunguitur oleo, ut signo sanctae crucis diabolo claudatur ingressus. Signantur et scapulae, ut undique muniatur. Item in pectoris et scapulae unctione signatur fidei firmitas et operum bonorum perseverantia.

It is the Christian, faithfully persevering in his baptismal vows, who needs not fear the Last Judgement.

There is ancillary documentation for the meaning of the line in another prosopopoeic poem of the Anglo-Saxon period that deals with the paradox of the Cross, once an instrument of terror, now a healing sign of hope. The *Ænigma* of Tatwine, the English Primate and leading southern 'intellectual' of the first half of the eighth century, have received less attention than they merit. His riddle 'De cruce Christi' in particular bears such obvious relationship to *The Dream of the Rood* that it may be cited in full.

> Versicolor, cernor, nunc nunc mihi forma nitescit,
> Lege fui quondam cunctis jam larvula servis,
> Sed modo me gaudens orbis veneratur et ornat;
> Quiqui meum gustat fructum jam sanus habetur.
> Nam mihi concessum est insanis ferre salutem.
> Propterea sapiens optat me in fronte tenere.

Among the obvious similarities of phrasing between the

Latin riddle and the Old English poem are the following: 'Geseah ic wuldres treow/ waedum geweorðode wynnum scinan' (14-15); 'Iu ic waes geworden wita heardost/leodum laðost' (87-88); 'ic haelan maeg/aeghwylcne anra' (85-86); 'þe him aer in breostum bereð beacna selest' (118). The final line of Tatwine's poem refers in a more immediately recognizable way to the baptismal mystery which is also in *The Dream of the Rood.*

The grace which the baptismal mystery implies is central to the meaning of *The Dream of the Rood,* and to the interpretation of the concluding section of the poem, which has so far found small favor with the critics. Dickins and Ross say that the 'last few lines, referring to the harrowing of Hell, have all the appearance of an addition.' And A. S. Cook, whose pronouncements should usually command respect, speaks in a similar vein.

> The concluding section, which has the air of an interpolation, or of an inartistic addition by the poet's own hand, is only about a twentieth of the whole. The poem is complete without it, and it seriously mars the unity of impression.

These arguments need answering, and Burrow has set out to answer them. With fine perception he notes that the 'transition to the Harrowing of Hell . . . is natural at this point as an amplification of Christ's "releasing" power. It is also convincing in the general economy of the poem.'

It is also possible to argue that the reference to the Harrowing is a logical reflection of the sequence of prayers addressed to Christ on the Cross in the monastic devotions codified in the *Regularis Concordia,* the well known *adoratio crucis.* We are fortunate in having an interlinear Old English gloss to the second oldest surviving text of these prayers, and this gloss, as might be expected, presents some interesting parallels with the poem. The final six petitions of the sequence run as follows: [1] *Domine Jesu Christe, adoro te in cruce ascendentem* [in rode astigendne]; (2) . . . *in crucem vulneratum* [on rode gewundudne]; (3) . . . *in sepulchro positum* [on byrgene geledne]; (4) . . . *descendentem ad inferos, liberantem captivos* [nyðer astigendne to hellwarum alysendne gehæfte]; (5) . . . *a mortuis resurgentem & ad caelos ascendentem* [fram deadum arisendne 7 to heofenum astigendne]; (6) . . . *venturum & judicaturum* [toweardne 7 to demenne].

Now the events in the life of Christ to which the prayers refer are in the order of their statement in the Creed, 'chronological' order as it were. With the exception of the sixth act of devotion, adoring Christ in his coming at the Doom, the prayers are parallel to and in the order of similar elements in *The Dream of the Rood.* As for the Doom, it is the explicit subject of a lengthy section (103 ff.), and the whole poem reverberates with eschatological echoes of those monastic aspirations so felicitously defined by Dom Colombas which characterize so much of early English religious literature, the Doomsday poems, the 'elegiac' poems, the apocalypticism at the heart of Bede, historian of 'the Sixth Age.' Any connection between such monastic spiritual exercises and *The Dream of the Rood* must remain speculative. Though we may presume that the petitions of the *adoratio crucis* antedate their codification in

the *Regularis Concordia,* we have no evidence. Still, there remains a more powerful response to the objection raised against the episode of the 'Harrowing.'

The answer is to deny the premise upon which it is founded. To be blunt, Dickins and Ross are mistaken in saying that lines 148 to the end 'clearly refer to the Harrowing of Hell.' Line 148b and line 149 do make such a reference, but the following lines (150-156), which conclude the poem, refer to an entirely different though conjugate event in the history of Our Lord, namely the Ascension. The eccentric punctuation adopted by Dickins and Ross leads them to deny that *siðfæt* means 'journey;' they translate it as 'expedition.' But Bosworth-Toller record its principal meaning as 'journey,' and the punctuation adopted by Cook and Krapp-Dobbie underscores what that journey is; it is the victorious journey of Christ to Heaven, *þær his eðel wæs,* that is, the Ascension.

Far from being irrelevant or tangential, the reference to Christ's glorious Ascension completes the poem's mystery of grace. It is the expected fulfillment of his earlier 'lifting up' in line 40 ('Gestah he on gealgan heanne'). It resolves the mystery of the Cross which is at once a gory gibbet and a jewel-encrusted ornament, the mystery of the brazen serpent in the desert. We may recall our text in St. John 3. 13-15.

> Et nemo ascendit in caelum, nisi qui descendit de caelo, Filius hominis, qui est in caelo. Et sicut Moyses exaltavit serpentem in deserto, ita exaltari oportet Filium hominis, ut omnis qui credit in ipsum non pereat, sed habeat vitam aeternam.

In another crucial 'monastic' text (Rom. 6. 4-6) St. Paul has said that the price of resurrection with Christ is the 'crucifixion of the old man.' In a profoundly eschatological discussion of the meaning of the monastic life, a modern Benedictine has argued that there is but a single mystery of the Christian vocation, the mystery of the Ascension. Christ's ascension of the Cross on Calvary, His Ascension into Heaven—these are the two visions which the Dreamer sees. In the eschatological mysticism of St. Benedict the two views are one: *per crucem ad lucem.* The Dreamer first sees the vision of a glorious cross, wrapped in light, covered with jewels, but this is a cross he cannot truly 'see' until he perceives the implications of the Crucifixion. Without the first ascension, there can be no second.

The controlling themes of *The Dream of the Rood* are eschatological. All the 'last things' are there: the death of spiritual crucifixion and the impending Doom, the Heaven to which the Dreamer aspires and the Hell spoiled by Christ. These themes have been prepared for from the opening lines of the poem. *To midre nihte* when, *literaliter,* the vision occurs, has associations beyond the commonplace, for it immediately suggests the Nocturns of the Benedictine Office.

> On uhtan we sculon God herian ealswa Dauid cwæð: 'Media nocte surgebam ad confitendum tibi super iudicia iustitie tue.' Dæt is: 'To middre nihte ic aras (and andette drihtenes doma rihtwisnesse).' Crist sylf bead þæt we georne wacian sceoldon; he cwæð: 'Vigilate ergo quia nescitis quando ueniet dominus'. Dæt bið: 'Waciað

georne forðam þe ge nyton hwænne eower drih-
ten cymð.

But the Christians of the early Middle Ages did know
'when' their Lord was to come again. It would be at midnight, announced by a glorious rood, the jewelled image
of which typically decorated the eastern apses of early medieval churches.

We know as well what some of them thought about as they
waited. From quite early times Benedictines employed a
series, or rather several different series, of unofficial meditations in conjunction with the canonical hours of the Office. A little poem written down in the fifteenth century
summarizes their nature thus:

> Haec sunt septennis Domino cur psallimus
>   horis:
> Prima flagris cedit, subducit tercia morte,
> Sexta tegit solem, sed nona vidit morientem.
> Vespera deponit, reddit completa sepulchro
> In medio noctis domita morte resurgit.

Rupert of Deutz has left us in his *De Divinis Officiis* a more
complete schedule of the meditations of his day. They include, for the Office *to midre nihte,* two which are of cardinal interest to this study. 'Bursting the gates of Hell, like
another Samson, Christ rose from the dead at midnight;'
and 'It is written that He will come again in the middle
of the night, as in Egypt when the Passover was celebrated
and the exterminator came.' It is not fortuitous that *The
Dream of the Rood* ends with allusions to the Harrowing
and the Ascension, nor irrelevant that the Dreamer awaits
the Doom with expectancy.

The Dream of the Rood, of course, is no mere patchwork
of phrases gleaned from theological treatises, and the texts
which I have collated are not offered as 'sources' in any
narrow sense. The poet who so brilliantly shaped the
structure of the Vercelli text was more than equal to the
task of giving original and satisfying expression to the traditional ideas with which he dealt. What I have tried to
suggest is that the poem is characterized by a cast of
thought and to some extent by a vocabulary that is not
merely vaguely 'Christian,' but which is specifically monastic in its spirituality. A leading authority on Anglo-
Saxon monasticism [Hugh Farmer, "The Studies of
Anglo-Saxon Monks (A. D. 600-800)," in *Los Monjes y los
Estudios,* 1963] has recently written that

> the doctrinal and theological implications of sev-
> eral surviving poems such as *The Dream of the
> Rood* are so deep that it seems unlikely that they
> were composed outside a monastic milieu.

The thematic ordering of the poem argues even more; for
it is no Caedmonian biblical paraphrase, no inspired redaction. It is a poem about the monastic life, the Christian
life *par excellence,* born of the deep spirituality of Anglo-
Saxon Benedictinism. We know from Alcuin that the *Regula Benedicti* was expounded in the vernacular for the
benefit of the monoglot monks in the Northumbrian
monasteries. *The Dream of the Rood* is, among other
things, a sophisticated verse exposition of the spiritual precepts of that document in which the cross is everywhere—
except in name.

This characterization of the poem does not exhaust its
being nor fully explain the poet's achievement. On the
other hand, I hope it will provide a fresh perspective about
a work whose richness has captivated several generations
of literary historians. English literature begins with the lay
brother Caedmon in the Celtic convent at Whitby. Ald-
helm, whose verse King Alfred admired, was a Benedictine. So, probably, was Cynewulf. If we consider Bede's
'Death Song' we can claim the greatest English man of letters of the Middle Ages. To this group of early English humanists, members of that monastic fraternity whose literary aspirations and achievements Dom Jean Leclercq has
so brilliantly taught us, we may add the anonymous author of *The Dream of the Rood,* an Anglo-Saxon monk in
whom the 'love of letters and the desire for God' combined
to produce a poem of extraordinary imaginative power.

Louis H. Leiter   (essay date 1967)

SOURCE: *"The Dream of the Rood:* Patterns of Transformation," in *Old English Poetry: Fifteen Essays,* edited by
Robert P. Creed, Brown University Press, 1967, pp. 93-
127.

[*In this essay, Leiter studies the transformation of the
poem's three characters: Christ, the Cross, and the Dreamer.*]

The Dream of the Rood is concerned with a process of salvation by means of radical transformation that involves
three actors in a universal spiritual crisis. Metamorphosis
informs the structure of the poem and gives life and significance to its aesthetic materials.

In presenting these transformations, the poet has recourse
to Christian tradition—to the Passion of Christ, the story
of the Cross, and the hoped-for conversion of fallen mankind. For poetic reasons the poet casts the Passion, the
drama of the Cross, and the salvation of the Dreamer into
a series of three almost identical dramatic metaphors that
reinforce each other contrapuntally. By this means he
achieves amplification, progression, and cohesion among
his metaphors. But the metaphors being dramatic, are also
dynamic: they are incremental, varied, and transmuted;
they progress through a series of dramatic climaxes. In
their final resolution they project a new life, a new state
of being, for the three performers—Christ, Cross, and
Dreamer.

The drama of the first two performers, Christ and Cross,
must be regarded in a special light, that is, not as exclusive
historical happenings, but as what might be called rehears-
als—actions that demonstrate a method, a way of achieving spiritual rejuvenation. But it is the Dreamer who,
through identification of his fate with the radically contrasted experiences—mundane and yet eschatological—of
Christ and Cross, validates and enlarges their common
fate.

The poem, then, is concerned with the religious experience, but not in the form of belief, or of conversion, or of
revelation, or of the nature of any of these, but religion in
the sense of change—human transformation. Hence metamorphosis is used quite deliberately and literally for two

The panels of the Ruthwell Cross, c. 8th century, now preserved in Dumfriesshire, on which parts of The Dream of the Rood *are inscribed.*

reasons: the transformations of the performers and, congruent with their change, the transformation of the structure, imagery, and thematic materials of the poem.

For these dramas the poet chose materials close at hand, experience from a daily life that was animated by memories of a pagan past and incidents from his encounter with biblical story. Then, taking the vocabulary of warfare of which he had intimate knowledge, he constructed the three identical dramas that form the poem: the defeat and paradoxical victory of Christ, the hewing down and raising up of the Cross, and the sleep and awakening of the stained and sinful Dreamer.

CHRIST

In the first of these dramatic metaphors the young hero, *frea . . . mancynnes* (33b), who is either king, prince, or lord, has been defeated in battle. This defeat the Cross points up by saying *heton me heora wergas hebban* 'they ordered me to lift up their criminals' (31b). The defeated hero proves he still has the hero's *ellen,* however, since he *efstan elne mycle* 'hastened with great boldness' (34a) and *Gestah he on gealgan heanne* 'ascended the high gallows' (40b). He is tortured, pierced with *deorcan næglum* 'dark nails' (46a), which leave *opene inwidhlemmas* 'open malicious wounds' (47a), treated ignominiously, while *Bysmeredon hie unc butu ætgædere* 'they mocked us both together' (48a). The prince, *weruda god* 'god of hosts' (51b), is then further tortured and executed, his death being *þearle þenian* 'violently extended[?]' (52a). *Weop eal gesceaft, / cwiðdon cyninges fyll* 'all creation wept, mourned the fall of the king' (55b-56a). Reinforcements come: *Hwæðere þær fuse feorran cwoman / to þam æðelinge* 'still eager ones came from afar to that prince' (57-58a), but these *hilderincas* 'warriors' (61b) find that they cannot save their lord. He is dead: *beheoldon hie ðær heofenes dryhten, ond he hine ðær hwile reste, / meðe æfter ðam miclan gewinne* 'there they beheld the lord of heaven, and he rested there for a time, tired after the great struggle [battle, or war]' (64-65a).

They bury him:

> Ongunnon him þa moldern wyrcan
> beornas on banan gesyhðe . . .
> gesetton hie ðæron sigora wealdend.
>
> (65b-67a)

> Then men began to make him a tomb in the sight
> of the murderers . . . in it they then put the lord
> of victories.

In this act can be seen a paradoxical foreshadowing of his return to life and eventual victory. Like the comitatus around a fallen prince—those around the burned Beowulf, for instance—the warriors, eager but mournful reinforcements, gather to sing funeral songs: *Ongunnon him þa sorhleoð galan* 'they then began to sing a dirge' (67b). The grief-stricken *mæte weorode* 'little band' (69b) remain with their lord: *syððan stefn up gewat / hilderinca* 'the cry of warriors went up' (71b-72a), until *Hræw colode, / fæger feorgbold* 'the body grew cold, the lovely abode of the soul' (72b-73a).

The poet continues to amplify the battle metaphor: now

physically defeated by the enemy, *strange feondas* (30b), but spiritually victorious, the warrior-hero-prince rises phoenix-like from the flames of death: *hwæðere eft dryhten aras / mid his miclan mihte mannum to helpe* 'yet again the lord arose with his great strength as a help to men' (101b-2). Consequently, *Hiht wæs geniwad / mid bledum ond mid blisse þam þe þær bryne þolodan* 'hope was renewed with blessedness and with joy to those who had earlier suffered from fire' (148b-49a). Like a warrior-prince, he returns from exile in the foreign country of his captors and executioners: the prince *cwom / . . . þær his eðel wæs* 'came . . . where his native land was' (155b-56b), where he will join his people *to symle* 'at the feast' (141a) of victory.

There are rather complex emotional overtones generated here for which this bare rehearsal of the cohesive metaphor of battle does not completely account. Doubtless the metaphor would serve to capture the emotions of a people to whom warfare was as familiar as their daily bread and catch them up in the excitement of its drama. Their memories and fears would be stirred, but the effect here goes deeper. By identifying with the protagonist of the clearly wrought struggle, the listeners would unconsciously submit to the mimetic powers of the metaphor, supported, to be sure, by the rhythm of the verse, for the poet has at his command means other than that of dramatic metaphor. For example, he achieves emotional heightening by repetition of half-lines, often beginning with the same word, as in the insistent *ongunnon . . . ongunnon* in the two lines *Ongunnon him þa moldern wyrcan* (65b) and *Ongunnon him þa sorhleoð galan* (67b). These two heavily emphasized and paralleled beginnings, echoing an earlier line in which the tree *ongan þa word sprecan* 'began to speak words' (27a), are supported and emphasized with two statements beginning similarly with very strongly dramatic verbs: *curfon hie ðæt of beorhtan stane* (66b) and *gesetton hie ðæron sigora wealdend* (67a).

Repetition, parallelism, shifting of the verb of action to the semantically (though not rhythmically) important initial position, and hints that the message of the Cross is the Word of Christ (*ongan þa word sprecan*) are all deliberate devices for underscoring the significance of the drama enacted in the cohesive metaphor of battle. At the same time they are fairly simple devices of a stylization that achieves emotional heightening precisely at the necessary moment in the battle metaphor. The warrior-hero is dead; his men have had the spirit knocked out of them. Then comes the cluster of sounds *on, un, mo, an, no, or, en, am* in the following lines:

> *Ongunnon* him þa *mo*ldern wyr*can*
> beor*nas on b*anan gesyhðe;   curf*on* hie ðæt of
>   beorh*t*an stane,
> gesett*on* hie ðær*on* sig*or*a weald*en*d.
>   *Ongunnon* him þa sorhleoð gal*an*
> earme *on* þa æfentide,   þa hie wold*on* eft
> si*ð*ian,
> meðe fr*am* þam mæran þeod*ne.*
>
> (65b-69a)

In their profound resonance they mime the importance of the climactic change. Thus dramatic ending and equally dramatic beginning demand and receive in various ways the proper aesthetic emphasis.

Not the least of the devices at the poet's command is that which he employs to emphasize the transformation from the paralysis accompanying grief to the activity accompanying release from grief. After using three images of stasis within the space of two lines—*limwerigne* (63a), *gestodon* (63b), and *reste* (64b)—to characterize the astonishment and moral perplexity of the witnesses of the dramatic execution, the poet immediately calls in verbs of action— *ongunnon, curfon, gesetton, ongunnon*—to signal a rebirth, a new beginning, of the spirit in the emotionally depleted men at the exact moment they entomb their warrior-hero-Christ. The transformation is mimed here rather than overtly presented; it is like an echo or the passing of a dark shadow that cannot but emotionally move the reader or listener.

The poet and the warriors of Christ seem to catch their breaths for one shocked moment; then, releasing them, they move into action. Through this action they inspire their defeated neighbors, much as the Cross does the Dreamer, with those breaths of hope without which they cannot rebuild their exhausted moral lives and achieve victory over death. The poet dramatizes this inspiration when he sings of the raising and adorning by the prince's *comitatus* of the felled and buried Cross. Spiritually changed by participation in the drama of hero-Christ, the men symbolically spiritualize the Cross by adorning it with jewels, thus making it worthy of its future office. In turn, the spiritualized Cross repeats their action when it appears to the Dreamer and ministers to him, admonishing him to minister to other men by carrying its sign in his breast, much as the poet now sings to his rapt audience.

When in the battle metaphor the poet uses *fyll* 'fall,' 'destruction,' or 'death,' in *Weop eal gesceaft, / cwiðdon cyninges fyll* 'all creation wept, mourned the fall of the king' (55b-56a), the word is precisely the one that enriches his battle metaphor with the necessary spiritual overtones. Literally, *fyll* refers to the disobedience and fall of Adam, the connotation needed at this juncture to link the death of warrior-Christ in the present drama with the fall of Adam in that old chaos of the Garden, the effect of which is still evident in the felled tree and prostrate speaker. The metaphorical *fyll, aheawen, licgende*, and *þa us man fyllan ongan / ealle to eorðan* (73b-74a) of the singer fuse Adam, Cross, tree, and Dreamer in one perpetually repeated drama of loss and redemption, much like the three detailed repetitions of the battle metaphor. The ***Rood*** poet could depend on his listeners' acquaintance with the doctrine that all mankind rebelled with Adam when he forfeited supernatural life by his transgression in tasting the forbidden fruit. Adam, the first Christ, was "the figure of him that was to come" (Rom. 5:14); "For since by man came death, by man came also the resurrection of the dead. For as in Adam all die, even so in Christ shall all be made alive" (I Cor. 15:21-22); "The first man Adam was made a living soul; the last Adam was made a quickening spirit" (I Cor. 15:45). Singing of the *cyninges fyll*, the poet could quite naturally depend on his audience's

hearing 'fall,' automatically recalling Adam, remembering the Dreamer—and making the proper identifications.

The poet constantly expands the battle metaphor through his use of fairly commonplace religious material until it links events in the distant past, Adam's fall, for instance, to events in the more recent past, the felling of the tree and the fall of Christ to the sleeping Dreamer, now lying stained with sins and forgetful of those old tragedies.

What is perfectly clear is the identification of the fall of Adam with the execution of Christ and of the drama of the tree bearing the forbidden fruit with the drama of the Cross bearing the redemptive body—the "firstfruits" of I Cor. 15:20-23: "But now is Christ risen from the dead, and become the firstfruits of them that slept. For since by man came death, by man came also the resurrection of the dead. For as in Adam all die, even so in Christ shall all be made alive. But every man in his own order: Christ the firstfruits; afterward they that are Christ's at his coming."

> þæt . . . is wuldres beam,
> se ðe ælmihtig god   on þrowode
> for mancynnes   manegum synnum
> ond Adomes   ealdgewyrhtum.
>   (97b-100)

that . . . is the tree of glory on which God Almighty suffered for the many sins of mankind and Adam's deed of old.

Because Adam sinned in the past, Christ must suffer now; because Adam-man still sins, Christ must re-enact and reverse that drama of the Fall by waging war (thus the central metaphor of battle) against man's Adamic self still enthralled by His old foe Satan. It was in this manner that legend and dogma saw in Adam an antitype to Christ and maintained that the tree whose fruit was forbidden Adam and Eve was the one that served as the Cross of the Crucifixion. The concept that Christ "in his own self bare our sins in his own body on the tree, that we, being dead to sins, should live unto righteousness: by whose stripes ye were healed" (I Pet. 2:24) lies behind the poet's use of the word *fyll* to dramatize Christ's death on the Cross, the evocation of Adam's name in line 100a, and the fallen Dreamer lying as though in death.

The Adam-Christ tradition persisted well into the seventeenth century with notable examples in Donne's *Hymne to God My God, in My Sicknesse*: "We thinke that Paradise and Calvarie, / Christs Crosse, and Adams tree, stood in one place." Or a somewhat more complex version in Crashaw's *Vexilla Regis, The Hymn of the Holy Crosse*:

> Hail, our alone hope! Let thy fair head shoot
> Aloft; and fill the nations with thy noble fruit.
>   The while our hearts and we
>   Thus graft our selves to thee;
> Grow thou and they. And be thy fair increase
> The sinner's pardon and the just man's peace.

Crashaw clearly fuses tree (crucifix), noble fruit (Christ), sinful man (Adam), with the Prince of Peace; and to that he grafts the just man so that all participate in one grand drama of salvation.

The subtle chemistry of ***The Dream of the Rood*** strengthens the contrasted identification of Adam and Christ by evoking the legend that saw a connection between Adam's forfeit of mankind to Satan and his ransom by Christ: *Gestah he on gealgan heanne, / modig on manigra gesyhðe, þa he wolde mancyn lysan* 'he ascended the high gallows bold in the sight of many, when he wished to redeem mankind' (40b-41).

Amplifying and reinforcing his basic battle metaphor by choosing the dramatic *lysan* 'redeem' or 'ransom,' the poet directs our attention to the reward demanded for captured warriors. Because it is biblical, 'redeem' also refers to Christ's incarnation in order to purchase forfeited man from that Satan whom the poet characterizes as the enemy: "Even as the Son of man came not to be ministered unto, but to minister, and to give his life a ransom for many" (Matt. 20:28).

An even more apt identification might be made in this manner among Dreamer, Cross-messenger, and Job, who, like the Dreamer, lies sorely wounded (though unlike Job, the Dreamer admits he is stained with sins): "Yea, his soul draweth near unto the grave, and his life to the destroyers. If there be a messenger with him, an interpreter, one among a thousand, to shew unto man his uprightness: Then he is gracious unto him, and saith, Deliver him from going down to the pit: I have found a ransom" (Job 33:22-24). The *Rood* poet will return to this idea at the end of the poem: *He us onlysde ond us lif forgeaf, / heofonlicne ham* 'He redeemed us [or released us] and gave us life, a heavenly home' (147-48a). That the Lord is a 'ransom' deepens our immediate experience with the familiar Christian materials by pointing to the dramatic metaphor of war and the reward that must be paid the enemy for worthy captives.

But in religious poetry literal fact usually points to spiritual significance. 'Ransom' encompasses sacrifice and redemption, the fundamental ritual of the poem—a ritual that we celebrate through the stained and fallen Dreamer, Cross, and Christ and conversely through the purified Christ, Cross, and Dreamer. Man like Christ and Cross must lose his life to save it: "He that findeth his life shall lose it: and he that loseth his life for my sake shall find it" (Matt. 10:39). In the Mass for the celebration of the finding of the Holy Cross the congregation repeats the prayer after the Gloria: "O God, we were reminded again of the mystery of your passion by the miraculous discovery of the cross of salvation. May we attain eternal happiness through the ransom price you paid for us on that tree of life; who lives and rules with God the Father." In this manner the Church Fathers identified Adam's eating of the forbidden fruit and the consequent forfeiture of man with the ransom paid by Christ on the Cross, seen metaphorically as "the tree of life."

The *Rood* poet strengthens his Adam-Christ identification by recourse to the legend that Adam or his skull or both were buried on Mt. Calvary. He alludes to it when he uses *beorg* in *hie me on beorg asetton* (32b). The word primarily denotes a mountain or hill, yet by its secondary meaning, 'barrow' or 'burial place,' it may direct our attention to the iconographical image of Adam's skull at the foot of the Cross. Because of Adam's fault the world has become a

cemetery very much like Ezekiel's valley of dry bones: "The hand of the Lord was upon me, and carried me out in the spirit of the Lord, and set me down in the midst of the valley which was full of bones, And caused me to pass by them round about. . . . Prophesy upon those bones, and say unto them, O ye dry bones, hear the word of the Lord. Thus saith the Lord God unto these bones; Behold, I will cause breath to enter into you, and ye shall live: . . ." (37:1-5). Because of Christ's supreme compassion, Golgotha, that place of the skull and hill of bones, along with the fallen world, the sinful Adam, and the Dreamer lying beneath the towering Cross, shall be redeemed.

The poet gives even greater coherence to the Adam-Christ and tree-Cross identification by employing the imagery of food and eating. Speaking of the execution of the captured warrior-Christ in the battle metaphor, he says *Deað he þær byrigde* 'he tasted death there' (101a) for *Adomes ealdgewyrhtum* 'Adam's deed of old' (100). Adam tasted the fruit; Christ tasted death; now man must perform the same bitter act:

> hwær se man sie,
> se ðe for dryhtnes naman　　deaðes wolde
> biteres onbyrigan,　　swa he ær on ðam beame
> dyde.
>
> (112b-14)

where is the man who is willing to taste bitter death for the Lord's name as he himself did earlier on the Cross.

But only from this willing act comes salvation: "For if we have been planted together in the likeness of his death, we shall be also in the likeness of his resurrection: Knowing this, that our old man is crucified with him, that the body of sin might be destroyed, that henceforth we should not serve sin. For he that is dead is freed from sin" (Rom. 6:5-7). To purchase salvation and the forfeited paradise, with its eschatological banquet like that at the end of *The Dream of the Rood,* man must taste bitter death as Christ tasted bitter death because Adam tasted the fruit that exiled us from a blissful kingdom. Christ above all men chose to taste the death that would open the way for exiled man. "But we see Jesus . . . by the grace of God should taste death for every man" (Heb. 2:9).

This ritualistic metaphor of spiritual transformation is amplified further when the Dreamer describes where the Cross will take him:

> þær is blis mycel,
> dream on heofonum,　　þær is dryhtnes folc
> geseted to symle . . .
>
> (139b-41a)

where there is great joy, happiness in heaven, where the Lord's people are placed at the feast . . .

Here at the end of the poem he emphasizes the emotionally charged transformation by contrasting his fallen world with that restored paradise through the simple device of repeating powerful parallelisms: *þær is blis mycel* (139b), *þær is dryhtnes folc* (140b), *þær is singal blis* (141b), *þær ic syþþan mot* (142b), and *þær his eðel wæs* (156b). To summarize the fusions and identifications thus far: As Adam tasted the fruit and brought death, so warrior-Christ tasted the fruit of death; and the Dreamer must taste death with and for his Lord (his present dark night of sleep) in order to taste an eternal feast of life after death.

Thus the fallen Dreamer, representing all sinful men, lying now stained with mortal sins, has been fused with the fallen Adam. Then the poet identifies the Dreamer with the man willing to accept that death for Christ that the Cross endured earlier. Finally, the Dreamer undergoes another transformation identifying him with Christ, who will return to heaven with þam þe þær bryne þolodan 'those who earlier suffered from fire' (149b) after the Harrowing of Hell, much as the Dreamer hopes to return to man's lost paradise where he will join the messianic banquet.

Ideas much like these are stated more didactically in *The Phoenix:*

Swa þæt ece lif	eadigra gehwylc
æfter sarwræce	sylf geceoseð
þurh deorcne deað,	þæt he dryhtnes mot
æfter geardagum	geofona neotan
on sindreamum,	ond siþþan a
wunian in wuldre	weorca to leane.
Þisses fugles gecynd	fela gelices
bi þam gecornum	Cristes þegnum
beacnað in burgum,	hu hi beorhtne gefean
þurh fæder fultum	on þas frecnan tid
healdaþ under heofonum,	ond him heanne blæd
in þam uplican	eðle gestrynaþ.

(381-92b)

So is it
With each of the blessed, bearing misery
And choosing the darkness of death for them-
    selves
In order to find eternal life
And the protection of God, repaying pain
On earth with endless glory and endless
Joy. For the Phoenix is very like
The chosen servants of Christ, who show
The world and its towns what comfort and plea-
    sure
Descends from our Father's solace, and how,
In this dangerous time, they can take His grace
As a certain sign of lofty glory
To be lived in that celestial land above.

More obviously in *The Phoenix* than in **The Dream of the Rood** not only Christ but the people suffering in the flames are identified with the immortal bird. We also observe that both Phoenix and Cross come to the chosen and both are seen as ministering agents of grace.

The poem employs a final image to present the dramatic transformation from a lower to a higher spiritual level: stripping, a simple symbolic gesture, reveals the true man. Traditionally the stained garment that is put aside symbolizes the false man, the old Adam, the heavy burden of sinful flesh. When Christ's foes captured him and brought him to the gallows for execution *Ongyrede hine þa geong hæleð, (þæt wæs god ælmihtig), / strang ond stiðmod* 'the young hero—that was God Almighty—stripped himself strong and resolute' (39-40a). The allusion is to the bibli-

cal text: "ye have put off the old man with his deeds; And have put on the new man, which is renewed in knowledge after the image of him that created him" (Col. 3:9-10). To disobey as the old Adam did is to put on the garments of sinfulness; the new Adam, Jesus Christ, must be stripped of those garments before crucifixion. Put off the old Adam and put on the new Christ, as in Shakespeare's "old Adam new-apparelled" (*Comedy of Errors,* IV, iii) and as in his *King Lear,* where the sinful old man is freshly clothed before he rises from what he thinks is the grave. In *Everyman* the hero, varying the symbolism of the ritual action, strips off the old garments, scourges himself, and puts on the robe of contribution:

> *Knowlege:* It is a garment of sorrowe;
>   Fro payne it wyll you borrowe:
>   Contrycyon it is
>   That getteth forgyenes;
>   He pleaseth God passyinge well.
> *Good Dedes:* Eueryman, wyll you were it for
>   your hele?
> *Eueryman:* Now blessyd be Iesu, Maryes sone,
>   For now haue I on true
>   contrycyon . . .

Ritualistic stripping transformed the tree, ravished from the woods, stripped of the fruit of Christ's body, and *steame bedrifenne* 'covered over with blood' (62a) into the vehicle of redemption. It becomes the guide to the heavenly banquet, after the little band around Jesus had found it and *gyredon me golde and seolfre* 'adorned me with gold and silver' (77), suggestive, perhaps of the prophet Malachi: "Behold, I will send my messenger, and he shall prepare the way before me: and the Lord, whom ye seek, shall suddenly come to his temple, even the messenger of the covenant, whom ye delight in: behold, he shall come, saith the Lord of Hosts. But who may abide the day of his coming? and who shall stand when he appeareth? . . . And he shall sit as a refiner and a purifier of silver: and he shall purify the sons of Levi, and purge them as gold and silver . . ." (3:1-3). The once stripped but now adorned Cross *leohte bewunden* 'surrounded with light' (5b) and bearing gems *swylce þær fife wæron / uppe on þam eaxlegespanne* 'there were five up on the shoulder-beam' (8b-9a) symbolizes, by contrasting the five bloody wounds with the five shining gems, the dynamic process of physical and spiritual transformation lying at the heart of the poem. Having been stripped, mocked, slain, buried, and resurrected, the Cross and Christ became one. The Cross, the first Adam's tree, served as a bloody gallows, but through consciously sharing warrior-Christ's fearful experience, it changed, like Ezekiel's valley of bones, into a quickening spirit, into a guiding sign:

>   syllicre treow
> on lyft lædan,   leohte bewunden,
> beame beorhtost.

(4b-6a)

a marvelous tree, stretching [leading] aloft, surrounded with light, the brightest of beams.

This sign *ærþan . . . him lifes weg / rihtne gerymde, reordberendum* 'opened the true way of life to the people' (88b-89). So neatly does the **Rood** poet's language enrich and amplify his basic metaphor that if we are not careful we might miss the significance of 'stretching' in the expression *on lyft lædan:* extension, expansion, or stretching in space, as the poet well knew, symbolizes at once both God's suffering on the Cross and his dominion over the universe. John Donne also knew this when in "A Valediction: Forbidding Mourning" he identified his lovers with the beatified and then declared that, although separated, their two souls:

> endure not yet
> A breach, but an expansion,
> Like gold to ayery thinnesse beate.

Now all of this points directly to the central drama of the Dreamer who, as he lies *mid sorgum gedrefed, / forht . . . wæs for þære fægran gesyhðe* 'stained with sins, sorely wounded with evil deeds' (20b-21a), shares the stripping-adornment imagery with the Cross and Christ, but he does this only by extension of previous resemblances, by, as we might say, final association. No specific image pictures the Dreamer's being stripped and adorned; nevertheless, he does rise from his defeat, no longer stained with wounds, but carrying in his breast the 'best of signs.' He is changed, transformed, into a man:

> blíðe mode,
> elne mycle,   þær ic ana wæs
> mæte werede.
>
> (122b-24a)

with great zeal, happy in mind, there where I was alone with little company.

In this, one of the many parallels linking the three major actors in the redemptive drama, the Dreamer thus reminds us that, like the Cross and warrior-Christ on Calvary, he has only a *mæte werede* 'a little company' with him.

The significant act of stripping and adorning functions ritualistically as a *metanoia* for the dreamer because it renders mimetically the biblical text that avows that it is necessary to strip off the old man Adam and ritualistically to adorn oneself with the Cross in order to release the new man Jesus Christ from his enthrallment in the dark prison of the human heart. To bear the Cross on the human body or to carry 'in one's breast,' as the Dreamer declares, 'the best of signs,' is dynamically and dramatically to suffer death on the Cross with Christ, while purging, by means of ritual lustration, the old enemy of mankind.

The poem thus seems to contain a vivid metaphor of war, capture, execution, and apparent death that leads paradoxically to a purgation and transformation of the protagonist of the metaphorical drama. The metaphor contains a redemptive truth stated as a perennial paradox: man may save his life by losing it; though the spirit be incarnate in the flesh, that flesh may undergo purification through suffering until such time as flesh and spirit become one in God. Furthermore, the mimetic action contained in this metaphor will, as though to reinforce its communal and ritual aspects, be repeated twice in the exfoliating design of the poem, with the Cross and Dreamer as protagonists.

From another point of view the metaphorical battle would dramatize a timeless transformation going on inside man always, a continuous inward process of defeat and victory,

much as the dream or vision is internal, personal, yet universal, a ritual of spiritual conversion. Creating that drama of salvation, like a profound and insistent glow, the imagery illuminates, with its literal meanings and subtle connotations, the significance to all men of the Dreamer's transformational experience.

THE CROSS

Defeated and captured as though in battle, the Cross *wæs aheawen holtes on ende, / astyred of stefne minum* 'was cut down at the edge of the wood, taken from my stem' (29-30a). *Genaman me ðær strange feondas* 'strong foes seized me there' (30b) and exiled it: *Bæron me ðær beornas on eaxlum, oððæt hie me on beorg asetton, / gefæstnodon me þær feondas genoge* 'men carried me on their shoulders, until they placed me on a hill, enemies enough fastened me there' (32-33a). Enslaved and ordered to perform their tasks, the Cross declares that they *geworhton him þær to wæfersyne, heton me heora wergas hebban* 'they made me into a spectacle for them, ordered me to lift up their criminals' (31). Commanded not to counterattack by its lord, the Cross says *Ealle ic mihte / feondas gefyllan, hwæðre ic fæste stod* 'I could have killed all foes, yet I stood fast' (37b-38a). Now the warrior-Cross is *þurhdrifan . . . mid deorcan næglum* 'pierced with dark nails' (46a) and wounded: *On me syndon þa dolg gesiene, / opene inwidhlemmas* 'the wounds are visible on me, the open malicious wounds' (46b-47a); *eall ic wæs mid strælum forwundod* 'I was all wounded with darts' (62b). Ignominiously mocked, *Bysmeredon hie unc butu ætgædere* 'they mocked us both together' (48a), the Cross is tortured: *Feala ic on þam beorge gebiden hæbbe / wraðra wyrda* 'I endured on that hill many cruel experiences' (50-51a). Then the Cross is killed, *Þa us man fyllan ongan / ealle to eorðan* 'people began to cut us down completely to the earth' (73b-74a), and buried, *Bedealf us man on deopan seaþe* 'they buried us in a deep hole' (75a).

Like the warrior-Christ, the Cross is raised and adorned with symbolic riches:

> Hwæðre me þær dryhtnes þegnas,
> freondas gefrunon,
> ond gyredon me   golde ond seolfre.
>
> (75b-77)

Still the disciples of the Lord heard of me and adorned me with gold and silver.

Though defeated, the Cross paradoxically becomes a *sigebeam* 'cross of victory' (127a) and returns to its native land, the kingdom of the spirit:

> ac ðurh ða rode sceal   rice gesecan
> of eorðwege   æghwylc sawl,
> seo þe mid wealdende   wunian þenceð.
>
> (119-21)

every soul who proposes to dwell with the Lord must seek the kingdom away from earth through the Cross.

Through a felicitous use of imagery the poet deepens our dramatic involvement with the fate of the Cross much as he did with the fate of Christ. The Cross refers to itself as a vehicle, a means of passage from this earth to the heavenly kingdom in the lines just quoted, while the Dreamer declares that the Cross *on þysson lænan life gefetige / ond me þonne gebringe þær is blis mycel* 'will fetch me from this transitory life and bring me where there is great joy' (138-39). The poet's language here would surely have evoked images of rituals and their emotional meanings, for it sounds very much like the Preface to the Holy Cross from the Mass that is read from Passion Sunday through Wednesday of Holy Week: "It is truly right and just, proper and helpful toward salvation, that we always and everywhere give thanks to you, O Lord, holy Father, almighty and eternal God; for you ordained that the salvation of mankind should be accomplished upon the tree of the cross, in order that life might be restored through the very instrument which brought death, and that Satan, who conquered us through the tree, might also be overcome by it."

If the instrument that brought death becomes the vessel of salvation, perhaps it will not be amiss to see that the secondary meaning of the words used for 'cross' express through a most familiar image its function as a vehicle of redemption. *Beam* (6a), *wudu* (27b), and *beam* (97b) can all mean 'ship' as well as 'cross,' and *sigebeam* (127a) could connote 'ship of victory' as well as 'cross of victory.' This conjecture would then be strengthened by reading *on lyft lædan* (5a) as 'leading aloft.' Without pressing the poetic idea too far, however, we might recall that St. Hippolytus in the third century wrote: "The world is a sea, in which the Church, like a ship, is beaten by the waves but not submerged." And we are all acquainted with the architectural nave (ship), the main body of the church in which the congregation gathers. In the sixteenth century Donne could still write *A Hymne to Christ* in which he evokes much the same idea:

> In what torne ship soever I embarke,
> That ship shall be my embleme of thy Arke,
> Whence sea soever swallow mee, that flood
> Shall be to mee an embleme of thy blood . . .

Donne's subtle poetic sensibilities complicate what is in **The Dream of the Rood** a simple idea by identifying the church with Noah's ark or the ark of the covenant, the sea with the Flood (sea-whale with poet-Jonah), and the universal lustration of the Flood with the purgation-regeneration of Christ's blood. *Gestigan* (34b) means 'to mount,' yet it also strengthens the connotations suggested here through its secondary meaning, 'to go on board,' as does *holmwudu* (91a) by suggesting an ocean ship. And all these link back to *on lyft lædan* (5a).

Much of what I have been calling attention to here—the Cross as vehicle—is part of the hymn *Crux Fidelis* sung in the Reproaches of the Good Friday Mass, and it seems to confirm what at first may appear to be pure conjecture: the tree-Cross, the adorned Cross, the food-tasting imagery, the wounds of sinfulness, the Flood as an antitype of the world's lustration through Christ's sacrifice. The hymn goes:

> See His side is open now,
> Whence to cleanse the whole creation
> Streams of blood and water flow.

Then all of this is united in the verse that reads:

> Tree which solely was found worthy
> Earth's great victim to sustain,
> Harbor from the raging tempest,
> Ark, that saved the world again,
> Tree with sacred blood anointed
> Of the lamb for sinners slain.

Here we have a marvelous series of transformations of tree to Cross, to harbor, to ark, to Cross, to doorposts anointed with the blood of the sacred passover lamb, and none of it causes the slightest confusion. Nor apparently did it in *The Phoenix,* where we must follow the rapid metamorphosis of the old phoenix to a corpse, to an apple, to a worm hatched as though from an egg (apparently referring to the brazen serpent lifted up in the wilderness, Jesus rather than Satan), to an eaglet, to an eagle, and finally, to a rejuvenated phoenix that is not only Jesus Christ but all mankind:

> Þonne fyr þigeð
> lænne lichoman;   lif bið on siðe,
> fæges feorhhord,   þonne flæsc ond ban
> adleg æleð.   Hwæþre him eft cymeð
> æfter fyrstmearce   feorh edniwe,
> siþþan þa yslan   eft onginnað
> æfter ligþræce   lucan togædre,
> geclungne to cleowenne.   Þonne clæne bið
> beorhtast nesta,   bæle forgrunden
> heaþorofes hof;   hra bið acolad,
> banfæt gebrocen,   ond se bryne sweþrað.
> Þonne of þam ade   æples gelicnes
> on þære ascan bið   eft gemeted,
> of þam weaxeð wyrm,   wundrum fæger,
> swylce he of ægerum   ut alæde,
> scir of scylle.   Þonne on sceade weaxeð,
> þæt he ærest bið   swylce earnes brid,
> fæger fugeltimber;   ðonne furþor gin
> wridað on wynnum,   þæt he bið wæstmum
> gelic
> ealdum earne,   and æfter þon
> feþrum gefrætwad,   swylc he æt frymðe
> wæs,
> beorht geblowen. . . .
>   Swa se fugel weorþeð
> gomel æhter gearum,   geong edniwe,
> flæsce bifongen.
>   (219b-59a)

> And then it's gone,
> Flesh and bone burned in the flames
> Of a funeral pyre. Yet, in time
> He returns, his life re-born after
> The flames drop lower, and his ashes begin
> To fuse together in a shrivelled ball,
> After that brightest nest is burned
> To powder and that broken body, that valiant
> Corpse, slowly starts to cool.
> The fire flickers out. The funeral
> Pyre sprouts a rounded apple
> Out of a bed of ashes, and that pellet
> Sprouts a wonderful worm, as splendid
> As though hatched from a lustrous, pale-shelled
>   egg.
> He grows, flourishing in the holy shade
> And soon the size of an eaglet, soon,
> Fattening on pleasure, as large in form
> As any proud-winged eagle. Then

His feathers return and he is as he was
At the beginning, blossomed brightly to life
And eternal beauty. . . .
So the Phoenix grows, dropping a thousand
Years and taking on youth.

Here the image of ashes reminds the listeners of Adam's original clay and hell's fire; the apple reminds them of the Fall and the fruit of the tree of life; the worm recalls Satan and the brazen serpent, Nehushtan-Christ. Yet these complexities enrich rather than confuse: Cross is both tree and vessel, Christ is both serpent and savior, phoenix is both God and man. Only these paradoxes are capable of suggesting the full nature of the spiritual experience. For the experience is not only profound and complex; it goes beyond the visible and the mundane, and this relating of images is an attempt to express what is hidden, inward, and miraculous.

In the *Crux Fidelis* and *The Phoenix* the very rapid transformations through which the poet carries the Cross and the bird become a device through which he forces individual images to bear a massive burden of meaning. In **The Dream of the Rood** the rapid transformations in such a passage as the following accomplish much the same thing, while at the same time serving as a graphic demonstration of the central transformational process dramatized in the battle metaphor:

> Eall ic wæs mid sorgum gedrefed,
> forht ic wæs for þære fægran gesyhðe.
> Geseah ic þæt fuse
>   beacen
> wendan wædum ond bleom;   hwilum hit
> wæs mid wætan
>   bestemed,
> beswyled mid swates gange,   hwilum mid
> since gegyrwed.
>
> (20b-23)

> I was all completely troubled with
> sorrows;
> I was afraid because of the beautiful vision. I saw
> the hastening sign
> Vary in hanging and colors; at times it was wet
> with moisture,
> Stained with the flow of blood, and at times
> adorned with treasures.

After the transfigured tree has become a cross, it is then imbued with the numinous. Miming possible future transfiguration for the similarly stained Dreamer, it also symbolizes the dramatic means by which man attains wholeness and salvation. By suffering with the Cross and Christ in a similar transformational experience, the Dreamer undergoes an identical metamorphosis and elevation of spirit.

This passage has vividly dramatized for the benefit of the Dreamer a visual presentation of the process of transformation, ranging from a depleted spiritual state ('stained with blood') to an exalted one (symbolized by 'adorned with treasure'). Similarly, transformation is also dramatized in the parallel phraseology of *hwilum hit wæs mid wætan bestemed* (22b) and *hwilum mid since gegyrwed* (23b), which strongly contrast the beginning and the end of the spiritual change. The **Rood** poet reinforced this il-

lumination of the Dreamer's inner vision by making him observe the changing light surrounding the Cross and by the gradual metamorphosis of his own insight through a series of 'I saw' phrases that dynamically pass from the Dreamer's 'I thought that I saw' to tree, to sign, to master, to God, in this manner: *Þuhte me þæt ic gesawe syllicre treow* (4); *Geseah ic wuldres treow* (14b); *Geseah ic þæt fuse beacen* (21b). But when the phrase is next repeated, it incorporates the image of God, and it is the Cross that speaks, because, having shared Christ's pain, it can truly say *Geseah ic þa frean mancynnes* (33b); *Geseah ic weruda god* (51b). "Seeing" in the rhythm of the transformation drama has become a metaphorical way of expressing involvement in suffering, death, burial, and resurrection. The next change occurs at the end of the drama of the Cross when the phrase undergoes a transformation itself and becomes *Ic þæt all beheold* 'I beheld all that' (58b)—"to behold" has taken on the additional meaning "to be involved in the painful experience itself." Because of all this the Cross plays the role of a *beacna* (118b) and towers in the heavens above the Dreamer who miraculously beholds, not at the end, but at the beginning of his own transformational experience, all the heavenly hosts gazing at the Cross: *Beheoldon þær engel dryhtnes ealle, / fægere þurh forðgesceaft* 'all the angels of the Lord, fair through all time, gazed on it there' (9b-10a). Parallelism of phraseology, stylization of syntax, and accretion to words of unfamiliar connotations strongly emphasize the steps through which the Dreamer passes in his spiritual transformation.

Nor is this all. Toward the end of the historical explanation that passes into the hortatory address to future action (and as a matter of fact suddenly transcends the battle metaphor), the Cross suddenly refers to 'Mother Mary' without any apparent preparation for the simile:

> Hwæt, me þa geweorðode   wuldres ealdor
> ofer holmwudu,   heofonrices weard!
> Swylce swa he his modor eac,   Marian sylfe,
> ælmihtig god   for ealle menn
> geweorðode   ofer eall wifa cynn.
>
> (90-94)

> Lo! Then the Prince of Glory, the Lord of Heaven,
> Honored me above the other trees of the forest
> Just as God Almighty for the sake of mankind
> Also honored his Mother Mary above
> All the race of women.

The various elements of the poem cohere so faithfully that we unconsciously expect and immediately understand the relationship of a Cross that opens the true way of life to the people and the Virgin Mary whom God honored *ofer eall wifa cynn*. We have seen that the **Rood** poet manipulated Adam's fall in such a manner as to fuse it with Christ's crucifixion, the tree with the Cross, the instrument of death with the vessel of salvation. Now, relying on the same technique, the poet apparently assumes that we will think of Eva, the mother of death and type of Mary. In **The Dream of the Rood** this identification and contrast of the two women is strengthened by the earlier evocation of the Adam-Christ contrast. The churchman, the poet, and the playwright had no difficulty in entertaining and enjoying such manipulations of names. They saw the salutation "Ave" made to the Mother Mary, who brought new life to man, as a reversal of Eva (*e vae* 'from woe'). Certainly something very much like this appears in the Breviary hymn *Ave, maris stella,* but perhaps its appearance in the drama will indicate its common currency. In the Hegge *Salutation and Conception* Gabriel descends to Mary and says:

> Ave, Maria, gratia plena, Dominus tecum!
> Heyl, fful of grace, God is with the!
>   Amonge alle women blyssyd art thu!
> Here this name Eva is turnyd Ave;
>   That is to say, with-owte sorwe ar ye now.
>
> Thow sorwe in yow hath no place,
>   yett of ioy, lady, ye nede more;
> Therefore I adde and sey "ful of grace,"
>   ffor so ful of grace was nevyr non bore.
>   (220-28)

And something very much like this appears in the Wakefield *Annunciation.*

The transformative, spirit-bearing Cross becomes the sign of rebirth for the Dreamer; the intercessive Mother Mary becomes the vessel of birth for Christ, the warrior-hero, and through him for all mankind. Mary, the Mother who reopened the gates of heaven, is linked with the Cross that performs the same function in **The Dream of the Rood** for the transformed Dreamer. The antiphon for the purification of the Blessed Virgin Mary begins, "Embrace Mary, for she is the very gate of heaven who brings to you the glorious king of the new light." In the Litany of the Virgin, the Mother of Christ is variously symbolized as "Vessel of Honor," "Ark of the Covenant," "Gate of Heaven," and "Morning Star." Gate and Cross, Virgin and tree are even more closely linked through the "root" image in the Compline, final antiphon to the Blessed Virgin Mary:

> Hail, Queen of Heaven!
> Hail, Lady of the Angels!
> Salutation to thee, root and portal,
> When the Light of the world has arisen.

Symbolized by the sky at daybreak, Mary, the Queen of Heaven, the Morning Star, in turn symbolizes the root from which the Son grows to become that tree of life whose fruit all men shall share in paradise—the eschatological banquet at the end of the poem.

Both Cross and Virgin "opened the true way for all people," and the Dreamer learns from their metamorphic experiences. When he rises transformed from his slumber of death, he will do as the Cross commands:

> þæt ðu þas gesyhðe   secge mannum,
> onwreoh wordum   þæt hit is wuldres beam,
> se ðe ælmihtig god   on þrowode
> for mancynnes   manegum synnum
> ond Adomes   ealdgewyrhtum.
>   (96-100)

> that thou tellest this sight to men, make clear by words that this is the tree on which God Almighty suffered for the many sins of mankind and for Adam's deed of old.

The poet validates to some extent this conjecture by link-

ing the Dreamer to the sinful Adam, for as Adam stained all mankind and closed the gates, the Dreamer, who has been transformed by his vision, will rise from his sleep (symbolic of indolence, ignorance, and at its worst, death from the woundings of sin) and like Christ and Cross bear the glad tidings of lustration to other men.

THE DREAMER

"For what else is Christ but the word, the sound of God? So the word is this upright beam on which I am crucified; and the sound is the beam which crosses it, the nature of man; but the nail which holds the center of the cross-beam to the upright is man's conversion and repentance."

All transformations and identifications have been for the benefit of the Dreamer, who must be provoked into the metamorphic experience, into a radical change from stained and fallen man into a spiritualized being. Not surprisingly, his transformation imitates and profoundly participates in the dramatic metaphor of war traced with the Cross and Christ. The metaphor of the Christian warrior is common property of the New Testament, Old English poetic tradition, and religious through the ages. It is found, for instance, in the secret prayer for the Mass celebrating the finding of the Holy Cross: "May the sacrifice we offer be pleasing to you, O Lord. Let it free us from all the evils of war and destroy the pitfalls prepared by our powerful enemy, so that we may be safely protected under the banner of your son's cross. Through the same Jesus Christ, our Lord." The post-Communion prayer reads: "We have been nourished by the food of heaven and refreshed by spiritual drink. Shield us from our evil enemies, O Almighty God, for you have commanded us to fight through to victory under the cross of your Son, the weapon of justice that will save the world. Through the same Jesus Christ, our Lord." Perhaps even more important for this poem is the appearance of the warrior-hero in the final victory of Christ as described in Revelation: "And I saw heaven opened, and behold a white horse; and he that sat upon him was called Faithful and True, and in righteousness he doth judge and make war. . . . And the armies which were in heaven followed him upon white horses, clothed in fine linens, white and clean" (19:11-14).

The dramatic portrayal of this metaphor of the warrior-Cross and the warrior-God no longer stained but "clothed in fine linens, white and clean" is duplicated with the Dreamer, now a warrior-hero, as the protagonist. His battle has already been waged when the poem opens, and he apparently has been defeated. Cut down by the enemy, he lies bleeding from his wounds in a death-sleep, *ic synnum fah* 'I stained with sins [or injuries]' (13b). He is grievously wounded, *forwunded mid wommum* 'sorely wounded with evil deeds' (14a), and suffers, *Eall ic wæs mid sorgum gedrefed* 'I was completely troubled with sorrows' (20b); *ic þær licgende lange hwile / beheold hreowcearig hælendes treow* 'lying there for a long time, I looked sorrowfully at the Cross' (24-25). Then follows a lacuna in the logical, dramatic development of the battle metaphor, but it is that gap that is of most importance for the dynamic transformation of the warrior-Dreamer.

The warrior, we should observe, frames the poem with his

visionary experience and his joyous future life after that vision ends. Within this frame, as within his mind, there occur the dramas of Christ and the Cross. Thus the experience of the Dreamer frames that of the Cross, and that of the Cross frames that of Christ, as though one had to pass through the agency of the Cross to reach the Lord. Precisely symbolic, the structures of the three frames—really three almost identical dramatic battle metaphors—point to Christ and his archetypal experience, the redemptive drama as the magnetic center, the spiritualizing and transformative power of the source of life. The second frame, the story of the Cross, points towards the nucleus that is Christ and outward towards the Dreamer, thus symbolizing something very much like an agent of grace.

Moving inward from the outer frame, we meet, first, the defeated Dreamer, then the defeated tree, and at the heart of the poem, the defeated Christ, followed by references to Adam (who seems to represent all that is gross, weighty, base, and stained in the Dreamer) and Mary (who represents all that releases, gives life, and fructifies in the Dreamer). Moving outward, then, from that transcendent center, we experience, first, the victory of Christ, then the victory of the Cross, and finally the victory of the Dreamer, who has been spiritualized by having lived through, while vicariously participating in, the vivid drama of that numinous center and its immediate frame. Within the frame of the Dreamer's experiences they— Cross and Christ—suffer battles, captures, executions, mockeries, burials; yet they suffer not so much for themselves but precisely for the transformation of the defeated warrior-Dreamer. Another way of stating this would be to say that the outer frame contains earthy, Adamic man, sunk in sin and evil deeds, asleep or dead, and in need of radical transformation. This objective outer frame is united with the subjective center—Cross and Christ as redemptive forces—through a dramatic participation of the Dreamer in the Eucharistic vision that takes place in his own sleeping mind as a kind of internal illumination. Personal, subjective, psychic, but sacramental, this process transforms the spirit of the Dreamer because the cohesive battle metaphors consistently reveal his identity with the fallen Adam, the paradoxical destructive-creative Cross, and the resurrected Christ.

Some seventy lines after the battle metaphor is apparently suspended, it is resumed. Reinforcements come to the wounded warrior-Dreamer with orders for salvation: *Nu ic þe hate, hæleð min se leofa, / þæt ðu þas gesyhðe secge mannum* 'now, my dear man, I order you to tell this vision to men' (95-96). Upon hearing this, the Dreamer is revived:

> Gebæd ic me þa to þan beame   bliðe mode,
> elne mycle,   þær ic ana wæs
> mæte werede.
>
> (122-24a)

There I prayed to the Cross with great zeal, happy in mind, there where I was alone with little company.

Like his Lord, he is exiled and must *rice gesecan / of eorðwege* 'seek the kingdom away from earth' (119b-20a) and return to his homeland: *Wæs modsefa / afysed on*

forðwege 'the heart was ready for departure' (124b-25a). In anticipation of his return the Dreamer looks, as he says:

> daga gehwylce   hwænne me dryhtnes rod,
> þe ic her on eorðan   ær sceawode,
> on þysson lænan   life gefetige . . .
>
> (136-38)

for the time when the Cross of the Lord, which I formerly saw here on earth, will fetch me from this transitory life . . .

Finally, the battle completed and victory won, the Dreamer will join in celebrating the feast of victory in his true homeland:

> ond me þonne gebringe   þær is blis mycel,
> dream on heofonum,   þær is dryhtnes folc
> geseted to symle,   þær is singal blis,
> ond me þonne asette   þær ic siþþan mot
> wunian on wuldre . . .
>
> (139-43a)

and then bring me where there is great joy, happiness in heaven, where the Lord's people are placed at the feast, where [there] is perpetual happiness, and will set me where I can afterwards live in glory . . .

The Dreamer now transformed in spirit and ransomed from the enemy, the price having been the suffering of Christ, the suffering of the Cross, and his own suffering and awakening, returns successfully to his native land and is given *heofonlicne ham* 'a heavenly home' (148a).

Formerly the poet emphasized the suffering and death of the protagonists, Christ and Cross. Now, in the case of the Dreamer, he places the emphasis on "cleansing" and "lifting," because Christ and Cross, by means of their dramas, have in a large measure carried the burden of agony for the Dreamer, though that is not to imply that he has not shared their pain. He may even have suffered it three times over if we judge the dramas to be purely mental. Strongly emerging imagery of resurrection thrusts itself prominently into the foreground, especially after the Dreamer has participated in the double dramas of Cross and Christ, until ultimately that imagery becomes apocalyptic vision. In describing the act of crucifixion, the poet's images are such that they evoke overtones of resurrection or ascension: *Gestah he on gealgan heanne* 'he ascended on the high gallows' (40b), says the Cross of Christ. *Ahof ic ricne cyning* 'I lifted up the powerful king' (44b); and by implication the Cross will lift up the fallen warrior-Dreamer. *Rod wæs ic aræred* 'I was set up a cross' (44a). *Ahofon hine of ðam hefian wite* 'they raised him from that heavy torture' (61a). Prefiguring the voice of the penitent Dreamer, who because of the ritualistic purification will not only go up but, obeying the commands of the Cross, will go out to all men, *stefn up gewat / hilderinca* 'the cry of warriors went up' (71b-72a). Because of the former agony the Cross will now *hlifige under heofenum* 'tower under heaven' (85a), moved *on lyft* 'on high' (5a). The *dryhten aras* 'Lord arose' (101b), and *He ða on heofenas astag* 'he then ascended into heaven' (103a). The imagery of resurrection (ascended, lifted, set up, raised, went up, towers on high, arose, and ascended) is then applied to the Dreamer when the Cross enjoins him to *rice gesecan / of eorðwege* 'seek the kingdom away from earth' (119b-20a). Displaying an emotional state consonant with resurrection, the Dreamer is *bliðe mode* 'happy in mind' (122b); the Cross will *gebringe þær is blis mycel, dream on heofonum* 'bring me where there is great gladness, joy in heaven' (139-40a). Likewise, his friends *lifiaþ nu on heofenum mid heahfædere* 'live now with God the Father in heaven' (134). And finally, Christ *mid manigeo com* 'came with a multitude' (151b). 'Seek,' 'happy,' 'bring,' 'arrive,' and 'live in heaven' are words and phrases that approximate emotionally the resurrection imagery and shadow forth the Dreamer's hopes for future life.

Christ offered himself in a voluntary act of love, but in the actual sacrifice he suffered an agonizing and bloody death. The division of God into divine being and human being and his return to himself in the sacrificial act (symbolized in his stripping off his earthly garments and embracing the Cross) hold out the comforting doctrine that in the center of the Dreamer's own darkness there lies a hidden light (symbolized by the structural frames, the movement from Dreamer to Cross to Christ, the evoked memories of Mary and Adam, and then by a reversal from Christ to Cross to Dreamer) which will once again be ignited by its source. The poet makes us see that this light (variously symbolized in the bright, shining Cross, but specifically in the body of Christ, 'that bright splendor,' whose tomb is of 'shining stone') actually wished to descend into darkness in order to deliver the 'stained' one who languished there, hidden in the gloomy underworld of his manifold sins and mortal enemies, and lead him to the source of light: *Hiht wæs geniwad / mid bledum ond mid blisse þamþe þær bryne þolodan* 'hope was renewed with blessedness and with joy to those who had earlier suffered from fire' (148b-49).

The Christ of Revelation cautions mankind to "Repent; or else I will come unto thee quickly, and will fight against them with the sword of my mouth. He that hath an ear, let him hear what the Spirit saith unto the churches; To him that overcometh will I give to eat of the hidden manna, and will give him a white stone, and in the stone a new name written, which no man knoweth saving he that receiveth it" (Rev. 2:16-17). Because the poet previously evoked Adam and his misdeeds, the stumbling block for all mankind is the old Adam in the flesh; but specifically for the Dreamer who lies 'stained with sins, . . . wounded with evil deeds,' is this true. Though the poet evokes this stumbling block only through implication—by linking the fallen Adam with the stained and recumbent Dreamer—the evocation of the 'shining stone' of the tomb of Christ might help us understand the accomplishment of the poet. Stone, earth, matter, and indeed, flesh pull man down and drag him into the underworld. Only when Christ as Spirit enters that base matter, that stained and sleeping flesh, only then does that rock tomb of man's body become spiritualized, become 'shining stone.' After all, the entire drama is one man's spiritual crisis. Thus the significantly charged symbol, the 'shining stone' that the Spirit enters, serves as the vehicle for the apocalyptic vision at the end of the poem, the great feast expected to usher in the messianic kingdom, where the Cross will:

> . . . gebringe   þær is blis mycel,
> dream on heofonum,   þær is dryhtnes folc
> geseted to symle . . .
>
> (139-41a)

And Christ says in Rev. 2:17, "To him that overcometh will I give to eat of the hidden manna." The victorious spiritualized Dreamer will join the chosen at the eschatological feast and partake of the hidden bread, Jesus Christ. The white stone signed with the name of the Lord will, like the Cross signed with the body of Jesus and adorned with shining stones, gold, and silver, assure his passage to the land of glory, where he, the Dreamer, will enjoy pleasure fully with the saints.

If the splendor of Christ's sacrifice reveals the way out of darkness, if the Virgin Mother opened that way, if the shining Cross becomes that way, now the Dreamer will also show the way by rehearsing the grand vision and singing the glory of the Son to other men:

> onwreoh wordum   þæt hit is wuldres beam,
> se ðe ælmihtig god   on þrowode
> for mancynnes   . . . synnum . . .
>
> (97-99)

make clear with words that this is the tree [wood, ship] on which God Almighty suffered for the sins of mankind . . .

His transformation accomplished, the Dreamer fuses with the Cross and Christ. Through his new devotion and willingness to sacrifice his stained ego, the Dreamer, transfigured into a ministering instrument of glory, becomes one with Christ in the mysterious metamorphic process of the poem.

In *The Dream of the Rood* the three dramatic battle metaphors become symbolic means of redemption; they help delineate the purification, consecration, and exaltation of the Dreamer; they serve as centers of organization, cohesion, and wholeness. By emotionally participating in the two dramatic experiences during a dream in the depths of the night, the Dreamer unites himself with the Cross and Christ, is purified and strengthened. He then reveals to us that the thrice-repeated metaphor is essentially one profound drama of self-transcendence.

The poet found the precise means for expressing transformation in this dramatic metaphor of battle, defeat, capture, death, and sudden and climactic *metanoia,* a turning of the dry bones of death into glorious rebirth. This vivid metaphor reproduces the Passion of Christ and dramatizes those means by which a man saves his life: the poet's rehearsal and amplification of the metaphor to include the lowly tree-Cross serves as an example to the benighted Dreamer that not only the good but also the despised, the evil, the fallen and stained may find salvation through an imitation of Christ. The third rehearsal of the transformative metaphor dramatizes the process of redemption on the human level, the miraculous purification, elevation, and spiritualization of the Dreamer.

The *Rood* poet supports, broadens, and strengthens his consistent and cohesive metaphors of battle with a multitude of other images to describe both poles of the transformative process, the initial condition of man suffering from the fires of hell and the final goal of man dwelling in glory. Variously figured, these incidental metaphors appear as fall/ascend, bow down/rise up, tremble/strengthen, transitory/permanent, dark of clouds/bright splendor, troubled with sorrows/renewed in hope, afraid/brave, sorrowful/joyful, spectacle/ritual, criminals' gallows/glorified Cross, enemies that mock/angels that gaze and adore, tree/Cross, blood and wounds/gold and silver, stained/cleansed, no friends on earth/company of saints in heaven, wounding/healing, ignored ritual/celebrated ritual, sing a dirge/tell a vision, and sinners carrying the Cross on their shoulders/Cross carrying the redeemed sinners to the kingdom of heaven. All these incidental metaphors, amplifications of the thrice-repeated cohesive one, dramatize a permanent truth, the living, dramatic, transformational paradox that a man must first lose his life to save it. This is to say that the incidental images fall into dialectical opposites that mirror the larger thematic concerns of the poem's central battle metaphors.

But in the strange metabolism of the language of *The Dream of the Rood* the poet has created other ways of expressing this truth. When speaking in the voice of the Cross, just before the spiritualized Dreamer awakens, the poet creates a syntactical pattern related to sin and death: *Adomes ealdgewyrhtum* (100), *Deað he þær byrigde* (101a), *deaðes wolde / biteres onbyrigan* (113b-14a). However, radically contrasted with that imagery of death, when the transformed and spiritualized Dreamer begins to speak once again, all is life: *Is me nu lifes hyht* (126b); *lifiaþ nu on heofenum* (134a), *on þysson lænan life gefetige* (138), *ond us lif forgeaf* (147b), etc. The poet's genius lies precisely in his ability to force his syntactical arrangements, as well as metaphors, similes, and the like, to support, emphasize, and dramatize his themes.

In the same manner he may also create a strong thematic dialectic among various syntactical elements, for instance, those beginning with an initial *on*. The first of these, *on lyft lædan* (5a), and the final, *on godes rice* (152b), are symbolic formulas for the reanimation of the spirit. Moreover, within the frame of these syntactical elements at the beginning and end of the poem the thematic conflict shifts, with emphasis first on one, then on the other, pole of the theme, only to be resolved in the final lines of the poetry. Schematized, the pattern looks like this: *on lyft lædan* (5a); *On me syndon þa dolg gesiene* (46b); *On me bearn godes* (83); *on þrowode / for mancynnes manegum synnum* (98b-99); *on þysne middangeard* (104a); *on domdæge* (105a); *on þyssum lænum life geearnaþ* (109); *on þysson lænan life gefetige* (138); *on þam gealgetreowe* (146a); *on þam siðfate* (150b); *on godes rice* (152b). The repetition of the same unit lifts it to a kind of symbolic structure expressive of the vicissitudes of the regenerative process.

Transformation animates the heart and spirit of the poem and the Dreamer. Christ, the second Adam, is transformed into man, into criminal, and then once again into spiritual being. The Rood, transformed from tree to gallows, to torture instrument, to dead and buried object, and finally to adorned Cross and enlightened messenger, towers above the fallen Adam in everyman, as a sign, a way, a vehicle of salvation. The Dreamer, identified with a

stained and sinning Adam, changes into a cleansed and spiritualized human being, from grief-stricken man to joyous man, into an announcer of the good news and glad tidings of salvation to other men; and finally he assumes the form of a man hopeful of joining his Lord at the messianic victory banquet and in the company of all the saints.

Faith H. Patten   (essay date 1968)

SOURCE: "Structure and Meaning in *The Dream of the Rood,*" in *English Studies,* Netherlands, Vol. 49, No. 1, 1968, pp. 385-401.

[*Here, Patten explores the analogies between the Dreamer and the Cross, the Cross and Christ, and Christ and the Dreamer. She also analyzes the allegorical and historical aspects of* The Dream of the Rood.]

The existence in *The Dream of The Rood* of two speakers and two points of view, the cross and the dreamer, appears at first aesthetically disturbing, by seeming to imperil the poem's unity. But, on the contrary, the two points of view provide the backbone of the poem's structure which, at once complex and unified, both creates and reveals the poem's meaning.

This structure divides into three parts (ll. 1-27, 28-121, 122-end), each governed by the relation between its own subject and the rood. The cross is the one element common and central to all three parts; it provides the poem's chief means of unification. The first of these three parts, the introduction (through l. 27), consists of the speaker's description of the rood's appearance to him in a dream. Its subject is the dreamer; its significance, the meaning of the cross to and for him. This meaning is indicated by those visible attributes of the cross that the dreamer immediately sees, but neither the dreamer nor the reader can, at this early point, grasp their full significance; they are symbols whose meanings are developed by the rest of the poem.

The rood has two opposing sets of attributes: it first appears wondrous, glorious, covered with gold and jewels, and surrounded with light (ll. 4-17), but presently, underneath the gold ornamentation, the dreamer perceives suffering and evil:

> Hwæðre ic þurh þæt gold   ongytan meahte
> earmra ærgewin . . .

He also perceives that the rood sweats blood from its right side:

> . . . þæt hit ærest ongan
> swætan on þa swiðran healfe.
>
> (19b-20a)

These two entirely different appearances of the cross have two effects on the dreamer. The first, one of contrast, occurs in l. 13:

> Syllic wæs se sigebeam,   ond ic synnum fah,
> forwunded mid wommum. . . .
>
> (13-14a)

This juxtaposition suggests that the dreamer recognizes his guilt and sin *because* the cross is a 'wondrous victory-beam'. The metrical, alliterative, and echoic characteristics of the line ('*syllic . . . sigebeam . . . synnum*') reinforce this hint. The dream-vision of the exalted rood has awakened him, while the rest of the world sleeps, to his own sins. But, since 'wommum' literally means 'scars' or 'stains' and figuratively 'defilement' or 'sin', the curious phrase 'forwunded mid wommum' is descriptive also of Christ. This phrase constitutes the first link in the analogy the poet develops between the dreamer and Christ. Christ's 'wommum' are visible, physical wounds, caused by human sins—both of mankind generally and of his crucifiers particularly—and hence become the symbol of human sins. Clearly, we are dealing with a poet who uses his rich language in a sophisticated and subtle manner, not in a primitive one: in a single image, he suggests, first, one of the main technical devices of the poem, the analogy between Christ and the dreamer; and, second, the cause and the theological significance of that relationship and analogy.

The dreamer's second reaction to the cross occurs in ll. 20b and 21a:

> Eall ic wæs mid sorgum gedrefed,
> forht ic wæs for þære fægran gesyhðe.

This reaction immediately follows the dreamer's perception of the rood's flowing blood, and of the misery beneath its gold (ll. 18-20a). The causal relationship here is even clearer than in the dreamer's first reaction: he is sorrowful and fearful because of the rood's agony and blood.

The cross's two different appearances are summed up in ll. 21b-23:

> Geseah ic þæt fuse beacen
> wendan wædum ond bleom;   hwilum hit
>   wæs mid wætan bestemed,
> beswyled mid swates gange,   hwilum mid
>   since gegyrwed.

The effect of these two contrasting appearances, and of the respective contrasting reactions of the dreamer, is to suggest two of the symbolic values of the cross. A literal, non-symbolic cross could not alternate between two different appearances, nor could it influence the emotional state of the beholder. As Professors B. F. Huppé and D. W. Robertson, Jr., remark [in *Fruyt and Chaf: Studies in Chaucer's Allegories,* 1963]:

> In such [dream] visions the sense level is dependent on the underlying meaning [i. e. the physical on the symbolic, or the literal on the allegorical]. Characters [the cross] act in accordance with the demands of meaning, not in accordance with the logic of external events.

Why and how the meanings of the cross influence the dreamer are the burden of the rest of the poem. We learn from this first part the causal nature of the relationship between the dreamer and the dream-cross, as the dream opens: the exalted and glorified cross calls attention to the abased and sinful condition of the dreamer, and the agonized and bleeding cross awakens the dreamer's fear and sorrow.

The second part of the poem (ll. 28-121) relates the story that embodies the relationship between Christ and the cross: the crucifixion. The meaning of this section inheres in the relationship of the cross to Christ, plus, in turn, the meaning of that relationship to the dreamer. The first two parts of the poem are thus structurally analogous: the cross is the central symbol in each, and from the relationship of the cross to its persona derives the meaning of each. This structural analogy casting Christ and the dreamer in parallel positions strengthens the parallel between them already suggested by 'wommum'. Further, as the dreamer in part one describes the cross, so the cross in part two describes Christ, suggesting through their similar functions an analogy between the dreamer and the cross, and between the cross and Christ. The symbolic significance of this set of analogies accumulates as the poem progresses and will be discussed later; I shall now examine the mechanics of the last one.

The description of Christ in the second part, like the description of the cross in the first part, reveals that he has two distinct natures. The first of these appears in the cross's first description of Christ:

> Geseah ic þa frean mancynnes
> efstan elne mycle   þæt he me wolde on gestigan.
>
> (33b-34)

This nature of Christ prevails throughout the crucifixion:

> Ongyrede hine þa geong hæleð,   (þæt wæs god ælmihtig),
> strang ond stiðmod.   Gestah he on gealgan heanne,
> modig on manigra gesyhðe,   þa he wolde mancyn lysan.
>
> (39-41)
>
> Geseah ic *weruda god*
> þearle þenian.   Þystro hæfdon
> bewrigen mid wolcnum *wealdendes hræw,* . . .
>   . . . .
>   . . . Weop eal gesceaft,
> cwiðdon *cyninges* fyll.   Crist wæs on rode.
> Hwæðere þær fuse   feorran cwoman
> to þam æðelinge. . . .
>
> (51b-58a)
>
> Genamon hie þær *ælmihtigne god,* . . .
>   . . . . .
> beheoldon hie ðær *heofenes dryhten.*
>
> (60b-64a)

These passages, all from the second part, all spoken by the cross, establish the divine, victorious, heroic nature of Christ. He is the 'lord of mankind', 'the young hero' or 'warrior', and He approaches the cross with eagerness, as though it were His bride, and the crucifixion with resolution, as though it were a battle. Indeed, it is called a 'mighty struggle'—'miclan gewinne' (l. 65a)—which, recalling the 'ærgewin' (l. 19a) that the dreamer perceived underneath the cross's decoration, adds to that obvious reference to the 'wickedness' of the crucifiers, the further meaning of the agony or struggle of the crucifixion itself.

After the crucifixion, the delineation of this nature of Christ is complete, and He is referred to *at the moment of his burial* as the 'lord of victories': 'gesetton hie ðæron sigora wealdend' (l. 67a). The poet thus chooses the moment of Christ's greatest apparent defeat to point out that He is actually supremely victorious: by means of the battle of crucifixion, the warrior has conquered death—indeed, His death is something too mysterious and holy to be spoken of without euphemism: 'ond he hine ðær *hwile reste, / meðe æfter ðam miclan gewinne*' (ll. 64b-65a).

Like the rood's, the first presentation of Christ has emphasized his valiant and superhuman qualities which enable Him to triumph over evil, pain, and death. But He was also a real human being, who suffered, died, and was buried. The first, and strongest, evidence of Christ's humanity is the blood that gushes from His side when He is on the cross; He is here called 'guma' (l. 49a), the Anglo-Saxon word for *man* which has probably the fewest connotations of anything other than human (cp. *æðelinge, hæleð, monn*). After His mighty struggle and the descent from the cross, Christ is described as 'limbweary' (l. 63a), a movingly human term, and then as 'worn out' (l. 65a). A subsequent phrase indicates at once Christ's humanity and divinity, and the distinction between them: 'Hræw colode, / fæger feorgbold' (ll. 72b-73a).

At least one critic, Rosemary Woolf, thinks that these two opposing but reconciled natures of Christ import the central meaning of the poem, which she ascribes to the historical situation:

> At the time when the poet wrote, the Church insisted on the co-existence of these two elements in Christ, divine supremacy and human suffering, with a vehemence and rigidity deriving from more than two centuries of heretical Christological dispute.

Miss Woolf traces through the poem this dichotomy between the heresy of the Monophysites, who held Christ's divine nature more important than His human, and the heresy of the Nestorians, who held the reverse; she consequently contends that the point of the poem is the reconciliation or balancing of these views. This is only initially convincing. There are too many elements, both of structure and of meaning, that are neglected and unexplained by this interpretation. An attempt to take all these elements into account reveals a much greater meaning that transcends, though it does not contradict, Miss Woolf's interpretation.

In part two the cross, which narrates the story, also has two natures. These result from the rood's self-identification with Christ, an identification which is the logical extreme of the main traditional symbolic referent of the cross. The double appearance that the cross presents to the dreamer in part one is then a preparation for its two natures and for their identification with Christ's two natures in the second part. From this symbolic value added in part two, meaning accrues incrementally to part one. The cross's initial appearance as the jewelled, luminous battle-standard and tree of glory we now recognize to be analogous to the warrior-king, the triumphant and victorious Christ. The rood's description of its glorification suggests Christ's ascension:

> Hwæðre me þær dryhtnes þegnas,
> freondas gefrunon,
> ond gyredon me   golde ond seolfre.
>
> (75b-77)

Then in explaining the reason it is worshipped, the cross makes explicit its analogy with Christ:

> Is nu sæl cumen
> þæt me weorðiað   wide ond side
> menn ofer moldan,   ond eall þeos mære
>   gesceaft,
> gebiddaþ him to þyssum beacne.   On me
>   bearn godes
> þrowode hwile.   Forþan ic þrymfæst nu
> hlifige under heofenum,   ond ic hælan mæg
> æghwylcne anra,   þara þe him bið egesa to
>   me.
>
> (80b-86b)

Line 82b repeats exactly line 12b, providing a clue to the incremental nature of the symbols and structure. We now know why 'all this glorious creation' in part one worships the cross: because 'on me bearn godes / prowode hwile' (83b-84a). This also explains the dreamer's feeling (in part one) of sinfulness and sorrow—he is there reacting to the symbolic meaning of the cross though he does not know consciously until part two (and neither do we) what that meaning is.

But, perhaps both to compensate for the greater emphasis in part two on Christ's lordliness and divinity rather than on his humanity, and to avoid the risks either of idolatry or blasphemy, the cross stops short of identifying its glorified self with the victorious Christ, and leaves the relationship one of analogy and symbol. The purpose of specifying the symbolic meaning of the jewelled cross is achieved anyway. But, on the other hand, the cross fully identifies itself with Christ's human nature, and thus extends our knowledge of it. As His death was related euphemistically, so what is mortal and weak in Him is narrated by means of a surrogate, the cross, in order to sustain His sacredness; whereas His divine nature can be fully and directly described, without surrogate.

The relationship between the degraded Christ and the cross, like that between the triumphant Christ and the cross, was foreshadowed in part one through the dreamer's perception of the agony beneath the gold, followed by his expression of sorrow (19-21). In part two the identification is completed by the cross's descriptions of its actions and feelings in phrases which personify the cross even more and are equally applicable to Christ. First, the cross is carried to the hill where 'gefæstnodon me þær feondas genoge' (33a). Next, after Christ has ascended the cross, it says: 'Ealle ic mihte / feondas gefyllan, hwæðre ic fæste stod' (37b-38). This assertion is a kind of metonymy for the power of Christ: it is He who could destroy His enemies, and prevent their destroying Him, but He chooses not to. This identification, extending our knowledge of Christ's humanity, thus strengthens the implication of lines 33b-34 that the crucifixion was an act of Christ's free will. The rood 'stands fast' in its triply agonizing office of bearing Christ: as persona, it feels its own pain; as the surrogate of Christ, it feels His pain; and as the instrument of His torture, it feels the pain of guilt. The cross reiterates its Christ-like resolution in line 43b: 'ac ic sceolde fæste standan', a phrase similar in tone to the description of Christ's ascent of the cross (40b-41a).

The identification of the cross with the suffering, human Christ is completed at the moment when Christ is most mortal, His divine spirit having departed:

> Þurhdrifan hi me mid deorcan næglum.   On
> me syndon þa dolg gesiene,
> opene inwidhlemmas. . . .
> Bysmeredon hie unc butu ætgædere.   Eall ic
> wæs mid blode bestemed,
> begoten of þæs guman siden,   siððan he
> hæfde his gast onsended.
>
> (46-49)

Notable here is the use of the word 'begoten' to describe the blood pouring from Christ, in ironic contrast to its use in line 7a to describe the victorious rood's gold covering. This suggests that the gold of the cross is analogous to Christ's baptismal blood. Also important is the contrast between the 'dark nails' and the gemmed, shining cross in part one and later in part two (77). The same contrast of imagery recurs at the moment of Christ's mortal death:

> Þystro hæfdon
> bewrigen mid wolcnum   wealdendes hræw,
> scirne sciman,   sceadu forðeode,
> wann under wolcnum.
>
> (52b-55a)

Immediately after the climax of the poem ('Crist wæs on rode') and before Christ's descent from the cross, the rood prepares us for the next stage of the Passion:

> hnag ic hwæðre þam secgum to handa,
> eaðmod elne mycle.
>
> (59b-60a)

Line 60a recalls ironically Christ's eager approach to the cross: 'efstan elne mycel' (34a); here, line 59 confirms the rood's zealous Christ-like submission mentioned first in 37b. Both Christ and the cross choose throughout the crucifixion to obey with zeal the dictates of sinful men.

After relating Christ's descent from the cross and His burial, the cross describes its own fate, still parallel to Christ's:

> Þa us man fyllan ongan
> ealle to eorðan.   Þæt wæs egeslic wyrd!
> Bedealf us man on deopan seaþe.
>
> (73b-75a)

This passage, ostensibly about the cross, actually tells us more about Christ. When the cross describes Christ directly, the tone is elegiac and gentle, deliberately calculated to de-emphasize the degradation of Christ's burial, and to soften the reader's despair. This has the result of sanctifying Christ: He clearly has a mortal aspect, but it must not be so described as to impair His necessary remoteness. But the bitter degradation of Christ in His death and burial is theologically important, and must not be omitted. The cross, as Christ's surrogate, necessarily feels this, and as narrator of the crucifixion tells it to the dreamer, hence to us. Sanctification and the presentation of degradation are both achieved, simultaneously, by the rood's relation of its own story, analogous to Christ's:

> Nu ðu miht gehyran,   hæleð min se leofa,
> þæt ic bealuwara weorc   gebiden hæbbe,
> sarra sorga.
>
> (78-80a)

Both the cross and Christ ultimately triumph, are resurrected from their degradation, and ascend to heavenly supremacy (80-85). The account of the crucifixion in part two, then, establishes an analogy between the glorified and divine aspects of Christ and the cross, and a symbolic identification between their mortal aspects. The second relationship suggests another analogy, that between the dreamer and the human aspects of both the cross and Christ, which is introduced by the device of the rood's personification and its narration of the crucifixion, a function parallel to the dreamer's narration of his vision. Each narrates and thus testifies to a great scene he has witnessed. We have already noticed signs of this analogy: (1) the effect of the word 'wommum' in linking the dreamer to Christ, imagistically equating the dreamer's sins with Christ's wounds and reminding us that Christ deliberately assumed the burden of human sins to save man; (2) the imagistic parallel between the dreamer's and Christ's 'wommum' and the cross's 'dolg gesiene' or 'opene inwidhlemmas', caused by the 'deorcan næglum'; (3) the parallel functions of Christ and the dreamer as subjects of their respective parts. There are at least three more elements in this third analogy. First, in line 59a, the cross describes its emotions toward the crucified Christ in a phrase almost identical to the dreamer's description of his emotions toward the bleeding cross:

> Dreamer: Eall ic wæs mid sorgum gedrefed . . .
>
> (20b)
>
> Cross: Sare ic wæs mid sorgum gedrefed . . .
>
> (59a)

This parallel in phrase and in function suggests an equivalence between the dreamer and the cross that works reciprocally: the dreamer's reaction helps to humanize the cross; the cross's reaction, by repeating the dreamer's, generalizes it into everyman's. Second, the rood uses the same term in reference to the dreamer and to Christ: it describes Christ when approaching the cross as 'þa geong hæleð' (39a); it begins its exhortation to the dreamer by calling him 'hæleð min se leofa' (78b); and it concludes its exhortation to the dreamer with the same phrase (95a). Third, the cross describes itself as 'mid strælum forwundod' (62b) recalling the dreamer's 'forwunded mid wommum' (14a). The relationship is quite close, since it is the 'wommum' (as human sins) which, by means of the arrows ('strælum'), are responsible for the rood's (and Christ's) wounds, and these in turn become the symbolic scars. At this point in the poem, then (up to line 84), analogies have been established between the cross and Christ, the cross and the dreamer, and the dreamer and Christ. The cross has become representative of three persons: the victorious and immortal Christ, who exists in eternity; the mortal, necessarily defeated Christ, who existed in history; and the dreamer, everyman, who, existing also in history, must follow the pattern of faith shown by Christ's life on earth, to achieve life in eternity.

The remainder (84-121) of the rood's speech strengthens these significations. The cross and Christ are again described as victorious (84-85, 101b-102), as mortal and subject to death (101a, 97b, 98a), and the dreamer is addressed as a representative of mankind (95b, 96) who, we learn (127-128b), is one who would 'taste bitter death as He did' (113b-114). But as the first part foreshadowed the symbolic meaning of the cross developed in the second part, so the end of the second part foreshadows the additional symbolic signification of the cross conveyed by the third part. Lines 84b and 85a recall the heavenly position of the cross in the beginning of the poem, analogous to the cross's location of Christ at the end of its story of the crucifixion: 'He ða on heofenas astag' (103a), followed immediately by the rood's account of the Second Coming and the Last Judgment (103b-109). The Christ of these lines is not the historical Christ of the Crucifixion, but rather the atemporal and eternal Christ. This difference in ontological status suggests the difference in symbolic value between the two Christs of the poem. The cross relates all this in order to make its final point:

> ac ðurh ða rode sceal   rice gesecan
> of eorðwege   æghwylc sawl,
> seo þe mid wealdende   wunian þenceð.
>
> (119-121)

The cross then goes on to associate itself with heaven and the life after death, suggesting that it, like Christ, has undergone an ontological change. We now see that the cross which appears to the dreamer is, ontologically, eternal and atemporal; but the cross it tells us about existed historically. Its appearance to the dreamer pledges a similar ontological change from mortality to immortality for those individuals who, like him, seek Christ by worshipping the cross.

The ultimate Christian goal of heaven and the means of achieving it, are the subject of the third part of the poem (122-end), in which the dreamer returns as direct speaker. His first words, 'Gebæd ic me þa to þan beame bliðe mode, / elne mycle' (122-123a), recall the rood's description of its own and Christ's zeal, thus adding another link in the analogy between the dreamer, and the cross and Christ. In lines 124 to 135a, the dreamer elaborates this desire, instigated by the vision, to be equally zealous in his worship of the cross in order to achieve heaven, and thus to provide an example for his fellow man. There follows (135b-144a) a full description of heaven, in its relation to the dreamer. The identification of the cross and Christ is echoed for the last time by the dreamer's verbally parallel statements about the cross, 'þe ic *her* [the cross] *on eorðan* ær sceawode' (137), and about Christ:

> Si me dryhten freond,
> se ðe *her on eorþan*   ær þrowode
> on þam gealgtreowe   for guman synnum.
>
> (144b-146)

The dreamer concludes with a picture of Christ's triumphal arrival in heaven 'where his home was' (156b) with the spirits He redeemed in the Harrowing of Hell:

> Se sunu wæs sigorfæst   on þam siðfate,
> mihtig ond spedig,   þa he mid *manigeo com,*
> gasta weorode,   on godes rice . . .
>
> (150-152)

In this last section, then, the cross is associated with heaven and the Last Judgment.

Now that the poem's internal structure has been examined, it is possible to see the significance of its sections. Its incremental structure operates on the four levels familiar from patristic scriptural exegesis: the structure, imagery, and meaning of the first part are tropological; of the second part, allegorical and historical; of the third part, anagogical. By the very nature of this scheme, the three structural blocks of the poem cannot and should not be kept entirely discrete. Each successive level incorporates the meaning established by the preceding level, and preceding levels tend to foreshadow the succeeding, thereby enriching the poem's meaning while ensuring its unity.

The relationship in the first part of the poem between the cross and the dreamer creates the tropological meaning. The dreamer's reactions to the two different appearances of the cross show that he understands only their tropological significance: they awaken him, the individual human being, to moral consciousness; he sorrows for his sins. Tropologically, the cross is that 'syllicre treow' (4b)—a significant word, meaning both 'tree' and 'faith'—by which each Christian soul must guide its earthly behavior. Now we can see the effect of the intricately established parallel between the dreamer, and the human natures of Christ and the cross. The cross makes this tropological meaning overt in the second part of the poem:

> Frineð he for þære mænige   hwær se man sie,
> se ðe for dryhtnes naman   deaðes wolde
> biteres onbyrigan,   swa he ær on ðam beame dyde.
>
> . . . . .
>
> Ne þearf ðær þonne ænig   anforht wesan
> þe him ær in breostum bereð   beacna selest.
>
> (112-118)

The pattern established by the mortal Christ must be imitated by each individual who would be a true Christian: as Christ is a 'hæleð' who overcomes sin and death in the battle of crucifixion, so must the dreamer become a 'hæleð' and conquer his own sin. As it is the cross which in lines 112-118 (quoted above) and in the use of the word 'hæleð' verbally draws the parallel between the dreamer and Christ, so it is the cross which, by identifying with both the dreamer and Christ, implies the central link by which the dreamer and Christ are paralleled. The rood, having suffered like Christ, comes in part one as Christ's surrogate to show the human being his own sins. But not until part two does the cross set forth, through its narration of the crucifixion, the way for each individual to conquer sin; and not until part three does the dreamer show us that he has learned 'to carry the beacon in his breast' (118), that is, to follow Christ's conduct:

> Is me nu lifes hyht
> þæt ic þone sigebeam   secan mote
> ana oftor   þonne ealle men,
> well weorþian.   Me is willa to ðam
> mycel on mode,   ond min mundbyrd is
> geriht to þære rode.
>
> (126b-131a)

The tropology, thus, operates in each section: in part one, it is the individual's recognition of his sinfulness; in part two, the establishing of a pattern for the individual life; in part three, the individual's acknowledgement of that pattern. But parts two and three emphasize, respectively, the other two levels more strongly than the tropological, and though part one includes images which later acquire allegorical and anagogical meaning, they have those meanings only in retrospect, thus making the poem's structure at once cyclic and incremental.

Though the second section foreshadows the description of heaven in the third, and helps to show the dreamer the Christian way of life, it is primarily allegorical, concerned with the faith of Christianity ('quid credas') institutionalized in the Church, and with the historical event from which that faith derives, the crucifixion. The two aspects of the cross described in the first part of the poem, and the two aspects of the cross and of Christ in the second part, create these two allegorical meanings. Christ the victorious hero, and the analogous 'victory-cross', symbolize the church militant, the church here on earth which conquers the infidel and in whom all who wish to be saved must believe. The appellative 'hæleð' for both Christ and the dreamer thus has ecclesiological as well as moral significance: each is a soldier in the service of the church militant. St. Ambrose in his commentary on the Gospels and St. Augustine in a sermon ascribed to him both provide authority for the metaphor of Christ as victor, and for the cross as the symbol of his victory; the Blickling Homily says: 'we ought to honor the holy victory sign of Christ's cross . . .'; and the vision of Constantine confirms the interpretation of the ornamented cross as symbolic of that faith which men must follow and of its institutionalization in the chuch militant; according to Eusebius, Constantine said

> that about mid-day, when the sun was beginning to decline, he saw with his own eyes the trophy of a cross of light in the heavens, above the sun, and bearing the inscription, CONQUER BY THIS. At this sight he himself was struck with amazement, and his whole army also, which happened to be following him on some expedition, and witnessed the miracle . . . And while he continued to ponder and reason on its meaning, night imperceptibly drew on; and in his sleep the Christ of God appeared to him with the same sign which he had seen in the heavens, and commanded him to procure a standard made in the likeness of that sign, and to use it as a safeguard in all engagements with his enemies. . . . At dawn of day he arose, and communicated the secret to his friends: and then, calling together the workers in gold and precious stones, he sat in the midst of them, and described to them the figure of the sign he had seen, bidding them represent it in gold and precious stones. And this representation I myself have had an opportunity of seeing. . . . The emperor constantly made use of this salutary sign as a safeguard against every adverse and hostile power, and commanded that others similar to it should be carried at the head of all his armies. . . . he sent for those who were acquainted with the mysteries of His doctrines,

and inquired who that God was, and what was intended by the sign of the vision he had seen.

> They affirmed that He was God, the only begotten Son of the one and only God: that the sign which had appeared was the symbol of *immortality,* and the *trophy of that victory over death* which He had gained in time past when sojourning on earth.

There is strong precedent here for the tradition of the cross as symbolic of Christ's victory on earth, and consequently as the token of spiritual conquest by the church. W. O. Stevens points out the importance for Anglo-Saxon England of the vision of Constantine and his subsequent victory over Maxentius in the name of Christianity by noting its similarity to the victory of Oswald over Cadwalla in 633:

> it is not likely that the influence of this victory upon the national feeling for the cross can be overestimated. The cross had delivered the Angles from their enemies in the hour of greatest need. It was the victory of Constantine repeated in England, and probably the obvious points of similarity in the two stories helped to make the legend of Constantine as popular as it evidently was. This victory of Oswald, as well as that of Constantine, formed the associations with the cross that made appropriate the familiar Old English epithet *sige-beacn,* the 'banner of victory.'

This signification of the cross as the emblem of the militant and institutionalized faith of Christianity emerges explicitly at the end of part two, the conclusion of the rood's speech:

> ac ðurh ða rode sceal   rice gesecan
> of eorðwege   æghwylc sawl,
> seo þe mid wealdende   wunian þenceð.
> (119-121)

These lines mean both that the individual must pattern his conduct on the cross, that is, on Christ's life, and that mankind must believe in the faith represented by the cross, and institutionalized by Christ in the church.

Another element contributing to the identification of the cross with the church is the cross's sex, which seems to be female. The first of two passages in which the rood assumes femininity is this:

> Hwæt, me þa geweorðode   wuldres ealdor
> ofer holmwudu,   heofonrices weard!
> Swylce swa he his modor eac, Marian sylfe,
> ælmihtig god   for ealle menn
> geweorðode   ofer eall wifa cynn.
> (90-94)

As Mary is the bride of God, so the cross is the bride of Christ, a traditional metaphor for the church. An indirect confirmation of this occurs by means of the parallel set up between Christ and Adam (100), in conjunction with the passage in which the cross describes itself as wet with the blood from Christ's side (48b-49). As woman was born from the side of Adam while he slept, so, says Augustine in his commentary on St. John, was the church born from the side of Christ in his flowing blood as he slept on the cross:

Propter hoc prima mulier facta est de latere viri dormientis ([*Gen.*] II, 22), et appellata est vita materque vivorum (*Id.* III, 20). Magnum quippe significavit bonum, ante magnum prævaricationis malum. Hic secundus Adam inclinato capite in cruce dormivit, ut inde formaretur ei conjux, quod de latere dormientis effluxit. O mors unde mortui reviviscunt! Quid isto sanguine mundius? quid vulnere isto salubrius?

The second passage suggesting the femininity of the cross is the sexual imagery in lines 39-42:

> *Ongyrede* hine þa geong *hæleð,* . . .
> strang ond stiðmod. . . .
> *Bifode* ic þa me se beorn *ymbclypte.*

Again, the cross is imaged as the bride of Christ, or the Church, which, allegorically, is born from the union of Christ and the cross, that is, from the crucifixion.

The effect that the jewelled cross has on the dreamer in part one now acquires additional meaning, ecclesiological and redemptive: it is not just the contrast between himself and the radiant goodness of the cross, it is also the Church, represented by the cross, which awakens the dreamer to his sinfulness. The allegory thus determines the tropology: the church, the organizer of society and the embodiment of Christian faith, determines the conduct of the individual:

> . . . ic him lifes weg
> rihtne gerymde,　　reordberendum.
>
> (88b-89)

The human, suffering nature of Christ and the cross indicates the historical level. The cross that speaks is the very cross that crucified the mortal Christ:

> þæt ic wæs aheawen　　holtes on ende,
> astyred of stefne minum.
>
> (29-30a)
>
> Rod wæs ic aræred.　　Ahof ic ricne cyning.
>
> (44)
>
> Hwæt, me þa geweorðode　　wuldres ealdor
> ofer holmwudu.
>
> (90-91a)

As Christ chose this particular tree, so that tree as cross chooses the dreamer to hear and to relate its story, a parallel which extends the tropology by reaffirming the link between the cross and the dreamer. Again, the allegory provides the pattern for the tropology.

The poem also suggests directly and indirectly the standard patristic allegorical interpretation of Christ as the fulfillment of Adam. The direct suggestion occurs in a passage that also reiterates the preceding point:

> onwreoh wordum　　þæt hit is wuldres beam,
> se ðe ælmihtig god　　on þrowode
> for mancynnes　　manegum synnum
> ond Adomes　　ealdgewyrhtum.
>
> (97-100)

As Adam was responsible for man's original sin and fall, so Christ is responsible for man's redemption. We have already noted one of the indirect links between Adam and Christ, the blood that gushed from Christ's side, analogous to the birth of Eve from Adam. Another is the strip-

ping of Christ. St. Ambrose describes Christ as a regal victor removing his clothes, and draws a parallel with Adam: as Adam defeated by sin sought to clothe himself, so Christ victorious over sin stripped himself:

> Nudum video: talis ergo ascendat qui sæculum vincere parat; ut sæculi adjumenta non quaerat. Victus est Adam qui vestimenta quæsivit: vicit ille qui tegumenta deposuit.

If Christ is the second Adam, the cross is allegorically the second tree, the redemptive fulfillment of the tree of life and the tree of knowledge. Stevens points out that identification of the cross as the tree of life is common in Anglo-Saxon literature, and quotes Bede's hymn on the Passion of St. Andrew in which he refers to Christ's being raised on the cross as 'Levatur in vitae arborem'. In his commentary on Psalm I, Bede asserts: 'Christ is called therefore the tree of life'. Stevens also quotes Bede's interpretation of the cross as parallel to the tree of knowledge:

> Doubtless in the same hour in which the first man touched the tree of prevarication, the second man ascended the tree of redemption, and that hour of the day which expelled the prevaricators from Paradise led the Confessor to Paradise.

Through this system of typology, the poem shows the 'fortunate' result made possible by the fall of man: the redemption of man by Christ's sacrifice and through Mary's intercession; both acts—sacrifice and intercession—being, in the poem, adumbrated through the versatile symbol of the cross's personification.

By the end of the second part of the poem the cross has explained to the dreamer the meaning of all its initial visible characteristics: its position in the heavens portends the anagogical apocalyptic cross that announces the Second Coming and the Last Judgment, which it then announces to the dreamer (ll. 101-109); its ornamentation and exaltation recall Constantine's vision and suggest, allegorically, the historical and ecclesiastical development of the faith of Christianity; its dampness and bloodiness suggest the history of the crucifixion, which, when told to the dreamer, has the tropological effect of awakening him to his sins, and the anagogical effect of directing him to eventual immortality in heaven. The poem exploits the cross as a symbol central to, and capable of expressing, all the levels of meaning which Christianity comprehends.

The ultimate symbolic value of the cross, foreshadowed by its appearance in the heavens in part one, and by the cross's assertion at the end of part two that it is the way to heaven (119-121), is anagogical, and is developed at length in part three. There are two aspects of the anagogical meaning. In the first, the cross is a symbol of the divine, eternal Christ, whose intercession leads man to God. The ultimate anagoge, 'dream on heofonum', is described in lines 135-144:

> ond ic wene me
> daga gehwylce　　hwænne me dryhtnes rod,
> þe ic her on eorðan　　ær sceawode,
> on þysson lænan　　life gefetige
> ond me þonne gebringe　　þær is blis mycel,
> dream on heofonum,　　þær is dryhtnes folc

geseted to symle,   þær is singal blis,
ond me þonne asette   þær ic syþþan mot
wunian on wuldre,   well mid þam halgum
dreames brucan.

This value of the cross subsumes the previous two: the anagogical Christ and thus the anagogical cross indicate the translation of the individual to heaven and the transformation of the church militant into the church triumphant, both of which are changes in ontological status analogous to the ontological change undergone by Christ and the cross. This repeated pattern implies the second nature of the dreamer, an equivalence to the divine and immortal aspects of Christ and the cross: by patterning his mortal life on Christ's, each individual will be analogously saved, and will achieve immortality. Thus the tropological and the allegorical are directed by the anagogical.

The second element of the cross's anagogical meaning is its description of the Second Coming and the Last Judgment:

> Hider eft fundaþ
> on þysne middangeard   mancynn secan
> on domdæge   dryhten sylfa,
> ælmihtig god,   ond his englas mid,
> þæt he þonne wile deman,   se ah domes geweald,
> anra gehwylcum   swa he him ærur her
> on þyssum lænum   life geearnaþ.
>
> (103b-109)

The cross, announcing the Last Judgment to the dreamer and thereby to mankind, sets it as the ultimate test for which we must prepare ourselves. The rood's final purpose in appearing to the dreamer, attainable technically only by means of the first person point of view, is to bear witness of heaven. The anagogical meaning of part two foreshadows the central meaning of part three.

In the final part, the dreamer does for the reader what in the second part the cross has done for the dreamer: by carrying out the command of the cross, the dreamer conveys to all mankind the meanings he himself has learned, and in expressing his desire for physical death and spiritual life with God, he sets the pattern for the Christian. His return as first-person narrator reinforces his parallel with the cross, and his desire for heaven reinforces his parallel with Christ. The subject of the last section is the dreamer (everyman) in relation to heaven, and is thus predominantly anagogical. The cross and Christ have already ascended to heaven, and become immortal; since he is analogous to them, the dreamer expects—and predicts—a similar change for himself (124b-125a, 135b-140a), and thus for all believers.

These ascensions, one potential and two actual, begin to show the poem's pattern of analogous action. The three levels parallel and imply each other. The story of Christ involves all three: in His incarnation He is the pattern of moralia for the individual; in His crucifixion He conquers original sin and its consequence of death, and this victory becomes that faith 'quid credas' and is institutionalized in the church militant; and after death, He harrowed Hell, ascended to Heaven, and will return on the Day of Judgment to lead the faithful to Heaven. This pattern is repeated in the poem first through the persona of the cross, which, crucified with Christ, is buried (75), 'resurrected' (76-77), and symbolically ascends triumphantly to heaven (80b-83, 85) whence it announces the Second Coming and the Last Judgment (103b-105). This progress of the cross, recounted factually in the poem, symbolizes allegorically the course of the Christian church: at first persecuted and forced underground, or 'buried', it was eventually 'resurrected', and became victorious as God's kingdom here on earth, the earthly counterpart of the atemporal church triumphant in heaven.

The dreamer also repeats the pattern: he is first sinful man, then he recognizes the meanings of the cross, and finally he envisions his future ascension to heaven. He understandably dwells on this aspect of the imitation of Christ, rather than predict the painful struggles, death, and burial, analogous to the crucifixion, attendant on following Christ. The life of the individual (the tropology), and the life of the church and of the historical Christ (the allegory), both follow the same course and are analogous. Furthermore, in *The Dream of The Rood,* the tropology—the cross in relation to the moral life of everyman—is central to the first part, but developed by the second and completed by the third; the allegory—the cross in relation to the church and to its history—is central to the second part, but is foreshadowed by the visible characteristics of the cross in the first part, and is directed by the anagogical values of the third; the anagoge—the cross in relation to heaven, when united to God—is central to the third part, but it subsumes the first two: the rood's position in the heavens in part one is anagogical, as is its prediction of the Last Judgment in part two.

The cross, literally by speaking the poem and figuratively by the meanings the poet develops in it, teaches the dreamer the way of Christian life and salvation. Structurally and symbolically the cross reveals incrementally all four levels. It is the literal, historical cross on which Christ was crucified; it is the sign that each Christian must bear in his heart and live by; it is the symbol of the faith, of all those crosses throughout the earth which symbolize the church militant; and it is the heavenly symbol of the church triumphant, of Christ's return from Hell to God; and because it is all these things, it is the instrument which leads man to God, and the pledge of life everlasting.

Much of the poem's complexity and emotional force derive from its use of the four levels, and from its genre, the dream vision. Indispensable to this genre is the persona who both acts and relates his experience. Through the very poem which narrates the dreamer's vision, the dreamer carries out the command presented by the dream: to bear witness to all mankind of the Christian faith by relating to men what he has learned. The persona's experience consequently becomes archetypal and propagandistic. The aim of the poem is to express a religious truth indirectly, by means of symbol and figure, so that through the intellectual exertion necessary to discover it, the reader will be both more aware of its value and more convinced of its truth.

This analysis has barely touched the richness and beauty of *The Dream of The Rood,* and it has not considered many of its sophisticated poetic devices. But, even from this examination of its language and philosophy, we can see that the **Rood** poet forged a complex, moving, and profound poem, one of the great monuments of English literature. **The Dream of The Rood** is the furthest thing imaginable from the patchwork, primitive effort it has frequently been considered.

John Canuteson   (essay date 1969)

SOURCE: "The Crucifixion and the Second Coming in *The Dream of the Rood*," in *Modern Philology,* Vol. 66, No. 4, May, 1969, pp. 293-97.

[*In the following essay, Canuteson compares the Crucifixion as portrayed in* The Dream of the Rood *with the Biblical descriptions of Christ's second coming.*]

Praise for **The Dream of the Rood** has been uniformly generous. Charles W. Kennedy [*The Earliest English Poetry,* 1943] declares that it deserves "pre-eminent distinction as a superb lyric presentation of a religious adoration which finds its symbol in the Cross." In discussing possible sources for the poem, [Bruce] Dickins and [Alan S.C.] Ross mention [in *The Dream of the Rood,* 1966] the beautiful imagery, and Margaret Schlauch has pointed out [in *"The Dream of the Rood* as Prosopopoeia," in *Essays and Studies in Honor of Carleton Brown,* 1940] the uniqueness in Old English literature of **The Dream of the Rood** by virtue of the poet's technique of *prosopopoeia:* "To endow the cross with power of locution was to use a device of unexampled effectiveness in making vivid an event about which, for all devout Christians, the entire history of the world revolved."

The "effectiveness," then, of the poem has been beyond dispute. Some scholars have tried to determine influences on the poem, most notably H. R. Patch [in his "Liturgical Influence in *The Dream of the Rood*," *PMLA* XXIV (1919)], who has found parallels in Latin liturgical hymns, Miss Schlauch, who has pointed out Latin poems using *prosopopoeia,* and most recently John V. Fleming ["*The Dream of the Rood* and Anglo-Saxon Monasticism," *Traditio* XXII (1966)], who finds in the poem "a figurative statement of the main principles of early Benedictine asceticism and a typically monastic view of salvation." But against all source studies of this poem we have the warning by Dickins and Ross that the probable source for the poem was the poet's own emotion.

We must agree with Miss Schlauch that one of the things that make the poem so vivid is the personification of the Cross. But the poet seems also to have another way of making the moment of the crucifixion—or the meaning of the Cross—vivid, and a way which is much more immediate than personification derived from Latin poetry. The poet connects the crucifixion with the second coming of Christ and eternal life. By examining several passages in the Bible dealing with eschatology, particularly the new Jerusalem and the bride of Christ passages, we can see that the poet is able to underscore the significance of the crucifixion by looking forward to the Day of Judgment and the mystical marriage of Christ and the Church.

It is noteworthy that the poet's vision occurs at night, when other men are at rest (ll. 1-3). Writing of the second coming of Christ, Paul tells the Thessalonians to be watchful, since "the day of the Lord so cometh as a thief in the night" (I Thess. 5:2). He also reminds them that they are "children of the light," not of darkness:

> 6. Therefore let us not sleep, as do others; but let us watch and be sober.
> 7. For they that sleep sleep in the night.

In the vision the Cross is seen in the air, enveloped in light—brightness is its most startling characteristic—and visible at the corners of the earth, which the Cross reaches as it stretches across the sky. Moreover, the Cross is beheld by the host of angels and by men throughout the world. In Matthew, the disciples press Christ for more information about the last days, particularly for the sign of the end (24:3). He replies that temporal signs will be tribulation on earth, and he adds:

> 27. For as lightning cometh out of the east, and shineth even unto the west; so shall also the coming of the Son of man be. . . .
> 30. And then shall appear the sign of the Son of man in heaven: and then shall all the tribes of the earth mourn, and they shall see the Son of man coming in the clouds of heaven with power and great glory.
> 31. And he shall send his angels with a great sound of a trumpet, and they shall gather together his elect from the four winds, from one end of heaven to the other.

If one substitutes *Christ* for the Cross in lines 4-12, he will see how closely this vision follows that of the second coming. The gold and the gems with which the cross is adorned (ll. 7, 16) may have their origin in another account of the second coming, the description of the new Jerusalem in Revelation 21. The city, descending from heaven with brilliant light "like unto a stone most precious" (vss. 10-11), is of "pure gold," and its twelve foundations are each of a different gem. The difference between the Cross of Calvary and the Cross "begoten mid golde" or between the old and the new Jerusalem is one of glorification, the transmutation which takes place on Judgment Day.

The Rood not only reminds us of the new Jerusalem but also of the bride of Christ, as the poet develops his imagery along familiar scriptural lines. Throughout the Old Testament, the allegorical use of marriage was to indicate the relationship of God with his people, for example, Isaiah 54:5, Jeremiah 3:14, and Hosea 2:19. In the New Testament, however, Christ replaces Jehovah as the bridegroom, and the Church replaces the Israelites as the bride. Christ refers to himself and to the fact that he will be taken away by the metaphor of the bridegroom in Matthew 9:15; John the Baptist denies that he is the expected savior and mentions Christ as the bridegroom in John 3:28-29. The notion that the Church was the bride of Christ was established by the time that Paul wrote his second letter to the Corinthians: "For I am jealous over you with godly jealousy: for I have espoused you to one husband, that I may present you as a chaste virgin to Christ" (11:2).

When Revelation was written, the bridegroom-bride metaphor had been fully developed in terms of the return of Christ and his marriage to the Church. The writer of Revelation uses it twice, the first time, in Revelation 19, rather simply:

> 7. Let us be glad and rejoice, and give honor to him; for the marriage of the Lamb is come, and his wife hath made herself ready.
> 8. And to her was granted that she should be arrayed in fine linen, clean and white: for the fine linen is the righteousness of saints.
> 9. And he saith unto me, Write, Blessed are they which are called unto the marriage supper of the Lamb. And he saith unto me, These are the true sayings of the Lord.

When he uses it the second time, in Revelation 21, the bride is the new Jerusalem: "And I John saw the holy city, new Jerusalem, coming down from God out of heaven, prepared as a bride adorned for her husband" (vs. 21).

That the personification of the Cross is amenable to interpretation as representing the Church seems possible on several grounds, not the least of which is the complete passivity of the Cross. It is angry and afraid—it wants to fell Christ's enemies, and it shakes when Christ mounts it—but in everything it exhibits a feminine submission. This passivity is dictated by submission to God's will (ll. 35-36); nevertheless, one feels that he is witnessing feminine behavior. By line 90, the Cross can compare its/her prominence to that of Mary herself:

> Hwæt, me þa geweorðode wuldres Ealdor
> ofer holtwudu, heofonrices Weard,
> swylce swa he his modor eac, Marian sylfe,
> ælmihtig God, for ealle menn
> geweorðode ofer eall wifa cynn.

In addition to this feminine passivity, other details seem to call attention to the Church as the bride of Christ. Dickins and Ross admit perplexity concerning the meaning of *wædum* in "Geseah ic wuldres treow/wædum geweorðod wynnum scinan" (ll. 14-15). They consider *streamers,* but state, "It is not at all clear what these are." By translating this passage, "I saw the cross of glory adorned with weeds shine with joys," and by taking the usual meaning of weeds as *clothes,* could not the sense be lifted from the description of the bride, "arrayed in fine linen," the joys being the heavenly bliss which awaits the faithful? *Weeds* in the sense of *clothes* must be the meaning in line 22 in which the cross changes from a covering of sweat to a covering of treasure:

> Geseah ic þæt fuse beacen
> wendan wædum 7 bleom: hwilum hit wæs
>   mid wætan bestemed,
> beswyled mid swates gange, Hwilum mid
>   since gegyrwed.

When the Cross begins to speak, it relates how it was cut down at the edge of the woods (l. 29) and commanded to bear criminals (l. 31). It was then set on a (different?) hill (l. 32), from which it saw the Lord of mankind "hasten, very much" toward it (ll. 33-34). Miss [Rosemary] Woolf has noted [in her "Doctrinal Influences on *The Dream of the Rood,*" *Medium Aevum* XXVII (1958)] a series of departures from scriptural accounts of the crucifixion in the Cross's speech, the first being that neither Christ nor Simon of Cyrene carries the cross: "That the cross is already in position and watches Christ advancing to it seems to be the poet's own variation." Other curious details follow.

> Ongyred ehine þa geong Hæleð, (þæt wæs
>   God ælmihtig),
> strang 7 stiðmod. Gestah he on gealgan
>   heanne,
> modig on manigra gesyhðe, þa he wolde
>   mancyn lysan.
> Bifode ic þa me se Beorn ymbclypte; ne
>   dorste ic hwæðre bugan to eorðan,
> feallan to foldan sceatum. Ac ic sceolde
>   fæste standan.
>
> [ll. 39-43]

The stripping and the ascent onto the cross are also not found in the scriptures. These three distinct departures from biblical accounts of the crucifixion are interpreted by Miss Woolf as emphasizing "the confidence of divine victory and the voluntariness of Christ's undertaking the Crucifixion."

For the second of the details, the stripping, Miss Woolf maintains that the author "was following a patristic tradition, to be found, for instance, in Ambrose's commentary on Luke, of Christ as Kingly victor removing his clothes. . . . In *The Dream of the Rood* Christ is very clearly a hero stripping himself for battle." For the third detail, the poet has, she suggests, directly translated *crucem ascendere,* one of two "conventional expressions" of Latin hymnody, the result being that "the young hero's advance, and ascent of the Cross, is at once painless and heroic, and is therefore a most admirable symbol of the divine nature of Christ." My quibble with Miss Woolf would be that the crucifixion could hardly be considered painless with all the references to *swat* and *blod,* and the understatement, "þurhdrifan hi me mid deorcan næglum" (l. 46). While the account does show Christ's willingness, indeed his eagerness, to embrace his fate, it also reveals the physical details of what happens to a man, rather than a god, on the Cross.

The pattern of the details in lines 33-43 indicates a purpose on the part of the poet which would not exclude Christ's willingness to die. He is seen "efstan elne mycle, þæt he me wolde on gestigan." Then he takes off his clothes and embraces the Cross. Christ is *strang* as well as *stiðmod;* he is also *modig*—all the things that a woman would see and appreciate in a husband. The Cross, moreover, is demure—she trembles when she is embraced. This whole passage is simply a logical extension of the implications of the marriage of Christ and the Church.

The two have now become one. The dark nails are driven through the Cross, and on it are the wounds visible (ll. 46-47). "Bysmeredon hie unc butu ætgædere." Miss Woolf observes: "The cross shares in all the sufferings of Christ, so that it seems to endure a compassion, in the sense in which that word was used in the Middle Ages to describe the Virgin's identification of her feelings with those of her Son in His Passion."

The Cross has reached a nearness to Christ that rivals that of Mary. The interesting statement follows, "Eall ic wæs mid blode bestemed, / begoten of þæs Guman sidan" (ll. 48-49). This passage may have a reference to the origin of the Church in it, since Augustine had observed:

> At the beginning of the human race the woman was made of a rib taken from the side of the man while he slept; for it seemed fit that even Christ and His Church should be foreshadowed in this event. For that sleep of the man was the death of Christ, whose side, as He hung lifeless upon the cross, was pierced with a spear, and there flowed from it blood and water, and these we know to be the sacraments by which the Church is "built up."

The vision of the Cross therefore is formulated in terms of the imagery of the second coming of Christ and the new Jerusalem, and a kind of marriage consummation takes place on the Cross. Lines 50-77 are taken up with more or less matter-of-fact details from the universal darkness on the day of the crucifixion to the finding of the buried Cross. In lines 78-94, the Cross points out her present state of veneration, and in lines 95 and following the Cross directs the poet to tell the vision to men:

> onwreoh wordum   þæt hit is wuldres beam,
> se ðe ælmihtig God   on þrowode
> for mancynnes   manegum synnum
> 7 Adomes   ealdgewyrhtum.
> Deað he þær byrigde.
>
> [ll. 97-101]

But the Cross does not stop with the crucifixion. Instead, she goes on to relate the resurrection and the ascension, and to outline the second coming, as if these things were included by implication in the account of the crucifixion.

> Hider eft fundaþ
> on þysne middangeard   mancynn secan
> on domdæge   Dryhten sylfa,
> ælmihtig God   7 his englas mid,
> þæt he þonne wile deman,   se ah domes
>   geweald.
>
> [ll. 103-7]

Furthermore, the question Christ will ask will involve the Cross: "Hwær se man sie, / se ðe for Dryhtnes naman deaðes wolde / biteres onbyrigan, swa he ær on ðam beame dyde" (ll. 112-14). At lines 117 and following we learn that no one needs to be afraid who before bears the "beacna selest" in his breast. The last words that the Cross speaks connect most clearly the Cross to eternal life:

> Ac ðþurh ða rode sceal   rice gesecan
> of eorðwege   æghwylc sawl,
> seo þe mid Wealdende   wunian þenceð.

The poet begins to speak again at line 122, reporting that he prayed to the Cross. His life apparently has been redirected by the vision, since

> Is me nu lifes hyht
> þæt ic þone sigebeam   secan mote . . .
>   min mundbyrd is
> geriht to þære rode.
>
> [ll. 126-31]

He thinks of his friends briefly, who "lifiað nu on heofenum mid Heahædere," and longs for the day when the Cross will bring him to heaven:

> þær is blis mycel,
> dream on heofonum,   þær is Dryhtnes folc
> geseted to symle [i.e. the wedding feast].
>
> [ll. 139-41]

For the poet there is an undeniable connection between the Cross of Calvary and heavenly life.

> Si me Dryhten freond,
> se ðe her on eorþan   ær þrowode
> on þam gealgtreowe   for guman synnum:
> he us onlysde,   7 us lif forgeaf,
> heofonlicne ham.
>
> [ll. 144-48]

Huppé details the structure of *The Dream of the Rood*:

The basic design of the *Dream of the Rood* is clear. It consists of four scenes: I, 1-23, the vision; II, 24-77, the narrative of the Cross; III, 78-121, the peroration and exhortation of the Cross; IV, 122-156, the dreamer's prayer to Cross and Christ. However, this relatively simple frame supports an elaborate rhetorical structure in which a series of striking antitheses is developed. The antitheses derive basically from the juxtaposition, the *communicatio idiomatum*, of the two aspects of Christ as God and man. In the Crucifixion, Christ suffered as man, but without diminishing his godhead. His passion is universal and particular, and the ignominy of his shameful death is the glory of his triumph over death. Without sin he died for sinners. The Cross, in turn, is the symbol of the mystery of the Redemption, the triumph of mortification. . . .

The thematic development of the poem is clear in outline, but what distinguishes this development is the elaborate artifice of echo and re-echo, of the pattern of incremental repetition within the ordering of the verse paragraph. The dream is like an illuminated page from the Book of Kells, recounting the Crucifixion.

Bernard F. Huppé, in his The Web of Words, *State University of New York Press, 1970.*

O. D. Macrae-Gibson   (essay date 1969)

SOURCE: "Christ the Victor-Vanquished in *The Dream of the Rood*," in *Neuphilologische Mitteilungen: Bulletin de la Société Néophilologique*, Vol. LXX, 1969, pp. 667-72.

[*In the excerpt below, Macrae-Gibson focuses on the transformations of the Christ-figure in* The Dream of the Rood.]

Since Rosemary Woolf's well-known article ["Doctrinal Influence on *The Dream of the Rood*," *Medium Aevum* 27 (1958)] it has been a commonplace of criticism of the poem that the active principle in Christ's approach to the crucifixion, that springing from his Godhead, is given by the poet to the figure of Christ; the passive principle, springing from his manhood, to that of the Cross. The way in which the Cross acts as surrogate for Christ in respect of "what is mortal and weak in Him" has recently been very fully examined by F. H. Patten [in her "Structure and Meaning in *The Dream of the Rood,*" *English Studies* 49 (1968)]. This does not mean that the images of Christ and of the Cross are unchanging in their significances through the poem; another recent article, ["*The Dream of the Rood:* Patterns of Transformation," *Old English Poetry: Fifteen Essays,* 1967] by L. H. Leiter, should be an effective counter to any such suggestion. The image of Christ, in particular, moves between the figures of the defeated and of the triumphant warrior.

Leiter, however, in his concern to demonstrate a parallel change of status in the three "characters" of the poem (Christ, Cross, and Dreamer) seems to me to have gone somewhat astray in his detailed analysis of the transformations which the Christ-figure undergoes. For Leiter the young hero Christ appears first as one who "has been defeated in battle. This defeat the Cross points up by saying *heton me heora wergas hebban*" (31b). Though "the defeated hero . . . still has the hero's *ellen* (34a) . . . , he is tortured, pierced with *deorcan næglum* (46a)", and only after his death does he rise to the quality of the victorious hero. The intention of the present article is to examine closely just what transformations in his Christ-figure the poet in fact works, and how he manages them.

First, then, the figure does *not* come on the scene as a warrior defeated in battle. The fact that those who set up the Cross *heton me heora wergas hebban* merely expresses their intention for it. The intention was not realised; the Cross did not become *fracodes gealga* (10b). The poet could not have meant the term *werg* to apply to Christ; it would have made of him not a heroic though defeated warrior but an accursed evil-doer. The Christ-figure appears as an active hero eagerly approaching for battle. The first six verbs used of Christ, in lines 34-42, all attribute action to him (*efstan, wolde gestigan, ongyrede, gestah, wolde lysan, ymbclypte*). The descriptions of him in the same passage, as *strang, stiðmod, modig,* and coming *elne mycle,* are not those of a defeated warrior, but of the mighty king (*ricne cyning*) of 44b. Active himself, he can command passivity in the Cross (35ff.). The Cross, on the other hand, attracts references using passives and negatives—*ic ne dorste* (35a), *wæs ic aræred* (44a), *ne dorste* (45b), *þurhdrifan hi me* (46a). Even where the Cross is the subject of an active verb the sense is not of outgoing action—*ic fæste stod* (38b), *bifode ic* (42a), *ic sceolde fæste standan* (43b). It is the Cross-figure, not the Christ-figure, which is made the object of the blows, wounds, and shame of lines 46-47a (a fact oddly passed over by Leiter, who treats them as helping to establish the defeated status of Christ on his entry into the poem).

The active image of Christ the Warrior being thus established, the transformations can begin. The first sign of a shift to passivity has already appeared in line 44b; then in line 48 the shame is extended to Christ in close linkage with the Cross, an extension bound to the first reference to Christ's death by the alliterative linking between their

joint shame and the blood from his side. The transformation to a suffering, passive, "defeated" Christ is not yet complete, however: his death is here made active on his part; he "sent out his spirit" (49b). A further stage in the transformation follows in lines 51b-55a. The reference to Christ is unfortunately uncertain both syntactically and semantically. If *þenian* means "stretch out" it may have Christ as its object or subject, in the latter case with "himself" or "his hands" as understood objects; alternatively it may be held to mean simply "exert himself". Moreover *þearle* may be taken as retaining the sense "cruelly" or as a simple intensive. The alliterative association, however, of *þearle þenian* with the darkness which covered Christ's body strongly suggests that the image is one of suffering rather than action; the bright radiance (whether this be taken as actually Christ's body or as the Sun which so familiarly represents the glory of the Son) disappears in dark shadow. This leads on to the final stage of this first transformation (though not without a hint of the reversal which is to come, for cloud and shadow can cover light, but not extinguish it), the direct presentation of the defeated warrior. Christ has suffered *fyll* (56a), after *hefig wite* (61a). He is dead, or he could not have a *bana* (66a); the tomb and the dirge are just (65b, 67b); the cold of death is on him (72b). The simple physicality of the fact is emphasised by the third-person reference to the cross in line 56b, not at this point the actor in the drama but the bare wood.

Patten, while agreeing that it is "the divine, victorious, heroic nature of Christ" which is first established, considers that "this nature of Christ prevails throughout the crucifixion" up to the point where "He is referred to *at the moment of his burial* as the 'lord of victories' "; her analysis, however, concentrates almost exclusively on the titles used to describe Christ, and takes no account of the other signs of a transformation of attitude to him which I have dealt with above. In keeping with this view, while accepting that the human aspect of the Christ-figure appears in the poem at the Deposition (notably in the description of him "as 'limbweary' (l. 63a), a movingly human term, and then as 'worn out' (l. 65a)"), she cannot accept that this extends to a direct, clear presentation of him as dead: "the tone is . . . deliberately calculated to de-emphasize the degradation of Christ's burial . . . This has the result of sanctifying Christ: He clearly has a mortal aspect, but it must not be so described as to impair His necessary remoteness." ". . . indeed, His death is something too mysterious and holy to be spoken of without euphemism: 'and he hine ðær *hwile reste* . . .' ". I can see nothing remote about *hræw colode* (72b), and the image of the warrior's "rest" is rather set in deliberate contrast to that of his death than introduced as a softening euphemism.

It is, in fact, one of three ways in which the image of the dead and defeated is modified. First, the incredible paradox that the passive figure is in fact Almighty, the figure lying low so that one looks down on it is the Lord of high heaven, the defeated figure is the Ruler of all victories, is stressed in the juxtaposition (to which Woolf has drawn attention) of these titles of the Divine Victor and descriptions of the human victim (lines 60b, 64a, 67a). The device in fact appeared as soon as the transformation of the Christ-figure began to appear. The first real action assigned to the Cross and the first suffered by Christ appear in the double paradox of line 44, in which a thing itself so passive as to be lifted up by men is yet so active as to lift up one who could need no lifting, since his domain is in the Highest. And then the solitary figure cruelly stretched out in line 52a (if that is the correct rendering) is the God of Hosts. Second, the point already mentioned, alongside the image of the dead and defeated warrior runs that of the warrior resting, after victory one would have said (lines 64b-65a and 69b); resting only for a while—the metrical stress on *hwile* (64b) is important. Third, it is three times indicated that what lay dead was body only. Two of the three indications are relatively unemphatic (*hræw* in lines 53b and 72b), but the remaining one is striking; the ordinary construction one might have expected in line 63b would be *him æt þæm heafdum*, but the poet brings in, and gives a main metrical stress to, *his lices*.

This last modification of the simple image of the dead looks forward to the resolution of the paradox of the victor-vanquished. The body appears vanquished; the spirit is engaged in victorious battle with Satan before the gates of Hell. The resolution is explicit, and the transformations of the Christ-figure are completed, in the conclusion of the poem as Christ comes victorious from that expedition with the host of spirits which, as *weruda God,* he properly leads. His divine titles are no longer set gainst his human sufferings; Almighty God is home, in his own *eðel* (156). For the purpose of the poet's transformation of his Christ-figure to this conclusion Christ's bodily resurrection would be intrusive; it is referred to in low key in the doctrinal passage of lines 98 ff., but it is not dramatically presented. Rather the emphasis is on the raising up of the Cross, to whom the power of God on earth is largely assigned in the later parts of the poem.

Carol Jean Wolf   (essay date 1970)

SOURCE: "Christ as Hero in *The Dream of the Rood,*" in *Neuphilologische Mitteilungen: Bulletin de la Société Néophilologique,* Vol. LXXI, No. 3, 1970, pp. 202-10.

[*In the following essay, Wolf examines the poet's "presentation of the Crucifixion as a battle"* in The Dream of the Rood, *focusing on theme and diction.*]

The unlettered singer who attempts to create songs embodying thematic material novel to his tradition encounters severe and sometimes insurmountable difficulties. With the option of creating original formulas virtually denied him, the artist must find the means of expressing these new ideas in the traditional verses developed slowly by generations of his predecessors in their treatment of stories long familiar both to themselves and to their audiences. That he does not always succeed in the task is clear from the failure of Yugoslavian bards to cope with the socio-political themes of Marxism. Problems similar to those faced by the Yugoslavian singers must have confronted the Anglo-Saxon scop who sought to express within his songs the novel subjects and themes brought to his island by Christianity, for he, too, worked within a tradition which, if not necessarily oral, at least utilized formulaic techniques surviving from an earlier epoch. Of the extant Old English verses, few offer greater testimony to the ability of these poets to effect a fruitful wedding of their heroic tradition to a Christian subject than those describing the crucifixion of Christ (33b-76a) in *The Dream of the Rood.*

Throughout the crucifixion passage, the *Rood*-poet uses the traditional language of Anglo-Saxon heroic poetry to depict Christ as a hero valiantly engaging in conflict. He emphasizes the Redeemer's heroism by describing Him as a warrior-lord, explicitly calling Him a young hero (39a), a warrior (42a), and a powerful king (44b). Christ appears, moreover, as the prince (58a) and the illustrious ruler (69a), titles which, as Robert E. Diamond has observed [in his "Heroic Diction in *The Dream of the Rood,*" in *Studies in Honor of John Wilcox,* 1958] are frequently applied to the heroes of *Beowulf.* Accordingly, when the *Rood*-poet uses such phrases to describe Christ he invests Him with the aura surrounding the traditional heroic figure.

However, the Christ of *The Dream of the Rood* is not a warrior-lord in name only, for the poet surrounds Him with the retainers who accompany the lord in the Germanic *comitatus.* When he describes Christ's ascent to the cross as an embrace ("me se beorn ymbclypte," 42a), the *Rood*-poet employs a verb strongly reminiscent of that used in *The Wanderer* to describe the lord-thane relationship: "þinced him on mode þæt he his mondryhten/*clyþþe* ond cysse," (41-42a, my emphasis). Throughout the passage he repeatedly indicates that the cross is indeed the thane of Christ. It does not dare to fall to the earth when Christ ascends it because to do so would be to disobey its lord's command (35-36a). Like a good thane, the cross would defend the prince but it must again restrain itself because of the master's word (37b-38). When the apostles come to care for the body of Christ, the cross bows down meekly with great zeal to deliver the corpse into their hands:

> Sare ic wæs mid sorgum gedrefed,   hnag ic
>   hwæðre þam secgum to handa,
> eaðmod elne mycle.   Genamon hie þær
>   ælmihtigne god,
> ahofon hine of ðam hefian wite.
>
> (59-61a)

The similarity of the phrase "eaðmod elne mycle" to the one utilized by the poet to describe Christ's hastening to the cross, "efstan elne mycle" (34a), serves to link the Lord and the cross. One might suspect, moreover, that the Anglo-Saxon audience would have been alert to the contrast suggested by the first words of each of the formulas. Christ, the lord, is actively hastening to the crucifixion, while the cross, after the conflict, is still obedient to the lord's command, passively submitting to being handled by the apostles, but submitting with zeal because he fulfills Christ's wishes by so doing.

The apostles who come to remove Christ's body from the cross also appear as retainers. The poet describes them as soldiers (59b) and as battle-warriors (61b). According to Albert S. Cook [in *The Dream of the Rood,* 1905], this term "hilderincas" appears only in four other poems in the entire corpus of Old English poetry, all war poems. Later in the passage, the "friends" who discover the cross (their relation to Christ is relatively comparable to that of the apostles) are specifically called thanes of the Lord (75b). By standing firm during the crucifixion, the cross obeys his lord's command and renders his proper service as a retainer to the prince. Similarly, the apostles who remove the corpse from the cross, prepare the sepulchre for their prince, and sing a dirge lamenting his death fulfill the retainer's duty of attending to the burial of his dead lord.

Just as the poet presents Christ as a warrior-lord, he transforms the crucifixion into a heroic conflict. With his use of "ðam miclan gewinne" (65a) to describe the crucifixion, he evokes a military aura, for "gewin" can mean "battle," "strife," and "contest" in addition to "agony." Similarly, the cross refers to the men who preside at the crucifixion as foes (38a) and describes itself as being wounded with arrows (62b). These "arrows" are most probably the nails with which Christ was fastened to the tree. However, by referring to them with the military "stræelum," the poet greatly enhances his presentation of the crucifixion as a battle. Moreover, Christ moves toward the cross as a hero preparing himself for conflict. Throughout the passage, He is an active, even eager agent:

> Geseah ic þa frean mancynnes
> efstan elne mycle   þæt he me wolde on gestigan.
> Þær ic þa ne dorste   ofer dryhtnes word
> bugan oððe berstan,   þa ic bifian geseah
> eorðan sceatas.   Ealle ic mihte
> feondas gefyllan,   hwæðre ic fæste stod.
> Ongyrede hine þa geong hæleð,   (þæt wæs god ælmihtig),
> strang ond stiðmod.   Gestah he on gealgan heanne,
> modig on manigra gesyhðe,   þa he wolde mancyn lysan.
>
> (33b-41)

The Christ of *The Dream of the Rood* is not crucified; rather, He willingly ascends the cross, exhibiting as He does so the traditional heroic qualities of strength, resolution, and boldness. All the verb constructions describing the movement toward the cross are active with Christ as their subject. Moreover, the verb "ongyrede" which the poet uses to describe Christ's stripping is similar to the "gyrede" which appears in numerous descriptions of warriors arming themselves for battle. Consequently, the phrase, although it ironically describes Christ's stripping, strongly suggests that Christ is indeed a hero preparing himself for an impending conflict.

The discussion thus far has centered on the diction of *The Dream of the Rood,* the picture of Christ as a hero engaging in a heroic conflict created by the poet's use of a multitude of individual heroic or military details in his description of the crucifixion. The formulaic poet has available to him, however, not only a traditional diction but also certain larger formulaic structures which he may use as the basis of his narrative. In a recent article, "Old English Formulaic Themes and Type-Scenes," Donald K. Fry defines two such formulaic structures as they appear in Anglo-Saxon narrative poetry:

> A type-scene in Old English formulaic poetry may be defined . . . as a recurring stereotyped presentation of conventional details used to describe a certain narrative event, requiring neither verbatim repetition nor a specific formula content; and a theme may be defined as a recurring concatenation of details and ideas, not restricted to a specific event, verbatim repetition, or certain formulas, which forms an underlying structure for an action or description.

Typical examples of type-scenes are banquets, sea-voyages, councils, approaches to battle, and battles. Examples of themes include the "hero on the beach" and exile. Two such formulaic structures appear in the *Rood,* the "approach to battle" and the "hero on the beach." By using these to describe the crucifixion and burial of Christ, respectively, the poet effectively reinforces his presentation of Christ as a hero and the crucifixion as a heroic encounter.

In another discussion of the "approach to battle" type-scene, Fry lists nine details which frequently recur in various combinations and orders in the descriptions of such scenes. These include the *assembly* and *preparation* of the troops for battle, the issuing of the leader's *command,* the *advance* of the forces to the battle-ground, their *bearing of equipment,* the presence of the *beasts of battle,* the combatants' *haste* to enter the fighting, their *attitude,* and their objectives or *intent.* Fry notes, however, that no one of the seventeen passages he analysed "includes all nine details [nor] does any one detail occur in all seventeen passages."

The description of Christ's movement to the cross in *The Dream of the Rood* (33b-41) contains many of these elements characteristic of the "approach to battle" type-scene. The whole passage is an advance to the conflict of the crucifixion depicting Christ's progress from when He is first seen by the cross to His actual embrace of the tree. As He approaches the hill, Christ is hastening with great zeal (34a). He intends to climb up onto the cross so that He might redeem mankind (34b, 41b). The cross's comment that he did not dare to bow or burst in disregard of the Lord's word (35-36a) implies that he has been commanded by Christ to stand firm. "Ongyrede hine þa geong hæleð" (39a) suggests preparation for battle, as was discussed above. In His approach to the cross, moreover, the Redeemer exhibits the heroic attitudes of resolution (40a) and boldness (41a).

In the earlier discussion of this passage, these features were considered merely as independent elements of the poet's heroic diction. The similarity of these details to the elements of advance, haste, intent, command, preparation, and attitude which appear in many "approach to battle" type-scenes suggests, however, that the poet's concatenation of these details may also be of significance. By paralleling his description of Christ's movement to the cross to the pattern of the "approach to battle" type-scene, the *Rood*-poet brings all the associations accruing to such scenes from their use in the traditional songs to bear upon this passage, revealing by structure as well as diction his conception of the crucifixion as a heroic conflict.

His use of the theme of the "hero on the beach" in his description of the burial of Christ operates similarly to heighten the heroic tone of the passage. David K. Crowne

["The Hero on the Beach: an Example of Composition by Theme in Anglo-Saxon Poetry," *Neuphilologishe Mitteilungen* LXI (1960)] was the first to isolate the "hero on the beach" theme, which he defines as a "stereotyped way of describing (1) a hero on the beach (2) with his retainers (3) in the presence of a flashing light (4) as a journey is completed (or begun)." Subsequent studies by Alain Renoir and Donald Fry have demonstrated that the hero need not be on the beach but may also be in a doorway, the essential condition being, according to Renoir, not his specific location but his position, as it were, between two worlds.

In *The Dream of the Rood,* the hero is neither a warrior on the beach nor one in a doorway but rather Christ in the sepulchre:

> Aledon hie ðær limwerigne,   gestodon him
>   æt his lices heafdum,
> beheoldon hie ðær heofenes dryhten,   ond he
>   hine ðær hwile reste.
> meðe æfter ðam miclan gewinne.   Ongun-
>   non him þa moldern wyrcan
> beornas on banan gesyhðe;   curfon hie ðæt
>   of beorhtan stane,
> gesetton   hie   ðæron   sigora   weal-
>   dend.   Ongunnon
>   him þa sorhleoð galan
> earme on þa æfentide,   þa hie woldon eft
>   siðian,
> meðe fram þam mæran þeodne.   Reste he
>   ðær mæte weorode.
>
> (63-69)

Resting as He is between the crucifixion and the resurrection, the Lord is clearly between two worlds, life and death. This rather tenuous connection of the sepulchre to the beach or doorway would hardly be sufficient to justify calling this a "hero on the beach" theme if the remaining elements did not correspond so closely to those isolated by Crowne. Most telling is the presence of the extraneous light in the bright stone of the sepulchre. The retainers are the apostles who remove the body of Christ from the cross and subsequently fashion the grave. Two sets of journeys center around the burial. Christ himself has just journied to the cross to redeem mankind. The apostles have completed one journey to Christ (they came hastening from afar), and they depart on another after singing a dirge for their Lord.

While the "approach to battle" type-scene enhances the *Rood*-poet's presentation of the crucifixion as a battle, the "hero on the beach" theme specifically reflects the heroism of Christ both by emphasizing His position as a warrior-lord and by associating Him once more with the heroic figures of the traditional stories. That the poet should choose to use this theme as the underlying structure for his description of the burial of Christ suggests that the Lord remains a hero even though He is apparently defeated in His battle, and, moreover, since Christ is soon to embark on another journey in His harrowing of hell (*Rood* 148a-156), that His death as man is merely the transition between the two journeys which He is making as God.

The *Rood*-poet's presentation of Christ as a hero valiantly engaging in combat has been severely criticized by Robert Diamond who finds the spirit of the poem inappropriate to the crucifixion and can only attribute the poet's use of heroic language to his being a prisoner of his tradition:

> There are not an infinite number of ways to express an idea in correct verses; there are only the traditional ways. While the poet can rely on the traditional diction to help him out of tight places in composing, he is also caught in the net of tradition, so to speak—he cannot compose in any other way. This applies not only to his actual choice of words, but to the themes and narrative techniques of his work.

Diamond errs, however, in assuming that an Anglo-Saxon formulaic poet treating the subject of the crucifixion had no alternative but to present it as a heroic encounter. Indeed, in the *Christ,* a work roughly contemporary with *The Dream of the Rood,* the Redeemer appears not as a hero but rather as a sacrificial victim.

The descriptions of the crucifixion in *Christ* 1090-1127 and 1428-1468 are strikingly devoid of the heroic material found in the *Rood.* Christ appears only as ruler (1096a) and lord (1108). These titles are so frequently used to refer to God in Anglo-Saxon religious poetry that unless they are surrounded as in *The Dream of the Rood* by a plethora of elements characterizing God as a warrior-lord, they lose their heroic significance entirely. Similarly, the crucifixion in *Christ* is a sacrifice rather than a battle. The cross is merely the holy tree (1093a). On it Christ suffers gloryless body-pain (1429b) and evil affliction (1452a). Moreover, the poet extensively describes the nature of these afflictions, the spectators' mockery of Christ, His being given a drink of vinegar and gall, and the crowning with thorns (1433-1445). Far from being an eager hero, the Redeemer appears as a victim. In both passages, He is hanged upon the cross (1093, 1446); He does not actively climb up onto it as in the *Rood.* He rather than the cross is meek-minded (1442a). Three verbs summarize the activity of Christ; He receives insults ("onfeng," 1436a, 1439a), suffers ("geþolade," 1434b, 1442b; "þolade," 1451b), and endures ("þrowade," 1117b, 1433b). This suffering, passive Lord is the antithesis of the mighty warrior presented by the *Rood*-poet. He is not fighting for mankind, but rather buying (1095b, 1462b) eternal life for man at the price of His own life.

If the tradition which fostered the poets of both *Christ* and *The Dream of the Rood* can permit such disparate descriptions of the crucifixion, the critic must hesitate before attributing the heroic diction of the *Rood* to the tyranny of this tradition. Assuredly the poet's presentation of Christ as a warrior-lord and the crucifixion as a battle strikingly transforms the Gospel narratives. He is not, however, the first to describe the event in heroic terms, for to Saint Paul Christ was not only the sacrificial lamb, but also the "captain of [our] salvation" who took upon Himself flesh and blood so that "through death he might destroy him that had the power of death, that is, the devil" (Hebrews 2.10, 14). Moreover, like Saint Paul, the *Rood*-poet presents Christ as a hero who emerges victorious from the conflict of the crucifixion.

Throughout the crucifixion passage, the *Rood*-poet minimizes the agonies endured by Christ. His transformation of the slayer-cross into a retainer of the Lord emphasizes its aiding Christ in the conflict rather than its being an instrument of His death. Similarly, this speaking cross describes the humiliations and agonies of the crucifixion as he, rather than Christ, endured them. He tells the dreamer that he, not Christ, endured many cruel fates on Calvary (50-51a). Describing the fastening of Christ to the tree, he explains how he himself was pierced with nails (46a). The mockery of the soldiers, the cross says, both he and Christ endured together (48a). When the Lord's side is pierced, the poet concentrates on the blood's covering the cross rather than on the Redeemer's wound (48-49a). While the poet of the *Christ* emphasizes the sacrificial nature of the crucifixion by vividly describing Christ's agonies, the **Rood**-poet attributes these sufferings to the cross, thus minimizing the sacrifice of Christ and preparing the way for his presentation of the crucifixion as a victory.

In his description of the death of Christ, the **Rood**-poet reveals that the apparent defeat of the crucifixion was, in reality, a divine triumph. He has called the crucifixion a conflict ("gewinne," 65a), using a term which in addition to connoting strife and agony can also mean "fruit of labors," "gain," or "profit." When he depicts the death of Christ, the poet presents all creation weeping for the fall of the King (55b-56a); yet he describes the Christ whom the apostles remove from the cross not as dead but rather as weary. He calls Him the limb-weary one (63a), one who is tired (65a), and presents Him as resting both before and after He is actually placed in the sepulchre (64b, 69b). Although such descriptions appear to be typical examples of Anglo-Saxon understatement, their use does permit the suggestion that what in human terms is burial becomes in divine merely repose for a time before the harrowing of hell and the resurrection. The "hero on the beach" theme carries with it, moreover, strong associations of victory. Almost invariably, the journey of the hero is either the prelude or the sequel to a triumph. Accordingly, when the poet uses this theme in his description of the burial of Christ, he reveals once more that the crucifixion which he presents is a glorious triumph rather than a sacrifice. The Christ whom the apostles place in the tomb is truly, as he declares, the ruler of victories (67a).

The Christian's knowledge of Christ's resurrection enables him to perceive that the sufferings and humiliations of the crucifixion are the occasion of Christ's victory over Satan and the death which he first brought into the world. By utilizing the formulaic techniques of Anglo-Saxon heroic poetry to present Christ as a conquering hero, the **Rood**-poet creates a work which embodies this vision of the significance of the crucifixion. In his skillful hands, the heroic and Christian tradition are so united as to produce one of the finest religious poems in the English language.

Edward B. Irving, Jr.   (essay date 1986)

SOURCE: "Crucifixion Witnessed, or Dramatic Interaction in *The Dream of the Rood,*" in *Modes of Interpretation in Old English Literature: Essays in Honour of Stanley B. Greenfield,* Phyllis Rugg Brown, Georgia Ronan Cramp-

ton, Fred C. Robinson, eds., University of Toronto Press, 1986, pp. 101-13.

[*In the following essay, Irving describes the treatment of the Crucifixion from the perspectives of the poem's two main characters, the Dreamer and the Rood.*]

Very few of the countless artistic representations of the Crucifixion in the Middle Ages have the capacity to seize our imaginations like the Old English poem we call **The Dream of the Rood.** Probably it is rivalled only in the visual arts. Other literary attempts in English to express the complex experience of suffering and witnessing that dominates the event seem to fall short of **The Dream of the Rood**'s special intensity. I think specifically of the later religious lyrics where the listener or reader is urged to meditate on the catalogued afflictions of Christ; or the more dramatic renditions where the listener or reader, taken into the scene as spectator or passer-by, is movingly addressed directly by a reproachful Christ from the cross (particularly in the 'O vos omnes' theme), or where pain is inflicted on Christ's passive body by a squad of irritable soldiers (York Crucifixion play) or (a close analogue) literary or dramatic works where the listener or reader is invited to share the helpless agony of Mary on Golgotha—this last often a dialogue between Christ's two natures, with Mary representing the suffering human and the majestic son on the cross the divine.

This essay will explore the process of dramatization and the psychology of the two main characters in the poem, especially in the first half of it, trying to isolate more clearly what, despite many excellent critical attempts, have never yet been quite satisfactorily defined: the operative elements in **The Dream of the Rood**'s massive emotional power. This attempt will not be quite satisfactory either, it goes without saying, but I hope it may advance our understanding and appreciation a small way by taking a slightly different approach; in any encounter with such a masterpiece, that may be worth doing.

From the very beginning of the poem and all the way on to its ending, we can see a clear process under way, a development away from confusion, or even from downright befuddlement, towards clarity, confidence, and certainty. A poem of progressive enlightenment must begin in the dark. It should be noted that this vision-poem starts with total non-vision, the blackness of sleep and midnight, though the enthusiastic tone of the opening lines in itself hints strongly at the prospect of ultimate success.

> Hwæt! Ic swefna cyst   secgan wylle
> h[w]æt me gemætte   to midre nihte,
> syðþan reordberend   reste wunedon.
>
>   (1-3)

Listen to me, I wish to tell the very best of visions, what I dreamed at midnight, when speech-bearers dwelt in their beds.

At once this darkness becomes semi-darkness, the dubious and impeded vision of the subjunctive: 'Þuhte me þæt ic gesawe / syllicre treow' ('it seemed to me that I might have seen a very strange tree'). This subjunctive form of the verb 'to see' later clarifies itself, as the features of the objects seen become more distinct, into the firmer indicatives of lines 14 and 21: 'geseah ic' ('I clearly saw') (giving the perfective prefix 'ge-' full value). There is still much paradox here, of course, since the more plainly the object is seen, the more details are made out, the less its nature seems to be understood.

It is a very strange Tree that the character I will henceforth call simply Dreamer thinks he might have seen, a Tree first perceived as an almost formless upward surge of light and power into the air, becoming some kind of signalling object, a 'beacen,' covered with brightly radiant gold and gems. That Dreamer does not yet know himself what this object is is implied by the very fact that he is at once contrasted with, and feels himself inferior to, certain others who do know—who identify it and show their reverence towards it. Hosts of angels behold it and know it, angels we see only after his (and our) eyes have been steadily guided upward to the cross-beam and then above. The angels thus seem to appear in that 'heavenly' space above the cross-bar where we see them depicted in early Christian art, bending towards or cradling Christ's serene and divine head, while below the cross-beam, in the mortal or 'earthly' space, blood flows from Christ's wounds or his legs may be twisted in pain.

This tree is then a public sight, drawing the attentive gaze of many. Yet it is not the most common kind of public sight that it might at first superficially resemble, the gallows of an ordinary criminal. Like Anglo-Saxon poets elsewhere, Dreamer proceeds in his definition of what he is looking at by first eliminating what the thing is *not*. If it were a mere gallows, it could never be the cynosure of the admiring gaze of the fair and the holy, and of all men and all nature.

But repetition of the word 'syllic' ('strange') in line 13 recalls us to the state of mind of the puzzled Dreamer who cannot view the tree as the rest of the universe apparently does; they know something he does not yet know. The tree's uncomfortable strangeness takes on new meaning through the way it now makes impact on Dreamer (an impact reinforced effectively by the alliteration of 'syllic' and 'synnum'):

> Syllic wæs se sigebeam,   ond ic synnum fah,
> forwundod mid wommum.
>
> (13-14a)

Strange was that potent tree and I stained with sins, desperately wounded with corruptions.

All that we have so far been told is that Dreamer sees the glorious beauty of the tree. Why then, from where, does he get this sudden overwhelming sense of sin? One might call it an abrupt and startling sense of self, as if the object of his vision had turned without warning into a mirror of blinding clarity. It would be much too rational to say flatly that he thinks along such lines as these: 'Because I'm not able to *see* what those angels are obviously looking at, since I don't know what it can be, I must be stained and sick with sin.' But that connection of ideas must be some part of it. Part of it too is his apparent intuition that beneath all that gold and glory is hidden something uglier, blood and wounds like his own, an ugliness he seems to sense the presence of even before we are told that he actu-

ally sees it. I am fumbling without much success after something important here. Perhaps Dreamer's puzzlement, and insight, and the flickering ambivalence of what he is straining so hard to see clearly (yet perhaps also resisting the implications of) are all better reflected in strictly poetic form resistant to paraphrase: for example, in pun-like turns on words and paradoxical echoes that bring out both positive and negative meanings, in 'fah' ('bright-coloured') and 'fag' ('marked with evil'), or in 'bewunden' ('wound about, adorned') and 'forwundod' ('desperately wounded'). Despite the difficulties of vision, or because of the effort they demand, or because of Dreamer's new self-knowledge, it is at this point, as I remarked earlier, that he shifts fully into the indicative and can analyse with more assurance the mysteries before him, or at least take them more firmly into his range of vision.

He looks hard at the object. He sees a tree of glory, covered with *clothing* (can it then be a human figure, somehow?), shining with joys (emotionally electrifying and positive), drenched in the light and jewels of honour and reverence. Words wrenched slightly askew from their expected meanings (like 'wædum,' 'clothing') keep telling us that this is a riddle-object before us, and that there are rules to the guessing-game one must play in identifying it. One rule is that the object is not to be called by its proper name, Rood, until the Rood itself, in lofty heroic style, names itself proudly, at the very moment when it ceases entirely to be a forest-tree and rises symbolically to become a cross, The Cross: 'Rod wæs ic aræred' ('Rood was I raised up' 44). It reminds us of how, at the appropriate stage in his advance into Denmark to take on the task of fighting the monster Grendel, another riddling heroic figure proclaims his identity: 'Beowulf is min nama' (*Beowulf* 343).

Now, though still far from being able to guess the riddle, Dreamer peers and scrutinizes anxiously, and not altogether in vain. His vision penetrates some distance.

> Gimmas hæfdon
> bewrigene weorðlice   weald[end]es treow.
> Hwæðre ic þurh þæt gold   ongytan meahte
> earmra ærgewin,   þæt hit ærest ongan
> swætan on þa swiðran healfe.
>
> (16b-20a)

Jewels had covered beautifully the tree of the ruler. But still I could perceive *through* that gold the ancient agony of wretched men, could perceive that it first began to bleed on the right side.

Dreamer speaks almost as if he had solved the riddle, breaking through a deceptive façade (jewels) to the bitter and ugly truth within. Not only does he seem to see through this mask of outward beauty in space, he seems also to peer back through time to some past history of suffering, as if the very past began to betray itself by bleeding, at the very moment when he saw it. The intense effort of perception has its immediate effect. His intuition forces him to confront himself in this glimpse of blood and agony. He is now, as he must be, paradoxically terrified of the beautiful sight: 'forht ic wæs for þære fægran gesyhðe' (21a).

Yet at this point he must stop. Without other help, he can see no more and can go no further in understanding either what is in front of him or the obscure emotions seething inside him. He can only lie passively watching the glimmering rapid transmutations of the lovely/hideous riddle-object before him: its changing of clothes and colours (hinting, though Dreamer does not yet know this, at Christ's garments, bruised skin, streaming blood); its abrupt shift from being soaked in blood-wetness to gleaming with treasure (with perhaps some constant quality of shininess as a common visual ground); its state of being 'fus,' restlessly unstable and always ready to be converted into something else at any moment.

To have the Rood itself (or, to name and personify our second character, Rood himself) furnish the needed help by explaining his own meaning to Dreamer seems to require, theologically speaking, that Dreamer first be in a state of repentance, as Robert Burlin has pointed out, citing the word 'hreowcearig' in line 25 as meaning 'repentant.' Such repentance involves complex feelings: Dreamer's bafflement, and his anxiety about his lack of understanding; his admiration for the Tree's remote and dazzling beauty; his flinching back from what he does partly discover about what is in front of him and what is within him; his silent childlike waiting in hope of some further guidance.

There is a clear and important transition from Dreamer's confused state to the beginning of Rood's autobiographical narrative, one that links the two characters. Rood seems at the outset of his story more than a little like Dreamer, unable to make full sense of the ironies and paradoxes of his own experience—or at least telling his story in a way to give that impression, for Rood always speaks in the present dramatic moment and without retrospective and authoritative understanding of the full meaning of the events in which he participates.

The first lines of Rood's speech place him in a somewhat misleading context:

> Ðæt wæs geara iu,   (ic þæt gyta geman),
> þæt ic wæs aheawen   holtes on ende,
> astyred of stefne minum.
>
>   (28-30a)

> That was very long ago—I still remember it—
> that I was hewn down at the forest's edge,
> moved from my trunk.

The first line is formulaic in an old tradition of heroic poetry. It is reminiscent, for example, of the opening of Beowulf's long speech before his doomed fight with the dragon, where the hero falls back on his early memories to strengthen himself for present action:

> Fela ic giogoðe   guðræsa genæs,
> orleghwila;   ic þæt eall gemon.
>
>   (2426-7)

> I survived many warlike encounters in youth,
> times of fighting. I remember all that.

The associations of such a formula might prepare us to think of Rood as a heroic figure but, as he tells what happened to him, we wonder whether he indeed plays any heroic role at all, for he seems disturbingly passive for a hero, allowing others to cut him down (warriors are 'hewn down' in Old English poetry just as trees are), carry him,

make evil use of him. His history thus is a close parallel to the preceding vision, where the glorious (heroic) Tree as Dreamer sees it is half the time scarred and blurred by marks of defeat and bloody agony. The placing of verbs at the crucial beginnings of verses in lines 30-3 ('astyred,' 'genamon,' 'geworhton,' 'heton,' 'bæron,' 'gefæstnodon') relentlessly stresses the series of brutal actions carried out *on* him, ironically reminding us of the many actions this hero is *not* carrying out himself. When Rood at last sees Christ approaching him to be crucified, the exertion of heroic will is largely transferred from the passive Rood to Christ ('he me wolde on gestigan,' 'he wanted to climb up on me' 34).

But it is important to see that, if Rood begins in some sense from where Dreamer is, there is almost immediately a movement in his case from merely inert passivity towards a tense and deliberate willing of such inaction, a willing so strong as to be a kind of action, as Rood comes to understand the incredible situation in which he has been placed. To the extent (a large extent) that he partakes of the role of hero, he must now endure the hardest fate a hero can suffer: to be blocked completely from taking any action. Action is the natural mode of the hero's being and his essential definition. To be thus blocked from it is to feel great pain. Familiar examples from *Beowulf* are King Hrothgar seething with helpless anger under Grendel's unrelenting attacks on his hall, or Hengest enduring the long winter in a foreign hall, prevented for a time by complex circumstances from avenging his king's death. Rood can neither defend his king nor avenge his death. Worse yet, unimaginably terrible, God his king has ordered him to be an accomplice, chief agent even, in the very torture and murder of God: Rood is given the technical term 'bana' ('bane,' or 'slayer') in line 66. Though Rood now feels this pain, he does not yet fully understand that what he now suffers is the new Christian heroism of the martyr rather than the old Germanic heroism. Literally uprooted Tree—a hero not allowed to be a hero—and figuratively uprooted Dreamer thus share a sense of disorientation.

Such a parallel between Rood and Dreamer seems a compelling one. The way Rood speaks at first shows full sympathy with Dreamer's confusion, as if he were implying something like: 'Even though I myself actually went through this experience, at first I couldn't understand it.' In Dreamer's original vision, the same paradox of blood and glory was laid out in spatial terms, side by side, or so nearly simultaneous as to seem to overlap in time; this is now matched by the more clearly temporal, step-by-step experience of Rood himself. Possibly there is a further parallel to Dreamer's humiliating sense of being stained by sins in Rood's compulsive returning to the topic of what he feels as his 'heroic sin,' that is, his failure to act to protect or avenge his lord. One might imagine Rood saying: 'I too have felt miserably guilty, just as you are feeling now.' Though Rood's narrative now moves rapidly into the heart of mystery, it must not move so rapidly that the merely human Dreamer cannot follow.

Although up till now I have been doggedly insisting on viewing the interaction between these two fictional characters on the level of literal drama and assuming that this level is of primary importance in the poem's effect on its audience, this artificially limited way of looking at the poem is bound to become intolerably strained, for obviously we cannot go on pretending that we really do not know anything about the symbolic (that is, 'real') meaning of the text. This is only to say, to put it in theatrical terms, that the dramatic irony of the scene is too highly developed to be ignored. If Dreamer and Rood do not know—or do not know clearly and fully at this point in the narrative time-line of the poem—we know, although it is not easy to state discursively and explicitly all that we know when we begin to lay out all the complexities the dramatic situation implies within a new and 'proper' framework of theological meaning. What does the Rood stand for? We can enumerate some things: Christ as man, a human sufferer pierced by dark nails and racked by conflicts and doubts; as son (an Isaac type dumbly obedient to the inexplicable demands of a father who seems to have forsaken him); as the innocent Paradisal world of non-human nature (the Tree as Peaceable Kingdom), violated and appalled by man's cruelty and forced, against nature, to torture nature's own creator; as a dignified and proud participant and witness/martyr; as an apostle-preacher giving us the most literally 'inside' version of the Crucifixion we could imagine; as an object-lesson in how this pride and this new kind of heroic achievement can grow precisely out of the enduring of abasement and humiliation. As has come to be generally recognized, making the figure of the Rood represent chiefly the passively suffering human dimension of Christ allows the actual character of Christ who appears in the poem to be one of pure heroic will, in part human courage but chiefly God's intense will to save mankind. Yet the theological information the poem provides is nothing Christians do not already know. In that sense they hardly need the poem. What makes the poem needed is the way it leads to understanding not through ideas but through feelings about ideas as they are acted out in dramatic time. The knowledge we gain must be experiential: like Dreamer and Rood, we come to know through sharing in suffering and suspense.

One chief way the nature, duration, and intensity of Rood's suffering is brought out is by the stylistic feature that is most striking in the first part of Rood's speech (28-73): extraordinarily heavy repetitions of certain words and phrases. Use of so rigorously limited a set of words in itself creates a feeling of psychological entrapment. As part of a spoken utterance, the repetitions vividly imitate the obsessive and reiterative mumblings of a shock-victim. 'I saw . . . but I didn't dare . . . I could have . . . but I didn't . . . I trembled . . . but I couldn't . . . they hurt me . . . but I couldn't hurt them.' Four times in only 13 lines the phrase 'ic ne dorste' (with minor variations) appears; each time it does, we are brought back from some new detail of horror and outrage to the small prison of paralysed action, Rood's tormented inability to take vengeance. Rood's every wish to act is blocked by the stern adversatives of necessity, 'hwæðre,' 'ac,' in a way at least vaguely analogous to the frustration of Dreamer's attempts to seize on the security of a single meaning for his vision of the Tree. However Rood feels, whatever occurs, he must remain fixed in his standing position. He cannot

bow, or break, or use his strength to crush the insolent 'enemies' who torment him and his beloved king. He must always stand fast, his only movement an anguished trembling in resonance with the anguished trembling of the earth itself convulsed in earthquake. The movements that surround Rood emphasize his immobility: Christ hurries to climb up and embrace him; dark nails are driven into him; blood streams down. Only at the end he moves just a little, bowing forward to let the disciples lift Christ's body down from the remorseful clutch of its wretched murderer and most faithful retainer.

Enduring physical and emotional pain is only part of Rood's role in this scene. He must also play the important role of eyewitness. Here again the repetitions are many: not only the 'geseah ic' of lines 33 and 51 and the 'ic þæt eall beheold' of 58, but Rood's showing forth of his deep wounds, still there to be inspected as evidence by Dreamer (here briefly playing the part of doubting Thomas to the resurrected Christ); the witnessing crowd of 'many' who observe Christ's courage in mounting the 'high gallows'; the watch or wake of the mourning disciples over Christ's cooling body; Rood's own witnessing (and this is surely an original detail) of the carving of the sepulchre from 'bright stone.' At all points, the event of the Crucifixion experience must be fully attested and publicly authenticated.

And its implications must be understood. Like Dreamer (as I have been arguing), Rood seems to move gradually towards such understanding, first from frightened passivity to violent conflict and horror, which reaches a climax in lines 46-9 describing the nailing, wounding, mocking, bleeding of Rood and King together, and then on towards summary statement, a stage that may begin in line 50:

> Feala ic on þam beorge   gebiden hæbbe
> wraðra wyrda.   Geseah ic weruda God
> þearle þenian.
>
> (50-52a)

> I have experienced many angry fates on that hill.
> I saw the God of Hosts stretched out in agony.

Such verses suggest at least some small measure of distance from the immediate pain, and a clearer and calmer view of what has been happening. As Rood looks about him in the lines that follow—is now *able* to look about him and beyond his own pain—he sees that darkness has fallen and that all Creation weeps, lamenting the King's fall. We recognize the 'cosmic' setting in which Rood first appeared in Dreamer's vision. Now Rood is able to name Christ for the first time in the poem, seeing and naming this scene as we ourselves see it: 'Crist wæs on rode' ('Christ was on the cross' 56). This same phrase is, incidentally, given special prominence in the runic verses from the poem selected to be carved on the Ruthwell Cross: it appears at the top of the west face. We should recall that that great stone cross is personified; all the passages on it come from Rood's speech.

Now the narrative slows down markedly in pace and intensity. Rood watches gravely as the disciples come to remove, mourn over, and bury Christ's body. Since they fill our field of vision while this goes on, they shift our attention away from Rood's vivid experiences towards what he is watching. After singing their own sorrow-song, the three personified crosses stand alone in a weeping group reminiscent of the three Marys of many pictures of the Crucifixion scene and of the later religious drama. Like Christ, the crosses are then brought to ground and buried; like Christ, Rood undergoes later resurrection and receives great honour. The actions here are spaced out and fewer; feelings are given more leisure for expression. We are moving towards Rood's calm interpretation of his own passionate story and his application of it to Dreamer, as the poem shifts down very noticeably from the intense narrative mode to the discursive and hortatory. Both modes would certainly have seemed equally important to the original poet and audience, but for many modern readers the interesting part of the poem is over at this point. Older editors often tried to jettison the last half as inept later addition or interpolation. But the poem cannot truly be over until Dreamer's questions are concretely answered, the dialogue is completed, and Dreamer's own response to the explanation made to him is registered. And so, point by point, the mysteries of the initial vision are explicitly made clear.

The experience undergone by Rood himself in being first lowered (humiliated, wounded, buried) and then raised to glory is first summarized for Dreamer as a 'personal' experience before it is explicitly extended to the experience of Christ and combined with it:

> On me Bearn Godes
> þrowode hwile.　　Forþan ic þrymfæst nu
> hlifige under heofenum,　　ond ic hælan mæg
> æghwylcne anra　　þara þe him bið egesa to
> me.
>
> (83b-86)

On me God's son suffered for a time, and so now glorious I tower under the heavens, and I can heal everyone who is in awe of me.

Here the Tree we saw in the earlier vision towering towards heaven and worshipped by all Creation reappears, but now we can see and understand why it soars so high—because God's son went so low. The suffering is exactly what brings the glory; there is no way pain can be separated from the splendour that inheres in the Incarnation. The rhythms of the pattern are compelling. I fell, I rose; I was tormented, I am worshipped, with the alliteration strongly marking this contrast of pain and glory in 'þrowode'/'þrymfæst' (84) and in 'leodum laðost'/'lifes weg' (88). The wounded and bewildered Rood has now become, despite and because of his own suffering, a healer and a guide for all men who seek him, enlightened and able to give enlightenment through his own ordeal. He makes his final reference to his natural origin in the forest in a crucial identification of himself with Mary, the natural member of the race of women who was, like him, elected by God to be 'theotokos,' God-bearer. Three strong epithets for God ('wuldres, Ealdor,' 'heofonrices Weard,' 'ælmihtig God') are massed in the sentence to emphasize the divine power that fused itself with these two earthly beings, woman and tree, in the Incarnation and in the Crucifixion.

The parallel with Mary seems to bring the Rood down closer to the world of men. Certainly for the rest of his speech his attention is entirely human-directed. Dreamer is instructed to describe the vision he has had to men and to identify to them the object of his vision ('þæt hit is wuldres beam,' 'that it is the tree of glory' 97) in explicit terms. God suffered on the rood expressly for the many sins of 'manncyn' and of Adam (98-100). God rose from death to help men, and he will return on Doomsday to seek mankind. He will search out and he will find each individual man on that day. Then the normal response of each person will be fear, exactly like—now we understand it!—the fear felt by Dreamer in the vision as he became conscious that his sins were exposed to God's view. In the new context we see such anxiety as an experience all must go through. Yet the scene of Judgment is put in consoling terms. Such fear is not to be feared. There will be no person there who will not be afraid, because every man was afraid to volunteer to die on the Cross. Against this background, the Rood's courage stands out absolutely. He has managed to transcend and vanquish the fear inherent in all ordinary beings, and has thus now become the true source of courage for all, worn as a crucifix on each man's breast at Judgment Day. Every soul can seek heaven through that symbol. The whole immense story, as in *Paradise Lost,* has now been internalized. Cosmic narrative and myth are contracted into one small but all-powerful talisman, the Rood as the Key to the Kingdom.

Dreamer's final lines can best be seen, in contrast with his profound disorientation at the opening, as a new orientation, a repointing and redirection of himself. As God's (and the Rood's) full attention is now blazingly directed upon the Dreamer, he is at once pulled magnetically towards the Rood, and continues to point towards it:

> Gebæd ic me þa to þan beame　　bliðe mode,
> elne mycle,　　þær ic ana wæs
> mæte werede.　　Wæs modsefa
> afysed on forðwege;　　feala ealra gebad
> langunghwila.
>
> (122-126a)

I prayed earnestly towards that tree with happy heart and great zeal, where I was alone with a tiny band. My mind was ready for the journey outward; I had lived through a great many times of misery.

It should be noted that Dreamer not only prays to and towards Rood but he is also 'imitating,' that is, he is using language that recalls Rood's story. The body of Christ was also abandoned by its friends, as Dreamer says he is, and left 'with a tiny band' (69); Rood too told us what he had lived through ('gebiden' 79). Dreamer is now intent on seeking the fulfilment of his life's hope in the 'sigebeam' and realizes that his protection depends entirely on the Rood ('geriht to þære rode' 131). His friends having already passed on to heaven, Dreamer waits for the time his friend Rood will return in reality, not merely in the mists of dream as before, and will bring him back to the great feast in God's hall. By viewing the Rood as rescuer, the Dreamer can place himself appropriately among those fabled waiters-in-hell, the Old Testament patriarchs who expect the arrival of Christ on the great day of the Harrowing of Hell. To those so long in burning and darkness (and Dreamer's painful experience during his vision may include him among these), the heroic Son appears to open up hell and lead them all in triumph back to his native land. That same young hero Rood once saw hastening fearlessly towards his execution is now the young king assuming his birthright in his own kingdom and sharing that birthright in glory with his ecstatic followers. All the elements of the initial vision are now in place and fully lighted. The poem ends here on a satisfactorily resolving chord.

I have tried to show that **The Dream of the Rood** differs from the common medieval lecture-dialogue of Platonic ancestry (Lady Philosophy explaining the universe to the prisoner Boethius, or Beatrice instructing Dante, or—in parody—the Eagle suffocating the hapless Chaucer in verbiage in *The House of Fame*) in that the lecturer is entitled to speak with ultimate authority only when he has first shared with his listener similar acute bewilderment and pain. In this poem the essential experience, the Crucifixion, is thus seen from two angles that meet in a single image of unparalleled spiritual and psychological richness.

Monica Brzezinski   (essay date 1988)

SOURCE: "The Harrowing of Hell, the Last Judgment, and *The Dream of the Rood*," in *Neuphilologische Mitteilungen: Bulletin de la Société Néophilologique*, Vol. LXXXIX, No. 3, 1988, pp. 252-65.

[Below, Brzezinski contends that the last few lines of The Dream of the Rood *refer to the Last Judgment rather than to the Harrowing of Hell.]*

The narrative structure of **The Dream of the Rood** has been described as a Chinese box-like arrangement in which the Dreamer's first-person report of his vision frames the speech of the Rood, which in turn encloses a description of the passion of Christ. This neat equation of the **Dream**'s structure with that of a Russian doll is, however, inadequate, as it neglects the concluding lines of the poem: the nested narratives are followed by a puzzling eight-and-a-half line coda which has been traditionally identified as "a brief and oblique allusion to the Harrowing of Hell." The interpretation of this passage as the Harrowing of Hell has presented a major obstacle to seeing **The Dream of the Rood** as a unified whole, an obstacle so great that some critics have termed the coda a later addition to the original poem, following [Albert S.] Cook's suggestion [in *The Dream of the Rood: An Old English Poem Attributed to Cynewulf,* 1905] that the last section "has either come here by accident, or that the poet's judgment was at fault. The poem should have ended with 148a, or perhaps better with 146." While more recent critics have judged the coda to be part of the original poem, and indeed integral to its meaning, they have not been able to define precisely what function the reference to the Harrowing performs in the poem as a whole. [J.A.] Burrow ["An Approach to *The Dream of the Rood*," *Neophilologus* 43 (1959)] sees the Harrowing as "an amplification of Christ's 'releasing power' " and "convincing in the general economy of the poem." [John V.] Fleming

concurs [in *"The Dream of the Rood* and Anglo-Saxon Monasticism", *Traditio* 22 (1966)], fitting the end of the poem into the "thematic unity" of the whole. [N.A.] Lee speaks eloquently [in his "The Unity of *The Dream of the Rood,"* *Neophilologus* 56 (1972)] for the unity of the **Dream,** but is not sure what lines 151b-156 refer to, and thus leaves "the interpretation of the remaining lines open for the present." Such attempts to argue for the unity of the poem, while well meant, are too general to convincingly include the coda in the overall structure of the poem. We are left with the questions any critic begins with: Why does the reference to the Harrowing occur here, at the end of the poem, and not where one might expect it, within the Rood's speech? Why does the poet not follow Cook's suggestion and end the poem at line 146, with the Dreamer's prophetic vision of eternal bliss? And why, instead of ending with this vision, as would seem appropriate, do we instead conclude with this flashback to Christ's life? By placing the "Harrowing of Hell" episode at the end of the poem, the poet has created a flaw in the chronological order of the poem, a warp in the temporal structure. I suggest that this time-warp was intended by the poet, and furthermore that **The Dream of the Rood**'s coda refers not to one event in salvation history, but to several; in addition, its main reference is not to the Harrowing of Hell, but to the Last Judgment. It alludes as well to the Harrowing, and to Adam's fall, and to the Ascension, and through these multiple references it acts as a frame for the entire poem, positioning the events described in the Dreamer's account within the larger frame of salvation history by pointing to both the beginning and to the end of temporal existence. By its multiple references, the coda also acts as a contrast to the chronological structure of the first 148 lines, in which events in salvation history are told in the order in which they occured in time. By contrasting two different narrative techniques, the chronological narrative of the major part of the poem with the "oblique" narrative of the coda, the poet compares two views of time, man's and God's.

While the last lines of the **Dream** traditionally have been interpreted, with some disagreement, as referring to the Harrowing of Hell, there is no firm evidence for this identification. There is no specific reference to Hell nor to a prison in which the devil keeps souls; there is no mention of Old Testament patriarchs who are allowed to enter heaven as a result of Christ's victory at the Crucifixion. The coda speaks of *þam-þe þær bryne þolodan* "those who there endured fire" (l. 149) and says of Christ that *þa he mid manigeo com, / gasta weorode, on godes rice* "then he came with many, with a company of souls, into God's realm" (ll. 151b-52), and therefore does bear some resemblance to traditional descriptions of the Harrowing. But while the **Dream**'s description does have these points in common with the traditional story, there is one major point at which the poem's version of the "Harrowing" departs from tradition. The primary importance of the Harrowing was that it was the first occasion when the Gates of Heaven were open to men, having been closed against mankind since Adam had fallen. The souls of the just who died before Christ's redemptive act were compelled to wait for Him before they could enter heaven, either in Hell itself or in Limbo. Yet the **Dream** portrays a number of saints already dwelling in heaven who are on hand to greet Christ on His triumphal entry. Christ's entrance acts as:

> . . . englum to blisse,
> ond eallum ðam halgum þam-þe on heofonum
> ær
> wunedon on wuldre, . . .
>
> (ll. 153b-54a)

If saints *ær wunedon on wuldre* "formerly dwelt in glory," the coda of *The Dream of the Rood* cannot refer literally and primarily to the Harrowing of Hell, as at that time only God and His angels lived in the eternal paradise. Lee recognizes this problem and attempts to solve it by saying *eallum ðam halgum* refers to the two Old Testament figures, Enoch and Elijah, who meet Christ on His return to heaven after the Harrowing in the Gospel of Nichodemus, Chapter IX; never having died, they are not subject to captivity by the devil and are permitted into heaven. [Robert Emmet] Finnegan more recently has suggested a similar solution [in "*The Gospel of Nicodemus* and *The Dream of the Rood*," *Neuphilologische Mitteilungen* 84 (1983)], stating that the phrase refers to the two patriarchs and to the Good Thief as well, since these three figures greet Christ in the Gospel of Nicodemus. Lee, however, admits that *eallum ðam halgum* is "rather an over-enthusiastic way" of referring to the two men (or even to three), and as an alternative suggests that *halgum* does not refer to saints at all, but to "holy spirits," i. e., to angels. It would seem, however, that this is not the case, as angels are specifically referred to in their own right, and *eallum ðam halgum* does not seem to be a variation on *englum*. As [A.D.] Horgan has recently pointed out [in his "*The Dream of the Rood* and Christian Tradition," *Neuphilologische Mitteilungen* 79 (1978)] in questioning the reference of *eallum,* the presence of *and* rules out the possibility of variation. The passage is thus a clear description of many saints on hand to welcome Christ back to heaven, and cannot refer to the Harrowing.

Because these lines in the coda cannot refer to the Harrowing of Hell, I suggest that the same details which seem to point toward the Harrowing in fact refer to another primary event in salvation history which has already been shown to be central to any understanding of the poem: the Last Judgment. A number of critics have concluded that an apocalyptic vision informs the whole poem and especially the concluding lines. Fleming, for example, says that the "whole poem reverberates with eschatological echoes," and [Fay] Patton ["Structure and Meaning in *The Dream of the Rood*," *English Studies* 49 (1968)] believes that in the last lines "the cross is associated with heaven and the Last Judgment." Lee, in a detailed study, analyzes the importance of the Last Judgment theme to the poem as a whole, showing that the Crucifixion and Last Judgment are connected with each other in the service of the Adoration of the Cross of Good Friday, specifically in an invocation that appears in the *Regularis Concordia;* there the Crucifixion is associated with the Deposition in the Tomb, the Harrowing of Hell, the Resurrection and Ascension, and finally with the Second Coming. Lee finds additional connections between the Last Judgment and the Crucifixion in the liturgy for two feasts associated with the Cross, the Invention of the Cross and the Exaltation of the Cross, in homiletic literature, in other Anglo-Saxon poems, and in iconography, as in the Ruthwell Cross. He concludes that the connection between Christ's death and "seeming defeat" at the Crucifixion and His final "actual victory" at the Last Judgment is a natural one. While Lee's work focuses on the central portion of the poem, Payne has demonstrated that the opening scenes of the **Dream,** the Dreamer's first vision of the Rood's approach, is in fact a vision of the approach of the Last Judgment, described with motifs borrowed from traditional depictions of the last days, such as that by Ephraem the Syrian. [Richard C.] Payne further suggests [in his "Convention and Originality in the Vision Framework of *The Dream of the Rood*," *Modern Philology* 73 (1976)] that the key to the meaning of **The Dream of the Rood** is not the Crucifixion scene, as has been traditionally thought, but instead the first scene, the Last Judgment.

Payne's suggestion appears to be well-founded. The theme of the Last Judgment is central to the meaning of the poem, which opens with one judgment scene and has another in the middle (ll. 103b-21). I suggest that there is in addition a third depiction of the Last Judgment in the poem, in the last eight-and-a-half lines. The three judgment scenes together create one unified movement within the poem. **The Dream of the Rood** opens with the Dreamer fearful for the state of his soul in the face of approaching judgment heralded by the Rood; it is in this fear that he imagines the horror of the Last Judgment as described in the middle section of the poem. This horror is described not in terms of his own individual fear, but rather in terms of the fear of any man at Doomsday: *Ac hie þonne forhtiaþ ond fea þencaþ / hwæt hie to Criste cweðan onginnen* "But they then fear, and little think of what they might begin to say to Christ" (ll. 115-16). But as soon as the Rood comforts the Dreamer by telling him that anyone who trusts in the Cross has little to fear, his terror is gone and instead he looks forward to death. Immediately after the Rood finishes speaking, he prays to it *bliðe mode* and then imagines, not the dread of Doomsday, but the joy of his own arrival in heaven at the end of his life:

> . . . ond ic wene me
> daga gehwylce hwænne me dryhtnes rod,
> þe ic her on eorðan ær sceawode,
> on þysson lænan life gefetige
> ond me þonne gebringe þær is blis mycel,
> dream on heofonum, þær is dryhtnes folc
> geseted to symle, þær is singal blis,
> ond me þonne asette þær ic syþþan mot
> wunian on wuldre, well mid þam halgum
> dreames brucan . . .
>
> (ll. 135b-44a)

Thus comforted and assured of his own salvation, the Dreamer in his last description of Judgment presents, not Judgment itself, but its results for those like himself who have already merited salvation and who have been admitted to heaven at their death. Reunited with their bodies at Judgment, they now re-enter heaven with Christ to enjoy unending bliss. The Dreamer's description in the coda of saints who *ær wunedon on wuldre* (ll. 154b-55) is virtually a repetition of his prior description of his own arrival in heaven, where he might *wunian on wuldre, well mid þam halgum mid þam halgum* (l. 143). The verbal repetition would seem to show that the Dreamer includes himself in the number of those saints who "dwelled already in glory." Because the Last Judgment for him and for his fellow saints is simply a break in their eternal bliss, he does not fear it, and thus he does not describe it; instead his description of the Last Judgment in the coda focuses on the triumph of Christ and His saints.

There are several objections to the suggestion that the last lines of *The Dream of the Rood* refer not to the triumph of Christ at the Harrowing of Hell but to His final triumph at the Last Judgment; the most obvious objection is that there is no actual judgment described in these lines. Yet while there is no explicit mention of any judgment here, there is no real need for one. The judging itself has already been described in the poem, in the middle section dealing with the Last Judgment, when Christ appears and questions the assembled masses concerning their lives. The third and last description of Judgment is a continuation of that action, and thus the actual judging need not be described again. In addition, by omitting the actual judging from the description in the coda, the poet is following a tradition which holds that there will be no judgment in the last days for those who have already been pronounced as just; the decision regarding a soul's consignment to either heaven or hell at the time of his death is a final one which will not be overturned at the end of the world. Accordingly, those admitted into heaven at the time of their particular judgment will not be included in the general, or Last, Judgment.

Augustine, in *De Civitate Dei,* Book XX, discusses the Last Judgment and various traditional beliefs concerning it in great detail. Before dealing expressly with the Last Judgment, he differentiates between the particular judgment God makes concerning each man, either during his life or at the moment of his death, and the general judgment that will occur at the end of the world:

> Iudicat etiam non solum universaliter de genere daemonum atque hominum, ut miseri sint propter primorum meritum peccatorum, sed etiam de singulorum operibus propriis quae gerunt arbitrio voluntatis . . . et homines plerumque aperte, semper occulte, luunt pro suis factis divinitus poenas sive in hac vita sive post mortem . . . Non igitur in hoc libro de illis primis nec de istis mediis Dei iudiciis, sed de ipso novissimo, quantum ipse tribuerit, disputabo, quando Christus de caelo venturus est vivos iudicaturus et mortuos.

Augustine then goes on to explain that those who have proved themselves in this life to be among the just will not take part in the Last Judgment, for that judgment is reserved for those condemned to eternal punishment. While the condemned will rise from the dead at the end of the world for judgment, the just need not do this because they have already been resurrected metaphorically in this life from the death of sin to a life of grace in Christ. Augustine develops his argument as a commentary on John 5:27-29:

> Ac deinde subiungens unde agimus: "Nolite," inquit, "mirari hoc, quia veniet hora in qua omnes qui in monumentis sunt audient vocem

eius et procedent, qui bona fecerunt in resurrectionem vitae, qui vero mala egerunt in resurrectionem iudicii." Hoc est illud iudicium quod paulo ante, sicut nunc, pro damnatione posuerat dicens: "Qui verbum meum audit et credit ei qui misit me habet vitam aeternam et in iudicium non veniet, sed transiit a morte in vitam," id est, pertinendo ad primam resurrectionem, qua nunc transitur a morte ad vitam, in damnationem non veniet, quam significavit appellatione iudicii, sicut etiam hoc loco ubi ait: "Qui vero mala egerunt in resurrectionem iudicii," id est damnationis. Resurgat ergo in prima qui non vult in seconda resurrectione damnari.

The Dreamer in *The Dream of the Rood* appears to be a textbook case of one such as Augustine describes, one who has risen from sin to life by putting his faith in God or, as in the poem, specifically in the Cross. The Dreamer's moment of particular judgment in this life is that described in the poem; it is the moment in which the Rood approaches him and speaks to him of Christ's death, resurrection, and Last Judgment. The question that the Rood puts in Christ's mouth at the Judgment is not just a rhetorical question but is rather the question which the Rood, as Judge, puts to the Dreamer:

> Frineð he for þære mænige hwær se man sie,
> se ðe for dryhtnes naman deaðes wolde
> biteres onbyrigan, swa he ær on þam became
>   dyde.
> Ac hie þonne forhtiaþ, and fea þencaþ
> hwæt hie to Criste cweðan onginnen.
> Ne þearf ðær þonne ænig anforht wesan
> þe him ær in breostum bereð beacna selest
>   (ll. 112-18)

While the Dreamer is imagining the Last Judgment, the moment is for him one of particular judgment: is he that man who would taste death for the Lord's name? Apparently he is; he also bears the best of signs on his breast. For it is clear that after this moment of judgment the Dreamer is no longer fearful of the Rood but instead finds all of his joy in it: *Is me nu lifes hyht / þæt ic þone sigebeam secan mote* (ll. 126b-27). Having placed his trust in the Rood and so having risen to everlasting life, he is confident that he will not be among those condemned at the Last Judgment.

The poet's emphasis on particular judgment rather than on the Last Judgment itself is not unusual in Old English poetry. [Graham D.] Caie, in his study *The Judgment Day Theme in Old English Poetry,* points out that in many Old English poems ostensibly dealing with the Last Judgment there is no scene describing the actual judging. Instead, the poems use the general context and metaphors of the Last Judgment to make the point that a man's fate depends not so much on the outcome of the Last Judgment as on the morality of his deeds, so that the act of judgment is not the operation of a single day but rather a "continual process during life." Caie's analysis of *Christ III* is especially relevant to a discussion of *The Dream of the Rood,* for the two poems share a number of important parallels: both open with the advent of the Last Judgment, which comes to surprise men asleep at midnight, and (as I argue) end with a scene of the Last Judgment which contains no actual description of judging. Caie observes, "The most interesting aspect of the poem is that, as is mentioned before (and in other Judgment poems), there is no actual judgment, no weighing of the souls and consultation in ledgers. For the judgment has already taken place and is taking place, the poet implies, in the present moment." This emphasis on the present moment would seem to be another parallel that *Christ III* shares with **The Dream of the Rood.** In the **Dream,** the focus of the whole poem, including the Rood's speech and its detailing of the Passion as well as the three Last Judgment scenes, is on the Dreamer and for his benefit. He must realize that the power of condemnation lies not with Christ nor with the Rood, but in himself. That one's fate is self-determined by one's actions is also shown in the middle Judgment scene in the **Dream.** Here too there is no actual judgment represented. Instead, Christ asks a question: He does not condemn but asks men, in the passage quoted above (ll. 112-18) if they will follow His example in their own actions. Their fate depends not on Christ's pronouncements but on their own deeds.

While Old English poetry does not describe the Last Judgment in terms of judging, the poems usually do employ a number of common motifs to depict the event, one of which is prominent in the last lines of **The Dream of the Rood:** the function of fire at the Last Judgment. While there are different traditions for representing the last days—and the **Dream** employs several of those traditions—almost all of them make use of the fire motif. Fire was one of the "Signs of Doom" which would herald the end of the world and the Second Coming of Christ; as one of the Signs of Doom it can be found in the psalms, the prophets, the New Testament, and of course in Revelation. But in the Old English tradition, fire would not only be a sign of the approach of Judgment Day, but it would also be the means through which judgment would be accomplished. Fire coming down from heaven would at once be the agent of punishment for the wicked, akin to the fires of hell, yet would also be a purifying agent to perfect the just—a purgatorial fire. It would cleanse the righteous yet flawed so that they would be worthy of eternal life. Augustine in his discussion of the Last Judgment develops the idea of a purifying fire in his commentary on Malachi 3:1-6:

> Ex his quae dicta sunt videtur evidentius apparere in illo iudicio quasdam quorundam purgatorias poenas futuras. Ubi enim dicitur: "Quis sustinebit diem introitus eius, aut quis ferre poterit, ut aspiciat eum? Quia ipse ingreditur quasi ignis conflatorii et quasi herba lavantium; et sedebit conflans et emundans sicut argentum et sicut aurum" . . . Nisi forte sic eos dicendum est emundari a sordibus et eliquari quodam modo, cum ab eis mali per poenale iudicium separantur, ut illorum segregatio atque damnatio purgatio sit istorum, quia sine talium de cetero permixtione victuri sunt. Sed cum dicit: "Et emundabit filios Levi et fundet eos sicut aurum et argentum; et erunt Domino offerentes hostias in iustitia, et placebit Domino sacrificium Iudae et Hierusalem," utique ostendit eos ipsos qui emundabuntur deinceps in sacrificiis iustitiae Domino esse placituros. . . . Filios autem Levi

et Iudam et Hierusalem ipsam Dei ecclesiam debemus accipere . . . qualis tunc erit . . . eis quoque igne mundatis quibus talis mundatio necessaria est, ita ut nullus omnino sit qui offerat sacrificium pro peccatis suis.

The motif of fire as purifying agent appears to be a popular one in Old English poetry. In many poems the fire of Doomsday has a dual function, punishing the damned and purifying the saved. In *Judgment Day II,* for example, the fire that burns on the last day appears to fulfill both these functions at the same time, so that, as Augustine explained, the purification is actually a punishment:

> ne se wrecenda bryne wile forbugan
> oððe ænigum þær are gefremman,
> buton he horwum sy her afeormad,
> and þonne þider cume, þearle aclænsed.
> (ll. 155-58)

This same motif of fire acting as an agent both of purification and of punishment also seems to be found in **The Dream of the Rood,** in the coda which follows the Dreamer's description of his joy in heaven after his death. After the Dreamer has described his arrival in heaven and the *singal blis* (l. 141) of the feast of the "Lord's folk," the poem shifts into its enigmatic last lines with the reference to fire:

> . . . Hiht wæs geniwad
> mid bledum ond mid blisse þam-þe þær bryne
> þolodan.
> (ll. 148b-49)

While the reference to "those who endured the fire there" has usually been interpreted, following Cook, as an allusion to "the spirits in prison who were released by the Harrowing of Hell," these lines contain a clue that this is not the real reference. The poet states that "bliss is *renewed*" for those who endured the fire. Yet the souls of the just consigned to Hell to wait for Christ had never experienced bliss; their first entry into heaven at the Harrowing is not a "renewal" at all but their first experience of the heavenly feast. The lines must therefore refer to souls which had previously experienced the beatific vision, then suffered in flames, and then been granted re-entry into the presence of God in heaven. These would then be the souls of the just admitted to heaven on the basis of their particular judgment, who then are re-united with their bodies at the Last Judgment. At that time both bodies and souls experience a final cleansing in purgatorial fire, and now being perfect re-enter heaven together with a triumphant Christ who has vanquished His demonic foe forever. The Dreamer imagines himself to be one of these privileged souls who endure the flames for a moment in order to become perfect. He does not dwell on the flames, any pain they may cause, or the imperfections they do away with, for these are not his concerns; rather his theme is the triumph of Christ along with His Church, and so the poet's emphasis is on Christ's triumphal mission.

The reference to the Last Judgment in the coda of **The Dream of the Rood** creates several complex temporal relationships within the poem which together work to bind it into a unified whole. On a purely literal level, this description of the Last Judgment is a simple continuation of the previous narrative. The Dreamer has completed the section of the poem in which he contemplates the state of his own soul by looking forward to his own reward in heaven. His inmost thoughts are *afysed on forðwege* (l. 125) and he looks forward in happy expectation to the time when the Rood will carry him off to dwell in glory. He caps his expectations with a description of the joys that he expects to partake of in heaven. Thus it is only in keeping with this chronological structure that the Dreamer's mind should look forward beyond his own death and reward to a time still further in the future in which he will be one of the saints present at Christ's triumphant return from His final victory. Because at this time the Dreamer will be just one of many saints united in the Communion of the Blessed, he describes this final triumph in an objective third-person, and not in the emotional first-person style of the rest of the poem. The reward here is not a personal one for his deeds as an individual, as it was after his particular judgment, but instead reflects on the glory of Christ united with all His saints. Thus the Dreamer does not appear here as an individual at all, but as one of many. As the logical fulfillment to the Dreamer's moment of particular judgment in the poem, and as a reference to the last event in salvation history, the Last Judgment is a fitting ending to the poem.

The use of the Last Judgment as the ending point of the poem also creates a frame for the whole of *The Dream of the Rood,* for this passage is parallel to and yet thematically different from the opening passage of the poem. That opening scene, in which the Rood first appears to the Dreamer, is, as Payne has shown, a vision of the approach of the Last Judgment; many of the motifs here, including the presence of adoring angels, are used in descriptions of the Last Judgment. The motif of the Rood itself, a cross extending into the air and covered with jewels and blood, is used in representations of the Judgment by other Old English poets, who picture a gigantic cross covered with blood and gore but still shining magnificently. The fact that the Dreamer's vision of the Rood is a signal of the Second Coming would explain his terror at the sign of the cross; he is not merely awed but thoroughly frightened, and for the specific reason that he is intensely aware of his own sinfulness: *Eall ic waes mid sorgum gedrefed; / forht ic wæs for þære fægran gesyhðe* (ll. 20b-21a) Clearly his state of terror is the same as that of those who in the Rood's description of Doomsday fear the word of the Lord (l. 111); he is afraid that the Second Coming has arrived to find him unfit for eternal life. But while the Dreamer's terror of Judgment parallels that of the damned in the Rood's speech, it is remarkably different from the bliss and joy with which he describes that same event in the coda. Leiter posits a number of tranformations in the poem—of the Rood from gallows to sign of victory; of Christ from defeated criminal to victorious hero; of the Dreamer from fallen Adam to a triumphant follower of Christ—but the major transformation is the change in the Dreamer's attitude toward the last days; he no longer fears damnation, for the Rood has come to tell him that, despite his sins, he will be saved if he *in breostum bereþ beacna selest* (l. 118). *The Dream of the Rood* fittingly ends where it began, with the Dreamer's fears for his own soul, but with those fears having been put to rest.

While the coda section has these narrative and thematic connections to the beginning and end of the "nested narratives" of the Dreamer's vision and the Rood's speech, it also contains within itself an even more complex set of temporal relationships. By referring to the Last Judgment, these lines point to the end of temporal existence. But the lines are ambiguous; they can also be interpreted as referring to several other events in salvation history. It is not without reason that they have been traditionally interpreted as referring to the Harrowing of Hell and that Fleming sees them as an allusion to the Ascension; these three events had usually been grouped together by Biblical exegetes as similar manifestations of Christ's power over the forces of sin and death. Through these ambiguous references to Christ's saving power, the poet has also created a reference to the time of Adam, the beginning of temporality, when Adam's fall created the necessity for salvation. The fall of Adam was especially connected with the Harrowing in tradition, for Christ at that time paid forever the wages due to the devil for original sin. The *Gospel of Nicodemus* illustrates the relationship between the two events by showing Adam as the first of the Old Testament figures to follow Christ out of Hell:

> Et extendens Dominus manum suam fecit signum crucis super Adam et super omnes sanctos suos, et tenens dexteram Adae ascendit ab inferis et omnes sancti secuti sunt Dominum.

and into Heaven:

> Dominus autem tenens manum Adae tradidit Michaeli archangelo, et omnes sancti sequebantur Michaelim archangelum, et introduxit omnes in paradysi gratiam gloriosam.

Thus by making this section purposefully ambiguous so that it can refer at once to the Last Judgment and to Adam's fall, the poet is able to refer at the same time to the two limits of temporal existence and to the central event of salvation history, Christ's redemption of mankind from Hell at the Harrowing. In a few economical lines he is able to sum up the important events of salvation: man's fall into sin, his redemption from punishment, and his final reward.

The economical narrative technique of the coda starkly contrasts with the expanding technique used in the main section of the poem. The Dreamer's momentary vision opens up to include the Rood's "biography," which in turn opens up to include a description of the Passion, Resurrection, and Ascension, and a prophecy of the Second Coming. Through this structural technique of embedding the poet shows that the story of the Rood and the life of Christ are central to the Dreamer's experience; they are at the center of the poem and are also central in importance. The Dreamer's life contains all of the elements of salvation history described by the Rood, in the sense that he has been directly influenced by them: through his participation in original sin he is prey to individual failings; he is saved by Christ's death but must undergo an individual judgment and a general purification before he can enter the reopened paradise. As the main portion of the poem is directed at the Dreamer, its purpose is homiletic. Its expanding structure is designed to drive home the point that the Dreamer need not fear the Last Judgment if he has faith in the Cross. The Rood's speech and the Passion narrative are embedded within the Dreamer's visionary experience; in this way the Dreamer's life is expanded to show how even a single moment in his life partakes of the entire expanse of salvation history.

The expanding structure of the poem, however, is quickly overturned once we get to the coda. Here the poem collapses in on itself; time, instead of expanding, becomes a vortex in which events separated by millenia seem to occur simultaneously. There is no longer any specific point in time to which we may refer, only a melange of past, present, and future expectation. The individual life of the Dreamer is no longer celebrated but is absorbed into the shared eternal reward of nameless saints. As such, the coda attempts to create the impression of the beatific vision. We view time not as man sees it, linearly, horizontally, but perhaps as God sees it—all of earthly time is a mere eight lines within the limitlessness of eternity, an infinity which frames temporal existence in the same way that the descriptions of the Last Judgment frame the **Dream** and yet remain at its heart. While the first 148 lines are a vision of time, the last eight are a vision of timelessness. Uniting time and infinity, past and future, expectation and reward, is the figure of the Rood. Just as the Rood's speech acts as intermediary between the Dream's consciousness and the Passion of Christ, it also acts as intermediary between time and eternity, as the herald of the end of the ages and the beginning of agelessness.

FURTHER READING

Bolton, W. F. "The *Book of Job* in *The Dream of the Rood*." *Mediaevalia: A Journal of Medieval Studies* 6 (1980): 87-103.
   Compares the themes and imagery in *The Dream of the Rood* with those found in the *Book of Job*.

Burlin, Robert B. "The Ruthwell Cross, *The Dream of the Rood* and the Vita Contemplativa." *Studies in Philology* LXV, No. 1 (January 1968): 23-43.
   Contends that "the contemplative life was a significant component of the intellectual and spiritual climate" that existed during the time of the composition of *The Dream of the Rood*.

Carragáin, Éamonn Ó. "Crucifixion as Annunciation: The Relation of *The Dream of the Rood* to the Liturgy Reconsidered." *English Studies* 63, No. 6 (December 1982): 487-505.
   Compares the Ruthwell Cross Crucifixion Poem with *The Dream of the Rood*, concluding that they both "sprang from an unbroken tradition of monastic devotion informed by experience of the liturgy."

Cook, Albert S., ed. Introduction to *The Dream of the Rood: An Old English Poem Attributed to Cynewulf*, pp. v-lix. Oxford: At the Clarendon Press, 1905.
   Analyzes the literary characteristics and theories of authorship of *The Dream of the Rood*.

Hieatt, Constance B. "Dream Frame and Verbal Echo in *The Dream of the Rood*." *Neuphilologische Mitteilungen* LXXII, No. 2 (1971): 251-63.
   Assesses the poet's use of the dream sequence as a literary device.

Horgan, A. D. "*The Dream of the Rood* and Christian Tradition." *Neuphilologische Mitteilungen* LXXXIX (1978): 11-20.
   Explores details common to the early Jewish-Christian *The Gospel of Peter* and *The Dream of the Rood*.

Kintgen, Eugene R. "Echoic Repetition in Old English Poetry, Especially *The Dream of the Rood*." *Neuphilologische Mitteilungen* LXXV, No. 2 (1974): 202-23.
   Assesses the use of the echo as a basic characteristic of Old English poetry, primarily in *The Dream of the Rood*.

Krapp, George Philip, ed. Introduction to *The Vercelli Book*, pp. xi-lxxx. The Anglo-Saxon Poetic Records: A Collective Edition, Vol. II. New York: Columbia University Press, 1932.
   Discusses the origin and contents of the manuscript of the Vercelli Book.

Lee, N. A. "The Unity of *The Dream of the Rood*." *Neophilologus* LVI, No. 4 (October 1972): 469-86.
   Argues that the second half of *The Dream of the Rood*, which is often neglected by critics, is an important part of the poem that reveals "a satisfying shape and coherence which becomes plainer when the traditional nature of the poet's material is understood."

Le Saux, Françoise. "Didacticism in *The Dream of the Rood*." *Études de Lettres* 2, No. 3 (April-September 1987): 167-77.
   Studies the didactic parallels between *The Dream of the Rood* and the Old English bestiary *Physiologus*.

Payne, Richard C. "Convention and Originality in the Vision Framework of *The Dream of the Rood*." *Modern Philology* 73, No. 4, Part 1 (May 1976): 329-41.
   Compares the beginning of *The Dream of the Rood* with descriptions of the Last Judgment found in other Old English eschatological poems and art.

Pope, John C., ed. "*The Dream of the Rood*." In his *Seven Old English Poems*, pp. 60-70. Indianapolis: Bobbs-Merrill Company, 1966.
   Praises *The Dream of the Rood* for "the depth and subtlety of its understanding" as well as "the art and imagination with which the speeches of dreamer and cross are invented, complexities of meaning and emotion are conveyed, order is maintained, and a significant progression is unfolded from beginning to end."

Raw, Barbara C. "*The Dream of the Rood* and Its Connections with Early Christian Art." *Medium Aevum* XXXIX, No. 3 (1970): 239-56.
   Compares the poet's portrayal of Christ and the Cross with the imagery and symbolism used in Palestinian and Mediterranean art.

———. "Biblical Literature: The New Testament." In *The Cambridge Companion to Old English Literature*, edited by Malcolm Godden and Michael Lapidge, pp. 227-42. Cambridge: Cambridge University Press, 1991.
   Compares *The Dream of the Rood* with the three poems known collectively as the *Christ*.

Savage, Anne. "The Place of Old English Poetry in the English Meditative Tradition." In *The Medieval Mystical Tradi-*

tion in England: Exeter Symposium IV, edited by Marion Glasscoe, pp. 92-110. Cambridge: D. S. Brewer, 1987.

Discusses the meditative aspect of *The Dream of the Rood*.

Shepherd, Geoffrey. "Scriptural Poetry." In *Continuations and Beginnings: Studies in Old English Literature*, edited by Eric Gerald Stanley, pp. 1-36. London: Thomas Nelson and Sons, 1966.

Explores *The Dream of the Rood* as biblical poetry, calling it "a highly successful poem: its words bare and shining; its structure strong and shapely; its material rich in associations with Christian art and Christian documents."

Stevens, William O. *The Cross in the Life and Literature of the Anglo-Saxons*. Yale Studies in English, edited by Albert S. Cook, Vol. XXIII. New York: Henry Holt and Company, 1904, 105 p.

Discusses the setting of *The Dream of the Rood* with respect to devotion to the Cross, debating whether the spirit of veneration was peculiar to "the poet of *The Dream of the Rood*, or whether it was more or less characteristic of the civilization" to which the poem belongs.

Taylor, P. B. "Text and Texture of *The Dream of the Rood*." *Neuphilologische Mitteilungen* LXXV, No. 2 (1974): 193-201.

Emphasizes the importance of ambiguous language in *The Dream of the Rood* and cites several specific examples.

Wrenn, C. L. "Cynewulf and the Christian Establishment." In her *A Study of Old English Literature*, pp. 122-38. London: George G. Harrap and Co., 1967.

Contends that *The Dream of the Rood* was not written by Cynewulf, stating that the poem "really stands quite by itself, as anonymous as it is unique."

Terence

c. 195/185 B. C.-159 B. C.

(Full name Publius Terentius Afer) Roman playwright.

INTRODUCTION

Terence is best known for the elegant language, symmetrical plots, and complex, sympathetic characterizations exhibited in his six comedies. Though he has for the most part been viewed as a respected and influential author, Terence has also been criticized by commentators from his own time onward for closely basing his plays on earlier Greek models—a practice some reviewers have interpreted as imitation or even plagiarism. Today most scholars agree that although Terence used the forms and themes of Greek New Comedy, he created a new type of play that transcended its antecedents. Gilbert Norwood, for example, has praised Terence for his "splendid principle of accepting the traditional framework and evolving from it in a thoroughly serious, permanently interesting, type of drama."

Biographical Information

Most of what is known about Terence's life is very uncertain and comes from a second-century biographical sketch by the Roman imperial biographer Suetonius, preserved in a commentary by Donatus, a fourth-century grammarian. Terence's exact date of birth is not known, but he was probably born in Carthage, North Africa, and brought to Rome as a slave when he was very young. He was then purchased by Terentius Lucanus, a Roman senator, who allowed Terence to be educated and eventually emancipated him; according to custom, Terence took his former owner's name upon being freed. Since Terence reportedly possessed great personal charm and soon demonstrated exceptional dramatic talent, he was quickly accepted into the circle of Scipio Aemilianus—a group of wealthy, well-placed young Roman aristocrats enamored of Greek culture and literature. This circle and their friends comprised Terence's main audience; he never enjoyed the widespread popularity of some of his contemporaries. In fact, a powerful critic of Terence's time, Luscius Lanuvinus, charged that Terence's plays were actually written by Scipio and his friends, and publicly accused Terence of plagiarizing the Greek dramatist Menander, and of "contaminating" his sources by mixing scenes and characters from various plays. In 159 B.C. Terence sailed for Greece, either to escape criticism at home or to become more familiar with the country. Some biographers claim that he was lost at sea on the way back, but the circumstances of his death remain unknown.

Major Works

Terence wrote six comedies, each of which has survived.

All of them are close adaptations or translations of Greek plays, two (*Hecyra*, or *The Mother-in-Law*, and *Phormio*) by Apollodorus, and the other four by Menander. The earliest, *Andria* (*The Girl from Andros*), recounts the travails of two young men, both in love, and both thwarted by their respective fathers. *The Mother-in-Law*, first produced in 165 B. C., failed three times before it was successfully produced in 160 B.C. *Heautontimorumenos* (*The Self-Tormentor*), like *The Girl from Andros*, treats the problems of two young lovers. Considered Terence's most technically accomplished play, *Eunuchus* (*The Eunich*) describes the situation of Chaerea, one of Terence's most-discussed characters, who marries a girl he had earlier raped. In *Phormio*, a young husband must contend with a wife whom he erroneously believes to be carrying someone else's child. Terence's last play, *Adelphoe* (*The Brothers*), compares two fathers—one too strict and one too lenient—and their two sons, in an exploration of the merits of different methods of childrearing. Terence's comedies are characterized by his pure, nearly perfect use of the Latin language, and by a sense of realism tempered by urbanity and restraint. Unlike earlier Roman dramatists who relied on raucous humor and vulgar language for comic effect, Terence favored correct, sophisticated speech and more use of dialogue than monologue. In characterization Terence also departed from earlier convention: rather than merely relying on stock character types, he made more use of irony and created more subtle, less predictable characters. Numerous critics have commented on Terence's humane and objective approach to characters and situations, citing his adherence to his well-known credo, "*homo sum: humani nil a me alienum puto*" ("I am human myself, so I think every human affair is my concern"). Although his models came from Greek New Comedy, Terence depicted a distinctly Roman society, with all its foibles and eccentricities intact. The world of his plays, unlike earlier Roman drama, is an amoral one, however; Terence is more interested in describing and dissecting moral dilemmas than in suggesting the proper ways to solve them. In terms of dramatic structure, Terence's main contribution was his development of the double plot device, which allowed for a more balanced and complex development of plot, character, and theme, and which he utilized in all his plays except *The Mother-in-Law*.

Textual History

Terence's plays are preserved in one incomplete ancient manuscript, the Codex Bembius, now located in the Vatican library. The number of extant manuscripts of his plays attests to Terence's enduring popularity despite his early quarrels with his critics: there are more that one hundred manuscripts dating from before the fourteenth century, and it is known that there were at least 446 complete editions of his comedies in existence prior to the year 1600. The medieval manuscripts have been traced to one original, probably dating from the fifth century. The first complete edition of Terence's works was printed in 1470. Modern translations of Terence's plays abound, the most notable among them being those by John Sargeaunt, Frank O. Copley, and the joint edition by Palmer Bovie, Constance Carrier, and Douglass Parker.

Critical Reaction

While in his own time Terence's plays were not popular with audiences, many ancient critics, for example Cicero and Julius Caesar, praised his graceful and correct handling of the Latin language. Caesar tempered his complimentary remarks by calling Terence a "half-Menander" and accusing him of a lack of comic vision. That charge and the question of whether Terence was an original playwright have been the two main areas of critical discussion concerning Terence's comedies. The majority of scholars aver that Terence's sense of comedy was very much intact, but admit that his plays sometimes strike audiences as somewhat monotonous or over-refined. Terence himself answered the charges of imitation in the prologues to his plays, including himself in the long, honorable tradition of younger writers paying tribute by copying their predecessors. Most critics believe that, while he was not an inherently original author, Terence artfully transformed the situations and themes of Greek New Comedy into a genuinely Roman milieu. In the Middle Ages there was a resurgence of interest in Terence's plays, and their texts served as the basis for Latin language curricula in schools and monasteries. The influence of Terence's comedies has

also been traced to works of the Renaissance and the eighteenth century. Today Terence commands admiration for his humanistic approach to his characters, for the new directions he made possible in drama through his introduction of double plots, and for the excellence of his Latin. As Betty Radice has written, "He created a Latin style which was an admirable counterpart to the natural rhythms of Hellenic Greek, less rhetorical and dense, simpler and purer than anything before."

PRINCIPAL WORKS

PLAYS

Andria 166 B. C. [*The Girl from Andros*]
Hecyra 165 B. C. [*The Mother-in-Law*]
Heautontimorumenos 163 B. C. [*The Self-Tormentor*]
Eunuchus 161 B. C. [*The Eunich*]
Phormio 161 B. C.
Adelphoe 160 B. C. [*The Brothers*]

PRINCIPAL ENGLISH TRANSLATIONS

The Comedies of Terence   (translated by Sidney G. Ashmore, sec. ed.)   1910
Terence. 2 vols.   (translated by John Sargeaunt; Loeb Classical Library edition)   1912
The Complete Roman Drama, Vol. II   (translated by George E. Duckworth)   1962
Terence: Comedies   (edited by Robert Graves, based on the translation by Lawrence Echard)   1963
Terence: The Comedies   (translated by Betty Radice) 1965
The Comedies of Terence   (translated by Frank O. Copley)   1967
The Complete Comedies of Terence   (translated by Palmer Bovie, Constance Carrier, and Douglass Parker) 1974

CRITICISM

Joseph Webbe   (essay date 1629)

SOURCE: An introduction to *The First Comedy of Pub. Terentius, Called Andria* by Terence, translated by Joseph Webbe, 1629. Reprint by The Scolar Press Limited, 1972, pp. iv-xviii.

[*In the following excerpt, Webbe lavishly praises Terence's style and language, advising that, if his readers wish to improve their conversational skills, they need only read Terence as a guide.*]

Two prime steps to perfection in any study, are *choyce* and *vse* of Authors. But how to chuse, and how to vse, are two great difficulties. Therefore to such as know nor, I will giue one Rule for both of them.

If any man commend an Author, or the way to vse him, looke vpon his perfection which commendeth them, in that particular in which they are commended. If he speake from priuate fancy, and shew no proofe thereof, neglect him. If from report of men sufficient; find out the Authors of that report, and iudge them by the Rule that's giuen you.

In our particular of pure Latinitie: They tell me, *Erasmus, Scaliger, Heinsius,* (with diuers other moderne and ancient Writers) commend our present Author, *Terence.* And this report by further inquisition I finde true; for though some of them were in yeeres, and cry'd vp for great Scholers, yet they would be alwayes reading him; admiring nothing more, than his sweet Language, and vnspeakeable aptnesse of nature therein.

I finde others repenting that they so lately began so much to loue him: others affirming, that the puritie of the Romane Tongue is not more fruitfully to be learned out of any other, than of *Terence.* Others denying that there are any more pleasing to be read, or more accommodated to the capacities of young beginners; or more profitable for matter of eloquence, or behauiour.

They affirme also, that as it is a great part of prudence to know the sundry humours and dispositions of men: so is it a gracefull thing to be able to deliuer the passions, or motions of their minde with efficacie; for that is it, that aboue all things maketh Language most delightfull; and that is it, that can by no meanes bee so well atchieued out of other Rhethoricians.

Further, whereas the finding out of Arguments, is the chiefest part among those that belong to Oratory; they constantly affirme, that the reading of *Terence* is a great furtherance to the attaining also of this abilitie, in any sort of learning whatsoeuer. And that therefore the Criticks did not without good cause by generall consent and voyce attribute Arte vnto this Author.

The qualitie of these persons, makes me beleeue their reports and commendations: but, hauing giuen rule to others, I would not my selfe be thought irregular. Wherefore, though I reuerently imbraced their speeches; yet I desired they might (for my greater iustification) bee sealed and subscribed by their actions. And thereupon examining their monuments of puritie in this Language, I found few that were not natiue Romanes, come neerer a natiue Romane puritie than they haue done.

Hence I conclude, if any man would better his discretion, or carriage in conwersation; or fitly deliuer to another what himselfe conceiueth, and that in Latine of the purest Authors: let him by our aduice make *choice* of *Terence* as his chiefe foundation.

So likewise about the *vse* of *Terence* in the point of Language. If any man say, he hath the true vse of reading, or learning him by himselfe, or of teaching him to others, and neither he nor his Scholars can rightly either write, or speake him: beleeue him not, for he's deceiued. But if a methode bee produced, by which you may so vse this Author, that both he and you, and I, and all men else may truly, and purely write and speake him, with as little theft as he, or you, or I speake English; and that an *Erasmus,* or a *Scaliger,* both will and must confesse it to bee reall;

be bold to relye vpon that method, to teach you how to vse your *Terence.* And let this be your Rule in *choyce* and *vse* of other Authors . . . .

The first vse is gotten by our claused Authors, and the frequent vse and repetitions of them: not of whole Comedies, Acts, Scenes, Prologues, or other entire Speeches, without booke; but of clauses onely: with which, I would haue a Scholar so familiar thorow all the Author, that as hee is able to tell you out of euery Grammar or Dictionarie, that (*manus*) is a hand, and a hand is (*manus:*) so out of *Terence, The Poet conceiued,* is, *Poëta credidit;* and *Poëta credidit,* is, *The Poet conceiued,* or the same sense with any other words expressed. And further than this, I desire not that any mans memory should be charged. And thus farre euery man that is, or will be master of a Language, is, and must be charged.

Make your selues therefore as familiar as you may, with *Terences* Clauses, by often reading and repeating them: for in this manner you shall not onely make that habit that I spake of, in the first vse of your Author, but you shall be so prepared for the second vse, as you will be able from the first day forward, to make euery day two or three exercises of that condition for puritie of Latine, congruitie, placing, phrase, and all other requisires; that I shall hold the best Master of England very bold, that takes vpon him to correct this Scholars Latine in the way of *Terence:* presupposing that hee writes truly as hee finds it printed, and that the print be not defectiue.

For this second vse is gotten by Eulogies or Clausularies, whereby not onely euery Child or woman that hath but English, may write good Latine: but whosoeuer would remember, or turne vnto any clause through his Author, he shall be able in an instant to find in what, and in how many places euery Clause is vsed. And therefore whensoeuer any Learners by this Method are questioned about their Latine, these Eulogies must be their refuge; whereby they shall be able at an instant to instifie themselues and writings by plaine, maine, and vnanswerable Authoritie, without the which, all other Arts or Methods that belong to Language, will be fruitlesse. And, by that time, that you are well acquainted with our *Terence:* you shall (if God permit) haue our *Eulogium,* or *Clausularium Terentianum,* fitted for this purpose, in the second vse of this our pure and pleasing stiled Author.

Lawrence Echard (essay date 1694)

SOURCE: A preface to *Prefaces to Terence's Comedies and Plautus's Comedies,* 1694. Reprint by William Andrews Clark Memorial Library, 1968, pp. i-xxiii.

[*Echard was one of the most respected translators of the works of Terence. Here, he presents an overview of Terence's style and works, noting that his only real fault was a lack of comic vision.*]

As for our Author, wherever Learning, Wit or Judgment have flourish'd, this Poet has always had an extraordinary Reputation. To mention all his Excellencies and Perfections were a Task too difficult for us, and perhaps for the greatest Criticks alive; so very few there are that perfectly understand all of 'em; yet we shall venture at some of the most Remarkable.

To begin with him in general, He was certainly the most Exact, the most Elaborate, and withal the most Natural of all Dramatick Poets; His Stile so neat and pure, his Characters so true and perfect, his Plots so regular and probable, and almost every thing so absolutely just and agreeable, that he may well seem to merit that Praise which several have given him, That he was the most correct Author in the World. To compare him with Plautus, the other great Latin Comedian, we may observe that Plautus had more Wit and Spirit, but Terence more Sense and Judgment; the former's Stile was rich and glaring, the latter's more close and even: Plautus had the most dazelling out-side, and the most lively Colours, but Terence drew the finest Figures and Postures, and had the best Design; the one pleas'd the Vulgar, but our Author the Better sort of People; the former wou'd usually set his Spectators into a loud Laughter, but the latter seal 'em into a sweet Smile that shou'd continue from the beginning to the end of the Representation: in short, Plautus was more lively and vigorous, and so fitter for Action; and Terence more grave and serious, and so fitter for Reading. Tho' Plautus's Beauties were very extraordinary, yet he had his Faults and Indecorums very frequent; but Terence's Excellencies (the possibly inferior to some of the others) were more general, better dispers'd, and closer continu'd; and his Faults so inconsiderable, and so very few, that Scaliger said, There were not three to be found throughout the Six Plays. So that our Author seems to want nothing to make him absolutely compleat, but only that same *Vis Comica* that Caesar wishes he had, and which Plautus was Master of in such a high degree We shall determine nothing between 'em, but leave 'em good Friends as we found 'em.

This may be sufficient for our Author's Excellencies in general; for his particular ones, we shall begin with his Stile, a thing he has been admir'd for in all Ages, and truly he deserves it; for certainly no one was ever more accurate, natural, and clear in his Expressions than be. But to be a little more particular in this Matter, we shall give you some few of our Author's Excellencies in this kind under three or four different Heads.

And first, We may observe of his Words, that they are generally nicely chosen, extreamly proper and significant; and many of 'em carry so much Life and Force in 'em, that they can hardly be express'd in any other Language without great disadvantage to the Original.

Another remarkable Beauty of his Stile appears in his Climaxes; where every Word is Emphatical, heightens the Sense, and adds considerably to what went before. And as for the Purity of his Language in general; we find it very much commended even by Tully himself. And One of the Moderns is not at all out of the way when he tells us: That the Latin Tongue will never be lost, as long as Terence may be had.

Our Author's Excellent Latin is now the greatest Cause of his Esteem, and makes him so much read in the World; but for certain, he that reads him purely for his Latin sake, does but a quarter read him; for 'tis his Characters and

Plots have so far rais'd him up above the rest of the Poets, and have gain'd him so much Honour among the Criticks in all Ages. His Stile, tho' so very extraordinary, in a great measure may be learnt by Industry, long Custom, and continnal Usage, and has been imitated to a high degree by several; and indeed this was but as rich Attire, and outward Ornaments to set off a more beautiful Body. But in his Characters and Manners there it is that be triumphs without a Rival; and not only Dramatick, but all other Poets must yield to him in that Point. For these are drawn exactly to the Life, perfectly just, truly proportionably, and fully kept up to the last; and as for their being natural, Rapin says, That no Man living had a greater insight into Nature than he. The more a Man looks into 'em, the more he must admire 'em; he'll find there not only such Beauty in his Images, but also such excellent Precepts of Morality, such solid Sense in each Line, such depth of Reasoning in each Period, and such close arguing between each Party, that he must needs perceive him to be a Person of strong Sense and Judgment. His Deliberations are most compleat, where all the several Accidents, Events, Dangers, Casualties, good and bad Consequences are fully summed up and clearly urg'd; so are the Answers of each Person as perfect, where every thing is so well fitted, so home, and so natural, that if one shou'd study upon 'em never so long, he cou'd scarce find any thing more to the purpose. He had a peculiar Happiness at pleasing and amusing an Audience, perpetually keeping 'em in a most even, pleasant, smiling Temper; and this is the most distinguishing part of his Character from the rest of the World; his Pleasantries were somewhat Manly, and such as reach'd beyond the Fancy and Imagination, even to the Heart and Soul of the Audience; and what is more remarkable yet, one single Scene shall please a whole day together; a Secret which few or no other Poet ever found out.

And as we have scarce found one Man in the World that equals him in his Characters, so we find but very few that cou'd come up to him in the Management (we mean his Art and Contrivance) of his Plots. We are sensible that many have been so foolish as to count his Plays a bare Bundle of Dialogues dress'd up in a neat Stile, and there all his Excellency to consist, or at least that they are very ordinary and mean; but such senseless Suppositions will soon vanish upon giving an Account of the Nature and Perfection of 'em. He well understood the Rules of the Stage, or rather those of Nature; was perfectly Regular, wonderful exact and careful in ordering each Protasis or Entrance, Epitasis or working up, Catastasis or heighth, and Catastrophe or unravelling the Plot; which last he was famous for making it spring necessarily from the Incidents, and neatly and dextrously untying the Knot, whilst others of a grosser make, would either tear, or cut it in pieces. In short (setting aside some few things which we shall mention by and by) Terence may serve for the best and most perfect Model for our Dramatick Poets to imitate, provided they exactly observe the different Customs and Manners of the Roman and English People; and upon the same account we beg leave to be a little more particular in this Matter, which dispos'd us very much to this Translation.

The Nature of his Plots was for the most part grave and

solid, and sometimes passionate a little, resembling our Modern Tragy-Comedies; only the Comical parts were seldom so merry; the Thinness and clearness of 'em somewhat resembling our Modern Tragedies, only more perfect in the latter, and not crouded with too many Incidents. They were all double except the *Hecyra,* or *Mother-in-Law,* yet so contriv'd that one was always an Under-plot to the other: So that he still kept perfectly to the first great Rule of the Stage, the Unity of Action. As for the second great Rule the Unity of Time (that is for the whole Action to be perform'd in the compass of a Day) he was as exact in that as possible, for the longest Action of any of his Plays reaches not Eleven hours. He was no less careful in the third Rule, The Unit of Place, for 'tis plain be never shifts his Scene in any one of his Plays, but keeps constantly to the same place from the beginning to the end. Then for the Continuance in the Action, he never fails in any one place, but every Instrument is perpetually at work in carrying on their several Designs, and in them the design of the whole; so that the Stage never grows cold till all is finish'd: And to do this the more handsomely and dextrously, he scarce ever brings an Actor upon the Stage, but you presently know his Name and Quality, what part of the Intrigue he's to promote, why he came there, from whence he came, why just at that time, why he goes of, where he's a going, and also what he is or ought to be doing or contriving all the time he's away. His Scenes are always unbroken, so that the Stage is never perfectly clear but between the Acts; but are continually joyn'd by one of the four Unions. Which according to Mon. Hedelin are these; Presence, Seeking, Noise, or Time; and when the Action ceaseth (that is, upon the Stage) and the Stage is clear'd, an Act is then finish'd. Then for Incidents, and the due Preparation of 'em, Terence was admirable: And the true and exact Management of these is one of the most difficult parts of Dramatick Poetry. He contrives every thing in such a manner so as to fall out most probably and naturally, and when they are over they seem almost necessary; yet by his excellent Skill he so cunningly conceals the Events of things from his Audience, till due time, that they can never foresee 'em; by this means they are so amus'd with the Actors Designs, that the Poets is unknown to 'em, till at list, being all along in the dark, they are surpriz'd most agreeably by something they never look'd for: And this is the most taking and the most delightful part of a Play. We might insist much more largely upon each of these Particulars, and upon several others, but at present we shall content our selves with saying that these Plots are all so very clear, and natural, that they might very well go for a Representation of a thing that had really happen'd; and not the meer Invention of the Poet.

There are two or three remarkable Objections against our Author which we can't but take notice of. First, 'tis said, That he has not kept to the Unity of Time in his *Heautontimoreumenos,* or *Self-Tormenter;* which contains the space of two days. Then, between the second and third Acts, there's an absolute failure of the Continuance of the Action. These are generally believ'd by several Men, and such as are famous too; and some to vindicate Terence the better have added another Mistake, That the Play was always acted two several times, the two first Acts one, and the three last another. But 'tis plain from all Circum-

stances, that the Action began very late in the Evening, and ended betimes in the Morning (of which we have said something in our Remarks at the end) so that the whole cou'dn't contain about Eleven hours; but as for that of the Cessation of the Action, 'tis answer'd two ways, either by the necessity of Sleep at that Interval, and consequently no Cessation, or (which is more probable) by the Persons being busie at the Treat at Chremes's House, that being a necessary part of the main Action. The two following are Mr. Dryden's Exceptions; where first he lays an Error to our Author's Charge in matter of Time. In the *Eunuch* (says he) when Laches enters Thais's House by mistake, between his Exit and the Entrance of Pythias, who comes to give ample Relation of the Disorder he has rais'd within, Parmeno who is left upon the Stage has not above five Lines to speak. In answer to this, Pythias makes no such ample Relation, but rather tells him what Disorders such a foolish Act of he was like to raise; and in truth it is not probable she shou'd stay above five or six Lines speaking, since after she saw her Cheat had taken, she cou'dn't keep her countenance within Doors, and was so eager to revenge her self by laughing at the Fool without. Besides here's an excellent Artifice of the Poets, for had she tarry'd longer, Parmeno might ha' been gone, and her Mirth qualified when she saw the good Fortune Chaerea had met withal. His other Exception is, that our Author's Scenes are several times broken. He instances in the same Play, That Antipho enters singly in the midst of the third Act, after Chremes and Pythias were gone off. As for this,' tis to be consider'd that Scenes are united by Time as well as Presence; and this is a perfect Union of Time, apparent to all who understand the Art of the Stage. A little farther he says, That Dorias begins the fourth Act alone; —She quits the Stage, and Phedria enters next. Here Dorias does not quit the Stage till three Scenes after, as appears by Pythias, bidding her carry in such things as she had brought with her from the Captain's Entertainment; but if she did, there wou'd be an Union of Time nevertheless, as there is in all other places, where the Scenes seem broken. Some make this Objection; that in the beginning of many Scenes, two Actors enter upon the Stage, and talk to themselves a considerable time before they see or know one another; Which (they say) is neither probable nor natural. Those that object this don't consider the great Difference between our little scanty Stage, and the large magnificent Roman Theatres. Their Stage was sixty Yards wide in the Front, their Scenes so many Streets meeting together, with all By-Lanes, Rows and Allies; so two Actors coming down two different Streets or Lanes cou'dn't be seen by each other, tho' the Spectators might see both, and sometimes if they did see each other they cou'dn't well distinguish Faces at sixty Yards distances. Besides upon several accounts it might well be suppos'd when an Actor enters upon the Stage out of some House, he might take a turn or two under the Portico's, Cloysters, or the like (that were usual at that time) about his Door, and take no notice of an Actor's being on the other side the Stage.

But since we propose our Master as the best Model for Dramatick Poets to follow, we ought in Justice to mention such things wherein he was any ways faulty, or at least where he ought not to be imitated. The first is, He makes his Actors in some places speak directly, and immediately to the Audience (of which that Monologue of Mysis in the first Act of the first Play is an instance) which is contrary to the Rules of Dramatick Poetry, or rather indeed of Nature; and this is the only real Fault that Terence was guilty of, as his want of *Vis Comica* was the only real Defect. His Plots were not always the best for Story, tho' for Contrivance, and wanted somewhat of Length and Variety, fully and compleatly to satisfie an Audience. Take 'em all together, they were too much alike to have always their deserv'd Effect of surprizing; which also gave a mighty Limitation to the Variety of his Characters; a great pity for a Man that had such an admirable Knack of drawing them to the Life. It were also to be wish'd that his Monologues or Discourses by single Persons, were less frequent, and sometimes shorter too; for tho' they are all of 'em full of excellent Sence, sound Reasoning, ingenious Deliberations, and serv'd truly to carry on the main Design; yet several parts of 'em, especially all Narrations, wou'd ha' been more natural as well as Artificial, if told by Persons of the Drama to one another. Then his Aparts or Asides (that is when one Actor speaks something which another that is present is suppos'd to not hear, tho' the Audience do) are sometimes too long to be perfectly natural. Whether he has not sometimes too much Elevation of Passion, or Borders too nigh upon Tragedy for such inferior Persons, we leave to others. These are the main things to be taken notice of by all that make use of him for a Model, besides all such as belong purely to the various Customs of Countries, and to the difference of Theatres; but those are obvious enough to all.

But there's still one great Objection against these Plays in general; that is, It Terence's Plays are so good as is pretended, why doesn't some Poet or other translate one or more of 'em for the Stage, so save himself the trouble of racking his Brain for new Matter. We own they wou'dn't take upon our Stage; but to clear all, we shall give these two Reasons: First, The Difference between the Romans and our selves in Customs, Humors, Manners and Theatres is such, that it is impossible to adopt their Plays to our Stages. The Roman Plots were often founded upon the exposing of Children, and their unexpected Delivery, on buying of Misses and Musick Girls; they were chiefly pleas'd to see a covetous old Father neatly bubbled by his Slave of a round Sum of Money; to find the young Spark his Son (miserably in want of Cash) joyn with the Slave in the Intrigue, that he may get somewhat to stop his Mistress's Mouth, whom he keeps unknown to his Father; to see a bragging Coxcomb wheadled and abus'd by some cunning Parasite; to hear a Glutton talk of nothing but his Belly, and the like. Our Plots go chiefly upon variety of Love-Intrigues, Ladies Cuckolding their Husbands most dextrously, Gallants danger upon the same account, with their escape either by witty Fetches, or hiding themselves in dark Holes, Closets, Beds, &c. We are all for Humour, Gallantry, Conversation, and Courtship, and shou'dn't endure the chief Lady in the Play a Mute, or to say very little, as 'twas agreeable to them: Our amorous Sparks love to hear the pretty Rogues' prate, snap up their Gallants, and Repartée upon 'em on all sides. We shou'dn't like to have a Lady marry'd without knowing whether she gives her consent or no, (a Custom among the Romans) but wou'd be for hearing all the Courtship, all the rare and fine

things that Lovers can say to each other. The second Reason of their not taking upon our Stage is this, tho' Terence's Plays are far more exact, natural, regular, and clear than ours, and his Persons speak more like themselves than generally ours do; yet (to speak impartially) our Plays do plainly excel his in some Particulars. First, in the great Variety of the Matter and Incidents of our Plots; the Intrigues thicker and finer; the Stories better, longer, and more curious for the most part than his: And tho' there's much confusion, huddle and precipitation in the generality of 'em; yet the great variety and number of Incidents tho' ill manag'd, will have several Charms, and be mighty diverting, especially to a vulgar Audience, like the Sight of a large City at a distance, where there is little of Regularity or Uniformity to be discern'd just by. Next, we do much excel Terence in that which we call Humour, that is in our Comical Characters, in which we have shewn and expos'd the several Humours, Dispositions, Natures, Inclinations, Fancies, Irregularities, Maggots, Passions, Whims, Follies, Extravagancies, & c. of Men under all sorts of Circumstances, of all sorts of Ranks and Qualities, of all Professions and Trades, and of all Nations and Countries, so admirably, and so lively, that in this no Nation among the Ancients or Moderns were ever comparable to us. Lastly, Our Comedies excel his in some Delicacies of Conversation; particularly in the Resinedness of our Railery and Satyr, and above all in Repartée. Some of these things (especially when mix'd with Humour) have made many an ordinary Plot take and come off well; and without a pretty quantity of some of 'em, our Plays wou'd go down very heavily . . . .

The Edinburgh Review (essay date 1882)

SOURCE: "The Comedies of Terence," in *The Edinburgh Review,* Vol. CLV, No. CCCXVIII, April, 1882, pp. 364-81.

[*In the following excerpt, the anonymous reviewer points out that, although Terence suffered from a lack of recognition because his plays did not satisfy popular audiences in his time, he remains "a well of Latin undefiled."*]

Terence at the outset of his career had had a hard, uphill battle to fight and many great difficulties to overcome. The average class of spectator in a Roman theatre was very much the same as that of an ordinary modern crowd—such, for instance, as the collection of the great Unwashed which visits the Crystal Palace on a Bank Holiday. There was certainly a sprinkling of nobility; but, there being no charge for admission, the vast majority belonged to the lower orders. Plautus, with his genuine fun and broad jokes, too often, at least in his imitators, degenerating into obscene buffoonery, had set a fashion which it was next to impossible for after writers to avoid. When, therefore, Cæcilius began to be a little too serious, he at once found it hard to get a hearing; and all, or nearly all, the Terentian prologues contain an entreaty to the audience to listen patiently to the end. And, notwithstanding the savage opposition which was raised, Terence was enabled by the influence and support of the young nobles, Scipio and his following, to keep the even tenor of his way; and he might have boasted, as Aristophanes had done some two and a half centuries before him, of the reformation which he had effected on the stage.

The coarseness of the mimes—popular pantomimic plays—was a most seductive counter-attraction to our author's chaste sobriety. These mimes, Ovid tells us, indecent as they were, were looked at and listened to by many of the Senate, by maidens ripe for marriage, by matrons, by men and by boys. Little wonder, then, that the uneducated crowd, the great Unwashed, found his plays cold. Yet even he has been found fault with for a passage in the **Brothers,** wherein the one of milder mood, carried away by the intensity of his feeling, expresses in round terms approval of the irregularities of youth. But we cannot too carefully distinguish the artist from the moralist. What he aimed at doing, Terence did well; and this was . . . to give his Roman audience a more or less faithful picture of society at Athens, as depicted in the plays of the late comedy. If this mode of reasoning were universal, we should be compelled to believe that Euripides sympathised with the sophistries of Odysseus, Shakespeare with the villany of Iago. Nor was the code of morals at a high level; Christianity had not yet touched ethics, and Terence is distinctly above, and not below, the high-water mark.

But his strong point, and an extremely strong point too, is the refined grace, the exquisite finish, the keen point of language and style. He is, indeed, a well of Latin undefiled. The elegant wit, in respect of which he vies with his Attic masters, may well make us marvel how the African slave attained such a thorough command over a language not his own. The old Greek proverb 'Nothing in excess' was never more effectively illustrated than in his writings; and throughout he approaches the severe beauty of Greek sculpture. Plautus sometimes verges upon buffoonery, Terence never. And it was, in fact, this perfection of style which laid him open to the calumny—if calumny it were—of being assisted by noble friends in the production of his plays.

With regard to their treatment of the Greek originals, whereas Plautus took little but the bare outline and filled it up from his own fertile imagination, Terence preserved with much more accuracy the Greek colouring: he never sends his dead bodies through the Metian gate at Rome, and his allusions to Roman customs are sparing, though by no means absent. If, however, he imitates the Greek at all closely, like Virgil, he borrows in so masterly a manner as to make the theft his own. 'Ars est celare artem;' and herein he most undeniably succeeds. If we had not known it in other ways, most assuredly his style would never have betrayed to us the fact that his work is not altogether original.

And yet Cæsar's epigram charging him with want of comic force is to some extent true; and it would be unjust to say that he has the freshness or power of Plautus. But humour of a keen, dry kind he has in plenty. If we may be allowed to make a comparison, he bears, roughly speaking, the same relation to Plautus that Thackeray, as a satirist, bears to Dickens. If he has less broad fun, he has as much pointed humour, and certainly greater delicacy of treatment. Plautus, as Horace tells us, imitated the bustle of Epicharmus; Terence's plays are all *statariæ*. Like Sophocles, he has the true dramatic tact of making each scene not only good in itself, but also conducive to the general action of the play; and he has a strong vein of that 'irony' which in dramatic excellence is so necessary a factor.

With regard to his want of originality, this he does not, any more than other Roman writers, attempt to conceal. When his enemies accuse him of plagiarism, he sets to the disproving of the charge not by attempting to show that the passage in question is his own, but that he has translated it word for word from the Greek. To this a rather curious parallel has occurred in our own times, when an adaptation from the French may be described as 'new.' And just so the **Mother-in-Law,** when reproduced a second or even third time, could still be called 'new.'

We have already said that the six comedies have come down to us in a condition more or less satisfactory. Yet perhaps Ritschl is not overstating the truth when he alleges that there is hardly a scene of the Terentian plays in which there is not some serious flaw, even after the labours of Bentley. We have, however, a most excellent manuscript, an uncial of not later than the fifth century of our era, known as the Bembine from having once belonged to the celebrated Cardinal Pietro Bembo. It is sadly mutilated, and has received shameful treatment even in comparatively modern times; but it is the only manuscript copy of Terence, not even excepting the Victorian—and many hundreds of such copies exist—which is not disfigured by the wholesale corruptions and interpolations of the unknown grammarian Calliopius. Unfortunately, one authority of undoubted value we are not able confidently to use. Donatus, a distinguished grammarian at Rome during the fourth century, besides preserving to us a life of Terence which he ascribes to Suetonius, wrote a full commentary on his plays. But the commentary is in so corrupt a state that it is out of our power to collect, so to speak, the scattered limbs. And yet a better edition might be made than has yet appeared, for after the lapse of centuries still the least bad edition is the *editio princeps* brought out at Rome by Conrad Sweynheym and Arnold Pannartz in the year A.D. 1472!

From his own day to our times the study of Terence has never languished; the early fathers of the Church read and studied him, and Erasmus learnt all the plays by heart. But slowly and surely the character of the text degenerated; and not until the famous edition of the 'British Aristarchus.' Richard Bentley, was any decided improvement made in this direction.

[To] end by the words of Melanchthon: 'I exhort all schoolmasters with all boldness to commend this author to the zealous study of youth. For I think that from him more help is gained for forming a judgment concerning the manners of men than from most works of philosophers. Nor will any other writer teach greater elegance in speaking, or steep the tongue of a boy in eloquence of a more useful kind.'

Lucius Ambivius answers Terence's slanderers (c. 163 B.C.):

As to the malignant rumours, by which [Terence] has been mangled, to the effect that he has combined many Greek plays and written few Latin ones, he doesn't deny having done this: he declares he does not repent and will do it again. He has the precedent of good writers, whose example he considers himself entitled to follow. As for the assertion of the malignant old playwright that his devotion to a literary calling is a sudden freak, in which he relies on the genius of his friends, not on his own abilities, on this it is your judgment and your opinion that will decide. I must appeal to you then not to let the remarks of the slanderers have more weight than the remarks of the candid. Be sure that you are candid, and allow those to rise in the world who give you the opportunity of seeing new plays free from certain faults. This is not to be taken to himself as a defence by him who the other day represented the people in the street making way for a footman on the run: why be slave to a madman? On his rival's faults our playwright will speak further on his production of other new plays unless that rival put an end to his abuse.

Lucius Ambivius, in a prologue to Terence's The Self-Tormentor, *translated by John Sargeaunt, William Heinemann, 1912.*

J. W. Mackail   (essay date 1895)

SOURCE: "Comedy: Plautus and Terence," in *Latin Literature,* Charles Scribner's Sons, 1895, pp. 14-26.

[*Mackail was an English critic, biographer, and educator whose books include* The Springs of Helicon *(1909) and* Studies in Humanism *(1938). Here, he comments on Terence's position in the history of Roman literature, noting that, while his style is not colorful, it exemplifies the best stylistic qualities of his era.*]

The Terentian comedy is in a way the turning-point of Roman literature. Plautus and Ennius, however largely they drew from Greek originals, threw into all their work a manner and a spirit which were essentially those of a new literature in the full tide of growth. The imitation of Greek models was a means, not an end; in both poets the Greek manner is continually abandoned for essays into a new manner of their own, and they relapse upon it when their imperfectly mastered powers of invention or expression give way under them. In the circle of Terence the fatal doctrine was originated that the Greek manner was an end in itself, and that the road to perfection lay, not in developing any original qualities, but in reproducing with laborious fidelity the accents of another language and civilisation. Nature took a swift and certain revenge. Correctness of sentiment and smooth elegance of diction became the standards of excellence; and Latin literature, still mainly confined to the governing class and their dependents, was struck at the root (the word is used of Terence himself by Varro) with the fatal disease of mediocrity.

But in Terence himself (as in Addison among English writers) this mediocrity is, indeed, golden—a mediocrity full of grace and charm. The unruffled smoothness of diction, the exquisite purity of language, are qualities admirable in themselves, and are accompanied by other striking merits; not, indeed, by dramatic force or constructive power, but by careful and delicate portraiture of character, and by an urbanity (to use a Latin word which expresses a peculiarly Latin quality) to which the world owes a deep debt for having set a fashion. In some curious lines preserved by Suetonius, Julius Caesar expresses a criticism, which we shall find it hard to improve, on the "halved Menander," to whom his own fastidious purity in the use of language, no less than his tact and courtesy as a man of the world, attracted him strongly, while not blinding him to the weakness and flaccidity of the Terentian drama. Its effect on contemporary men of letters was immediate and irresistible. A story is told, bearing all the marks of truth, of the young poet when he submitted his first play, *The Maid of Andros,* for the approval of the Commissioners of Public Works, who were responsible for the production of plays at the civic festivals. He was ordered to read it aloud to Caecilius, who, since the death of Plautus, had been supreme without a rival on the comic stage. Terence presented himself modestly while Caecilius was at supper, and was carelessly told to sit down on a stool in the dining-room, and begin. He had not read beyond a few verses when Caecilius stopped him, and made him take a seat at table. After supper was over, he heard his guest's play out with unbounded and unqualified admiration.

But this admiration of the literary class did not make the refined conventional art of Terence successful for its immediate purposes on the stage: he was caviare to the general. Five of the six plays were produced at the spring festival of the Mother of the Gods—an occasion when the theatre had not to face the competition of the circus; yet even then it was only by immense efforts on the part of the management that they succeeded in attracting an audience. *The Mother-in-Law* (not, it is true, a play which shows the author at his best) was twice produced as a dead failure. The third time it was pulled through by extraordinary efforts on the part of the acting-manager, Ambivius Turpio. The prologue written by Terence for this third performance is one of the most curious literary documents of the time. He is too angry to extenuate the repeated failure of his play. If we believe him, it fell dead the first time because "that fool, the public," were all excitement over an exhibition on the tight-rope which was to follow the play; at the second representation only one act had been gone through, when a rumour spread that "there were going to be gladiators" elsewhere, and in five minutes the theatre was empty.

The Terentian prologues (they are attached to all his plays) are indeed all very interesting from the light they throw on the character of the author, as well as on the ideas and fashions of his age. In all of them there is a certain hard and acrid purism that cloaks in modest phrases an immense contempt for all that lies beyond the writer's own canons of taste. *In hac est pura oratio,* a phrase of the prologue to *The Self-Tormentor,* is the implied burden of them all. He is a sort of literary Robespierre; one seems to catch the premonitory echo of well-known phrases, "degenerate condition of literary spirit, backsliding on this hand and on that, I, Terence, alone left incorruptible." Three times there is a reference to Plautus, and always with a tone of chilly superiority which is too proud to break into an open sneer. Yet among these haughty and frigid manifestoes some felicity of phrase or of sentiment will suddenly remind us that here, after all, we are dealing with one of the great formative intelligences of literature; where, for instance, in the prologue to the lively and witty comedy of *The Eunuch,* the famous line—

Nullumst iam dictum quod non dictum sit prius—

drops with the same easy negligence as in the opening dialogue of *The Self-Tormentor,* the immortal—

Homo sum: humani nihil a me alienum puto—

falls from the lips of the old farmer. Congreve alone of English playwrights has this glittering smoothness, this inimitable ease; if we remember what Dryden, in language too splendid to be insincere, wrote of his young friend, we may imagine, perhaps, how Caecilius and his circle regarded Terence. Nor is it hard to believe that, had Terence, like Congreve, lived into an easy and honoured old age, he would still have rested his reputation on these productions of his early youth. Both dramatists had from the first seen clearly and precisely what they had in view, and had almost at the first stroke attained it: the very completeness of the success must in both cases have precluded the dissatisfaction through which fresh advances could alone be possible.

This, too, is one reason, though certainly not the only one, why, with the death of Terence, the development of Latin comedy at once ceased. His successors are mere shadowy names. Any life that remained in the art took the channel of the farces which, for a hundred years more, retained a genuine popularity, but which never took rank as literature of serious value. Even this, the *fabula tabernaria,* or comedy of low life, gradually melted away before the continuous competition of the shows which so moved the spleen of Terence—the pantomimists, the jugglers, the gladiators. By this time, too, the literary instinct was beginning to explore fresh channels. Not only was prose becoming year by year more copious and flexible, but the mixed mode, fluctuating between prose and verse, to which the Romans gave the name of satire, was in process of invention. Like the novel as compared with the play at the present time, it offered great and obvious advantages in ease and variety of manipulation, and in the simplicity and inexpensiveness with which, not depending on the stated performances of a public theatre, it could be produced and circulated . . . .

George Meredith   (essay date 1897)

SOURCE: "On the Idea of Comedy and of the Uses of the Comic Spirit," in *An Essay on Comedy and the Uses of the Comic Spirit,* edited by Lane Cooper, 1897. Reprint by Charles Scribner's Sons, 1918, pp. 73-155.

[*Meredith was a respected nineteenth-century British poet, novelist, and critic. His creative works, though they are considered to lack a philosophical framework, reflect the ideas of his age: they embody a profound belief in evolution and in the essential goodness of humanity. In the following excerpt, he briefly comments on Terence, focusing especially on his "beautiful translucency of language."*]

Of the six comedies of Terence, four are derived from Menander; two, the **Hecyra** and the **Phormio,** from Apollodorus. These two are inferior, in comic action and the peculiar sweetness of Menander, to the **Andria**, the **Adelphi**, the **Heauton Timorumenos,** and the **Eunuchus;** but Phormio is a more dashing and amusing convivial parasite than the Gnatho of the last-named comedy. There were numerous rivals of whom we know next to nothing (except by the quotations of Athenaeus and Plutarch, and the Greek grammarians who cited them to support a dictum) in this, as in the preceding periods of comedy in Athens; for Menander's plays are counted by many scores, and they were crowned by the prize only eight times. The favorite poet with critics, in Greece as in Rome, was Menander; and if some of his rivals here and there surpassed him in comic force, and outstripped him in competition by an appositeness to the occasion that had previously in the same way deprived the genius of Aristophanes of its due reward in *Clouds* and *Birds,* his position as chief of the comic poets of his age was unchallenged. Plutarch very unnecessarily drags Aristophanes into a comparison with him, to the confusion of the older poet. Their aims, the matter they dealt in, and the times, were quite dissimilar. But it is no wonder that Plutarch, writing when Athenian beauty of style was the delight of his patrons, should rank Menander at the highest. In what degree of faithfulness Terence copied Menander—whether, as he states of the passage in the **Adelphi** taken from Diphilus, '*verbum de verbo*' in the lovelier scenes (the description of the last words of the dying Andrian, and of her funeral, for instance)—remains conjectural. For us, Terence shares with his master the praise of an amenity that is like Elysian speech, equable and ever gracious; like the face of the Andrian's young sister:

Adeo modesto, adeo venusto, ut nil supra.

The celebrated '*flens quam familiariter,*' of which the closest rendering grounds hopelessly on harsh prose, to express the sorrowful confidingness of a young girl who has lost her sister and dearest friend, and has but her lover left to her—'she turned and flung herself on his bosom, weeping as though at home there'—this our instinct tells us must be Greek, though hardly finer in Greek. Certain lines of Terence, compared with the original fragments, show that he embellished them; but his taste was too exquisite for him to do other than devote his genius to the honest translation of such pieces as the above. Menander, then; with him, through the affinity of sympathy, Terence; and Shakespeare and Molière, have this beautiful translucency of language. And the study of the comic poets might be recommended if for that only . . . .

Theodor Mommsen   (essay date 1908)

SOURCE: "Literature and Art" in *The History of Rome, Vol. IV,* translated by William Purdie Dickson, Charles Scribner's Sons, 1908, pp. 219-60.

[A German historian, writer, and politician, Mommsen is known for his authoritative work in several areas of Roman studies, particularly Roman law. His Römische Geschichte *(1856;* The History of Rome), *acclaimed as a masterful synthesis, reflects Mommsen's conviction that history should be made intelligible and relevant to the reader. Mommsen received the Nobel Prize for literature in 1902. In the following excerpt, he presents a brief overview of Terence's contribution to Roman literature, emphasizing his elegant language and refined sense of style.]*

[Terence] is one of the most interesting phenomena, in a historical point of view, in Roman literature. Born in Phoenician Africa, brought in early youth as a slave to Rome and there introduced to the Greek culture of the day, he seemed from the very first destined for the vocation of giving back to the new Attic comedy that cosmopolitan character, which in its adaptation to the Roman public under the rough hands of Naevius, Plautus, and their associates it had in some measure lost. Even in the selection and employment of models the contrast is apparent between him and that predecessor whom alone we can now compare with him. Plautus chooses his pieces from the whole range of the newer Attic comedy, and by no means disdains the livelier and more popular comedians, such as Philemon; Terence keeps almost exclusively to Menander, the most elegant, polished, and chaste of all the poets of the newer comedy. The method of working up several Greek pieces into one Latin is retained by Terence, because in fact from the state of the case it could not be avoided by the Roman editors; but it is handled with incomparably more skill and carefulness. The Plautine dialogue beyond doubt departed very frequently from its models; Terence boasts of the verbal adherence of his imitations to the originals, by which however we are not to understand a verbal translation in our sense. The not unfrequently coarse, but always effective laying on of Roman local tints over the Greek ground-work, which Plautus was fond of, is completely and designedly banished from Terence; not an allusion puts one in mind of Rome, not a proverb, hardly a reminiscence; even the Latin titles are replaced by Greek. The same distinction shows itself in the artistic treatment. First of all the players receive back their appropriate masks, and greater care is observed as to the scenic arrangements, so that it is no longer the case, as with Plautus, that everything needs to take place on the street, whether belonging to it or not. Plautus ties and unties the dramatic knot carelessly and loosely, but his plot is droll and often striking; Terence, far less effective, keeps everywhere account of probability, not unfrequently at the cost of suspense, and wages emphatic war against the certainly somewhat flat and insipid standing expedients of his predecessors, *e. g.* against allegoric dreams. Plautus paints his characters with broad strokes, often after a stock model, always with a view to the gross effect from a distance and on the whole; Terence handles the psychological development with a careful and often excellent miniature-

painting, as in the *Adelphi* for instance, where the two old men—the easy bachelor enjoying life in town, and the sadly harassed not at all refined country-landlord—form a masterly contrast. The springs of action and the language of Plautus are drawn from the tavern, those of Terence from the household of the good citizen. The lazy Plautine hostelry, the very unconstrained but very charming damsels with the hosts duly corresponding, the sabre-rattling troopers, the menial world painted with an altogether peculiar humour, whose heaven is the cellar, and whose fate is the lash, have disappeared in Terence or at any rate undergone improvement. In Plautus we find ourselves, on the whole, among incipient or thorough rogues, in Terence again, as a rule, among none but honest men; if occasionally a *leno* is plundered or a young man taken to the brothel, it is done with a moral intent, possibly out of brotherly love or to deter the boy from frequenting improper haunts. The Plautine pieces are pervaded by the significant antagonism of the tavern to the house; everywhere wives are visited with abuse, to the delight of all husbands temporarily emancipated and not quite sure of an amiable salutation at home. The comedies of Terence are pervaded by a conception not more moral, but doubtless more becoming, of the feminine nature and of married life. As a rule, they end with a virtuous marriage, or, if possible, with two—just as it was the glory of Menander that he compensated for every seduction by a marriage. The eulogies of a bachelor life, which are so frequent in Menander, are repeated by his Roman remodeller only with characteristic shyness, whereas the lover in his agony, the tender husband at the *accouchement,* the loving sister by the death-bed in the *Eunuchus* and the *Andria* are very gracefully delineated; in the *Hecyra* there even appears at the close as a delivering angel a virtuous courtesan, likewise a genuine Menandrian figure, which the Roman public, it is true, very properly hissed. In Plautus the fathers throughout only exist for the purpose of being jeered and swindled by their sons; with Terence in the *Heauton Timorumenos* the lost son is reformed by his father's wisdom, and, as in general he is full of excellent instructions as to education, so the point of the best of his pieces, the *Adelphi,* turns on finding the right mean between the too liberal training of the uncle and the too rigid training of the father. Plautus writes for the great multitude and gives utterance to profane and sarcastic speeches, so far as the censorship of the stage at all allowed; Terence on the contrary describes it as his aim to please the good and, like Menander, to offend nobody. Plautus is fond of vigorous, often noisy dialogue, and his pieces require a lively play of gesture in the actors; Terence confines himself to "quiet conversation." The language of Plautus abounds in burlesque turns and verbal witticisms, in alliterations, in comic coinages of new terms, Aristophanic combinations of words, pithy expressions of the day jestingly borrowed from the Greek. Terence knows nothing of such caprices; his dialogue moves on with the purest symmetry, and its points are elegant epigrammatic and sententious turns. The comedy of Terence is not to be called an improvement, as compared with that of Plautus, either in a poetical or in a moral point of view. Originality cannot be affirmed of either, but, if possible, there is less of it in Terence; and the dubious praise of more correct copying is at least outweighed by the circumstance that, while the younger poet reproduced the agreeableness, he knew not how to reproduced the merriment of Menander, so that the comedies of Plautus imitated from Menander, such as the *Stichus*, the *Cistellaria*, the *Bacchides*, probably preserve far more of the flowing charm of the original than the comedies of the *"dimidiatus Menander."* And, while the aesthetic critic cannot recognize an improvement in the transition from the coarse to the dull, as little can the moralist in the transition from the obscenity and indifference of Plautus to the accommodating morality of Terence. But in point of language an improvement certainly took place. Elegance of language was the pride of the poet, and it was owing above all to its inimitable charm that the most refined judges of art in aftertimes, such as Cicero, Caesar, and Quinctilian, assigned the palm to him among all the Roman poets of the republican age. In so far it is perhaps justifiable to date a new era in Roman literature—the real essence of which lay not in the development of Latin poetry, but in the development of the Latin language—from the comedies of Terence as the first artistically pure imitation of Hellenic works of art. The modern comedy made its way amidst the most determined literary warfare. The Plautine style of composing had taken root among the Roman *bourgeoisie;* the comedies of Terence encountered the liveliest opposition from the public, which found their "insipid language," their "feeble style," intolerable. The, apparently, pretty sensitive poet replied in his prologues—which properly were not intended for any such purpose—with counter-criticisms full of defensive and offensive polemics; and appealed from the multitude, which had twice run off from his *Hecyra* to witness a band of gladiators and rope-dancers, to the cultivated circles of the genteel world. He declared that he only aspired to the approval of the "good"; in which doubtless there was not wanting a hint, that it was not at all seemly to undervalue works of art which had obtained the approval of the "few." He acquiesced in or even favoured the report, that persons of quality aided him in composing with their counsel or even with their cooperation. In reality he carried his point; even in literature the oligarchy prevailed, and the artistic comedy of the exclusives supplanted the comedy of the people: we find that about 620 the pieces of Plautus disappeared from the set of stock plays. This is the more significant, because after the early death of Terence no man of conspicuous talent at all further occupied this field.

Cicero (106 B.C.-43 B.C.) praises Terence's style:

Thou, Terence, who alone dost reclothe Menander in choice speech, and rendering him into the Latin tongue, dost present him with thy quiet utterance on our public stage, speaking with a certain graciousness and with sweetness in every word.

Cicero, quoted in Ancilla to Classical Reading, *by Moses Hadas, Columbia University Press, 1954.*

J. Wright Duff (essay date 1909)

SOURCE: "The Theatre and the Masters of Comedy" in *A Literary History of Rome,* revised edition, Ernest Benn Limited, 1960, pp. 148-62.

[*Duff was an English classical scholar whose books include* A Literary History of Rome: From the Origins to the Close of the Golden Age *(1909) and* Writers of Rome *(1923). In the following excerpt from the revised edition of the former work, he provides an overview of Terence's plays and style.*]

It was the achievement of the young African, P. Terentius Afer (c. 195?-159 B.C.), to put upon Roman comedy the highest Hellenic polish. For his career our fullest source of knowledge is the interesting *Life of Terence* excerpted from Suetonius's work *De Poetis* and luckily preserved by Donatus in his commentary upon Terence. Suetonius is at pains to quote his authorities-some of them more than once-Fenestella, Nepos, Porcius, Volcatius, Varro, C. Memmius, Santra, Q. Cosconius, Afranius, Cicero, and Caesar. Besides Donatus's brief addendum there are Jerome's notes based on Suetonius, Terence's own prologues, and the *didascaliae* upon his plays. Neither his race nor the date of his birth can be stated decisively. His birth at Carthage, recorded by Suetonius, does not prove Phoenician blood: his cognomen 'Afer' rather suggests that he belonged to some native tribe conquered by the Carthaginians. Since his whole life falls between the second and the third Punic conflict, his slavery at Rome was certainly not due to capture in war. He may have been a regular purchase from a Carthaginian master or a victim of kidnappers. In any case he was educated by his Roman owner, a senator, Terentius Lucanus, and manumitted. His African origin was conceivably his initial recommendation to Africanus the Younger and through him to Laelius and other members of the Scipionic circle. Their patronage of the talented youth led to aspersions on his character and insinuations that the plays he produced were theirs. His first play, the *Andria,* was performed in 166 B.C. The six which he composed before his departure for Greece in 160 B.C. have all survived. At that date, according to the best texts of Suetonius, he had not yet entered his twenty-fifth year. This would imply that Terence made his mark with a stage-play of finished style in his eighteenth year: and this is well-nigh incredible. Though he was Scipio's 'contemporary' *(aequalis),* the term may be vaguely used, and there is no need to ascribe to him the same birth-year, 185 B.C. Indeed, there is the evidence of Fenestella and of Santra [cited by Suetonius in his *Life of Terence]* that he was senior to Scipio and Laelius.

As a dramatist his fortune was made on the afternoon when in humble attire *(contemptiore uestitu)* and unknown to the poets' college he presented himself, by order of the aediles, before Caecilius at dinner to read his first play to him. He had not gone far before the stranger's stool was exchanged for a place at table, and the whole was received enthusiastically after dinner. His fortunes, however, were chequered. If the *Eunuchus* was repeatedly staged and commanded unprecedented earnings, the *Hecyra* was fated to have its audience slip away to the superior allurements of rope-dancing and to fare little better at its next presentation five years later. If his refinement delighted his exalted friends, he had to face carping criticisms of the kind rebutted in his prologues. Indeed, one recorded reason for that journey to Greece from which he never returned was his disgust at the allegation that he published other men's work as his own. The more likely reason reminds one of the quest after Hellenic perfection in which Virgil's life closed. Terence desired to study at first hand the ways of the people who were the subject of his dramas. His death in 159 is wrapped in mystery. Was he lost at sea, as one account ran, homeward bound with a stock of plays adapted from Menander in Menander's own country, or did he die in Arcadia broken-hearted over the lost manuscripts of his latest plays?

The chronology of the plays presents vexed questions. It is important for an appreciation of the prologues. The prologue to the *Hecyra,* for instance, belongs to its complete presentation at the Roman Games of 160 B.C., and not to the original date of production, 165 B.C. Regarding the order of the plays and the occasions of their presentation, there are certain discrepancies, among the *didascaliae* of the best MS., the Codex Bembinus, the *didascaliae* in the Calliopian MSS., and the information in Donatus. There discrepanicies are partly due to presentations at different dates. Arranged according to their first performance, the plays are *Andria,* 166 B.C.; *Hecyra,* 165 (interrupted; resuscitated unsuccessfully in 160 for the funeral games of Aemilius Paulus, at which the *Adelphi* was presented, and completely presented later in the year at the Roman Games in September); *Heauton Timorumenos,* 163; *Eunuchus,* 161; *Phormio,* 161; *Adelphi (Adelphoe),* 160. The commonest occasion was the Megalensian festival in April.

Metrical arguments *(periochae . . .)* of twelve iambic senarii were prefixed to the plays by C. Sulpicius Apollinaris of Carthage, the probable author of the non-acrostic summaries of Plautus's plots and a teacher under whom Gellius studied. The prologues have the great value of personal and critical interest. Unlike some of the Plautine prologues, they are genuine utterances by the dramatist. They give information about the Greek source of the play, they request a favourable hearing, they indulge, with one exception, in recriminations against spiteful old Luscius. The one prologue which is not polemic, that to the *Hecyra,* has the interest of revealing certain difficulties besetting artistic comedy. It is in his prologues that Terence answers charges of plagiarism as an artist should:

> *Nullumst iam dictum quod non sit dictum prius,*

—and of 'contaminating' Greek plays by citing the precedent of Naevius, Plautus, and Ennius in their free departures from rigid translation. In answer to the charge that he had resorted to *belles lettres* with insufficient training *(repente ad studium hunc se adplicasse musicum)* and to the recurrent allegation of borrowed plumes *(amicum ingenio fretum haud natura sua),* his appeal is from biased to unbiased judgement. Tact prompted him to repel but faintly the suggestions of his indebtedness to the Scipionic circle. It was, he could urge, his highest glory to please the noble houses whose services were their country's unfailing

resource. At most Terence received stimulus and friendly criticism from his cultured coterie, and one may as confidently deny Scipionic or Laelian authorship of the comedies under his name as one denies a Baconian origin for Shakespeare's plays. Criticasters panting after excitement were sure to find in him 'thinness of dialogue and triviality of style' *(tenui esse oratione et scriptura leui).* They got their answer in his claim that he avoids extravagances and improbabilities. His aim, stated elsewhere, is to compose a drama of the quiet *(stataria)* type. There is in him a fine contempt for cheap and trite means of winning popular applause. Filled with a lively sense of the overpowering seductions of rope-dancing, boxing *(pugilum gloria),* and gladiatorial fights, it is in the higher interests of comedy that he devotes part of the later prologue of the *Hecyra* to an appeal for such support as will hearten the author himself in the teeth of venomous backbiting and encourage the actor-manager in dramatic enterprise.

About his sources there is no doubt . . . . His decided preference for Menander's plots brought Terence much of Menander's spirit. It accounts for the chief features of his dramatic qualities.

His plays, then, confront us with the same society as Plautus put on the stage, but the spirit is different. At every turn in criticising Terence the comparison with Plautus is inevitable. But the head and front of the contrast appears on the most cursory survey of Terence's plays. With him the scene is uniformly Athens, and we are seldom tempted to imagine ourselves in Rome. A slight sketch will reveal his dramatic world. *The Lady of Andros* does not herself appear, though the secret love between her and young Pamphilus is the hinge of the action. He is in danger of being forced to renounce his *inamorata* and marry at his father's dictation a neighbour's daughter beloved by his friend. The daring tactics suggested by his slave compensate in some degree for the absence of the romantic, and are much more entertaining than the half-expected discovery that the fair Andrian is in reality a daughter of the very neighbour with whose house an alliance was sought. In the *Hecyra,* or *The Innocent Mother-in-Law,* a bride during her husband's absence quits his house, not because of any disagreement with his mother, but because of a mishap in her past, for which, as it turns out, her own husband had been responsible. There is nothing comic in the play, but a good deal of the sentimental. The play might well be entitled *Why the Bride Went Back to her Home;* for that is the puzzle which affects in different ways the bridegroom, his mother, and the fathers of the two parties. The self-sacrificing part played by the courtesan in reuniting the separated pair betokens an unusual, but quite Terentian, tenderness in such a character.

The *Heauton Timorumenos,* or *Self Tormentor,* is a father who imposes penitential hardships on himself out of remorse for the strictness which has driven his son abroad. His elderly neighbour, who preaches at him when the play opens, needs to be reminded of his own theories before the close; for his own son repays his indulgence and encouragement of frank confidences by escapades far more extravagant than those of his self-exiled comrade, whom he is now sheltering on his secret return. The blindness of the old neighbour to his own son's misconduct facilitates the slave's trick which cheats him out of money to serve the young scapegrace. In true Terentian manner, when all comes out the mother's love is pitted against the hot anger of the father. More in the manner of the New Comedy, the profligate must be conventionally settled in life. Forgiveness is conditional on his marriage. Conventionally, too, he accepts the terms, but with a touch of fresh realism demurs to his mother's first suggestion: 'What! that red-haired girl, with cat eyes, blotchy face, and tip-tilted nose? I can't, father!' and he is allowed to pick a more acceptable bride.

In the *Eunuchus,* or *Sham Eunuch,* an Ethiopian slave is being sent by Phaedria to his mistress, Thais. Phaedria's brother disguises himself as the slave to pursue his amour with a girl in Thais's establishment. The girl is traced by her brother, proved to be free-born, and united to her lover. At a parasite's instigation, an inglorious bargain is struck between Phaedria and a soldier for shares in Thais's favours. This makes the least pleasing consummation in Terence, and recalls the final scenes in Plautus's *Asinaria* and *Bacchides.*

The *Phormio,* or *A Parasite's Brains to the Rescue,* dramatises the help in love rendered to two youths who are cousins. The parasite Phormio, in collusion with Antipho, one cousin, engineers a legal quirk by which Antipho receives an order of court to marry a pretty and lonely mourner with whom he has fallen in love. Cousin Phaedria is desperately found of a music-girl, but as desperately devoid of means. Phormio's smartness in getting money and the double life led by Antipho's uncle, Chremes, secure happiness for the youth. Sympathy is with the parasite when old Chremes, by endeavouring to maltreat him, brings about merited exposure in the eyes of his wife.

The title of *Adelphi* is doubly appropriate. It applies to the elderly brothers, Micio, the good-natured townsman, and Demea, the stern countryman. It applies also to the young brothers, Demea's sons, the frankly extravagant rake Aeschinus, and that supposed model Ctesipho. Psychologically, the play rivets attention. The forbearance of Micio, the effect of his system of upbringing on character, the blustering reproofs of his brother, the antithesis in disposition between the youths, prove how successfully Terence can dispense with external incident. It is impossible not to like Micio. He is far more gentlemanly than Plautus's Periplecomenus. His riotous nephew and adopted son, too, has sparks of shame and gratitude, and honours him as a better man in the sight of heaven. For the greater part of the play our sympathies are enlisted for Micio, who can take the ravings of his moralising brother philosophically and talk calmly over the training of Demea's lads. But with the astonishing *volte-face* made by Demea, Terence seems to change psychology for something very like extravaganza. It is the drollest thing in Terence. The countryman suddenly alters his system of life. He recognises the fresh lessons of facts, age, experience *(res, aetas, usus).* Strictness does not pay. Laxity does. He contrasts his own unpopularity with his brother's popularity. He resolves to try geniality. 'If it can be done by giving presents and honouring people, I'll not be behindhand.' He begins practis-

ing affability on two slaves. Then, in his new *rôle* of the easy-going father, he tells Aeschinus not to worry over preparations for his marriage, and recommends he should start without flute-player or wedding-hymn, and knock down the wall between the houses to bring the bride in with less trouble! Next, he coolly suggests that Micio must really marry the bride's mother! She has nobody to look after her. It is now the turn of the old bachelor to quake. He makes an amusing struggle for freedom, but—a victim to his easy-going principles—succumbs and reluctantly agrees to marry. The bride's relative, Hegio, must, like her mother, have something: so the now irresponsible Demea makes the offhand proposal that Hegio should have a 'little field' of Micio's. After arranging all this at Micio's expense, Demea rubs merrily into him his former remark that the common blemish of old age is over-attention to money and property: 'we ought to shun this blot' *(hanc maculam nos decet ecfugere).* But Demea's humour is not yet ended. He insists that the slave, Syrus, be freed-he is so sharp at marketing, and at providing questionable company for his young master, that he deserves a good turn, *pour encourager les autres (prodesse aequomst: alii meliores erunt).* Syrus having expressed a wish that his wife Phrygia should be freed, Demea of course seconds this heartily. Finally, Demea tells Micio he must produce ready money for his new freedman to start in life. Thus Demea has brought Micio's facile system *ad absurdum.* The last word lies with Demea. 'I have shown,' he says in effect, 'that your reputation as a jolly good fellow is based not on principles of sound justice, but on giving people their own way. Now,' he remarks to the youths, 'if you wish me to restrain you in pursuits the consequences of which you are too young to foresee, I am ready to render that service.' And Aeschinus, the slackly brought up' youth, agrees that his father knows more of what is right and proper *(plus scis quod opus factost).* Thus the whole conclusion has the surprising quality of paradox.

The Terentian characters are more subtle, more refined, more humane than those of Plautus. The same society reappears—more amiable, but less virile. At heart it is no better, but fuller concessions are made to outward appearance. A woman's purity or a child's life may go for little, and a veneer may gloze over excesses, and yet something is gained in the realm of feeling. Youths exhibit increased affection for fathers, slaves increased respect for masters. The prevailing urbanity reflects Terence's own circle, and stamps him the dramatist of the aristocracy, as Plautus was the dramatist of the people. Nothing jars in the considerate politeness of Chremes in the *Andria* when he declines to renew his daughter's engagement to Simo's son. Similar courtesy permeates the interviews of the fathers of the separated pair in the *Hecyra.* Such fathers in general treat their sons rationally, and expect regard and open confidence in return. Micio roundly scolds his adopted son for his misconduct, but he recognises all the time that 'if serious, it is human,' and he wins the young man's real gratitude. A son in Terence does not wish the death of a father who crosses his passion—he may go the length of wishing him three days in bed without serious injury to health. Most Terentian sons are more deferential than Clitipho in the *Heauton Timorumenos,* who does not listen to his father *(surdo narret fabulam),* and jests over his father's indiscreet revelations in his cups. The relations of master and man have palpably improved. It is unusual to find in Terence such fierce threats as are hurled at Davos in the **Andria.** This very Davos, distrusted as much too smart *(mala mens, malus animus),* is the one who reminds Pamphilus of his duty to his father. Slaves receive fair treatment. The cynical defiance of torture is not ridden to death as in Plautus. The soldier lies and boasts more plausibly. The parasite also is more real. Gnatho of the **Eunuchus** is not such a grotesque figure as the Plautine gourmandisers, for his studied flattery and its success are not so very impossible in actual life; while Phormio has independent brains and deserves his reward. A parallel refinement in the courtesan has taken place. The most repulsive type has given place to one capable of genuine feeling, hurt when her affection is doubted, lonely though she has gallants, and devoted to her foster-sister. Humility in the presence of a matron and the virtue of self-sacrifice are still nobler traits. Thais in the **Eunuchus** and Bacchis in the **Hecyra** have touches almost prophetic of *La Dame aux Camélias.* Broadly, the elemental problem of sex retains too much of the conventional in its treatment to become romantic. Chaerea's passion in the **Eunuchus** is abnormally furious for Terence. A more representative lover is Pamphilus, who reveals his love for Glycerium at the funeral scene in the **Andria,** and declares that death alone will part him from his beloved. Here, as elsewhere, Terence practises restraint. Rhapsodical passion could not be so consonant with his spirit as the tamer gallantry of Phaedria in the **Eunuchus,** whose motto that 'It is something to love, even if you're out of the lists' may explain his acquiescence in the claims of his military rival. In such social circumstances, marriage at the close of a play is frequently a retarded reparation for an act of brutality.

Terence's polished repression was purchased at the expense of energy. There is an absence of impetuosity in action, less caricature among characters, fewer freaks of language, as compared with Plautus. But the gain in regularity has meant a loss of vigour, colour, daring. Terence substitutes a minuter psychology and a more pervading sentimentality for the broad strokes of Plautus, but he is tame in proportion. No one character, no one scene, no one play, stands out with such pre-eminent distinctness as several in Plautus do, although there is a pervading sense of finish. It is characteristic that there should be recurrent *motifs,* and confusingly recurrent names of personages in different plays. The author did not elaborate in the direction of individuality, and his characters are not abiding creations. In other dramatic qualities and artifices Plautus and Terence differ widely. The imperfectly constructed plots, the extravagant and irrelevant episodes, the provoking tautologies, the teasing postponements of a piece of news, the unfettered anachronisms, have gone, but with them also much of Plautus's robust strength and rollicking humour. There is no hearty laughter in Terence. One must pay for better workmanship. The kernel of the matter lies in Caesar's criticism—Terence lacked the full share of *uis comica.* He was an artist; Plautus, an untutored genius.

The style of Terence is the perfection of lightness and clearness. A foreigner, he wrote Latin with an Attic grace.

The purity of his idiom, remarked by Caesar, had been from the first guaranteed by rumours of Scipionic authorship. Hitting the mean between the florid and the simple style, he was for Varro the model of *mediocritas,* as Pacuvius was of *ubertas* and Lucilius of *gracilitas.* Critics, English and French, have noted his Addisonian qualities. One might almost parody the sentence with which Johnson closes his *Life of Addison* and declare—Whoever wishes to attain a Latin style, familiar but not coarse, and elegant but not ostentatious, must give his days and nights to the dramas of Terence. Certainly Terence possesses the merits of the best English literature of the eighteenth century—'regularity, uniformity, precision, and balance.' Like the eighteenth century, he eschews the vulgar and polishes to *finesse* the choice language of aristocratic culture. Here again the contrast with Plautus is decided. Taste renounces his common colloquialisms and slang, as it renounces his almost barbaric exuberance of puns and alliterations. The goal is correctness rather than variety, refinement rather than originality. As in the eighteenth century, there is no horror of the commonplace, provided it be rendered in consummate form:

> What oft was thought, but ne'er so well expressed.

This is the secret of Terence's wealth of phrases eminently quotable for pith, point, or balance. They often give final literary expression to some experience or to shrewd homespun wit . . . . Much of the definitely proverbial and reflective in Terence came from the Greek, and received a fresh lease of life from the brevity and force of his translation.

The humour of Terence is essentially quiet. He has genial satire for extremes. The too strict brother, who propounds a system of precepts and a 'mirror of morality,' he parodies in the slave's culinary mirror—the bright saucepan to test kitchen-work. The too indulgent brother he ridicules by pushing his system to its utmost bounds. Terence's humour is the outcome of that Menandrian moderation which tempers his whole outlook. He would hold with his own cheerful Micio that life is a game, and the bad in it must be mended with skill—not with passionate invective. If a character has to be laughed at, there is nothing ill-natured, just as there is nothing boisterous, in the laugh. So Ctesipho—the 'Joseph Surface' of Terence—who is content that his brother should be suspected for his sake, is let off lightly. The Terentian humour is seen to advantage in the clever little scene in the **Phormio** designed to satirise the advice of friends—those 'prophets of the past' as Byron calls them. And without possessing Plautus's humour, Terence has the saving grace of being able to jest at his own art. A mock realism of effect is introduced in the **Hecyra** by contrasting the life of his play with the tricks of the stage. 'No need for so much as a whisper,' says Pamphilus, who has the best of reasons for hiding from his father the manner of his getting a young lady's ring, 'we don't want this to happen exactly as in comedies, where everybody knows everything.'

The prosody of Terence, though more 'regular' than that of Plautus, follows the same fundamental principles: that is, the accent of spoken Latin plays a dominant part in regulating scansion. There is a marked decrease in the variety of metres. They are prevailingly iambic (senarian or septenarian) and trochaic (septenarian) to suit less or more animated dialogue. Lyric measures other than trochaic octonarians are rare. The musical accompaniments for the portions sung were provided by 'Flaccus, the slave of Claudius.' It is recorded that four sorts of flutes, differing in length and key, were employed by him.

A drama so consistently Hellenic in manners and style was too subtly artistic to hold the populace. With Terence comedy became aristocratic and gradually withdrew from the theatre. His appeal was to the refinement of his day; and at all times he is best appreciated in the study. His classic purity was a potent influence on literature. It won not panegyrists only but imitators. Cicero is particularly fond of quoting Terence. Horace found in him much that was congenial, and borrowed his phrases freely. To Quintilian he was 'elegantissimus,' and this very elegance made him appear insidiously dangerous in the eyes of those Fathers of the Church who denounced his world of lustful intrigue. Yet it was the nun Hrosvitha who imitated his plays in the tenth century; and in the sixteenth Schoon ('Schonaeus') of Gouda wrote his *Terentius Christianus*, six plays in Terentian style upon subjects drawn from Holy Writ, in which the pagan and the biblical are quaintly blended. The influence of Terence was maintained by being studied and acted in the schools of the Middle Ages; it acted powerfully on Erasmus, Melanchthon, and scholars of their time. The influence was widened by translation into different vernaculars, and from the Renaissance onwards, his plays, by example, contributed to inculcate, especially in France, a regard for the 'unities' of the drama. Indeed, it is in France, the home of the best modern prose and the best modern conversation, that Terence has since the seventeenth century gained his most sympathetic admirers, and most firmly fastened his hold upon literary taste . . . .

Gilbert Norwood   (essay date 1923)

SOURCE: "Conclusion" in *The Art of Terence*, Basil Blackwell, 1923, pp. 131-52.

[*Norwood was an American classical scholar whose books include* Greek Comedy *(1932) and* Pindar *(1945). In the following excerpt from his well-regarded monograph on Terence, he summarizes Terence's career, praising especially the playwright's humanist impulse and declaring him* "the most Christian writer of pagan antiquity."]

[Terence] is an attractive, a tantalizing, almost a mysterious figure. A native of Africa, not a Carthaginian but of Libyan birth, and possibly a mulatto or a quadroon (as Suetonius' description, *mediocri statura, gracili corpore, colore fusco,* might suggest), he was brought in childhood to Rome and became the slave of one Terentius Lucanus, a senator. This excellent man, little dreaming that by his good nature he was conferring a notable benefit upon posterity, gave the lad a sound education, and ultimately his freedom and his own name. Terence enjoyed the intimacy of Scipio Africanus Minor and his circle, especially the amiable Caius Laelius, produced six plays, journeyed to Greece with the intention (it appears) of collecting more works of Menander, and died without returning to Rome, at the age of thirty-one or even less. Such are the only facts of importance at our command; they seem to provide small help towards explaining his achievement in dramatic composition, or the notable circumstance that this African stripling, who learned Latin as a foreign tongue, could use it with an elegance and purity which quickened the coarsegrained Roman language with Attic elasticity and charm.

The story does, however, contain one apparent clue. It was reported in his own day, and later, that to his friendship with the Scipionic circle Terence owed much of his success. These accomplished young nobles, fond of theatrical displays and imbued with a taste for Greek literature, had a hand in his writings, we are to suppose, and to them a considerable part of the credit (how great is not precisely indicated) must be transferred. We find in the poet's own prologues allusion to this story. The earlier is in *Self-Punishment:*

> tum quod malivolus vetus poeta dictitat, repente
> ad studium hunc se adplicasse musicam,
> amicum ingenio fretum, haud natura sua: ar-
> bitrium vostrum, vostra existumatio valebit.

The later and more striking occurs in *The Brothers:*

> nam quod ita dicunt malivoli, homines nobilis
> hunc adiutare adsidueque una scribere:
> quod illi maledictum vehemens esse existumant,
> eam laudem hic ducit maxumam, quom illis pla-
>   cet,
> qui vobis univorsis et populo placent,
> quorum opera in bello, in otio, in negotio
> suo quisque tempore usust sine superbia.

Three facts are plain. Firstly, the report has gained wider currency as time advances: in the earlier play Luscius Lanuvinus alone is mentioned (though not by name) as a traducer, whereas in the later work a number of ill-wishers appear. Secondly, the precise wording of the charge is that 'men of high birth are his helpers and constant collaborators.' Thirdly, Terence is careful neither to rebut nor to admit the accusation, and in *The Brothers* remarks that it is no disgrace, but a great credit to himself, that he is 'favoured by' (*placet*) men who 'have won the favour of' (*placent*) the whole nation by their distinguished services; he is appealing dexterously though disingenuously to the principle *laudari a laudato.* The first of these facts is of small importance. Again, that Terence scrupulously avoids denying or accepting the statement, though highly interesting, leads us in fact nowhere; for it suits equally both the truth and the falsity of the charge. Were it false, he would be little disposed, considering his desire for popularity and the opposition he was meeting, to refuse so strong a claim upon popular favour. Were it true, he would have no wish either to fix publicly upon distinguished nobles a practical interest in theatrical composition which they clearly desired to conceal, or to deprive himself of that considerable credit which on any showing belonged to him.

We are therefore compelled to judge the second fact—the existence of the charge itself—on its own merits. What is

Wall niche with masks for The-Mother-in-Law, *from an early manuscript of the play.*

its intrinsic probability? Are we to believe that Scipio and Laelius were indeed the poet's 'continual collaborators,' that he is little more than the mouthpiece of others, that he stood to them in a relation which some allege Shakespeare to have held towards Bacon? Considered in the abstract, such an arrangement was quite possible. But there is no trustworthy external evidence that it existed. Even the contemporary statement does not prove itself; granted that some were jealous of Terence, and that he was an associate of cultivated noblemen, the charge was in any case certain to be made. Nor is there any internal evidence. Where in these six comedies can one point out unevenness of style, inequalities of versification, suspicious excrescences in structure, or (above all) arresting allusions to contemporary Roman policy, events, opinions, eminent persons? It is difficult to believe that the sprightly Laelius would never have inserted some racy piece of 'topical' fun, some witty satire, had Terence been nothing but a secretary and not free to leave his characters and events so generalized that some readers have deplored the absence of all local colour and other such specific features of interest. As it is, these comedies show nothing in their subject-matter which would enable us to date them; in this respect Terence's collaborator might as well have been Hadrian as Scipio. If these works come from various hands, they are a curiosity perhaps unique in literature. Such partnership is far from unknown; but the scholar confidently distinguishes the contributions of Fletcher from those of Beaumont, and in a single play, (*Eastward Ho,* for example) finds not infrequently evidence of even three co-operating dramatists. But the six works before us defy the keenest scalpel.

It is nevertheless plain that Terence wrote in the first instance for a coterie, and we may easily suppose that one or another of his patrons from time to time suggested some Greek play as a model or as containing material which he could turn to account; he may even have received advice as to ideas which he should throw into dramatic form. So much we may safely assume, but assuredly, not that the suggestions were always, or ever, adopted; though it naturally cannot be denied that he may have used hints such as that which John Crowne received from Charles the Second and which resulted in *Sir Courtly Nice,* or may have obeyed a friendly wish, as Shakespeare obeyed Elizabeth in composing *The Merry Wives of Windsor.* The important facts are that he wrote for a coterie, and that he passed beyond its influence. The first is proved by his own prologues, by his custom of giving Greek titles to his plays—*Hecyra* instead of *Socrus,* for example, is a curious affectation—and by the boldness wherewith he rebukes the low taste of the *populus stupidus:* he feels that supporting him is a solid, if small, party of cultivated friends. That he passed beyond this, that he did not remain merely the poet of a clique, is the most striking feature of his career.

Instead of becoming a poet of esoteric 'cachet' and producing a subtly artificial 'vintage' calculated only for highly-sophisticated palates, Terence steps forth from the Scipionic circle, determined to be a Roman dramatist. He will take a place in the history of Latin art, and announces

to the world the reform of Comedy. A well-known critic [J. W. Mackail, *Latin Literature*] has written:

> In all of them (the Terentian prologues) there is a certain hard and acrid purism that cloaks in modest phrases an immense contempt for all that lies beyond the writer's own canons of taste. *In bac est pura oratio,* a phrase of the prologue to *The Self-Tormentor,* is the implied burden of them all. He is a sort of literary Robespierre; one seems to catch the premonitory echo of well-known phrases, "degenerate condition of literary spirit, backsliding on this hand on that, I, Terence, alone left incorruptible." Three times there is a reference to Plautus, and always with a tone of chilly superiority which is too proud to break into an open sneer.

This is all true, but the writer evidently condemns it as discreditable or misguided in Terence. Others will regard our poet as completely justified in his opinions and his tone, the only cause for wonder being that a dramatist possessing both youth and genius (a combination rarely productive of discretion in criticism) should have expressed himself so urbanely. He is defending himself against the tasteless indifference of the multitude and the pedantic censure of rivals; he is also proclaiming a new and fruitful method of writing comedy. The whole situation reminds one strongly of Marlowe and his prologue to *Tamburlaine the Great:*

> From jigging veins of rhyming mother-wits,
> And such conceits as clownage keeps in pay,
> I'll lead you to the stately tent of war,
> Where   you   shall   see   the   Scythian
> Tamburlaine . . .

There is the same self-confidence, defiance, artistic theorizing, the same promise and the same splendid fulfilment.

Hence each of these six prologues contains matter invaluable to the literary historian. We have discussed the alleged collaboration of Scipio and his friends. Another theme is the poet's defence of his method and style. Thus the prologue to *The Girl of Andros* tells us that some objected to *contaminatio;* do they not realize that they are herein accusing Naevius, Plautus, and Ennius, the authorities whom Terence follows? So in *Self-Punishment* he says his detractors complain that by this practice he has made few Latin out of many Greek plays: 'quite so; I am not ashamed of that and shall do it again, since I am thereby following good examples.' In *The Eunuch* there is an elaborate defence against the charge of plagiarism from Naevius and Plautus. His own method of composition is well described in *Self-Punishment: statariam agere ut liceat per silentium, and in hac est pura oratio.* At other times he returns the onslaught with damaging criticism of his censor's own work. *The Girl of Andros* merely hints at this; in *Self-Punishment* an example of rowdyism on the stage is pilloried, with the threat that more rebukes are to follow unless the adversary mends his ways. Accordingly in *The Eunuch* he ridicules a blunder in legal procedure, and in *Phormio* a piece of sensational pathos unsuited to comedy. Lastly, there are remarks on the audience. In the prologues to *The Mother-in-Law* he is naturally bitter against the 'stupidity' of the spectators who have twice caused the play to fail; it seems, too, that this result was partly caused by the annoyance or scandalized hostility which the work aroused in women. The poet appeals for a fair hearing. 'Give me,' he exclaims in an early work, 'a chance to grow: I give you a chance to see new and flawless plays.' But although he has assuredly grown by the time he composes **The Mother-in-Law,** we find his actor-manager Ambivius Turpio hinting that detraction has so discouraged Terence that he has been on the point of retiring from the theatre. This same prologue contains the splendid appeal:

> vobis datur
> potestas condecorandi ludos scaenicos.
> nolite sinere per vos artem musicam
> recidere ad paucos.

These words may reveal something of that haughtiness discussed above, but they are nevertheless the unmistakable language of an artist who, refusing to content himself with a clique of intellectuals, would reform popular comedy and give the whole Roman people a taste for sound art. It proved to be *vox clamantis in deserto.* Quintilian centuries later confessed that comedy was the 'lame dog' of Latin literature.

Here, before we quit this theme, his literary career, some general remarks may be added . . . concerning his style. There is comparatively little in Latin which has kinship with it; but often in Horace, in the letters of Cicero and Pliny, we have this sense of well-balanced worldly experience uttering itself in diction unforced and limpid. Congreve's style exhibits the same mastery of unexcited brilliance. Thackeray, especially perhaps in *Esmond,* has much of the quiet Terentian vigour in dialogue as in character-drawing. Marivaux, as Pichon has admirably observed, resembles the Roman poet, not only in the conduct of his drama, but also in his dialogue. Balzac, perhaps more than any other, recalls his ingratiating pungency, his skill in slowly cumulative effect, his expression of sheer humanity. Throughout, the diction of Terence makes upon us the impression of patient and tranquil resourcefulness,

> As a cunning workman, in Pekin,
> Pricks with vermilion some clear porcelain vase,
> An emperor's gift—at early morn he paints,
> And all day long, and, when night comes, the
>   lamp
> Lights up his studious forehead and thin hands.

Of some such pale porcelain, or wrought ivory, delicately tinged with subtly-blent colours, this mode of language may remind us, or of that frail spiritual St. Jerome pictured by Cosimo Tura, kneeling in rapture upon the sand as his eyes, frame, and nervous fingers pass into something ethereal that transcends the flesh under the radiance of the indwelling and transmuting soul.

Let us turn now to gather an appreciation of his strictly dramatic talent, and deal first with two great defects which may plausibly be alleged against Terence here. Julius Caesar thought him but a 'half-Menander' because his *purus sermo,* his *lenia scripta,* are not supported by *vis comica.* Also, it was remarked . . . that many readers will find too much sameness in the general effect of the six plays.

Vis comica means one of two things: power, forcefulness, dramatic pungency as seen in comedy, of whatever type the comedy may be; or that 'comic' force which illuminates and refreshes by means of racy humour and fun in action, the whole plot being a well-constructed joke. In the first kind a magnificent example is the work of Molière; in the second, the *Frogs* (let us say) of Aristophanes. That Terence, save in the curious and unsuccessful 'battlescene' of **The Eunuch,** never attempted the latter type is manifest; but it is clear that in the former he is a master fully equal to Molière. Of what, then, is Caesar complaining? The obvious answer might seem to be that he prefers comedy, of which the *Frogs* is possibly the best existing specimen, or rather that he confines *vis comica* to this type, and that he blames Terence for lack of excellence therein. But, as a fact, he blames him in comparison with Menander, not with Aristophanes. It seems an inevitable dilemma that we must either suppose Menander to have shown an Aristophanic quality for which there is no other evidence—the other available evidence, of course, is entirely against such a belief—or suppose that Terence, in Caesar's view, had no *vis* even of Menander's kind. Whichever horn of the dilemma we choose, Caesar must be set down as the worst of critics.

The other charge, an excessive sameness in the general effect, must be admitted as fairly true . . . . [There are] marked differences between the plays in psychology and construction; but it cannot be denied that there is small variation from one to another in the ordinary fabric of diction. This evenness of surface seems a mark of the Comedy of Manners—both Molière and Congreve show it too—and in Terence the defect is aggravated by the extremely brief catalogue of proper names which he would appear to have at his disposal. It is probably an inheritance from Menander, and may remind us how Greek literature after the fifth century, despite its elegance and high value, does tend strongly towards monotony of texture. Isocrates, for example, cannot be read for more than half an hour without effort. Menander, if we may judge from his copious though comminuted remains, shared this slipperiness of surface. It is, finally, due (to no small degree in Terence, and no doubt in his Greek predecessors) to an almost total absence of picturesqueness in the details of events or stage management—such things as the caskets in Portia's house, Perdita's distribution of the flowers, and countless other such beauties. *In hac est pura oratio.*

We may next summarize the progress in dramatic power shown by these works when viewed chronologically. The **Andria** is a plain love-story, obtaining the complication necessary for drama from the elementary facts that Glycerium is supposed not of free Attic birth and that Pamphilus therefore does not tell his father the truth when marriage with another woman is suggested. Among these facts we do not include the interests of Charinus because they are not necessary to the complication here spoken of. But they are interesting as proof that Terence's duality-method is in his mind from the outset of his career; so much so that he has given us in Charinus a character not found in Menander's play.

Self-Punishment deals with the same love-story, helped out technically by the father's peculiar connexion therewith and by another youth's liaison with a courtesan. In ***The Eunuch*** we find the same story, but shown in its very inception; it is helped out both technically and morally by a similar liaison, the courtesan being now of first-rate importance. ***Phormio*** shows the love-match again, but as a legal marriage; the courtesan-element is present, but slight, owing most of its interest to the part played in connexion with it by Phormio, who dominates the whole action, including the factor contributed by the bigamy of the heroine's father. In ***The Mother-in-Law*** the two familiar elements again appear, but very differently handled. The love-match which has begun, as in ***The Eunuch,*** and at the end continues in affectionate marriage, as in ***Phormio,*** is here shown combined with the liaison far more closely than hitherto, the courtesan being the former mistress of the husband himself. Moreover, the ***senes,*** who are usually somewhat distant from the technical centre of gravity, here not only develop into two elderly married couples, but, since this is a drama of more normal life and more permanent elements, stand at the very heart of the action. ***The Brothers*** exhibits once again the more reputable and the less reputable love-affair, superficially with the same baldness as in ***Self-Punishment,*** but employing it to raise the whole problem of the true relation in which fathers should stand to their sons. Throughout, then, is to be observed the same starting-point, two love-affairs. In the ***Andria*** this *motif* is faint and poor, since the suit of Charinus is so feebly handled; the three succeeding plays give it a strong but obvious interest; in the two final masterpieces it serves as occasion for a noble study of family life; in the ***Hecyra*** the root-interest being purely domestic and internal, while in the ***Adelphoe*** the family interest leads us outward to consider its import for society at large.

Terence's splendid principle of accepting the traditional framework and evolving from it a thoroughly serious, permanently interesting, type of drama, becomes instantly evident from this survey. But the double love-entanglement is not the sole, though it is the most striking, example of this. It will have been noticed how steadily the *senex* develops in psychology and structural value, from the ***Andria,*** where he is mere machinery to further or thwart a marriage, right through to the ***Adelphoe,*** where he is himself the very heart of the interest. In the earlier period he is seen entirely from the outside—a permanent and dangerous feature of the landscape; in the later we are admitted into his soul and can watch him from every angle. Another instance of this development is the *rôle* assigned to the confidential slave. Davus in the ***Andria*** presents the traditional type, the playwright's ostensible agent to keep things moving; his part is very long, he exhibits the normal cunning, fears, and resource, meddles with everything and orchestrates everyone's emotion. Syrus in ***Self-Punishment*** is much the same, but his part is not quite so extensive, and the set-back which he meets in the middle of the play (the revelation of Antiphila's parentage) is more serious than that faced by Davus (Simo's determination to turn the pretended marriage-scheme into earnest).

The Eunuch marks a notable development. Parmeno is fairly important, in particular because he suggests the stratagem to Chaerea. But Terence is careful to rob him of the credit: Chaerea jumps at the plan, while Parmeno seeks nervously to withdraw. Moreover he is deluded by Pythias so utterly that he reverses the customary situation by divulging the whole affair to his old master and embroils himself unnecessarily. In ***Phormio,*** Geta is technically still lower: though he performs good service, it is merely as an underling to the magnificent Phormio, and long before the end he is forgotten. The Parmeno of ***The Mother-in-Law*** is merely pitiable: he is constantly ordered off the stage so as not to impede the action, and his being kept in the dark at the end is the exact negation of the *rôle* traditionally given to such characters. In ***The Brothers,*** however, Syrus is better treated; for example, he succeeds in postponing Demea's discovery of Ctesipho's secret.

In this manner one might pass from his handling of tradition to his advance in characterization as a whole . . . It is enough to recall one class of examples, which also reveal once more his power of self-improvement. Terence seems to dwell with especial delight on the idea of a noble and amiable courtesan. In the ***Andria*** Chrysis does not appear on the stage at all; she is dead before the play opens, but her goodness and gentle wisdom suffuse the scenes with a glow of distant sunshine. ***The Eunuch*** presents a very similar creation, but there Thais in her own person pervades and directs the action, a figure structurally analogous to Phormio. Bacchis in ***The Mother-in-Law*** is one of the noblest, most authentic, most loveable characters in Roman literature; and her share in the plot, though less active than that of Thais, is no less momentous.

The last element in his dramatic development is one which has been mentioned more than once, but which is so vital that it calls for final summary here. It is the method of employing two problems or complications to solve each other. This conception appears already in the ***Andria,*** fully understood (perhaps) but badly executed. Charinus and his interests do not genuinely affect the situation of Pamphilus. ***Self-Punishment*** exhibits the method in full vigour, but the interweaving impresses us less with a sense of subtlety and appropriateness than with a feeling of strain due to over-complication and obtrusive cleverness, since the instrument is employed both by Syrus and by Menedemus. Terence purges this excessive elaboration away in ***The Eunuch,*** but in doing so gravely weakens the effect of his second problem, the love-affair of Chaerea; striking or curious as are the scenes to which that affair gives rise, the genuine interaction of the two interests is limited to this, that Chaerea's amour is made, during the last few minutes of the play and behind the scenes, to extract from the father his acquiescence in the liaison of Phaedria and Thais. ***Phormio*** shows the principle at last perfected; it might seem capable of no new development. But the playwright is not content with this triumph of mere elegance in intrigue. His broad vivid interest in life takes up the consummate method and employs it upon new tasks. Thus in ***The Mother-in-Law*** the two problems hinge upon one man only, their interaction securing, not a joyful marriage and a success of gallantry, but the permanent happiness of a young couple already married, the satisfaction of their parents, and the future of their child; in **The Brothers** the same two problems lead us quite beyond themselves to a broad consideration of life itself, based on discussion of the relations between old and young.

If, finally, we ask what idea about human life is impressed upon his work, we may find our way to such a generalization by setting out from one simple fact: if we ignore Gnatho and Thraso, who belong to the feeble pseudo-Plautine scenes of **The Eunuch,** we observe that all Terence's people are good. It is not meant that they are 'moral' or show no grave weaknesses; taking that sense of the word 'good,' we must condemn almost all his people. But there is no Terentian character (with the two exceptions already named) whose heart is not sound, whom the reader feels it would be impossible to respect, from whom he would object to receive an obligation if need arose. We do not forget or except the Bacchis of **Self-Punishment,** who (though the least admirable of all) is heard on her first appearance uttering to Antiphila words of wistful admiration and envy:

> edepol te, mea Antiphila, laudo et fortunatam
> iudico, id quom studuisti, isti formae ut mores
> consimiles forent,

and the rest. The other *meretrices* need no defence; and a study of the slaves and of Phormio, not to mention the fathers, mothers, and sons, will lead us to the same conclusion. 'Contempt is a sentiment that cannot be entertained by comic intelligence.'

But the most arresting example is provided by the *lenones*. It is easy to misjudge this class. If we take a modern view, translate *leno* by 'pandar,' and imagine a wretch who makes money by dragging the innocent into shame and keeping them there, we shall go astray. These things, as cold facts, were true of the ancient *leno;* but here, as elsewhere, we must cultivate the historical imagination. His conduct may have been as bad then as now, absolutely considered; relatively, it was far less heinous. The recognition of slavery makes an immense difference. The women under his control were allowed on all hands to be his property; if he purchased them legally, he could employ them as he did with precisely as much right as others employed male slaves to toil in mines or cultivate a farm. It is not to be denied that his trade was despised, but a regular trade it was. He was regarded in the same light, not as a modern *leno,* but as a modern money-lender. It was conceivable that he should be a tolerably acceptable fellow-citizen, though he is of course often represented as falling ignominiously short of this, the chief reason perhaps being that the plays in which he appears demand objectionable features in him so as to create or increase the difficulties of the 'hero.' But it is notable that, vigorous as is the abuse cast upon him, none of the modern accusations is to be found. His great crimes are rapacity and fraud, as numberless passages in Plautus testify; all the sneers—*si leno est homo* and the rest—amount to that when the speaker comes to details. Terence has made of him a tradesman. Read the scenes in **Phormio** and **The Brothers** where Dorio and Sannio appear, and imagine for an instant that the former is a horse-dealer, the latter a dog-fancier; what objection can be offered to anything they do or say? Only

this, that Dorio in the **Phormio,** after agreeing to a date by which Phaedria is to pay, proposes to sell the girl before the fixed day to a person who has made a more attractive offer. (This is undoubtedly sharp practice, and brings Dorio nearer to the Plautine *lenones.* Sannio is quite free from such offence: here again we observe development.)

That these two men deal in other merchandise than dogs or horses is terrible and vile, but that fact is plainly the shame of the whole civilization which recognizes them. Sudden incursions of irrelevant, though superior, morality are unfair. Dorio is a man of business. Before the question of date is mentioned, we read:

> *Antipho:* heia, ne parum leno sies.
>   numquid hic confecit?
> *Phaedria:* hicine? quod homo inhumanissumus:
>   Pamphilam meam vendidit.
> *Antipho:* quid? vendidit?
> *Geta:* ain vendidit?
> *Phaedria:* vendidit.
> *Dorio:* quam indignum facinus, ancillam aere
>   emptam meo!

All the logic, all the business attitude which Phaedria himself is perfectly ready to accept when it suits his own purpose, are on Dorio's side. As for his colleague in **The Brothers,** his case is even stronger. Aeschinus coolly robs him of his property, and Demea, when the news comes to his ear, rightly considers Sannio as the victim of an outrage. It is, then, the plain truth that in Terence everyone (save always Thraso and Gnatho) is, despite lapses, on the whole and in his situation, sound, worthy of respect, what our colloquial language calls 'decent.' If we contrast his method with that of Dickens, to whom it is fashionable to attribute an almost morbid charity, and contemplate his Pecksniffs, Quilps, Chadbands, Carkers, we shall appraise duly the breadth and insight of the heathen dramatist.

But what of the sexual morality expressed by these plays, and the tinge even of lubricity in **Self-Punishment** and **The Eunuch**? Most readers are unlikely to go wrong with regard to the general tone. Terence adopts a standard less strict than ours, but not in itself surprising or unworkable. Intimacy with a courtesan on casual terms is in his works a serious fault which is, however, by no means damning; it corresponds to reckless gambling or occasional drunkenness in our own day. Cohabitation based on mutual affection is considered by him, naturally, as far less censurable. The great objection to it is its unwisdom—so many unhappy or awkward results may arise. But such unions are 'morally' equivalent to marriage; *pro uxore habere* is a phrase more than once employed by Terence. Such women were really in the situation of those in our own country a few years ago who 'married' their deceased sisters' husbands; the union was simply ignored by the courts. With the best will in the world, a foreign woman could not in Athens marry a citizen: such 'marriages' were illegal. As for the lubricity shown by two passages, it is a passing feature. In **Self-Punishment** it is very slight; in **The Eunuch** it is a blot, but may be partly condoned as marking the character of Chaerea and so giving peculiar value to the change of heart which Thais works in him. A significant comment on the whole subject is, as we saw, the sound-hearted attitude which prevails regarding the possibility of children.

This impression, that all his persons are good, rests on the central fact about Terence. He is interested most of all, not in virtue or vice, or 'problems' or 'movements,' but in people. His subject is mere humanity; hence the notable frequency in his pages of *homo, humanus,* and other such words. He knows that the key to life is not the application of standards, but clear-sighted sympathy. From this knowledge flows that 'sweet reasonableness' which moulds his dramatic structure, his characterization, and his diction alike. Hence flows also his fondness for moralizing. He is one of the few writers whose sententiousness we can not merely tolerate but enjoy; many will even find that the passages which cling most firmly to their memory are Micio's words concerning the game of life—*quasi quom ludis tesseris*—or the slave's homily, at the opening of **The Eunuch,** on the unreason of lovers. Terence is, in fact, the Horace of the theatre. Their affinity lies not only in this apt and pleasant moralizing: it is seen too in their diction—elastic, dignified, elegant; in their exquisitely clear understanding of their own purpose; in their perception of precisely how much they can, and how much they cannot, perform; in their unaffected relish for human nature. Something of all this Horace may actually have imbibed from Terence: the Terentian echoes in his work, though not numerous, are remarkable.

Terence is the most Christian writer of pagan antiquity. It is not difficult to find in Greek, even in Latin, literature authors who surpass him in profundity of thought and feeling, in beauty of language, in wideness of appeal. But in this noble realization that 'We are members one of another' he comes nearest to St. Paul, nearer even than those memorable passages of the *Republic* where Plato bases the efficiency, the happiness, the very life of society upon the doctrine of human fellowship. In Plato this is an intellectual conviction with a political outcome; in Terence it is an instinctive conviction with a moral outcome. For Plato it is an engine of statesmanship; for Terence it is a way of life. So does it come about that our poet, though practising a form of his art where characters especially tend to stereotype themselves, yet takes each person on his own merits, presenting us with sympathetic fathers, noble courtesans, honest slave-dealers. The trade-catalogue of theatrical humanity is to him of no value save as a starting-point. But this voyage of discovery in quest of unexpected virtues must bring to light many weaknesses. Terence depicts these without lessening our faith in the essential goodness of human beings, but they strengthen his passion for human fellowship. It is precisely because we are weak that we need others; and, still more germane to his business, since we observe others' faults so much more keenly than our own (a fact often noted in Terentian comedy) the prime necessity for us is that we should stand together; we dare not suppose that we know ourselves well enough for safety. Hence comes his famous maxim, *homo sum: humani nil a me alienum puto:* hence, too, the fact that his plots not only contain two interests, but as a rule actually consist of the duality. Hence, in truth, comes also the characteristic that his plays on the surface read so much alike, that his persons have a sometimes confusing family-resemblance. For, in the last analysis, Terence has only one stage-character, and his name is *Homo.*

Gilbert Norwood   (essay date 1932)

SOURCE: "Plot-Structure in Terence" in *Plautus and Terence,* 1932. Reprint by Cooper Square Publishers, 1963, pp. 141-80.

[*In the following excerpt from his reconsideration of Terence, Norwood presents a detailed examination of the plot structure of Terence's comedies.*]

From first to last Terence devotes great attention to plot, but does not at first succeed: in fact we cannot regard him as a master of construction till **Phormio.** In the two latest plays he employs the perfected method with still greater ease, boldness and versatility.

The **Andria** shows grave faults amid undoubted merits. Simo's change of purpose provides a delightful entanglement. Having urged his son's acceptance of a marriage that Simo himself does not really wish, he is so pleased by Pamphilus' feigned eagerness that he decides to turn the sham into earnest. As he expounds this change of plan to Davus, Pamphilus' valet, we can imagine the slave's jaw dropping as he realizes that Pamphilus' pretended acceptance (devised by Davus) has been to convincing. Still more sophisticated comedy is found in the scene of the midwife. The stage-convention, it will be remembered, was that all business, however domestic or indeed secret, should be transacted in the street or at the doorway. Terence naturally chafed at such nonsense, and here he hits back beautifully. After Glycerium's baby is born, the midwife comes out and, as usual, bawls her instructions from the door-step—"give her a bath at once" etc. (483 ff.). Simo has already begun to overreach himself with a too cunning idea that Glycerium's confinement is a figment of Davus. The midwife's action confirms it. "Instead of telling them in the bedroom what the patient needed, she waited till she got outside and shouted from the pavement to the women inside! Oh, Davus! Do you despise me as much as that? Do you think me a proper dupe for such obvious plots? You might have taken some pains about it, so that, if I found out, I might think you had at any rate some fear of me" (490 ff.). This is wit indeed. Simo's reproach, uttered less in anger at the supposed conspiracy than in grief at its badness, gives help to the construction; and in the same moment it utters trenchant satire on a stupid stage-convention. Terence has used his very limitations: a method which seems to ruin dramatic art is turned into a novel and effective means of construction.

But the flaws are much greater. Little need be said about Sosia, the "protatic" character. Such people, as we have seen, were never expelled from the theatre: Terence himself uses them in later plays, and they flourish even today. There are far more serious things. We gradually realize that the contriving slave himself makes no real contribution to the plot. Of course Davus provides much incidental excitement and fun, but what does he perform? In reality he is but a fifth wheel on the coach. He produces a device that looks formidably knowing and subtle, that Pamphilus should pretend compliance with Simo's plan of a marriage with Philumena. But what is the outcome of this master-piece? Firstly, Byrria's discovery, which leads nowhere (see the next paragraph). Further, Simo's sudden idea of turning the sham marriage into earnest; but that too comes to nothing at last. As for Davus' elaborate orchestration of Chremes, Mysis, and the baby, it is impossible—at any rate for one reader—to explain the deliberate bungling that he introduces. Nor does he in any way help to bring about the *peripeteia,* Crito's arrival, which involves the recognition of Glycerium as Chremes' daughter and therefore a possible wife for Pamphilus.

Further, Charinus (the second lover) and his man Byrria are structurally useless. They look important, to be sure: Charinus wishes to marry Philumena, and Byrria abets him. But the two love-interests do not genuinely affect one another in action. When Byrria discovers that Pamphilus, after assuring Charinus that he does not wish to marry Philumena, tells Simo (untruthfully) that he does, this supposed discovery of Pamphilus' deception of Charinus ought to produce counter-plots of Charinus that shall affect the Pamphilus-Glycerium affair. But no: hearing Byrria's news, Charinus—quite sensibly, of course—straightway confronts Pamphilus and is at once told the facts. Byrria's discovery could be deleted without loss, and a little further thought will show that the rest of the Charinus-Byrria part could follow it.

But could it? Here, if anywhere in the study of Roman drama—nay, of drama in general—it is worth while to attempt the extreme of caution and particularity. Careful study, or rather balanced thinking, here will show us just how Terence worked. These Charinus-scenes have been proved structurally useless to the "question of the play"—what is to become of the Pamphilus-Glycerium affair in face of Simo's determination that Pamphilus shall marry Philumena? On this side, then, the play is bad. But, as often, the bungle reveals the writer's purpose far better than would success. For *ars est celare artem:* conversely, an artistic breakdown exhibits the artist's method. So does it come about that the adventure of peering over a poet's shoulder is here more delightful than at any other moment of Terence's career.

These scenes are useless. Then why does the playwright put them in? "Put in" is exactly correct: Terence has obtruded them upon his "original," the *Andria* of Menander. Donatus writes on v. 301: "These characters are not in Menander: Terence has added them to the play . . ." Why? Few assumptions are less dangerous than that Menander's plot was soundly constructed. Therefore, if Terence takes the initiative so drastically, it is certain that to him the intended matter must have seemed in some way vital. Donatus tells us his idea of the reason: "Terence has added them to the play lest it should be too painful to leave Philumena scorned or unbetrothed while Pamphilus marries another." This is excellent, so far as it goes. But does it meet the objections we have raised against the Charinus-scenes? Yes and no. The "question of the play," we have just said, is Pamphilus' trouble; the climax, or *peripeteia,* is Crito's revelation that Glycerium is Chremes' daughter; the solution, or dénouement, is the satisfaction both of Pamphilus and of Simo by a marriage with Glycerium.

That is, Philumena (strictly in herself) is of no importance: she exists merely to help provide the "question." On the other side, if we raise our eyes from mere charts or machinery, we may ask what becomes of Philumena when Pamphilus "deserts" her: we should like to "see her settled." Hence the insertion of Charinus to make ready for this; hence, too, the spurious variant of the final scene, which dilates upon Philumena's marriage. The most exact statement is that Charinus has an excuse for his presence, but he is a bungle because he does not help the real plot.

That is to say, in the *Andria* we are present at the birth of a notable dramatic expedient. In all his plays Terence bifurcates the plot—thinks it out and works it out in two parts that are necessary to each other. This device must by no means be confused with the underplots familiar in Elizabethan drama. It is not merely that the two parts of a Terentian comedy together form the whole as two gloves make a pair: they are complementary, as is one blade of a pair of scissors to its companion. This duality-method is the centre, the focus, of Terentian art and the Terentian spirit: both his vivid moral sense and his magnificent dramatic talent lead him to this principle of duality in unity. So far as can be learned, it is entirely his own—another, and the most impressive, proof of his originality not merely in play-conception but in play-construction also. For he actually recasts his "original" in order to secure this dualism. He tells us this concerning the *Heautontimorumenos* in so many words, though few care to listen. So in the *Andria:* that duality-method which is good in *Self-Punishment,* excellent in *Phormio,* magnificent in *The Brothers,* is here crudely thrust upon us. It works badly, but its very badness makes it unmistakable. The improvement to which so many allusions have been made is clearest of all in this basic element of Terentian art.

Self-Punishment, the author tells us in his prologue (v. 6), is a "two-fold play made out of a single plot"—*duplex quae ex argumento facta est simplici.* That he should so handle a "single" or "simple" Menandrian comedy as to secure the duality-structure shows how vital it was in his eyes. His skill here shows a decided advance on the *Andria.* The two groups—Clinia, his father Menedemus, and his mistress Antiphila; Clitipho, his father Chremes, and his mistress Bacchis—are of tolerably equal importance. The love-troubles of Clinia and of Clitipho settle one another by an admirable interlocking that far transcends the mere juxtaposition of the preceding drama.

Menedemus, before the action opens, is so enraged by Clinia's keeping a mistress that by his reproaches he has caused his son to go off to the wars. But he misses Clinia, and soon deeply repents his own harshness: in order to punish himself, he toils early and late with spade and ploughshare, old though he is. Thus, when Clinia returns, Menedemus is eager to indulge him; but his old neighbour Chremes, fearing that this new extreme may spoil Clinia, induces him to pretend that he is still harsh and to allow himself, as if unconsciously, to be swindled out of the money that Clinia needs. This odd arrangement helps Clitipho, whose mistress Bacchis, being vastly more expensive than Antiphila, is in pretence substituted for her with disconcerting but laughable results. Nevertheless, the duality-scheme is not perfect. Not only should it secure Clinia's permanent happiness with Antiphila—she proves, as a matter of fact, to be Chremes' daughter and marries Clinia: it should also put the Clitipho-Bacchis affair on a "satisfactory" footing. This does not happen: Bacchis vanishes after the Third Act, and Clitipho agrees to marry a lady not hitherto mentioned. This lapse in technique is due to the irremediably undesirable character of Bacchis.

The mining and countermining is marvellously deft but not flawless. Clinia and his slave Syrus know nothing (apparently) about Menedemus' complete change of mind as to Clinia's extravagance; yet they coolly transfer Bacchis and her retinue to his house. Also, there are one or two blind alleys in the discussions concerning all these machinations. But the chief defect is the complexity itself. Terence has been too clever. Perhaps no one is able, perhaps no one except Terence himself ever has been able, to give from memory a complete and accurate account of this plot: far more to the purpose, it may be doubted whether any Roman auditor could follow it. Menedemus is to know that he is not being fooled as Chremes thinks he is, and is to tell Chremes, so as to fool him, that he is not being fooled as he intended to allow himself to be. The stalwart sons of Romulus must have found this trying. Even a modern reader, who can go as slowly as he wishes, must keep his wits about him. Menander wrote the play "simple"; it is Terence who has introduced this eye-defeating complexity.

In the arrangement or development we observe a brilliant novelty. Terence takes the conventional idea, a slave's device to extract from the old master funds for his young master's amour. He also adopts the equally familiar discovery that the heroine is of free Athenian birth and so may legally marry her lover. But he sets this discovery in the centre of the action, not at the close as usual, thus dislocating the traditional procedure by forcing Syrus to begin his money-plots afresh. Nor has Syrus a moment to lose: he only just prevents Clinia from revealing Clitipho's connexion with Bacchis by departing without her to Menedemus' house, despite the foregoing pretence that Bacchis is his mistress, not Clitipho's.

The **Eunuch** exhibits a queer yet fascinating jumble of qualities. Consider first our main topic of plot-construction. Repenting (it would seem) the extreme elaboration, the ruthlessly close interweaving, that marks **Self-Punishment,** Terence here aims at a simplicity that shall yet follow his duality-method. Such success was not to be attained till **Phormio.** Here he has improved his notion of structure without, however, carrying it quite adequately into practice. The parts that in **Self-Punishment** interlocked too tightly can here be heard rattling as they hang together.

The two correlative interests are Phaedria's jealous passion for the courtesan Thais and Chaerea's rape of Pamphila followed by his desire to marry her. The interweaving consists herein, that Pamphila is a protégée of Thais and that Chaerea gains his opportunity by impersonating the eunuch whom Phaedria presents to Thais. So far, this is an excellent bifurcation of interest, as easy to follow as anything (properly to be called a complication) can well

be. But Terence has practised *contaminatio.* What has just been described corresponds to the *Eunuch* of Menander. Into this, as he notes in his prologue, he has inserted the soldier and parasite from Menander's *Flatterer.*

These scenes of Thraso and his hanger-on Gnatho form a considerable part of our comedy. Most of them are curiously out of key with the rest of Terence's work: apparently in an evil hour he tried to imitate Plautus. For it seems plain that the one reason for this element is the wretched battle-scene where Thraso deploys his followers in front of Thais' door: that is why we have so often been told of Thraso's fancy for Pamphila, which otherwise has no point or result. And when the battle does arrive, it is a fiasco not only for the soldier (of course) but for the playwright also. Having set his heart on a scene of boisterous farce, he leads up to the rally with some elaboration and then allows all the fun to slip through his fingers. Plautus would have done it much better; in *Ralph Roister Doister* it is carried through with capital fun and boundless verve.

Why, then, is this written in at all? Thraso restores Pamphila to Thais, but why need they have been separated? Only to give Thraso a *locus standi.* Again, Thais' wish to conciliate him is made her excuse for temporarily dismissing Phaedria; but there is no reason in the main plot for such dismissal. Chaerea's outrage could not have been committed had not Thais left home—to dine with Thraso; but why such elaboration to secure her absence, which could easily have been caused and arranged otherwise in three lines? Evidently Terence sets great store by this element, seeing that he takes such pains to force them into the action. Why? The explanation is found in that disgusting final scene, where Thraso is induced by his longing for Thais' society unconsciously to finance the liaison between her and Phaedria. Terence is insisting on his duality. Chaerea's affair is settled by a discovery that Pamphila is of free Athenian birth. Thais is not, but she has shown herself throughout a wise, resourceful, and charming woman. Therefore Phaedria is to be permanently happy with her, a result secured by a steady and quasi-respectable concubinage. Funds for this can be secured only through Thraso. On moral grounds we may condemn this vigorously; at present we are to observe that Thraso proves necessary to the duality-method. The dualism would have been perfect had Thais been legally possible as a wife for Phaedria.

The main plot is masterly. Thais' dismissal of Phaedria brings out beautifully his jealous passion and the loving patience of his mistress. Chaerea's plan to impersonate the eunuch, and its outcome, are brutal and heartless, but they give excellent dramatic results. His success engenders in him a sincere love: when he learns that Pamphila can marry him he bursts into a rhapsody of delight. Further, the discovery of his offence brings out the sound character of Thais as does nothing else. Throughout the comedy she shows herself a worthy successor of Chrysis in the **Andria** and foretells the noble Bacchis of the **Hecyra,** but her great moment comes when she rebukes this reckless young scoundrel (864 ff.):

> *nec te dignum, Chaerea, fecisti: nam si ego digna*
> *hac contumelia sum maxume, at tu indignus qui*
> *faceres tamen.*

"Chaerea, you have done what is unworthy of you. Even if I entirely deserve this insult, you should have been above inflicting it." Chremes, again, Pamphila's brother, is used to throw light upon Thais: his drunken vacillation, when the "battle" threatens, is turned to firmness by her encouragement. At the close she gains even the father's affection. Another delightful feature is the passage (968 ff.) where tradition is made to stand on its head. Pythias, seeking revenge on Parmeno, terrifies him by her account of the punishment about to be inflicted upon Chaerea. In panic he reveals everything to his old master on his own initiative—a laughable reversal of the trite system whereby the *senex* threatens flogging and other horrors in order to extract the scandalous truth.

In *Phormio* Terence's constructive skill reaches perfection. We shall observe in the two following plays that this skill is applied with greater resourcefulness and flexibility, as with deeper feeling and richer wisdom, but he has now at last gained complete mastery of his instrument. He has learned the double lesson of *Self-Punishment* and of the *Eunuch.* All is beautifully orchestrated, so that even a spectator could follow every detail with comfort: the various interests of Antipho, Phaedria, Demipho and Chremes, dominated and driven by Phormio with pervasive activity and tireless ingenuity, make this comedy a delight, not a puzzle. The duality-method also is here at length perfected. Antipho, son of Demipho, dreads being compelled to give up his beloved wife Phanium and marry his cousin, daughter of Demipho's brother Chremes. Phaedria, son of Chremes, is in love with Pamphila, a slave owned by Dorio, and is at his wits' end for money to buy her freedom, for she is about to to be sold to the usual officer and taken by him away from Athens. These two difficulties are made to solve one another by the talent and impudence of Phormio, one of the most engaging scoundrels in the rich annals of the stage.

Before the play opens he has brought about Antipho's marriage, while Demipho and Chremes are abroad, by pretending to be Phanium's relative and so bound, under Attic law, either to find her a husband or to marry her himself. He therefore brought a lawsuit against Antipho to compel him as next-of-kin to marry her. Antipho intentionally lost the case and took her though she had no dowry. Demipho on his return is furious at Antipho's apparent supineness. The young husband in terror hides and Phaedria defends him to Demipho, who exclaims (267) *tradunt operas mutuas*—"they help each other turn and turn about": the words are a capital description of Terence's method. Demipho and Chremes offer Phormio five *minae*—the legal minimum—to take Phanium back. This he contemptuously refuses; but we shall find that the offer gives him an idea. Next, our attention is transferred to Phaedria and his trouble about Pamphila. He pleads abjectly with Dorio for three days' grace in which to find the thirty *minae* for her purchase, but the slave-dealer is obdurate. Then Antipho intercedes—*tradunt operas mutuas*—and, with Geta, prevails on Dorio to allow them until tomorrow morning. Phormio evolves a scheme to extract the required thirty *minae* from the two fathers. He sends Geta to report to them that Phormio would have been glad to marry Phanium himself, but she has no dowry and he

has debts. So he has become engaged to a lady who has a dowry. Now, if Demipho will pay him what he needs (thirty *minae!*), he will break off his engagement and marry Phanium. Demipho is enraged, but Chremes is so eager to see Antipho his daughter's husband that he volunteers to pay, out of the rents of his wife's property which he has just brought home from Lemnos. Phormio receives the money, pays Dorio, and delivers Pamphila to Phaedria, whose difficulty is now overcome.

But what of Antipho? We are told (705 ff.) that Phormio will find some excuse for not taking Phanium from him after all. But is the scheme handsome enough? Surely so lame and precarious a solution would be unworthy of a fine worker like Phormio. The requisite brilliance is made possible by an opportune discovery that he is not the only rascal in the play. Chremes has throughout been nervously intent on a marriage between Antipho and his daughter. But who is she? We learn that she is not the child of his Athenian wife Nausistrata. His voyage to Lemnos had for its object not only the collection of Nausistrata's rents, but also a visit to his wife and their daughter, who had however left for Athens. Chremes is a bigamist. It is this Lemnian girl whom he wished Antipho to marry, since his brother's son would be less likely to make trouble about his bigamy. When the two fathers go in to arrange for Phanium's dismissal, it is found that Phanium is the very daughter in question. Thus Antipho's marriage is safe, and is now at once used to help Phaedria's amour—*tradunt operas mutuas.*

In a scene of delicious light comedy Demipho and Chremes coolly ask Phormio to return the thirty *minae,* since Phanium is not leaving Antipho after all. Phormio protests against this shilly-shallying and calls on them to send him his "wife." Demipho scoffs bitterly, but Phormio blandly goes on to explain that he has another woman's cause to defend. Amid the agitated groans of Chremes he airily discourses of Lemnos and bigamy: he will reveal all to this wronged lady Nausistrata. Chremes is for leaving him in possession of the money, but Demipho urges him to desperate courage and they fall upon their too-virtuous opponent. He cries aloud for Nausistrata, who comes out and learns everything. Chremes is utterly humiliated and Phaedria is allowed to keep Pamphila—Chremes' own wife asks him (1040 f.): "Do you think it a scandal for a young man to have one mistress when you have two wives?"

The *Mother-in-Law* is unique among Terentian plays in one particular at least: indeed it would probably be hard to find many parallels in the whole of dramatic literature. That peculiarity is the splendid boldness and success wherewith it accepts traditional theatrical data and proceeds charmingly and skilfully to stand tradition on its head. That is why it failed in Rome and is despised or ignored by modern critics. Mr. Shaw did the same thing when he wrote *Arms and the Man.* What could his innocent audiences make of a play that, starting well with the resplendent military hero (in the cavalry, of course), the idolatrous fiancée awaiting his glorious return, the amusing parents, and the commonplace soldier of the defeated side, suddenly went off the rails and destroyed itself, depicting hero and heroine as shams, the unromantic people as genuinely mature and effective human beings? But Mr. Shaw luckily survived, and continued his work. Today most of us understand what he was driving at thirty-seven years ago. The *Hecyra* provides a close analogy with the Shavian play, but unluckily Terence died young. At its first appearances the audience did not hear it to the end owing (among other causes) to the vociferous protests of the ladies in the audience, who, no doubt, were scandalized by the charm and strength attributed to a courtesan. Only at the third attempt was it performed in full, shortly before its author left Rome for ever, as it proved. He could not, like Mr. Shaw, impose himself gradually upon the public by many years of sparkling trenchant original work that pursued this method of constructive disillusionment.

In brief, this is a most beautiful play, composed with such perfect mastery that it is probably unequalled in its own kind; but certain unconventional qualities have prevented many readers from appreciating its peculiar charm. These unconventional features shall be considered first.

First, this is no comedy at all as comedy is understood by enthusiasts for Plautus, by those who "go to the theatre to enjoy themselves" (meaning either a surfeit of guffaws or a drench of sentimentality), by those who understand by comedies about the relations of the sexes either the airily fanciful like *The Admirable Crichton* or the pornographic like *Le Vieux Marcheur*. Such theatre-goers have often much right on their side. But there are more sorts of comedy than one, or two. The *Hecyra,* judged by the standards both of the Globe Theatre and of the Palais Royal, is certainly an execrable play. But Terence is not attempting to write like Shakespeare or like Rip; this should be absurdly obvious, but it seems to need saying. Our play is pathetic high comedy, not unlike the *comédie larmoyante* evolved by La Chaussée, though it enormously surpasses any work of that forcible-feeble rhetorician. As a result, though the dialogue is aglow with wit in the sense of brilliant aptness, jokes are very rare. Perhaps Pamphilus' hurried description (440 f.) of his imaginary acquaintance is the only example:

> *magnus, rubicundus, crispus, crassus, caesius, cadaverosa facie.*

> "Tall, ruddy, curly-haired, burly, gray-eyed—he looks like a corpse."

Next, although traditional characters tread the stage, they act (as we have already said) in defiance of tradition. Terence openly rejoices in this break with stereotyped puppets, machine-made situations: more than once he actually remarks that he is flouting theatrical convention. At the close Pamphilus says (866): "Don't let us manage this affair as they do in the comedies"—*placet non fieri hoc item ut in comoediis.* Indeed, whoever else does not enjoy this play, Terence did. Probably his "slim feasting smile" was least slim while he dealt with Parmeno. That luckless henchman knows well enough what the audience expects of a "knavish valet"; but every time he tramps dutifully onto the stage, his pockets crammed with amulets, his brain agog with cunning devices, his mouth full of *hem, quid ais, heus,* he is ordered off again to make room for the play. This happens repeatedly: the centurions and their

wives knew no more what to make of it than their descendants appreciated Saranoff's cavalry-charge, but its preliminary recital must have caused a glorious hour round Scipio's dinner-table. Laches, again, is a very poor specimen of the comic heavy father. He does indeed insult his wife now and then, bringing back a moment's cheer to the bewildered auditor; but on the whole we perceive with growing alarm and resentment that he is a much better man than his son, the "hero," and shows real commonsense, a reasonable grip of the situation. No doubt he loses all sense of theatrical decency because from beginning to end no one makes any attempt to swindle him—enough to unnerve any comic father.

But the least conventional of all is Bacchis. Her defection is not in the least laughable, for Terence is expending all his delicate yet powerful art on the creation of a beautiful character. But here, no less than in Parmeno, he is perfectly aware how he is treating tradition. In the first words of the play he puts forward Syra to lecture young Philotis on the correct practice of a courtesan—the "vampire" method so incessantly depicted today and even then familiar. Bacchis proceeds to do exactly the opposite: some might even say that Terence has over-emphasized her revolt from rule. She is more than willing to help bring Pamphilus' wife back to him, and cheerfully tramples on professional rules in doing so (774 ff.):

> *Pamphilo me facere ut redeat uxor oportet: quod si perficio, non paenitet me famae,*
> solam fecisse id quod aliae meretrices facere fugitant.

"It is my duty to see that Pamphilus' wife returns to him. If I do this, I shall not be sorry to have the repute of doing what all other courtesans shrink from." Before this climax, her self-control, discretion and kindness have induced him to learn, and love his wife; and now her courage in facing Philumena brings about the discovery that entirely closes the breach between husband and wife and between their parents. She is a splendid and delightful woman, the fulfilment of Chrysis and Thais. Her interview with Laches makes a superb scene. He expects a woman of Syra's school, to be overawed and bribed: he finds a vibrant spirited personality (734 f.):

> *ego pol quoque etiam timida sum, quom venit in mentem quae sim,*
> *ne nomen mihi quaesti obsiet; nam mores facile tutor.*

"Indeed, I am nervous too, when I consider what I am—lest the name of my trade should injure me: for my conduct I can defend easily." Before this wonderful scene closes, a great figure has been added to the world's drama.

The third and last peculiarity of the *Hecyra* concerns plot-structure. In outline the story runs thus. Pamphilus, despite his passion for Bacchis, was induced by his father Laches to marry Philumena, daughter of Phidippus; but he has been her husband only in name. He seeks Bacchis, but she has ignored him; this, and Philumena's sweet patience, have turned his heart to his wife. But he has to go to Imbros on business, leaving his wife with his parents, Laches and Sostrata. Later, Philumena left them for Phidippus and Myrrina, and refused to return, alleging illness. Laches thinks his wife to blame for this estrangement. Pamphilus comes home, definitely in love with Philumena: he is convinced that he must choose between her and Sostrata. He hears that Philumena is ill, rushes in, and finds that she has been delivered of a child, which he knows cannot be his. Myrrina appeals to him. Her daughter (she explains) was outraged by some man unknown, before her marriage: that is why she left Laches' house; Pamphilus alone "knows" that he himself is not the father: let him keep the secret; the child shall be exposed. To this Pamphilus agrees, but he is determined not to take his wife back; this refusal puzzles Laches and Phidippus. Soon Phidippus discovers his grandchild and informs Laches. Pamphilus refuses to take Philumena back even despite the birth of the child, and makes the supposed quarrel between Sostrata and Philumena his excuse. Sostrata and Laches offer to withdraw from Athens, but even this does not alter his intent. The fathers in angry amazement conclude that this obstinacy can be due only to the continued ascendancy of Bacchis. Laches sends for her and insists that she give his son up. Bacchis tells him the facts, which he asks her to convey to the ladies. She goes within for this purpose, and discovers by means of a ring that Philumena's unknown assailant was Pamphilus himself. All ends happily.

But no such bald summary can do justice to the flawless mastery of construction here, the gracious charming flexibility whereby character moulds plot and plot reveals character. Consider the different reasons that cause Bacchis to confront Philumena: you will find character after character slowly giving up their essence under your contemplation. Perhaps the most beautiful device is that the same event, the child's birth, makes Laches still more eager to receive Philumena back and Pamphilus still more resolute not to agree—both for excellent reasons. So might one continue to enjoy now the quiet beauty, now the thrilling deftness, again the lingering fragrance, of this matchless drama.

The peculiarity whereof we spoke at first concerns the duality-method. What becomes of it here, in one of the two finest works that Terence has left? It seems to vanish, for we find but one pair of lovers. Evanthius points out this discrepancy in his essay *On Tragedy and Comedy* [in K.M. Westaway, *The Original Element in Plautus,* 1917]. "This further quality in Terence seems to merit praise, that he has chosen for treatment richer subject-matter, drawn from double interests (*ex duplicibus negotiis*). For, except the *Hecyra,* which has only the love-affairs of Pamphilus, the other five have two young men apiece." But a little consideration will show the duality-method at work here, and most dextrously. The uniqueness lies in the interweaving. Whereas the other comedies exhibit two pairs of lovers and two love-difficulties entangled, here the two difficulties exist indeed but concern the same man and woman. The problems are Pamphilus' estrangement from his wife and Philumena's plight owing to the offence of an unknown man. Then these two affairs beautifully merge by the identification of Pamphilus with the offender. The plot-complication is no less consummate than the character-drawing.

The Brothers exhibits Terence's most highly elaborated use of the duality-method, in a manner entirely different from the novelty of the *Hecyra.* Here we find two pairs of interests, not one pair as in all the five preceding works.

First, as in *Phormio,* the two love-affairs, of Aeschinus and Pamphila, of Ctesipho and "Bacchis," are employed to solve one another. Aeschinus, on behalf of his timid brother Ctesipho, abducts Bacchis from the slave-dealer: this, becoming known, causes Pamphila's mother to believe that he is deserting Pamphila for Bacchis, and her resistance brings Aeschinus' liaison to the ears of his "father" Micio, who therefore arranges the marriage of Aeschinus and Pamphila when their situation was otherwise hopeless. Thus Ctesipho's affair produces the solution of the Aeschinus-Pamphila predicament. On the other side, Ctesipho's difficulty is solved by his brother's trouble. For his father, Demea, is induced to acquiesce in his liaison by Aeschinus' appeal, and this appeal has weight exactly because Demea has already decided to beat Micio at his own game of indulging youthful folly; this indulgence, finally, has been shown above all, and to Demea's continued annoyance, in favouring Aeschinus' affair with Pamphila.

Secondly, Demea and Micio form a separate couple with conflicting interests. One of Demea's sons, Aeschinus, has been adopted by his bachelor uncle Micio and educated in Athens on a system of indulgence and mutual confidence. The other, Ctesipho, has stayed with Demea and has been brought up in the country on a system of severity and repression. Each of the "fathers" believes firmly in his own method and criticizes his brother's: the kernel of the play is the clash between these systems. Here is duality again, applied to a quite different theme from the love-escapades of the five earlier comedies, another couple of which is found here also, but as the outcome of these more fundamental educational doctrines. Demea and Micio are admirably contrasted. The latter has been already described. Demea is not less good, though less novel. He is the traditional *senex* of a thousand comedies, with the addition of will-power and sagacity. His outcries against the corruption of Aeschinus and the system that has induced it are justified and effective. At the close he dominates the stage in scenes richly comic, rather touching, altogether wise and instructive.

The value and attractiveness of this climax are caused by the duality-method once more, but applied to new material. Micio's failure and Demea's failure are both repaired by the lessons that each can read the other. Both the competing systems are mistaken. A good number of modern plays have been founded on the *Adelphoe,* among them Molière's *L'École des Maris,* Shadwell's *Squire of Alsatia,* Garrick's *Guardian,* Fielding's *Fathers,* Cumberland's *Choleric Man,* and Colman's *Jealous Wife.* In all these one of the rival theorists confesses that the other has been justified by results, and in all except Fielding's the victor is the person who corresponds to Micio; for the theatre has usually sought to please sons rather than fathers. Terence has been wiser than his successors. Here, as indeed throughout his brief career, technique and knowledge of human nature reinforce and irradiate each other. He knows that extreme and theoretical notions of dealing with men and women, especially the young, cannot produce a sound life. Both these youths have been corrupted. Aeschinus after all has concealed his amour from the sympathetic Micio, and lets matters drift until Pamphila's happiness is in danger. He has no backbone: the system has only made him reckless and insolent, as we observe in that disgusting interview between him and the slave-dealer. He is a bumptious, bullying pseudo-fashionable oaf—the worst kind of oaf. Ctesipho is no worse and no better. Secretive and utterly self-indulgent like his brother, he is also a poltroon: the scene (537-553) where he hides behind the door from his father, too timid to show himself, too nervous to carouse at his ease within, and hysterically whispering to the contemptuous slave who stands between him and detection, is a complete exposure of his depravity.

We return to the climax. A solution of all these troubles, a sound relationship between father and son, is wisely allotted by the playwright to Demea, not Micio, partly through a sense of dramatic balance, Demea having suffered so acutely, partly because he has always realized more deeply the need for a permanently sound way of life for the two youths. First, since Micio has continuously "scored off " him, he determines to beat Micio at his own game, not for the mere fun of the thing but to demonstrate that anyone can grow popular if with an air of *bonhomie* he lets other people have exactly what they want. (Here he is—very naturally—not altogether just to Micio.) This demonstration makes a rather wonderful scene or two, for it is richly farcical and yet all its details proceed from a moral theory and a moral purpose.

He begins with extreme affability to the slaves; next, when Aeschinus complains of the tedious preparations for the wedding, Demea with a wave of the hand exclaims (906): "Let it all go: knock down the back-wall between the gardens and bring your bride through to our house at once, mother, servants and all." These unusual rites come to Micio's ears, as well they may, and he hurries out to expostulate with Demea, who is quite ready for him. "We ought to help this family," he explains. "Why, of course," replies his unconscious victim. "Very well," rejoins the benevolent Demea. "The bride's mother has no one left to look after her. *You* should marry her." Micio splutters in helpless indignation; Aeschinus joins his voice to Demea's; and Micio, now for years accustomed to give way to his "son," surrenders. This is an admirable comic rendering of a serious moral thesis, an appropriate application of his own methods. Moreover, it not only secures the excellent Sostrata's future: it withdraws Micio from that irresponsible detachment that renders so many elderly bachelors a public danger. Meanwhile, Demea sweeps triumphantly onwards: this poor kinsman Hegio . . . "let *us* give him that little farm of *yours* . . . don't you remember what you told me yourself: that in old age we are too fond of money? We must avoid that fault." Demea is congratulating himself on hoisting his brother with his own petard—*suo sibi gladio hunc iugulo* (958)—when Syrus bustles in to announce that the back-wall is down. Demea's eye gleams. Why should the "contriving valet" go unrecompensed? Has he not crowned his faithful services by helping to abduct Bacchis? *Non mediocris hominis*

haec sunt officia (966)—"only a remarkable man could have shown such diligent loyalty": Syrus receives not only his freedom but that of his wife also and a "loan" into the bargain. All this settled, Micio in a stupor asks his brother (984 f.): "What on earth has changed your character all of a sudden?" Demea answers gravely and trenchantly, then turns to Aeschinus with a solution of the whole rivalry between the two systems. Both are wrong: we need a compromise between them. This conclusion is obvious to us modern people, who advise, and mostly seek to attain, a blend of elderly wisdom and enlightened sympathy for the young. But it was less obvious to ancient Europe. Micio's system was the vogue in the Athens of Menander, Demea's in the Rome of Terence. This compromise is a real contribution to practical morality.

Thus the duality-method reaches its height in this final work of the Terentian genius: the result arises from neither one doctrine nor the other, but only from their interaction. And, as we saw, the same technique is applied to the love-affairs. Moreover, the two sets of duality—if an ugly phrase will be forgiven—are perfectly interwoven, since of course the love-affairs demonstrate the failure of the two competing theories if they do compete instead of blending. It is this exquisitely close yet perfectly intelligible structure, and, within it, the admirable balancing of all the four men, that makes **The Brothers** a perfect master-piece of high comedy.

. . . . .

Last of all, something ought to be said concerning topics, themes, or even the "message" of Terence; for here we come upon a chief reason for the frequent opinion that, for all his eloquence, Terence is somewhat pallid, diluted, monotonous. The truth is, he has no topics at all in the usual sense: it would be impossible to prepare any dissertation upon "Politics in Terence" or "The Attitude of Terence towards Sculpture and Painting." The charge of pallor and the rest is in some degree true, as it is true of many others who keep closely to the business of intellectual social comedy. This high urbanity, this slightly fastidious elegance, this chastity of outline in thought and phrase, would consort ill with eloquent outbreaks on politics or atheism, sudden perils or exploits, and frolics, jesting, or horseplay. But, even so, why should not Terence have varied the vivacity, the gusto, of one comedy as compared with another? This, to be exact, he has done in the Thraso-scenes of **The Eunuch** and in the flippancy of Micio. But the first are not successful, and the second is a minor element in **The Brothers.** In this respect Terence assuredly falls below Menander. Even though we possess no complete play of Menander, we cannot mistake the difference in tone between *Arbitration* and *The Girl of Samos*. Whether Terence, had he been granted, like his predecessor, another twenty-five years of life, would have developed in this regard, is a natural but useless inquiry. We may indeed observe that his last scene is not merely delightful but novel—a profoundly important theory of conduct expounded by means of light fun. Such a description might be applied without too offensive pedantry to some portions of *Henry the Fourth*: who knows what Terence might have achieved at fifty? But we shall of course guard against denying any weakness in him on the strength of a plea that he might later have outgrown it. He remains, on this side of dramatic excellence, a junior Menander.

Let us return to our discussion of topics, or lack of them. We said that Terence has none in the usual sense, nothing like Plautus' frequent allusions to public institutions, law, and commerce. Still we can extract—nay, we cannot fail to observe—an important idea concerning human nature itself. And, so far is he from merely obtruding themes or instruction, that his one theory about life has created his dramatic method. His plays are not simply the vehicle of this idea: they *are* the idea, expressed not only by dialogue and action but also by the very shape of his work. This governing idea of Terence is the mutual dependence of human beings. Again and again he causes his people to exclaim that we are sure to err if we walk by ourselves, that others see more wisely in our affairs than we can, that the true life is a life of mutual helpfulness. In his plays the villain is not a slave-dealer or a harsh father or a rapacious courtesan. To heap all the blame for an awkward or agonizing predicament upon the broad shoulders of some artificial bogey ablaze with theatrical fiendishness is easy drama—too easy—but disastrously bad ethics. The real "villain" for Terence is the short-sighted pride that the best of us shows when he seeks to walk alone: the true life is found, not by the excogitation of ethical standards but by human sympathy. That is why *homo* and its cognates are so frequent in his writing. His most famous sentence is also his most emphatic assertion that our great need is not virtue, not wisdom, so much as a sense of humanity— *homo sum: humani nil a me alienum puto:* "nothing human do I count alien to me, for I too am human." Nothing alien, nothing "no business of mine"—this feeling explains Hegio's sturdy championship of his kinswoman, the self-sacrifice of Bacchis, Chremes' expostulation with his neighbour's remorseless toil. Sympathy is the basis of Terentian morals. That is why Terence as a playwright invented and developed the duality-method whereof we have said so much: his plots consist of two problems that solve each other, just as in life one man needs and helps his neighbour. It is the central excellence of Terence that in his work truth and the expression of truth become one and the same.

Edith Hamilton   (essay date 1932)

SOURCE: "The Comic Spirit in Plautus and Terence" in *The Roman Way*, W. W. Norton & Company, Inc., 1932, pp. 47-63.

[*A German-born classical scholar, essayist, and translator, Hamilton is best known as an explicator of ancient cultures for the modern reader. Her studies include* The Roman Way (1932) *and* Spokesmen for God: The Great Teachers of the Old Testament (1949). *Below, she compares the style of Terence with that of his predecessor, Plautus.*]

[Plautus and Terence] are the founders of our theatre. Their influence has been incalculable. The two main divisions of comedy under which all comic plays except Aristophanes' can be grouped, go back to the two Roman playwrights. Plautus is the source for one, Terence for the

other. The fact is another and a vivid illustration of how little the material of literature matters, and how much the way the material is treated. Both dramatists deal with exactly the same sort of life and exactly the same sort of people. The characters in the plays of the one are duplicated in the plays of the other, and in both the background is the family life of the day, and yet Plautus' world of comedy is another place from Terence's world. The two men were completely unlike, so much so that it is difficult to conceive of either viewing a play of the other with any complacency. Plautus would have been bored by Terence, Terence offended by Plautus. Precisely the same material, but a totally different point of view, and the result, two distinct types of comedy.

Plautus was the older by a generation. His life fell during a restless period when Rome was fighting even more than usual. He could have taken part in the Second Punic War and the wars in the east which followed it, but whether he did or not is pure conjecture. All that is actually known about him is that he was the son of a poor Umbrian farmer, that he worked once in a mill and wrote three of his plays there, and that he was an old man when he died in 184 B.C. But it is impossible to read him without getting a vivid impression of the man himself. A picture emerges, done in bold strokes and unshaded colors, of a jovial, devil-may-care vagabond, a Latin Villon; a soldier of fortune who had roamed the world hobnobbing with all manner of men, and had no illusions about any of them; a man of careless good humor, keen to see and delighting to laugh at follies, but with a large and indulgent tolerance for every kind of fool.

Terence was a man of quite another order. He was born a slave in one of Rome's African colonies and brought up in a great Roman house where they recognized his talents, educated and freed him. These talents, too, found him a place in a little circle of young men who were the intelligentsia and the gilded youth of Rome combined. The leader was the young Scipio, but the elegant Laelius, no mean poet, and the brilliant Lucilius, the inventor of satire, were close seconds, and it was an astonishing triumph that the former slave, once admitted, proved inferior to none of them. It requires no imagination to realize his pride and happiness at being made one of their number. When envious people declared that his grand friends wrote his plays for him, he answered proudly that he boasted of their help.

It was a very youthful company. Terence is said to have died before he was twenty-six and they were all much of an age. The plays show nothing more clearly than that the audience they were primarily written for was this little band of close friends and not the vulgar crowd. Every one is laid in the Utopia of a young man about town in Republican Rome. Undoubtedly the members of the group in their bringing up had had a great deal required of them in the way of the antique Roman virtues. The father and mother of the day, as Plautus shows them, were not given to overindulgence, and Scipio Africanus Maior, the young Scipio's grandfather by adoption, must have been a man very much to be reckoned with in the family circle, while the ladies of the Scipio household were notable for their practice of the domestic virtues. The redoubtable Cornelia

Typical slaves with scarves: an illustration from a manuscript of Phormio.

herself was his aunt and her jewels were his cousins. No doubt at all he and his friends had had to walk a narrow path with watchful guardians on either side.

But under Terence's guidance, art, the liberator, set them free. He took them away to an enchanted world where fathers were that they ought to be and young men had their proper position in the world. Plautus' fathers were hard on their sons and—more intolerable still—the young fellows were held up to ridicule. Terence altered all this delightfully. For the most part his fathers are of an amiability not to be surpassed. "Does my darling son want that pretty flute girl? The dear boy—I'll buy her for him at once." "Extravagant do you call him? Well, all young men are like that. I was myself. I'll gladly pay his debts." There is never any joking at that sort of thing. Such sentiments are the part of a rightminded man. Indeed, there are no jokes at all where the young men are concerned. They are all wonderfully serious and completely noble and accorded the deepest respect. Plautus' young lover on his knees before the door that shuts in his ladylove, undoubtedly moved the audience to laughter when he declaimed:

> Hear me, ye bolts, ye bolts. Gladly I greet you,
> I love you.

> Humbly I pray you, beseech you, kneel here before you to beg you,
> Grant to a lover his longing, sweetest bolts, fairest and kindest.
> Spring now like ballet-girls dancing, lift yourselves up from the door-post.
> Open, oh open and send her, send her to me ere my life blood
> Drains from me wasting with waiting.

But who would laugh at Terence's estimable young man, so admirably concerned for his love:

> I treat her so? And she through me be wronged, made wretched,
> She who has trusted love and life, her all, to me?
> So will I never do.

They are all like that. Whatever the audience thought of them, they were certainly not amused. But whereas Plautus was out to get a laugh by any and every means possible, Terence had an entirely different object in view. Plautus talked directly to the spectators when the action failed to get a response, calling out to the man in the back row not to be so slow to see a joke, or to the women in front to stop chattering and let their husbands listen, or making an actor warn another,

> Softly now, speak softly.
> Don't disturb the pleasant slumbers of the audi-
> ence, I beg.

His object was to amuse. But Terence's mind was bent upon the approval of what he thought the most fastidious, polished people that ever there had been, and he worshipped where they did, at the shrine ever dearest to youth, good taste, as laid down by the canons of each youthful circle, "the thing," which is and isn't "done." Plautus makes fun of everyone, gods included. Terence has few comic characters, and they are in general confined to the lower classes. One catches a glimpse of an English public-school feeling for good form in that little circle of serious young men of which he was so proud a member. Making gentlemen ridiculous was simply not "done." Fortunately, in the circumstances, Terence's sense of humor was such that it could be perfectly controlled. No doubt to him Plautus was a terrible bounder—Plautus, the comedian pure and simple, who when he is not funny, is nothing at all. Terence is a serious dramatist, able to write an amusing scene; but seldom choosing to do so. His interest is in his nice people, above all his nice young men, and in their very well-bred-man-of-the-world doings. It is not to be presumed that Plautus knew anything about well-bred men, and no one ever had less concern for good taste. His quality is Rabelaisian—diluted—and certainly he would have been as much disconcerted by Terence's fine friends as they would have been uncomfortable with him.

With dissimilarities so marked it is not surprising that they disagreed about the whole business of drama-making. The fundamental question of how to secure dramatic interest each solved in his own way, completely unlike the other's. They constructed their plays differently and two forms of comedy, widely divergent from each other, were the result.

There are only two main sources for dramatic interest in a comedy. The first is the method of suspense and surprise, depending upon plot or upon the reaction of character to character, or to situation. But the second method is precisely the reverse: it acts by eliminating suspense and making surprise impossible. The dramatic interest depends upon the spectators knowing everything beforehand. They know what the actor does not. It is a method found in both tragedy and comedy; it is common ground to the sublime and the ridiculous. The Greeks who made great use of it, called it irony. Nothing in tragedy is more tragic. Œdipus invokes an awful curse upon the murderer of his wife's first husband:

> I charge you all: Let no one of this land
> Give shelter to him. Bar him from your homes,
> A thing defiled, companioned by pollution.
> And solemnly I pray, may he who killed,
> Wear out his life in evil, being evil.

And we know it is he himself he is cursing, he is the murderer; he killed his father, he married his mother. This is tragic irony. It lies at the very foundation of Greek tragedy. The audience knew beforehand what the action of each play would be. They sat as beings from another world, foreseeing all the dire results of every deed as it took place, but perceiving also that thus it must be and not otherwise.

The feeling of the inevitability of what is being done and suffered upon the stage, of men's helplessness to avert their destiny, which is the peculiar power of Greek tragedy, depends in the last analysis upon irony, upon the spectators' awareness and the actors' unconsciousness of what is really happening. The darkness that envelops mortal life, our utter ignorance of what confronts us and our blinded eyes that cannot see the ruin we are bringing down upon ourselves, is driven home so dramatically and with such intensity as is possible to no other method.

The use of it may be as comic as it is tragic. We, the audience, are in the secret that there are two men who look exactly alike. The poor, stupid actors do not dream that it is so. How absurdly unable they are to escape their ridiculous mishaps, and what a delightfully superior position our omniscience assures to us.

We cannot trace back the use of the suspense method. Plot is as old as the very first story-teller and the interest of what the effect will be of a situation or of one character upon another is at least as old as Homer and the Bible. But irony begins with Greek tragedy, and, as far as our evidence goes, comic irony begins with Roman comedy. Among the fragments we have of Menander there are two in which irony is evident, but in neither passage is it used humorously. It is found so used for the first time in Plautus. If he was indeed the originator of it, if it was he who perceived to what comic uses tragic irony could be turned, he deserves a place in literature far higher than that now given him. Irony is his chief source of dramatic interest and he is a master of it. It follows, of course, that he offers nothing notable in plots. Suspense is automatically shut out when irony is used. Plautus' plots, when he has one, are extremely poor, and there is a distressing similarity between them. But no one ever put irony to better comic use. His usual way is to explain the action of the piece in a very long and exceedingly tiresome prologue, but the result of the detailed explanation is that the spectators are free to give their entire attention to the absurdities they are now in a position to see through.

In the *Amphitryon,* it will be remembered, Jupiter is in love with Amphitryon's wife, Alcumena. When Amphitryon is away at war Jupiter assumes his form to gain access to Alcumena. Mercury, who guards the house whenever Jupiter is in it, under the form of Amphitryon's slave, Sosia, absent with his master, speaks the prologue, and explains in minutest detail all that is going to take place throughout the play. Jupiter and Amphitryon will look exactly alike, he warns the audience, and so will he and Sosia, but in order that they may have no bother as to which is which, Jupiter will have a bright gold tassel hanging from his hat and

> I shall wear this little plume on mine,
> Note well: the other two are unadorned.

With this the play begins. The scene is a street at night before Amphitryon's house where Mercury stands on guard. To him enters his duplicate, Sosia, sent ahead by Amphitryon to prepare his wife for his unexpected return. It is too dark for Sosia to see how Mercury looks. As he goes up to the door the latter stops him.

MERCURY May I know where you come from, who you are, and why you're here? Just you tell me.

SOSIA Well, I'm going in there. I'm the master's slave. Do you know it all now? Just you tell me.

MERCURY Is that your house?

SOSIA Haven't I said so?

MERCURY Then who is the man that owns you?

SOSIA Amphitryon. General commanding the troops. He's got a wife—name Alcumena.

MERCURY What stuff are you giving me? What's your name?

SOSIA It's Sosia. My father was Davus.

MERCURY Well, you've got your cheek. You're Sosia? You? What's your name? Didn't know I was he? Eh? *(Strikes him.)*

SOSIA Oh, you'll kill me!

MERCURY You'll find if you keep this up there are things a whole lot worse than dying. Now, say who you are.

SOSIA I'm Sosia, please—

MERCURY He's mad.

SOSIA I'm not. Why, you rascal. Didn't a ship bring me in from the battlefield this very night? Didn't my master send me here to our house? And you say I'm not—Well, I'll go straight in to my mistress.

MERCURY Every word a lie—I'm Amphitryon's slave. We stormed the enemy's city, Killed the king—cut his head off, Amphitryon did.

SOSIA *(awestruck)* He knows it all. *(pause, then recovering)* Just you tell me If you are me, when the fight was on, where were you? What were you doing?

MERCURY A cask full of wine in the tent and my own pocket flask. What d'you think I'd be doing?

SOSIA *(overwhelmed)* It's the truth. Wretched man that I am. *(shakes head, then suddenly holds lantern up so that the light falls on Mercury)* Well, well. He's as like me as I myself was. Oh, immortal gods! When was I changed? Did I die? Have I lost my memory? Did they leave me behind in foreign parts? I'm going straight back to my master. *(Runs off, and re-enters following Amphitryon who is completely nonplussed at the report of what has happened.)*

AMPHITRYON *(angrily)* The boy's drunk. You, speak up. Tell the truth, where you got the stuff.

SOSIA But I didn't.

AMPHITRYON *(uneasiness getting the better of his anger)* Who's that man you saw?

SOSIA I've told you ten times. I'm there at the house and I'm here, too. That's the straight truth.

AMPHITRYON *(trying to persuade himself it's all nonsense, but uncomfortable)* Get out. Take yourself off. You're sick.

SOSIA I'm just as well as you are.

AMPHITRYON Ah, I'll see that you aren't. If you're not mad, you're bad.

SOSIA *(tearfully)* I tell the truth. You won't hear me. I was standing there in front of the house before I got there.

AMPHITRYON You're dreaming. That's the cause of this nonsense. Wake up.

SOSIA No, no. I don't sleep when you give me an order. I was wide awake then—I'm wide awake now. I was wide awake when he beat me. He was wide awake too. I'll tell you that.

AMPHITRYON *(gruffly)* It'll bear looking into. Come on then.

This is the way Plautus handles comic irony. Molière follows him closely. In his *Amphitryon* the dialogue between Mercure and Sosie is essentially a reproduction of the Latin and no one can say that the great master of comedy used the device at any point more skillfully than the Latin poet.

Playwright after playwright took it over from him. Shakespeare's ironical play, *The Comedy of Errors,* is not as close a parallel to Plautus' *Menaechmi* as Molière's is to the *Amphitryon,* but the entire play is only a variation on Plautus' theme. Scenes in Shakespeare and Molière where the comedy depends upon irony are so many, to run through them would mean making a résumé of a large part of their comedies. The basis of the fun in *Much Ado About Nothing* is the spectators' knowledge of the plot against Beatrice and Benedick. The great scene in *L'Avare* is funny because we know the miser is talking about his money box and the young man about his lady-love, while each supposes the other has the same object in mind. Here, too, Molière drew directly from Plautus. Whether the latter first employed the method or whether he got it from the Greek New Comedy, it is certain that its use upon our own stage goes directly back to him.

Terence never used it. It seems strange at first sight that he did not, but upon consideration reasons appear. A plot intricate enough to supply a full measure of suspense and surprise can be enjoyed only by an intelligent and attentive audience, especially when programmes, outlines, synopses of scenes, all the sources of printed information, have to be dispensed with. Plautus' audience was not up to that level; Terence's was—the real audience he wrote for, his little circle of superior people. Plautus had to hold the attention of a holiday crowd, and hold it too, as he says in many a prologue, against such competitors as chattering women and crying babies. No method of playwriting requires so little effort on the part of the spectator as comic irony. Comedies based upon it are merely a succession of funny scenes strung on the thread of a familiar story. There was sound sense in Plautus' preference for it, and equally good reason for Terence's rejection. His audience enjoyed using their minds on an ingenious plot. He could dispense with the obviously comic and follow his own strong bent toward character and situation. The germ of the novel lies within his plays. His plots are never poor. Perhaps the best of them is that of the ***Mother-in-Law,*** where the suspense is excellently sustained to the very end. Indeed, as the curtain falls the two chief characters pledge each other to keep the solution of the mystery to their own selves. "Don't let's have it like the comedies where everyone knows everything," one of them says.

It is a good story throughout and the characters are well drawn. Nevertheless when the play was presented to the public it failed. The prologue, spoken at a second presentation, declares the reason was that

> A rope-dancer had caught the gaping people's
>   mind.

Yet another prologue—for still another presentation, presumably—says that the theatre was thrown into an uproar by the announcement of a gladiatorial show, and the play could not proceed. Clearly the road of the early dramatist in Rome was not an easy one, but there is never a hint that Plautus found it hard. Perhaps he had the happy faculty of not taking himself too seriously, and merely went along with the crowd when such occasions worked havoc with his play. One feels sure that even so he would have enjoyed the rope-dancer. But the young playwright, hardly more than a boy, felt poignantly the hurt to his feelings and the wrong to his genius. Every one of his prologues contains an attack upon his critics or his public. They are fearfully serious productions, warranted to make any audience restless and any other show irresistibly attractive, but to his own inner circle, those very sober and cultured young men, no doubt they appeared admirably distinguished from the well-worn, old-fashioned method of appeal to the vulgar.

The marked difference between the two writers is another proof of the Roman character of Roman comedy. Plautus and Terence owed something, no doubt, much perhaps, to their Greek originals, but much more to their own selves. They were Roman writers, not Greek copyists, and the drama they bequeathed to the world which still holds the stage today, is a witness to the extent of our legacy from Rome.

Julius Caesar (100 B.C.-44 B.C.) isolates a flaw in Terence's style:

Thou too, even thou, art ranked among the highest, thou half-Menander, and justly, thou lover of language undefiled. But would that they graceful verses had force as well, so that thy comic power might have equal honor with that of the Greeks, and thou mightest not be scorned in this regard and neglected. It hurts and pains me, my Terence, that thou lackest this one quality.

Julius Caesar, quoted in Ancilla to Classical Reading, *by Moses Hadas, Columbia University Press, 1954.*

Benedetto Croce   (essay date 1936)

SOURCE: "Terence" in *Philosophy, Poetry, History: An Anthology of Essays,* translated by Cecil Sprigge, Oxford University Press, London, 1966, pp. 776-801.

[*An Italian educator, philosopher, and author, Croce developed a highly influential theory of literary creation and a concomitant critical method. In defining the impetus and execution of poetry, Croce conceives of the mind as capable of two distinct modes of thought, which he terms cognition and volition. Cognition mental activity is theoretical and speculative, while volition is the mind's practical application of ideas originating in the cognitive realm. Croce's literary theories had a profound impact on the criticism of the first* half of the twentieth century, particularly in his emphasis on judging the totality of a work within a context created by its own existence as a separate, independent entity. In the following essay written in 1936, he addresses several of the charges traditionally levelled at Terence by critics, asserting that his comedies remain interesting and vital to the modern reader.]

The Roman critics discerned as a weakness in Terence his lack of the power, or virtue, of comedy. This adverse opinion is found in some celebrated verses attributed to Caesar, and is perhaps the reason why the grammarian Volcatius Sedigitus, in drawing up a hierarchy of the comic poets, assigned to Terence only the sixth place, Caecilius getting the first and Plautus the second. The author of these verses deplored the fact that because in him comic power was not superadded *(adjuncta)* to his verses, sweet or delicate *(lenibus)* as they were, therefore Terence was held of little account *(despectus)* and could not equal the Greeks, remaining a *dimidiatus Menander.* And because none the less Terence inspired in him sympathy and affection he sighed: *"Atque utinam",* and lamented: *"Unum hoc maceror et doleo tibi deesse, Terenti."* But how can one love a poet while feeling that something substantial is missing in him? Is not that which we admire in a poet precisely that which is essential, the soul, the poetry, which is either there or not there? That *purus sermo* and *lenitas* in his composition, was it not the manifestation of the poetry itself, in the appropriate and necessary tone? But if that which was found lacking in him was not an essential, but an "adjunct", something whose presence or absence was equally possible, why lament so much over its absence? Why call the poet of one's affections a "half man", which is as much as to say a eunuch?

Not one of the many who have quoted those verses seems to me to have asked these reasonable questions. Whoever had done so could not perhaps have found any answer except this, which rises out of the root of the matter, namely that the author of the verses was caught up in the theory of the "genres tranchés", the clear-cut poetical genres, according to which comedy was no comedy unless it was comic and mirth-provoking. But this theory conflicted painfully with the author's own feelings, and while he would not sacrifice the theory, neither would he fully sacrifice his feelings, whence the inner contradiction in the judgement contained in the verse. It was very similarly that Francesco De Sanctis felt the power of Machiavelli's *Mandragola,* but in view of Machiavelli's abstention from working up a gaily confidential atmosphere around the plot and the characters, treating them rather with an air of disgust and detachment, De Sanctis concluded that the work was an artistic failure because it was not a comedy. But if in fact it were a tragedy where would the harm be? (So I myself once enquired [in *Poesia popolare e poesia d'arte,* 1946].) And no more would there be any harm if Terence's comedy were not comedy but something else. Surely there is nothing strange about such a suggestion, now that the links between Euripides' tragedies and the New Comedy have so often been recognized and stressed. One finds in some literary histories a similarity traced between the comedy of Terence and the "bourgeois" comedy of the sixteenth century, as indeed was recognized at the time by an Italian writer, Signorelli, who in the *Hecyra* found "an excellent model for tender comedy such as calls for a poet of sensitive and delicate heart. This sort of comedy", he added, "has across the Alps degenerated into an unpersuasive and halting *comédie larmoyante*" [Pietro Napoli Signorelli, *Storia critica dei teatri antichi e moderni*, 1813. A first succinct edition appeared in 1771]. But perhaps these comparisons across the centuries are better avoided lest one fall into the way of infecting the spontaneous and naive sentiment of the Roman poet (a sentiment not lacking in Roman restraint) with the *sensiblerie* of the Enlightenment.

Terence was still more adversely judged by critics and historians of the nineteenth century. Roman comedy, indeed Roman poetry in general, and together with this the comedy of the Italian Renaissance, and other art forms of that epoch, were despised as unoriginal because evidently modelled upon Greek comedy. As though the art of a later age were not always, in one way or another, based upon what went before! The critics and historians in question did not altogether deny this, but in their view the Roman poets ought to have based themselves on such indigenous traditions as the Atellan mimes (described by Valerius Maximus as *genus delectationis italica severitate temperatum*), and the Renaissance Italians should have sought their basis in the religious plays, so rich in profane and comic elements, and the popular farces. By so doing both would have been in line with the Romantic theory of the organic and autochthonous development of literature and of everything else, a theory which in its zeal for nice explanations of the facts seemed to require the facts to fall in with its own view of how they should have come about. If they erred against nature by failing to do so, all the worse for them, and they were duly arraigned and punished. The only thing would have been to tell Plautus and Terence to their faces that they must refrain from reading those seductive authors Menander, Diphilus, and Apollodorus, and to tell Bibbiena and Machiavelli not to read the two Romans but to fix their attention on strolling players and the actors of the sacred confraternities, on the Macci, the Pappi, the Bucconi, the Dossenni. They of course would have shrugged their shoulders at this preposterous proposal that they should drop the works which spoke to their mind and feelings and artistic sense and abase themselves to bear company with popular and plebeian mimes whose very existence they had forgotten.

This false idea of originality which clamours for an art unrelated to the art which went before it, for a purely national or purely provincial art, is now rarely found in the criticism and history of modern literatures, but it persists or at least lingers on in regard to ancient literature, without heed for the results of the long and now antiquated discussions of other times on the independence of French from Greek tragedy and so on.

The other adverse judgement levelled against Terence suggests that the pleasure he gives us, the reputation he enjoys, are all due to our having no access to the Greek originals from which he more or less freely translated. If ever the ignorance is made good by the discovery of those originals, then, it is suggested, the pleasure will cease, the bor-

rowed glory will slip away. Well, let us for argument's sake assume that the dramas of Terence are just translations, very fine translations, no doubt, exquisitely phrased in pure Latin. Why should the discovery of the originals impair their reputation? The Greek text of Homer is known but this does not render Vincenzo Monti's Italian version of the *Iliad* less admirable, it being beautiful in itself as well as a medium serving the needs of those unable to read Homer himself. Shakespeare's English text is known to the Germans, but Schlegel's German translation remains a classic. Beautiful translations are always the work of some poetic spirit who embraces the original and warms it with his own life. Why should the fact that Terence's "translations" stand to some extent in lieu of the lost Greek comedies be viewed as a weakness and detract from their merit? August Wilhelm Schlegel, with his cultivated dislike or Romantic prejudice against everything Roman and Italian, in his lectures on dramatic poetry made no more than a bare and disdainful allusion to Plautus and Terence ("no creative artists"), but spread himself on the Greek comedy, forgoing mention of the two authors still living in their works in order to treat of authors whose works are non-existent (in Schlegel's time much less of them had been discovered than now). But numberless are the blunders of critics who, when discoursing of art, often forget the subject of their discourse. One almost blushes to recall them and to confute them. For example the charge is blunderingly laid against Terence that the dramas which pass under his name are really by Scipio or Laelius, or by one of the two in collaboration with Terence. Antiquity too had its "Baconians", the sort of people who would attribute Shakespeare's dramas to the most unpoetical of lords of his time if thereby they could wrest them from the poor actor, "sweet William". In antiquity such people wished to strip the wreath of Apollo from the brow of an African, a slave, a freed-man, and the initiated whispered it around that this wreath properly belonged to illustrious personages who, disdaining or blushing to appear before the public as theatrical authors, had brought in some poor fellow of their acquaintance to stand for them. That Terence's comedies should be the fruit of a collaboration must seem unlikely to anyone who appreciates what style is. But even were it so, and even if the author's name has been deliberately falsified, what has that to do with a judgement on poetry? Are we giving marks to Terence in an examination or competition, and trying to make sure that his answers have not been cribbed from another candidate? Professors, when they engage in criticism, find it difficult to drop the attitude of the examiner. This accounts for a certain suspicion and disapproval shown by them towards Terence.

So I have for the sake of argument accepted the worst that the critics can or could bring against the works of Terence—that they are translations and not written by Terence—and I have shown that it has no significance for the appreciation and judgement of the works themselves as poetry. That does not mean that I myself think they are straight translations from Greek originals. Terence, of course, himself says that he took this or that comedy from Menander or another Greek. The old stage directions confirm this and name the other Greek, Apollodorus. The approved and required method in the Roman theatre was to take the schemes or frames of the Greek comedies and to keep their location in Greece. In fact, to judge from Terence's apologies, it seems to have been considered improper to fuse two or more of these well-known schemes together, though once one was adopted great liberty was allowed in tacitly recasting it, introducing variations, and extra episodes and personages. However, what matters for us is not the frame, but the embroidery, not the argument or fable, but the flow of poetry infused in it. This was understood during the many centuries of European literature in which the word "imitation" had a significance, at the same time humble and noble, as the acceptance of a traditional outline to serve as a frame to support the embroidery, the creation of beauty.

But in later times the philologians, untrained for the judgement of art, if not actually deaf to poetry, gave great and primary importance to the canvas, and ended by glorifying the weaving of the canvas itself with the scientific-sounding but in this context unscientific term of "technique". So nowadays, instead of enquiring after poetry, they pronounce judgement and allot retribution on the good or bad technique of the work, with an air of knowing the job, which, since we are here discussing drama, would mean being expert stage-managers or actor-managers, with a sound knowledge of theatrical continuity and effect. It was therefore inevitable, when some papyrus discoveries brought to light several long fragments of Menander and a good part of one of his comedies, that they should soon weight up and pass judgement that the "technique" of Menander was superior to that of Terence, whom they regard as little better than a bungler. Be that as it may (and personally I feel this also to be a prejudiced assessment), the point is that the canvas or technique in poetry is a secondary matter. I will here enlist the assertion of this simple truth, so hard to put across to the stiff minds of the philologians, made by Michel de Montaigne in reference precisely to Terence. Montaigne had a great affection for the Roman comic poet, calling him "admirable à représenter au vif les mouvements de l'âme et la condition de nos mœurs". Montaigne had little use for those whose interest lay and was centred in the plot, the accidents, the complications, the diverting adventures. "Il en va de mon aucteur tout au contraire: les perfections et beautez de sa façon de dire nous font perdre l'appetit de son subject: sa gentillesse et sa mignardise nous retiennent partout; il est partout si plaisant, *liquidus puroque simillimus amni,* et nous remplit tant l'âme de ses graces que nous en oublions celles de sa fable" [*Essais*]. As Montaigne says, we forget it, or rather we take no heed of it. What does it matter to us that the usual slave, the Know-all or Think-of-all, produces the usual shrewd devices for getting cash for the young master and hoodwinking the old? What does it matter that the sweetheart turns out to be a daughter of the old man's friend and marriage supplies a happy ending? Our eye follows something which arises out of this tale and leaves it behind and dances above it.

Moreover, it is improbable that Terence's plays are mere or even free translations of Greek plays, with at the most some well-conceived changes of detail, but having no originality save that poetic quality which always pertains to the work of the artistic translator or adaptor, and without

which he could not accomplish it. But the scholars wish to deny Terence the authorship even of the changes of detail. Where the sources relate that a given character or scene was introduced by Terence, they reply that these are too fine and masterly to be flour from the mill of Terence, and that the old commentator must have made a mistake or has been misunderstood or his text meddled with, since those sections also are certainly by Menander or some other Greek comediographer overlooked by the commentator. This seems to me, I confess, arguing in a vicious circle. In any case the fact is that Terence and Plautus had before them more or less the same models: and what a difference divides their two temperaments and respective dramatic output! In the plays of Terence there is a unity of feeling, a steady and coherent personality, an artistic chastity and nobility, a shyness about leaving his own range and breaking or straying into those of others. Translators, on the contrary, are usually versatile, and in this versatility display their artistic sensitiveness and their prowess. Why did Terence compose only "sex comoedias"? Probably because "son verre n'était pas grand mais il buvait dans son verre". The tale, so often foolishly repeated, originating in the misreading of a page of Suetonius, that after publishing his six comedies, Terence went on a trip to Greece where he translated and adapted no fewer than a hundred and eight comedies of Menander, but was shipwrecked and died of grief for the loss of the *novas fabulas* among his baggage, might smack of mockery at the smallness of his literary output. But the relation of Terence to Menander may be other than the modern grammarians suppose. The right idea may be that which is perhaps suggested in a well-known passage of Saint Jerome, who knew and valued both authors, and advised enquiring students to accept as the four standards of poetical style Homer and Virgil, Menander and Terence, a hint, maybe, that as Virgil stands to Homer so—in the other couple, for whom, as Petrarch remarked, the "altitudo stili" of the epic does not obtain—Terence stands to Menander.

In truth, the increased but by no means voluminous stock which we now have of Menander's writings is far from confirming the view of Terence as being merely a graceful and gifted translator. Rather, it serves to emphasize the differing features of the lively, impetuous, smiling Greek, so agreeable and witty, though he can also be warm-hearted and pathetic as with Glycera and the soldier of the *Perikeiromene* and Abrotonon and Carisio of the *Epitrepontes;* and on the other hand of Terence, with his deep humanity and feeling, not easily moved to mirth and laughter. Maybe further discoveries of other Menander plays, permitting a fuller valuation of Menander's personality, will indicate a closer connexion between the two authors, but at this moment I do not think that there is ground for going beyond what was already known because recounted by Terence himself: that Terence took some plots from Menander. The copious literature, still piling up, which busies itself with cataloguing all the scenes which he took from Menander, with the changes and adaptations which he introduced, is altogether conjectural and sterile, and, frankly, seems to me just so much scholarly raving. If *tantus amor* spurs on the scholars to acquire knowledge of this sort (as though there were not already an excess of it in regard to other poets, and very little of it—as has been found—of any use for the interpretation of the poets), then on with the business of digging up more papyri, and mean-while, a little patience!

Still less does the comparative study of the new fragments authorize conclusions as to a superiority of Menander as a true poet over Terence as a mere man of letters, or of Menander as a creative mind over Terence as a mechanical mind. Or is one to try and take seriously the absurd pastime in which the philological scholars, taking on the air of philosophers, and thus degenerating into bad philosophers, have begun to indulge with such zeal and pleasure, the game of supposing that the discussion of certain moral, political, or other concepts underlies the poets's works, constituting what is with heavy emphasis called their "problems"? By such devices a German scholar [K. Stavenhagen, in *Hermes,* XLV (1910)] showed the gulf which divides an "artist of genius" like Menander and a "clever comedy writer" like Terence, or rather, (since even this rank was denied to him) Terence's immediate model Apollodorus of Karystos. Just think of it: Menander in the *Epitrepontes* felt and propounded, according to this scholar, the moral problem of the duty of chastity for the male, equally with the female, before marriage. This tremendous and sublime problem Terence-Apollodorus threw aside for the petty pleasure of changing the scene and resolving a "technical problem". Our Italian Pasquali, hotly pursuing the German, put the essential greatness of Menander in this self-revelation in the *Epitrepontes* as a "thinker absorbed in problems of social ethics" including a problem such as that of pre-matrimonial male chastity which is "eminently modern, Kantian, Ibsenic"; and although Menander "did not actually solve it" (alas, he sighs, it has not even yet been solved), yet, we are told, he was able to develop it in the way that Ibsen would have done, which Pasquali proceeds to divine and describe. In reality, this problem belongs not to the Kant of philosophy, but if at all to the Kant of the casuistic exercises, and the mental atmosphere of this problem is lacking in Ibsen. (Nora in the *Doll's House* has nothing to do with the case.) Where it is found is in such an abstract and insipid moralist as Björnson, whose drama on the subject (*The Glove* of 1883) Pasquali should, if necessary, have called in to support his odd thesis. It would be superfluous here to explain once again that the existence of a conceptual problem (moral, political, or otherwise) so far from confirming the presence confirms the absence of poetry: and in any case not only is the problem in question not enunciated in Menander's comedy, but the particular case cited by the German scholar and his Italian follower does not arise. What Carisio reproaches himself with is a fault quite different from that of not having retained the flower of chastity to offer to his bride.

I have confuted these distorted judgements which it is now fashionable to pile up against the art of Terence, in the interests of truth and logic. In the same way the preceding objections and reserves which I expressed on the theory that Terence was a mere translator are the fruit of a methodic doubt and critical caution. Yet once again I will be prepared for the sake of argument to admit the improbable hypothesis that the six comedies attributed to Terence are simple translations from Greek comedies. For that is not the point. Translations or originals, these six comedies are present and expressive and they reveal to us the soul of a poet having his own accent, his own music, his own prevailing feeling. The reader of poetry asks the critic to remove the obstacles and help him to enjoy the poetry; that, and nothing else. Other questions, even if they are sensible and soluble, yet since they relate to something outside and apart from the poetical work, do not meet the reader's need, but on the contrary overlook it, and are therefore tiresome or at least otiose. I suggest that after so much irrelevant comment it is time to tackle that which alone is relevant. It is time, after lingering so long with his scholarly commentators, to turn directly to himself, and to learn from him his "dominating feeling", which fortunately is something very dear and precious-human goodness. The human goodness in question can be more closely described as one which is well aware of human weaknesses, but would rather trace and observe the spontaneous awakening and development of the finer affections, thereby placing bounds upon those which are less noble and pure, so as to offset them and elude their dominance.

The first and most obvious example of this is the manner of his treatment of the shameless wench, the "meretrix mala" of the other comic dramatists. Terence never shows this character as totally and utterly "mala". With him, she always exhibits some inclination to good and generous behaviour, some disposition or longing for virtue, some feeling of humility regarding her position. Terence seems not to believe that a human being can be radically wicked, and seems unwilling to exclude any one of them from the pale of humanity.

Thus we hear of the young Chrysis migrating from Andros to Athens under the spur of need and neglect at home. She has no thought or desire of vice, indeed at first she lives by the hard work of spinning and weaving. Then she yields to the temptations which beset youth and beauty where the helps and hindrances of family and social links are lacking. She yields to the lure of pleasure and sinks gradually to the position of a courtesan. But she still arouses feelings of friendship and strong affection, and when near to death she is in a position to call on a young man who is like a brother to her, and to entrust a young girl whom she has treated as a sister to his faith and honour, placing her hand in his as in that of a husband, friend, brother, father, in fact as the representative of all institutions and moral relations. The young man, who was never her lover, follows her bier weeping with the others, and his father too, responding to these marks of gentleness which he sees with pleasure in his son, joins in the mourning.

Bacchis, in the *Hecyra,* had been warmly loved by young Pamphilus. But Pamphilus, at his father's orders, marries against his own will. He leaves his bride untouched, with the firm intention of restoring her as a virgin to her parents, and he continues his amour with the other. The lover, now that she no longer has the young man all to herself, becomes ill-tempered and overbearing, so that by contrast the gentle yieldingness of the bride wins him over, and little by little he shifts his love and ends by dropping Bacchis. But the bewildered relatives, at the height of the painful and hopeless tension between the young husband and wife, suspect that Pamphilus is still in the sway of his old mistress. Pamphilus' father proceeds to question her and is ready to pass on to threats. But Bacchis takes no malevolent pleasure in the troubles of the young couple and their families, harbours no vengeful feelings against the lover who has left her or the bride who is the cause of this, but says truthfully that Pamphilus is no longer visiting her. The father asks her to repeat this to his women-folk, and she, who is no better than she should be, feels a mingled pride and shyness at being required to appear before a bride who must necessarily look on her with hostility, in a respectable house which in itself is a reproach and humiliation for her; and she knows that no other girl in her position would do it. But her good heart prevails, and a sort of natural honesty, and she goes. As luck will have it, at the encounter she is able to produce evidence which, much better than her own statement, cuts the knot and allays the painful tension between the young husband and wife. And great is her joy.

> *Quantam obtuli adventu meo laetitiam Pamphilo*
>   *hodie!*
> *Quot commodas res attuli! Quot autem ademi*
>   *curas!*
> *Gnatum ei restituo, paene qui harum ipsiusque*
>   *opera periit:*
> *uxorem, quam nunquam ratus posthac se habi-*
>   *turum, reddo:*
> *qua re suspectus suo patri et Phidippo fuit,*
>   *exolui . . .*

She rejoices and congratulates herself upon being the one chosen to dispel such great troubles, to bring about so much joy in a family which certainly did not expect this from her. At this point one of those excellent scholars who cannot admire one poet without running down another, affirms that Bacchis is "much inferior" to Abrotonon in the *Epitrepontes,* whom Terence must have had in mind, because Bacchis "talks too much of her generosity, laying on an excessive air of modesty", particularly in the verses just quoted, whereas Abrotonon "who felt that she had served as a decoy for herself, instead of indulging in self-praise, works out her plans carefully and proceeds to put them into action without talking too much about herself." Here there are misstatements of fact, for if Abrotonon had quickly lost the affections of Carisios, Bacchis, too, after repeated declarations of love and a long attachment had been abandoned by Pamphilus. And if Bacchis is pleased with what she has done, but neither asks nor expects a reward, Abrotonon had in mind the reward of winning her freedom. Nor is it possible to point to a passage in which Bacchis "lays on an excessive air of modesty" and at the same time "talks too much of her own generosity". The satisfaction which she shows, even if she wears it a little bit like a halo, becomes her well, for the poet never claimed to be depicting a woman of exquisite fineness and austere perfection. Let us, however, ignore these details. The point is that poetically the two characters are quite different. Abrotonon is a poor creature, a little *cocotte* usually down on her luck, who cannot herself make out how Carisios came to pick her up, and comically complains that he does not even want her company at meals and has already left her in "unmarried purity" for as long as three

days. She is also a good creature who makes haste and takes pains to discover whether the exposed child is or is not the son of Carisios, and who was its mother. All this she does and says pleasantly, shrewdly, and amusingly. What has this to do with Bacchis? Bacchis refuses to be like the other courtesans with their cold crude selfishness, their hatred and vengefulness against anyone who has escaped from their clutches and is no longer any use to them. Her behaviour at that meeting, I think, has no need to be judged by these moralizing scholarly gentlemen, for it had already been fittingly judged and understood and felt by young Pamphilus in his expression of warm gratitude and tenderness when after her saving action she comes up to him with a plain greeting.

O Bacchis, mea Bacchis, servatrix mea!

He calls her "his" Bacchis, "his" in a different sense from before, "his" as she now speaks to his heart; his old feeling for her being restored and purified, and changed in its quality and savour. The words which they now exchange are not those of the former lovers, but of two beings who have been raised on to another plane. He still finds in her the charm that renders her delightful to look at and speak with wherever it may be, while she still admires in him the manners and the mind which make of him the most charming young man in the world. And she wants him to be happy in his new condition and affectionately recommends him to be good to his wife, who well deserves this "Recte amasti, Pamphile, uxorem tuam". The wife, whom she has just seen for the first time strikes her as most charming, "perliberalis". The two leave their common past behind them and find each other on a new and higher level in the present.

There is a similar kindly disposition, at bottom, in Bacchis' girl friend Philotis, who, though amazed and outraged by Pamphilus' desertion of Bacchis, rejects the lesson inferred by the old hag that girls should feel no pity for any man; but should despoil them, mutilate them, injure them all, not excepting anyone, when they hold them in their power. What, asks Philotis "eximium neminem habeam?"—not even one of them? And to the old woman's repeated arguments she objects again. "Tamen pol eandem injuriumst esse omnibus", as if to say that one could not and should not be as vindictive as that.

The other Bacchis (the character in the *Heautontimorumenos*) is shown as a courtesan in the full display and zeal of one greedily pursuing her business interests. Yet she too feels the need to explain to young Antiphila, who is on her way to meet her bridegroom, that she behaves like this not out of sheer viciousness but because she is caught up helplessly in the logic of her situation. "Nam expedit bonas esse vobis: nos quibuscum est res, non sinunt." It is the selfishness of the male, she means, which brings this about, seeking nothing else but voluptuous beauty and turning the back when this fades. And Thais in the **Eunuchus,** Thais whose name thanks to Dante has come in the Italian language to designate the most shrewish sort of whore, is in Terence just one of those who follow the iron logic of the life to which they have given themselves, and think and provide against future woes. But she is not a bad woman. Thais, in her way, feels affectionately for young

Phaedria, and if she courts the soldier, it is because she expects to win from him the gift of a young slave whom she hopes to restore to the bosom of her family and thus to gain for herself some goodwill to console her solitude in the city. I recall how in the expurgated text of Terence (that of Monsignor Bindi) which I was given at school the episode of Bacchis' success in getting herself by that means received into the household and home of Laches "in clientelam et fidem", contrary to good family morality, received a pained comment on the lines that the "corruption of those pagan times" could alone excuse Terence. The good Monsignor Bindi had already transformed Phaedria and Thraso into two suitors for "the hand of Thais", which Phaedria had the good luck to obtain! For all that Monsignor Bindi understood and enjoyed his Terence much more sensibly than many modern scholars.

In view of this handling of the figure of the courtesan in the Terentian plays I cannot help wondering that these eminent scholars have missed the occasion for congratulating not of course Terence (that mere "santo pequeño"), but Menander, on the discovery and exploration of the "problem" of the "redemption" of the fallen woman, foreshadowing a favourite theme of the French Romantics. As a matter of fact they have not wholly overlooked this, and let us hope that they will follow it up with their customary intuitive penetration into broad issues and delicacy of interpretation of particulars. Thus Lafaye says that Terentius-Apollodorus "semble avoir voulu, comme les romantiques, rajeunir les types traditionnels en leur prêtant des sentiments contraires à l'idée que l'on se faisait généralement: de là la bonne courtisane, fine, sensible, désintéressée. According to this critic Terence was unconventional for love of novelty, not, then, in a Romantic but at most in a Baroque spirit. For the Romantics were drawn to paradoxical characterizations by the spirit of revolt against society with its conventions and laws. But in truth it was neither the spirit of revolt nor a Baroque love of the amazing and the bizarre that guided the straightforward and delicate Terence.

Naturalness, indulgence, goodness of heart pervade other scenes and other characters also in the plays of Terence. Nowhere in the pages of Giovanni Boccaccio - eager expert though he was in all the paths which natural love finds for surmounting hindrances, winning its ends by the subtlest tricks and eluding all precautions - is there any such humane moral atmosphere as in the first scene of the *Andria.* The father has very sensibly decided that the best way of deterring young Pamphilus from getting into mischief is to leave him entirely free; and observing him in his youthful occupations and amusements, his delight in horses and hunting, his interests too in philosophers and their disputations, and his social activities, is delighted to see him behaving temperately and tactfully, surrounded by popularity and affection. The father observes that he also frequents the house of Chrysis, joining in talks and supper-parties but without committing himself or scorching himself with the flames of love. The father is pleased with this too, for his son's and his own sake, and when he sees the boy distressed at the death of this woman, he approves of that proper sentiment and joins respectfully in his grief and tears. But at the funeral he sees among the

other women one that he does not know, a pretty, shy, attractive girl, who they tell him is the dead woman's sister. This is somewhat of a shock. A veil drops from his mind, there is a flash of comedy in this dissipation of a comfortable illusion, leaving him surprised, but at the same time seriously concerned. Tut-tut - so that is at the root of the affair, is it?

> *Attat, hoc illud est,*
> *hinc illae lacrimae, haec illast misericordia!*

The two young persons' love soon after reveals itself infallibly without any need of words from them or from others when, as the flames lick the pyre and the girl ventures too close, Pamphilus, greatly alarmed,

> *adcurrit: mediam mulierem complectitur:*
> *"Mea Glycerium" inquit "quid agis? quor te is*
> *perditum?"*
> *Tum illa, ut consuetum facile amorem cerneres*
> *rejecit se in eum flens quam familiariter.*

Four verses which are a picture in themselves, a poem of inconsolable grief, of watchful loving care, as the woman gives way to her feelings and seeks and finds comforting protection from the man she loves. The youth is worthy of this trusting abandon, he feels the responsibility which falls on him for this girl who has given herself to him, whom if he were to throw aside in order to fulfil the marriage arranged for him by his father, he would not only consign to utter despair, but would expose her to corruption in the corrupt world, so that for his fault that innocent and charming nature would be ruined:

> *Hem, egone istuc conari queam?*
> *Egon propter me suam decipi miseram sinam,*
> *quae mihi suom animum atque omnem vitam*
> *credidit,*
> *quam ego animo egregie caram pro uxore ha-*
> *buerim!*
> *Bene et pudice eius doctum atque eductum sinam*
> *coactum egestate ingenium inmutarier?*

The vow made to the dying Chrysis was sacred, and he will not loosen his grip upon that hand which she placed in his, and which he gripped as he swore the oath.

Quite a different note of passion is portrayed in young Phaedria (in the *Eunuchus*), a passion without ethical content, all feeling and desire, greedy and violent, steadily persistent, however badly the woman behaves and however much he himself tries to free himself from the coils. Phaedria and Thais, one may say, are on the same level. Parmeno sums up his situation for him, and tells him what to do:

> *Quid agas? nisi ut te redimas captum quam queas*
> *minumo: si nequeas paululo, at quantum queas:*
> *et ne te adflictes . . .*

This tries to compromise between her preference for him and her own needs and ambitions which require her to give some satisfaction also to the other man, the rich soldier who was formerly her lover. In her words there is a resignation bordering upon melancholy:

> *Ne crucia te, obsecro, anime mi, Phaedria.*

Non pol, quo quemquam plus amem aut plus dili-
   gam,
  eo feci: sed ita erat res, faciundum fuit.

And Phaedria ends by acquiescing, in order not to have to sever relations with the woman, only begging and insisting that he is not to be kept waiting more than two days, during which he goes off to his farm, but cannot stay there more than an hour or two before he is back in the town hanging round Thais. Once again Parmeno cannot resist philosophic reflections on the oddity of poor mankind, and sees no remedy:

Di boni, quid hoc morbist? adeon homines in-
   mutarier
ex amore, ut non cognoscas eundem esse! Hoc
   nemo fuit
minus ineptus, magis severus quisquam, nec
   magis continens . . .

Phaedria, that is to say, was not a blind and crude slave of the senses, but a man who had fallen into a net and was struggling in it and simply drawing it tighter. For the moment he was in the sway of an inebriation which one day, however, would be dissolved.

In the same spirit (I use this expression advisedly, for surely those pretended eulogies of a poet, be it Terence, Menander, or any other, for depicting "daily life as it really is in itself" or for "competing with nature and beating her at her own game" are quite senseless), in the same spirit, I say, the dramatist delineates the passionate old man Menedemus (in the *Heautontimorumenos*), that father who cannot forgive himself for having by his strictness caused his son to go off on military service, and now himself works furiously on the land, anxiously avoiding the slightest pleasure or relaxation, for that would seem to him time stolen from the son whom his behaviour had thrown into the fatigues and harshness of military life. The contrast in the educational methods of the two fathers in the *Adelphoi* is not, as some moralizing commentators would have it, designed to inculcate the lesson of avoidance of extremes, but serves to illustrate and to express wonderment at the variety of human conduct and its unforeseeable consequences. Terence really does not know what to think of the two respective methods and takes sides for neither, least of all for a schoolmaster's synthesis of the two. Demea, who has seen his strict methods frustrated in the outcome, proceeds to adopt the opposite method which he previously denounced and opposed, but does so in a mood of angry exasperation as if wishing it to do its worst, and to end in disaster. He violently exaggerates the easy-going methods of his brother, punishing him by forcing him also to practise his indulgence on a new and widened scale, and making him reel with the mounting measure of his liberalities. He wishes thereby to demonstrate to him that the praise and the advantages which he has hitherto enjoyed were not won *ex aequo et bono,* but simply by yielding to the interests and passions of others. War-weary, he drops the reins and spurs his horse to a precipitous and disorderly gallop, but all the time he clings to the opinion that his method was the right one and will have to come into its own again. On the other side the indulgent brother does not really cease to believe in his method, or consent to forswear it. There is no ques-

tion, then, of a "problem" or an educational programme, but simply of a clash of temperaments and feelings, and a tangle of chances, eluding all educational theory.

Alongside of the contrast between the two father-brothers, the two mothers are shown in the *Hecyra* as placed in different circumstances, indeed, calling for different attitudes, but equally disposed for self-effacing maternal sacrifice, one for her son and the other for her daughter. This harmonious correspondence between the minds of two mothers has astonishingly been dubbed a mere "duplication", and more or less blamed on the usual presumption that Terence must always and in everything be inferior to the great Menander. The unfortunate Philumena, too, innocent victim who confides the secret of her shame to the mother only, concealing it from husband and father, must, it seems, be judged inferior to Pamphila of the Epitrepontes. But in truth these girls and brides of the Terentian comedies are delineated in their innocency with delicate simplicity. I will end this brief series of illustrations of Terence's handling of the human affections with a reference to the parasite in the *Eunuchus,* so different a figure from the cut-and-dried caricatures of the other comic writers (Ergasilus in the *Captivi* of Plautus, for example). He is as amusing as a Casanova when he sets forth his guiding principle that fools are sent into the world solely for the benefit of clever fellows. Since the world contains such a soldier as Thraso, living on boasts, longing to be recognized as brave, far-sighted, clever, brilliant, why not at his side a Gnatho to humour him and so make a living for himself? There can be no question of altering him, changing him for the better. The utmost that would be possible would be to leave this rich soil uncultivated, unharvested, for someone else to exploit, and that would be a pity. So Gnatho follows up the soldier's boasts with approval, applause, epigrams, confirmations and corollaries of what he says, laughs at the quips which Thraso thinks must be amusing, bears with endless repetitions of the soldier's exploits, asks to have them repeated as though he had forgotten the details and would love to hear them again. But Thraso is also the poor fellow who, however much he is wronged and fooled, cannot give up Thais, but creeps back to her and as usual recalls the example of his peers in heroism. "Qui minus quam Hercules servivit Omphalae?" Gnatho approves: "Exemplum placet." Gnatho's masterpiece as a knowing and competent man of the world is when he gets the warrior, and himself too, accepted into the new combine formed by Phaedria and Thais, by dint of the prudent counsel that Thais is too extravagant to be kept by one man and that since a partner must be found none could be better than this rich spendthrift fool who is already on the spot. Even Thraso and Gnatho are not villains, they are poor devils who get on as best they can. True, Pasquali complains that Terence has spoiled the delicate delineation of Thais by Menander (in a comedy which is lost so that no one can say what that delineation was: a new proof of the abounding but peculiar imagination of the scholars). He spoiled it, according to Pasquali, in this last scene "quite unworthy of the charming creature (Thais)" and thereby, "though he may not have offended the majority of the spectators, he certainly must have offended the more refined even of his contemporary readers", for the scene was a contradiction "not only by logical but by psychological and artistic" standards, and "Terence's *Eunuch* thus ends on a note of disharmony". If Dante treated poor Thais with unmeasured contempt, Pasquali seems to have become captivated by her wiles and to have forgotten, as amorous dreamers do, what she really was and what she is shown to be by the words of Phaedria and Parmeno and in her own words to them. On the other hand Pasquali also displays an erudite moral zeal blind to the feelings which, in all their gradations and complications and interplay, are the stuff of life and the stuff of poetry too, which is free of such scruples and niceties. Whatever the unknown Thais of Menander's unknown comedy may have been like, Terence's Thais is quite all right as she is, and excites our human understanding and compassion.

These are the mainsprings of the poetry of Terence's comedies, among which the palm used to be given to the *Eunuchus,* so full of life and with a good deal more of that comic and sometimes farcical element in it than in the other comedies, where this is slight or almost wanting. Perhaps it would be better to give the first place to the *Hecyra,* followed by the *Eunuchus,* the *Andria,* the *Adelphoi,* the *Heautontimorumenos,* and last, because having more the character of a mere comedy of intrigue, the *Phormio.*

Thanks to the kindly feeling which he shows in observing and depicting human life, and an occasional touch of something like Christian charity - and by no means, therefore, simply for his excellent Latin - Terence had his warm admirers in antiquity and was among the most read Roman authors in the Middle Ages, and was as dear to Petrarch as afterwards to Montaigne, Erasmus, and Carlo Borromeo, and for his mildness and suavity and artistic clarity seemed almost the Virgil of the Roman comic theatre. In later times familiarity with him, as with all Latin authors, has declined, with the particular assistance in his case of the depreciatory attitude of the professional scholars. But whoever reopens his pages will find his attraction undiminished, and will forget the passage of the centuries.

Henry Ten Eyck Perry   (essay date 1939)

SOURCE: "Roman Imitators: Plautus and Terence" in *Masters of Dramatic Comedy and Their Social Themes,* Cambridge, Mass.: Harvard University Press, 1939, pp. 49-78.

[*Perry was an American educator and author. In the following excerpt, he examines the themes of Terence's plays in the context of Roman comedy, concluding that he refined the plots and characters that he borrowed from other playwrights to make them more serious and more humane.*]

Terence is much more like Menander than Plautus is, four of his six plays being based on works by Menander and all of his dramas giving the effect of imitation more than of creative vitality. Unlike Plautus, he had no hesitancy in wringing every possible tear from Menander's situation of the long-lost child. He makes use of it in all but one of his comedies. Plautus is at bottom concerned with the humorous complications that get in the way of his lovers and frequently with the absurd per'sons who stand in their paths; Terence is obsessed with the harshness of fate. After he

has developed throughout five acts the misery that it causes, he finally permits its patient victims to be rewarded, not always inevitably, with unexpected happiness.

What is exceptionally non-Plautine in the *Cistellaria* is typically Terentian in the *Girl from Andros (Andria)*, the first of Terence's plays, produced in 166 B.C. These two plays have the same basic plot, the love of a young man for a girl who turns out to be the sister of his fiancée. In the *Girl from Andros* a slave tries to break off the formal engagement, but his efforts are worse than useless. If it were not for the romantic discovery of the Andrian's birth, the hero would probably have had to give up the girl with whom he was in love and by whom he had already had a child. In the *Self-Tormentor (Heauton Timorumenos)* of 163 B.C. the hero has not lived with the girl whom he loves, but again the revelation of the heroine's birth is necessary to clear up all the complications of the plot. The *Eunuch (Eunuchus)*, 161 B.C., shows the young man anticipating Wycherley's Horner in *The Country Wife,* by posing as a eunuch so that he may secure access to a mistress; libertine though he is, he is anxious to continue the liaison, and the discovery that the girl is freeborn makes marriage with her possible for him. In the *Phormio* (also 161 B.C.) the hero has already taken the girl as his wife and later finds that she is his own cousin, whom his father had intended him to marry. In all these cases the proof that the heroine is freeborn straightens out an intrigue which has progressed to the varying stages of first love, physical violence, parenthood, or marriage.

Terence's fifth play, the *Mother-in-Law,* has a curious history. It was originally produced in 165, which would make it his second piece in chronological order, but it failed and was taken off the boards. In 161 it was performed again, probably in its present form, but it was not until 160 that it finally met with success. As the play now stands, its central plot is a combination of those used in the *Eunuch* and the *Phormio.* As in the former, the hero has attacked the girl; as in the latter, he has married her. The denouement reveals that the unfortunate girl and his wife are one and the same person, a fact which he himself did not previously know. This situation is like that in the *Epitrepontes* of Menander, and the heroes of the two plays are equally sensitive and upright in intention. The young man in the *Mother-in-Law* finds it difficult to give up Bacchis, the courtesan with whom he has lived up to the time of his marriage and who is herself a noble creature. She refuses to let her lover visit her after he is married, she assures his wife and mother-in-law that her intrigue with him is over, and by so doing she is the instrument of the discovery essential to a happy outcome of the plot. She does not appear on the stage until the last act, but her brief scenes establish her as the most unselfish courtesan in Latin comedy, a striking contrast to the two mercenary sisters in Plautus whose names are also Bacchis.

Another attractive figure in the *Mother-in-Law* is the hero's mother. Fearing that the success of her son's marriage is endangered by her presence, she resolves to sacrifice herself by retiring to the country out of her daughter-in-law's way. She is the mother-in-law or *hecyra* who gives her name to the play, unless this title, like those of the

Thraso attacks the house of Thais: illustration from an early manuscript of The Eunich.

Self-Tormentor and the *Brothers* (*Adelphoe*), can bear two interpretations. The hero's mother is thought to be the first obstacle to the happiness of the married pair, and the heroine's mother is considered the second one; but as a matter of fact neither of them is responsible for the original misunderstanding, which is brought about by the wife's having given birth to a child before the marriage was consummated. When it is proved that the husband is also the father of the child, the bad luck that has pursued all the characters is dispelled in time for a happy ending. The one comic twist in the story is that the two fathers-in-law are kept in the dark as to the true state of affairs. They blame the trouble first on one of their wives and then on the other, and even at the end they are not enlightened as to its cause. The hero says that it is not necessary to tell everyone everything, as is customary in most comedies, and it is arranged that the unsavory facts of the case shall be concealed by the husband and wife, the wife's mother, and the husband's former mistress. The ironic way in which the fathers are fooled by the women in the *Mother-in-Law* is the only amusing incident in a drama that is otherwise extremely grave in tone.

The *Mother-in-Law* is the most solemn of Terence's comedies, with the possible exception of the *Girl from Andros*, and that early play has its comic moments in the vain at-

tempts of a slave to help the lovers by trickery. The scheming slave is naturally a much less important figure in the sentimental dramas of Terence than in the boisterous farces of Plautus. In the *Mother-in-Law,* he is pathetically powerless. At the end of the play he is almost as ignorant of what has occurred as are the fathers. In the *Self-Tormentor* he has slightly more to do, by suggesting the plot which temporarily comes to the aid of the second lover. All Terence's dramas except the *Mother-in-Law* have two pairs of lovers whose fortunes are at stake, and it is generally the affair of the secondary hero which provides the comic situations needed to sustain the serious primary action. Terence's plays would not fall into the sphere of comedy if in all of them there were not occasional opportunities for laughter, or at least for quiet smiles.

The hero's jealous friend in the *Girl from Andros* is not sufficiently prominent to produce much merriment, but the secondary hero of the *Self-Tormentor* is amusing in his efforts to get money enough to buy the favors of the courtesan whom he loves. He succeeds for a time, but finally his ruses are discovered by his father, who threatens to disinherit him unless the son will agree to reform his conduct and settle down in matrimony. He does not like the first girl proposed for him, but he is willing to accept his father's second choice for a suitable but not very joyful marriage. In a true comedy the son would not only have secured the money for the courtesan by cheating his father, but he would have been left with her at the final curtain to enjoy his momentary happiness. His repentance is much less plausible than that of the reformed spendthrift in Plautus' *Trinummus,* who was not in love with any specific courtesan, and this abrupt reformation is a striking evidence of how unwilling Terence was to let the events of his plays work themselves out to a logical comic conclusion.

The outcome of the secondary plot of the *Eunuch* is no better prepared for than is that of the *Self-Tormentor,* but its unexpected turn is in the direction of comedy instead of towards conventional morality. The brother of the supposed eunuch is in love with a courtesan who really cares for him, and his father agrees to the liaison; but even a sincere courtesan has expensive tastes that must be gratified. At the end of the play the courtesan's lover agrees to share his mistress's favors with Thraso, a wealthy captain who has been pursuing her, with the result that the secondary plot of the *Eunuch* closes in a sardonic mood. Thraso is the best example of the Terentian *miles gloriosus,* differing from the similar figure of Plautus in that he boasts of his wit rather than of his valor. Terence's conception is characteristically more subtle than Plautus', but Thraso lacks the astonishing verve of Pyrgopolynices.

To the secondary plot of the *Phormio* Terence gives an ending that is in accordance with the best traditions of classic comedy. The hero of this part of the play is in love with a slave-girl owned by a *leno* and is successful in obtaining the money necessary to secure her. The *leno* is not tricked, as is generally the case in Plautus, but fairly receives the money, which is wrung from the hero's father by the taunts of his jealous wife. The agent in this transaction is Phormio, a parasite, who plays the part generally taken by the clever slave in Plautus. Terence here challenges his predecessor on his own grounds, and he has succeeded in creating a drama as truly comic as any by Plautus. The double plot in the *Phormio* is a little too complicated to follow easily, but its parts are fitted together with the technical skill of which Terence was a master. In the course of his career he had gradually developed from the romantic author of the *Girl from Andros* into a comic dramatist able to evolve original variations on the traditional theme of a crafty servant deceiving a father in the interest of a pair of young lovers.

The father is the principal dupe in the *Phormio* and, as we have seen, the main humor of the *Mother-in-Law* comes from the ignorance in which its old men are left at the close of the intrigue. Is it possible that Terence introduced that comic touch into the earlier and more sentimental version of his play when he rewrote it for a second production? This surmise is given additional weight when we observe the importance of old men in Terence's last comedy and master-piece, the *Brothers* of 160 B.C. In this piece the dramatist avoids the romantic discovery which plays a strategic part in his first five dramas and concentrates his interest on the lovers and their fathers. Both young heroes are really the sons of Demea, but Demea's brother, Micio, has adopted one of them, to whom he acts as a father. Both

of the sons are engaged in love affairs; with the aid of the benevolent Micio each of them finally secures the girl of his choice. The element of intrigue in the *Brothers* is largely superficial and does not engage the main attention of Terence.

The point of this play is the contrasted characters of Micio and Demea. Micio lives in the city, where by knowing the ways of the world he has been able to accumulate a large fortune. He has not been contaminated by his experiences, however, and maintains a kindly spirit toward his fellow men. He is especially sympathetic with his adopted son and gives him everything he desires. Demea, on the other hand, has always lived in the coutry, where he has learned cautious habits from the necessity of supporting a wife and family. He is suspicious and grasping, and he rules his son with a rod of iron. The two methods of life, particularly the two ways of bringing up children, are the opposing forces in the *Brothers.*

In the first meeting between the two brothers at the beginning of the play, the problem is clearly stated: Is it better in this world to be kind or to be careful? Micio is always tolerant toward the escapades of youth, for would not he and Demea have acted in the same free and easy way when they were young, if they had had the necessary funds? Demea complains of the way Micio has spoiled his adopted son and feels that his own strict attitude towards his boy has been far more successful. He has apparent evidence on his side, because the adopted son has just been discovered to have taken part in a disreputable adventure. Still Micio refuses to blame the young man, and in due time learns that the boy's outrageous actions have sprung from high-minded motives.

Demea is much slower to find out the true facts of the case; when the two old men meet at the end of the fourth act, he is at a disadvantage from his ignorance of the situation. As a result he is inexpressible shocked by his brother's complacent philosophy and unimpressed by its splendid phrasing: "Human life is like a game of dice; if the throw which you most want does not turn up, you must by your skill make the most of the one which has fallen by chance,"

> ita vitast hominum quasi quom ludas tesseris;
> si illud quod maxume opus est iactu non cadit,
> illud quod cecidit forte, id arte ut corrigas.

Micio mischievously refuses to explain to Demea why he can be satisfied with the present state of his adopted son's affairs, but Demea soon finds out the truth, which does not redound to the credit of his own son. This turn of affairs leads into the third scene between the brothers at the beginning of the fifth act, in which Micio is clearly the victor. Facts are now on his side: his adopted son has shown a certain degree of nobility, and Demea's training has brought his son to grief. Micio is able to preach to his brother and remind him that if extravagance is the vice of youth, avarice is the vice of age: "O my dear Demea, in all other things we judge more rightly with age; old age brings to men only this one defect: we all pay more attention to money than we need to."

If the *Brothers* ended at this point Micio would be completely vindicated, as is the corresponding character in Thomas Shadwell's *The Squire of Alsatia,* but Terence has a surprise in store for his audience. Often in his comedies a new element is introduced with great effect into the final scene, but never more successfully than in the case of Demea. He proves to be a more subtle and complex character than Micio, for, whereas Micio does not understand Demea's point of view, Demea comes to realize the value of Micio's. Since his treatment of his own son has not restrained the boy from sowing wild oats and has made him dislike his father, Demea resolves to imitate Micio's course of action. He suddenly assumes benevolence and prosecutes it to an absurd extreme. He becomes very polite to his servants; he advises that the wall between two adjacent houses be demolished in the interests of friendship; he persuades Micio to marry an impoverished neighbor, and he urges his brother to free a slave and advance him money. When asked why he has completely changed his attitude, Demea explains that he is simply trying to show where Micio's position logically leads: undiscriminating kindness is sure to cause acts of folly. Demea has not been converted by the action of the play; he has merely been forced to see the weakness of his own views and as a result to appreciate the grain of truth in his brother's code of action. He finds that basically Micio's ideas are as absurd as his own, and that, when all is said and done, there is not much to choose between them.

Such is Terence's conclusion in regard to the problem that he stated at the beginning of the play. The golden mean has triumphed, and any extreme is shown to be dangerous and absurd. The dramatist's approach to the specific question raised in the *Brothers* is unmistakable. How far he intended that Demea should finally come to share his views is left in fascinating ambiguity. The old gentleman berates his brother for too great indulgence and selfishness in his easy course of life. Then he turns to the boys and assures them that as for himself he will never fall in with all their inclinations, adding, "But if in those matters where because of your youth you have too little wisdom, where your desires are too immoderate, where you take too little counsel, you would have me reprove and correct and aid you at the proper time, here I am to do it for you."

This statement may mean that hereafter Demea will temper severity with sympathy, or it may mean that Demea will revert to his original position, having shown by his own foolish conduct the fallacy in Micio's behavior. For the time being he lets his son have his way, and the comedy comes to a happy ending; but there is a sting in the happiness that leaves no one entirely satisfied. Demea was wrong and Micio was wrong, but the tolerance of Micio comes off a shade worse than the worldly wisdom of Demea. In the *Brothers* Terence has risen above his own innate kindliness and taken a detached view of human imperfections.

The *Brothers* is probably the best comedy written in the Latin language. The breadth of its wisdom and the depth of its feeling set it far above the more obviously uproarious farces of Plautus. Only once, in the *Aulularia,* does Plautus arrange matters so that incongruous incidents seem to spring directly from men's weaknesses. Euclio's avarice is

his outstanding characteristic; in fact, it is so outstanding that it becomes impossible to regard the miser as a credible figure. In spite of minor efforts to give life to his characters, Plautus is primarily an entertainer, sympathizing little with human beings and striving at all costs to make his audiences laugh. The playgoers of his day were, to judge from his prologues, a miscellaneous and ill-behaved group of people, who cared little for the nuances of life; if they were not entertained in the theater, they would not listen to the play. Plautus had a genius for amusing them. He could construct a complicated plot that would entangle unpleasant old men, vicious slave-dealers, or boastful soldiers. His comic gift extended beyond skill in plot construction to the adroit handling of individual scenes and the writing of brilliant dialogue. He was adept at the use of words and never missed an opportunity for a pun or a double meaning. His immense fertility of comic invention was unflagging; sometimes there does not seem to be sufficient relief from the continuous merriment in his plays.

Terence took a more serious view of life and erred in the opposite direction. His early plays are hardly comedies at all, if by a comedy is meant a humorous picture of human society. They are stories of adventure, which end happily but in which disaster is constantly threatened. Gradually the dramatist developed an increased sense of gaiety, possibly urged on by the failure of his second play, the *Mother-in-Law.* Terence also had to consider his audience, but his prologues suggest that he was far less concerned with pleasing them than Plautus was. Terence was a Carthaginian slave who had been freed by his Roman master and introduced into the most cultivated social circles of his day. He was the friend of Scipio Africanus Minor and Gaius Laelius, and these men are supposed to have helped him in composing his dramas. Whether they did so or not, Terence seems to have cared more for winning their praise than for appealing to the many-headed mob. The fact that he was a foreigner by birth may have made it easier for him to assimilate Greek culture than if he had been a native Roman. The detachment from his audience which his situation gave him influenced his writing both for good and bad. It made his plays more like those of Menander and less a purely Roman product. It enabled him to devote such attention and care to the purity of his language that Terentian Latin became a byword through the Middle Ages and that his comedies were kept alive during a religious period in spite of the worldly nature of their subjects. It caused his plays to be more refined, and less amusing, than those of Plautus; it made him less a pure comedian and more thoroughly a literary artist.

The quality of human sympathy which prevented Terence from seeing life as an unrelieved comic phenomenon made it possible for him once, in the *Brothers,* to surpass anything that his predecessor had done. The characters of Micio and Demea, especially Demea, have more vital reality than Euclio remotely suggests. For one thing, the contrast between the brothers in Terence is much more striking than that between Euclio and his foil, the generous Megadorus. Micio and Demea embody in themselves the opposing forces that are at work in the *Brothers;* the conflict between Euclio and Megadorus seems more superficial than structurally fundamental. Moreover, Terence understood his characters and was anxious to have his audience do so. Plautus was a much less humane person. His lack of humanity reveals itself in the unnaturalness of the exaggerated figures in his plays. They make up in number and variety for what they lack in carefully observed detail, but they move on a lower artistic plane than Terence's most masterly creations.

The broad sweep of Plautus and the refined sensitivity of Terence both emphasize the personalities of old men. Micio and Demea, Euclio, and Periplecomenus in the *Boasting Soldier* are the most memorable figures created by the two dramatists. They stand out from the rank and file of colorless lovers, intriguing servants, and foolish dupes. They help or hinder the lovers, they are themselves deceivers or deceived, but they maintain their own individualities irrespective of the plots in which they appear. That this should be so depends partly upon social conditions in Greece and Rome, where the older generation exerted a powerful influence upon the lives of younger people. Old men held the purse strings and exacted obedience to parental authority as the price of their compliance with youthful inclinations. They could not be laughed off the stage as palpably absurd, like boasting soldiers; they could not be treated as utterly despicable, like slave-merchants. They must be given a certain amount of consideration, and yet they should not be allowed exclusive domination over the lives of the young.

Old age has its power and respect is due to it, but it also has its foibles and peculiarities. An old man who keeps youthful impulses in a decaying body is ridiculous, and so is one who has succumbed to the lure of worldly treasure. He who has lived his life without affections is no less badly balanced than he who loves his fellow men and women without discrimination. Advancing years have pitfalls for men of whatever temperament, and a comic dramatist must be expected to make the most of them. Plautus shows us old men who err by being too selfish, Terence shows us old men who err by being too blind; they unite in ridiculing old age as that period in life when a man's personality, having reached its fullest development, is at its most rigid and absurd. Social comedy under the conditions prevalent at Rome in the pre-Christian era had come to the conclusion that youth is always right and that with age comes a loss of the perspective essential to appreciating the proper human values.

George E. Duckworth   (essay date 1952)

SOURCE: "Methods of Composition" in *The Nature of Roman Comedy: A Study in Popular Entertainment,* Princeton University Press, 1952, pp. 177-208.

[*In the following excerpt from his highly-regarded study of Roman comedy, Duckworth explains the notion of* contaminatio *(imitation of earlier authors) as it applies to Terence.*]

In Homeric scholarship the Higher Critics have used repetitions and contradictions as a means of distinguishing Homeric passages from those which they believed to be earlier traditional material or later additions; so also in the study of Roman comedy scholars have attempted to sepa-

rate the Roman elements from the Greek and have sought in repetitions and inconsistencies arguments to support various theories of composition. During the past half century they have endeavored particularly to prove that many of the plays of Plautus were composed by contamination, which they believe provides the most satisfactory explanation of the difficulties in the plays . . . . [Contaminatio is] the method of composition employed by Terence and assigned by him to Plautus. In the prologue to the *Andria* Terence states (13 ff.):

> The poet admits that he has transferred from the *Perinthia* to the *Andria* such passages as suited him and has used them as his own. His enemies blame him for having done this and maintain that plays should not thus be contaminated . . . . When they accuse him, they are accusing Naevius, Plautus, and Ennius, whom our dramatist accepts as authorities, and whose carelessness (*neclegentia*) he desires to imitate rather than the obscure accuracy of his critics.

This passage is important for several reasons: it is one of the two passages—the other one being *Heaut.* 17—in which Terence applies the verb *contaminare* to his use of Greek originals; it is the only passage in Roman literature which ascribes to Plautus the same procedure; it is a passage which has perhaps been mistranslated and misinterpreted in the light of modern theory. Is it correct to translate *contaminari non decere fabulas* (*And.* 16) as [John] Sargeaunt does [in his edition of Terence]: "two plays ought not thus to be combined into one"? There is need here for clarification both of the meaning of the word and the nature of the process.

As used by modern scholars, contamination signifies the joining or working together of material from two (or more) Greek originals to form one Latin play. Typical definitions are the following: "By *contaminatio* is meant the practice of inserting in a Latin translation of one Greek play a scene derived from another Greek play", "*contamination* means the process of fusing two Greek originals together, or grafting a portion of one on the other, in order to produce one Latin play." The second definition, it will be noted, refers to two different methods of composition: (1) the process of adding a small portion from a second original; this was the procedure of Terence who borrowed the opening scene for his *Andria* from Menander's *Perinthia,* added to his *Eunuchus* from Menander's *Colax* the characters of the soldier and his parasite, and inserted in his *Adelphoe* a scene from Diphilus' *Synapothnescontes;* (2) the process of combining two plots from two Greek originals into one Latin play. Plautine comedies which contain two deceptions (e. g., the *Miles* and the *Poenulus*) have been considered the result of such fusion or interweaving but there is no evidence in Terence that Plautus ever combined two Greek plays in this fashion.

The noun *contaminatio* occurs neither in Plautus nor in Terence but *contaminare,* although not in Plautus, is found in three passages in the younger playwright (*And.* 16, *Heaut.* 17, *Eun.* 552). The original meaning of *contaminare,* related etymologically to *tangere, contingere,* is "to touch," "to defile by contact," "to soil," "to pollute." This is clearly the meaning of the verb in *Eun.* 552:

. . . ne hoc gaudium contaminet uita aegritu-
dine aliqua.
. . . lest life pollute this pleasure with some distress.

The other two passages bear the same sense: Lanuvinus
had accused Terence of soiling Greek plays by adding
parts from a second orginal; in **And.** 13 ff. Terence admitted the procedure and appealed to the example of his predecessors; in **Heaut.** 16 ff. he referred again to the criticism
that

> he has contaminated (i. e., spoiled) many Greek
> plays while writing a few Latin ones.

A Greek play was defiled (in the eyes of literal translators)
if alien matter was added to it from another source; perhaps also the second original was spoiled for later adaptation if a part of it was inserted into another play. It should
be noted that to speak of a Latin comedy as being "contaminated" is highly inaccurate; it was always the Greek
play that suffered injury. This use of *contaminare* in Terence is supported by the commentary of Donatus, who defines the verb as *manibus luto plenis aliquid attingere, pol-
luere, foedare, maculare.* The added phrase, *ex multis
unam non decere facere,* "that one ought not to make one
play from many," is not a definition of *contaminare,* but
an interpretation by the commentator which has been
wrongly understood by modern scholars.

There is thus little evidence that *contaminare* meant to
Terence anything more than "soil" or "defile"; he was engaging in a method of composition which seemed to his
critics to be injurious to the Greek originals; he did not
deny the charge but claimed that others before him had
done the same. If Terence is telling the truth, his words
mean that contamination in Plautus was limited to insertions such as he himself had made; if Plautus had ever
combined two Greek originals into one play—a much
more thoroughgoing type of reworking—any indication of
such a procedure must be found in the plays themselves.
Beare [in his *The Roman Stage*] goes even further in his
attempt to discredit the external evidence for contamination in Plautus, slight as that evidence is; he believes that
Terence is not telling the truth, or rather, that he is confusing his audience by giving them the false impression that
his method of treating the Greek originals had been the
practice of the earlier playwrights whereas actually it was
something new. Beare's argument in brief is this: to Lanuvinus, who favored close literal translation, Terence's insertion of material from a second source indicated a freedom in the use of the Greek originals; Plautus likewise had
taken liberties with his models, adding and omitting in a
somewhat careless fashion for the purpose of comic effect;
thus, since *contaminare* meant "to stain" or "to soil" or
"to change for the worse," both playwrights could be
called contaminators and so Terence says (**And.** 20) that
he would rather imitate the carelessness (*neclegentia*) of
his predecessors than the "obscure accuracy" of his critics; but both here and in **Heaut.** 20. f. he gives his audience
the impression that the earlier playwrights had also inserted material from a second original.

Beare's theory is ingenious. It is not beyond the bounds
of possibility that Terence defended his literary procedure

by telling a direct lie and, if this is the case, we have no
reliable testimony of any sort to connect Plautus with the
process of contamination. On the other hand, if we accept
Terence's statement at its face value, all we learn is that
Plautus and others did occasionally add scenes from a second Greek model. The extent to which Plautus "contaminated" is still unknown. But in the absence of more definite external evidence scholars turn to a minute examination of the plays themselves; assuming the flawlessness of
the lost originals, they list all the imperfections, repetitions, and contradictions which they can find, and point
to these as proof of Plautus' clumsiness in combining the
different parts of two or more Greek plays.

An immense amount of effort and ingenuity has been expended on the subject of contamination in Plautus (and,
to a lesser degree, in Terence) during the past half century.
Scholars, mostly German, have written dozens, even hundreds, of books, pamphlets, and articles on the composition of the various plays. In 1920 Michaut [in *Plaute*]
pointed out that at one time or another every play of Plautus, with the exception of the *Asinaria, Cistellaria, Menaechmi,* and *Mostellaria,* had been believed to show traces
of *contaminatio,* but he argued strongly against the acceptance of these views. The plays more generally thought to
derive from two or more originals include the *Amphitruo,
Casina, Miles, Poenulus, Pseudolus,* and *Stichus,* but even
here there has seldom been complete agreement among
the proponents of contamination. The structure of the
Amphitruo does not necessarily imply that a play about
Zeus' "long night" with Alcumena has been combined by
Plautus with another play dealing with the birth of Hercules. The *Stichus* can hardly come from three different originals, as Leo assumes, if the first two sections of the play
contain passages which resemble fragments from the same
Menandrian original; the conclusion of the comedy with
its festal song and dance may be Greek, or Plautus may
have developed it under the influence of Italian farce; so,
too, the very farcical and ribald ending of the *Casina:* does
it come from the original of Diphilus (Jachmann) or from
a second Greek comedy (Fraenkel) or from Italian farce
or mime (Leo)? Does the *Pseudolus* come from two different sources, as Hough and others have assumed, or has
one deception, that of the *senex,* been omitted from the
one original? Or is it not more likely that the wager with
Simo in *Pseud.* 535 ff. anticipates just the sort of conclusion that we have in the play, the payment of the twenty
minae by Simo when Ballio is successfully tricked? The
Poenulus with its double intrigue and possible minor flaws
has been explained by Leo and Jachmann as resulting
from the fusion of two originals but Fraenkel limited contamination in the play to the insertion of a single scene,
and more recently it has been maintained that the first deception by Collybiscus and the *aduocati* is the invention
of Plautus. The *Miles* likewise has two deceptions, the second of which has wrongly been considered unnecessary;
references to the twin sister are firmly embedded in the
second part of the play and there is no evidence that the
passageway through the wall was constructed for the purpose of escape; it is a far more satisfactory conclusion to
have the soldier send Philocomasium away of his own volition and to give up Palaestrio at her request. The play as

it stands seems a much better comedy than either of the two originals postulated by Leo and others.

There are several basic weaknesses in the methods of the scholars favoring contamination: (1) they explain by *contaminatio* many features of the plays which are more properly attributed to the staging of plays with a limited cast, to conventions of ancient comedy, to the playwright's desire for clarity or humor; (2) they ascribe to Plautus or Terence all real or imagined weaknesses in the plays and assume that the originals were free from repetitions and inconsistencies—a most unlikely assumption; since, as Bowra says [in his *Tradition and Design in the Iliad*, 1930], "all authors contradict themselves, many contradict themselves violently"; (3) they believe that the Roman playwrights had little originality and no ability to compose scenes or episodes of any value, so that any additions or insertions must necessarily betray the crude and faulty workmanship of the Roman playwright; (4) above all, they fail to look upon the plays as comedy created for the amusement and delight of spectators. Even an audience far more critical and cultured than the Romans of the second century B.C. would fail to notice most of the minor flaws and difficulties which the modern scholar, poring over the text, discovers by a logical and unimaginative investigation of details.

In recent years more and more voices have been raised against this type of technical approach to comic drama. Harsh, after showing that many of the criteria are faulty and that inartistic features usually assigned to Roman playwrights occur in many Greek plays also, concludes [*American Journal of Philology* 58 (1937)]: "the method of distinguishing Roman workmanship from Greek by means of logical analysis and theoretical standards of dramatic technique must definitely and finally be abandoned. The many years devoted to the problem by scholars have proved fruitful mainly in respect to the incidental results produced and to the stimulus given general studies in the field. Doubtless it would be advisable to relegate to the background consideration of contamination and Roman originality in future studies of Plautus and Terence." Enk agrees that the theories of the scholars seem in general without foundation; he does not deny the existence of contamination in Plautus but limits it to the addition of single scenes, i. e., the method of Terence in the **Adelphoe,** and he finds only three instances in the plays where Plautus apparently made such insertions: *Mil.* 813 ff. (the Lurcio scene), *Pseud.* Act 1, Scene 3, and *Stich.* Act v. [*Revue de Philologie* 64 (1938)]. Beare considers none of these passages convincing. His view that modern scholars have been misled by Terence's statement in the **Andria**-prologue leads him to an extreme position: for solving the difficulties in the plays, "almost any proposed solution, however farfetched, lies nearer at hand than a theory of contamination. An *a posteriori* proof of contamination cannot be got out of the materials at our disposal; but for the statement of Terence, scholars would scarcely have wasted their time in spinning these cobwebs" [*American Journal of Philology* 66 (1940)].

Thus many of the conclusions of Leo, Fraenkel, Jachmann, and others have been discredited; the pendulum has

swung in the opposite direction but, like most healthy reactions, it has perhaps gone too far. Most scholars today would hesitate to deny contamination to Plautus as completely as Beare does. Hough, for instance, has . . . [in *American Journal of Philology* 58 (1937)] supported the use of a second original for both the *Asinaria* and the *Captivi.* But the intricate combining and interweaving of two Greek plays cannot be definitely proved for any Plautine comedy. That the playwright made many insertions and additions is not to be doubted; if this new material came from a different Greek source, we have contamination in the Terentian sense; Plautus, however, may have added passages and scenes of his own invention. The older view that Plautus, though a comic genius and a master of Latin, was incapable of composing a scene of merry dialogue (e. g., the Lurcio scene in the *Miles*) would claim few adherents today. If ever the sands of Egypt should deliver up to us the complete original of the *Miles* or the *Poenulus* or some other controversial play, the difficulties with which scholars have been struggling would be solved—but such a fortunate discovery seems at least highly improbable. Meanwhile, critics would do well to admit that the answers to many problems of structure and composition cannot be determined with any degree of certainty. There is no evidence that *contaminatio,* any more than *retractatio,* was ever as common in the second century B.C. as many scholars have believed.

Suetonius (c. 69-c. 140) relates an anecdote about Terence:

. . . [Terence] wrote six comedies, and when he offered the first of these, the *Andria,* to the aediles, they bade him first read it to Caecilius. Having come to the poet's house when he was dining, and being meanly clad, Terence is said to have read the beginning of his play sitting on a bench near the great man's couch. But after a few lines he was invited to take his place at table, and after dining with Caecilius, he ran through the rest to his host's great admiration. . . .

Suetouius, quoted in Ancilla to Classical Reading, *by Moses Hadas, Columbia University Press, 1954.*

John Gassner   (essay date 1954)

SOURCE: "Menander, Plautus, and Terence" in *Masters of the Drama,* third revised edition, Dover Publications, Inc., 1954, pp. 92-104.

[*Gassner, a Hungarian-born American scholar, was a great promoter of American theater, particularly the work of Tennessee Williams and Arthur Miller. He edited numerous collections of modern drama and wrote two important dramatic surveys,* Masters of Modern Drama *(1940) and* Theater in Our Times *(1954). In the following excerpt from the revised edition of the former work, Gassner discusses Terence's place in the development of Roman theater, pointing out that "he not only knew his limitations but gloried in them . . . ."*]

The three-quarters of a century which intervened between Plautus and the next important writer of Roman comedy produced a stratification of taste to which no artist could fail to respond. Drunk with conquest, the Roman populace developed an insatiable taste for rude farces and acrobatics, while the aristocracy was increasingly Hellenized much to the regret of such an unrelenting puritan as Cato the Censor who resented the relaxing influence of the Greeks. In other words, the taste of the lower orders became coarser while that of the upper classes became more refined, even to the point of attenuation.

Terence was not the people's poet but the darling of the aristocracy. He could never have written plays for the former, because he felt alien to them. Publius Terentius Afer was a Phoenician or Semite and a native of Carthage, where he was born about 190 B.C. Brought to Rome as a slave, he was carefully educated by a master who quickly recognized his talent and emancipated him. His personal grace, as well as his literary ability, made the young alien an amiable companion of the cosmopolitans of high society. He not only knew his limitations but gloried in them, declaring that it was his chief aim to please the *boni* or elect.

His output was meager not only because he was lost at sea when he was at about the age of thirty, but because he was such a scrupulous stylist. From his first play the **Andria,** written at the age of nineteen, to his last work the **Adelphi,** his development was primarily in the direction of polish and more polish. It is little wonder that the art of Greece was his sole interest and that he devoted himself to capturing the spirit of his originals with practically no concession to popular taste. He had gone to Greece, probably in order to be closer to the fountain of his inspiration, when he met his untimely death. Nor is it any wonder that his work continued to be considered a model of Latin purity of style, that he won the admiration of Cicero and Horace, and that he was the only classic playwright whom the medieval churchmen of Western Europe could tolerate.

Taking for his springboard the comedies of Menander, who was with a single exception his life-long model, Terence felt free to adapt them as he pleased, thereby courting the charge of *contaminatio* although he justified his practice by pointing to the work of his predecessors as Ennius, Naevius, and Plautus. He was, he claimed, a creative writer in the freedom with which he used his material instead of following the *obscura diligentia* of some of his plodding contemporaries and of one of his detractors. Still he not only confined himself to the *palliatae* or dramas of Greek subjects and backgrounds, but tried to equal the delicacy of the works he revered, cultivating their refinement of sentiment to the point of depriving most of his comedies of vigor and movement.

Terence does not laugh as much as smile, and instead of ridicule he employs irony. Among the Roman playwrights he is perhaps the only one who aimed at perfection rather than at instant pleasure. His characterization is relatively subtle, and his dialogue combines grace with economy. For colloquial speech he who wrote under the patronage of the aristocracy reveals no taste. But his diction and syntax have a fascination and poetry of their own, a limber and yet restrained beauty which can hardly be conveyed in translation. It is instructive to compare such translated lines as "When you link a son to you by kindness, there is sincerity in all his acts; he sets himself to make a return, and will be the same behind your back as to your face" with the spare original:

> *ille quem beneficio adiungas ex animo facit, studet par referre, praesens absenque idem erit.*

The gulf that yawns between such art and the taste of the impatient Roman populace was, of course, too wide to allow him much popularity. Time and again in his prologues Terence complains that "the uproar drove our company from the stage" (Phormio); that "I have never been allowed a silent hearing . . . in flocked the people with uproar and clamor and a struggle for seats with the result that I could not hold my ground," and that "the people's thoughts were preoccupied by a rope-dancer" (**Hecyra** or **The Mother-in-Law**).

As in the case of Plautus, it is unnecessary to review all his plays to observe the quality of the dramatic output. **The Eunuch (Eunnuchus)**, for instance, tells the story of Thais, a courtesan who takes a girl under her wing while she herself is in love with a young man of good family. She receives the girl as a gift from an admirer Thraso, a bragging and fatuous old soldier. At the same time she takes into her house a eunuch presented to her by her lover Phaedria. But the latter's younger brother, having fallen in love with her young charge, takes the place of the eunuch and seduces the girl, a serious misdemeanor when she is discovered to be free-born. All ends well, of course; Phaedria drives off the boastful soldier and his retinue, and wins Thais for himself, while her protégée marries the younger brother. The humor derives largely from the discomfiture of the *miles gloriosus,* the vainglorious but essentially cowardly soldier who has so many counterparts in Elizabethan drama. Sentiment, however, is the predominant note of the comedy. Thais is a very worthy person despite her station, her charge is a delightful girl, Phaedria is a spirited and well-intentioned lover, and his younger brother has the excuse of youth and infatuation for the ruse by which he enters the house and wins the *ingenue.*

In **The Mother-in-Law,** which recalls *The Arbitration* of Menander, a husband suspects his wife of gross misconduct when she gives birth to a child during his absence, but discovers in the end that his wife was the girl he had assaulted earlier and that he is actually the father of the presumably illegitimate infant. The play is light and genial; even the courtesan Bacchis, who says of her profession that "it is not in our interest to have marriages happy," is not without saving grace when she enables the man who has been visiting her to discover his wife's innocence. As usual, the action is carefully developed and the audience is kept in suspense.

Perhaps the most delightful of Terence's works, however, is **Phormio,** named after the parasite who advances the action and supplies much of the comic effect. This, the only comedy not adapted by Terence from Menander but from the other New Comedy playwright Apollodorus, is the liveliest of his plays. Phormio is supplemented by the intriguing slave Geta, another ancestor of Molière's resourceful servants and Beaumarchais' Figaro. Molière, in fact, utilized **Phormio** in one of his earliest works *Les Fourberies de Scapin,* just as Terence's **Andria** was used by Molière's successor Baron in *Adrienne* and by Richard Steele in *The Conscious Lovers.* The bigamous old man of **Phormio,** Chremes, had a wife in Lemnos who came to Athens and died there, leaving her young daughter helpless. The girl attracts Antipho, Chremes' brother's son, who falls in love with her and marries her with the assistance of Phormio and a servant. Both his father and his uncle Chremes are highly indignant, until the latter learns that the girl is his daughter. Complications are added by a parallel love affair on the part of Chremes' son who is restrained by his father with doubtful consistency. The old men, especially the susceptible Chremes, are amusing portraits, and Phormio is truly memorable.

Phormio's insolence and resourcefulness are equaled only by his love of sponging on others: "Think of it!" the parasite declares. "You come scot free to your patron's dinner, all perfumed and shining from the bath, with a heart free from care, when he's drowned with worry and eaten up with expenses. While everything's done to your liking, he's snarling. You can laugh, drink your wine before him, take the higher seat; and then a puzzling banquet's set spread." Asked what a puzzling banquet is, he replies, "That's when you're puzzled what to help yourself to first." After having exposed Chremes to his wife, Phormio who has thus paid him in good coin for mistreating him congratulates himself, "Now she's got something to din into his ears just as long as he lives." He is also richer by thirty pieces of gold at the end for having consented to marry Antipho's girl whom the lad's father had tried to remove from the field. Moreover, in winning the favor of Chremes' wife, Phormio now has another place where he can always get a free dinner. . . .

After Terence's death the Roman drama deteriorated rapidly. Neither Plautus nor Terence had a permanent theatre in which to present their plays: they wrote for a platform stage. Theatrical display now became the rage, especially when Rome became a monarchy and a rapidly decaying one after the death of Julius Caesar, who was himself a discriminating critic and was not even satisfied with Terence whom he called a "half-Menander." The engineering genius of Rome expressed itself in marble theatres and an abundance of stage machinery. The populace had little regard for the drama itself, vastly preferring elaborate shows, gaudy processions of captives and slaves, circuses, and mimic sea-fights in Naumachiae so elaborate that they defy description. True drama no longer flourished in a nation whose economic and political policies had impoverished the people to the point of pauperism and dependence on a dole, while the ruling classes frittered away their energy in debauchery and the struggle for tyrannical power. Opium is what the masses needed to forget their condition, and it is opium they received in the spectacle of gladiators slashing each other to death. Butchery took the place of comedy.

By the time the Roman empire collapsed under the weight of its economic contradictions and its glories crumbled away in corruption, only pantomimists and jugglers or ac-

robats, known as *mimes,* were left. Little better than vagabonds, they satisfied a crude desire for entertainment during the Dark Ages but remained beyond the pale of respectability. The theatre in Europe had to be built anew, out of fresh material and with new forces, and it was ironically the historic task of the Catholic Church to foster beginnings in an art which it was the first to despise but which it could not ultimately resist. Once more, as in Greece, Rome, and almost everywhere on man's planet, the drama had to be cradled anew in the rites of religion.

Robert Graves   (essay date 1962)

SOURCE: A foreword to *The Comedies of Terence,* edited by Robert Graves, Aldine Publishing Company, 1962, pp. ix-xiv.

[*A highly versatile man of letters, Graves was an English poet, novelist, translator, and critic. He was first associated with the Georgian war poets during World War I, but afterward followed a more nontraditional yet highly ordered line, being influenced during the 1920s and 1930s by the American poet Laura Riding. Working outside the literary fashions of his day, Graves established a reputation which rests largely on his verbal precision and strong individuality as a poet. He is also considered a great prose stylist, and is well known for such historical novels as* I, Claudius *(1934) and* Wife to Mr Milton *(1943). In the excerpt below, he briefly introduces the plays of Terence, pointing out that they call attention to some of the less positive aspects of classical civilization.*]

Terence, like Plautus, wrote a pure Latin, and closely followed the rule of the Dramatic Unities first framed by Aristotle, and since accepted both in Greece and Rome. These comprised unity of action, meaning that sub-plots must materially assist the development of the main plot; unity of time, which restricted all action to the period of a single day; and the unity of place, which allowed no shifting of scene. Moreover, because the Roman audience was slow-witted, each new character had to announce his business or be announced by some other character as soon as he entered: thus everyone knew not only his name and position, but what part of the plot he had to fulfil, why he came, from where, and with what purpose, and all that went on in his mind. This convention made performances even more artificial.

We cannot tell precisely what liberties Terence took with his Romanization of Menander, whose reputation had for two centuries stood as high as Homer's: because *The Dour Man,* the single complete play still extant, is not one from which Terence borrowed. We can only compare him with Plautus, who handled farcical situations in a livelier way, was less careful of the Unities, and had a greater command of language. Terence set himself a standard of literary perfection and artistic restraint which so commended him to scholars and grammarians that his collected plays were used as a text-book in Roman schools and, like Virgil's poems, remained part of the curriculum even when the Christian Church reformed national education. It is regrettable that the very terseness of his Latin makes an accurate modern English rendering read drily and flatly . . .

. Nor can we blame Terence for this. He knew his trade, being a master of the dramatic surprise, and though the turnings and twistings of the plot provide admirable theatre, the Romans, unlike (say) the Elizabethans, preferred penny plain to twopence coloured in dramatic entertainment. His plays continued to be staged before appreciative audiences for three hundred years.

A revival of Terence in English must, I believe, be based on the translation made in 1689, with fascinating vigour, by a young Cambridge student Laurence Echard (1670-1730)—later Dr Echard, Prebendary of Lincoln, Archdeacon of Stow, and author of a well-known *History of England.* Echard firmly held to the Aristotelian Unities, which had been revived by the French dramatists of his day, and frowned on the wild, un-Classical English drama. "The non-observance of dramatic rules,' he observes in his Preface, 'has occasioned the miscarriage of so many excellent geniuses of ours, particularly that of the Immortal Shakespeare.' Yet he saw that Terence's plays could be made vastly more readable if dressed up in the language of Restoration Comedy. He wrote that Terence's bluntness of speech was unsuited to the manners and gallantry of his own times, but that he had taken it upon himself to correct this defect and, in some places, had lent a scene greater humour than it originally contained—'but all the while we have kept so nigh to our author's sense and design that we hope our additions can never be justly called a fault.' Even so he despaired of getting the popular London theatres to stage the plays, 'because,' he wrote,

> of the difference betwixt the Romans and ourselves in customs, humours, manners and theatres. The Roman plots were too often founded on the exposing of newborn children and their unexpected rescue, or on the buying of mistresses and music-girls. The spectators were pleased to see a covetous old father cheated of a round sum by his slave; to watch the young spark, his son, miserably in want of cash, join with the slave in the intrigue, so that he might get something to stop the mouth of his mistress whom he keeps without the father's knowledge; to find a bragging soldier wheedled or abused by a cunning parasite; to hear a glutton talk of nothing but his belly, and the like. Our plots nowadays turn chiefly upon variety of love intrigues between married couples, ladies very dexterously cuckolding their husbands, gallants in danger upon the same account, with their escape either by witty excuses or hiding themselves in dark holes or closets. We are all for gallantry in conversation and shouldn't endure the chief lady in the play to be a mute, as Terence makes her. Our amorous sparks love to hear the pretty rogues prate, snap up their gallants and repartee them on all sides. We shouldn't like to have a lady married without knowing whether she gives her consent or no—a custom among the Romans— but would be for hearing all the rare and fine things that lovers can say to each other in the way of courtship.

The fact was that since freedom of speech had been curtailed at Athens even before the death of Aristophanes, Menander's courageous predecessor, and no topical reference could thereafter be safely made to any contemporary event or character, the theatre had been reduced to plots involving certain stock bourgeois types. The debauched young spark, the gave old father, the distressed mother, the confirmed bachelor, the good-natured, expensive courtesan, the parasite, the boastful soldier, the greedy bawdmaster, the scheming slave, and an occasional sour old woman . . . All parts were played, as on the Elizabethan stage, by men or boys; but because public morality banned tender love between members of the same sex, Terence could not supply his heroine with a speaking part, even when the plot hinged on the hero's love for her. And the scene (without props or curtain) must always be a street in front of three houses where the principal characters lived.

Difficulties caused by the need for introducing actors who, though visible to the audience, were supposedly invisible to one another, were overcome it seems by use of a *siparium,* or folding screen, which could be interposed between them and which let hidden characters deliver audible asides. Terence, by the way, never allowed the 'stage to grow cold' between Acts, for fear his audience might drift away during intermissions and come struggling back late; or even, as they had done at the *première* of **The Mother-in-Law,** visit the neighbouring Circus to watch a tight-rope act and never come back at all. The division into Acts can therefore be disregarded, though intermissions may have been marked by songs to flute accompaniment, as the title pages suggest.

I have followed Echard's example in not translating Terence's prologues, which are concerned either with begging the audience to behave decently, or with dramatic squabbles which would be of historical interest only if Terence had mentioned names, which he refrained from doing.

Under the early Roman Empire, an enormous increase in the size of the unroofed theatres, and a lack of any contrivance to magnify the sound of actors' voices, or any control on the audience's hubbub, put an unbearable strain on the cast. Only people seated close to the orchestra could follow the turns of an intrigue; those behind had either to know each stock play by heart, or guess what was happening from the actors' miming. To distinguish one character from another, each wore a different-coloured dress: white for an old man, multi-coloured for a young spark, yellow for a courtesan, purple for the rich, red for the poor, a short tunic for a slave, and so on . . . But this was not enough: by the second century A.D., the rival attractions of chariot racing, gladiatorial shows and opera, had killed comedy altogether.

Nevertheless, I can see no reason why **The Eunuch,** for instance, could not be recast as a modern musical-though, of course, by a breach of Terence's cherished Unities-with great success. Meanwhile, let me repeat, if any of his plays are performed in the original, this should be done by gentlemen in periwigs, ladies in jewelled stomachers, and lacqueys of the period fixed by Echard's translation. I follow his English pretty faithfully-the seventh edition (1729), 'revised and corrected by Dr Echard, Sir R. L'Estrange and others'-but whenever he uses contemporary slang now obsolete, and words that no longer preserve their seventeenth-century meaning have substituted clearer language of the same date. Sometimes, also, where he has missed the sense of the Latin, or worked from a corrupt text, I make the necessary amendment.

It is extraordinary that Terence was praised so long by educated Christians for his moral values. How could they have swallowed the heartless, vicious rape of virgins-by the heroes of **The Mother-in-Law** and **The Eunuch**-condoned as pardonable whims of youth? Or (in **The Mother-in-Law** again) the cruelty of a husband who forces his wife to expose her infant daughter, condoned as economic prudence? Or, in **The Eunuch,** the sympathy demanded from the audience for two well-bred young sparks who plan to maintain a courtesan at the expense of a rich soldier whom she cheats?

It was a fascination with the strange forms that popular entertainment takes in different civilizations, which made me choose [to edit this edition of Terence's plays]. A close reading of Terence is a fine corrective to any idea that may still be current, about the glory that was Greece and grandeur that was Rome during the Hellenistic period; and an assurance that, in some respects at least, this age is not so morally depraved after all.

W. Beare   (essay date 1964)

SOURCE: "Terence" in *The Roman Stage: A Short History of Latin Drama in the Time of the Republic,* revised edition, Methuen & Co. Ltd., 1964, pp. 91-112.

[*Beare's* The Roman Stage, *first published in 1950 and later revised, is a critically-acclaimed survey of Roman drama and its theatrical milieu. Here, he offers detailed examinations of* The Girl from Andros *and* The Eunich *and their Menandrian sources, concluding that a "deepening of sentiment . . . [is] Terence's chief claim to originality."*]

We gather from Terence's own words that he was accused of weakness of style, of accepting literary help from others, of entering on his profession as dramatist without proper preparation, of stealing characters and passages from old Latin plays, of 'spoiling' or taking liberties with his Greek originals. Terence's style was indeed something new on the Roman stage. That he accepted literary help from his noble friends is perhaps unlikely, and even if true would have little relevance to our opinion of the plays as we have them; we can understand, however, that tact would forbid him to give a direct rebuttal to this charge. The other two accusations, however spiteful, have this much basis in fact: Terence deliberately departed from his Greek originals. Earlier Latin dramatists had indeed

Illustration from a twelfth-century edition of The Girl from Andros.

translated with considerable freedom, as we have seen in the case of Caecilius. But Terence was the first, perhaps the only, Latin dramatist who deliberately tried to produce a Latin play which would be artistically superior to its Greek original. This he nowhere states, but it is implicit in much that he says. The *Andria* opens a new chapter in Latin literature.

Andria. The scene, as in all Terence's plays, is in Athens. The three houses shown on the stage are those of the old gentleman Simo (and his son Pamphilus), the girl Glycerium and the young gentleman Charinus. Simo wishes Pamphilus to marry Philumena, daughter of Chremes. But Pamphilus has secretly formed a liaison with Glycerium, a poor but modest girl who had recently come from Andros to Athens with her supposed sister Chrysis. Chrysis, after having been forced by poverty to become a courtesan, has now died. In the opening scene Simo confides to his freedman Sosia the news that Chremes, hearing of the entanglement with Glycerium, has refused to give Philumena to Pamphilus (who was to have wedded her this very day) (line 102); however, Simo has not told Pamphilus of this, as he wishes to test his filial obedience. But Davus, Pamphilus' servant, who has divined that the wedding is off, advises Pamphilus to call Simo's bluff by professing his readiness to do what his father wishes. To complicate matters, Charinus is in love with Philumena, and privately begs Pamphilus to put the wedding off. But Simo now manages to talk Chremes round, and Pamphilus finds himself faced with immediate marriage to Philumena, while we listen to the cries of Glycerium as she lies in the pangs of childbirth. Davus redeems his blunder by getting Glycerium's bewildered maid, Mysis, to put the baby down in front of Simo's door just as Chremes arrives on the scene. Chremes' suspicions return with redoubled force, and he again withdraws his consent. Now a new character appears, Crito, Chrysis' cousin, looking for Glycerium, who, it turns out, is not the sister of Chrysis, but the lost daughter of Chremes. Accordingly Pamphilus may marry her, and in the final scene he promises Charinus that he will put in a good word for him with Chremes.

Donatus tells us that Terence has made certain alterations in translating Menander's *Andria*. Menander's play had opened with a monologue of the old man; Terence has turned this into a dialogue by adding Sosia, who is a 'protatic' character—that is, he will not appear again after this 'protasis' or opening scene. Furthermore, Terence has added Charinus and his servant Byrria, for these two 'are not in Menander'.

As has been said, the plot of the *Andria* turns on Simo's intention to marry Pamphilus to Philumena. Pamphilus has never even seen Philumena; we find him wondering (line 250) whether she is a monster of ugliness, whose parents are trying to get rid of her. It is quite in keeping with New Comedy and with Greek life that marriage should be arranged between two young people who have never met. But Charinus, the young gentleman added to the play by Terence, is passionately in love with the young lady Philumena; and his slave Byrria mentions her good looks and physical desirability and assumes that this explains Pam-

philus' apparent willingness to marry her (lines 428-30). We are not told how Charinus has made her acquaintance. Her father, though anxious to find a husband for her, seems never to have heard of this very eligible suitor (an incongruity which the author of the spurious alternative ending tried to explain away). Apparently Terence has here introduced a situation foreign to what we know of New Comedy, but presumably possible in Roman life. He must, then, have invented Charinus, and with him his slave Byrria—and this is the natural interpretation of what Donatus says. The two characters have no influence on the main plot, and the scenes in which they appear could be altered without difficulty so as to eliminate them altogether. But the *reason* for the introduction of Charinus may have been not, as Donatus suggests, to supply Philumena (who never appears on the stage) with a husband, but to provide an interesting contrast in character and situation to Pamphilus. The second love-plot is stated by Donatus to be an addition made by Terence to Menander's *Andria*; he also tells us that each of Terence's plays except the *Hecyra* contained two young men; of cf. Evanthius De Fab. 3.9: 'Terence chose richer plots containing a double intrigue'.

These changes, then, and others as well, were made by Terence when translating Menander's [*Andria*]. He now came up against the hostility of Luscius Lanuvinus, an elderly and perhaps not very successful dramatist, who saw his livelihood threatened by this young protégé of the great. I find no reason to believe that Luscius was actuated by any higher motive than jealousy; any slander which would put Terence out of business was good enough for him. Luscius somehow got to know that Terence had departed from his ostensible original. There was indeed no law against this; but Luscius thought that by reporting Terence's procedure in as malicious terms as he could find he might damage his reputation by that most baffling of slanders, a half-truth. He accordingly began to protest to all who would listen that Greek plays should not be 'spoiled'. The word he used for 'spoil' was 'contaminare'.

This charge put Terence in a dilemma. He felt that he must reply to it, in order to secure a fair hearing for his play; accordingly he found himself forced to write a prologue. Yet how was he to meet the charge in terms which the Roman crowd could understand? They had been promised a version of a play by Menander; he was now accused of intending to give them something different. Of what use would it be to embark on an explanation which, if honest, was bound to be technical and puzzling? Some brief and intelligible reply was needed, which would make the changes he undoubtedly had made seem as innocent as possible.

What he says in the prologue is this. Menander wrote two plays, the [*Andria*] and the [*Perinthia*] alike in plot and differing merely in dialogue. The poet (Terence) has borrowed from the [*Perinthia*] what was suitable and has inserted it in his *Andria*. His enemies attack him for this, saying that plays should not be spoiled. Their charge shows their own ignorance; in accusing Terence they are accusing Naevius, Plautus and Ennius, whose 'carelessness' Terence professes that he would rather imitate than the 'dull carefulness' of his critics.

Modern students, almost without exception, suppose that Terence has been accused of the very thing which he boasts of doing—namely, the borrowing of material from a second Greek play—and moreover that it is this procedure which he ascribes to Naevius, Plautus and Ennius. We are told that contaminare could mean 'to combine' Greek plays; that such combination was the established practice of the Roman dramatists; that Terence was being accused of combining plays; and that he defended himself by saying that he had in fact combined plays, thus following the 'careless' example set by the great masters of the past, including Ennius, who had died only three years before the production of the **Andria.** This explanation breaks down at almost every step. The verb contaminare means 'spoil'; if Terence had been merely following established practice, where was the sting in saying that he had done so?; yet if this was in fact the charge, how could he hope to defend himself by admitting it? and how could the combination of plays be equated with carelessness?

Donatus gives us to understand that he read through the two Greek plays (in order, it would seem, to check what Terence says about them). Apart from the opening scence, he could find only two short passages in which they resembled each other. Apparently he failed altogether to find in Terence's translation any passage which resembled anything in the *Perinthia.* Donatus was naturally puzzled. Why, he asks, should Terence accuse himself of doing something which he has not done? He can only suggest that the reference is to the opening scene. For here, though the wording is 'almost identical' in the two Greek plays, the scene is a monologue in Menander's *Andria,* while in the *Perinthia* it is a dialogue: the senex is talking to his wife. Terence's senex speaks to his freedman Sosia (who appears only in this scene). Donatus seems to mean that Terence is indebted to the *Perinthia* for the idea of using dialogue rather than monologue. In substituting dialogue for monologue Terence is no doubt aiming at greater dramatic effect; similarly in the **Eunuchus** he introduces Antipho in order that Chaerea may be able to tell someone of his adventure instead of soliloquizing, as in Menander. But it is really unthinkable that the conversation of patron and client was exactly like that of husband and wife. The one example of borrowing which Donatus claims to have discovered turns out to be no example at all.

Plainly Donatus was not satisfied. He read on, still looking for passages borrowed from the *Perinthia,* and could find none; but near the end of the **Andria** (959-61) he found a three-line illustration of general application which reminded him not indeed of the *Perinthia,* but of a passage in a third play of Menander, the *Eunuchus* (unfortunately he does not quote the Greek), and he exclaims with what seems like relief, 'this is what is meant by the remark that plays should not be contaminated'.

Of course there may have been resemblances which Donatus failed to notice. Two of our extant fragments of the *Perinthia* resemble passages in Terence's **Andria.** These would be verbal borrowings; and verbal borrowings are precisely what Terence seems to admit. But it appears

from Donatus' words that these borrowings were not very striking. Many modern scholars hold that the added characters, Charinus and Byrria, came from the *Perinthia;* and as we shall see when we come to the prologue to the **Eunuchus,** Terence there admits—indeed proclaims—that he has added two characters to his **Eunuchus** from another Greek play. But Charinus' rôle is simply to be in love with the young lady whom the principal lover (Pamphilus) is being forced to marry. Charinus is dependent on Pamphilus: Pamphilus could do without Charinus. Those who suppose that Charinus and Byrria were taken from the *Perinthia* must further suppose that the principal lover is also taken from the *Perinthia.* It is claimed that there was a slave named Pyrrhias (=Byrria) in the *Perinthia.* There is indeed a slave in the *Perinthia* whose name apparently ends in -rias; but he belongs to old Laches, and we find him bringing faggots with which the intriguing slave Daos is to be burned alive.

The only other reference to this charge of 'spoiling' Greek plays is in Terence's next prologue, that to the **Heautontimorumenos.** Evidently his critics had not been silenced; their charge was now that he had 'spoiled many Greek plays in making only a few Latin plays'. This charge may have been based on his own words in the prologue to the **Andria:** in effect his critics are saying 'when we accuse you of spoiling your Greek model, your reply is that you have spoiled not *one* model but *two'.* He replies that he does not deny what he has done; that he will go on doing it, and that he has good example. Thus once more we seem to be faced with a dilemma: either the charge brought against Terence is pointless, or his defence consists of an admission of the charge.

If we cling to the common-sense view that ordinary Latin words probably have their ordinary meaning even in Terence, we may still agree that Terence is unlikely to have admitted that he had 'spoiled' his Greek models. This was indeed the charge against him, but he only quotes it in Oratio Obliqua. His defence is not that he has spoiled Menander's plays, but that he is giving his hearers more Menander than he had promised. 'Carelessness', again, cannot have seemed an admirable quality to him; if he pretends to admire the 'careless' dramatists of the past, he is being less than candid. Nor could 'carelessness' have achieved the one type of alteration which he admits in his own case—the combining of two Greek plays. When Plautus omits a passage in a play which he is translating, Terence calls that 'carelessness'. (*Ad.* 14). The one thing in which Terence can honestly claim to resemble the old dramatists, as contrasted with the pedantic Luscius, is that they took liberties with their originals. Terence also intends to take liberties with *his* originals; but the changes which *he* makes will be careful and artistic. When he taunts Luscius (**Eun.** 7 ff.) with 'turning good Greek plays into bad Latin plays by good translation and bad writing', he implies that in his view 'good' (i. e. close) translation is not enough.

Nevertheless the **Heauton Timorumenos (Self-Tormentor)** seems to be a straight translation from Menander . . . .

The play opens with an evening scene (one of the finest

scenes in Latin comedy). We see two old men, Chremes and Menedemus, walking home together from the 'country' side-entrance. Chremes' questioning elicits from Menedemus a confession that he has been 'punishing himself' by heavy toil on his farm for having by harsh treatment driven his son Clinia to run away and enter military service abroad. Menedemus enters his house, and Chremes is about to enter his, when his son Clitipho comes out, and we learn that he is sheltering Clinia, who has come back from abroad. Preparations are being made in Chremes' house for supper; and presently there arrive two guests whom Chremes does not expect: Bacchis, a courtesan, who is Clitipho's extravagant mistress, and her friend Antiphila, the modest girl whom Clinia loves. The slave Syrus persuades Bacchis to pose as Clinia's mistress, so as to deceive Chremes into admitting her to his house. A night passes; next morning Chremes reports to Menedemus the presence of Clinia and his mercenary mistress Bacchis. Menedemus, overjoyed to have Clinia back, is willing to endure all the extravagances of Bacchis if he can keep his son at home. There is much mystification, but in due course Antiphila is discovered to be the daughter of Chremes, and Chremes' self-importance is deflated when he finds that Bacchis is the mistress, not of Menedemus' son, but of his own. The complications of the plot are difficult to follow on the stage, or even in the study; but there is evidence that the play was produced more than once, and we must applaud the public who could appreciate it.

Eunuchus. The courtesan Thais has two lovers, Phaedria and the braggart captain Thraso, who is attended by his parasite Gnatho. Thraso has offered to present Thais with a virtuous and beautiful maiden, Pamphila, a foundling who had been brought up with Thais but was afterwards sold by a miserly uncle. Phaedria intends to give Thais a eunuch, Dorio. Phaedria's younger brother Chaerea sees Pamphila being brought by Gnatho to Thais' house, is inflamed, and, at the suggestion of the slave Parmeno, puts on the eunuch's clothes and enters Thais' house while Thais is out at a party given by Thraso. A new character now appears, Chremes, a cautious young gentleman who has received a mysterious summons from Thais; he is sent off to look for her at Thraso's house. Chaerea comes out of Thais' house and relates his adventure to a friend, Antipho, who has come to look for him. They go off in order that he may change his clothes at Antipho's house. Thais' maid returns from Thraso's house with the news that Chremes' arrival there has provoked the soldier to a storm of jealousy; while the discovery that Pamphila has been violated throws Thais' house into turmoil. Presently Chremes (slightly intoxicated) appears, soon followed by Thais; she tells him that Pamphila is his sister, and that Thraso intends to carry the girl off by force. They defend the house against an assault by Thraso and his followers; then Chaerea returns, learns that the girl whom he has outraged is free-born, and promises to make what reparation he can by marrying her. Gnatho induces Phaedria to consent to an arrangement whereby he will share Thais with Thraso, and so in the end all parties are satisfied.

We gather from the prologue that, after the aediles had bought the play, a preliminary performance was given in their presence. Luscius Lanuvinus had contrived to see the play in manuscript, and was present at its performance. The play began. Suddenly he cried out that Terence was a thief: he had stolen two characters, the captain and the parasite, from an old Latin play, the *Colax,* translated from the Greek by Naevius and (? or) Plautus. There was no law of copyright in Rome; still, the charge of theft was an ugly one. Terence's defence is that he took these characters not from the old Latin play (the very existence of which was unknown to him) but from its Greek original, the *Kolax* of Menander. And if one must not bring 'the same' characters on the stage a second time, how is one to treat of the stock themes of comedy, or indeed to write a play at all?

It seems that Terence agrees with his critics that he has added two characters from another play, which they have correctly identified. Yet this cannot be true: it must be either more or less than the truth. If by dramatic characters we mean the words that they utter, it is manifest that these are related to the context, and that to import into one play all the words uttered by a major character in another play would necessitate consequential changes in the new context. If we try to imagine the *Eunuchus* without the captain and parasite, it is plain that the plot would fall to pieces. Therefore Menander's *Eunuchus* cannot have been simply Terence's *Eunuchus* without the two added characters; we must find others to take their places in the plot. Moreover, if Terence took over from the *Kolax* all the words uttered by the captain and the parasite, he must have taken over with them a large portion of the plot. There is quite a simple solution of this problem; it is to suppose that Menander's *Eunuchus* had its own captain and parasite, and that all that Terence did was to add certain touches which characterized the captain and parasite of Menander's *Kolax*. The entrance monologue of Gnatho and the dialogue of Thraso and Gnatho give us the touches which we want. Gnatho describes himself in his monologue as a new kind of parasite, one who attaches himself to would-be wits and plays upon their vanity; the soldier appears in the dialogue as just such a would-be wit, who prides himself not on his exploits in war or love so much as on his skill in repartee. But in the rest of the *Eunuchus* Thraso seems to be very much the stock type of captain, Gnatho the traditional parasite. So Terence's borrowings from the *Kolax* are reduced to a few lines unconnected with the plot of his *Eunuchus.* But why did he not explain all this to his audience? Because there was no time to go into such technical matters; what was needed was a brief and apparently intelligible reply to the charge, and that is what he gave.

In truth it would be easier to invent new characters than to introduce them ready-made from another play. We are assured by Donatus that Terence did in fact invent the character of Antipho in order to convert Menander's monologue into dialogue. The scene in which Chaerea describes how he violated Pamphila was famous in antiquity, and is indeed of considerable dramatic power; but its effect is largely due to its dialogue form. There is no reason to doubt Donatus' evidence here; yet many scholars will clutch at any theory rather than concede so much original power to the Latin poet.

There is one other passage in which Terence refers to the changes which he has made in his Greek original. This is in the prologue to his most famous play, the *Adelphi.* Demea and Micio are two elderly brothers; Micio is a genial bachelor, Demea is the care-worn father of two sons, Aeschinus and Ctesipho. Aeschinus has been adopted by his uncle, who has given him every freedom, hoping by indulgence to win his confidence; Ctesipho has been kept under strict surveillance by his cross-grained father. Thus the play strikes a modern note by giving us a comparative study of two methods of education. Neither system is successful; both the young men find sweethearts for themselves without consulting their elders. Aeschinus, the stronger character, breaks into a pimp's house and carries off the wench Bacchis in order to hand her over to his timid brother, whose mistress she is; but his action is open to misconstruction, and news of it distresses Pamphila, the poor but virtuous girl whom Aeschinus loves. When Micio learns Aeschinus' secret, he consents to Aeschinus' marriage with Pamphila; but when Demea discovers that he has been deceived by Ctesipho, he realizes that his stern methods have been a failure, and turns the tables on Micio by treating everyone liberally at his expense.

It would seem that in the [*Adelphoi* B.] of Menander the carrying off of Bacchis by Aeschinus had been merely reported. In Terence's play this happens on the stage. In the prologue Terence tells us that Diphilus wrote a play called the [*Sunapothnēskontes*] (translated by Plautus as the *Commorients*) in which a young man carries off a wench from a pimp; this passage had been omitted by Plautus owing to his 'carelessness', and Terence has incorporated it in his *Adelphi,* translating the Greek 'word for word'. He asks the public to judge whether this is a theft, as his critics allege, or, as he holds, the turning to good account of what Plautus had neglected.

It appears that the accusations brought against Terence were inspired not by artistic ideals but by spite. There is little likelihood that Luscius had set before himself a new and higher standard of fidelity to his original. Even Terence's reference to Luscius' 'good translation' may have been introduced sarcastically, or as a mere antithesis to 'bad writing'. Unacknowledged borrowing from various sources was a frequent practice among ancient writers. Afranius tells us frankly that his supposedly 'native' comedies contained material borrowed from whatever source he thought suitable, whether Greek or Latin. Few Roman dramatists would have felt qualms about inserting in their plays, whether translations or original compositions, an effective line or passage which they had come across in their reading. But this haphazard procedure was never recognized as a specific method of literary composition. Of large-scale fusion of originals, of the combination of two Greek plots into one Latin plot, we have no examples, even in Terence.

He was, in a limited sense, an original dramatist forced by circumstances to pose as a mere translator. As a dramatist he could not afford to ignore the general public, but his opinion of their taste is revealed in his petulant reference to the 'populus studio stupidus' who left the *Hecyra* to see a rope-dancer. His admitted object is to write plays of a high artistic standard, sine uitiis. Though he professes to admire and imitate the great careless masters of the past, we may be sure that his standards were very different from theirs. His repeated reference to Plautus' 'carelessness' in dealing with his originals is itself a criticism; yet his boast that his own plays are 'faultless' suggests that, for him, mere translation of the Greek original is not enough. Donatus frequently points out alterations introduced by Terence; sometimes he enlivens a scene by turning monologue into dialogue, sometimes he makes his characters behave more naturally than in the Greek play (for example Micio, the comfortable old bachelor of the *Adelphi,* is allowed by Terence at least to protest before he is pushed into marriage), sometimes he adapts his original to Roman customs and feelings. Donatus' comments are supported by the evidence of the fragments preserved from the Greek originals. While toning down difficult allusions to peculiarly Greek institutions, Terence refuses to introduce anything specifically Roman or Italian. He adds no topical references, no allusions to contemporaries; there is little word-play, little buffoonery; the language is restrained; the metrical effects are subdued. Reading Terence we find ourselves in a world which is neither characteristically Greek nor aggressively Italian, but independent of place and time.

Terence's great interest is humanity. The keynote of his dramatic technique is contrast of character. In the *Heautontimorumenos,* the *Phormio* and the *Adelphi* we have contrasted pairs of old as well as of young men. In the *Hecyra* we have a study of two elderly couples. In the *Eunuchus* there is a double love-plot. The addition of the abduction-scene in the *Adelphi* may have been intended to bring into bold relief one side of Aeschinus' character, as conceived by Terence. Donatus tells us that in Menander's [*Eunouchos*] Chremes was a 'rustic'; in Terence's play he is effectively portrayed as a timid creature, who has to be roused to action by the encouraging words of a courtesan! Indeed one of the things that struck ancient critics was the nobility of Terence's courtesans. In character-drawing, according to Varro, Terence was first among Latin writers of comedy.

We have seen that Terence treated his originals with some freedom. Exactly what liberties he took we cannot always divine. There may have been more divergencies than those mentioned by Donatus; for that matter, Donatus occasionally points out where Terence's text *agrees* with the Greek originals, and it is impossible to suppose that Donatus has given all the examples of such agreement. Apart from the addition of characters in the *Andria* and the *Eunuchus* and the insertion of a whole scene in the *Adelphi,* the changes made seem to have been slight. One of Terence's objects may have been to extend the use of surprise as an element in drama. Ancient drama, on the whole, does not seem to have aimed at surprise effects; in tragedy the myths were already known: in comedy, where the plot was invented by the dramatist, the danger of puzzling the audience had to be taken into account. Plautus, adapting Greek plays for a Roman audience, often wearies us with the pains he takes to explain each turn of the plot beforehand. Terence expects more of his audience. Perhaps his total avoidance of preliminary explanations of the plot (such as Menander had thought necessary, at least in his *Perikeiromene*) is connected with a desire to startle his audience, and even at times to mystify them a little. The revelation of Chremes' bigamy (in the ***Phormio***), Pamphilus' discovery (in the ***Hecyra***) of what is really the matter with Philumena, the extraordinary trick played by Davus (in the ***Andria***) in making the unwitting Mysis act the desired part much more effectively than she could have done had he previously disclosed his intentions, Demea's sudden abandonment of his previous way of life (in the ***Adelphi***) and the success with which he turns the tables on Micio—these scenes (which may indeed be purely Greek in origin, but are unlike anything in Plautus) are not only 'dramatic' in our sense of the word; well acted, they must have been excellent 'theatre'. Practical details of staging may sometimes be a little obscure; the movements of characters are not made as clear to us as they are by Plautus, who was above all things a man of the theatre. In command of rhythm and metre, in flow of language, in farcical power and animal spirits, admittedly Plautus is the superior of Terence. Nevertheless it would be altogether wrong to regard Terence as indifferent to the applause of the crowd. He seems to be telling the truth when he says (***And.*** 3) that his aim from the start had been 'to please the people'. What he would not do was to write down to them. He could not but be influenced by the tone of the society in which he moved, the phil-Hellenic Roman aristocracy of the second century. The kingdoms of the world seemed to lie at their feet; and some at least among them tried to temper power with humanity, with sentiment. Plautus had lived in the bleak yet bracing air of the struggle with Hannibal. Though he admires courage, even religion and virtue (as we see in his portrait of Alcumena), he is free from sentimentality. He sees life like one of his own heroines (***Ps.*** 343):

> sine ornamentis, cum intestinis ombinus.

Menander's most famous and perhaps most melancholy line, 'he whom the gods love dies young', reads in Plautus (*Bacch.* 816 f.) like a proverbial remark given a farcical setting. Terence's most famous line is also presumably taken from Menander (H.T. 77):

> homo sum: humani nil a me alienum puto.

In Menander's play this remark may have been nothing more than a characterizing touch indicating Chremes' inquisitiveness; but few readers of the line in Terence's play will take it in so limited a sense.

In this deepening of sentiment I would find Terence's chief claim to originality. The outlines may be less sharp than in Menander; but there seems to be a gain in feeling. To some extent we may agree with those who find in him the herald of the new humanitas, the new urbanitas, which was to refine, if not to ennoble, the harsh realities of Roman power. Nowhere is this more evident than in the first scene he wrote, the opening scene of the ***Andria,*** which Cicero admired so much, and which must have gained so much from being cast by Terence into dialogue form. The art of Terence is like the beauty of Glycerium in her tears:

> et uoltu, Sosia,

adeo modesto, adeo uenusto, ut nil supra!
'so modest, so winning of feature, that nothing could excel her!'
Good manners, good feeling find their fitting expressions (43 f.):
istaec commemoratio
quasi exprobratiost immemoris benefici.

'That reminder of a kindness you have done me amounts to a reproach of ingratitude.' There are the memorable halflines: ne quid nimis (61), a version, of course, of a Greek proverb, 'nothing too much', but put in the mouth of the added character Sosia, and therefore presumably not from the Greek original; and again the famous hinc illae lacrimae (126). Comedy is speaking now, not in the racy idiom of the marketplace, hearty, cynical, uninhibited, but in the quiet, courteous phrases, the meaning silences, of the salon. Life is a serious matter; it cannot be successfully lived without tenderness as well as wisdom. This may not be Christianity, as that word is understood in the north of Europe, but it is at least humane.

The dramatist was an artist, not a teacher; yet many who saw the ***Adelphi*** may have felt that it had a message for them. Here in Rome, where the spirit of old Cato was putting up a losing fight against the incoming Hellenism, they were looking at a play which depicted the results of two contrasted forms of education. Yet even in this, his last play, Terence has added a scene of rougher quality, showing Aeschinus and his slave carrying off Bacchis regardless of the protests of Sannio, who is threatened in the traditional comic style with a 'smack on the jaw'. So we see Terence trying to the last to carry with him both sections of the public, in spite of the widening gulf which would soon destroy the famous Roman unity admired by Polybius.

The study of Terence raises problems affecting our whole outlook on comedy and its relation to life. In dealing with these large themes it is easy to carry a sound argument too far, and in correcting the extreme views of others to be led ourselves into an opposite extreme. These are faults arising from the very nature of research. Ancient plays were not, I think, *pièces à thèse:* modern dissertations indubitably are. Is the ***Adelphi*** a picture of an actual situation in the Rome of the second century B.C.? or alternatively in the Athens of the fourth century B.C.? Is Demea Cato? or is Micio Demetrius of Phalerum? Either view is perhaps defensible; but we can hardly hold *both*. Indeed the whole character of New (and Roman) Comedy seems to have been determined by the need to avoid offending the rulers of the State; and political allusions subtle enough to escape the notice of authority would probably have been missed by most of the audience too. Is Terence a moral teacher? or are his plays also examples of that 'immoral morality' which Mommsen (*Hist. of Rome*) found in Menander? Should a dramatist show courtesans better than they are in real life (like Thais in the ***Eunuchus*** and Bacchis in the ***Hecyra***)? Is Plautus' pitiless cynicism a more honest and less dangerous guide? Is Chaerea's rape of Pamphila presented with unnecessarily luscious detail? Which play would do a young man more good, the ***Eunuchus*** or the ***Truculentus***?

What we must keep before us is the central fact that Plautus and Terence were both playwrights, and that as playwrights they must have shared the same aim—to please their public. They are indeed different; we are conscious of the difference, it might almost be said, in every line. Where they agree (and differ from their originals), the agreement may be regarded as due to their Roman background. According to Duckworth the one feature which their plays have in common is 'mental error, or misapprehension'. I would add that (in contrast to their Greek originals) they share the freer Roman outlook on sex, the Roman zest for life, the optimism inspired by Rome's victory. For all its fascination, New Comedy reflects a played-out world. In Latin comedy the element of enjoyment is more prominent. We must not exaggerate the difference between Plautus and Terence; there is plenty of moralizing in Plautus (e. g. in the *Trinummus* and the *Captivi*), there is plenty of quiet humour in Terence (e. g. in the ***Phormio*** and the ***Adelphi***); and both the moralizing and the humour are meant to be enjoyed. Plautus is farcical, exuberant, extravagant; he aims at immediate effects; Terence is thoughtful; his words are carefully chosen, his general design is more steadily kept in view. A Plautine character may say almost anything at any time: Terence's characters are more consistent, if less striking. Terence builds up his effects more carefully, and for that reason he is superior, I think, not only in surprise but also in irony.

Terence's appeal is to the reflective; but this does not mean that his plays were a failure on the stage. To the end of the Republic, and even in imperial times, they were known to the theatre-going public; Quintilian seems to refer to contemporary performances of Terence's plays, and the illustrations in the manuscripts have been thought to suggest that their connexion with the stage reaches to even later times.

We may wonder why of all the Republican dramatists only Plautus and Terence have survived. The reason may be that later ages found them particularly good *reading*. Each in his own way was admitted to be a master of style. If Plautus was more amusing, Terence was more polished and more philosophic; he was also easier to understand.

Abess Hroswitha of Gandersheim (10th century) on using Terence's comedies as a model:

There are some who cleave to the sacred pages but who, though they spurn other writings of the gentiles, read the fictions of Terence all too frequently, and in taking pleasure in the sweetness of his discourse are sullied by familiarity with wicked matters. Wherefore I, the Strong Voice of Gandersheim, have not, while others cultivate him in perusal, refused to imitate him in utterance, to the end that by that same fashion of discourse by which the foul bawdiness of lewd women are set forth, the admirable chastity of holy virgins should be celebrated, according to the capacity of my small gifts.

Hroswitha of Gandersheim, quoted in Ancilla to Classical Reading, *by Moses Hadas, Columbia University Press, 1954.*

The excellence of the manuscript tradition is evidence of his popularity in late antiquity and the Middle Ages. Few Latin authors are in less need of a commentator. Free from difficult expressions or topical allusions, written in the easy, graceful Latin of aristocratic Rome, his plays retain their attraction because they invest the themes of daily life with a certain nobility.

Frank O. Copley   (essay date 1967)

SOURCE: An introduction to *The Comedies of Terence,* translated by Frank O. Copley, The Bobbs-Merrill Company, Inc., 1967, pp. vii-xxi.

[*Below, Copley discusses Terence's dramatic method and his treatment of several literary motifs in his comedies.*]

Like the plays of his predecessor Plautus, all the comedies of Terence are adaptations from the Greek New Comedy, a relatively simple type of play concerned with the problems, personal and circumstantial, into which an affluent and leisured society is likely to fall. The treatment accorded these problems and predicaments ranged from the broadest, coarsest caricature to the gentlest, most sensitive social satire, but in all cases the characters were general and typical in nature rather than individual and specific. With this simple form and content and with these characters, in whom the audience might see many who resembled their neighbors but none who could be positively identified, the New Comedy provided the Romans with a model far more susceptible of imitation than did the Old Comedy, which, with its dances, its elaborate costumes and stage settings, was highly complex in form. Furthermore, it was characterized by attacks on familiar public figures and by violent castigation of specific public policies, a freedom of expression such as the Romans were never to learn to tolerate on their own stage. In any event, the Old Comedy, represented for us by the works of Aristophanes, (ca. 445-ca. 387 B.C) was and always will be completely inimitable. It was great of its kind, but it was so peculiarly the expression of the great fifty years (480-430 B.C) of Athenian power and glory, that no other age has ever succeeded in creating anything quite like it.

By contrast, the New Comedy has been a richly productive literary form; it was the parent not only of the Roman comedy, but also, through that comedy, of all continental comedy, particularly the French, the Italian, and the Spanish; and it even influenced the lustily independent Shakespeare. It is generally agreed that the greatest writer of New Comedy was Menander (342-291 B.C). Four of Terence's plays are based on originals by him: ***The Woman of Andros, The Self-Tormentor, The Eunuch,*** and ***The Brothers.*** The other two, ***Phormio*** and ***The Mother-in-Law,*** were adaptations of plays by a somewhat later writer, Apollodorus (300-260 B.C). Until very recently, the works of Menander, Apollodorus, and other writers of the New Comedy were known to us only through the adaptations made of their plays by Plautus and by Terence, or through fragments garnered from other authors and from papyri. When, less than ten years ago, the complete text of Menander's *Dyskolos* was discovered, it was hoped that new and further light would be shed on the nature of the

New Comedy; unfortunately the *Dyskolos* turned out to be an early and rather minor effort of Menander, and while it is not lacking in interest, it is hardly to be regarded as truly representative of his work.

Terence's method, like that of his Roman predecessors, was not simply to translate the Greek plays that were his models, but rather to adapt them for the Roman stage. But whereas Plautus was likely to use a free hand in introducing original matter, Terence, more conscientiously, did not. The age in which he lived, in contrast to that of Plautus a generation earlier, was characterized by a devotion to all things Greek that bordered on Hellenomania; reflections of this not entirely healthy attitude are to be seen in the attacks made on it by Terence's younger contemporary, the satirist Lucilius. Wholesome or not, it appears to have been Terence's deliberate aim to create in Latin, and on the Roman stage, a drama that would present a Greek world to the Roman audience. This does not mean that Terence had no originality whatever, or that he slavishly copied the plays of Menander and Apollodorus. A sensitive literary artist, he must have realized that slavish imitation would have resulted in plays that to his audiences would have seemed not Greek but merely grotesque. We may be sure that Terence handled his Greek models freely enough to ensure that his Roman audiences would know what the plays were intended to say and to mean.

In the plays of both Plautus and Terence, the scene is always Greek, the characters and the society depicted on the stage are Greek; costumes, customs, institutions, social conventions, even such matters as law and coinage are Greek. Terence is more careful and conscientious than Plautus, however, in preserving this Greek atmosphere down to the most minute details. It is only fair to note that there were playwrights in Italy who attempted to create a native Italian theater, but for reasons now difficult to fathom, this theater was never a success and died almost as soon as it was born. It is sometimes charged that the Italians lacked the originality to create a successful theater of their own. A more likely reason for the failure of the native theater, however, was the Roman's deepseated dislike of what he fancied to be the indignities of the stage. Intensively, almost fanatically proud of his national garment, the toga, and extremely sensitive to any real or imagined slight to his customs, institutions, and personalities, he was unwilling to run the risk of putting them on the stage, where they might be subject to ridicule. He preferred a theater in which the only fools were Greek fools. In any event, the only form of drama, whether comic or tragic, which was to achieve any success in Rome was that which produced an exclusively non-Roman world upon the stage. Far from finding this a restriction upon his talents, Terence seems to have looked upon it as a laudable aim; honor for him lay in the production on the stage of a play in which the only non-Greek element was the Latin language.

The first permanent theater building in Rome about which we know anything is the one constructed by Pompey in 55 B.C. The theaters in which Plautus and Terence produced their plays were temporary structures, probably consisting of nothing more than rough wooden benches set up in a natural amphitheater with a temporary stage constructed of wood. The general form of the theater, nevertheless, remained the same at all periods. The orchestra was semicircular, not circular as in the Greek theater, and was used for seating the more distinguished members of the audience. The stage itself had a fairly high platform, and was long and narrow-120 to 180 feet long, and perhaps 20 feet wide. Unusual stage sets sometimes were used, as in the *Rudens* of Plautus, in which the scene is laid on a seashore. In general, however (and in Terence, always), the scene consists of two or three house fronts, each with a door opening onto the stage, which itself represents a street. In Terence this is always a street in Athens. Entrance onto the stage could be made through the house doors and from either end of the stage; by convention, the entrance on the audience's right led to the center of town, and that on the audience's left, toward the harbor. On the stage, front and center, was an altar, relic of the days when the drama was a religious celebration. In Terence's plays, there are no indoor scenes: all the action is so constructed that it can be staged realistically and logically out-of-doors.

Costumes on the Roman stage seem to have been more or less standardized: white was worn by the free characters—old man, young man, married woman; gray was worn by slaves, and yellow by the *meretrix,* the young woman not to be demeaned by the label "prostitute," but rather termed, in modern editions, a "courtesan." Masks were not worn in Terence's time, although they seem to have been used in the later revivals of his plays. White wigs were worn by older men and women, dark brown or black wigs by young men, red wigs by slaves, blond by courtesans. In Terence's time women did not appear on the stage; women's parts were played by young boys. The plays were acted by troupes of professional actors, most or all of whom would have been slaves, headed by a producer-actor who, in some instances at any rate, may have been their owner. The actors had to be non-Romans; Roman citizens were forbidden by law to appear upon the stage.

The plots of the New Comedy were reasonably varied, moving as they did through a fairly wide range of the personal and circumstantial problems faced by Greek upper-middle-class society; nonetheless, they do exhibit a kind of basic or standard plot, which appears in play after play and was followed by both Plautus and Terence. This plot involves a young man who has fallen in love with a courtesan but for one reason or another is unable to find the funds to pay for her favors, or in some instances to purchase her for his own exclusive enjoyment. The young man himself is usually pleasant but neither bright nor forceful enough to find a way in which to solve his predicament. The solution falls to the clever slave, who by trickery, deceit, and temporizing manages to extract the sum from the young man's father, from the slave-dealer himself, or sometimes from some other character, such as the soldier, who, either wealthy or a spendthrift, is a favorite object of ridicule in this kind of comedy. When the necessary sum has been obtained and the girl or her services paid for, the play ends. The story is a thin one, and what interest it possesses is provided by the slave's clever schemes, the working out of which provides enough suspense and sheer fun to keep the audience interested.

In a common variation of this theme, the young man falls in love not with a courtesan but with a young virgin who is held as a slave by a pimp. The young man's intentions in this instance are strictly dishonorable, for he would like to make this young girl his mistress. However, before this fate befalls her—or, at any rate, before she has been compelled to dispense her favors with some impartiality among the patrons of the house in which she lives—she is discovered to be an Athenian citizen, and the play ends with the young man properly marrying her. In a still further variation of the discovery theme, the heroine is not a slave at all, but a citizen girl, the daughter of a poor but honest widow. One night, walking alone through the streets of the city, she is seized and raped by a drunken young man who manages to escape without revealing his identity. The girl becomes pregnant, but once again, just as all appears lost, her attacker is identified as the respectable young man who has been pining for her but, because she is penniless, never expected to be allowed to marry her. Once the identities have been properly established on both sides, the young man marries the girl whom he has so roughly misused, and the play reaches its usual happy ending. In all six of Terence's plays, the story ends with one or another sort of discovery, and with the marriage of the hero and heroine.

If these stories appear to have very little to do with love as we like to think of it, and if the discovery element in particular seems to hang by a very thin thread of coincidence, a number of sociological facts should be kept in mind. In the first place, extramarital relationships, at least before marriage, were not forbidden by ancient society, and in general were viewed with a kind of amused tolerance. All that was asked of the young man was that he exercise a certain degree of discretion. He was not to flaunt his affair before the eyes of respectable society but to conduct it in a quiet and reasonable way, confining his attentions to women who were not citizens, and remembering always that some day he must put the affair aside and dutifully marry the citizen girl whom his parents had chosen for him. His premarital fling with the noncitizen lady must never be allowed to take on aspects of permanence; it must always be recognized by both parties that inevitably the day would come when the two must go their separate ways. If this kind of affair seems to us commercial and cold-hearted, in that the girl is always the loser in the matter, we may be certain that the girls in question understood and accepted the situation and, since their livelihood depended on the institution, asked of the young man only that he show them affection, consideration, and a reasonably well-lined purse for the duration of the affair. Although as they grew older and their attractions faded these girls may well have ended as common prostitutes, they were not regarded as such. Rather, since they were not citizens, they were looked on simply as professional entertainers of men who could not marry the young men who sought their favors. They quite willingly entered into a kind of semipermanent cohabitation, in which a certain degree of loyalty and faithfulness, as well as of affection, was to be expected from both parties. The girls involved

in this trade were often well-educated in literature and philosophy, and trained to play the flute and lyre, and to sing and dance. In Greek society, at least, they may well have been more interesting companions than the citizen women who were qualified to become wives; the latter were rarely educated beyond the barest essentials, and they were taken in marriage primarily for the sake of their social standing, their fortunes, and their potential value as housekeepers and childbearers. They must have been rather a dull lot, and it is scarcely surprising that they rarely, if ever, mingled socially with their husbands. It was to the noncitizen women—the *hetaerae* (Latin *meretrices*)—that the average Greek male resorted when he wished pleasant feminine company. With these girls his social evenings were passed, and toward them he experienced any romantic feelings he may have had. In point of fact, virtually all ancient love literature is concerned with this relationship. Feelings of a romantic sort had little if anything to do with the stiff and formal courtship that preceded the arranged marriages of antiquity. Ancient society accepted the courtesan as inevitable, and perhaps as entirely desirable.

As for the discovery motif, it need be remembered only that in antiquity birth records were not as systematically kept as they are today. One needs to recall, too, the rather brutal method of birth control practiced by the ancients: unwanted children were simply cast out to die. Social values being what they were, these unwanted children were more often female than male; it is not hard to imagine that the pimps might have sent their slaves wandering through the streets and fields around any Greek city looking for abandoned female babies whom they might bring home and educate for the trade. It is equally easy to imagine that the distraught mother, ordered by her husband to dispose of an unwanted girl-child, might have left with her baby trinkets of some sort—a bracelet, a necklace, a brooch—in the fond hope that the child might live, and that the mother might, on some future day, recognize her through these pitiful tokens.

As for the rape incident, we need only remember that ancient paganism recognized a number of orgiastic festivals, the chief feature of which was drunkenness and brawling; in some—the fertility festivals—it might well have been mandatory for the young men participating in the ceremonies to have sexual intercourse with any women they chanced to meet during the period of the festivities. When such festivals were in progress, sensible girls stayed at home; if one of them was foolish enough to go out in the street, she had no cause for surprise if she became the object of unwanted attentions. Greek society did not forgive her for having an illegitimate child, even though it had been conceived in the name of some religious ceremony; the young man's action, however, was dismissed with a shrug of the shoulders and with the ancient equivalent for "boys will be boys." These circumstances, therefore, though dramatic conventions to some degree, had realistic roots and should serve to remind us that the typical plots of the New Comedy were neither as contrived nor as unrealistic as they may appear to be.

All Terence's plays end, as we have seen, with hero and heroine very properly getting married; this note of moral rectitude is quite characteristic of Terence, who in his gentle way tends to be something of a critic of ancient society. Apart from providing a morally proper ending to his plays, he creates characters all of whom—particularly the slaves and the women—show evidence of social protest. Whoever the formal protagonist in any of the plays may be, the real hero in every instance is a slave. It is the slave who turns out to be not only intelligent but honest, loyal, warmhearted, generous—in short, to have the full stature of a man. Often he contrasts strongly with the formal hero, who is likely to be weak-kneed, spineless, and, if not unintelligent, certainly unimaginative. All Terence's courtesans, too, are good women. Even when they are frankly businesswomen, engaging in the trade for the money they hope to make from it, they emerge as honest and sensible, and at their best they are kind, generous, and affectionate. Again by contrast, the respectable women either remain entirely off-stage or, if present, say little or nothing, never revealing themselves as anything but quite ordinary and unexciting. These contrasts can hardly be accidental, especially when we recall that Terence himself had been a slave and knew what was meant by that condition; his manly slaves and womanly courtesans are Terence's protests against a society that was entirely too inclined to be callous to the human pretensions of slaves and other noncitizens.

Second only to Terence's penchant for social reform is his interest in personal, or what we would call psychological, problems, particularly those that are involved in the father-son relationship. In every one of the six plays this relationship is subjected to some degree of study. In *The Woman of Andros,* we see Pamphilus tormented by conflicting loyalties toward his father, whose patience and good will Pamphilus deeply appreciates; toward Glycerium, to whom he feels bound by a deep mutual affection; and toward the dead Chrysis, Glycerium's friend and protector. Pamphilus had made a solemn promise to Chrysis to protect Glycerium from all harm. Simo, on *his* side, is equally attached to his son, and the play studies the strain that is placed upon this father-son relationship by misunderstanding, misinformation, and willfulness. The moral, if the play has one, seems to be that father and son should not permit loyalty and affection to degenerate into hypersensitivity, should always be honest each with the other, and should make certain that they have been correctly informed before passing judgment. *The Brothers* tussles with the ancient problem of the best way to bring up a son, whether by love, patience, and good will, or by strict rule and discipline. In the end the play reaches no specific conclusion. The gentle and generous Micio is made to look a fool, while Demea, the stern disciplinarian, is revealed as a heartless hypocrite; and neither of the two sons comes out very well. Ctesipho remains a sorry scapegrace, bettered neither by the discipline of Demea nor by the good humor of Micio; and Aeschinus, who seems about to prove Micio's philosophy right by turning into a gentleman like his adoptive father, turns instead at the very end of the play to join forces with Demea in discomfiting Micio. For centuries scholars have wondered what Terence meant to be the lesson of this play; perhaps the lesson is that there is no sure way. In *The Mother-in-Law* we see a rather spoiled young man brushing his father aside as of

little consequence but showing deep devotion to his mother—perhaps too deep, since at one point he prefers her to his wife. *The Self-Tormentor* deals with the agonies of a father who is overcome with guilt at what he mistakenly imagines to have been his cruelty toward his son. When the son returns, however, he seems none the worse for his experience and certainly wastes little time in appreciation for the sacrifices his father has made in his behalf. The play is in fact very uneven. Beginning with a most provocative investigation into the guilt feelings to which a father may fall prey, it trails off into the standard boy-girl plot, undistinguished save for a rather cleverly contrived ending in which the two fathers in the play exchange roles. In *Phormio* and *The Eunuch,* the father-son relationship is treated in a rather conventional way; in fact, in *The Eunuch,* the father plays a very slight part. In *Phormio,* the relationship is given an interesting turn when the old man's wife reminds him that his own bigamous behavior has left him in a poor position to censure his son for keeping a mistress.

Whatever else may be said about Terence's plays, in form they are nearly perfect. Exits and entrances are properly motivated; plots are brought in reasonable fashion to a logical conclusion; every scene is functional, every speech contributes to the progress of the story. No lines are wasted on gratuitous jokes. The characters are carefully portrayed and logically developed. There is little boisterous humor and virtually no violence. No situations that would have been regarded as immoral by the ancients are portrayed; there are no off-color jokes and relatively few references to sex. Essentially the plays are quiet, polished, and restrained in action and in tone; they probably make better reading than they did acting, and therefore, it would not be surprising if Terence sometimes had trouble holding his audience's attention. Comparisons between Plautus and Terence are almost inevitable. At the risk of oversimplification, I should say that Plautus was the master comedian to whom the theater was everything, whereas Terence was the master craftsman whose primary concern was to make his plays as nearly perfect as he could. Perhaps this devotion to formal perfection made Terence, rather than Plautus, the great teacher of succeeding generations of playwrights. For all their rich borrowings from Plautus, Terence's plays are, in the end, the ones from which Molière, Goldoni, and other figures of the later European stage learned. And we must not forget that in the ninth century, when Hrosvitha, Abbess of Gandersheim, wished to construct edifying plays for the sisters to peruse and to act, it was to Terence, not to Plautus, that she turned for her model . . . .

Douglass Parker   (essay date 1974)

SOURCE: An introduction to *The Eunich* by Terence, translated by Douglass Parker, in *The Complete Comedies of Terence: Modern Verse Translations,* edited by Palmer Bovie, Rutgers University Press, 1974, pp. 147-52.

[*In the following essay, Parker discusses influences on* The Eunich, *concluding that Terence's individuality is evident in the play's "reasoned confusion of viewpoints [and] contradiction of attitudes, that mark the best comedy."*]

Portrait of Terence from a Carolingian manuscript in the Bibliothèque Nationale, Paris.

Success dies hard. **The Eunuch** was Terence's most successful play during his lifetime, earning an immediate second production and a considerably increased royalty. It has yet to be forgiven this by critics who, equating excellence with unpopularity, prefer the **Hecyra's** double failure as an index of attainment. Since this is not a universal standard, they find themselves faced with a thorny problem: **The Eunuch** is fast and funny, and, in fact, an excellent case can be made for its being Terence's best play. How to dispose of it? The answer is simple and somewhat sinister: Call it "Plautine."

The precise meaning of this epithet is not so obvious as might at first appear, but its connotations are clear enough: When used by a pro-Terentian (or pro-Menandrean) critic, it implies that the play is a sort of regrettable mistake, an attempt at pit-pandering by a playwright who should have known better, and usually did. And, when picked up and employed by an anti-Terentian, it passes implicit judgment against his other five plays. Either way the poet loses.

And loses yet another way: In making **The Eunuch,** Terence modified Menander's *Eunouchus* considerably to admit two characters, the soldier Thraso and the parasite Gnatho, from another play by the same Greek author—the *Kolax* ("Toady" or "Yes-Man"). Unfortunately, literary politics compelled him to admit this in his prologue. I say "unfortunately," not because this defense of dramatic *contaminatio* failed (it did not), but because, by his rather detailed admission, he supplied critics of two millennia later with their most substantial handle for the reconstruction of lost Greek plays. Thus armed, they have prodded joyously for a century or so, descrying the necessarily seamless excellence of the originals through the gaps they

make in the Roman poet's necessarily shoddy composition.

The play, of course, however categorized or tortured, has not changed, and annoyance at its criticism may seem ill-taken. After all, "Plautine" can be a perfectly accurate and unexceptionable, if somewhat otiose, synonym for Donatus' *motoria:* it must be granted that fast and furious fun is not exactly a characteristic Terentian virtue (though the **Phormio** abounds in it). And there is certainly nothing wrong per se with the attempted recovery of Menandrean comedies. But, as it happens, the two practices described above have interacted to form a barrier to the proper understanding of just what Terence has done in this play, "Plautine" becoming a rug under which to sweep, unexamined, any difficulties in taste, *Quellenforschung* a sieve with which **The Eunuch** is axiomatically strained of any real dramatic unity.

To take the first point: Many critics who are not bothered by the hot-blooded rape of Pamphila become quite upset at the play's ending—the projected *ménage à trois* that involves the cold-blooded diddling of Thraso. If this does not signal a blast against the morality of the playwright, it is generally resolved by recourse to the adjective "Plautine." Such a situation obtains at the end of Plautus' *Asinaria* and *Bacchides* and unsettles no one; why should it here? But this begs the question; the unease remains undissolved. And that such a reaction from his audience might have been a reasoned dramatic aim of Terence is an observation that rarely occurs; the poet is evidently the prisoner of the style he has chosen.

Or the second point: Gnatho's bravura disquisition on his new method of coney-catching (Act II, Scene 2) is the longest and most memorable speech in the play; it should logically have something to do with the over-all action. But the seeker after Menander, anxious to pin something down for good, is all too ready to overstate his case for its derivation from the *Kolax* by declaring that the speech's only function is to delineate the character of the parasite.

These are not random points, but both are intimately bound up with the meaning of **The Eunuch,** and the critic neglects them at his peril. The play, whatever its genealogy, is more than farce, more than loose-knit romp; it is a serious dramatic exploration, all of a piece.

Returning to the ending, to call it "Plautine" merely intensifies the problem: Why should critics who are proof against anything written suddenly be found muttering about "the dubious morality of **The Eunuch's** conclusion"? Why should otherwise hardheaded translators feel impelled to give their readers the perfectly gratuitous (and unfounded) intelligence that, when Gnatho proposes milking Thraso, Phaedria accepts the suggestion "reluctantly"? In sum, why should a phenomenon that passes without objection in a play by Plautus cause unease when it occurs in a play by Terence? Provisionally, the only possible answer would appear to be that Terence has somehow employed it in a different fashion. And he has; he has indulged in one of his most effective practices: Taking a comedic *datum* and, by a change in its context, pushing it beyond the bounds of comfortable acceptability, he has achieved that bite which is distinctly his own.

The change involved is one in "characterization"—a bad word for critics, but no matter. Terence has humanized and deepened the stock *personae* of New Comedy, not greatly, but enough to involve the audience with them at a different level, a level where hackneyed situations acquire a new and distressing reality through their participants. Upset at *The Eunuch's* conclusion arises, not from abstract disapproval of confidence-games or *ménages à trois,* but from a directed feeling that *these* lovers ought not to be doing such a thing to *this* soldier. Therefore Phaedria must be "reluctant." Therefore at least one critic has suggested (I am not making this up) that Terence's ending must derive, not from Menander's *Eunouchos,* but from his *Kolax,* since Thais, taken from the former play, is really too noble to be party to such an arrangement, even in prospect. Ridiculous remedies, arising from misreadings, but they locate the ailments: Phaedria, the lovestruck and ineffectual *adulescens* who possesses enough self-knowledge to see his weakness but not to avoid it; Thais, the whore with, not a heart of gold, but an overlay of altruism—they really should behave better.

For the object of the diddling is to be Thraso, and to dupe him is not to take a deserved revenge on a monster, but to shoot a very sorry fish in a very small barrel. In the abortive siege of Thais's house he has demonstrated his purely military futility, but other deficiencies have emerged as well. It is really ironic that this character should have supplied English with an adjective—*thrasonical*—to describe vaingloriousness; Thraso is the first *miles gloriosus* whose *words* completely fail him. He fumbles for quotations, relies on ludicrously inept repartee, goes gauche at the sight of Thais. He needs only poverty to match the most inept specimen of the breed, Armado in *Love's Labour's Lost*—like him, a would-be Hercules who cannot fight; like him, a hopeless lover who solicits instruction from an unqualified source; like him, total prisoner of a rhetoric that his opponents can use more effectively in fun than he can in earnest. Stupid and defenseless, a man rattling around in a monster's role, he resembles Armado in one more, one most important particular: Sincerely in love, he is the only person in the play actually willing to make a sacrifice for his love. And his sacrifice, to everyone else's profit, constitutes the ending of *The Eunuch.*

To return to the second point raised earlier—Gnatho's speech in Act II, Scene 2—it is certainly obvious that the ending proceeds, logically and inevitably, from the enlightened self-interest set forth in the parasite's *nouom aucupium.* It marks, in fact, the conversion of the principal members of the play's cast to Gnatho's way of life: Thraso, giving in to a hopeless love, will be gulled by almost everyone in sight.

This way of life is itself an answer to Parmeno's sarcastic comment on love's (and life's) vicissitudes in Act I, Scene 1:

> Incerta haec si tu postules
> ratione certa facere, nihilo plus agas
> quam si des operam ut cum ratione insanias.

> No mind can reduce this mess
> To any controllable order; you're better off
> To spend your effort devising a plan to go mad
> on.

And a method for madness is what Gnatho supplies; more specifically, a blueprint for subservience. All of the principal characters in the play, one way or another, are in search of dependence and its fruits: Chaerea, who puts on the weeds of slavery and unmanliness to gain his beloved; Thais, whose regard for her "sister," however touching, is a means to patronage; Phaedria, whose ideal love can always be altered by practical consideration. Even Parmeno, whose moral disapproval is strongest, is not immune; he may think that the information he gives to Chaerea's father is done in the boy's best interest, but his own admission and Pythias' accusation show the truth. When the crunch comes, try as he will, his guiding impulse is to save himself:

> Huius quidquid factumst, culpa non factumst mea.

> Whatever happened, it wasn't my fault that it happened.

In this play as elsewhere, comic characters are rarely to be taken at their own evaluation.

The Eunuch, then, from Phaedria's initial whines to Thraso's invitation to the slaughter, is a study of the workings of dependency in which all noble motives, except for that of the play's standard butt, shrink alarmingly to one ignoble motive—the one unblushingly practiced and preached by that two-dimensional caricature from the older style of comedy, Gnatho:

> Me huius quidquid facio id facere maxumo causa mea.

> Whatever I do, I do from pure self-interest.

A most unpleasant motif for a cynical sermon—but it is not offered as such. Its effect is to counterpoint and bind together the play's farcical fun, to weave its strands to a not-quite-happy end, to produce in the audience that reasoned confusion of viewpoints, that contradiction in attitudes, that mark the best comedy. And it is in this achievement, proceeding from the play's *Gestalt* rather than from any part of it, that we can see the playwright's excellence: The fun may be Plautine, the characters and plot may be Menandrean, but the totality is Terence's own.

R. H. Martin   (essay date 1976)

SOURCE: An introduction to *Adelphoe* by Terence, edited by R. H. Martin, Cambridge University Press, 1976, pp. 1-41.

[*Below, Martin supplies a summary of the development of Roman comedy to Terence's time, and then goes on to discuss the sources, themes, characters, and style of the* The Brothers.]

Although there is evidence of dramatic entertainment in Rome and other Italian towns from an early date, formal literary drama came to Rome only in the third century

B.C., when in September of the year 240 at the *ludi Romani* there was performed a Latin play, translated from the Greek by Livius Andronicus, a *semigraecus* from Tarentum. Rome had just brought the First Punic War to a successful conclusion, and the *ludi Romani* of that year were celebrated on a grander scale to mark the nation's pride and joy at that success. The inclusion of a dramatic entertainment in the games is noteworthy, for it was to remain the Roman practice that the performance of plays, both comedies and tragedies, should take place on important public occasions—this is true no less of performances at funeral games (*ludi funebres*) than at the annual *ludi scaenici*. The fact that Andronicus presented Latin versions of Greek plays chosen from the repertory of New Comedy is also significant. A Roman audience, while recognising the unchanging human traits portrayed on the stage, could—like an English audience watching French farce (or even Molière)—observe with amused superiority the foibles and weaknesses of characters who were not Romans. Livius not only established the translation into Latin of Greek New Comedy as a new genre, the *fabula palliata:* in an important matter of technique he took a decisive step. The metres he chose were essentially those of Greek drama, modified to the needs of Latin, above all in the freedom with which he admitted long syllables where the Greek metrical scheme demanded a short. The example that Andronicus set in this respect was followed by all subsequent writers in the genre.

Within a quarter of a century war against Carthage was resumed and continued unbroken, for the most part on Italian soil, until Hannibal was defeated at Zama in 202 B.C. and the Carthaginians sued for peace, which was granted in the following year. The period of the Hannibalic war might seem to be scarcely conducive to the development of organised dramatic entertainment, but it was during this time that Plautus, another non-Roman (he was a native of Sarsina in Umbria) established himself as the foremost writer of the *fabula palliata*. Unlike Livius, Plautus confined himself to this one genre and, although many of the 130 or so plays attributed to him a century later were not genuine, his literary output was considerable; the twenty plays that survive, together with fragments of a twenty-first, may well be identical with the twenty-one plays whose authenticity Varro declared to be generally acknowledged, but Varro makes it clear that there were a number of other genuine plays. Only two of Plautus' plays can be firmly dated, the *Stichus* (200 B.C.) and *Pseudolus* (191), but internal evidence suggests that some at least of his plays were written before the end of the Second Punic War, and if, as a statement of Cicero seems to imply, Plautus was an old man when he wrote the *Pseudolus,* his earliest plays might go back to the first years of the war. The plays of Plautus are drawn from a wide range of Greek authors—Demophilus, Diphilus, Menander, and Philemon are attested—and they also show a wide range of plots and characters. But though their ultimate parentage is Greek, plot, language, and metre are handled with such freedom and self-assurance that the result cannot be regarded as mere translation. The extent to which Plautus departs from his Greek models seems to vary considerably from play to play, but at times his relationship to his models is certainly no closer than is Shakespeare's *Comedy of*

Errors to its model, the *Menaechmi* of Plautus. From the viewpoint of a more sophisticated age Plautus might be justly criticised for insufficient attention to careful construction and artistic finish, but, whatever their shortcomings, his plays were a success. For into the carefully organised structure of Greek New Comedy Plautus infused just that degree of native vigour that a Roman audience required. The gusto that Plautus contributed to his plays is matched by the range and vividness of the characters and themes he encompassed. Major roles are given to such characters as the braggart soldier, the unsavoury *leno,* the dinner-seeking parasite, and the scheming slave, while the comic potential of scenes, and even whole plays, involving mistaken identity is fully exploited. In part this reproduces characteristics of the Greek originals—though the choice that Plautus made is itself indicative of the breadth of his interests—but in part too the Latin plays show a new emphasis that has been contributed by Plautus himself. Certainly the manner in which the role of the *callidus seruus* is emphasised is demonstrably the result of Plautine addition or alteration. The fact that the society that was being depicted was Greek may have made such comic exaggerations more acceptable to a Roman audience, but it should be remembered that the native Italian *fabula Atellana* had already accustomed them to grossly exaggerated stock characters.

The period of about twenty years that elapsed between the death of Plautus and the first play of Terence was bridged, in the realm of comedy, by Caecilius Statius, an Insubrian Gaul from Milan or nearby. Although only fragments of his plays survive, he is a writer of some importance. It is to him, not to Plautus, that a Republican critic, Volcacius Sedigitus, gives first place in a list of writers of Roman comedy, while Varro writes 'in argumentis Caecilius poscit palmam'. What survives of Caecilius does not allow us to make any judgements on his plots, but a chapter of Aulus Gellius (2.23) permits us to compare three passages (in total just over thirty lines) of Menander's Πλόκιον with Caecilius' Latin version. The technique is very similar to that of Plautus. Instead of literal translation there is compression, addition, substitution; a monologue in iambic trimeters is converted into a polymetric monody. Alliteration and assonance are freely employed - not only in the polymetric section. The affinity that Caecilius shows with Plautus in language and style is all the more notable, since he markedly differs from him in some other respects. We know the titles of more than forty of his plays, and over a third of them are based on Menandrean originals, a significant increase over Plautus and a step in the direction of the later practice of Terence. It is probable that he did not adopt the practice of so-called *contaminatio,* which Plautus certainly used in some of his plays, for the praise that Varro gives him for his plots seems to imply that the structure of his plays closely adhered to that of their Greek originals.

Between Caecilius and Terence there are two direct links. Suetonius' life of Terence, which is quoted almost in its entirely by Donatus, records a touching incident. After Terence had written his first play, the **Andria,** he submitted it to the aediles, who were to be responsible for the conduct of the *ludi* at which Terence hoped his play might be produced. The aediles instructed him to take his manuscript and read it to Caecilius, who, presumably, would give the aediles an expert opinion on whether the play deserved to be produced. Terence found Caecilius at dinner, and, being himself poorly dressed, was asked to sit on a separate bench. But after he had read only a few lines, Caecilius asked him to join him at table as his guest, whereupon Terence read the rest of the play *non sine magna Caecilii admiration.* Since Caecilius died in 168 B.C. and the commonly accepted date for the production of the **Andria** is 166, the story may be apocryphal, but, if so, it is *ben trovato,* for there is a real sense in which the young poet, who was to draw four of his six plays from Menander, continues the tradition of Caecilius. Another link between Caecilius and Terence is certain. The second prologue of Terence's **Hecyra** is spoken by L. Ambivius Turpio, the actor-manager (and producer) of all Terence's plays. Now an old man, he recalls his younger days, when his vigorous efforts were needed to secure a hearing for Caecilius' plays in the face of attempts by adversaries to prevent the plays being performed. The unnamed *aduorsarii* are those professional rivals whose hostility to Terence is a recurring theme of his prologues. Professional jealousy might show itself in many ways, but its underlying cause was economic. The number of occasions on which comedies could be publicly performed was limited, and playwright and actor-manager had a common interest in having a play accepted, and in carrying through its successful performance. Certainly in the case of Terence, as probably in the case of Caecilius, at the outset of his career professional jealousy came from 'established' writers, who saw their livelihood and position threatened by a new and younger talent. The similarity of language of **Hec.** 21-3 (referring to Caecilius) and **Ph.** 16-18 (referring to Terence) is striking:

> ita poetam [sc. Caecilium] restitui in locum
> prope iam remmotum iniuria aduorsarium
> ab studio atque ab labore atque arte musica.
> (**Hec.** 21-3)

> is sibi responsum hoc habeat, in medio omnibus
> palmam esse positam qui artem tractent musi-
>   cam.
> ille ad famem hunc [sc. Terentium] a studio
>   studuit reicere.
> (**Ph.** 16-18)

In the case of Terence the battle was fought largely under the banner of literary and aesthetic principles, and it is possible that those who opposed Caecilius used similar tactics. But if this is so, our sources tell us nothing of it. What is clear is that ultimately Caecilius won both popular success in the theatre and the approval of qualified critics; so, in Volcacius Sedigitus' canon he was ranked higher than Plautus. And if there is any truth in the story of his meeting with Terence, the aediles must have referred Terence to him because they regarded him as the doyen of comic playwrights.

By the time that Terence began to write, the cultural climate had changed considerably from what it had been in Plautus' day. A number of factors in this change can be identified. In the period immediately after the end of the Second Punic War there was a continuing increase in the number of occasions on which dramatic performances were given. This affected both audience and playwrights. The former became more demanding and more sophisticated in their expectations, the latter were compelled not only to select their models with greater care, but also to consider how to handle those originals, particularly whether translation was to be freer or more literal. A decision on this problem might involve theoretical considerations, but an important factor was the fact that other forms of entertainment were available at the *ludi;* the prologues to the **Hecyra** tell how the competing attractions of tightrope walkers, boxers, and gladiators caused Terence's audience to vanish. Since the *ludi* were occasions for conspicuous display by those who gave them, they too had an interest in seeing that only such plays were chosen as would make a good impression on the audience at large. Such a consideration need not necessarily lead to an appeal to the lowest levels of taste, but the desire to avoid exhibiting a failure—ancient Roman audiences seem to have been as vocal in showing their disapproval as modern ones—must have influenced the choice of author and play. But there is one factor above all that affects the generation after Plautus' death: the increasing influence of Greek culture on Rome as a result of Rome's military and political involvement with Greece. That influence could be welcomed or opposed: it could not be ignored.

Two figures illustrate the opposing views. M. Porcius Cato ('Cato the Censor') denounced the luxury and moral enervation he observed in contemporary Rome, and proclaimed that Rome would be ruined by Greek culture and education. Cato, himself a *nouus homo,* was a particularly vigorous opponent of the philhellenic policy and sympathies of many of Rome's hereditary aristocracy, especially Scipio Africanus. This philhellenism was equally conspicuous in L. Aemilius Paullus, who brought to an end the war against Perseus, king of Macedon, by his victory at Pydna in 168 B.C.—the year of Caecilius' death. One result of the Roman victory in Greece was the deportation from Achaea of one thousand of its leading citizens, who included the historian Polybius. Polybius had the good fortune, though a hostage, to become the close friend of the sons of Aemilius Paullus, one of whom, after his adoption by the son of Scipio Africanus, bore the name of Publius Cornelius Scipio Aemilianus. Associated with Scipio Aemilianus was a group of *nobiles* who are generally referred to as 'the Scipionic Circle'. These men shared a common interest in Greek culture, especially its literature and philosophy. Their interest in literature extended to its patronage, and Terence is the earliest writer to be linked with the names of Scipio and his friend, C. Laelius. From details concerning the life of Scipio Aemilianus, including those recorded by his contemporary and intimate friend, Polybius, we get the fullest picture of a philhellenic aristocrat of the time during which Terence wrote his plays. Our concern, however, is not with details of Scipio's life, but with him as an outstanding representative of philhellenism.

So, when Terence began writing, the prevailing taste among writers of the *palliata* was markedly different from what it had been in the days of Plautus. Terence was bound, in any case, to face opposition from established writers, since his success might endanger their livelihood. But it is clear from his prologues that they also took issue with him on the proper way to 'translate' Greek plays. It is important to gain some understanding of their respective views. Caecilius had taken a significant step in the direction of showing preference for Menander in his choice of Greek plays, but his manner of translating seems to have remained essentially Plautine. But after Plautus' death there had clearly been a definite move towards a theory of greater fidelity to the Greek original, and with the death of Caecilius the advocates of this type of translation might have hoped to come into their own. To the realisation of this hope Terence's advent posed a threat. Though at times he speaks of his adversaries in the plural, there is one, described by him as a *maleuolus uetus poeta,* to whom we can give a name, and about whose writing we have some detailed information. This is Luscius of Lanuvium, already an old man in 166 and, quite possibly, hoping to inherit Caecilius' position as the acknowledged leading writer of *palliata.*

The charges that were levelled against Terence are those of plagiarism (*furtum* 'literary theft'), the practice of *contaminatio,* feeble writing, and dependence on noble patronage. As regards the last charge, it was easy for the suspicion to arise—whether justified or not—that Terence's plays were not accepted for production simply on their merits. If production was linked to a public occasion, who could say what might be achieved if an aristocratic patron dropped a word in the ear of the officials who were to preside over the games? And when, as was the case with the **Adelphoe,** Terence was on friendly terms with the heirs responsible for giving the *ludi funebres* in memory of L. Aemilius Paullus, the choice of him as playwright must have seemed to many to have been prearranged. The allegations of plagiarism and *contaminatio* to some extent hang together, for the plagiarism which is complained of consists of incorporating into the **Eunuchus** and **Adelphoe** scenes taken from other Greek plays already translated into Latin, and it is to this combination of elements from different plays that the word **contaminatio** is traditionally applied. Behind these accusations lies the feeling that the integrity of the Greek original should be respected in translation, at least as far as the unitary nature of the plot was concerned. Whether Luscius also advocated close fidelity to the Greek cannot be demonstrated conclusively, since we possess at most three lines from his comedies. But it seems to be implied by Terence's jibe (**Eun.** 7-8) that Luscius *bene uortendo et easdem scribendo male / ex Graecis bonis Latinas fecit non bonas,* where *bene uertere* (apparently 'faithful translation') is said to produce bad plays.

Luscius' other objection is to Terence's style. In **Ph.** 4-5 Luscius has said (according to Terence) that in Terence's plays 'the language is thin and the writing slight' (*tenui esse oratione et scriptura leui*). To this Terence answers that at least he has never written a play in which a young man sees a deer in flight, pursued by hounds, and earnestly imploring his aid. Clearly Terence is describing a scene in one of Luscius' plays and criticising it on the ground that situation and language are out of keeping with the tone of comedy. What emerges from these exchanges is that Ter-

ence and Luscius have one thing in common: in keeping with the spirit of the times they both sought to provide Latin comedy that was more deeply hellenised than in preceding generations. But on the way in which that objective was to be achieved they differed radically. Luscius believed in the maximum fidelity to his Greek originals, but welcomed originals that gave scope for the melodramatic, including apparitions and semi-tragic incident: Terence was prepared to handle Greek originals with some freedom, but he selected those originals in such a way as to exclude themes that seemed inconsistent with his conception of comedy. In one vital respect we may be sure that Terence proved his superiority over his adversaries; refusing to adhere to a principle of over-exact translation, he had the genius to perfect a pure Latin style that was, not a replica, but a masterly equivalent of the Attic elegance of Menander. In the list of the 'top ten' Latin writers of comedy complied by Volcacius Sedigitus about 100 B.C. we may be surprised to find Terence placed only sixth. Luscius, however, fares still worse: he is placed last but one.

Terence chose his Greek models with great care. Not only did he confine his choice to Menander and a close follower of Menander, Apollodorus of Carystus, but—with the exception of the **Hecyra** (and to a lesser extent the **Eunuchus**)—he selected plays that were constructed basically on the same formula: a young man is in love with a girl, but is unable to marry her, either because, though freeborn, she is poor and therefore unacceptable as a daughter-in-law to his father, or because she is ostensibly a courtesan. The obstacles to marriage (of which parental disapproval is the commonest) are eventually overcome, often by the unexpected discovery that the girl is the eligible daughter of a near neighbour or relation. The way is thus open for the traditional 'happy ending'. To this central core of the play a complication is added by the fact that the young man has a friend (or brother) who is also involved in an unsuccessful love affair, though in his case the girl is mostly a practising courtesan, which puts a permanent liaison with her out of the question. Great ingenuity may be displayed in the way in which this subplot is interwoven with the main plot.

But though the young man's love affair is the pivot on which the plot turns, the relationship between him and the girl he loves is not normally depicted on the stage. However strange this may seem to a modern audience, it arises naturally from two circumstances affecting Greco-Roman dramatic production. Since the action that was depicted took place out of doors—the Greek and Roman theatre never showed a house interior—and since in Athens an unmarried girl of good family did not normally appear out of doors unattended, opportunities for the young lovers to appear together on the stage were almost non-existent. Instead, a large amount of the humour of Terence's plays comes from the conflict and the misunderstandings that arise within the family circle, especially between father and son. Though double plots of the kind just described were to be found among Menander's plays, they represent only one of the types of plot he uses, and it is clear that Terence must have had a conscious preference for plays with double plots, in which the relationship between father and son played a conspicuous part. Though the *Hecyra,* unlike the other five plays, does not have a double plot, problems of family relationships are at its centre; the young man, Pamphilus, has to contend with mother and father and both parents-in-law in his attempt to conceal what he believes to be his wife's guilty secret. The *Eunuchus* has a double plot involving the love affairs of two brothers, but here, contrary to Terence's practice elsewhere (and, apparently, greatly to the enjoyment of his Roman audience), the play evolves essentially from the relationship between the elder brother and a *bona meretrix,* Thais.

By selecting plays which gave him the opportunity to bring out certain facets of human character, particularly in the sphere of family relationships, Terence had chosen to concentrate on those aspects of Menander's writing that could most readily be understood by the Romans. In so doing Terence emphasised what was most universal and basic in its human appeal, and although we have no extended passage where Terence can be directly compared with his Greek original, a number of small points are noted in Donatus' commentary, which show Terence omitting or generalising details that are too localised to be immediately comprehensible to a Roman audience. In this process some loss of clarity and focus may arise, but it was largely this emphasis on the universal in human nature that gave Terence his appeal not only throughout the Middle Ages, but also among vernacular writers of comedy in the countries of western Europe after the Renaissance. A good illustration of this generalising process is shown by a passage from the opening scene of Terence's *Hautontimorumenos,* where good fortune has preserved two separate fragments that give us just over five consecutive lines of Menander's original. The speaker is Chremes, a *senex,* who is interested in everybody else's affairs, and who, consequently, fails to see what is going on under his own nose. It is he who, to justify poking his nose into other people's business, speaks Terence's most famous line: *homo sum: humani nil a me alienum puto* (*Ht.* 77). Shortly before this he has found his neighbour, Menedemus, hard at work on the land—no sort of occupation for a prosperous Athenian gentleman. Wondering why his neighbour should behave in this strange way, he asks him (61-4):

> nam pro deum atque hominum fidem quid uis tibi aut
> quid quaeris? annos sexaginta natus es
> aut plus eo, ut conicio; agrum in his regionibus
> meliorem neque preti maioris nemo habet;

Menander's version is:

> . . . ('By Athene! You're out of your mind, though you're old enough to know better! For I reckon you're a good sixty years. And, by Zeus! you've got the finest estate in Halae - or at least one of the three finest; and, best of all, there's no mortgage on it.')

It is in lines 63b-4 that Terence shows his generalising tendency most clearly. The reference to the deme of Halae is dropped, as having no significance to a Roman audience. So too the detail about mortgage is omitted, for the Romans did not have the Attic practice of marking mort-

gaged land with a pillar *in situ.* Two items, then, that locate the scene in time and place are dispensed with: Terence's sentence can refer to any time, anywhere. But Terence also drops the precise-pernickety . . . ('or at least one of the three') of Menander, which so exactly hits off the fussiness of the busybody.

The omission of local colour and the restricted range of plots and characters he chose offer some justification to those who feel that, compared with Plautus, Terence is lacking in verve. But even in the sphere of structure and incident Terence is more than a *Menander dimidiatus.* From statements in his prologues and from information given by Donatus in his commentary on the plays it is clear that Terence felt it desirable or necessary to introduce elements that would appeal to a Roman audience. The introduction of Charinus and his slave into the *Andria,* which allows further scope for the elements of surprise and intrigue, for dramatic confrontation and comic misunderstanding, is evidence of this intention from the outset of Terence's career, as is also his conversion of the play's opening scene from Menandrean monologue to a dialogue between Simo and his freedman, Sosia. If he had been in any doubt about the need to make some concessions to Roman taste, the failure of his *Hecyra* would have brought it home to him. It is no accident that the play which won him his greatest success was the *Eunuchus,* for it is the only one of his plays in which a *miles gloriosus* appears, and we know from the prologue to the play that the figure of the *miles,* with his attendant *parasitus,* was introduced into the play by Terence from another play of Menander (the *Kolax*) by the process of *contaminatio.* And again in his last play, the *Adelphoe,* he incorporates a scene of knockabout comedy from Diphilus' *Synapothnescontes.* In it a *leno,* who, apart from the *miles gloriosus,* is the character in the *fabula palliata* most fitted to be the butt of ridicule, is subjected to a good deal of physical and verbal indignity. It is not difficult to imagine how such a scene would appeal to an audience that was ready to rush off to see boxers, tightrope walkers, and gladiators.

Terence, then, had an individual contribution to make to his craft. His own temperament as well as the literary tastes of his patrons led him to attempt a new and finer interpretation of the Hellenic spirit of his models, above all the Attic grace of Menander. If he avoided for the most part the robust humour of an earlier generation, he avoided also the arid literalness of a Luscius Lanuvinus. As he sought to combine Greek and Latin elements in his plays, the task of the modern reader must be to attempt to assess them as a Greco-Roman phenomenon. But to be able to do so we must be prepared to try to separate the Greek and Roman strands in that interwoven whole. Until recently scholars, convinced of the superiority of Greek New Comedy, and tending to regard the Latin plays as inferior imitations, generally used the plays of Terence only as an aid to reconstructing the missing Greek originals. To regard Terence's plays, instead, as in some sense new creations is not to imply that they are superior to their Greek models, but it does imply a shift of emphasis. It is worth trying to assess the merits of Terence's plays in their own right: to do so it is not only legitimate but necessary to employ all the evidence that our ever-increasing remains of New Comedy can afford.

. . . . .

In the **Adelphoe** Terence returns to a theme he had already handled in the **Hautontimorumenos.** In that play, as in the **Adelphoe,** there are two contrasting old men, each with a son of marriageable age. Menedemus (the 'Self-Tormentor' of the title) is overcome with remorse because his constant criticism of his son for associating with a freeborn but penniless girl has driven the boy to leave home: now the father is prepared to do anything to have his son back again. An inquisitive neighbour, Chremes, is only too ready to explain to him where he has gone wrong in dealing with his son, and when Menedemus' son returns home, Chremes is equally free with the advice he offers for the future. The plot becomes extremely complicated. Menedemus agrees to allow himself to become the victim of a deception, so that his son may obtain money from him without realising that his father is parting with it willingly. Chremes undertakes to assist in this deception, but is himself deceived into supporting his own son's affair with an expensive courtesan, whom *he* believes to be the mistress of Menedemus' son. When the truth comes out, Menedemus, who so far has been prepared to bow to Chremes' superior wisdom, realises (V i) that it is not he, but Chremes, who is the real fool (see esp. 874-8): Chremes, on the other hand, flies into a rage and shows exactly the same lack of self-control that he had earlier criticised in Menedemus. But Chremes' discomfiture does not last long. Before the play ends, he has reasserted his parental control by putting an end to his son's liaison with the courtesan and forcing him to agree to a respectable marriage. Although the contrasting characters of the *senes* in the **Hautontimorumenos** do not lack credibility, the action of the second half of the play is so contrived that it seems to spring more from the demands of the plot than from the free choice of the *senes.* Consequently their characters are somewhat lacking in depth, and the play's outcome is wholly conventional.

In the **Adelphoe** the relative importance of plot and character is reversed; the plot is basically simple, the characters more complex and interesting. Demea and Micio, both *senes,* are brothers. Demea has married and had two sons. The elder of these, Aeschinus, he has given to his brother to adopt, while he brings up Ctesipho, accustoming him (he believes!) to the hard and rigorous life of the country. Micio, by contrast, is an easy-going city bachelor, and he brings up his adopted son with a liberality that Demea regards as culpable indulgence. Unknown to his father, each young man is engaged in a love affair; Aeschinus loves a poor, fatherless girl, who, as the play begins, is about to bear his child, while Ctesipho is enamoured of a courtesan, the property of a slave-dealer (*leno*). But since the timid Ctesipho lives in dread of his domineering father, Aeschinus forcibly abducts the courtesan on his brother's behalf. When Demea hears of the abduction, he believes that Aeschinus has taken the girl for himself, and regards it as demonstrating the folly of Micio's failure to exercise adequate discipline over his adopted son. Subsequently Demea learns that Aeschinus has also seduced a freeborn girl, and when Micio, who by now

knows that it is Ctesipho who is interested in the courtesan, takes the matter coolly, Demea is convinced that Micio has taken leave of his senses. Up to this point in the play - about three-quarters of the way through - the direction in which the plot has been moving is quite clear: one incident after another conspires to make Demea appear ridiculous. The climax is reached when (between 782 and 788) Demea learns that the courtesan is the *amica* of Ctesipho, not Aeschinus. After a scene (V iii) in which Micio with difficulty pacifies his brother, Demea performs a complete volte-face. Since his own way of bringing up his son has failed, he decides to outdo Micio in affability and generosity, hoping thereby to gain the affection that he has hitherto failed to win. In the final scenes of the play, Demea's new policy succeeds beyond expectation. Ironically, the generosity he now practises is mostly to be paid for by Micio, who has also to agree to marry his son's future mother-in-law. In the play's closing lines a bewildered Micio asks his brother what has caused this amazing change of heart. To this Demea replies that he has acted in this way to show how easy it is to win apparent affection by extravagant generosity and compliance with other people's wishes.

Demea's volte-face and the consequences that flow from it give a new impetus to the play and raise interesting and important questions for its interpretation, which will be considered shortly. But until the point where Demea announces his decision to alter his ways the basic simplicity of the plot allows ample room for the poet to develop the character of the play's main figures. As a result, even before Demea's volte-face, which would be bound to force the problems upon the attention of the audience, the conflicting views of Demea and Micio have been brought out with far greater clarity and dramatic effectiveness than those of Chremes and Menedemus in the **Hautontimorumenos**—indeed in that play there is little real conflict between the two *senes,* for until the dénouement in the fifth Act Menedemus readily accepts that Chremes 'knows best'. In the **Adelphoe** the conflict of views between Demea and Micio lies at the heart of the play. So the opening scenes (Micio's monologue and a dialogue between Micio and Demea) not only introduce us to the two brothers and launch the action of the play, but also clearly enunciate the opposing theories of education that the two brothers uphold. From the outset the audience is made curious to see which system of education is going to prove successful. Until the last act of the play it is Micio's system that shows the better results, but from that point onwards Demea's change of attitude seems to turn the play on its head, and Micio is reduced to a position where he can do nothing but say 'yes' to a series of increasingly outrageous demands. A startled audience can scarcely fail to ask what this sudden reversal means, and because the way in which young people are brought up, and the relationship between the generations are topics of continuing interest to civilised society, the **Adelphoe** has an interest and importance additional to its merits as comic entertainment.

When dramatists such as Molière and Shadwell in the seventeenth century wrote plays based on the **Adelphoe,** the genial character of Micio claimed their sympathy, and the final humiliation that was inflicted on him in Terence's play was discarded or altered. The ending of the play was first critically discussed in the latter part of the eighteenth century by Lessing in a number of essays included in *Hamburgische Dramaturgie*. In the hundredth of these he wrote, 'Micio's final aberration is contrary to all probability, and must inevitably offend the more discriminating spectator.' Having diagnosed the problem Lessing offered his own solution. On *Ad.* 938 Donatus' commentary says *apud Menandrum senex de nuptiis non grauatur: ergo Terentius [euretikos]* (= 'by his own invention'), and Lessing interpreted this as meaning that in Menander's play Micio was 'not troubled' about a marriage, that is, did not marry. Thus, according to Lessing, the indignity of Micio's being forced to marry the elderly mother of his son's bride-to-be is to be ascribed to Terentian innovation. Though Lessing, in fact, misunderstands Donatus' *grauatur* ('makes difficulties'), he has put his finger on the crucial point from which any modern interpretation of the *Adelphoe* must start, namely, the attempt to establish how Terence's version differs from that of Menander.

Direct evidence of the text and contents of Menander's *[Adelfoi]* is confined to about a dozen fragments, totalling some twenty lines in all, with the addition of some further passages in Donatus' commentary where reference is made to Menander, but without quoting any Greek. Of these passages three are of special importance. Donatus . . . confirms that Micio professed satisfaction (presumably in a monologue) at being a bachelor; fr. 11 (= *Ad.* 866) guarantees that in Menander too Demea delivered a 'change of heart' monologue; lastly, Don. on *Ad.* 938 (quoted in the previous paragraph) establishes that in Menander's play Micio offers no opposition when it is proposed that he should marry the elderly widow, Sostrata.

But the limited direct evidence about Menander's play can be supplemented by the knowledge we gain about Menander from his other plays and from testimony about him. All Menander's plays are pervaded by an attitude of respect for moderation and good sense. At first reading this might seem to be no more than an expression of the common Greek ideal of . . . ('nothing to excess'). But there is another, more specific reason for the prominence given to this attitude in Menander. According to Diogenes Laertius, Menander was a pupil of Theophrastus, who succeeded Aristotle as head of the Peripatetic school of philosophy, and particularly developed its teaching in the field of ethics. The application of the Aristotelian theory of the golden mean to the analysis of character—an interest which Theophrastus continued in his brief (extant) work, the *Characters*—directly influenced Menander's thinking. The comic figure is, above all, one who deviates excessively in one direction or the other from the mean of right conduct. From c. 6 of Bk. 3 to the end of Bk. 4 of the *Nicomachean Ethics* Aristotle discusses a series of 'moral virtues' and their corresponding vices, in each case a vice of excess and a vice of defect (see 2.8.1). A number of these virtues and vices are of particular relevance to the comedies of Menander. Man is a social animal, and there is a general virtue concerned with social intercourse, to which the name . . . ('friendliness') is applicable. The man who carries friendliness too far is called 'obsequious' . . . or, if he has an ulterior motive, 'flatterer'

. . . : or, if he is deficient in friendliness, he is 'surly' . . . and 'quarrelsome' . . . (4.6.9). It is noteworthy that the names for a man who is guilty of the vice of excess or the vice of deficiency corresponding to [friendliness] are, respectively, [flatterer] and [quarrelsome], for these are the titles of two of Menander's plays. Two other virtues (with their vices) are of still more direct relevance to the *Adelphoe*. Liberality is defined as 'observing the due mean in money matters'. The corresponding vice of deficiency is illiberality or meanness, that of excess is prodigality or profligacy. With regard to anger too it is possible for a man to show excess or deficiency or the true mean. Though Aristotle finds it difficult to put a name to these qualities, there is no doubt of their existence: in English it is only for the quality of excess that a precise word is available—'irascibility'—though 'lack of spirit', or, perhaps, 'spinelessness' might do to describe its opposite vice.

In the *Adelphoe* it is clear that surliness, quarrelsomeness, irascibility, and illiberality are qualities displayed by Demea until his change-of-heart monologue. In the succeeding scenes he switches to the opposite vices of excessive affability and prodigality, until the last dozen lines of the play, when he explains to Micio that his switch to the opposite extreme has been a deliberate charade designed to show his brother that he too had failed to hit the true mean. There can be little doubt that this is the impression that Terence leaves (and, presumably, intended to leave) with his audience; at the end of the play Demea has the upper hand, and Micio can do no more than acquiesce in whatever his brother proposes. But did Menander too end his play with the triumph of Demea and the discomfiture of Micio, or have we here a striking example of Terentian alteration and innovation? It is generally agreed that, if Menander's Micio came off 'second best' at the end of the play, there are likely to be indications in the first four acts that Micio's conduct is open to criticism as representing a deviation from the Aristotelian mean. Is this the case? Are we to regard Micio as friendly, or as obsequious? As gentle . . . , or lacking in spirit? As liberal, or as profligate? These questions do not admit of an easy answer, and scholars are divided in their opinions about them. But it is one of the features that give the *Adelphoe* its continuing interest that each new reader (or spectator) can and must make up his own mind on these issues. To do so requires a detailed study of Terence's play and it is in the commentary that such an investigation is best conducted. But attention may be drawn here to some of the general considerations that are likely to influence a decision.

The opening scene, in typical Menandrean fashion, does at least three things at once. It introduces us to Micio as an individualised personality, it begins the exposition of the plot, and it allows Micio to discourse on the different theories he and his brother have on the way to bring up their respective sons. One sentence is particularly revealing. In lines 65-7 Micio argues that a father's authority will be more effective if it is based on *amicitia* than if it is founded on *uis*. It is possible that *amicitia* here corresponds to the Greek [friendliness], which (as we have seen) is an Aristotelian virtue. But this does not necessarily mean that Menander (or Terence) intends us to approve of Micio, for 'the devil can cite Scripture', and Micio may be using good philosophical doctrine as a cloak for his own laziness. The following scene (I ii) between the two brothers gives us a first sample of Demea's irascibility. Unable to pacify him, Micio finally gets him to agree that each shall look after his own son, and not interfere with the way the other brings up his son. Demea departs for the forum, and Micio, left alone, reveals to the audience in a monologue that he is indeed concerned about the new report of Aeschinus' disorderly conduct; he too leaves for the forum, anxious to have a word with his son. It is important to note that at this point in Terence's play the audience does not yet know that Aeschinus' abduction of the 'music-girl' was undertaken on his brother's behalf; as a result it is likely to take a less favourable view of the success of Micio's educational principles than it would have done if it had known the true motive for Aeschinus' violent action. In Menander's play, on the other hand, it is generally agreed that the audience was put in possession of this vital information not later than the end of the first act.

The succeeding scenes (II i-iv), which introduce us to Aeschinus, Ctesipho, Syrus, and the *leno* from whom Aeschinus has abducted Ctesipho's *amica*, also pose problems, for they include the scene or scenes which Terence inserted in Menander's play from the *Synapothnescontes* of Diphilus. How far the introduction of an element of 'thug comedy' disturbs the ethos of Menander's play it is difficult to say, for it is likely that in Menander too the *leno* had cause to complain with equal vigour of his rough handling by Aeschinus—even though that rough handling did not, in Menander, take place on the stage.

After two scenes (III i-ii) in which we learn of Aeschinus' own involvement with 'the girl next door' the next section of the play (to IV ii) belongs to Demea, who is on the stage for 200 of the next 230 lines. He is twice completely hoodwinked by Syrus, who feigns admiration for the success which has attended Demea's system of bringing up his son. It is by no means certain, though it is possible, that these scenes are intended to convey the poet's condemnation of Demea's system of education; the outwitting of the father of the young man in love is a basic ingredient of many plays of the genre, and does not in itself imply disapproval of the values that the father seeks to uphold. It is more revealing to compare III iv, in which Demea meets with Hegio, and IV iii, in which Hegio meets Micio. Only a careful scrutiny of both scenes can show whether there is validity in Rieth's argument that the comparison shows greatly to Demea's disadvantage. At line 586 Demea is sent off on his second, and longer, wild goose chase. During his absence Micio and Aeschinus meet, and harmony is restored between them, after Micio has good-humouredly got a little of his own back on Aeschinus for his earlier deception of his father. At the end of the meeting Aeschinus, left alone on the stage, delivers a short panegyric (707-12) on Micio's generosity, and proclaims his intention never again to do anything that will incur his disapproval. Rieth [in his *Die Kunst Menanders in den "Adelphen" des Terenz*] takes this declaration at its face value, and accordingly believes that it is impossible that in the last scenes of Menander's play Aeschinus should aid and abet Demea in getting Micio to agree to do things that are

contrary to his better judgement. Another interpretation is possible: Aeschinus' present good intentions towards Micio are simply forgotten when Demea offers him a course of action that is more to his liking.

When Demea, having been misdirected by Syrus, returns from his vain attempt to find his brother, there follow in quick succession (IV vii, V iii) two meetings between the two brothers. In the first Demea finds that Micio, far from being perturbed by Aeschinus' seduction of Pamphila, has agreed to their marriage. Since Demea still believes that the music-girl is Aeschinus' *amica,* he concludes that Micio must be out of his mind. Nevertheless, he abides by the agreement made by Micio and him in I ii that each father should look after his own son, and when Micio urges him to put on a cheerful face for Aeschinus' wedding, he utters no word of objection. When, after a brief interval, the brothers meet again, the storm has already broken: Demea has discovered his son, Ctesipho, with the music-girl inside Micio's house. To Demea's accusation that Micio has broken the compact between them that each should look after his own son only, Micio can offer no effective answer. His excuse, that it is right for friends to share and share alike, is feeble. Yet on a higher and more general plane Micio puts a good case. In deciding what is the best way to bring up a boy, Micio argues, account must be taken of his nature. A boy who has a generous nature (*liberum ingenium atque animum* (828-9)) can be allowed considerable freedom in his conduct. Aeschinus and Ctesipho, he is sure, have that basic character, and their actions should be judged accordingly. The fact that the argument is aristocratic, not egalitarian, does nothing to discredit the assumption that the view may derive from Menander, for the restrictive nature of Athenian citizenship in Menander's age tended to an élitist view of society. On the other hand, Micio's ability to expound wholesome philosophical doctrine is not proof that he had practised what he preaches. His insistence that Demea need not worry over the expense incurred by the peccadilloes of their sons is meant to allay what he believes to be Demea's chief anxiety, but it may possibly also reveal an inability to realise that Demea's concern is not only—or indeed primarily—financial. It is dramatically fitting that his rebuke of Demea, 'Old age makes men too keen on money', is turned against him by Demea in the penultimate scene of the play (833-4—953-4).

Demea's monologue in V iv (855-81) marks a crucial turning point in more ways than one, for not only does he resolve to alter his ways, spending instead of saving, and saying 'yes' to everyone: with his change of heart the roles that he and Micio play are dramatically altered. Hitherto Demea has, time after time, been the victim of his own misunderstanding or other people's deception—Syrus rightly says of him (548), *primum ait se scire: is solus nescit omnia*—whereas Micio, even if he does not control events, is quick to adjust to them, making the best of whatever fortune brings (cf. 739-41). But from V iv to the end of the play Demea, who is on the stage throughout, dictates events, and does so almost entirely at the expense of Micio, whose whole function henceforth seems to be to implement Demea's orders. Such at least is his role in Terence's play. Rieth argues that in Menander Micio could not have been humiliated in this way. There are, he believes, two specific arguments that support this general thesis:

(1) There is a direct conflict between Demea's attitude in his monologue (V iv) and the explanation he gives for his actions at the very end of the play (986f.). In his monologue there is not the slightest hint that his change of heart is anything but a genuine resolve. But in 986f. he tells Micio that it was a pretence, adopted to teach his brother a lesson. Since it is alien to the convention of Greco-Roman drama that a character should deliver a monologue that deliberately deceives the audience about his motives, and since the essence of V iv seems to be guaranteed for Menander by fr. 11 (quoted in 866n.), it should follow that the explanation given in *Ad.* 986f. comes, not from Menander, but from Terence.

(2) Donatus' comment on *Ad.* 938 (see p. 19 above) entitles us to look for Terentian addition in this part at least of V viii. Rieth's suggestion that 934 (better 933b)-46 comes from Terence may be near the truth, for it would eliminate precisely those lines where Micio offers strenuous opposition to the suggestion that he should marry. There is, it should be added, no evidence that any other passage in the final scene is not in essence derived from Menander.

If (as Rieth argues) 934-46 and 984ff, are Terentian additions, and it is accepted that the final scene of Menander's play is fairly represented by *Ad.* 924-33+947-83, the sequence of events in Menander would be:

(i) Demea (abetted by Aeschinus?) proposes that Micio should marry Sostrata; Micio accepts without demur.

(ii) Demea (abetted by Aeschinus?) proposes that Micio should grant Hegio the lease of a plot of land, rent-free. Since 953-4 picks up 833-4, it is highly probable that in Menander too Demea quoted Micio's own proverb against him, and did so because Micio was showing some reluctance to accept Demea's suggestion.

(iii) Demea proposes that Syrus should be set free 'for services rendered'. By now the situation is moving into the realm of the absurd, for though Syrus' services are enumerated as giving instruction in wine, women, and extravagant living (964-8), Micio after only a brief hesitation agrees to do as Demea suggests.

(iv) It is now Syrus' turn to ask for a favour - that his 'wife', Phrygia, also should be set free: her service was to have acted as wet-nurse to Micio's grandson! As Micio questions whether this merits the proposed reward, Demea for the only time offers to put his hand in his own pocket to meet the cost.

(v) Lastly, Demea proposes that Syrus should receive a small loan. Very reluctantly, under pressure from Demea and Aeschinus, Micio promises to think about it later.

There can be no good reason to deny any of the above five incidents to the Menandrean original. On that assumption the Menandrean Micio was compelled to consent to a series of requests that become progressively more outrageous, and even if he yielded with a better grace than his

Terentian counterpart, it is clear that in Menander's last act, as in Terence's, Micio fails to sustain the ideal of the Aristotelian mean. If this is the case, a final speech by Demea, explaining to his brother the error of his ways, would be by no means incompatible with what has gone before. On the other hand, there is nothing to prove that Menander's Demea did deliver such a speech. It is conceivable that the play ended rapidly after 982 with Micio saying, 'I'll think about that later: but now let us go inside to celebrate Aeschinus' wedding.' An ending on these lines would save Micio from total humiliation, and it would be in keeping with Menander's general pattern, that at the play's end a willing concord should be reestablished within the family. But there is not one whit of evidence that this is how Menander's play ended, and it should be pointed out that much of what Demea says in his final speech in Terence is sound Aristotelian doctrine. Thus, just as Micio at the beginning of the play had criticised Demea for straying from the mean (*praeter aequomque et bonum*) (64) in the direction of *duritas,* so now in 987-8 Demea accuses his brother of deviating *ex aequo et bono* in the direction of *assentari, indulgere, largiri.* In place of this excessive permissiveness Demea offers an alternative policy: he is prepared both to criticise and assist, as the occasion seems to demand. Aeschinus, who at 707-11 had been prepared to do all he could to show himself worthy of Micio's trust and generosity, immediately accepts Demea's offer. Since, however, the policy that Demea now offers is neither that of extreme severity nor extreme indulgence, the play, as it stands in Terence, ends on a note of moderation, which, as was observed earlier is both typically Menandrean and typically Peripatetic: so we are left with the impression that the desirable mean has hitherto not been achieved by either Demea or Micio.

Understanding of the Peripatetic ethical doctrines which influenced Menander's thinking can aid the interpretation of the **Adelphoe,** but it must be remembered that a play is not a philosophical treatise. Seneca's Stoicism, Racine's Jansenism, Brecht's Marxism are all relevant to the understanding of their plays, but any 'lesson' they may convey is incidental to their main aim, which is to be dramatically effective. Comedy, including that of Menander and Terence, is an artefact designed to throw light on the human condition, especially by making fun of human foibles and shortcomings. It is intrinsically improbable that that aim

---

Michel de Montaigne in praise of Terence (1580-88):

As for Terence, that model of the refined elegancies and grace of the Latin tongue, I find him admirable in his vivid representation of our manners and the movements of the soul; our actions throw me at every turn, upon him; and I cannot read him so often that I do not still discover some new grace and beauty.

Michel de Montaigne, in his Essays of Montaigne, *translated by William Carew Hazlitt, Reeves and Turner, 1877.*

will be attained by introducing a character who personifies the author's own ideal of human excellence; indeed, when a character claims to have discovered the quintessence of human perfection, it is likely that he is riding for a fall. Such, probably, is the case with Micio in the *Adelphoe.* That his fine principles come unstuck is no condemnation of the principles themselves: it is the nature of human beings never fully to realise their ideals, and much of the humour of comedy comes from seeing the gulf that exists between what men profess and what they achieve.

Betty Radice　(essay date 1976)

SOURCE: An introduction to *Terence: The Comedies,* translated by Betty Radice, Penguin Books, 1976, pp. 11-29.

[*Radice was an English educator who, as joint editor of the Penguin Classics series, translated such works as Pliny's* Letters, The Letters of Abelard and Heloise, *and Desiderius Erasmus's* Praise of Folly. *In the following excerpt, she presents an overview of Terence's career.*]

Comedy is a more intellectual and sophisticated art than tragedy, and on the stage it depends for its effects on verbal exchange. Its characters must be wholly articulate, and if it is to succeed it needs an equally articulate, civilized audience, who can respond not with hilarity so much as with a delighted amusement. Audiences of this kind evidently existed for comedy to flourish in fifth-century Athens, in Hellenistic Greece, in Elizabethan and Restoration England, in the Paris of Louis XIV, eighteenth-century Venice, and in Edwardian London, but Rome of the second century B.C. gave small encouragement to a young man who had all the requisites to make him a great writer of comedy. Terence died young, and could be judged a failure in his own day, but the originality he showed in his treatment of his Greek models had a lasting influence on the history of western drama. The six plays of Terence are his complete works and were preserved in a single corpus from an early date. Attached to each play is an authentic author's prologue, a personal apologia of unique literary interest, and several of the medieval MSS. are headed by a production notice giving the date of the play's composition and details of the first production. There is also a Life of Terence ascribed to Suetonius with an addition by the grammarian Aelius Donatus, preserved with Donatus's very full commentaries on the plays. It would seem that a lot is known about Terence and his work and no early author was more quoted by poets and prose-writers alike; yet he remains one of the most problematic of ancient authors, and there were conflicting accounts of him within a century of his death.

Plautus is said by Cicero to have died in 186 B.C. so that all his plays were first written in the years of austerity at the end of the second Carthaginian war and in the changed social conditions produced by the rapid increase of an urban and slave population. They were all taken from Greek New Comedy of Menander and his contemporaries, and military service must have brought many Romans in contact for the first time with the more sophisticated Greek cities of South Italy and Sicily; but Roman society was still parochial and puritanical, based on the close ties of family life. There was nothing in it to correspond with the *jeunesse dorée* of the Hellenistic world, young men in debt to pimps and mistresses, their elders worldly-wise, and their servants as pert and resourceful as a Figaro or Scapin. Plautus took the stock characters of comedy, 'a running slave, virtuous wives and dishonest courtesans, greedy spongers and braggart soldiers' (*The Eunuch,* 36-8), but he could not risk outraging Roman morality by humanizing them. Sometimes the result is caricature, but at his best Plautus created something more vigorous and exuberant than his original, mixing Roman with Greek elements and developing the comic potentiality of a scene in whatever way his sense of theatre suggested. As well as being a master of *vis comica* he has a gift for verbal extravaganza and metrical technique like that of Aristophanes; and the high spots of his plays are often his musical *cantica.*

Some twenty years after Plautus's death Terence brought out his *Andria,* and from the opening conversation between an Athenian gentleman and his trusted freedman it is immediately apparent that his aims are quite different. There is no formal prologue to describe the plot, and the use of dialogue to explain the situation is Terence's improvement on his Greek model. The tone is light but sympathetic towards young love, the language is direct and natural, and the whole scene has been beloved and quoted by literary critics from Cicero down to Sainte-Beuve, who compares some of its phrases with Andromache's smiling through her tears. Terence is consistent throughout his six plays in avoiding what is too Greek or too Roman, and this gives them their timeless quality. He creates a beautifully simple, fluid style of Latin to match the lucidity of Hellenistic Greek. He can handle genuine problems with perception and show people as much the same then as now-mixed in their motives, muddled in their intentions, but, like the young men in *The Brothers,* good at heart. In 'translating' Greek comedy into a different world, Terence's achievement was to take over the typical irascible father, irresponsible youth, courtesan and slave-dealer, and present them as individuals caught up in a complex plot which sets them at cross-purposes and has many comic possibilities when no one is in full possession of the truth until the final *dénouement;* in the meantime much is revealed about the persons involved by means of their reactions to the confusion. At the same time Terence's tolerant attitude to his characters is moral and serious. A young man seduces a girl, but 'there were excuses . .. it is human nature'. Yet he is not allowed to shirk the consequences and leave her in the lurch. A strict father believes he is doing the best thing for his son; but if he makes no allowances for youth he lives in a fool's paradise. A woman can be scorned by her neighbours as a professional courtesan and later show real generosity and an almost maternal affection to her former lover. It is easy to see why his words *homo sum: humani nil a me alienum puto* (*The Self-Tormentor* 77) have been so often quoted out of context with application to Terence himself.

It is also understandable that he has never had wide popular appeal, especially for those unwilling to accept the conventions of formal comedy, where the situations are always relatively stereotyped so as to provide a recognizable framework in which wit can sparkle and intrigue unfold. Some of his double plots and counterplots make great demands upon the concentration of a reader, let alone a theatre audience, and even as early as Cicero and Horace he was more quoted for his humanity and style than for his stagecraft. And in his concern for writing Latin which combines elegance with conversational ease, he makes no attempt to vary it for his different characters. Slaves speak as impeccably as their masters, and only Phormio is allowed more colourful phrases. In his own day he met with instant criticism from his older rivals, and in comparison with Plautus he was judged to be a half-size Menander lacking vigour.

Four of Terence's plays were modelled on Menander's, two (**Phormio** and **The Mother-in-Law**) on plays by Apollodorus of Carystus. (Only three of the twenty-one extant plays of Plautus can be certainly said to follow Menander.) Opinions differ widely on the question how much in a play by Terence is original and how much directly due to the Greek model: T. B. L. Webster in *Studies in Menander* quotes Terence as evidence for the content of lost plays, while Gilbert Norwood in *The Art of Terence* is unwilling to allow anything to Menander at all. The larger surviving fragments of Menander are sufficient to show that his high reputation in antiquity was well deserved; he was a master of plot, of dialogue, of metre, and a creator of characters who are more than mere types. His tolerance and humanity are such as we find in Terence, and both authors are quotable for their observations on life and its problems. What they say may not be strikingly original but it always gives pleasure because it rings true.

It is certain that Terence was never a *translator* of Greek comedies; he has sharp words to say in his prologues about people who were. Moreover, Donatus says more than once in his commentaries that he has read the Greek original, for the purpose of comparison, and in the case of **Andria** that he has studied both the plays cited in the prologue in order to estimate how Terence had used them. He sometimes quotes a line in Greek to show that Terence took it over word for word, but the very fact that he singles out these passages shows that they were comparatively rare. Elsewhere he remarks on Terence's improvement on his original-the opening scene, in dialogue, of **Andria,** for instance. From the six remarkable prologues to the plays in which Terence answers his critics, it is possible to see what he set out to do. He was accused of writing thin dialogue, of stealing characters and scenes from earlier Latin plays, of accepting unacknowledged help from his noble patrons, and of tampering with his Greek originals by picking and choosing from more than one for each of his plays, thus rendering them useless to other translators. Instead of formally refuting the charges, Terence counter-attacks. His critic, he says, is a competent translator with no stage sense, whose fidelity to the text only turns a good Greek play into a bad Latin one. The question of plagiarism in his own work does not arise; he has only made use of stock situations and characters and ignored the plays of his Roman predecessors. 'Nothing in fact is ever said which has not been said before.' He is proud of his 'noble friends', and dismisses the charge that they helped him with his plays as no more than a 'spiteful accusation'. He has no

intention of courting popularity by noisy crowd scenes or animals on the stage; all he asks for is an attentive audience. And if 'spoiling' plays (*contaminare*) means selecting what he wants from any source he likes, that is precisely what the great Plautus did and what Terence proposes to do.

Much has been written about the precise meaning of *contaminatio*. The general meaning of the verb is 'pollute' or 'soil', and in its specialized sense it appears twice in Terence's prologues and nowhere else. Luscius Lanuvinus is quoted as protesting that this upstart young dramatist is 'soiling' or 'spoiling' Greek plays, and again as charging Terence with 'spoiling' Greek plays for others by using more than one to make a single Latin play. It seems very unlikely that so strong a word used pejoratively could mean no more than 'combine'. Luscius surely means that Terence makes a Greek play useless to a straight translator if he picks bits out to incorporate in another play. Terence's reply is that he intends to revert to the freedom and inventiveness of the earlier dramatists, seeing that pedantic accuracy in translation can never create a living Roman play.

The portrait of Terence which emerges from the prologues is one of a conscious artist, impatient of criticism which he feels to be malicious, and confident (as gifted young men must be) that he has it in him to do good work. He is self-assured and intolerant of the second-rate, but he is as sensitive and eager for appreciation as one of his own young men. He says more than once that his main concern is to give pleasure, and he knows very well that a play can never come to life without the support of its audience. Hence his repeated pleas for a fair hearing to enable a young man to make his way in the world, and his tone of hurt surprise in reference to the repeated failure of **The Mother-in-Law.** (No doubt he was well aware that in many ways it was his best-constructed play.) He certainly thought he was bringing something new to the stage, and it must be allowed that he did. Whatever Terence owed to Greek New Comedy, and however confused and contradictory were the traditional accounts of his life collected by Suetonius, it remains a matter of astonishment to his latter-day admirers, as it was to their Roman predecessors, that six plays of such assurance and maturity could be written in as many years at that point in Rome's history by a young man who was apparently an obscure foreign immigrant, but had the power and personality to win the support of the leading actor-producer and be recognized as a dangerous rival by established older playwrights.

His chief original contribution was the double plot, and this enabled him to enlarge on his major interest, the effect of plot on character, and the contrasted reactions of different types of character to the same situation. He could then draw carefully diversified portraits of closely connected persons, the two young men and the two old fathers in **The Brothers,** the two neighbours in **The Self-Tormentor,** the three young men in **The Eunuch,** and end his plays with two resolutions of plot, each acting as a foil to the other: one young man enjoys a socially acceptable and legal marriage when the true identity of his bride is known, while the other is allowed only a temporary liaison with a *meretrix,* less romantic and less seriously taken by his elders. He created a Latin style which was an admirable counterpart to the natural rhythms of Hellenistic Greek, less rhetorical and dense, simpler and purer than anything written before . . . . He settled comedy more firmly in the real world by removing the formal expository prologue (which Plautus kept) and dispensing with divine intervention, thus retaining an element of suspense and making his plays more logical. He moved away from caricature in his minor characters, and was more sympathetic towards old people—the father is never a mere dupe nor the mother a figure of fun—and more interested in women as persons. **The Mother-in-Law** is essentially a woman's play. He was the creator of serious or problem comedy, and became a major influence on European drama from the earliest days of the Renaissance.

A few names of other writers of *fabulae palliatae* (adaptations of Hellenistic comedies played in Greek dress) are known, the last being that of Turpilius who died as a very old man in 103 B.C. Only titles of plays survive; perhaps no one could handle material with Terence's inventiveness. *Fabulae togatae* using Italian themes lasted longer and left about six hundred quoted lines and seventy titles. There are three known writers, Titinius, L. Afranius, and T. Quinctius Atta, who is said to have died in 77 B.C. But as mimes, burlesques and sophisticated versions of the native Atelline farce took over the stage from true comedy, what was written under the Empire was intended for reading aloud to an invited audience. Juvenal starts his first Satire with a protest against the tedium of such readings, and Pliny writes enthusiastically of a young friend's gifts as a playwright without any suggestion that his plays might be staged. It is significant that when Quintilian wishes to illustrate a comment on the acting of comedy he quotes from Terence's **Eunich** and nothing later.

Terence continued to be studied and quoted for his humanity and purity of style down to the last days of the Empire, and when scholarship took refuge in the monasteries, he was one of the authors whose works were carefully preserved complete. The Codex Bembinus of the fourth or fifth century is still the best manuscript we have; in it only most of **Andria** and parts of **Hecyra** and **Adelphoe** are missing. Donatus's commentary is preserved in a sixth-century compilation, intact but for **Heauton Timorumenos.** The archetype of all the later MSS. of Terence is dated to the fifth century, and the extant versions range from the ninth to the twelfth centuries, some of the earliest being illustrated by miniature drawings. All this goes to show the loving care bestowed on Terence, whose Latin served as a model of clarity and style. As his plays had long since left the stage, they escaped the censure of the Fathers of the Church who attacked the brutality and indecency of the mime and stage spectacles of the later Empire. That Terence was read and enjoyed we know from St Augustine and Ammianus Marcellinus, and from St Jerome who complained that the ancient comedies could distract the devout from their bibles. In the tenth century, an aristocratic Saxon nun, Hrotsvitha of Gandersheim, even wrote plays on sacred subjects in the manner of Terence, in an attempt to purge him of his worldliness; the resultant literary curiosity proves how well she knew her model, though she believed he wrote prose.

With the coming of the Renaissance, the popular pageants and morality plays encouraged by the western Church gradually yielded to the discipline of classical tragedy and comedy, with Seneca, Plautus, and Terence as the greatest influence on European drama. In Italy the movement started with learned works in classical style like the *Philodoxius* of Alberti; then came actual performances of such plays, such as those sponsored in the Rome of Sixtus IV by the antiquarian Pomponius Laetus. Finally, the ancient dramatists reached a wider public through direct translation, with some of the great principalities of North Italy leading the way. In 1496 we find the Marquis of Mantua writing to his father-in-law, Hercules I of Ferrara, for copies of the plays of Plautus and Terence translated and played at Ferrara, and there are performances also recorded at Milan under Lodovico Il Moro. Ariosto is known to have translated **Andria** and **The Eunuch.** The presses of Venice produced both verse and prose translations of Terence and selections from Plautus; then original comedy began to be written in Italian, and by the mid sixteenth century the movement was spreading over western Europe. Spain provides one of the earliest examples of classical comedy in de Rojas' dramatized novel, *La Celestina,* and later in the plays of Lope de Vega and his contemporaries. The first English comedy, *Ralph Roister Doister,* written by Nicholas Udall about 1553, is directly modelled on Plautus's *Braggart Soldier* and Terence's **Eunuch.** In 1598 the first English translation, that of Richard Bernard, was published in Cambridge; accurate, lively, and free from verbal conceits, it is still one of the most readable. But the best of the Elizabethan comedies have an element of fantasy which is a distinguishing mark of English comedy at its best and something quite alien to the Latin-Italian style. Shakespeare realizes his powers in comedy when he moves away from the formal pattern of *The Two Gentlemen of Verona* and *The Comedy of Errors* towards the greater poetic depth and freedom of *As You Like It* and *Twelfth Night.* With the post-Restoration dramatists, Wycherley, Vanbrugh, and, above all, Congreve, there is a return to true classic comedy in a somewhat coarsened form; to be followed in the next century by Goldsmith and Sheridan writing with more polish in the same style. The greatest of these plays, *The Way of the World,* is prefaced by Congreve's personal tribute to Terence. But as Diderot pointed out, the characters in English classic comedy tend to become caricatures; in his opinion there have been only two comic dramatists with the gift of drawing characters in depth, with sympathy and without exaggeration, placing them in situations designed to reveal both their individuality and their timelessness: Terence and Molière. The great writers of English comedy have not written for the stage—they are among the poets, essay-writers, and novelists, Chaucer, Addison, Fielding, and Jane Austen.

Terence has had his most sympathetic admireres since the seventeenth century in France, where his humanism and his sense of style had greatest influence. This is apparent from the tributes of critics such as Montaigne, Diderot, and Sainte-Beuve, but his true spiritual descendant is of course Molière. In Molière we find the true humanistic approach - sanity and common sense, freedom from cant and exaggerated sentiment, an understanding of the sufficiency of the world and man's part in it. He can use comedy as a medium for a sustained social commentary, and his essential seriousness can lift it to its highest level so that under the impact of laughter we are made to feel the truth of his judgement on us all. Terence may be limited by the convention that he must 'translate' light Greek comedy into a different world of thought and sentiment, but he is as much the creator of Aeschinus, Demea, and Bacchis as Molière is of M. Jourdain and Céliméne.

For those whose interests were wider and deeper than the study of dramatic comedy Terence had great appeal, especially for the Renaissance humanists in their aim to reconcile the best of pagan learning with the Christian ideal. He was read and quoted by Petrarch, by Politian, who studied the Bembine codex, by Boccaccio, and later by Colet, founder of St Paul's School as the realization of his theories of a Christian education on a classical basis. Erasmus worked on his *Adages* through the years in order to discuss the wisdom of antiquity transmitted through its proverbs and to show that its moral aspirations were not in conflict with the Christian ethic. He had learned the plays by heart in youth, and quoted from them repeatedly, both in his letters and in his published writings; there are more than 250 references and quotations in the *Adages* alone.

Terence was used as a teaching manual of Latin composition until comparatively recent times, and in the early days of the English grammar schools the scholars gave regular performances of Roman comedies. The foundation statute of 1561 for Westminster School said that it should present a play every Christmas, and the second headmaster 'brought in the reading of Terence for the better learning the pure Roman style'. Bernard's translation was printed with the Latin text, with extensive notes on points of grammar and interpretation for the guidance of the children to whom he was tutor. It is our loss that nineteenth-century educationists thought that Terence's urbanity would corrupt schoolboys, and laid down a curriculum of Roman history and oratory and Augustan poetry, to the neglect of the apposite words, free-moving syntax and nimble repartee of colloquial classical Latin. It does not need a very profound knowledge of Latin to enjoy an exchange like that of *Adelphoe* 413 ff. (*The Brothers*).

Roman comedy took over its stage conventions from Greek New Comedy. The back of the stage showed the doors of two or three houses, and the side exits led to the country on the spectators' left and the town centre or market place (the forum) on the right. Whether the harbour should be thought of as on the right or left is disputed; the ancient evidence is not clear about Greek practice nor do we know how far Roman playwrights would follow it. All stage action took place in the open street, and though characters talk to people in the houses through the open door, nothing was allowed to be seen of the interior. The greater breadth of stage made it easier to accept the convention that characters only saw and heard what the author intended. The style of acting was declamatory, with formalized gestures, costume was stereotyped, and actors were probably masked in the Greek fashion to indicate typical characters: 'running slave, angry old man, greedy sponger, shameless impostor and rapacious slave-dealer' (*The Self-Tormentor* 37-9). Though Terence made little use of the sung aria in which Plautus had excelled, his spoken dialogue of six-foot iambics alternate with longer lines of mixed iambics and trochaics, which were rhythmically recited to the musical accompaniment of the pipe player. These passages are called by Donatus *mutatis modis cantica*. Perhaps Terence had no gift for writing lyric metre, or he may have considered it unsuitable for his more serious comedy.

The music for the plays was composed by a slave, Flaccus, named with his master Claudius in the production notices (*didascaliae*). The instrument was the *tibia* (Greek *aulos*), an oboe-style reed instrument (not a flute), translated as 'pipe'. Such pipes were played in pairs, held in the mouth of the player by a band passing over his head. *Tibiae pares*, of equal length, were evidently played in unison; those which were unequal were apparently tuned to play in harmony, one playing the melody, the other an accompaniment. It is generally thought that the longer (curved) one of lower pitch supplied the melody and the shorter (straight) one a kind of descant. It is not certain whether the longer pipe was held in the right or left hand: probably in the right. Usually the same combination was used throughout a play, but *The Self-Tormentor* starts with unequal pipes and changes to equal pipes at l. 410—perhaps to mark the lapse of time and change of mood in the play. The true arias are thought to have been mimed by the actor while sung by a professional singer standing by the *tibicen;* he is probably to be identified with the *cantor* who invites the audience to applaud at the end of each play.

Modern editors, following the manuscripts, divide the plays into five acts and each act into several scenes. The scene-divisions date from the earliest manuscripts and are no more than headings which list the characters on the stage whenever a new character enters, and sometimes when he leaves the stage as well. Neither scene—nor act—divisions were the work of the playwright, as Donatus and the early commentators knew; Donatus remarks that *The Eunuch* was played continuously for fear that bored members of the audience might leave their seats, and Plautus in his short preface to *Pseudolus* indicates that a long non-stop performance was about to begin. Elsewhere Donatus seems to think it desirable to divide a play by Terence into five acts, doubtless thinking that Horace's ruling (in *Ars Poetica*) that a play must have five acts to be successful should be applied to the *fabula palliata*. This was to become the rigid five-act law of Renaissance drama. Greek plays were of course divided into sections by choral passages, though the chorus declined from its position of dramatic importance. New Comedy seems generally to have been divided into five acts by non-dramatic choral interludes, marked in the MSS. only by the word 'chorus'. As Terence made no use of a chorus, it was left to the grammarians to decide how to divide up his plays into five acts — with often very unsatisfactory results.

There is something elusive about comedy which makes it difficult to define, and that part of the *Art of Poetry* is lost where Aristotle gave it full treatment. He left only a provisional distinction between tragedy and comedy, the one dealing with the fate of an individual and stirring the emotions, and the other depicting social groups and aiming at a sense of the ridiculous. The writer of comedy may point his finger at wrong ideas, as Shaw did, or at social pretensions and sentimental notions, like Congreve and Sheridan. He can be as brilliant as Wilde, as romantic as Synge, or as caustic as Maugham; his interest may be primarily in character, as Jonson in *Volpone,* or in intrigue of plot as in *Figaro.* But if he is not to write satire his handling of characters must be kindly, he must know people as they really are to avoid burlesque, and retain a sense of proportion to keep free of exaggeration and farce. He needs a natural optimism if his purpose is not sick comedy; as Meredith put it, 'To love comedy you must know the real world, and know men and women well enough not to expect too much of them, though you may still hope for good.' In his famous essay *On Books,* Montaigne wrote: 'As for Terence, who personifies the charm and grace of the Latin tongue, I am astounded by the lifelike way in which he depicts ways of thought and states of manners which are true of us today; at every turn our actions send me back to him.' This is still true, for, though the six plays are short and undeveloped by modern standards, each one expresses in a different way Terence's own most quoted line: *Homo sum: humani nil a me alienum puto.* 'I am human myself, so I think every human affair is my concern.'

F. H. Sandbach   (essay date 1977)

SOURCE: "Terence" in *The Comic Theatre of Greece and Rome,* W. W. Norton & Company, Inc., 1977, pp. 135-47.

[Sandbach is a well-known English classicist. In the following essay, he explores Terence's plays in the light of their Greek models, asserting that, while in some ways Terence did "enrich" Menander's comedies, his style has been "too equable, [lacking] the ebb and flow which gives life to the Greek poet's writing and enables him to mirror every kind of emotion."]

Publius Terentius Afer was believed by later Romans to have been born at Carthage, brought to Rome as a slave, and given a liberal education by his owner, Terentius Lucanus, who soon set him free. They may have had good reason for this belief, or the story may have grown from his name. Afer means a member of the dark native races of North Africa; an African would be a slave, and a manumitted slave took the middle name of his master. But the name After does not of necessity indicate a place of origin or a servile birth; it is attested as a Roman family name. If Terence did come from Africa, the excellence of his Latin is noteworthy but not unparalleled; Livius Andronicus, the father of Latin literature, was a Greek; Caecilius, the leading writer of comedy when Terence was young, is said to have been a slave from Gaul. Men who have won literary fame in languages not their own are not common in the modern world, but some can be named.

In his own lifetime Terence was charged with having received help in his dramatic work from friends who be-

Illustration from a 1493 French edition of The Mother-in-Law.

longed to the best families. In the prologue to his last play, **Adelphoe (Brothers)**, he wrote:

> Those ill-wishers say that men of famous families help him and constantly write along with him. They think this a violent aspersion, but he regards it as the height of praise if he is approved by men who have your unanimous approval, and that of the people too, men whose services everyone has on occasion used in war, in peace, in business.

This is typically elusive and evasive. Terence neither admits the charge nor denies it. If he had confessed it to be true, as it may well have been, it might have been thought that he had but a small share in the dramas which went under his name, that he was a mere front for some nobles; if it were false and he had declared it so, the great men involved might not have welcomed their loss of literary glory, however undeserved.

Later it became widely believed that these men included the younger Scipio and Gaius Laelius, and ignorance of the fact that he was not their junior allowed the scandalous suggestion that their motive was pederasty. This charge may be dismissed, but a literary association need not attract the same disbelief. Terence's plays were produced in the years 166 to 160, when Scipio was about eighteen to twenty-four years of age. It is by no means unlikely that the young aristocrat, interested in Greek culture, should have dabbled in play-writing, although he would not have wished to be thought a professional dramatist, or that Terence, for anything we know not very much older, should have accepted his collaboration and patronage.

It must be emphasised, however, that very probably ancient guess-work invented the connection with Scipio and his friends; no reliable evidence seems to have survived, since one Santra, probably a contemporary of Cicero's, suggested a trio of older personages, arguing that if Terence had needed help, he would not have gone to men younger than himself. Nevertheless the accepted guess may have been sound, it may have been supported by oral tradition, and it may also be significant that **Adelphoe,** the prologue to which mentions these alleged collaborators, was performed at the funeral games of L. Aemilius Paullus, and Scipio organised those.

In any case the support of powerful men, whoever they were, with literary interests, would make it easier to understand the nature of Terence's plays, which make few concessions to popular taste. When he began to write, less than thirty years had passed since the death of Plautus, and it would not seem that the majority of the audience had greatly changed. The first two performances of *Hecyra* (*The Mother-in-Law*) were failures, and the prologue to the third, spoken by the leading actor, Turpio, explains why:

> Once again I am bringing you **The Mother-in-Law,** a play I have never been allowed to act in silence; disaster has swamped it. Your appreciation, if it can be allied to our efforts, will put an end to that disaster. On the first occasion when I began to act it, the great renown of some boxers (expectation of a tight-rope walker was

thrown in), friends getting together, a clatter of conversation, women's penetrating voices, made me leave the theatre all too soon . . . I brought it on again: the first act was liked, and then there came a rumour that gladiators were on the programme; the people came flocking in, rioting and shouting, fighting for places: when that happened, I could not keep my place.

Yet, unlike Plautus, Terence made almost no attempt to put in something for everybody in his audience. His plays give the impression of being what spectators ought to like rather than what they would enjoy. Although there are more long lines spoken to the music of the pipe than in Menander, the songs in varied meters, which had diversified the plays of Plautus and seem still to have been used by Caecilius, are no longer present. There are no indecencies, no puns, no slanging-matches, no gloatings over corporal punishments. Instead there is concentrated action, moving steadily forward, and dialogue that is often rapid and generally needs unremitting attention if the thread is not to be lost. Terence's plays resemble those of Menander rather than those of Plautus. In fact four of his six are adaptations of Menandrean originals and the other two are taken from Apollodorus of Carystus, a less-gifted follower of the great Athenian.

Anyone who wished to argue that Terence was not overtaxing the capability of his public might appeal to the fact that Caecilius had already shown a similar preference for plays by Menander. But so far as we can see, he was not true to Menander's spirit. Aulus Gellius, a writer of miscellanies in the second century AD compares three pairs of passages by the two authors and exclaims at Caecilius' lack of taste. In one the Latin author introduces the old joke that the husband of a rich wife wishes her dead, and makes him imagine her boasting to her contemporaries and relatives that she has in her old age forced her husband to give up his young mistress, a thing *they* could not have done when they were still in their first youth; in another he causes the husband's friend to crack a coarse jest about her bad breath, wishing to raise a laugh, so Gellius says, more than to provide words suitable for the character. Gellius accuses him of descending to the level of the mime. Caecilius' changes were not merely a matter of adding familiar motifs that would appeal to the more simpleminded. In these passages, at least, he dealt freely with the Greek, with which he kept no more than a minimal necessary relation. He seems to have felt no commitment to maintain a colloquial style: other fragments show that he often made great use of alliteration, a device which must have had a popular appeal, much as early drama in England used rhyme, still found in parts of our pantomimes.

Terence on the other hand attempted to transfer Menander to the Roman stage without changes and additions obviously inconsistent with the qualities of the Greek. In his prologues he speaks of 'literary art' and tells the spectators that they have a chance of 'bringing distinction to the dramatic festival'. But his admiration for Menander did not make him rest content with mere translation. Virgil was to be credited with the epigram that it was easier to steal his club from Hercules than a line from Homer; but it was his ambition not only to borrow from Homer but to improve on him wherever he could. Similarly Terence may have been aware that he could not hope to reproduce all Menander's merits, but he could try in some ways to better him.

The most obvious of his changes, and one which must have immediately struck anyone who knew the original plays, was to abandon the convention of the expository prologue. He retained a prologue, but used it for quite different purposes. Spoken by an actor, perhaps always by the principal actor, in his own person, not that of the character he was to represent, it gives the name of the play, as had been done in some of the Plautine prologues; twice Menander is mentioned as the original author, but once it is said that there is no need to name either the dramatist or the man he is translating, since the majority of the audience will already know. Presumably the minority, if it was a minority, did not care. But the greater part of the prologue is given over to a defence of Terence's use of his originals and to counter-attacks on a critic, an older writer of comedies; he is not named, but can be identified as one Luscius from Lanuvium.

An earlier move towards making the prologue a place for literary criticism has been seen in a fragment from some Greek author in which the god Dionysus complains of long-winded deities who set out all the facts, which the spectators fail to take in. He then proceeds to what promises to be a detailed exposition of the background to his play; the contrast between his theory and his practice is amusing. But it was Terence who took the decisive step of separating the prologue from the play and expressing in it seriously meant views on dramatic methods. This was to have long-lasting effects in the European theatre. One may compare the prologues to Ben Jonson's *Volpone* or *Every Man in His Humour.* Even when there is nothing more than mere *captatio benevolentiae,* as in Dekker's *Shoemaker's Holiday,* or witty trifling, as in Goldsmith's *She Stoops to Conquer,* a line of descent goes back to Terence, who established this form of independent introduction.

In the prologue to *Andria* (*A Woman from Andros*), which is based on Menander's play of the same title, he says that he had been attacked by his older rival for transferring to it matter from Menander's *Perinthia* (*A Woman from Perinthos*); his critics maintain that plays should not be 'spoiled' or 'adulterated'. He replies that he has the precedent of Naevius, Plautus and Ennius, whose 'negligence' he prefers to rival rather than the 'obscure carefulness' of the critics. It seems that he charges them with practising a fidelity to their models of which the public, who were not students of Greek drama, could not be aware, while they accuse him of spoiling plays by introducing foreign matter. He defends himself by declaring that his predecessors had also adulterated their plays.

A play may be 'adulterated' in various ways; he had done it in a particular manner, that of blending parts of two different comedies to make a new one. [In a footnote, the critic adds, "Some modern scholars use the word for adulteration, *contaminatio,* in this restricted sense, as a technical term."] So far as *Andria* is concerned, the fourth-century scholar Donatus was unable to identify much borrowing

from *Perinthia,* but in two other plays also, *Eunuchus* and *Adelphoe,* Terence adopted this procedure of blending two originals, as their prologues explain. Its effects are clearly visible in both but they are easier to understand in the latter. In Menander's play the young hero had before it opened abducted a girl from a slave-trader on behalf of his brother, who loved her. Terence found in a play by Diphilus a lively scene of just such an abduction, which Plautus in his adaptation had for some reason omitted. He decided to enliven his play by using this scene, translated (so he unconvincingly alleges) word for word, to represent by stage-action what was only narrated in Menander.

This involved him in various difficulties. First, Diphilus' scene was enacted outside the slave-trader's house at the moment of the theft; his efforts to prevent it very naturally led to violence. In the play of Menander, and therefore in that of Terence, the slaver's lodging was not represented on the stage, so the scene had to be transferred to the street outside the house of the young man, whose raiding party he had followed. This necessitated some alterations of wording, but even so the exchanges remain more suitable to the earlier occasion. Secondly, Terence was obliged to introduce this scene after the opening monologue, which leads into a duologue where the young men's father indignantly reports that the theft has become the talk of the town. Clearly he cannot have learned this before the son had had time to bring the girl home; there is an absurdity in the time-sequence, which had to be ignored.

Thirdly, by causing the slaver to follow on the heels of the raiding party, Terence brings him to the young man's house before he is needed there by the plot of Menander's play, and he has to stand about, awkwardly forgotten, during scenes of explanation between the two brothers. There is perhaps a fourth point. The scene taken from Diphilus ends with an assertion by the young man that the girl is really a free woman and no slave. Nothing more is heard of this, and it is not clear whether, Terence, unwilling to abandon a fine climax, left a loose end, or whether he believed it would be understood that the claim was a false one and no more than a move to embarrass her owner.

This will serve to illustrate the difficulties which may beset the transference of a scene from one play to another. Nevertheless at one time many scholars believed that it had been extensively practised by Plautus. He was even supposed to have fused whole plays together, to make one Latin play out of two Greek. Today some hold that he cannot be proved ever to have resorted to either device. Certainly he 'adulterated' his originals by adding matter of his own invention; this kind of adulteration was not that for which Terence was reprehended, and Terence may be suspected of disingenuously sheltering behind him. Yet one need not deny that Plautus may well have found inspiration for some of his supplements in plays other than the one he was at the moment adapting, even if what he acquired was a suggestion rather than a model to be translated.

Terence's reasons for giving up the expository prologue are unknown, and no more can be done than speculate about them. Perhaps he found it unrealistic to make a character unashamedly explain the opening situation to the audience. But that is not altogether convincing, since in *Adelphoe,* his last play, much of the exposition is contained in a long opening monologue composed as an address to the audience, not as a piece of reflection; and he shows no objection to narrative monologues in the body of his plays. Perhaps he thought that more was to be gained by allowing the spectators to share the characters' surprise as facts were brought to light than by giving them a superior comprehensive view from the first. Either way of writing is defensible; each of the two forms of drama brings its own gains and losses. But it is to be noticed that the Terentian method of construction has predominated in the theatre ever since his day.

It is however one thing to write an original play in this manner, another to convert a drama written in the other way to the new fashion. In so far as an expository prologue contained information about the background necessary to make the characters' actions intelligible, this had to be conveyed, when the prologue was dropped, to the audience in some other way. On the whole Terence solved the problem not unskillfuly; he succeeded in introducing explanations where they were needed.

Terence had a way with personal names that may be seen as significant of his relation to his models. Most are known from Greek New Comedy, and almost all are suitable for use over and over again. In fact Terence duplicated even more than Menander had done; in his six plays there are three old men called Chremes, three hetairai called Bacchis, three married women called Sostrata. Yet he seems regularly to have replaced the name in the Greek original by a new one. Thus he at once declared his adherence to Greek dramatic methods and his own originality in handling his models.

A complete picture of the changes he made is impossible because so little detail is known of the Greek plays he adapted. A very little is given by Donatus and something can be deduced from study of his plays' structure and knowledge of Menander's methods of writing. But there are several cases where his object can be divined; it was to enrich the original material by additions that were Greek in spirit, sometimes taken from a Greek play, but likely to have a popular appeal. It has been seen how the *Adelphoe* gained a scene of lively action and some rough-and-tumble; let us consider the other two Menandrean dramas to which additions are certain.

Andria has a young man, Pamphilus, who is in love with a poor unprotected girl, Glycerium, but whom his father wishes to marry a neighbour's daughter, Philumena. He consents to this match, believing there to be an obstacle which will prevent it. Terence added a motif, perhaps of his own invention, perhaps taken from some other play, in the shape of a youth who is Pamphilus' friend and who loves Philumena. His jealousy is an easily understood emotion and the extra complication for Pamphilus provides the spectators with a further source of interest. This is a more likely way to explain the addition than Donatus' suggestion that it was done to avoid disappointment for Philumena (who never appears on the stage) when Glycerium turns out to be another daughter of the neighbour and so an eligible bride for Pamphilus.

The most pervasive additions are those made to *Eunuchus,* where there have been introduced the figures of Thraso and Gnatho, a soldier and his parasite, taken on Terence's own admission from *Kolax,* another play by Menander, which had a totally different plot. Thraso is made the rival of a rich young man, Phaedria, for a courtesan, Thais, and replaces some other rival, perhaps a less colourful soldier, perhaps a merchant, in Menander's *Eunuchos.* But Gnatho makes an additional character, except inasmuch as at his first entrance he replaces a slave who brought the 'heroine' to Thais' house as a gift from the rival. His entrance monologue, describing his technique of flattery, is very amusing, but the entertainment is bought at the expense of letting his charge stand about in the street with nothing to do while he delivers it.

A second amusing scene is provided by the sixty lines with which Thraso makes his first entrance. More than half of this has no connection with the plot of *Eunuchus,* but exemplifies his tasteless boasting, to which he is egged on by the malicious Gnatho, whose irony he is too stupid to understand. This is certainly based on material taken from *Kolax,* although it cannot be determined how closely that play was followed. Although the latter part of the scene continues the same manner and characterisation, it is essential to the plot: Thraso boorishly invites Thais to dinner and Gnatho suggests to him a method of making her jealous which the audience will know to be certain to cause her great embarrassment; Gnatho is clever enough to guess that it will be very unwelcome to her. This must be Terence's composition, even if he was able to find some material for it in Menander's plays.

In the following passage Phaedria's slave brings Thais his master's gift of a slave-girl and a eunuch. Unknown to Phaedria, his younger brother has substituted himself disguised for the eunuch. Terence has made changes here, necessitated by the removal of the rival of Menander's *Eunuchos,* whose place is taken by Thraso and Gnatho. Their extent is not to be determined, but one exchange is undoubtedly based on *Kolax:* Gnatho suddenly bursts out laughing, and when asked why, replies that he had just thought of the soldier's quip at the expense of a man from Rhodes; this had been mentioned in the earlier part of the previous scene, and was an adaptation of a joke preserved in a fragment of that play.

Thraso and Gnatho next appear in the 'siege-scene', where an abortive move is made to storm Thais' house in order to recover the soldier's gift to her. This again is not only amusing, as the parasite's malice and the soldier's cowardice interact, but also has lively action on the stage, as the 'troops', who consist of four slaves, are disposed. Some of the material may be taken from *Kolax;* that is no more than a guess, but it is certain that this scene is a lively replacement of some less noisy attempt at recovery in Menander's *Eunuchos.*

The two characters from *Kolax* are seen again at the end of the play. Gnatho arranges a pact between Phaedria and the soldier that they should share Thais' favours; it will be an effect of this that it will be the soldier who pays. Phaedria agrees moreover that Gnatho should transfer to his patronage. Although the matter is disputed, I have no doubt that those are right who see here a Terentian ending. In the earlier part of the play Phaedria has been portrayed as intensely jealous of Thraso, and Thais has promised to abandon the soldier so soon as she has secured the 'heroine', whom she hopes to restore to her parents. The pact is brutally inconsistent with this relation between them; moreover it utterly disregards the position of Thais. She is an independent and good-hearted courtesan, sincerely concerned to reunite the girl with her family, although not without self-interest, since she hopes that in their gratitude they will take her under their protection; this protection she has now attained. It is absurd that she should be disposed of behind her back, as if she were a slave, and condemned to the embraces of the ridiculous soldier, in order that Phaedria should enjoy her for nothing. It is a minor absurdity that he should saddle himself with the support of the dangerous Gnatho.

Very possibly this ending was taken from *Kolax,* where Thraso's rival in love was, unlike Phaedria, an impecunious young man, and the object of their attentions a slave, whose inclinations it may not have been necessary to consult. Terence's belief that the conclusion he gave to his ***Eunuchus*** would be welcomed by the Roman audience, who would enjoy its ingenuity, the solider's foolish acceptance of a bad bargain, and the young man's combination of success with economy, is based on a difference between Greek and Roman society. In Terence's time at least the *meretrix* had an opprobrious name, and was despised and tolerated as a necessary evil; the Greek hetaira must not be sentimentalised, but by her name she was 'a companion' and she was accepted as a useful member of the community. The best kind of hetaira, of which Thais is one, could be a woman of some wealth, an independent mind and self-respect. This was something not understood at Rome.

Another play the end of which some think Terence adapted in an attempt to meet Roman taste is ***Adelphoe;*** I believe them to be right. The theme is that of a contrast between two methods of bringing up a son, the one permissive, the other restrictive. Neither proves to be entirely successful but Micio, the father who practises the former method, is, until the last act, presented in a favourable light as generous, realistic and humane; when he has occasion to give his son an understanding reproof, the young man accepts it and reflects that their relation is more like that of brothers or friends than that usual between father and son, and determines to do nothing that would be against his wishes. The other father, his brother, who is harsh and without joy in life, finds himself in ridiculous situations and is at a loss when faced with a moral problem over which Micio has no hesitation: although it is not the match he would have chosen, he never doubts that his son should marry the poor girl whom he loves and who has borne him a child.

In the last act this martinet declares in a monologue that he sees that indulgence is the way to win popularity and that he will adopt that course for the brief spell of life that is left him. He proceeds in some amusing scenes to practise a new-found affability and generosity, not at his own expense but at that of his brother, whom he provides with a widow as a wife. In Terence's play the permissive parent

feebly resists, but is so accustomed to letting people have their way that he has to accept this bride. Donatus remarks that in Menander he raised no objection to the marriage, and if he did not resist this, the heaviest of all the demands made on him, it is unlikely that he made any difficulties about any of the others, none of which are unreasonable. In Terence his ineffective objections are designed to show a lack of will.

Finally his brother says that the object of his apparent change of character was to show that the other's popularity did not depend on what was right and good and a true way of life, but on complaisance and indulgence. He offers himself as one with the knowledge to reprehend, correct, and where suitable support the young; thereupon the permissively educated son declares that he will accept his guidance. Although Molière, Lessing and Goethe all felt that this ending was wrong, orthodoxy interprets it as supporting the view that the right form of education is a mean between the strict and the permissive. However much this may appeal to those who subscribe to that view, I do not believe that this was the play's intended message. The reason for the martinet's change of front must be given by the monologue; it was to win popularity. It is a dramatic necessity that the speaker of a monologue utters what he believes to be the truth. What he here says is quite inconsistent with putting on an act for a short time with the intention of exposing the weakness of his brother's way of life. It follows that Terence has altered the balance of the end of the play, to bring down the scales on the side of the man whose stern hard-working parsimonious austerity accorded more with Roman ideals than did his easy-going life-enjoying brother.

Other ways in which Terence enriched Menander were comparatively superficial. In ***Eunuchus*** the stage was made fuller by dividing a single part into two characters, Pythias and Dorias [the critic adds in a footnote, "This is not universally accepted."], and in other plays a character is sometimes kept on after the point at which he must have left in the Greek. Breaking of the three-actor rule together with the fact that he takes no substantial part in the second scene is the evidence for this change. Sometimes his continued presence allows him to overhear a monologue by someone else, a situation which Terence not infrequently contrives.

He also tried to reduce the number of non-speakers on the stage. Slaves, who in a Greek play would be given orders which they carried out in silence, are by him allowed a line or two. It is hard to say whether the motive was realism or simply a desire to make the scene more lively. He has been credited with realism, but on insufficient grounds. If, as Donatus seems to have believed but many modern scholars deny, he introduced Antipho into ***Eunuchus*** to provide a hearer for the young man's account of the rape he had perpetrated in his disguise as a eunuch, the reason was not a dislike on principle of monologues, which are of frequent occurrence. Perhaps he felt it to be unsuitable for the transgressor to confide directly to the audience what many of them must regard as a crime.

Nowhere can the words of Terence be compared with any extended passage of a Greek model; this prevents appreciation of the changes he made in the details of language. He seems to have broken speeches up, made the exchanges more rapid and multiplied interjections. What can be done is to observe how he differs from Plautus and even Caecilius.

Plautus exploited the natural genius of Latin for assonance, alliteration and full-blown, almost tautological, expression. Terence set to work with remarkable success to reproduce the merits of Menander's style, its simplicity, flexibility and concision, although Latin was an inadequate instrument for this purpose, having a limited vocabulary, if vulgar words were excluded, and a restricted ability to express nuances. Terence was praised by Julius Caesar as a 'lover of pure speech'. 'Pure speech' was that practised by the conventional educated upper classes, and may have been the nearest equivalent to Menander's standard in Greek. Terence used this kind of Latin with great skill, making next to no use of foreign words, and attaining speed by his brevity. Not only did he avoid repetitiousness, he often truncated sentences by leaving out a verb or a subject which could be understood, or could even reduce them to a single word.

The result is admirable and Caesar could compare him with Menander; but he called him a 'Menander halved', and regretted that he lacked 'power' or 'force' (*uis*), and spoke of his 'gentle' writings. What this means is perhaps that his writing is too equable, it lacks the ebb and flow which gives life to the Greek poet's writing and enables him to mirror every kind of emotion.

Sander M. Goldberg   (essay date 1982-83)

SOURCE: "Terence and the Death of Comedy," *Comparative Drama*, Vol. 16, No. 4, Winter 1982-83, pp. 312-24.

[*Goldberg is the author of several articles on Terence and a monograph,* Understanding Terence *(1986). In the following essay, he explores Terence's role in the demise of Roman comedy, arguing that "Terence had made it too alien to be taken seriously at Rome."*]

The creative age of Roman comedy died with a man named Turpilius in 103 B.C. That was actually half a century after the death of Terence, the last great writer of stage comedy at Rome, and nearly a whole century before Latin literature reached maturity in the time of Augustus. The golden age of Roman comedy is thus quite clearly divorced from the golden age of Roman literature itself, but something more than a minor literary genre died with Turpilius. The very interest in stage comedy that had survived the change in conditions from Aristophanes to Menander and the change in culture from Greece to Rome died with a whimper late in the second century B.C. No further comedy of literary stature was written in antiquity, and the ancient tradition lay dormant until revived by the Italian humanists of our own fourteenth century. What happened? Why did the Romans lose interest in stage comedy? The death of a genre is as common an occurrence in the history of literature as it is complex, and there can be no simple answer to such a question. Yet some of the responsibility must lie with Terence, the author who brought to Roman comedy both a peak of sophistication

and an end of creative vitality. What was it about his achievement that brought the development of ancient comedy to a halt?

Since all Roman drama, both tragic and comic, evolved from Greek forms, it may prove helpful to begin with the place of drama in Athenian culture. The constant, creative re-working of old myths that gave fifth-century tragedy its intellectual tension and vitality established drama as a legitimate medium for serious thought, and tragedy's profound appeal enriched the substance of Athenian comedy even as the comic poets parodied its mannerisms. The Old Comedy of Aristophanes took not only such useful stage devices as narrative soliloquies and *ex machina* endings from tragedy, but also a sense of urgency that led to the building of comic fantasies around matters of cultural, political, or intellectual substance. The so-called New Comedy of the following century represented the culmination of dramatic development at Athens and was thus heir to both the technical and intellectual traditions of tragedy and comedy. Menander, the best known but long-lost master of New Comedy, has recently been restored to us by the minor miracle of papyrology, and it is now plain that his domestic comedies, although certainly not pointed fantasies in the old style, are not simply trivial restatements of established *topoi* either. They too have a respectable intellectual base, using the romantic plots of lost children and obstructed marriages to explore legitimate problems of social and family relationships. In such plays as *The Shorn Girl (Perikeiromene)* and *The Hated Man (Misoumenos)* Menander created soldiers who lose their traditional swagger and confront genuine problems of integration into civilian society. *The Arbitrants (Epitrepontes)* deals with a young husband in agony over his wife's apparent infidelity who finds that her fault is no more than his own. Young Charisios was himself the pre-nuptial rapist, and he discovers his own moral failing in an emotional climax that, like Aristotle's best kind of tragic plot, combines a sudden realization with an abrupt reversal in the direction of the play's action.

Such comedies have many serious moments, and to signal them Menander's characters frequently strike a tragic pose or speak in tragic style, but the dramatist's purpose is not parody. Menander aims instead to borrow some of tragedy's seriousness by assuming its manner. A play called *The Man from Sikyon (Sikyonios)*, for example, has a messenger's speech that shares the function and echoes the language of a similar speech in Euripides' *Orestes* without ridiculing the tragic prototype. Meter and staging combine for a different kind of tragic effect in *Dyskolos* when Knemon, the misanthropic grouch of the title, is brought out of his house after nearly drowning in a well. His rescue leads him to renounce the misanthropy that had isolated him from society and prevented the marriage of his daughter, and it is crucial to the play's success that we take this scene of recantation seriously. If we do not listen carefully to Knemon's words and perceive both the honesty and the difficulty of his apology, the subsequent action of the play makes little sense. We must appreciate both the depth and the limitations of the change that has come over him. Menander signals the importance of this moment by structuring his scene to recall similar moments in tragedy. After the disaster within, Knemon appears in tableau, wheeled out like Sophocles' Ajax and Euripides' Heracles, and as often happens in tragedy, the meter changes to trochaic tetrameters to mark the coming climax. These are the only devices required to suggest seriousness to an audience steeped in the tragic tradition and attuned to its nuances. Menander draws upon established classics, adding something old and grand to something light and new.

Things were a little different at Rome, though tragedy and comedy also developed side by side and the tragedians' skill should not be underestimated. Crowds shouted in excitement when Pylades tried to sacrifice himself for his friend in Pacuvius' tragedy *Orestes Enslaved (Dulorestes)*. When the ghost of Deiphilus roused his sleeping mother to avenge his murder in *Iliona*, his words reduced audiences to tears. Scenes of madness seem to have been especially popular. Pacuvius, in an unidentified play, showed Orestes beset by the Furies as he left the sanctuary of Apollo. A brilliant scene in Ennius' *Alexander* portrays Cassandra's prophetic madness, and in *Alcmeo* the Furies appear to Alcmaeon after he has murdered his mother, Eriphyle.

> Come! Come! They are here. They seek me.
> Bring me aid. Drive the plague from me,
> this flameful force that tortures me.
> Darkly dressed, with fire they come.
> They stand about with glowing torches.

Scenes of this kind no doubt inspire Plautus' Menaechmus II as he routs the poor father-in-law of Epidamnus with feigned madness (*Men.* 826-88). The young man claims to hear Bacchus and then Apollo urging him to violence. Then he sees a chariot before him, mounts, and prepares a journey to perdition. His speech is a tumble of vivid, sequential images, and his actions are as lively as those of the truly possessed heros from the Roman tragic stage. Plautus recognized the effectiveness of the tragic style and embraced it with enthusiasm. Menaechmus' vision is comic rather than tragic largely because it is so incongruous.

Incongruity is central to the effect of all Plautus' tragic echoes, whether they parody specific tragic postures or simply elevate the tone at moments of high emotion. Plautus always plays on the outward form of tragedy, borrowing its manner for a momentary effect. He does this brilliantly, but nowhere is tragedy more than a source of humor for him. His echoes are never very subtle and never integral to a play's meaning in the way that Knemon's tragic pose shapes our understanding of *Dyskolos*. When Plautus plays light off against serious, his aim is invariably to make a funny scene still funnier. The reasons for this are both technical and intellectual.

Roman tragedy had its own distinct vocabulary and its own type-scenes, but the underlying structure of dramatic verse and the stock of technical devices were the same for the two genres. They shared the same stage apparatus from the beginning. There were no equivalents of Porson's bridge and no clearly felt norms of resolution and caesura to distinguish the spoken meters, nor can we identify organic differences between tragic and comic lyrics. Ennius'

favorite lyric meters in his tragedies were the same anapests, bacchiacs, and cretics that Plautus favored. Nor did the Latin language offer dramatists the dialectical variation that enriches and distinguishes Greek tragic diction. The difference in sound between the two dramatic styles was largely on the surface. This made the mannerisms and melodrama of Roman tragedy easy for comic dramatists to incorporate as parody, but the very similarity of the tragic and comic styles made more subtle allusions difficult to achieve.

For the most part, of course, this hardly mattered. Menandrean comedy needed the subtle effects of tragic echoes because it was assuming some of tragedy's seriousness. It represented nearly two centuries of dramatic development and played before audiences steeped in its traditions. Roman comedy did not shoulder a similar burden. Its sophistication was largely technical, the ability to have characters speak and act effectively on the stage, and it achieved this technical virtuosity in two generations by developing those elements of Greek New Comedy best suited to broad musical theater. The most elaborate plots of intrigue and recognition, the most clever slaves, most memorable villains, and most brilliant lyrics that survive are thus products of this Roman half of the tradition. Yet the very success of the comic formula posed a problem for any later dramatist who sought a return to New Comedy's more serious side.

P. Terentius Afer (Terence) was such a dramatist. He was perhaps two generations younger than Plautus. He came to Rome not as an enterprising Italian provincial on the make, but as a foreigner, a slave in a senatorial household, and his interest in theater proved to be a good deal more literary than Plautus' had been. Plautus, like Shakespeare and Molière after him, was a practical man of the theater, an actor as well as a playwright, who not only was conscious of but clearly enjoyed his role as a popular entertainer. Terence was more bookish, more conscious of the literary tradition, and perhaps less concerned with the commercial tradition of Roman comedy. Whereas Plautus and such dramatists as Naevius and Caecilius had deliberately broadened the appeal of Greek New Comedy by expanding its musical element and augmenting the place of slapstick and foolishness in its characters and plots, Terence deliberately chose models from among the most sedate of the Greek authors and sought to reproduce their effects. Menander was apparently his favorite model, but when it came to bringing Menander's kind of seriousness to the Roman stage, Terence could not actually follow his model very closely. The tragic echoes that worked so well for Menander could not work equally well for Terence. His audiences were not attuned to hear them. Roman audiences were not uncouth and not inexperienced, but they did come to the theater with a limited range of experience and with limited expectations. Roman tragedy did not provide Terence with the wealth of associations and with the model for serious thought in drama that Attic tragedy had offered Menander. He nevertheless persisted in the effort to write "serious" plays in the sense that Menander's plays plays are serious: the dramatic action challenges the values and self-concepts of the characters and draw us into their dilemmas through echoes of our own experience.

This was something new to Roman comedy. Though such Plautine plays as *Amphitruo* and *Captivi* may touch on important social issues, they remain essentially plays about particular, rather absurd characters caught up in their own delightfully improbable situations. Terence sought to keep a more generalized seriousness at the center of his plays, but to preserve this Greek type of focus while producing plays successfully at Rome necessitated changes in the Greek models. Favorite Greek techniques for developing serious themes had the wrong connotations or no connotations at all. Menander's tricks of meter and staging to echo tragic seriousness without trace of parody had no immediate Roman equivalents. Simple translation of Menander's subtleties would have been entirely without significance to Roman audiences or, if recognized at all, would have been interpreted as signals of humor rather than of dramatic intensity. Terence had to strive for a serious tone analogous to, but not identical with Menander's tone. He needed to build on the special strengths of his own Roman tradition, and this is what he consistently did.

In one way or another, each of Terence's six plays shows the signs of a Greek play tailored to the exigencies of the Roman stage, but our best course is probably to look at a single play in some detail to see how Terence accommodates its serious theme to Roman requirements. *Adelphoe (The Brothers)* was Terence's last play and probably his most ambitious one. It involves two sets of brothers, Micio and Demea and Demea's two sons, Aeschinus and Ctesipho. Aeschinus has been raised since infancy by his bachelor uncle Micio and has assumed Micio's urbane, easy-going manner. Demea, a stern and tight-fisted farmer, has sought to raise Ctesipho to be like himself. Neither father gets quite what he expects. Ctesipho, contrary to Demea's principles, falls in love with a slave girl, and Aeschinus, despite Micio's cheerful indulgence, fears to admit that he has gotten a free-born but penniless girl pregnant. He has also stolen Ctesipho's slave girl from her pimp to make a present of her to his brother. In the course of the play both Micio and Demea pay the price of their own self-righteous confidence. Micio learns the disadvantages of leniency, and Demea learns its benefits. Ctesipho is bullied by both father and brother, and Aeschinus, while getting his own girl, learns to respect his natural father. This effort to portray complex relationships, to load the play with difficult and serious questions of right conduct, is what makes it so ambitious, and some have argued that Terence does not really pull it off. His plot lurches now and then as it strains to show the limitations of both Micio and Demea, and we are never completely sure which—if any—characters deserve our sympathy. This complexity is not all Terence's doing. *Adelphoe* is based on a play by Menander, and we can be fairly sure that the Greek original dealt seriously with the nature of father-son relationships, for this is a recurring theme in Menander's extant work. The subject matter of *Adelphoe* is therefore Menander's subject, but Terence has made important changes that affect the impression the play makes on the stage. The changes themselves are easy to identify. The real question is why Terence made them.

The play opens with a worried Micio fretting over the whereabouts of Aeschinus. Demea then appears to tell him that Aeschinus has abducted a slave girl, and we promptly see the young man in action. Micio and Demea leave the stage. Aeschinus enters accompanied by his slave, the girl, and the pimp Sannio, who is screaming for the return of his stolen property. The pimp is mocked, beaten, and eventually sent packing with neither the girl nor her full market value in coin. Terence tells us in his prologue that he has introduced this scene of bullying the pimp into his Menandrean model from a different play by the quite different Greek dramatist Diphilus. It is a fast-moving bit of slapstick that happens to create certain difficulties for the play's proper sequence of events, but Terence pays the structural price because it does more than simply enliven a moralistic play with broad action. Micio's initial worry was accompanied by a confident statement of his permissive views on child-raising. This scene with the pimp is our first look at his son, and Aeschinus' haughty and violent manner immediately suggests a flaw in that enlightened philosophy. Terence deliberately excludes from his early exposition any mention of the fact that Aeschinus is acting for his brother. We are forced to confront his violence as Micio and Demea do, without any knowledge to excuse or soften it, and we come away with the picture not of a decent young man working unselfishly in his brother's interest, but of an arrogant bully eager to display his power at any cost. Ctesipho, weakest of the four brothers, then simply accepts what is offered. By the play's end, Micio too, despite his sophistication and glib self-confidence, is also forced to accept what is offered. His very success at winning the affection of the two boys is the basis of his eventual downfall. Demea comes to see the practical advantages of permissiveness and contrives a way to indulge his sons at his brother's expense. He announces a change of heart, promptly purchases the boy's admiration, and forces Micio to pay the bills. Micio is compelled to part with money, slaves, and finally his prized bachelor life. The play ends with Demea and Aeschinus forcing Micio to take a wife, and this is the second major change Terence has made in his Greek original. Menander's Micio also married, but according to the fourth-century commentator Aelius Donatus, "in Menander's play the old man did not make trouble about the marriage." Why does Terence make *this* change? To bring the play's end in line with its beginning. He wants to make it quite clear that Micio is being forced to act against his will. The suave old man who began the play as the fretting victim of his son Aeschinus ends it as the victim of his brother Demea.

Not many moderns have liked this ending. Since the time of Lessing, critics arrested by Micio's initial speech on child-raising have sought to interpret the play as a conflict not between Micio and Demea themselves, but between their opposing philosophies of education. While both Demea and his ideas are too crusty to be loved, the debonair Micio's call for trust between father and son and his belief in a relationship based on friendship *(amicitia)* rather than authority *(imperium)* are easily admired. His impatience and ridicule of the harsh Demea are easily shared. Micio often sounds like the play's hero, yet Terence's ending is surely a victory for Demea. Micio loses money, his bachelorhood, and—much the most important—his son. Aeschinus comes away with new respect for his natural father. He calls Demea *pater* in the play's last few lines and for the first time willingly does what he is told. Those who have listened too hard to Micio—and liked too much what they have heard—find this finale surprising and perplexing. Thus Lessing, whose moralistic taste in comedy made him a careful listener of dramatic speech, was very troubled by the ending of *Adelphoe*. "Micio," he wrote in 1768, "has shown himself to be so amiable, so full of good sense, with so much knowledge of the world, that this final extravagance of his is contrary to all probability and must inevitably offend the more refined spectator." Lessing was himself a practical man of the theater and no mean critic of ancient literature. Why was Terence willing to risk offending so sensitive a critic? Why does he seem to lead us in one direction only to push us suddenly off in another? The answers lie not so much in Terence as in ourselves, or rather in our own response to *Adelphoe* as opposed to the response of a Roman audience. We need to recognize how Terence tailored his play to the Roman idea of theater and to Roman techniques for putting meaning into dramatic action.

We bring to the theater a curious blend of ancient Greek and distinctly modern values. Like the Greeks, we enjoy the rhetoric of drama. We may be more willing than they to put decisive action on the stage itself, but we preserve their practice of interpreting what characters do in terms of what they say. We want action to have meaning, and we look for that meaning in speech. Without its soliloquies, a tragedy like *Macbeth* would strike us as a mean and sordid little melodrama. Without their wit, neither Congreve nor Sheridan would have much claim to our attention. If Shavian characters could not declaim, their actions would be inexplicable. Roman audiences saw the relative merits of speech and action differently. They perceived not only scenes, but whole plays in terms of movement. The significant moments of a Roman play are most likely to be moments of intense action: the priestess Cassandra whirling across the stage in prophetic frenzy, the ghost of Deiphilus demanding revenge, the parasite Curculio elbowing aside an imaginary crowd, the pimp Ballio marshalling his girls and sending them off to market. The characters of Plautus, and in this he is typically Roman, are always doing things. They sing, dance, meet and flee from each other, get into fights and make love. They certainly talk a great deal, but never standing still. The Roman taste for melodrama and love of colorful stage business meant that audiences sought a play's meaning less in what the characters said than in what they did.

Plautus was happy to oblige that taste, and in adapting the comparatively loquacious comedy of Menander to Roman conditions, Terence himself could not afford to forget it. Nor did he. His changes in the Greek *Adelphoe* are all designed to intensify events on the stage and to create not a conflict of ideas as developed by speech, but a conflict of personalities as developed by action. His two sets of brothers are distinguished not by the severity or leniency they profess in speech, but by the strength or weakness they demonstrate through action. The older brothers Demea and Aeschinus are strong and active. Micio is their victim from the beginning and pays the price of his weakness. He can, and he does, talk circles around his brother,

but ultimately his words are no match for his brother's deeds. As revealed by the plot, Micio's "philosophy" consists not of guiding Aeschinus but of yielding to him, and not a single action of *Adelphoe* actually justifies his principles. Yet when Demea suddenly discovers the advantages of leniency, the result is quite different because he is an active character. He alters the play's direction by announcing not a new set of principles but a new course of action. He seizes the initiative and brings both his brother and his sons to heel. *Adelphoe* rewards action, mocks passivity, and may in the process lead us to weigh our own principles against our own practices.

Terence's play creates distinct individuals whose foibles and frustrations, unexpected failures, and sudden successes mirror the experiences of all parents and all children. We are not ourselves quite as absolute as Micio and Demea, not quite as expensively troublesome as Aeschinus and Ctesipho, and not very likely to find ourselves in quite their predicaments, but their difficulties as children, siblings, and parents are at least analogous to our own experiences in those same social roles. New Comedy's ability to develop stylized situations that create sympathetic resonances in its audiences lies at the root of its perennial appeal. This is the mimetic power that had led the Alexandrian critic Aristophanes of Byzantion to inquire of Menander and Life which had imitated the other, and Terence has worked hard to develop a similar strength. He centers his play squarely on the domestic concerns of its plot, brings its family relationships to the fore, and in the process encourages us to read our own concerns into those of his characters. *Adelphoe* as a play has no simple ending because the questions it raises about family life itself have no simple answers. Terence's art, too, is truly mimetic. He has put on the stage what Thornton Wilder was to call "the generalized occasion." He has brought Menander's kind of seriousness to Roman drama, but consider the cost.

Menander had generalized his dramatic occasions largely by putting emphasis on character. His men and women are challenged by the stage events, forced to respond to them, and eventually change and grow as a result of them. The double tradition of Athenian comedy and tragedy made available a host of devices—prologues, monologues, asides, tragic echoes, carefully wrought contrasts between serious and light elements—by which Menander expanded New Comedy's range and distracted his audiences from the harsh and formalized realities of its plots. His plays develop new, sometimes unexpected meanings. The love plot of *Dyskolos,* a simple story of boy meets girl when read in synopsis, becomes a portrait of misanthropy and its consequences as developed on the stage. The romance of *The Woman of Samos* moves from the brutal consequences of sexual jealousy to a sensitive study of trust and obligation. The sordid domestic tension of *The Arbitrants* forms the background for an exploration of moral affectation. The message in each case is neither sordid nor mean, and in each case Menander has taken care to create pleasant, often quite admirable characters. The urbane Sostratos of *Dyskolos* is simple but sweet. His rustic counterpart Gorgias commands respect. Old Demeas of *The Woman of Samos* impresses us with his powers of self-criticism, and

Charisios of *The Arbitrants* eventually faces up to the shallowness of his moral Posturing. We learn to like these characters, and because we like them we accept and even become engrossed in their situations. Thus the basic structures of Menander's comedy, though artificial, never make us uncomfortable.

What do we find in Terence's **Adelphoe?** Where Menander's view of his characters was affectionate, Terence's view is necessarily ironic. By making stage action the primary vehicle for meaning, he reveals the conventional roles and situations of New Comedy for what they are. He never lets us forget that his dramatic material is built upon the self-indulgence, obtuseness, and moral failings of his characters. We may sympathize with the problems of **Adelphoe,** but not with its characters. We tolerate Micio's fall precisely because we have been taught to distrust him. Demea is no more likable in triumph than he was in defeat. The willful, spoiled Aeschinus enjoys the fruits of his misdeeds without ever facing the fact that they *were* misdeeds. Ctesipho escapes our moral scrutiny only because his weak personality largely escapes our notice. What has happened to the wry but engaging humanity of the Greek models?

The Romans themselves never forgot that their *comoedia palliata* was essentially a foreign art form. Though the characters of Plautus and Terence spoke colloquial Latin, they remained stock figures of the Greek stage acting in Greek settings and wearing Greek dress. Menander's characters reflected his own people; there was no such immediacy for Roman audiences. Plautus deliberately juxtaposed the different *mores* of Greece and Rome to create a delightfully fantastic comedy from the resulting incongruities. He made the very Greekness of his genre a subject of fun, and in the process put considerable distance between his characters and his audience. Terence's attempt to capture the seriousness of Greek models created a comedy that was less fantastic, but no less alien to his audience. His famous avoidance of specific Greek, references may make his characters sound less obtrusively Greek, but they are not therefore any more Roman. Though their problems may echo Roman problems, their solutions do not reflect acceptable Roman solutions. Terence's irony is clever and incisive, but it is also remote and unpleasant. What then could attract later Roman authors to this kind of literature?

Perhaps the most striking thing about the history of Greek drama in the two centuries between Aeschylus and Menander is the remarkable flexibility of its forms and themes. Comedy and tragedy at Athens worked together to explore a wide range of issues with great interest for their society, and their partnership succeeded so well that at tragedy's death sometime in the fourth century, comedy was resilient enough to meet the continuing challenge alone. Thus Menander, and thus the legacy bequeathed to Terence. At Rome, however, tragedy and comedy never formed such a partnership. They went their separate ways, limiting rather than broadening the range of problems they addressed. The subsequent history of Latin literature reveals many authors who, like Terence, were interested in human relationships and the moral dilemmas those relationships can pose, but none was a comic dramatist. Plautus had made comedy too absurd and Terence had made it too alien to be taken seriously at Rome. When later authors sought Greek models for their work, they chose genres—epic, elegy, history, and oratory come readily to mind—whose forms were easily divorced from their original Greek milieu. Terence continued to be admired as a stylist and read as a school text, but his experiment with "serious" comedy had no successors. He was the last pioneer of the ancient stage. Within a century of his death Roman literature had achieved greatness, but ancient comedy as a creative genre was gone for good.

David Konstan   (essay date 1983)

SOURCE: "*Phormio*: Citizen Disorder" in *Roman Comedy,* Cornell, 1983, pp. 115-29.

[*In the following essay, Konstan probes the tension between private emotion and public social codes in* Phormio, *observing that this dual subject constitutes one of the main themes of the play.*]

Terence particularly favored such plots as the frame story in [Plautus's] *Cistellaria,* based on the elementary triangle of stubborn father, enamored son, and maiden apparently ineligible for marriage. Thus R. H. Martin remarks, in the introduction to his excellent school edition of the **Phormio** [*Terence: Phormio,* 1959]:

> The following elements of plot are found in all Terence's plays except the **Hecyra.** Two young men, often brothers, are engaged in love affairs. One of them loves a courtesan, the other wishes to marry a young woman, who is either poor but freeborn, or ostensibly a courtesan. The father opposes his son's marriage or even wants him instead to marry the daughter of a friend or relation. The young woman turns out to be freeborn or the daughter in question, and all ends well.

In a general way, the **Phormio** may be seen to fit this pattern. Antipho is in love with and, in his father's absence, has actually married a poor young woman called Phanium; his father, Demipho, is opposed to the match, because he intends the boy to marry his niece, the daughter of his brother Chremes; by means of a recognition scene, it is discovered that the niece is none other than Phanium, Antipho's bride, thereby bringing about the congruence of the father's wishes with the son's.

A closer look at the structure of the **Phormio,** however, questions the simplicity of this analysis. For the play falls into two distinct parts or movements, each of which appears to have its own theme and resolution. The two parts are joined by an elegant turn of the plot, and in their synthesis the proper significance of the **Phormio** emerges.

From a conversation between two slaves, Geta and Davus, we learn at the beginning of the play that the girl with whom Antipho has become infatuated is an Athenian citizen (114). As a result, he is unable to arrange the kind of irregular liaison that might have been formed with a woman of inferior status. He is obliged, if he will have her, to take her as his wife, but recognizes in her poverty a social barrier his father will not ignore. As Geta says: "Would he give him a maiden dowerless and common? Never!" (*ille indotatam virginem atque ignobilem daret illi? numquam faceret,* 120-21). Since it was scarcely possible for an Athenian youth to marry against the wishes of his father—while at Rome, it was entirely out of the question, since the boy would be *in patria potestate,* in the power of his father, and therefore without the status of a person before the law—it was necessary to devise a stratagem that would prevent Demipho from annulling the arrangement upon his return. This purpose is accomplished according to the advice of Phormio, who plays a role technically known as a parasite, that is, a free man of no property who lives by his wits at the expense of others. Phormio's scheme is to pass himself off as a friend of the girl's father, who had been, he will allege, a relative of Demipho's; according to Attic law, the nearest kin is obliged to marry an orphaned maiden, or provide five hundred drachmae for her dowry.

The action begins when Geta announces to the fainthearted Antipho and his cousin, Phaedria, the imminent arrival of Demipho. Antipho flees in panic, and Geta and Phaedria are left to handle his defense. Their argument is well rehearsed: Antipho's natural modesty tied his tongue in court; Geta, as a slave, was unable to testify; neither had the resources to raise or borrow the money necessary to provide a dowry and wed the girl to some other suitor. Finally, Demipho demands an interview with Phormio himself. Phormio is in no way daunted by Demipho and the three elders he brings with him as witnesses and counselors; he refuses to discuss the case, reminding Demipho that the law does not allow double jeopardy (403-6). The ruse thus proves entirely successful, and with it the plot is brought to a stalemate. Demipho is trapped, so long as Phormio refuses to negotiate. The action is set in motion again through a subplot involving an affair of Phaedria's with a lute girl called Pamphila. Before examining this transition, we may review the basic elements in the first movement of the comedy.

The issue that divides father and son is one of social class or caste. When Demipho denies any connection or acquaintance with Phanium's father, Phormio rejoins: "Really? Aren't you ashamed? But if he had left an estate of ten talents, you'd promptly summon up your lineage mindfully all the way back to your grandfather and great-grandfather" (392-95). The theme is familiar in new comedy, and central to such plays as Menander's *Samia* and Terence's *Adelphoe.*

The prejudice of the father and the passion of the son are essentially correlative motives. Demipho endorses a customary exclusiveness; Antipho's desire, like that of young men generally in the comic tradition, is heedless of status and defies the respect for conventional boundaries characteristic of the older generation. The dramatic function of passion is thus determined in relation to the particular norms that contain it, here the restrictions pertaining to class, represented by Demipho. This relationship between the father and son is captured in their names: Demipho suggests something like "voice of the people," Antipho, "voice of the opposition." In general, names with the root

dēm, meaning "the people" or "the community," are reserved for figures of authority. Put another way, we may say that while love is a personal emotion, it acts in tension with a social code, and this polarity of rule and passion constitutes the theme of the play.

Phormio's cunning abuse of the law relating to orphaned women succeeds, as we have seen, in baffling Demipho. In effect, Antipho has triumphed over his father, achieving the union he desires in spite of his father's opposition. But this victory does not furnish a comic closure. Ordinarily, in new comedy, the point is not the mere discomfiture of the paterfamilias and his conservative ideals. Rather, the denouement reestablishes the harmony of the group, reconciling the interests of father and son. Without this harmony, Antipho's success appears not as a resolution of the tension but as a standoff, demanding some further action or revelation to complete the story. Let us consider, moreover, the ways in which the complication might be satisfactorily resolved. We usually think of the recognition scene as the favored device in situations of this sort: Unexpected tokens or testimony reveal the eligibility of the girl. But in fact this means is normal only in questions of citizenship or civic status. Where the obstacle is simply a matter of wealth, the reconciliation was conventionally achieved through a change of heart or a revelation of true feelings in the blocking character. In Menander's *Samia,* for example, where a young man has had a child by the daughter of a humble neighbor, it turns out that the two fathers had independently decided to arrange the match between them. In Terence's **Adelphoe,** based on a play by Menander, Micio insists that his son meet his responsibilities by marrying the impoverished young woman who has borne his child. The difference in the treatment of themes of class and citizenship reflects the ideology of the classical city-state. The discriminations that separate members of the community from outsiders—whether strangers, slaves, resident aliens, or otherwise illegitimate or disfranchised individuals—were sanctified by law and custom, and their abrogation was a serious matter. Divisions based on wealth, on the other hand, were felt to strike at the solidarity of the community and were therefore regarded as the baleful effects of prejudice and greed. Their proper resolution is thus alteration of character or opinion. To reveal a poor citizen as an heiress or heir would imply that boundaries of class are in principle absolute and unbridgeable, like the boundaries that delimit the community, and this would be incompatible with the spirit of civic unity that reigns in comedy. In the **Phormio,** as we shall see, the problem assumes an entirely different form because of the supervention of the second movement of the play.

The argument we have been analyzing occupies the first two acts into which the **Phormio** is conventionally divided. Geta had indicated, in his conversation with Davus, that Phaedria had conceived a passion for a lute girl while his father, Chremes, the brother of Demipho, was abroad. In the third act we learn that Pamphila's master, Dorio, has sold her to a foreign soldier, but if Phaedria can raise the sum of thirty minae within a day, he can preempt the contract (531-33; 557). In the fourth act, Phormio rises once more to the occasion by pretending that he will marry Phanium himself if Demipho will provide a dowry of thirty minae. This sum he will lend to Phaedria, until the lad can collect the like amount from his friends (703). Then he will return both the money and the girl to Demipho on the pretext that the omens are against the marriage, thereby saving at a single stroke Antipho his bride and Phaedria his concubine. The transfer of the money to Phormio is accomplished by the beginning of Act V.

The second stage of the intrigue occupies a considerable part of the action in the **Phormio** (all of Act III; Act IV except for the first scene; and four scenes—two through five, omitting an intercalary scene following number three—in the final act). Nevertheless, Phaedria's affair remains a subplot rather than a second plot for two reasons. First, it never achieves the confrontation and resolution that occur between Antipho and Demipho. Indeed, after the third act, Phaedria disappears from the play. To be sure, he gets his money and his girl, but the machinations in his behalf on the part of Geta and Phormio occur in the new context that arises with the second movement of the play, in which Phaedria's problem is overshadowed by quite different concerns. The subordination of Phaedria's complication is a good illustration of the essentially correlative nature of passion in new comedy: Without an articulated opposition from Chremes, it recedes to an ancillary status in the drama. The second reason is that the exchange of the thirty minae and the right to wed Phanium serve formally to facilitate the second movement, which requires that Demipho and Chremes work to recover the girl for Antipho. We may now examine this unusual conversion of the plot in detail.

In the first scene of the fourth act, it is disclosed, through a dialogue between Chremes, who has just arrived home, and Demipho, that Chremes has been maintaining on the island of Lemnos the daughter of a bigamous marriage. The purpose of his trip was to fetch the girl, since he and his brother have conspired to marry her to Antipho in order to conceal his conduct from his legitimate wife, Nausistrata, whose dowry is the sole source of his wealth (586-87). With this brief conversation, the entire structure of the plot is transformed. Demipho's objection to Phanium is now revealed as unrelated to her poverty; he was not motivated by avarice or class feeling, but by his desire to protect his brother's domestic peace and security. The issue of class was only virtual, based on Antipho's natural assumption that this would be the basis of his father's anger. When it emerges that Demipho's opposition stems not from conventional prejudices but from private contingencies, the meaning of Antipho's passion is correspondingly reduced from a challenge, albeit personal and accidental, to public norms to a matter of individual disobedience. Thus the issue shifts from social boundaries, which had been represented by parental authority, to authority itself, without that embeddedness in communal values by which it is legitimized. With the disclosure of Demipho's true motives, the play beings anew, because the obstacle has been altered, and the obstacle is the essence of the comic tension. To be sure, Demipho remains the blocking figure, and this sustains the continuity of the narrative, but here we may see once again and most clearly how the conflict in comedy is located not simply in the struggle between the characters but in the complex of values and impulses which they enact.

For the rest of Act IV, Demipho and Chremes continue their efforts to end the marriage between Antipho and Phanium, and finally accede to Phormio's demand for thirty minae as her dowry. However, the change in focus from class division to domestic imbroglio opens the way to a recognition scene, which comes at the beginning of Act V: Chremes encounters Sophrona, the nurse of his Lemnian daughter, and learns that she is the very girl whom Antipho has taken as his wife. Naturally, the brothers make haste to recover the thirty minae, which have already been transferred to Phormio, but the parasite, informed of the circumstances by Geta, sees a way to press his advantage: He will give up his claim to Phanium only on condition that the dowry remain with him, as compensation for the one he lost when he broke off—he pretends—a previous engagement in their behalf (927-29). Phormio's real purpose, as he reveals in an earlier soliloquy, is to relieve Phaedria once and for all of his financial anxieties and to enjoy the utter duping of the two old men (885-86). When the brothers hesitate to concede, Phormio informs them that he is apprised of their secret, and is prepared to reveal it to Chremes' wife. Chremes is inclined to submit, Demipho to resist the extortion, now that the truth is out in any case and must soon reach the ears of Nausistrata. The plot has here arrived at an ambiguous juncture, at which it might develop in either of two ways, depending on whether Chremes and Demipho can come to terms with Phormio. Here, we may evaluate the significance of both the second movement, and the shift in content from the first part to the second, for in this transformation resides the theme of the play as a whole.

The action following the revelation of Phanium's relationship to Chremes has an unusual twist: Father and uncle striving to recover for the son the object of his enamorment. This situation is contrived by the placement of the recognition scene in the subplot: Had it occurred earlier, Chremes and Demipho would still have been in possession of the girl and their money; later, and Phormio's intention to renounce Phanium would have been realized. This inversion of dramatic vectors, in which the two old men suddenly are made to swing round and contend for the girl they have just contrived to be rid of, may be taken as an image of a deeper reversal of roles on the thematic level. Because Demipho and Chremes are abetting a marriage for private rather than social reasons—reasons which they must conceal, for they have their source in a violation of the conjugal code—they are more in the position customarily occupied by the wayward young lover than that of the stern, old-fashioned paterfamilias. This reversal stands out most clearly when we see the play as a whole, projecting the argument of the second movement upon that of the first.

Let us look once at the characteristic paradigm of ancient new comedy; we have observed that, in the formal pattern of separation and union of lovers structuring virtually every play in the genre, the differentiating principle essentially lies in the nature of the obstacle, and further that this obstacle is best understood as a code of values or motives represented in the blocking character. The opposition of the father, then, is normally predicated on the status rules of the city-state, and the recognition is designed to remove an apparent violation by bringing the woman into the community. In the *Phormio,* however, the discovery of Phanium's identity appears to have the reverse effect. In the first part of the play, where the central issue is class, the citizenship of the girl is not in doubt. But in the second part, when she is revealed as the illegitimate daughter of Chremes' Lemnian mistress, Phanium's civic status would seem most precarious. In real life, of course, her citizenship would be crucial, since she would, at Athens or at Rome, be ineligible for connubial rights as a foreigner. Commentators have therefore been concerned to explain away the contradiction. Thus, Bond and Walpole, in their note to line 114, where Phanium's nurse asserts her citizenship, remark: "The Lemnian mother must have been of genuine Athenian extraction: otherwise Phanium could only have been made legitimate by a vote of the citizens or by proclamation at the meeting of the *phratries.* The penalty for a false claim of citizenship was very heavy" [John Bond and Arthur Sumner Walpole, eds., *The Phormio of Terence,* 3d ed., 1964; orig. 1889]. This kind of solution, I believe, is beside the point. The character Phanium serves different functions in the two parts of the play. In the first, she must be a citizen, since her status is critical to Phormio's scheme of forcing her marriage to Antipho. In the second, where the focus is on Chremes' domestic difficulties, the technical point of citizenship can remain moot. The decision of the court in favor of Phormio's suit may of course be construed as internal evidence in support of Phanium's claims, but her foreign birth, the bigamous marriage of her parents, and the need to preserve secrecy concerning her identity all create an aura of illegitimacy which is both the dominant and relevant aspect for the later developments in the plot. Rather than attend too nicely, therefore, to the legal status of Phanium, we might better consider the implications of the shift in story paradigms from one in which her status is secure and significant to a second in which it is dubious and peripheral.

The plot of the *Phormio* advances from the conventional world of comedy, where order and authority are respected, even if in the breach, to a topsy-turvy situation in which everyone is involved in a transgression of the rules. The fathers had been perceived as defenders of the boundaries, but with the revelation of their true motives, the tension between impulse and custom which had informed the first movement gives way to a morally ambiguous opposition, where fathers and sons alike evade the social code and undermine its distinctions. Thus the recognition scene seems perverse: Instead of resolving the issue of class with which the *Phormio* began, it merely provides for the convergence of Antipho's and Demipho's private intentions. Since Demipho's reasons for desiring the marriage are if anything more scandalous than Antipho's, Phanium comes off the worse for the revelation of her identity.

That the play displaces rather than mends the violation of convention is thematically significant. In the archetypal story forms of ancient new comedy, the denouement normally accommodated apparent dislocations in the social structure by revealing that the actual state of affairs was as it should be. The principle was not unlike the Persian belief concerning parricide, according to the report of Herodotus: "They say that no one has ever killed his own father or mother, but that every time such things have happened, it is absolutely necessary that upon close examination they would be discovered to involve either supposititious or adulterous children. For they say that it is against reason that a true parent should die at the hands of his own child" (1.137). John K. Davies, in his article "Athenian Citizenship" [*Classical Journal* 73 (1977-78)], analyzes this pattern in the plays of Menander:

> If one stands back from the wild complexities of Menandros' plots, they can be seen to share one primary characteristic—an intense, even obsessive awareness of the status boundaries separating citizen from foreigner, citizen from slave, well-born from low-born, legitimate from illegitimate, wife from concubine, wealthy man from poor man from beggar. Plot after plot is exploring this sensitive area and mediating a transition from one status to another—always, of course, in the fantasy, in an upwards direction. For example, the cardinal fact of *Heros* and *Epitrepontes* is that young man rapes girl, and they subsequently marry without knowing that the other was the person involved, while the children born of the rape are exposed. However, they then turn up, to cause embarrassments and suspicions till the heavy use of the *gnorismata* [i. e., recognitions] motif makes everything straightfoward again between virtuous wife, mortified and repentant husband, and (after all) legitimate children. Or again the *Sikyonios,* where Stratophanes is in love with Philoumene but (a) he though rich is a Sikyonian and therefore a foreigner, and (b) she, though upperclass Athenian by origin, had been kidnapped and sold as a slave, and though Stratophanes knows her real status it will be hard to get it publicly recognized. Difficulty (a) disappears when it emerges that Stratophanes was 'really' an Athenian all the time: difficulty (b) vanishes when Stratophanes' parasite Theron tries to find someone to impersonate her father and just happens, as it were, to stumble upon the one man, Kichesias, who can perform that role without pretense. Since so much depends on citizenship, while for fifteen years of Menandros' adult lifetime Athens was powerless to determine her own citizenship criteria, his obsession with the theme is understandable: he was dealing with something of crucial contemporary importance. Of course, in his fantasies things come right in the end without the need for action and change, since the plots consist of discovering what is the case, which is what the participants want. In that sense Menandros is deeply escapist, since for the facts once discovered not to be as the participants want them to be would constitute a recipe for neurosis, tragedy, or revolution.

Clearly, the *Phormio* is a different kind of play. The transition of status is not upward but sideways at best. The characters get what they want, but not because they discover what is the case, for what is the case at the end is as incompatible with public norms as it was at the beginning. When Demipho and Chremes learn the identity of Phanium, they are as much at pains as before to keep her real position concealed.

The facts, however, do not remain a secret, since Phormio denounces the whole affair to Nausistrata, just when it seemed that the last loose end of the plot had been tied. Herbert Charles Elmer, in the introduction to his commentary on the play [*P. Terenti Phormio,* 1901], wonders about the reasons for this coda:

> To one feature of the play, critics may, perhaps, take exception. Why does not Phormio, after having sufficiently bantered the old men and compelled them, by threatening to tell Nausistrata of the secret marriage, to give up all claim to the money already paid him,—why does not Phormio content himself with this result? Why does he, by carrying out his threat, again set at stake what he has won? He must indeed have foreseen that he would not be able to carry out his plan without exposing the secret of Phaedria. The play might well have come to a rapid close after vs. 947, when all the complications had come to a happy termination.

To this question, which is plainly an important one for the theme since it touches on the action just where it exceeds the plot, Elmer offers the following series of responses:

> Still, it is quite in harmony with the bold, determined character of Phormio, that he improves the opportunity for the spirited scene which follows; and again the demands of justice, as it were, required that Chremes should be made to pay the penalty of his faithlessness and illbecoming conduct. For Phaedria there was the prospect of winning his mother as an ally in his love-affair, and for Phormio that of becoming a permanent guest in the house of Chremes.

Elmer does not, however, seem altogether satisfied with his own explanation, for he adds: "Whatever may be said regarding this addition from an artistic point of view, it may at any rate be said that the play is thereby enriched by a very effective scene."

The exposure of Chremes and Demipho forecloses a hypocritical accommodation to public sentiment and obliges the characters to confront openly the improprieties related to Phanium's situation. Chremes and Demipho in other ways have betrayed a concern with appearances. Chremes, for example, was at pains earlier to make the repudiation of Phanium as seemly as possible, both by providing her a dowry and by assuaging her distress through the offices of Nausistrata. When Demipho protests against this officiousness, Chremes replies: "It is not enough to have done your duty if public opinion does not approve it; I want this to happen in accord with her own wishes too, so that she doesn't spread the word that she has been kicked out" (724-25). Later, when the brothers are trying to recover their money from Phormio, Demipho explains his change of heart about Phanium as a scruple for his reputation: "He [i. e. Chremes] convinced me not to give her to you. 'For what will people say,' he said, 'if you do it? Before, when it could have been done honorably, she wasn't given; to drive her out now is foul.' Pretty much the same things which you were accusing me of a while back to my face"

(910-14). Demipho is being dishonest here of course, but the excuse reveals what he and his brother think of as a persuasive consideration. In the end, however, the strongwilled Demipho decides to face disclosure rather than endure the mockery of Phormio (955-56), and Chremes reluctantly follows suit.

For all her distress, Nausistrata will finally forgive her husband, in accord with the requirements of the genre. But before she grants her pardon, Phormio slips in a word about Phaedria's affair, and his need for thirty minae (1038-39). Chremes is taken aback, but Nausistrata turns on him at once: "Does it seem so wrong to you that your son, a young man, has one girlfriend, when you have two wives? Shameless! With what countenance will you rebuke him? Answer me!" (1040-42). Chremes meekly submits, but Nausistrata goes further, putting the whole matter before the judgment of her son (1045-46); a moment later, it is Phormio she elects as arbiter: "Phormio, from now on to the best of my ability I shall do and say whatever you want" (1050-51), and then, at his suggestion, she invites him in to dinner as a final insult to her husband. The play closes with the matron, the youth, and the parasite in command, while the two old men are humbled and obedient.

The **Phormio** began with a son in dread of his father; it ends with a father at the mercy of his son. This reversal mirrors the progression from the first movement of the play to the second, in which the fathers have lost their role as guarantors of social exclusiveness and restraints and are shown themselves to be transgressors. In the ancient citystate, adult propertied males constituted the citizen body. Normally, they are the repository of those values by which distinctions of status are maintained. The lapse in the moral authority of Demipho and Chremes produces a certain blurring of the boundaries, a relaxation in the conventional structures. The old men are obliged to be more tolerant once their own motives are publicly known to be compromised, while Nausistrata, Phaedria, and Phormio—all of them disfranchised in varying degrees—have less of a stake in preserving the traditional social codes. When Nausistrata learns that Chremes has changed his mind about evicting Phanium, though she does not yet know the reasons why, she remarks: "It's much better this way for everybody, I think, than what you started to do— that the girl should stay. For when I saw her, she seemed a thoroughly fine girl *(perliberalis)"* (814-15). Nausistrata judges by her sense of the person and is indifferent to considerations of class. Radical divisions of status are tempered by a spirit of humanity.

This spirit of humanity presides over the opening scenes of the play, where the slaves Geta and Davus are portrayed seriously and sensitively, and endowed with a generosity and good faith, despite their straitened circumstances, which put to shame the greed and casuistry of their masters. But the figure who best incarnates the challenge to the narrow exclusivism of the conservative citystate ideology is the parasite, Phormio himself. Many have acclaimed the subtlety and artistry of the characterization in the **Phormio,** and certainly the personality for whom Terence named the play is done with special brilliance and verve. Phormio is clever, bold, generous, loyal, independent, and ironic. He is, like many another of his métier in comedy, proud of his style of life (see especially lines 326-45). It is not that of a respectable citizen, and Phormio's social status is most dubious. Yet without question he is the hero of the comedy, in whose hands Antipho and Phaedria rest their fate. He manipulates each stage of the action successfully and in the end triumphs personally over Demipho and Chremes. His encouragement of love and disdain for conventional barriers suit perfectly his ambiguous station in society. Phormio's victory is also a victory for his point of view, that of a marginal person who is prepared to improvise with laws and customs in order to facilitate passionate, if not quite socially acceptable, unions. He is fixer, who bends the rules and softens the lines that define the social structure. Each time his work is vindicated: The fathers turn out to desire the marriage he has brought about, although for personal reasons of their own; Phaedria is indulged in his affair by a broad-minded mother and a crestfallen father. Phormio's invitation to dinner and elevation to arbiter of the household's destiny are the confirmation of his wisdom. With the inner dislocation of the old structure, the old men cede place to a new type: Phormio, rootless and humane, is at the moral center of gravity of his play and the society it represents.

Walter E. Forehand   (essay date 1985)

SOURCE: "Terence and His Influence" in *Terence,* Twayne Publishers, 1985, pp. 120-30.

[*In the following excerpt, Forehand first summarizes his conclusions about the style and themes of Terence's plays, then discusses Terence's influence on later drama.*]

Terence has left us six plays upon which to base our evaluation of him. If, as the tradition affirms, this is the total output of his short life, we are in a position to survey his work without the worrisome question of how we would modify our opinions if we had more complete evidence. His reputation as a comic dramatist has withstood the test of critical opinion through the centuries; his theatrical soundness is evidenced by the influence he has had on playwrights since the Middle Ages, who turned to him for the most practical of reasons, that he provided characters, themes, and comic formulae useful for reaching their own audiences . . . .

Since antiquity Terence has been especially prized in two areas, the refinement of his style and the care with which he fashioned characters. It is difficult to demonstrate how one must conclude that style is excellent and characters are handled well without resorting to close analysis of specifics. We can, however, delineate Terence's chief strengths without going on at great length.

Terence's Latin is a model for educated speech of the second century before our era. His language is idiomatic and appropriately chosen to fit mood and character. Nor is it only the opinion of modern scholastics. Roman critics were quick to cite his excellence in use of language. Whereas his older second-century B.C. colleague Plautus reveled in highly lyrical passages and extravagant verbal effects, Terence was controlled. Though less lyrical, he managed spoken meters skillfully and reproduced the idiom of the educated upper class in smooth dramatic poetry. Thus, not only has he been used as a model for school children in search of a good Latin style, but those playwrights well versed in Latin have found him a study in dialogue construction.

At another level, Terence managed the pace of his dialogues with great craft. It has long been a canon of good dramatic structure that material should not exist for its own sake, but should contribute to character or plot or theme, preferably to all at once. Both within the individual scene and in the ordering of scenes Terence's touch is deft. His plays are all quite short, none over 1,100 lines. Yet he managed to get the most out of each scene so that we are left with complete, well-turned plots and characters effectively developed. Such was his control of when, how, and with whom characters should speak.

Ever since the Roman scholar Varro credited Terence with Roman comedy's best characters, critics have given our poet high marks for his handling of character. The French critic Diderot might have been speaking for the critical tradition at large when he wrote, in his essay "Praise of Terence":

> What man of letters has not read his Terence more than once and does not know him almost by heart? Who has not been struck by the truth of his characters and the elegance of his diction? Wherever in the world one carries his works, if there are libertine children and angry fathers, the children will recognize in the poet their follies and the fathers their reprimands.

Certainly, Terence emulated models which had carefully drawn characters, but he did not follow any model slavishly and his own skill in this area was considerable, so that his characters are always prominent in our consideration of a play.

Terence's genre, in fact, puts special constraints upon the playwright, for it relies totally on stock types for each play. No character in Terence is, then, wholly unique. There are old men, young men, slaves, matrons, courtesans; but no carpenters, insurance salesmen, maniacs, or the like. The skillful playwright, however, turns this to his advantage.

Since the basic outlines of a role are recognized immediately by an audience, the playwright can create most of his characters quickly so that he can concentrate on "individualizing" a specific example of a type, needing only spare space to accomplish much. Terence was masterful at this manipulation of his genre, and was able not only to fashion "interesting" stock characters but to make them function in the larger framework of his theme.

One technique he favored was the use of pairs from which comparisons might be made to reveal the nature of each role. Thus, for example, we develop our opinion of Micio and Demea, the two old men in *The Brothers,* from seeing them constantly in relation to one another. The same is true of Menedemus and Chremes in *The Self-Tormentor.* Terence also accentuates the strength of one important character by placing it against the weakness of a less sig-

The characters of The Self-Tormentor, *from a 1503 edition of Terence's works.*

nificant, similar figure, as, for example, the young man Pamphilus in *The Girl from Andros,* who gains stature from comparison with his friend Charinus, or Aeschinus, the strong-willed young man in *The Brothers,* who is seen in relation to his brother Ctesipho.

Often minor figures are given just the touch of personality necessary to raise them from the level of dramatic ciphers to characters who enrich the overall texture of the play. Thus Bacchis, the courtesan, and Antiphila, the ingenue, in *The Self-Tormentor* have minor roles, and each is a stock type, but in their interaction they gain depth and help to place the actions of others in perspective. The serving girl Pythias, who might well have remained a nondescript slave, exhibits a strength of purpose that accentuates the theme of *The Eunuch* in such a way as to make it a significantly better play. Minor female characters such as Nausistrata, the deluded wife in *Phormio,* and Myrinna, one of the wives in *The Mother-in-Law,* are likewise used effectively to show the injustices in these plays; male characters such as Hegio in *The Brothers* and Crito in *The Girl from Andros* become effective instruments for giving credibility to information or individuals.

Because his plays lacked expository prologues and so needed to develop character and situation internally, Terence expended special effort on his opening scenes. In three of these he made use of protatic characters, introduced as foils for a principal figure and then allowed to drop form the play: Sosia, the freedman who talks with Simo at the beginning of *The Girl from Andros;* Geta, the slave who talks with Davus to open *Phormio;* Philotis, the young courtesan, and Syra, the old maid, who are prominent in the first scenes of *The Mother-in-Law.* These minor figures are developed just enough to provide from their interactions with major characters important thematic and character information, and the care with which they are employed is sound testimony to Terence's skills.

If Terence has been prized for his characters, he must nonetheless be singled out also among the playwrights, ancient and modern, of the New Comic tradition for the richness of his themes. Except for *Phormio,* his plays develop ideas worthy of serious comment and consideration . . . .

To the extent that the plays of New Comedy deal with the foibles of everyday people, they may be thought to "hold the mirror up to nature." It is possible, then, to find in almost any play elements that can be seen as corrective satire or models for moral edification. The fact that bourgeois problems are lifelike, however, is not by itself sufficient reason to take the situations of these plays seriously.

Hence, there has been a tendency in modern times to judge New Comedy more on style than content. Aristophanes depicts specific social and political problems; New Comedy thrives on generalities. But to the ancients New Comedy was considered highly instructive; Menander above all others was thought to provide a view of existence from which we could profit, but no less a conservative Roman than Cicero was interested in Terence's plays for the examples he might find there. And, as the passage from Diderot quoted above would suggest, serious critics in other eras have found Terence worthy of their careful consideration.

In fact, Terence is at pains to elevate issues which in other circumstances might have remained at a level of trivial importance to a genuinely serious plane. This very tendency has often been adduced as a criticism of his comedy. He can wax subtle, so that his plays often have rather little of the obvious humor we associate with the comic stage. The advantages of less obvious humor and of profounder moods must be weighed against this loss of verve and a tendency to moralize. Not all critics have found that balance in Terence's favor.

Taken as a whole, however, theme remains in the opinion of most a strength of Terentian comedy. He does not write philosophical plays dedicated to expounding a systematic view of life, albeit philosophical ideas in common circulation in the Hellenistic world are found in his work. Rather, when he has completed his presentation, the characters have been rich enough, and the complications of their interactions sufficiently understood, so that we see a common problem in greater depth. The focus is not on theoretical social, political, or psychological issues, but the investigation of ordinary interpersonal situations.

The single most common situation in New Comedy is that of a young man in love but unable to pursue his affair happily, primarily because of his father, who will not pay the expenses or disapproves of the relationship. It is not surprising, then, to find fathers and sons in all of Terence's plays. In his treatments, however, we are shown important rather than routine aspects of their relationships.

The Girl from Andros, The Self-Tormentor, and *The Brothers* all make the father-son relationship their central concern. Miscommunication is generally the cause of problems, arising both from faulty parenting and from the generation gap. In *The Girl from Andros* old Simo is so fearful that Pamphilus is ruining his life by devoting himself to Glycerium that he cannot grasp that his son's character is really quite solid. He is dominated by his fears and becomes obsessed with forcing his son into a relationship with a more acceptable girl so that he loses his sense of balance. Ironically, the son acts more responsibly than the father, and only the typical ending in which Glycerium is found to be an acceptable marriage partner after all can salvage the situation.

The Self-Tormentor presents a different sort of problem. One father, Menedemus, is so remorseful at having been too unyielding and thereby driving his son into the army that he racks himself daily with hard labor; his neighbor, Chremes, is the repository of all good advice and is eager to help Menedemus manage his relationship when his son suddenly returns. With typical comic irony, however, Chremes is in need of advice himself when he becomes aware that his own son is pursuing an affair with an extravagant courtesan. Again, lack of communication between well-meaning parents and their sons creates conditions dangerous to all their happiness.

The Brothers is the *locus classicus* for the father-son theme. Here, opposing extremes of childraising are at issue: Micio's permissiveness is pitted against his brother

Demea's strictness. The play is so constructed that these relationships become tightly entwined. The children, Aeschinus and Ctesipho, are both the natural children of Demea. Aeschinus was adopted by Micio, however, and so there are two sets of brothers and two father-son relationships to provide many contrasts. Micio thinks Demea regressive, while Demea believes his brother is ruining Aeschinus. In the end neither father is totally vindicated. Ctesipho's independence has not prospered under Demea's handling. Instead, he has tried to hide his juvenile foibles and has made a mess. Aeschinus has fared better, but he too is not perfect. Furthermore, neither father communicates as well with his son as one would like. Ctesipho is afraid to reveal himself to Demea at all, and Aeschinus is not totally frank with Micio. Terence contrives to show us that both approaches must be tempered. He favors liberality generally, but warns against the dangers of assuming too much when dealing with adolescents.

In the final analysis, it is indicative of the strength with which Terence manages his themes that we do not find a heavily moralizing tone. Rather, he has taken comic commonplaces and focused our attention on them, especially through the interactions of well-drawn characters, in such a way that we ponder the situations with some seriousness despite the comic atmosphere and the stock nature of the plot.

We must conclude upon examining Terence's plays as a whole that the father-son relationships we have just reviewed are only one aspect of a larger concern with human relationships in general. Some commentators have felt, in fact, that Terence's interest is in the nature of a philosophical position, that men should practice *humanitas,* or "humaneness," toward one another. There is no need, however, to claim any organized philosophical approach for Terence in order to affirm that he was especially interested in the way people treat one another and the ironies inherent therein.

Each of the plays (except *Phormio*) examines human interactions under difficult conditions. We have noted the father-son relationships in *The Girl from Andros, The Self-Tormentor,* and *The Brothers.* In *The Girl from Andros* we see further how concern and love for others are expressed by different people. Ironically, the son, Charinus, is more effective in his protective love for Glycerium than is his father in his efforts to protect his son, for Simo, constrained by his own opinions of correct behavior, cannot separate his own frustrations from his view of his son. So, Simo cannot see how capable his son really is. For comparison, incidentally, we see Simo's friend Chremes find a much more satisfactory balance between concern for his daughter and for his friend's problems.

The Eunuch presents a counterpoint to genuine love in a play which shows the effects of human selfishness. Its characters profess devotion, but upon any close scrutiny we see them follow their own interests. The centerpiece for this examination is the callous rape of Pamphila by young Chaerea, who then claims without remorse that he is deeply in love with her. This message is softened by boisterous scenes which keep us well within the comic world, but

Terence orchestrates them in such a way that the ending leaves us aware of the irony in what the characters say.

In *The Self-Tormentor* Terence explores the irony of a man, like Chremes, who is so interested in the affairs of others that he cannot see his own problems. We are edified by watching the relationships between fathers and sons in the play, but standing beyond this theme is the spectacle of Chremes falling into one of life's more common traps.

Terence's most ambitious effort in examining human relationships is *The Mother-in-Law* . . . . [It has been difficult] for critics who have discussed its dramatic viability. And yet, the play contains some of Terence's most attractive characters and the richest mixture of human relations of all his works. *The Mother-in-Law* shows us people being unjust to one another because of a willingness to believe wrong information or to form faulty conclusions rather than to trust the goodness of those close to them. Thus, everyone is confused by the strangeness of the situation. Philumena must feign reasons for leaving her mother-in-law when she finds herself pregnant. Pamphilus cannot accept the psychological burden placed on him by his young wife's problems, though he loves her a great deal; furthermore, he is caught between wife and mother. The old men are all too eager to assume that their children's problems stem from a mother-in-law's interference. Terence evokes pity, concern, and indignation as the play progresses, and it is only careful blending of comic elements with these somber concerns that keeps us attuned to the comic mood. In the end the genuine love and concern which the characters also show toward one another triumph in what remains Terence's most mixed comedy, but a truly interesting play.

Terence's influence on Western comic drama has been immense. He survived through the ages whereas his Greek predecessors did not, or, in the case of Aristophanes, were not rediscovered until the influence of the Roman playwrights had established itself firmly. Plautus, his immediate predecessor on the Roman stage, may rival him in influence, but in those periods when tastes favored urbane, sophisticated comedy, Terence was considered the master both for practicing dramatists and theorists alike.

Our survey of Terence's influence must be quite brief. Certainly, many sources are available which deal with his influence at greater depth, both in general and specific terms. Here we will discuss briefly only two features of his influence, his place as a theoretical model and the direct use made of his plays by some later writers.

The history of Terence as a model for drama is long and rich. It begins in the tenth century with a nun in Saxony, one Hrotsvitha, who wrote several plays to elucidate Christian virtues for the good of Christian maidens; she used as her model the comedies of Terence. In the Renaissance the notion that plays based on his comedies could be effective as moral statements was revived, and Terence was so favored as a model that scholars speak of a "Christian Terence."

In the sixteenth century not only practicing playwrights, especially in Italy, but schoolmasters and critics as well turned to the Roman dramatists, especially Terence, for evidence to support their dramatic theories. The *editio princeps* of his plays published in 1470 made him generally available, and the ancient commentaries on his work survived, especially that of Donatus. Thus, Terence became a model against which to measure the theories of Aristotle and Horace, and the Terentian commentators also gained stature as theoreticians. As Marvin Herrick puts it [in his *Comic Theory*],

> the Athenian Aristophanes was too vulgar, too indelicate; the Roman Plautus was sometimes too vulgar and often too "irregular." The later Roman poet, Terence, offered safer and more familiar ground upon which schoolmasters and critics could expatiate on art, on manners, and on morals.

Terence was a favorite source for the playwrights of the later English stage, who often waxed theoretical about their work. William Congreve (1670-1729), for example, specifically states that he was the inheritor of Terence's stage; he was typical of those writing comedy of manners in this era.

In the eighteenth century, the great Frenchman of letters, Denis Diderot (1713-1784) credited Terence as a near-perfect model for the aspiring comic playwright. He wrote several essays on drama in which he cited Terence frequently as illustrative of his notions of how comedy should function. Diderot's impact on practicing playwrights and critics throughout Europe was considerable. His fondness for Terence is best expressed in his short essay "Praise of Terence" (ca. 1769): "Young poets, alternately turn the pages of Molière and of Terence. Learn from the one to draw, from the other to paint." Diderot felt secure that Terence's lack of comic energy was more than compensated for by his refined diction and his great skill in character portrayal.

It is an old saw that good playwrights borrow, great playwrights steal. Even a quick glance through literary history confirms that comic dramatists have always been alert to good material and willing to appropriate it regardless of its source. The list of works which have used Terence's plays directly is quite long, and the reputations of their authors great. We need cite only a few examples to give a clear idea of the extent of his influence.

Molière has two works based closely on plays of Terence. *The Brothers* was the principal model for *The School for Husbands* (1661); *Phormio* provided the core (around which was wound material from many other places) for *The Trickeries of Scapin* (1671). In fact, Plautus appealed to the great Frenchman more than did Terence, but the influence of Terence's dramatic style on his work was significant. For example, *The Miser* (1668) was based on Plautus's *The Pot of Gold*, again with material from several other sources. Now, *The Pot of Gold* has what Terence would have called a "simple" plot, that is, it has one love affair. Molière made his play "double," as Terence might have said, that is, he introduced neat pairs of characters in two intertwined love affairs. Terence made great use of such technique, and became a prime model for such composition for later playwrights. Thus, in *The Miser* Molière followed a tradition going back to Terence: he turned a

single plot into a double one and in the process "Terenced" Plautus.

Terence's influence on Shakespeare is less direct. The Englishman, like Molière, seems to have gone to Plautus more. We can feel confident, however, that Terence had an effect on Shakespeare's dramatic thinking, for he must have read him quite as much as Plautus.

In England during the seventeenth and eighteenth centuries, when the stage was filled with comedy, Terence found many admirers. We have mentioned Congreve's "spiritual" affinity to him. More direct influence can be found in *The Squire of Alsatia* (1688), by Thomas Shadwell, or Richard Steele's *The Conscious Lovers* (1722), the first based on *The Brothers*, the second on *The Girl from Andros*. Other examples might be easily cited from an era in which the most popular comedies were akin in theme and character to the bourgeois atmosphere of Terence's plays.

In modern times Terence, as well as Roman comedy in general, has lost the position of direct influence on practicing playwrights, though Roman drama is still taught in history of drama courses. Occasional revivals have been successful, but they are novelties that are meant as adaptations. The heirs of Terence have had their influence, however, and comedy of manners is still very popular whether in the theater, at the movies, or on the television "sitcom." Terence remained a basic author in the schools until perhaps fifty years ago. No one at the opening of Oscar Wilde's *The Importance of Being Earnest* (1895) would have missed the humor arising from the careful reincarnation of Terence's brand of New Comedy. The bourgeois situation, the "duality" construction with its two interconnected love affairs, and the improbable recognition scene can be understood immediately as coming from Terence as much as from Wilde's predecessors on the British stage.

Joseph Trapp responds to Caesar's criticism of Terence (1742):

But granting that Terence was no way remarkable for his Talent at Wit and Repartee, yet (with Submission to so great a Judge [as Julius Caesar]) so sharp and severe a Censure seems more than he deserves. For there are many, and those of the best Taste, who are more pleas'd with a Writer, that perpetually keeps up an agreeable Smile, and an easy Chearfulness; than one, who is every now and then throwing them into Fits of Laughter, and violent Emotions.

Joseph Trapp, in his Lectures on Poetry Read in the Schools of Natural Philosophy at Oxford, *Garland Publishing, 1970.*

A. J. Brothers   (essay date 1988)

SOURCE: An introduction to *Terence: The Self-Tormentor*, edited and translated by A. J. Brothers, Aris & Phillips Ltd, 1988, pp. 1-26.

[*Below, Brothers surveys characterization and plot devices in* The Self-Tormentor, *and also explores some of Terence's sources for the play.*]

It has long been part of scholarly practice to attempt to understand the relationship of the Roman comedies to their lost Greek originals, and to try to pinpoint the additions, omissions and alternations of the Roman dramatists and recover the original Greek form - to play, in fact, 'hunt the New Comedy' with the text of a Terence (or Plautus) play. Though this type of activity has its limitations, particularly if carried out to the exclusion of other studies, it is nevertheless not merely legitimate but interesting and valuable.

Such investigations are always difficult, because we have so little to go on. With [Terence's **The Self-Tormentor**], the problem is perhaps worse than usual, since we do not have Donatus' commentary and so do not possess, as we do for the other five of Terence's plays, the rather sparse information, varying greatly in quality, which he can provide about Terentian workmanship; we do, however, have the less helpful commentary of Eugraphius. We have some fragments of Menander's play, preserved (not as are most of the fragments of the other originals) by Donatus, but by chance quotation elsewhere; however, not all of these obviously match up with the Latin text. We also have the prologue, where lines 4-6 are crucial, but we have seen that that evidence may not be straightforward. Lastly, we have the play itself, which we can examine for internal evidence of change - though . . . "we must at all times beware of assuming that Terence was so unskilled that his points of alteration will always be obvious to us if only we look for them hard enough".

In the prologue (6) Terence says of his version of the play *duplex quae ex argumento facta est simplici* "which from being a single plot has been turned into a double play". The seemingly inescapable interpretation of this (especially since all of Terence's other plays except **Hecyra** involve the love affairs of two couples) is that the Roman poet has 'doubled' the play by increasing the pairs of lovers from one to two; attempts to interpret the line without assuming that it entails some such 'doubling' do not succeed. However, if one attempts to remove one of the pairs (presumably Clitipho and Bacchis, since Clinia, as son of the self-tormentor of the title, and Antiphila, for whose sake he incurred his father's displeasure, must have been in Menander), the entire fabric of the play falls apart. Two themes in particular, the pretence that Bacchis is Clinia's and not Clitipho's, and the cock-and-bull story that Antiphila is surety for a debt owed to Bacchis, ensure that the affairs of Clitipho and Bacchis are so closely interwoven with those of Clinia and Antiphila that they cannot be divorced from one another without the plot totally disintegrating. And if the plot does disintegrate in this way, it means that all elements involving Bacchis (and possibly Clitipho and Chremes too) would derive from Terence and not Menander's *Heautontimorumenos;* and this in turn means that Terence largely rewrote the play from line 223 onwards (if he introduced Bacchis) or totally (if he introduced the other two as well). Quite apart from the nature of the existing Menander fragments making this ex-

tremely unlikely, it would mean that Menander's *Heautontimorumenos,* containing only the Menedemus / Clinia / Antiphila element, would have been dramatically very thin. It is the virtual certainty that this hypothesis of almost total re-writing by Terence is therefore wrong which has led scholars to try to interpret line 6 in such a way that they need not say that Terence has 'doubled' the play. This, as I have said, seems quite impossible, and so the argument returns to its starting point.

However, there is another way of looking at the 'doubling' of a play. It concerns the introduction of extra characters, not into the plot, but into the action of the play as presented on stage. There seems to be good internal evidence for believing that in his adaptation Terence has made Antiphila and Bacchis speaking characters, when in Menander they either did not appear on stage at all or were non-speaking parts. If this is true, then in the Greek original there were two pairs of lovers in the plot, but only the young men were given full roles in the action; Terence, however, for reasons of his own, decided to give the women something to say as well. He therefore took from Menander a single plot in the sense that he only used one play and did not add characters from his own head or from another original; but he 'doubled' the play in the sense that he showed all four lovers with speaking parts, whereas Menander had shown only two. Clearly, this is not 'doubling' in the obvious sense; the additions are to the action only and not to the plot, the chief change is not a second pair of lovers but two women provided for the two men, and the extra writing consists of just two short scenes not half the play. But the statement in line 6 is not absolutely untrue, though it is exaggerated and misleading - perhaps deliberately so. R.C. Flickinger mentions "the deliberate policy of teasing and bewilderment which is pursued throughout the prologue" [*Philological Quarterly* 6 (1927)]. Perhaps by saying that he had made a single plot double, Terence was hoping to trap Luscius; he had 'doubled', but not in the way he hoped his critic would think.

Briefly, arguments for suspecting the change are that Bacchis only appears in two short scenes (381ff., 723ff.), Antiphila only in the former, and that there are grounds for thinking that Terence, not Menander, was the author of these.

381ff. divides easily into two (381-97; 398-409). The first part consists largely of a monologue by Bacchis which shows her to be much more respectable and considerate than previous description (223ff.) has led us to expect and than the picture of her given later (455ff.) will show; the second part, where Bacchis makes little contribution, is the reunion of Clinia and Antiphila (awkwardly delayed by Bacchis' speech). It seems that Terence wanted to depict this reunion on stage, and felt that in doing so he could give Bacchis something to say which would reinforce the audience's high opinion of Antiphila - even though what she said was out of keeping with her character. This view of the scene entails that Terence must also have altered the end of the previous scene (376ff.).

In 723ff. nothing essential is done apart from what is said will happen at the end of the previous scene and what we are told has happened at the start of the next - the transfer of Bacchis and her *grex ancillarum* "retinue of maids" from Clitipho's house to Clinia's. The rest is merely a humorous threat by Bacchis to leave, which is immediately averted by Syrus' assurance that he will obtain the money Bacchis wants. The scene is also awkward dramatically, with doubts about Clinia's exit and an impossibly short time allowed for the transfer of the *grex*. If this scene is Terentian, then Terence created Phrygia, Bacchis' maid, who only appears here.

Both scenes involve movements by Bacchis and her *grex*. It is probable that in Menander these movements were 'masked' by choral interludes. When Terence dispensed with the chorus, for two of its four appearances he substituted these scenes.

Other changes have been suspected. If Menander's original had an explanatory prologue, the long exposition scene in Terence (53ff.) may have been expanded with some information originally there. Chremes' supposed exit at 170 to visit his neighbour Phania, where the Oxford Text marks a *saltatio convivarum* "dance of supper-guests", has been thought by some to mark the place of a Greek choral interlude or deferred prologue; his hurried exit to put off some business with neighbours (502) and his rapid return (508) have seemed so odd to others that they have been held to mark Terentian alteration. Another difficulty has been found in the spread of the action over two days with a night interval, which has been though un-Greek and therefore Terentian; and yet another has been the ending, which some have felt too untypical. Other theories about change, based on scenes where in Terence more than three characters speak, are now seen to have less force than was thought. Finally, the fact that Menedemus, the self-tormentor of the title, is not for long the centre of attention and the focus for intrigue in the play has been taken by some as evidence of wholesale rewriting by Terence of the type already indicated. This has been seen to be unlikely; and the argument from the title of Menander's and Terence's plays is in fact spurious, since in this type of drama titles are not necessarily good guides to content.

. . . . .

In the early part of this century, the attention paid to the relationship of the plays of Terence (and Plautus) to their Greek originals took precedence over appreciation of the plays as they stand. The Roman dramas were regarded merely as pale reflections of their Greek predecessors, useful mainly as a means of learning about Greek New Comedy, and they were not given full consideration as independent art. More recently, however, the emphasis has shifted, and this imbalance is being corrected; no doubt this change has been assisted by the discovery of enough New Comedy to provide a basis for fruitful first-hand study. It has been rightly said that "research could be more profitably directed into what the comedies of Plautus and Terence have themselves to offer than into their uncertain relationships with lost sources." We must always remember that Terence wrote for the Roman stage and that his audience regarded *The Self-Tormentor* as a Roman play.

In the prologue (36) Terence calls his play *stataria*, "containing more talk than action". But, though it does not contain vigorous action like the siege in *Eunuchus* (771ff.) or exaggerated cameos like the pimp or the "running slave" in *Adelphi* (155ff., 299ff.), the "talk" nevertheless produces a fast-moving and complicated play. The twists and turns of the plot, as Syrus proves ever more inventive about getting money for Clitipho's mistress each time he is thwarted, leave the audience (or reader) breathless and perhaps confused. Such confusion is deliberate. The spectator is meant to be amazed by the frequent changes of direction brought about by Syrus' unending ingenuity; he is not necessarily meant to keep up with him every step of the way. One is reminded of Sandbach's comment that "close attention was necessary to follow Menander's dramas"; this is no less true of Terence's adaptation of this Menander play.

The "talk" also produces excellent character-drawing. The chief example is Chremes; but, apart from the interest centred on him, Menedemus, Syrus, Clitipho, Clinia and Sostrata are also characters fully, sensitively and sympathetically drawn.

It is Chremes, rather than the 'self-tormentor' Menedemus, who is the central character of the play and the victim of deception and trickery by Syrus, Clitipho and Clinia for much of its duration. Menedemus' problems begin to be resolved as early as 182, when the audience learns that his son Clinia has returned from abroad; and, but for Chremes' snap decision (199) not to reveal Menedemus' true feelings to his own son Clitipho, who is Clinia's close friend, they would have been swiftly settled. By contrast, Chremes' problems are only just beginning with the first mention of Clitipho's affair with the courtesan Bacchis (223) and Syrus' sudden revelation that Bacchis is on her way to Chremes' house (311). Thereafter the gradual but steady resolution of Menedemus' worries (assisted by the recognition of Clinia's love, Antiphila, as Chremes' daughter) becomes almost a sub-plot as interest centres on the increasing state of self-deception into which Chremes drifts until he is finally forced to confront the truth about his son's affair (908), and tries to salvage what he can of his self-sought reputation for sound judgement at the end of the play.

There are several ways of looking at Chremes' character. One, now largely discredited, regards him as someone whose genuine interest in and regard for others, typified by the sentiments of 77, is a model of human sympathy. Another sees him as a busybody, too anxious to take a hand in other people's affairs and to preach to them, when he cannot even keep his own house in order. A third sees him as something of both: "inquisitive, opinionated, self-satisfied, and insensitive, yet genuinely moved by the other man's situation and ready to extend his unwanted help".

The first view, at least, cannot be right. It is surely the essence of the comedy that a rather unpleasant man gets his 'comeuppance', not that a good one comes to grief through honest refusal to believe ill of his son. And the whole irony of the situation is that Chremes is too busy intervening in other people's affairs to notice what is going on under his nose, not that his genuine concern for others does not leave him time to see what is happening. The unattractive side to his character is underlined by his treatment of his wife Sostrata, whose words he mockingly imitates (622), and to whom he is rude and overbearing (624, 630, 632ff., 1006ff., 1018ff.) . Moreover, his judgement, on which he prides himself, is unsure; his decision to keep Clitipho (199) and Clinia (436) in the dark about Menedemus' feelings is misconceived and prolongs his neighbour's unhappiness, while his encouragement of Syrus' mischief (533ff.) merely rebounds on himself. Only when he has been made to look a complete fool at the end of the play and his moral authority has been seriously impaired, does he allow himself (with rather bad grace, 1053) to be persuaded to forgive his son.

How far one accepts the view which combines both traits depends upon the interpretation put on several passages. For example, are Chremes' words at 159-60 genuine encouragement or empty platitude? Is his dinner invitation (161ff.) anything more than a desire to play Lord Bountiful? Is his expression of sorrow at 167-8 sincere or perhaps a little too perfunctory? Is his wish to be first to tell Menedemus (184ff., 410ff.) prompted by concern for his neighbour or eagerness for credit as a bringer of good news? I tend to take the less charitable, more jaundiced view; but the reader must decide, and even Chremes' sternest critic must accept that the complaints he makes about Clitipho at 1039ff. are fully justified.

Menedemus is altogether more attractive. His vivid accounts of how he drove Clinia away (96ff.) and afterwards in remorse chose a life of hard labour and rejected all pleasure and relaxation (121ff.) combine with the picture of his continued misery (420ff.) to excite our sympathy; his ready acknowledgement of how wrong he was (99ff., 134, 158) arouses respect for his candour and creates an impression of his essential good nature. And towards the end of the play this impression is reinforced by a contrast drawn with Chremes: whereas Menedemus behaved as he did towards Clinia with nobody to advise him otherwise, Chremes acts in precisely the same manner towards Clitipho even though he has the lesson of Menedemus before him and even though Menedemus (932) and Sostrata (1013) warn him of the trouble he will cause. It is only with difficulty that Chremes is persuaded to relent - and it is fair and honest Menedemus, wiser for his recent sufferings, who in his new-found happiness finds time to come outside and reconcile his neighbour with his son (1045ff.). It is small wonder that we earlier shared this appealing character's resentment at Chremes' curiosity (75-6), just as later (897, 914) we felt we could allow him to have a little fun at the expense of his discomfited *adiutor. . . monitor et praemonstrator* "helper, counsellor and guide".

Syrus, one of Chremes' slaves particularly attached to Clitipho, is the next most important figure in the action after Chremes; from him stems all the intrigue aimed at securing for his young master enough money for him to continue to enjoy Bacchis' favours. As in many plays of this type, the young men prove rather unimaginative and helpless when confronted with problems; it is the slaves who make all the running, and Syrus is the *servus callidus* "cunning slave" *par excellence,* quick-witted, bold, full of ideas and never downcast. In this he is contrasted to Clinia's slave

Dromo, whom he calls *stolidus* "pretty stupid" (545) and whom earlier Clitipho had felt should be accompanied by Syrus when Clinia sent him to fetch Antiphila (191).

As a schemer, Syrus enjoys freedom of action, not waiting for instructions; it comes as a complete shock to Clitipho (311) that he has taken the amazingly bold step of bringing Bacchis along with Antiphila, intending to pretend to Chremes (332-3) that she is Clinia's. His task is now to find the wherewithal to keep Bacchis there, and this search, which occupies his mind until money is secured at 831, shows his ingenuity at its best. He starts (512-3), as is natural, by planning to get the money out of his own master Chremes, but is deflected from this by a golden opportunity presented by Chremes himself (546-7) into attempting to get it from Menedemus. He pretends (599ff.) that Antiphila is surety for a debt owed to Bacchis, and proposes (608ff.) to tell Menedemus that she is a captive from Caria and to persuade him to buy her from the courtesan. When Chremes tells him that Menedemus will not agree, Syrus replies that there is no need for him to; but, although pressed to explain, he does not (610ff.). This is one of a number of occasions where the exact nature of what Syrus has in mind is not explained. Such instances are devices intended to boost our opinion of the slave's cleverness. There is no need to suppose that Terence (or Menander) worked out what these unexpressed plans were, and the audience had no need to know; it is sufficient to be told that Syrus' fertile brain has produced them.

The discovery that Antiphila is Chremes' daughter ruins Syrus' plan of getting Menedemus to purchase her. We are amused to see his despair as it collapses (659-60, 663) and vastly impressed by the speed with which he thinks up another (668-78). This one, he boasts (709ff.), is his masterpiece, because he will achieve his aim simply by telling the truth. He persuades Clinia to allow Bacchis, still supposedly Clinia's, to transfer to Menedemus' house, and gets him to tell his father the truth - that Bacchis is Clitipho's and that he himself wants to marry Antiphila. When Menedemus later duly tells this to his neighbour (847, 852-3), Chremes does not believe it; he has already been duped by Syrus (767ff.), and thinks it is a ruse for Clinia to get money for Bacchis out of Menedemus under the pretence that it is needed for his wedding. However, Syrus' plan again fails, because Chremes refuses to cooperate (779) in pretending to betroth Antiphila to Clinia. But in an instant the slave comes bouncing back; he returns (790ff.) to the story of the debt and says that Chremes must pay it since his newly-discovered daughter is surety. Without a murmur Chremes agrees; Syrus has at last got money for Clitipho to give to Bacchis, and he has got it from Chremes himself, the person he had originally intended to defraud. And his crowning glory is that he persuades Chremes to let Clitipho take it to Bacchis himself (799-800).

The complexities of all this are enormous, but the plot construction which brings them about is masterly. In the end we have a situation where Chremes is confronted with the truth and refuses to believe it; but when presented with the nonsense about Antiphila and the debt, he swallows it whole and pays up. Syrus' triumph is complete.

When the truth eventually comes out and Chremes' anger erupts, another side to this likeable rascal emerges; he is genuinely sorry for getting Clitipho into such trouble (970), and attempts to take his share of the blame (973-4). When this is brushed aside, there is one more service his cleverness can do for his young master, and his final trick plays a major part in bringing about a reconciliation between father and son. By suggesting to Clitipho that the extent of Chremes' anger is due to the fact that he is not his parents' real son (985ff.), and by prompting him to ask Chremes and Sostrata what his true parentage is (994-6), Syrus ensures that Sostrata will be shocked into helping her son obtain his father's pardon. We have seen that Menedemus is influential in achieving this; but so is Sostrata, and it is Syrus' ingenious move (cf. 996-7) which, though it causes Clitipho some short-term pain, nevertheless helps to ensure that his father does forgive.

Clinia and Clitipho are not so instrumental in the advancement of the plot; young men in this type of comedy tend to protest at the actions or plans of their slaves (Clitipho 311ff., 589, 810ff.; Clinia 699, 713), or be exaggeratedly grateful for them (Clitipho 825), rather than be initiators themselves. Standing in awe of their fathers (Clinia 189, 433-5) and complaining - but not doing much - about them (Clitipho 213ff.), they entrust the resolution of their troubles entirely to their slaves (Clitipho 350-1). Our two young men provide good examples of the extremes of despair and elation between which they can swiftly alternate (Clinia 230ff., 244, 246ff., 308; Clitipho 805ff., 825). They are also appealing characters, particularly in their mutual friendship (182ff.) and support (358-60) - facets upon which Syrus plays (688ff.).

Perhaps the most attractive figure of all, despite her comparatively small role, is Sostrata, who is excellently drawn. Devout (1038), endearingly superstitious (650-2, 1015), self-deprecatory (649-50) and devoted to her family (1029ff., 1060-1), she has to put up with a lot from her husband, but not without protest (1003ff., 1010-1), and she knows how to handle him (623-4, 631-2, 644ff.). And she takes equal credit with Menedemus for reconciling Chremes and Clitipho at the end of the play.

The complexities of the plot, with its frequent changes of direction, make for a fast-moving play, which in turn combines with the skillfully-executed character drawing to produce good theatre. But there are some weaknesses in the construction, many of which have been held, rightly or wrongly, to be evidence of Terential workmanship . . . . Among others which have been identified are the contrast between the two older men's only recent acquaintance (53ff.) and their sons' long friendship (183-4), the awkwardness of the empty stage at 873-4, and the contrast between Chremes' threats against Syrus (950ff.) and his actual words to his face (974ff.). It need hardly be said that such comparatively minor inconsistencies and awkwardnesses, though evident to a careful reader, would have been scarcely noticeable to the audience as it was swept along by the quickly changing pattern of events being enacted on the stage . . . .

Dwora Gilula   (essay date 1991)

SOURCE: "Plots Are Not Stories: The So-Called 'Duality Method' of Terence," in *Reading Plays: Interpretation and Reception,* edited by Hanna Scolnicov and Peter Holland, Cambridge University Press, 1991, pp. 81-93.

[*In the essay below, Gilula examines Terence's use of dual plots and characters in the context of his* The Girl from Andros.]

Terence was praised in antiquity for the excellence of his plot construction. Donatus deemed as praiseworthy the existence of two love affairs (*bini amores*) in all Terence's plays but the **Hecyra,** and Evanthius commended the richness of Terence's plots (*locupletiora argumenta*) constructed of double affairs (*ex duplicibus negotiis*), likewise observing that all the plays except the **Hecyra** feature two young men in love. Terence's plays continued to be read, admired and even sometimes imitated in the Middle Ages, and the Renaissance comedy was modelled principally on his comedies. Herrick, who examined the leading commentaries on Terence from the fourth-century work of Donatus and on, has shown that Terence was considered a master of dramatic structure and his comedy monopolized the sixteenth-century discussion of comic theory: the 'dramatic' rules established for comedy mostly derived from the practice of Terence. On the issue of the double action, Donatus's observation was usually repeated and the double structure commended for the enriching of the action. Even after the interpretation of the single action recommended by Aristotle and Horace became established, the double plot continued to be practised in the Renaissance comedy, which, as is well known, influenced comedies of later periods. It is therefore interesting to note the change of attitude among modern scholars and critics towards Terence's plots.

Legrand, [in his *The New Greek Comedy,* 1917], for example, required the two love affairs to be of equal importance and tightly connected one with the other, using these two arbitrarily selected qualities of the double plot as a norm of evaluation. Accordingly, the **Phormio** received poor marks for having the two love affairs 'run parallel and without influence upon one another for too long a time' (i. e., they are not tightly connected), and the **Andria** was criticized, since 'one of the lovers becomes a matter of indifference to the spectators', and thus fails the requirement of 'equal importance'.

These requirements are based on an Aristotelian conception of dramatic unity and transfer Aristotle's critical method and criteria from tragedy to comedy. The double plot is regarded as artistically satisfying only if it fulfils the requirements of one action which evolves according to the rules of probability and necessity. The greater the extent of the causal interaction of its two issues the nearer will the double plot be to a representation of one action, whereas their equality makes sure that neither may be regarded as a subplot. Such requirements not only demand that plots of comedies should conform with the plots of tragedies, but they also ignore, or criticize, plots with two issues of varying importance, or plots with other, not causal interconnections.

Legrand's normative approach was adopted by Norwood [in his *The Art of Terence,* 1923], who augmented it with yet another requirement. He was the first to coin the term 'the duality method', defining it as 'the method of employing two problems or complications to solve each other'. Since Norwood believed in evolution and in intellectual progress, he deemed early works as immature and discerned in Terence's comedies a constant ascending line of improvement towards perfection. Thus, he proclaimed the *Andria* immature, which coincides with Legrand's view, but disagreed with Legrand's negative evaluation of the *Phormio,* which, being a later play, should reveal traits of artistic perfection. In this he was followed by Duckworth [in his *The Nature of Roman Comedy,* 1952], who also canonized 'the duality method', which, thanks to him, came to be taken almost for granted by others.

An amusing illustration of such a normative approach is the following criticism of the *Andria:* 'Charinus and his love for Philumena do not suit the standards for the dual plot as defined by Norwood and as practised by Terence in his later plays, particularly the Phormio'. Surely it is not Terence who has to suit Norwood's, or any other scholar's, standards. Normative evaluation based on arbitrarily selected or invented *ad hoc* dramatic qualities is unhelpful. What is needed is an understanding of the actual ways in which Terence's plots are constructed, an understanding which can be achieved through an unbiased reading of the plays, without any preconceived attitudes.

For quite a long time scholars and critics of the Roman comedy were chiefly interested in establishing the degree of originality in Terence's use of his Greek models and in their speculative reconstruction, to the relative neglect of other questions. Bent on finding contradictions, inconsistencies and other proofs of Terence's inferior workmanship, scholars used a methodology borrowed from Homeric studies. This contributed a great deal no doubt to the lack of interest in characteristics specific to the dramatic genre. Plays were treated in a way similar to that used in examining epic narrative as texts to be read, not as scripts to be performed. This attitude, more than anything else, has affected the treatment of dramatic plots, either single or double.

In this [essay] I propose to examine the question of 'the duality method' through a reading of one play, the *Andria,* Terence's first comedy.

A typical summary of any of the Terentian double plot comedies by scholars who subscribe to 'the duality method' tells the story of the two love affairs, stressing the degree of their importance and their interconnections. Duckworth, for example, summarizes the plot of the *Andria* as follows:

> In the *Andria,* Pamphilus—passionately devoted to his mistress Glycerium—does not wish to marry Chremes' daughter, who is beloved by Charinus, and Pamphilus assures Charinus that he has nothing to fear. When Davus' plans go astray, Charinus' hopes are temporarily shattered but the recognition of Glycerium as Chremes' daughter solves the problem of both

young men, and Charinus is free to marry Philumena.

Factually, this is a correct summary, but it is construed of various elements of unequal dramatic standing. It tells the story of the *Andria.* But while a play has a story to tell, the story of a play does not necessarily coincide with its dramatic stage plot, namely with the words and deeds of the characters who enact before the audience the actual stage events. The dramatic stage plot differs from what the formalists call *syuzet,* which is the order and presentation of the events in a narrative. It may contain narrative elements which describe past events in a non-chronological order, but these are described in a direct discourse by one of the characters and form a part of a present tense stage event. The sum of all present tense stage events is the dramatic stage plot.

Readers of a dramatic text who wish to construct its dramatic stage plot must think in terms of performance and take into account only what the play's characters are to say and do on stage before an audience. What is narrated by the *dramatis personae* as being said and done elsewhere are narrative elements incorporated into the present tense stage event, but with a different mode of existence. In order to construct a dramatic stage plot of a play, one has to compose a short story, namely to substitute the play's dialogues with a narrative. But, since plays are not texts conceived in terms of a narrative medium, they usually defy attempts at extrapolating their plots by playing tricks on the summarizing narrator. For it is easy to narrate what is narrated, and it seems almost natural to perform the transformation of the dialogue into narrative by adulterating it with actual narrative elements picked out of the dialogue itself. The result is a story of the play not at all representative of its dramatic stage plot. Since stories are not plots, substituting one for the other leads to erroneous analyses of the plays misrepresented in such a way.

Duckworth's previously quoted summary of the *Andria*'s plot is a fine example of such a story. It not only misrepresents what actually happens on stage, but also distorts the nature of the *Andria*'s dramatic conflict, for it creates the false impression that the two love affairs are equally important and that they are the main interest of the dramatic plot, that, in fact, the *Andria* is a romantic comedy. Terence's comedies, however, are not romantic dramas, but intrigue plays in which the emphasis is not one the lovers themselves but on the persons who plan to bring them together or set them apart. The two young men are not the main protagonists of the play and the girls do not appear on stage at all. If the importance of a character is commensurate with the length of his role, the first role belongs to the slave Davus, the second to the head of the household, the *senex* Simo, and only the third to his son Pamphilus. The same conclusion is bound to be reached if the importance of a character is measured in terms of the dramatic conflict he originates or in which he is involved. Even a brief glance at what actually happens in the *Andria* reveals that the action stems from a conflict between Simo and Davus.

The antecedents to the play's dramatic conflict are described by Simo in the exposition: his wealthy friend

Chremes, who, impressed by Pamphilus's allegedly exemplary behaviour, had offered Simo a marriage deal, had withdrawn his generous offer after a rumour reached him of Pamphilus's affair with the *meretrix* Glycerium. Simo plans to find out the truth and test his son's obedience by pretending that the marriage is to take place as arranged. He also hopes to fool his slave Davus into believing that the marriage is real, so that his schemes against it will be wasted harmlessly. Simo's main concern is that it will be not his son but Davus who will foil his plans. He deduces his son's unwillingness to get married from Davus's fear, and it is Davus whom he orders to see to it that his son will consent to the marriage. When Simo warns Davus not to try to pull any smart tricks, it is clear that it is now Davus's turn to do exactly what he is warned not to, that is to show how clever and inventive he is.

Thus, from the onset of the play, it is obvious that the two protagonists who advance the action are Simo and Davus and not Pamphilus, the *adulescens* in love. When Pamphilus is brought on stage for the first time (Act I, Scene 5), it is not to offer a course of action but to clarify his position, which up till then has been reported by a third party. In order to appraise correctly the schemes devised on his behalf, the audience has to hear directly from him what is his attitude to Glycerium and the proposed marriage, but it is Davus, not Pamphilus, who acts. His scheme counteracts Simo's, and in spite of all its (prepared) unexpectedness it neatly parallels Simo's stratagem: it is a bluff pitted against a bluff. Davus has found Simo out, correctly guessed his aim, and consequently advised Pamphilus to agree to the pretended marriage in order to avoid disobedience and to embarrass his plotting father. Pamphilus does whatever he is advised to do.

Both Simo and Davus are prompted to action by mutual disbelief, both constantly stand on guard and examine each other's moves. The chief comic ingredient of these situations is that each schemer, confident of his own cleverness, is led to a false assessment of events, disbelieving what is true and vice versa. Simo is, of course, only too happy to believe that his son is willing to marry Philumena. But, when Davus in his eagerness to eliminate all doubts overplays his hand with the explanation that Pamphilus's sadness is caused by Simo's close-fisted preparations for the marriage, Simo's suspicions are alerted (What is the old plotter (*veterator*) up to? 467), but his assessment of the events is false. Simo believes that the birth of Glycerium's child (his grandson) is staged in order to scare off Chremes. Not only is he led to disbelieve what is true, but, conditioned to explain events according to his expectations, he also jumps to the false conclusion that he has succeeded in fooling Davus exactly as he had planned, namely that his scheme of the pretended marriage actually helped him to uncover and to annul Davus's machinations.

Davus is quick to take advantage of Simo's mistaken conclusions and immediately proceeds to exploit his disbelief: You are right, you have detected the truth. The baby is not Glycerium's baby, she ordered it to be brought to break the marriage which is to her disadvantage but which Pamphilus now wants. Since it falls in line with his reasoning,

Simo believes Davus, takes his son's promise as a firm basis for further action, and proceeds as he initially planned. He persuades Chremes to change his mind again and to agree to the marriage (III, 3). Since Davus fooled Simo into believing that he, Davus, is not fooling him at all, Simo feels free to tell him about his initial plan of the pretended marriage. Now Davus is really gloating over his success, which reaches its peak in his ironic comment: Such cleverness! I could never have guessed it (589).

Immediately, however, he learns that the situation has been reversed. Simo, although fooled and outwitted, has actually achieved his goal, whereas Davus, the arch-schemer, finds out that his cleverness, instead of averting the marriage has helped to bring it about. Thus, for Davus, the first round ends with a setback: he must devise a new manoeuvre. It is surprisingly funny and structurally ingenious that Simo himself is the source of inspiration for this second stratagem. Davus decides to use the baby to scare off Chremes and stages an encounter with the slave-girl Mysis for him to witness (IV, 4). His scheme consists of two cleverly combined and balanced parts. Davus knows that the baby is the baby of Glycerium and Pamphilus, but by pretending that he believes it was brought by a midwife to deter Chremes he hopes to evoke a strong denial from the simpleton Mysis which will convince Chremes to believe the opposite. He also hints that Glycerium is an Athenian citizen with whom a marriage can be contracted. Although this is true, Davus considers it to be false. He adds it nevertheless in order to increase the baby's potential as a deterrent.

Davus's carefully planned and executed scheme—the funniest farcical stage scene of the entire comedy—is a great success. This time, the breaking of the second marriage offer (like the second marriage offer itself) is part of the actual dramatic stage plot and not of its expository antecedent narrative. In this way, the incidents of the dramatic action, by paralleling the narrated events of the exposition, achieve a unified continuity of the entire narrated and acted out sequence of events.

By pressuring Chremes, Davus succeeds in overturning Simo's plans. According to the best tradition of comedy in the battle of wits between the master and his slave, it is the slave who has the upper hand in the end. The final virtual power, however, is in the hands of the vanquished. The victor is at the mercy of the defeated. This part of the plot is neatly rounded off by Simo's carrying out his initial threat. He arranges for a physical punishment of Davus for not taking heed of his warning.

The arrival of Crito from Andros leads to the *anagnorisis* or recognition scene. His credibility is established by Chremes, whose acquaintance he is, and the entire episode is integrated into the mainstream of the plot by Simo's attitude of disbelief. Simo's doubting of Crito's integrity and his suspecting of yet another ruse iterates his former disposition and the attitude he displayed in all the previous instances which the audience has witnessed.

From the above short analysis it is clear that the opposition with which Simo and Davus meet, impersonated for each in the person of the other (the dramatic opposing forces), causes them constantly to alter their plans up to the turning-point of the play and its resolution. It is an intrigue plot, in which the complicating factor is the outwitting of the antagonist, not a romantic comedy, in which the lover himself takes a part and forwards the action. The chief ingredients of such a comedy are lacking: there is no courtship, no chase, seduction, persuasion, capture of hearts or conquest, in a word there is a lack of the chief ingredient, the battle of the sexes.

It is no wonder that the adherents of 'the duality method', who tend to upgrade the importance of the love stories, entirely misconstrue the **Andria's** dramatic plot structure. Norwood considers Davus a spurious character, 'a fly in the wheel', and 'a fifth wheel on the coach'. He is, also on this point, blindly followed by Duckworth, who writes: 'Davus . . . [is] a bungler whose suggestions and schemes confuse everyone but actually accomplish little.'

The secondary plot of the young Charinus and his slave Byrria is linked to the main plot, the Simo—Davus battle of wits, through causal and analogous means. Charinus is in love with Chremes' daughter Philumena, the girl whom Pamphilus, his friend, tries not to marry. This unique plot aspect of the **Andria**—in all the other double plot comedies of Terence each young man is linked with a separate young lady—is used as a causal connection of the two plot issues throughout the entire play sequence. Any fluctuation in Pamphilus's fate directly affects Charinus and repeatedly justifies his appearance on stage. This causal link also serves as an analogous combining element for the tying together and delineating of the actions and reactions of the two young men and their slaves. For even more important from the point of view of the plot structure is yet another unusual feature of the Charinus—Byrria plot element, the fact that Charinus does not have a family. As the only fatherless young man in the Terentian comedies he is also the only *adulescens* who does not need to secure his father's consent to a marriage. It precludes his plot issue from developing into a traditional intrigue plot in which a schemer slave outwits a *senex* for the sake of an *adulescens* in love. Where there is no *senex,* there is no room for any plotting with his fooling or persuasion as its goal. Thus, the inertness of Byrria is not only understandable but actually necessary.

Prevented from being a schemer, Byrria is not a mirror-image of Davus but rather his antithesis. He is represented as hindered from action by contemplation and by weighing of consequences. His cleverness, and clever he is, is not externalized in creative machinations but expressed in proverbial formulations of practical wisdom. The relations between Charinus and Byrria, presented as different from the relations between Davus and Pamphilus, provide the dramatic justification for Byrria's inaction. When Byrria proposes a course of action, Charinus refuses to accept it and accuses him of never giving him good advice. When Pamphilus urges Charinus and Byrria to devise a way for marrying Philumena while he will endeavour to avoid the marriage, it is immediately made clear that nothing will be done: Charinus is represented as quite satisfied with Pamphilus's declaration of intents (*sat habeo* 335). This is dramatized by Charinus's prompt dismissal of Byrria,

which highlights the incompatibility of the pair. Consequently the next scene (II, 2) presents the dependence of the two *adulescentes* on the doings of one scheming slave, and ends with an analogous situation: Davus repeats Pamphilus's advice and urges Charinus to forward his case on his own, for no marriage for Pamphilus need not necessarily mean a marriage for Charinus. The repetition underlines Charinus's future inaction and the continuing lack of initiative. He is expected, as before, to be satisfied with whatever is planned by Davus and done by Pamphilus. It is, therefore, in line with these aroused expectations that his only line of action is to send the passive Byrria to find out Pamphilus's whereabouts (II, 5).

As a result, the causal connection between the two plot issues is highly effective. Charinus's mistaken accusation of Pamphilus as interested in marrying Philumena (IV, 1) has an ironic effect and adds to Pamphilus's accumulating heap of misfortunes exactly at the right point in plot-time, whereas Davus's promise to extricate Pamphilus by a new stratagem from the spot into which he 'succeeded' in putting him bears hope also for Charinus. And again, this scene's end parallels that of the previous one: Davus refuses to act on behalf of Charinus and the latter departs conveying the impression of continuing inaction. Finally, in the closing scene of the play, Charinus is represented as ultimately taking the route of action previously advised by Davus, to plead with the girl's father through his friends. The advice itself is unusual and stems from the unusual feature of Charinus's lack of family. Young men do not negotiate their marriages in comedies, it is done by their fathers. But now, once Pamphilus is found to be Chremes' son-in-law, Charinus can use his good offices for the achieving of his desire (V, 5). The approval of Pamphilus's marriage to Glycerium, with its entailed huge dowry, turns him from a dependent lover into a rich *pater familias* whose authority is instrumental in bringing about a happy ending of Charinus's plot issue. Consequently, the Charinus—Byrria plot issue is intertwined into the main plot issue also through the thematic dependence of an *adulescens* on an able slave, albeit not his own, as well as by the contrasting analogy with Byrria, which enhances Davus's scheming ability and rounds off his characterization as an all-knowing, all-providing factotum with a finger in each and every pie.

As befits intrigue plots, the resolution of Charinus—Byrria's plot occupies but a tiny fraction of the play's actual stage time. The resolution of the main plot, although somewhat longer, is still far shorter and less prominent than the intrigues through which it has been achieved. Moreover, both resolutions are foreshadowed and expected. What is new and unknown are the stage situations leading to them. What Styan writes on the Restoration comedy [in his *Restoration Comedy in Performance*, 1986] is applicable, without much change, also to the Menandrean comedies of Terence: 'the comedies were not constructed like modern well-made plays. The outcome of each play was more or less known for the unexciting thing it was, and there were to be no surprises.'

The chief requirement of Norwood and his followers for the Terentian double plot, that its two problems solve each other, is a theoretical construct of a reader, neat, clean and nice, but hardly stage-oriented. For a spectator, resolutions do not exist throughout the entire stage time devoted to the plot sequences; they merely terminate them. Obviously readers' constructs of dramatic plots have all the characteristics of an end product of a silent reading process. They resemble the constructs of plots of narrative fiction, whose readers need not consider the different essences of the plot's various component elements and the different degree of their stage prominence.

To sum up: from the above analysis of the actual stage happenings of the **Andria** it may be concluded that both the plots are plots of intrigue, each of a different quality: one based on action, the other on inaction. The secondary plot highlights by a contrasting analogy the parallel but opposite elements of intrigue in the main plot. The modern tendency to define Terentian double plots in terms of love interests and call them romantic comedies obscures the intrigue elements and shifts the focus away from the stage action as viewed by spectators.

Before Legrand and others voiced their normative requirements, Donatus and other students of Terence described the Terentian double plot structure (see above) as pleasing in its variety. Thus, for example, Gibaldi Cinthio wrote (in 1554):

> double structure . . . has made the plays of Terence succeed wonderfully. I call that plot double which has in its action diverse kinds of persons of the same station in life, as two lovers of different characters, two old men of varied nature, two servants of opposite morals, and other such things as they may be seen in the **Andria** and in the other plots of the same poet, where it is clear that these like persons of unlike habits make the knot and the solution of the play very pleasing. [in Herrick, *Comic Theory in the Sixteenth Century,* 1964]

What enriches the dramatic plot is the addition of a second set of characters whose interests and goals multiply the original problems thus adding further angles and possibilities of comparison. Where there are two sets of lovers, fathers and slaves, with two sets of problems, their very presence on stage as part of the actual dramatic action enriches the play. But a rich plot is chiefly a plot which richly activates the spectators' minds. Interest is created and tension is increased not only when the audience's mind is occupied with what is presented on stage but also with what is not. When one plot is acted out on stage the audience does not entirely forget the other, but rather tends to think that actions of the other plot presumably take place at the same time somewhere else. Thus, a double plot is *ipso facto* richer than a single issue plot. It is no wonder, then, that later comedies, and especially farcical comedies, mirrored the Terentian double plot and even multiplied it.

Dana F. Sutton   (essay date 1993)

SOURCE: "Terence" in *Ancient Comedy: The War of the Generations,* Twayne Publishers, 1993, pp. 109-22.

[*In the essay below, Sutton discusses Terence's use of real-*

ism in The Brothers, *concluding that his plays were unpopular because "at their very heart is a philosophy of life that is incompatible with the innate outlook of ancient comedy."*]

Terence is a comic poet rather neglected in our times. The amount of criticism and scholarship devoted to him is not especially great or penetrating. Even more symptomatic is the fact much modern criticism regards Plautus and Roman Comedy as nearly synonymous, with Terence shoved firmly into the background on the occasions when he is considered at all. Reasons for this lukewarm attitude are not difficult to discern. Plautus fits in very well indeed with modern ideas of what comedy is and ought to be, but Terence does not. His plays are not especially funny, and they are certainly not uproariously joyous and life-affirming. Nor are they pugnaciously antinomian in the manner of Aristophanes and Plautus. There is nothing hilariously cathartic about them. Thus they are difficult to accommodate to modern critical theories, or readers' expectations, about the nature of ancient comedy or of comedy in general.

Terence was willing to reproduce the quieter and more thoughtful tone of his Greek New Comedy models. Most of the specific adaptive and Romanizing touches we find in Plautus are missing. To the extent that Plautus borrowed an outlook and specific features from Italian farce-forms, Plautine comedy is firmly anchored in native Roman soil. Terence's plays are unrelentingly Hellenistic.

Plautus' audience was the holidaymaking Roman people gathered in the Forum. Terence also ostensibly wrote for the kind of theatergoers described in the prologues of some of his plays, but in reality he enjoyed the patronage of progressive, enlightened, and thoroughly Hellenized patricians, Scipio Africanus (the conqueror of Carthage) and his circle. He was not so dependent on popular reception of his work, and he had good reason to concentrate more on catering to the tastes of his patrons. Insofar as he wrote for their consumption, in presenting works reflecting Hellenistic values he was therefore in the position of a man preaching to the converted, and his plays are shaped to appeal to a sophisticated intellectual elite whose idea of comedy may well have been shaped by firsthand contact with the kind of Greek originals from which Terence was working.

If much in Plautine comedy invites a specifically Freudian interpretation, the same is scarcely true of Terence, particularly as he does not invite the spectator to side with sons in their contentions against their fathers in the same straightforward way. One might be tempted to explain this difference between the two playwrights in terms of their personal psychic dispositions, but such an explanation would probably be both superficial and impertinent. For Plautus the especial interest of the Oedipal situation was that it could be co-opted as a powerful sociopolitical metaphor. Terence was not, and was not obliged to be, so concerned with the conflict of Hellenistic and traditional Roman values, and so had no similar use for the Oedipal metaphor.

Instead, he took a wholly different (and much more sophisticated) tack. In some of his tragedies Euripides employed the trick of placing ordinary characters in traditional heroic situations that are highly stressful, where their consequent behavior can be studied. Naturally, they cannot conduct themselves in heroic ways, and so they act out of their weaknesses and foibles rather than out of their strengths, and their motivations are those of recognizable men and women. Critics both admiring and hostile (beginning with Aristophanes, especially in *The Frogs*) have observed that the veneer of mythology-based tragedy often wears very thin in his plays and that he was groping toward a new kind of realistic melodrama.

Terence adopts the comic equivalent of Euripides' strategy. The world of pure comedy is usually populated with simply conceived and one-dimensional characters. He, on the other hand, places three-dimensional human beings in traditional comic situations, and so his plays may be called "psychological" in a very different sense than those of Plautus. They are concerned with the exploration of realistically depicted character. Pure comedy portrays its characters in blacks and whites. This is why I have repeatedly talked about a comedy's *dramatis personae* being divided into two camps. We find a hero, whose enterprise we cheer, and his friends and supporters ranged against his opponents, whose defeat we hope for and applaud. Each character can readily and unambiguously be assigned to one of these sides. And the hero's ultimate victory is decisive and uncomplicated, with the result that the spectator feels unmixed pleasure and relief at the happy outcome.

There is little room for shades of nuanced gray in this formula, nor is there any tolerance for the message that ostensibly happy resolutions may not be as uncomplicated as they first seem. There is, in short, something eternally cartoonlike about pure comedy's simplistic representations of life, just as there is about its pasteboard characters. Terentian comedy defies this tradition. Here too, his strategy is to reproduce traditional comic situations, but in the more complex and nuanced terms of realistic representation.

It does not matter whether you choose to resent Terentian realism as a betrayal of the proper business of comedy or applaud it as a step in the direction of urbane sophistication. The result in either case is the same: he devised a new kind of drama at Rome featuring a transvaluation of traditional comic values, a dissolution of the barrier between comedy and reality. In this transformed world, characters who are neither wholly admirable or totally ridiculous can act out of complex and sometimes self-contradictory motives. They can change and grow over the course of a play. The meaning of a play's events can be equally complex and ambiguous, no less so than the meaning of the events of real life. Terence's very different aims and methods are fully illustrated by *Adelphoe* (140 B.C.—all of Terence's plays were produced between 146 and 140 B.C.). In this play, traditional stock New Comedy characters and situations are readily visible, and the reader will immediately see analogues to elements from plays already studied here. Nevertheless, each of these appears in transmuted form so

that they simultaneously strike us as familiar and as startlingly new.

Adelphoe (*The brothers*) is based on a like-named play by Menander. The premise of the play is that a gentleman named Demea has two sons, Aeschines and Ctesipho. He also has a brother, Micio, who is a childless bachelor. Therefore he has allowed Micio to adopt Aeschines, keeping Ctesipho for himself. As Micio explains in his address to the audience at the beginning of the play, he and Demea have been very different kinds of men since boyhood. Demea has always been frugal and hard-working, and lives in the country. He himself, on the other hand, is an easygoing city dweller who has always devoted himself to a life of ease. He is very devoted to Aeschines, and since his primary concern is that the boy love him in return (49f.) he has brought him up very permissively: "I do not regard it is necessary that he do everything in obedience to my paternal authority" (51f.). Rather, he has encouraged the boy to hide nothing from his father, as his theory is that if a son gets in the habit of lying to his father, he will behave dishonorably toward everyone else: "I believe it is preferable to rear sons with tact and liberality, rather than govern them by intimidation" (58).

But, he tells us, Demea is disturbed by this policy. He rebukes his brother for letting the son carouse, chase women, run up bills. But Micio persists in his theory that:

> [Demea] is unreasonably harsh. In my opinion, he is badly mistaken to think that paternal authority is weightier or more enduring than a father's control based on friendship. This is my feeling and what I have persuaded myself: a man who is only forced to do his duty by impending evil, is only afraid as long as the threat hangs over him. If he thinks he can get away with it, he goes back to his natural-born ways. But he whom you join to yourself out of friendship is eager to repay you and will be the same when he's in your presence and when he's not. It's a father's job to accustom his son to doing right voluntarily rather than out of fear. This is the difference between a father and a master, and the man who doesn't know how to do this must confess that he's incompetent at child rearing. (64ff.)

Demea enters and chides Micio for Aeschines' wild behavior. Smugly, he contrasts him with the thrifty and sober Ctesipho who remains down on the farm (94ff.). Micio retorts (98ff.) that there's no crime in the sowing of adolescent wild oats. If Demea were a human being, he'd let Ctesipho do the same. For there's only one alternative: for the boy to await Demea's hoped-for demise and then behave similarly when he is a man (109f.). He himself subsidizes Aeschines' behavior. It's his own money, and Demea has no right to complain about how he chooses to spend it.

Demea reiterates that he is troubled about Aeschines. Micio maintains each father must stick to the rearing of his own boy, for to do otherwise would be to rescind Aeschines' adoption. Demea grudgingly agrees, and leaves. His departure creates an abrupt change of attitude in Micio. He confesses to the audience that there is much in what Demea says. He was too proud to confess as much in his presence, but in fact he too is disturbed by Aeschines' profligate behavior. Recently Aeschines announced that he was tired of whoring and desired to marry. But now, it seems, he is up to his old tricks. He himself must go and find out what is really happening.

In the next scene Aeschines enters, accompanied by a girl named Bacchis. He has forcibly taken her away from a pimping slave-dealer named Sannio, and although this gentleman pursues them expostulating he refuses to give her back. He is sure the girl is actually freeborn and has made up his mind to rescue her.

He takes her in the house leaving Sannio to fulminate. Syrus, Micio's slave, manages to calm him down. Then Ctesipho reenters, and greets Aeschines in the most friendly and grateful way. As the scene progresses it is gradually revealed to the audience that Bacchis is actually Ctesipho's girlfriend and that Aeschines has rescued her on his brother's behalf. At the end of the scene, Ctesipho goes into the house to join her.

In the next scene the plot grows more complex. Micio has for a next-door neighbor a widow named Sostrata. It seems that her daughter Pamphila is about to give birth. Aeschines, the father, has promised to marry her, but now her slave Geta bursts in and with high indignation informs her how Aeschines has liberated a slave-girl. Geta of course thinks that the boy has done this for his own benefit and his moral sensibilities are outraged. Although most of his imprecations are directed against Aeschines, he has a choice remark left over for Micio (314): "I'd kill that old man for producing such a rascal!" Sostrata is thrown into despair at this development. The girl's reputation is ruined, she has no dowry, and so she will be destitute. There's only one ray of hope. Aeschines gave her a ring, which she can produce as evidence if he denies his responsibility. Geta is to go tell the whole story to Hegio, a friend of her late husband who has always served as her protector.

The next scene begins with the entrance of a wrathful Demea. He has learned about Aeschines' abduction of the girl and, even worse, has gotten wind of the fact that Ctesipho had a hand in the escapade. Syrus comes along and, although he knows the truth, does not disabuse the old man (392ff.):

> SYR. There's a world of difference between you and Micio (and I'm not just saying this because you're here). You're nothing but wisdom, he's just a bunch of dreams. Would you allow your boy to carry on like this?
>
> DEM. Let him? Wouldn't I smell it out six months before he started anything?

Syrus goes on to tell him a cock-and-bull story about how upset Ctesipho became with Aeschines because of the escapade, how he hit him with a steady barrage of moral maxims. Demea hears all this reassuring stuff about his boy with great self-satisfaction.

Demea is about to go off to his farm, where he imagines Ctesipho awaits him, when Hegio comes in. Hegio is understandably upset about Aeschines' supposed abandonment of Pamphila, and taxes Demea about it as the girl's birth-shrieks can be heard offstage. All Demea can do is promise to refer the matter to Micio's attention.

After they leave Ctesipho and Syrus reenter. Ctesipho is disturbed because he is supposed to be at home on the farm but he wants to spend the night with Bacchis. Syrus tells him not to worry. He can invent some lie to explain his absence to Demea, and all he has to do to pacify the old man's anger is feed him some more lies about what a paragon of virtue Ctesipho is. Shortly thereafter, Ctesipho departs and Demea enters. Syrus is as good as his word. He pretends that Ctesipho has just administered a beating both to himself and to Bacchis because Aeschines' malfeasances had put him into a towering rage. Demea is naturally delighted to hear this and is not too careful about investigating the lies Syrus makes up to explain Ctesipho's absence.

They exit and Micio and Hegio enter. Micio has learned the truth about Aeschines' abduction of Bacchis and pacifies Hegio by relating the actual story. When they leave the stage a highly distraught Aeschines enters. He has gone to Sostrata's house to visit Pamphila and has been rudely turned away because they think he has acquired Bacchis for himself and is in the process of breaking his promises. He is shattered. He wants to tell the women the truth.

As he is summoning the nerve to knock at Sostrata's door Micio arrives. Although he knows the truth, he informs the audience in an aside that he'll have a little fun with Aeschines as a means of repaying him for not confiding in him about the whole situation. So he innocently asks the boy why he is standing at Sostrata's door. He is overjoyed to observe that Aeschines is capable of blushing (643), but to continue his deception he makes up a story that, since her father is dead, Pamphila is about to be married off to her nearest male kin. To be sure, her mother has some make-believe story about the girl having a baby by some unknown man, and so she is opposed to such a marriage. Nevertheless, this appointed husband is right now on his way to Athens in order to claim the girl.

Aeschines is of course upset yet again. He expostulates that this arrangement is downright dishonorable: think how the nameless young father of Pamphila's child will feel when she is taken away from it! Micio replies that no unfairness has been committed: after all, there was no wedding. Aeschines cannot take any more of this, and so he breaks down in tears. This causes Micio to drop his pretenses: he reveals that he knows the whole story. Father and son profess their deep love for each other, and Aeschines admits to feelings of shame over his behavior during this episode.

After this touching interview between father and son, Aeschines exits to prepare for his wedding and Demea enters. He starts to take Micio to task for Aeschines' behavior: in the past he has merely debauched girls like Bacchis; now he seems to be taking after honest freeborn Athenian girls. Micio receives this news with irritating equanimity. He professes not to be at all disturbed by the impending marriage of Aeschines to Pamphila. No point in getting upset over things you can't change; you just have to reconcile yourself to the throw of the dice.

This response has no calming effect on Demea. What, he asks, will happen to Bacchis? With equal blandness Micio announces that she will remain in the house. This horrifies his brother, who broadly hints at the arrangement's sexual implications (750ff.):

> DEM. I presume that you will arrange things so
> as to have a singing partner.
> MIC. Why not?
> DEM. And I suppose you will go a-dancing with
> these women.
> MIC. Fine.
> DEM. Fine?
> MIC. And you can dance along with us, if the
> need arises.

And so Micio (who of course knows the truth about Ctesipho and Bacchis) goes on teasing Demea, much as he has already teased Aeschines. Demea gives up in exasperation: the whole household is ruined by its excessive prosperity, and Micio is off his head.

Micio leaves and a drunken Syrus comes out. Demea takes this as further evidence of how Micio has let his household go to rack and ruin. He tries to talk to Syrus, but they are interrupted by another slave calling to Ctesipho within. So Demea learns that his son is not at the farm, but in Micio's house drinking. When Micio appears, he tries to remonstrate, but Micio gives him a lecture (896ff.). Demea can stick to his frugal habits, but his own money is a kind of bonus for the boys to enjoy. There's no need for worry; they can be trusted. He sees in them the qualities one wants. They are wise and intelligent; they display deference, mutual affection, and generosity. Even though they may be sowing their wild oats, they can easily be brought back to probity. Demea might think that they are spendthrifts, but the great fault of old age is an overconcern with money.

This produces a remarkable change of heart in Demea. As soon as Micio departs, he enters into a long soliloquy, worth quoting in full:

> No man can have a plan for his life so well worked out that reality, age, and experience cannot modify by teaching you. You are ignorant of that you imagine you know, and what at first you hold to be true is disproved by experience. This has now happened to me. For now that my life has nearly run its course I'm abandoning the austere life style I have always followed. Why? By experience I have discovered that nothing is better for a man than tolerance and kindness. The truth of this can easily be ascertained by looking at the situation of me and my brother. He is mild, tranquil, never offends anybody, has a smile for one and all. He has lived for himself at his own expense. Everybody greets him affectionately. But I, a harsh farmer, severe, stingy, and truculent, took a wife. Plenty of trouble there! Fathered two sons—more trouble. When I worked hard to provide for them, I wore out my life in striving. Now that I've reached old age, here's the reward they give me for my hard work—their dislike. This brother of mine reaps

the rewards of fatherhood without any effort. They adore him but shun me. They confide all their plans to him; they love him. They both stay with him, while I'm deserted. They pray for his long life, but I suppose they're hoping for my death. Thus he makes them both his own sons cheaply, although they have been brought up by me at great expense. I get all the bother; he gets the pleasure. So come now, let us take the opposite track. Since he's issuing me a challenge, let's see if I can talk pleasantly and act kindly. I also want to be loved and be well thought of by my boys. If this requires generosity and tolerance, I'll not be behindhand. The money will run out, but at my advanced age that scarcely matters. (855ff.)

And, so it appears that Demea has undergone a change of heart, a veritable transformation of the personality such as that experienced by Cnemon in *Dyscolus*. But the sequel shows that matters are not so simple. At first sight it seems that such will be the case, as Demea greets first Syrus, and then another slave named Geta, with unwonted affability, treating them virtually as equals. After he has done so, he says in a self-satisfied aside, "I am gradually winning the lower classes over to my side" (898). Then he meets Aeschines, and with an uncharacteristic display of emotions announces that he is his son's father both by birth and by nature, and that he loves him more than his own eyes (902f.).

But matters quickly swerve in a different direction. Demea is increasingly generous. When Aeschines complains that the wedding is being delayed, Demea airily responds that there is no problem—just break down the wall separating Micio's house from Sostrata's and combine the families into one. In an aside to the audience Demea reveals his real thinking (911): of course he can be as generous as he wants, for he is purchasing his own new popularity with Micio's money.

Micio, finding out that the wall is being demolished, breaks out of the house in fury, but Demea in his newly benign way convinces him that he should indeed support Sostrata's family. Indeed, with Aeschines breathlessly seconding him, he proposes all sorts of ways in which Micio can be generous: an estate for Hegio, freedom for Syrus, his wife, and Geta. Come to think of it, Micio ought to settle down and marry Sostrata.

Micio is of course appalled, both by seeing his money evanesce and at the prospect of losing his bachelor freedom to marry a woman he frankly regards as "a decrepit hag" (938). Finally, when he has finished rubbing Micio's and Aeschines' noses in this outburst of extravagant generosity, he brings home the lesson in a speech at 985ff.:

> I'll tell you why I acted thus. In order to show to you that the reason these boys think you are liberal and affable, Micio, does not come from the way you live your life or for any good and reasonable reason, but because of your permissiveness, your indulgence, and your open purse. And now, Aeschines, if my life style is hateful to you because I do not give in to you completely on every matter, just and unjust alike, I'm done with the subject. Spend, squander, do what you

like. But because of your youth you are heedless in your desires and excessively eager, and you may wish me to reprove and correct you on occasion as well as support you. If so, here I am at your service.

Aeschines can only say that henceforth he will defer to Demea. Demea says that he will allow Ctesipho to keep Bacchis—but that this must be his last fling. Micio chimes in this is right, and the play thus ends.

The issue explored in *Adelphoe,* the proposition that upbringing shapes character and that differing forms of upbringing create different products, is distinctly reminiscent of the theme of *The Clouds,* although one of the play's special jokes is that *Adelphoe* suggests that the products of different upbringings needn't be so very different after all. Since we are shown two allegedly contrasting products of conservative and liberal, old-fashioned and modern upbringings, *Adelphoe* even more sharply recalls *The Banqueteers.* Perhaps this is no accident. In a more general sense, the play very certainly is a commentary on a host of comedies of the *Mostellaria* type that favorably contrast liberality and hedonism, located in the city, with repressive conservatism, situated in the countryside.

To the extent that *Adelphoe* is conceived as a commentary on these two Aristophanic plays and perhaps other comedies treating the same theme, its message is that things are not so simple as comedy traditionally represents them.

This is true regarding both the play's central issue and its characters. Given the history of ancient comedy, one would predict both that it would show that different methods of child rearing would produce different kinds of young men, and that the more tolerant method would be represented as unquestionably superior. In that sense, the spectator expecting to see yet another rehearsal of comedy's standard lesson about the superiority of the young at heart and the fun-loving has lit up an exploding cigar. The play explores the limitations and deficiencies of tolerant liberality and strongly suggests that a hedonistic approach to life is not without its own shortcomings. The play's critical attitude toward liberalism and hedonism is startlingly new and different.

In *Adelphoe* we are shown a familiar cast of characters. Many of its major characters have generic equivalents in *Mostellaria.* In accordance with comedy's usual antiauthoritarian and fun-loving outlook, the position represented by Micio would normally be characterized as entirely in the right, and that represented by Demea would be given some manner of unsympathetic representation. Demea himself, in the tradition of such characters as Theopropides in *Mostellaria,* would be portrayed as an agelast and would be assigned some such unpleasant traits as dourness, excessive austerity, or obtuseness, and Micio, a fun-loving older man of the Simo type, would be presented as a decidedly more attractive human being. The play would conclude with the decisive and uncomplicated triumph of the fun-loving characters and the values they represent.

But in accordance with Terence's program of heightened realism, representing life in something resembling its full

complexity, things do not work out this way. There is plenty to be said in favor of Demea's conservative approach and his philosophy of child rearing. In agreement with this revised way of regarding the situation, Demea is given a sympathetic characterization. There is nothing pathological about him, and for a "repressive" comic father he is, very uncharacteristically, not shown as either stupid or insensitive. Indeed, by the end of the play we appreciate that he is its most intelligent character. He conceives and executes a plan for turning the tables on Micio and teaching him and the two boys a valuable lesson about hedonism's limitations. Although Micio already seems to have some doubts about the wisdom of keeping such a loose rein on adolescent men, he keeps his reservations to himself. Demea pushes the issue to extremes to make Micio confront the issue squarely. But it is the mark of Demea's tact and intelligence that he manages to do so in such a way that Micio is not subject to undue humiliation and so that no attempt is made to alienate the boy's affections or interfere with their love lives. *Adelphoe* is not a comedy that ends with a typical reconciliation of its characters, because no such reconciliation is needed. Demea has engineered a solution in which everybody (even plenty of secondary characters) wins.

Adelphoe is populated with a set of characters quite unlike any we have previously encountered. They are equipped with a remarkable repertoire of emotions. They blush; they cry; they are capable of feeling and of expressing deep affection. The need to be loved is recognized as a necessary human desire. There is no room here for Oedipus. This is the only comedy we have read in which the relation of a son (or at least an adopted son) and his father is portrayed as loving rather than antagonistic, so that we are shown the possibility that a *familia* can be held together by bonds of affection rather than by upward-directed loyalty and downward-directed authoritarianism. His characters are moved by genuine feelings (although Terence is no mawkish sentimentalist). They are capable of learning and growing, and an important part of Terence's interest in psychological analysis is the representation of human character evolving in response to changing circumstance. In *Dyscolus* this can be said of the central character, but in *Adelphoe* the observation holds good not just for Demea but also for those who are educated by his trick.

There is, in short, an unusual degree of sophistication in *Adelphoe.* Neither its issues nor its characters are represented in a simplistic or one-sided way. Terence has converted comedy into an instrument for a more serious and realistic exploration of life's problems and of human nature. Comedy perennially pokes fun at sacred cows, but it turns out that ancient comedy has a certain sacred cow of its own. In *Adelphoe* Terence calls into question a view that constitutes the central feature of ancient comedy's characteristic world-view: uncritical and reflexive endorsement of hedonism. "Yes, but life does not really work like that" is not a message characteristic of comedy, and when this comment is made about hedonism the result is rather devastating. If comedy is a subversive literary form, Terence turns the tables and writes a kind of drama meant to subvert comedy itself. And so there is a fine symbolism in the fact that *Adelphoe* (together with the *He-*

cyra, produced in the same year, just prior to Terence's death) happens to be the last ancient comedy to be written surviving from antiquity.

In his recent book on Terence [*Understanding Terence,* 1986], Sander M. Goldberg observes that the death of Terence meant, for all intents and purposes, the death of comedy at Rome. This presents the literary historian with a puzzle. Why did Roman comedy cease to flourish at a time when Roman literature as a whole was, if not still quite in its infancy, at least in its early and rather ungainly adolescence? Probably any number of causes might be discovered for comedy's early demise, but surely part of the responsibility (or should one say the blame?) falls on Terence himself. Goldberg plausibly suggests that Terence's innovations had the effect of alienating comedy from itself. Thus an argument might be constructed parallel to that of Aristophanes in *The Frogs* (revived by Nietzsche in *The Birth of Tragedy)* that Euripides' innovations had the effect of killing Greek tragedy. Some of the innovations in question were rather similar to those introduced by Terence: use of drama as a subtle tool for the critical examination of issues and exploration of character, coupled with a new toleration of moral ambiguities. Probably the motivation was also somewhat similar for both playwrights. Although they were still ostensibly writing for production in the popular theater, they were (much more than their respective predecessors) writing plays to be seen and read by a rising class of educated intellectuals; in Terence's case this was the Scipionic circle.

Goldberg's essential complaint is that Terence's ironical probing of character and social relationships took the fun out of comedy. He could have added that, since the quest for fun and freedom is the great ground-theme of ancient comedy, adoption of a detached and critical attitude toward hedonism, coupled with the insight that those who would put the brakes on fun-seeking are not necessarily in the wrong, is not only uncomic but down-right anti-comic. The construction of a critique of hedonism may well be a sign of deeper wisdom and increased moral and intellectual sophistication. But it is fatal to the spirit of comedy. Thus the difficulty with Terence is not just that his plays are insufficiently hilarious or lacking in comic energy, as modern critics often complain. The real problem is that at their very heart is a philosophy of life that is incompatible with the innate outlook of ancient comedy. After Terence, there really was nowhere for comedy to go.

FURTHER READING

Arnott, Geoffrey. "*Phormio Parasitvs*: A Study in Dramatic Methods of Characterization." *Greece & Rome* XVII. No. 1 (April 1970): 32-57.
> Study of Terence's characterization techniques, focusing on the eponymous character of Phormio.

Ashmore, Sidney G. Introduction to *P. Terenti Afri Comoediae: The Comedies of Terence*, by Terence, translated by Sidney G. Ashmore, pp. 1-68. New York: Oxford University Press, 1910.

Introduction to various aspects and attributes of the Roman theater of Terence's time.

Austin, James Curtiss. "The Significant Name in Terence." *University of Illinois Studies in Language and Literature* VII (1921): 401-532.
> Explores Terence's choice of character names, asserting that the majority are "etymologically appropriate to their predicament" and "bear both type and individual significance."

Bieber, Margaret. "The Roman Plays at the Time of the Republic." In her *The History of the Greek and Roman Theater,* pp. 147-60. Princeton: Princeton University Press, 1961.
> Briefly discusses Terence in relation to Roman comedy, calling him "a refined, subtle, cultured, and morally eminent poet."

Brothers, A. J. "The Construction of Terence's *Heautontimorumenos*." *Classical Quarterly* 30 (1980): 94-119.
> Detailed discussion of Terence's style in *The Self-Tormentor*, focusing especially on plot construction.

Earl, D. C. "Terence and Roman Politics." *Historia* XI (1962): 469-85.
> Explores Terence's attitude toward Roman politics as seen in his plays and concludes that he was largely apolitical.

Flicklinger, Roy C. "A Study of Terence's Prologues." *Philological Quarterly* VI, No. 3 (July 1927): 235-69.
> Extensive study of Terence's prologues, noting that "each in turn admirably reflect the situation in which they were composed and the psychology of the playwright as it varied with the change of his fortunes from festival to festival."

———. "On the Originality of Terence." *Philological Quarterly* VII, No. 2 (April 1928): 97-114.
> Traces the degree to which Terence adhered to his original sources for each play and concludes that "his crowning acheivement . . . was that his language never betrays this . . . but ever seems the spontaneous expression in choice Latin of the ideas which he sought to convey."

Frank, Tenney. "Terence's Contribution to Plot-Construction." *American Journal of Philology* XLIX, No. 4 (1928): 309-22.
> Detailed examination of the ways in which Terence consciously structured his plots to suit his comic purposes.

Goldberg, Sander M. "The Dramatic Balance of Terence's *Andria*." *Classica et Mediaevalia* XXXIII (1981-82): 135-43.
> Study of *The Girl from Andros* that supports Goldberg's thesis that Terence "is interested not so much in action nor even in individuals as in the relationships among a set of characters, and his artistic strength lies in his sensitive portrayal of people caught up in webs of conflicting obligations."

Gomme, A. W. "Menander." In his *Essays in Greek History and Literature,* pp. 249-95. Oxford: Basil Blackwell, 1937.
> Respected monograph that includes passing references to Terence and comparisons between his works and those of Menander.

Greenberg, Nathan A. "Success and Failure in the *Adel-*

phoe." Classical World 73, No. 4 (December 1979-January 1980): 221-36.

Discusses comic and farcical aspects of *The Brothers* and their effect on the interpretation of the theme of parental authority in the play.

Henry, G. Kenneth G. "The Characters of Terence." *Studies in Philology* 12 (1915): 55-98.

Exploration of Terence's characterization techniques. Henry asserts that "the strength of Terence's characters lies in their unity and moderation. Nothing is overdrawn. Nothing is forced or twisted to bring the character within the limits of the scheme."

Konstan, David. "*Hecyra.*" In his *Roman Comedy*, pp. 130-41. Ithaca, N. Y.: Cornell University Press, 1983.

Discusses *The Mother-in-Law* as a problem play because it "challenges and confounds" the norms and conventions of Roman comedy. For Konstan's study of *Phormio*, see essay dated 1983, above.

————. "Love in Terence's *Eunich*: The Origins of Erotic Subjectivity." *American Journal of Philology* 107, No. 1 (Spring 1986): 369-93.

Suggests that "the tension between love and constraint or interest" in Terence's *Eunich* acts as "a harbinger as well as a moment in the history of love that found expression in the elegists of the Augustan principate, and, after another transformation, in the medieval tradition of courtly love."

Laidlaw, W. A. *The Prosody of Terence: A Relational Study.* London: Oxford University Press, 1938.

A detailed, technical look at Terence's use of meter and accent in his prose.

Levin, Richard. "The Double Plots of Terence." *The Classical Journal* 62, No. 1 (October 1966): 301-05.

Discusses Terence's dual plot mechanism and its influence on later drama.

Lloyd-Jones, Hugh. "Terentian Technique in the *Adelphi* and the *Eunichus.*" *The Classical Quarterly* LXVIII, No. 2 (November 1973): 279-84.

Defends *The Brothers* and *The Eunich* from charges of inconsistency and tampering with the ending of both plays to suit Roman taste.

Ludwig, Walther. "The Originality of Terence and His Greek Models." *Greek, Roman, and Byzantine Studies* 9, No. 1 (Spring 1968): 169-82.

Explores Terence's handling of Menander's plays in adapting them, defending his standing as a "creative poet."

Mattingly, Harold B. "The Terentian *Didascaliae.*" *Athenaeum* XXXVII, Nos. I-II (1959): 148-73.

A detailed examination of Terence's *didascaliae* (official records of performances) with the aim of seeing what they tell us about Terence's life and career.

McGarrity, Terry. "Thematic Unity in Terence's *Andria.*" *Transactions of the American Philological Association* 108 (1978): 103-14.

Explores the continuity of theme in *The Girl from Andros*, arguing that Terence's two additions to Menander's basic plot "develop and support" his theme.

————. "Reputation vs. Reality in Terence's *Hecyra.*" *Classical Journal* 76, No. 1 (October/November 1980): 149-56.

Discusses the gap between expectations set up by the plot of *The Mother-in-Law* and actual performance in Terence's comedy.

Robbins, Edwin W. *Dramatic Characterization in Printed Commentaries on Terence 1473-1600.* Urbana: University of Illinois Press, 1951, 122 p.

Explores the influence of Terence's comedies on the development of sixteenth-century drama, especially with respect to characterization.

Saylor, Charles F. "The Theme of Planlessness in Terence's *Eunichus.*" *Transactions of the American Philological Association* 105 (1975): 297-311.

Focuses on *The Eunich* as a critique of "the planning and calculation prevalent in New Comedy and its Roman offspring."

Segal, Erich, and Moulton, Carroll. "*Contortor Legum*: The Hero of the *Phormio.*" *Rheinisches Museum für Philologie* 121, Nos. 3-4 (1978): 276-88.

Explores *Phormio* as a parody of the law.

Wright, John. "Terence." In his *Dancing in Chains: The Stylistic Unity of the Comoedia Palliata*, pp. 127-51. Papers and Monographs of the American Academy in Rome, Vol. XXV. Rome: American Academy in Rome, 1974.

Asserts that Terence rejected the traditions of Roman comedy in order to forge his own, individualistic style.

CLASSICAL AND MEDIEVAL LITERATURE CRITICISM

INDEXES

How to Use This Index

The main references

Calvino, Italo
1923-1985.....CLC 5, 8, 11, 22, 33, 39,
73; SSC 3

list all author entries in the following Gale Literary Criticism series:

BLC = Black Literature Criticism
CLC = Contemporary Literary Criticism
CLR = Children's Literature Review
CMLC = Classical and Medieval Literature Criticism
DA = DISCovering Authors
DC = Drama Criticism
HLC = Hispanic Literature Criticism
LC = Literature Criticism from 1400 to 1800
NCLC = Nineteenth-Century Literature Criticism
PC = Poetry Criticism
SSC = Short Story Criticism
TCLC = Twentieth-Century Literary Criticism
WLC = World Literature Criticism, 1500 to the Present

The cross-references

See also CANR 23; CA 85-88;
obituary CA 116

list all author entries in the following Gale biographical and literary sources:

AAYA = Authors & Artists for Young Adults
AITN = Authors in the News
BEST = Bestsellers
BW = Black Writers
CA = Contemporary Authors
CAAS = Contemporary Authors Autobiography Series
CABS = Contemporary Authors Bibliographical Series
CANR = Contemporary Authors New Revision Series
CAP = Contemporary Authors Permanent Series
CDALB = Concise Dictionary of American Literary Biography
CDBLB = Concise Dictionary of British Literary Biography
DLB = Dictionary of Literary Biography
DLBD = Dictionary of Literary Biography Documentary Series
DLBY = Dictionary of Literary Biography Yearbook
HW = Hispanic Writers
JRDA = Junior DISCovering Authors
MAICYA = Major Authors and Illustrators for Children and Young Adults
MTCW = Major 20th-Century Writers
NNAL = Native North American Literature
SAAS = Something about the Author Autobiography Series
SATA = Something about the Author
YABC = Yesterday's Authors of Books for Children

Literary Criticism Series
Cumulative Author Index

Aldiss, Brian W(ilson)
  1925- .... **CLC 5, 14, 40**
  See also CA 5-8R; CAAS 2; CANR 5, 28;
  DLB 14; MTCW; SATA 34

Alegria, Claribel 1924- .... **CLC 75**
  See also CA 131; CAAS 15; HW

Alegria, Fernando 1918- .... **CLC 57**
  See also CA 9-12R; CANR 5, 32; HW

Aleichem, Sholom .... **TCLC 1, 35**
  See also Rabinovitch, Sholem

Aleixandre, Vicente 1898-1984 ... **CLC 9, 36**
  See also CA 85-88; 114; CANR 26;
  DLB 108; HW; MTCW

Alepoudelis, Odysseus
  See Elytis, Odysseus

Aleshkovsky, Joseph 1929-
  See Aleshkovsky, Yuz
  See also CA 121; 128

Aleshkovsky, Yuz .... **CLC 44**
  See also Aleshkovsky, Joseph

Alexander, Lloyd (Chudley) 1924- .. **CLC 35**
  See also AAYA 1; CA 1-4R; CANR 1, 24,
  38; CLR 1, 5; DLB 52; JRDA; MAICYA;
  MTCW; SATA 3, 49

Alfau, Felipe 1902- .... **CLC 66**
  See also CA 137

Alger, Horatio, Jr. 1832-1899 ..... **NCLC 8**
  See also DLB 42; SATA 16

Algren, Nelson 1909-1981 .... **CLC 4, 10, 33**
  See also CA 13-16R; 103; CANR 20;
  CDALB 1941-1968; DLB 9; DLBY 81,
  82; MTCW

Ali, Ahmed 1910- .... **CLC 69**
  See also CA 25-28R; CANR 15, 34

Alighieri, Dante 1265-1321 .... **CMLC 3**

Allan, John B.
  See Westlake, Donald E(dwin)

Allen, Edward 1948- .... **CLC 59**

Allen, Paula Gunn 1939- .... **CLC 84**
  See also CA 112; 143; NNAL

Allen, Roland
  See Ayckbourn, Alan

Allen, Sarah A.
  See Hopkins, Pauline Elizabeth

Allen, Woody 1935- .... **CLC 16, 52**
  See also AAYA 10; CA 33-36R; CANR 27,
  38; DLB 44; MTCW

Allende, Isabel 1942- .... **CLC 39, 57; HLC**
  See also CA 125; 130; HW; MTCW

Alleyn, Ellen
  See Rossetti, Christina (Georgina)

Allingham, Margery (Louise)
  1904-1966 .... **CLC 19**
  See also CA 5-8R; 25-28R; CANR 4;
  DLB 77; MTCW

Allingham, William 1824-1889 ... **NCLC 25**
  See also DLB 35

Allison, Dorothy E. 1949- .... **CLC 78**
  See also CA 140

Allston, Washington 1779-1843 .... **NCLC 2**
  See also DLB 1

Almedingen, E. M. .... **CLC 12**
  See also Almedingen, Martha Edith von
  See also SATA 3

Almedingen, Martha Edith von 1898-1971
  See Almedingen, E. M.
  See also CA 1-4R; CANR 1

Almqvist, Carl Jonas Love
  1793-1866 .... **NCLC 42**

Alonso, Damaso 1898-1990 .... **CLC 14**
  See also CA 110; 131; 130; DLB 108; HW

Alov
  See Gogol, Nikolai (Vasilyevich)

Alta 1942- .... **CLC 19**
  See also CA 57-60

Alter, Robert B(ernard) 1935- ...... **CLC 34**
  See also CA 49-52; CANR 1

Alther, Lisa 1944- .... **CLC 7, 41**
  See also CA 65-68; CANR 12, 30; MTCW

Altman, Robert 1925- .... **CLC 16**
  See also CA 73-76; CANR 43

Alvarez, A(lfred) 1929- .... **CLC 5, 13**
  See also CA 1-4R; CANR 3, 33; DLB 14,
  40

Alvarez, Alejandro Rodriguez 1903-1965
  See Casona, Alejandro
  See also CA 131; 93-96; HW

Amado, Jorge 1912- ..... **CLC 13, 40; HLC**
  See also CA 77-80; CANR 35; DLB 113;
  MTCW

Ambler, Eric 1909- .... **CLC 4, 6, 9**
  See also CA 9-12R; CANR 7, 38; DLB 77;
  MTCW

Amichai, Yehuda 1924- ...... **CLC 9, 22, 57**
  See also CA 85-88; MTCW

Amiel, Henri Frederic 1821-1881 .. **NCLC 4**

Amis, Kingsley (William)
  1922- .. **CLC 1, 2, 3, 5, 8, 13, 40, 44; DA**
  See also AITN 2; CA 9-12R; CANR 8, 28;
  CDBLB 1945-1960; DLB 15, 27, 100, 139;
  MTCW

Amis, Martin (Louis)
  1949- .... **CLC 4, 9, 38, 62**
  See also BEST 90:3; CA 65-68; CANR 8,
  27; DLB 14

Ammons, A(rchie) R(andolph)
  1926- .... **CLC 2, 3, 5, 8, 9, 25, 57**
  See also AITN 1; CA 9-12R; CANR 6, 36;
  DLB 5; MTCW

Amo, Tauraatua i
  See Adams, Henry (Brooks)

Anand, Mulk Raj 1905- .... **CLC 23**
  See also CA 65-68; CANR 32; MTCW

Anatol
  See Schnitzler, Arthur

Anaya, Rudolfo A(lfonso)
  1937- .... **CLC 23; HLC**
  See also CA 45-48; CAAS 4; CANR 1, 32;
  DLB 82; HW 1; MTCW

Andersen, Hans Christian
  1805-1875 .. **NCLC 7; DA; SSC 6; WLC**
  See also CLR 6; MAICYA; YABC 1

Anderson, C. Farley
  See Mencken, H(enry) L(ouis); Nathan,
  George Jean

Anderson, Jessica (Margaret) Queale
  .... **CLC 37**
  See also CA 9-12R; CANR 4

Anderson, Jon (Victor) 1940- .... **CLC 9**
  See also CA 25-28R; CANR 20

Anderson, Lindsay (Gordon)
  1923- .... **CLC 20**
  See also CA 125; 128

Anderson, Maxwell 1888-1959 ..... **TCLC 2**
  See also CA 105; DLB 7

Anderson, Poul (William) 1926- .... **CLC 15**
  See also AAYA 5; CA 1-4R; CAAS 2;
  CANR 2, 15, 34; DLB 8; MTCW;
  SATA 39

Anderson, Robert (Woodruff)
  1917- .... **CLC 23**
  See also AITN 1; CA 21-24R; CANR 32;
  DLB 7

Anderson, Sherwood
  1876-1941 .... **TCLC 1, 10, 24; DA;
  SSC 1; WLC**
  See also CA 104; 121; CDALB 1917-1929;
  DLB 4, 9, 86; DLBD 1; MTCW

Andouard
  See Giraudoux, (Hippolyte) Jean

Andrade, Carlos Drummond de ...... **CLC 18**
  See also Drummond de Andrade, Carlos

Andrade, Mario de 1893-1945 ..... **TCLC 43**

Andreas-Salome, Lou 1861-1937 ... **TCLC 56**
  See also DLB 66

Andrewes, Lancelot 1555-1626 .... **LC 5**

Andrews, Cicily Fairfield
  See West, Rebecca

Andrews, Elton V.
  See Pohl, Frederik

Andreyev, Leonid (Nikolaevich)
  1871-1919 .... **TCLC 3**
  See also CA 104

Andric, Ivo 1892-1975 .... **CLC 8**
  See also CA 81-84; 57-60; CANR 43;
  MTCW

Angelique, Pierre
  See Bataille, Georges

Angell, Roger 1920- .... **CLC 26**
  See also CA 57-60; CANR 13, 44

Angelou, Maya
  1928- .... **CLC 12, 35, 64, 77; BLC; DA**
  See also AAYA 7; BW 2; CA 65-68;
  CANR 19, 42; DLB 38; MTCW;
  SATA 49

Annensky, Innokenty Fyodorovich
  1856-1909 .... **TCLC 14**
  See also CA 110

Anon, Charles Robert
  See Pessoa, Fernando (Antonio Nogueira)

Anouilh, Jean (Marie Lucien Pierre)
  1910-1987 ..... **CLC 1, 3, 8, 13, 40, 50**
  See also CA 17-20R; 123; CANR 32;
  MTCW

Anthony, Florence
  See Ai

Anthony, John
  See Ciardi, John (Anthony)

Anthony, Peter
  See Shaffer, Anthony (Joshua); Shaffer,
  Peter (Levin)

Anthony, Piers 1934- . . . . **CLC 35**
   See also AAYA 11; CA 21-24R; CANR 28;
   DLB 8; MTCW

Antoine, Marc
   See Proust, (Valentin-Louis-George-Eugene-)
   Marcel

Antoninus, Brother
   See Everson, William (Oliver)

Antonioni, Michelangelo 1912- . . . . . **CLC 20**
   See also CA 73-76; CANR 45

Antschel, Paul 1920-1970
   See Celan, Paul
   See also CA 85-88; CANR 33; MTCW

Anwar, Chairil 1922-1949 . . . . **TCLC 22**
   See also CA 121

Apollinaire, Guillaume . . **TCLC 3, 8, 51; PC 7**
   See also Kostrowitzki, Wilhelm Apollinaris
   de

Appelfeld, Aharon 1932- . . . . **CLC 23, 47**
   See also CA 112; 133

Apple, Max (Isaac) 1941- . . . . **CLC 9, 33**
   See also CA 81-84; CANR 19; DLB 130

Appleman, Philip (Dean) 1926- . . . . . **CLC 51**
   See also CA 13-16R; CAAS 18; CANR 6,
   29

Appleton, Lawrence
   See Lovecraft, H(oward) P(hillips)

Apteryx
   See Eliot, T(homas) S(tearns)

Apuleius, (Lucius Madaurensis)
   125(?)-175(?) . . . . **CMLC 1**

Aquin, Hubert 1929-1977. . . . . **CLC 15**
   See also CA 105; DLB 53

Aragon, Louis 1897-1982 . . . . **CLC 3, 22**
   See also CA 69-72; 108; CANR 28;
   DLB 72; MTCW

Arany, Janos 1817-1882 . . . . **NCLC 34**

Arbuthnot, John 1667-1735 . . . . **LC 1**
   See also DLB 101

Archer, Herbert Winslow
   See Mencken, H(enry) L(ouis)

Archer, Jeffrey (Howard) 1940- . . . . **CLC 28**
   See also BEST 89:3; CA 77-80; CANR 22

Archer, Jules 1915- . . . . **CLC 12**
   See also CA 9-12R; CANR 6; SAAS 5;
   SATA 4

Archer, Lee
   See Ellison, Harlan

Arden, John 1930- . . . . **CLC 6, 13, 15**
   See also CA 13-16R; CAAS 4; CANR 31;
   DLB 13; MTCW

Arenas, Reinaldo
   1943-1990 . . . . **CLC 41; HLC**
   See also CA 124; 128; 133; HW

Arendt, Hannah 1906-1975 . . . . **CLC 66**
   See also CA 17-20R; 61-64; CANR 26;
   MTCW

Aretino, Pietro 1492-1556 . . . . **LC 12**

Arghezi, Tudor . . . . **CLC 80**
   See also Theodorescu, Ion N.

Arguedas, Jose Maria
   1911-1969 . . . . **CLC 10, 18**
   See also CA 89-92; DLB 113; HW

Argueta, Manlio 1936- . . . . **CLC 31**
   See also CA 131; HW

Ariosto, Ludovico 1474-1533 . . . . **LC 6**

Aristides
   See Epstein, Joseph

Aristophanes
   450B.C.-385B.C. . . . . **CMLC 4; DA; DC 2**

Arlt, Roberto (Godofredo Christophersen)
   1900-1942 . . . . **TCLC 29; HLC**
   See also CA 123; 131; HW

Armah, Ayi Kwei 1939- . . . . **CLC 5, 33; BLC**
   See also BW 1; CA 61-64; CANR 21;
   DLB 117; MTCW

Armatrading, Joan 1950- . . . . **CLC 17**
   See also CA 114

Arnette, Robert
   See Silverberg, Robert

Arnim, Achim von (Ludwig Joachim von
   Arnim) 1781-1831 . . . . **NCLC 5**
   See also DLB 90

Arnim, Bettina von 1785-1859 . . . . **NCLC 38**
   See also DLB 90

Arnold, Matthew
   1822-1888 . . . . . **NCLC 6, 29; DA; PC 5;**
                                    WLC
   See also CDBLB 1832-1890; DLB 32, 57

Arnold, Thomas 1795-1842 . . . . . . **NCLC 18**
   See also DLB 55

Arnow, Harriette (Louisa) Simpson
   1908-1986 . . . . **CLC 2, 7, 18**
   See also CA 9-12R; 118; CANR 14; DLB 6;
   MTCW; SATA 42, 47

Arp, Hans
   See Arp, Jean

Arp, Jean 1887-1966 . . . . **CLC 5**
   See also CA 81-84; 25-28R; CANR 42

Arrabal
   See Arrabal, Fernando

Arrabal, Fernando 1932- . . . **CLC 2, 9, 18, 58**
   See also CA 9-12R; CANR 15

Arrick, Fran . . . . **CLC 30**

Artaud, Antonin 1896-1948 . . . . . **TCLC 3, 36**
   See also CA 104

Arthur, Ruth M(abel) 1905-1979 . . . . **CLC 12**
   See also CA 9-12R; 85-88; CANR 4;
   SATA 7, 26

Artsybashev, Mikhail (Petrovich)
   1878-1927 . . . . **TCLC 31**

Arundel, Honor (Morfydd)
   1919-1973 . . . . **CLC 17**
   See also CA 21-22; 41-44R; CAP 2;
   CLR 35; SATA 4, 24

Asch, Sholem 1880-1957 . . . . **TCLC 3**
   See also CA 105

Ash, Shalom
   See Asch, Sholem

Ashbery, John (Lawrence)
   1927- . . . . . . **CLC 2, 3, 4, 6, 9, 13, 15, 25,**
                                       41, 77
   See also CA 5-8R; CANR 9, 37; DLB 5;
   DLBY 81; MTCW

Ashdown, Clifford
   See Freeman, R(ichard) Austin

Ashe, Gordon
   See Creasey, John

Ashton-Warner, Sylvia (Constance)
   1908-1984 . . . . **CLC 19**
   See also CA 69-72; 112; CANR 29; MTCW

Asimov, Isaac
   1920-1992 . . . . . . **CLC 1, 3, 9, 19, 26, 76**
   See also BEST 90:2; CA 1-4R; 137;
   CANR 2, 19, 36; CLR 12; DLB 8;
   DLBY 92; JRDA; MAICYA; MTCW;
   SATA 1, 26, 74

Astley, Thea (Beatrice May)
   1925- . . . . **CLC 41**
   See also CA 65-68; CANR 11, 43

Aston, James
   See White, T(erence) H(anbury)

Asturias, Miguel Angel
   1899-1974 . . . . **CLC 3, 8, 13; HLC**
   See also CA 25-28; 49-52; CANR 32;
   CAP 2; DLB 113; HW; MTCW

Atares, Carlos Saura
   See Saura (Atares), Carlos

Atheling, William
   See Pound, Ezra (Weston Loomis)

Atheling, William, Jr.
   See Blish, James (Benjamin)

Atherton, Gertrude (Franklin Horn)
   1857-1948 . . . . **TCLC 2**
   See also CA 104; DLB 9, 78

Atherton, Lucius
   See Masters, Edgar Lee

Atkins, Jack
   See Harris, Mark

Atticus
   See Fleming, Ian (Lancaster)

Atwood, Margaret (Eleanor)
   1939- . . . . . **CLC 2, 3, 4, 8, 13, 15, 25, 44,**
                           84; DA; PC 8; SSC 2; WLC
   See also AAYA 12; BEST 89:2; CA 49-52;
   CANR 3, 24, 33; DLB 53; MTCW;
   SATA 50

Aubigny, Pierre d'
   See Mencken, H(enry) L(ouis)

Aubin, Penelope 1685-1731(?) . . . . **LC 9**
   See also DLB 39

Auchincloss, Louis (Stanton)
   1917- . . . . **CLC 4, 6, 9, 18, 45**
   See also CA 1-4R; CANR 6, 29; DLB 2;
   DLBY 80; MTCW

Auden, W(ystan) H(ugh)
   1907-1973 . . . . . . **CLC 1, 2, 3, 4, 6, 9, 11,**
                                14, 43; DA; PC 1; WLC
   See also CA 9-12R; 45-48; CANR 5;
   CDBLB 1914-1945; DLB 10, 20; MTCW

Audiberti, Jacques 1900-1965 . . . . . . **CLC 38**
   See also CA 25-28R

Audubon, John James
   1785-1851 . . . . **NCLC 47**

Auel, Jean M(arie) 1936- . . . . **CLC 31**
   See also AAYA 7; BEST 90:4; CA 103;
   CANR 21

Auerbach, Erich 1892-1957 . . . . **TCLC 43**
   See also CA 118

Augier, Emile 1820-1889 . . . . **NCLC 31**

August, John
See De Voto, Bernard (Augustine)

Augustine, St. 354-430 . . . . **CMLC 6**

Aurelius
See Bourne, Randolph S(illiman)

Austen, Jane
1775-1817 . . . . **NCLC 1, 13, 19, 33; DA; WLC**
See also CDBLB 1789-1832; DLB 116

Auster, Paul 1947- . . . . **CLC 47**
See also CA 69-72; CANR 23

Austin, Frank
See Faust, Frederick (Schiller)

Austin, Mary (Hunter)
1868-1934 . . . . **TCLC 25**
See also CA 109; DLB 9, 78

Autran Dourado, Waldomiro
See Dourado, (Waldomiro Freitas) Autran

Averroes 1126-1198 . . . . **CMLC 7**
See also DLB 115

Avison, Margaret 1918- . . . . **CLC 2, 4**
See also CA 17-20R; DLB 53; MTCW

Axton, David
See Koontz, Dean R(ay)

Ayckbourn, Alan
1939- . . . . **CLC 5, 8, 18, 33, 74**
See also CA 21-24R; CANR 31; DLB 13; MTCW

Aydy, Catherine
See Tennant, Emma (Christina)

Ayme, Marcel (Andre) 1902-1967 . . . **CLC 11**
See also CA 89-92; CLR 25; DLB 72

Ayrton, Michael 1921-1975 . . . . **CLC 7**
See also CA 5-8R; 61-64; CANR 9, 21

Azorin . . . . **CLC 11**
See also Martinez Ruiz, Jose

Azuela, Mariano
1873-1952 . . . . **TCLC 3; HLC**
See also CA 104; 131; HW; MTCW

Baastad, Babbis Friis
See Friis-Baastad, Babbis Ellinor

Bab
See Gilbert, W(illiam) S(chwenck)

Babbis, Eleanor
See Friis-Baastad, Babbis Ellinor

Babel, Isaak (Emmanuilovich)
1894-1941(?) . . . . . . **TCLC 2, 13; SSC 16**
See also CA 104

Babits, Mihaly 1883-1941 . . . . **TCLC 14**
See also CA 114

Babur 1483-1530 . . . . **LC 18**

Bacchelli, Riccardo 1891-1985 . . . . . **CLC 19**
See also CA 29-32R; 117

Bach, Richard (David) 1936- . . . . **CLC 14**
See also AITN 1; BEST 89:2; CA 9-12R; CANR 18; MTCW; SATA 13

Bachman, Richard
See King, Stephen (Edwin)

Bachmann, Ingeborg 1926-1973 . . . . . **CLC 69**
See also CA 93-96; 45-48; DLB 85

Bacon, Francis 1561-1626 . . . . **LC 18**
See also CDBLB Before 1660

Bacon, Roger 1214(?)-1292 . . . . . . **CMLC 14**
See also DLB 115

Bacovia, George . . . . **TCLC 24**
See also Vasiliu, Gheorghe

Badanes, Jerome 1937- . . . . **CLC 59**

Bagehot, Walter 1826-1877 . . . . . . **NCLC 10**
See also DLB 55

Bagnold, Enid 1889-1981 . . . . **CLC 25**
See also CA 5-8R; 103; CANR 5, 40; DLB 13; MAICYA; SATA 1, 25

Bagrjana, Elisaveta
See Belcheva, Elisaveta

Bagryana, Elisaveta
See Belcheva, Elisaveta

Bailey, Paul 1937- . . . . **CLC 45**
See also CA 21-24R; CANR 16; DLB 14

Baillie, Joanna 1762-1851 . . . . **NCLC 2**
See also DLB 93

Bainbridge, Beryl (Margaret)
1933- . . . . **CLC 4, 5, 8, 10, 14, 18, 22, 62**
See also CA 21-24R; CANR 24; DLB 14; MTCW

Baker, Elliott 1922- . . . . **CLC 8**
See also CA 45-48; CANR 2

Baker, Nicholson 1957- . . . . **CLC 61**
See also CA 135

Baker, Ray Stannard 1870-1946 . . . **TCLC 47**
See also CA 118

Baker, Russell (Wayne) 1925- . . . . . . **CLC 31**
See also BEST 89:4; CA 57-60; CANR 11, 41; MTCW

Bakhtin, M.
See Bakhtin, Mikhail Mikhailovich

Bakhtin, M. M.
See Bakhtin, Mikhail Mikhailovich

Bakhtin, Mikhail
See Bakhtin, Mikhail Mikhailovich

Bakhtin, Mikhail Mikhailovich
1895-1975 . . . . **CLC 83**
See also CA 128; 113

Bakshi, Ralph 1938(?)- . . . . **CLC 26**
See also CA 112; 138

Bakunin, Mikhail (Alexandrovich)
1814-1876 . . . . **NCLC 25**

Baldwin, James (Arthur)
1924-1987 . . . . . . **CLC 1, 2, 3, 4, 5, 8, 13, 15, 17, 42, 50, 67; BLC; DA; DC 1; SSC 10; WLC**
See also AAYA 4; BW 1; CA 1-4R; 124; CABS 1; CANR 3, 24; CDALB 1941-1968; DLB 2, 7, 33; DLBY 87; MTCW; SATA 9, 54

Ballard, J(ames) G(raham)
1930- . . . . **CLC 3, 6, 14, 36; SSC 1**
See also AAYA 3; CA 5-8R; CANR 15, 39; DLB 14; MTCW

Balmont, Konstantin (Dmitriyevich)
1867-1943 . . . . **TCLC 11**
See also CA 109

Balzac, Honore de
1799-1850 . . . . **NCLC 5, 35; DA; SSC 5; WLC**
See also DLB 119

Bambara, Toni Cade
1939- . . . . **CLC 19; BLC; DA**
See also AAYA 5; BW 2; CA 29-32R; CANR 24; DLB 38; MTCW

Bamdad, A.
See Shamlu, Ahmad

Banat, D. R.
See Bradbury, Ray (Douglas)

Bancroft, Laura
See Baum, L(yman) Frank

Banim, John 1798-1842 . . . . **NCLC 13**
See also DLB 116

Banim, Michael 1796-1874 . . . . . . **NCLC 13**

Banks, Iain
See Banks, Iain M(enzies)

Banks, Iain M(enzies) 1954- . . . . **CLC 34**
See also CA 123; 128

Banks, Lynne Reid . . . . **CLC 23**
See also Reid Banks, Lynne
See also AAYA 6

Banks, Russell 1940- . . . . **CLC 37, 72**
See also CA 65-68; CAAS 15; CANR 19; DLB 130

Banville, John 1945- . . . . **CLC 46**
See also CA 117; 128; DLB 14

Banville, Theodore (Faullain) de
1832-1891 . . . . **NCLC 9**

Baraka, Amiri
1934- . . . . **CLC 1, 2, 3, 5, 10, 14, 33; BLC; DA; PC 4**
See also Jones, LeRoi
See also BW 2; CA 21-24R; CABS 3; CANR 27, 38; CDALB 1941-1968; DLB 5, 7, 16, 38; DLBD 8; MTCW

Barbellion, W. N. P. . . . . **TCLC 24**
See also Cummings, Bruce F(rederick)

Barbera, Jack (Vincent) 1945- . . . . . . **CLC 44**
See also CA 110; CANR 45

Barbey d'Aurevilly, Jules Amedee
1808-1889 . . . . **NCLC 1; SSC 17**
See also DLB 119

Barbusse, Henri 1873-1935 . . . . **TCLC 5**
See also CA 105; DLB 65

Barclay, Bill
See Moorcock, Michael (John)

Barclay, William Ewert
See Moorcock, Michael (John)

Barea, Arturo 1897-1957 . . . . **TCLC 14**
See also CA 111

Barfoot, Joan 1946- . . . . **CLC 18**
See also CA 105

Baring, Maurice 1874-1945 . . . . **TCLC 8**
See also CA 105; DLB 34

Barker, Clive 1952- . . . . **CLC 52**
See also AAYA 10; BEST 90:3; CA 121; 129; MTCW

Barker, George Granville
1913-1991 . . . . **CLC 8, 48**
See also CA 9-12R; 135; CANR 7, 38; DLB 20; MTCW

Barker, Harley Granville
See Granville-Barker, Harley
See also DLB 10

Barker, Howard 1946- . . . . **CLC 37**
See also CA 102; DLB 13

Barker, Pat 1943- . . . . **CLC 32**
See also CA 117; 122

Barlow, Joel 1754-1812 . . . . **NCLC 23**
See also DLB 37

Barnard, Mary (Ethel) 1909- . . . . **CLC 48**
See also CA 21-22; CAP 2

Barnes, Djuna
1892-1982 . . . **CLC 3, 4, 8, 11, 29; SSC 3**
See also CA 9-12R; 107; CANR 16; DLB 4,
9, 45; MTCW

Barnes, Julian 1946- . . . . **CLC 42**
See also CA 102; CANR 19; DLBY 93

Barnes, Peter 1931- . . . . **CLC 5, 56**
See also CA 65-68; CAAS 12; CANR 33,
34; DLB 13; MTCW

Baroja (y Nessi), Pio
1872-1956 . . . . **TCLC 8; HLC**
See also CA 104

Baron, David
See Pinter, Harold

Baron Corvo
See Rolfe, Frederick (William Serafino
Austin Lewis Mary)

Barondess, Sue K(aufman)
1926-1977 . . . . **CLC 8**
See also Kaufman, Sue
See also CA 1-4R; 69-72; CANR 1

Baron de Teive
See Pessoa, Fernando (Antonio Nogueira)

Barres, Maurice 1862-1923 . . . . **TCLC 47**
See also DLB 123

Barreto, Afonso Henrique de Lima
See Lima Barreto, Afonso Henrique de

Barrett, (Roger) Syd 1946- . . . . **CLC 35**

Barrett, William (Christopher)
1913-1992 . . . . **CLC 27**
See also CA 13-16R; 139; CANR 11

Barrie, J(ames) M(atthew)
1860-1937 . . . . **TCLC 2**
See also CA 104; 136; CDBLB 1890-1914;
CLR 16; DLB 10, 141; MAICYA;
YABC 1

Barrington, Michael
See Moorcock, Michael (John)

Barrol, Grady
See Bograd, Larry

Barry, Mike
See Malzberg, Barry N(athaniel)

Barry, Philip 1896-1949 . . . . **TCLC 11**
See also CA 109; DLB 7

Bart, Andre Schwarz
See Schwarz-Bart, Andre

Barth, John (Simmons)
1930- . . . . . . **CLC 1, 2, 3, 5, 7, 9, 10, 14,
27, 51; SSC 10**
See also AITN 1, 2; CA 1-4R; CABS 1;
CANR 5, 23; DLB 2; MTCW

Barthelme, Donald
1931-1989 . . . . . . **CLC 1, 2, 3, 5, 6, 8, 13,
23, 46, 59; SSC 2**
See also CA 21-24R; 129; CANR 20;
DLB 2; DLBY 80, 89; MTCW; SATA 7,
62

Barthelme, Frederick 1943- . . . . **CLC 36**
See also CA 114; 122; DLBY 85

Barthes, Roland (Gerard)
1915-1980 . . . . **CLC 24, 83**
See also CA 130; 97-100; MTCW

Barzun, Jacques (Martin) 1907- . . . . **CLC 51**
See also CA 61-64; CANR 22

Bashevis, Isaac
See Singer, Isaac Bashevis

Bashkirtseff, Marie 1859-1884 . . . **NCLC 27**

Basho
See Matsuo Basho

Bass, Kingsley B., Jr.
See Bullins, Ed

Bass, Rick 1958- . . . . **CLC 79**
See also CA 126

Bassani, Giorgio 1916- . . . . **CLC 9**
See also CA 65-68; CANR 33; DLB 128;
MTCW

Bastos, Augusto (Antonio) Roa
See Roa Bastos, Augusto (Antonio)

Bataille, Georges 1897-1962 . . . . **CLC 29**
See also CA 101; 89-92

Bates, H(erbert) E(rnest)
1905-1974 . . . . **CLC 46; SSC 10**
See also CA 93-96; 45-48; CANR 34;
MTCW

Bauchart
See Camus, Albert

Baudelaire, Charles
1821-1867 . . . . . **NCLC 6, 29; DA; PC 1;
WLC**

Baudrillard, Jean 1929- . . . . **CLC 60**

Baum, L(yman) Frank 1856-1919 . . . **TCLC 7**
See also CA 108; 133; CLR 15; DLB 22;
JRDA; MAICYA; MTCW; SATA 18

Baum, Louis F.
See Baum, L(yman) Frank

Baumbach, Jonathan 1933- . . . . . . **CLC 6, 23**
See also CA 13-16R; CAAS 5; CANR 12;
DLBY 80; MTCW

Bausch, Richard (Carl) 1945- . . . . . . **CLC 51**
See also CA 101; CAAS 14; CANR 43;
DLB 130

Baxter, Charles 1947- . . . . **CLC 45, 78**
See also CA 57-60; CANR 40; DLB 130

Baxter, George Owen
See Faust, Frederick (Schiller)

Baxter, James K(eir) 1926-1972 . . . . **CLC 14**
See also CA 77-80

Baxter, John
See Hunt, E(verette) Howard, Jr.

Bayer, Sylvia
See Glassco, John

Baynton, Barbara 1857-1929 . . . . . **TCLC 57**

Beagle, Peter S(oyer) 1939- . . . . **CLC 7**
See also CA 9-12R; CANR 4; DLBY 80;
SATA 60

Bean, Normal
See Burroughs, Edgar Rice

Beard, Charles A(ustin)
1874-1948 . . . . **TCLC 15**
See also CA 115; DLB 17; SATA 18

Beardsley, Aubrey 1872-1898 . . . . . **NCLC 6**

Beattie, Ann
1947- . . . . **CLC 8, 13, 18, 40, 63; SSC 11**
See also BEST 90:2; CA 81-84; DLBY 82;
MTCW

Beattie, James 1735-1803 . . . . **NCLC 25**
See also DLB 109

Beauchamp, Kathleen Mansfield 1888-1923
See Mansfield, Katherine
See also CA 104; 134; DA

Beaumarchais, Pierre-Augustin Caron de
1732-1799 . . . . **DC 4**

**Beauvoir, Simone (Lucie Ernestine Marie
Bertrand) de**
1908-1986 . . . . **CLC 1, 2, 4, 8, 14, 31, 44,
50, 71; DA; WLC**
See also CA 9-12R; 118; CANR 28;
DLB 72; DLBY 86; MTCW

Becker, Jurek 1937- . . . . **CLC 7, 19**
See also CA 85-88; DLB 75

Becker, Walter 1950- . . . . **CLC 26**

Beckett, Samuel (Barclay)
1906-1989 . . . . . . **CLC 1, 2, 3, 4, 6, 9, 10,
11, 14, 18, 29, 57, 59, 83; DA; SSC 16;
WLC**
See also CA 5-8R; 130; CANR 33;
CDBLB 1945-1960; DLB 13, 15;
DLBY 90; MTCW

Beckford, William 1760-1844 . . . . **NCLC 16**
See also DLB 39

Beckman, Gunnel 1910- . . . . **CLC 26**
See also CA 33-36R; CANR 15; CLR 25;
MAICYA; SAAS 9; SATA 6

Becque, Henri 1837-1899 . . . . **NCLC 3**

Beddoes, Thomas Lovell
1803-1849 . . . . **NCLC 3**
See also DLB 96

Bedford, Donald F.
See Fearing, Kenneth (Flexner)

Beecher, Catharine Esther
1800-1878 . . . . **NCLC 30**
See also DLB 1

Beecher, John 1904-1980 . . . . **CLC 6**
See also AITN 1; CA 5-8R; 105; CANR 8

Beer, Johann 1655-1700 . . . . **LC 5**

Beer, Patricia 1924- . . . . **CLC 58**
See also CA 61-64; CANR 13; DLB 40

Beerbohm, Henry Maximilian
1872-1956 . . . . **TCLC 1, 24**
See also CA 104; DLB 34, 100

Beerbohm, Max
See Beerbohm, Henry Maximilian

Begiebing, Robert J(ohn) 1946- . . . . . **CLC 70**
See also CA 122; CANR 40

Behan, Brendan
1923-1964 . . . . **CLC 1, 8, 11, 15, 79**
See also CA 73-76; CANR 33;
CDBLB 1945-1960; DLB 13; MTCW

Behn, Aphra
1640(?)-1689 . . . . **LC 1; DA; DC 4; WLC**
See also DLB 39, 80, 131

Behrman, S(amuel) N(athaniel)
1893-1973 . . . . **CLC 40**
See also CA 13-16; 45-48; CAP 1; DLB 7,
44

Besant, Annie (Wood) 1847-1933 ... **TCLC 9**
See also CA 105

Bessie, Alvah 1904-1985.......... **CLC 23**
See also CA 5-8R; 116; CANR 2; DLB 26

Bethlen, T. D.
See Silverberg, Robert

Beti, Mongo............... **CLC 27; BLC**
See also Biyidi, Alexandre

Betjeman, John
1906-1984 .... **CLC 2, 6, 10, 34, 43**
See also CA 9-12R; 112; CANR 33;
CDBLB 1945-1960; DLB 20; DLBY 84;
MTCW

Bettelheim, Bruno 1903-1990 ...... **CLC 79**
See also CA 81-84; 131; CANR 23; MTCW

Betti, Ugo 1892-1953 .... **TCLC 5**
See also CA 104

Betts, Doris (Waugh) 1932-.... **CLC 3, 6, 28**
See also CA 13-16R; CANR 9; DLBY 82

Bevan, Alistair
See Roberts, Keith (John Kingston)

Bialik, Chaim Nachman
1873-1934 .... **TCLC 25**

Bickerstaff, Isaac
See Swift, Jonathan

Bidart, Frank 1939- .... **CLC 33**
See also CA 140

Bienek, Horst 1930-........... **CLC 7, 11**
See also CA 73-76; DLB 75

Bierce, Ambrose (Gwinett)
1842-1914(?) .... **TCLC 1, 7, 44; DA;**
SSC 9; WLC
See also CA 104; 139; CDALB 1865-1917;
DLB 11, 12, 23, 71, 74

Billings, Josh
See Shaw, Henry Wheeler

Billington, (Lady) Rachel (Mary)
1942- .... **CLC 43**
See also AITN 2; CA 33-36R; CANR 44

Binyon, T(imothy) J(ohn) 1936- .... **CLC 34**
See also CA 111; CANR 28

Bioy Casares, Adolfo
1914- ...... **CLC 4, 8, 13; HLC; SSC 17**
See also CA 29-32R; CANR 19, 43;
DLB 113; HW; MTCW

Bird, C.
See Ellison, Harlan

Bird, Cordwainer
See Ellison, Harlan

Bird, Robert Montgomery
1806-1854 .... **NCLC 1**

Birney, (Alfred) Earle
1904- .... **CLC 1, 4, 6, 11**
See also CA 1-4R; CANR 5, 20; DLB 88;
MTCW

Bishop, Elizabeth
1911-1979 ...... **CLC 1, 4, 9, 13, 15, 32;**
DA; PC 3
See also CA 5-8R; 89-92; CABS 2;
CANR 26; CDALB 1968-1988; DLB 5;
MTCW; SATA 24

Bishop, John 1935-.............. **CLC 10**
See also CA 105

Bissett, Bill 1939-................ **CLC 18**
See also CA 69-72; CAAS 19; CANR 15;
DLB 53; MTCW

Bitov, Andrei (Georgievich) 1937-... **CLC 57**
See also CA 142

Biyidi, Alexandre 1932-
See Beti, Mongo
See also BW 1; CA 114; 124; MTCW

Bjarme, Brynjolf
See Ibsen, Henrik (Johan)

Bjornson, Bjornstjerne (Martinius)
1832-1910 .... **TCLC 7, 37**
See also CA 104

Black, Robert
See Holdstock, Robert P.

Blackburn, Paul 1926-1971 ...... **CLC 9, 43**
See also CA 81-84; 33-36R; CANR 34;
DLB 16; DLBY 81

Black Elk 1863-1950 .... **TCLC 33**
See also CA 144

Black Hobart
See Sanders, (James) Ed(ward)

Blacklin, Malcolm
See Chambers, Aidan

Blackmore, R(ichard) D(oddridge)
1825-1900 .... **TCLC 27**
See also CA 120; DLB 18

Blackmur, R(ichard) P(almer)
1904-1965 .... **CLC 2, 24**
See also CA 11-12; 25-28R; CAP 1; DLB 63

Black Tarantula, The
See Acker, Kathy

Blackwood, Algernon (Henry)
1869-1951 .... **TCLC 5**
See also CA 105

Blackwood, Caroline 1931- ...... **CLC 6, 9**
See also CA 85-88; CANR 32; DLB 14;
MTCW

Blade, Alexander
See Hamilton, Edmond; Silverberg, Robert

Blaga, Lucian 1895-1961 .... **CLC 75**

Blair, Eric (Arthur) 1903-1950
See Orwell, George
See also CA 104; 132; DA; MTCW;
SATA 29

Blais, Marie-Claire
1939- .... **CLC 2, 4, 6, 13, 22**
See also CA 21-24R; CAAS 4; CANR 38;
DLB 53; MTCW

Blaise, Clark 1940-.............. **CLC 29**
See also AITN 2; CA 53-56; CAAS 3;
CANR 5; DLB 53

Blake, Nicholas
See Day Lewis, C(ecil)
See also DLB 77

Blake, William
1757-1827 ..... **NCLC 13, 37; DA; WLC**
See also CDBLB 1789-1832; DLB 93;
MAICYA; SATA 30

Blasco Ibanez, Vicente
1867-1928 .... **TCLC 12**
See also CA 110; 131; HW; MTCW

Blatty, William Peter 1928-........ **CLC 2**
See also CA 5-8R; CANR 9

Bleeck, Oliver
See Thomas, Ross (Elmore)

Blessing, Lee 1949-.............. **CLC 54**

Blish, James (Benjamin)
1921-1975 .... **CLC 14**
See also CA 1-4R; 57-60; CANR 3; DLB 8;
MTCW; SATA 66

Bliss, Reginald
See Wells, H(erbert) G(eorge)

Blixen, Karen (Christentze Dinesen)
1885-1962
See Dinesen, Isak
See also CA 25-28; CANR 22; CAP 2;
MTCW; SATA 44

Bloch, Robert (Albert) 1917-...... **CLC 33**
See also CA 5-8R; CANR 5; DLB 44;
SATA 12

Blok, Alexander (Alexandrovich)
1880-1921 .... **TCLC 5**
See also CA 104

Blom, Jan
See Breytenbach, Breyten

Bloom, Harold 1930- .... **CLC 24**
See also CA 13-16R; CANR 39; DLB 67

Bloomfield, Aurelius
See Bourne, Randolph S(illiman)

Blount, Roy (Alton), Jr. 1941- ..... **CLC 38**
See also CA 53-56; CANR 10, 28; MTCW

Bloy, Leon 1846-1917........... **TCLC 22**
See also CA 121; DLB 123

Blume, Judy (Sussman) 1938-... **CLC 12, 30**
See also AAYA 3; CA 29-32R; CANR 13,
37; CLR 2, 15; DLB 52; JRDA;
MAICYA; MTCW; SATA 2, 31, 79

Blunden, Edmund (Charles)
1896-1974 .... **CLC 2, 56**
See also CA 17-18; 45-48; CAP 2; DLB 20,
100; MTCW

Bly, Robert (Elwood)
1926- .... **CLC 1, 2, 5, 10, 15, 38**
See also CA 5-8R; CANR 41; DLB 5;
MTCW

Boas, Franz 1858-1942.......... **TCLC 56**
See also CA 115

Bobette
See Simenon, Georges (Jacques Christian)

Boccaccio, Giovanni
1313-1375 .... **CMLC 13; SSC 10**

Bochco, Steven 1943-............. **CLC 35**
See also AAYA 11; CA 124; 138

Bodenheim, Maxwell 1892-1954 ... **TCLC 44**
See also CA 110; DLB 9, 45

Bodker, Cecil 1927- .... **CLC 21**
See also CA 73-76; CANR 13, 44; CLR 23;
MAICYA; SATA 14

Boell, Heinrich (Theodor)
1917-1985 .... **CLC 2, 3, 6, 9, 11, 15, 27,**
32, 72; DA; WLC
See also CA 21-24R; 116; CANR 24;
DLB 69; DLBY 85; MTCW

Boerne, Alfred
See Doeblin, Alfred

Bogan, Louise 1897-1970... ⌐LC **4, 39, 46**
See also CA 73-76; 25-28ᴿ CANR 33;
DLB 45; MTCW

Brathwaite, Edward (Kamau)
1930- .... **CLC 11**
See also BW 2; CA 25-28R; CANR 11, 26;
DLB 125

Brautigan, Richard (Gary)
1935-1984 .... **CLC 1, 3, 5, 9, 12, 34, 42**
See also CA 53-56; 113; CANR 34; DLB 2,
5; DLBY 80, 84; MTCW; SATA 56

Braverman, Kate 1950- .... **CLC 67**
See also CA 89-92

Brecht, Bertolt
1898-1956 ...... **TCLC 1, 6, 13, 35; DA;**
DC 3; WLC
See also CA 104; 133; DLB 56, 124; MTCW

Brecht, Eugen Berthold Friedrich
See Brecht, Bertolt

Bremer, Fredrika 1801-1865 ..... **NCLC 11**

Brennan, Christopher John
1870-1932 ....**TCLC 17**
See also CA 117

Brennan, Maeve 1917-.............. **CLC 5**
See also CA 81-84

Brentano, Clemens (Maria)
1778-1842 .... **NCLC 1**

Brent of Bin Bin
See Franklin, (Stella Maraia Sarah) Miles

Brenton, Howard 1942- .... **CLC 31**
See also CA 69-72; CANR 33; DLB 13;
MTCW

Breslin, James 1930-
See Breslin, Jimmy
See also CA 73-76; CANR 31; MTCW

Breslin, Jimmy .... **CLC 4, 43**
See also Breslin, James
See also AITN 1

Bresson, Robert 1907- .... **CLC 16**
See also CA 110

Breton, Andre 1896-1966... **CLC 2, 9, 15, 54**
See also CA 19-20; 25-28R; CANR 40;
CAP 2; DLB 65; MTCW

Breytenbach, Breyten 1939(?)- .. **CLC 23, 37**
See also CA 113; 129

Bridgers, Sue Ellen 1942- .... **CLC 26**
See also AAYA 8; CA 65-68; CANR 11,
36; CLR 18; DLB 52; JRDA; MAICYA;
SAAS 1; SATA 22

Bridges, Robert (Seymour)
1844-1930 .... **TCLC 1**
See also CA 104; CDBLB 1890-1914;
DLB 19, 98

Bridie, James..................... **TCLC 3**
See also Mavor, Osborne Henry
See also DLB 10

Brin, David 1950-................ **CLC 34**
See also CA 102; CANR 24; SATA 65

Brink, Andre (Philippus)
1935- .... **CLC 18, 36**
See also CA 104; CANR 39; MTCW

Brinsmead, H(esba) F(ay) 1922- .... **CLC 21**
See also CA 21-24R; CANR 10; MAICYA;
SAAS 5; SATA 18, 78

Brittain, Vera (Mary)
1893(?)-1970 .... **CLC 23**
See also CA 13-16; 25-28R; CAP 1; MTCW

Broch, Hermann 1886-1951...... **TCLC 20**
See also CA 117; DLB 85, 124

Brock, Rose
See Hansen, Joseph

Brodkey, Harold 1930-............ **CLC 56**
See also CA 111; DLB 130

Brodsky, Iosif Alexandrovich 1940-
See Brodsky, Joseph
See also AITN 1; CA 41-44R; CANR 37;
MTCW

Brodsky, Joseph .. **CLC 4, 6, 13, 36, 50; PC 9**
See also Brodsky, Iosif Alexandrovich

Brodsky, Michael Mark 1948- ..... **CLC 19**
See also CA 102; CANR 18, 41

Bromell, Henry 1947-.............. **CLC 5**
See also CA 53-56; CANR 9

Bromfield, Louis (Brucker)
1896-1956 .... **TCLC 11**
See also CA 107; DLB 4, 9, 86

Broner, E(sther) M(asserman)
1930- .... **CLC 19**
See also CA 17-20R; CANR 8, 25; DLB 28

Bronk, William 1918-.............. **CLC 10**
See also CA 89-92; CANR 23

Bronstein, Lev Davidovich
See Trotsky, Leon

Bronte, Anne 1820-1849.......... **NCLC 4**
See also DLB 21

Bronte, Charlotte
1816-1855 ... **NCLC 3, 8, 33; DA; WLC**
See also CDBLB 1832-1890; DLB 21

Bronte, (Jane) Emily
1818-1848 .... **NCLC 16, 35; DA; PC 8;**
WLC
See also CDBLB 1832-1890; DLB 21, 32

Brooke, Frances 1724-1789 .... **LC 6**
See also DLB 39, 99

Brooke, Henry 1703(?)-1783 .... **LC 1**
See also DLB 39

Brooke, Rupert (Chawner)
1887-1915 ...... **TCLC 2, 7; DA; WLC**
See also CA 104; 132; CDBLB 1914-1945;
DLB 19; MTCW

Brooke-Haven, P.
See Wodehouse, P(elham) G(renville)

Brooke-Rose, Christine 1926- ...... **CLC 40**
See also CA 13-16R; DLB 14

Brookner, Anita 1928-...... **CLC 32, 34, 51**
See also CA 114; 120; CANR 37; DLBY 87;
MTCW

Brooks, Cleanth 1906-1994 .... **CLC 24**
See also CA 17-20R; 145; CANR 33, 35;
DLB 63; MTCW

Brooks, George
See Baum, L(yman) Frank

Brooks, Gwendolyn
1917- ...... **CLC 1, 2, 4, 5, 15, 49; BLC;**
DA; PC 7; WLC
See also AITN 1; BW 2; CA 1-4R;
CANR 1, 27; CDALB 1941-1968;
CLR 27; DLB 5, 76; MTCW; SATA 6

Brooks, Mel..................... **CLC 12**
See also Kaminsky, Melvin
See also DLB 26

Brooks, Peter 1938-.............. **CLC 34**
See also CA 45-48; CANR 1

Brooks, Van Wyck 1886-1963...... **CLC 29**
See also CA 1-4R; CANR 6; DLB 45, 63,
103

Brophy, Brigid (Antonia)
1929- .... **CLC 6, 11, 29**
See also CA 5-8R; CAAS 4; CANR 25;
DLB 14; MTCW

Brosman, Catharine Savage 1934-.... **CLC 9**
See also CA 61-64; CANR 21

Brother Antoninus
See Everson, William (Oliver)

Broughton, T(homas) Alan 1936- - ... **CLC 19**
See also CA 45-48; CANR 2, 23

Broumas, Olga 1949-.......... **CLC 10, 73**
See also CA 85-88; CANR 20

Brown, Charles Brockden
1771-1810 .... **NCLC 22**
See also CDALB 1640-1865; DLB 37, 59,
73

Brown, Christy 1932-1981 .... **CLC 63**
See also CA 105; 104; DLB 14

Brown, Claude 1937- .... **CLC 30; BLC**
See also AAYA 7; BW 1; CA 73-76

Brown, Dee (Alexander) 1908- .. **CLC 18, 47**
See also CA 13-16R; CAAS 6; CANR 11,
45; DLBY 80; MTCW; SATA 5

Brown, George
See Wertmueller, Lina

Brown, George Douglas
1869-1902 .... **TCLC 28**

Brown, George Mackay 1921-.... **CLC 5, 48**
See also CA 21-24R; CAAS 6; CANR 12,
37; DLB 14, 27, 139; MTCW; SATA 35

Brown, (William) Larry 1951-...... **CLC 73**
See also CA 130; 134

Brown, Moses
See Barrett, William (Christopher)

Brown, Rita Mae 1944-..... **CLC 18, 43, 79**
See also CA 45-48; CANR 2, 11, 35;
MTCW

Brown, Roderick (Langmere) Haig-
See Haig-Brown, Roderick (Langmere)

Brown, Rosellen 1939-............ **CLC 32**
See also CA 77-80; CAAS 10; CANR 14, 44

Brown, Sterling Allen
1901-1989 .... **CLC 1, 23, 59; BLC**
See also BW 1; CA 85-88; 127; CANR 26;
DLB 48, 51, 63; MTCW

Brown, Will
See Ainsworth, William Harrison

Brown, William Wells
1813-1884 .... **NCLC 2; BLC; DC 1**
See also DLB 3, 50

Browne, (Clyde) Jackson 1948(?)-... **CLC 21**
See also CA 120

Browning, Elizabeth Barrett
1806-1861 ..... **NCLC 1. ⸱⸱ DA; PC 6;**
WLC
See also CDBLB 1832-1890; DLB 32

Cable, George Washington
1844-1925 . . . . **TCLC 4; SSC 4**
See also CA 104; DLB 12, 74

Cabral de Melo Neto, Joao 1920-. . . **CLC 76**

Cabrera Infante, G(uillermo)
1929- . . . . **CLC 5, 25, 45; HLC**
See also CA 85-88; CANR 29; DLB 113;
HW; MTCW

Cade, Toni
See Bambara, Toni Cade

Cadmus and Harmonia
See Buchan, John

Caedmon fl. 658-680. . . . . **CMLC 7**

Caeiro, Alberto
See Pessoa, Fernando (Antonio Nogueira)

Cage, John (Milton, Jr.) 1912- . . . . . **CLC 41**
See also CA 13-16R; CANR 9

Cain, G.
See Cabrera Infante, G(uillermo)

Cain, Guillermo
See Cabrera Infante, G(uillermo)

Cain, James M(allahan)
1892-1977 . . . . **CLC 3, 11, 28**
See also AITN 1; CA 17-20R; 73-76;
CANR 8, 34; MTCW

Caine, Mark
See Raphael, Frederic (Michael)

Calasso, Roberto 1941- . . . . **CLC 81**
See also CA 143

Calderon de la Barca, Pedro
1600-1681 . . . . **LC 23; DC 3**

Caldwell, Erskine (Preston)
1903-1987 . . . . **CLC 1, 8, 14, 50, 60**
See also AITN 1; CA 1-4R; 121; CAAS 1;
CANR 2, 33; DLB 9, 86; MTCW

Caldwell, (Janet Miriam) Taylor (Holland)
1900-1985 . . . . **CLC 2, 28, 39**
See also CA 5-8R; 116; CANR 5

Calhoun, John Caldwell
1782-1850 . . . . **NCLC 15**
See also DLB 3

Calisher, Hortense
1911- . . . . **CLC 2, 4, 8, 38; SSC 15**
See also CA 1-4R; CANR 1, 22; DLB 2;
MTCW

Callaghan, Morley Edward
1903-1990 . . . . **CLC 3, 14, 41, 65**
See also CA 9-12R; 132; CANR 33;
DLB 68; MTCW

Calvino, Italo
1923-1985 . . . . . **CLC 5, 8, 11, 22, 33, 39,**
73; SSC 3
See also CA 85-88; 116; CANR 23; MTCW

Cameron, Carey 1952- . . . . **CLC 59**
See also CA 135

Cameron, Peter 1959- . . . . **CLC 44**
See also CA 125

Campana, Dino 1885-1932. . . . . . . **TCLC 20**
See also CA 117; DLB 114

Campbell, John W(ood, Jr.)
1910-1971 . . . . **CLC 32**
See also CA 21-22; 29-32R; CANR 34;
CAP 2; DLB 8; MTCW

Campbell, Joseph 1904-1987 . . . . . . **CLC 69**
See also AAYA 3; BEST 89:2; CA 1-4R;
124; CANR 3, 28; MTCW

Campbell, Maria 1940-. . . . . **CLC 85**
See also CA 102; NNAL

Campbell, (John) Ramsey 1946- . . . . **CLC 42**
See also CA 57-60; CANR 7

Campbell, (Ignatius) Roy (Dunnachie)
1901-1957 . . . . **TCLC 5**
See also CA 104; DLB 20

Campbell, Thomas 1777-1844 . . . . **NCLC 19**
See also DLB 93; 144

Campbell, Wilfred . . . . **TCLC 9**
See also Campbell, William

Campbell, William 1858(?)-1918
See Campbell, Wilfred
See also CA 106; DLB 92

Campos, Alvaro de
See Pessoa, Fernando (Antonio Nogueira)

Camus, Albert
1913-1960 . . . . **CLC 1, 2, 4, 9, 11, 14, 32,**
63, 69; DA; DC 2; SSC 9; WLC
See also CA 89-92; DLB 72; MTCW

Canby, Vincent 1924-. . . . . **CLC 13**
See also CA 81-84

Cancale
See Desnos, Robert

Canetti, Elias 1905- . . . . . . **CLC 3, 14, 25, 75**
See also CA 21-24R; CANR 23; DLB 85,
124; MTCW

Canin, Ethan 1960-. . . . . **CLC 55**
See also CA 131; 135

Cannon, Curt
See Hunter, Evan

Cape, Judith
See Page, P(atricia) K(athleen)

Capek, Karel
1890-1938 . . . . . **TCLC 6, 37; DA; DC 1;**
WLC
See also CA 104; 140

Capote, Truman
1924-1984 . . . . . . **CLC 1, 3, 8, 13, 19, 34,**
38, 58; DA; SSC 2; WLC
See also CA 5-8R; 113; CANR 18;
CDALB 1941-1968; DLB 2; DLBY 80,
84; MTCW

Capra, Frank 1897-1991. . . . . **CLC 16**
See also CA 61-64; 135

Caputo, Philip 1941-. . . . . **CLC 32**
See also CA 73-76; CANR 40

Card, Orson Scott 1951- . . . . **CLC 44, 47, 50**
See also AAYA 11; CA 102; CANR 27;
MTCW

Cardenal (Martinez), Ernesto
1925- . . . . **CLC 31; HLC**
See also CA 49-52; CANR 2, 32; HW;
MTCW

Carducci, Giosue 1835-1907. . . . . . **TCLC 32**

Carew, Thomas 1595(?)-1640. . . . . . . **LC 13**
See also DLB 126

Carey, Ernestine Gilbreth 1908- . . . . **CLC 17**
See also CA 5-8R; SATA 2

Carey, Peter 1943- . . . . **CLC 40, 55**
See also CA 123; 127; MTCW

Carleton, William 1794-1869. . . . . . . **NCLC 3**

Carlisle, Henry (Coffin) 1926-. . . . . . **CLC 33**
See also CA 13-16R; CANR 15

Carlsen, Chris
See Holdstock, Robert P.

Carlson, Ron(ald F.) 1947-. . . . . **CLC 54**
See also CA 105; CANR 27

Carlyle, Thomas 1795-1881 . . **NCLC 22; DA**
See also CDBLB 1789-1832; DLB 55; 144

Carman, (William) Bliss
1861-1929 . . . . **TCLC 7**
See also CA 104; DLB 92

Carnegie, Dale 1888-1955 . . . . **TCLC 53**

Carossa, Hans 1878-1956. . . . . **TCLC 48**
See also DLB 66

Carpenter, Don(ald Richard)
1931-. . . . . **CLC 41**
See also CA 45-48; CANR 1

Carpentier (y Valmont), Alejo
1904-1980 . . . . **CLC 8, 11, 38; HLC**
See also CA 65-68; 97-100; CANR 11;
DLB 113; HW

Carr, Emily 1871-1945. . . . . **TCLC 32**
See also DLB 68

Carr, John Dickson 1906-1977 . . . . . . **CLC 3**
See also CA 49-52; 69-72; CANR 3, 33;
MTCW

Carr, Philippa
See Hibbert, Eleanor Alice Burford

Carr, Virginia Spencer 1929-. . . . . . . **CLC 34**
See also CA 61-64; DLB 111

Carrier, Roch 1937-. . . . . **CLC 13, 78**
See also CA 130; DLB 53

Carroll, James P. 1943(?)-. . . . . **CLC 38**
See also CA 81-84

Carroll, Jim 1951- . . . . **CLC 35**
See also CA 45-48; CANR 42

Carroll, Lewis . . . . **NCLC 2; WLC**
See also Dodgson, Charles Lutwidge
See also CDBLB 1832-1890; CLR 2, 18;
DLB 18; JRDA

Carroll, Paul Vincent 1900-1968. . . . **CLC 10**
See also CA 9-12R; 25-28R; DLB 10

Carruth, Hayden
1921- . . . . . . **CLC 4, 7, 10, 18, 84; PC 10**
See also CA 9-12R; CANR 4, 38; DLB 5;
MTCW; SATA 47

Carson, Rachel Louise 1907-1964 . . . **CLC 71**
See also CA 77-80; CANR 35; MTCW;
SATA 23

Carter, Angela (Olive)
1940-1992 . . . . . . **CLC 5, 41, 76; SSC 13**
See also CA 53-56; 136; CANR 12, 36;
DLB 14; MTCW; SATA 66;
SATA-Obit 70

Carter, Nick
See Smith, Martin Cruz

Carver, Raymond
1938-1988 . . . **CLC 22, 36, 53, 55; SSC 8**
See also CA 33-36R; 126; CANR 17, 34;
DLB 130; DLBY 84; MTCW

Chaviaras, Strates 1935-
See Haviaras, Stratis
See also CA 105

Chayefsky, Paddy . . . . CLC 23
See also Chayefsky, Sidney
See also DLB 7, 44; DLBY 81

Chayefsky, Sidney 1923-1981
See Chayefsky, Paddy
See also CA 9-12R; 104; CANR 18

Chedid, Andree 1920-. . . . . CLC 47
See also CA 145

Cheever, John
1912-1982 . . . . . . CLC 3, 7, 8, 11, 15, 25,
64; DA; SSC 1; WLC
See also CA 5-8R; 106; CABS 1; CANR 5,
27; CDALB 1941-1968; DLB 2, 102;
DLBY 80, 82; MTCW

Cheever, Susan 1943-. . . . . CLC 18, 48
See also CA 103; CANR 27; DLBY 82

Chekhonte, Antosha
See Chekhov, Anton (Pavlovich)

Chekhov, Anton (Pavlovich)
1860-1904 . . . . . TCLC 3, 10, 31, 55; DA;
SSC 2; WLC
See also CA 104; 124

Chernyshevsky, Nikolay Gavrilovich
1828-1889 . . . . NCLC 1

Cherry, Carolyn Janice 1942-
See Cherryh, C. J.
See also CA 65-68; CANR 10

Cherryh, C. J. . . . . CLC 35
See also Cherry, Carolyn Janice
See also DLBY 80

Chesnutt, Charles W(addell)
1858-1932 . . . . TCLC 5, 39; BLC; SSC 7
See also BW 1; CA 106; 125; DLB 12, 50,
78; MTCW

Chester, Alfred 1929(?)-1971. . . . . . . CLC 49
See also CA 33-36R; DLB 130

Chesterton, G(ilbert) K(eith)
1874-1936 . . . . TCLC 1, 6; SSC 1
See also CA 104; 132; CDBLB 1914-1945;
DLB 10, 19, 34, 70, 98; MTCW;
SATA 27

Chiang Pin-chin 1904-1986
See Ding Ling
See also CA 118

Ch'ien Chung-shu 1910-. . . . . CLC 22
See also CA 130; MTCW

Child, L. Maria
See Child, Lydia Maria

Child, Lydia Maria 1802-1880 . . . . NCLC 6
See also DLB 1, 74; SATA 67

Child, Mrs.
See Child, Lydia Maria

Child, Philip 1898-1978 . . . . CLC 19, 68
See also CA 13-14; CAP 1; SATA 47

Childress, Alice
1920- . . . . CLC 12, 15; BLC; DC 4
See also AAYA 8; BW 2; CA 45-48;
CANR 3, 27; CLR 14; DLB 7, 38; JRDA;
MAICYA; MTCW; SATA 7, 48

Chislett, (Margaret) Anne 1943-. . . . CLC 34

Chitty, Thomas Willes 1926-. . . . . . . CLC 11
See also Hinde, Thomas
See also CA 5-8R

Chomette, Rene Lucien 1898-1981
See Clair, Rene
See also CA 103

Chopin, Kate . . . . TCLC 5, 14; DA; SSC 8
See also Chopin, Katherine
See also CDALB 1865-1917; DLB 12, 78

Chopin, Katherine 1851-1904
See Chopin, Kate
See also CA 104; 122

Chretien de Troyes
c. 12th cent. - . . . . CMLC 10

Christie
See Ichikawa, Kon

Christie, Agatha (Mary Clarissa)
1890-1976 . . . . . . CLC 1, 6, 8, 12, 39, 48
See also AAYA 9; AITN 1, 2; CA 17-20R;
61-64; CANR 10, 37; CDBLB 1914-1945;
DLB 13, 77; MTCW; SATA 36

Christie, (Ann) Philippa
See Pearce, Philippa
See also CA 5-8R; CANR 4

Christine de Pizan 1365(?)-1431(?) . . . . LC 9

Chubb, Elmer
See Masters, Edgar Lee

Chulkov, Mikhail Dmitrievich
1743-1792 . . . . LC 2

Churchill, Caryl 1938-. . . . . CLC 31, 55
See also CA 102; CANR 22; DLB 13;
MTCW

Churchill, Charles 1731-1764. . . . . LC 3
See also DLB 109

Chute, Carolyn 1947-. . . . . CLC 39
See also CA 123

Ciardi, John (Anthony)
1916-1986 . . . . CLC 10, 40, 44
See also CA 5-8R; 118; CAAS 2; CANR 5,
33; CLR 19; DLB 5; DLBY 86;
MAICYA; MTCW; SATA 1, 46, 65

Cicero, Marcus Tullius
106B.C.-43B.C. . . . . CMLC 3

Cimino, Michael 1943-. . . . . CLC 16
See also CA 105

Cioran, E(mil) M. 1911-. . . . . CLC 64
See also CA 25-28R

Cisneros, Sandra 1954-. . . . . . CLC 69; HLC
See also AAYA 9; CA 131; DLB 122; HW

Clair, Rene. CLC 20
See also Chomette, Rene Lucien

Clampitt, Amy 1920- . . . . CLC 32
See also CA 110; CANR 29; DLB 105

Clancy, Thomas L., Jr. 1947-
See Clancy, Tom
See also CA 125; 131; MTCW

Clancy, Tom. . . . . CLC 45
See also Clancy, Thomas L., Jr.
See also AAYA 9; BEST 89:1, 90:1

Clare, John 1793-1864 . . . . NCLC 9
See also DLB 55, 96

Clarin
See Alas (y Urena), Leopoldo (Enrique
Garcia)

Clark, Al C.
See Goines, Donald

Clark, (Robert) Brian 1932-. . . . . CLC 29
See also CA 41-44R

Clark, Curt
See Westlake, Donald E(dwin)

Clark, Eleanor 1913- . . . . CLC 5, 19
See also CA 9-12R; CANR 41; DLB 6

Clark, J. P.
See Clark, John Pepper
See also DLB 117

Clark, John Pepper 1935- . . . . CLC 38; BLC
See also Clark, J. P.
See also BW 1; CA 65-68; CANR 16

Clark, M. R.
See Clark, Mavis Thorpe

Clark, Mavis Thorpe 1909-. . . . . CLC 12
See also CA 57-60; CANR 8, 37; CLR 30;
MAICYA; SAAS 5; SATA 8, 74

Clark, Walter Van Tilburg
1909-1971 . . . . CLC 28
See also CA 9-12R; 33-36R; DLB 9;
SATA 8

Clarke, Arthur C(harles)
1917- . . . . . . CLC 1, 4, 13, 18, 35; SSC 3
See also AAYA 4; CA 1-4R; CANR 2, 28;
JRDA; MAICYA; MTCW; SATA 13, 70

Clarke, Austin 1896-1974. . . . . CLC 6, 9
See also CA 29-32; 49-52; CAP 2; DLB 10,
20

Clarke, Austin C(hesterfield)
1934-. . . . . CLC 8, 53; BLC
See also BW 1; CA 25-28R; CAAS 16;
CANR 14, 32; DLB 53, 125

Clarke, Gillian 1937-. . . . . CLC 61
See also CA 106; DLB 40

Clarke, Marcus (Andrew Hislop)
1846-1881 . . . . NCLC 19

Clarke, Shirley 1925-. . . . . CLC 16

Clash, The
See Headon, (Nicky) Topper; Jones, Mick;
Simonon, Paul; Strummer, Joe

Claudel, Paul (Louis Charles Marie)
1868-1955 . . . . TCLC 2, 10
See also CA 104

Clavell, James (duMaresq)
1925-. . . . . CLC 6, 25
See also CA 25-28R; CANR 26; MTCW

Cleaver, (Leroy) Eldridge
1935-. . . . . CLC 30; BLC
See also BW 1; CA 21-24R; CANR 16

Cleese, John (Marwood) 1939- . . . . . CLC 21
See also Monty Python
See also CA 112; 116; CANR 35; MTCW

Cleishbotham, Jebediah
See Scott, Walter

Cleland, John 1710-1789 . . . . LC 2
See also DLB 39

Clemens, Samuel Langhorne 1835-1910
See Twain, Mark
See also CA 104; 135; CDALB 1865-1917;
DA; DLB 11, 12, 23, 64, 74; JRDA;
MAICYA; YABC 2

Cleophil
See Congreve, William

Endo, Shusaku 1923- . . . . . **CLC 7, 14, 19, 54**
See also CA 29-32R; CANR 21; MTCW

Engel, Marian 1933-1985 . . . . **CLC 36**
See also CA 25-28R; CANR 12; DLB 53

Engelhardt, Frederick
See Hubbard, L(afayette) Ron(ald)

Enright, D(ennis) J(oseph)
1920- . . . . **CLC 4, 8, 31**
See also CA 1-4R; CANR 1, 42; DLB 27;
SATA 25

Enzensberger, Hans Magnus
1929- . . . . **CLC 43**
See also CA 116; 119

Ephron, Nora 1941- . . . . **CLC 17, 31**
See also AITN 2; CA 65-68; CANR 12, 39

Epsilon
See Betjeman, John

Epstein, Daniel Mark 1948- . . . . **CLC 7**
See also CA 49-52; CANR 2

Epstein, Jacob 1956- . . . . **CLC 19**
See also CA 114

Epstein, Joseph 1937- . . . . **CLC 39**
See also CA 112; 119

Epstein, Leslie 1938- . . . . **CLC 27**
See also CA 73-76; CAAS 12; CANR 23

Equiano, Olaudah
1745(?)-1797 . . . . **LC 16; BLC**
See also DLB 37, 50

Erasmus, Desiderius 1469(?)-1536 . . . . **LC 16**

Erdman, Paul E(mil) 1932- . . . . **CLC 25**
See also AITN 1; CA 61-64; CANR 13, 43

Erdrich, Louise 1954- . . . . **CLC 39, 54**
See also AAYA 10; BEST 89:1; CA 114;
CANR 41; MTCW

Erenburg, Ilya (Grigoryevich)
See Ehrenburg, Ilya (Grigoryevich)

Erickson, Stephen Michael 1950-
See Erickson, Steve
See also CA 129

Erickson, Steve . . . . **CLC 64**
See also Erickson, Stephen Michael

Ericson, Walter
See Fast, Howard (Melvin)

Eriksson, Buntel
See Bergman, (Ernst) Ingmar

Eschenbach, Wolfram von
See Wolfram von Eschenbach

Eseki, Bruno
See Mphahlele, Ezekiel

Esenin, Sergei (Alexandrovich)
1895-1925 . . . . **TCLC 4**
See also CA 104

Eshleman, Clayton 1935- . . . . **CLC 7**
See also CA 33-36R; CAAS 6; DLB 5

Espriella, Don Manuel Alvarez
See Southey, Robert

Espriu, Salvador 1913-1985 . . . . **CLC 9**
See also CA 115; DLB 134

Espronceda, Jose de 1808-1842 . . . **NCLC 39**

Esse, James
See Stephens, James

Esterbrook, Tom
See Hubbard, L(afayette) Ron(ald)

Estleman, Loren D. 1952- . . . . **CLC 48**
See also CA 85-88; CANR 27; MTCW

Eugenides, Jeffrey 1960(?)- . . . . **CLC 81**
See also CA 144

Euripides c. 485B.C.-406B.C. . . . . **DC 4**
See also DA

Evan, Evin
See Faust, Frederick (Schiller)

Evans, Evan
See Faust, Frederick (Schiller)

Evans, Marian
See Eliot, George

Evans, Mary Ann
See Eliot, George

Evarts, Esther
See Benson, Sally

Everett, Percival L. 1956- . . . . **CLC 57**
See also BW 2; CA 129

Everson, R(onald) G(ilmour)
1903- . . . . **CLC 27**
See also CA 17-20R; DLB 88

Everson, William (Oliver)
1912-1994 . . . . **CLC 1, 5, 14**
See also CA 9-12R; 145; CANR 20; DLB 5,
16; MTCW

Evtushenko, Evgenii Aleksandrovich
See Yevtushenko, Yevgeny (Alexandrovich)

Ewart, Gavin (Buchanan)
1916- . . . . **CLC 13, 46**
See also CA 89-92; CANR 17; DLB 40;
MTCW

Ewers, Hanns Heinz 1871-1943 . . . **TCLC 12**
See also CA 109

Ewing, Frederick R.
See Sturgeon, Theodore (Hamilton)

Exley, Frederick (Earl)
1929-1992 . . . . **CLC 6, 11**
See also AITN 2; CA 81-84; 138; DLB 143;
DLBY 81

Eynhardt, Guillermo
See Quiroga, Horacio (Sylvestre)

Ezekiel, Nissim 1924- . . . . **CLC 61**
See also CA 61-64

Ezekiel, Tish O'Dowd 1943- . . . . **CLC 34**
See also CA 129

Fadeyev, A.
See Bulgya, Alexander Alexandrovich

Fadeyev, Alexander . . . . **TCLC 53**
See also Bulgya, Alexander Alexandrovich

Fagen, Donald 1948- . . . . **CLC 26**

Fainzilberg, Ilya Arnoldovich 1897-1937
See Ilf, Ilya
See also CA 120

Fair, Ronald L. 1932- . . . . **CLC 18**
See also BW 1; CA 69-72; CANR 25;
DLB 33

Fairbairns, Zoe (Ann) 1948- . . . . **CLC 32**
See also CA 103; CANR 21

Falco, Gian
See Papini, Giovanni

Falconer, James
See Kirkup, James

Falconer, Kenneth
See Kornbluth, C(yril) M.

Falkland, Samuel
See Heijermans, Herman

Fallaci, Oriana 1930- . . . . **CLC 11**
See also CA 77-80; CANR 15; MTCW

Faludy, George 1913- . . . . **CLC 42**
See also CA 21-24R

Faludy, Gyoergy
See Faludy, George

Fanon, Frantz 1925-1961 . . . . . **CLC 74; BLC**
See also BW 1; CA 116; 89-92

Fanshawe, Ann 1625-1680 . . . . **LC 11**

Fante, John (Thomas) 1911-1983 . . . **CLC 60**
See also CA 69-72; 109; CANR 23;
DLB 130; DLBY 83

Farah, Nuruddin 1945- . . . . **CLC 53; BLC**
See also BW 2; CA 106; DLB 125

Fargue, Leon-Paul 1876(?)-1947 . . . **TCLC 11**
See also CA 109

Farigoule, Louis
See Romains, Jules

Farina, Richard 1936(?)-1966 . . . . **CLC 9**
See also CA 81-84; 25-28R

Farley, Walter (Lorimer)
1915-1989 . . . . **CLC 17**
See also CA 17-20R; CANR 8, 29; DLB 22;
JRDA; MAICYA; SATA 2, 43

Farmer, Philip Jose 1918- . . . . **CLC 1, 19**
See also CA 1-4R; CANR 4, 35; DLB 8;
MTCW

Farquhar, George 1677-1707 . . . . **LC 21**
See also DLB 84

Farrell, J(ames) G(ordon)
1935-1979 . . . . **CLC 6**
See also CA 73-76; 89-92; CANR 36;
DLB 14; MTCW

Farrell, James T(homas)
1904-1979 . . . . **CLC 1, 4, 8, 11, 66**
See also CA 5-8R; 89-92; CANR 9; DLB 4,
9, 86; DLBD 2; MTCW

Farren, Richard J.
See Betjeman, John

Farren, Richard M.
See Betjeman, John

Fassbinder, Rainer Werner
1946-1982 . . . . **CLC 20**
See also CA 93-96; 106; CANR 31

Fast, Howard (Melvin) 1914- . . . . . . **CLC 23**
See also CA 1-4R; CAAS 18; CANR 1, 33;
DLB 9; SATA 7

Faulcon, Robert
See Holdstock, Robert P.

Faulkner, William (Cuthbert)
1897-1962 . . . . . **CLC 1, 3, 6, 8, 9, 11, 14,
18, 28, 52, 68; DA; SSC 1; WLC**
See also AAYA 7; CA 81-84; CANR 33;
CDALB 1929-1941; DLB 9, 11, 44, 102;
DLBD 2; DLBY 86; MTCW

Fauset, Jessie Redmon
1884(?)-1961 . . . . **CLC 19, 54; BLC**
See also BW 1; CA 109; DLB 51

Forche, Carolyn (Louise)
    1950- . . . . **CLC 25, 83; PC 10**
    See also CA 109; 117; DLB 5

Ford, Elbur
    See Hibbert, Eleanor Alice Burford

Ford, Ford Madox
    1873-1939 . . . . **TCLC 1, 15, 39, 57**
    See also CA 104; 132; CDBLB 1914-1945;
    DLB 34, 98; MTCW

Ford, John 1895-1973. . . . . **CLC 16**
    See also CA 45-48

Ford, Richard 1944- . . . . **CLC 46**
    See also CA 69-72; CANR 11

Ford, Webster
    See Masters, Edgar Lee

Foreman, Richard 1937-. . . . . **CLC 50**
    See also CA 65-68; CANR 32

Forester, C(ecil) S(cott)
    1899-1966 . . . . **CLC 35**
    See also CA 73-76; 25-28R; SATA 13

Forez
    See Mauriac, Francois (Charles)

Forman, James Douglas 1932-. . . . . . **CLC 21**
    See also CA 9-12R; CANR 4, 19, 42;
    JRDA; MAICYA; SATA 8, 70

Fornes, Maria Irene 1930-. . . . . . **CLC 39, 61**
    See also CA 25-28R; CANR 28; DLB 7;
    HW; MTCW

Forrest, Leon 1937- . . . . **CLC 4**
    See also BW 2; CA 89-92; CAAS 7;
    CANR 25; DLB 33

Forster, E(dward) M(organ)
    1879-1970 . . . . . **CLC 1, 2, 3, 4, 9, 10, 13,
    15, 22, 45, 77; DA; WLC**
    See also AAYA 2; CA 13-14; 25-28R;
    CANR 45; CAP 1; CDBLB 1914-1945;
    DLB 34, 98; DLBD 10; MTCW;
    SATA 57

Forster, John 1812-1876 . . . . **NCLC 11**
    See also DLB 144

Forsyth, Frederick 1938-. . . . . . **CLC 2, 5, 36**
    See also BEST 89:4; CA 85-88; CANR 38;
    DLB 87; MTCW

Forten, Charlotte L. . . . . **TCLC 16; BLC**
    See also Grimke, Charlotte L(ottie) Forten
    See also DLB 50

Foscolo, Ugo 1778-1827. . . . . **NCLC 8**

Fosse, Bob . . . . **CLC 20**
    See also Fosse, Robert Louis

Fosse, Robert Louis 1927-1987
    See Fosse, Bob
    See also CA 110; 123

Foster, Stephen Collins
    1826-1864 . . . . **NCLC 26**

Foucault, Michel
    1926-1984 . . . . **CLC 31, 34, 69**
    See also CA 105; 113; CANR 34; MTCW

Fouque, Friedrich (Heinrich Karl) de la Motte
    1777-1843 . . . . **NCLC 2**
    See also DLB 90

Fournier, Henri Alban 1886-1914
    See Alain-Fournier
    See also CA 104

Fournier, Pierre 1916- . . . . **CLC 11**
    See also Gascar, Pierre
    See also CA 89-92; CANR 16, 40

Fowles, John
    1926- . . . . **CLC 1, 2, 3, 4, 6, 9, 10, 15, 33**
    See also CA 5-8R; CANR 25; CDBLB 1960
    to Present; DLB 14, 139; MTCW;
    SATA 22

Fox, Paula 1923-. . . . . **CLC 2, 8**
    See also AAYA 3; CA 73-76; CANR 20,
    36; CLR 1; DLB 52; JRDA; MAICYA;
    MTCW; SATA 17, 60

Fox, William Price (Jr.) 1926- . . . . . **CLC 22**
    See also CA 17-20R; CAAS 19; CANR 11;
    DLB 2; DLBY 81

Foxe, John 1516(?)-1587 . . . . **LC 14**

Frame, Janet . . . . **CLC 2, 3, 6, 22, 66**
    See also Clutha, Janet Paterson Frame

France, Anatole . . . . **TCLC 9**
    See also Thibault, Jacques Anatole Francois
    See also DLB 123

Francis, Claude 19(?)- . . . . **CLC 50**

Francis, Dick 1920- . . . . **CLC 2, 22, 42**
    See also AAYA 5; BEST 89:3; CA 5-8R;
    CANR 9, 42; CDBLB 1960 to Present;
    DLB 87; MTCW

Francis, Robert (Churchill)
    1901-1987 . . . . **CLC 15**
    See also CA 1-4R; 123; CANR 1

Frank, Anne(lies Marie)
    1929-1945 . . . . **TCLC 17; DA; WLC**
    See also AAYA 12; CA 113; 133; MTCW;
    SATA 42

Frank, Elizabeth 1945-. . . . . **CLC 39**
    See also CA 121; 126

Franklin, Benjamin
    See Hasek, Jaroslav (Matej Frantisek)

Franklin, Benjamin 1706-1790. . . **LC 25; DA**
    See also CDALB 1640-1865; DLB 24, 43,
    73

Franklin, (Stella Maraia Sarah) Miles
    1879-1954 . . . . **TCLC 7**
    See also CA 104

Fraser, (Lady) Antonia (Pakenham)
    1932- . . . . **CLC 32**
    See also CA 85-88; CANR 44; MTCW;
    SATA 32

Fraser, George MacDonald 1925-. . . . **CLC 7**
    See also CA 45-48; CANR 2

Fraser, Sylvia 1935- . . . . **CLC 64**
    See also CA 45-48; CANR 1, 16

Frayn, Michael 1933-. . . . . . **CLC 3, 7, 31, 47**
    See also CA 5-8R; CANR 30; DLB 13, 14;
    MTCW

Fraze, Candida (Merrill) 1945-. . . . . **CLC 50**
    See also CA 126

Frazer, J(ames) G(eorge)
    1854-1941 . . . . **TCLC 32**
    See also CA 118

Frazer, Robert Caine
    See Creasey, John

Frazer, Sir James George
    See Frazer, J(ames) G(eorge)

Frazier, Ian 1951-. . . . . **CLC 46**
    See also CA 130

Frederic, Harold 1856-1898. . . . . . **NCLC 10**
    See also DLB 12, 23

Frederick, John
    See Faust, Frederick (Schiller)

Frederick the Great 1712-1786 . . . . . . **LC 14**

Fredro, Aleksander 1793-1876. . . . . **NCLC 8**

Freeling, Nicolas 1927- . . . . **CLC 38**
    See also CA 49-52; CAAS 12; CANR 1, 17;
    DLB 87

Freeman, Douglas Southall
    1886-1953 . . . . **TCLC 11**
    See also CA 109; DLB 17

Freeman, Judith 1946-. . . . . **CLC 55**

Freeman, Mary Eleanor Wilkins
    1852-1930 . . . . **TCLC 9; SSC 1**
    See also CA 106; DLB 12, 78

Freeman, R(ichard) Austin
    1862-1943 . . . . **TCLC 21**
    See also CA 113; DLB 70

French, Marilyn 1929-. . . . . . **CLC 10, 18, 60**
    See also CA 69-72; CANR 3, 31; MTCW

French, Paul
    See Asimov, Isaac

Freneau, Philip Morin 1752-1832. . **NCLC 1**
    See also DLB 37, 43

Freud, Sigmund 1856-1939 . . . . **TCLC 52**
    See also CA 115; 133; MTCW

Friedan, Betty (Naomi) 1921-. . . . . . **CLC 74**
    See also CA 65-68; CANR 18, 45; MTCW

Friedman, B(ernard) H(arper)
    1926- . . . . **CLC 7**
    See also CA 1-4R; CANR 3

Friedman, Bruce Jay 1930-. . . . **CLC 3, 5, 56**
    See also CA 9-12R; CANR 25; DLB 2, 28

Friel, Brian 1929-. . . . . **CLC 5, 42, 59**
    See also CA 21-24R; CANR 33; DLB 13;
    MTCW

Friis-Baastad, Babbis Ellinor
    1921-1970 . . . . **CLC 12**
    See also CA 17-20R; 134; SATA 7

Frisch, Max (Rudolf)
    1911-1991 . . . . . **CLC 3, 9, 14, 18, 32, 44**
    See also CA 85-88; 134; CANR 32;
    DLB 69, 124; MTCW

Fromentin, Eugene (Samuel Auguste)
    1820-1876 . . . . **NCLC 10**
    See also DLB 123

Frost, Frederick
    See Faust, Frederick (Schiller)

Frost, Robert (Lee)
    1874-1963 . . . . **CLC 1, 3, 4, 9, 10, 13, 15,
    26, 34, 44; DA; PC 1; WLC**
    See also CA 89-92; CANR 33;
    CDALB 1917-1929; DLB 54; DLBD 7;
    MTCW; SATA 14

Froude, James Anthony
    1818-1894 . . . . **NCLC 43**
    See also DLB 18, 57, 144

Froy, Herald
    See Waterhouse, Keith (Spencer)

Fry, Christopher 1907-. . . . . **CLC 2, 10, 14**
    See also CA 17-20R; CANR 9, 30; DLB 13;
    MTCW; SATA 66

Gelber, Jack 1932- . . . . CLC 1, 6, 14, 79
  See also CA 1-4R; CANR 2; DLB 7

Gellhorn, Martha (Ellis) 1908- . . CLC 14, 60
  See also CA 77-80; CANR 44; DLBY 82

Genet, Jean
  1910-1986 . . . CLC 1, 2, 5, 10, 14, 44, 46
  See also CA 13-16R; CANR 18; DLB 72;
  DLBY 86; MTCW

Gent, Peter 1942- . . . . CLC 29
  See also AITN 1; CA 89-92; DLBY 82

Gentlewoman in New England, A
  See Bradstreet, Anne

Gentlewoman in Those Parts, A
  See Bradstreet, Anne

George, Jean Craighead 1919- . . . . . . CLC 35
  See also AAYA 8; CA 5-8R; CANR 25;
  CLR 1; DLB 52; JRDA; MAICYA;
  SATA 2, 68

George, Stefan (Anton)
  1868-1933 . . . . TCLC 2, 14
  See also CA 104

Georges, Georges Martin
  See Simenon, Georges (Jacques Christian)

Gerhardi, William Alexander
  See Gerhardie, William Alexander

Gerhardie, William Alexander
  1895-1977 . . . . CLC 5
  See also CA 25-28R; 73-76; CANR 18;
  DLB 36

Gerstler, Amy 1956- . . . . CLC 70

Gertler, T. . . . . CLC 34
  See also CA 116; 121

Ghalib 1797-1869 . . . . NCLC 39

Ghelderode, Michel de
  1898-1962 . . . . CLC 6, 11
  See also CA 85-88; CANR 40

Ghiselin, Brewster 1903- . . . . CLC 23
  See also CA 13-16R; CAAS 10; CANR 13

Ghose, Zulfikar 1935- . . . . CLC 42
  See also CA 65-68

Ghosh, Amitav 1956- . . . . CLC 44

Giacosa, Giuseppe 1847-1906 . . . . . . TCLC 7
  See also CA 104

Gibb, Lee
  See Waterhouse, Keith (Spencer)

Gibbon, Lewis Grassic . . . . TCLC 4
  See also Mitchell, James Leslie

Gibbons, Kaye 1960- . . . . CLC 50

Gibran, Kahlil
  1883-1931 . . . . TCLC 1, 9; PC 9
  See also CA 104

Gibson, William 1914- . . . . CLC 23; DA
  See also CA 9-12R; CANR 9, 42; DLB 7;
  SATA 66

Gibson, William (Ford) 1948- . . . CLC 39, 63
  See also AAYA 12; CA 126; 133

Gide, Andre (Paul Guillaume)
  1869-1951 . . . . TCLC 5, 12, 36; DA;
              SSC 13; WLC
  See also CA 104; 124; DLB 65; MTCW

Gifford, Barry (Colby) 1946- . . . . CLC 34
  See also CA 65-68; CANR 9, 30, 40

Gilbert, W(illiam) S(chwenck)
  1836-1911 . . . . TCLC 3
  See also CA 104; SATA 36

Gilbreth, Frank B., Jr. 1911- . . . . CLC 17
  See also CA 9-12R; SATA 2

Gilchrist, Ellen 1935- . . CLC 34, 48; SSC 14
  See also CA 113; 116; CANR 41; DLB 130;
  MTCW

Giles, Molly 1942- . . . . CLC 39
  See also CA 126

Gill, Patrick
  See Creasey, John

Gilliam, Terry (Vance) 1940- . . . . CLC 21
  See also Monty Python
  See also CA 108; 113; CANR 35

Gillian, Jerry
  See Gilliam, Terry (Vance)

Gilliatt, Penelope (Ann Douglass)
  1932-1993 . . . . CLC 2, 10, 13, 53
  See also AITN 2; CA 13-16R; 141; DLB 14

Gilman, Charlotte (Anna) Perkins (Stetson)
  1860-1935 . . . . TCLC 9, 37; SSC 13
  See also CA 106

Gilmour, David 1949- . . . . CLC 35
  See also CA 138

Gilpin, William 1724-1804 . . . . . . NCLC 30

Gilray, J. D.
  See Mencken, H(enry) L(ouis)

Gilroy, Frank D(aniel) 1925- . . . . CLC 2
  See also CA 81-84; CANR 32; DLB 7

Ginsberg, Allen
  1926- . . . . . . CLC 1, 2, 3, 4, 6, 13, 36, 69;
              DA; PC 4; WLC 3
  See also AITN 1; CA 1-4R; CANR 2, 41;
  CDALB 1941-1968; DLB 5, 16; MTCW

Ginzburg, Natalia
  1916-1991 . . . . CLC 5, 11, 54, 70
  See also CA 85-88; 135; CANR 33; MTCW

Giono, Jean 1895-1970 . . . . CLC 4, 11
  See also CA 45-48; 29-32R; CANR 2, 35;
  DLB 72; MTCW

Giovanni, Nikki
  1943- . . . . . . CLC 2, 4, 19, 64; BLC; DA
  See also AITN 1; BW 2; CA 29-32R;
  CAAS 6; CANR 18, 41; CLR 6; DLB 5,
  41; MAICYA; MTCW; SATA 24

Giovene, Andrea 1904- . . . . CLC 7
  See also CA 85-88

Gippius, Zinaida (Nikolayevna) 1869-1945
  See Hippius, Zinaida
  See also CA 106

Giraudoux, (Hippolyte) Jean
  1882-1944 . . . . TCLC 2, 7
  See also CA 104; DLB 65

Gironella, Jose Maria 1917- . . . . CLC 11
  See also CA 101

Gissing, George (Robert)
  1857-1903 . . . . TCLC 3, 24, 47
  See also CA 105; DLB 18, 135

Giurlani, Aldo
  See Palazzeschi, Aldo

Gladkov, Fyodor (Vasilyevich)
  1883-1958 . . . . TCLC 27

Glanville, Brian (Lester) 1931- . . . . . . CLC 6
  See also CA 5-8R; CAAS 9; CANR 3;
  DLB 15, 139; SATA 42

Glasgow, Ellen (Anderson Gholson)
  1873(?)-1945 . . . . TCLC 2, 7
  See also CA 104; DLB 9, 12

Glaspell, Susan (Keating)
  1882(?)-1948 . . . . TCLC 55
  See also CA 110; DLB 7, 9, 78; YABC 2

Glassco, John 1909-1981 . . . . CLC 9
  See also CA 13-16R; 102; CANR 15;
  DLB 68

Glasscock, Amnesia
  See Steinbeck, John (Ernst)

Glasser, Ronald J. 1940(?)- . . . . CLC 37

Glassman, Joyce
  See Johnson, Joyce

Glendinning, Victoria 1937- . . . . CLC 50
  See also CA 120; 127

Glissant, Edouard 1928- . . . . CLC 10, 68

Gloag, Julian 1930- . . . . CLC 40
  See also AITN 1; CA 65-68; CANR 10

Glowacki, Aleksander
  See Prus, Boleslaw

Glueck, Louise (Elisabeth)
  1943- . . . . CLC 7, 22, 44, 81
  See also CA 33-36R; CANR 40; DLB 5

Gobineau, Joseph Arthur (Comte) de
  1816-1882 . . . . NCLC 17
  See also DLB 123

Godard, Jean-Luc 1930- . . . . CLC 20
  See also CA 93-96

Godden, (Margaret) Rumer 1907- . . . CLC 53
  See also AAYA 6; CA 5-8R; CANR 4, 27,
  36; CLR 20; MAICYA; SAAS 12;
  SATA 3, 36

Godoy Alcayaga, Lucila 1889-1957
  See Mistral, Gabriela
  See also BW 2; CA 104; 131; HW; MTCW

Godwin, Gail (Kathleen)
  1937- . . . . CLC 5, 8, 22, 31, 69
  See also CA 29-32R; CANR 15, 43; DLB 6;
  MTCW

Godwin, William 1756-1836 . . . . . . NCLC 14
  See also CDBLB 1789-1832; DLB 39, 104,
  142

Goethe, Johann Wolfgang von
  1749-1832 . . . . NCLC 4, 22, 34; DA;
              PC 5; WLC 3
  See also DLB 94

Gogarty, Oliver St. John
  1878-1957 . . . . TCLC 15
  See also CA 109; DLB 15, 19

Gogol, Nikolai (Vasilyevich)
  1809-1852 . . . . NCLC 5, 15, 31; DA;
              DC 1; SSC 4; WLC
  See also DLB 94

Goines, Donald
  1937(?)-1974 . . . . CLC 80; BLC
  See also AITN 1; BW 1; CA 124; 114;
  DLB 33

Gold, Herbert 1924- . . . . CLC 4, 7, 14, 42
  See also CA 9-12R; CANR 17, 45; DLB 2;
  DLBY 81

Goldbarth, Albert 1948- . . . . CLC 5, 38
  See also CA 53-56; CANR 6, 40; DLB 120

Goldberg, Anatol 1910-1982 . . . . **CLC 34**
See also CA 131; 117

Goldemberg, Isaac 1945- . . . . **CLC 52**
See also CA 69-72; CAAS 12; CANR 11,
32; HW

Golding, William (Gerald)
1911-1993 . . . . **CLC 1, 2, 3, 8, 10, 17, 27,
58, 81; DA; WLC**
See also AAYA 5; CA 5-8R; 141;
CANR 13, 33; CDBLB 1945-1960;
DLB 15, 100; MTCW

Goldman, Emma 1869-1940 . . . . . . **TCLC 13**
See also CA 110

Goldman, Francisco 1955- . . . . **CLC 76**

Goldman, William (W.) 1931- . . . . **CLC 1, 48**
See also CA 9-12R; CANR 29; DLB 44

Goldmann, Lucien 1913-1970 . . . . . . **CLC 24**
See also CA 25-28; CAP 2

Goldoni, Carlo 1707-1793 . . . . **LC 4**

Goldsberry, Steven 1949- . . . . **CLC 34**
See also CA 131

Goldsmith, Oliver
1728-1774 . . . . **LC 2; DA; WLC**
See also CDBLB 1660-1789; DLB 39, 89,
104, 109, 142; SATA 26

Goldsmith, Peter
See Priestley, J(ohn) B(oynton)

Gombrowicz, Witold
1904-1969 . . . . **CLC 4, 7, 11, 49**
See also CA 19-20; 25-28R; CAP 2

Gomez de la Serna, Ramon
1888-1963 . . . . **CLC 9**
See also CA 116; HW

Goncharov, Ivan Alexandrovich
1812-1891 . . . . **NCLC 1**

Goncourt, Edmond (Louis Antoine Huot) de
1822-1896 . . . . **NCLC 7**
See also DLB 123

Goncourt, Jules (Alfred Huot) de
1830-1870 . . . . **NCLC 7**
See also DLB 123

Gontier, Fernande 19(?)- . . . . **CLC 50**

Goodman, Paul 1911-1972 . . . . **CLC 1, 2, 4, 7**
See also CA 19-20; 37-40R; CANR 34;
CAP 2; DLB 130; MTCW

Gordimer, Nadine
1923- . . . . **CLC 3, 5, 7, 10, 18, 33, 51, 70;
DA; SSC 17**
See also CA 5-8R; CANR 3, 28; MTCW

Gordon, Adam Lindsay
1833-1870 . . . . **NCLC 21**

Gordon, Caroline
1895-1981 . . . **CLC 6, 13, 29, 83; SSC 15**
See also CA 11-12; 103; CANR 36; CAP 1;
DLB 4, 9, 102; DLBY 81; MTCW

Gordon, Charles William 1860-1937
See Connor, Ralph
See also CA 109

Gordon, Mary (Catherine)
1949- . . . . **CLC 13, 22**
See also CA 102; CANR 44; DLB 6;
DLBY 81; MTCW

Gordon, Sol 1923- . . . . **CLC 26**
See also CA 53-56; CANR 4; SATA 11

Gordone, Charles 1925- . . . . **CLC 1, 4**
See also BW 1; CA 93-96; DLB 7; MTCW

Gorenko, Anna Andreevna
See Akhmatova, Anna

Gorky, Maxim . . . . **TCLC 8; WLC**
See also Peshkov, Alexei Maximovich

Goryan, Sirak
See Saroyan, William

Gosse, Edmund (William)
1849-1928 . . . . **TCLC 28**
See also CA 117; DLB 57, 144

Gotlieb, Phyllis Fay (Bloom)
1926- . . . . **CLC 18**
See also CA 13-16R; CANR 7; DLB 88

Gottesman, S. D.
See Kornbluth, C(yril) M.; Pohl, Frederik

Gottfried von Strassburg
fl. c. 1210- . . . . **CMLC 10**
See also DLB 138

Gould, Lois . . . . **CLC 4, 10**
See also CA 77-80; CANR 29; MTCW

Gourmont, Remy de 1858-1915 . . . . **TCLC 17**
See also CA 109

Govier, Katherine 1948- . . . . **CLC 51**
See also CA 101; CANR 18, 40

Goyen, (Charles) William
1915-1983 . . . . **CLC 5, 8, 14, 40**
See also AITN 2; CA 5-8R; 110; CANR 6;
DLB 2; DLBY 83

Goytisolo, Juan
1931- . . . . **CLC 5, 10, 23; HLC**
See also CA 85-88; CANR 32; HW; MTCW

Gozzano, Guido 1883-1916 . . . . **PC 10**
See also DLB 114

Gozzi, (Conte) Carlo 1720-1806 . . **NCLC 23**

Grabbe, Christian Dietrich
1801-1836 . . . . **NCLC 2**
See also DLB 133

Grace, Patricia 1937- . . . . **CLC 56**

Gracian y Morales, Baltasar
1601-1658 . . . . **LC 15**

Gracq, Julien . . . . **CLC 11, 48**
See also Poirier, Louis
See also DLB 83

Grade, Chaim 1910-1982 . . . . **CLC 10**
See also CA 93-96; 107

Graduate of Oxford, A
See Ruskin, John

Graham, John
See Phillips, David Graham

Graham, Jorie 1951- . . . . **CLC 48**
See also CA 111; DLB 120

Graham, R(obert) B(ontine) Cunninghame
See Cunninghame Graham, R(obert)
B(ontine)
See also DLB 98, 135

Graham, Robert
See Haldeman, Joe (William)

Graham, Tom
See Lewis, (Harry) Sinclair

Graham, W(illiam) S(ydney)
1918-1986 . . . . **CLC 29**
See also CA 73-76; 118; DLB 20

Graham, Winston (Mawdsley)
1910- . . . . **CLC 23**
See also CA 49-52; CANR 2, 22, 45;
DLB 77

Grant, Skeeter
See Spiegelman, Art

Granville-Barker, Harley
1877-1946 . . . . **TCLC 2**
See also Barker, Harley Granville
See also CA 104

Grass, Guenter (Wilhelm)
1927- . . . . . **CLC 1, 2, 4, 6, 11, 15, 22, 32,
49; DA; WLC**
See also CA 13-16R; CANR 20; DLB 75,
124; MTCW

Gratton, Thomas
See Hulme, T(homas) E(rnest)

Grau, Shirley Ann
1929- . . . . **CLC 4, 9; SSC 15**
See also CA 89-92; CANR 22; DLB 2;
MTCW

Gravel, Fern
See Hall, James Norman

Graver, Elizabeth 1964- . . . . **CLC 70**
See also CA 135

Graves, Richard Perceval 1945- . . . . **CLC 44**
See also CA 65-68; CANR 9, 26

Graves, Robert (von Ranke)
1895-1985 . . . . . . **CLC 1, 2, 6, 11, 39, 44,
45; PC 6**
See also CA 5-8R; 117; CANR 5, 36;
CDBLB 1914-1945; DLB 20, 100;
DLBY 85; MTCW; SATA 45

Gray, Alasdair 1934- . . . . **CLC 41**
See also CA 126; MTCW

Gray, Amlin 1946- . . . . **CLC 29**
See also CA 138

Gray, Francine du Plessix 1930- . . . . **CLC 22**
See also BEST 90:3; CA 61-64; CAAS 2;
CANR 11, 33; MTCW

Gray, John (Henry) 1866-1934 . . . . **TCLC 19**
See also CA 119

Gray, Simon (James Holliday)
1936- . . . . **CLC 9, 14, 36**
See also AITN 1; CA 21-24R; CAAS 3;
CANR 32; DLB 13; MTCW

Gray, Spalding 1941- . . . . **CLC 49**
See also CA 128

Gray, Thomas
1716-1771 . . . . . . **LC 4; DA; PC 2; WLC**
See also CDBLB 1660-1789; DLB 109

Grayson, David
See Baker, Ray Stannard

Grayson, Richard (A.) 1951- . . . . **CLC 38**
See also CA 85-88; CANR 14, 31

Greeley, Andrew M(oran) 1928- . . . . **CLC 28**
See also CA 5-8R; CAAS 7; CANR 7, 43;
MTCW

Green, Brian
See Card, Orson Scott

Green, Hannah
See Greenberg, Joanne (Goldenberg)

Green, Hannah . . . . **CLC 3**
See also CA 73-76

Guy, Rosa (Cuthbert) 1928-........ **CLC 26**
See also AAYA 4; BW 2; CA 17-20R;
CANR 14, 34; CLR 13; DLB 33; JRDA;
MAICYA; SATA 14, 62

Gwendolyn
See Bennett, (Enoch) Arnold

H. D. .... **CLC 3, 8, 14, 31, 34, 73; PC 5**
See also Doolittle, Hilda

H. de V.
See Buchan, John

Haavikko, Paavo Juhani
1931-................... **CLC 18, 34**
See also CA 106

Habbema, Koos
See Heijermans, Herman

Hacker, Marilyn 1942- .... **CLC 5, 9, 23, 72**
See also CA 77-80; DLB 120

Haggard, H(enry) Rider
1856-1925 .... **TCLC 11**
See also CA 108; DLB 70; SATA 16

Haig, Fenil
See Ford, Ford Madox

Haig-Brown, Roderick (Langmere)
1908-1976 .... **CLC 21**
See also CA 5-8R; 69-72; CANR 4, 38;
CLR 31; DLB 88; MAICYA; SATA 12

Hailey, Arthur 1920- .... **CLC 5**
See also AITN 2; BEST 90:3; CA 1-4R;
CANR 2, 36; DLB 88; DLBY 82; MTCW

Hailey, Elizabeth Forsythe 1938-... **CLC 40**
See also CA 93-96; CAAS 1; CANR 15

Haines, John (Meade) 1924-....... **CLC 58**
See also CA 17-20R; CANR 13, 34; DLB 5

Haldeman, Joe (William) 1943-..... **CLC 61**
See also CA 53-56; CANR 6; DLB 8

Haley, Alex(ander Murray Palmer)
1921-1992 .... **CLC 8, 12, 76; BLC; DA**
See also BW 2; CA 77-80; 136; DLB 38;
MTCW

Haliburton, Thomas Chandler
1796-1865 .... **NCLC 15**
See also DLB 11, 99

Hall, Donald (Andrew, Jr.)
1928- .... **CLC 1, 13, 37, 59**
See also CA 5-8R; CAAS 7; CANR 2, 44;
DLB 5; SATA 23

Hall, Frederic Sauser
See Sauser-Hall, Frederic

Hall, James
See Kuttner, Henry

Hall, James Norman 1887-1951 ... **TCLC 23**
See also CA 123; SATA 21

Hall, (Marguerite) Radclyffe
1886(?)-1943 .... **TCLC 12**
See also CA 110

Hall, Rodney 1935- .... **CLC 51**
See also CA 109

Halleck, Fitz-Greene 1790-1867 .. **NCLC 47**
See also DLB 3

Halliday, Michael
See Creasey, John

Halpern, Daniel 1945- .... **CLC 14**
See also CA 33-36R

Hamburger, Michael (Peter Leopold)
1924-..................... **CLC 5, 14**
See also CA 5-8R; CAAS 4; CANR 2;
DLB 27

Hamill, Pete 1935-............... **CLC 10**
See also CA 25-28R; CANR 18

Hamilton, Clive
See Lewis, C(live) S(taples)

Hamilton, Edmond 1904-1977....... **CLC 1**
See also CA 1-4R; CANR 3; DLB 8

Hamilton, Eugene (Jacob) Lee
See Lee-Hamilton, Eugene (Jacob)

Hamilton, Franklin
See Silverberg, Robert

Hamilton, Gail
See Corcoran, Barbara

Hamilton, Mollie
See Kaye, M(ary) M(argaret)

Hamilton, (Anthony Walter) Patrick
1904-1962 .... **CLC 51**
See also CA 113; DLB 10

Hamilton, Virginia 1936-......... **CLC 26**
See also AAYA 2; BW 2; CA 25-28R;
CANR 20, 37; CLR 1, 11; DLB 33, 52;
JRDA; MAICYA; MTCW; SATA 4, 56,
79

Hammett, (Samuel) Dashiell
1894-1961 .... **CLC 3, 5, 10, 19, 47;
SSC 17**
See also AITN 1; CA 81-84; CANR 42;
CDALB 1929-1941; DLBD 6; MTCW

Hammon, Jupiter
1711(?)-1800(?) .... **NCLC 5; BLC**
See also DLB 31, 50

Hammond, Keith
See Kuttner, Henry

Hamner, Earl (Henry), Jr. 1923- ... **CLC 12**
See also AITN 2; CA 73-76; DLB 6

Hampton, Christopher (James)
1946-........................ **CLC 4**
See also CA 25-28R; DLB 13; MTCW

Hamsun, Knut .... **TCLC 2, 14, 49**
See also Pedersen, Knut

Handke, Peter 1942- .. **CLC 5, 8, 10, 15, 38**
See also CA 77-80; CANR 33; DLB 85,
124; MTCW

Hanley, James 1901-1985 ... **CLC 3, 5, 8, 13**
See also CA 73-76; 117; CANR 36; MTCW

Hannah, Barry 1942-.......... **CLC 23, 38**
See also CA 108; 110; CANR 43; DLB 6;
MTCW

Hannon, Ezra
See Hunter, Evan

Hansberry, Lorraine (Vivian)
1930-1965 ...... **CLC 17, 62; BLC; DA;
DC 2**
See also BW 1; CA 109; 25-28R; CABS 3;
CDALB 1941-1968; DLB 7, 38; MTCW

Hansen, Joseph 1923-............. **CLC 38**
See also CA 29-32R; CAAS 17; CANR 16,
44

Hansen, Martin A. 1909-1955..... **TCLC 32**

Hanson, Kenneth O(stlin) 1922- .... **CLC 13**
See also CA 53-56; CANR 7

Hardwick, Elizabeth 1916- .... **CLC 13**
See also CA 5-8R; CANR 3, 32; DLB 6;
MTCW

Hardy, Thomas
1840-1928 ...... **TCLC 4, 10, 18, 32, 48,
53; DA; PC 8; SSC 2; WLC**
See also CA 104; 123; CDBLB 1890-1914;
DLB 18, 19, 135; MTCW

Hare, David 1947- .... **CLC 29, 58**
See also CA 97-100; CANR 39; DLB 13;
MTCW

Harford, Henry
See Hudson, W(illiam) H(enry)

Hargrave, Leonie
See Disch, Thomas M(ichael)

Harjo, Joy 1951- .... **CLC 83**
See also CA 114; CANR 35; DLB 120

Harlan, Louis R(udolph) 1922-..... **CLC 34**
See also CA 21-24R; CANR 25

Harling, Robert 1951(?)- .... **CLC 53**

Harmon, William (Ruth) 1938-..... **CLC 38**
See also CA 33-36R; CANR 14, 32, 35;
SATA 65

Harper, F. E. W.
See Harper, Frances Ellen Watkins

Harper, Frances E. W.
See Harper, Frances Ellen Watkins

Harper, Frances E. Watkins
See Harper, Frances Ellen Watkins

Harper, Frances Ellen
See Harper, Frances Ellen Watkins

Harper, Frances Ellen Watkins
1825-1911 .... **TCLC 14; BLC**
See also BW 1; CA 111; 125; DLB 50

Harper, Michael S(teven) 1938- .. **CLC 7, 22**
See also BW 1; CA 33-36R; CANR 24;
DLB 41

Harper, Mrs. F. E. W.
See Harper, Frances Ellen Watkins

Harris, Christie (Lucy) Irwin
1907-...................... **CLC 12**
See also CA 5-8R; CANR 6; DLB 88;
JRDA; MAICYA; SAAS 10; SATA 6, 74

Harris, Frank 1856(?)-1931....... **TCLC 24**
See also CA 109

Harris, George Washington
1814-1869 .... **NCLC 23**
See also DLB 3, 11

Harris, Joel Chandler 1848-1908 ... **TCLC 2**
See also CA 104; 137; DLB 11, 23, 42, 78,
91; MAICYA; YABC 1

Harris, John (Wyndham Parkes Lucas)
Beynon 1903-1969
See Wyndham, John
See also CA 102; 89-92

Harris, MacDonald................. **CLC 9**
See also Heiney, Donald (William)

Harris, Mark 1922- .... **CLC 19**
See also CA 5-8R; CAAS 3; CANR 2;
DLB 2; DLBY 80

Harris, (Theodore) Wilson 1921-.... **CLC 25**
See also BW 2; CA 65-68; CAAS 16;
CANR 11, 27; DLB 117; MTCW

Hemingway, Ernest (Miller)
1899-1961 .... **CLC 1, 3, 6, 8, 10, 13, 19, 30, 34, 39, 41, 44, 50, 61, 80; DA; SSC 1; WLC**
See also CA 77-80; CANR 34;
CDALB 1917-1929; DLB 4, 9, 102;
DLBD 1; DLBY 81, 87; MTCW

Hempel, Amy 1951- .... **CLC 39**
See also CA 118; 137

Henderson, F. C.
See Mencken, H(enry) L(ouis)

Henderson, Sylvia
See Ashton-Warner, Sylvia (Constance)

Henley, Beth .... **CLC 23**
See also Henley, Elizabeth Becker
See also CABS 3; DLBY 86

Henley, Elizabeth Becker 1952-
See Henley, Beth
See also CA 107; CANR 32; MTCW

Henley, William Ernest
1849-1903 .... **TCLC 8**
See also CA 105; DLB 19

Hennissart, Martha
See Lathen, Emma
See also CA 85-88

Henry, O. .... **TCLC 1, 19; SSC 5; WLC**
See also Porter, William Sydney

Henry, Patrick 1736- .... **LC 25**
See also CA 145

Henryson, Robert 1430(?)-1506(?).... **LC 20**

Henry VIII 1491-1547............. **LC 10**

Henschke, Alfred
See Klabund

Hentoff, Nat(han Irving) 1925- ..... **CLC 26**
See also AAYA 4; CA 1-4R; CAAS 6;
CANR 5, 25; CLR 1; JRDA; MAICYA;
SATA 27, 42, 69

Heppenstall, (John) Rayner
1911-1981 .... **CLC 10**
See also CA 1-4R; 103; CANR 29

Herbert, Frank (Patrick)
1920-1986 ...... **CLC 12, 23, 35, 44, 85**
See also CA 53-56; 118; CANR 5, 43;
DLB 8; MTCW; SATA 9, 37, 47

Herbert, George 1593-1633 .... **LC 24; PC 4**
See also CDBLB Before 1660; DLB 126

Herbert, Zbigniew 1924- .... **CLC 9, 43**
See also CA 89-92; CANR 36; MTCW

Herbst, Josephine (Frey)
1897-1969 .... **CLC 34**
See also CA 5-8R; 25-28R; DLB 9

Hergesheimer, Joseph
1880-1954 .... **TCLC 11**
See also CA 109; DLB 102, 9

Herlihy, James Leo 1927-1993 ...... **CLC 6**
See also CA 1-4R; 143; CANR 2

Hermogenes fl. c. 175- .... **CMLC 6**

Hernandez, Jose 1834-1886...... **NCLC 17**

Herrick, Robert
1591-1674 .... **LC 13; DA; PC 9**
See also DLB 126

Herring, Guilles
See Somerville, Edith

Herriot, James 1916- .... **CLC 12**
See also Wight, James Alfred
See also AAYA 1; CANR 40

Herrmann, Dorothy 1941-........ **CLC 44**
See also CA 107

Herrmann, Taffy
See Herrmann, Dorothy

Hersey, John (Richard)
1914-1993 .... **CLC 1, 2, 7, 9, 40, 81**
See also CA 17-20R; 140; CANR 33;
DLB 6; MTCW; SATA 25;
SATA-Obit 76

Herzen, Aleksandr Ivanovich
1812-1870 .... **NCLC 10**

Herzl, Theodor 1860-1904....... **TCLC 36**

Herzog, Werner 1942- .... **CLC 16**
See also CA 89-92

Hesiod c. 8th cent. B.C.- .... **CMLC 5**

Hesse, Hermann
1877-1962 .... **CLC 1, 2, 3, 6, 11, 17, 25, 69; DA; SSC 9; WLC**
See also CA 17-18; CAP 2; DLB 66;
MTCW; SATA 50

Hewes, Cady
See De Voto, Bernard (Augustine)

Heyen, William 1940- .... **CLC 13, 18**
See also CA 33-36R; CAAS 9; DLB 5

Heyerdahl, Thor 1914-............ **CLC 26**
See also CA 5-8R; CANR 5, 22; MTCW;
SATA 2, 52

Heym, Georg (Theodor Franz Arthur)
1887-1912 .... **TCLC 9**
See also CA 106

Heym, Stefan 1913- .... **CLC 41**
See also CA 9-12R; CANR 4; DLB 69

Heyse, Paul (Johann Ludwig von)
1830-1914 .... **TCLC 8**
See also CA 104; DLB 129

Hibbert, Eleanor Alice Burford
1906-1993 .... **CLC 7**
See also BEST 90:4; CA 17-20R; 140;
CANR 9, 28; SATA 2; SATA-Obit 74

Higgins, George V(incent)
1939- .... **CLC 4, 7, 10, 18**
See also CA 77-80; CAAS 5; CANR 17;
DLB 2; DLBY 81; MTCW

Higginson, Thomas Wentworth
1823-1911 .... **TCLC 36**
See also DLB 1, 64

Highet, Helen
See MacInnes, Helen (Clark)

Highsmith, (Mary) Patricia
1921- .... **CLC 2, 4, 14, 42**
See also CA 1-4R; CANR 1, 20; MTCW

Highwater, Jamake (Mamake)
1942(?)- .... **CLC 12**
See also AAYA 7; CA 65-68; CAAS 7;
CANR 10, 34; CLR 17; DLB 52;
DLBY 85; JRDA; MAICYA; SATA 30, 32, 69

Hijuelos, Oscar 1951- ...... **CLC 65; HLC**
See also BEST 90:1; CA 123; HW

Hikmet, Nazim 1902(?)-1963....... **CLC 40**
See also CA 141; 93-96

Hildesheimer, Wolfgang
1916-1991 .... **CLC 49**
See also CA 101; 135; DLB 69, 124

Hill, Geoffrey (William)
1932- .... **CLC 5, 8, 18, 45**
See also CA 81-84; CANR 21;
CDBLB 1960 to Present; DLB 40;
MTCW

Hill, George Roy 1921- .... **CLC 26**
See also CA 110; 122

Hill, John
See Koontz, Dean R(ay)

Hill, Susan (Elizabeth) 1942- .... **CLC 4**
See also CA 33-36R; CANR 29; DLB 14, 139; MTCW

Hillerman, Tony 1925-............ **CLC 62**
See also AAYA 6; BEST 89:1; CA 29-32R;
CANR 21, 42; SATA 6

Hillesum, Etty 1914-1943 .... **TCLC 49**
See also CA 137

Hilliard, Noel (Harvey) 1929-...... **CLC 15**
See also CA 9-12R; CANR 7

Hillis, Rick 1956-................ **CLC 66**
See also CA 134

Hilton, James 1900-1954......... **TCLC 21**
See also CA 108; DLB 34, 77; SATA 34

Himes, Chester (Bomar)
1909-1984 .... **CLC 2, 4, 7, 18, 58; BLC**
See also BW 2; CA 25-28R; 114; CANR 22;
DLB 2, 76, 143; MTCW

Hinde, Thomas .... **CLC 6, 11**
See also Chitty, Thomas Willes

Hindin, Nathan
See Bloch, Robert (Albert)

Hine, (William) Daryl 1936- .... **CLC 15**
See also CA 1-4R; CAAS 15; CANR 1, 20;
DLB 60

Hinkson, Katharine Tynan
See Tynan, Katharine

Hinton, S(usan) E(loise)
1950- .... **CLC 30; DA**
See also AAYA 2; CA 81-84; CANR 32;
CLR 3, 23; JRDA; MAICYA; MTCW;
SATA 19, 58

Hippius, Zinaida .... **TCLC 9**
See also Gippius, Zinaida (Nikolayevna)

Hiraoka, Kimitake 1925-1970
See Mishima, Yukio
See also CA 97-100; 29-32R; MTCW

Hirsch, E(ric) D(onald), Jr. 1928-... **CLC 79**
See also CA 25-28R; CANR 27; DLB 67;
MTCW

Hirsch, Edward 1950- .... **CLC 31, 50**
See also CA 104; CANR 20, 42; DLB 120

Hitchcock, Alfred (Joseph)
1899-1980 .... **CLC 16**
See also CA 97-100; SATA 24, 27

Hitler, Adolf 1889-1945.......... **TCLC 53**
See also CA 117

Hoagland, Edward 1932-.......... **CLC 28**
See also CA 1-4R; CANR 2, 31; DLB 6;
SATA 51

Hoban, Russell (Conwell) 1925- .. **CLC 7, 25**
See also CA 5-8R; CANR 23, 37; CLR 3;
DLB 52; MAICYA; MTCW; SATA 1,
40, 78

Hobbs, Perry
See Blackmur, R(ichard) P(almer)

Hobson, Laura Z(ametkin)
1900-1986 .... **CLC 7, 25**
See also CA 17-20R; 118; DLB 28;
SATA 52

Hochhuth, Rolf 1931- .... **CLC 4, 11, 18**
See also CA 5-8R; CANR 33; DLB 124;
MTCW

Hochman, Sandra 1936- .... **CLC 3, 8**
See also CA 5-8R; DLB 5

Hochwaelder, Fritz 1911-1986...... **CLC 36**
See also CA 29-32R; 120; CANR 42;
MTCW

Hochwalder, Fritz
See Hochwaelder, Fritz

Hocking, Mary (Eunice) 1921- ..... **CLC 13**
See also CA 101; CANR 18, 40

Hodgins, Jack 1938-............. **CLC 23**
See also CA 93-96; DLB 60

Hodgson, William Hope
1877(?)-1918 .... **TCLC 13**
See also CA 111; DLB 70

Hoffman, Alice 1952-............ **CLC 51**
See also CA 77-80; CANR 34; MTCW

Hoffman, Daniel (Gerard)
1923- .... **CLC 6, 13, 23**
See also CA 1-4R; CANR 4; DLB 5

Hoffman, Stanley 1944-............ **CLC 5**
See also CA 77-80

Hoffman, William M(oses) 1939- ... **CLC 40**
See also CA 57-60; CANR 11

Hoffmann, E(rnst) T(heodor) A(madeus)
1776-1822 .... **NCLC 2; SSC 13**
See also DLB 90; SATA 27

Hofmann, Gert 1931-............. **CLC 54**
See also CA 128

Hofmannsthal, Hugo von
1874-1929 .... **TCLC 11; DC 4**
See also CA 106; DLB 81, 118

Hogan, Linda 1947- .... **CLC 73**
See also CA 120; CANR 45

Hogarth, Charles
See Creasey, John

Hogg, James 1770-1835.......... **NCLC 4**
See also DLB 93, 116

Holbach, Paul Henri Thiry Baron
1723-1789 .... **LC 14**

Holberg, Ludvig 1684-1754 .... **LC 6**

Holden, Ursula 1921-............. **CLC 18**
See also CA 101; CAAS 8; CANR 22

Holderlin, (Johann Christian) Friedrich
1770-1843 .... **NCLC 16; PC 4**

Holdstock, Robert
See Holdstock, Robert P.

Holdstock, Robert P. 1948-........ **CLC 39**
See also CA 131

Holland, Isabelle 1920- .... **CLC 21**
See also AAYA 11; CA 21-24R; CANR 10,
25; JRDA; MAICYA; SATA 8, 70

Holland, Marcus
See Caldwell, (Janet Miriam) Taylor
(Holland)

Hollander, John 1929- ...... **CLC 2, 5, 8, 14**
See also CA 1-4R; CANR 1; DLB 5;
SATA 13

Hollander, Paul
See Silverberg, Robert

Holleran, Andrew 1943(?)-........ **CLC 38**
See also CA 144

Hollinghurst, Alan 1954-.......... **CLC 55**
See also CA 114

Hollis, Jim
See Summers, Hollis (Spurgeon, Jr.)

Holmes, John
See Souster, (Holmes) Raymond

Holmes, John Clellon 1926-1988.... **CLC 56**
See also CA 9-12R; 125; CANR 4; DLB 16

Holmes, Oliver Wendell
1809-1894 .... **NCLC 14**
See also CDALB 1640-1865; DLB 1;
SATA 34

Holmes, Raymond
See Souster, (Holmes) Raymond

Holt, Victoria
See Hibbert, Eleanor Alice Burford

Holub, Miroslav 1923-............. **CLC 4**
See also CA 21-24R; CANR 10

Homer c. 8th cent. B.C.- ..... **CMLC 1; DA**

Honig, Edwin 1919-............. **CLC 33**
See also CA 5-8R; CAAS 8; CANR 4, 45;
DLB 5

Hood, Hugh (John Blagdon)
1928- .... **CLC 15, 28**
See also CA 49-52; CAAS 17; CANR 1, 33;
DLB 53

Hood, Thomas 1799-1845....... **NCLC 16**
See also DLB 96

Hooker, (Peter) Jeremy 1941-...... **CLC 43**
See also CA 77-80; CANR 22; DLB 40

Hope, A(lec) D(erwent) 1907- .... **CLC 3, 51**
See also CA 21-24R; CANR 33; MTCW

Hope, Brian
See Creasey, John

Hope, Christopher (David Tully)
1944- .... **CLC 52**
See also CA 106; SATA 62

Hopkins, Gerard Manley
1844-1889 .... **NCLC 17; DA; WLC**
See also CDBLB 1890-1914; DLB 35, 57

Hopkins, John (Richard) 1931-...... **CLC 4**
See also CA 85-88

Hopkins, Pauline Elizabeth
1859-1930 .... **TCLC 28; BLC**
See also BW 2; CA 141; DLB 50

Hopkinson, Francis 1737-1791 ...... **LC 25**
See also DLB 31

Hopley-Woolrich, Cornell George 1903-1968
See Woolrich, Cornell
See also CA 13-14; CAP 1

Horatio
See Proust, (Valentin-Louis-George-Eugene-)
Marcel

Horgan, Paul 1903- .... **CLC 9, 53**
See also CA 13-16R; CANR 9, 35;
DLB 102; DLBY 85; MTCW; SATA 13

Horn, Peter
See Kuttner, Henry

Hornem, Horace Esq.
See Byron, George Gordon (Noel)

Horovitz, Israel 1939- .... **CLC 56**
See also CA 33-36R; DLB 7

Horvath, Odon von
See Horvath, Oedoen von
See also DLB 85, 124

Horvath, Oedoen von 1901-1938... **TCLC 45**
See also Horvath, Odon von
See also CA 118

Horwitz, Julius 1920-1986......... **CLC 14**
See also CA 9-12R; 119; CANR 12

Hospital, Janette Turner 1942-..... **CLC 42**
See also CA 108

Hostos, E. M. de
See Hostos (y Bonilla), Eugenio Maria de

Hostos, Eugenio M. de
See Hostos (y Bonilla), Eugenio Maria de

Hostos, Eugenio Maria
See Hostos (y Bonilla), Eugenio Maria de

Hostos (y Bonilla), Eugenio Maria de
1839-1903 .... **TCLC 24**
See also CA 123; 131; HW

Houdini
See Lovecraft, H(oward) P(hillips)

Hougan, Carolyn 1943- .... **CLC 34**
See also CA 139

Household, Geoffrey (Edward West)
1900-1988 .... **CLC 11**
See also CA 77-80; 126; DLB 87; SATA 14,
59

Housman, A(lfred) E(dward)
1859-1936 ...... **TCLC 1, 10; DA; PC 2**
See also CA 104; 125; DLB 19; MTCW

Housman, Laurence 1865-1959 ..... **TCLC 7**
See also CA 106; DLB 10; SATA 25

Howard, Elizabeth Jane 1923- ... **CLC 7, 29**
See also CA 5-8R; CANR 8

Howard, Maureen 1930- ..... **CLC 5, 14, 46**
See also CA 53-56; CANR 31; DLBY 83;
MTCW

Howard, Richard 1929- ...... **CLC 7, 10, 47**
See also AITN 1; CA 85-88; CANR 25;
DLB 5

Howard, Robert Ervin 1906-1936... **TCLC 8**
See also CA 105

Howard, Warren F.
See Pohl, Frederik

Howe, Fanny 1940- .... **CLC 47**
See also CA 117; SATA 52

Howe, Irving 1920-1993.......... **CLC 85**
See also CA 9-12R; 141; CANR 21;
DLB 67; MTCW

Howe, Julia Ward 1819-1910 ..... **TCLC 21**
See also CA 117; DLB 1

Howe, Susan 1937-............... **CLC 72**
See also DLB 120

Howe, Tina 1937-................ **CLC 48**
See also CA 109

Johnson, Charles (Richard)
1948- .... **CLC 7, 51, 65; BLC**
See also BW 2; CA 116; CAAS 18;
CANR 42; DLB 33

Johnson, Denis 1949- .... **CLC 52**
See also CA 117; 121; DLB 120

Johnson, Diane 1934- .... **CLC 5, 13, 48**
See also CA 41-44R; CANR 17, 40;
DLBY 80; MTCW

Johnson, Eyvind (Olof Verner)
1900-1976 .... **CLC 14**
See also CA 73-76; 69-72; CANR 34

Johnson, J. R.
See James, C(yril) L(ionel) R(obert)

Johnson, James Weldon
1871-1938 .... **TCLC 3, 19; BLC**
See also BW 1; CA 104; 125;
CDALB 1917-1929; CLR 32; DLB 51;
MTCW; SATA 31

Johnson, Joyce 1935- .... **CLC 58**
See also CA 125; 129

Johnson, Lionel (Pigot)
1867-1902 .... **TCLC 19**
See also CA 117; DLB 19

Johnson, Mel
See Malzberg, Barry N(athaniel)

Johnson, Pamela Hansford
1912-1981 .... **CLC 1, 7, 27**
See also CA 1-4R; 104; CANR 2, 28;
DLB 15; MTCW

Johnson, Samuel
1709-1784 .... **LC 15; DA; WLC**
See also CDBLB 1660-1789; DLB 39, 95,
104, 142

Johnson, Uwe
1934-1984 .... **CLC 5, 10, 15, 40**
See also CA 1-4R; 112; CANR 1, 39;
DLB 75; MTCW

Johnston, George (Benson) 1913- ... **CLC 51**
See also CA 1-4R; CANR 5, 20; DLB 88

Johnston, Jennifer 1930- .... **CLC 7**
See also CA 85-88; DLB 14

Jolley, (Monica) Elizabeth 1923- ... **CLC 46**
See also CA 127; CAAS 13

Jones, Arthur Llewellyn 1863-1947
See Machen, Arthur
See also CA 104

Jones, D(ouglas) G(ordon) 1929-.... **CLC 10**
See also CA 29-32R; CANR 13; DLB 53

Jones, David (Michael)
1895-1974 .... **CLC 2, 4, 7, 13, 42**
See also CA 9-12R; 53-56; CANR 28;
CDBLB 1945-1960; DLB 20, 100; MTCW

Jones, David Robert 1947-
See Bowie, David
See also CA 103

Jones, Diana Wynne 1934- .... **CLC 26**
See also AAYA 12; CA 49-52; CANR 4,
26; CLR 23; JRDA; MAICYA; SAAS 7;
SATA 9, 70

Jones, Edward P. 1950- .... **CLC 76**
See also BW 2; CA 142

Jones, Gayl 1949- .... **CLC 6, 9; BLC**
See also BW 2; CA 77-80; CANR 27;
DLB 33; MTCW

Jones, James 1921-1977.... **CLC 1, 3, 10, 39**
See also AITN 1, 2; CA 1-4R; 69-72;
CANR 6; DLB 2, 143; MTCW

Jones, John J.
See Lovecraft, H(oward) P(hillips)

Jones, LeRoi .... **CLC 1, 2, 3, 5, 10, 14**
See also Baraka, Amiri

Jones, Louis B. .... **CLC 65**
See also CA 141

Jones, Madison (Percy, Jr.) 1925- ... **CLC 4**
See also CA 13-16R; CAAS 11; CANR 7

Jones, Mervyn 1922- .... **CLC 10, 52**
See also CA 45-48; CAAS 5; CANR 1;
MTCW

Jones, Mick 1956(?)- .... **CLC 30**

Jones, Nettie (Pearl) 1941- .... **CLC 34**
See also BW 2; CA 137

Jones, Preston 1936-1979 .... **CLC 10**
See also CA 73-76; 89-92; DLB 7

Jones, Robert F(rancis) 1934- .... **CLC 7**
See also CA 49-52; CANR 2

Jones, Rod 1953- .... **CLC 50**
See also CA 128

Jones, Terence Graham Parry
1942- .... **CLC 21**
See also Jones, Terry; Monty Python
See also CA 112; 116; CANR 35; SATA 51

Jones, Terry
See Jones, Terence Graham Parry
See also SATA 67

Jones, Thom 1945(?)- .... **CLC 81**

Jong, Erica 1942- ...... **CLC 4, 6, 8, 18, 83**
See also AITN 1; BEST 90:2; CA 73-76;
CANR 26; DLB 2, 5, 28; MTCW

Jonson, Ben(jamin)
1572(?)-1637 .... **LC 6; DA; DC 4; WLC**
See also CDBLB Before 1660; DLB 62, 121

Jordan, June 1936- .... **CLC 5, 11, 23**
See also AAYA 2; BW 2; CA 33-36R;
CANR 25; CLR 10; DLB 38; MAICYA;
MTCW; SATA 4

Jordan, Pat(rick M.) 1941- .... **CLC 37**
See also CA 33-36R

Jorgensen, Ivar
See Ellison, Harlan

Jorgenson, Ivar
See Silverberg, Robert

Josephus, Flavius c. 37-100 ...... **CMLC 13**

Josipovici, Gabriel 1940- .... **CLC 6, 43**
See also CA 37-40R; CAAS 8; DLB 14

Joubert, Joseph 1754-1824 .... **NCLC 9**

Jouve, Pierre Jean 1887-1976 ...... **CLC 47**
See also CA 65-68

Joyce, James (Augustine Aloysius)
1882-1941 ...... **TCLC 3, 8, 16, 35; DA;
SSC 3; WLC**
See also CA 104; 126; CDBLB 1914-1945;
DLB 10, 19, 36; MTCW

Jozsef, Attila 1905-1937......... **TCLC 22**
See also CA 116

Juana Ines de la Cruz 1651(?)-1695 ... **LC 5**

Judd, Cyril
See Kornbluth, C(yril) M.; Pohl, Frederik

Julian of Norwich 1342(?)-1416(?) .... **LC 6**

Just, Ward (Swift) 1935- .... **CLC 4, 27**
See also CA 25-28R; CANR 32

Justice, Donald (Rodney) 1925- .. **CLC 6, 19**
See also CA 5-8R; CANR 26; DLBY 83

Juvenal c. 55-c. 127 .... **CMLC 8**

Juvenis
See Bourne, Randolph S(illiman)

Kacew, Romain 1914-1980
See Gary, Romain
See also CA 108; 102

Kadare, Ismail 1936- .... **CLC 52**

Kadohata, Cynthia................. **CLC 59**
See also CA 140

Kafka, Franz
1883-1924 .... **TCLC 2, 6, 13, 29, 47, 53;
DA; SSC 5; WLC**
See also CA 105; 126; DLB 81; MTCW

Kahanovitsch, Pinkhes
See Der Nister

Kahn, Roger 1927- .... **CLC 30**
See also CA 25-28R; CANR 44; SATA 37

Kain, Saul
See Sassoon, Siegfried (Lorraine)

Kaiser, Georg 1878-1945 .... **TCLC 9**
See also CA 106; DLB 124

Kaletski, Alexander 1946- .... **CLC 39**
See also CA 118; 143

Kalidasa fl. c. 400- .... **CMLC 9**

Kallman, Chester (Simon)
1921-1975 .... **CLC 2**
See also CA 45-48; 53-56; CANR 3

Kaminsky, Melvin 1926-
See Brooks, Mel
See also CA 65-68; CANR 16

Kaminsky, Stuart M(elvin) 1934- ... **CLC 59**
See also CA 73-76; CANR 29

Kane, Paul
See Simon, Paul

Kane, Wilson
See Bloch, Robert (Albert)

Kanin, Garson 1912-.............. **CLC 22**
See also AITN 1; CA 5-8R; CANR 7;
DLB 7

Kaniuk, Yoram 1930- .... **CLC 19**
See also CA 134

Kant, Immanuel 1724-1804 ...... **NCLC 27**
See also DLB 94

Kantor, MacKinlay 1904-1977 ...... **CLC 7**
See also CA 61-64; 73-76; DLB 9, 102

Kaplan, David Michael 1946- ...... **CLC 50**

Kaplan, James 1951- .... **CLC 59**
See also CA 135

Karageorge, Michael
See Anderson, Poul (William)

Karamzin, Nikolai Mikhailovich
1766-1826 .... **NCLC 3**

Karapanou, Margarita 1946- .... **CLC 13**
See also CA 101

Karinthy, Frigyes 1887-1938 ...... **TCLC 47**

Karl, Frederick R(obert) 1927- ..... **CLC 34**
See also CA 5-8R; CANR 3, 44

Leiber, Fritz (Reuter, Jr.)
  1910-1992 . . . . **CLC 25**
  See also CA 45-48; 139; CANR 2, 40;
  DLB 8; MTCW; SATA 45;
  SATA-Obit 73

Leimbach, Martha 1963-
  See Leimbach, Marti
  See also CA 130

Leimbach, Marti . . . . **CLC 65**
  See also Leimbach, Martha

Leino, Eino . . . . **TCLC 24**
  See also Loennbohm, Armas Eino Leopold

Leiris, Michel (Julien) 1901-1990 . . . **CLC 61**
  See also CA 119; 128; 132

Leithauser, Brad 1953- . . . . **CLC 27**
  See also CA 107; CANR 27; DLB 120

Lelchuk, Alan 1938- . . . . **CLC 5**
  See also CA 45-48; CANR 1

Lem, Stanislaw 1921- . . . . **CLC 8, 15, 40**
  See also CA 105; CAAS 1; CANR 32;
  MTCW

Lemann, Nancy 1956- . . . . **CLC 39**
  See also CA 118; 136

Lemonnier, (Antoine Louis) Camille
  1844-1913 . . . . **TCLC 22**
  See also CA 121

Lenau, Nikolaus 1802-1850 . . . . . . **NCLC 16**

L'Engle, Madeleine (Camp Franklin)
  1918- . . . . **CLC 12**
  See also AAYA 1; AITN 2; CA 1-4R;
  CANR 3, 21, 39; CLR 1, 14; DLB 52;
  JRDA; MAICYA; MTCW; SAAS 15;
  SATA 1, 27, 75

Lengyel, Jozsef 1896-1975 . . . . **CLC 7**
  See also CA 85-88; 57-60

Lennon, John (Ono)
  1940-1980 . . . . **CLC 12, 35**
  See also CA 102

Lennox, Charlotte Ramsay
  1729(?)-1804 . . . . **NCLC 23**
  See also DLB 39

Lentricchia, Frank (Jr.) 1940- . . . . . . **CLC 34**
  See also CA 25-28R; CANR 19

Lenz, Siegfried 1926- . . . . **CLC 27**
  See also CA 89-92; DLB 75

Leonard, Elmore (John, Jr.)
  1925- . . . . **CLC 28, 34, 71**
  See also AITN 1; BEST 89:1, 90:4;
  CA 81-84; CANR 12, 28; MTCW

Leonard, Hugh . . . . **CLC 19**
  See also Byrne, John Keyes
  See also DLB 13

Leopardi, (Conte) Giacomo (Talegardo
  Francesco di Sales Save
  1798-1837 . . . . **NCLC 22**

Le Reveler
  See Artaud, Antonin

Lerman, Eleanor 1952- . . . . **CLC 9**
  See also CA 85-88

Lerman, Rhoda 1936- . . . . **CLC 56**
  See also CA 49-52

Lermontov, Mikhail Yuryevich
  1814-1841 . . . . **NCLC 47**

Leroux, Gaston 1868-1927 . . . . **TCLC 25**
  See also CA 108; 136; SATA 65

Lesage, Alain-Rene 1668-1747 . . . . **LC 2**

Leskov, Nikolai (Semyonovich)
  1831-1895 . . . . **NCLC 25**

Lessing, Doris (May)
  1919- . . . . . **CLC 1, 2, 3, 6, 10, 15, 22, 40;**
  DA; SSC 6
  See also CA 9-12R; CAAS 14; CANR 33;
  CDBLB 1960 to Present; DLB 15, 139;
  DLBY 85; MTCW

Lessing, Gotthold Ephraim
  1729-1781 . . . . **LC 8**
  See also DLB 97

Lester, Richard 1932- . . . . **CLC 20**

Lever, Charles (James)
  1806-1872 . . . . **NCLC 23**
  See also DLB 21

Leverson, Ada 1865(?)-1936(?) . . . . **TCLC 18**
  See also Elaine
  See also CA 117

Levertov, Denise
  1923- . . . . . . **CLC 1, 2, 3, 5, 8, 15, 28, 66**
  See also CA 1-4R; CAAS 19; CANR 3, 29;
  DLB 5; MTCW

Levi, Jonathan . . . . **CLC 76**

Levi, Peter (Chad Tigar) 1931- . . . . . **CLC 41**
  See also CA 5-8R; CANR 34; DLB 40

Levi, Primo
  1919-1987 . . . . **CLC 37, 50; SSC 12**
  See also CA 13-16R; 122; CANR 12, 33;
  MTCW

Levin, Ira 1929- . . . . **CLC 3, 6**
  See also CA 21-24R; CANR 17, 44;
  MTCW; SATA 66

Levin, Meyer 1905-1981 . . . . **CLC 7**
  See also AITN 1; CA 9-12R; 104;
  CANR 15; DLB 9, 28; DLBY 81;
  SATA 21, 27

Levine, Norman 1924- . . . . **CLC 54**
  See also CA 73-76; CANR 14; DLB 88

Levine, Philip 1928- . . **CLC 2, 4, 5, 9, 14, 33**
  See also CA 9-12R; CANR 9, 37; DLB 5

Levinson, Deirdre 1931- . . . . **CLC 49**
  See also CA 73-76

Levi-Strauss, Claude 1908- . . . . **CLC 38**
  See also CA 1-4R; CANR 6, 32; MTCW

Levitin, Sonia (Wolff) 1934- . . . . **CLC 17**
  See also CA 29-32R; CANR 14, 32; JRDA;
  MAICYA; SAAS 2; SATA 4, 68

Levon, O. U.
  See Kesey, Ken (Elton)

Lewes, George Henry
  1817-1878 . . . . **NCLC 25**
  See also DLB 55, 144

Lewis, Alun 1915-1944 . . . . **TCLC 3**
  See also CA 104; DLB 20

Lewis, C. Day
  See Day Lewis, C(ecil)

Lewis, C(live) S(taples)
  1898-1963 . . . . . **CLC 1, 3, 6, 14, 27; DA;**
  WLC
  See also AAYA 3; CA 81-84; CANR 33;
  CDBLB 1945-1960; CLR 3, 27; DLB 15,
  100; JRDA; MAICYA; MTCW;
  SATA 13

Lewis, Janet 1899- . . . . **CLC 41**
  See also Winters, Janet Lewis
  See also CA 9-12R; CANR 29; CAP 1;
  DLBY 87

Lewis, Matthew Gregory
  1775-1818 . . . . **NCLC 11**
  See also DLB 39

Lewis, (Harry) Sinclair
  1885-1951 . . . . . **TCLC 4, 13, 23, 39; DA;**
  WLC
  See also CA 104; 133; CDALB 1917-1929;
  DLB 9, 102; DLBD 1; MTCW

Lewis, (Percy) Wyndham
  1884(?)-1957 . . . . **TCLC 2, 9**
  See also CA 104; DLB 15

Lewisohn, Ludwig 1883-1955 . . . . . . **TCLC 19**
  See also CA 107; DLB 4, 9, 28, 102

Lezama Lima, Jose 1910-1976 . . . **CLC 4, 10**
  See also CA 77-80; DLB 113; HW

L'Heureux, John (Clarke) 1934- . . . . **CLC 52**
  See also CA 13-16R; CANR 23, 45

Liddell, C. H.
  See Kuttner, Henry

Lie, Jonas (Lauritz Idemil)
  1833-1908(?) . . . . **TCLC 5**
  See also CA 115

Lieber, Joel 1937-1971 . . . . **CLC 6**
  See also CA 73-76; 29-32R

Lieber, Stanley Martin
  See Lee, Stan

Lieberman, Laurence (James)
  1935- . . . . **CLC 4, 36**
  See also CA 17-20R; CANR 8, 36

Lieksman, Anders
  See Haavikko, Paavo Juhani

Li Fei-kan 1904-
  See Pa Chin
  See also CA 105

Lifton, Robert Jay 1926- . . . . **CLC 67**
  See also CA 17-20R; CANR 27; SATA 66

Lightfoot, Gordon 1938- . . . . **CLC 26**
  See also CA 109

Lightman, Alan P. 1948- . . . . **CLC 81**
  See also CA 141

Ligotti, Thomas 1953- . . . . **CLC 44; SSC 16**
  See also CA 123

Liliencron, (Friedrich Adolf Axel) Detlev von
  1844-1909 . . . . **TCLC 18**
  See also CA 117

Lilly, William 1602-1681 . . . . **LC 27**

Lima, Jose Lezama
  See Lezama Lima, Jose

Lima Barreto, Afonso Henrique de
  1881-1922 . . . . **TCLC 23**
  See also CA 117

Limonov, Eduard . . . . **CLC 67**

Lin, Frank
See Atherton, Gertrude (Franklin Horn)

Lincoln, Abraham 1809-1865..... **NCLC 18**

Lind, Jakov .... **CLC 1, 2, 4, 27, 82**
See also Landwirth, Heinz
See also CAAS 4

Lindbergh, Anne (Spencer) Morrow
1906- .... **CLC 82**
See also CA 17-20R; CANR 16; MTCW;
SATA 33

Lindsay, David 1878-1945 .... **TCLC 15**
See also CA 113

Lindsay, (Nicholas) Vachel
1879-1931 .... **TCLC 17; DA; WLC**
See also CA 114; 135; CDALB 1865-1917;
DLB 54; SATA 40

Linke-Poot
See Doeblin, Alfred

Linney, Romulus 1930- .... **CLC 51**
See also CA 1-4R; CANR 40, 44

Linton, Eliza Lynn 1822-1898.... **NCLC 41**
See also DLB 18

Li Po 701-763 .... **CMLC 2**

Lipsius, Justus 1547-1606 .... **LC 16**

Lipsyte, Robert (Michael)
1938- .... **CLC 21; DA**
See also AAYA 7; CA 17-20R; CANR 8;
CLR 23; JRDA; MAICYA; SATA 5, 68

Lish, Gordon (Jay) 1934-........ **CLC 45**
See also CA 113; 117; DLB 130

Lispector, Clarice 1925-1977...... **CLC 43**
See also CA 139; 116; DLB 113

Littell, Robert 1935(?)- .... **CLC 42**
See also CA 109; 112

Little, Malcolm 1925-1965
See Malcolm X
See also BW 1; CA 125; 111; DA; MTCW

Littlewit, Humphrey Gent.
See Lovecraft, H(oward) P(hillips)

Litwos
See Sienkiewicz, Henryk (Adam Alexander
Pius)

Liu E 1857-1909................ **TCLC 15**
See also CA 115

Lively, Penelope (Margaret)
1933- .... **CLC 32, 50**
See also CA 41-44R; CANR 29; CLR 7;
DLB 14; JRDA; MAICYA; MTCW;
SATA 7, 60

Livesay, Dorothy (Kathleen)
1909- .... **CLC 4, 15, 79**
See also AITN 2; CA 25-28R; CAAS 8;
CANR 36; DLB 68; MTCW

Livy c. 59B.C.-c. 17 .... **CMLC 11**

Lizardi, Jose Joaquin Fernandez de
1776-1827 .... **NCLC 30**

Llewellyn, Richard
See Llewellyn Lloyd, Richard Dafydd
Vivian
See also DLB 15

Llewellyn Lloyd, Richard Dafydd Vivian
1906-1983 .... **CLC 7, 80**
See also Llewellyn, Richard
See also CA 53-56; 111; CANR 7;
SATA 11, 37

Llosa, (Jorge) Mario (Pedro) Vargas
See Vargas Llosa, (Jorge) Mario (Pedro)

Lloyd Webber, Andrew 1948-
See Webber, Andrew Lloyd
See also AAYA 1; CA 116; SATA 56

Llull, Ramon c. 1235-c. 1316..... **CMLC 12**

Locke, Alain (Le Roy)
1886-1954 .... **TCLC 43**
See also BW 1; CA 106; 124; DLB 51

Locke, John 1632-1704 .... **LC 7**
See also DLB 101

Locke-Elliott, Sumner
See Elliott, Sumner Locke

Lockhart, John Gibson
1794-1854 .... **NCLC 6**
See also DLB 110, 116, 144

Lodge, David (John) 1935-........ **CLC 36**
See also BEST 90:1; CA 17-20R; CANR 19;
DLB 14; MTCW

Loennbohm, Armas Eino Leopold 1878-1926
See Leino, Eino
See also CA 123

Loewinsohn, Ron(ald William)
1937- .... **CLC 52**
See also CA 25-28R

Logan, Jake
See Smith, Martin Cruz

Logan, John (Burton) 1923-1987..... **CLC 5**
See also CA 77-80; 124; CANR 45; DLB 5

Lo Kuan-chung 1330(?)-1400(?)...... **LC 12**

Lombard, Nap
See Johnson, Pamela Hansford

London, Jack .. **TCLC 9, 15, 39; SSC 4; WLC**
See also London, John Griffith
See also AITN 2; CDALB 1865-1917;
DLB 8, 12, 78; SATA 18

London, John Griffith 1876-1916
See London, Jack
See also CA 110; 119; DA; JRDA;
MAICYA; MTCW

Long, Emmett
See Leonard, Elmore (John, Jr.)

Longbaugh, Harry
See Goldman, William (W.)

Longfellow, Henry Wadsworth
1807-1882 .... **NCLC 2, 45; DA**
See also CDALB 1640-1865; DLB 1, 59;
SATA 19

Longley, Michael 1939-........... **CLC 29**
See also CA 102; DLB 40

Longus fl. c. 2nd cent. - .... **CMLC 7**

Longway, A. Hugh
See Lang, Andrew

Lopate, Phillip 1943- .... **CLC 29**
See also CA 97-100; DLBY 80

Lopez Portillo (y Pacheco), Jose
1920- .... **CLC 46**
See also CA 129; HW

Lopez y Fuentes, Gregorio
1897(?)-1966 .... **CLC 32**
See also CA 131; HW

Lorca, Federico Garcia
See Garcia Lorca, Federico

Lord, Bette Bao 1938- .... **CLC 23**
See also BEST 90:3; CA 107; CANR 41;
SATA 58

Lord Auch
See Bataille, Georges

Lord Byron
See Byron, George Gordon (Noel)

Lorde, Audre (Geraldine)
1934-1992 .... **CLC 18, 71; BLC**
See also BW 1; CA 25-28R; 142; CANR 16,
26; DLB 41; MTCW

Lord Jeffrey
See Jeffrey, Francis

Lorenzo, Heberto Padilla
See Padilla (Lorenzo), Heberto

Loris
See Hofmannsthal, Hugo von

Loti, Pierre .... **TCLC 11**
See also Viaud, (Louis Marie) Julien
See also DLB 123

Louie, David Wong 1954- .... **CLC 70**
See also CA 139

Louis, Father M.
See Merton, Thomas

Lovecraft, H(oward) P(hillips)
1890-1937 .... **TCLC 4, 22; SSC 3**
See also CA 104; 133; MTCW

Lovelace, Earl 1935-............. **CLC 51**
See also BW 2; CA 77-80; CANR 41;
DLB 125; MTCW

Lovelace, Richard 1618-1657........ **LC 24**
See also DLB 131

Lowell, Amy 1874-1925 .... **TCLC 1, 8**
See also CA 104; DLB 54, 140

Lowell, James Russell 1819-1891 .. **NCLC 2**
See also CDALB 1640-1865; DLB 1, 11, 64,
79

Lowell, Robert (Traill Spence, Jr.)
1917-1977 ... **CLC 1, 2, 3, 4, 5, 8, 9, 11,
15, 37; DA; PC 3; WLC**
See also CA 9-12R; 73-76; CABS 2;
CANR 26; DLB 5; MTCW

Lowndes, Marie Adelaide (Belloc)
1868-1947 .... **TCLC 12**
See also CA 107; DLB 70

Lowry, (Clarence) Malcolm
1909-1957 .... **TCLC 6, 40**
See also CA 105; 131; CDBLB 1945-1960;
DLB 15; MTCW

Lowry, Mina Gertrude 1882-1966
See Loy, Mina
See also CA 113

Loxsmith, John
See Brunner, John (Kilian Houston)

Loy, Mina .... **CLC 28**
See also Lowry, Mina Gertrude
See also DLB 4, 54

Loyson-Bridet
See Schwob, (Mayer Andre) Marcel

Lucas, Craig 1951-............ **CLC 64**
See also CA 137

Lucas, George 1944-............ **CLC 16**
See also AAYA 1; CA 77-80; CANR 30;
SATA 56

Lucas, Hans
See Godard, Jean-Luc

Lucas, Victoria
See Plath, Sylvia

Ludlam, Charles 1943-1987 .... **CLC 46, 50**
See also CA 85-88; 122

Ludlum, Robert 1927- .... **CLC 22, 43**
See also AAYA 10; BEST 89:1, 90:3;
CA 33-36R; CANR 25, 41; DLBY 82;
MTCW

Ludwig, Ken..................... **CLC 60**

Ludwig, Otto 1813-1865......... **NCLC 4**
See also DLB 129

Lugones, Leopoldo 1874-1938 .... **TCLC 15**
See also CA 116; 131; HW

Lu Hsun 1881-1936 .... **TCLC 3**

Lukacs, George .... **CLC 24**
See also Lukacs, Gyorgy (Szegeny von)

Lukacs, Gyorgy (Szegeny von) 1885-1971
See Lukacs, George
See also CA 101; 29-32R

Luke, Peter (Ambrose Cyprian)
1919-...................... **CLC 38**
See also CA 81-84; DLB 13

Lunar, Dennis
See Mungo, Raymond

Lurie, Alison 1926-....... **CLC 4, 5, 18, 39**
See also CA 1-4R; CANR 2, 17; DLB 2;
MTCW; SATA 46

Lustig, Arnost 1926-............ **CLC 56**
See also AAYA 3; CA 69-72; SATA 56

Luther, Martin 1483-1546.......... **LC 9**

Luzi, Mario 1914-............... **CLC 13**
See also CA 61-64; CANR 9; DLB 128

Lynch, B. Suarez
See Bioy Casares, Adolfo; Borges, Jorge
Luis

Lynch, David (K.) 1946-.......... **CLC 66**
See also CA 124; 129

Lynch, James
See Andreyev, Leonid (Nikolaevich)

Lynch Davis, B.
See Bioy Casares, Adolfo; Borges, Jorge
Luis

Lyndsay, Sir David 1490-1555 ...... **LC 20**

Lynn, Kenneth S(chuyler) 1923-.... **CLC 50**
See also CA 1-4R; CANR 3, 27

Lynx
See West, Rebecca

Lyons, Marcus
See Blish, James (Benjamin)

Lyre, Pinchbeck
See Sassoon, Siegfried (Lorraine)

Lytle, Andrew (Nelson) 1902-...... **CLC 22**
See also CA 9-12R; DLB 6

Lyttelton, George 1709-1773........ **LC 10**

Maas, Peter 1929- .... **CLC 29**
See also CA 93-96

Macaulay, Rose 1881-1958 ..... **TCLC 7, 44**
See also CA 104; DLB 36

Macaulay, Thomas Babington
1800-1859 .... **NCLC 42**
See also CDBLB 1832-1890; DLB 32, 55

MacBeth, George (Mann)
1932-1992 .... **CLC 2, 5, 9**
See also CA 25-28R; 136; DLB 40; MTCW;
SATA 4; SATA-Obit 70

MacCaig, Norman (Alexander)
1910-..................... **CLC 36**
See also CA 9-12R; CANR 3, 34; DLB 27

MacCarthy, (Sir Charles Otto) Desmond
1877-1952 .... **TCLC 36**

MacDiarmid, Hugh
.... **CLC 2, 4, 11, 19, 63; PC 9**
See also Grieve, C(hristopher) M(urray)
See also CDBLB 1945-1960; DLB 20

MacDonald, Anson
See Heinlein, Robert A(nson)

Macdonald, Cynthia 1928-...... **CLC 13, 19**
See also CA 49-52; CANR 4, 44; DLB 105

MacDonald, George 1824-1905..... **TCLC 9**
See also CA 106; 137; DLB 18; MAICYA;
SATA 33

Macdonald, John
See Millar, Kenneth

MacDonald, John D(ann)
1916-1986 .... **CLC 3, 27, 44**
See also CA 1-4R; 121; CANR 1, 19;
DLB 8; DLBY 86; MTCW

Macdonald, John Ross
See Millar, Kenneth

Macdonald, Ross..... **CLC 1, 2, 3, 14, 34, 41**
See also Millar, Kenneth
See also DLBD 6

MacDougal, John
See Blish, James (Benjamin)

MacEwen, Gwendolyn (Margaret)
1941-1987 .... **CLC 13, 55**
See also CA 9-12R; 124; CANR 7, 22;
DLB 53; SATA 50, 55

Macha, Karel Hynek 1810-1846.. **NCLC 46**

Machado (y Ruiz), Antonio
1875-1939 .... **TCLC 3**
See also CA 104; DLB 108

Machado de Assis, Joaquim Maria
1839-1908 .... **TCLC 10; BLC**
See also CA 107

Machen, Arthur.................. **TCLC 4**
See also Jones, Arthur Llewellyn
See also DLB 36

Machiavelli, Niccolo 1469-1527 .. **LC 8; DA**

MacInnes, Colin 1914-1976...... **CLC 4, 23**
See also CA 69-72; 65-68; CANR 21;
DLB 14; MTCW

MacInnes, Helen (Clark)
1907-1985 .... **CLC 27, 39**
See also CA 1-4R; 117; CANR 1, 28;
DLB 87; MTCW; SATA 22, 44

Mackay, Mary 1855-1924
See Corelli, Marie
See also CA 118

Mackenzie, Compton (Edward Montague)
1883-1972 .... **CLC 18**
See also CA 21-22; 37-40R; CAP 2;
DLB 34, 100

Mackenzie, Henry 1745-1831 .... **NCLC 41**
See also DLB 39

Mackintosh, Elizabeth 1896(?)-1952
See Tey, Josephine
See also CA 110

MacLaren, James
See Grieve, C(hristopher) M(urray)

Mac Laverty, Bernard 1942-....... **CLC 31**
See also CA 116; 118; CANR 43

MacLean, Alistair (Stuart)
1922-1987 .... **CLC 3, 13, 50, 63**
See also CA 57-60; 121; CANR 28; MTCW;
SATA 23, 50

Maclean, Norman (Fitzroy)
1902-1990 .... **CLC 78; SSC 13**
See also CA 102; 132

MacLeish, Archibald
1892-1982 .... **CLC 3, 8, 14, 68**
See also CA 9-12R; 106; CANR 33; DLB 4,
7, 45; DLBY 82; MTCW

MacLennan, (John) Hugh
1907-1990 .... **CLC 2, 14**
See also CA 5-8R; 142; CANR 33; DLB 68;
MTCW

MacLeod, Alistair 1936- .... **CLC 56**
See also CA 123; DLB 60

MacNeice, (Frederick) Louis
1907-1963 .... **CLC 1, 4, 10, 53**
See also CA 85-88; DLB 10, 20; MTCW

MacNeill, Dand
See Fraser, George MacDonald

Macpherson, (Jean) Jay 1931-...... **CLC 14**
See also CA 5-8R; DLB 53

MacShane, Frank 1927-.......... **CLC 39**
See also CA 9-12R; CANR 3, 33; DLB 111

Macumber, Mari
See Sandoz, Mari(e Susette)

Madach, Imre 1823-1864........ **NCLC 19**

Madden, (Jerry) David 1933- .... **CLC 5, 15**
See also CA 1-4R; CAAS 3; CANR 4, 45;
DLB 6; MTCW

Maddern, Al(an)
See Ellison, Harlan

Madhubuti, Haki R.
1942-.......... **CLC 6, 73; BLC; PC 5**
See also Lee, Don L.
See also BW 2; CA 73-76; CANR 24;
DLB 5, 41; DLBD 8

Maepenn, Hugh
See Kuttner, Henry

Maepenn, K. H.
See Kuttner, Henry

Maeterlinck, Maurice 1862-1949 ... **TCLC 3**
See also CA 104; 136; SATA 66

Maginn, William 1794-1842....... **NCLC 8**
See also DLB 110

Mahapatra, Jayanta 1928-........ **CLC 33**
See also CA 73-76; CAAS 9; CANR 15, 33

Mahfouz, Naguib (Abdel Aziz Al-Sabilgi)
1911(?)-
See Mahfuz, Najib
See also BEST 89:2; CA 128; MTCW

Mahfuz, Najib . . . . **CLC 52, 55**
See also Mahfouz, Naguib (Abdel Aziz
Al-Sabilgi)
See also DLBY 88

Mahon, Derek 1941- . . . . **CLC 27**
See also CA 113; 128; DLB 40

Mailer, Norman
1923- . . . . . . **CLC 1, 2, 3, 4, 5, 8, 11, 14,
28, 39, 74; DA**
See also AITN 2; CA 9-12R; CABS 1;
CANR 28; CDALB 1968-1988; DLB 2,
16, 28; DLBD 3; DLBY 80, 83; MTCW

Maillet, Antonine 1929- . . . . **CLC 54**
See also CA 115; 120; DLB 60

Mais, Roger 1905-1955 . . . . **TCLC 8**
See also BW 1; CA 105; 124; DLB 125;
MTCW

Maistre, Joseph de 1753-1821 . . . . **NCLC 37**

Maitland, Sara (Louise) 1950- . . . . . . **CLC 49**
See also CA 69-72; CANR 13

Major, Clarence
1936- . . . . **CLC 3, 19, 48; BLC**
See also BW 2; CA 21-24R; CAAS 6;
CANR 13, 25; DLB 33

Major, Kevin (Gerald) 1949- . . . . **CLC 26**
See also CA 97-100; CANR 21, 38;
CLR 11; DLB 60; JRDA; MAICYA;
SATA 32

Maki, James
See Ozu, Yasujiro

Malabaila, Damiano
See Levi, Primo

Malamud, Bernard
1914-1986 . . . . . . **CLC 1, 2, 3, 5, 8, 9, 11,
18, 27, 44, 78, 85; DA; SSC 15; WLC**
See also CA 5-8R; 118; CABS 1; CANR 28;
CDALB 1941-1968; DLB 2, 28;
DLBY 80, 86; MTCW

Malaparte, Curzio 1898-1957 . . . . . **TCLC 52**

Malcolm, Dan
See Silverberg, Robert

Malcolm X . . . . **CLC 82; BLC**
See also Little, Malcolm

Malherbe, Francois de 1555-1628 . . . . . **LC 5**

Mallarme, Stephane
1842-1898 . . . . **NCLC 4, 41; PC 4**

Mallet-Joris, Francoise 1930- . . . . . . **CLC 11**
See also CA 65-68; CANR 17; DLB 83

Malley, Ern
See McAuley, James Phillip

Mallowan, Agatha Christie
See Christie, Agatha (Mary Clarissa)

Maloff, Saul 1922- . . . . **CLC 5**
See also CA 33-36R

Malone, Louis
See MacNeice, (Frederick) Louis

Malone, Michael (Christopher)
1942- . . . . **CLC 43**
See also CA 77-80; CANR 14, 32

Malory, (Sir) Thomas
1410(?)-1471(?) . . . . **LC 11; DA**
See also CDBLB Before 1660; SATA 33, 59

Malouf, (George Joseph) David
1934- . . . . **CLC 28**
See also CA 124

Malraux, (Georges-)Andre
1901-1976 . . . . . . **CLC 1, 4, 9, 13, 15, 57**
See also CA 21-22; 69-72; CANR 34;
CAP 2; DLB 72; MTCW

Malzberg, Barry N(athaniel) 1939- . . . **CLC 7**
See also CA 61-64; CAAS 4; CANR 16;
DLB 8

Mamet, David (Alan)
1947- . . . . **CLC 9, 15, 34, 46; DC 4**
See also AAYA 3; CA 81-84; CABS 3;
CANR 15, 41; DLB 7; MTCW

Mamoulian, Rouben (Zachary)
1897-1987 . . . . **CLC 16**
See also CA 25-28R; 124

Mandelstam, Osip (Emilievich)
1891(?)-1938(?) . . . . **TCLC 2, 6**
See also CA 104

Mander, (Mary) Jane 1877-1949 . . . **TCLC 31**

Mandiargues, Andre Pieyre de . . . . . . **CLC 41**
See also Pieyre de Mandiargues, Andre
See also DLB 83

Mandrake, Ethel Belle
See Thurman, Wallace (Henry)

Mangan, James Clarence
1803-1849 . . . . **NCLC 27**

Maniere, J.-E.
See Giraudoux, (Hippolyte) Jean

Manley, (Mary) Delariviere
1672(?)-1724 . . . . **LC 1**
See also DLB 39, 80

Mann, Abel
See Creasey, John

Mann, (Luiz) Heinrich 1871-1950 . . . **TCLC 9**
See also CA 106; DLB 66

Mann, (Paul) Thomas
1875-1955 . . . . **TCLC 2, 8, 14, 21, 35, 44;
DA; SSC 5; WLC**
See also CA 104; 128; DLB 66; MTCW

Manning, David
See Faust, Frederick (Schiller)

Manning, Frederic 1887(?)-1935 . . . **TCLC 25**
See also CA 124

Manning, Olivia 1915-1980 . . . . . . **CLC 5, 19**
See also CA 5-8R; 101; CANR 29; MTCW

Mano, D. Keith 1942- . . . . **CLC 2, 10**
See also CA 25-28R; CAAS 6; CANR 26;
DLB 6

Mansfield, Katherine
. . . . **TCLC 2, 8, 39; SSC 9; WLC**
See also Beauchamp, Kathleen Mansfield

Manso, Peter 1940- . . . . **CLC 39**
See also CA 29-32R; CANR 44

Mantecon, Juan Jimenez
See Jimenez (Mantecon), Juan Ramon

Manton, Peter
See Creasey, John

Man Without a Spleen, A
See Chekhov, Anton (Pavlovich)

Manzoni, Alessandro 1785-1873 . . **NCLC 29**

Mapu, Abraham (ben Jekutiel)
1808-1867 . . . . **NCLC 18**

Mara, Sally
See Queneau, Raymond

Marat, Jean Paul 1743-1793 . . . . **LC 10**

Marcel, Gabriel Honore
1889-1973 . . . . **CLC 15**
See also CA 102; 45-48; MTCW

Marchbanks, Samuel
See Davies, (William) Robertson

Marchi, Giacomo
See Bassani, Giorgio

Margulies, Donald . . . . **CLC 76**

Marie de France c. 12th cent. - . . . . **CMLC 8**

Marie de l'Incarnation 1599-1672 . . . . **LC 10**

Mariner, Scott
See Pohl, Frederik

Marinetti, Filippo Tommaso
1876-1944 . . . . **TCLC 10**
See also CA 107; DLB 114

Marivaux, Pierre Carlet de Chamblain de
1688-1763 . . . . **LC 4**

Markandaya, Kamala . . . . **CLC 8, 38**
See also Taylor, Kamala (Purnaiya)

Markfield, Wallace 1926- . . . . **CLC 8**
See also CA 69-72; CAAS 3; DLB 2, 28

Markham, Edwin 1852-1940 . . . . . . **TCLC 47**
See also DLB 54

Markham, Robert
See Amis, Kingsley (William)

Marks, J
See Highwater, Jamake (Mamake)

Marks-Highwater, J
See Highwater, Jamake (Mamake)

Markson, David M(errill) 1927- . . . . **CLC 67**
See also CA 49-52; CANR 1

Marley, Bob . . . . **CLC 17**
See also Marley, Robert Nesta

Marley, Robert Nesta 1945-1981
See Marley, Bob
See also CA 107; 103

Marlowe, Christopher
1564-1593 . . . . . **LC 22; DA; DC 1; WLC**
See also CDBLB Before 1660; DLB 62

Marmontel, Jean-Francois
1723-1799 . . . . **LC 2**

Marquand, John P(hillips)
1893-1960 . . . . **CLC 2, 10**
See also CA 85-88; DLB 9, 102

Marquez, Gabriel (Jose) Garcia
See Garcia Marquez, Gabriel (Jose)

Marquis, Don(ald Robert Perry)
1878-1937 . . . . **TCLC 7**
See also CA 104; DLB 11, 25

Marric, J. J.
See Creasey, John

Marrow, Bernard
See Moore, Brian

Marryat, Frederick 1792-1848 . . . . **NCLC 3**
See also DLB 21

Marsden, James
  See Creasey, John

Marsh, (Edith) Ngaio
  1899-1982 .... CLC **7, 53**
  See also CA 9-12R; CANR 6; DLB 77;
  MTCW

Marshall, Garry 1934- .... CLC **17**
  See also AAYA 3; CA 111; SATA 60

Marshall, Paule
  1929- .... CLC **27, 72; BLC; SSC 3**
  See also BW 2; CA 77-80; CANR 25;
  DLB 33; MTCW

Marsten, Richard
  See Hunter, Evan

Martha, Henry
  See Harris, Mark

Martial 40-104 .... PC **10**

Martin, Ken
  See Hubbard, L(afayette) Ron(ald)

Martin, Richard
  See Creasey, John

Martin, Steve 1945- .... CLC **30**
  See also CA 97-100; CANR 30; MTCW

Martin, Violet Florence
  1862-1915 .... TCLC **51**

Martin, Webber
  See Silverberg, Robert

Martindale, Patrick Victor
  See White, Patrick (Victor Martindale)

Martin du Gard, Roger
  1881-1958 .... TCLC **24**
  See also CA 118; DLB 65

Martineau, Harriet 1802-1876.... NCLC **26**
  See also DLB 21, 55; YABC 2

Martines, Julia
  See O'Faolain, Julia

Martinez, Jacinto Benavente y
  See Benavente (y Martinez), Jacinto

Martinez Ruiz, Jose 1873-1967
  See Azorin; Ruiz, Jose Martinez
  See also CA 93-96; HW

Martinez Sierra, Gregorio
  1881-1947 .... TCLC **6**
  See also CA 115

Martinez Sierra, Maria (de la O'LeJarraga)
  1874-1974 .... TCLC **6**
  See also CA 115

Martinsen, Martin
  See Follett, Ken(neth Martin)

Martinson, Harry (Edmund)
  1904-1978 .... CLC **14**
  See also CA 77-80; CANR 34

Marut, Ret
  See Traven, B.

Marut, Robert
  See Traven, B.

Marvell, Andrew
  1621-1678 ..... LC **4; DA; PC 10; WLC**
  See also CDBLB 1660-1789; DLB 131

Marx, Karl (Heinrich)
  1818-1883 .... NCLC **17**
  See also DLB 129

Masaoka Shiki................. TCLC **18**
  See also Masaoka Tsunenori

Masaoka Tsunenori 1867-1902
  See Masaoka Shiki
  See also CA 117

Masefield, John (Edward)
  1878-1967 .... CLC **11, 47**
  See also CA 19-20; 25-28R; CANR 33;
  CAP 2; CDBLB 1890-1914; DLB 10;
  MTCW; SATA 19

Maso, Carole 19(?)- .... CLC **44**

Mason, Bobbie Ann
  1940- .... CLC **28, 43, 82; SSC 4**
  See also AAYA 5; CA 53-56; CANR 11,
  31; DLBY 87; MTCW

Mason, Ernst
  See Pohl, Frederik

Mason, Lee W.
  See Malzberg, Barry N(athaniel)

Mason, Nick 1945- .... CLC **35**

Mason, Tally
  See Derleth, August (William)

Mass, William
  See Gibson, William

Masters, Edgar Lee
  1868-1950 ...... TCLC **2, 25; DA; PC 1**
  See also CA 104; 133; CDALB 1865-1917;
  DLB 54; MTCW

Masters, Hilary 1928- .... CLC **48**
  See also CA 25-28R; CANR 13

Mastrosimone, William 19(?)-...... CLC **36**

Mathe, Albert
  See Camus, Albert

Matheson, Richard Burton 1926-... CLC **37**
  See also CA 97-100; DLB 8, 44

Mathews, Harry 1930- .... CLC **6, 52**
  See also CA 21-24R; CAAS 6; CANR 18,
  40

Mathews, John Joseph 1894-1979... CLC **84**
  See also CA 19-20; 142; CANR 45; CAP 2

Mathias, Roland (Glyn) 1915-...... CLC **45**
  See also CA 97-100; CANR 19, 41; DLB 27

Matsuo Basho 1644-1694........... PC **3**

Mattheson, Rodney
  See Creasey, John

Matthews, Greg 1949- .... CLC **45**
  See also CA 135

Matthews, William 1942-.......... CLC **40**
  See also CA 29-32R; CAAS 18; CANR 12;
  DLB 5

Matthias, John (Edward) 1941-...... CLC **9**
  See also CA 33-36R

Matthiessen, Peter
  1927- .... CLC **5, 7, 11, 32, 64**
  See also AAYA 6; BEST 90:4; CA 9-12R;
  CANR 21; DLB 6; MTCW; SATA 27

Maturin, Charles Robert
  1780(?)-1824 .... NCLC **6**

Matute (Ausejo), Ana Maria
  1925- .... CLC **11**
  See also CA 89-92; MTCW

Maugham, W. S.
  See Maugham, W(illiam) Somerset

Maugham, W(illiam) Somerset
  1874-1965 ...... CLC **1, 11, 15, 67; DA;
  SSC 8; WLC**
  See also CA 5-8R; 25-28R; CANR 40;
  CDBLB 1914-1945; DLB 10, 36, 77, 100;
  MTCW; SATA 54

Maugham, William Somerset
  See Maugham, W(illiam) Somerset

Maupassant, (Henri Rene Albert) Guy de
  1850-1893 .... NCLC **1, 42; DA; SSC 1;
  WLC**
  See also DLB 123

Maurhut, Richard
  See Traven, B.

Mauriac, Claude 1914-............ CLC **9**
  See also CA 89-92; DLB 83

Mauriac, Francois (Charles)
  1885-1970 .... CLC **4, 9, 56**
  See also CA 25-28; CAP 2; DLB 65;
  MTCW

Mavor, Osborne Henry 1888-1951
  See Bridie, James
  See also CA 104

Maxwell, William (Keepers, Jr.)
  1908- .... CLC **19**
  See also CA 93-96; DLBY 80

May, Elaine 1932- .... CLC **16**
  See also CA 124; 142; DLB 44

Mayakovski, Vladimir (Vladimirovich)
  1893-1930 .... TCLC **4, 18**
  See also CA 104

Mayhew, Henry 1812-1887 ...... NCLC **31**
  See also DLB 18, 55

Maynard, Joyce 1953-............ CLC **23**
  See also CA 111; 129

Mayne, William (James Carter)
  1928- .... CLC **12**
  See also CA 9-12R; CANR 37; CLR 25;
  JRDA; MAICYA; SAAS 11; SATA 6, 68

Mayo, Jim
  See L'Amour, Louis (Dearborn)

Maysles, Albert 1926- .... CLC **16**
  See also CA 29-32R

Maysles, David 1932-............. CLC **16**

Mazer, Norma Fox 1931- .... CLC **26**
  See also AAYA 5; CA 69-72; CANR 12,
  32; CLR 23; JRDA; MAICYA; SAAS 1;
  SATA 24, 67

Mazzini, Guiseppe 1805-1872 .... NCLC **34**

McAuley, James Phillip
  1917-1976 .... CLC **45**
  See also CA 97-100

McBain, Ed
  See Hunter, Evan

McBrien, William Augustine
  1930- .... CLC **44**
  See also CA 107

McCaffrey, Anne (Inez) 1926-...... CLC **17**
  See also AAYA 6; AITN 2; BEST 89:2;
  CA 25-28R; CANR 15, 35; DLB 8;
  JRDA; MAICYA; MTCW; SAAS 11;
  SATA 8, 70

McCann, Arthur
  See Campbell, John W(ood, Jr.)

Merritt, E. B.
See Waddington, Miriam

Merton, Thomas
1915-1968 .. **CLC 1, 3, 11, 34, 83; PC 10**
See also CA 5-8R; 25-28R; CANR 22;
DLB 48; DLBY 81; MTCW

Merwin, W(illiam) S(tanley)
1927- ...... **CLC 1, 2, 3, 5, 8, 13, 18, 45**
See also CA 13-16R; CANR 15; DLB 5;
MTCW

Metcalf, John 1938-............. **CLC 37**
See also CA 113; DLB 60

Metcalf, Suzanne
See Baum, L(yman) Frank

Mew, Charlotte (Mary)
1870-1928 .... **TCLC 8**
See also CA 105; DLB 19, 135

Mewshaw, Michael 1943-.......... **CLC 9**
See also CA 53-56; CANR 7; DLBY 80

Meyer, June
See Jordan, June

Meyer, Lynn
See Slavitt, David R(ytman)

Meyer-Meyrink, Gustav 1868-1932
See Meyrink, Gustav
See also CA 117

Meyers, Jeffrey 1939- .... **CLC 39**
See also CA 73-76; DLB 111

Meynell, Alice (Christina Gertrude Thompson)
1847-1922 .... **TCLC 6**
See also CA 104; DLB 19, 98

Meyrink, Gustav .... **TCLC 21**
See also Meyer-Meyrink, Gustav
See also DLB 81

Michaels, Leonard
1933- .... **CLC 6, 25; SSC 16**
See also CA 61-64; CANR 21; DLB 130;
MTCW

Michaux, Henri 1899-1984 ...... **CLC 8, 19**
See also CA 85-88; 114

Michelangelo 1475-1564........... **LC 12**

Michelet, Jules 1798-1874....... **NCLC 31**

Michener, James A(lbert)
1907(?)- .... **CLC 1, 5, 11, 29, 60**
See also AITN 1; BEST 90:1; CA 5-8R;
CANR 21, 45; DLB 6; MTCW

Mickiewicz, Adam 1798-1855 ..... **NCLC 3**

Middleton, Christopher 1926- ...... **CLC 13**
See also CA 13-16R; CANR 29; DLB 40

Middleton, Richard (Barham)
1882-1911 .... **TCLC 56**

Middleton, Stanley 1919-........ **CLC 7, 38**
See also CA 25-28R; CANR 21; DLB 14

Migueis, Jose Rodrigues 1901- ..... **CLC 10**

Mikszath, Kalman 1847-1910 ..... **TCLC 31**

Miles, Josephine
1911-1985 .... **CLC 1, 2, 14, 34, 39**
See also CA 1-4R; 116; CANR 2; DLB 48

Militant
See Sandburg, Carl (August)

Mill, John Stuart 1806-1873 ..... **NCLC 11**
See also CDBLB 1832-1890; DLB 55

Millar, Kenneth 1915-1983 .... **CLC 14**
See also Macdonald, Ross
See also CA 9-12R; 110; CANR 16; DLB 2;
DLBD 6; DLBY 83; MTCW

Millay, E. Vincent
See Millay, Edna St. Vincent

Millay, Edna St. Vincent
1892-1950 ..... **TCLC 4, 49; DA; PC 6**
See also CA 104; 130; CDALB 1917-1929;
DLB 45; MTCW

Miller, Arthur
1915- .... **CLC 1, 2, 6, 10, 15, 26, 47, 78;**
DA; DC 1; WLC
See also AITN 1; CA 1-4R; CABS 3;
CANR 2, 30; CDALB 1941-1968; DLB 7;
MTCW

Miller, Henry (Valentine)
1891-1980 .... **CLC 1, 2, 4, 9, 14, 43, 84;**
DA; WLC
See also CA 9-12R; 97-100; CANR 33;
CDALB 1929-1941; DLB 4, 9; DLBY 80;
MTCW

Miller, Jason 1939(?)- .... **CLC 2**
See also AITN 1; CA 73-76; DLB 7

Miller, Sue 1943- .... **CLC 44**
See also BEST 90:3; CA 139; DLB 143

Miller, Walter M(ichael, Jr.)
1923- .... **CLC 4, 30**
See also CA 85-88; DLB 8

Millett, Kate 1934-.............. **CLC 67**
See also AITN 1; CA 73-76; CANR 32;
MTCW

Millhauser, Steven 1943-....... **CLC 21, 54**
See also CA 110; 111; DLB 2

Millin, Sarah Gertrude 1889-1968 .. **CLC 49**
See also CA 102; 93-96

Milne, A(lan) A(lexander)
1882-1956 .... **TCLC 6**
See also CA 104; 133; CLR 1, 26; DLB 10,
77, 100; MAICYA; MTCW; YABC 1

Milner, Ron(ald) 1938-....... **CLC 56; BLC**
See also AITN 1; BW 1; CA 73-76;
CANR 24; DLB 38; MTCW

Milosz, Czeslaw
1911- ... **CLC 5, 11, 22, 31, 56, 82; PC 8**
See also CA 81-84; CANR 23; MTCW

Milton, John 1608-1674... **LC 9; DA; WLC**
See also CDBLB 1660-1789; DLB 131

Minehaha, Cornelius
See Wedekind, (Benjamin) Frank(lin)

Miner, Valerie 1947- .... **CLC 40**
See also CA 97-100

Minimo, Duca
See D'Annunzio, Gabriele

Minot, Susan 1956- .... **CLC 44**
See also CA 134

Minus, Ed 1938-................. **CLC 39**

Miranda, Javier
See Bioy Casares, Adolfo

Mirbeau, Octave 1848-1917....... **TCLC 55**
See also DLB 123

Miro (Ferrer), Gabriel (Francisco Victor)
1879-1930 .... **TCLC 5**
See also CA 104

Mishima, Yukio
.... **CLC 2, 4, 6, 9, 27; DC 1; SSC 4**
See also Hiraoka, Kimitake

Mistral, Frederic 1830-1914 ...... **TCLC 51**
See also CA 122

Mistral, Gabriela............ **TCLC 2; HLC**
See also Godoy Alcayaga, Lucila

Mistry, Rohinton 1952-........... **CLC 71**
See also CA 141

Mitchell, Clyde
See Ellison, Harlan; Silverberg, Robert

Mitchell, James Leslie 1901-1935
See Gibbon, Lewis Grassic
See also CA 104; DLB 15

Mitchell, Joni 1943-.............. **CLC 12**
See also CA 112

Mitchell, Margaret (Munnerlyn)
1900-1949 .... **TCLC 11**
See also CA 109; 125; DLB 9; MTCW

Mitchell, Peggy
See Mitchell, Margaret (Munnerlyn)

Mitchell, S(ilas) Weir 1829-1914 .. **TCLC 36**

Mitchell, W(illiam) O(rmond)
1914- .... **CLC 25**
See also CA 77-80; CANR 15, 43; DLB 88

Mitford, Mary Russell 1787-1855.. **NCLC 4**
See also DLB 110, 116

Mitford, Nancy 1904-1973........ **CLC 44**
See also CA 9-12R

Miyamoto, Yuriko 1899-1951 ..... **TCLC 37**

Mo, Timothy (Peter) 1950(?)- ...... **CLC 46**
See also CA 117; MTCW

Modarressi, Taghi (M.) 1931-...... **CLC 44**
See also CA 121; 134

Modiano, Patrick (Jean) 1945-..... **CLC 18**
See also CA 85-88; CANR 17, 40; DLB 83

Moerck, Paal
See Roelvaag, O(le) E(dvart)

Mofolo, Thomas (Mokopu)
1875(?)-1948 .... **TCLC 22; BLC**
See also CA 121

Mohr, Nicholasa 1935-...... **CLC 12; HLC**
See also AAYA 8; CA 49-52; CANR 1, 32;
CLR 22; HW; JRDA; SAAS 8; SATA 8

Mojtabai, A(nn) G(race)
1938- .... **CLC 5, 9, 15, 29**
See also CA 85-88

Moliere 1622-1673 .... **LC 10; DA; WLC**

Molin, Charles
See Mayne, William (James Carter)

Molnar, Ferenc 1878-1952........ **TCLC 20**
See also CA 109

Momaday, N(avarre) Scott
1934- .... **CLC 2, 19, 85; DA**
See also AAYA 11; CA 25-28R; CANR 14,
34; DLB 143; MTCW; NNAL; SATA 30,
48

Monette, Paul 1945-.............. **CLC 82**
See also CA 139

Monroe, Harriet 1860-1936....... **TCLC 12**
See also CA 109; DLB 54, 91

Monroe, Lyle
See Heinlein, Robert A(nson)

Montagu, Elizabeth 1917- . . . . NCLC 7
See also CA 9-12R

Montagu, Mary (Pierrepont) Wortley
1689-1762 . . . . LC 9
See also DLB 95, 101

Montagu, W. H.
See Coleridge, Samuel Taylor

Montague, John (Patrick)
1929- . . . . CLC 13, 46
See also CA 9-12R; CANR 9; DLB 40;
MTCW

Montaigne, Michel (Eyquem) de
1533-1592 . . . . LC 8; DA; WLC

Montale, Eugenio 1896-1981. . . CLC 7, 9, 18
See also CA 17-20R; 104; CANR 30;
DLB 114; MTCW

Montesquieu, Charles-Louis de Secondat
1689-1755 . . . . LC 7

Montgomery, (Robert) Bruce 1921-1978
See Crispin, Edmund
See also CA 104

Montgomery, L(ucy) M(aud)
1874-1942 . . . . TCLC 51
See also AAYA 12; CA 108; 137; CLR 8;
DLB 92; JRDA; MAICYA; YABC 1

Montgomery, Marion H., Jr. 1925- . . CLC 7
See also AITN 1; CA 1-4R; CANR 3;
DLB 6

Montgomery, Max
See Davenport, Guy (Mattison, Jr.)

Montherlant, Henry (Milon) de
1896-1972 . . . . CLC 8, 19
See also CA 85-88; 37-40R; DLB 72;
MTCW

Monty Python
See Chapman, Graham; Cleese, John
(Marwood); Gilliam, Terry (Vance); Idle,
Eric; Jones, Terence Graham Parry; Palin,
Michael (Edward)
See also AAYA 7

Moodie, Susanna (Strickland)
1803-1885 . . . . NCLC 14
See also DLB 99

Mooney, Edward 1951-
See Mooney, Ted
See also CA 130

Mooney, Ted . . . . CLC 25
See also Mooney, Edward

Moorcock, Michael (John)
1939- . . . . CLC 5, 27, 58
See also CA 45-48; CAAS 5; CANR 2, 17,
38; DLB 14; MTCW

Moore, Brian
1921- . . . . CLC 1, 3, 5, 7, 8, 19, 32
See also CA 1-4R; CANR 1, 25, 42; MTCW

Moore, Edward
See Muir, Edwin

Moore, George Augustus
1852-1933 . . . . TCLC 7
See also CA 104; DLB 10, 18, 57, 135

Moore, Lorrie . . . . CLC 39, 45, 68
See also Moore, Marie Lorena

Moore, Marianne (Craig)
1887-1972 . . . . CLC 1, 2, 4, 8, 10, 13, 19,
47; DA; PC 4
See also CA 1-4R; 33-36R; CANR 3;
CDALB 1929-1941; DLB 45; DLBD 7;
MTCW; SATA 20

Moore, Marie Lorena 1957-
See Moore, Lorrie
See also CA 116; CANR 39

Moore, Thomas 1779-1852. . . . . . . NCLC 6
See also DLB 96, 144

Morand, Paul 1888-1976 . . . . CLC 41
See also CA 69-72; DLB 65

Morante, Elsa 1918-1985. . . . . . . CLC 8, 47
See also CA 85-88; 117; CANR 35; MTCW

Moravia, Alberto . . . . . . CLC 2, 7, 11, 27, 46
See also Pincherle, Alberto

More, Hannah 1745-1833 . . . . NCLC 27
See also DLB 107, 109, 116

More, Henry 1614-1687. . . . . LC 9
See also DLB 126

More, Sir Thomas 1478-1535 . . . . LC 10

Moreas, Jean. . . . . TCLC 18
See also Papadiamantopoulos, Johannes

Morgan, Berry 1919- . . . . CLC 6
See also CA 49-52; DLB 6

Morgan, Claire
See Highsmith, (Mary) Patricia

Morgan, Edwin (George) 1920- . . . . . CLC 31
See also CA 5-8R; CANR 3, 43; DLB 27

Morgan, (George) Frederick
1922- . . . . CLC 23
See also CA 17-20R; CANR 21

Morgan, Harriet
See Mencken, H(enry) L(ouis)

Morgan, Jane
See Cooper, James Fenimore

Morgan, Janet 1945- . . . . CLC 39
See also CA 65-68

Morgan, Lady 1776(?)-1859. . . . . . NCLC 29
See also DLB 116

Morgan, Robin 1941-. . . . . CLC 2
See also CA 69-72; CANR 29; MTCW

Morgan, Scott
See Kuttner, Henry

Morgan, Seth 1949(?)-1990 . . . . CLC 65
See also CA 132

Morgenstern, Christian
1871-1914 . . . . TCLC 8
See also CA 105

Morgenstern, S.
See Goldman, William (W.)

Moricz, Zsigmond 1879-1942 . . . . . TCLC 33

Morike, Eduard (Friedrich)
1804-1875 . . . . NCLC 10
See also DLB 133

Mori Ogai . . . . TCLC 14
See also Mori Rintaro

Mori Rintaro 1862-1922
See Mori Ogai
See also CA 110

Moritz, Karl Philipp 1756-1793 . . . . . . LC 2
See also DLB 94

Morland, Peter Henry
See Faust, Frederick (Schiller)

Morren, Theophil
See Hofmannsthal, Hugo von

Morris, Bill 1952-. . . . . CLC 76

Morris, Julian
See West, Morris L(anglo)

Morris, Steveland Judkins 1950(?)-
See Wonder, Stevie
See also CA 111

Morris, William 1834-1896 . . . . NCLC 4
See also CDBLB 1832-1890; DLB 18, 35, 57

Morris, Wright 1910-. . . CLC 1, 3, 7, 18, 37
See also CA 9-12R; CANR 21; DLB 2;
DLBY 81; MTCW

Morrison, Chloe Anthony Wofford
See Morrison, Toni

Morrison, James Douglas 1943-1971
See Morrison, Jim
See also CA 73-76; CANR 40

Morrison, Jim . . . . CLC 17
See also Morrison, James Douglas

Morrison, Toni
1931-. . CLC 4, 10, 22, 55, 81; BLC; DA
See also AAYA 1; BW 2; CA 29-32R;
CANR 27, 42; CDALB 1968-1988;
DLB 6, 33, 143; DLBY 81; MTCW;
SATA 57

Morrison, Van 1945- . . . . CLC 21
See also CA 116

Mortimer, John (Clifford)
1923- . . . . CLC 28, 43
See also CA 13-16R; CANR 21;
CDBLB 1960 to Present; DLB 13;
MTCW

Mortimer, Penelope (Ruth) 1918-. . . . CLC 5
See also CA 57-60; CANR 45

Morton, Anthony
See Creasey, John

Mosher, Howard Frank 1943-. . . . . . CLC 62
See also CA 139

Mosley, Nicholas 1923-. . . . . CLC 43, 70
See also CA 69-72; CANR 41; DLB 14

Moss, Howard
1922-1987 . . . . CLC 7, 14, 45, 50
See also CA 1-4R; 123; CANR 1, 44;
DLB 5

Mossgiel, Rab
See Burns, Robert

Motion, Andrew 1952-. . . . . CLC 47
See also DLB 40

Motley, Willard (Francis)
1909-1965 . . . . CLC 18
See also BW 1; CA 117; 106; DLB 76, 143

Motoori, Norinaga 1730-1801 . . . . NCLC 45

Mott, Michael (Charles Alston)
1930- . . . . CLC 15, 34
See also CA 5-8R; CAAS 7; CANR 7, 29

Mowat, Farley (McGill) 1921- . . . . . CLC 26
See also AAYA 1; CA 1-4R; CANR 4, 24,
42; CLR 20; DLB 68; JRDA; MAICYA;
MTCW; SATA 3, 55

Moyers, Bill 1934-. . . . . CLC 74
See also AITN 2; CA 61-64; CANR 31

Mphahlele, Es'kia
See Mphahlele, Ezekiel
See also DLB 125

Mphahlele, Ezekiel 1919-..... **CLC 25; BLC**
See also Mphahlele, Es'kia
See also BW 2; CA 81-84; CANR 26

Mqhayi, S(amuel) E(dward) K(rune Loliwe)
1875-1945 .... **TCLC 25; BLC**

Mr. Martin
See Burroughs, William S(eward)

Mrozek, Slawomir 1930-........ **CLC 3, 13**
See also CA 13-16R; CAAS 10; CANR 29;
MTCW

Mrs. Belloc-Lowndes
See Lowndes, Marie Adelaide (Belloc)

Mtwa, Percy (?)-................ **CLC 47**

Mueller, Lisel 1924-.......... **CLC 13, 51**
See also CA 93-96; DLB 105

Muir, Edwin 1887-1959 .... **TCLC 2**
See also CA 104; DLB 20, 100

Muir, John 1838-1914 .... **TCLC 28**

Mujica Lainez, Manuel
1910-1984 .... **CLC 31**
See also Lainez, Manuel Mujica
See also CA 81-84; 112; CANR 32; HW

Mukherjee, Bharati 1940-......... **CLC 53**
See also BEST 89:2; CA 107; CANR 45;
DLB 60; MTCW

Muldoon, Paul 1951-.......... **CLC 32, 72**
See also CA 113; 129; DLB 40

Mulisch, Harry 1927-............ **CLC 42**
See also CA 9-12R; CANR 6, 26

Mull, Martin 1943-.............. **CLC 17**
See also CA 105

Mulock, Dinah Maria
See Craik, Dinah Maria (Mulock)

Munford, Robert 1737(?)-1783 .... **LC 5**
See also DLB 31

Mungo, Raymond 1946-.......... **CLC 72**
See also CA 49-52; CANR 2

Munro, Alice
1931-........ **CLC 6, 10, 19, 50; SSC 3**
See also AITN 2; CA 33-36R; CANR 33;
DLB 53; MTCW; SATA 29

Munro, H(ector) H(ugh) 1870-1916
See Saki
See also CA 104; 130; CDBLB 1890-1914;
DA; DLB 34; MTCW; WLC

Murasaki, Lady................ **CMLC 1**

Murdoch, (Jean) Iris
1919-...... **CLC 1, 2, 3, 4, 6, 8, 11, 15,**
22, 31, 51
See also CA 13-16R; CANR 8, 43;
CDBLB 1960 to Present; DLB 14;
MTCW

Murnau, Friedrich Wilhelm
See Plumpe, Friedrich Wilhelm

Murphy, Richard 1927-........... **CLC 41**
See also CA 29-32R; DLB 40

Murphy, Sylvia 1937-............ **CLC 34**
See also CA 121

Murphy, Thomas (Bernard) 1935-... **CLC 51**
See also CA 101

Murray, Albert L. 1916-.......... **CLC 73**
See also BW 2; CA 49-52; CANR 26;
DLB 38

Murray, Les(lie) A(llan) 1938- ..... **CLC 40**
See also CA 21-24R; CANR 11, 27

Murry, J. Middleton
See Murry, John Middleton

Murry, John Middleton
1889-1957 .... **TCLC 16**
See also CA 118

Musgrave, Susan 1951-........ **CLC 13, 54**
See also CA 69-72; CANR 45

Musil, Robert (Edler von)
1880-1942 .... **TCLC 12**
See also CA 109; DLB 81, 124

Musset, (Louis Charles) Alfred de
1810-1857 .... **NCLC 7**

My Brother's Brother
See Chekhov, Anton (Pavlovich)

Myers, Walter Dean 1937- ... **CLC 35; BLC**
See also AAYA 4; BW 2; CA 33-36R;
CANR 20, 42; CLR 4, 16, 35; DLB 33;
JRDA; MAICYA; SAAS 2; SATA 27, 41,
71

Myers, Walter M.
See Myers, Walter Dean

Myles, Symon
See Follett, Ken(neth Martin)

Nabokov, Vladimir (Vladimirovich)
1899-1977 ..... **CLC 1, 2, 3, 6, 8, 11, 15,**
23, 44, 46, 64; DA; SSC 11; WLC
See also CA 5-8R; 69-72; CANR 20;
CDALB 1941-1968; DLB 2; DLBD 3;
DLBY 80, 91; MTCW

Nagai Kafu.................... **TCLC 51**
See also Nagai Sokichi

Nagai Sokichi 1879-1959
See Nagai Kafu
See also CA 117

Nagy, Laszlo 1925-1978........... **CLC 7**
See also CA 129; 112

Naipaul, Shiva(dhar Srinivasa)
1945-1985 .... **CLC 32, 39**
See also CA 110; 112; 116; CANR 33;
DLBY 85; MTCW

Naipaul, V(idiadhar) S(urajprasad)
1932-.......... **CLC 4, 7, 9, 13, 18, 37**
See also CA 1-4R; CANR 1, 33;
CDBLB 1960 to Present; DLB 125;
DLBY 85; MTCW

Nakos, Lilika 1899(?)-........... **CLC 29**

Narayan, R(asipuram) K(rishnaswami)
1906-................. **CLC 7, 28, 47**
See also CA 81-84; CANR 33; MTCW;
SATA 62

Nash, (Fredric) Ogden 1902-1971 .. **CLC 23**
See also CA 13-14; 29-32R; CANR 34;
CAP 1; DLB 11; MAICYA; MTCW;
SATA 2, 46

Nathan, Daniel
See Dannay, Frederic

Nathan, George Jean 1882-1958 ... **TCLC 18**
See also Hatteras, Owen
See also CA 114; DLB 137

Natsume, Kinnosuke 1867-1916
See Natsume, Soseki
See also CA 104

Natsume, Soseki .... **TCLC 2, 10**
See also Natsume, Kinnosuke

Natti, (Mary) Lee 1919-
See Kingman, Lee
See also CA 5-8R; CANR 2

Naylor, Gloria
1950-............ **CLC 28, 52; BLC; DA**
See also AAYA 6; BW 2; CA 107;
CANR 27; MTCW

Neihardt, John Gneisenau
1881-1973 .... **CLC 32**
See also CA 13-14; CAP 1; DLB 9, 54

Nekrasov, Nikolai Alekseevich
1821-1878 .... **NCLC 11**

Nelligan, Emile 1879-1941....... **TCLC 14**
See also CA 114; DLB 92

Nelson, Willie 1933-.............. **CLC 17**
See also CA 107

Nemerov, Howard (Stanley)
1920-1991 .... **CLC 2, 6, 9, 36**
See also CA 1-4R; 134; CABS 2; CANR 1,
27; DLB 6; DLBY 83; MTCW

Neruda, Pablo
1904-1973 ..... **CLC 1, 2, 5, 7, 9, 28, 62;**
DA; HLC; PC 4; WLC
See also CA 19-20; 45-48; CAP 2; HW;
MTCW

Nerval, Gerard de 1808-1855...... **NCLC 1**

Nervo, (Jose) Amado (Ruiz de)
1870-1919 .... **TCLC 11**
See also CA 109; 131; HW

Nessi, Pio Baroja y
See Baroja (y Nessi), Pio

Nestroy, Johann 1801-1862...... **NCLC 42**
See also DLB 133

Neufeld, John (Arthur) 1938- ...... **CLC 17**
See also AAYA 11; CA 25-28R; CANR 11,
37; MAICYA; SAAS 3; SATA 6

Neville, Emily Cheney 1919-....... **CLC 12**
See also CA 5-8R; CANR 3, 37; JRDA;
MAICYA; SAAS 2; SATA 1

Newbound, Bernard Slade 1930-
See Slade, Bernard
See also CA 81-84

Newby, P(ercy) H(oward)
1918-.................... **CLC 2, 13**
See also CA 5-8R; CANR 32; DLB 15;
MTCW

Newlove, Donald 1928-............ **CLC 6**
See also CA 29-32R; CANR 25

Newlove, John (Herbert) 1938-..... **CLC 14**
See also CA 21-24R; CANR 9, 25

Newman, Charles 1938-.......... **CLC 2, 8**
See also CA 21-24R

Newman, Edwin (Harold) 1919- .... **CLC 14**
See also AITN 1; CA 69-72; CANR 5

Newman, John Henry
1801-1890 .... **NCLC 38**
See also DLB 18, 32, 55

Newton, Suzanne 1936-........... **CLC 35**
See also CA 41-44R; CANR 14; JRDA;
SATA 5, 77

O'Donovan, Michael John
1903-1966 .... CLC **14**
See also O'Connor, Frank
See also CA 93-96

Oe, Kenzaburo 1935- .... CLC **10, 36**
See also CA 97-100; CANR 36; MTCW

O'Faolain, Julia 1932- .... CLC **6, 19, 47**
See also CA 81-84; CAAS 2; CANR 12;
DLB 14; MTCW

O'Faolain, Sean
1900-1991 .... CLC **1, 7, 14, 32, 70;**
SSC **13**
See also CA 61-64; 134; CANR 12;
DLB 15; MTCW

O'Flaherty, Liam
1896-1984 .... CLC **5, 34;** SSC **6**
See also CA 101; 113; CANR 35; DLB 36;
DLBY 84; MTCW

Ogilvy, Gavin
See Barrie, J(ames) M(atthew)

O'Grady, Standish James
1846-1928 .... TCLC **5**
See also CA 104

O'Grady, Timothy 1951- .... CLC **59**
See also CA 138

O'Hara, Frank
1926-1966 .... CLC **2, 5, 13, 78**
See also CA 9-12R; 25-28R; CANR 33;
DLB 5, 16; MTCW

O'Hara, John (Henry)
1905-1970 .... CLC **1, 2, 3, 6, 11, 42;**
SSC **15**
See also CA 5-8R; 25-28R; CANR 31;
CDALB 1929-1941; DLB 9, 86; DLBD 2;
MTCW

O Hehir, Diana 1922- .... CLC **41**
See also CA 93-96

Okigbo, Christopher (Ifenayichukwu)
1932-1967 ..... CLC **25, 84;** BLC; PC **7**
See also BW 1; CA 77-80; DLB 125;
MTCW

Olds, Sharon 1942- .... CLC **32, 39, 85**
See also CA 101; CANR 18, 41; DLB 120

Oldstyle, Jonathan
See Irving, Washington

Olesha, Yuri (Karlovich)
1899-1960 .... CLC **8**
See also CA 85-88

Oliphant, Laurence
1829(?)-1888 .... NCLC **47**
See also DLB 18

Oliphant, Margaret (Oliphant Wilson)
1828-1897 .... NCLC **11**
See also DLB 18

Oliver, Mary 1935- .... CLC **19, 34**
See also CA 21-24R; CANR 9, 43; DLB 5

Olivier, Laurence (Kerr)
1907-1989 .... CLC **20**
See also CA 111; 129

Olsen, Tillie
1913- .... CLC **4, 13;** DA; SSC **11**
See also CA 1-4R; CANR 1, 43; DLB 28;
DLBY 80; MTCW

Olson, Charles (John)
1910-1970 ..... CLC **1, 2, 5, 6, 9, 11, 29**
See also CA 13-16; 25-28R; CABS 2;
CANR 35; CAP 1; DLB 5, 16; MTCW

Olson, Toby 1937- .... CLC **28**
See also CA 65-68; CANR 9, 31

Olyesha, Yuri
See Olesha, Yuri (Karlovich)

Ondaatje, (Philip) Michael
1943- .... CLC **14, 29, 51, 76**
See also CA 77-80; CANR 42; DLB 60

Oneal, Elizabeth 1934-
See Oneal, Zibby
See also CA 106; CANR 28; MAICYA;
SATA 30

Oneal, Zibby .... CLC **30**
See also Oneal, Elizabeth
See also AAYA 5; CLR 13; JRDA

O'Neill, Eugene (Gladstone)
1888-1953 ...... TCLC **1, 6, 27, 49;** DA;
WLC
See also AITN 1; CA 110; 132;
CDALB 1929-1941; DLB 7; MTCW

Onetti, Juan Carlos 1909-1994 ... CLC **7, 10**
See also CA 85-88; 145; CANR 32;
DLB 113; HW; MTCW

O Nuallain, Brian 1911-1966
See O'Brien, Flann
See also CA 21-22; 25-28R; CAP 2

Oppen, George 1908-1984 .... CLC **7, 13, 34**
See also CA 13-16R; 113; CANR 8; DLB 5

Oppenheim, E(dward) Phillips
1866-1946 .... TCLC **45**
See also CA 111; DLB 70

Orlovitz, Gil 1918-1973 .... CLC **22**
See also CA 77-80; 45-48; DLB 2, 5

Orris
See Ingelow, Jean

Ortega y Gasset, Jose
1883-1955 .... TCLC **9;** HLC
See also CA 106; 130; HW; MTCW

Ortiz, Simon J(oseph) 1941- .... CLC **45**
See also CA 134; DLB 120

Orton, Joe .... CLC **4, 13, 43;** DC **3**
See also Orton, John Kingsley
See also CDBLB 1960 to Present; DLB 13

Orton, John Kingsley 1933-1967
See Orton, Joe
See also CA 85-88; CANR 35; MTCW

Orwell, George
.... TCLC **2, 6, 15, 31, 51;** WLC
See also Blair, Eric (Arthur)
See also CDBLB 1945-1960; DLB 15, 98

Osborne, David
See Silverberg, Robert

Osborne, George
See Silverberg, Robert

Osborne, John (James)
1929- .... CLC **1, 2, 5, 11, 45;** DA; WLC
See also CA 13-16R; CANR 21;
CDBLB 1945-1960; DLB 13; MTCW

Osborne, Lawrence 1958- .... CLC **50**

Oshima, Nagisa 1932- .... CLC **20**
See also CA 116; 121

Oskison, John Milton
1874-1947 .... TCLC **35**
See also CA 144

Ossoli, Sarah Margaret (Fuller marchesa d')
1810-1850
See Fuller, Margaret
See also SATA 25

Ostrovsky, Alexander
1823-1886 .... NCLC **30**

Otero, Blas de 1916-1979......... CLC **11**
See also CA 89-92; DLB 134

Otto, Whitney 1955-............. CLC **70**
See also CA 140

Ouida .... TCLC **43**
See also De La Ramee, (Marie) Louise
See also DLB 18

Ousmane, Sembene 1923- .... CLC **66;** BLC
See also BW 1; CA 117; 125; MTCW

Ovid 43B.C.-18(?).......... CMLC **7;** PC **2**

Owen, Hugh
See Faust, Frederick (Schiller)

Owen, Wilfred (Edward Salter)
1893-1918 ...... TCLC **5, 27;** DA; WLC
See also CA 104; 141; CDBLB 1914-1945;
DLB 20

Owens, Rochelle 1936-............. CLC **8**
See also CA 17-20R; CAAS 2; CANR 39

Oz, Amos 1939- ... CLC **5, 8, 11, 27, 33, 54**
See also CA 53-56; CANR 27; MTCW

Ozick, Cynthia
1928- .... CLC **3, 7, 28, 62;** SSC **15**
See also BEST 90:1; CA 17-20R; CANR 23;
DLB 28; DLBY 82; MTCW

Ozu, Yasujiro 1903-1963 .... CLC **16**
See also CA 112

Pacheco, C.
See Pessoa, Fernando (Antonio Nogueira)

Pa Chin .... CLC **18**
See also Li Fei-kan

Pack, Robert 1929-............... CLC **13**
See also CA 1-4R; CANR 3, 44; DLB 5

Padgett, Lewis
See Kuttner, Henry

Padilla (Lorenzo), Heberto 1932- ... CLC **38**
See also AITN 1; CA 123; 131; HW

Page, Jimmy 1944-............... CLC **12**

Page, Louise 1955-............... CLC **40**
See also CA 140

Page, P(atricia) K(athleen)
1916- .... CLC **7, 18**
See also CA 53-56; CANR 4, 22; DLB 68;
MTCW

Paget, Violet 1856-1935
See Lee, Vernon
See also CA 104

Paget-Lowe, Henry
See Lovecraft, H(oward) P(hillips)

Paglia, Camille (Anna) 1947-....... CLC **68**
See also CA 140

Paige, Richard
See Koontz, Dean R(ay)

Pakenham, Antonia
See Fraser, (Lady) Antonia (Pakenham)

451

Perelman, S(idney) J(oseph)
     1904-1979 ... **CLC 3, 5, 9, 15, 23, 44, 49**
     See also AITN 1, 2; CA 73-76; 89-92;
     CANR 18; DLB 11, 44; MTCW

Peret, Benjamin 1899-1959 .... **TCLC 20**
     See also CA 117

Peretz, Isaac Loeb 1851(?)-1915 ... **TCLC 16**
     See also CA 109

Peretz, Yitzkhok Leibush
     See Peretz, Isaac Loeb

Perez Galdos, Benito 1843-1920 ... **TCLC 27**
     See also CA 125; HW

Perrault, Charles 1628-1703 .... **LC 2**
     See also MAICYA; SATA 25

Perry, Brighton
     See Sherwood, Robert E(mmet)

Perse, St.-John .... **CLC 4, 11, 46**
     See also Leger, (Marie-Rene Auguste) Alexis
     Saint-Leger

Peseenz, Tulio F.
     See Lopez y Fuentes, Gregorio

Pesetsky, Bette 1932- .... **CLC 28**
     See also CA 133; DLB 130

Peshkov, Alexei Maximovich 1868-1936
     See Gorky, Maxim
     See also CA 105; 141; DA

Pessoa, Fernando (Antonio Nogueira)
     1888-1935 .... **TCLC 27; HLC**
     See also CA 125

Peterkin, Julia Mood 1880-1961 .... **CLC 31**
     See also CA 102; DLB 9

Peters, Joan K. 1945- .... **CLC 39**

Peters, Robert L(ouis) 1924- .... **CLC 7**
     See also CA 13-16R; CAAS 8; DLB 105

Petofi, Sandor 1823-1849 .... **NCLC 21**

Petrakis, Harry Mark 1923- .... **CLC 3**
     See also CA 9-12R; CANR 4, 30

Petrarch 1304-1374 .... **PC 8**

Petrov, Evgeny .... **TCLC 21**
     See also Kataev, Evgeny Petrovich

Petry, Ann (Lane) 1908- ...... **CLC 1, 7, 18**
     See also BW 1; CA 5-8R; CAAS 6;
     CANR 4; CLR 12; DLB 76; JRDA;
     MAICYA; MTCW; SATA 5

Petursson, Halligrimur 1614-1674 .... **LC 8**

Philipson, Morris H. 1926- .... **CLC 53**
     See also CA 1-4R; CANR 4

Phillips, David Graham
     1867-1911 .... **TCLC 44**
     See also CA 108; DLB 9, 12

Phillips, Jack
     See Sandburg, Carl (August)

Phillips, Jayne Anne
     1952- .... **CLC 15, 33; SSC 16**
     See also CA 101; CANR 24; DLBY 80;
     MTCW

Phillips, Richard
     See Dick, Philip K(indred)

Phillips, Robert (Schaeffer) 1938-... **CLC 28**
     See also CA 17-20R; CAAS 13; CANR 8;
     DLB 105

Phillips, Ward
     See Lovecraft, H(oward) P(hillips)

Piccolo, Lucio 1901-1969 .... **CLC 13**
     See also CA 97-100; DLB 114

Pickthall, Marjorie L(owry) C(hristie)
     1883-1922 .... **TCLC 21**
     See also CA 107; DLB 92

Pico della Mirandola, Giovanni
     1463-1494 .... **LC 15**

Piercy, Marge
     1936- .... **CLC 3, 6, 14, 18, 27, 62**
     See also CA 21-24R; CAAS 1; CANR 13,
     43; DLB 120; MTCW

Piers, Robert
     See Anthony, Piers

Pieyre de Mandiargues, Andre 1909-1991
     See Mandiargues, Andre Pieyre de
     See also CA 103; 136; CANR 22

Pilnyak, Boris .... **TCLC 23**
     See also Vogau, Boris Andreyevich

Pincherle, Alberto 1907-1990 ... **CLC 11, 18**
     See also Moravia, Alberto
     See also CA 25-28R; 132; CANR 33;
     MTCW

Pinckney, Darryl 1953- .... **CLC 76**
     See also BW 2; CA 143

Pindar 518B.C.-446B.C. .... **CMLC 12**

Pineda, Cecile 1942- .... **CLC 39**
     See also CA 118

Pinero, Arthur Wing 1855-1934 ... **TCLC 32**
     See also CA 110; DLB 10

Pinero, Miguel (Antonio Gomez)
     1946-1988 .... **CLC 4, 55**
     See also CA 61-64; 125; CANR 29; HW

Pinget, Robert 1919- .... **CLC 7, 13, 37**
     See also CA 85-88; DLB 83

Pink Floyd
     See Barrett, (Roger) Syd; Gilmour, David;
     Mason, Nick; Waters, Roger; Wright,
     Rick

Pinkney, Edward 1802-1828 ..... **NCLC 31**

Pinkwater, Daniel Manus 1941-.... **CLC 35**
     See also Pinkwater, Manus
     See also AAYA 1; CA 29-32R; CANR 12,
     38; CLR 4; JRDA; MAICYA; SAAS 3;
     SATA 46, 76

Pinkwater, Manus
     See Pinkwater, Daniel Manus
     See also SATA 8

Pinsky, Robert 1940- .... **CLC 9, 19, 38**
     See also CA 29-32R; CAAS 4; DLBY 82

Pinta, Harold
     See Pinter, Harold

Pinter, Harold
     1930- ..... **CLC 1, 3, 6, 9, 11, 15, 27, 58,
     73; DA; WLC**
     See also CA 5-8R; CANR 33; CDBLB 1960
     to Present; DLB 13; MTCW

Pirandello, Luigi
     1867-1936 ...... **TCLC 4, 29; DA; WLC**
     See also CA 104

Pirsig, Robert M(aynard)
     1928- .... **CLC 4, 6, 73**
     See also CA 53-56; CANR 42; MTCW;
     SATA 39

Pisarev, Dmitry Ivanovich
     1840-1868 .... **NCLC 25**

Pix, Mary (Griffith) 1666-1709 ...... **LC 8**
     See also DLB 80

Pixerecourt, Guilbert de
     1773-1844 .... **NCLC 39**

Plaidy, Jean
     See Hibbert, Eleanor Alice Burford

Planche, James Robinson
     1796-1880 .... **NCLC 42**

Plant, Robert 1948- .... **CLC 12**

Plante, David (Robert)
     1940- .... **CLC 7, 23, 38**
     See also CA 37-40R; CANR 12, 36;
     DLBY 83; MTCW

Plath, Sylvia
     1932-1963 ..... **CLC 1, 2, 3, 5, 9, 11, 14,
     17, 50, 51, 62; DA; PC 1; WLC**
     See also CA 19-20; CANR 34; CAP 2;
     CDALB 1941-1968; DLB 5, 6; MTCW

Plato 428(?)B.C.-348(?)B.C.... **CMLC 8; DA**

Platonov, Andrei .... **TCLC 14**
     See also Klimentov, Andrei Platonovich

Platt, Kin 1911- .... **CLC 26**
     See also AAYA 11; CA 17-20R; CANR 11;
     JRDA; SAAS 17; SATA 21

Plick et Plock
     See Simenon, Georges (Jacques Christian)

Plimpton, George (Ames) 1927-..... **CLC 36**
     See also AITN 1; CA 21-24R; CANR 32;
     MTCW; SATA 10

Plomer, William Charles Franklin
     1903-1973 .... **CLC 4, 8**
     See also CA 21-22; CANR 34; CAP 2;
     DLB 20; MTCW; SATA 24

Plowman, Piers
     See Kavanagh, Patrick (Joseph)

Plum, J.
     See Wodehouse, P(elham) G(renville)

Plumly, Stanley (Ross) 1939- ...... **CLC 33**
     See also CA 108; 110; DLB 5

Plumpe, Friedrich Wilhelm
     1888-1931 .... **TCLC 53**
     See also CA 112

Poe, Edgar Allan
     1809-1849 ..... **NCLC 1, 16; DA; PC 1;
     SSC 1; WLC**
     See also CDALB 1640-1865; DLB 3, 59, 73,
     74; SATA 23

Poet of Titchfield Street, The
     See Pound, Ezra (Weston Loomis)

Pohl, Frederik 1919- .... **CLC 18**
     See also CA 61-64; CAAS 1; CANR 11, 37;
     DLB 8; MTCW; SATA 24

Poirier, Louis 1910-
     See Gracq, Julien
     See also CA 122; 126

Poitier, Sidney 1927- .... **CLC 26**
     See also BW 1; CA 117

Polanski, Roman 1933- .... **CLC 16**
     See also CA 77-80

Poliakoff, Stephen 1952- .... **CLC 38**
     See also CA 106; DLB 13

Police, The
See Copeland, Stewart (Armstrong);
Summers, Andrew James; Sumner,
Gordon Matthew

Pollitt, Katha 1949- .... **CLC 28**
See also CA 120; 122; MTCW

Pollock, (Mary) Sharon 1936-..... **CLC 50**
See also CA 141; DLB 60

Pomerance, Bernard 1940-........ **CLC 13**
See also CA 101

Ponge, Francis (Jean Gaston Alfred)
1899-1988 .... **CLC 6, 18**
See also CA 85-88; 126; CANR 40

Pontoppidan, Henrik 1857-1943 ... **TCLC 29**

Poole, Josephine .... **CLC 17**
See also Helyar, Jane Penelope Josephine
See also SAAS 2; SATA 5

Popa, Vasko 1922-.............. **CLC 19**
See also CA 112

Pope, Alexander
1688-1744 .... **LC 3; DA; WLC**
See also CDBLB 1660-1789; DLB 95, 101

Porter, Connie (Rose) 1959(?)- ..... **CLC 70**
See also BW 2; CA 142

Porter, Gene(va Grace) Stratton
1863(?)-1924 .... **TCLC 21**
See also CA 112

Porter, Katherine Anne
1890-1980 ...... **CLC 1, 3, 7, 10, 13, 15,**
27; DA; SSC 4
See also AITN 2; CA 1-4R; 101; CANR 1;
DLB 4, 9, 102; DLBY 80; MTCW;
SATA 23, 39

Porter, Peter (Neville Frederick)
1929- .... **CLC 5, 13, 33**
See also CA 85-88; DLB 40

Porter, William Sydney 1862-1910
See Henry, O.
See also CA 104; 131; CDALB 1865-1917;
DA; DLB 12, 78, 79; MTCW; YABC 2

Portillo (y Pacheco), Jose Lopez
See Lopez Portillo (y Pacheco), Jose

Post, Melville Davisson
1869-1930 .... **TCLC 39**
See also CA 110

Potok, Chaim 1929-....... **CLC 2, 7, 14, 26**
See also AITN 1, 2; CA 17-20R; CANR 19,
35; DLB 28; MTCW; SATA 33

Potter, Beatrice
See Webb, (Martha) Beatrice (Potter)
See also MAICYA

Potter, Dennis (Christopher George)
1935-1994 .... **CLC 58**
See also CA 107; 145; CANR 33; MTCW

Pound, Ezra (Weston Loomis)
1885-1972 ...... **CLC 1, 2, 3, 4, 5, 7, 10,**
13, 18, 34, 48, 50; DA; PC 4; WLC
See also CA 5-8R; 37-40R; CANR 40;
CDALB 1917-1929; DLB 4, 45, 63;
MTCW

Povod, Reinaldo 1959-............. **CLC 44**
See also CA 136

Powell, Anthony (Dymoke)
1905-........... **CLC 1, 3, 7, 9, 10, 31**
See also CA 1-4R; CANR 1, 32;
CDBLB 1945-1960; DLB 15; MTCW

Powell, Dawn 1897-1965 .... **CLC 66**
See also CA 5-8R

Powell, Padgett 1952-............. **CLC 34**
See also CA 126

Powers, J(ames) F(arl)
1917- .... **CLC 1, 4, 8, 57; SSC 4**
See also CA 1-4R; CANR 2; DLB 130;
MTCW

Powers, John J(ames) 1945-
See Powers, John R.
See also CA 69-72

Powers, John R. .... **CLC 66**
See also Powers, John J(ames)

Pownall, David 1938-............. **CLC 10**
See also CA 89-92; CAAS 18; DLB 14

Powys, John Cowper
1872-1963 ....**CLC 7, 9, 15, 46**
See also CA 85-88; DLB 15; MTCW

Powys, T(heodore) F(rancis)
1875-1953 .... **TCLC 9**
See also CA 106; DLB 36

Prager, Emily 1952-............. **CLC 56**

Pratt, E(dwin) J(ohn)
1883(?)-1964 .... **CLC 19**
See also CA 141; 93-96; DLB 92

Premchand...................... **TCLC 21**
See also Srivastava, Dhanpat Rai

Preussler, Otfried 1923-........... **CLC 17**
See also CA 77-80; SATA 24

Prevert, Jacques (Henri Marie)
1900-1977 .... **CLC 15**
See also CA 77-80; 69-72; CANR 29;
MTCW; SATA 30

Prevost, Abbe (Antoine Francois)
1697-1763 .... **LC 1**

Price, (Edward) Reynolds
1933- .... **CLC 3, 6, 13, 43, 50, 63**
See also CA 1-4R; CANR 1, 37; DLB 2

Price, Richard 1949- .... **CLC 6, 12**
See also CA 49-52; CANR 3; DLBY 81

Prichard, Katharine Susannah
1883-1969 .... **CLC 46**
See also CA 11-12; CANR 33; CAP 1;
MTCW; SATA 66

Priestley, J(ohn) B(oynton)
1894-1984 .... **CLC 2, 5, 9, 34**
See also CA 9-12R; 113; CANR 33;
CDBLB 1914-1945; DLB 10, 34, 77, 100,
139; DLBY 84; MTCW

Prince 1958(?)-................. **CLC 35**

Prince, F(rank) T(empleton) 1912-.. **CLC 22**
See also CA 101; CANR 43; DLB 20

Prince Kropotkin
See Kropotkin, Peter (Aleksieevich)

Prior, Matthew 1664-1721.......... **LC 4**
See also DLB 95

Pritchard, William H(arrison)
1932-..................... **CLC 34**
See also CA 65-68; CANR 23; DLB 111

Pritchett, V(ictor) S(awdon)
1900-....... **CLC 5, 13, 15, 41; SSC 14**
See also CA 61-64; CANR 31; DLB 15,
139; MTCW

Private 19022
See Manning, Frederic

Probst, Mark 1925- .... **CLC 59**
See also CA 130

Prokosch, Frederic 1908-1989.... **CLC 4, 48**
See also CA 73-76; 128; DLB 48

Prophet, The
See Dreiser, Theodore (Herman Albert)

Prose, Francine 1947-............. **CLC 45**
See also CA 109; 112

Proudhon
See Cunha, Euclides (Rodrigues Pimenta) da

Proulx, E. Annie 1935- .... **CLC 81**

Proust, (Valentin-Louis-George-Eugene-)
Marcel
1871-1922 ... **TCLC 7, 13, 33; DA; WLC**
See also CA 104; 120; DLB 65; MTCW

Prowler, Harley
See Masters, Edgar Lee

Prus, Boleslaw 1845-1912 .... **TCLC 48**

Pryor, Richard (Franklin Lenox Thomas)
1940-..................... **CLC 26**
See also CA 122

Przybyszewski, Stanislaw
1868-1927 .... **TCLC 36**
See also DLB 66

Pteleon
See Grieve, C(hristopher) M(urray)

Puckett, Lute
See Masters, Edgar Lee

Puig, Manuel
1932-1990 ... **CLC 3, 5, 10, 28, 65; HLC**
See also CA 45-48; CANR 2, 32; DLB 113;
HW; MTCW

Purdy, Al(fred Wellington)
1918-................**CLC 3, 6, 14, 50**
See also CA 81-84; CAAS 17; CANR 42;
DLB 88

Purdy, James (Amos)
1923-............ **CLC 2, 4, 10, 28, 52**
See also CA 33-36R; CAAS 1; CANR 19;
DLB 2; MTCW

Pure, Simon
See Swinnerton, Frank Arthur

Pushkin, Alexander (Sergeyevich)
1799-1837 .... **NCLC 3, 27; DA; PC 10;**
WLC
See also SATA 61

P'u Sung-ling 1640-1715 .... **LC 3**

Putnam, Arthur Lee
See Alger, Horatio, Jr.

Puzo, Mario 1920-......... **CLC 1, 2, 6, 36**
See also CA 65-68; CANR 4, 42; DLB 6;
MTCW

Pym, Barbara (Mary Crampton)
1913-1980 .... **CLC 13, 19, 37**
See also CA 13-14; 97-100; CANR 13, 34;
CAP 1; DLB 14; DLBY 87; MTCW

Pynchon, Thomas (Ruggles, Jr.)
1937- ..... CLC **2, 3, 6, 9, 11, 18, 33, 62,**
72; DA; SSC 14; WLC
See also BEST 90:2; CA 17-20R; CANR 22;
DLB 2; MTCW

Qian Zhongshu
See Ch'ien Chung-shu

Qroll
See Dagerman, Stig (Halvard)

Quarrington, Paul (Lewis) 1953-.... CLC **65**
See also CA 129

Quasimodo, Salvatore 1901-1968 ... CLC **10**
See also CA 13-16; 25-28R; CAP 1;
DLB 114; MTCW

Queen, Ellery................... CLC **3, 11**
See also Dannay, Frederic; Davidson,
Avram; Lee, Manfred B(ennington);
Sturgeon, Theodore (Hamilton); Vance,
John Holbrook

Queen, Ellery, Jr.
See Dannay, Frederic; Lee, Manfred
B(ennington)

Queneau, Raymond
1903-1976 ....CLC **2, 5, 10, 42**
See also CA 77-80; 69-72; CANR 32;
DLB 72; MTCW

Quevedo, Francisco de 1580-1645.... LC **23**

Quiller-Couch, Arthur Thomas
1863-1944 .... TCLC **53**
See also CA 118; DLB 135

Quin, Ann (Marie) 1936-1973....... CLC **6**
See also CA 9-12R; 45-48; DLB 14

Quinn, Martin
See Smith, Martin Cruz

Quinn, Simon
See Smith, Martin Cruz

Quiroga, Horacio (Sylvestre)
1878-1937 .... TCLC **20; HLC**
See also CA 117; 131; HW; MTCW

Quoirez, Francoise 1935-........... CLC **9**
See also Sagan, Francoise
See also CA 49-52; CANR 6, 39; MTCW

Raabe, Wilhelm 1831-1910 .... TCLC **45**
See also DLB 129

Rabe, David (William) 1940-... CLC **4, 8, 33**
See also CA 85-88; CABS 3; DLB 7

Rabelais, Francois
1483-1553 .... LC **5; DA; WLC**

Rabinovitch, Sholem 1859-1916
See Aleichem, Sholom
See also CA 104

Radcliffe, Ann (Ward) 1764-1823 .. NCLC **6**
See also DLB 39

Radiguet, Raymond 1903-1923 .... TCLC **29**
See also DLB 65

Radnoti, Miklos 1909-1944 .... TCLC **16**
See also CA 118

Rado, James 1939-............... CLC **17**
See also CA 105

Radvanyi, Netty 1900-1983
See Seghers, Anna
See also CA 85-88; 110

Rae, Ben
See Griffiths, Trevor

Raeburn, John (Hay) 1941-........ CLC **34**
See also CA 57-60

Ragni, Gerome 1942-1991 .... CLC **17**
See also CA 105; 134

Rahv, Philip 1908-1973 .... CLC **24**
See also Greenberg, Ivan
See also DLB 137

Raine, Craig 1944- .... CLC **32**
See also CA 108; CANR 29; DLB 40

Raine, Kathleen (Jessie) 1908- ... CLC **7, 45**
See also CA 85-88; DLB 20; MTCW

Rainis, Janis 1865-1929.......... TCLC **29**

Rakosi, Carl..................... CLC **47**
See also Rawley, Callman
See also CAAS 5

Raleigh, Richard
See Lovecraft, H(oward) P(hillips)

Rallentando, H. P.
See Sayers, Dorothy L(eigh)

Ramal, Walter
See de la Mare, Walter (John)

Ramon, Juan
See Jimenez (Mantecon), Juan Ramon

Ramos, Graciliano 1892-1953 ..... TCLC **32**

Rampersad, Arnold 1941-.......... CLC **44**
See also BW 2; CA 127; 133; DLB 111

Rampling, Anne
See Rice, Anne

Ramuz, Charles-Ferdinand
1878-1947 .... TCLC **33**

Rand, Ayn
1905-1982 ...... CLC **3, 30, 44, 79; DA;**
WLC
See also AAYA 10; CA 13-16R; 105;
CANR 27; MTCW

Randall, Dudley (Felker)
1914- .... CLC **1; BLC**
See also BW 1; CA 25-28R; CANR 23;
DLB 41

Randall, Robert
See Silverberg, Robert

Ranger, Ken
See Creasey, John

Ransom, John Crowe
1888-1974 .... CLC **2, 4, 5, 11, 24**
See also CA 5-8R; 49-52; CANR 6, 34;
DLB 45, 63; MTCW

Rao, Raja 1909- .... CLC **25, 56**
See also CA 73-76; MTCW

Raphael, Frederic (Michael)
1931- .... CLC **2, 14**
See also CA 1-4R; CANR 1; DLB 14

Ratcliffe, James P.
See Mencken, H(enry) L(ouis)

Rathbone, Julian 1935- .... CLC **41**
See also CA 101; CANR 34

Rattigan, Terence (Mervyn)
1911-1977 .... CLC **7**
See also CA 85-88; 73-76;
CDBLB 1945-1960; DLB 13; MTCW

Ratushinskaya, Irina 1954-........ CLC **54**
See also CA 129

Raven, Simon (Arthur Noel)
1927- .... CLC **14**
See also CA 81-84

Rawley, Callman 1903-
See Rakosi, Carl
See also CA 21-24R; CANR 12, 32

Rawlings, Marjorie Kinnan
1896-1953 .... TCLC **4**
See also CA 104; 137; DLB 9, 22, 102;
JRDA; MAICYA; YABC 1

Ray, Satyajit 1921-1992........ CLC **16, 76**
See also CA 114; 137

Read, Herbert Edward 1893-1968.... CLC **4**
See also CA 85-88; 25-28R; DLB 20

Read, Piers Paul 1941- ...... CLC **4, 10, 25**
See also CA 21-24R; CANR 38; DLB 14;
SATA 21

Reade, Charles 1814-1884 .... NCLC **2**
See also DLB 21

Reade, Hamish
See Gray, Simon (James Holliday)

Reading, Peter 1946- .... CLC **47**
See also CA 103; DLB 40

Reaney, James 1926- .... CLC **13**
See also CA 41-44R; CAAS 15; CANR 42;
DLB 68; SATA 43

Rebreanu, Liviu 1885-1944 .... TCLC **28**

Rechy, John (Francisco)
1934- .... CLC **1, 7, 14, 18; HLC**
See also CA 5-8R; CAAS 4; CANR 6, 32;
DLB 122; DLBY 82; HW

Redcam, Tom 1870-1933 .... TCLC **25**

Reddin, Keith..................... CLC **67**

Redgrove, Peter (William)
1932- .... CLC **6, 41**
See also CA 1-4R; CANR 3, 39; DLB 40

Redmon, Anne..................... CLC **22**
See also Nightingale, Anne Redmon
See also DLBY 86

Reed, Eliot
See Ambler, Eric

Reed, Ishmael
1938- ... CLC **2, 3, 5, 6, 13, 32, 60; BLC**
See also BW 2; CA 21-24R; CANR 25;
DLB 2, 5, 33; DLBD 8; MTCW

Reed, John (Silas) 1887-1920 ...... TCLC **9**
See also CA 106

Reed, Lou....................... CLC **21**
See also Firbank, Louis

Reeve, Clara 1729-1807 .... NCLC **19**
See also DLB 39

Reich, Wilhelm 1897-1957........ TCLC **57**

Reid, Christopher (John) 1949-..... CLC **33**
See also CA 140; DLB 40

Reid, Desmond
See Moorcock, Michael (John)

Reid Banks, Lynne 1929-
See Banks, Lynne Reid
See also CA 1-4R; CANR 6, 22, 38;
CLR 24; JRDA; MAICYA; SATA 22, 75

Reilly, William K.
See Creasey, John

Reiner, Max
    See Caldwell, (Janet Miriam) Taylor
    (Holland)

Reis, Ricardo
    See Pessoa, Fernando (Antonio Nogueira)

Remarque, Erich Maria
    1898-1970 . . . . **CLC 21; DA**
    See also CA 77-80; 29-32R; DLB 56;
    MTCW

Remizov, A.
    See Remizov, Aleksei (Mikhailovich)

Remizov, A. M.
    See Remizov, Aleksei (Mikhailovich)

Remizov, Aleksei (Mikhailovich)
    1877-1957 . . . . **TCLC 27**
    See also CA 125; 133

Renan, Joseph Ernest
    1823-1892 . . . . **NCLC 26**

Renard, Jules   1864-1910 . . . . **TCLC 17**
    See also CA 117

Renault, Mary . . . . **CLC 3, 11, 17**
    See also Challans, Mary
    See also DLBY 83

Rendell, Ruth (Barbara) 1930- . . **CLC 28, 48**
    See also Vine, Barbara
    See also CA 109; CANR 32; DLB 87;
    MTCW

Renoir, Jean   1894-1979 . . . . **CLC 20**
    See also CA 129; 85-88

Resnais, Alain   1922- . . . . **CLC 16**

Reverdy, Pierre   1889-1960 . . . . **CLC 53**
    See also CA 97-100; 89-92

Rexroth, Kenneth
    1905-1982 . . . . . . **CLC 1, 2, 6, 11, 22, 49**
    See also CA 5-8R; 107; CANR 14, 34;
    CDALB 1941-1968; DLB 16, 48;
    DLBY 82; MTCW

Reyes, Alfonso   1889-1959 . . . . **TCLC 33**
    See also CA 131; HW

Reyes y Basoalto, Ricardo Eliecer Neftali
    See Neruda, Pablo

Reymont, Wladyslaw (Stanislaw)
    1868(?)-1925 . . . . **TCLC 5**
    See also CA 104

Reynolds, Jonathan   1942- . . . . **CLC 6, 38**
    See also CA 65-68; CANR 28

Reynolds, Joshua   1723-1792 . . . . **LC 15**
    See also DLB 104

Reynolds, Michael Shane   1937- . . . . **CLC 44**
    See also CA 65-68; CANR 9

Reznikoff, Charles   1894-1976 . . . . **CLC 9**
    See also CA 33-36; 61-64; CAP 2; DLB 28,
    45

Rezzori (d'Arezzo), Gregor von
    1914- . . . . **CLC 25**
    See also CA 122; 136

Rhine, Richard
    See Silverstein, Alvin

Rhodes, Eugene Manlove
    1869-1934 . . . . **TCLC 53**

R'hoone
    See Balzac, Honore de

Rhys, Jean
    1890(?)-1979 . . . . **CLC 2, 4, 6, 14, 19, 51**
    See also CA 25-28R; 85-88; CANR 35;
    CDBLB 1945-1960; DLB 36, 117; MTCW

Ribeiro, Darcy   1922- . . . . **CLC 34**
    See also CA 33-36R

Ribeiro, Joao Ubaldo (Osorio Pimentel)
    1941- . . . . **CLC 10, 67**
    See also CA 81-84

Ribman, Ronald (Burt)   1932- . . . . **CLC 7**
    See also CA 21-24R

Ricci, Nino   1959- . . . . **CLC 70**
    See also CA 137

Rice, Anne   1941- . . . . **CLC 41**
    See also AAYA 9; BEST 89:2; CA 65-68;
    CANR 12, 36

Rice, Elmer (Leopold)
    1892-1967 . . . . **CLC 7, 49**
    See also CA 21-22; 25-28R; CAP 2; DLB 4,
    7; MTCW

Rice, Tim   1944- . . . . **CLC 21**
    See also CA 103

Rich, Adrienne (Cecile)
    1929- . . . . **CLC 3, 6, 7, 11, 18, 36, 73, 76;
                                                        PC 5**
    See also CA 9-12R; CANR 20; DLB 5, 67;
    MTCW

Rich, Barbara
    See Graves, Robert (von Ranke)

Rich, Robert
    See Trumbo, Dalton

Richards, David Adams   1950- . . . . . . **CLC 59**
    See also CA 93-96; DLB 53

Richards, I(vor) A(rmstrong)
    1893-1979 . . . . **CLC 14, 24**
    See also CA 41-44R; 89-92; CANR 34;
    DLB 27

Richardson, Anne
    See Roiphe, Anne (Richardson)

Richardson, Dorothy Miller
    1873-1957 . . . . **TCLC 3**
    See also CA 104; DLB 36

Richardson, Ethel Florence (Lindesay)
    1870-1946
    See Richardson, Henry Handel
    See also CA 105

Richardson, Henry Handel . . . . **TCLC 4**
    See also Richardson, Ethel Florence
    (Lindesay)

Richardson, Samuel
    1689-1761 . . . . **LC 1; DA; WLC**
    See also CDBLB 1660-1789; DLB 39

Richler, Mordecai
    1931- . . . . **CLC 3, 5, 9, 13, 18, 46, 70**
    See also AITN 1; CA 65-68; CANR 31;
    CLR 17; DLB 53; MAICYA; MTCW;
    SATA 27, 44

Richter, Conrad (Michael)
    1890-1968 . . . . **CLC 30**
    See also CA 5-8R; 25-28R; CANR 23;
    DLB 9; MTCW; SATA 3

Riddell, J. H.   1832-1906 . . . . **TCLC 40**

Riding, Laura . . . . **CLC 3, 7**
    See also Jackson, Laura (Riding)

Riefenstahl, Berta Helene Amalia   1902-
    See Riefenstahl, Leni
    See also CA 108

Riefenstahl, Leni . . . . **CLC 16**
    See also Riefenstahl, Berta Helene Amalia

Riffe, Ernest
    See Bergman, (Ernst) Ingmar

Riggs, (Rolla) Lynn   1899-1954 . . . . **TCLC 56**
    See also CA 144

Riley, James Whitcomb
    1849-1916 . . . . **TCLC 51**
    See also CA 118; 137; MAICYA; SATA 17

Riley, Tex
    See Creasey, John

Rilke, Rainer Maria
    1875-1926 . . . . **TCLC 1, 6, 19; PC 2**
    See also CA 104; 132; DLB 81; MTCW

Rimbaud, (Jean Nicolas) Arthur
    1854-1891 . . . . . **NCLC 4, 35; DA; PC 3;
                                                           WLC**

Rinehart, Mary Roberts
    1876-1958 . . . . **TCLC 52**
    See also CA 108

Ringmaster, The
    See Mencken, H(enry) L(ouis)

Ringwood, Gwen(dolyn Margaret) Pharis
    1910-1984 . . . . **CLC 48**
    See also CA 112; DLB 88

Rio, Michel   19(?)- . . . . **CLC 43**

Ritsos, Giannes
    See Ritsos, Yannis

Ritsos, Yannis   1909-1990 . . . . . **CLC 6, 13, 31**
    See also CA 77-80; 133; CANR 39; MTCW

Ritter, Erika   1948(?)- . . . . **CLC 52**

Rivera, Jose Eustasio   1889-1928 . . . **TCLC 35**
    See also HW

Rivers, Conrad Kent   1933-1968 . . . . . . **CLC 1**
    See also BW 1; CA 85-88; DLB 41

Rivers, Elfrida
    See Bradley, Marion Zimmer

Riverside, John
    See Heinlein, Robert A(nson)

Rizal, Jose   1861-1896 . . . . **NCLC 27**

Roa Bastos, Augusto (Antonio)
    1917- . . . . **CLC 45; HLC**
    See also CA 131; DLB 113; HW

Robbe-Grillet, Alain
    1922- . . . . . . **CLC 1, 2, 4, 6, 8, 10, 14, 43**
    See also CA 9-12R; CANR 33; DLB 83;
    MTCW

Robbins, Harold   1916- . . . . **CLC 5**
    See also CA 73-76; CANR 26; MTCW

Robbins, Thomas Eugene   1936-
    See Robbins, Tom
    See also CA 81-84; CANR 29; MTCW

Robbins, Tom . . . . **CLC 9, 32, 64**
    See also Robbins, Thomas Eugene
    See also BEST 90:3; DLBY 80

Robbins, Trina   1938- . . . . **CLC 21**
    See also CA 128

Roberts, Charles G(eorge) D(ouglas)
    1860-1943 . . . . **TCLC 8**
    See also CA 105; CLR 33; DLB 92;
    SATA 29

Roberts, Kate 1891-1985 . . . . **CLC 15**
See also CA 107; 116

Roberts, Keith (John Kingston)
1935- . . . . **CLC 14**
See also CA 25-28R

Roberts, Kenneth (Lewis)
1885-1957 . . . . **TCLC 23**
See also CA 109; DLB 9

Roberts, Michele (B.) 1949- . . . . **CLC 48**
See also CA 115

Robertson, Ellis
See Ellison, Harlan; Silverberg, Robert

Robertson, Thomas William
1829-1871 . . . . **NCLC 35**

Robinson, Edwin Arlington
1869-1935 . . . . **TCLC 5; DA; PC 1**
See also CA 104; 133; CDALB 1865-1917;
DLB 54; MTCW

Robinson, Henry Crabb
1775-1867 . . . . **NCLC 15**
See also DLB 107

Robinson, Jill 1936- . . . . **CLC 10**
See also CA 102

Robinson, Kim Stanley 1952- . . . . . . **CLC 34**
See also CA 126

Robinson, Lloyd
See Silverberg, Robert

Robinson, Marilynne 1944- . . . . **CLC 25**
See also CA 116

Robinson, Smokey . . . . **CLC 21**
See also Robinson, William, Jr.

Robinson, William, Jr. 1940-
See Robinson, Smokey
See also CA 116

Robison, Mary 1949- . . . . **CLC 42**
See also CA 113; 116; DLB 130

Rod, Edouard 1857-1910 . . . . **TCLC 52**

Roddenberry, Eugene Wesley 1921-1991
See Roddenberry, Gene
See also CA 110; 135; CANR 37; SATA 45

Roddenberry, Gene . . . . **CLC 17**
See also Roddenberry, Eugene Wesley
See also AAYA 5; SATA-Obit 69

Rodgers, Mary 1931- . . . . **CLC 12**
See also CA 49-52; CANR 8; CLR 20;
JRDA; MAICYA; SATA 8

Rodgers, W(illiam) R(obert)
1909-1969 . . . . **CLC 7**
See also CA 85-88; DLB 20

Rodman, Eric
See Silverberg, Robert

Rodman, Howard 1920(?)-1985 . . . . . **CLC 65**
See also CA 118

Rodman, Maia
See Wojciechowska, Maia (Teresa)

Rodriguez, Claudio 1934- . . . . **CLC 10**
See also DLB 134

Roelvaag, O(le) E(dvart)
1876-1931 . . . . **TCLC 17**
See also CA 117; DLB 9

Roethke, Theodore (Huebner)
1908-1963 . . . . . . **CLC 1, 3, 8, 11, 19, 46**
See also CA 81-84; CABS 2;
CDALB 1941-1968; DLB 5; MTCW

Rogers, Thomas Hunton 1927- . . . . . **CLC 57**
See also CA 89-92

Rogers, Will(iam Penn Adair)
1879-1935 . . . . **TCLC 8**
See also CA 105; 144; DLB 11

Rogin, Gilbert 1929- . . . . **CLC 18**
See also CA 65-68; CANR 15

Rohan, Koda . . . . **TCLC 22**
See also Koda Shigeyuki

Rohmer, Eric . . . . **CLC 16**
See also Scherer, Jean-Marie Maurice

Rohmer, Sax . . . . **TCLC 28**
See also Ward, Arthur Henry Sarsfield
See also DLB 70

Roiphe, Anne (Richardson)
1935- . . . . **CLC 3, 9**
See also CA 89-92; CANR 45; DLBY 80

Rojas, Fernando de 1465-1541 . . . . . . **LC 23**

**Rolfe, Frederick (William Serafino Austin
Lewis Mary)** 1860-1913 . . . . . **TCLC 12**
See also CA 107; DLB 34

Rolland, Romain 1866-1944 . . . . . . **TCLC 23**
See also CA 118; DLB 65

Rolvaag, O(le) E(dvart)
See Roelvaag, O(le) E(dvart)

Romain Arnaud, Saint
See Aragon, Louis

Romains, Jules 1885-1972 . . . . **CLC 7**
See also CA 85-88; CANR 34; DLB 65;
MTCW

Romero, Jose Ruben 1890-1952 . . . **TCLC 14**
See also CA 114; 131; HW

Ronsard, Pierre de 1524-1585 . . . . **LC 6**

Rooke, Leon 1934- . . . . **CLC 25, 34**
See also CA 25-28R; CANR 23

Roper, William 1498-1578 . . . . **LC 10**

Roquelaure, A. N.
See Rice, Anne

Rosa, Joao Guimaraes 1908-1967 . . . **CLC 23**
See also CA 89-92; DLB 113

Rose, Wendy 1948- . . . . **CLC 85**
See also CA 53-56; CANR 5; NNAL;
SATA 12

Rosen, Richard (Dean) 1949- . . . . **CLC 39**
See also CA 77-80

Rosenberg, Isaac 1890-1918 . . . . . . **TCLC 12**
See also CA 107; DLB 20

Rosenblatt, Joe . . . . **CLC 15**
See also Rosenblatt, Joseph

Rosenblatt, Joseph 1933-
See Rosenblatt, Joe
See also CA 89-92

Rosenfeld, Samuel 1896-1963
See Tzara, Tristan
See also CA 89-92

Rosenthal, M(acha) L(ouis) 1917- . . . **CLC 28**
See also CA 1-4R; CAAS 6; CANR 4;
DLB 5; SATA 59

Ross, Barnaby
See Dannay, Frederic

Ross, Bernard L.
See Follett, Ken(neth Martin)

Ross, J. H.
See Lawrence, T(homas) E(dward)

Ross, Martin
See Martin, Violet Florence
See also DLB 135

Ross, (James) Sinclair 1908- . . . . **CLC 13**
See also CA 73-76; DLB 88

Rossetti, Christina (Georgina)
1830-1894 . . . **NCLC 2; DA; PC 7; WLC**
See also DLB 35; MAICYA; SATA 20

Rossetti, Dante Gabriel
1828-1882 . . . . **NCLC 4; DA; WLC**
See also CDBLB 1832-1890; DLB 35

Rossner, Judith (Perelman)
1935- . . . . **CLC 6, 9, 29**
See also AITN 2; BEST 90:3; CA 17-20R;
CANR 18; DLB 6; MTCW

Rostand, Edmond (Eugene Alexis)
1868-1918 . . . . **TCLC 6, 37; DA**
See also CA 104; 126; MTCW

Roth, Henry 1906- . . . . **CLC 2, 6, 11**
See also CA 11-12; CANR 38; CAP 1;
DLB 28; MTCW

Roth, Joseph 1894-1939 . . . . **TCLC 33**
See also DLB 85

Roth, Philip (Milton)
1933- . . . . . . **CLC 1, 2, 3, 4, 6, 9, 15, 22,
31, 47, 66; DA; WLC**
See also BEST 90:3; CA 1-4R; CANR 1, 22,
36; CDALB 1968-1988; DLB 2, 28;
DLBY 82; MTCW

Rothenberg, Jerome 1931- . . . . **CLC 6, 57**
See also CA 45-48; CANR 1; DLB 5

Roumain, Jacques (Jean Baptiste)
1907-1944 . . . . **TCLC 19; BLC**
See also BW 1; CA 117; 125

Rourke, Constance (Mayfield)
1885-1941 . . . . **TCLC 12**
See also CA 107; YABC 1

Rousseau, Jean-Baptiste 1671-1741 . . . **LC 9**

Rousseau, Jean-Jacques
1712-1778 . . . . **LC 14; DA; WLC**

Roussel, Raymond 1877-1933 . . . . . **TCLC 20**
See also CA 117

Rovit, Earl (Herbert) 1927- . . . . **CLC 7**
See also CA 5-8R; CANR 12

Rowe, Nicholas 1674-1718 . . . . **LC 8**
See also DLB 84

Rowley, Ames Dorrance
See Lovecraft, H(oward) P(hillips)

Rowson, Susanna Haswell
1762(?)-1824 . . . . **NCLC 5**
See also DLB 37

Roy, Gabrielle 1909-1983 . . . . **CLC 10, 14**
See also CA 53-56; 110; CANR 5; DLB 68;
MTCW

Rozewicz, Tadeusz 1921- . . . . **CLC 9, 23**
See also CA 108; CANR 36; MTCW

Ruark, Gibbons 1941- . . . . **CLC 3**
See also CA 33-36R; CANR 14, 31;
DLB 120

Rubens, Bernice (Ruth) 1923- . . . **CLC 19, 31**
See also CA 25-28R; CANR 33; DLB 14;
MTCW

Santiago, Danny .... **CLC 33**
See also James, Daniel (Lewis); James,
Daniel (Lewis)
See also DLB 122

Santmyer, Helen Hoover
1895-1986 .... **CLC 33**
See also CA 1-4R; 118; CANR 15, 33;
DLBY 84; MTCW

Santos, Bienvenido N(uqui) 1911-... **CLC 22**
See also CA 101; CANR 19

Sapper .... **TCLC 44**
See also McNeile, Herman Cyril

Sappho fl. 6th cent. B.C.-.... **CMLC 3; PC 5**

Sarduy, Severo 1937-1993 .... **CLC 6**
See also CA 89-92; 142; DLB 113; HW

Sargeson, Frank 1903-1982 .... **CLC 31**
See also CA 25-28 ; 35; CANR 38

Sarmiento, Felix F   arcia
See Dario, Rub

Saroyan, William
1908-1981 ..... **CLC 1, 8, 10, 29, 34, 56;**
DA; WLC
See also CA 5-8R; 103; CANR 30; DLB 7,
9, 86; DLBY 81; MTCW; SATA 23, 24

Sarraute, Nathalie
1900- .... **CLC 1, 2, 4, 8, 10, 31, 80**
See also CA 9-12R; CANR 23; DLB 83;
MTCW

Sarton, (Eleanor) May
1912- .... **CLC 4, 14, 49**
See also CA 1-4R; CANR 1, 34; DLB 48;
DLBY 81; MTCW; SATA 36

Sartre, Jean-Paul
1905-1980 .... **CLC 1, 4, 7, 9, 13, 18, 24,**
44, 50, 52; DA; DC 3; WLC
See also CA 9-12R; 97-100; CANR 21;
DLB 72; MTCW

Sassoon, Siegfried (Lorraine)
1886-1967 .... **CLC 36**
See also CA 104; 25-28R; CANR 36;
DLB 20; MTCW

Satterfield, Charles
See Pohl, Frederik

Saul, John (W. III) 1942- .... **CLC 46**
See also AAYA 10; BEST 90:4; CA 81-84;
CANR 16, 40

Saunders, Caleb
See Heinlein, Robert A(nson)

Saura (Atares), Carlos 1932-....... **CLC 20**
See also CA 114; 131; HW

Sauser-Hall, Frederic 1887-1961.... **CLC 18**
See also CA 102; 93-96; CANR 36; MTCW

Saussure, Ferdinand de
1857-1913 .... **TCLC 49**

Savage, Catharine
See Brosman, Catharine Savage

Savage, Thomas 1915- .... **CLC 40**
See also CA 126; 132; CAAS 15

Savan, Glenn 19(?)- .... **CLC 50**

Sayers, Dorothy L(eigh)
1893-1957 .... **TCLC 2, 15**
See also CA 104; 119; CDBLB 1914-1945;
DLB 10, 36, 77, 100; MTCW

Sayers, Valerie 1952-............. **CLC 50**
See also CA 134

Sayles, John (Thomas)
1950-................. **CLC 7, 10, 14**
See also CA 57-60; CANR 41; DLB 44

Scammell, Michael .... **CLC 34**

Scannell, Vernon 1922- .... **CLC 49**
See also CA 5-8R; CANR 8, 24; DLB 27;
SATA 59

Scarlett, Susan
See Streatfeild, (Mary) Noel

Schaeffer, Susan Fromberg
1941-................. **CLC 6, 11, 22**
See also CA 49-52; CANR 18; DLB 28;
MTCW; SATA 22

Schary, Jill
See Robinson, Jill

Schell, Jonathan 1943-............ **CLC 35**
See also CA 73-76; CANR 12

Schelling, Friedrich Wilhelm Joseph von
1775-1854 .... **NCLC 30**
See also DLB 90

Schendel, Arthur van 1874-1946... **TCLC 56**

Scherer, Jean-Marie Maurice 1920-
See Rohmer, Eric
See also CA 110

Schevill, James (Erwin) 1920-....... **CLC 7**
See also CA 5-8R; CAAS 12

Schiller, Friedrich 1759-1805 .... **NCLC 39**
See also DLB 94

Schisgal, Murray (Joseph) 1926-..... **CLC 6**
See also CA 21-24R

Schlee, Ann 1934-................ **CLC 35**
See also CA 101; CANR 29; SATA 36, 44

Schlegel, August Wilhelm von
1767-1845 .... **NCLC 15**
See also DLB 94

Schlegel, Friedrich 1772-1829 .... **NCLC 45**
See also DLB 90

Schlegel, Johann Elias (von)
1719(?)-1749 .... **LC 5**

Schlesinger, Arthur M(eier), Jr.
1917- .... **CLC 84**
See also AITN 1; CA 1-4R; CANR 1, 28;
DLB 17; MTCW; SATA 61

Schmidt, Arno (Otto) 1914-1979.... **CLC 56**
See also CA 128; 109; DLB 69

Schmitz, Aron Hector 1861-1928
See Svevo, Italo
See also CA 104; 122; MTCW

Schnackenberg, Gjertrud 1953-..... **CLC 40**
See also CA 116; DLB 120

Schneider, Leonard Alfred 1925-1966
See Bruce, Lenny
See also CA 89-92

Schnitzler, Arthur
1862-1931 .... **TCLC 4; SSC 15**
See also CA 104; DLB 81, 118

Schor, Sandra (M.) 1932(?)-1990 ... **CLC 65**
See also CA 132

Schorer, Mark 1908-1977 .... **CLC 9**
See also CA 5-8R; 73-76; CANR 7;
DLB 103

Schrader, Paul (Joseph) 1946-...... **CLC 26**
See also CA 37-40R; CANR 41; DLB 44

Schreiner, Olive (Emilie Albertina)
1855-1920 .... **TCLC 9**
See also CA 105; DLB 18

Schulberg, Budd (Wilson)
1914-..................... **CLC 7, 48**
See also CA 25-28R; CANR 19; DLB 6, 26,
28; DLBY 81

Schulz, Bruno
1892-1942 .... **TCLC 5, 51; SSC 13**
ee also CA 115; 123

Schulz, Charles M(onroe) 1922- .... **CLC 12**
See also CA 9-12R; CANR 6; SATA 10

Schumacher, E(rnst) F(riedrich)
1911-1977 .... **CLC 80**
See also CA 81-84; 73-76; CANR 34

Schuyler, James Marcus
1923-1991 .... **CLC 5, 23**
See also CA 101; 134; DLB 5

Schwartz, Delmore (David)
1913-1966 ...... **CLC 2, 4, 10, 45; PC 8**
See also CA 17-18; 25-28R; CANR 35;
CAP 2; DLB 28, 48; MTCW

Schwartz, Ernst
See Ozu, Yasujiro

Schwartz, John Burnham 1965- .... **CLC 59**
See also CA 132

Schwartz, Lynne Sharon 1939-..... **CLC 31**
See also CA 103; CANR 44

Schwartz, Muriel A.
See Eliot, T(homas) S(tearns)

Schwarz-Bart, Andre 1928-....... **CLC 2, 4**
See also CA 89-92

Schwarz-Bart, Simone 1938-........ **CLC 7**
See also BW 2; CA 97-100

Schwob, (Mayer Andre) Marcel
1867-1905 .... **TCLC 20**
See also CA 117; DLB 123

Sciascia, Leonardo
1921-1989 .... **CLC 8, 9, 41**
See also CA 85-88; 130; CANR 35; MTCW

Scoppettone, Sandra 1936-........ **CLC 26**
See also AAYA 11; CA 5-8R; CANR 41;
SATA 9

Scorsese, Martin 1942- .... **CLC 20**
See also CA 110; 114

Scotland, Jay
See Jakes, John (William)

Scott, Duncan Campbell
1862-1947 .... **TCLC 6**
See also CA 104; DLB 92

Scott, Evelyn 1893-1963.......... **CLC 43**
See also CA 104; 112; DLB 9, 48

Scott, F(rancis) R(eginald)
1899-1985 .... **CLC 22**
See also CA 101; 114; DLB 88

Scott, Frank
See Scott, F(rancis) R(eginald)

Scott, Joanna 1960- .... **CLC 50**
See also CA 126

Scott, Paul (Mark) 1920-1978.... **CLC 9, 60**
See also CA 81-84; 77-80; CANR 33;
DLB 14; MTCW

Shepard, Jim 1956-............. **CLC 36**
See also CA 137

Shepard, Lucius 1947-............. **CLC 34**
See also CA 128; 141

Shepard, Sam
1943-......... **CLC 4, 6, 17, 34, 41, 44**
See also AAYA 1; CA 69-72; CABS 3;
CANR 22; DLB 7; MTCW

Shepherd, Michael
See Ludlum, Robert

Sherburne, Zoa (Morin) 1912-...... **CLC 30**
See also CA 1-4R; CANR 3, 37; MAICYA;
SAAS 18; SATA 3

Sheridan, Frances 1724-1766........ **LC 7**
See also DLB 39, 84

Sheridan, Richard Brinsley
1751-1816 ... **NCLC 5; DA; DC 1; WLC**
See also CDBLB 1660-1789; DLB 89

Sherman, Jonathan Marc.......... **CLC 55**

Sherman, Martin 1941(?)-......... **CLC 19**
See also CA 116; 123

Sherwin, Judith Johnson 1936-... **CLC 7, 15**
See also CA 25-28R; CANR 34

Sherwood, Frances 1940-.......... **CLC 81**

Sherwood, Robert E(mmet)
1896-1955 .... **TCLC 3**
See also CA 104; DLB 7, 26

Shestov, Lev 1866-1938 .... **TCLC 56**

Shiel, M(atthew) P(hipps)
1865-1947 .... **TCLC 8**
See also CA 106

Shiga, Naoya 1883-1971........... **CLC 33**
See also CA 101; 33-36R

Shilts, Randy 1951-1994 .... **CLC 85**
See also CA 115; 127; 144; CANR 45

Shimazaki Haruki 1872-1943
See Shimazaki Toson
See also CA 105; 134

Shimazaki Toson................. **TCLC 5**
See also Shimazaki Haruki

Sholokhov, Mikhail (Aleksandrovich)
1905-1984 .... **CLC 7, 15**
See also CA 101; 112; MTCW; SATA 36

Shone, Patric
See Hanley, James

Shreve, Susan Richards 1939-...... **CLC 23**
See also CA 49-52; CAAS 5; CANR 5, 38;
MAICYA; SATA 41, 46

Shue, Larry 1946-1985........... **CLC 52**
See also CA 145; 117

Shu-Jen, Chou 1881-1936
See Hsun, Lu
See also CA 104

Shulman, Alix Kates 1932-...... **CLC 2, 10**
See also CA 29-32R; CANR 43; SATA 7

Shuster, Joe 1914-............. **CLC 21**

Shute, Nevil..................... **CLC 30**
See also Norway, Nevil Shute

Shuttle, Penelope (Diane) 1947-..... **CLC 7**
See also CA 93-96; CANR 39; DLB 14, 40

Sidney, Mary 1561-1621 .... **LC 19**

Sidney, Sir Philip 1554-1586.... **LC 19; DA**
See also CDBLB Before 1660

Siegel, Jerome 1914- .... **CLC 21**
See also CA 116

Siegel, Jerry
See Siegel, Jerome

Sienkiewicz, Henryk (Adam Alexander Pius)
1846-1916 .... **TCLC 3**
See also CA 104; 134

Sierra, Gregorio Martinez
See Martinez Sierra, Gregorio

Sierra, Maria (de la O'LeJarraga) Martinez
See Martinez Sierra, Maria (de la
O'LeJarraga)

Sigal, Clancy 1926-............... **CLC 7**
See also CA 1-4R

Sigourney, Lydia Howard (Huntley)
1791-1865 .... **NCLC 21**
See also DLB 1, 42, 73

Siguenza y Gongora, Carlos de
1645-1700 .... **LC 8**

Sigurjonsson, Johann 1880-1919... **TCLC 27**

Sikelianos, Angelos 1884-1951 .... **TCLC 39**

Silkin, Jon 1930- .... **CLC 2, 6, 43**
See also CA 5-8R; CAAS 5; DLB 27

Silko, Leslie (Marmon)
1948-............... **CLC 23, 74; DA**
See also CA 115; 122; CANR 45; DLB 143

Sillanpaa, Frans Eemil 1888-1964... **CLC 19**
See also CA 129; 93-96; MTCW

Sillitoe, Alan
1928-......... **CLC 1, 3, 6, 10, 19, 57**
See also AITN 1; CA 9-12R; CAAS 2;
CANR 8, 26; CDBLB 1960 to Present;
DLB 14, 139; MTCW; SATA 61

Silone, Ignazio 1900-1978 .... **CLC 4**
See also CA 25-28; 81-84; CANR 34;
CAP 2; MTCW

Silver, Joan Micklin 1935- .... **CLC 20**
See also CA 114; 121

Silver, Nicholas
See Faust, Frederick (Schiller)

Silverberg, Robert 1935-......... **CLC 7**
See also CA 1-4R; CAAS 3; CANR 1, 20,
36; DLB 8; MAICYA; MTCW; SATA 13

Silverstein, Alvin 1933-........... **CLC 17**
See also CA 49-52; CANR 2; CLR 25;
JRDA; MAICYA; SATA 8, 69

Silverstein, Virginia B(arbara Opshelor)
1937-....................... **CLC 17**
See also CA 49-52; CANR 2; CLR 25;
JRDA; MAICYA; SATA 8, 69

Sim, Georges
See Simenon, Georges (Jacques Christian)

Simak, Clifford D(onald)
1904-1988 .... **CLC 1, 55**
See also CA 1-4R; 125; CANR 1, 35;
DLB 8; MTCW; SATA 56

Simenon, Georges (Jacques Christian)
1903-1989 ...... **CLC 1, 2, 3, 8, 18, 47**
See also CA 85-88; 129; CANR 35;
DLB 72; DLBY 89; MTCW

Simic, Charles 1938-... **CLC 6, 9, 22, 49, 68**
See also CA 29-32R; CAAS 4; CANR 12,
33; DLB 105

Simmons, Charles (Paul) 1924-..... **CLC 57**
See also CA 89-92

Simmons, Dan 1948-.............. **CLC 44**
See also CA 138

Simmons, James (Stewart Alexander)
1933-..................... **CLC 43**
See also CA 105; DLB 40

Simms, William Gilmore
1806-1870 .... **NCLC 3**
See also DLB 3, 30, 59, 73

Simon, Carly 1945-.............. **CLC 26**
See also CA 105

Simon, Claude 1913-....... **CLC 4, 9, 15, 39**
See also CA 89-92; CANR 33; DLB 83;
MTCW

Simon, (Marvin) Neil
1927-.......... **CLC 6, 11, 31, 39, 70**
See also AITN 1; CA 21-24R; CANR 26;
DLB 7; MTCW

Simon, Paul 1942(?)- .... **CLC 17**
See also CA 116

Simonon, Paul 1956(?)- .... **CLC 30**

Simpson, Harriette
See Arnow, Harriette (Louisa) Simpson

Simpson, Louis (Aston Marantz)
1923-................. **CLC 4, 7, 9, 32**
See also CA 1-4R; CAAS 4; CANR 1;
DLB 5; MTCW

Simpson, Mona (Elizabeth) 1957-... **CLC 44**
See also CA 122; 135

Simpson, N(orman) F(rederick)
1919-..................... **CLC 29**
See also CA 13-16R; DLB 13

Sinclair, Andrew (Annandale)
1935-..................... **CLC 2, 14**
See also CA 9-12R; CAAS 5; CANR 14, 38;
DLB 14; MTCW

Sinclair, Emil
See Hesse, Hermann

Sinclair, Iain 1943-.............. **CLC 76**
See also CA 132

Sinclair, Iain MacGregor
See Sinclair, Iain

Sinclair, Mary Amelia St. Clair 1865(?)-1946
See Sinclair, May
See also CA 104

Sinclair, May.................. **TCLC 3, 11**
See also Sinclair, Mary Amelia St. Clair
See also DLB 36, 135

Sinclair, Upton (Beall)
1878-1968 ...... **CLC 1, 11, 15, 63; DA;
WLC**
See also CA 5-8R; 25-28R; CANR 7;
CDALB 1929-1941; DLB 9; MTCW;
SATA 9

Singer, Isaac
See Singer, Isaac Bashevis

Singer, Isaac Bashevis
1904-1991 .... **CLC 1, 3, 6, 9, 11, 15, 23,
38, 69; DA; SSC 3; WLC**
See also AITN 1, 2; CA 1-4R; 134;
CANR 1, 39; CDALB 1941-1968; CLR 1;
DLB 6, 28, 52; DLBY 91; JRDA;
MAICYA; MTCW; SATA 3, 27;
SATA-Obit 68

Souster, (Holmes) Raymond
1921- .... **CLC 5, 14**
See also CA 13-16R; CAAS 14; CANR 13,
29; DLB 88; SATA 63

Southern, Terry 1926- .... **CLC 7**
See also CA 1-4R; CANR 1; DLB 2

Southey, Robert 1774-1843 .... **NCLC 8**
See also DLB 93, 107, 142; SATA 54

Southworth, Emma Dorothy Eliza Nevitte
1819-1899 .... **NCLC 26**

Souza, Ernest
See Scott, Evelyn

Soyinka, Wole
1934- .... **CLC 3, 5, 14, 36, 44; BLC;**
DA; DC 2; WLC
See also BW 2; CA 13-16R; CANR 27, 39;
DLB 125; MTCW

Spackman, W(illiam) M(ode)
1905-1990 .... **CLC 46**
See also CA 81-84; 132

Spacks, Barry 1931- .... **CLC 14**
See also CA 29-32R; CANR 33; DLB 105

Spanidou, Irini 1946- .... **CLC 44**

Spark, Muriel (Sarah)
1918- .... **CLC 2, 3, 5, 8, 13, 18, 40;**
SSC 10
See also CA 5-8R; CANR 12, 36;
CDBLB 1945-1960; DLB 15, 139; MTCW

Spaulding, Douglas
See Bradbury, Ray (Douglas)

Spaulding, Leonard
See Bradbury, Ray (Douglas)

Spence, J. A. D.
See Eliot, T(homas) S(tearns)

Spencer, Elizabeth 1921- .... **CLC 22**
See also CA 13-16R; CANR 32; DLB 6;
MTCW; SATA 14

Spencer, Leonard G.
See Silverberg, Robert

Spencer, Scott 1945- .... **CLC 30**
See also CA 113; DLBY 86

Spender, Stephen (Harold)
1909- .... **CLC 1, 2, 5, 10, 41**
See also CA 9-12R; CANR 31;
CDBLB 1945-1960; DLB 20; MTCW

Spengler, Oswald (Arnold Gottfried)
1880-1936 .... **TCLC 25**
See also CA 118

Spenser, Edmund
1552(?)-1599 .... **LC 5; DA; PC 8; WLC**
See also CDBLB Before 1660

Spicer, Jack 1925-1965 ...... **CLC 8, 18, 72**
See also CA 85-88; DLB 5, 16

Spiegelman, Art 1948- .... **CLC 76**
See also AAYA 10; CA 125; CANR 41

Spielberg, Peter 1929- .... **CLC 6**
See also CA 5-8R; CANR 4; DLBY 81

Spielberg, Steven 1947- .... **CLC 20**
See also AAYA 8; CA 77-80; CANR 32;
SATA 32

Spillane, Frank Morrison 1918-
See Spillane, Mickey
See also CA 25-28R; CANR 28; MTCW;
SATA 66

Spillane, Mickey .... **CLC 3, 13**
See also Spillane, Frank Morrison

Spinoza, Benedictus de 1632-1677 .... **LC 9**

Spinrad, Norman (Richard) 1940- ... **CLC 46**
See also CA 37-40R; CAAS 19; CANR 20;
DLB 8

Spitteler, Carl (Friedrich Georg)
1845-1924 .... **TCLC 12**
See also CA 109; DLB 129

Spivack, Kathleen (Romola Drucker)
1938- .... **CLC 6**
See also CA 49-52

Spoto, Donald 1941- .... **CLC 39**
See also CA 65-68; CANR 11

Springsteen, Bruce (F.) 1949- ...... **CLC 17**
See also CA 111

Spurling, Hilary 1940- .... **CLC 34**
See also CA 104; CANR 25

Squires, (James) Radcliffe
1917-1993 .... **CLC 51**
See also CA 1-4R; 140; CANR 6, 21

Srivastava, Dhanpat Rai 1880(?)-1936
See Premchand
See also CA 118

Stacy, Donald
See Pohl, Frederik

Stael, Germaine de
See Stael-Holstein, Anne Louise Germaine
Necker Baronn
See also DLB 119

Stael-Holstein, Anne Louise Germaine Necker
Baronn 1766-1817 .... **NCLC 3**
See also Stael, Germaine de

Stafford, Jean 1915-1979 ... **CLC 4, 7, 19, 68**
See also CA 1-4R; 85-88; CANR 3; DLB 2;
MTCW; SATA 22

Stafford, William (Edgar)
1914-1993 .... **CLC 4, 7, 29**
See also CA 5-8R; 142; CAAS 3; CANR 5,
22; DLB 5

Staines, Trevor
See Brunner, John (Kilian Houston)

Stairs, Gordon
See Austin, Mary (Hunter)

Stannard, Martin 1947- .... **CLC 44**
See also CA 142

Stanton, Maura 1946- .... **CLC 9**
See also CA 89-92; CANR 15; DLB 120

Stanton, Schuyler
See Baum, L(yman) Frank

Stapledon, (William) Olaf
1886-1950 .... **TCLC 22**
See also CA 111; DLB 15

Starbuck, George (Edwin) 1931- .... **CLC 53**
See also CA 21-24R; CANR 23

Stark, Richard
See Westlake, Donald E(dwin)

Staunton, Schuyler
See Baum, L(yman) Frank

Stead, Christina (Ellen)
1902-1983 .... **CLC 2, 5, 8, 32, 80**
See also CA 13-16R; 109; CANR 33, 40;
MTCW

Stead, William Thomas
1849-1912 .... **TCLC 48**

Steele, Richard 1672-1729 .... **LC 18**
See also CDBLB 1660-1789; DLB 84, 101

Steele, Timothy (Reid) 1948- .... **CLC 45**
See also CA 93-96; CANR 16; DLB 120

Steffens, (Joseph) Lincoln
1866-1936 .... **TCLC 20**
See also CA 117

Stegner, Wallace (Earle)
1909-1993 .... **CLC 9, 49, 81**
See also AITN 1; BEST 90:3; CA 1-4R;
141; CAAS 9; CANR 1, 21; DLB 9;
DLBY 93; MTCW

Stein, Gertrude
1874-1946 ...... **TCLC 1, 6, 28, 48; DA;**
WLC
See also CA 104; 132; CDALB 1917-1929;
DLB 4, 54, 86; MTCW

Steinbeck, John (Ernst)
1902-1968 ...... **CLC 1, 5, 9, 13, 21, 34,**
45, 75; DA; SSC 11; WLC
See also AAYA 12; CA 1-4R; 25-28R;
CANR 1, 35; CDALB 1929-1941; DLB 7,
9; DLBD 2; MTCW; SATA 9

Steinem, Gloria 1934- .... **CLC 63**
See also CA 53-56; CANR 28; MTCW

Steiner, George 1929- .... **CLC 24**
See also CA 73-76; CANR 31; DLB 67;
MTCW; SATA 62

Steiner, K. Leslie
See Delany, Samuel R(ay, Jr.)

Steiner, Rudolf 1861-1925 .... **TCLC 13**
See also CA 107

Stendhal
1783-1842 ..... **NCLC 23, 46; DA; WLC**
See also DLB 119

Stephen, Leslie 1832-1904 .... **TCLC 23**
See also CA 123; DLB 57, 144

Stephen, Sir Leslie
See Stephen, Leslie

Stephen, Virginia
See Woolf, (Adeline) Virginia

Stephens, James 1882(?)-1950 ...... **TCLC 4**
See also CA 104; DLB 19

Stephens, Reed
See Donaldson, Stephen R.

Steptoe, Lydia
See Barnes, Djuna

Sterchi, Beat 1949- .... **CLC 65**

Sterling, Brett
See Bradbury, Ray (Douglas); Hamilton,
Edmond

Sterling, Bruce 1954- .... **CLC 72**
See also CA 119; CANR 44

Sterling, George 1869-1926 .... **TCLC 20**
See also CA 117; DLB 54

Stern, Gerald 1925- .... **CLC 40**
See also CA 81-84; CANR 28; DLB 105

Stern, Richard (Gustave) 1928- ... **CLC 4, 39**
See also CA 1-4R; CANR 1, 25; DLBY 87

Sternberg, Josef von 1894-1969 ..... **CLC 20**
See also CA 81-84

Suskind, Patrick
See Sueskind, Patrick
See also CA 145

Sutcliff, Rosemary 1920-1992 ..... **CLC 26**
See also AAYA 10; CA 5-8R; 139;
CANR 37; CLR 1; JRDA; MAICYA;
SATA 6, 44, 78; SATA-Obit 73

Sutro, Alfred 1863-1933 .... **TCLC 6**
See also CA 105; DLB 10

Sutton, Henry
See Slavitt, David R(ytman)

Svevo, Italo .... **TCLC 2, 35**
See also Schmitz, Aron Hector

Swados, Elizabeth 1951- .... **CLC 12**
See also CA 97-100

Swados, Harvey 1920-1972 .... **CLC 5**
See also CA 5-8R; 37-40R; CANR 6;
DLB 2

Swan, Gladys 1934- .... **CLC 69**
See also CA 101; CANR 17, 39

Swarthout, Glendon (Fred)
1918-1992 .... **CLC 35**
See also CA 1-4R; 139; CANR 1; SATA 26

Sweet, Sarah C.
See Jewett, (Theodora) Sarah Orne

Swenson, May
1919-1989 .... **CLC 4, 14, 61; DA**
See also CA 5-8R; 130; CANR 36; DLB 5;
MTCW; SATA 15

Swift, Augustus
See Lovecraft, H(oward) P(hillips)

Swift, Graham 1949- .... **CLC 41**
See also CA 117; 122

Swift, Jonathan
1667-1745 ...... **LC 1; DA; PC 9; WLC**
See also CDBLB 1660-1789; DLB 39, 95,
101; SATA 19

Swinburne, Algernon Charles
1837-1909 ...... **TCLC 8, 36; DA; WLC**
See also CA 105; 140; CDBLB 1832-1890;
DLB 35, 57

Swinfen, Ann .... **CLC 34**

Swinnerton, Frank Arthur
1884-1982 .... **CLC 31**
See also CA 108; DLB 34

Swithen, John
See King, Stephen (Edwin)

Sylvia
See Ashton-Warner, Sylvia (Constance)

Symmes, Robert Edward
See Duncan, Robert (Edward)

Symonds, John Addington
1840-1893 .... **NCLC 34**
See also DLB 57, 144

Symons, Arthur 1865-1945 .... **TCLC 11**
See also CA 107; DLB 19, 57

Symons, Julian (Gustave)
1912- .... **CLC 2, 14, 32**
See also CA 49-52; CAAS 3; CANR 3, 33;
DLB 87; DLBY 92; MTCW

Synge, (Edmund) J(ohn) M(illington)
1871-1909 .... **TCLC 6, 37; DC 2**
See also CA 104; 141; CDBLB 1890-1914;
DLB 10, 19

Syruc, J.
See Milosz, Czeslaw

Szirtes, George 1948- .... **CLC 46**
See also CA 109; CANR 27

Tabori, George 1914- .... **CLC 19**
See also CA 49-52; CANR 4

Tagore, Rabindranath
1861-1941 .... **TCLC 3, 53; PC 8**
See also CA 104; 120; MTCW

Taine, Hippolyte Adolphe
1828-1893 .... **NCLC 15**

Talese, Gay 1932- .... **CLC 37**
See also AITN 1; CA 1-4R; CANR 9;
MTCW

Tallent, Elizabeth (Ann) 1954- ..... **CLC 45**
See also CA 117; DLB 130

Tally, Ted 1952- .... **CLC 42**
See also CA 120; 124

Tamayo y Baus, Manuel
1829-1898 .... **NCLC 1**

Tammsaare, A(nton) H(ansen)
1878-1940 .... **TCLC 27**

Tan, Amy 1952- .... **CLC 59**
See also AAYA 9; BEST 89:3; CA 136;
SATA 75

Tandem, Felix
See Spitteler, Carl (Friedrich Georg)

Tanizaki, Jun'ichiro
1886-1965 .... **CLC 8, 14, 28**
See also CA 93-96; 25-28R

Tanner, William
See Amis, Kingsley (William)

Tao Lao
See Storni, Alfonsina

Tarassoff, Lev
See Troyat, Henri

Tarbell, Ida M(inerva)
1857-1944 .... **TCLC 40**
See also CA 122; DLB 47

Tarkington, (Newton) Booth
1869-1946 .... **TCLC 9**
See also CA 110; 143; DLB 9, 102;
SATA 17

Tarkovsky, Andrei (Arsenyevich)
1932-1986 .... **CLC 75**
See also CA 127

Tartt, Donna 1964(?)- .... **CLC 76**
See also CA 142

Tasso, Torquato 1544-1595 .... **LC 5**

Tate, (John Orley) Allen
1899-1979 .... **CLC 2, 4, 6, 9, 11, 14, 24**
See also CA 5-8R; 85-88; CANR 32;
DLB 4, 45, 63; MTCW

Tate, Ellalice
See Hibbert, Eleanor Alice Burford

Tate, James (Vincent) 1943- ... **CLC 2, 6, 25**
See also CA 21-24R; CANR 29; DLB 5

Tavel, Ronald 1940- .... **CLC 6**
See also CA 21-24R; CANR 33

Taylor, Cecil Philip 1929-1981 ..... **CLC 27**
See also CA 25-28R; 105

Taylor, Edward 1642(?)-1729 .... **LC 11; DA**
See also DLB 24

Taylor, Eleanor Ross 1920- .... **CLC 5**
See also CA 81-84

Taylor, Elizabeth 1912-1975 ... **CLC 2, 4, 29**
See also CA 13-16R; CANR 9; DLB 139;
MTCW; SATA 13

Taylor, Henry (Splawn) 1942- ...... **CLC 44**
See also CA 33-36R; CAAS 7; CANR 31;
DLB 5

Taylor, Kamala (Purnaiya) 1924-
See Markandaya, Kamala
See also CA 77-80

Taylor, Mildred D. .... **CLC 21**
See also AAYA 10; BW 1; CA 85-88;
CANR 25; CLR 9; DLB 52; JRDA;
MAICYA; SAAS 5; SATA 15, 70

Taylor, Peter (Hillsman)
1917- ...... **CLC 1, 4, 18, 37, 44, 50, 71;**
                                          SSC 10
See also CA 13-16R; CANR 9; DLBY 81;
MTCW

Taylor, Robert Lewis 1912- .... **CLC 14**
See also CA 1-4R; CANR 3; SATA 10

Tchekhov, Anton
See Chekhov, Anton (Pavlovich)

Teasdale, Sara 1884-1933 .... **TCLC 4**
See also CA 104; DLB 45; SATA 32

Tegner, Esaias 1782-1846 .... **NCLC 2**

Teilhard de Chardin, (Marie Joseph) Pierre
1881-1955 .... **TCLC 9**
See also CA 105

Temple, Ann
See Mortimer, Penelope (Ruth)

Tennant, Emma (Christina)
1937- .... **CLC 13, 52**
See also CA 65-68; CAAS 9; CANR 10, 38;
DLB 14

Tenneshaw, S. M.
See Silverberg, Robert

Tennyson, Alfred
1809-1892 .. **NCLC 30; DA; PC 6; WLC**
See also CDBLB 1832-1890; DLB 32

Teran, Lisa St. Aubin de .... **CLC 36**
See also St. Aubin de Teran, Lisa

Terence 195(?)B.C.-159B.C. ...... **CMLC 14**

Teresa de Jesus, St. 1515-1582 ...... **LC 18**

Terkel, Louis 1912-
See Terkel, Studs
See also CA 57-60; CANR 18, 45; MTCW

Terkel, Studs .... **CLC 38**
See also Terkel, Louis
See also AITN 1

Terry, C. V.
See Slaughter, Frank G(ill)

Terry, Megan 1932- .... **CLC 19**
See also CA 77-80; CABS 3; CANR 43;
DLB 7

Tertz, Abram
See Sinyavsky, Andrei (Donatevich)

Tesich, Steve 1943(?)- .... **CLC 40, 69**
See also CA 105; DLBY 83

Teternikov, Fyodor Kuzmich 1863-1927
See Sologub, Fyodor
See also CA 104

Torsvan, Traven
See Traven, B.

Tournier, Michel (Edouard)
1924- . . . . **CLC 6, 23, 36**
See also CA 49-52; CANR 3, 36; DLB 83;
MTCW; SATA 23

Tournimparte, Alessandra
See Ginzburg, Natalia

Towers, Ivar
See Kornbluth, C(yril) M.

Townsend, Sue 1946- . . . . **CLC 61**
See also CA 119; 127; MTCW; SATA 48,
55

Townshend, Peter (Dennis Blandford)
1945- . . . . **CLC 17, 42**
See also CA 107

Tozzi, Federigo 1883-1920. . . . . . . **TCLC 31**

Traill, Catharine Parr
1802-1899 . . . . **NCLC 31**
See also DLB 99

Trakl, Georg 1887-1914 . . . . **TCLC 5**
See also CA 104

Transtroemer, Tomas (Goesta)
1931- . . . . **CLC 52, 65**
See also CA 117; 129; CAAS 17

Transtromer, Tomas Gosta
See Transtroemer, Tomas (Goesta)

Traven, B. (?)-1969 . . . . **CLC 8, 11**
See also CA 19-20; 25-28R; CAP 2; DLB 9,
56; MTCW

Treitel, Jonathan 1959- . . . . **CLC 70**

Tremain, Rose 1943- . . . . **CLC 42**
See also CA 97-100; CANR 44; DLB 14

Tremblay, Michel 1942- . . . . **CLC 29**
See also CA 116; 128; DLB 60; MTCW

Trevanian . . . . **CLC 29**
See also Whitaker, Rod(ney)

Trevor, Glen
See Hilton, James

Trevor, William
1928- . . . . **CLC 7, 9, 14, 25, 71**
See also Cox, William Trevor
See also DLB 14, 139

Trifonov, Yuri (Valentinovich)
1925-1981 . . . . **CLC 45**
See also CA 126; 103; MTCW

Trilling, Lionel 1905-1975 . . . . **CLC 9, 11, 24**
See also CA 9-12R; 61-64; CANR 10;
DLB 28, 63; MTCW

Trimball, W. H.
See Mencken, H(enry) L(ouis)

Tristan
See Gomez de la Serna, Ramon

Tristram
See Housman, A(lfred) E(dward)

Trogdon, William (Lewis) 1939-
See Heat-Moon, William Least
See also CA 115; 119

Trollope, Anthony
1815-1882 . . . . . . **NCLC 6, 33; DA; WLC**
See also CDBLB 1832-1890; DLB 21, 57;
SATA 22

Trollope, Frances 1779-1863 . . . . . **NCLC 30**
See also DLB 21

Trotsky, Leon 1879-1940 . . . . **TCLC 22**
See also CA 118

Trotter (Cockburn), Catharine
1679-1749 . . . . **LC 8**
See also DLB 84

Trout, Kilgore
See Farmer, Philip Jose

Trow, George W. S. 1943- . . . . **CLC 52**
See also CA 126

Troyat, Henri 1911- . . . . **CLC 23**
See also CA 45-48; CANR 2, 33; MTCW

Trudeau, G(arretson) B(eekman) 1948-
See Trudeau, Garry B.
See also CA 81-84; CANR 31; SATA 35

Trudeau, Garry B. . . . . **CLC 12**
See also Trudeau, G(arretson) B(eekman)
See also AAYA 10; AITN 2

Truffaut, Francois 1932-1984 . . . . . . **CLC 20**
See also CA 81-84; 113; CANR 34

Trumbo, Dalton 1905-1976 . . . . **CLC 19**
See also CA 21-24R; 69-72; CANR 10;
DLB 26

Trumbull, John 1750-1831 . . . . . . **NCLC 30**
See also DLB 31

Trundlett, Helen B.
See Eliot, T(homas) S(tearns)

Tryon, Thomas 1926-1991 . . . . **CLC 3, 11**
See also AITN 1; CA 29-32R; 135;
CANR 32; MTCW

Tryon, Tom
See Tryon, Thomas

Ts'ao Hsueh-ch'in 1715(?)-1763 . . . . . . **LC 1**

Tsushima, Shuji 1909-1948
See Dazai, Osamu
See also CA 107

Tsvetaeva (Efron), Marina (Ivanovna)
1892-1941 . . . . **TCLC 7, 35**
See also CA 104; 128; MTCW

Tuck, Lily 1938- . . . . **CLC 70**
See also CA 139

Tu Fu 712-770 . . . . **PC 9**

Tunis, John R(oberts) 1889-1975 . . . **CLC 12**
See also CA 61-64; DLB 22; JRDA;
MAICYA; SATA 30, 37

Tuohy, Frank . . . . **CLC 37**
See also Tuohy, John Francis
See also DLB 14, 139

Tuohy, John Francis 1925-
See Tuohy, Frank
See also CA 5-8R; CANR 3

Turco, Lewis (Putnam) 1934- . . . **CLC 11, 63**
See also CA 13-16R; CANR 24; DLBY 84

Turgenev, Ivan
1818-1883 . . . . . . **NCLC 21; DA; SSC 7;
WLC**

Turgot, Anne-Robert-Jacques
1727-1781 . . . . **LC 26**

Turner, Frederick 1943- . . . . **CLC 48**
See also CA 73-76; CAAS 10; CANR 12,
30; DLB 40

Tutu, Desmond M(pilo)
1931- . . . . **CLC 80; BLC**
See also BW 1; CA 125

Tutuola, Amos 1920- . . . **CLC 5, 14, 29; BLC**
See also BW 2; CA 9-12R; CANR 27;
DLB 125; MTCW

Twain, Mark
. . . **TCLC 6, 12, 19, 36, 48; SSC 6; WLC**
See also Clemens, Samuel Langhorne
See also DLB 11, 12, 23, 64, 74

Tyler, Anne
1941- . . . . **CLC 7, 11, 18, 28, 44, 59**
See also BEST 89:1; CA 9-12R; CANR 11,
33; DLB 6, 143; DLBY 82; MTCW;
SATA 7

Tyler, Royall 1757-1826 . . . . **NCLC 3**
See also DLB 37

Tynan, Katharine 1861-1931 . . . . . . **TCLC 3**
See also CA 104

Tyutchev, Fyodor 1803-1873 . . . . . **NCLC 34**

Tzara, Tristan . . . . **CLC 47**
See also Rosenfeld, Samuel

Uhry, Alfred 1936- . . . . **CLC 55**
See also CA 127; 133

Ulf, Haerved
See Strindberg, (Johan) August

Ulf, Harved
See Strindberg, (Johan) August

Ulibarri, Sabine R(eyes) 1919- . . . . . **CLC 83**
See also CA 131; DLB 82; HW

Unamuno (y Jugo), Miguel de
1864-1936 . . . . **TCLC 2, 9; HLC; SSC 11**
See also CA 104; 131; DLB 108; HW;
MTCW

Undercliffe, Errol
See Campbell, (John) Ramsey

Underwood, Miles
See Glassco, John

Undset, Sigrid
1882-1949 . . . . **TCLC 3; DA; WLC**
See also CA 104; 129; MTCW

Ungaretti, Giuseppe
1888-1970 . . . . **CLC 7, 11, 15**
See also CA 19-20; 25-28R; CAP 2;
DLB 114

Unger, Douglas 1952- . . . . **CLC 34**
See also CA 130

Unsworth, Barry (Forster) 1930- . . . . **CLC 76**
See also CA 25-28R; CANR 30

Updike, John (Hoyer)
1932- . . . . . . **CLC 1, 2, 3, 5, 7, 9, 13, 15,
23, 34, 43, 70; DA; SSC 13; WLC**
See also CA 1-4R; CABS 1; CANR 4, 33;
CDALB 1968-1988; DLB 2, 5, 143;
DLBD 3; DLBY 80, 82; MTCW

Upshaw, Margaret Mitchell
See Mitchell, Margaret (Munnerlyn)

Upton, Mark
See Sanders, Lawrence

Urdang, Constance (Henriette)
1922- . . . . **CLC 47**
See also CA 21-24R; CANR 9, 24

Uriel, Henry
See Faust, Frederick (Schiller)

Uris, Leon (Marcus) 1924- . . . . **CLC 7, 32**
See also AITN 1, 2; BEST 89:2; CA 1-4R;
CANR 1, 40; MTCW; SATA 49

Voltaire
1694-1778 ... **LC 14; DA; SSC 12; WLC**

von Daeniken, Erich 1935- .... **CLC 30**
See also AITN 1; CA 37-40R; CANR 17, 44

von Daniken, Erich
See von Daeniken, Erich

von Heidenstam, (Carl Gustaf) Verner
See Heidenstam, (Carl Gustaf) Verner von

von Heyse, Paul (Johann Ludwig)
See Heyse, Paul (Johann Ludwig von)

von Hofmannsthal, Hugo
See Hofmannsthal, Hugo von

von Horvath, Odon
See Horvath, Oedoen von

von Horvath, Oedoen
See Horvath, Oedoen von

von Liliencron, (Friedrich Adolf Axel) Detlev
See Liliencron, (Friedrich Adolf Axel) Detlev von

Vonnegut, Kurt, Jr.
1922- ...... **CLC 1, 2, 3, 4, 5, 8, 12, 22, 40, 60; DA; SSC 8; WLC**
See also AAYA 6; AITN 1; BEST 90:4; CA 1-4R; CANR 1, 25; CDALB 1968-1988; DLB 2, 8; DLBD 3; DLBY 80; MTCW

Von Rachen, Kurt
See Hubbard, L(afayette) Ron(ald)

von Rezzori (d'Arezzo), Gregor
See Rezzori (d'Arezzo), Gregor von

von Sternberg, Josef
See Sternberg, Josef von

Vorster, Gordon 1924- .... **CLC 34**
See also CA 133

Vosce, Trudie
See Ozick, Cynthia

Voznesensky, Andrei (Andreievich)
1933- .... **CLC 1, 15, 57**
See also CA 89-92; CANR 37; MTCW

Waddington, Miriam 1917- .... **CLC 28**
See also CA 21-24R; CANR 12, 30; DLB 68

Wagman, Fredrica 1937- .... **CLC 7**
See also CA 97-100

Wagner, Richard 1813-1883....... **NCLC 9**
See also DLB 129

Wagner-Martin, Linda 1936-....... **CLC 50**

Wagoner, David (Russell)
1926- .... **CLC 3, 5, 15**
See also CA 1-4R; CAAS 3; CANR 2; DLB 5; SATA 14

Wah, Fred(erick James) 1939-..... **CLC 44**
See also CA 107; 141; DLB 60

Wahloo, Per 1926-1975 .... **CLC 7**
See also CA 61-64

Wahloo, Peter
See Wahloo, Per

Wain, John (Barrington)
1925-1994 .... **CLC 2, 11, 15, 46**
See also CA 5-8R; 145; CAAS 4; CANR 23; CDBLB 1960 to Present; DLB 15, 27, 139; MTCW

Wajda, Andrzej 1926-............ **CLC 16**
See also CA 102

Wakefield, Dan 1932-............. **CLC 7**
See also CA 21-24R; CAAS 7

Wakoski, Diane
1937- .... **CLC 2, 4, 7, 9, 11, 40**
See also CA 13-16R; CAAS 1; CANR 9; DLB 5

Wakoski-Sherbell, Diane
See Wakoski, Diane

Walcott, Derek (Alton)
1930- .... **CLC 2, 4, 9, 14, 25, 42, 67, 76; BLC**
See also BW 2; CA 89-92; CANR 26; DLB 117; DLBY 81; MTCW

Waldman, Anne 1945-............. **CLC 7**
See also CA 37-40R; CAAS 17; CANR 34; DLB 16

Waldo, E. Hunter
See Sturgeon, Theodore (Hamilton)

Waldo, Edward Hamilton
See Sturgeon, Theodore (Hamilton)

Walker, Alice (Malsenior)
1944- .... **CLC 5, 6, 9, 19, 27, 46, 58; BLC; DA; SSC 5**
See also AAYA 3; BEST 89:4; BW 2; CA 37-40R; CANR 9, 27; CDALB 1968-1988; DLB 6, 33, 143; MTCW; SATA 31

Walker, David Harry 1911-1992.... **CLC 14**
See also CA 1-4R; 137; CANR 1; SATA 8; SATA-Obit 71

Walker, Edward Joseph 1934-
See Walker, Ted
See also CA 21-24R; CANR 12, 28

Walker, George F. 1947-....... **CLC 44, 61**
See also CA 103; CANR 21, 43; DLB 60

Walker, Joseph A. 1935-.......... **CLC 19**
See also BW 1; CA 89-92; CANR 26; DLB 38

Walker, Margaret (Abigail)
1915- .... **CLC 1, 6; BLC**
See also BW 2; CA 73-76; CANR 26; DLB 76; MTCW

Walker, Ted.................... CLC 13
See also Walker, Edward Joseph
See also DLB 40

Wallace, David Foster 1962-....... **CLC 50**
See also CA 132

Wallace, Dexter
See Masters, Edgar Lee

Wallace, (Richard Horatio) Edgar
1875-1932 .... **TCLC 57**
See also CA 115; DLB 70

Wallace, Irving 1916-1990...... **CLC 7, 13**
See also AITN 1; CA 1-4R; 132; CAAS 1; CANR 1, 27; MTCW

Wallant, Edward Lewis
1926-1962 .... **CLC 5, 10**
See also CA 1-4R; CANR 22; DLB 2, 28, 143; MTCW

Walpole, Horace 1717-1797......... **LC 2**
See also DLB 39, 104

Walpole, Hugh (Seymour)
1884-1941 .... **TCLC 5**
See also CA 104; DLB 34

Walser, Martin 1927-............. **CLC 27**
See also CA 57-60; CANR 8; DLB 75, 124

Walser, Robert 1878-1956........ **TCLC 18**
See also CA 118; DLB 66

Walsh, Jill Paton.................. CLC 35
See also Paton Walsh, Gillian
See also AAYA 11; CLR 2; SAAS 3

Walter, Villiam Christian
See Andersen, Hans Christian

Wambaugh, Joseph (Aloysius, Jr.)
1937- .... **CLC 3, 18**
See also AITN 1; BEST 89:3; CA 33-36R; CANR 42; DLB 6; DLBY 83; MTCW

Ward, Arthur Henry Sarsfield 1883-1959
See Rohmer, Sax
See also CA 108

Ward, Douglas Turner 1930-....... **CLC 19**
See also BW 1; CA 81-84; CANR 27; DLB 7, 38

Ward, Mary Augusta
See Ward, Mrs. Humphry

Ward, Mrs. Humphry
1851-1920 .... **TCLC 55**
See also DLB 18

Ward, Peter
See Faust, Frederick (Schiller)

Warhol, Andy 1928(?)-1987........ **CLC 20**
See also AAYA 12; BEST 89:4; CA 89-92; 121; CANR 34

Warner, Francis (Robert le Plastrier)
1937- .... **CLC 14**
See also CA 53-56; CANR 11

Warner, Marina 1946-............ **CLC 59**
See also CA 65-68; CANR 21

Warner, Rex (Ernest) 1905-1986.... **CLC 45**
See also CA 89-92; 119; DLB 15

Warner, Susan (Bogert)
1819-1885 .... **NCLC 31**
See also DLB 3, 42

Warner, Sylvia (Constance) Ashton
See Ashton-Warner, Sylvia (Constance)

Warner, Sylvia Townsend
1893-1978 .... **CLC 7, 19**
See also CA 61-64; 77-80; CANR 16; DLB 34, 139; MTCW

Warren, Mercy Otis 1728-1814... **NCLC 13**
See also DLB 31

Warren, Robert Penn
1905-1989 .... **CLC 1, 4, 6, 8, 10, 13, 18, 39, 53, 59; DA; SSC 4; WLC**
See also AITN 1; CA 13-16R; 129; CANR 10; CDALB 1968-1988; DLB 2, 48; DLBY 80, 89; MTCW; SATA 46, 63

Warshofsky, Isaac
See Singer, Isaac Bashevis

Warton, Thomas 1728-1790........ **LC 15**
See also DLB 104, 109

Waruk, Kona
See Harris, (Theodore) Wilson

Warung, Price 1855-1911........ **TCLC 45**

Westall, Robert (Atkinson)
1929-1993 .... **CLC 17**
See also AAYA 12; CA 69-72; 141;
CANR 18; CLR 13; JRDA; MAICYA;
SAAS 2; SATA 23, 69; SATA-Obit 75

Westlake, Donald E(dwin)
1933- .... **CLC 7, 33**
See also CA 17-20R; CAAS 13; CANR 16,
44

Westmacott, Mary
See Christie, Agatha (Mary Clarissa)

Weston, Allen
See Norton, Andre

Wetcheek, J. L.
See Feuchtwanger, Lion

Wetering, Janwillem van de
See van de Wetering, Janwillem

Wetherell, Elizabeth
See Warner, Susan (Bogert)

Whalen, Philip 1923- .... **CLC 6, 29**
See also CA 9-12R; CANR 5, 39; DLB 16

Wharton, Edith (Newbold Jones)
1862-1937 ...... **TCLC 3, 9, 27, 53; DA;
SSC 6; WLC**
See also CA 104; 132; CDALB 1865-1917;
DLB 4, 9, 12, 78; MTCW

Wharton, James
See Mencken, H(enry) L(ouis)

Wharton, William (a pseudonym)
.... **CLC 18, 37**
See also CA 93-96; DLBY 80

Wheatley (Peters), Phillis
1754(?)-1784 .... **LC 3; BLC; DA; PC 3;
WLC**
See also CDALB 1640-1865; DLB 31, 50

Wheelock, John Hall 1886-1978 .... **CLC 14**
See also CA 13-16R; 77-80; CANR 14;
DLB 45

White, E(lwyn) B(rooks)
1899-1985 .... **CLC 10, 34, 39**
See also AITN 2; CA 13-16R; 116;
CANR 16, 37; CLR 1, 21; DLB 11, 22;
MAICYA; MTCW; SATA 2, 29, 44

White, Edmund (Valentine III)
1940- .... **CLC 27**
See also AAYA 7; CA 45-48; CANR 3, 19,
36; MTCW

White, Patrick (Victor Martindale)
1912-1990 .. **CLC 3, 4, 5, 7, 9, 18, 65, 69**
See also CA 81-84; 132; CANR 43; MTCW

White, Phyllis Dorothy James 1920-
See James, P. D.
See also CA 21-24R; CANR 17, 43; MTCW

White, T(erence) H(anbury)
1906-1964 .... **CLC 30**
See also CA 73-76; CANR 37; JRDA;
MAICYA; SATA 12

White, Terence de Vere
1912-1994 .... **CLC 49**
See also CA 49-52; 145; CANR 3

White, Walter F(rancis)
1893-1955 .... **TCLC 15**
See also White, Walter
See also BW 1; CA 115; 124; DLB 51

White, William Hale 1831-1913
See Rutherford, Mark
See also CA 121

Whitehead, E(dward) A(nthony)
1933- .... **CLC 5**
See also CA 65-68

Whitemore, Hugh (John) 1936- ..... **CLC 37**
See also CA 132

Whitman, Sarah Helen (Power)
1803-1878 .... **NCLC 19**
See also DLB 1

Whitman, Walt(er)
1819-1892 ..... **NCLC 4, 31; DA; PC 3;
WLC**
See also CDALB 1640-1865; DLB 3, 64;
SATA 20

Whitney, Phyllis A(yame) 1903- .... **CLC 42**
See also AITN 2; BEST 90:3; CA 1-4R;
CANR 3, 25, 38; JRDA; MAICYA;
SATA 1, 30

Whittemore, (Edward) Reed (Jr.)
1919- .... **CLC 4**
See also CA 9-12R; CAAS 8; CANR 4;
DLB 5

Whittier, John Greenleaf
1807-1892 .... **NCLC 8**
See also CDALB 1640-1865; DLB 1

Whittlebot, Hernia
See Coward, Noel (Peirce)

Wicker, Thomas Grey 1926-
See Wicker, Tom
See also CA 65-68; CANR 21

Wicker, Tom .... **CLC 7**
See also Wicker, Thomas Grey

Wideman, John Edgar
1941- .... **CLC 5, 34, 36, 67; BLC**
See also BW 2; CA 85-88; CANR 14, 42;
DLB 33, 143

Wiebe, Rudy (Henry) 1934- ... **CLC 6, 11, 14**
See also CA 37-40R; CANR 42; DLB 60

Wieland, Christoph Martin
1733-1813 .... **NCLC 17**
See also DLB 97

Wiene, Robert 1881-1938 .... **TCLC 56**

Wieners, John 1934- .... **CLC 7**
See also CA 13-16R; DLB 16

Wiesel, Elie(zer)
1928- .... **CLC 3, 5, 11, 37; DA**
See also AAYA 7; AITN 1; CA 5-8R;
CAAS 4; CANR 8, 40; DLB 83;
DLBY 87; MTCW; SATA 56

Wiggins, Marianne 1947- .... **CLC 57**
See also BEST 89:3; CA 130

Wight, James Alfred 1916-
See Herriot, James
See also CA 77-80; SATA 44, 55

Wilbur, Richard (Purdy)
1921- .... **CLC 3, 6, 9, 14, 53; DA**
See also CA 1-4R; CABS 2; CANR 2, 29;
DLB 5; MTCW; SATA 9

Wild, Peter 1940- .... **CLC 14**
See also CA 37-40R; DLB 5

Wilde, Oscar (Fingal O'Flahertie Wills)
1854(?)-1900 .... **TCLC 1, 8, 23, 41; DA;
SSC 11; WLC**
See also CA 104; 119; CDBLB 1890-1914;
DLB 10, 19, 34, 57, 141; SATA 24

Wilder, Billy .... **CLC 20**
See also Wilder, Samuel
See also DLB 26

Wilder, Samuel 1906-
See Wilder, Billy
See also CA 89-92

Wilder, Thornton (Niven)
1897-1975 ...... **CLC 1, 5, 6, 10, 15, 35,
82; DA; DC 1; WLC**
See also AITN 2; CA 13-16R; 61-64;
CANR 40; DLB 4, 7, 9; MTCW

Wilding, Michael 1942- .... **CLC 73**
See also CA 104; CANR 24

Wiley, Richard 1944- .... **CLC 44**
See also CA 121; 129

Wilhelm, Kate .... **CLC 7**
See also Wilhelm, Katie Gertrude
See also CAAS 5; DLB 8

Wilhelm, Katie Gertrude 1928-
See Wilhelm, Kate
See also CA 37-40R; CANR 17, 36; MTCW

Wilkins, Mary
See Freeman, Mary Eleanor Wilkins

Willard, Nancy 1936- .... **CLC 7, 37**
See also CA 89-92; CANR 10, 39; CLR 5;
DLB 5, 52; MAICYA; MTCW;
SATA 30, 37, 71

Williams, C(harles) K(enneth)
1936- .... **CLC 33, 56**
See also CA 37-40R; DLB 5

Williams, Charles
See Collier, James L(incoln)

Williams, Charles (Walter Stansby)
1886-1945 .... **TCLC 1, 11**
See also CA 104; DLB 100

Williams, (George) Emlyn
1905-1987 .... **CLC 15**
See also CA 104; 123; CANR 36; DLB 10,
77; MTCW

Williams, Hugo 1942- .... **CLC 42**
See also CA 17-20R; CANR 45; DLB 40

Williams, J. Walker
See Wodehouse, P(elham) G(renville)

Williams, John A(lfred)
1925- .... **CLC 5, 13; BLC**
See also BW 2; CA 53-56; CAAS 3;
CANR 6, 26; DLB 2, 33

Williams, Jonathan (Chamberlain)
1929- .... **CLC 13**
See also CA 9-12R; CAAS 12; CANR 8;
DLB 5

Williams, Joy 1944- .... **CLC 31**
See also CA 41-44R; CANR 22

Williams, Norman 1952- .... **CLC 39**
See also CA 118

Williams, Tennessee
1911-1983 ..... **CLC 1, 2, 5, 7, 8, 11, 15,
19, 30, 39, 45, 71; DA; DC 4; WLC**
See also AITN 1, 2; CA 5-8R; 108;
CABS 3; CANR 31; CDALB 1941-1968;
DLB 7; DLBD 4; DLBY 83; MTCW

Wright, Judith (Arandell)
1915- . . . . CLC 11, 53
See also CA 13-16R; CANR 31; MTCW;
SATA 14

Wright, L(aurali) R. 1939- . . . . CLC 44
See also CA 138

Wright, Richard (Nathaniel)
1908-1960 . . . . CLC 1, 3, 4, 9, 14, 21, 48,
74; BLC; DA; SSC 2; WLC
See also AAYA 5; BW 1; CA 108;
CDALB 1929-1941; DLB 76, 102;
DLBD 2; MTCW

Wright, Richard B(ruce) 1937- . . . . . . CLC 6
See also CA 85-88; DLB 53

Wright, Rick 1945- . . . . CLC 35

Wright, Rowland
See Wells, Carolyn

Wright, Stephen Caldwell 1946- . . . . CLC 33
See also BW 2

Wright, Willard Huntington 1888-1939
See Van Dine, S. S.
See also CA 115

Wright, William 1930- . . . . CLC 44
See also CA 53-56; CANR 7, 23

Wu Ch'eng-en 1500(?)-1582(?) . . . . LC 7

Wu Ching-tzu 1701-1754 . . . . LC 2

Wurlitzer, Rudolph 1938(?)- . . . CLC 2, 4, 15
See also CA 85-88

Wycherley, William 1641-1715 . . . . LC 8, 21
See also CDBLB 1660-1789; DLB 80

Wylie, Elinor (Morton Hoyt)
1885-1928 . . . . TCLC 8
See also CA 105; DLB 9, 45

Wylie, Philip (Gordon) 1902-1971 . . . CLC 43
See also CA 21-22; 33-36R; CAP 2; DLB 9

Wyndham, John . . . . CLC 19
See also Harris, John (Wyndham Parkes
Lucas) Beynon

Wyss, Johann David Von
1743-1818 . . . . NCLC 10
See also JRDA; MAICYA; SATA 27, 29

Yakumo Koizumi
See Hearn, (Patricio) Lafcadio (Tessima
Carlos)

Yanez, Jose Donoso
See Donoso (Yanez), Jose

Yanovsky, Basile S.
See Yanovsky, V(assily) S(emenovich)

Yanovsky, V(assily) S(emenovich)
1906-1989 . . . . CLC 2, 18
See also CA 97-100; 129

Yates, Richard 1926-1992 . . . . . CLC 7, 8, 23
See also CA 5-8R; 139; CANR 10, 43;
DLB 2; DLBY 81, 92

Yeats, W. B.
See Yeats, William Butler

Yeats, William Butler
1865-1939 . . . . . TCLC 1, 11, 18, 31; DA;
WLC
See also CA 104; 127; CANR 45;
CDBLB 1890-1914; DLB 10, 19, 98;
MTCW

Yehoshua, A(braham) B.
1936- . . . . CLC 13, 31
See also CA 33-36R; CANR 43

Yep, Laurence Michael 1948- . . . . . . CLC 35
See also AAYA 5; CA 49-52; CANR 1;
CLR 3, 17; DLB 52; JRDA; MAICYA;
SATA 7, 69

Yerby, Frank G(arvin)
1916-1991 . . . . CLC 1, 7, 22; BLC
See also BW 1; CA 9-12R; 136; CANR 16;
DLB 76; MTCW

Yesenin, Sergei Alexandrovich
See Esenin, Sergei (Alexandrovich)

Yevtushenko, Yevgeny (Alexandrovich)
1933- . . . . CLC 1, 3, 13, 26, 51
See also CA 81-84; CANR 33; MTCW

Yezierska, Anzia 1885(?)-1970 . . . . . CLC 46
See also CA 126; 89-92; DLB 28; MTCW

Yglesias, Helen 1915- . . . . CLC 7, 22
See also CA 37-40R; CANR 15; MTCW

Yokomitsu Riichi 1898-1947 . . . . . . TCLC 47

Yonge, Charlotte (Mary)
1823-1901 . . . . TCLC 48
See also CA 109; DLB 18; SATA 17

York, Jeremy
See Creasey, John

York, Simon
See Heinlein, Robert A(nson)

Yorke, Henry Vincent 1905-1974 . . . CLC 13
See also Green, Henry
See also CA 85-88; 49-52

Yoshimoto, Banana . . . . CLC 84
See also Yoshimoto, Mahoko

Yoshimoto, Mahoko 1964-
See Yoshimoto, Banana
See also CA 144

Young, Al(bert James)
1939- . . . . CLC 19; BLC
See also BW 2; CA 29-32R; CANR 26;
DLB 33

Young, Andrew (John) 1885-1971 . . . . CLC 5
See also CA 5-8R; CANR 7, 29

Young, Collier
See Bloch, Robert (Albert)

Young, Edward 1683-1765 . . . . LC 3
See also DLB 95

Young, Marguerite 1909- . . . . CLC 82
See also CA 13-16; CAP 1

Young, Neil 1945- . . . . CLC 17
See also CA 110

Yourcenar, Marguerite
1903-1987 . . . . CLC 19, 38, 50
See also CA 69-72; CANR 23; DLB 72;
DLBY 88; MTCW

Yurick, Sol 1925- . . . . CLC 6
See also CA 13-16R; CANR 25

Zabolotskii, Nikolai Alekseevich
1903-1958 . . . . TCLC 52
See also CA 116

Zamiatin, Yevgenii
See Zamyatin, Evgeny Ivanovich

Zamyatin, Evgeny Ivanovich
1884-1937 . . . . TCLC 8, 37
See also CA 105

Zangwill, Israel 1864-1926 . . . . TCLC 16
See also CA 109; DLB 10, 135

Zappa, Francis Vincent, Jr. 1940-1993
See Zappa, Frank
See also CA 108; 143

Zappa, Frank . . . . CLC 17
See also Zappa, Francis Vincent, Jr.

Zaturenska, Marya 1902-1982 . . . . CLC 6, 11
See also CA 13-16R; 105; CANR 22

Zelazny, Roger (Joseph) 1937- . . . . . CLC 21
See also AAYA 7; CA 21-24R; CANR 26;
DLB 8; MTCW; SATA 39, 57

Zhdanov, Andrei A(lexandrovich)
1896-1948 . . . . TCLC 18
See also CA 117

Zhukovsky, Vasily 1783-1852 . . . . NCLC 35

Ziegenhagen, Eric . . . . CLC 55

Zimmer, Jill Schary
See Robinson, Jill

Zimmerman, Robert
See Dylan, Bob

Zindel, Paul 1936- . . . . CLC 6, 26; DA
See also AAYA 2; CA 73-76; CANR 31;
CLR 3; DLB 7, 52; JRDA; MAICYA;
MTCW; SATA 16, 58

Zinov'Ev, A. A.
See Zinoviev, Alexander (Aleksandrovich)

Zinoviev, Alexander (Aleksandrovich)
1922- . . . . CLC 19
See also CA 116; 133; CAAS 10

Zoilus
See Lovecraft, H(oward) P(hillips)

Zola, Emile (Edouard Charles Antoine)
1840-1902 . . . . . . TCLC 1, 6, 21, 41; DA;
WLC
See also CA 104; 138; DLB 123

Zoline, Pamela 1941- . . . . CLC 62

Zorrilla y Moral, Jose 1817-1893 . . NCLC 6

Zoshchenko, Mikhail (Mikhailovich)
1895-1958 . . . . TCLC 15; SSC 15
See also CA 115

Zuckmayer, Carl 1896-1977 . . . . CLC 18
See also CA 69-72; DLB 56, 124

Zuk, Georges
See Skelton, Robin

Zukofsky, Louis
1904-1978 . . . . CLC 1, 2, 4, 7, 11, 18
See also CA 9-12R; 77-80; CANR 39;
DLB 5; MTCW

Zweig, Paul 1935-1984 . . . . CLC 34, 42
See also CA 85-88; 113

Zweig, Stefan 1881-1942 . . . . TCLC 17
See also CA 112; DLB 81, 118

Literary Criticism Series
Cumulative Topic Index

This index lists all topic entries in the Gale Literary Criticism Series *Classical and Medieval Literature Criticism, Contemporary Literary Criticism, Literature Criticism from 1400 to 1800, Nineteenth-Century Literature Criticism,* and *Twentieth-Century Literary Criticism.*

CMLC Cumulative Nationality Index

CMLC Cumulative Title Index

483

Title Index

Title Index

Title Index

CMLC Cumulative Critic Index

Gerow, Edwin
Kālidāsa **9**:130

Ghazoul, Ferial Jabouri
Arabian Nights **2**:61

Gibb, H. A. R.
Arabian Nights **2**:28

Gibbon, Edward
Augustine, St. **6**:10

Gibbs, J.
Apuleius **1**:13

Gibbs, Marion E.
Wolfram von Eshcenbach **5**:347, 429

Gifford, William
Juvenal **8**:6

Gilson, Etienne
Abelard **11**:17
Augustine, St. **6**:44
Averroës **7**:18, 26
Bacon, Roger **14**:86
Meister Eckhart **9**:42, 60

Gilula, Dwora
Terence **14**:389

Girard, René
The Book of Job **14**:191
Sophocles **2**:408

Gladstone, W. E.
Iliad **1**:297

Godwin, William
Poem of the Cid **4**:225

Goethe, Johann Wolfgang von
Kālidāsa **9**:130
Longus **7**:217
Menander **9**:227
Sophocles **2**:303

Goldberg, Sander M.
Menander **9**:276
Terence **14**:372

Goldin, Frederick
The Song of Roland **1**:251

Golding, Arthur
Ovid **7**:287

Goldsmith, Margaret E.
Beowulf **1**:134

Gollancz, I.
Sir Gawain and the Green Knight **2**:186

Göller, Karl Heinz
Morte Arthure **10**:418

Gombrowicz, Witold
Inferno **3**:131

Gomme, A. W.
Menander **9**:259

Good, Edwin M.
The Book of Job **14**:206

Goodell, Thomas Dwight
Aeschylus **11**:112

Goodheart, Eugene
The Book of Job **14**:171

Goodrich, Norma Lorre
Arthurian Legend **10**:100, 108

Gordis, Robert
The Book of Job **14**:175

Gordon, E. V.
Hrafnkel's Saga **2**:86

Gosse, Edmund
Beowulf **1**:73

Gottfried von Strassburg
Gottfried von Strassburg **10**:246, 249, 258
Wolfram von Eschenbach **5**:291

Gradon, Pamela
Beowulf **1**:138

Grahn, Judy
Sappho **3**:494

Grane, Leifn
Abelard **11**:25

Granrud, John E.
Cicero, Marcus Tullius **3**:205

Gransden, Antonia
Anglo-Saxon Chronicle **4**:21

Grant, Michael
Aeschylus **11**:175
Apuleius **1**:26
Cicero, Marcus Tullius **3**:285, 291
Josephus, Flavius **13**:240
Livy **11**:367
Ovid **7**:405

Graves, Robert
Aeneid **9**:394
Apuleius **1**:20
Iliad **1**:361
Menander **9**:236
Terence **14**:341

Gray, Wallace
Iliad **1**:405

Green, D. H.
Wolfram von Eschenbach **5**:391

Green, Peter
Juvenal **8**:68
Ovid **7**:419
Sappho **3**:438

Greenberg, Moshe
The Book of Job **14**:196

Greene, Thomas
Aeneid **9**:399

Greenfield, Stanley B.
Beowulf **1**:119
The Dream of the Rood **14**:243

Gregory, Eileen
Sappho **3**:495

Grene, David
Aeschylus **11**:220

Grierson, Herbert J. C.
Beowulf **1**:90

Griffin, Jasper
Iliad **1**:392

Grigson, Geoffrey
Sei Shōnagon **6**:300

Grimm, Charles
Chrétien de Troyes **10**:141

Groden, Suzy Q.
Sappho **3**:436

Groos, Arthur
Wolfram von Eschenbach **5**:423

Grossman, Judith
Arabian Nights **2**:57

Grossvogel, Steven
Boccaccio, Giovanni **13**:114

Grube, G. M. A.
Aristophanes **4**:136
Cicero, Marcus Tullius **3**:258

Gruffydd, W. J.
Mabinogion **9**:159

Grunmann-Gaudet, Minnette
The Song of Roland **1**:248

Guardini, Romano
Augustine, St. **6**:95
The Book of Psalms **4**:414

Guarino, Guido A.
Boccaccio, Giovanni **13**:52

Gudzy, N. K.
The Igor Tale **1**:485

Gunkel, Hermann
The Book of Psalms **4**:379

Gunn, Alan M. F.
Romance of the Rose **8**:402

Guthrie, W. K. C.
Plato **8**:321, 360

Hackett, Jeremiah M. G.
Bacon, Roger **14**:99, 110

Hadas, Moses
Aeschylus **11**:150
Apuleius **1**:23
Aristophanes **4**:121
Hesiod **5**:98
Juvenal **8**:45
Plato **8**:304
Sappho **3**:417
Seneca, Lucius Annaeus **6**:378, 385

Hägg, Tomas
Longus **7**:262

Haight, Elizabeth Hazelton
Apuleius **1**:18

Haines, C. R.
Sappho **3**:397

Haley, Lucille
Ovid **7**:310

Hallam, Henry
Bacon, Roger **14**:16
Poem of the Cid **4**:225

Hallberg, Peter
Hrafnkel's Saga **2**:124
Njáls saga **13**:339

Hallett, Judith P.
Sappho **3**:465

Halleux, Pierre
Hrafnkel's Saga **2**:99, 102

Halverson, John
Beowulf **1**:131

Hamilton, Edith
Aeschylus **11**:128
Aristophanes **4**:109
Sophocles **2**:328
Terence **14**:322

Hamori, Andras
Arabian Nights **2**:51

Handley, E. W.
Menander **9**:243, 276

Hanning, Robert
Marie de France **8**:158

Hanson-Smith, Elizabeth
Mabinogion **9**:192

Hardison, O. B., Jr.
Mystery of Adam **4**:203

Hardy, E. G.
Juvenal **8**:17

Hardy, Lucy
Boccaccio, Giovanni **13**:30

Harris, Charles
Kālidāsa **9**:81

Harrison, Ann Tukey
The Song of Roland **1**:261

Harrison, Robert
The Song of Roland **1**:220

Harsh, Philip Whaley
Menander **9**:216

Hart, Thomas R.
Poem of the Cid **4**:306

Hartley, L. P.
Murasaki, Lady **1**:422

Hastings, R.
Boccaccio, Giovanni **13**:59

Hatto, A. T.
Gottfried von Strassburg **10**:259
Nibelungenlied, Das **12**:194

Havelock, Eric A.
Hesiod **5**:111, 150
Iliad **1**:382, 386

Hay, John
Khayyám **11**:261

Haymes, Edward R.
Nibelungenlied, Das **12**:244

Headstrom, Birger R.
Boccaccio, Giovanni **13**:35

Hearn, Lafcadio
Khayyám **11**:258

Hegel, G. W. F.
Aristophanes **4**:46
The Book of Job **14**:157
Inferno **3**:12
Plato **8**:225
Sophocles **2**:297

Heidegger, Martin
Plato **8**:295
Sophocles **2**:376

Heidel, Alexander
Epic of Gilgamesh **3**:310

Heine, Heinrich
Bertran de Born **5**:10

Heinemann, Frederik J.
Hrafnkel's Saga **2**:120, 123

Heiserman, Arthur
Apuleius **1**:46
Longus **7**:254

Herder, Johann Gottfried von
The Book of Psalms **4**:355
Kālidāsa **9**:102

Herington, John
Aeschylus **11**:210

Critic Index

Critic Index